Four Fields

ALSO BY TIM DEE

The Running Sky: A Birdwatching Life
The Poetry of Birds (co-editor with Simon Armitage)

Tim Dee

Four Fields

COUNTERPOINT
BERKELEY

Library of Congress Cataloging-in-Publication Data Is Available

ISBN 978-1-61902-461-8

Cover design by Julia Connoly
Interior Design by Palimpsest Book Production Ltd, Falkirk, Stirlingshire

Counterpoint Press
2560 Ninth Street, Suite 318
Berkeley, CA 94710
www.counterpointpress.com

Printed in the United States of America
Distributed by Publishers Group West

10 9 8 7 6 5 4 3 2 1

husbandry

for Claire

CONTENTS

A man keeps and feeds a lion. The lion owns a man.

Diogenes

Home Field

I was driving home in the dark. The stop-start charms of the A14. Lorries, boxy with containers heaving into the night, metal bergs not long off the sea struggling over the land, Stonehenge and Easter Island heads to be delivered to the interior. Body shunts and heart attacks on every incline. The Midlands up in front. Dusk had taken the fields next to the hurrying road out of sight. The lit trench was all. I was thinking of nothing, as you must to survive, when stems of grass suddenly glanced in my beams and crowded at my windscreen, their straight thin bars of strobing light tinkling against the glass. Somewhere in front of me a hay lorry was travelling and throwing behind it this green storm. The traffic slowed. As I braked, the hectic sprinkle fell away and I could see in my headlights and then feel beneath my tyres that the whole of the road's surface was covered in the thinnest spread of hay. A cigar butt or two of the stuff must have bounced from the back of the lorry and split on the road. We were all driving on grass. It brought a smile to my face. I might have strayed into some nativity scene of straw carried into a church and spread across a stone floor to make a point. I might have drifted into the story of the Princess and the Pea. The road had been transported or turned over into a kind of field and the grass was announcing itself in our ungreen and ungrowing world. My car and all the cars and lorries around me inched forward over the strange luxury beneath our tyres and, though the hay blades were thin and crushed thinner, I could still feel the new field under me with its tiny ridges and furrows briefly repossessing the road.

Throughout my life much of my happiness has come from being outside. That brief smile on the A14 was declaring it. I became a serious birdwatcher at the age of seven in 1968. I've grown less serious with time but, ever since my childhood, going out *into the field* has been part and parcel of what I do. The *field* might mean the fields of a farm but it can also mean anywhere that birds live and especially places where you deliberately look for them. Mostly this has been away from towns and cities, but not always: a back garden would do on a good day, or a park. My wanting to see birds simplified the world: if you didn't go out, you didn't see anything; if you did go out, regardless of what you saw, you seemed to have been somewhere and to have done something. Thoreau used the same phrase having spent a day kneeling to the earth to collect fallen sweet chestnuts in October 1857. Any day out for me, any day in the field, was better than a day indoors – I think that is what Thoreau meant too. Being outside was never a waste of time: even a day in July in a wood in the middle of England at the year's green midnight, when no birds sing; even an expedition in February with a grumpy girlfriend to an urban sewage farm; even a day with only a pitiful species list or wet feet to show for your efforts. Without any fieldwork of this kind, life inside stalled. Long before I read it, I knew the damp grey constriction – in my chest and between my eyes – of the first page of *Jane Eyre*: 'There was no possibility of taking a walk that day.'

Indoors, looked at from the field, seemed at best to be talk about life instead of life itself. Rather than living under the sun it fizzed – if it fizzed at all – parasitically or secondarily, with batteries, on printed pages, and in flickering images. I realised this around 1968 in my seven-year-old way. At the same time, however, I learned that I needed the indoor world to make the outdoors be something more than simply everything I wasn't. I saw it was true that indoor talk helped the outdoor world come alive and could of itself be living and lovely, too. Words about birds made birds live as more than words. Jane Eyre, held inside by bad weather, takes Thomas Bewick's *History of British Birds* to the window and reads looking out into the wind and rain.

A yellowhammer on a flaming gorse a mile from my childhood home, my first ring ouzels on spring migration on the grassed bank of a slurry pit – these birds, once found and named (real, flighty, not interested),

2

started something off like a shock into living. The world leaned on me, as it were, and the green gears of outside became part of the machinery of my mind, and 'a language of my whole life', as Ted Hughes described animals in his. Ever since, being in the field, following the field's seasons and its birds, and, at the same time, moving words from indoors out, and outdoors in, has more or less dominated my years.

Without fields – no us. Without us – no fields. So it has come to seem to me. 'This green plot shall be our stage,' says Peter Quince in *A Midsummer Night's Dream*. Fields were there at our beginning and they are growing still. *Earth* half-rhymes with *life* and half-rhymes with *death*. Every day, countless incarnations of our oldest history are played out in a field down any road from wherever we are. Yet these acres of shaped growing earth, telling our shared story over and over, are so ordinary, ubiquitous and banal that we have – mostly – stopped noticing them as anything other than substrate or backdrop, the green crayon-line across the bottom of every child's drawing. It is in the nature of all commonplaces that they are overlooked, in both senses of the word: fields are everywhere but we don't see them for they are too familiar and homely; being the stage and not the show, they are trodden under-foot, and no one seeks them out, no one gives a sod. For Walt Whitman, prairie-dreamer of the great lawn of men, grass fitted us and suited; it was a 'uniform hieroglyphic'. It grew and stood for us and, because it goes where we are, we tread where it grows. Yet because it meant everything it could easily mean nothing.

Might it be possible to look again and to see the grass and the fields afresh? Our making of fields, first of all from that grass, has tied us to nature more than any other human activity. The relationship is rooted yet simple, ancient yet living. Fields offer the most articulate description and vivid enactment of our life here *on earth*, of how we live both within the grain of the world and against it. We break ground to lay founda-tions, sow seeds and begin life; we break ground to harvest life, bury our dead and end things. Every field is at once totally functional and the expression of an enormous idea. Fields live as proverbs as well as fodder and we reap what we sow.

3

'The fields!' urged John Ruskin, early conjuror of cultural land-scapes, 'follow but forth for a little time the thoughts of all that we ought to recognize in those words.' What follows here is an attempt to say some more about the fields in my life; to understand why these four fields mean as much to me as they do and how they have given me the sentimental education, the heart's journey, that they have; to explore what they have meant to others; to discover the common ground they make, the *midfield*; to walk and work them in the only way I know, to name their birds and to read their words; to remember their other workers, their makers, mappers, gleaners, fighters; to count their flowers and to smell them; to link wild fields to factory fields; to argue that the most meaningful green squares might be the most banal, the most beautiful meadows the most ruined; to learn how they all work and how they all fail; to find the future of some in their past and, in others, their present enduring through change; to dive into their grass and sneeze alive, to lie in their grass and feel it a grave; to enlist every acre.

My beginning is the simple discovery of a simple truth. The outside places that I like are the places that I know. And being born in the 1960s and growing up in southern England, the places I know best, apart from the A-roads and the paved and heaped-up world of towns and cities, are the man-made fields close to home in between them. A *terra cognita*.

I hardly know a single wild place. There is none left in England. 'Natural England' is a government department. I am not actually sure that you can know a wild place. Not knowing how to be in a rain-forest, I couldn't wait to get out of the only one I have ever been in. I am equally frightened of the open sea. In 1972, I thought I was going to drown when the father of a schoolfriend lost his nerve as we sailed a little dinghy off the Isle of Sheppey and the sea slopped over the side of the boat. The nearest I have come to divorcing my wife was just last year when she scampered on ahead and left me frozen in terror on a (humiliatingly) small cliff on Table Mountain above Cape Town.

For Claire the mountain isn't wild – it is her outside place, a mountain as it happens, and which begins at the end of the street where she grew up. I would say the same for most of the fields in this book. They are places where I find myself. My plots and theirs overlap. I am not a farmer but like almost all of us I am a fieldworker. Jane Eyre peers at Thomas Bewick's Arctic vignette of 'forlorn regions of dreary space' and makes the English weather outside her window speak. Seamus Heaney digs with his pen as outside his window his father lifts potatoes with a spade. The plough was the first constellation in the night sky that I learned. It remains the only one I can point to reliably.

In what follows I want a field to mean most often a man-made outside place, but my definitions will run wild at times and be close-cropped at others, my facts and my metaphors (those carried into and out of the fields) will change with every ground. Come with me, then, as I plough my own furrow, but forgive me, knowing that we all must.

The word *field* is almost as big and elusive as its neighbour *nature*. And fields are talk of nature as well as ways of talking to nature. One of our oldest words, speaking of one of the first things we made and one of our oldest concepts, is alive and growing still. Fields are ordinary, universal, tamed and practical, but they are also none of those things or their opposite; they are strange, particular, wild, and as far beyond money as human-inflected things can be. The hedged allotment and the open prairie coax different poems as well as different meals. Kept places keep us in all sorts of ways. Fields are pay dirt but also the greatest land art on the globe. There is a story that John Ruskin once took a plough into an art lecture at Oxford to ensure his students – who, like me, might have known the plough of the night sky better – would recognise what one of the most effective sculptural tools ever invented by man looked like.

What is predictable in a field is never quite understood and what is extraordinary about them often seems familiar. 'Visionary dreariness', Wordsworth reported in *The Prelude*, and fields mist with the same negative capability or paradoxical potential. A fallow field is life in waiting. But so are all fields. In their ubiquity and in their endless difference, they are places of continuity and of security but also of risk and of transformation. In a dream scene in the Taviani brothers' film

The Night of San Lorenzo, a troop of Italian partisans in World War Two hides below the ripe wheat of a field and then, moments later, stands up armoured as Virgilian heroes to fight the Black Shirts with pitchforks. A bread field becomes a battlefield. In a ballad sung by Nic Jones, a smart lady is tempted and lies outdoors all night with seven yellow gypsies. A green field becomes a seamy bed of grass. Who wouldn't smile?

For a year or so around my tenth birthday I was perhaps the only subscriber in Croydon to *Farmers Weekly*. Before I fell in fully with birds, I had wanted to be a zookeeper or a farmer. But I have never had a field of my own nor worked in one. I have never cut hay nor driven a tractor. Once I rode on a horse. It tried to throw me into a puddle. More recently, I abandoned a walk across a fen field because a herd of cows was gathered at its gate and I was frightened to cross into their bulky company. I don't like milk, fatty meat, gravy, thick butter, or runny eggs.

For a few months in my twenties I had a girlfriend who was a farmer's daughter. We ended in a mess, strung out in different cities in different countries, but the beginning of our end happened I think near our very beginning, in her bed in her old childhood bedroom down the farmhouse corridor from her parents' room. Not that anyone was asleep, except for me; not that anyone was even in their bedrooms, except for me. Me – the visitor who knew about the early whitethroat singing in the hawthorns along the farm hedge but who wasn't expected or even invited to join the rest of the family out in the lambing barn in the middle of the night. Shifts had been allocated: my girlfriend's visit, even with a new boy, didn't excuse her, and when they weren't pulling lambs from ewes, or forking bloody straw from the cobbles, or cutting the fleece off dead lambs to wrap others that had been orphaned at birth so they might be fostered by the mothers of the dead, she and her family were behind the lines at the big range in the farmhouse kitchen on tea-making duty (the slab-tongue of milk into a mug), or cutting crumbling ham slices for midnight sandwiches (a brick of butter oiling its own dish). Eventually the farmer's daughter came back to bed and she smelled of the ewes and the lambs, of birth and afterbirth, of grass and wool, of everything that I wasn't, and I smelled of nothing at all, and we were never to work.

I had though, aged six, loved my little silvery-grey rubber milk churns that were part of my Britains toy farm set. I also loved how I could have a Ford tractor (blue) and a Massey Ferguson one (red) and could fix on the back of either my Lely Snipe Rotary Tedder (four words I have never written in that order until now nor uttered to anyone ever but which I know to be as indelibly true as anything in this world). When you steered the tractor with your finger the tines on the tedder spun round. And at the same time, in the next field, made with plastic drystone walls that clicked together, you could have a one-inch tall shepherd carrying a crook in one hand and a lamb in the other, and put next to him a shire horse with great feathered feet, some tiny saddleback piglets, and a blonde girl wearing wellingtons and a short 1960s sky-blue dress who spooned maize for chickens or ducks forever. And I loved it, and her for getting it for me, when my mother persuaded a greengrocer to part with some of his plastic display grass so that I might lay out on the proper ground my whole farm, barns, fences, tractors, farmers, animals, and so be installed in heaven, irked only by a problem of scale that meant that the blades of greengrocer grass came too high up the sides of my livestock and they tended to fall over in it.

I did the falling over, on a family holiday to Skye in Scotland, when I was ten. My sister and I were encouraged to feed two orphaned lambs with bottles of fresh milk from the farm cow. The lambs were small and stood only to our knees, but they butted us with surprising force, knocking me over in their haste and my nervousness. I got up and patted them, and their fleece was thick and my fingers came away greased with lanolin. The next time I knew that same strange ointment was holding for a quick minute in my surprised arms the oily purple body of my first son, just after he was born and before he was dried and delivered to his mother's breast. On Skye, my sister and I were dragged around the sheepfold by the amazing suck of the lambs on their teated bottles which they pulled at as if everything they needed was in the milk. I next knew that sensation when after his first feed I slipped my finger into the warm wet pucker of my baby's mouth and felt concentrated there all of his world.

The farmer's wife did the milking on Skye. She was a farmer too, though we have no word for her despite her centuries of toil. 'The farmer wants a wife', was the end of the round we sang at school of cattle and chattels. The wife followed 'the farmer wants a sheep' and 'the farmer wants a pig'. One morning she invited me into the byre to watch her milking. The Old English *byre* is related to *bower*, which is related to the German *Bauer* or birdcage. Sure enough, as I followed her muddy boots, swallows flew in and out above us, cutting into the dark, twittering one quick tune as they arrived and another slightly amended one as they left. The cowshed was heavy with the catching smell of sweet-grass-made-shit, a half-dirt-half-dream smell, rising up out of an old world that you find, even aged ten, you know already. I stood against the stone doorway and watched.

The farmer's wife pulled the pail of new milk towards me from between the cow's dirty legs. She had leaned in there on a little low stool, her cheek pressed against the cow's flank, a great black furry wall, while her hands moved on the swaying full moon of udder. The jet of milk rattled like peas at first in the empty bucket and then, as it frothed and filled, like nothing so much as the sound of my own desperate peeing after a run home from school. And, like my pee accidentally touched, it was surprising for being warm, almost hot. In the dark of the byre, the brightest things were all the same washed creamy colour: the farmer's hands, her cow's udder, and the rising disc of milk. 'Try it,' she said, and I knew I should even though I already knew that it wasn't for me. I drew her enamel cup through the bubbles and they burst into tiny flecks of curd that fell back on to the skin of the milk. I wanted to pour it direct to my throat but it covered the inside of my mouth in a warm chalky paint. As it went down it pulled just below my ears, at the place where my jaw was joined to my head. One mouthful was enough. I gave up on *Farmers Weekly* not long after.

Two grass truths I have learned anyway. Like anyone in the temperate world I lived these without knowing them. If you cut grass it doesn't die. If you eat its tops it doesn't mind, because it grows from near its base at what is called an intercalary meristem. This is the joint-like node on the stalk, the bump you feel beneath your fingers when you pluck a stem from the side of a path. Grasses and intercalary meristems are inseparable. In the growth tissue at the meristem, rapid cell division occurs and pushes the grass upwards. A simple and beautiful adaptation has brought us to where we are: hay can be cut, lawns mown, plains grazed. Herbivores – grass-croppers – drove this evolution. Grazing by buffalo maintained the prairie. A savannah is a wildebeest.

The second unknown known: our bodies are grass. We are grass 'carnified' as Thomas Browne said: 'all those creatures we behold, are but the hearbs of the field, digested into flesh in them, or more remotely carnified in our selves'. A cow eats grass and makes milk; a steer eats grass and becomes beef. We toast our cheese and barbecue our burgers and wrap the ensemble in a bread roll made of grass. The three great food crops of the north (now of the whole world) are grasses: rice, corn and wheat. They made us but we made them, as well. We have more than grown up together. Our domestication of the wild has drawn the wild after us. The transubstantiation of the earth works on.

Grass, like us, is young, fresh and green across many time zones. Our bodies are grass, and our days, as the Psalmist said, are 'as' grass. Grass has been a metaphor for our short life as long as we have known it. Land plants have been around for more than 400 million years but grasses evolved only 50 or 60 million years ago. The world's grasslands are young landscapes. Grass has dominated the temperate northern hemisphere only in the last 10,000 to 12,000 years. We appeared in these places about the time they became grasslands. And grass itself seems endlessly young while endlessly dying. Nowhere do its blades grow older than any autumn makes them. A meadow is a year.

Fields are not often famous for what they are. But begin to make a list of those you recall and it is hard to stop. South of the High Atlas Mountains of Morocco there is pitifully little grass. In this rock-desert the soil is thin. The last fields before the Sahara are here. Some giant has unpacked, tearing impatiently at a parcel, and the surface of the

Earth is littered like a new planet with the debris of its making, with black shattered stones that might have fallen from above or sliced their way up from beneath. They are hot from the sun or with the smoulder of the core. In the hills east of N'kob, a Berber family was making a field near a dry riverbed, clearing stones and raising low walls from them, twisting thorns into shrunken hedges. Seeing my friend Mark and me looking for scrub warblers, they said hello and invited us for tea. The young mother, forever pulling her headscarf across her shy smiling face, bent to a pile of thorn twigs and made a fire from them under a soot-blackened kettle. Her two teenage boys brought more kindling. Their father stooped lightly to their field, with a familiarity that made the stones at his feet seem like his crop. He collected an armful as he walked through the cleared place he was making and dropped the stones at the field edge, then crouched to the kettle and leaned in to his wife. I smiled and bent too. We had no language in common. The boys were picking at a thorn; in the next bush along I could see a scrub warbler, my first ever, carrying smaller twigs for its own purposes. The new field beyond the little fire of sticks and its three hearthstones ran for no more than fifty feet in one direction and thirty in the other. There were still many stones to clear. The soil without the stones was as dry and as hard as the stones. The mother shook green tea leaves from a box into their blue enamelled teapot and took a rough block of sugar from the folds of her clothes and passed it to her husband. He hit it with a stone and dropped shattered angular chunks into four blue tea glasses. The boys had to wait while Mark and I drank. The warbler came closer and scolded us with a call as dry as the grey thorn it hid among. The family would try to grow a few lines of wheat here, for couscous. When the kettle had finished a small cooking pot replaced it on the tiny flames; in the pot were a few slices of potato in dilute harissa, their lunch.

Two days later we came down from the mountains into Marrakesh, descending through white storks and cattle egrets planing to their roosts, and arriving as the high violet dusk gave way to a night of blue velvet above the Djemaa el-Fna, the teeming square at the heart of the old medina. There was drumming and singing and a thousand mopeds.

Wood smoke from the grills thickened the air and the lanterns of the cafes floated in it like so many full moons. We ate and then walked into the souk, losing ourselves within moments between the beetling cliffs of goods bursting from the fronts of crowded stalls that deepened giddily beyond like tunnels without end. There were reclining torsos of pungent leather bags, star clusters of verdigris-stained copper lamps, forests of rusty carpets. The vendors were packing up, getting everything that had been laid out in front of their stalls back into the narrow spaces beyond. We were chased down alleys by the judder of metal roller-blinds and we stumbled out of the maze to stop in front of the smallest unit of any that we had passed: a lit green cave, fluorescent bright and deeply scented, a mint stall. The mint-man in a khaki greatcoat was tiny-faced and old and he stood (there was only standing room) framed or wrapped by bunch after bunch of countless serrated green leaves in a sweet and clean-smelling cloud. For the female customer ahead of us, he selected eight or so handfuls from beneath a freshening wet sack at the front of his stall. We spoke briefly (me in halting French) and she said that the carrier bag of mint she had bought was all for tea, would keep in the fridge, and would last about a week. We smiled at the green man in his green cave, the smallest, freshest and greenest field in the world, and walked on out into the riot of the dusty old city.

At the other end of Europe, a few months later, I slept in the final field before the Atlantic.

After the last of the mainland fell away behind us, there was an hour and a half of open water. The sea rolled and slapped the boat. The engines churned, roaring when the propellers rose out through the swell. The seabirds thinned. I tried not to be sick. More slapping, the sea's leer and its bully lean. Then the auks came again, flying ahead of us now, towards where we were going. Slowly out of the marine-blue rose a low grey whaleback. It calmed my guts, grew up, and turned island-green. The engines were cut and we sunk down in the boat, finding our level in the sea at the base of a cliff. We landed in a tender, clambering down to the sea's surface, touching it as we gripped the dinghy, then scrambled up again, wet rocks, then dry, then grass. We dragged barrels of fresh water up the rough slope, its green rising in front of me to fill my sweating eyes, as the salt sea had done minutes before. At the top, I threw my bags from my back and found myself sitting in a field – fifty miles out into the ocean west of Cape Wrath, and the only field on North Rona.

I pitched my tent in a grassed ditch at what looked like the field edge. Away from its cliffs most of the top of the island is grass; on its gentlest slope looking back towards the mainland is the remains of its one field. My friend Kathleen had a bunk in the hut where seal scientists stay. No one has lived on North Rona since 1844; no one could live there now. It and its neighbour, Sula Sgeir, twelve miles off to the south-west, are like accidental islands, crumbs brushed from the table of the mainland and lodged in the sea. Even huddling into the bank there is no real shelter to be had from the wind. But once, under the same oceanic barrage, the island was farmed. The ditch was dug to raise an adjacent bed of soil in order to grow things to eat. Dug and re-dug between the eighth century and the nineteenth, the lazy bed (a mean name far removed from the effort needed to make it) marks the land still, just as it did on the day it was cut from the turf and soil. It is part of a beautiful sinuous geometry, a delta of green corduroy, which drains furrows and ridges, runs and rigs, down the island's sloping southern flank to the sea. It is as human a mark as we have made anywhere before or since.

There is an unmanned lighthouse on Rona now, and the hut is used by the seal people for a few weeks of the year. Both buildings are too recent to look anything other than garish and temporary, ludicrously – and vulnerably – square-angled and blocky in this place of rounded and winded things. The grass blows into a permanent wave along the lazy beds; the ruined houses and chapel in the old village with their turf roofs and drystone walls curve out of and back into the land as if they have grown from it. Storm petrels and Leach's petrels now breed in burrows they dig between the stones of the village.

The ditches, like the ruins, are an imposition on Rona; they mark a clearance, an enclosure, something made in our scale, and yet the space they create has found some natural equivalence in the scale of the island and so of the Earth. The human space has become a landscape that endures even in its ruin. A centre, somehow, even on the edge. The ripples of green man-made lines spilling down the grass-topped island seem good. If marks have to be made, they seem to be the best marks to make. Thus fields anywhere and everywhere: old but apt; imposed but giving; made in proportions that fit the Earth and us, which bring us together, that allow us to belong, that take the oldest and most searching human measurement – how much land does a man need? – and say, this can be yours, these acres, this plot, your field, man's not nature's, but the best thing of man, and the thing of his that is nearest to becoming nature.

After a midsummer night of the snag and fret of half-light and sea wind, I lay in my sleeping bag with my head out of the tent looking up at the sky. A migrant swallow flew above me along the shelter of the ditch, seeking – as I had – the calmed air made by people shifting earth hundreds of years ago. It fed, as it flew, on the insects that gathered in the windless lee. The sea had stilled to the south and tracks and furrows had stretched to meander across its surface, oiled smooth in places, more choppy in others, marking deeper currents beneath, and the way the sea, even in its continuousness, drifts and ripples variously under the wind and around the land. It looked like a field of grass.

If you were not a commoner or a parishioner in early-modern England and you wanted to rent part of a common field or hire rights to pasture, you might seek someone called a *fieldsearcher*, who would act as an agent on your behalf. Without fields of my own, these chapters are my *fieldsearches*. The field to which I return most often is currently rough grazing land at Burwell in the Cambridgeshire fens, one mile from where I live. This field was once a fen and the intention of its current owners is that it will be fen again, one day. The other three are foreign plots that I have known (in part) across some years: far afield, but not. The first of these is in Zambia on an old colonial farm. This particular field once grew tobacco but is at present overgrown with grasses and scrub. I have already written a little about these Zambian fields. Since those first words the farmer has died (he is buried near his old crops) and I have married Claire, the woman who showed me the field, the farm and the farmer. The second foreign field is a battlefield, and the remnant shortgrass prairie and adjacent croplands, in Montana in the USA where Sioux and Cheyenne warriors killed George Custer and his party in June 1876, in a battle which as much as anything was a fight over grass. The last field is in the abandoned village of Vesniane in the Exclusion Zone near the exploded nuclear reactor at Chernobyl in Ukraine. Until April 1986 it was a meadow grazed by cows. When I went there, the last thing I saw was an empty aluminium milk churn lying on its side, in the open doorway of a ruined byre at the field edge.

Each of these four fields has been turned over in one way or another for as long as they have been fields – it's in their nature. But now each is at a more angled point in its life. Fields cut from cleared scrub are abandoned back to thorns and thickets. Wild grasslands have become battlefields and then the holding place for the dead of those battles. Pasture is poisoned. A plot will be unplumbed. Territory, ownership, the exploitation of land, its meaning and value, the grass itself – all has been and is being argued over. There are tangled human voices in each field but there is also the sound of the grass. Just as fields aren't famous, grass isn't heroic of itself. It works anonymously. But I am trying to hear that as well. In John Clare's great poem 'The Lament of Swordy Well' a put-upon, enclosed field talks back. It's worth listening.

I'll begin by taking us once again to the worst so we might get it behind us. The road, encore. The anti-field. A place that is not even a place, which is the opposite of where you want to be, but where you find yourself again and again. I grow old even thinking about it, even as I tell you. This time we will walk up to it, in order to best catch the sting of its slap, but so that we might also have a means of escape. Stand at the last field edge before the asphalt. In front of you is a main road, the A14 once more, sunk into the ditch of a cutting. You don't see it until you arrive at the lip of its wound but you have heard it already, forever, the crenellated din of combustion and hardware passing without end. If you are lucky it sounds like a sea heard from the top of a cliff; more likely it puts a boxed fever into the brain, a swarfed headache driving between your ears. You have been here many times before; indeed, part of you lives here, though you are never at home. Your car will dip below the earth's surface, angle down the slipway, and latch on. But today, on foot, turn your back on the road and walk west down the green path through the wheat fields. Right now you must start away from here.

The dual carriageway of the A14 marks the eastern edge of the English fields of this book. The road forms the county border between Suffolk and Cambridgeshire and also the upland end of the parish of Swaffham Prior where Claire and I live. From the house it takes half an hour to walk to the main road, up a farm lane or along a footpath on the top of a chalk dyke (the Anglo-Saxon Devil's Dyke or Ditch). Depending on the wind's quarter I hear the road between five and fifteen minutes after leaving the front door. Once, when I was near, a crash had stopped the traffic on both sides and I could hear skylarks singing in Suffolk, otherwise I have never heard it quiet. Every day it fights its fight, dug into its trench.

Halfway into the last field before the traffic, a lesser whitethroat rattling from the final hedge stole into my ears. After that the road silenced all apart from itself. I flushed a skylark and it rose nervously and banked to avoid having to fly over the cars. I saw its beak open but couldn't hear its call. In the last wide fields of Cambridgeshire that run to the road there were forty hares spread through the young wheat in twos and threes. The sun streamed through their long black ears flushing them blood-pink. Such ears for such noise. At the road, parallel with it, is a hedged bridleway, just twenty feet from the metal run of traffic. I have never seen any person or horse there. A dead mole was on the path, lying with its head pointing towards the road, *unsoiled* – encumbered by being above the earth and to be buried in the air. It looked, as D. H. Lawrence said of a mole in his story 'Second Best', 'like a very ghost of joie de vivre'. It was earless and its eyes were lost into its soft fur, giving its front a blank and incomplete look. Its mouth grinned half open and showed two tiny canines, ivory needles against its sooted snout. Its fleshy hands and feet hung at its four corners like pink flags.

I turned from the mole and the road and headed west. If you look from the Suffolk hills to the Cambridgeshire fens, the sky leaps up above you and doubles in height. In the spring on days of silvery cloud-less sheen it seems higher still and able to further flatten the fields beneath it. The country before me opened but it also disappeared, thinning at the horizon about ten miles away to a level green line. This is a fen effect. Shining green ground hurries like dark water spilled across a tabletop to fill the flat space. The width of the view tugs at the corners of your eyes, its shallowness makes you frown. There is a lot of light to take in and not much else.

I heard a bee flying past my ear. The chalk hills behind me (though they would barely count as hills anywhere but here) made a bony barn of stone and they shouldered the dyke back towards the main road. Ahead, where the bee had gone, the fens were a soft and glistening skin, streaming from beneath me, cambered at either edge, an offering of earth, thin and damp but vividly alive. The green squares of the farms of Burwell, Reach and Swaffham Prior were chopped and trimmed by their hedges and ditches and, rolled hard under the silver-blue noon, they receded like Euclid's geometry or Alice's chessboard. Descending towards them and the fen beyond from the last few feet of altitude on the dyke was like watching from the windows of a landing aeroplane, when distance and spread shrink and narrow until you arrive on the ground as if buried by the near edge of things. But there were consolations: new weather came and conversation. A skylark got up from the path ahead, climbing over a field, its wings and throat rippling in one continuous action of flight and song. A lapwing shadowed a buzzard. Cowslips on the bank shook in the wind like smeared butter. There were swallows laying their slates, one over the other, up above my head. They sang as they worked.

The village of Reach marks the fen end of the dyke. It finishes on the village green but the dyke line continues beyond the cluster of houses and joins another man-made pathway running across the flat fen: Reach Lode, a cut waterway draining west. Though my feet remained dry I had crossed into a world of wet. I felt it beneath me. The calcified spine of the dyke was replaced by stoneless earth banks held together by the lush green grass and the soft dampness of the soil itself. Back on the dyke the molehills had been pale and powdery and bumped with nubs of chalk and blades of flint. A hundred steps away on the banks of the lode they were soft and peaty, smooth and sticky, and as black as mole fur.

My fen field begins here, the first of the four in this book. From here, there is not much to look at. It is the same closer up. But the field, once a stretch of fenland, has worked its way into my life, as have the three others. All four are grassed at the moment. They are real fields: a few hundred acres standing for the world. They could be walked, mapped, mown and known. Each has lived, at least for some time, as an apparently flat and plain place but also as a living sheet on which people sketched or screened various dreams for a while. Yet regardless of their fieldworkers' attentions, each also holds on to its own life, and remains itself even as it is harvested or grazed, preserved or abandoned. All fields are places of outlasting transience. They reset time. Each has a past but each lives in the present; each has a biography but is still a work in progress.

It happens that the same species of bird, the swallow (known internationally these days as the barn swallow), flies and feeds over all my four fields, and I love the bird and our world for that, though that doesn't make the grass beneath the swallows the same. The fields have some things in common but much that is particular. They are site-specific, idiomatic and accented; they are shaped by what they are near and speak of where they are. We made them and we were made by them. 'The land has been humanised, through and through', D. H. Lawrence wrote of rural Italy as he might have of all fields, 'and we in our own tissued consciousness bear the results of this humanisation.' I wonder if there are any two fields in Britain that are identical? I doubt it. I've been keeping watch. I know there are no ways into a field, no field-gateways in the world, that are the same. But I also know in no field anywhere do you feel properly lost.

And yes, as well as being a book of four fields, I want this to be a book *for* fields, a work of advocacy as much as of observation. My field love is different from my swallow love. Swallows I love for not being us, for not knowing they are swallows, for quickening the air while flying so closely and so swallowishly about our lives. I love fields for what they are, parcels of the earth we have gathered to us (almost always beautifully, could there be an *ugly* field?), but also for the picture they give us of ourselves (not always beautiful), the way all fields tell of how we have orphaned ourselves from the world – how hard we must work for even a whisper of Eden – but also how best we can be at home in it.

WINTER FEN

Life moves. A year neither starts nor finishes. I went out.

In a field next to Burwell Fen a lit fuse of winter wheat ran bright along the hard earth, its green mocking the cold. Overhead eight white winter swans lowered out of the north sky, cut from its freezing grey canvas, a family of whoopers from Russia flying like a washing line of flapping linen and yelping to one another as they pitched and juddered to a stop in the field. Their booted black feet kicked up the cold peat as they settled, and their long necks straight away dowsed the green where they ate.

A storm beyond the horizon had chased the swans south and was moving on the fen. Ten herring gulls with cold fish eyes and heads of shaved ice sat on another run of the wheat field, as white on the green as mushrooms. In the next-door field, 800 fieldfares spread over the threadbare flint-olive winter turf. Never before had I seen so many together. Each had its allotted grass and bounced over it at the same speed and in the same direction as its neighbour. The flock moved with the tact of a herd. Every few minutes the leading edge of the birds sensed they had come to the rim of something and rose into a flex of grey-brown flight which drew their followers up after them until, fifty yards or so further on, they all landed again, spaced as before, and resumed taking in the grass beneath them.

Even in the winter, because of the lifting and carrying of water, the once great swamp of the fens is now mostly dry. Slub – the evocative fen word for mud – is not what it once was. Drains beneath the grass vein the ground, while pumps and ditches and a thousand cuts (reaches, eaus and lodes, conduits and leams, fosses and sewers, washes and sluices) fetch rain and river water from the fields and beyond and bear it away. For the fens to function as a place for us, their water must be sent somewhere else and turned into the sea's problem. The pumping is non-stop; this country must bail itself out forever if it is to remain country; if the sea broke in and came down from where it rides now, fifty miles to the north, all would drown.

To walk on the flat worn grass of Burwell Fen in the winter is to cross a seabed. Both the North Sea at the Wash and the nearby water are over my head. The zero contour circles the fen and the land dips further at its centre to lie six and a half feet below sea level, the lowest place for miles. To step below the waterline in these fields is to sense a keeping back of a wetter truth across the wider fens: it was once sea here and then was kept from being always-sea by being sometimes-sea, and part of the great porous edge-of-sea that the fens were until we bested them, or tried to.

The wringing of water from the spongy fens and its portage away has put them further under. After hundreds of years of drainage the land has shrunk and lies *against* nature, below the sea but also below the rivers and drains that take its water away. The soil is drying and wasting, six feet every sixty years: 'by the height of a man' it was said sixty years ago, 'in the life of a man'.

Yet even in the time I have known them, the fens ran wet for part of every year and spread their own inland floodlit waters. That we still think of them as *fens* declares the dripping fact. And this is still a wet place in waiting. As fast as we build our dams the fens run back, rippling without contours, flat but edgy, a place where planned outcomes never quite happen and where human intentions forever come up against falling water. No one has nailed them. In an otherwise locked-down southern England, they seem like a work still in progress. Unfinished, you might say, or unfished.

Half a mile from my home, there is a road through the fields to the fens called Commercial End. It's a cul-de-sac. The tarmac ends. Farmers use the track that remains, and dog walkers, and birdwatchers like me. Today the village turns its back on the fens, and the road to town is king. But once the people faced them as if the entire world came to the village from there. And it did. Commercial End is a road, but the oldest villagers remember it as a hythe or a quay. Coal came here from the north-east of England by boat; wine, bricks and timber were also landed. Less than sixty years ago a way to the sea began here.

From the quay at Commercial End you once could have stepped on to a boat and not walked on land again until you were in Cape Town, Odessa, or Nantucket. The sense of the fens as the beginning of the sea is hidden now but still lies locked at their heart. The flat land asks us to feel the marine in it again and again. There doesn't seem to be much to the earth here. The world is spread thinly. The sky does most of the work. You can watch rain from far off steering over the land, and so look around you in time. At the horizon, which is only the horizon because I am five foot ten, the fen peters out, edged but not ended – a bank or a line of willows is merely in the way. Being there would be the same as being here. If I was five foot eleven I could see more, but not much. To see further I would need a mast or a crow's nest.

There is a story from hundreds of years ago that is told and repeated in various histories of the fens about a sea fish, a cod, taken to market in 1626 from the Wash to Cambridge, splashing in a wooden barrel of seawater as the boat that carried it and others sailed inland from the salt to the sweet. Keeping fish fresh by carrying them alive to market was not unusual. A hundred years later, in 1724, Daniel Defoe noted horse-drawn wagons hauling fish through the fens: 'tench and pike, pearch and eels ... [in] ... great butts fill'd with water'. But Cambridge was also a port and much arrived there by boat. The coat of arms of the town – fifty miles from the North Sea at the Wash – included three ships and two seahorses. The city market was busy and barges and boats from the sea often blocked the Cam. When the cod was opened at a fish-woman's stall, a book wrapped in a piece of canvas fell from the fish's guts. It was 'much soyled and defaced, and couered ouer with a kind of slime & congealed matter'. The mess on the gutting slab was given the name of *Book-Fish*.

Someone's book, an inland indoors thing, had fallen overboard and been swallowed into the belly of a fish, and so carried across the lost sea of the fens to a city of stone and readers. The book was made up of three separate religious texts that had been written in prison by an early-sixteenth-century protestant reformer called John Frith: 'The Preparation to the Cross and to Death', 'A Mirrour, or, Glasse to know thy selfe' and 'A Briefe Instruction, to teach a person willingly to die, and not to feare death'. It was a sort of fish-supper, or *Compleat Angler*, for the soul.

The last great thaw in the northern hemisphere began 11,000 years ago. Calculations made of the former extent and thickness of the ice suggest that, after it melted, the sea level rose eustatically (uniformly around the world) by 300 feet. Many fields were lost beneath the waves. Previously, when the sea was locked away in ice to the north, the bed of what we now know as the North Sea made a 'great lowland plain' of dry accessible land, riddled with the rivers Rhine, Thames and Trent (each far longer then than now). In those days a horse might walk east and unhindered from the grass-topped western cliff edge of Ireland all the way through Europe and Asia, across the grassed Bering Bridge and on to the valley of the Greasy Grass River in the middle of the Great Plains of North America.

In the summer of 1929 the fishermen of the *Colinda* out from Yarmouth, trawling between the Leman and Ower Banks, north-east of the Norfolk coast, dredged up from 120 feet of salt water a piece of what they called *moorlog*, the brown fibrous remains of freshwater peat. Breaking it open they found what they thought was a 'harpoon', a pointed piece of worked bone some inches long, serrated on one side with well-fabricated teeth. In fact it was a farm tool, not a fish tool: a Danish Mesolithic implement dating from around 6500 BC, a time when the seabed was worked as a field.

The book lost overboard and carried inland in the belly of a cod here finds its echo or half-rhyme: a man's hand-tool from the land, lost and left, first within the earth and then buried at sea, netted to the surface and carried ashore.

* * *

Other books have come from the earth of the fens over which the cod and its book sailed. Two appeared in the middle of the Second World War made from the few flat acres of Adventurers' and Burwell Fens. At a time of national crisis, when the very earth of Britain was under threat, the fen soil was tilled variously into service. The copies I have of the two are printed on thin but precious wartime economy paper, onion skin to the touch. They are oppositional documents, enemies of one another, and record a battle over a single fen – what it meant, what it was for, and how people might live from it. The battle, in some ways, pitched onions against fish.

The two books, Eric Ennion's *Adventurers Fen* and Alan Bloom's *The Farm in the Fen*, are about precisely the same place: the fen and the fields one mile north-west of where I live. Thirty years ago, as a visiting student birdwatcher, I saw a barn owl overtaken by a hunting male hen harrier there, and this secured the place as always worth watching. Today as I travel towards it, as I have done hundreds of times in the last few years, even when it is still hidden by its surrounding earthen aqueducts carrying away its water, I find I am raising it in my mind's eye and wondering what it will hold.

Snowlight on the fen after an overnight fall. Its white gold spread evenly, a universe of snow: nothing excluded, everything covered. Fields transformed into rooms, walled and ceilinged in muting pink. The whole fen padded. Not a whisper of wind. I talked to myself as if at home as I walked across the sheeted floor. Below me, a dentist packing a tooth, or the squeak of kapok. The sun, an old orange light bulb, eventually leaked through the ceiling, a stain from upstairs. My eyes burned with the spirit glare of reflected snow: the white razorlight pressing from the ground was brighter than the sky. All about me the stopped air ticked like a tube-train rail. Some sort of crystal set had been lowered over the fen. Tiny live-wire *seeps* of meadow pipits came across the frost. Hares moved off stiff-backed with their odd, humping limp. Their long hind legs afflict them with a kind of virile disability, as if to walk were always more taxing than to run.

The snow had come with wind. In the village, the north-east side of both church towers was white; it was the same with the willows on the road, the lower legs of the pylons on the fen, and the reed flags along the ditch: a carpet, flicked from one angry quarter only, had crept up the walls of the room. There were some pigs in a field, in the snow they looked like naked people. Under a hawthorn thrushes had gathered, arriving on hurried flights – the snow made everything fly as if startled into the air. The birds came whiffling down into a space too small for them, crowding into a clear patch of ground the size of a spread handkerchief: two blackbirds and two fieldfares with a redwing more nervous at the edge of the ring. With the desperation of displaced people they had half abandoned and half redoubled their territoriality. The blackbirds – a male and a female – launched themselves upwards from standing jumps to snatch berries from the thin low-slung branches above them. I saw them come back down on the earth with the frozen haws, the colour of old blood, jammed in their beaks. They threw their heads back and swallowed. The fieldfares and the redwing waited.

Thirty years ago, in what seems now like an ancient Elizabethan winter of iron cold and hard freeze, the fens flooded and then fixed: a new Greenland cast in ice. I came out of Cambridge with friends, nudging a car down a slippery road, and we stopped and I put on borrowed Dutch skates and slid across the utter quiet of a frozen field. An iced mist tinkled from one side of the flood to the other. Our voices and the scratch of our skates came back to us. I grew bolder and undid the brass buttons on my old khaki greatcoat, trying to make a sail or wings to catch any wind but there was none. We were somehow inside an outside place.

The flood was only a foot deep and it had frozen solid, and apart from a few milky clouds it had set clear. Clear like old glass is clear: yellowish, a little bumpy and not quite true. Moving out over the fen was like being able to slide over the roof of a Victorian greenhouse. Even as it was freezing the water had passed across the field and the icing flood had stirred the grass until it was fixed in rippling waves and looked like a long-exposure photograph taken as a tide rises into a weedy rock pool. There were imprisoned bubbles strung through the grass stems like wall-eyed pearls. The ice had trapped the earth's breathing.

Burwell is the nearest village to Burwell Fen and Adventurers' Fen. It had an unfinished *burh* or castle that was built on the orders of King Stephen in 1144 to oversee the rebellious Geoffrey de Mandeville who was pillaging across the fens from his captured base at Ely. The castle duly drew Geoffrey in and he attacked it from its watery side but was mortally wounded in the process. The Adventurers came long after the village and its castle were founded, and maybe never *came* at all: they were the investors who put money into fen drainage in the 1600s, the backers of delvers, dykers and ditchers, the fen equivalent of hedge-funders or enclosers. A document from 1717 marks a drained fen as *Adventure land*. But long before (and long since) the fens were (and have remained) risky places for pillage or adventure, indeed for almost every project undertaken on their shifting ground.

Nonetheless the *fens* are almost entirely *Fens* now. Naming them and draining them began at the same time. The capital men made capital Fens. Fen scale became human; they were branded, like wild horses, with a big letter that cut straight ditches and right angles in their swamp and made their wet someone's. Yet once it was all one fen, not just these acres west of Burwell, but for dozens of miles in all directions, and all of it without edge but for the hills to its sides and the sea at its mouth. Lower-case fens were wider, wilder and unbound. They slipped more fishily from the grasp, wanting wet, and beyond all measuring. And in the little letter something of the creep of water over land survives if only in the imagination: f is for flood.

The *fen* is the haunt of Grendel, the grim demon, and other monsters in *Beowulf*. Our word comes from the same Old English (Anglo-Saxon) *fen*, meaning marsh, dirt or mud. The word is shared across the swamp-lands of Europe with Old Frisian, Old Saxon, Middle Dutch, Old High German, Old Icelandic and Gothic: all the places where the living have liked to put the unwanted living and other, deader, bodies in bogs.

The commonality of wetness, uncertain footing, and the ordinary stuff that surrounds us but which clings unclean, can be traced still further back to both the words for marsh or mud in Sanskrit, *páñka-s* or *paṅka*, and Indo-European, *pen-* or *pon-*.

When it came into language, in what is now Cambridgeshire, the fen world was divided into two. Later the terms could be defined and discussed, originally they were lived as fact: there were winter grounds and there were summer grounds. Something solid was sought beneath the wet: winter grounds were places where you could stand in the winter and not drown; summer grounds were wetter places that were only dry enough during the summer months. Any map, to begin with, was thinly filled. Appearing out of the wet, parcels of land were identified when they meant something, earning a name if they could be visited to graze animals or mow hay or dig peat or cut litter (reeds and sedge and other marsh plants) before the water returned and it all became fen again. The following summer the names would come back as the drowned land rose once more, like mud- or sandbanks lifted into being as a tide falls.

Once draining began and took hold over centuries, the fens thickened with names and kept them through the year. *Fen* itself became one of the commonest suffixes to place names in Cambridgeshire. As well as Sedge, Turf, Mow and Cow Fen, there was Rushfenne, Oxefen, Hoggesfenne, Bullockes Fenne, but also Snytefen (snipe fen) and Purfenne (bittern fen). From around 1200 the word *feld* for field appears commonly on maps and documents. Fens were called fields when they were drained and brought into use. In the fens the word field doesn't have the old meaning of 'open country' – *fen* meant that. *Field* meant, as in our modern sense, a somehow 'enclosed area': Grasfeld, Pesefeld, Whetefeld, Stubbilfeld, Cleyfeld, Chalkfeld, Peetfeld, Smethefeld (smooth), Clenefeld (free of weeds), Wildefeld, Medowefeld, Falowfeld, Somerfeld, Honiefeld (sticky), Brenfeld (burned), Foxfeld, Sparwefeld (sparrow), Finechefeld, Crowfeld, Hartfeld.

Though they are all around me, I don't know any of these fields within Burwell or Adventurers' Fen by name. The fields still have them, farmers call their acres something, and there are signs on the fens where the nature reserves begin and end. But the fields that I know, I call by other names: the field where the pylons march like winter trees; the field where we saw three owls – a little, a tawny and a barn – in three quick minutes; the whinchat ditch; the badger field; the field where the car crashed into the tree; the magic field where Ade, the birdman, sees rare plovers; the fly-tip lane; the crane field.

A dun day after a thaw. The grassy fen at Burwell looked like a dead lake. Several inches of snow had covered the ground for more than a week and in that time the earth hadn't received its usual junk from above. When the melt came anything that had arrived on the snow's surface was just beginning to be incorporated into it, like a body being moved through a glacier, but now it was dumped greasily about the flattened, school-dinner grass: snapped teazels, blown straw, blue string, the body of a herring gull, and a cattle-tramped discus of ice on the hard bare earth around a gate, like a jellyfish on a beach.

Sounds travelled again. A light aeroplane fiddled. The rim of the fen bumped with gunshots. Padded jackets were going after pheasants and machines were scaring pigeons. A string of skylarks settled ahead of me, the end of the line looping close to the leader, tying a knot. Roe deer sat down on the fen once more like sandcastles. The cables sagged lower between the pylons and dripped as I walked beneath them.

On Tubney Fen, the stymied pool melted from its middle and ducks, survivors of the freeze, crowded in to talk: the soft frog pulse of teal, *whew*ing wigeon, the *crick crack* of gadwall and shoveler. Around midday they fell quiet and drowsy. Across the unruffled water I watched one after another look over its shoulder and twist its head over its back and tuck it between its wings and its body. They were folding themselves away to sleep: their bills hidden, one eye buried in feathers, the other, a button flat to the sky, shutting in the warmth of the thaw.

The next day, in the inch of spring sun, the plough-pressed ridges of turned soil along the bare fields shone like fish-scale, and the water in the lodes rainbowed with clay oils: some marrow was moving again through the buttery land beneath the peat.

* * *

27

I went to Peterborough on the western side of the fen basin to inspect the reduced world of the shrunken fens, walking eastwards down the slightest of inclines to Holme Fen. Nearby, in 1851, Whittlesey Mere was drained, the last fen mere to have its plug pulled. The year before it had been one of the largest lakes in England. When its water had gone, a green-painted iron column, said to be from the Crystal Palace Exhibition hall, was sunk into the ground half a mile from the south-west margin of the mere, on the peat fen at Holme. It was hammered in until it disappeared, twenty-two feet pushed deep into the damp skin of the earth. The column's base rested on solid clay, its top was level with the surface peat.

The water was pumped from Whittlesey in a matter of days. Locals strapped planks to their feet to walk on the mud and gather the fish that were drowning in air. Eels and others were taken by the ton from the drying mere to Birmingham and Manchester. When it was fully drained the lakebed gave up a censer and an incense boat, which the last Abbot of Ramsey had lost in his watery flight from the Dissolution Commissioners of Henry VIII. The skeleton of a *grampus* (a dolphin of some species, possibly a killer whale) was also found, a leftover from more marine times. The water birds of Whittlesey went with its water. Previously, eight punt-gunners had made a living shooting its ducks. Three thousand wildfowl had been taken from the decoy on Holme Fen in one week. Eight bitterns or *butterbumps* had been shot on Whittlesey in one day.

Holme Fen now is thick with sickly looking silver birches that thin at their tops to scratchy headaches. Trains on the east coast mainline shake past, drumming the ground and making the treetops judder. The green metal column at the wood edge is surrounded by taller birches like a lamp post in an overgrown town. And, like the trees but not quite as fast, it is pulling up out of the soil. Its crown is now twelve feet clear of the earth, an iron-green stick in the birch-crowded sky.

All those who were once alive and have died since, you think, and all that rot, the corruption of what Thomas Browne called the *aftergrave*, but so much less earth to keep the bodies in: where did it all go? The column grows at Holme out of the death of the surrounding soil, revealed by the earth's loss and wastage, like a fossil tree exhumed, a bog splinter of rust, and alive only in its long dying because of the quicker death and vanishing of that which once blackly cloaked it underground. The column hasn't grown. The earth – the world, here – has shrunk.

Between the trains, the woods at Holme Fen were quiet. One great spotted woodpecker called. *Quit.* A party of tits dabbed through the sticky treetops like Christmas lights, feeble against the day. I took a last look at the post. The plug is still in but around it the cold black bath has drained away.

The first of the two books about Burwell and Adventurers' Fens was *Adventurers Fen* by E. A. R. Ennion, published in 1942. Eric Ennion was born in 1900 and grew up in Burwell. His father was the general practitioner in the village and Ennion also trained as a doctor but spent much of his adult life as a naturalist and painter of birds. His line drawings illustrate his book: he makes a perfect black-tailed godwit out of twenty strokes of a pen; his drake tufted duck, smaller than my smallest fingernail, is dense with duckishness. After the war Ennion was prominent in the founding and running of some of the first bird observatories and field-studies centres in Britain. But it is as an artist that he is remembered today. His eye comes from the fens. You would know this after a single hour on what remains of his home patch. The splash of light across flat land and the wateriness of water is everywhere in his paintings. He used watercolours almost exclusively and his pictures, especially of watery birds in watery places – ducks, waders, kingfishers, wagtails – are all fluid. Everything depicted is close to dissolving into his paper with a thin silvery wash. Nothing stands still. Each bird seen has been moving through water-lit air up until the very moment he has caught it. He can paint the nothing of the wind as well.

Ennion was a proper birdman, a seasoned looker, and one reason why his pictures still seem fresh and valuable is that he repeatedly caught the ineffable this-ness of the birds that he painted, their quintessence, instress or jizz. In 1972, when I was ten, the RSPB magazine, *Birds*, featured an interview with Ennion and a double-page colour spread of a superb painting that drenched me then and which I can still recall: a party of around twenty spotted redshanks (I'd never seen one in 1972) have just landed in a pool of clear water at Minsmere (a much desired but unvisited destination for me then) and are swimming after fish fry. Most of the birds are upending like ducks, each is angled and moving differently, many are reflected on the water and some are visible beneath the surface with their eyes intent and their beaks widening after the tiny fish. Ennion's painterly modesty – an austere palette and thin watercolours – has a remarkably strong effect, recreating the spangled sensation of surfacing after a dive into a lake. No other bird painting has gone in so deep or stayed so fresh – so *undried* – in my mind.

In Ennion's terms, Adventurers' Fen runs almost to the back gardens of Burwell. His chapters give a little history of the villages and wildlife of the parishes round about, but his book is mostly an elegy for the fen and the wet and wild decades between the First World War and the Second when what had previously been half-drained reverted to swamp. It is an elegy because, as part of the war effort, the fen was drained once again and dried and ploughed to agricultural land. Hence the second book got from these fields. *The Farm in the Fen* appeared in 1944 and is by Alan Bloom. It takes over where Ennion leaves off. Before the war, Alan Bloom had a nursery further west in Cambridgeshire (he has a perfect name for a plantsman), but he wanted more land (for plants at first and then for crops) and he felt that sodden acres of fenland languishing 'unimproved' were a crime in hungry wartime Britain.

Ennion loved the world of wet for its implacable and unownable spread, its enabling recklessness and the wild gifts that brought; Bloom needed to make a living and wanted the soil to turn for him, and the water be made useful, and only the things that he had nominated to grow (both functional and beautiful). In this way the two men were enemies, but I see them set down on the fen as one: its little acres so lovingly and humanly known, its oozy truculence so accurately and tellingly told.

I never met Alan Bloom, but I did once, aged thirteen, sit in a classroom to listen to Eric Ennion talk of turning the wetlands of his life (Adventurers' Fen, the Northumberland coastline, the water-meadows around Flatford Mill) into field sketches and watercolours. He held in his small, doctorly, hands a portfolio, and opened it in front of us to show, in one wet sheet or watery fresco after another, the fixtures he had managed, superbly, to take down in the slippery world. He propped his pictures against his chest, slipping from one saturated scene to the next, surrounded, as it now seems, by the costume or weeds of his defeat. His suit was ruddy worsted: an old ploughed field flecked with flints and the sown stars of scarlet pimpernel and bird's foot trefoil. A field of his enemy, in this way, the nurseryman Mr Bloom, who came himself, marvellously, in his later years to look like *his* opposing field: a gardener who got wilder as he got older and jumped the fence, grew his white hair until it was Crazy Horse long, and slung a brassy earring above his cheek like a gypsy moon.

The fog was everywhere but thickest on the fen, for that is the lowest ground and the air knows it – the land has been underwater before. The sky leaked. Through its emulsion, I couldn't make out much, but I heard snipe as they crisped up and away, one after another, four flushing ahead from the wet grass, two to my side, and I imagined their gimlet bills worming a hole through the day. An invisible lapwing called. The bare elder in the middle of the fen reared like branching coral. The grass at my feet pulsed. The mist and the moist earth became one. I caught again the strike of snipe wings and they burned like sedge-lamps for an instant before they faded, melding with the curtained ring of fog that kept pace with me. If just once you could reach this and part it you might find the snipe on the far side chatting amongst themselves in sunlight, loosening their upholstered tweeds, smoking.

On a rare-bird twitch one winter weekend in the late 1970s I travelled from Bristol to a field near Canterbury in Kent. It was cold. The dawn was slow to come; the day concussed with fog. My friends and I walked along a farm track between cabbages and steamed in our coats like horses. Around our moving feet the cabbages were vividly bright, those just a few yards beyond cold-cooked to grey. Somewhere beyond the beyond was a vagrant male great bustard, a refugee from central or eastern European grasslands in all probability, and, wonderfully, after an hour or so an amateurish breeze got up between a few cabbage stalks and nudged the fog just enough for the walking bird to appear, sandy brown, vast, and as improbable as a camel. There is a story that in 1801 on Salisbury Plain a man wrestled for an hour with a great bustard that was attacking his horse. Watching the looming bird stepping heavily in and out of the Kentish fog I could believe it.

What Eric Ennion calls Adventurers' Fen is now more commonly known as Burwell Fen. The names have been somewhat muddied over the last hundred years. Bloom uses both. Here, I call the grounds between Reach and Burwell Lode, Burwell Fen, and the smaller fen to the north of Burwell Lode that abuts on to Wicken Fen, Adventurers'. Most present-day maps say the same.

It is not surprising that the names of the two adjacent fens have slipped across the water and between the peat. For some decades in the last century they were farmed together; at times they were both swampy places; at other times Burwell was farmed and Adventurers' was fen. Both are now owned and managed by the National Trust. They have signs as well as names. Adventurers' Fen has been a rough grazed part-fen since Alan Bloom's attempt to farm it stopped at the end of the Second World War. It is currently fenced and is a mix of scrawny grass and reedy pools; Highland cattle graze it and snipe live in it. Burwell Fen is being newly returned, via grazing, to fenland after a longer period under the plough. It too was undertaken during the war.

To date, Burwell Fen is the most substantial expression of what the National Trust calls the 'Wicken Vision', its project for the *rewilding* of the fens. Wicken Fen was the first nature reserve to be owned by the Trust. The fen was taken into care in 1899. Now the Trust is trying to collect adjacent farm properties south from Wicken whenever possible. The plan is to buy somewhere between 10,000 and 15,000 acres of the fens towards Cambridge and take them out of arable farming and return them to wetter grounds, reducing the amount of drainage, raising the water table, and converting the fields to swampier places, thereby coaxing back the *bogbumpers*: the bitterns, the crakes, the cranes and all the rest.

From the air or on a map Burwell Fen is an isosceles triangle, like a green slice of cake narrowing west. The lodes flowing away from the villages of Reach and Burwell form its two long sides. The point of the fen triangle is made where the lodes join to flow on together towards the River Cam at Upware. At this sharp corner there is a captured pond on the fen, separate from the waters flowing on either side of it. Common terns breed on the pond and kingfishers fish. Behind it are some debauched willows at the site of an old building, long gone, called Pout Hall. Green woodpeckers and little owls like this place. The remainder of the fen back towards Reach and Burwell is a series of rough open fields, half fenced, half ditched. As well as collapsed winter grass there is some sedge, a line or two of shivering reeds, dark patches of stiff thistles and burrs and smaller stains of nettles and docks. Young beef cattle have been grazed on Burwell Fen since it was taken out of more active agricultural service in preparation for its *rewetting*. They share the grass with roe deer. A near-ruined corrugated-iron barn is sinking in the middle of the fields. The base of the triangular fen is a lesser ditch, dry at the moment, running between the lodes. Further east of that, the rough fields end and a few arable plots – rape and wheat in recent years – take over until the scrubby-wooded edges of Burwell village appear.

Perhaps nowhere in fenland truly is drained, but Burwell Fen has been particularly wet. It was a low place even in the terms of the wider low country and it functioned for hundreds of years as a kind of soak-away for the surrounding slightly higher fens. Its acres were among the very last to be drained. Wicken Fen has never been drained. The village of Wicken just to the north gets its name from *wicha*, meaning a dairy farm. It is mentioned in the Domesday Book of 1086 and reminds us that it would be wrong to think there haven't always been people *close* to the fens. Nowadays, thanks to the Adventurers and then to the farm in the fen and its wartime labours, you can drive out of Burwell to both fens (and so on to Wicken too) on a metalled dead-end lane called Factory Road (some maps call it Little Fen Drove). Along it, between the village and the fens, there is an old brick kiln, an electricity station approached by heavy swags of cabling, and a cardboard factory. There is also a hedge of wild plum trees where lesser whitethroats sing in late April, and a ditch at a field edge that seems to be a memory lane for migrant wheatears and whinchats, capturing a few of them for a day or two most springs and autumns. One December morning not long after dawn, I watched an elderly Indian man in a belted winter coat marching briskly down the road from the village, flushing dopey pheasants from the verge as he went. One hundred yards behind him, his wife (I assume) followed, her pink sari blowing tightly around her and then flapping like a flag in the licking wind as she hurried towards the fen and her husband. Both were wearing bright-yellow trainers.

Adventurers' and Burwell Fens both lie in Burwell parish. Parishes on this eastern edge of the fens are mostly shaped as long thin strips running roughly east to west. They commonly have three parts. Westernmost is the fen, once the lowest and the wettest third, a peatland of waterlogged grass and reeds, criss-crossed with waterways and flood-prone and sometimes submerged for months. It was once the way to the sea. The middle part rises slightly on chalky loam to the east and was the beach to the fen. This was the place to live and to build your churches, shops and pubs. Burwell had ten in Ennion's day, nowadays the village has four, perhaps three: one is boarded up and its wall lettering that had announced it as The Crown was reconfigured as *Whore* for a week or two by some village jokers before being removed altogether. The soil in this middle third of the parish is paler than the peat, stony and drier, but there are freshwater springs bubbling through the chalk. The easternmost part of the parish rises higher again towards Suffolk. Its sandy boulder clay once grew forest or heath. It was bustard country then. For a long time only the skirt-land around the villages beside their springs would have been laid out in fields: the fen was too wet, the heath too dry and forested.

Lodes were cut or co-opted from streams, probably by the Romans, and straightened further in the eighteenth and nineteenth centuries. They took water from the eastern uplands down on to the fens' innumerable channels, eventually feeding to rivers and so to the sea at the Wash. Before the fens were drained the villagers' lives mostly faced the water. Villages had hythes or quays on their lodes and people travelled west by boat. Paths, among them the Icknield Way linking East Anglia with the Thames valley and the Wiltshire downs, cut south-west to north-east along the parishes' eastern edges making a corridor for feet between the heath and the fen.

For most of these parishes wet feet were the norm, hence webbed feet the myth. Fen people stuffed fresh grass in their boots to cool their toes in the summer, but they still preferred them dry. In Burwell, Ennion remembered, 'most able men would live with one foot on dry land and the other aboard a boat'. Their houses echoed the shape of the parish, long and thin, boat-like, running from the dry into the wet, their east gable-end to the road, their west fen-end looking towards the water. People built barges in their back gardens and launched them from there, transforming a terrestrial animal into a marine one: 'it seemed as if some great dinosaur were being assembled . . . and slowly the gaunt frame *turned into a whale* as they nailed on the barge's thick plank skin and tarred it all over a shining black'.

After the fens were drained the villagers looked in the same direction as before – west, always west – but now their lives faced the grass. At the bottom of their gardens, as in a dry dock, their old boats rotted in the peat, while the old hythes were still visible as a 'green depression in a field'.

'The only fish that can swim backwards is an eel,' Hilaire Belloc wrote in one of his fenland essays. Perhaps this isn't true but the eel is certainly the best fen fish for the sometimes salt, sometimes sweet waters; for the once dry land now drowned now dry again; for wet grass turned elver; for Ely, island of eels. Aristotle thought eels grew out of the mud. Izaak Walton, writing from the wet heart of the fen-fixing seventeenth century, wasn't so sure and kept his options slippery: the 'putrefaction of the earth' might breed them or 'divers other ways'. Eels have skin not scales and the very largest ever caught in the fens (which weighed

35

twenty-five pounds) was not hooked but *shot*. In cold winters they were thought to clamber from the water into soft earth to sleep. In the severest weather they were known to climb into a stack of hay in a meadow on dry ground and bed themselves there. Turf cutters wore eel-skin garters to fend off rheumatism. At one time in Ely, eels were a destination, a punishment for the wicked: St Dunstan, who re-established the monastery there in 970, insisted on the celibacy of his priests and 'all those who disobeyed the order of the saint were, with their wives and children, transformed into eels'. In other times eels were a crop. They fed the people. Eel-cake, Walton said, was eaten 'like as bread'. And being valuable they were transformed into money. In the medieval fens there was a currency in *fish-silver*, also called *phisshe-silver*. Debts, rentals and tithes were paid in *eel-stickes* (twenty-five eels per stick). These bundles, in their vain suggestion of the straightening of the sinuous, are paradigmatic tokens of man's efforts in the fens. As if you could clasp an eel. Or keep one in your purse.

A dull near-colourless midwinter day hung with badges of the times. A day for a Flat Earth Society. Ely Cathedral, a gunmetal tanker run aground across the fens, was the only bright thing in the ring of grey. Because it is taller than anything else, the body of the church pulled the sun from further away, capturing the weather that was over the horizon, living longer in the little light. In Burwell old dogs wobbled in tight green coats. The posh horses in Reach were saddled in blankets. At the row of houses along Factory Road people had driven their cars right up to their living-room windows and wrapped them in black tarpaulins. At Upware handwritten signs offered 'Horse Carrots' and 'Home Growen Vegetables' between garish roadside shrines: a failed bonfire of MDF and Formica; the seaweed mess of discarded clothes spilling from split carriers; and dog turds picked up and bagged in blue, but tossed and hanging as scrotal ornaments in a bald blackthorn. The two streets of fen bungalows looked like Atlantis inland, sunken castles, moated and overgrown by their firs and flags, with dark hedges of leylandii and the snapping cross of St George periscoping above.

Few people lived out on the fen proper. Even today, despite the

36

pumps and the drains, the nuzzling drone of machines and the straight dug lines, there are not many houses at sea level or below it. The parish shape still applies and it has sunk into the mind of the place even if it is no longer necessary to live by it in order to keep floodwater from lapping at your bed. If you plan to stop on the fens it remains best to be ready to move on quickly. You must either fortify your house with fir trees and barking dogs or live in something with wheels. Nowhere in the flatlands is fixed and the area feels *gypsy* to this day. *Pikeys*, they call them in Burwell from the token security of the village's one or two brown contour lines lifting it out of the wet, though at the moment the gypsies are likely to be Polish or Lithuanian. At the field edge next to some leeks near Tubney Fen, five mouldy white caravans were parked like great skulls dug from the black peat around them. On the east edge of Burwell Fen a kind of wagon train outspanned on the soggy prairie with huts and trucks pulled into a forlorn circle. I watched a man struggling over the grass towards the camp with a fridge somehow tied to the back of his bicycle. Piebald and skewbald ponies are tethered nearby, horsepower under the pylons. A recycled advertising banner for Benetton clothes of a girl's face looking skywards had been lashed as a roof of sorts to one of the huts. I saw gulls jink to one side of it as they looked down when flying over the thirty-foot lipstick pout.

Towards dusk the sky crowded with air-minded birds. For grey weeks in winter the whole day is tilted towards its end, and the sky always promises more life than the land. As the light fails, everything appears to be heading home. Twelve waxwings hurried over Upware in a flying brown diamond looking for last berries in the hedges. Nine magpies pranged into a single ash tree. Buzzards clenched on fence posts like dark fists. Gulls planed sensibly overhead. A great assembly of rooks and jackdaws was noisily underway on the fen, restive and festive before their roost; a cormorant steered through the tumbling corvids like their lizard king. A raven, a fen rarity, croaked once along the sky edge, its black hammered far away in some ancient smithy and still cooling. Below it, lapwings plotted a ploughed field, heads into the wind, crested like isobars. When I got too close the birds rose as soft black smuts.

Their round wings looked like feathered hooves pushing at the sky. As they climbed I noticed golden plovers among them, slighter and paler, cutting their own channels in the air. And strings of starlings flew between both waders, twisting through the flock, dotting and dashing it like punctuation. They had been mixed haphazardly across the field, but each species took to the sky at the moment its own blood did, regardless of what its immediate neighbours were up to. The golden plovers went first, then the lapwings, last the starlings, and the field was cleared like a game of pelmanism, the spaces where each species had stood opening around the remaining birds until eventually they all left and the field was emptied.

I don't know any sexier lines in literature than the sequence in Book VII of Milton's *Paradise Lost* that describes the sixth and last day of creation when animals crawl out of the soil into life. Among other things, the poem explains how Adam was made out of dust, how the human race fell into farming and scrabbling around in the dirt (for both a living and as a place to keep our dead), and how we will all end up down there. But its most sensational lines – writing you feel as well as read – are about the earth turning and its birthing of cattle, lions, leopards, lynx, tigers, deer and an elephant. It is amazingly done: ductile and mimetic of movement in a rather woozy half-awake tense that perfectly captures a coming into the light as, with the strange and oddly erotic sense of a film being run backwards, the decay and rot of things to dust and dirt is played in reverse. Life shakes free of the dark and creatures are disinterred before us as the earth quakes alive:

> . . . out of the ground uprose
> As from his lair the wild beast where he wons
> In forest wild, in thicket, brake, or den;
> Among the trees in pairs they rose, they walked:
> The cattle in the fields and meadows green:
> Those rare and solitary, these in flocks
> Pasturing at once, and in broad herds upsprung.
> The grassy clods now calved; now half appeared

The tawny lion, pawing to get free
His hinder parts, then springs as broke from bonds,
And rampant shakes his brinded mane; the ounce,
The libbard and the tiger, as the mole
Rising, the crumbled earth above them threw
In hillocks; the swift stag from under ground
Bore up his branching head: scarce from his mould
Behemoth biggest born of earth upheaved
His vastness: fleeced the flocks and bleating rose,
As plants: ambiguous between sea and land
The river horse and scaly crocodile.

There is a fen poem in here as well. Every animal comes as a vivid impression, like a field note, of how seen things look, of how creatures stand up and move through grass as much as how they might grow out of its soil: cattle getting to their feet, a stag lifting its head into view, and blind Milton imagining or remembering how a lion rises. The lines also evoke for me all that primal fen traffic of becoming and disappearing, of wet and dry, soil and water, winter and summer, of everything (not only the river horse and the scaly crocodile) being uncertain and ambiguous between sea and land.

I like to think of Wordsworth remembering these lines in his sonnet 'London, 1802' and recalling that Milton, like him a sometime Cambridge resident, detected the fens north of the city: 'Milton! thou should'st be living at this hour: / England hath need of thee: she is a fen / Of stagnant waters . . .'

Neither Milton nor Wordsworth saw the value of pilgrimages to the wet flats but, whatever Wordsworth was remembering, Milton is cast in his poem as a dynamic operator, the sort who might coax flesh and blood from the soil, a moral and emotional dowser for natural flowing life. 'Thou hadst a voice', Wordsworth says, 'whose sound was like the sea.'

On the fen, lapwings marked their patch, mopping at the wet sky, something in their heads making them window-clean the same spot over and over. Golden plovers are differently nervous. At any one time a stipple of them through the field was fretting with doleful calls that piped softly through the big-eyed flock, their wings flexing open in panic as if they'd seen a ghost. Alarm parties went up on short flights but they were wary of rising or angling their bodies too obviously above the skyline. There were peregrines over the fields: even I sensed them, like a bee down my shirt the moment before it stings; and here was one now throwing down the grey anvil of itself through its prey, lowering all of the sky as it arrived, squeezing time into a tight ball and tripping up the light. Only then, but then obviously, did I see the meat in front of me. Thirty woodpigeons, just now stolid on the green, were smashed apart and directed hellwards, shell-shocked mad men grabbing at their dressing gowns as they rose in panic in their day room, pushing their chairs from under them in a clatter, always too slow and stupefied by the peregrine's unavoidable terms and conditions. The falcon turned, looking as ever casual and at ease, and moved, an intensifier of the air, spinning the globe beneath it, from the grass field to the bare soil where the nervous golden plovers were now due their terror. The pigeons had splattered into the sky, as if hit from above, and dispersed; the plovers coalesced, pulled in on themselves, wanting a herd and wanting to be in its heart, and they turned over as one, like fish pulled in a net, their tightening quicksilver making the hunting peregrine for the first time look lame. It rampaged on, freaking out a crow and a hare as it went. Through binoculars I could see the pigeons a mile off, collapsing into a wood. The lapwings, far and away the most visible edible things, had escaped, and they lifted into the sky again, crosspatch and cleaning it once more.

Attempts to drain Burwell Fen continued over many hundreds of years. The Romans, as well as building the lodes, may well have tried to drain the fen around the channels they were digging. Ennion believes they did. In the medieval period before 1300, villagers from Burwell enclosed and drained the fenland that was near their houses. Ennion thinks Bishop Morton of Ely, one of the succession of wealthy and powerful local clerics (although possibly half-eel beneath his vestments), also had a go at the wider fen in the fifteenth century. But the most concerted and most successful drainage, for a time at least, was undertaken in the seventeenth century when the Adventurers were active. The 'rigid grid' of field shapes on the fen is evidence, the landscape historian Christopher Taylor wrote, of 'massive drainage and reclamation'. In the mid 1600s, the Adventurers were allotted 2,600 acres of fen in four blocks from Burwell south towards the village of Lode. A drain was cut connecting the blocks south to north and by the early eighteenth century the majority of the fenland in Burwell parish was enclosed and drained as best it could be. But the peat shrank and the fen surface lowered and water turned sluggish and hard to shift. A drainage commission was proposed in 1766 but by then the landowners of Burwell didn't want their fen drained any more. The still-deep peat was too valuable as a fuel resource and they thought drainage would destroy it. Landowners to the south were keener on drier fields and the villages henceforth split and went their own ways.

Over the next hundred years various new drains were dug, wind was co-opted to help, and pumps set running so that the flow of the water across the wider area was manually changed about. The Romans had started this by turning the natural south-west to north-east drainage through right angles by digging the lodes, the Adventurers corrected this with their purpose-built drain, but then in the eighteenth and nineteenth centuries wind-pumps on the banks of the Cam pulled the water at right angles again from its original flow.

Burwell Fen had got wetter, and despite its value for peat cutting the landowners woke up in the nineteenth century and decided they wanted it drained. But they were too late and the adjacent waters on the neighbouring fens were already being whipped into shape in ways that couldn't help Burwell, so the Burwell drainage commission, set up in 1841, had to cut a new drain – called the Engine – following the line of Burwell Lode to their own steam pump at Upware: 'this proved to be', Christopher Taylor says, 'a serious mistake, for they were in effect trying to make water run uphill'. It didn't work and most of the fen was waterlogged by the time Eric Ennion moved to Burwell as a four-year-old boy in 1904. When he first knew the fen a few years later the

Adventurers' field shapes were more than part-hidden, there were flooded turf pits, peat-shrouded bog oaks crumpled the surface, and the place was sodden: it looked like it might have done in the fifteenth century before the great drainage years began.

Though it was a swamp it was alive with people. The locals had long known how to use its wet. Before he gets to the birds in his book, Ennion describes a productive and busy fen, a part-wild part-farmed place crowded in a way that is inconceivable nowadays. There were always people in every field and on every fen. Even with today's caravans of vegetable pickers and the travellers' stalled wagon train on Burwell Fen, it is hard to picture the place moving with working people: reeds and sedge scythed for thatching; ducks and fish trapped for food; peat dug for fuel; litter or what Ennion calls the 'welter' of marsh plants cut for coarse hay. As a boy Ennion was on the fen so often that he was on personal terms with some of its fish. He could tell one chub from another by the slight variations in their shape and by the differing patches of white fungus on their scales. There were eels, tench, perch, roach and bream too and also the mysterious (and now extinct throughout Britain) eel-pout or burbot, a kind of freshwater cod, with three long feelers stroking its face, one over each eye and one under its chin.

Peat or turf was dug from the fen in spring, the pits growing to about six turves or three feet wide, and about three beckets (turf-spades) or four and a half feet deep. When floods came the pits filled readily. Reeds grew on the wetter part of the fen. After winter frosts stripped them of their flags, old stems of four years or more were cut for roofing and younger stems were mixed with litter for fodder. If the bottom of the reed was dry or glazed with ice it could be cut with a scythe; if wet, a reed hook – a short, toothed sickle – was used. Coopers sought the bulrushes on the fen, their long round stems were dried and placed between barrel staves where, on contact with beer or whatever else filled the barrels, the stems would swell and keep the joints watertight. Sedge was cut in the autumn by scythe and brought home by a broad-beamed boat, haystacks of it pulled up the lodes across the fen on a 'float'. The navigable lodes were kept clear by a reeve and other men who were employed to *rode* the waterways. Two men on either bank of the lode, dragging back and forth a jagged chain fixed with knives, cut waterweed and emergent vegetation. They were mowing underwater so that another crop could sail on the surface. The sedge was used for cattle bedding and as an alternative thatching material. It could last for forty or fifty years and was more durable than reeds. At the end of the summer any uncut litter died down to add itself to a future layer of peat, which could build up, Ennion said, 'by a foot every twenty years'. Osiers from willows on the fen were cut for baskets, eel traps and faggot binds; thicker branches made good scythe handles. To keep the stick swollen and the fastenings firm between harvests scythes would be stored under the fen water, like moon-slivers of rusting silver. The blade was easily rubbed clean when needed once more. The tool wanted to be wet. 'During dinner hour scythes were kept out of the sun', Ennion wrote, 'the fittings might work loose if the stick got dry. They were laid in the ditch border or heaped with an armful of litter.'

There are fen emblems and parables too of swampy metamorphoses in this: the way water goes into and out of things and breeds by itself, the parthenogenesis of wet. A bulrush in the barrel holds wetness in by its wetness, and shows how waterproofing can be done by water, an osmotic soak being best for brokering edges. A scythe stick is sent underwater having been cut from the wet fen and kept damp on the same ground under a rick of vegetation that it itself has helped to cut.

Molecatchers also had a use for willows. The soft fen earth swam with moles. Their tunnelling business made work for men. The moles' 'scribbling' was so successful at undermining banks and putting holes in dykes that each and every expert floodsman was sought out and killed. A four-foot stick of willow or elder was cut for the spring device in an underground mole trap. The stick was replanted in the buried trap and its angle at the fen surface told the moleman when the trap had sprung. The mole, caught and killed with 'a tap on the snout', was often strung up by its feet on the stick, which was replanted for a second time in the fen as a sort of combined gibbet and sandwich board for the moleman, a warning to others and an advertisement of success. John Clare, on the western edge of the fens, wrote of moles being 'hung . . . for traitors' and 'sweeing to the wind / On the only aged willow that in all the field remains'. The mole-stick often rooted and lived on: a new tree growing with a mole-fruit rotting in its crown. In Arthur Randell's deep-dug autobiography from 1970, *Fenland Molecatcher*, we find this and more: 'there were, in time, quite a number of willow trees growing in Magdalen Fen which had been "planted" in this way, and I still know, today, where there are three willows and two elders which began as mole sticks'. Thirty-five years on, I have an explanation for what I once saw on the bank of a Norfolk river on the eastern fen edge: four separate whittled branches stuck in the soil three feet apart, and on them four beaten-up furry black flags, four pairs of front feet rowing at the air like tiny human hands, with fingernails and creased palms, and four fleshy but dry pink noses pointing to the peat.

There were more days of ice before the winter was over. Thin hours of bruised sunlight, the skate scratches of contrails on the cold sky otherwise scoured of cloud, and a canine wind that blued my bent knuckles, even in their gloves. The parching air burned and the saturated ground stiffened. Mud foundered iron-hard, or 'frawn' as Eric Ennion remembered it on his winter doctor's round walking from Burwell towards Upware and the 'lonely yellow square' of a single lit window of a house on the fen. Crossing the same fields, frozen peat rattled at my feet like clinker and there were carrots scattered in the black like severed fingers. The ducks disappeared and the deer hobbled. To stop my legs slipping from under me, even on this flatness, I had to shuffle as if chained at the ankles. Everywhere the ice spoke glassily of its conquests: in reedy ditches the water froze muddy brown, in grassy ditches it was khaki, puddles on the fen solidified to bones, on the lode the wind had blown the freeze to a skin of chopped ginger. As the water thickened there, moorhens were forced out of it and up the banks, where their cumbersome reed-green legs and giant clammy feet looked like some hauled-up deep-sea by-catch. On the frozen bank otter prints crossed with hares' and both circled stone-hard molehills. The jewelled toolkit of a kingfisher flew along the lode, plumbed still to the iced trench and seeking a way through the thick vitrine that kept it from its bullheads and minnows.

Now, in the frost, the grass died to the colour of a mistle thrush's back: dead brown. Chaffinches gathered at the beet-clamp by the cattle pen on the edge of the fen, drawn there by the grains still lodged in the straw bales that walled the beets. They were hungry and, forced by hunger to shed their fear, they moved close to my feet. Like workers allowed back into the remains of a crop, they hovered at the straw, gleaning.

Around 1910 the business on Ennion's Adventurers' Fen shifted as demand for its natural produce declined. A decade of agriculture followed. Coal was preferred to turf for fuel, new roofs were tiled not thatched: 'the reedbeds stood unwanted in the fen and no one cut the sedge'. Previously the water on the fen had been part-baled by the engine at Upware and two creaky and inefficient wind-pumps on the fen edge. Now the wet was more fully banished. A new drain was dug and a tractor-driven pump installed. The fen dried out sufficiently to be planted. Its sedge was ploughed in and its deeper clay married with the top peat to 'lighten the one and stop the other blowing away'. A row of cottages called New Zealand – because they were so far from anywhere – was built, tucked in against Reach Lode on the south side of the fen. Wheat, barley, mustard, potatoes and beets followed.

The First World War was hungry but the farmed fen was short-lived. The wheat did well for a few years on the new turned soil but not for long: the peat was too light and began to blow away, it hadn't been ploughed deep enough to mix with the clay beneath it, and because of the dry surface the wheat couldn't be rolled and therefore properly bedded. Wind and rain bashed about the top-heavy stalks. And then 'the Bailiff of Bedfordshire' – floods from the Bedfordshire watershed – was always a likely visitor and, as Ennion said, 'he was to come yet again'. Daniel Defoe making his *Tour* labelled the fens 'the sink of no less than thirteen Counties', and much of central England's river water exits the country through them. The Bailiff duly called in 1920. The following decade was one of agricultural recession: after only a few seasons under the plough the fen sank back into itself, the pump wore out, winter floods took longer to drain, harvests were spoiled, cut wheat wasn't even collected and 'many a sheaf lay sprouting on the sodden ground'.

By 1930 only a hundred acres of the fen (at its corner nearest the village) was still arable land. From then until the start of the Second World War, nature reasserted itself and wildlife came back. Swallowtail butterflies reappeared. And during what remained of the harvest turtle-doves came 'in their hundreds to feast on the seeds and cool their pink toes in the mud at the sides of the drain'. The 1930s was the last decade of part-wild original swamp and part-worked man-made fenland: probably the best recent environment for nature. The National Trust might have those unloved years in its mind's eye as a model for its rewilding plans. I have never seen a swallowtail on the fens. They are extinct now. One recent September I did see two turtledoves cooling their toes just as Ennion described it, but I haven't seen more than two at any time since the 1980s.

In the winter of 1936–7 a great flood rolled from bank to bank of the fen and topped up its ground-water. Reeds began to spread, fields became reedbeds, divided only by open ditches of water that were too deep for them to grow in. The hollies that had been planted at New Zealand drowned, and the cottages there were abandoned. Their wooden floors were 'smashed by horses wandering through downstairs rooms'. Little owls took over the lease – they, at least, are still there in the patch of scrub that New Zealand now is (or was; the National Trust has recently cut the scrubby copse to the ground). The owls nested in the ruins and spat out pellets containing the beaks and crushed skulls of starlings.

Ennion says he knew every inch of the new fen and he records – and draws – Montagu's harriers and hen harriers, a vagrant lesser yellowlegs from North America, and he sees a water rail swimming (I have seen this once – it is like being privy to some secret ceremony that brings the skulking bird not only out of the reeds but into the water to swim like a high-class passenger on the Titanic, proud and hopeless). A colony of black-headed gulls painted the fen with white squawks; bitterns returned to breed like swaying reeds gathered into a stook. In 1938 black-necked grebes nested, and Ennion describes pushing his punt out on to the fen and lying all day under its canvas cover to sketch them. Spring waders passed through on migration, joining the fen to other flashes, marshes, rivers, seas and oceans, flying from Africa to Siberia and landing en route only where their feet might be covered with water. He watched and sketched, beautifully, a party of bar-tailed godwits: 'As if overtired they couldn't settle comfortably: waders always fidget when they sleep. Later they rose and circled to gain height. They flew steadily north till my glasses could find them no longer. Where were they bound? The Yenesi? Whence had they come? The Nile?'

The godwits disappear and the book ends abruptly soon after: one sentence, there is a brilliant observation (the stare of a kingfisher), and the next, a goodbye. The fen has been drained and dug to farmland once again. 'Nature cannot let sentiment usurp her laws: that is for us to feel. Adventurers Fen in all its loveliness has gone but nature goes on elsewhere.'

Ennion's old fen at Burwell is a good place now for owls. In the willed abandonment of the fields here the crops have gone and for some years rough grass has grown on Burwell Fen. More water is expected soon but for several winters the fallow has fed many things. I counted seventy roe deer on one afternoon scan. Barn owls have bred in the ruined buildings at the centre of the fen, and it is rare to walk the banks around it and not see at least one. Most winters, migrant short-eared owls from further north and east join the resident barn owls adding a sheaf of sedge to their straw. One December day thirteen were seen working the fen.

The pallor and intent of hunting barn owls configure them as winter's thing even in the heavy hum of summer evenings. They are paler than everything else around them. Outside they are all sangfroid, within they seem to burn with heat, and their eyes are like portholes on to an oven. Tawny owls – darker and more severely nocturnal – are leafed and summery by comparison; they are brown bags of soft air, bark and foliage made feathers, hewn from the woods. Barn owls, in the middle of the day, in the hovering ghost dance of their mothy obviousness, are like a moon in the sky at noon, a lantern by which to see the night, even in daylight. In their scull and swoop above the dead grass, they fly as if their wings were stiff-wired and subject to some force from below that meets and matches their hollow-boned lift. They hunt by a kind of laying-on of wings, crossing and recrossing the fen until the hidden contents of the grass are shown to them.

Short-eared owls also quarter and dive in a crash into the grass after voles. Their yellow jelly eyes burn bright. The warmth of their brown back and wings flushes like a heart above the cold fen. Their flying is easier, longer and looser winged than the barn owls', less intense, less hungry perhaps. I watched two jousting in flight, weaving around one another, their legs dangling like thick socks come out of wellingtons. Another was harried right at the edge of daylight by a late-flying kestrel and both birds towered high into the sky, the owl yapping in distress at the fluster, escaping higher, odd and gawky.

Soon enough the night comes to meet the birds. The winter sky lifts and abandons the earth to darkness. One short afternoon on the fen I felt the light being taken as the owls became part of the dusk. A short-eared owl's hare-brown back and upper wings turned to grass; nearby a barn owl's burnt cream float became the mist that rose out of the grass. As the light thickened, the dark crept along the ground, just where the owls flew. At the fen edge it was darkest of all. This middle distance, the rim of the near, is the first to declare for night.

I turned for home. A little egret appeared from nowhere and circled overhead, a nervous white towel. Looking for somewhere to sleep, it lowered its black legs towards a ditch of black water and its dangling yellow feet flashed suddenly above my head like a bunch of bananas. Two hidden nearby pheasants called their *ko-kocks* and I felt their invisible horse-shudder of wings. Lapwings lifted from the field and tumbled along, hugging close to its surface, hurrying to resettle. Last flights after lights out seem panic-stricken for all. All except for the crows, rooks and jackdaws that sail on blackly into the black, flying their history as it seems, knowing where they're going.

* * *

48

Nowadays the fens are hard to love. Love, rather, is difficult for what we have made of them. Though it has owls, Burwell Fen is a straight-sided, flat and unmistakably man-made place. At the moment it doesn't really qualify as a fen. It is just some fields. Its neighbour, the nature reserve at Wicken Fen where no Adventurers ever set foot, is a shaggy place by comparison, with large reedbeds, bold mosquitoes, booming bitterns, but also a problem. It is turning into a wood. Being the only undrained place for miles around is not easy. Its peat was deep – sixteen to eighteen feet thick in places – and protected, but when the adjacent fens were drained Wicken suffered as well. It wasn't big enough to make its own rules. The fens share a common wetness and when all those around you are sucked dry you do not escape.

Wicken proves that nowhere in crowded, man-altered, southern Britain can natural processes create and sustain a natural landscape. How then could we best live with the fens in the future? Might we redefine our tenancy over that which we have subjugated? To this end something new has crept out of the drying earth – an almost posthumous chapter in nature-conservation thinking. Our tangle with the place is to be declared – how we made the fens, altered them, ruined them even; and then, demonstrating that we have finally understood this, some knowing and kindly repairs will be proposed. The new ethos extols prefixes and is another film running backwards: rewetting, rewilding, unfarming, the undoing of doing, the managed retreat from management, the letting go via legislation of what we once ruled. And all of it will be offered with a curious half-devoted half-nervous face put forward to show how we might still love this place.

This floats all sorts of questions about projected or imagined environments. How does land management, even managed retreat, live with a dynamic landscape? Who sets the year for the climax of creation? If trees have to be felled to maintain the fen, then in what way is the fen now anything other than a farmed place? In any case, for some, dry might be better than wet. Nightingales and woodcock have liked the trees at Wicken. And I liked them both. But I also thrilled to an invisible spotted crake cracking its unworldly whiplash in a new patch of reeds through several June nights one year. Whatever we do, whether we drain or we wet, we remain thoroughly and forever implicated. To return is always as difficult as to go on.

Some of the first notions of what an ecosystem might mean – how lives work by being meshed with other lives, life alongside life – were teased out at Wicken Fen by the botanists Arthur Tansley and Harry Godwin in the early 1920s. The fen then was still naturally reedy and wet, or at least still living the long losing of its nature. Now neighbouring Burwell Fen will get wetter once again. But to replicate nature – to build an ecosystem – involves a lot of pipes. I've seen them on the fen. Taps must be turned on in order that the big field might shine its sheet of winter water once more.

Sometimes I don't mind this thought, sometimes I do. There are days when the fen feels continuous with the thronged banality of southern England: a supermarket mind, a bird list that stops at pheasants and woodpigeons, local radio news, and eventless rain. Trying to come up for air through this weather, the projected fen-future sounds like cant and looks like spin, the nonce words alerting us to the sleight of hand: *rewilding* will be a trick involving no less human interference and delivering no wilder life. And – warming my bile – isn't there something oddly self-regarding and tonally superior about the leaving of the scene as it is proposed: the bowing and scraping and walking backwards that draws more attention to the departed than to the empty stage? And isn't that a nonsense anyway? There can be no true leaving. We cannot just stop and clear off. Instead, some sort of facility is being made and, though the public noise is all about access and community benefits, what is being offered can sound, even with value-adding booming bitterns, like a reduced version of the place. In substantial part this is because wisdom about the land and any feeling for it – contact or occupancy of any kind – is being siphoned off as the sole province of experts and managers. What the former dairy farmers of Wicken know will no longer be admissible; new landowners have decided that their ecosystem was the wrong one. Rewilding will not then return the remade fens to the farmers or indeed to anyone; we have all forfeited our rights to be in them in any way that isn't mediated. Ordinariness will be banished along with muddy feet. A new sort of alienation has already been devised: the tristesse of the birdwatching hide. I can feel it now in the strange log cabin that has been erected on Tubney Fen. Nothing seen from its shelter seems as real as it does when seen from under the sky.

On sunnier days I've had still blacker thoughts. Thinking of that emptying stage, it can seem that the corporatized language boostering a one-hundred-year vision for thousands of acres has released something unexpectedly metaphysical on to the fen: an idea of life after us and life without us. Curiously, for all the positive-sounding future and for all the management needed to get there, what is proposed is a description of our profound separation from the fens and the fields, a terminal version of pastoral. Behind the new picnic tables and the bike racks an exclusion zone is being conjured, an enclosure beyond enclosure, the darkest arcadia. I could put that differently. And on good days, on and off the fen, I do. Let the water come, but let us be allowed to step into it as well, as we surely have and must for it all – wet and dry – to mean anything.

Winter is long but the end of summer and the beginning of spring press at it from both sides. In the village churchyard in mid November I had watched a red admiral sunning itself as it clung to the lettering cut into the slate gravestone of Edwin Muir, the sometime worker in a bone factory, translator of Kafka, and great poet of horses, the describer of 'that long-lost, archaic companionship' between humans and other animals. Then, the day after the midwinter solstice, from the middle of a blackthorn in the lane beyond the gravestones, a blackbird was whispering subsong, like a message sent on ahead from the coming spring. In the haunch of winter, as Shakespeare had it, the summer bird is singing the lifting up of day. June's ghost talked through the silver of finch calls and the tinsel of a dunnock. Near the blackbird a great tit sang for the first time in its life. The sun had warmed the hedge enough and the bird within it. A handle turned in its throat, its biddable brain was stoked, and the extra spoonful of light after the shortest day pulled its beak apart. After three cranks its squeak was tuned into sawing song as if it had never been silent.

Rooks, too, are early starters. Along the eastern edge of the fens where taller trees thrive in the villages, there are rookeries. Like a photographic negative of seabirds, whites for blacks, the rooks crowd their high sea-cliff trees and sail out over the waters of the fen like black gannets. At Burwell, there are three rookeries, or perhaps a single exploded one, scattered in the churchyard and in trees nearby. In Bottisham, there is a rookery in beeches at Bottisham Hall, near where Leonard Blomefield lived in the early nineteenth century and kept his *Naturalist's Calendar*. Blomefield records his rooks returning to their nest trees to roost after they have raised their young on a mean date of 2 July. Their spring starts then. They pair up in the early autumn. Every day through the winter they visit their old nests and sit beside them as they might at a bedside. On dull days you can often mistake the nest in the tall trees for the bird and the bird for the nest, until they get up to front the wind above the trees with their smoky paddle of wings, before returning to their vigil, warming their black stick bundle through the season.

An oil-painted day came after weeks of watercolour. A wet and greasy sun fingered into the western sky in a broadside of light. Mildness bowled about. Insects appeared. The hedges steamed, and the dung heap at the field edge next to the fen smoked thickly and, doing so, seemed old, an inexplicable and happy survival from some ancient world. I walked home through the fields like a bird scarer, flushing woodpigeons and pushing them ahead of me, out from the field I was in and on to the next. Pale fire was coming into the willows along the fly-tipping lane. A roebuck sprang up in front of me with new velveted antlers like gloved hands. I passed an old orchard, and I stopped because I had seen that there were fresh leaves like mouse-ears on the apple trees. And then, news out of Africa: a wheatear leapt up from the sheep's grass at the dyke's end, its white rump an invitation card, bouncing away like nothing that had lived in the fields or on the fen through the winter.

HONEYGUIDE

I grew up with no sense of what a farm in Africa meant. I didn't know there were any. I think most of the people around me would have thought the same. Karen Blixen's opening words to *Out of Africa* drew attention to this common misperception by, exotically, stating its opposite: 'I had a farm in Africa.' In my childhood, butter and lamb came from New Zealand, bacon and wheat from Canada, but nothing as far as I knew was from Zambia. From Kenya there was just ground and bitter coffee. A crushed bean from a bush didn't suggest a farm to me. It came in vacuum-sealed tins that hissed when you opened them. We had it on special occasions and I didn't like it. I remember the palaver of the percolator. Otherwise, I knew the Masai kept cattle and secured them in thorn kraals each night against predators. They drank their cows' blood, tapped from the living animals, and I used to wonder whether it tasted more like a nosebleed or black pudding. Those humped cows and their vampire masters seemed the extent of African farming to me. This was dumb even for a seven-year-old – a continent of people mostly existing at subsistence levels means there must be more farming by more people in Africa than anywhere else in the world. But those ordinary farmers were absent from any accounts I knew, and my wider confusion about what farms could be ran deep.

The first time I flew from London to Cape Town, I looked down and saw how fields, such as I thought them, barely made it across the Mediterranean. The sand of the Maghreb and then the bones of the mountains dust them out of existence. The swaddle of equatorial forests smothers the ground, permitting only rare clearings. Further south is a steaming tangle of vegetation and swamp. Only into coastal southern

Africa, the strip of temperate Africa beyond Africa, do anything like regular recognisable fields return. As I was born in Europe, a child of enclosure and settlement, a farm still means to me something other than the farming of Africa that happens between the Atlas Mountains and the Cederberg – its scratched livings, unfenced cattle, children minding goats, and tiny stands of maize next to simple one-room houses. There are big farms now of course, and rich local farmers as well as international business interests busily growing profits as they feed the world from the soil of the poorest places, but Africa still farms and feeds itself as it has done for thousands of years – those children around the goats, forever. Put it this way: throughout most of Africa the word *countryside* remains meaningless. Habitats are being degraded, forests are cut to nothing, lakes fouled, fetid shanties grow as large as cities, but the whole continent is still living *in* nature. In Africa there is only *bush*. And it runs, scratchily real and as a landscape of the mind, for 7,500 miles from north to south.

Everything here is under the sun. We'd left the fields and were almost home when we heard the call. A dirt track snaking back to the farm-house had put us on the edge of an old tobacco plot. The call came again, *chakka chakka chakka chakka*, loud over the toil of the four-wheel drive. We stopped. Once more the bird shouted against the judder of the switch off. It had come closer, and this time Lazaro, who works in the fields of the farm and knew what he was hearing, was already out of the car and answering it, his mouth full of whistling and tutting and Tonga chatter. We're coming, *kacheka kacheka*, he said. Lazaro had seen the *kacheka*, as well. Fumbling with binoculars I had managed a glimpse of a brown flycatcher-sized bird with pale undersides, far smaller than its stone-sieving call would suggest. It dropped from a high branch towards us through the air in a mock fall, fanning its tail to show white outer feathers and twisting upon itself. Having successfully caught our eyes as well as our ears, it flew on ahead. We were hooked.

A bird calls with some news for someone who is passing. Across Africa, south of the Sahara, the same bird has called to people for thousands of years for the same reason. The hunter coming home, the herdsman driving his goats, the woman carrying water from a well, her son walking back from school – all of them at one time or another have looked up to listen, and knowing what the honeyguide's call meant, they moved towards the bird and followed it. Because they have done this, the bird has kept calling and will call to you if you pass, as it called to me. It knows us for what we are. Sweet-toothed.

The honeyguide's chatter is good news. Sweet news. It has found a wild bees' nest, a hive of honey, with a combed stack running slowly with its sweet warm sap. But the prize is locked in the dark of a hollow tree. The bird has seen the bees going in and out of their hole; it knows what that means and, remembering how things are, it has gone in search of help. It loves to eat beeswax but it is not a woodpecker. Instead, the honeyguide employs us as its tool. A chimpanzee will strip the leaves from a fine twig and poke it into a narrow hole from where termites run, before sliding the stick and the insects it has disturbed through its lips. We are to play the part of the stick for the honeyguide. It will hunt, we will gather. And, as he walked towards the bird, answering its call, because he knew the deal, Lazaro had an axe in his hand.

The field edge here in southern Zambia was no longer clearly an edge at all. The field might be a field no more. Spindly but confident saplings were already advancing across it, breaking from the thirty-foot-wide wooded corridor that doubled as field edge and track-way. The bush is coming back. The new trees reached towards four old termite mounds, wooded islands rising from the tall yellow grass, never taken into the field when it grew tobacco. Pythons thicken there beneath knotted dark-leaved trees and the honeyguide calls from the canopy. Unless someone cuts at the trunks, old and new, the clearing will soon disappear, its open green eye shutting to something darker, older and shaded. Today, the honeyguide doesn't mind. People are still passing, but what will happen if Lazaro is no longer available to listen?

Perhaps humans are not essential to honeyguide happiness; perhaps there are other ways to wax. Can't they do it without us, as they must have done when we were otherwise occupied and only good for putting twigs in termite holes? No evidence exists but some have speculated that honeyguides once used honey badgers as their field labourers. It might be that the birds sacked the badgers when it became clear that people had learned, presumably by watching the badgers and the birds, and had rapidly become better at the job. It's hard to know because it is hard to watch a honeyguide without it watching you. And if we are watched and there is honey to be had, we are to be pressed into service.

For now, Lazaro was talking back to the bird. He said, in words I found myself assuming the honeyguide understood: show us what you have found. The bird obliged, thinking we were obliging it. Lazaro stepped into the field barefoot from the car, and moved his axe from his hand and slid it down his neck inside the back of his shirt until its shaft lay straight along his spine and its head faced out from above his collar. This was in preparation for tree climbing, but it also allowed him to roll and light a cigarette as he walked towards the bird. His paper was a scrap of old newspaper; his tobacco – flakes and filaments of brown crumbled leaf and stem – came from the next field. Last year's crop, planted, tended, cut and dried – all on the farm in the fields about us. His lit cigarette sent up thick grey smoke, like a smouldering bonfire of damp leaves and grass, and for a moment his faun-face was lost in a cloud. He looked out on the same scene as me but as if from another country.

After each call the honeyguide flew on 200 yards or more, sometimes straight, sometimes zigzagging, through the field trees and hedge until it reached the more continuous miombo woodland at the back of the farm. As we caught up with it there, instead of flying on, it came closer to us, buzzing about the treetops, swooping down nearer to the ground. 'One honeyguide', Lazaro said, 'showed me four hives; one hive then another then another; and sometimes, because it is interested, it showed us other things as well, a snake or a dead animal in the bush.'

Climbing wasn't necessary. The bees' nest this honeyguide had found, and brought us to, was at the foot of a *muyongolo* or snake-bean tree. Lazaro gathered twigs and a few strands of dry grass, fire was set, and smoke made to coil round the trunk. I saw the soles of his bare feet as he knelt; they looked like the cracked earth. He dug a little in the sandy soil to expose the base of the tree and hacked at it.

Smoking grass was held to the gash. Bees started seething at two exit holes higher up the trunk, driven from their comb by the smoke rising, through their nest, up the chimney of the tree. Swirled in smoke himself, with half-stunned half-furious bees crawling over his head, Lazaro reached his hand into the hole he had made and pulled out the *buchi*, the wild honey. The comb came twisting like snakeskin. It was eighteen inches long and three inches wide, a dripping tongue. He pulled at it, laughing and breaking it apart. A rope of honey ran from the chunk in his left hand to that in his right. It stretched, glooped, broke, and spilled to the ground. Something precious and potent was being desecrated so that we might eat. Lazaro passed me a piece of the chambered wafer. I felt its tug back from where I was taking it. On my palm it looked like a block of flats at sunset. There is a similar building, Soviet-style, in the centre of Lusaka. The comb itself was the colour of our fingernails, but the honey that drained from it was a uniform and clear golden-brown varnish that coated everything it flowed over. I sucked it from my fingers: the sun itself had been distilled, the forest and the field captured and concentrated. Something beyond sweetness caught at the back of my tongue and throat and burned there with the rasp of pollen or a balm that stung. I picked off two bees glued to the comb by their own honey and drowned in it in the chaos of excavation, and bit into three stories of the apartment block. In my mouth the comb was all texture. I pressed the sweetness from its gum and what was left was too chewy to swallow. I spat it out as Lazaro stuffed more dripping mess into his mouth. He ate it all. Today was a quick opportunistic feast for him, a raid on a sweet shop; on other occasions he puts the comb on a plate of bark and carries it home for his family. Now, he placed one piece back into the hollow tree, so that the bees might return, sealed the smoke hole he had made with a wedge of bark, and on the ground placed a last lump of comb for the honeyguide. In our honey lust we had lost sight of the honey bird. It had stopped calling, but sat silently in a tree a few yards away, watching us doing its bidding.

We walked back towards the car, out through the wood and across two fields. One was scrubby, the other dry and near bald; every green thing had been scorched back into the earth. It was hot. The blue of the sky was the colour of sensation, not of contemplation. It did not calm the eyes so much as stretch and drain them. The air sizzled. Birdsong was heat-flattened to weary purrs and static pulses. Drops of honey, trapped in the stubble on my chin, dried to scabs. Flies moved to any damp creases at my nostrils, lips and eyes. Underfoot the old rind of the earth crackled, like metal swarf, with a scrunch of seedpods and the foil-scuff of dead leaves. Poachers had burned all the grass to encourage new lawns which might lure antelope. The baked soil crumbled at the surface and chinked. It was impossible to imagine the stuff of honey being made in this dead field.

All things look blasted and ruined in the dry season but on the Major's farm it was worse. The Englishman had died and his Zambian widow was sick. The farm had failed. The Major had run out of cash some years back and no crops had been planted in the last season. A stoical orchard of guavas produced a few fruit but that was all. There was one prepared but unplanted field on the farm. It took eighty litres of tractor fuel to plough, and used the last of the money; there was nothing left for seedlings. There would be no tobacco that year or perhaps ever again. Royce, the dying widow, had spoken to the workers; they were free to go as they hadn't been paid since May and it was now November. It was remarkable that they were still there, that they had survived on so little, but the uncertainties of upheaval had kept most families in the compound. Lazaro, who had lived there all his forty-two years, and the other tied-hands (their homes, such as they were, came with the job) eked out a living as best they could from their one-room huts in the shadow of the idle tobacco barns. Lazaro and his family lived off *nshima*, maize-flour porridge, garnished with an occasional rat, optimistically known as 'relish'. His cigarette, as rare a treat as honey, was built from tiny threads of leftover tobacco salvaged from the barn.

Walking back, we came across a lorry pulled off the track into the trees. A gang of men around it fell quiet and looked up in surprise as we crossed their path. They were wearing town clothes and were cutting at the thicket with axes and saws, throwing branches on to the flatbed. The wood was leaving the farm, though not in order to keep the fields alive.

Perhaps we should have confronted the wood thieves. But the farm seemed beyond rescue. No one was working in its fields any longer. The farmhouse wasn't a home. The building where the Major had lived was a near-empty shell, blown of life. His fabulous egg collection and bird skins had been boxed up and shipped out and the house had been stripped. Any remaining furniture had been pushed to the room edges. On the walls, the framed family trees had been taken down, leaving stains and ghost outlines where the pictures once hung. Outside, the tractor's wheels had been stolen. It sat on its axles like a stone lion. The Major's museum for his dead birds and their dead eggs was never finished and its doors were open, the heat and dust of days bowling into the sanctuary like any other abandoned outbuilding. Old charcoal ash blew into the grass in grey drifts from the four iron ovens at the base of the tobacco-drying barn. Inside the building, green tobacco was once cured by being hung on a vaulted lattice of wooden slats and struts six shelves high. Hot air smoked and rose through the indoor forest. The cure took a week; the leaves like a sort of cud in the barn's gut, drying in the body of the building. Stepping through the low door and looking up now was like finding yourself in the skeleton of a huge extinct animal among a gantry of its bones. The smell of cooked grass was all that remained.

In the orchard, the guavas dropped from the trees and baked in their skins in the grass below. Waiting, without hope, the workers were mostly too nervous to gather the fruit themselves. Back at the farm we ate peanut-butter sandwiches that Claire had made. She was employing Lazaro as a nest-finder for her scientific fieldwork on honeyguides, studying not their honeyguiding skills but their co-evolution with the host birds they parasitise. They live, like cuckoos, by laying their eggs in other birds' nests and leaving the rearing of their young to other parents.

At the Major's, the honeyguides' wet-nurses were mostly little bee-eaters. The nest-finders call them 'John Deeres' because they are the same green and yellow as the tractors. In Tonga they are called *hatwili*

– the ones who follow the small flies. They feed on the bees that make the wax the honeyguide loves. They breed in the fields or their remnants, digging tunnels in the sandy soil, hollowing out a nest chamber two or three feet down a narrow passageway. Often they will dig into an aardvark's hole, excavating their tunnel within the roof of the ready-made burrow.

We walked back through the fields to examine a nest for signs of honeyguides. Lazaro had spotted adult bee-eaters going in and out of a hole earlier in the week. He picked a long thin stem of yellowing grass from the ground, stripped it of its seed head by passing it through his closed fist, and crouched at the entrance of the aardvark hole where a much smaller dark circle opened off it. He pushed the grass into this hole, feeling with it until, three feet in, it reached a wall of sand and could go no further. He pulled the stem out and laid it like a thin tawny arrow on the bare surface of the field above the hole. With a mattock, he dug at the earth a foot back from where the grass marker ended, scooping up palmfuls of sandy soil, slowing his actions the deeper he got, until eight inches down, the sand began to drain beneath his hands and he knew he had reached the nest chamber. He tamped the walls of the shaft he had dug and carefully picked his way towards the floor of the nest, clearing any sand that had fallen into it. There was no built structure under his hand. The female little bee-eater, having dug out the chamber, simply lays her eggs beneath her in the scrape she makes in the dust of the hole.

Hot light beat in on the nest for the first time. We peered over the rim, but seemed to have come to the wrong place, pushed at a door we were not supposed to, opened it on to the aftermath of a battle. There were two dead bodies, bald, blind bee-eater chicks, each an inch long, splayed headlong and limp in the sand, little gobs of meat, half pink, half yellow. They were bruised on the head, neck, thighs and back. In the middle of the scrape, a boxer in a ring, a cock in its pit, panting in the heat and from its exertions, was a living chick, bald, blind but bigger, a honeyguide. Grains of sand armoured the black blisters where its eyes were pushing through its skin, its bill hung to one side, and at the end of it, under the bright smash of sunlight, I could see a needle-fine hook pointing down from the tip of its upper mandible. A dinosaur tooth. It is the only tool of its own a greater honeyguide ever needs. Just a day or so old, still blind and, in any case, in the total darkness of the burrow, the chick had sensed movement alongside itself or heard the begging calls of the fresh-hatched bee-eaters. Then, with this sharp weapon at the centre of its being, the honeyguide pursued its foster-siblings in a frenzy of killing, puncturing their bodies, dragging them from side to side, clinging to them over and over in order to dash them down again and again, until their blood ran beneath their skin. The attacks continue until each chick is dead.

Something about the way we broke in on this scene, the bird's sweet communitarian name, and the minute severity of the hook on the tip of its bill took me somewhere else altogether: some other trespassing; a witnessed moment of the arrival into a safe round world of a sharp point from outside. Around his fourth month in the womb, there were worries for Lucian, my second son. An amniocentesis was arranged and while his mother lay on her back, a doctor inserted a needle, guided first by his experience and then, when the needle's tip broke through the wall of her womb, by its image on a screen at the bedside. Some amniotic fluid would be drawn for examination and testing. As I watched the needle in the womb on the screen, thinking how straight it was in a world of curves, our baby's newt hand, creamy fingers and thumb, came slowly swimming out from the dark and reached – with what looked like generous curiosity – towards the new pointed arrival in its cave world.

In the hole in the field were the corpses of the little bee-eaters, forgotten now, tiny sandbags pushed beyond the edge of a dug-out. We stared at the victor, an inch and a half long, a bald, blind king, exposed in the chamber of its horrors and triumph, whose first action on hatching was to seek warmth and life by reaching for whatever was adjacent and killing it. The chick must have been doing this as, earlier, we walked a foot above it across the ashy earth, led on by a promise of sweetness, sung by an adult honeyguide, calling its call, speaking of the reasonableness of shared enterprise, making us feel at home in the fields.

Looking up, I saw one of the parent little bee-eaters sitting quietly on a branch of a tree, beyond the circle of the old field, in much the same way as the adult honeyguide looked on as we plundered the honey. The bee-eater seemed to be waiting for us to finish so it could return to its nest and the young it thought it had. Lazaro carefully repaired the roof of the nest chamber and we stood up and moved away. The bee-eater called a quiet *chip chip* as it left its perch and flew above us, circling its hole in the ground.

There are more ways to farm than we might think. The honeyguide isn't interested in snakes and dead animals in the same way as we might be. But its attention to the fields and the trees, their bees and their bee-eaters, and its fruitful and violent diligence in those places, enlarges the meaning of the farm. We can know the fields through the magnifying lens the honeyguide gives us, if we grasp how to use it and choose to do so. There is now no ploughing at the Major's, yet the soil there is being turned constantly.

At one unmarked point, as we headed home, we crossed a boundary and strayed on to another property. Behind a rampant hedge was a house, netted with creepers and vines. A farmer lived there; he was old and didn't come out as we approached. Lazaro knows him as Mr Kandondo, the white man who loves black women. I asked what his English name was but Lazaro couldn't remember. It was not needed and had got lost in the bush somewhere.

We neared the Major's house and passed a large shaggy termite mound with, at its base, a bare hummock of new-turned reddish earth like a snout of moraine. It was the Major's grave. He lies at the edge of a field on his farm. Lazaro and the other farm workers who dug his burial hole also cut at termite mounds to use their soil for bricks. The fields of the farm are not totally abandoned. The mounds are valuable. Termites are extraordinary fieldworkers themselves: farmers, engineers, industrial experts as well as geniuses of demolition. Their mounds are hardened compost heaps made from chewed wood and other vegetation. Seeing what termites have built, human farm workers have learned to make homes from the termites' house. They shave slices from the mound, cutting it open like a peat bog. The termite chew is mixed with water, poured into a wooden frame, and baked to bricks in a kiln itself built from cooked termite chew. The finished bricks make houses that look like harder, darker boxes of the original mound. Rain wears away at the bricks and eventually it will return them to where they came from, but for now Lazaro lives in a house made by termites, and both he and his late employer lie beneath the soil of the farm.

Claire and I headed down the dirt road towards another farm. Bruce, our host, a white farmer on the property west of the Major's, said he would drive us to look at the dam and the reservoir at the edge of his land. His car was an old station wagon, grumpy about starting. The front windscreen was cracked in four places and shuddered as we went. The hazard lights flashed on and off as they wished. Four dogs came with us. Two huge brown beasts that would not stay in the boot of the car and blundered over to the back seat, peering from Bruce's shoulders, dribbling on to his shirt. And two Jack Russell terriers that sat on his lap, resting their heads on his arm. In order to avoid disturbing them, he steered as if taking his driving test, his hands at ten-to-two on the wheel.

On the way to the dam, Bruce showed us some of his fields. He talked as he drove. Farming is hard. His poly-tunnels for bringing on tobacco seedlings had to be abandoned because of a mystery disease. Many young plants in the fields were struggling. They were flowering too soon and were feeble. The night before, 700 older tobacco plants had been cut, slashed and ruined. Two men were tracked by Bruce's workers but their trail went cold in some woodland. Most likely they were attacking Bruce's crop because the pension scheme he devised for his workers had partly gone wrong. The authorities had supported him but his labour force had been left resentful and many wanted out of the scheme but couldn't get at their money. A ring-tail Montagu's harrier drifted over a wheat field, silencing us for a moment. The wheat hadn't done well and the world price fell as Bruce was planting. He hadn't planted further acres. A neighbouring field was burnt. That was a mistake. A cattle herders' campfire got out of control. Bruce has bought movable electric fences for his cattle, believing Africa is 'overgrazed but under-stocked' and wanting cattle to be encouraged to eat all the available fodder by being confined rather than roaming in bigger fields where they can pick and choose the most palatable grasses. He'd been trying this for two years, but hadn't yet got the system right. He wasn't a cattle specialist. He now thought he needed more manure on his farm, but didn't have enough manuring animals. Too much scrub had grown up. Goats might have been the answer. He'd have liked the Kalahari red variety, as they would be easy to spot if they were rustled. Fifty would have been good but he could only afford fifteen. There again, the goats he already had hadn't eaten much scrub. Now he needed sheepdogs to keep the goats on the move and to stop them eating the cows' grass.

We arrived at the dam and the dogs burst from the car along the banks of the reservoir. Bruce walked and talked. The village chief and headman took a lot of persuading about the wisdom of the dam, though Bruce was paying for the pump and the irrigation scheme. Relations were still strained; the benefits slow to show. As we got to the edge of the village on the shore, the big dogs went berserk, hurtling off like terrifying tubular robots, running down the local scrawny mongrels. Bruce shouted. Floris and Demi charged on.

The village side of the reservoir had hardly any large trees. Because the villagers on the chief's land remain tenants and do not own their trees, they cut down any they can. 'If your village owns a wood, you learn the value of the wood. If you are on your own, you know only the value of a single tree as fuel for cooking and firewood.' Bruce urged the chief to give land to the people, but the chief was reluctant. Not enough African farmers have experience of farming at increasing densities of population. The common practice has been to move on having exhausted the land, but now 'Africa has been used up'. A balloon would help. Bruce was building one. It would be twenty feet in diameter and fly a mile high over his farm and his neighbours'. The plan was for a camera slung beneath it to take photographs, showing the villagers how many trees they have and what their land looks like from the air, in the hope that they might attend to its survival.

It was dark now, I couldn't see more than a few steps in front of me and I tripped over my feet in the long grass. A million night insects were scratching at the damp and the dew around the water. We stopped talking and finally the dogs returned to Bruce's side, frothing with the bliss of their exertion. They love him.

It is hard not to. Bruce walking back along his dam against the skyline and jouncing with his dogs was tall, energetic, intense and indefatigable: a young Tolstoy on his estate. Walking through the ruins of the Major's farm just an hour before, I'd thought how loveless it seemed, how its fields had failed through a lack of care, as its poor owner became mired in bitter thoughts, locked in his terminal illness, cheered only by his harvest of blown birds' eggs and dead birds' skins, and by his scrutiny of the decay of avian and human genealogies, the end of lines. On Bruce's farm it's the opposite; there is, perhaps, too much love and a farmer who is trapped by the sweetness of his ideas. On my last visit to the Major before he died, at his request, I had brought him a jar of Olde English marmalade and sticks of sealing wax for his will; on this trip to see Bruce I had carried a hundred yards of ultra-light balloon fabric from Britain. Three different packages, assorted tools for assorted lift-offs.

Everywhere in the wild grass of the Masai Mara in southern Kenya, the shortest route is found between the earth and the mouth. The answer is always grass. Six elephants walked through tall yellow grass that reached to the bellies of the smaller animals, to the knees of the larger. Their haunches rocking, they paced as if they had an appointment at the end of the world, as Karen Blixen said. And they reaped as they went, their tusks like pitchforks, and the rest of their bodies like various loaves of bread. Three miles away, a line of giraffe necks appeared from the grass, all else was hidden. Five canted masts. Ten yards away a female cheetah and her two cubs, with rouged cheeks and whiskers, fed on a Thomson's gazelle, the meat of its exposed muscles drying from crimson to rust as we watched. The downy ridge of hairs along one cub's spine waved in the light just as the grass next to it did. Two barn swallows dipped to nip at the flies the kill had brought out. A baboon sat and ate, picking hand over hand at fresh grass stems; it wiped its face with one palm, its other fist wrapped round a hank of grass, pausing midway towards its mouth. A shining hippopotamus, tagged on its flanks with emerald reed-stalk calligraphy, wobbled from one wet patch of grass to another. Grant's gazelles and topi looked up from their cropping, jaws sliding, top over bottom, bottom under top; quern mouths.

Arriving in the Mara is to enter a grassed universe. The plain widens in the Rift until you are nowhere other than simply here, in the middle of the grassiest place you've ever been. The earth stretches generously over its equatorial miles. I have never seen so many blades of grass in one *field of view*. Like all the flat places, the plains, the fens, the steppe, it works on your eyes first with a scene so wide it pulls at their corners and a view so deep it furrows the brow.

Let the Mara then *be* one field. The sun splashed down between great cakes of cloud on to countless communities of grass-life: spread acres of tall grass and of short, herd after herd of mixed animals, browns and blacks and fawns, scattered trees and their tethered shadows. Every yellow, every green, every brown surrounded me, running from my feet to the edge of the world. Beneath the grass the land rises and falls; it is worn in places where rock pushes through and cut in others where rivers channel wet across it; but overall the business of what is beneath is muted and what prevails is the surface. Over all: the grass which covers everything is not just superficial – it becomes the Earth as well as growing from it, for the movement and shape of the land rhymes with the movement and shape of its outgrowth; the grass is both the world's body and its gesture. Mara in Maa, the Masai language, means dotted or spotted, patchy or chequered. It is also the word for cheetah, leopard and giraffe. It suggests the entire view and its contents.

In the grass were corpses. Thousands beyond counting. So many in one place that, there and then, the plain effected a revision of everything I knew about death. Almost all were wildebeest. Dead young and dead old, alike. They hadn't come here to die, but since they were here, they would die here and because they live here in hundreds of thousands, the dead gathered at the feet of the living. In places, for every standing animal, there was a shadow at its hooves, a skeleton, a skull, a mummified body, brown bags of bones, old overcoats shed in the heat. I didn't see anything die but I have never seen so many dead. The new dead steamed as vultures stoked at open ribcages. The old dead liquefied under the sun in a meltdown to meaty molasses. Bones blurred in a hymn of flies. Grass grew livid from beneath, through bleached bone houses. Grass grew livid from within, pulling up from ruptured guts; a last meal germinated, juiced into life by rot. A wildebeest grazed on the grass that sprouted from the stomach of a wildebeest.

The same sun blared evenly down over everything. The air above the grass was either rancid or chalky. There were meals of bone to be had and there were dead eyes to be drunk. The vultures were fat. Hyenas too. Where the grass was long, sometimes only a rib or a horn was visible above it, the ruins of a city lost in a jungle; where it was short, whitewashed collapses of bones daubed the plain with tents of spines and skulls like an abandoned camp. Death's organising genius is to be disorganised, to make a shambles everywhere. The very scatter of bodies was frightening. A skull where all else had gone; a complete skeleton without a skull; three legs arranged like the spokes of a cart-wheel; a splay of yellow teeth rolled like dice across baize; the skin and hair of a wildebeest looking as good as new, its interior a hollowed cave of gore; a new corpse plaited through an older one; a skull resting within a ribcage. And, all the time, the grass growing all about, and the living stepping through the dead to eat it.

What is it that pulls the herd of living and dead together? What moves the congress across the plain? Grass, exhausted, trampled and cropped beneath hooves. Grass, longer, fresher, greener, ahead. The smell of grass beyond the smell of the dead. The smell of green beyond the brown river. A glimpse of lions, yellow in the yellow grass. The push of teeth at the heels of the herbivores. Like a rising flood, a blunt front of wildebeest reached us; the advancing line, half a mile deep, billowed into the grass of the plain. Behind it, a solid scrum, a continuous, interlocked shunt of 50,000 parts. The earth raised by five feet for miles into a moving brown crust. The first animals flushed yellow-throated longclaws from the grass that flew up above and tried to settle again but could find no space to land between the wildebeest. I couldn't see where the herd ended. The horizon was made of animals.

The beards at their chins are the colour of the grass that strokes them. Nose to tail, flank to flank, walking, eating, walking and eating. Nothing prepared me for the epic ordinariness of the herd, the mind-wipe of its pedestrian repetitiveness, the same again and again in front of me, moving from right to left, passing and passing, plain as the plain itself, like wind through grass and made from both and becoming both. The wildebeest moved in a cloud of audible near-quiet, with only an occasional husky *gnu*, or adenoidal cough, marking their progress and showing the bigger silence of the others, while behind everything, and making its wildtrack and weather, was the breathing of the herd and their steps through the grass.

The grass was no greener on the southern side of the Mara River, but animals were beginning to gather on its northern bank. As they did, so did we, slotting our car between the other tourist vehicles on the south side. To overlook the herd, we had taken a clattering iron bridge thirty miles downstream and driven back to the river edge. To arrive in the same place, the wildebeest must get wet. The southbound crossings of the Mara begin in August and end in October and through those months in every recent year 1.5 million wildebeest have swum 200 yards from one bank to the other. Most of them will have already swum north in June or July. They come then, with their calves of the year, in pursuit of grass, up from the Serengeti in Tanzania. *Serengit* in Maa means *endless plain*. The same grass continues across the border; the Masai Mara is simply the northern field of the Serengeti.

Shifting weather, above all the movement of rain across this vast area, draws grass up from the ground at different times. The wildebeest and other herbivores follow the rain and eat. The sun dries the plain around them from salad to hay. By August the Mara is looking wan, by October it is time to return south where the rains have revived the stubble the animals left behind in June or July. They track towards green and away from yellow, moving under a circling smear of cloud as it blows hundreds of miles over the savannah. Old pastures are swapped for new, hooves and mouths making those grasses old in turn. The herd scent moisture in the air, they can smell rain from thirty miles away. They walk towards the weather they want and the grass that the rain is making.

They walk, except for the 200 yards of the Mara River where the earth falls away beneath them and they pluck at muddy water with their thin legs, trying to gallop over it, finding themselves ploughing through it. The river, on the day we watched it, was deep and fast and iron red. It had been raining further upstream. Clouds were milking the sky to the north. But the time had come for the herd opposite. Further back, across the plain, were lines of wildebeest, pencilled through the grass. Their hooves had trodden a delta of paths that gathered, as at the neck of an hourglass that is as narrow-waisted as the wildebeest themselves, to drain into the water at the crossing.

When they move towards the river the wildebeest tie themselves into a thread often only one animal thick, a single file of one-track minds, nose to tail. Behind them, grazing animals spread out in loose ruminant meanders. It is hard to see how and when the graze turns into the trek. Feet apart, as if different species, some continue to eat while others are set on passage. The lines coming to the bank picked up speed into a rocking-horse canter with apparent resolve, but a parallel pathway opened of animals running from the river with the same sense of purpose. Had they given up? Would they cross later, or elsewhere? The oncoming wildebeest reached the top of the gently shelving slope that led down to the beach. The riverside was empty, but many had already crossed and the bare sandy soil was pockmarked with hoof prints right to the water's edge. On our side of the river twenty wildebeest, a mixture of adults and young, having heard the animals arrive opposite, ran past us, returning to the top of the bank, which is steeper here, like a low sand cliff. They looked back over the water they had crossed at those who were to follow and mooed. The sound – encouragement or the pain of separation – didn't bridge the river. The animals that must cross had stalled. Having hurried to the edge they stopped, as if waking from a trance. How did we get here? Why did we come?

All of a wildebeest lives in its ugly nervy head, its long goatish face, boxer's nose, lawnmower mouth, flattened grey horns and thickset heavy shoulders slung with a straight black cumbrous mane lying over a brindled neck. At its rear, the animal is something else, petite and unfinished and edible. Those nearest the river tossed their heads, turned and moved away from the water. No thanks. The rank behind them – the file had thickened at the waterside to the width of about twenty animals – walked down to the river and did the same, spinning round and moving back up the bank, causing a jam. A startle spread through the herd and they all turned and moved up the slope. But more arrivals were pushing through the reluctant animals and, four times, individuals broke from the front of the herd and stepped right to the water's edge before wheeling back, their decision rippling through the animals behind and prompting all to retreat. Another line made it down the slope to the river. They all turned except for a calf, still brown where all around were grey. It moved to the edge, dithered for a moment, and then launched into the water with a skittish lunge of splayed legs, bared teeth and flaring eyes. The tap was opened. Previously cautious animals streamed back to the edge and jumped in, one after another at first and then in a broader line of divers along the riverside.

The crossing was terrifying to watch. Each wildebeest takes twenty seconds to cover the yards but, in that time, they look far from home. Entering the slapping river they seem stripped naked, forced to endure a swimming lesson by an instructor who, for all his severities and cruelties, sits nowhere but in their own heads. Within two plunges they are sodden and out of their depth, broadsided by the brown swirling current, blinded by spray and the splashes of panicking neighbours. Midstream the lives of the animals seem wrenched from themselves and violently transformed. Their faces, accustomed to look down, made for living downwards, must now strain up, marked with struggle and anxiety, to keep clear of the water. As we watched, one swimmer turned round and went back headlong into those behind it. Freaked by this spin, they all turned and the chain was broken.

The last animal ahead of the recusant reached the bank beneath us. It clambered shakily up the crumbling sandy wall. The moaning encouragers had moved off and the last swimmer tried to pick up speed to follow, dripping water, its loose hair darkened and plastered to its grey body and dribbling the last of the river from it. It looked shattered but it must keep going, for just there, ten yards away, between our trucks and the wildebeest, were four lions standing around like Nazi SS officers.

After the first yards of trampled mud at the bank a beautiful corridor of grass ran away from the river, curving around a low domed hill and opening beyond to a broad plain dotted with acacias. Having crossed the Mara, the wildebeest head towards the grass, to spread in the bulb of its hourglass, and resume their chewing. But the grass road is fringed on either side by a natural hedge of longer tangled stems. Here there were more lions, all females, and they tussled with one another as, in a catty mixture of animus and apathy, they took up positions in the hedge. The day was heating up and they had already eaten. Sleep kept on creeping over them but meat kept on passing as well. The wildebeest must run to avoid being taken to one side and pulled down into the grass by hot sharp mouths.

The last swimmer was alone and a crouching lion in a gap in the hedge pulled her head below her tensed shoulders and dropped her lower jaw. The wildebeest might or might not have seen the lion but it hurried on, picking up speed, trying to catch the tails of the animals in front of it. The moment passed and its taut specifics slackened. The swimmer reached the other wildebeest and re-entered the herd; the lion loosened her muscles and lay down in the grass, flattening a yellow bed of straw.

The dead hadn't finished with us. We drove back to the bridge over the Mara and this time we stopped. The bridge is just south of a bend in the river, and a succession of wildebeest bodies that had drowned in their crossing attempt had spun from the turbid flow and eddied at the shore into a gruesome flotilla. There were more than a hundred corpses along fifty yards of bank. In death they had arrived on the side of the river they died trying to get to. The uncrossable crossed. At the shore the corpses bumped into one another, nuzzling tenderly in whirlpools, like calves to mothers. The sugar-slime smell of decay was so thick it seemed animated; particulates furred my tongue, I tasted sweetmeats on the air. In the water, some bodies were still supple and flowing and seemed to manoeuvre as the river buffeted them; others were stiff and bloated, like dirty anchored buoys. Some were still recognisably mammal; others were ballooning hairless haggis-bags. Any visible eyes looked iced with green cataracts. Any anuses bulged with a pink plug of distended rectum. On the beach there were bones from earlier tides; midstream was one skull washed clean by the swirl and rot of the river, its body behind still apparently ready for life if only it could be untangled from the rocks that had snagged it.

Negotiating the pontoon of glutted bodies were two monitor lizards, walking from haunch to haunch, licking their lips, and tasting the cooking smells. Marabous waded through the shallows of ox-tail soup, digging deep into submerged bodies, pulling up skin, gristle, and viscera that they juggled into the best position with their huge canoe-bills before swallowing. White-backed and Rüppell's griffon vultures were more squeamish about the water, and gripped on to hairy corpses in order to dig lusciously into more ruined animals after drowned lights, their heads coming out shining red with wet blood. A common sandpiper surfed on the back of a slow drifting corpse, daintily picking at the insects that crawled over its drying skin. A vast crocodile – Francis, the man who guards the bridge with a 1930s Enfield rifle, knew him as Solomon – gorged on wildebeest, lay half out of the water, one yellowing canine poking up at the front of its yard-long head, anchoring him to the bank.

Further out into the centre of the river there were many bodies still riding the rapids and bucking through the breaking water. Seventeen went past in ten minutes and, if that is typical, 2,500 therefore each day. A couple embraced, locked together by entangled legs. One sailed past on its back, its feet curving stiffly upwards like an ornate table. Another was steered into a whirlpool by the useless rudder of its horns. New ways to be dead came past every minute. The corpse of a hippo-potamus floated round the bend, an incidental casualty among the failed swimmers; some vast continent of death, the biggest uncooked sausage ever made.

* * *

I dreamed about the river that night, my face pushed into roiling water with monstrous bodies coming at me like malign bumper cars, tumbling in free-fall but torqued and glutinous. I woke: hot, knotted and twisted into my sleeping bag. Months later, on the other side of Africa, at Ameib in the Erongo Mountains in central Namibia, I re-ran the dream in a drier place, at the edge of another wild field, this time counting falling elephants.

I fell asleep in a cave. I'd climbed over hot rocks on a day stunned by the sun and lay down to rest on a smooth tongue of granite at the shaded mouth of Phillips cave. As my eyes adjusted to the dim, I could make out a train of creatures walking across the stone ceiling over my head: a chalky white elephant coming through the straw-lemon rock, and next to it another with, in its belly, a red antelope, then a line of ochre human stick-figures, a dark oryx with elongated horns emerging from a rust streak, an ostrich, a giraffe's neck crossing another line of people. I tracked the parade back and forth and as I did I could feel my eyelids pebbling with tiredness and the cosset of the warm stone beneath me. In a minute I was gone, the cave slid over me, its elephants the last things I saw.

When I woke the animals swam on into focus, floating out from the rock, crystallised from its grits and sparkle. It seemed they came *through* the roof of the cave, as if the painter had seen the living things surging from their own centre to surface on the stone. As my eyes got used to the light, the animals drifted, walking without anything beneath their feet, and overlapping one another, a projection of depth without space, a herd moving and adding animals as it passed without leaving any behind, elephants, oryx, people all together, the draught of life still in their steps.

Stone tools found in the cave date to the southern African Late Stone Age, probably around 5,400–5,700 years ago, but no one has conclusively aged the Bushmen paintings nor said what they were for. Looking up at them is to see the stony logic of the illogicality of dreams; to see truths and the uses to which those truths have been put; to see facts (the species are readily identifiable and depicted moving as their living counterparts move in the valley below the cave) but also beliefs; to see tricks of the eye and tricks of the light, but also tricks of the mind; to take in the observed and its setting but also the observer. The pictographs are accounts of how nature writes itself – an antelope's stride, the curl of an elephant's trunk – but also of how people write it, and of how different that is; they are shockingly man-made things in a stone room amidst miles of wild. I imagine the Bushmen painters making the frieze of images, aware of the gulf between those they painted and those they saw, driven by wanting to articulate the gap and interested in trying to close it. They are indoor versions of outdoor things whose shadows are cast, as in Plato's cave, on a stone wall, but which are cast here not by the sun but by human minds. The painted elephants, the antelope, the oryx are more than food; the pictures more than a shopping list or a propitiatory offering. This is not just the hunting and gathering of the wild, but an enclosing of it within an idea, a human settlement among and around nature, and evidence that farming began in the mind before it started in the fields.

The elephants seemed to be ambling above me, floating in their rippling sea of rock. I noticed, for the first time, a small red one as well as the two white, and wondered at the difference. I imagined the painters falling asleep under their paintings like me and then waking to see the cave roof like a night sky, with animals instead of stars. I thought of a Chagall picture with people and animals lifted from the earth and blown, without harm, through space. The cave is a refuge overlooking a vast spread of bush and weather. By comparison it seems an intimate place, not so different from the inside of a head, and good for storing things, including ideas. Lying there, looking up, I could see how it might have been the same for the painters too. The very concept of mind might have evolved from living in caves, their interiority allowing for internal life. It was calm and still there and quieter than outside as well as cooler. Sound changed – the cave's room acoustic, its chambered feel, allowed for indoors talking and softer human utterance. Bushmen clicks would work especially well, their echoes encouraging conversation. Cave talk is like night talk, dimmed but close.

Under the eaves, I sat up and looked out at the ends of the day.

Ameib, the outward side of the mountains here, means The Green Face. The inward run of the Erongo range is all rock and it gathered below me to a wide amphitheatre of granite known as the Bull's Party. It is named for the huge balls of weathered stone that perch on plinths of the same rock, like vast worn skulls or giant dislocated ball-joints, a stone bone-yard three miles across. There are dozens of boulders and thousands of smaller round rocks. On one, below the cave, was a Damara rockrunner, a stone-specialist bird, endemic to Namibia, looking like a large, brightly patterned rufous and rust wren and, here, like a ball of hot rock hurrying over the cooler, older domes. It flew to a closer stone and scattered lizards on a boulder at the cave mouth. On the ceiling, near the paintings, rock martins had slung two mud hammocks. Beneath their nests was a spatter of droppings. Further along, dassie or rock hyrax urine had chalked the stone in a similar colour to the white elephants. There is more than one way to paint a cave.

Just below, back out in the sun, was a tiny front garden. The granite is smooth but not totally flat, and rainwater – and perhaps urine too – had gathered in depressions and hollows and rubbed at the rock until it flaked and gritted. Seeds had found moisture and minerals and purchase. Long-stemmed green grass sprouted from one coffin-shaped gouge. Its feathered heads trapped the dipping sunlight, making a small lanterned meadow. Beyond it and far below, the great swatch of plain ran from the foot of the mountains like carpet from a wall, implacable, unfenced, open miles of mottled bare earth and grasses and scrub. I could see zebras and giraffes through my binoculars. The slanting sun picked at the breath of dust, sprinkling its smoke with pinpricks of brilliance, sharpening the view rather than misting it. Every moving thing was revealed and caught in the last of the lowering light. Every animal threw a lengthening dark shadow across the earth but also a bright corona that snagged in the air. At the very moment the sun, lighting the view and its contents, showed the separation of things, singling out animals moving far apart across wide spaces, the same light spilled and streamed everything together. At six-fifteen in the evening, I could see fifteen giraffes, at least five miles away, with their necks above the thorn scrub holding the sun in warm orange bars. Nearer, two mountain zebras grazed in the shadows, their white stripes seeming to move more than their black ones. To my side, dark slack shapes of granite-dusted dassies had emerged from their hiding cracks to sing their sundown songs like sad hens.

As the sun dropped it pushed shadows further and further, until the mountain's shadow, the shadow from the cave, reached the giraffes, and then the Earth's shadow, night, reached the horizon in its daily dreamy ambush, collecting everything together, sifting everything into dark. I lowered my binoculars and could see nothing with my naked eye. The animals were lost from view. I knew they were still there but the dark had folded them into its corral. As I watched, the images of the elephants and the antelopes on the cave wall came again to me, floating out of the rock.

By the time we had walked back to our tent the full night was upon us. Its sky so crowded with stars it took me close to tears. The seeming emptiness of Namibia invites you to think about these things: the night being no lonelier than the day; the plain no more open than the cave.

For two weeks in the desert I slept at snake-level, on the ground, knapping the corners of my body, my shoulders, elbows, hips and ankles, making arrowheads of my bones. Beneath my thin camping mat, there was always some worn aggregate of sand or grit. If stray strands of grass were caught under the tent, by the morning they were flattened into zigzags like lightning strikes or broken stems of dry spaghetti.

We drove one day for three hours along a hundred miles of one desert road and saw neither a single car nor a building. Where else is there so little soil or vegetation, where else so much exposed rock? Where else is so apparently field-less, so man-less? When we asked an old Afrikaner in a shop for a corkscrew he waited long seconds before he answered, looking far over my shoulder deep into the dusted distance of his store. The whole country looks back at you in the same way.

The sea is a few dozen miles to the west but the place has dried up. An ocean has been baulked. The land seems ancient, on the far side of the green rush of life, long finished with all that oozes. It is too hot to move, too hot to stand still. Mica and quartz dazzle you from below but to look up would be madness. You must walk to create your own breeze, but strides breed sweat. Every step is hamstrung. I felt the fat melting from me. To expose a liquid in this heat is to kill it. Our wine dregs dried to cave-paint rust. I stepped away from pissing in the sand and, as my shadow cleared the wet patch beneath me, it disappeared as quickly as breath from a mirror. On a dirt track was a dead puff adder squashed to a slack S of amber dust, a last glisten of wet at its open jaw. In the dry grass Ludwig's bustards panted, their pink mouths quivering in the heat. From the hot sand lizards raised their feet one at a time against the sun's battering monologue.

We travelled through the country, winded by its scale, drunk on its level, blinded by its light. The surface of the Earth has been reduced and salted, rubbed away to a worn-out old cloth drained of colour. The soil is thin; the grass is thinner. Everything is pulled gaunt against bone, stretched at a heel or knee or elbow or brow. It seems tired; reverted in its withered collapse to some simplified dried shape. It is like looking at the stone a lithograph has been cut from – not at the print, but at the printer. Here, just into Lüderitz province, all the hills from which the valleys run are at the same height, flat topped, like army haircuts. The hillsides and the valley floors are uniformly empty all the way down. A dead-straight road rolled over the lip of what seemed to be the floor of a valley, the lowest part of the outside of the Earth, but which, as we descended, was revealed to be part of a plateau. What I thought was down was up. At its parched mouth, a valley broadened and opened into an impossibly wide plain, dipping lower, blurring into sand, sky, and invisibility, all one in the heat. I could see ostriches miles away like black weather balloons trembling in the haze. I was never in an emptier place, never felt so obviously on a ball of stone rolling through space.

There were no surface rocks in this valley. The distribution of loose stones in Namibia is magically or madly mysterious. In places there are so many, in others so few. The summoning and banishment, the gatherings and clearings of talus and scree, of rocks piled neatly in peaks, of dust dusted and of naturally swept fields suggests a strict and particular plan beyond our comprehension, a plan that is legible but unintelligible. There are porcupine cairns of a million un-climbable fragments, and, just 300 yards away across open grass, huge single boulders like slumbering giant tortoises. The valley floor here is made of sand. Grass grows over it in snaking lines, following the ripple of wind and dune. The sand settles in the valley like a filled bath, its surface calming after the taps have been switched off. Except here they never are. Mountains dry-rot to sand, and the sand returns to bury its shrunken, stooped parents. Dunes are mountains made from the ruins of mountains. In the next valley the countless stones on the hard earth look planted, as if they were sown yesterday; nothing hides their freshness, but perhaps they have been lying there for thousands or millions of years, incubated under the sun and kindled by the wind and dust to shine like dark coal-stars.

Only in the short dawns or dusks can you lift your eyes and see. Much remains hidden. Invisible, a Rüppell's korhaan, a small bustard the colour of dry grass, dribbled its liquid croak. A sundowner: a cork eased from the neck of a bottle and followed by a glug. A common tit-babbler stowed in its bundle of mimicry the sound of water droplets, an almost-cure for drought. As I walked, lark after lark brushed up grasshopper-dry ahead of me, a thread of tattered browns through a desert of brown scrub, brown grass, brown rock, brown sand. There being so many larks in the desert, everything moves towards the condition of lark. Each bird is a slight and dusted survivor, a desert father or niche farmer, occupying subtly different landscapes and living in what they know: a karoo lark, then a black-eared sparrow-lark, a karoo long-billed lark, a grey-backed sparrow-lark, a lark-like bunting, a spike-heeled lark, a Stark's lark, and, just before dark, a dune lark, its back the same colour as the red sand it had walked on, lifting like thrown sand from the dune into its song flight, a shower from an open beak that scratched like grass, carried easily through the dry air, hooked to it like a seed head, then dried itself before reaching the ground. The desert given wings.

In half an hour the sun hurried behind the dunes. The mountains and the plain softened briefly, pastel-rubbed like sea-washed glass, and then disappeared into the dark; the skyline along the west held an ember-rift of orange, but it thinned from overhead, and the black from above descended the sides of the sky's dome to join the black from below. For minutes it seemed very dark and then the starlight came. Nothing is more beautiful. A field, in the fieldless place, growing at night. The entire sky was stuffed with stars like spectral pollen. They lay thick and deep and ran down to the ground: the Milky Way arching its voluptuous leash. After the lone tyrant sun of the day, barging all over, came the democracy of night, ancient lights, a myriad silver pin-suns. Their waltzing spangle said you are there and we are here, here and there and everywhere; a concert of stars spun through space, distant, open-mouthed, silent yet shouting; now is yesterday, here was tomorrow. The shock comes, once again, at the demonstration of so much *other*, a star for every lark, a star for every grain of sand. And once again, the oldness of the view, the way looking up shreds your life, strips it back, joins you to all those who have looked up, millennia of watchers, a star for every gazer.

You could, it seemed, step from one to another along the warming crowded stretch overhead, where the stars flowed and swam together and turned from jewellery into cloth. It seemed so, yet the stars teach only rock-like cold-blood. There is no human kindness in the Milky Way and no stride long enough to tread the star chamber. We might be at a party, but we weren't invited. I looked down at the sand at my feet. I had been walking around our tent looking up. There was a puff adder squeezing under a fence, alive this time, chunky and muscled, just beyond the end of my flip-flops. It looked like a businessman's tie thrown on the floor of a hotel bedroom. Brown sand against brown sand. I could see far-away stars reflected in its green-gold chips of eyes. Perhaps it could see the same in mine.

The next night we stayed at an old farmstead called Stellarine. We had the bliss of a bed, and slept under a roof, keeping the stars from us. Though we were seventy miles inland from the Atlantic there was probably no one sleeping between the sea and us. It is all sand. The desert runs out of the ocean up the cold and misted beach, shrugging off the sharks and fur seals in the waves and the wrecked ships driven on to the shore. The beach rises and dries and becomes desert. A great buckled blowing, hundreds of miles long, a hundred miles wide, with flat feet and flyaway skin, accumulating and drifting, rising and plunging like nothing but itself. It is, in all sorts of ways, an unsettling place. Movement is its life. En route through it, as the Bushmen always were, a living might be possible. En route, the European would-be settlers could temporarily outspan or remove the yoke or harness from their animals and sleep. En route was one thing; to root was harder. Farming is and always has been tough here. South of the South African border with Namibia you pass a sign to a place called Douse-the-Glim. There doesn't seem to be anywhere down the dirt road to which the sign points. As it says, put out the light and give up hope. Nearby is Moedverloor, or loss of heart.

The dunes begin at the back of the house at Stellarine. This was once the furthest into the desert, the nearest to the ocean, that it was possible to farm, but the sand has won and pushed its warm rust east into the fields. It heaps at the low walls surrounding the house. There had been a farm on this site since the turn of the twentieth century. Jacob van Lill was the original farmer. His wife was Stella. The farm was named for her not the night sky. They had six children. The van Lills grazed sheep for their skins and wool. In the early 1960s a good fleece from Stellarine was worth two pounds and five shillings. The sheep were fat-tailed central Asian karakuls. Their name carries the promise of water. They share it with an oasis in Uzbekistan and two lakes in Tajikistan. Karakul wool, or rather the pelt of newborn lambs, makes astrakhan collars and hats. For a time the farm worked, but low rainfall meant livestock rearing was always hard. When nearby water supplies dried up, bore holes to aquifers had to be dug further and further out west into the desert. The sheep were pushed into an oven. Wrapped in their greasy fleeces they boiled in the sun, while overgrazing led to a drastic deterioration of the land. In the early 1980s a severe drought finished the farming off.

Now oryx and springbok come to the old water-troughs, trekking across the plain to drink at the back gate of the farm. I woke in the morning and watched them from my bed. The oryx is all frump and resignation. Its progress to and from the water is a definition of weary stubbornness. They make you think of the farmers in their overcoats arriving here with their ox-carts. Hot and heavy and trying hard to conceal their anxieties on a great trek that never ends. Yes, I am going over there; yes, I know the sun is boiling the plain; yes, it smacks at my skull; yes, I am wearing an unwieldy crown of horns too long for my head; but, yes, I will doggedly cross this thinning grass; why, I don't know, but I must. Through the broken heavy plod of oryx came springbok, moving like a corps de ballet, light on their feet, frisky in their stotting and pronking, never too hot to jump, cooling themselves as they went.

On the verandah of the old farmhouse a familiar chat came looking for insects. I love this bird for its colour, its name and for the reason it got its name. It came, familiarly, around us as it has come around people in caves and on farms for thousands of years, moving into spaces we had taken as our own. It is intensely drab, soft dusty brown throughout, except for a warmer brown tail, the part of itself that it does not see. As it landed its wings flicked and every few hops it made them flick again. Sunlight passed through the bird's raised feathers and scattered in the same way it shone through the grass heads nodding in the hot wind. The chat flicks its wings as a card player shuffles a pack: beneath his fingers but beyond his mind. It flicks its wings, as a starling paddles its when it sings or a redstart quivers its tail, unthinkingly and yet with an action that defines it.

In Afrikaans the familiar chat is a *spekvreter* or bacon-eater. It came around the trekkers and ate the ox fat they used to grease their cartwheels. The van Lills would have known it. On the verandah of their farm we ate local salami for breakfast and I tossed scraps to the chat. Even in the shade, the dabs of fat liquefied and ran through the meat. Grease sweats away here without a *spekvreter*. This is the land of biltong and rusk, a place where things cook dry rather than rot.

In the oven-warm wind, I walked from under the verandah towards the oryx and springbok. My shoes filled like flowerpots with the sand's soft sift. Beneath a camel thorn was a mummified orphan, a springbok calf, its dead tongue withered in its skull, its stiff and juiceless board of skin lying propped on the sand. Some bones had escaped from the manila file of its body and fallen to its feet like kindling. Running across the sand between the dead springbok and the tree trunk was a black dung beetle. It carried its dry turd ball, a springbok pellet, towards its desert sewage farm. The ball was clasped between the beetle's back legs; it ran using only its front legs, and the dung ploughed a little furrow behind it as it went towards its burrow.

Hoisted up into the far side, the desert side, of the tree was a hayrick. A vast communal nest of sociable weavers. The farm no longer has human sounds but it chatters and scratches with farming life. The birds, patterned in desert camouflage of greys, browns and blacks, have lifted a mighty forkful of grass twenty feet into the air, weaving it brilliantly into the thorns. They carried the grass stem-by-stem, one blade at a time, each held in their beaks like a single whisker. I have watched them gather it and begin starter homes in other trees and on telephone poles. Here the nest was old, its upperside a dome of greying grass twenty feet across, and its underside, brighter, less bleached grass with dozens of tunnels plaited into the thatch. All the straws at each tunnel mouth were woven to splay centrifugally outwards at the same angle like a flash photograph of a fiery wheel. Like rookeries, the communal nesting places seem to be raised mostly in sight of neighbours. I could see a further three weaver townships across the plain along the edge of the dunes. At dawn and dusk the ricks glow like low suns, a solar system of floating grass.

For their nests, the sociable weavers harvest only the stems of the Bushmen grass. Below the birds' nest live tiny ants, no longer and no thicker than a dash. Cutters and harvesters, a colony of *Messor denticornis*, they snip Bushmen grass heads from their stems for food and carry them one by one underground to thresh and store in granaries they have built. The chambers are kept dry so the hulled seeds don't germinate. The chaff is taken back to the surface and dumped carefully along the rim of a growing ruff of husks that rings each nest entrance hole.

These mounds with their single dark eyes in their centre are scattered through the short grass like cushions. They are crisp at their outer rims and pale and fading like the sociable weavers' nest, the colour gone to the universal non-colour of dust and old grass. Bushmen and others once knew how to steal the stored seeds from the ants, to make porridge from them, or beer, or a stronger liquor called *poka*.

At Palmwag, 370 miles north of Stellarine, there was less sand and more scrub but there were still plenty of harvester ants. There were bigger ruminants too. We rounded a corner of a dirt road and arrived mid stand-off in a war over cud between a cow and a small herd of elephants. All had been intent on their browse, the elephants curling their trunks round great hanks of grass and gathering it tightly from the earth, the cow dribbling with pleasure at the same stand of lush green, until it looked up and started bellowing at the knees of the elephants. They stopped their harvest to retaliate with blasts from their trumpets. One dropped a tube of hay bricks behind it as it moved off. It rolled towards us and I could see within it the same stems of grass a harvester ant would cut or a sociable weaver select for its nest.

The empty quarter isn't. It only seems that way. There are arrowheads and axes scattered through the plain, man-made things on their slow journey back to the condition from where they started. And the land is farmed; the plain is a field. But because there is apparently so little in the foreground, our eyes are always being drawn further and wider. The plain proposes a kind of nomadism of looking. As we drove towards the coast we startled an oryx. It is continually surprising how large animals can remain unseen in acres of flat and treeless country until you are almost upon them. In its panic it ran alongside the car, outstripping us but heaving with terror and unable to flee because there was a fence at the roadside as there had been for much of a hundred miles. I hadn't noticed it, until the oryx, which also hadn't, ran up against it. Snorting, with flared nostrils and streaming eyes, it turned and breasted the fence, stumbling into a crash of horns and legs and dust; a galloping nomad unable to see the wire, unable to believe a fence would stop it. The Bushmen cave painters in Namibia abandoned painting around the time a different people, herders who were more farmers than hunter-gatherers and more settled, arrived on the plains. Various fences, real and understood, stopped the animals coming through the rock. In 1985 one of the last recorded phrases of the /Xam Bushmen language, as remembered by an old gardener called Hendrik Goud on a South African farm near Gifvlei, were interpreted as /hu kwa koa se: /ke / / a. This was translated as, 'Here come the Boer, we must hurry away', or better still: 'Run, here come the farmers.'

In June 2011, in Zambia, Lazaro killed Stanley Munkombwe with his axe. Stanley was a fellow farm worker and honeyguide follower and nest finder. Lazaro attacked him in an argument about thievery in a field of maize that both men were guarding. He was sentenced to five years' hard labour. Claire, who visits him in gaol, reports that he still talks of the fields on the old farm by name: R4 and R3, Number 12, and Shangwondo and Mubanga.

SPRING FEN

New weather redecorates the room. You go to bed, as Hardy has it in *Under the Greenwood Tree*, among nearly naked branches and wake next morning among green ones. Rise and put on your foliage, is Robert Herrick's less pyjama'd version of the same transformation. Spring grows on the world.

First the light changes. A lid lifts. In the black poplar on the fen a mistle thrush sang, throwing out everything it had saved through the winter. Fen skies are wider and open higher in March than in February and they are bluer and whiter. The angle of the Earth's orbit of the sun does it, but the effect is felt overhead in the species of sky. I watched clouds at odds with each other barge together above the fen, seasons in battle. Mizzling curtains of rain messed with wedding cakes of cumulus. The motor of the year turns in this.

Looking out for swallows from the bank of Reach Lode, I was about the same height as the first fields that rose away to the east where the fen ends. But in the low sun streaming from behind me the grass plots there on the rising ground seemed to lift and tilt. Because these fields are hedged rather than ditched, they looked like framed paintings of soft rumpled green hung on the edge of the day. It is in this light and during these spring weeks that the lines and dips of old ridges and furrows appear through the grass, all gentle and snowy, and the new green reveals the farmers and the farming that lie behind it.

One of these floating fields at the end of the Devil's Dyke lures migrant wheatears every spring and, sensing or sharing the draw, I hurried there to see three bright males working the short grass. Close up, all the snowy folding had gone, and the green was still wintery thin, with chalk obvious beneath it. The light had played a trick and yet the birds had come back, or another generation of them had found the same inducements in the same field. I wondered if these birds (old timers or newcomers) had travelled with something like a *feeling* for this grass, and if so whether a sense-memory was being topped up? And what happens when they leave? They printed their feet into its late-winter turf but maybe they fly north carrying something other than its first spring insects with them: some fold-away version of the field, its essence or co-ordinates, its value or its taste, its reason? In this way, the wheatear would *be* the field at the end of the Devil's Dyke wherever it was, and the field (and every other field the bird stopped in) would get out and about and travel the world. If the light was right, it might even be possible for those of us grounded below the birds to catch the traces walked by their little feet into the thin March grass, year after year, like those ghost-ridges and furrows from the old days that appear in the early spring.

The wheatears faced north with their black eye-stripes like compass needles all looking the same way. Cold air did fierce battle with the warming evening light and four swallows came flying low in a black line over the wheatears, my first of the year. They pushed into the wind, their heads drawn down to their shoulders like polar explorers; the birds cowed and roped as Wilson, Bowers, Oates and Evans, a different magnet to the wheatears' drawing them on, keeping them from dropping down to the grass, seeding their minds with home.

I turned south to the village and the shelter of its still-bare trees and the jam of blackbird song came warm as I walked towards it. The cumulus rafted on overhead, piling themselves upon themselves. For days in early spring these clouds mass before the leaves burst below them. The sky tutors the earth in this way, showing the shapes of summer trees, the towering black poplars, skulled willows, keyed ashes, shaggy oaks. When the trees open and fill at last, any clouded sky looks suddenly old, grey haired beyond the green, and it stays this way throughout the summer, getting older still.

In 1980 I went to university in Cambridge believing that incest was more prevalent in the fens than anywhere else in the country. The epicentre of consanguineal sex was the village of Soham. Or so it lodged in my mind. I had never been there or stopped for any length of time anywhere else in the fens and I am not sure where I had picked up the notion. I wasn't, however, alone in my delusion. For hundreds of years Cambridge had lived *under* the fens. In the summer, wind dry-choked with pollen and thrips blew the flatlands into town and, in the winter, wet fog coming off the shadow-swamps seemed to drip-feed all sorts of myths and fantasies, stories of webbed feet and incest.

Another version of the same impulse – the simultaneous capturing and holding-off of a place, believed close enough to mark the place you were in – could be heard ten times a day some winters in Cambridge. It still can. I learned it in my first weeks in the city. The wind in Cambridge was cold, it was said, because it blew directly from the Urals. This was almost but not quite a joke. The wind did often blow wolfish from the east but no one in the city could really say where it came from. Nor did anyone in the Urals think they were breathing on Cambridge. What was designated as an import was actually invented in situ. In a flat place it is hard to believe in mountains but, as a remote opposite of Cambridge, the Urals sounded plausible, and they took on an imaginary truth that made them and their wind more than an almost-joke and raised them, fantastically, into local life. The mountains became, in this way, a hinterland of the city.

I arrived in Cambridge already bogged with fen baggage no less nonsensical. I knew the people of the fens couldn't have webbed feet – I was a birdwatcher and strong on my ducks – but unconsciously I had given headroom to a mishmash of other prejudices and received ideas. Fen people, the wind and the fog said, were the last peasants of England, trapped throwbacks like gypsies who couldn't move. The isolated population was genetically raddled. Ignorance and poverty had condoned father-and-daughter sex and other too-close-to-the-bone breeding liaisons. Shaking with marsh-ague or poleaxed by opium taken to alleviate their pains, the runtish people crouched under dwarfing skies. In the summer the wind blew them around a dust bowl. In the winter the same soil, now glutinous mud, clung to their short legs and sucked them in.

This gallery of grotesques was nothing more than the local encore of a yokel pantomime, a situation-comedy done in broad Mummerset. Versions of it arise everywhere. The neighbours just across the fields are always the strangest of people. We are too much alike to permit any other truth. But it is striking how strong and how shared these fen caricatures were. Why should that be? I think the place itself is the substantial reason, particularly its apparent emptiness. It was the place, or rather the lack of it, in my mind's eye, not its villagers, that had allowed Soham to be the incest capital. The village barely occurs between the peat and the sky. The fens all around it look like an open stage asking for some scenery. Their unemphatic mundanity makes them (still, as it always has) into a place where a kind of negative capability of landscape operates. Where less becomes more. Where the landscape itself is thin but the weather is wide. Where the prospects are so low that small things loom tall. Where you might mistake a windmill for a giant. Where things are so boring they become interesting.

There is energy in all this. At a first glance the fens might seem surrendered and banal. They are flat and farmed. Their drained soil is turned to our advantage. Every inch of them represents a human victory over the wet. Look a little longer though and you can see how unfinished they are and how they declare it themselves. The ghost of water is everywhere – its presence, its absence, its removal and its defiance – and it wetly mirrors everything dry. Fen flatness is not beautiful. Man and nature have wrestled and their business has resulted in a curiously abrasive and uncouth emptiness: an ordinariness that refuses to be just tame. The eradication of wild detail in so worked and so low a place gives off the opposite of familiarity. Each field, even the dreariest square, has the smack of itself. That they are all man-made redoubles their power to disconcert. They cannot be left alone if we want them to remain as they are; yet they cannot be subjugated no matter how much we lean on them. Though they are edged and boxed and rolled, they will not stop where we would have them stop. And the people living in the fens, even the commuters of today who shuttle its A-roads, are still under the fen regime. In the space here, between how we would configure them and how they will be, in the contrary weirdness of the deeply human but deeply resistant land, a kind of fen pastoral has taken root and grown up. And so: webbed feet and the fishing in your own family's pond.

Every student day I walked through a reduced or playground version of the fens. Fen fields and ditches ran almost to the centre of Cambridge. On either side of the straightened River Cam, the college gardens and grounds of The Backs were reclaimed and drained swamp just like the fens to the north. That cod with the book in its belly had arrived not far from here. The autumn mist that hung above the conduits and culverts, and which seemed able to detect or remember where old water had once flowed, came with the fen. Even the punts on the river began life as fishing boats for shallow water and as a way of lying down on that water in order to steal up on ducks.

Severed from their source yet still ghosting the world they were born in, the micro-fens of the city are diagrams of nature mastered; 'enclosed within the garden's square / A dead and standing pool of air' (as Marvell's 'The Mower against Gardens' has it). The Backs are a double-dream of connection and control brought into a half-life and laid out in lawns and flowerbeds. And, mastered also at the expense and exclusion of people. At King's College, cattle are still often to be seen on the grazing meadow just over the river from the college buildings, looking like bovine extras with walk-on parts in that same fen pantomime. No cowherd walks among them at King's and the trailer that brings the animals to the field doesn't hang around getting in the way of the view. Instead, it was possible, when I was a student, to see either Raymond Williams or John Barrell, two great critics of the comforts and deceits of artistic arcadias, passing the field of lowing kine as they walked to the University Library where they were doing their best to reframe the old georgics and bucolics of literature, and to revise our understanding of them by – broadly – putting people back into the picture.

I came, like almost anyone born in Britain in the last hundred years, to the peasantry through books. It began romantically. I was beguiled by Levin among his serf haymakers in *Anna Karenina* and enjoyed the photograph of Tolstoy in his peasant smock, fashion model for all hay writers. Long before university I had cherished a child's-size fisherman's smock of orange canvas that my parents had bought for me on a family holiday to Cornwall – it had deep pockets in the front and I'd imagined stuffing twitching mackerel into them even though I was always frightened of the sea and had never caught a fish. It was similar with hay. It made me sneeze. At university, I also loved John Berger's *Pig Earth*, new then, with its stories of the haymakers of the Savoie and the photograph of Berger – such a good pastoral name too – in a hay field. If that shepherd had started a commune I would have joined the flock. But I only had to walk through Cambridge market, 500 steps from the cows at King's, and thronged then with people from fen villages shopping and selling vegetables, leeks and celery stuck with black peat, to know that Tolstoy's or Berger's truth, if that is what it was, couldn't apply around me any longer. Likewise, nor could that more ugly version of the fantasy fens that I had somehow imbibed en route to living on the edge of them. The woman who cleaned my room in college took the bus in from Manea in the fens every day. Her husband gardened the college grounds. I didn't enquire after their sex life but she seemed thoroughly ordinary and, for weeks, kindly overlooked my stowaway girlfriend. Between my bedder, Raymond Williams, and later a stone curlew, I eventually woke up to where I was.

I took a train to Ely and walked east to Soham and then caught a bus back. No signs of incest, but the bus made the tallest thing for miles; even the people at the bus stop craned over the fields. I knew little of the history of those fields but, unlike so much of the rest of Britain, they seemed new. The ground had been settled with squares of wheat and rape and fenced by ditches of water. More water was being carried in straight channels raised, improbably, above the roads and as high as the bus. Following the hemmed flow even the gulls were forced to turn chicanes or right angles in the sky. All this was unlikeable as much as unlikely but I couldn't pass it by.

Along the eastern miles of the fens, among carrot fields at Lakenheath, there was a square-edged poplar plantation being grown for matchsticks. Above it the sky shook with planes ferrying cruise missiles between the nearby British and American airbases. Nesting in the box of matches were golden orioles, the only ones breeding in Britain. They belled my name, *dee-o*, and burned like yellow candles with black wicks among the green leaves. Stone curlews lived a few fields away, on an old rabbit warren rising from the fen. They walked about like slow lizards in the haze, their goat eyes yellow and bulbous as if myxi-sick.

Nothing seemed quite wild, yet nothing was fully tamed either. The soil was special pitch-black like the stuff you got in grow-bags from garden centres, except it was everywhere and almost greedy, running up over the grass as if it hadn't sanctioned its growing. Raindrops bounced little chits of it up the legs and over the back of feeding lapwings, like black fur. The rain thickened to a summer storm and I was caught out in it and felt like a tree. How stupid to be so tall and obvious, lost in the flat and shown up by it at the same time. I scrambled down a bank and hid in some reeds, underneath thunder and shrunken in the wash.

On Remembrance Sunday, in the autumn of the same student year, I cycled from Cambridge to Ely through Swaffham Bulbeck, Burwell and Soham, accidentally tracking war memorial ceremonies in the villages as I rode. There were church bells, wreathes and old soldiers wearing berets and medals and talking and smoking and standing about in the brittle light. In Burwell, one man, who must have been in his late eighties, wore a black furry jerkin. His medals, pinned to it, shone out from the fur like eyes. Slowly, he walked to the memorial and stood in front of it, with his feet apart, his stiff legs and mole-fur waistcoat redolent of a time when farm workers from the fens went to fight in the fields of France: digging for shelter as they had dug peat or ploughed furrows; eyeing what Isaac Rosenberg called the 'sleeping green' between the opposing trenches; feeding horses as they had at home; living, as they knew how, in the open air and close to the ground, in sodden hedgeless fields under the same astonishing expanse of sky; and keeping company for a while with those who would be mown down under that sky, like 'autumn corn before the cutter' as a witness to the first day of the Somme described what he had seen. Mole-men out in the light.

On 4 November 1914, Franz Kafka recorded in his diary some of the experiences of a brother-in-law (a soldier for Austro-Hungary) newly returned from the eastern front: 'Story about the mole burrowing under him in the trenches which he looked upon as a warning from heaven to leave that spot. He had just got away when a bullet struck a soldier crawling after him at the moment he was over the mole.' Six weeks before he was killed, Edward Thomas wrote in his war diary from northern France on 25 February 1917: 'Does a mole ever get hit by a shell?' Sixty-nine didn't come back to Burwell and their names are recorded in little carved trenches on the village war memorial. At the end of his play, when they have met on the beach at Dover, broken Lear says to blinded Gloucester: 'You see how this world goes.' Gloucester replies: 'I see it feelingly.'

All those I saw are dead now. Much has changed in thirty years. Another generation of ordinariness has arrived in the fens. There are newer soldier deaths to remember; the villages are dormitories for bigger towns; the volume of traffic makes cycling off designated tracks dangerous; in the fen nearest to where I live, migrant workers pick most of the leeks, gathering around what looks like a slow-moving portable office block suspended above the field. But the flatness and its thin potency remain: the determining sky ('chief organ of sentiment', as John Constable called it not so many fields away) and the equally striking refusal of the place beneath to be fixed. To fix the fens – to perform repairs thought of as necessary and thereby to bring them towards some solid state – has been the desire of people forever who have lived in or dreamed of its villages and fields, their grass, soil and water. In some ways this is functional and familiar – we might call it farming – in others it is strange, idealised or hopeless. It has made an unbeautiful human place from acres of ground that will not ultimately settle. There again, their not settling has been the making of the fens, keeping the most turned-over and dug-out place inviolably itself.

In early spring just before the green wheat came in the ploughed field, the opened soil folding along the surface of the earth looked like the crust of a loaf of bread. The furrows were like ribs scored in dough that crack open from below as the bread rises. Ploughmen and bakers must have noticed this many times. In the same field woodpigeons, fat already, moved with the heaviness of tanks up and down each ridge and trench. The spring-bright birds have a white neck-plate with a turnip-green patch above and, as they waddled, the feathers of the plate split and glistened also like the turned soil, magnesium bright at the surface, dark and unlit in the cracks. Some trapped charged air gathers there; the same warm spring static that comes in the purr of a catkin or the humming spark of the bumblebee's bum.

The next day a blue sheet dried in the western wind over the whole of the fens. On the chalky fields behind the village a green flush opened like mould on an old bone. The wheatears had longer grass at their feet. The nap that comes gentle at the sharp edges of the trees fuzzed tenderly at the air, warm and quick. Everything that was and will be wood was furred. The brightness of midday polished the bone-axe beaks of the rooks walking the fens and turned the sheen on their wings from black to glassy white. Songs rose from the fields like a freshet or a spring: skylarks mirroring the bright sky, the simple washed tune of a chaffinch in the hedge unfolding like young water making its way downhill.

There followed a week of air warm enough to feel continuous with skin and blood. But then the wind moved hard into the north-east and slapped down a dish-cloth sky. The birds stopped singing. It rained and made a sodden silence of the fields. Tree trunks, black with wet, were papered with leaves that had fallen after only days of life. Grass blades were bent awry by watery lenses. Cattle lay down, as if defeated, in the cold air of the fen field. Overnight, ruined blossom dropped along the hedges. The demolition of the year began before swifts had arrived into its skies.

It has always been like this and always will be. But other birds had started and couldn't stop. Through the rain a cuckoo flew along the lode with what must have been a reed warbler's egg jammed in its beak, its head wobbling as if surprised by what it had done; a second cuckoo crossed the first, calling its tongue-swallowing yelp as if another egg was gagging its throat. This bird, in its long-winged whickering flight, was chased by chaffinches, pulled out of the farmhouse trees by the *gowk* charmer, a wolf in a skirt, like a folk tale being flown across the fen.

* * *

94

The fens have been cast forever as a place needing repairs. Their story might have gone a different way in the middle of the great fen-fixing seventeenth century had Charles I built Charlemont, his projected Venice or St Petersburg-like city with a Versailles-like palace near Manea, and thereby come to rule the country from a flat fen. When Cornelius Vermuyden's first attempt to drain the Great Level with spades, wheelbarrows and horses had failed, and the Adventurers under Francis, Fourth Earl of Bedford, were near ruined, Charles declared himself the Sole Undertaker and plans were made for 'an eminent town in the midst of the Level', a fen city, 'the design whereof he drew himself'. It never happened. In the Civil War the captured king was bundled across the fens to prison in a hunting box or lodge in Newmarket, in a richly inverted ballet of power and pursuit. Later, Charles the would-be undertaker was beheaded. Charlemont Drive is now a cul-de-sac near the railway station on the edge of Manea. But in the imagined fixing Charlemont offered – the planting of the centre of the nation in a bog (the *mont* being all of fifteen feet above sea level) – we have another epigrammatic definition of all fen projects, Canute-moments in the tides of men, from the earliest dryings to the proposed rewettings of today.

Adventurers in the fens have repeatedly dreamed of combining one sort or another of moated castle (safety underwritten by wet) with the wholesomeness of drainage (swapping webbed feet for dry socks). That this combination is irreconcilable is a further fen truth. That Manea was also the site for a utopian commune inspired by Robert Owen is a fen joke. Robert made a little more progress than Charles. In 1838 at Colony Farm on Manea Fen, a follower of Owen started a 150-acre commune for between 100 and 200 colonists. Money was abolished, a windmill, cottages and a school were built, the communitarians wrote and read a newspaper called *The Working Bee* and dressed in suits of Lincoln Green. It didn't work. After a couple of years the Cambridgeshire Community Number One was abandoned.

* * *

From my bed at five in the morning I could hear the jackdaws trying their flint-knapping calls around the church towers in the village, testing whether yesterday's echo will be today's as well. At the front door the new air tasted unbreathed, birdsong alone had taken possession of it. But by the time I was properly out, the sun was already rubbing its white burn into the sky over the chalk hills at the edge of the fen. The incoming day had almost finished its work. The shadows running west from the village and its trees shrank back as the sun rose. Its splash turned up the birdsong and with that came the sensation of the day waking, the covers of night falling from the shoulder of the Earth as it rolled eastwards into the sunrise.

Dawn song through the northern hemisphere is continuous in the spring – it being always dawn somewhere, at every minute of every day, in May. If we could travel with those first splashes of sunlight we would hear the waking music of the whole of the top of the world beginning again and again and on and on for a month. As the sun touches each new yard of earth, song unfurls from it and sings it into life: the eastern thrushes at the Great Wall and through the taiga; the redwings and the fieldfares that ate and rested in the fens in the winter, now back in their birches; the bluethroats in the reed-lines around Moscow; the redstart in a tree in the centre of Yalta below which the Tatars come to sell honey; the thrush nightingale in a ditch outside Tallinn; the collared flycatchers of the Buda Hills; and here a common nightingale in the scrim of a hawthorn brake near the end of the Devil's Dyke – the relay of the day held for a moment in the water droplets and fabric-tears of its music.

From the shrinking pool on Baker's Fen at Wicken at six in the morning, twenty-three bar-tailed godwits clambered up into the air, a mixture of old-shirt grey and old-brick red, winter and summer plumage – the ratio changing each day as they make their passage from the Atlantic coast of Africa to the tundra of Russia. As if they were picking up the thread they had stitched to get them to Wicken, they wheeled as they climbed to the point from where I had seen them drop ten minutes earlier to the shallow dish of wet. Sky-hooked once again they moved confidently, flying with the whole of their bodies and heading urgently into the wind, determinedly north-north-east, seeking their tether, and following the same airway as Eric Ennion's birds nearly a hundred years ago. In the same sky, homing airforce planes, sand brown, mud grey, dead green, banked over the fen into the sun stream, turning into the wind as they descended towards the American bases, seeking their earth over the county border.

This was the story of the day: the necessary and sought tie to the world at a time of flight. In a square of ploughland a pair of lapwings had settled. Their winter flocks have broken apart and each bare acre has tugged two birds to its soil. In this the lapwings are ahead of the golden plovers, which, like the godwits, are still away from home. The same fingered-flights of plovers that were gloved with lapwings until just a month ago now swirl around the black and white breeding pair. The two species have become strangers to one another. *Wypes*, lapwings used to be called on the fens. And in their territorial agitation the birds cast their short-stringed kite flights above the furrows, tilting the earth to them and away, writing with their rounded wings a hurried looping script above the fen. Somewhere below them are their eggs: 'dingy dirty green', John Clare called them, 'deep blotched with plashy spots of jockolate stain'. The golden plover flocks will split up themselves when they reach their hilltops and tundra breeding grounds. Already some are carried north by their plumage. Most are still tan-coloured above and silvery-grey below, but a few have stepped on into their summer suits, with their neck, throat, breast and belly feathers new moulted to a peat-black bulbed flask painted down their fronts, and their backs prickling with a stone-top graphic of orange and green lichen. The season is stretching into its various clocks.

Yesterday it hadn't been here, today it was: a male whitethroat had arrived from the 10 million umbrella thorn trees of the northern Sahel to find one hawthorn on the fen edge. The bird settled to its summer anchor and the place grew up around it. The arrow-flight of its lengthy linear journey bent into tiny circular display sallies made once a minute through every day for six weeks. It had flown 5,000 miles in order to fly fifteen feet. On its song flights it launched from its thorn perch over domed-planets of cow parsley, but each time it was pulled back to its tree, the cursive script of its journey matching the length of its scratchy tune. The next tree along the ditch was an elder and it held another singing male whitethroat. Because it must, this bird adventured out towards the other but was pulled back by its tether. Between the white-throats a reed warbler, also not long installed, sang alone in its stand. Its song made a crowd out of its chopped and fretted mimicry, the sound of the world as it might be known from a summer cage of reeds.

Above the fen, twelve snipe chased one another in a dispute over women and living space. They flew like swifts, horizontal and furious, and then broke apart to work up their own wooing speeches and aggro gestures. Each male described his ambition in the air, drumming above his territory on the fen and marking its borders upwards. In the spring, tugged by the sun, these swamp-loving hunkered birds transform them-selves into little horses and ride the sky. The males dance and bleat, calling *chip chip chip chip* on and on as if they are loosening something tight, their beaks screwdriving up, their whole bodies rocking from side to side. Moor-lambs, snipe were called in the Lincolnshire fens; the goat of the air is what *Gabhar-athair*, one of their many Gaelic names, means. They climb until their calls thin to the edge of the audible back on the earth or when their twisting bodies become too small to see and then they turn downwards and fall sideways back through the sky. As they do they fan their tails and part the outermost feathers so that, in their headlong dive, the rushing air rippling over their wings sounds through their spread plumage and their bodies sing. The sky then drums with a woolly thrum like a slow mosquito at your ear. The horseplay gallops on through spring moonlit nights. Drumming is among the very best sounds of the fens; a shaking of one of its membranes, like a bittern's boom ('his bump', John Skelton called it), that is heard in your chest and which vibrates there like the heart's foghorn.

One man went to mow. And let him stand for all men, that is for all those who sought thinking through haymaking and harvesting, sparing

98

those poor anonymous millions who more simply, more exhaustingly, just had to *do* it, to mow in order to live. Since the first poems of Greece, Western writing has been drawn to lines of mowers strung across a field and, among the cutting men, there have been those who went to mow seeking something other than a swath of aromatic drying grass. Pastoral literature grew up in these fields. It cut two paths out of them. Some pastoral is an account of the fall of man (farming wasn't needed in Eden or during the Golden Age) and the repeated and commonplace repairs that can be made around that fall (wholesome good lives, grass that grows again, wool that can be cut without killing a sheep). Some pastoral writes a darker arcadia, a place or a mood that can only be known at the point of severance from it, that can only be lost even at the moment of its apparent possession (death is a condition of life no matter how sweet the roses smell).

The pastoral in William Empson's far-sighted formulation in *Some Versions of Pastoral* is characterised as being an intellectual or emotional position or cast of mind as well as a literary trope. It is a way of thinking and of feeling. A pastoral scene – imagined, written, dreamed, painted, sung – first of all is a description of separation that takes in both sides. A poet looks at a mower or a shepherd and thinks, 'I am in one way better, in another not so good.' We like scything peasants because we imagine their life makes a shape in the world that we desire but at the same time we are glad we don't have to cut grass in order to live. What Nietzsche called the 'pathos of distance' is at the heart of pastoral. The mower seems like the *echt man* or the *ur-man*, living a life of *soft* primitivism, organic and sustainable. But he is also stuck outdoors with straw in his hair and mud on his feet, struggling with *hard* primitivism. Empson goes on to say that his definition of pastoral 'may well recognize a permanent truth about the aesthetic situation'. In the fens, and in the fields more widely, I think it goes further still, beyond the aesthetic and deep into life. 'I am in one way better, in another not so good' speaks of our current relationship with everything natural that isn't us, with modernity, urban living, nature craving and with our estrangement from much of the planet, and with the drained world that we have dug for ourselves, north of Cambridge and south of the Wash.

Here is our mower – now looking impossibly old – Hilaire Belloc, wing-collared, high Catholic, advocate of conservative agrarianism and friend of the fens, arriving at his field (not in the fens) with his scythe in 1906. '[M]y own field', he says, 'my scythe'. Possession was important for him, though not essential for others. Some hay writers or turf accountants have been landlords determined to divest themselves of what they owned (Tolstoy). Some have been willing tourists into indentured labour (John Stewart Collis – who wrote on Tolstoy as well as on the plough and its pleasures). Some have scythed as young men or as holiday workers and recalled it later as writers (D. H. Lawrence: 'you could have seen me high on the load, or higher on the stack, like a long mushroom in my felt hat, sweating with my shirt neck open'; and John Fowles in the memorably blazing opening chapter of *Daniel Martin*). Some have less directly but no less intently walked and watched fields into meaning, making grassy versions of Philip Sidney's (the poet of *Arcadia*) poetic curriculum vitae that said '[m]y sheep are thoughts' (Richard Jefferies, Thomas Hardy). One, John Clare (and a handful of less well-known others too), cut hay to live at times, so to put food on the table of his crowded cottage, but also made a version of hay in words to try to communicate how he lived, and to hold on to what he knew he was losing – a way of life but also, in his case, his mind.

Belloc is certain he has no such doubts. Perhaps he protests too much about the healthiness of what he is doing. His field is an unidentified secret place, locked in a valley in southern England, 'remote from ambition and from fear'. It is hidden and he further hides it, as he must, for hand-mowing was already moribund when 'The Mowing of a Field' was published in 1921 (a year before T. S. Eliot's *The Waste Land*). A scythe swinging through time and sickles hissing through wheat – the ancient pastoral verities were losing their anchorage in the real world. The cutting, gathering and carrying of grass and grain were being mechanised and therefore the metaphorical gleam that the blade and the severed stems laid into the human mind was dimming. Our once common tools for the alteration of the earth, our harrows, sickles and scythes, had fashioned a sharp-pointed armoury for our imaginations, but without a real scythe, why should we fear the reaper?

Scything had only a decade or so left in Britain, but Belloc's anxiety about its disappearance is literary rather than agricultural. Even a few years earlier when Edward Thomas wrote about a ploughman (in 'As the team's head-brass'), he was separate from the scene: he sat and watched the man and his horses; he didn't need to (nor could he any longer legitimately or literarily) grab hold of the reins. But Belloc's sense of arriving in a fifth and final act, and catching the last trembling shimmer of halcyon, old world days, is a recurring given in hay writing. The land of cockayne is always slipping with the sun behind the hill in Samuel Palmer colours, and with it the shepherd and his fold, the goodly crop, the hare hiding in the last sheaf, the sweep of the scythe.

Anxieties about these sunsets come as often as the sun falls. There are no arcadias that are deathless. The very first cave paintings of animals would have flickered into life around the leaping shadows of a burning torch in the midst of a black hole. The pictures weren't how the animals looked in the light of day outside. From Hesiod and Theocritus onwards, from the invention of poetic fieldsman, hard on the goat heels of the birth of farming itself, part and parcel of pastoral is the impossibility of recovering any unblemished arcadia, or Golden Age, or Eden. Already in Virgil is the endless fact that a joined world with simple abundant treasure, the natural giving of the earth, is no longer ours to be had. The shepherd cannot pipe until his flock is folded. Fields without fieldwork don't work. Virgil's *Eclogues* and the *Georgics*, like Hesiod's *Works and Days* and Theocritus's *Idylls*, were new but they told old stories.

While all the poems were being written, generation after generation were working in the fields, of course. No matter how little the poems meant to the fieldworkers, through this adjacency, the poetry of the imagined communion was repeatedly vivified by the life going on outside, by real contact with harvests, animals, weather, the earth. Even fantastical pastoral poetry can read like valuable documentary realism in this way. William Langland's agricultural parable-making worked for the fifteenth century but also speaks through the years to us: the poor ploughman hanging on his plough, wearing knobby shoes and clothes slobbered in mire, his wife at his side, wrapped in a winnowing sheet, barefoot, and three tiny children in rags at the edge of the field, crying. D. H. Lawrence's pastoral, the farm so brilliantly created in *The Rainbow*, comes from farms he knew in the Midlands a couple of counties away from Langland's fields. It doesn't seem odd to me that both speak to my memory of reading *Farmers Weekly* in the 1970s. I was naïve in many ways and romantic in others, but the endless truths of mud and grass, of seeds and milk, of work and death remain. 'Nature is never journalistic,' the poet W. S. Graham said – a warped and wonderful fringe-pastoralist himself – and its not being newsy has allowed the pastoral to keep it company. The specifics of pastoral will change from age to age, even a decade-old copy of magazines like *Country Living* or *Resurgence* (two contrary but not unconnected contemporary catalogues of pastoral dreams) seem dated and ancient but the bigger picture persists. Pastoral lives on, powered now as before by being not just about the good old days (although it often lives there) and not just about losing touch with the earth (though it likes to garden both with bare hands and in gloves). Its spark-plug energy, as Empson discovered, comes from being always about the gaps between things: the town and the country, the rich and poor, the sick and the healthy, the cerebral and the manual, the viewer and the participant. It is further charged by being nearly always invoked at the moment of its leaving or its loss. The green flash at sundown is how the pastoral has worked for 2,500 years: blink and you'll miss it, but it was once all fields around here.

We might write the rules of hay pastoral. The field to be mowed is as close to Eden as we are permitted to get. The acres must be old but recalled vividly from childhood or other impressionable days. Belloc's field is being revisited from an 'exile', he says, that was dirtied by life and the world – 'cities and armies . . . a confusion of books . . . and horrible great breadths of sea'.

The grass must be ready for the scythe and the writer-mower must show that he (I don't know of a woman haymaker) knows this himself: 'it is just before, or during, or at the very end of that [spring week of] rain – but not later – that grass should be cut for hay'. Hocus-pocus of this kind is required proof of earth-knowledge, with nods and silent obeisance paid to Thomas Tusser and other almanacs of farm lore as well as to Hesiod and Virgil. You can catch an echo of this today when you hear the 'Agricultural Story Editor' being credited at the end of an episode of *The Archers* on BBC Radio 4. What is that? Another name for God?

Having asserted the (pseudo) facts the usufruct can be enjoyed: without wasting the substance of the harvest, ancient metaphorical truths are stooked before us, as at an agricultural show: 'what we get when we store our grass is not a harvest of something ripe, but a thing just caught in its prime before maturity: as witness that our corn and straw are best yellow, but our hay is best green. So also Death should be represented with a scythe and Time with a sickle; for Time can take only what is ripe, but Death comes always too soon.'

After any dalliance with capitalised concepts, practicalities must be underlined; tools are holy objects and are to be venerated as well as well-kept: 'there is an art also in the sharpening of a scythe, and it is worth describing carefully'. The hay essayist builds an icon in words, smitten with the hard matter to hand: half a page on whetting, another half on listening to your scythe in order to know when it is blunt.

The morals of mowing must be delineated: bad mowing is clumsy, formless and isolating; good mowing is a stepping through the now into an ancient but continuing rhythmic and balanced embrace: 'the scythe [will] mow for you if you treat it honourably and in a manner that makes it recognize its service'. But don't – despite the details here detailed – think too much. Indeed, you must unthink yourself in the field in order to mow well. Tolstoy struggled with this and beautifully and honestly recorded his difficulties in his diary and made Levin falter in the same way in *Anna Karenina*. Belloc gives us an unthinker who is rather more homiletic and pleased with himself: 'be thinking of anything at all but your mowing, and be anxious only when there seems some interruption to the monotony of the sound. In this mowing should be like one's prayers – all of a sort and always the same . . .'

Honour the hayseeds, 'the permanent root of all England' or wherever, the first farmers, the taciturn but wise natural-men. Capture them by taking down their noises ('Ar') but let them laugh at you and your smockery, your *nostalgie de la boue*, your Marie Antoinetting with the scythe so that you both play 'the comedy that we [are] free men'. Mention, if necessary, Cobbett and Bottom ('Methinks I have a great desire to a bottle of hay: good hay, sweet hay, hath no fellow').

Mow from the outside to the middle of the field, listen for the whisper of the stems as they are scythed, then, under the dipping sun, pause when at last there is 'nothing left but a small square of grass, standing like a square of linesmen who keep their formation, tall and unbroken, with all the dead lying around them when a battle is over and done'. Wipe your brow. Drink cider from cool earthenware flagons, drink ale, drink kvass. Pick up the corpses of corncrake chicks sliced in two by your mowing. Set your dog on the hare in the last stand and run the fleeing animal down in the stubble. Rake what you have cut into cocks. Sling your scythe on your shoulder and walk through the windrows and the aftermath to follow the farm track home in the red dust of the harvest sunset.

In 1847, at the age of nineteen, Tolstoy inherited Yasnaya Polyana, the estate where he had been born, near Tula, south of Moscow. The 5,400 acres of woods and fields came with 330 male serfs and their families. Long before he put on peasants' clothes (the *tolstovka* is still the name for the rather fancy loose smock-like shirt that he made famous), or started making his own shoes (offering them to his literary friends, much to their horror), or became a vegetarian (his lonely soup tureen for his special meatless meals is the saddest thing you can see at the museum of his Moscow town house), Tolstoy had grappled with what best to do for his fields and his fieldworkers and how to make his estate into a complete and happily, wholesomely, answering world. First he took up beekeeping and planted apple trees. At Yasnaya Polyana, after I watched a party of schoolchildren and their teachers blithely scrumping armfuls of apples from the orchards, I stole one myself, an Antonovka, from a basket of them, filled outside the stables in preparation for the horses' dinner on their return from the fields (the last clover hay was still being mown when I was there in September, and it was brought back to the farm by horse and cart). It tasted unripe and sour and not at all great, but I was told that, as a cooker, it transforms borscht and is perfect for stuffing a goose. The linen-coloured honey, set hard in a plastic yoghurt pot, that I bought from the beekeeper in the wooden greenhouse at the side of the old Tolstoy home was much nicer: a grown-up taste of a sweetness that didn't cloy, smoked through with the toasted smell of late summer.

For a time, Tolstoy was interested in technology, and attempted to modernise the farming on his estate with agro-gadgets and scientific growing. He tried raising cabbages on an industrial scale, built a distillery, diversified with sheep, and imported fashionable breeds of Japanese pigs. He designed a mechanical threshing machine and had one built to his own specifications. It made a big noise in the fields but threshed nothing. 'Master, our young master!', Henri Troyat, the first biographer of Tolstoy that I read, imagined the peasants respectfully saying, 'and when his back was turned they called him a madman'.

Frustrated, deflated and already (and characteristically) bored, Tolstoy moved on from machines to minds. He started a kind of hedge-school at Yasnaya Polyana, teaching the children of his peasants by devising things for them to read. He researched and began to publish an ABC, illustrated with huge simple copyable letters and woodblock prints. Typically for Tolstoy, though, the project was abandoned before he got, in effect, to the end of the alphabet. He was always hurrying on to the next thing, except when he stopped in the fields.

Trying to simplify himself in all departments, Tolstoy gave up wearing socks and invented a one-piece romper suit that he could climb into and button up from within. His wife, Sofya, was not impressed by peasant chic and continued to embroider L. T. in red letters in his underwear. But, incognito in his body bag, Tolstoy was able to eavesdrop on his peasants out on the estate and it was thus that he overheard them talking of their hatred for the nobility. In his earlier days, when more heavily dressed, he had once tried to impress some young ladies by diving fully clothed into a lake. Bogged down, he got into difficulties and had to be rescued by some peasant women who were haymaking nearby and who dragged him to the shore with their rakes. Everything Tolstoy did seems to have turned into a parable along the way.

Sex with his serfs (he had a son called Timofey with one) and scything with them were what survived longest in Tolstoy's pastoral. He was addicted to both: the contact with the skin of the earth. To begin with the master was seigneurial about his rights and it was no accident that he could install himself at the heart of the simple, hard won, hard worn, physical world that he championed. He wanted to learn from the peasants, but then he wanted to teach them what they already knew. He wanted to scythe but he wanted always to watch himself scythe, even as he declared the bliss of the loss of his selfhood. He was a permanent *thinker* even though he knew thinking could be oppressive; he was always, as he put it, 'thinking that he was thinking about what he was thinking about'. To be lost in action was what he wanted, to be lost in thought was where he was; once, thinking, he reached for a piece of bread when fishing and ate instead a handful of worms, his bait.

But as he grew, even though his ideas got less orthodox, he became subtler, cleverer, and more self-aware. Tolstoy, the master and the boss-farmer, might not have directly heard his peasants laughing at him, and he rushed from fad to fad and tried on different shirts for different personalities – but increasingly Tolstoy, the more private man and writer, returned candidly upon himself, and was harder on his own failings than anyone else could have been. In his diary he shows a far deeper self-knowledge than any of his peasant play-acting would suggest, even if sometimes the self-treatments he proposed eluded him. In his fiction he made his characters, above all Levin in *Anna Karenina* (almost a match for Tolstoy's own Lev with just a couple of extra letters), inhabit a world so fully realised that all their external actions and internal thoughts were lit by the comedy of truth. Sensing, even as he stumbled with his scythe, something of what his peasants were thinking of him, enables Levin to grow and to harvest or mow *himself* and, thereby, know himself better. And through this he (both Levin and Lev) saw the yearning for selfless belonging for what it was – a selfish dream.

'The gentleman must be mowed,' the old harvest song has it, and among Tolstoy's best diary entries are his field notes, his honest mappings of the passage of his life and mind across various open places, a weathered mix of bright noticing and clouded judgement, of moving forwards and backwards, in time and out of step, into and out of the grass:

20 April 1858: 'the grass is pushing through'; 10–13 May: 'drooping bird cherry in the workers' calloused hands . . . Caught a glimpse of Aksinya . . . Her neck is red from the sun . . . I'm in love as never before'; 14 June: 'All day in the fields. A wonderful night. A dewy white mist. Trees in the mist. The moon behind the birch trees and a corncrake; no more nightingales'; 15–16 June 'Had Aksinya . . . but I'm repelled by her;' 15 June–19 July: 'I'm not writing, not reading, and not thinking. I'm wholly absorbed in the estate. The battle is still in full swing. The peasants are trying it on and putting up a fight;' 20–22 July: 'Mowing . . . The idea occurs to me of describing this summer. What form would it take?'

At the house at Yasnaya Polyana, one of the small downstairs rooms with a low cellar-like curved ceiling served as a study for Tolstoy and also as his dressing room for scything. Rooms decorated in the folksy 'Russian style' were fashionable in the late nineteenth century. Olga Ivanovna, the narcissistic and wannabe artist in Chekhov's story 'The Grasshopper' (she is jumpy like a grasshopper) has peasant woodcuts, bark-shoes and sickles on the wall of her dining room with a scythe and a rake standing in one corner. She entertains her art-celebrity friends surrounded by these tools. Tolstoy did actually play with his toys. In a display case in his room there is a copy of two small blue ink sketches of the Count at his labours. They look like a page torn from a Brueghel notebook. In the same case is a totem, a scythe blade, one that Tolstoy used, displayed like the cursive stroke of one of the giant letters from his ABC, or the long metal flight feather, a primary, of a huge bird, a crane or a bustard or an eagle: escape tools of one sort or another here boxed and half-buried in the cellared room.

Imagine being a child of Tolstoy, woken in your bedroom at Yasnaya Polyana every morning by the sound of your father harnessing himself to a sledge outside the back door so that he – rather than any animal or any servant – might drag a barrel to the well, fill it with water for the household, and drag it back again. Imagine hearing how your embarrassing dad attended a party in town but was mistaken for an old peasant in sheepskins and told to wait outside. Imagine having a father, who didn't believe in using reins when in philosophical conversation, and who went for a ride in a cart with a holy fool of a follower, who didn't believe in using the whip. The recovery of the overturned cart from the ditch and the extrication of the thinkers took some doing. But then the same thinker also kept what was called the *Letter Box* at Yasnaya Polyana, where moans or boasts, confessions or apologies, jokes and news from all the family were encouraged and posted and which, every Sunday, would be read aloud by those in residence. Imagine, then, hearing your father read one note that he had written headed 'Bulletin of the Patients of the Yasnaya Polyana Lunatic Asylum' which reported of himself: 'His hallucinations consist in thinking that you can change other people's lives by words. General symptoms: discontent with the whole existing order of things, condemnation of everyone except himself, and irritable garrulity quite irrespective of his audience; frequent transitions from fury and vexation to an unnatural and lachrymose sentimentality. Special symptoms: busying himself with unsuitable occupations, such as cleaning and making boots, mowing hay, etc. Treatment: complete indifference of all surrounding the patient to what he says . . .'

There were years when Tolstoy didn't mow but the cutting comes around and, despite his posted confession, the harvests and the people in the fields operate on him repeatedly as a steadying corrective to his wayward self, while also (and also repeatedly) setting running some marvellous imaginative motor that never stopped, even during his last decades of fiction-hatred and self-castigation. One day, on a visit to Yasnaya Polyana, Turgenev saw him carrying bales of straw on his back and concluded he was 'lost to literature', but that was not true:

11 August 1893: A blue haze; the dew seems to be sewn on to the grass, bushes and trees to the height of a *sazhen* [seven feet]. Apple trees are bowed beneath their weight. From a log cabin comes the fragrant smoke of fresh brushwood. And over there, in a bright-yellow field, the dew is already drying out on the fine oat stubble and work has begun, binding, carting, scything and, in a violet-coloured field, ploughing. Everywhere along the roads and caught in the branches of the trees are torn off broken ears of corn. Gaily dressed young girls are weeding a dewy flowerbed and quietly singing, and man-servants in aprons are bustling about. A lap dog is warming itself in the sun. The gentlemen haven't got up yet.

As the years went on, outdoors life at Yasnaya Polyana remained similar; a little more hay and a little less love in the haystacks, but otherwise much the same, hay being good where life, especially indoors life, was mostly bad. A walk through a field, laying waste to it, came for Tolstoy to represent the opposite of all the mess and chaos of humans, a way of putting to one side the sex and women and drinking and gambling and art-making that derailed him and, beyond that, the wider curse of wealth and grand families and, wider still, the deluded vanities of the church and the state and almost every other person, as it came to seem, that lived, or had, or would:

4 June 1884: I'll do some mowing and stitch some boots. Tomorrow I'll get up at 5. But I don't yet undertake not to smoke. Mowed for a long time. We had dinner. Then I went to stitch boots until late in the evening. Didn't smoke. Around me the same parasitic life goes on. June: Recapitulation. I've been trying to change my habits. I've been getting up early. Doing more physical work . . . I don't drink any wine at all, don't put sugar in my tea and don't eat meat. I'm still smoking, but not so much; 25 June: Got up early. Was five rows behind the peasants but did my stint. Worked all day. Had no dinner; 30 June: I don't notice how I sleep and eat, and I'm strong and am composed spiritually. But at night there

are sensual temptations; 3 July: Got up at six. They had already done four rows each. I mowed with a terrible effort.

6 July 1890: In the evening I'll go and cut the rye. In the morning I argued again with Helbig about art ... Harvested the hay. Then the Zinovyevs came. I feel depressed with dead people; 10 July: Went for a bathe. Came back; the table was set for thirty people. The Ofrosimovs and Figners. Then music and singing. Terrible, pointless, it got on my nerves. Two pathetic machines and trumpets – people eating and making a nasty smell.

Tolstoy knew, nonetheless, that he made his own smell just as pungently as his houseguests. By 1889 he had already begun to worry that mowing had become, like his cigarettes, an addictive, almost masochistic, luxury. The more he mowed, the more he wanted from it, until either no cut was enough or every cut was self-lacerating. It was as if he knew he had ruined scything by taking part in it. And the mowers around him came to seem like fallen people, the prisoners of modernity. So the inklings of a further escape rose up in him, a dream of open country that would take him both backwards and beyond farming:

27 July 1889: Agriculture, which is replacing the nomadic conditions I experienced in Samara, is the first step towards wealth, luxury, dissipation and suffering ... We must make a conscious effort to return to the simple tastes of that time.

When he finally left Yasnaya Polyana in 1910 on his half-mad, half-wretched escape attempt, he started on foot towards the more open east. That he ended up falling ill on a train and then dying next to a railway station is one of the many indignities that the world outside Yasnaya Polyana seemed to have ready for Tolstoy whenever he left the two round towers at the park gate and joined the public road.

I had to make a spring journey by train on a fine day from Edinburgh Haymarket to Bristol Temple Meads. All the way down the country, there were fields being cut for the first haying of the year. In places the grass had already been lifted from the fields and hurried away in black plastic, as if it were evidence of something wrong; in others it lay drying in lines and the windrows or swaths rendered its late home an old picture, no matter what machines and geometries had constructed it. All the good green had gone in one mowing and the fields were ridged with the fallen. An old world was laid before me. For the first hour after the mowing, the tented grass is what you see, but quickly the aftermath, the fog of living grass coming through the cut, begins its work. The mown stems shrink and silver and sink. The beheaded but vigorous shoots rally and pull up through the dead, as green as they can.

Somewhere in the Midlands one tiny field had been spared or overlooked. Last year it had grown a single tubular bale of hay that had sat uncollected in the middle of its half-acre. This year new grass had grown vigorously at the bale's base and some cut stems in its top had seeded and sprouted. The grey face of the dead head now had shaggy green hair as well as a luxuriant green-knight ruff growing and spreading out from beneath it. That one field alone had escaped. But brambles were already fingering from its hedges. It might have only one more year left as runaway grass before the scrub closed it down. Everywhere else the hay fields were shorn and their grass surrendered. And like that they were half-lovely and half-not. My year falters hereabouts. I die a little more now than at any other season. The best has come so quickly and is taken so fast. And I cannot see those fields without thinking of my children's first haircuts, the plank on the chair in the barber's and the clippers and the scissors coming at their grown-out soft blond fur.

Back at home I went out to cut the lawn. The clatter of the wonky old mower struggled against thick and juicy stems, its rusty grasshopper mouth straining in a toothless chew. Every ten pushes or so it gave up, having tangled itself to a halt, knotted with the grass blades that it sought to cut. I knelt to the mess, unpicking the grass from the mower, and my hands came up dyed green and sweet-scented with sap. For the rest of the day, I had grass stains on my palms, and for the rest of the week, I had green cuticles.

Near the back door I dumped a heap of the longer stems of the drying cut grass on its way to the compost. A female blackbird found it and wanted it for her nest. Over the afternoon while I pottered down the garden she made repeated purposeful journeys to and from the pile every five minutes or so. On each visit she selected grass strands that were eight inches long or more. I could see her looking and choosing. She pulled at the pile and she gathered the stems she wanted with her beak. She worked fast but with care. It was beautiful to watch. She had to hold on to each strand as she plucked the next. It looked a little like shepherding peas on a fork. In the time that I watched her she got better at the task. Either that or I watched her less closely once I knew what she was about. When she had a beakful – sometimes fifteen strands were enough, once she took twenty-two – she flew down the garden towards her nest, jinking past me with her new whiskers trailing below her. In the time she was away, she tedded and turned the strands and stems until she could plait and weave them into her nest, making a wheel of hay which she would curve round her incubating body like a grass skirt. Then she came again to the heap.

A marvellous day opened on the fen, the greenest of the year, and foaming with tender brightness. It ran on and on, hot and cloudless for sixteen hours, but softened by the wind from the east and by the air filling with willow down and poplar seeds, mayflies and birds. The fields were full and working. The shaking leaves on the trees appeared to taste the air in the wind. Butterflies tumbled in the lower sky like stamps from an album. All of the wet of the rainy spring was held in the lush green that had raised the surface of the fen by a foot or more. The blue above surged but was not so harsh that I couldn't look up into it. And much was happening there. Above the lode that runs between Wicken and Burwell Fens there were ten or more hobbies hawking for insects, their sleek wings and long tails printing trident-shaped cut-outs all over the sky. In their yellow claws hanging from their red trousers they caught dragonflies, and other insects too small to see from the ground. And then, like all the best birds, they stopped in the air, pulling up into it and breaking from their stream-lines as they bent their heads forward between their wings to pass their prey from their feet to their bill in an exquisitely athletic gourmet action. To watch this treading of the air is almost as good as seeing swifts mate on the wing: the loved world made lovelier still.

There were other bright things below the hobbies. At the pond at Pout Hall the common terns had come back to breed. The bird incubating on the little gravel island was hot under the sun and panted, opening its red bill like a pair of bloody pliers. A kingfisher flying like a giant blue bee steered straight towards the dark foliage of the huge black poplar on the bank of the lode and disappeared, apparently taken inside the tree. Cuckoos called all across the fen, deepening the place, summoning the curve of the Earth in their deep-throated song. And on the flat turf fields at the fen edge four yellow wagtails ran after insects and, doing so, disturbed orange-tip butterflies and both yolk-bright things leaped into the blue, embossing the sky.

Around the fen, blossom thickly dressed from the thorns. Whitethroats and lesser whitethroats scratched and rattled in relay from the bushes like burrs snagged in underwear. Rape pollen gathered in the corners of my eyes, sticky as moth dust. On the pool at Tubney Fen two pairs of avocets had managed four chicks between them thus far. Four other young had already disappeared into the compost of the season since I last visited. On land the surviving babies looked like melting dirty snow-balls. When the field of cows arrived through the evening mist of butter-cups to drink at the waterhole, the young avocets floated away from the huge animals like thistledown hovercraft. The cows sank up to their knees on the shore. As each began to drink it pissed in a great split carrier-bag wallop. The hot plunge drilled into the mud. A coot scuttled from its nearby nest, assembling its seaweed legs from the twisted wreath of green reeds. As the cows drank, their calves latched on to their bagpipe udders. A drake shoveler paddled close to the cows' legs, dabbled and then surfaced, its spatula bill running with water, like the baleen of a whale.

* * *

113

The lapwing knows, and the eel must too, but no human, resident or stranger, quite grasps how to get into the fens or what that would mean. Are they geology or mindset? The outside looking in or the inside looking out? A room, or weather? A draining board, or a granary? A dustbowl, or a floodplain? A delta of catchments, or the sea deferred? They fall between. In books they often turn up at the end, beyond systematics and topologies, overlooked and under-loved, half-lands and etceterative places. 'Sunk' as Defoe says, in his *Tour*, of Ancaster, the Roman village on the Lincolnshire fen edge, 'out of knowledge'. In the 1950s, after writing of its few acres, Eric Ennion and Alan Bloom – the two rivals for the projected fixings of Adventurers' Fen – both attempted panoptic accounts. Ennion wrote *Cambridgeshire* (1951) for a series called 'The County Books' and Bloom, for 'The Regional Books', wrote *The Fens* (1953). Ennion ends his book lamenting the disappearance of wild fenland lost to farmland, Bloom lamenting that drained and farmable fens will without 'constant vigilance' return to 'wild nature'.

'I had almost forgotten *Marsh-Earths*,' John Evelyn writes in his *Terra: A Philosophical Discourse of Earth*, a book written in 1676 from the centre of the open-horizon century, 'which though of all other, seemingly, the most churlish, a little after 'tis first dug, and dryed (when it soon grows hard, and chaps,) may with labour, and convenient exposure, be brought to an excellent temper; for being the product of rich Slime, and the sediment of Land-Waters, and Inundations, which are usually fat, as also the rotting of Sedge, yea, and frequently of prostrated Trees, formerly growing in or near them, and in process of time rotted (at least the spray of them) and now converted into mould, becomes very profitable Land: But whether I may reckon this among the natural Earths, I do not contend.'

Up until its last paragraph, John Henry Gurney's book *Early Annals of Ornithology* (1921) painstakingly attempts to lasso scientifically the flightiest of histories (birds seen by poets rather than through binoculars, Homer's eagles, quails in the Bible, the meaning of 'gannet'). The final words are about Thomas Pennant (the naturalist and traveller and Gilbert White's correspondent) and a heronry in the Lincolnshire fens at 'Cressi Hall', six miles from Spalding (and twenty-five from Defoe's Ancaster). They are telling words, even in their retreat into the wet unknown. The truth must be out there but where? Gurney, elsewhere oftentimes number-cruncher, mapper, and fly-poster of facts, admits defeat. And so the herons disappear into the fens: 'On less competent authority so many as eighty nests on one oak tree would hardly have been accepted as credible, nor has Pennant's counting met with a modern parallel in England. Lincolnshire heronries appear to have been larger than at the present day, but it is hardly likely that the birds themselves were more numerous. Pishey Thompson, a local historian, writes of a very large tree at Leake, in the same neighbourhood, which was literally covered with Heron's nests, but he does not tell us how many, or whether anybody counted them.'

BUFFALO

For one summer day, outside the little town of Interior (population: 94), in the Badlands of South Dakota, I walked along animal trails through dry grass and the scratch of low scrub. Meadowlarks kept me company. Until you get to an edge here you feel you are on the floor of the Earth, flat and low. Then the ground gives way and, beyond gulches and canyons of bare earth, the busy washing away of the world, are dropped and sunken miles of more grass blowing into the distance. Through binoculars I could see a small herd of buffalo moving a mile below me and three miles out, their backs rippling through the silvery-green. They looked like surfacing whales shiny with brine, watched from a cliff top, and swimming far out to sea.

In the early evening storm clouds put a lid over the plain. A line of bikers passed me on the road on their way to a rally at Sturgis, their engines panting like tired horses with loose lips, the last riders of a late cavalry. In the end of the light I went down to the buffalo. There were twenty pushing up against the fence of the national park. Their dark eyes wept with dirty pollen and their dark brown fur, old pipe tobacco at their heads and shoulders, was deep-scored with the tattoo of the barbed wire. They had open acres behind them in which to roam but they had all gathered tightly together into a wheel of hot dusty wool and sniffed at the thick air beyond their enclosure. On the other side of the fence were five black cows avoiding their eyes. Next to the buffalo, they looked modern, compact and close-shaved, but also rather gormless. In another field, three brown horses stood and stared, shifting their weight from hoof to hoof.

A single fence, a line across the land, means that nowhere is truly unfenced any longer in North America. One fence is all it took. I walked to my car through a run of grass, between the fields, keeping my eye out for rattlesnakes and pushing legions of grasshoppers ahead of me. Prairie dogs whistled from the open mouths of their sandy burrows. Rain spotted the earth just as I got back to the road near a sign that said: 'Caution – Prairie Dogs Have Plague! Keep People and Pets in Vehicles.' Someone had used the yellow square for a rifle target.

I camped nearby that night. A thin bar of electric light spilled from the toilet block but everywhere else was very dark. Once for a few moments the clouds opened, and a shooting star and a hunting night-hawk moved in quick succession across the gap above me. Then the rain came and I hid in my tent, the sky flashing on and off with lightning and then pile-driving with thunder, a riot that kept me awake for an hour and made the horses whinny in the Indian rodeo field next door.

I lay there and imagined the undoing of it all. First the lightning leaping back into the sky, the clouds sucked into the dark blue night. Then, across the plain below and stretching ever wider, the United States united, unfenced and unfarmed; wire twanging from its staples, posts returned to pine trunks; hay sprung from its bale and replanted as grass, the juice coming again into it. Earth in the ploughed fields tamping back its own furrows, the glister of wet soil gone; seeds springing up into a sower's hand; the crust of the badlands made good without a scar; grass touching grass across thousands of miles into a single spread. Barn swallows, before barns, coursing the lawns for insects; a grasshopper that never stopped; and across this open land, flapping flags of skin and fur rushing at mounds of meat and wrapping them, the buffalo kneeling up from the ground and moving away through the grass. Smoke drawn back into the barrels of rifles, arrows taken to sticks, feathers and flints. The railway tidied into reversing boxcars; other buffalo pulled up a cliff like a smoking waterfall; wheels rolled from the skeletons of carts; the continent remembering the drum of unshod hooves. An Indian climbing down from the bare back of a horse; animals in the grass losing the smell of people in their noses, the Europeans at sea losing the green smell of the new world and sailing backwards over the horizon.

I stirred in the early morning and, as I turned over, a half-squashed grasshopper crept stunned from my side.

Later the same day, in midsummer haze, piebald and skewbald Crow ponies swam as they grazed next to the Little Bighorn battlefield in Montana. In the hot wind, bowling from all around, their colours slid from them, and their long manes and tails rippled in concert with the grass. They stepped towards the wire that kept them from the stone markers indicating where fighters from both sides fell in the battle that killed Custer in June 1876. Around the markers were visitors, with guides (Crow in their National Parks uniforms and others) explaining what happened here. At every step the ponies flushed dozens of grass-hoppers that leapt up like dusty spray in all directions, some sailing through the wire fence, others falling back into the grass on the horses' side of the hill.

What happened, in the end, *was* the wire. The Plains Indians, who forced Custer from his horse and held him here, the Sioux and others who won the battle to secure their way of life, the Crow who had fought with Custer, all of them lost everything within a few short years. Fields came from the east and with them fences. 'We use nails to stir the tea,' wrote Wallace Stevens, poet and unlikely dude-rancher, on his western adventure in 1903. The blowing prairie was wired, its herds hobbled and its nomads stalled. The settlement and farming that followed, the opening of the West, marked an end not a beginning. At the very moment it was taken into white possession the space closed.

Many of the Sioux's battles throughout their history had been about grass. Two of the three Sioux groups, the Yankton and the Teton (also called Lakota), were agriculturalists. Pushed south into the Great Plains by the Santee Sioux (themselves fleeing war with the Ojibwa around Lake Superior), all three Sioux groups, acquiring horses and surrounded by buffalo, abandoned farming and moved through the grass. They traded buffalo products for maize with farming Indians ('dust scatterers' they derisively called them – the Hidatsa, Mandan, Arikara, and

Pawnee) but they raided these tribes too, eventually driving them into alliances with the US military.

The Sioux's conflict with the United States was similarly centred on farming and fencing. The First Treaty of Fort Laramie in 1851, negotiated between the Plains Indians and the US government, restricted the Santee to reservations and encouraged them to take up agriculture. They didn't like it and in 1862 starvation threatened their reservation in what is now Minnesota (it remains a reservation and the site of the state's first casino). A white trader, Andrew Myrick, refused the Sioux credit saying, 'Let them eat grass.' His remark (as well as his name, perhaps) was one of the inciting factors in what became known as the Sioux Uprising. He was killed. His killers stuffed hanks of grass into his mouth and his opened stomach.

On 1 August 1867 near Fort C. F. Smith, forty-five miles south-west of the Little Bighorn, between 500 and 800 Lakota Sioux and Cheyenne warriors attacked six settlers cutting hay. Almost all battles have been in fields; this was a fight explicitly about what was in the field. Twenty-one soldiers from the Fort assisted the settlers and were able to defeat the Indians with the help of new breech-loading rifles and a howitzer. The engagement, part of Red Cloud's War, is known as The Hayfield Fight.

In 1870 Red Cloud, the Lakota Sioux leader, met President Grant in Washington, DC, and spoke. 'The white people have surrounded me and left me nothing but an island. When we first had this land we were strong. Now we are melting like snow on the hillside while you are growing like spring grass.'

In 1875 Red Cloud spoke again to a United States senate commission who had arrived in the Black Hills. Gold had been found during the previous year: Custer, sent after it, had said the hills were filled with gold 'from the grass roots down'. The government wanted to negotiate a lease of the area from the Sioux or buy the hills outright for 6 million dollars. Red Cloud said he would not accept payment of less than 70 million dollars and beef herds to last seven generations. 'I want a sow and a boar, and a cow and a bull, and a hen and a cock, for each family. I am Indian and you want to make a white man out of me . . . Maybe you white people think that I ask too much . . . but I think those hills extend clear to the sky, and that is the reason I ask so much . . . I have been in to white people's houses and I have seen nice black bedsteads and chairs and I want that kind of furniture . . . and a sawmill . . . a mower and a scythe.'

These abrupt and violent passages from grass as a universal given to the man-made farm, from the grazed to the scythed, from bending stems to wire fences, from the mobile to the settled, are all evidence of a people forcibly estranged from what had been their familiar place. The Sioux encounter with white America effected, for them, an alienation at home. In large part this was externally dictated – the Indians were basically caged – but it was also internally grown. I don't mean the Sioux were complicit with their own destruction, but it is hard not to feel their deep shock over meeting this new and devastatingly successful way of being on the land. Nature was being bundled into stooks and ricks; wild things were given hard edges and turned into money. Industrial metals were driven into the ground like weapons: tethers, posts and ploughs. The grass was suddenly greener. But there was a fence where there hadn't been one before.

Grass still covers the battlefield at the Little Bighorn and stretches as far as you can see. Its green persistence makes it hard to mourn a prairie. To my lazy eye it still looks *good*. Green and watered coulees meander through buttery hills under a bone-yellow sky. There seems more than enough grass to go round. Yet that is what the battle was about. Grass and its fencing. The conjuring of proleptic fields. Today, despite the green and despite what the plains grow, the world here is curtailed and depleted, and in many places speaks only of the end of things. Standing in the battlefield makes you look into the distance and eventually something arrives through the heat shimmer and grass gloss of July. Nowhere else that I know has the enclosing of wild grass seemed so humanly germane (summer in Montana is beautifully, humanly made) yet so precisely terminal (to know anything of this place's past is to know how much death lies just below its surface). Or, perhaps, nowhere else other than these Elysian fields and those in Las

Vegas – Las Vegas, that is, which means *the meadows*, las vegas, that is, that aren't.

For some it was like this two hundred years ago in England. The closing off of the wild drew attention to a world that had been lost, not just fenced. The quarried ground at Swordy Well in Northamptonshire, a broken place on its knees, answered back through John Clare's poem from the 1830s. 'And me they turned inside out / For sand and grit and stones / And turned my old green hills about / And pickt my very bones.' But it is different in Montana. Much of England had already been harrowed by 1800 and most enclosure was of already man-made open fields. Those who were fenced out were among the millions who crossed the Atlantic. Forty-four per cent of the 839 men of the 7th Cavalry at the Little Bighorn were foreign-born. Among them two were born 'at sea', two in Hungary, one in Russia, 128 in Ireland, and fifty-three in the United Kingdom. Smith 1st, Smith 2nd, Smith 3rd, reads the roll call of the dead. None of the white dead were born within 200 miles of the battlefield. A closer parallel with Montana would be the time in Britain when the old woods were cut for the first plough, but that was long ago, the raw materials were different and the land itself hardly remembers. In North America the old world lived until my grandfather's time. In Montana wild grass grew recently enough for us all to feel its passing. And the fences still operate today, putting a brake on a land that seems – despite its posthumous atmosphere – not reconciled to stopping.

Custer didn't want to dismount. Prairie riding was a delicious species of bliss. Another plains sailor, James Silk Buckingham, described the waving green as 'the bosom of a new Atlantic'. Westering through interior seas of grass to the rim of the world, Custer liked the way the wind through his hair cooled his neck, the way the land flowed away from the saddle, the way his buckskin joined the world-skin. He titled his autobiography *My Life on the Plains*. He travelled in a laughing and festive mood with his friends and family as well as his own cook, a sixteen-man band, and his pack of staghounds. But, forced to get off, he made his history out of standing, and now he settles in my mind somewhat like the tractor seats awaiting their farmers that are fixed in front of the slot machines at Caesar's Palace in Las Vegas. Ploughing your own furrow brings a harvest of indignities. Settling is to be ill at ease.

Custer stopped here. Many of his cavalrymen shot their own horses in order to hide behind them. And for a while Custer's body disappeared into this ground, his scarecrow straw hair combed with prairie soil; his dead mouth plugged with it. Everything is said to go very quiet after a battle. The meadowlarks that sit today on the death markers and bend their oriole bluegrass through the hot air would have stopped singing for an hour in the madness of the fight. Watching them, I wondered, as Edward Thomas did of moles in the trenches, if any were killed in the crossfire. As soon as the guns fell silent the birds would have started up again. In late June there is work to be done and the prairie sparkles with its workers' music. Custer would have been buried to lark song.

Though he hunted as he crossed the plains, bringing down wolves and bagging a bear, and was a keen amateur taxidermist (able to do a full elk), Custer was also a nature lover of sorts. He kept a pelican and a porcupine (which shared his marital bed on occasions). He allowed a field mouse to live in the inkwell on his desk and let it run up his sleeve and scurry through his grassy hair. He made over the cavalry's hospital tent for his travelling menagerie (a hawk, two owls, toads, rattlesnakes and a petrified tree trunk, a prairie bog oak). And there is a story that he once 'altered the regimental line of march to avoid disturbing a meadowlark's nest'. Sitting Bull, chief among Custer's enemies at the Little Bighorn, also had poignant dealings with the ecosystem. Before the battle he 'sang a thunder song, smoked, and prayed for knowledge of things to come'. He filled buckskin pouches with tobacco and willow bark and fastened these offerings to sticks, which he planted in the ground of the valley of the Little Bighorn. Later the same night he dreamed of soldiers falling on an Indian village like so many thousand grasshoppers. And after the fight, and not long before he died, a Sioux-speaking meadowlark appeared to him in a dream and told him that his own people would kill him. The bird's words came true in 1890 at Standing Rock when he was shot by two Indian Agency policemen.

* * *

Without the last 150 years breathing all over it, the prairie might have endured. But the worm cannot forgive the plough. 'Busting the sod' or 'breaking out' the land does as it describes. Turn over the grasses and topsoil of the prairie and it is no longer prairie. Rescue is hard. Grasslands are soil manufactories. But they need grass to do it. There was often more than ten feet of topsoil beneath the prairie surface. Most of any grass is underground; roots spread for miles allowing it to live in drought conditions and to survive fire. One square-yard sod of big bluestem, the once dominant native grass of tallgrass prairie, contained twenty-five miles of roots. To sever the roots is to destroy the surface of the earth. When the first horses pulled ploughs through the prairie, the sound of grass roots cracking and snapping on the blades was so loud it was described as being like 'a fusillade of pistols'.

Almost the entire prairie has now gone, the grass and its soil and everything following. Less than five per cent of the original tallgrass prairie (the eastern prairie type) remains. A few unploughed acres rise above the surrounding land, like the islands of wet undrained fens in Cambridgeshire that are higher than the farmland around them. Less than half of the original mixed and shortgrass prairies remain. One of the ironies that the straw-headed Custer bequeathed to the world is that the best surviving shortgrass prairie in southern Montana is at the Little Bighorn battlefield. Though the fight was over the grass, and though the battle dead have been buried and reburied beneath it, the 700 acres have never been ploughed. Nor has grazing been permitted on the Custer battlefield since 1891 or on the adjacent Reno-Benteen site since 1954. On ungrazed high plains, 250 plant species have been found at a single location; on ranches where the ground is unploughed but nonetheless grazed, the count drops to forty or so species. In a valley of old grass ploughed to wheat or alfalfa the crop replaces an ecosystem with a monoculture.

Below the battlefield across the shallow doodling river, Crow farmers were cutting wheat. The Little Bighorn is now at the heart of the Crow Reservation. Swallows cast a net in the air above the field to take its flies. The chaff from the combine blew up towards me through the trees of the little wood where Major Marcus Reno got into trouble in the Custer fight in 1876 and was forced into the timber. Reno's scout, Bloody Knife, was hit in the head by a bullet, and his brains wet Reno's face. The shrapnel of splinters killed forty men there.

Specks of straw stuck to my sweating forehead. There was a sign in front of me: *The removal of objects from the battlefield or adjacent Indian lands is illegal.* Later, when I rinsed my face in the visitor centre, three stowaway grasshopper legs swirled into the sink along with the chaff. The fold of their joints was the same angle as the crook in the grass stems that they had lived among and the same as the bend in the leg of the meadowlarks that had sung over them.

Some of Reno's men got out of the wood but didn't make it back up the hill. Those who did were besieged for two days; theirs was the longest of battles at the Little Bighorn. On the hilltop they dug 'rifle trenches' as best they could with forks, spoons and coffee cups to get as close to the ground and as far out of harm's way as possible. Soldiers used the molehills of a prairie dog town, little hummocks of turned earth, for breastworks. Some were buried in their own trenches afterwards. Lieutenant Edward S. Godfrey remembered fighting from the little scuffed up and scraped places: 'The excitement and heat made our thirst almost maddening. The men were forbidden to use tobacco. They put pebbles in their mouths to excite the glands, some ate grass roots, but did not find relief; some tried to eat hard bread, but after chewing it awhile would blow it out of their mouths like so much flour.' Several were so exhausted in their trenches they fell asleep holding their guns.

Grass stems scribble at the death markers on the battlefield. The low hills are planted with white marble stones, scattered in places, clustered elsewhere. The stones take you to specific minutes in June 1876. Those showing the outcome of the fight between Captain Myles Keogh and Crazy Horse struck me especially. In a scrape of grass in a shallow basin below a ridge, they look like a disturbed clutch of eggs – with some death markers practically touching, others tossed aside. This man died alone, these close enough to have held hands. Beyond the markers are open acres with nothing, escapes that never were. There are darker red granite memorials for Indian deaths too, though fewer of them are known (and fewer died: between forty and a hundred). These have been erected only in the last decade or so. Each, the white stone for the white man or red for the red, marks a last breath. Cornered in an open field and clobbered, cut down with axe or arrow or bullet, people fell to the ground. Here he died; right here, where now, as then, the grasshopper goes and the meadowlark sings. I am used to trudging to fixed stony monuments and reading the text – the words and the stone being all there is left – but these scattered markers shook me awake; a tombstone is after the fact, these stones mark the crossing places. Or so we think.

The markers were erected in 1890. Photographs from before show a chaos of human and horse bones across the abattoir of the battlefield. Some bodies were moved and many were mutilated after death. Ravens and eagles, coyotes and wolves, burying beetles and worms, all would have done their work as well. In 1866 in another battle in Red Cloud's War, ten years before the Little Bighorn, Crazy Horse and nearly 2,000 other Lakota, Santee and Cheyenne warriors killed eighty-one men of William J. Fetterman's command near Fort Phil Kearny (one hundred miles south-east of the Little Bighorn). It has been estimated that the Indians fired 40,000 arrows in the fight. Private John Guthrie was deputed to gather up the dead: 'We walked on top of their internals and did not know it in the high grass. Picked them up, that is their internals, did not know the soldier they belonged to, so you see the cavalry man got an infantry man's gutts and an infantry man got a cavalry man's gutts . . .'

Chapter twenty-three of Genesis tells the story of Abraham seeking to bury his wife Sarah in the land of the Hittites, where he describes himself as a 'sojourning settler'. Custer and the other immigrant dead were not intending to become settlers right away on the battlefield at the Little Bighorn but they had to be buried. The Hittites grant Abraham a cave at the far end of a field (the word is *sadeh*, 'a flexible term for territory that stretches from field to steppe'). The desire to bury our dead meaningfully and live among them – to put down roots

125

– is one reason to stop moving and settle. Some corner of a foreign field is not enough; Abraham buys the cave to bury his dead wife.

On the Crimean steppe, Scythian horse-riding nomads dug huge earthworks and raised conical burial kurgans, like lighthouses in the sea of grass, defying the rolling flow of the land itself. Inside they stowed their dead kings but also their dead king's horses and lots of gold. It was time to stop moving.

White America had similar ideas. The tension between the desire to push on, the sense that better things lie over the next hill, and the urge to make camp – to open the ground and live on it – run through the interleaved history of Americans and American grass. Landless but enclosed people left one continent for another and there sought fences. Out of Europe came bodies and minds that had registered what hedging meant, that understood the wish to be bordered, and that admired the pioneer but loved also to sit down. In Montana and elsewhere these incoming undertakers met a landscape that couldn't think like that, and inhabitants who had been shaped by living in the place: who had taken on its qualities, no more nor less than the immigrants who, even as they broke free of their European cages, had brought their fenced minds with them. We, the Europeans, wanted the grass the Indians had, and if we could convince ourselves that they didn't actually own it (since they weren't subduing the earth enough, as God commanded man to do in Genesis) it made taking it from them that much easier.

One summer in Montana I saw the Last Stand twice and I met six Custers. One, in buckskin, handed me his business card in a long caravan purring with its air conditioning at the back of a white farmer's field beyond Hardin. 'The people come out,' he said, 'they can actually handshake George Armstrong Custer, they can get an autograph; that goes a long way in saying they've touched a piece of history.' Another Custer, in cavalry uniform, handed me his card the next day. He'd just died and was husky as we spoke, 'I'm wore down,' he said. When not Custer he was Steve Alexander, a linesman running wires across the plains for an energy company. We were sitting on the temporary wooden bleachers erected on a Crow farm at the edge of the battlefield.

126

Restagings of the Last Stand happen all around but are not permitted on the sacred ground itself. 'You believe that I look like Custer because I convince you that I am Custer, but if you take my picture and put it up against Custer there is probably not that much of a correlation, but this is as close as you'll ever be to the man, you will never find another person who will be able to portray him in this manner, who has put as much time into it. The ring I'm wearing is the West Point ring of June of 1861; I have cinnamon oil in my hair; I carry a toothbrush in my pocket because Custer always carried a toothbrush in his pocket.' As we were talking, next to us, an Indian pony rider was being reprimanded for still wearing his socks. They were white. A brisk middle-aged woman was telling him to take them off the next time he rode. He asked her if he could keep his glasses on. She thought for a moment and said, 'Uh huh, that's OK; but make sure when you fall off next time that you stay down; don't go getting up too quick.'

Custer was thirty-six when he was killed. He was shot twice, beneath the heart and in the left temple. One account has him not scalped (his hair, despite all stories, was short on his last campaign) but sitting up and stripped naked except for his white socks with his thigh gashed so he couldn't ride horses again in the afterlife. Another says two Cheyenne women found his body and pushed the point of their sewing awls into each of his ears. 'This was done to improve his hearing.' A third report describes arrows driven into his groin (just because). He stopped, the last straw, in the sandy soil of the battlefield for a year. Then he (or the 'double handful' of bones that remained of him) was dug up and taken to what was thought holier ground, 1,000 miles east at West Point in New York State. But by then the resident alien had turned the green hills about and marked the earth forever.

'When the last stand was made, the Long Hair stood like a sheaf of corn with all the ears fallen around him,' said Sitting Bull. At the Little Bighorn the 7th Cavalry Custer battalion lost 210 men, and in the fighting further north along the ridge the Reno-Benteen battalion lost fifty-three. Indians, coming from their village and splashing across the river, looked like bees hurrying from a hive, Kill Eagle, a Blackfoot, said. The battle, according to another Indian, looked like 'thousands of dogs might look if all of them were mixing in a fight'. But the heart of it lasted, a third Indian warrior remembered, 'no longer than a hungry man needed to eat his dinner'. 'It was as easy as killing sheep,' Rain, a Sioux, said.

Though Custer and the 7th Cavalry were trounced, the Indians didn't linger at the scene of their victory. They gathered their dead and left the valley as soon as they could. Their possession of the place was as fleeting as it ever was. Late in the afternoon of the battle day, its little hour of blood already passed, the great joined camp of Indians at the riverside gathered their few things and began to leave. Reno's surviving men watched them through binoculars. First they set fire to the prairie around their tepees, so that flames swirled from its sweet grass, and smoke clouded the campsite. And through the smoke, 7,000 people and their horses and dogs moved west up the grassed ridges of the valley towards the distant Big Horn Mountains. The crowd stretched for five miles over the prairie. Charles Windolph, a member of H Company, recalled: 'It was like some Biblical exodus; the Israelites moving into Egypt; a mighty tribe on the march.'

I stood in the valley of the Little Bighorn and looked at it also from its eastern rim where the surviving cavalrymen would have watched the departing Indians. Having been there makes it strange to know that just a few years later some of those same Indians walked again a few yards from where I sit now in the evening of a wet English day. Extraordinarily quickly after the real event, Sioux fighters and even Sitting Bull himself were recruited to appear in various stagings of the battle promoted by and usually starring Buffalo Bill. Sitting Bull charged between one and two dollars for his signature as he travelled the world. On tour he wore goggles fashioned from green wire and found stairs difficult, never having known them previously. Presented with a telephone, he would offer his best (and only) English: 'Hello' and 'You bet!' One of Buffalo Bill's Wild West Show tours in 1891 visited Bristol. When not in the fens I live there and write in a room that looks out on to the Gloucester Road. This was the road taken by the cavalcade of performers from the railway station at Temple Meads to their performing grounds at Horfield. They walked from the train, field names everywhere, to get to their battlefield show, drumming up business as they went. I have often looked up from my table and out across the street to imagine the sound of Indian feet and Indian hooves, and the eighteen buffalo they also had with them, all passing my window.

Once the Indians had gone, the earth at the Little Bighorn became one great lodging for the white men. The first soldiers who came upon the battlefield after the fight mistook the naked bodies of Custer and his troop for skinned buffalo carcasses. The sun had already blackened the dead, the stench was nauseating. The smell of dead men persisted for the whole summer, it was said. The Indians had dismembered some bodies, many were stripped and many, like Custer, had been mutilated after death. Across the battlefield the fallen were 'disembowelled, with stakes driven through their chests, with their heads crushed in, and many of them with their arms and legs chopped off'. Most received only a shallow grave, a scoop of soil taken from beneath the body poured back on top of it. Officers were buried more deeply than ordinary men: 'to keep the wolves from digging them up'. The earth isn't hard to scuff. By late June the short prairie grasses are drying in Montana, their first green already silvering under the sun, the soil is fine and easily shaken from the roots. The summer of 1876 was unseasonably wet but most of the rain fell after the battle. Indians did not bury their dead, so the Custer graves were the very first turnings of the prairie turf.

Those who survived the battle but were wounded were evacuated at the same time as its dead were buried. The injured were carried on litters and stretchers made, in some cases, by tearing apart Sioux burial scaffolds that had been built adjacent to the battlefield. For fifteen miles they were taken through the grasslands to a steamer, the *Far West*, which waited at the confluence of the Bighorn and Little Bighorn Rivers. There the bleeding were laid on deck on a bed of freshly cut grass.

A year later in 1877, the bones and other scraps and remnants of almost all the officers and the civilians were removed from the battlefield. They were buried back east, nearer, as it seemed, the centre of things. Custer's remains were never returned to where he died.

In 1879 a military expedition was sent to the battlefield to tend to its graves and to collect still more bones. It was long claimed that the only official survivor of the Custer battle on the United States government side was a 'claybank' coloured horse called Comanche that had been ridden by Captain Keogh. The horse was shot seven times in the battle including through both of its back legs and a hoof but it survived. One bullet went through Keogh's knee and on into Comanche's flank. Many horses (and even a yellow bulldog) actually survived the battle, but many also died, often shot by their own riders. In 1879 the shambles of horse bones and human bones that was scattered across the hillsides was gathered into a heap and topped with a pyramid of logs. This – the Cordwood Monument – was the first memorial built on the ridge that became known as Last Stand Hill. One horse skeleton was identified as Custer's. Its hooves were removed and fashioned into four inkwells. Comanche lived to be twenty-nine and was stuffed when he died.

In 1881 all the remaining shallow graves on the battlefield were opened and dug over, and their contents placed in a new mass grave around the base of the new granite memorial that replaced the bone and log affair. Lieutenant Charles Roe of the 2nd Cavalry reported on his work: 'A trench was dug, into which were gathered all remains of those who fell in that fight . . . and deeply buried at the foot of the monument.' Thirty-nine horses, 'all sorrels of C Company', were buried at this time just beyond the humans in another pit near the memorial. This mass grave was discovered in 1941 when pipes were being laid and ten horse skeletons were uncovered.

The biggest cluster of the 1890 white stone death markers is across a hundred-yard square of the grass slope just below the crest of Last Stand Hill and the memorial. These are the only close-fenced markers on the battlefield. Custer's stone is in the middle of a field of comrades who are sown around him in death like so many bags of flour. The well-known *Last Stand* oil painting of 1890 by Frederic Remington shows this as well: Custer in the middle of a corral of men curved against the Indians who are circling like wolves. But both stones and picture are in fact fictions, early restagings of the battle. It is thought Custer actually died slightly to one side of most of his men nearer the hilltop on what is now a square of mown lawn around the granite memorial. The commemoration of the event has obscured the event itself and Custer is forced to play his part in a simulacrum a little way off.

A larger military cemetery on the edge of the battlefield was founded in 1886. It is a great depot for the dead, housing 4,950 dead soldiers and others from conflicts the USA was involved in from the Indian Wars up until Vietnam. It seems strange to have gathered the dead and to bury them on top of others' last moments but the blood shed in 1876 sacralised the soil for many, making it a good place, super-special, super-sad, to stake a claim. Though the cemetery is considered 'closed' it is still waiting for a few relatives of some of the already dead who had booked family plots. They are permitted to arrive in their own time.

Below the plots and the battlefield I could see silvery cottonwood trees hugging the banks of the Little Bighorn River and, beyond them, Crow ponies that had been let on to the aftermath of a cropped field to graze. On the far side of the valley a long coal train appeared on the railway tracks. I walked one section of the graveyard and still the same train was drawing down the line. There were hundreds of wagons, each filled with the same shaped mound of black coal. The whole stretched for perhaps four miles and the wild klaxon of the train's locomotive ran back over the coal wagons like smoke and met its echo from the answering dry hills.

In the cemetery those who had been previously buried in the army forts of Montana, Wyoming and the Dakotas were reburied here when those places were abandoned. As a consequence civilians are buried next to soldiers, and soldiers next to children. Some died unnamed at birth and are marked bluntly with a dash, a surname, and the carved word *Child*. Vincent Charley, the Swiss farrier in D Company of the 7th Cavalry, is buried here; he was shot through the hips at the Little Bighorn and tried to crawl after his retreating comrades. His body was later found with a stick rammed down his throat. Corporal John Noonan is buried here. He didn't fight at the Little Bighorn. He shot himself in 1878 after his wife died. She was known as Mrs Nash and had survived several soldier husbands but on her death she was discovered to be a man. Corporal Noonan couldn't take the ridicule that followed. John Burkman, Custer's orderly, is buried here. He was devoted to his boss and would hear no ill word said of him. He'd wanted to ride with Custer on 25 June but his commander had sent him back to the pack train. Lonely and adrift in his later years he moved to Billings in Montana so he could at least be close to the scene of the end of his hero. He shot himself in 1925. Captain Fetterman, or what remained of him, is buried here. His 'internals' were among those of his command of eighty-one that proved so difficult to unjumble when their tangled corpses were found in 1866.

In 1893 the first battlefield superintendent arrived at the Little Bighorn site. He built a house ('one of the first permanent structures in eastern Montana') and looked after the graves. The Crow, who had recovered their lands around the battlefield by this time, called him the 'ghost herder'. They believed that as he lowered the flag in the cemetery in the evening the soldiers' spirits rose from the graves and when he raised the flag the next morning the spirits hurried back underground.

I returned to the spot on the Custer battlefield where Keogh and Crazy Horse fought and Comanche the horse took his hits. It was near closing time and I was the last person out on the road. Far to the west there was lightning and a grey mess of rain. The nearer air began to sizzle in expectation. In the evening sky above me, Venus pushed through like a first match struck and then the silver dust of the night came prickling overhead all the way along the battle ridge from Last Stand Hill. Away from the storm, unvexed clouds lay quiet around the sky, darkening it where they ran, marshalling yards for the night. A female northern harrier bucked along beside me, silent over the grass and the death markers. The meadowlarks began to wind down and just as I turned to leave, a nighthawk appeared right at the roadside, flapping fast and ghostly over the grass, part of the dark coming into the end of the day.

The next day I drove south, reading signs as I went: American telegrams, letters from the people – *Native Eggs, Crawfish, Reiki for Horses, Worms and Frogs, Sewing for Babies, Support our Troops*. On the Sioux reservation at Pine Ridge there were different messages. Nailed to a telephone pole was a narrow plank, written on it in white lettering, *Jesus Saves*. Some miles further, on a different road but in what seemed the same hand, in red paint this time, an arrow pointed right, as if for the next turning, *Hell* →.

If the Little Bighorn is the beginning, Wounded Knee is the end of the end. In the shiny tubes of hay in the fields around the Little Bighorn is the terminus for the life of grass on the plains. At Wounded Knee – and Pine Ridge where it lies – is the end-station of a people. The massacre of Lakota Sioux there (between 150 and 300 were killed, no one can agree exact numbers) by the revived 7th Cavalry in December 1890 seems cruelly continuing, with the living forced to exist in a permanent day of the dead.

The graveyard for the Indians in the Pine Ridge Reservation is a wretched place. I have been there twice – fifteen years apart – and nothing seemed to have happened in the interim. The dead neither got deader nor had the living moved on. It is a stopped place for a stopped people. At the foot of a low hill is a dusty car park ringed with empty trinket stalls. One advertised 'cold pop'. The sign that describes the massacre and the end of the Ghost Dance movement is the same as before, except 'Massacre' has been stapled over an earlier word, perhaps 'Battle'. A thin man, looking like a sick bear with a smashed-in mouth, walked out of the grass giving me permission to take photographs if I wanted to and offering to sell me a dream-catcher for ten dollars 'for gas'. Fifteen years before a younger version of the same man offered me the same hopeless tat. The cemetery is on top of a hill. The mass grave for the victims of the massacre is fenced with grey wire mesh. It looked like what it is – a filled-in ditch. The fence was broken in places and old posies of plastic flowers had blown and bleached through its wire. There were two more Sioux with dream-catchers for sale at the gate to the cemetery. The girl said she was an artist. Her teeth were in a terrible state.

I asked her about Ghost Dancing but couldn't make much sense of her answer. She knew it had some connection to her people but was keener to explain the sacred colours of the Sioux that she had used in her jewellery. In the late 1880s, when most Indians were already cooped on reservations, the Ghost Dance movement travelled through many tribes. Half invented and half adapted by a Paiute Indian called Wovoka, who had a vision during a solar eclipse, it varied in its religious and millenarian aspects but commonly offered escape routes from the end of the world: a native messiah was expected, white men would be removed from the plains and buried under a new layer of earth, the buffalo would be restored to the Indians, and the Indian dead would walk abroad once more – up from the ground. A people with nowhere to go had devised a fake passport. The Sioux sent a delegate to check out Wovoka. When he looked into Wovoka's hat, he 'saw the whole world'.

Ghost Dancing took its adherents through exhaustion into trance. They would shuffle and dance themselves silly until they fell down into the dust and into a seeing state. Many reported visiting distant stars and meeting long dead relatives. 'Sometimes they brought back white, greyish earth – a piece of the morning star – as proof.' Some Sioux thought that symbols of the dance painted on their shirts made them bulletproof. There are historians that believe this idea of protective holy clothing migrated into Ghost Dancing from the Mormon underwear known as the Temple Garment. Meanwhile, non-sacred all-in-one underwear, known as a Union Suit, was de rigueur for many settlers at this time (and has been used in many recent cowboy films as an icon of authenticity). It is striking to think of these various extra skins or body bags, trying to contain the swelling population of the Great Plains at the end of the nineteenth century. The Ghost Shirts make for an especially sad thread in the story. The Union Suit keeps you together, intact and preserved, as you occupy a new space and open its soil. The Temple Garment saves you from yourself, sealing the fleshly horrors of the body beyond your own reach. The Ghost Shirt tries to erect a barrier, a first and last fence for an Indian, between body and bullets. It didn't work. Supposed evidence of where you had been in your dreams, the shirt became a way-marker for where you were going. And a target.

Ghost Dancing frightened nearby white settlers, agitated the Indian police on the reservations, and provoked the United States cavalry. In a botched arrest in the Standing Rock Agency, north of Pine Ridge, Sitting

Bull was killed. Buffalo Bill, his sometime employer, had been sent to bring him in. Circus masters can become policemen, just as cowboy actors can turn president. Events got out of hand. Guns went off. The grey circus horse Buffalo Bill had given Sitting Bull sat down in the chaos and started performing his tricks, kneeling on his haunches and delicately raising one hoof after another, just as he did on tour when the pop-guns sounded. History restaged as farce was repeating itself as tragedy. After the killing some surviving Sioux moved south, joining Spotted Elk (also known as Big Foot) and others and all heading, at midwinter 1890, to Pine Ridge to seek shelter with Red Cloud. Intercepted by the 7th Cavalry, they were forced to camp at Wounded Knee and the next day they were ordered to surrender their weapons. Some accounts say this prompted a Ghost Dance and a medicine man called Yellow Bird said that the Ghost Shirts would stop the cavalry's bullets. Shooting began. 'We tried to run but they shot us like we were buffalo,' said Louise Weasel Bear. The wounded (Indians and troopers alike) were taken to a church at Pine Ridge and laid on pews covered in hay. A photograph shows the body of Spotted Elk lying stiff and frozen in the snow on the hillside, his eyes half closed, his long and delicate fingers locked into a grip of something in front of him no longer there or invisible. He is wearing an overcoat and heavy trousers and has a scarf wrapped around his head as if he had a toothache. I cannot see a Ghost Shirt.

I bought a dream-catcher from the girl at the cemetery gates. With the money in her hand she immediately walked away down the hill in a kind of purposeful drift off the track and through the grass. People walk in the reservation like nowhere else I have seen in the USA. People walk there as they do across Africa in order to get to places they need to go to. Other people sit on the ground, again like no one else in North America. Some lie on it. A few miles from the cemetery, south of Pine Ridge, across the state line in Nebraska, there is a liquor store. The street has no paved sidewalk and dirt runs up to the broken wooden buildings. Scabby dogs, slung with raw pink teats, ran recklessly across the street; barn swallows stitched their way along it. For hundreds of yards on either side of the store there were people in various stages of collapse. I was shocked again by how absolutely the scene replicated one that I remembered from fifteen years earlier. Were these the children of those I saw before? One figure – it was impossible to tell if it was a man or a woman – was lying on its back, feet together and arms splayed, like a crucifix nailed to the earth. Others crouched in huddles, leaning against trees or ruined storefronts. The faces I could see as I walked and then drove past looked orphaned; they seemed open but bewildered, as if they were surprised by their own demolition and were caught up in some dream and dazzled by daylight.

Unadopted is what many of the village signs say around the reservation. Buffalo Corral was one. Surrounding a house, once a mobile home, was a stockade of dead cars and old coin-operated laundry machines. Down a telescope it would look like the orbital rings of some failed white-goods planet. The Indian Wars had turned into junkyard opera. The outer crap was older, among it a Buick grassed up through its broken guts to its empty windows. Closer to, the house was circled with more recent rubbish, the washing machines like a string of pulled teeth, and the verandah, one time definition of rest, piled impossibly with stuff, semi-rotten, rained on and snow-softened, and faded to the universal weathered brown. Out front three children took their parts, riding bareback on ponies towards two pickups that had stopped by the road edge. A medicine show masque between the opera's acts. The flatbeds of the trucks were wrapped in neon-pink paper and hand-painted signs: *Mustangs don't do drugs; I had a daughter; now I have a prostitute because of Meth; Breast-feed your children; Get help.*

I drove on to Sidney, Nebraska. I went looking for dinner but found only a bar where a covers band was playing 'Don't Fear the Reaper'. The twenty-year-old vocalist leapt about to the crash of drums.

There are other Indians. I wanted to meet some who had taken a different path through the grass after it was fenced. Back in Montana and thanks to Tim McCleary, a white man who teaches Crow students at Little Big Horn College and speaks Crow and knows more Crow lore and history than most Indians, I met Bill Yellowtail of the Crow tribe in a Dairy Queen in Hardin. Bill is a cowboy Indian – a rancher, among other things. He opted for a caramel ice cream, Tim chose a more lurid event streaked with red and paved with a rainbow of hundreds and thousands. I'd eaten a buffalo burger for lunch so was off all solids and sucked instead at a bucket of lemonade. Our talk between mouthfuls and friendly laughter was however, as it might have been in Pine Ridge, of the end of a people.

Bill was heading away from the Crow Reservation the next day but ten minutes after our meeting he had invited me to travel with him that evening to his ranch home tucked into the first hills of the Big Horn Mountains at the head of Lodge Grass Creek, a tributary off the valley of the Little Bighorn River. He drove and we talked and then we sat at the house he is building on his family's land and talked some more. We slept and then he shepherded me up a small mountain on what he called a 'Japanese Quarter Horse'. A first-timer on a quad bike, all I had to do was follow the old-timer on his, but still I crashed the gears, my beast bucked and I unwisely allowed the steering to decide its own route, twice having to be rescued when I thought the angle I was climbing was untenable. Bill was smilingly patient throughout. My day with him was full of jokes. He laughs like Yogi Bear.

The view from the top was good. For a thirty-mile spread, dry deer-brown grass flowed below us in rippling warm plenitude. Far away across the green gash of the Little Bighorn the land rose again on a blue horizon to the lone hill of the Crow's Nest where Custer scouted ahead and misread the scene in June 1876. The entire country of a people was laid out there, every feature holding a story from the past and Bill, though he half-pretended not to, knew them all. Coming down was harder than going up. I became attentive to Bill's waistline. By concentrating on his jeans and hugging close to his bike I managed to stay on mine, follow him and stay alive as we controlled our fall down the mountainside. No forty-four-inch-waist Levi's could be more inspirational.

Bill is an unusual Indian. 'I choose to identify myself as a Crow though it would be altogether easier not to be an Indian.' His father was Crow and his mother Scots-Irish. He graduated from Dartmouth College. He was a Montana State Senator from 1985 to 1993. He

137

has served on the board of the National Audubon Society. He was Angler of the Year in 1991 in *Fly Rod and Reel* magazine. He has a university job. He doesn't speak the language of his people. Most strange of all is that he is an Indian rancher and part of a settled Indian family who took up the farming all the Plains Indians were pressed to do by the US government at the end of the catastrophic nineteenth century.

In the Dairy Queen, Bill showed me his Crow identity card. Among its facts: his height, six foot four inches, and his 'blood degree', which has him as 13/32 Crow. If that second number is 25 or lower, you are not, officially at least, a Crow. Tim remembered Tom Morrison who was more Crow than many but wasn't allowed a Crow identity since he was also seventy-five per cent Irish. He had reddish hair, grey eyes and alabaster skin but was raised by a Crow grandmother and Crow uncles. His spoken Crow was celebrated for its archaisms and much sought by language collectors. The only English words he knew were *Hello* and *Jesus*.

Both of Bill's grandmothers arrived into Crow country at the same time around 1887. One was a Scottish-Irish homesteader coming from Missouri to settle on the Wyoming–Montana border along the Big Horn Mountains. The other was a Crow restored to her ancestral homelands – which the tribe had lived in since at least the fifteenth century – in the aftermath of the Little Bighorn battle (she could remember hearing the news of the death of Custer) and the subsequent clearing of the occupying *'mean-and-nasty-Sioux* – all one word to a Crow'.

The grandmothers' sons become friends and partners in a cattle business and their respective children, a son (Crow) and a daughter (European), found one another. Their love was risky and unusual at a time when there was pitifully little assimilation or accommodation between the contending peoples of the plains. The Crow faced an abject future and white Americans commonly behaved like a vengeful army. The young couple had to marry in secret, 150 miles away from the reservation. But they came back to settle on Bill's father's allotted property (all Crow had been given parcels of land on the reservation when it was established). His mother, the white girl, was welcomed by the Crow, although his father, the Indian boy, was not made to feel so at home by the white settlers.

'My mongrel pedigree!' Bill groaned. Not only was his mother white, his family put the paleface on even more thickly by taking up the white man's calling to become ranchers, 'a minority within a minority'. There are not many Crow (12,000 'enrolled members' of the tribe at the moment) and there are very few ranching Crows. The idea of an Indian cowboy, though such creatures have existed for nearly 150 years, is still hard to take for many in the Crow nation. It is a foreign concept or, as it sounds, a contradiction in terms. Bill and others like him have been accused of 'becoming white'. Some of this reaction comes from various inherited or received ideas. White ranchers think they are supermen; cattle herders came first to the plains and were often rather grand or even aristocratic. Farmers came later and were usually poorer small-time operators. The Crow are differently prejudiced. Horse people scorn those who run cattle. Sheep are even worse; Bill knows them as 'prairie maggots'. Farmers are not even included in the debate. There might also be some economic jealousy at work – Bill and his family are well-off in Crow terms. But overall the Crow suspicions about ranching and farming speak of a continuing anxiety in the people themselves about their very legitimacy. The wounds suffered by the fenced nomads have not healed and, worse still, they are being kept painfully open by the sanctioned victimhood (the Indian as evolutionary drop-out) of the present.

This is particularly sad since the Crow are known for their historical efforts to become farmers and ranchers. Among Plains Indians they were early adopters of the settled life. At the end of the nineteenth century, with the buffalo gone, the wars played horribly out and the reservation supposedly secure, many Crow followed their leaders, like Plenty Coups, and wondered if they might make farmers of themselves as the United States government would have them. The Crow are supposed never to have killed a white man in anger and in the Indian Wars they scouted for them, including for Custer at the Little Bighorn. The Sioux were a greater enemy to the Crow than the white man. The rival Indians had driven them from their buffalo hunting grounds and the Crow were keen to get back to their grass. But even so, even as the white man's trusted red men, they ended up jilted then broken then ruined, just like the Sioux.

Perhaps the Crow felt encouraged to try farming simply because they saw defeat coming anyway, having already scouted for and supped with the devil and tasted his tinned meats. Various so-called agreements in the early 1880s tied the Plains Indians to the new reservations. The Crow term for the 1883 rule that stopped them moving translates as 'Living Within A Line Drawn On The Ground'. They became semi-sedentary, most still lived in tepees for a time and horses remained important, but houses were built and the government doled out rations and slaughtered cattle to replace the buffalo. At Crow Agency, the tiny capital of the reservation, a flour mill was set up. The US government hoped the Crow might grow wheat to feed themselves. In Crow the name for Crow Agency is 'The House Where *They* Grind'. The Indians took the ground flour but didn't take to growing wheat. At Pryor, on the western edge of the reservation, Plenty Coups tried to set an example to his people and started eating biscuits made from the free flour. He also planted vegetables and moved into a log homestead house. You can visit it today and see a sweat lodge in the garden like a gazebo and some of the items the chief – named for the many enemies he had touched with his coup stick – once offered for sale in his pitiful Crow version of a corner shop.

In 1887 the Dawes or General Allotment Act allocated each Indian a parcel of their reservation land. A year before, from the other end of the great grass swath around the northern hemisphere, Tolstoy had asked 'How Much Land Does a Man Need?' in his marvellous story-parable of greed and trickery. The Crow and other Indians were told that forty acres was their lot. Tolstoy's answer is a six-foot grave after his covetous peasant-farmer Pakhom drops dead trying to outwit some Bashkirs of their land. The Bashkir were the Plains Indians of the steppes, semi-nomadic cattle-herding, beekeeping people from the flat-lands around the Urals. They drank kumiss and played pipes. Pakhom is an ambitious accumulator from elsewhere. He wants to own the earth. He sells foals and 'half his bees' to buy land, stepping on to an escalator of acquisitiveness, selling and owning and selling again. He learns that the Bashkirs' 'beautiful grassy steppe' can be bought for a few trinkets, 'a chest of tea and vodka for anyone who wanted it'. The Bashkirs take his gifts and tell him he can have as much land as he can walk around in a day, so long as he carries a spade to dig a hole at every turning and lifts the turf to mark his circuit. Pakhom is excited and starts early 'across the virgin soil, flat as the palm of one's hand, black as poppy-seed, with different kinds of grass growing breast high in the hollows'. This Tolstoy knew directly for, in the richly complicating background to the story, he himself had bought land cheaply from the Bashkirs and for several summers went for kumiss cures and to read Herodotus on the Scythians, dragging his family to the blasted plain to sleep on heaps of feather grass strewn across the mud floor of the hut-house on his land. Pakhom hurries, walking hastily around his would-be field edge until, increasingly desperate as he tries to enclose a larger area than he can circumnavigate, he begins to panic and run. As he joins his circle, under the watchful eyes of the Bashkirs, he collapses and dies. His servant buries him with his own spade.

At the museum in Hardin is a hand-drawn three-quarter-inch to one-mile map of the allotted lands of the Crow Reservation made in 1907 by Carl Rankin at Crow Agency. Most of the indicated forty-acre allotments are along the fertile river valleys, the Little Bighorn and others; some of the rising arid plains between the rivers are still marked 'unsurveyed'. Below the map is a list of the allotted. There are hundreds of names, each having their boxy tombstone plot numbered on the grid above. I filled a page in my notebook: Medicine Porcupine, Kills On Her Own Ground, Small Head, Balls, Bird Child, Sits Down Far Away, Three Wolves, Spies Well On Camp, Old Horse, Big Elk, Strikes The Enemy, The Wet, Strong Leg, She Sees It, Hoop That Moves, Mrs Mary M. Humphrey, Bad Baby, Like A Beaver, Lies In Bed With A Man, Her Medicine Is Medicine, The Other Heart, Wolf Looks Up, Fire Weasel, Shot in the Hand, Puts On A Hat, Walks In The Water.

To turn the Indians into farmers, to plough and run cattle, 'boss-farmers' were appointed on the reservation. These were government employees, sometime Indians from elsewhere, appointed by the Indian agent in charge. Some of these men were better at their job than others; just as some Crow were more receptive to change than others. Horses could be taken to water but not necessarily made to drink. For some boss-farmers and agents, horses themselves were an issue. One superintendent at Crow Agency, Charles H. Asbury, thought European-style farming was the only way for the Crow and wanted to outlaw as many native practices as possible. His assimilating severities still pain Crow memories today. He wanted to ban the Tobacco Society, the Crow organisation that sacralised their belief that happiness could be guaranteed so long as treasured and holy tobacco seeds were gathered, looked after, planted and grown. Asbury also didn't like horses and insisted a Crow farmer would need only two. In three years the Crow horse herd shrank from 40,000 to 2,000. The people's money, transport and definition for the previous 200 years were slaughtered or sent east by rail to be canned.

Asbury's successor as agent was a relative of Bill's, Robbie Yellowtail, and a Crow. He brought the horses back and there are still hooves all across the Crow lands wherever there are Indians. In the broken-down town and villages, horses are tethered outside people's houses. Nowhere else in the United States apart from here and the Sioux reservation at Pine Ridge have I seen people riding in order to get somewhere. Somewhere, though, turns out to be nowhere. At Crow Agency I watched some Indians riding their ponies up the paved streets and to the edge of the fields beyond them. The riders might own those fields but they almost never will be the farmers of them. When they got to the field edge, where the grass begins, they turned their ponies around and rode them back down the road.

There were some successful Crow farmers and ranchers in the early years of the reservation but the life didn't take hold and many left the land that they had been allotted. Instead of becoming farmers the Indians themselves were to be farmed. Within a few years of granting Indians their own land, the federal government wanted Crow territory opened to non-Indians. From his wooden shop at Pryor, Plenty Coups resisted. The 1920 Crow Act half protected the reservation and half prepared it for its journey out of Crow hands. All of the reservation was allocated to the then-living Crow; even babies were given land in their name. But Indians were henceforth permitted to lease their land to non-Indians: they didn't have to become farmers after all, they could become landlords instead. White ranchers and farmers moved in and leased land cheaply and the process of leasing is still in place today, with many Crow being a strange enfeebled type of absent landowner.

I picked up Raymond de la Forge who was hitching with his ten-year-old son, Raymond Junior, just outside the Little Bighorn battlefield and drove them through the Crow lands to the Northern Cheyenne Reservation that joins it to the east. Raymond is a Crow carpenter and separated from Raymond Jnr's Cheyenne mother. By stopping to give them a ride I was assisting in complying with the terms of young Raymond's childcare order that has him shuttling back and forth between his parents. They got into the car with nothing but themselves. I have never seen an Indian carrying a bag. As we drove and Raymond Jnr finished his can of fizzy drink on the back seat, his dad gestured vaguely to either side of the road. He had an allotment to the left hereabouts on some grazing benchlands above a river and he had another in some juniper timber, he thought, that rose in the hills to the right towards the Big Horn Mountains. 'White men' leased both plots. Raymond had never been to either place and couldn't remember how much rent his land earned him or his family, though he knew it wasn't much. His carpentry paid his bills, but he had to do that in Colorado, and if it weren't for his son he wouldn't have been standing by the road in his old country.

Nowadays much more of the Crow Reservation is farmed or ranched by non-Crows than by Crows. Leasing has turned into ownership and agriculture has become industry. The prime river valley croplands that grow wheat, barley and sugar-beet (corn in some areas too) and the upland rangelands and wheat fields are either owned or leased by non-Crow farmers. As he drove me to his anomalous ranch (it has no name and no sign, 'nothing that would say – look at me') Bill pointed out the farms up the Little Bighorn valley, the small grassy places where some Indian families (the Real Birds, the Moccasins, the Not Afraids) reared rodeo horses or bucking bulls, and the irrigated and fenced fields and tight-run rangelands where a millionaire farmer from Salt Lake City or billionaire corporations from who knows where make their money. Great, wheeled irrigation arms were drawing green circles of alfalfa on the valley bottom and corn grew there because so much water and other care was lavished on it. We passed Bill's mother's childhood home. Bill's grandfather had to keep a fire going outside that house all night when his cows were calving to keep the wolves from helping themselves. The white wooden house is still there; it is now owned by the Salt Lake City man.

The wolves have gone, but in keeping with his contrary-rancher-counter-Crow way Bill would happily see them back and running across his dirt road and over his cranky fences. The Yellowtail ranch is a far cry from the valley farms. The Salt Lake alfalfa is cut four times a year. Bill can 'hay' his un-irrigated crop just once. Ranching is hard on the scale Bill and his brother and sister do it. The ranch went bust in the 1980s and they can no longer afford to own land as well as cattle, so their species-rich and never-ploughed high prairie grass is let to a cow-man who trucks his herd of Herefords in and then trucks them out and away some months later to a feed-lot elsewhere where they fatten further on corn.

Bill regrets not speaking his father's language but doesn't think of himself as forced to speak the words of his conquerors. His life simply went another way. Moreover, he thinks the Crow, as a people, are too happy to cast themselves as irreparably wounded by their history. 'There is no better victim than an Indian victim,' Bill said. 'Even the Jews feel sorry for us! I don't want to relate to that. My grandparents were hardy, hearty and independent, and walking proof that in the transition time victimhood and dependency were not a condition of being an Indian. But as well as apparently being genetically the saviours of the earth, now, genetically we are its greatest victims.'

As we had driven towards the mountains up the Little Bighorn valley, passing Crow Agency, the battlefield, and then the small Indian villages, I had asked Bill if he could explain the mess his people make. I wanted to be told that I had misread what I had seen at Pine Ridge and saw here, the rag-and-bone forecourts slipping past the car windows, the squalor and the broken-down fabric of the lives of those who live among the crap. But Bill couldn't offer any better news: 'We speak most passionately about how we are the genetic environmentalists, but our very living space defies that. But I am not sure, though, that many Crow can deal with the psychological dissonance involved in contemplating that. It's pretty devastating.'

It is. What I saw of the reservation seemed not like a home for the Crow but more like a *field-hospital* where a people have been installed after a battle. The wounded are still too sick to move. Some manage to get on their ponies but don't travel far. Some wave their arms at passing cars and get out as best they can. Some travel no further than a few hundred yards. Dying, as they might say, within a line that is drawn on the ground. In Crow Agency one car passed us without a bonnet, its barrelling engine wobbling like an exposed heart. The roadsides in Montana, as in South Dakota at Pine Ridge, are skewered with white crosses marking fatal crash sites. Meadowlarks perch on them to sing. Larks and markers. They thicken noticeably around Indian places.

The Crow are poor and under-educated. There is seventy per cent unemployment on the reservation. The sorts of things the people can afford to buy don't last. But they who had nothing cannot let go of the nothing they now have. In the old nomadic times family refuse would be dropped outside each tepee but the rubbish was biodegradable and the Crow would move every three days. They were known for being a very clean people. They had to be; their enemies would smell them otherwise. Nowadays everybody smells clean but everybody stays put.

Crow life on the reservation is village life, but the villages are not villages, as many would think them. The idea of a village as being not only adjacent to but also intimately connected to the surrounding land seems not to exist in contemporary Crow country. No Crow village, not even Crow Agency, has a road that doesn't end in a field, but these apparent openings to rurality belie the truth. Crow life is as deracinated, as *ungrassed*, as any city life. Although they live no more than one hundred yards from the grass it is as if it isn't there. Nature deficit disorder, if it exists, is rampant in the Crow lands and never more acute for occurring in the midst of what has been commemorated as the birthplace of sustainable living, the home of those able to be at home even as they moved seasonally in a wholesome wheel across the land, like its buffalo and its weather and its birds; the birds whose name the people took, the *Apsáalooke*, the children-of-the-long-beaked-bird.

Bill dropped me off at my car and continued on his way to his university life in Bozeman. I drove back down some of the Crow roads. They were quiet without his talk and his laughter. A hot wind came heavily through the open windows. It smelled baked. I watched the birds that flew up around the car. There was a magic forty-five miles between the Crow villages of Pryor and St Xavier. Midway there, the road runs alone or rather on its own and for itself. Every ten miles or so there is a ranch gate, the name of the place given often by no more than a brand mark burned into a post, but no houses or farmsteads are visible and along the top of a series of broad-backed ridges through these rolling rangelands the road snakes like a flexing spine.

The grass stretched on, the wind now moving mazily across it, fetching and carrying light just as it does over the surface of the sea. Watching the swaying and seething, the fish flash and the weedy green turns, I saw how an aerial acre of wind crossed the plain, how the grass lived the weather. The same gust came up through the car window and raked my hair into dusty furrows. I slowed to keep pace with a male northern harrier as it flew parallel to me, hunting at between ten and fifteen miles per hour with its downcast owl-face interrogating the grass. I adopted its methods and its speed, a prairie lick.

It took me three hours to dawdle along the road, stopping every few hundred yards to look at the fields, pulling over to walk out into them, waving at the cattle five miles away on a ridge, trying to talk some prairie dogs into a meeting. In places the metallic ripple of a cattle-grid took away the fences. Then the grass, running from either side of me, made an even bigger scene, as close to the once high prairie as I might get.

Birds the same colour as the earth and its outgrowth came to the ground to be part of it. How does the earth itself paint the life above in its own shades? Over the cattle-grid I'd been delivered into the lark-lands of America. The grey smudge of a Sprague's pipit; horned larks with sand-brown backs, perfect matches for the soil beneath them, and yellow and black ear-tufts, prickling up like sharp thistle-heads; lark sparrows, streaked and drawn like a bottle of grass; and lark buntings, the females a thicker wetter grass than the lark sparrows, the males darker than anything for miles, with bright white panels on their black wings. Between the lark buntings and lark sparrows were western meadowlarks. Every higher stem or tussock stretching into the blue haze appeared to have one sitting on it, each like a hank of the grass with one yellow flower head pinned to their breast like a medal of spring. They panted like farmyard chickens in the sun but their songs, a liquid in-and-out breath with a following tumble of cooling water, came through the dust and the heat like a drink.

Fences strung to the roadside once more and under the same blue sky the grass changed to wheat, dry still but more intense in its ripeness, golden with its held grain. Two colours only, Ian Frazier says, would be needed to paint the plains: gold and blue. There was wire at the road but beyond it on both sides ran the largest cropped fields I have ever seen. One kept going next to me for five miles. The combines were busy, each raising its own weather of field-dust and wheat chaff, some clouds caught the light and travelled bright as a headdress, others were thick and baffled the sun like an animal skin. I thought of the fields being taken in, all of them through the metal grasshopper 'header' of the machine, their grain grown and harvested and lifted from them without once being touched by anything human. That night, in a restaurant in Hardin, I watched an exhausted team of custom harvesters (the travelling gangs who take their combines from Texas to Canada following the cutting seasons) lifting slices of a shared pizza and, even as they did, falling asleep one by one at their table, until four of the five slept while the remaining young man pushed the sleepers' beer and soda glasses away from them and rescued their drooping pizza from their drowsy hands.

Half a block away from the sleeping harvesters, I met the granddaughter of Thomas D. Campbell, the epic wheat farmer of Montana, outside the old German hotel. She had spotted me looking at a historic marker nailed to the wall and introduced herself. In the first half of the twentieth century, Campbell, farmer of the world's largest wheat farm, harvested in the Crow Reservation on leased land or land he had bought from the Indians. His family had first grown wheat in South Dakota in 1876, the year of the Custer battle. He was born in 1882 in a settler's sod house in North Dakota. By 1926 he had 95,000 acres of wheat in Montana. His tractors changed the place even more than Custer succeeded in doing; breaking the sod, and turning prairie ground for the first time in its history, and then ploughing its native grasses back into it, quite possibly for them never to return. The various prairie blades were hopeless before the plough blades. The winning was dangerously easy.

Campbell was a genius of mechanisation and of the industrialisation of agriculture. His fields were brashly vast, a single furrow in one of them is said to have run for five miles. Such earthworks, such scarification, might rival any marks our species has made on the face of the planet. But the bigger the cut, the deeper the wound. In drought years in the 1930s, soil that had broken from the opened plains blew away, some dust clouds made it to the east coast, news from the interior, like the Plains Indians visiting the president. Some fell through an open window on to a desk in Washington, DC, even as those around the desk were discussing erosion and drought and bad farming, and some of the dust went further east again, three hundred miles out above the Atlantic where it fell as dry prairie rain on the ocean's saltwater fields.

A few years later Campbell had his hand in another rainstorm. He was an inventor as well as industrial ploughman. In the Second World War he was credited with part-developing the napalm firebomb used in the Pacific theatre: seeds of sticky invasive pain that were scattered on people and their places from above. Odysseus acting strange in order not to go to war and sowing his home fields with salt might have devised such madness, such madnesses.

In the three hours on the Crow road only one car passed me but as it did it killed a cliff swallow. I was an accessory. The birds nested along the road in drainage culverts that ran beneath its surface every mile or so. When the road was straight I could see the next colony of the birds half a mile ahead, an *air field* of swallows flying and feeding, close above their breeding tunnel. Barn swallows joined them, though they must have been further from home. As my car drew towards the other oncoming vehicle, an old clapped-out coupe with an even older Indian at the wheel, we pushed the air between us. This must have agitated its insects for it excited the swallows. For a few seconds the near sky around our cars was crowded with the birds, blue-black and rust-red, and they flew low to the road. One went too low and then too close to the approaching car and was drawn under its front. I saw the bird pulled up towards the engine and fall back to the road instantaneously dead even before the car had passed over it. I stopped and walked back and picked it up. In my hands it was still warm. Its eyes began to dry and then slowly shut as I was holding it. Its smoky-grey belly had been split open and its intestines had burst. The colour of its insides was midway between the warm buff of its rump and the brick-red of its throat. It cooled even as I held it and I laid it back down on the road-side while the birds it had left behind twittered and busied themselves over my head and on out across the grass.

At Pryor I stood in the shade of Plenty Coups's log-house-cum-shop and looked towards the stream. I spotted a male yellowthroat, a warbler, sherbet-yellow all over apart from a perfect bank-robber black mask wrapped round its face. It flew busily through the brush after a bird twice or maybe three times its size, a cowbird chick, lumpen, dusty brown and demanding. Cowbirds are called cowbirds because they associate with cattle; they live in fields at the hooves of herds, feeding on insects disturbed by the animals and are tolerated beneath the cattle's feet because they eat irksome biting flies and other nuisances. They are able to move with moving animals across country and through the season because they are also brood parasites; they live like cuckoos or honeyguides, dumping their eggs in other birds' nests. The yellowthroat had been tricked into believing it must adopt the imposter and was raising the cowbird as its own. The cowbird has found a way to wipe its foster parent's mind. The chick begged and the yellowthroat hurried to fill the cowbird's open beak. The yellowthroat's own chicks were nowhere to be seen, were perhaps dead or, at best, back in their nest, feeble, underfed and out-competed by the giant incomer. The big brown baby was taking up all of the yellowthroat's day.

In an old mess-house from one of the Campbell farm complexes on the Crow lands, now installed in the outdoor museum at Hardin, there are photographs of the same building or one very similar. A print shows visiting Soviet agronomists in the 1930s sitting along a bench at a table eating their lunch. These men ('two hundred sod busters') came halfway round the world to be taught by Campbell or to learn by example how to make their collective farms grow during the desperate decade of famine and terror in the USSR. Campbell himself travelled several times to the Soviet Union, knew Lenin and then Stalin, advised on the first Five Year Plan in 1929, and continued until the 1950s to tutor the world's other great wheat grower in how to 'start from scratch on unplowed endless steppe'. After the 1950s he stopped going east, and the Soviets didn't come west any more. Spaces, meanwhile, were cleared deep into the soils of the Montana wheat fields and grasslands in order to plant intercontinental ballistic missiles that were to be aimed at the heads of the children of those who had walked the same fields twenty years before, learning how to turn the soil of the east-west plains into bread. For cannot pruning hooks be beaten into spears and ploughshares into swords?

Fred E. Miller, the one-eyed and highly sympathetic photographer of the Crows between 1898 and 1912, took several pictures of Curley, Custer's Crow scout. Curley had escaped the battlefield, he said, by galloping away with a blanket over his head. Miller's last portrait is a masterpiece. Curley stands in soft abundant summer grass that stretches to a pale horizon. Behind him is a row of trees, young plums perhaps, in the beginnings of an orchard. In the long exposure their foliage has shimmered into a blur and bright stars of light speckle the leaves like fruit. Behind the trees is the side of a wooden barn or house. The horsemen of the plains have become farmers; its scouts have turned fruit pickers. An invisible tree beyond the frame throws some shadow over the foreground grass and on to Curley's lower half. He stands looking straight at the camera, his eyes squeezed in the bright light. He appears older than in any of the other portraits I've seen although I think the picture was taken around 1898 and he still had twenty-five years of life ahead of him. His face has lost its young man contours and his chest has got heavier and dropped on to the beginnings of a belly. His hair, a quiffed pompadour, gives him a touch of an old rocker. A striped blanket that he wears like a loose skirt obscures his legs. In his left hand he holds a pale version of a reservation hat. At his right side stands his daughter Dora who was also called Bird Another Year. She was born in 1893 when Curley was already forty. She looks about five here. Like her dad she has two pigtails framing her round cheeks. She is wearing a long dress with a dark shirt that is sewn with elk's teeth down its sleeves and all across the breast. The teeth are white and roughly circular like ancient coins, each about half an inch in diameter. At least 150 spread across her shirt. They make a pattern like the lark bunting's wings that I saw near Pryor. She looks apprehensive as she peers from under her fringe at the camera but Curley's right hand is gently resting on her shoulder, bringing her to him, holding her still.

The young fruit trees, the new farmyard and the old Indian man in front of them holding his daughter clad in elk teeth are all markers of the same violent rupture, the grass-fight and the plough-down, that dragged the bodies of the 7th Cavalry through the soil of the battlefield in the years after 1876, that tried to make the Crow settled farmers of that soil, and then eventually in 1923 planted Curley's own body in the same earth that had eaten the white men's flesh and fed the plum trees. The white man's guide died not wanting to be known for what he'd done in 1876 but was buried all the same in the soil of the battlefield beneath a white tombstone in the military cemetery, one of a line among many lines of pulled teeth grimacing across the grass. The Crows otherwise didn't bury their dead in the ground. They feared the entrapment of the earth and placed their loved ones in a coffin or wrapped them in material and then took them out on to the prairie, to places the dead had loved, to a hillside or the banks of the Little Bighorn, and there they raised them for sky burial, six or more feet off the ground, on stilted biers or scaffolds they called *ghosts*. Birds – vultures and ravens mostly – would eat the bodies. Fred Miller took six mesmerising photographs of these rickety launch pads, and his pictures of the Crow ghosts surpass even his portraits of the living.

SUMMER FEN

The moment the music stops, the maypole-year collapses about itself, stepping out of its green finery, trampling its own juices into the soil. The festival is done, the tent abandoned in the swamp where the field once was.

At midsummer, rain fell from dawn until after dusk, and then again on the morning after the longest day. I stood at the back door and looked out. The general synopsis: marine. The whole busted flush of the sodden country to be rafted out into the Western Approaches and given there a drubbing. Whales expected inland, ships on the horizon. 'Summer,' Coleridge said once to Charles Lamb, 'has set in with its usual Severity.'

I went out in a raincoat and shorts. Cloud-wool clagged about my head. In the garden slugs worked as beavers, felling one tomato plant after another. Rank veg basted my legs and peppered them with seeds. I found a snail in my pocket.

Further out at sea, the sky had clamped itself to the fen, and pressed it low under its pedal of cloud. Fresh squalls came building, bellying, and bursting above me every five minutes. A downpour hurried off a field of beet leaves sounding them like umbrellas. A tight-packed wheat field made a machine hiss. When the rain was heavy the lode was tin-tacked; when it eased, the water puckered with frog lips. It burped once as a sunken parcel of disturbed dead reeds was hurried to the surface by the furious knocking at the door. I could smell beer as I passed barley, borscht from a bare peat field, and Vichyssoise between leeks and potatoes.

A blackbird sang a hooded version of its song from the brambles out into the seasonless rainlight. Young goldfinches and meadow pipits got wet in the kelpy grass, their pale pink skin showing through their waterlogged feathers, making them look cold and wormy, like pickled birds in a jar. Cows lay about the fen like walruses, dirty and thick-skinned. An old wet carpet smell came off their backs. One stood up to deliver a copious piss, then lay down in the lake it had made. It rained on and the water began to creep to the top of the banks, and the grass at Burwell Fen flashed.

One of Thomas Browne's shorter works is described by Samuel Johnson in his life of Browne as 'a letter "on the fishes eaten by our Saviour with his disciples, after his resurrection from the dead," which contains no determinate resolution of the question, what they were, for indeed it cannot be determined. All the information that diligence or learning could supply, consists in an enumeration of the fishes produced in the waters of Judea.' This isn't a fen matter but it contains a fen truth. The last-fish-supper is not the answer. The fens and their facts slip and slide, sink and swim. Nor was this the end of Browne's fish thoughts. In 1662 the antiquarian William Dugdale wrote a rather tedious survey of fen projects from the Romans onwards, a *History of Imbanking and Drayning*. His book is mostly book-based – Dugdale was a reader and a compiler not a digger or a paddler through the earth – but he did send Browne a bone from a great and apparently marine fossil fish that had been found at Conington Down in the far south-west of the fens near Cambridge. With the bone came questions. How did the twenty-foot fish get into the fens? Were they once covered with sea? Dugdale knew there were marine silts in the fens as well as freshwater peat and that both lay often on clayey soil, and it was in this soil that he thinks the fish foundered. How could it get beneath the sea-soil? He asks Browne: 'when, or on what occasion, it was that the sea flowed over all this . . .'

From Norwich, Browne wrote back to Dugdale several times. He knew many things and had many ideas about things he didn't know. He reared ostriches. He coined the word *antediluvian* (as well as *electricity, precarious* and *hallucination*). He noted the first inland gannet in Norfolk, reporting a bird storm-wrecked and 'kild by a greyhound neere swaffam'. He knew otters were caught in marshy places and could be trained to serve for 'turnspits', being harnessed in such a way so that kebabs of meat rotated as they cooked. He knew the world of the drenched and drowned, the quaggy and the mired, fen and carr, the rescued and the doomed. He kept a stuffed pelican and a bittern in his house. He called mankind 'that great and true Amphibium'. He was superbly that himself.

Browne indentified Dugdale's petrified fishbone as a vertebra, 'solid, according to the spine of fishes' though 'too big for the largest dolphins, porpoises, or swordfishes, and too little for a true or grown whale'. He also knew that there are three layers of earth in fenland: 'ancient & proper soyle', 'siltie soile' and 'fenny soile'; but he would not commit himself to an explanation. In October 1660, he responded to Dugdale saying, 'in points of such obscuritie, probable possibilities must suffice for truth'. A floodful of fruitful doubts, the negative capability once again of the place and of the times, rises in Browne and he delivers a most exquisite evasion of certainty touching on elephants' bones and giants, the great Deluge and Flood, inexplicable seashells on Alpine peaks, and the recent use of whalebones for buildings. He is further troubled by the confusion that may be caused in the future by a maverick citizen of Norfolk who instructed that he should be buried wrapped up in the horned hide of an ox: 'How this may hereafter confound the discoverers, and what conjectures may arise thereof, it is not easy to conjecture. Sir, your servant to my power, Tho. Browne.'

On the western fens along the Nene Washes the corncrake has come back. Captive-bred birds were acclimatised in outdoor cages to the grass, its worm- and snail-foods, and to the sky-map overhead. Released into the summer, they knew they must fly south for the winter to the great tawny spread of grass through southern Africa. The following spring, because they had left the fields at the Washes, they wanted to return to where they started and some did. Those homed males called their hoarse double rasp, *crex crex*, and brought down totally wild birds, untouched by man, that were flying north over the fens. Generations of corncrakes might have been doing this – flying the same skies on spring migration – for a hundred years, without hearing anything of themselves calling them down from below. The new-partnered birds bred, the man-planted and the crake-captured together, and the wider fortunes of the species may yet revive.

Common cranes, an ancient fen bird, are back in their old haunts as well. They have bred on the Washes too. I saw one walking through the grey of a ploughed field just south of Burwell Fen one early summer day. The same colour as the soil, it also looked appropriately big in the wide spaces, a pylon bird, and it made me feel how I'd missed its scale and the fitting purchase it offered on the place. Its great beak out-did the rooks' bone-bill and looked like an ancient fen tool; its bum-end was muddied and dishevelled from sitting in fen earth; its stilted legs and wide-pattened feet were accustomed to stepping through wet. Cranes' feet not human webbed feet are true fen feet, the *pied de grue*, or the fen pedigree. Then it took off, with neither the mute swan's lumpen judder into flight, nor the 'big boan'd' bustard's stampede (see the twenty-fifth song of Michael Drayton's 'Poly-Olbion'), but with a triple-jumper's hop, skip and leap – the fen being long enough for its slow-motion hurdling into the air. Airborne, it was magnificent and, apt for fen skies, showed no shrinkage. A grey heron will fold itself away in a flying shrug; the crane, with everything fully extended, neck ahead and legs behind, seemed to frighten the sky into keeping it aloft. Peat from its feet fell back to the earth like exhaust fumes. The air-beating vans of its wings whacked at the grey tent of itself and kept it going in its slow transporter-plane climb. Migrating cranes were once believed to carry corncrakes on their backs. I could imagine it. My fen hero joined the stack of airforce heavies and headed east towards Lakenheath and out of sight.

In the list of lost fen things – the smell of 10,000 working horses, skateable fields, peat smoke, the punt-gun's sonic boom, mole gibbets, swallowtail butterflies – the sound of corncrakes must be the noisiest absence. It is one of the most missing birds in Britain. Since 1900 its population collapse has been more dramatic than any other bird species in our islands. During the last quarter of the nineteenth century the bird bred in every county of Britain and Ireland. Many people leaving their work in the fields on a May evening would have walked home to the sound of corncrakes. On the fens they were especially common:

the wet grass was ideal habitat. In the county in the 1880s 'nearly every small grass meadow had its pair'. Everyone sleeping between Cambridge and Lincoln – or trying to – would then have known the corncrake's call. Once started, the males will commonly sing their cracked come-hithers throughout the night.

Three times in my life I have been kept awake by corncrakes. On Coll, the island in the Inner Hebrides, which is now one of the last strongholds of the birds in Britain, I heard males calling through a chatter of adjacent sedge warblers, the whickering of snipe above, and the moaning of seals just offshore. On the Hortobágy of Hungary, about as far from a seal as you can get in Europe, I tried to sleep out one short summer night until the syncopated irritations of mosquito music and corncrake call seemed to get inside my head as well as all around it, and I had to seek insulated shelter in the spidery waiting room of a village railway station. And, aged ten on my first holiday in northern Scotland, I saw what I subsequently discovered was a rare thing. My parents rented a cottage at Oldshoremore in Sutherland. A walled potato patch ran around its backyard and from our first evening until our last we attended a corncrake concert. The light dipped but never fully went, the potato leaves grew heavier and darker through the night, and the raucous singers (or was it just a single running soloist?) kept up their song. It was so hidden in the gloom that on the first night we didn't know who or what the performers were – a vast frog, some sort of clunking machine, synchronised grasshoppers? – until the crofter asked us the next morning if the corncrakes had kept us up.

They sang on. Knowing what they were didn't help us sleep. The singing, which is not singing at all, is loud. The male takes his voice for a walk; one minute it came from one corner of the potatoes and the next from another. Even sung from the same place, the bird twisted his head and shouted like a strobing lighthouse, throwing his voice through all points of the compass. Nor was it continuous and eventually soporific like a soundbed of grasshoppers: it started; threw itself; moved; started again; stopped; started.......; started...; started.....; started..............; started. We listened every night having no choice, and I remember lying in bed, beneath an open window, and the birds' craking

157

seeming to blow the thin curtains above me. We didn't see them until our final morning when, on a pile of cut potato stems at the back of the patch, first one and then another appeared, each like a little inconsequential chicken, brown and streaked all over. Both stomped a bit on their potato mound. The male then walked off the heap and as it did threw back its head and opened its pink beak as if to drink in the damp Sutherland sky and instead croaked its crake-trumpet and out and up came its name, *Crex crex*.

A sighting like this is rare. The birds are not often seen in the open. At the time, simply putting feathers around the call was exciting enough. And, indeed, since then I have only seen corncrakes for fleeting moments. They no longer breed in western Sutherland. The potato patch is still there; I went a couple of years ago to have a look and a listen, but it was silent. Even as a ten-year-old neophyte birdman I knew something was up with the species. The birds were deep into their decline in the 1970s. A kind of out of date thing anyway, they were undone above all by the mechanisation of haymaking. Machines cut the heads off incubating birds and cut their downy black chicks in two. My potato pair were unusual; most corncrakes do everything that they do in the breeding season in fields of grass. And although haymaking was late in Sutherland, and the grass was still cut, raked, and stooked by hand – the key essentials for the survival of nesting corncrakes – the fields there couldn't hold on to their birds.

Their life in these plots and yards has followed ours in them. The bird is tied to us. The Clearances of the human population from the Highlands were responsible also for the removal of the corncrake from there. When people were taken from the land and their hay fields, and arable crops in mountain straths were converted to sheepwalks, the corncrakes also disappeared, having nowhere to hide or to run to. Further south and closer to the fens, Marvell's 'tawny mowers' in his poem 'Upon Appleton House' accidentally carve corncrakes when massacring, as he says, the grass. Their scythes come up bloody from the sliced chicks and the 'orphan parents' call in dismay with what Marvell hears as a 'death-trumpet' or a 'sourdine in their throat'. Sourdine (from the Italian *sordino*) means a mute on a trumpet that produces a hoarse effect. It is a perfect summoning of the corncrake's call, as a last post or rusty taps, and proves Marvell must have been very familiar with the sound.

But there is something else about corncrakes that exacerbates their otherworldliness. It is not their fault, and I have no science to prove it, but it is something I cannot help feeling. They don't appear to be fully resolved on life. 'A sort of living doubt', John Clare called the corncrake and its music in 'The Landrail', his poem from the fen edge on the bird. Though it calls like a little god of the fields it is nowhere to be seen. They are full-time hideaways. At no point in their lives do they elect to break from cover. I have heard corncrakes for perhaps one hundred hours of my life, but I have seen them for no more than one hundred seconds. And I get this sense that before we messed with them and their places, they were already removing themselves, as if something hadn't quite worked for them as a species.

The skulking bird is also a reluctant flier, yet somewhere along its lifeline it has become a migrant, addicted equally to concealing vegetation thousands of miles apart, pretty much at opposite ends of the grassed world. Not long after my family and I watched the corncrakes at Oldshoremore, the parent birds would have done a midnight flit and lifted into the sky, their yellow-brown chicken feet trailing beneath them, their babies back in the potatoes. Somehow they would have steered south, flying now when for months they had only walked, crossing the sea now when for months they had crept at soil level under leaves of grass and potato stems. And somehow, even less fathomable, the young birds, knowing that they must, would later climb alone into the same following sky.

When I read about this aged ten it conjured an absolutely terrifying world. That same holiday, for similar reasons, I lost my briefly held head for heights. On Handa Island, I discovered that cliffs were out of bounds to me. In a swirl of vertigo, the seabirds I was intent on loving were lifted from me and taken into the air, as young guillemots still not able to fly leapt from their breeding ledges hundreds of feet to the sea below. For the corncrakes, all I could imagine was exhausted young birds falling unseen into the sea at night with the tiniest of splashes as they hit the water and it opened its wet embrace around them and took them down.

In David Thomson's magnificent account of seal legends in Scotland and Ireland, *The People of the Sea*, he asks an old crofter on South Uist what spells the seals are under, such that at times they become people and people become them. The crofter replies: 'it is given to them that their sea-longing shall be land-longing and their land-longing shall be sea-longing'. When I read this, decades after the potato patch, I thought straight away of those corncrakes. I still know of no better way of explaining and describing the driving migratory imperative that lifted the streaky groundsmen from the earth and took them over the water.

I haven't seen the corncrakes on the fens. Nor even heard them. It rained so much in the spring of the year when I had set my heart on a night of rasping that the room of the Washes flooded, and even if the creeping land bird hadn't abandoned the sudden sea-place it had certainly shut up. I did, though, at the other end of the same year, and at the other side of the corncrakes' life, watch one in early morning light along a farm track near Lazaro's honeyguides in southern Zambia: a wintering corncrake high-stepping from the long wet grass on to the red-rutted way and, stretching its wings like a brown cape, shaking the dew of the night from its body, telling me in its silent purposeful walk out of sight that, while I might be, it was anything but doubtful.

At the Temple of Heaven in Beijing on a cold autumn morning I once saw dozens of elderly men in grey suits carrying square bamboo cages. Crouching on the floor of each was a single sandy-brown, chunky-headed and black-collared Mongolian lark. The larks and their keepers walked between squadrons of tai chi dancers and bright fluttering kites tethered on sticks. The cages swung in the men's hands until they gathered on a square of open grass to the side of the circular Hall of Prayer for Good Harvests. The men put their cages on the park benches and greeted their friends, their breath smoking into the cold air. The larks, seeing others of their own, began to sing. Like all lark song, it was some sweet, burbling twitter mixed with drier notes. The specific sand and dust of their home-ground made music. It rolled on, between the cages, sky song kept down to earth, while the men, after their hellos, fell increasingly silent as their birds took over.

Skylarks were a bird I looked for even before I became a birdwatcher. Near my home when I was a boy, the wooded North Downs of Surrey opened to grassy hilltops. One of the first things I remember doing on my own, aged about seven, was cycling to a place we knew as Viewpoint and hunting for skylarks as they sang above me until, by listening, I found their singing dot in the sky, the colourless scribble of an impossible gnat. Best of all was to do this when lying down, when grass stems leaned over your face and the damp of the soil crept through your shirt. I would turn my head, the grass brushed loud in my ear and I could hear that the sprinkle of song fell more to one side of me than the other. I looked in that direction, again the song was offset, and again I turned towards it. Clouds stretched my eyes. The sky toppling over me brought the sensation of falling upwards towards the birds. I think of this every time I pass gasometers that have deflated, leaving a circular gantry and metal steps curling around the sunken gas-tank's nothing, holding the shape of what was there, the stairs climbing into the open air. Being on the top stair might be like falling towards the skylarks. With my hand at my forehead I shielded my eyes, a gesture that always seems old to me, like an explorer's in a new land or a sailor's at sea. But my ears had found it: up there in another realm, little more than a drift of air, spilling music around it without stopping as if it were breathing the sky in and out.

One reason we love birds is that they move in some ways as we do. They walk with two feet on the ground. Watch starlings crossing a lawn and you might be seeing people in a park. Then they fly and flying seems superbly different to walking, unencumbered and free. But, like walking, it is also essentially a continually averted falling. Our bodies – starlings' and mine – must work to keep us from the ground. Birds that don't appear to struggle to stay up or that have passages of flight where they are able to stop in the sky seem special because they have broken beyond gravity's pull. The lark above me on the fen now was all effort but didn't show it; its wings appeared to tremble with music not exertion. It rose as if the fountain of song it was spilling was pushing it from underneath. Having found its level in the sky it settled there and made its way through open country.

As the day warmed, a second and then a third lark rose with a rippling electrical call, breaking from the field to sing, to give themselves airs, each in earshot of each, a raised descanting chorus that moved over the grass like the searchlight beams that stream from the sun through gaps in the cloud. Both larks and light are aimed at the earthed world: the sun comes down on to the field, the larks sing their occupancy of the grass beneath them, but both are also glimpses of a life lived upwards, where we cannot go.

Wordsworth would have known The Backs when he was a student at Cambridge. He could have shot snipe as others did over the land now occupied by Downing Terrace, then known as The Marsh. But he wrote of the countryside, from where the garden fens were sequestered, only in passing ('level fields / Far from those lovely sights and sounds sublime'), or as a blank space for the screening of generic thoughts ('I looked for universal things; perused / The common countenance of earth and sky'). Perhaps the fens were too flat and too boring, too farmed and fielded already. Or were they too wet and too messy? *Fen* remained a dirty word for him, which was why he enjoined the shade of Milton to tidy the place up. But if he had explored them, he might have done for the molecatchers and eel men what he did for the solitary reaper and the leech gatherer. As it is, instead of romantic heroes buzzing with feeling and natural truth, the fens have come down to us as a sideshow of freaks. Old, unhappy, far-off things made jolly.

Missing their Wordsworth the fens got butterfly collectors, character-hunters and outward-bound chaps like the student members of the self-styled Republic of Upware in the mid nineteenth century, among them Samuel Butler, later author of *Erewhon*. They sought out the fens as a nowhere place, a quaint holiday site of specialness, of primitive energies and untutored wisdoms. They loved to fish and hunt and sail and skate and to learn field-craft and plunder tales from the canny rustics. Tennyson came out by boat to see the sunken sights of the *drown* of 1861 and wrote a poem about beer. Invoking Virgil's *Georgics*, others wrote doggerel: 'The wide, wide fens are drear and cold / And drear and cold the weather / But the skies are light and the fens are bright / When warm hearts meet together.' They recorded what they shot as well: '8th March 1852 Fell in with a flock of rare linnets *Linaria montium* [they mean twite] and shot about 50. Lunched, adjourned to the Fen and killed four [short-eared] owls *Strix brachyotus*.'

James Wentworth Day thought the republic 'hilarious'. His *History of the Fens* appeared in 1954; it was written in six weeks, he says, and joined his twenty-six other titles. He was perhaps the most incorrigible of the many writers (almost *all* writers before 1960) who milked and mined the fens for the characters those students would have loved to patronise. Much 'country writing' across Britain was imprisoned by this two-dimensional dehumanising of its own people; in the fens, with very few exceptions, it seems to have been endemic.

Dates and details were kept vague, but it always helped if you could sketch in at least the illusion of a direct encounter. Fowlers in Wentworth Day's book were 'near savages' who lived on Adventurers' Fen in peat hovels with horn-paned windows and lay about eating water rats on couches of sheepskin. Tom Harrison was one of them, the 'last' (of course) of the punt-gunners: 'a hermit of the fens, a man of the prim-itive wild . . . in his veins ran the wild blood of Hereward's Saxons'. Our author had a particular thing for the Saxons: Hilaire Belloc, fen prospector likewise, made a fetish of the Normans – there is no truth here. On Adventurers' Fen, Harrison netted lapwings, noosed redshanks, darted jack pike and, knowing 'the workings of the eel in the mud', stabbed them with a glaive ('pure Saxon'). He was part paid for his catch with laudanum for his ague.

A fitting rig of your own was required to even begin to match such a fenman. Wentworth Day had dug deep into the peat to collect 'the mandible of a small pterodactyl dredged from the bed of the Cam at Upware . . . together with the heel bone of what Sir Arthur Keith, the distinguished anthropologist, definitively identified as a "tree-climbing woman".' He also announced 600 years of fenland ancestry and his ownership of 'a few hundred acres of Adventurers' Fen' (he bought this, 'my fen' he says, in 1935). Perhaps he didn't feel the need to dress up.

In any case the entomologist Lord Walsingham, who went butterfly collecting at Wicken in the early 1900s (those extinct swallowtails . . .), had probably upstaged the whole century and the entire fen playground with his mole-fur jacket, snakeskin waistcoat and a cap made out of a hedgehog.

Along with the witch-doctor togs and the high old heels, the fens themselves were cast as a character: the misty embodiment of archaic nationhood. 'I bought the fen to preserve it,' Wentworth Day says, 'to save for all time the essential Englishness of it.' Quite what that would be is never disclosed but the Saxons are involved, providing, 'an indefinable background'. In addition, Wentworth Day recruited a home guard to defend his patch. His roster of friends and staff, though, are even more lost in time than the tree-woman or the auroch, also dug up from Burwell Fen, with a Neolithic polished-stone axe embedded in the great blackened forehead of its buffalo-like skull. Watch the parade as the film runs, once again, backwards: 'Lord Lloyd, dark, incisive, and gay, the greatest Proconsul of his age; Ralph Okeover Curzon, who would get up at two o'clock in the morning and cheerfully motor sixty miles to be in his butt before dawn; the present Duke of Manchester, an old friend of many Fenland forays; "Chubb" Leach, the Newmarket trainer, a boyhood friend for whom no day is too cold, no water too deep; Sir Jocelyn Lucas, that engaging man-of-all-work, Member of Parliament, Master of Hounds, gallant soldier . . . and overlording it all was Ernest Parr, my keeper, quiet, sunburned, tough as old iron, with the water-wisdom of an otter, the eye of a hawk . . .'

But it was all for nothing. In the war, farm-improvers or 'little Hitlers', raucous with 'bureaucratic self-praise' and severe in their 'extravagant, ruthless, soulless form of "efficiency"', drained his fen thereby 'destroying not only the beauty of the English countryside [but] killing the spirit, the soul, and the independence of the countryman'.

When we hear the word *countryman* we might reach for our eel-glaive but, in any case, the fen was long drained and growing leeks and potatoes by the time Wentworth Day wrote his dead letter to old England. The three books on Adventurers' Fen appeared within twelve years of one another. All are rather quiet about the nearby writers. Alan Bloom mentions neither Ennion nor Wentworth Day. Ennion, first on the scene, doesn't call any other writer by their name. Wentworth Day, with his *opera buffa* Adventurers' Fen and his 600-year stare, talks of 'Dr Ennion's . . . charming little book'.

At last the rain stopped. Under the dry zinc of the sun the days grew heavy with the smell of nettles and heated with ragwort crowns and rosebay spikes. Flies hummed the fields. The stubby ponies tethered in the lee of a hawthorn were hypnotised by the buzzing. Only their trembling flanks said they were alive. Sheep cooked in their fleeces. There were grey stockings of dried mud on the cows' legs. Nobody had anything to say. The larks had finished and the rooks and crows were silent and moved like black damper felts over the ground. The erotics of the year here were remaindered to the close scrambling drone of a bumblebee into a pale purple foxglove, the pansy-dark tongue-spots on the flower's lip quivering beneath the bee's boozy crawl like moulds in a dish. The fen had never seemed so inland, so quiet, so far from the sea. Somewhere offshore, through the days and nights, puffins swirled between the wings of gannets. Above the fen, an afternoon woodpigeon climbed a rotting stair, stumbled and slipped.

As a child, I liked to stand on summer days for minutes at a time inside the thin tent made by a bed sheet drying on a washing line. The cool shaded fresh interior and the warm burnished smell of the outside made the summer for me. The hot quilted week on the fen after the soaking gave me something of the same. Towards Upware, a second haying was underway. Walking the field twice, in the morning and then in the afternoon, I tasted its drying, from bleeding green stem-juice to the dusted grey biscuit of hay.

Ruined mallards sat around the fen pools: the boys, demobbed, looking like girls, the girls like they were wearing their brothers' old clothes. This annual catastrophe, a fag-end anti-masque, is politely called *eclipse* plumage by birdwatchers. Both sexes moult but the drakes have the most to lose. Their spring flash and quack must give way to unemployed loafing while their new feathers grow. An old pillow had been shaken out over the fen, the water was clogged and messy with shed plumage, medals of the blown season. The men, in their underwear, peered at their reflections.

There was an emerald-green fly on a dead shrew on the fen track, the finger of a glove with a jewelled ring worn on top. The fly flew and the shrew moved. From under its snout appeared its puppeteer, a corpse-burying beetle, fastidious sexton in orange and black scrubs, busy shaving the body beneath, or laying its eggs, or doing whatever it must. Shaking itself free of its prize it paused and cleaned its feelers with its front legs, the left feeler stroked by the front left leg, the right by the right. The tiny morsel's sugary rot rose above it in a little scented tower about a foot high and four inches wide. A day later I walked the same track. There was nothing to smell or see.

I had waited for the last frost before I planted my maize in the garden, but the first swifts above the house distracted me and I forgot to dig and the corn went in late.

The village next to ours is Swaffham Bulbeck. There, between 1820 and 1831, Leonard Blomefield kept, and eventually published, *A Naturalist's Calendar*. It is a list of species – of birds, flowers, trees, insects, agricultural crops, amphibians and one or two bats – and the 'Mean, Earliest and Latest' dates of their occurrence in and around the fen village.

Phenological documents like this are of immense value in charting not only lost species but also cycles and rhythms of animal populations and climate change. We know how bad things are because of the banal entries in gardeners' diaries that have recorded, over many years, the first annual mowing of back garden lawns. The dates have crept earlier and earlier.

Blomefield was born Leonard Jenyns, but later changed his name. Blomefield is perfect for his book. He lived near Bottisham Hall, on the edge of Swaffham Bulbeck, where he held the living. From 1818 to 1854 he was the vicar at St Marys. The beech trees, along the edge of the park of the hall, are a good place to see little owls (which Blomefield didn't know, as they were yet to be introduced and established in the country) and tawny owls (his mean date for 'hoots' was

2 February). His father had inherited the hall from Soame Jenyns, author of *A Free Inquiry into the Nature and Origin of Evil*, which much provoked Samuel Johnson for its mealy dealings with serious things. Leonard seems to have been a rather cautious and singular man. He was invited to travel on the *Beagle* as the ship's naturalist, but turned down the offer, suggesting Charles Darwin took the job instead. He knew Darwin from beetle-catching expeditions they had shared to the fens (Darwin's fen beetles, pinned and labelled in a box, are on show at the University Zoology Museum in Cambridge).

Blomefield's own interest in order and systematics started early. At Eton he reported arranging his belongings 'with great particularity' and was nicknamed '*Methodist*' – 'This I did not like but it was true all the same.' Also at school, terrified that he might never see the book again, he copied out nearly the whole of *The Natural History of Selborne*.

My copy of Blomefield's *A Naturalist's Calendar* is small and khaki, like an army manual, but the list within is the poem of a green man. The book's title page describes him not as the author of the *Calendar* but its *keeper*. The earliest a song thrush began singing in Swaffham Bulbeck was 1 January. The pipistrelle bat was 'last seen abroad' on 31 December. Blomefield has wonderful sightings from the late-summer fens to record: the appearance of both the ghost moth and the goat moth, the hatching of hen harriers, the shining of glow worms. Many of his noted creatures are no longer found on the fens, but the list doesn't read as an elegy. Blomefield knew so much, and had noted so much, that to be in the field with him must have been like walking out with a recording angel who could channel the song of the earth. If we could take down the world like this, in long- and shorthand, we might, it seems, save it and ourselves.

His mean date for the cessation of blackbird song is 16 July. Wheat is cut on a mean date of 30 July; mushrooms abound; the stridulous notes of the great-green *acrida* grasshopper are heard, and all else falls quiet. And then, on a mean date of 8 August, the last swifts are seen.

In October 1974 Georges Perec sat for three days in various cafes around a square in Paris, the Place Saint-Sulpice. He noted down what he saw – pigeons, people, traffic – as a birdwatcher might keep a tally from a hide. Subsequently, he wrote a short book on what he'd been doing for those days called *An Attempt at Exhausting a Place in Paris*. He had had in mind an investigation into 'what happens when nothing happens' or a study of what he called the *infraordinary*. His fifty pages list the activities and scenes that he witnessed one after the other. It is wilfully banal and humdrum stuff and the square is drained of drama. His commonest entries are for the buses that cross in front of him. They prompt the most continuous passage of writing in the book:

> why count the buses? probably because they are recognisable and regular: they cut up time, they punctuate the background noise; ultimately they're foreseeable.
>
> The rest seem random, improbable, anarchic; the buses pass by because they have to pass by, but nothing requires a car to back up, or a man to have a bag marked with a big 'M' of Monoprix, or a car to be blue or apple-green, or a customer to order a coffee instead of a beer.

Not that it's important but I remember what I was doing in October 1974. My field days were in jeopardy. My young teenage life was rather bleak. My parents were rough-riding an unhappy relationship while my sister, in love with horses and ponies, was lost to me. I was at a school twenty miles from where we lived. Instead of teaching me how best to count buses or other useful skills, the teachers seemed more interested in making sure that my hair didn't creep below my ears. Kept from weekend birdwatching by Saturday classes and oceans of homework, I took up trainspotting on my long rail journeys to and from school. It didn't work. I needed something to identify, to count, and to write down, but I needed whatever it was not to come predictably towards me trapped by its own metal rails. Not even Clapham Junction with its great snake-head of tracks was wild enough. I left the school and moved to another where they had a Field Club and I joined it at once.

Perec's book is fascinating mostly because it is a failure. The place cannot be exhausted. But the book's failure makes it happier than it would have been had it succeeded. Perec sits in his cafes trying to be objective and empirical but finds he is part of the scene. What he notes down is increasingly conditioned by what he has already noticed and by what he already knows. To begin with he sees more than he knows but rapidly he knows more than he sees. He discovers, as the Russians have it, that life isn't a walk across an open field. On first glance what might have looked like a *tabula rasa* is soon shown to have a history, as do those people who are traversing it, and so does he who is observing. His first sightings are as bald as can be, a time and motion project, but within minutes he is working on what has already become a phenological poem: now is different from then; that has changed; this is new. Everything thickens.

I think of Perec, a rare specimen of a now near-extinct species – the hardcore but playful literary avant-garde – starting out as a kind of regular birdwatcher trying to work his local patch but discovering, having gone into the field, as much about himself as about the movements of the gulls he watches, and, as he does so, discovering that the gulls are also infinitely more complicated than they seemed at first. These complications and his elucidations of them change him as well as shaking out the birds into Caspian and yellow-legged along with the herrings and lesser black-backeds. As he watches the gulls, the diary of his heart and his carefully written bird list become interleaved, and when he gets up to go he has just one notebook in his hand.

The more we know, the more there is to know, and the more it all joins up. The harder we look, the less straightforward seeing becomes. At the end of his life Linneaus, the greatest namer the natural world has known since Adam, no longer knew what he himself was called. Leonard Blomefield, anxious about putting things in their proper place and struggling to order Swaffham Bulbeck's bird song and flowering successions, might have found the Galápagos too much to take in. His decision not to go on the *Beagle* was probably the right one, but it has also left us with a theory that makes sense of everything (Darwin's) and a transcendental account of life in a few fen acres written as a list of names and numbers (his). After (what proved to be) the wild life of Saint-Sulpice, Georges Perec wrote a 600-page account of an imaginary Parisian apartment and made, in *Life: A User's Manual*, an ordering of the domestic world into his origin of species.

On 8 January 1964 Elizabeth Bishop wrote to her fellow poet Anne Stevenson about Charles Darwin, one of her favourite authors. Her thoughts in her letter have much to say about her own poetics yet also, accidentally but brilliantly, capture Perec and Blomefield too, and find the whole unlikely gang on the same bus: 'reading Darwin one admires the beautiful solid case being built up out of his endless heroic *observations*, almost unconscious or automatic – and then comes a sudden relaxation, a forgetful phrase, and one feels the strangeness of his undertaking, sees the lonely young man, his eyes fixed on facts and minute details, sinking or sliding giddily off into the unknown'.

Those gulls are being shaken out these days in the Cambridgeshire fens and on its gravel pits, rubbish tips and reservoirs. Species are being split and there are new and obscure featherings to learn. Caspian and yellow-legged gulls didn't exist by name when I was sorting out my birds, and this has made it hard for me to believe that I could pull them from the world around me into knowable life. I have never consciously seen either in Britain, but I have promised myself that I will one day work them out. And my maize? Late planted in the lacklustre summer, it never grew higher than its first foot.

The big projects to fix the fens always ran alongside smaller and more local negotiations for living with them. The Romans tried to do what they did everywhere, rolling out their strict and straight brand. Their tidying of the place was unsurpassed for 1,500 years, but the fens were slippery and tricky even for Rome. Their causeways had to crook and curve and meanwhile, as their lost silverware dulled in the peat, the *custom of the fen* grew up – a looser, more pliant give and take, saturated usually, dissolved sometimes, knowing always. It was an ambience not a fact and denoted a lived environment, an accreted neighbourhood of shifting uses that had become patterned into habits. You could see it in the common sense of the commoners over their common wealth. Like a conversation preserved across centuries, it was a muttered and reinterpretable agreement between a people and their place. It blew in the wind and the words got carried away, but when it worked it was like the best of farming or like seeing how wild animals live. Life goes wrong and comes right and goes round again as another year brings another chance.

The wet demanded adaptations. And although the people didn't think of themselves as oddities until outsiders repeatedly cast them in that role, their strategies for survival were tailored to amphibian life. On census forms, fen natives were usually denoted as labourers or peat cutters; local differences alone separated them from other farm workers up or down the Roman roads. Only others dressed them as full-time stilt-walking fen *slodgers* or plover-trapping eel-stabbers. It is true they sometimes worked this way, but that wasn't all that they did. Some did catch waders with nets and some did use stilts to navigate flooded fields: in the fourteenth century a boy walking on pattens or stilts into a marsh, looking for ducks' eggs, was drowned; in 1610 Isaac Casaubon watched one stilted man and a single small boy drive 400 cattle to pasture. Summer grounds, also called *half-lands*, were often reached by boat. But on them, fen people grew hay and grazed cattle like anywhere.

Parts of the fens have been a near-industrial agricultural landscape for many centuries. Medieval fenland was remarkably organised. Fishing rights were arranged with such precision in some fens that the night was divided into eight separate bank-side sessions. Minute regulations also controlled peat cutting, intercommoning between villages, and the maintenance of ditches. In the presentments and inquisitions of medieval courts, the failure of individuals to play their part in the common upkeep is repeatedly noted. When the custom of the fen had been ignored and things had gone bad, the arraigning documents were jammed with Fen-Latin verbs: *obstruitur, inundantur, submergunter*. The detailing of what was neglected and went wrong intimates what was otherwise done well and went right. In order that water might flow for all, your channel had to be kept clean, your *clowes* (sluice or floodgate) cleared, your sewer sorted.

Through the seventeenth century, as the fens were mangled most severely and clobbered closer to submission by outsiders, the people who had lived on and from them became identified with the recalcitrant non-complying swamp. Obstreperous Lincolnshire fen people were said to 'live at large, and prey, like pikes, upon one another'. Straight lines were demanded, meanders and porosity were threatening signs of a backwards or dangerous character. Some fen dwellers rioted against drainage, threw down ditches, broke open sluices, and found common ground with parliament in the Civil War years. Cromwell's own fen tide went in and out: the fenman was first against drainage (his national reputation was made as a defender of fen commoners who opposed drainers), then, when in charge, turned in favour. The unknown writer of the *Anti-Projector* from around 1653 described how the fens provided a livelihood for 'many thousand cottagers', with those locals gathering 'reeds, fodder, thacks, turves, flags, hassocks, segg, fleggweed for fleggeren, collors, mattweede for churches, chambers, beddes and many other fenn commodytyes of greate use both in towne and countreye'. The alternative, the Anti-Projector declared, was 'Cole-seed and Rape', and what were they 'but Dutch commodities and but trash and trumpery'. A Dutch-engineered landscape prevailed, however: Vermuyden and the Adventurers had their way and the waters began to obey, for a time at least. A poem of 1685, attributed to Samuel Fortrey, toots the drainers' triumph from the height of the Restoration years of zealous surveying, embanking and pumping. The poem lumped the bogtrotters with the bog, and suggested the wild man would be tamed like the waters he had stilted across. The floods were new 'muzled', rivers 'govern'd', streams dammed with 'bridles' and, as a consequence, 'there shall a change of Men and Manners be' so that 'Souls of Sedge shall understand Discourse'.

As I read the old fen books I began keeping a list of flood dates – of *drowns* as they are called in the fens – until I realised I was writing down almost every year in some decades. Floods were part of ordinary fen life, part of the custom of the fen. Flooding water was once thought of as 'mother' to the fens. For this reason, some people resisted drainage just as the fens did themselves. Their livelihood looked better to them wet. Parts of the medieval fens were more valuable in their half-natural condition than they would have been drained to winter grounds. They were highly productive bogs. For centuries the meadow grasses of a seasonally flooded summer ground were worth more than an arable field. A heath, William Cobbett wrote, might be more valuable for the bees it feeds than for anything that might come of its enclosure. It was the same on the fens. Eels paid their way. So did the sedge.

An astonishing aerial photograph of the great flood of March 1947 east of the Ouse Washes shows three farms, Causeway, Doles and New Willow, as three trinket clusters of matchboxes and sugar cubes in a vast grey plain of sheeted water. That year the banks couldn't hold the flood, but the same year the farmers there grew bumper crops out of what had been drowned fields. In a flood in 1918, around the Little Ouse, Frank Harrison carried his eight pigs, one by one, upstairs to safety in the bedroom of his cottage. In 1613 when the sea flooded the silt-fen at Terrington, some took to the church for its protecting height and some to their haystacks. In 1861 a windmill took off, sailing across the flooded fens it had failed to drain. In another flood a sea boat was driven inland and came to rest on the roof of a fen house; three sailors saved themselves by clinging to the chimney. Elsewhere old boats were used to shore up banks and keep the water from making the land a sea. Attacking Hereward, when the Isle of Ely was still an island, the Normans built a pontoon bridge by inflating the skins of drowned cattle. Stone for fen churches came by boat and sometimes didn't make it. The huge blocks destined for Ramsey Abbey were tipped from their ferry by a storm. Each weighing a ton, they sank to the flooded fen floor and are now stuck on the long-drained fields of nearby Engine Farm like a henge dropped from the sky. In June 1693, around the town of March, 30,000 acres were underwater: 'where wee should be now plowing the fowles of the ayre are swimming'. Another photograph shows men trying to harvest standing up to their waists in water in a field. Each stook of wheat rises like a straw mountain peak from a sea.

There is no doubting the severities of the floods and the casualties they caused, and even a regular crisis is hard to prepare for, but the flooded fens were part of fen life for centuries, and people lived alongside the water with their own expert if sometimes sunken knowledge. Fen people once understood the fields, wet or drained, in ways we cannot fathom. The custom of the fen has all but disappeared. The closest we can get to it nowadays is the flooding Washes and their man-made creation each winter (or flood-time) of a wet broadway twenty miles long and half-a-mile wide that stops the nearby rivers from flooding the fens. Vermuyden planned the Washes so that 'the water, in time of extremity, may go in a large room to keep it from rising too high'. The image is telling. Looking at the banked waters, the housed wet, spilling over the fields into the Nene Washes near Whittlesey, or the Ouse Washes between the Old and New Bedford Rivers west of Ely, it is possible to see some late lingering reflection of how the wider fens looked and how they worked. No fen river, even as they are routed and managed today, can carry its winter load without further help. On the Washes a sanctioned flood is floated in front of us. Water is ushered into a room. The flood flattens the flat place still further. Field lines and fence posts grow like the raised stitching of the earth. Whooper swans scull over half-sunk gates. Gulls slide and dip over the drowned grass as over the sea. And then, two months later, cattle graze in the lush summer meadows that the Washes become after the winter water flows on. The grass there is thicker and greener than any I have ever seen elsewhere on the fens.

A story is told about a punishment reserved for those who most severely ignored or denied the custom of the fens. A penalty at the disposal of the medieval Court of Sewers for those who neglected or deliberately breached locally raised and vital banks was to have the offender buried alive. The culprit would become part of the defences he had ignored or wrecked. He was to be bound and planted into the gap he had created, peat doing for a concrete overcoat. Can we believe this happened? Like a lot of fen stories and their near-neighbours – the Dutch boy at the dyke and Canute at the waves, or the fens themselves as flow country with their endless brokering of the dry and the wet, of land and water – no one knows where this story begins or where it might end, or where, if anywhere, its truth lies among other fen burials and disinterments, the melting of solids, the fixings of the eel and the bog, the swimming of mole and mist.

The blackbird in the rain was the last I heard singing for the year. Through June, birdsong drains sweetly and slowly to the reductions of midsummer. In the bushes hidden blackbird fledglings take over, with their punctured-tyre *pseep* noises. One day all you hear is flies and you struggle to remember what has gone. In the village, I caught the last juice of blackcap from the sloes, the beak-snap of a spotted flycatcher on its sallies from the gravestones, and the tinnitus of goldcrests – the white noise of a hangover – from the cedar in the churchyard. Then – unheard and unnoticed at first – space opened in the hedges. From now on, if the sun is to come back before the winter, it will be in the legs of grasshoppers or the dry wheezing calls of young starlings. They flock as soon as they leave the nest and then crash about in gangs, flying the tattered matt flags of the season that they share with young rooks and crows. You can see this even in May. Long before the school summer holidays begin the winter is signed up. Only the woodpigeon tries again and again his cracked tuba. He sounds far away and out of date: a lullaby sung on an iron-lung. Through the summer his sorry song tightens the chest as old grass shrinks taut over the field and harvest chaff and thistledown come to stuff the air. The Earth, the whole planet, is slung out on its slingshot arc and on the fen you feel it, coasting without power, all traction spent.

Swifts make July bearable, almost rescuing the month, swinging through its otherwise hammock-slump on scything wings. But, by the third week, the village birds are done with its rooftops, the skittering and screaming is over, the beetling scuttles into the crannies and the bale-outs from the eaves no more. If they come over our house they are higher and quieter than before. In the first days of August most hunt out above the fields, rigging the wind and fattening on flies. Ant-flights one day steered them over the fen in a brilliant black frenzy. Black-headed gulls gathered for the insect bonanza as well, clomping about the sky, pulled and tugged after the aerial morsels; wooden spoons to the swifts' steel blades.

That same evening I lay on my back in the middle of the field and looked up. The winged ants had lifted in the still of the afternoon but now the wind had risen and with it the late light grew ruddy and loose. The gulls sloped off into it, turning gold as they went, but the swifts were still there flying above me in the way they always fly, describing their continual motion, their permanent entrance into the sky: endlessly, effortlessly, blackly uncoiling, always moving yet always there. Above me were birds that wouldn't make contact with anything that touched the Earth for at least ten months. One swift that summered in Oxford was known throughout its life. It lived to be eighteen and in those years had flown 2 million miles, the equivalent of four round trips to the moon.

James Ferguson, the eighteenth-century Scottish astronomer and instrument maker, began his life as a farm labourer. Aged ten, in 1720, he minded the sheep on a neighbour's farm in Banffshire. He was a precocious astronomer and already fascinated by the night sky that cloaked him on his way to and from his long days in the fields. In his autobiography he described how, with his flock folded, he would lay a blanket on the sheep-turf and would lie on his back and hold beads on strings over his head to measure star distances and patterns in the fields of space. These measurements he then transferred to paper star-maps that he had spread beside him on the grass. The reckoning of swifts' flight is no easier but just as alluring as Ferguson's celestial calibrations: how a handspan might make a light year; how a bird that lives in my neighbour's roof might fly to the moon and back.

Above me the swifts were quiet. So quiet they seemed to silence the air. They seem to darken their surroundings as well, their blackness spilling from them. They sleep on the wing. There are beautiful black and white photographs of radar screens blooming into life at night, capturing swifts leaving London in all directions to sleep in the sky. The night-screen is black, the birds appear greyish white. The image looks like winter breath parsleying on a pane of glass. The birds I saw lifting themselves into the sky beyond my eyes were probably preparing to sleep. In their sleep-flight they rock from one side to the other as if they were being swung in a cradle. It is thought this motion is prompted by a sleep pattern that dims and then alternates brain activity. First the left side of the swift sleeps and then its right. The sleeping half begins to fall through the air, the waking half corrects the fall. *Nocturnal harmonic oscillatory orientation* is the term given for the shuttle of the bird through the loom of the night. Flying above the Earth they move around the world as it moves around – beneath and above – them, their globe-curved heads like little planets, half-lit, half-dark, swaying above the swaying earth, the bending grass, and the curved reeds.

One year, out on the Wash, from a boat riding the mixing waters of the North Sea and half the rivers of eastern England, I watched two swifts slicing like flung peat between three gannets, cruciform flints, all piling south towards the fens. Neither gannet nor swift is a bird of the fields. Both are useless if set down on the earth. Once, on ploughland far from the sea, I saw a storm-wrecked gannet looking like an abandoned wedding dress. Once, in a field after a thunderstorm, I found a swift grounded – a dropped glove. Both birds are wrong for my story, but both, between them, are sentries keeping watch when airborne. Lie in your summer bed in Britain and know that gannets are flying around the island's every edge and swifts are flying above your head. The light walking on the sea. The dark swimming through the air.

Midnight on the fen, a half-hearted dark in the dog days of the year: all quiet and still but for the leaning air of summer which came over me like cow breath. Everything was here – the fen was flat but full – and yet the engine of the place seemed elsewhere. Whatever was once noisy and colourful and fresh in these same fields was worn out and run down. Labouring up through clouds a slice of moon cheese sweated into the muzzy sky. I looked as far across the murky plain as I could. There was little to see. The horizon was flat with a few trees hanging at its end like dark chandeliers. But the smell was strong – a low-tide vegetable ooze with a salted edge. The sea.

The sea is not here but it once was and perhaps will be once again. At the dead end of the road, where the tarmac stops and the grass begins, I slipped off my shoes and socks and waded out. Most of the fields there were lying under wheat, almost ready for harvest, their gold gone to grey and in the dark they looked like tiles of worn carpet. But I went on to paddle in a grass field, one of the few. Where cattle had stood, its earth was warm, wormy and black under my toes; further out the grass bit at my feet like insects and a few tired dribbles of dew brushed my shins. It smelt: green but old. Cabbage not lettuce. Rot not ripe.

The sky misted taking the feeble stars still further away. From invisible clouds it started to rain. The long-buried sea stirred in its basket of sleep. Just before the first drops, I felt the field breathe in and hold a deep quiet for a moment. Then I heard the rain as it hit the sleeping grass at my feet and the earth sighed. The grass stems bowed beneath each tiny wet punch. Away across the fields, in the almost dark, a hidden quail called twice like a damp electrical contact fizzing in the night: *wet-my-lips, wet-my-lips,* a fen prayer signalled over the waves of green.

As a crop grows, tight-packed and uniform, it closes a field, like bread rising in a loaf tin. Then the harvest cut comes that releases the ground and, with it, the itch of all its welcome irregularities. By the end of the dry week the fields next to the fen were transformed in this way and it was the same for every mile around. The corn-top of the world had been lowered by two feet, close-cropped and clear-felled. With the wheat taken, the soil, its earthenware, was to be seen once again. And the ruins, the leftovers, seemed more homely than what had grown before.

The farmers drove their cars into the half-done fields and left them there while they were combining, stopping every other hour, walking across the toast and marmalade stubble and straw. They sat with the radio on, smoking and texting in their cars, the last fade of the linen cloth carried at noon to the field, a jug of cider, thick-cut sandwiches, and a snooze in the shade.

The combine started up again like a taxiing jumbo. The field was shaken and heated and shouted at. The machines made their noisy, partnered dance around the square. All the years, all the people, the barefoot bending to the ground, the cutting, the raking, the stooking, the threshing, all is now put so quickly through those metal mouths into those playground-bright trundling bellies. I stood and watched the harvester make light of the harvest, and the field was done in an hour.

All night the combines drove on across the fens with dragon roars

178

and bright lamps, as if this gold rush was an emergency, and the molten gush from the Earth's core must be tapped and capped at any price. In the floodlit dark between the roaring engines I heard lapwings bleating anxiously around the stubble fields, woken and inconsolable.

SWALLOW

Afterwards I threw away my rucksack and a pair of socks: I had put my bag down on the ground in some dusty places and grass seeds had got woven into the knit of my ankles. I should really have binned my jeans as well. My fingernails grew unbitten for a week. I put my contact lenses in with diligence, eyeballing them for flecks of alien grit. On the third day my throat ran with mucus before drying to chalk and I thought I'd been delivered to the end in double-quick time but, after a hot night of dire imaginings, a regular cold took hold and I shivered on and off through the rest of my stay.

Chernobyl is flat, as flat as the fens. Its horizons are local and edged with trees. Rarely does the view extend more than half a mile in any direction. The green at the rim of things curls up the sides of the sky. Nowhere can you stand on a hill and feel that, like the Little Prince, you are on the outer edge of the planet and towering over its curve. Everywhere you are held in the bottom of a shallow spreading basin. Somewhere there must be a gradient, something that tilts or rolls or drains, but you do not feel anything of that here. Somewhere, you remember, there is sea too, but here that would only be a rumour or, at best, a defrosted fish finger in the canteen of Chernobyl town.

Any and all wide views close down when you arrive at the checkpoint barrier across the road two hours by car north of Kiev. Before the Exclusion Zone that begins here, flat fields had been coursing next to the road for miles, tangled with old grasses or stubbly with wheat straw, each already finished for the year. At the fenced border of the Zone, a tall wild hedge of shaking aspens at right angles to the road squared off the last field and from there on to the plant, a further forty-five minutes away, only trees crowded to the roadside.

The red and white barrier had the English word *nice* printed on it several times. I don't know why. No one goes into the Zone who doesn't have business with it. And nice is not the word. We waited for our papers to be processed. A redstart sang half a phrase of song and then called from a pine next to the road on the Kiev side of the barrier. Its orange gape opened a cave in its black throat. As it sang, its silvered back and warm red tail trembled against the scabby bark of the branch. At the same moment, on the Zone side of the barrier, a black redstart called from the corrugated roof of the policemen's hut and shook its dustier back and rustier tail. The fountain sparkle of one bird passed into the metered buzzing of the other, their tails quivering like needles across the line. The policeman raised the barrier.

Hemmed by pine and birch we drove towards the heart of the Zone. Staring into the trees I caught glimpses of open space, flashes of yellower light through the green dark of the woods. There were villages half-hidden, and industrial sites, and then a town. A lead-grey pipe crossed above the road like a gateway and we passed under it.

We drove on to somewhere flat somewhere else in the trees. We did this for five days. Away from the town we saw no one for there was no one to see. At fifteen or so places we stopped and collected plants, bugs and grasshoppers. We wanted variations and aberrations. Radiation levels were metered and noted. Leonid was at the wheel of his old saloon; our minder, Igor, issued directions from the passenger seat and helped with paperwork at the two or three other barriers we met. On the back seat with me was Anders Pape Møller, a Danish scientist based in Paris, and Tim Mousseau, a biology professor from South Carolina. There wasn't much talk. They were both on their second study trip to Chernobyl this year alone. Between their weeks in the Exclusion Zone they had had a summer holiday to Fukishima in Japan on a first visit to assess whether they might be able to start gathering biological data in the shadow of the devastated power station.

Above the redstarts at the first checkpoint there were barn swallows calling as they cut around the government buildings, and for the rest of our stay there were loose gangs of the birds over our heads almost everywhere in the Zone. Often they were the only birds that we saw or heard for an hour or more. Their lovely chittering flights, warm, sociable and unhindered, seemed to come from another time and place, the best of a summer farm thrown up into the autumn air above a forest. There are no longer wires between the telephone poles at the roadsides of Chernobyl, and the poles themselves have often rotted and fallen like trees in a swamp, snapped at their knees. The swallows must make their gatherings on the top twigs of limes or birches or on the loose tiles of the collective farm buildings and houses in the abandoned villages. As you approach, the birds shake from these places like dead leaves or brick dust.

Later in the week the weather closed. The swallows stayed on and flew lower. Even dulled and reduced, the air where they lived came increasingly to seem like a place you wanted to be. A place where you might revise your life upwards, lift your head and see beyond the trees and beyond the Zone to a freer and more open space less poisoned than the place we have been given. By their flights and calls through this air the swallows advertised it as habitable. But the swallows of Chernobyl are sick. The air might be their zone but the insects they take from that air pull the birds heavily down to earth.

We know this thanks to Anders. Most springs since 1991 he has come to study swallows here; for twenty years before that, and continuing to this day, he has also followed swallows breeding on Danish farms. His father was a dairy farmer and Anders has known swallows domestically since he was a child. His scientific research is among the longest continuing study of a bird by a single scientist ever. 'Someone', he said, 'did' common gulls for almost as long and there was a 'Finnish count' who worked on pied flycatchers for forty-three years, 'but he had a chauffeur and a servant to carry his stepladder'. Anders has ringed 50,000 birds himself – every one passing through his hands and many of them swallows. And those birds at Chernobyl join the swallows he knows from Jutland and elsewhere. Cradling so many in his palm to fix rings on their legs and take measurements and samples has allowed him to look deeply into the birds, understanding them as a species, but also and inevitably registering their individual characters. 'I have known hundreds of swallows personally,' he said, with half a joke, as ever, playing over his face, 'and it is not my fault.'

His voice is dry and quiet. You have to lean in to hear him and he leans away as you come close. In the car he sits still; in the field he walks with steady steps and a straight back. His hands are small and tremendously calm. When they are not working he holds them, I noticed, in a way that suggests an old painting, a still life, as if they are not solely or fully his. He is mordantly funny but doesn't laugh out loud very often, nor does he even grin, but something like a smile is always hovering at the tight corners of his mouth. As a scientist he is extraordinarily productive. A monograph on the swallow by another ornithologist flits between Anders's studies, with half the book indebted to things he has seen and thought about and its bibliography thick with the thin man's name and his references. He is fiercely clever – the only scientist I have met who I imagine lives fully in the stark light of what his behavioural ecology teaches him, its iron severities and truths, its granulated accounts of love and desire. Being a Danish dairyman's son contributed to this, he said, and Anders also told me that he was a teenage reader of Kierkegaard and, at the same time, debated vehemently with his local priest. In rural Denmark in the 1960s you were, he said, included in a list of believers in your parish unless you demonstrated that you weren't one. He duly did. Forty years on I found myself momentarily pitying the priest. It is still easy to feel stupid in Anders's company. I did that but I also liked him very much. Another possible reaction to his cleverness is to turn against him. Some biologists have done this. There was a spat a few years ago with serious consequences that ended with him being accused of manipulating his data. His ringing permit was revoked in Denmark. He was to be kept from his swallows. An academic tribunal subsequently cleared him of all the charges but watching him walk through the abandoned farms under the shadow of the reactor in the Exclusion

Zone, it is hard not to think that Chernobyl and its hot and testing seriousness is answering all of this, and that there is proving to be done in the remains of its fire. However, that is not the end of things. Anders's work with Tim Mousseau in Ukraine goes far beyond the personalities of the two men and whatever local motivations I might guess at. After repeated journeys in and out of the sick place and the painstaking accumulation there of evidence and understanding, they are now writing what amounts to a book of the end of things, nothing less than a Revelation and an Apocalypse.

This summer, between the poisoned places, Anders returned to Denmark and its swallows with gadgets that human runners wear on their wrists to record their heart rate. Previously, with birds in his hand he had noticed that when another swallow flew over calling or singing he could feel the held bird's heart racing against his fingers. Some hearts pumped harder than others. This year he sat in his car in assorted Danish cattle-yards clutching swallows he had netted and holding the runners' gadget against their chests while the car cassette machine played various swallow contact calls and alarm notes and songs. The length and complexity of the electric bubbling at the end of the male swallow's song indicate his testosterone levels. Listening birds, especially males, reacted strongly to the beefiest messages. But no two birds were the same; each swallow was either more agitated than the next or less. These variations offer glimpses of what nowadays are being called bird personalities. An individual might be defined by the way its blood is pumped. By your pulse we shall know you. Indeed, if you go ringing great tits, you can feel a whole society travelling through your hands in a single morning. Some come easily out of the net and lie meek in your palm, others attack like dwarf woodpeckers drilling at your fingers and drawing blood. Every bird is different. In Anders's hands some swallows flinched more than others when they heard alarm notes. These variations may well indicate how successful these individuals are likely to be as parents or long-distance migrants or as birds struggling to live in inhospitable places. Every bird being different, the more swallows you know the closer you get to the truth. There can never be enough data but each bird handled

184

narrows the gap even by the tiniest amount, a feather's width. This is what brings Anders and Tim back to Chernobyl when so many have left. As well as its book of the dead they are working on the map of its life.

In Chernobyl the swallow variations are vertiginous to contemplate. Every living thing is more or less ill, that is true of all life everywhere, but in the great sick room of the Zone this given comes to mean something far darker. The long dying that is life is horribly truncated there. Gerontologists talk of *twisted growth* in elderly humans as a way of understanding how we age into death. In Chernobyl you do not grow old with twisted growth, you are born with it.

To my eyes there seemed to be plenty of swallows in the Zone, but the map-makers know how to see beyond this seeming. Everything is to do with counting and the more that can be counted the better. By your pulse, but also by your neighbour's pulse, we shall know how things are. Good or bad. At Chernobyl another pulse, the throb of invisible radioactive particles, complicates the picture, marking it brightly and terrifyingly if you know how to look. The radiation released when the nuclear reactor at the power plant exploded in April 1986 ruined the woods and fields, villages and farms, fishponds and towns. I could see that. There is nobody there and trees grow up through the village bus stops, libraries and schools. But the ruin goes on, thriving as it ruins, and there is much to be learned from how those events are putting a kind of continuing stop on life. There is, it turns out, a gradient in this flat place, Chernobyl is a sink: it takes life in but gives next to no life out.

Radiation has triggered variations that no swallow personality can possibly cope with. It is eating them alive. Anders has been ringing birds since he was fifteen but before he started working at Chernobyl he had never seen a visible tumour on any bird. Of the 3,000 swallows he has handled to date in the Zone, at least fifteen had external growths blackly bursting from their bodies like cankered fruits. The red throats of other swallows were blotched with partial albinism, and others had asymmetric outermost tail feathers. Anders has also held birds whose toes pointed in the wrong direction, whose beaks wouldn't close, whose eyes were deformed by cloudy lenses. Cataracts increase in a human population exposed to higher than normal levels of radiation. A near-blind bird is a soon-dead bird.

Overall, fifteen to twenty per cent of the swallows in the Zone show aberrations or mutations. Every fifth or sixth swallow that flew over me was blighted in some way. One in ten of all birds of all species are afflicted in the Zone. From the ground I couldn't see the thinning red on the throats of the damaged swallows, nor the tail streamers that curl, but they were there. Aberrant birds seem able to breed (sperm has been collected from males and brood patches have been seen on females), but no one has yet watched the young of these birds or counted how many leave the nest. But it is known that their survival rate is low. Adult swallows show a bewitching loyalty to places familiar to them. We love them for this. Pulled by a rough half-moon of spit and mud, they try to come back to the same nest in the same barn that they previously bred in. Half the adult swallows elsewhere in Ukraine return at least once to breed (the exact number is 0.49). In Chernobyl only one in five makes it back the summer after it hatches (0.28 to be precise). If they don't return to where they started in all likelihood they are dead.

Getting back is not enough. There is neither escape, nor home-coming. The clocks of those swallows that do return are running down. In radiation-contaminated areas swallows are breeding two weeks later than birds in cleaner fields. This is bad. Though springs are warmer, encouraging birds to nest earlier, mutations are holding back breeding. Early birds get everything. Returning breeders, birds that have survived the winter, are much more likely to have hatched early themselves. Leaving late because you hatched late is almost certainly a death sentence. Anders glanced at the swallows above us. 'It is not good to be a slow starter if you have to fly to southern Africa on wings this big.' He spread his thumb and forefinger apart into the outline of a five-inch swallow curve. 'The old is dying,' Antonio Gramsci wrote of a different place and another time, 'and the new cannot be born; in this interregnum a great variety of morbid symp-toms appear.'

*   *   *

'Don't chew the grass or put anything else in your mouth, and wipe your feet whenever you leave the field.' Anders offered no further safety advice. He and Tim both laughed when I asked if they had any extra health checks after their visits. My five days in the Zone, they said, would radiate me no more than a single X-ray at the dentist. But in the Red Forest on our second day, they encouraged me to put on a thin white bodysuit over my jeans and shirt so that, when I stooped to the ground, the creases of my denim knees wouldn't fill with radioactive grains of sand.

I was kneeling in order to pin down my grasshopper victims in a butterfly net – my contribution to the week's work: forty grasshoppers from each site we visited in the Zone. After the first day of looking I began to be able to do the job: attend to what you would otherwise ignore; follow whatever filament of moving light flicks ahead of you as you walk; watch for where it stops moving and, at that place, something slight will have been added to a stem of grass or will have scratched a new mark on the ground; go there quickly and quietly and if possible without a shadow. For five days I peered down for hour after hour. Never have I looked so intimately at grass before, never scrutinised the places it pulls up from the earth, never felt so many dry feet on my fingertips.

There were bigger grasshoppers. I saw two the size of locusts, and others beautifully cryptic, their bodies dark chocolate brown with cream tramlines like the back of a great snipe. Some brighter ones too, paintbox green mantises with lashless professorial eyes, and others with cornflower-blue skin stretching from their legs into papery wings that helped them flee. But the grasshoppers I had been deputed to catch were half-an-inch long and the colour and texture of old grass; some had a little brighter green on their bellies, some a rye-red – those colours, you only really saw when you were holding them between your fingers.

Every day my hands smelled dimly of silage and my thumbs and fingers were stained brown from the tobacco-spit that bubbled at the grasshoppers' tight-lipped faces. The sodden chew was their last mouthful. I put them in a plastic bag. Every time I opened it to add a new recruit, those already captured leapt upwards, kicking off from the backs of others, or managing to get some grip where their spit had stuck on the slippery walls. Once one escaped, sailing free back to the field, but for all the others being caught was the beginning of the end. The bag sat on the table in the tent that Leonid and Igor erected for Tim and Anders at every stop. For a while, as the grasshoppers jumped within, it twitched; the clicks of their legs against the plastic like the ticks of the radiation meter next to them. Having finished his other tasks at each site – the dissection and photography of evening primrose flower heads (an American native, here an invasive weed) – Tim would take the hoppers from the bag one at a time. Their genes, like the primroses', were to be plumbed. In deft doctorly gestures he manoeuvred the animals between his fingers on to their backs and with the blades of a pair of surgical scissors snipped their bodies in three or four places. Their legs kicked a few more times, each kick with less certainty, drawing last hieroglyphs in the air, before they were posted into small glass tubes filled with liquid preservative. The three of us sat in the tent for a moment after the final delivery. Tim recalled doing his master's degree and how his dreams at the time became sinister distortions of his fieldwork that required him to pull the legs off more than 20,000 crickets. Anders admitted that he 'wasn't good with blood', and that the snip of Tim's scissors across the camping table took him back to the sound of his wife being cut to allow their first child to be born.

The grasshoppers were easy to catch on sunny days in the Zone in areas of lower radiation; they were hardest in the blasted clearings of the Red Forest, one of the hottest radiation spots. Highly contaminated ground here might have at best only one grasshopper every square metre; a similar area of clean grass might accommodate one hundred. The Red Forest is a mix of pines and birch (some originally planted, some wild growth) and clearings (some natural, some enforced). It is the nearest woodland to the west of the vast yards of reactors, chimneys, cooling towers, ponds and pylons at Chernobyl. All of these are now defunct and the trees are growing closer to the fences and wires.

In the aftermath of the explosion and nuclear fire that burned for ten days in 1986, the forest was the first dropping-off point for the radiation cloud. Its trees turned red. The wind blew towards the west and rain fell and both sowed radionuclides over the land. In particular, isotopes of three ductile silvery-white metals drifted where the air took them and sank where it left them: caesium (at Chernobyl, caesium-137), discovered in mineral water in 1860 and named for the sky-blue electromagnetic radiation that it emits; strontium (strontium-90), named by Humphry Davy in 1808 after the Scottish village Strontian where it was first discovered; and plutonium, the baby of the family, synthesized in 1940, though identified subsequently in nature, and named after the former (now dwarf) planet and the god of the underworld. Of the last of these, the isotope now found in the Exclusion Zone (plutonium-239) has a half-life of 24,100 years.

In the Red Forest, the birch trees are doing better than the pines. Birch seems to possess some superior ability to repair its own DNA. In the abandoned fields around the villages and collective farms a little further away from the reactor, it is the flimsy and short-lived but pushy birch that first steals a march across the grass. In the Red Forest I walked among birches half my age and three times my height, the wispy children of Chernobyl. The open acres of thin sandy soil scattered with a few of these rangy trees might have been in the Brecks of East Anglia, except that this was a clearing made by the explosion – the trees that grew here once were killed by radiation. Many of them still lay on the ground, preserved in death since 1986, their grey trunks wrapped in a fogged and brittle marquetry. Fall-out was so potent in these woods that for a time it destroyed microbial activity as well as most other living things. Rot was killed, decay arrested and the dead kept immutably dead. There were no friendly worms. Death, needing no colleagues, moved as an absolute master through these woods and fields, armed solely with itself, raining death beyond death down over the trees and grass, keeping everything dead. Dante, genius complicator of hell, would have understood; Achilles trapped in Hades too, a permanent king in the underworld wanting to be a ploughboy above and make things grow; and perhaps also the architects of the gulag, those men who devised death sentences given cruelly warped names like *twenty-five years without the right of correspondence.*

Even wrapped in my everything-proof suit I felt nervous in the Red Forest. It was ineffably strange: to be in a calm clearing that could kill you, where soil is dangerous, where the air might violate you, where standing under a blue sky is risky, where dust is lord of everything's future. I had walked only a few yards but had arrived on to an orphaned planet where nothing speaks to nothing. I started moving with flat feet, making deliberate low footfalls to try not to kick up the sandy earth. This made the grasshoppers hard to catch. The counter ticked hot at more than one hundred microsieverts per hour. Humans prefer their background radiation level at less than one. A little whirlwind got up from nowhere, as if looking for a Tarkovsky film, and brushed past me, picking up pine needles and then turning back with its cargo to stipple my white suit. My eyes smarted in the brilliance of the day. I began to imagine I could feel my own porosity, the soft membranes of my body, and the weather moving through me, the air coming inside and laying ash on my tongue.

Eight ravens came wheeling above me, each arriving separately but lingering, and calling hoarsely as I crouched to collect grasshoppers. A breeze riffled the birch leaves, already yellow and old. Older still, curled pages of bark scrolled from their trunks. Birches, wherever they are, look like they have got into the tree business rather too quickly. Here they leaned into some hopeless sickbed vigil at the edge of the pines. But the pines are beyond help, for in the Red Forest they have gone mad.

Eyes down for grasshoppers I nearly bumped into a standing stone of grey concrete, a twenty-foot-high stele marked 1941–1944 in fading black numerals. Fallen to the foot of this lost memorial was a tin crest, like a cheap fruit bowl, embossed with a wheat sheaf and knotted leaves and 'CCCP'. A pine tree scratched at the concrete and I could see weird sprouting balls of needles, dense and black like sea urchins, hanging from the ends of the tree's branches. Some malignity had driven extreme levels of needle over-production; another had concentrated these like angry iron filings leaving the rest of the branch twig-less and bald. At its dirty fingertips, the tree had grown its own wreaths.

Back at the car, Igor had laid on the bonnet a mushroom that he had picked in the woods. It had a cap three inches across, the colour of a brown envelope, and a chunky cheese stalk. On such a day in such a place it looked one-legged. Outside the Zone, the weekend before we started, Igor had been collecting mushrooms to eat. He pursues four species; one is dried, and three are bottled after being boiled with herbs and spices. They see him through the winter. On the way from Kiev to Chernobyl, men clutching black bin bags had been walking from the roadside into the woods. A lorry driver clambered back into his cab with mushrooms thickening both his hands to boxing fists. In many lay-bys and the forecourts of petrol stations, vendors squatted on the oily earth, next to blue and pink plastic buckets piled high with more mushrooms. Others, some as wide as eight inches in diameter, were laid head to the road on tea towels. All the mushrooms have high concentrations of radioactive isotopes, both in and out of the Zone, and the Ukrainians eat them throughout the year. This is not a good idea. Ingesting radiation is much the best way to absorb it. A single particle of plutonium can give you lung cancer: your own mushroom cloud.

In the autumn of 1986, four months after the disaster at Chernobyl, I moved to Budapest to study for a year. In the Nagycsarnok, the big covered market on the Pest bank of the Danube, a white-coated man with thick-rimmed glasses was often stationed behind a stall. You could show this mushroom doctor what you had collected in the Buda Hills and he would identify the species, separating the edible from the poisonous. He wrote authenticating chits so that the old men and women who got off the trams and trolley buses with baskets of mushrooms might sell them from the small tables at the back of the market. This little area was one of the best things I saw in the workers' state. The capitalist concession to the last peasants in the communist city. I liked the little altars of honey and herbs, of two eggs and ten mushrooms, and the ancients steadying themselves behind the tables. I bought jars of honey and its gloopy sunshine to light the winter, but I was always wary of the mushrooms, even with the doctor's notes. The first autumn after the explosion, and nearer to Chernobyl than I had ever been before, I wrote in my diary wondering about radiation and how it might be laid invisibly into everything that was banked so richly through the market: carp like old shoes lying in tanks of dirty water, glistening seams of pig fat, headcheese, huge bruised apples, collapsing curds, strings of hot paprika like dried tongues, barrels of chopped vinegary cabbage that made you wince as you passed, and buckets and baths of plums and grapes smoking in their own bloom.

I didn't know at the time, but the radiation had blown north and west of Budapest and the food I'd left behind in Britain was probably more at risk of contamination, but in any case my fears moved on and landed elsewhere. A mix of curiosity and trepidation had drawn me to Hungary. It was a European country but one that had made me a target through the cold war, that I had grown up in, and that had the where-withal to kill me. I half knew this was crazy but I also knew that I wanted something from the same angled light that had cast these distortions and refractions as it passed through the curtain (made of who knew what?) across Europe. I went east to see myself more sharply, but of course I carried my own bent light with me. A vagrant, even a vagabond, even a master's student, always comes from somewhere. The novelty and remoteness of Hungary then – I heard no English spoken except in my head for weeks at a time – revived and refocused two almost invisible madnesses that had clouded my childhood and teenage years. These were not my madness – they were the world's: the fear of poison and the fear of the bomb, bad stuff forged from the dust of life, brightness falling from the air turning everything dark.

At school when I had learned about the Earth, it was obvious that it was imperilled, and that we had poisoned it and, not content with that, were on the brink of destroying it. All my school projects were about extinctions and pollution. Aged ten I wrote about mercury in Antarctic penguins; I filled test tubes with pond water and sent them for analysis; I learned the word *epitaph* reading a book about dead elm trees. My favourite bird book of the time, J. A. Baker's *The Peregrine*, was a toxic account of a sick and self-hating man stalking wintering falcons in Essex ('a dying world, like Mars, but glowing still') during the decade the species came close to global oblivion. Agricultural insecticides, DDT and Dieldrin, were wracking the birds' bodies with poison, thinning their eggshells, and, in one of several gothic moments in the book, sending them falling to Earth on their backs, their yellow talons and legs clutching hopelessly at the sky.

This, I thought, was how the world would end. If the chemicals didn't crawl up the food chain to get us, then the nuclear blast surely would. I imagined the coming flash at the horizon and the burning wind. When I was thirteen a schoolmaster confiscated a hippy ring with a mandala design that I liked and the silver and black CND badge I'd tried to wear on my lapel. I never got them back. I watched *The Survivors*, a television serial about the aftermath of a catastrophic chemical weapons spillage, as if it was a manual for life, knowing, though, that I wasn't a winner and would have fallen at the first scything.

In the Zone, we drove back from the Red Forest to our hostel. There are two in Chernobyl town itself, one for Ukrainian visitors and one known as the Foreign Experts Hostel. It costs one hundred dollars a night to stay; the toilet paper has the colour and feel of woodchip wallpaper and comes in solid rolls, like a cut log of birch. The wind blew elsewhere in April 1986 and, although it is less than five miles from the plant, the town survives, the only living streets in the Zone. But it is a strange thing, oddly flat like a film set. As we drove I asked Tim and Anders if they remembered where they were when the reactor exploded. Tim, who was in Canada at the time, had no memory of the day; it barely featured in North American news bulletins. Anders knew exactly the place: 'a cabin made of moss and twigs,' beyond Uppsala in Sweden, 'hidden from the world' but under the same skies that bowled over Chernobyl. With a student, he was watching the extraordinary display of a male capercaillie, the giant woodland grouse of northern Europe, a boreal troll-turkey. Its name, coming out of Gaelic, means the horse of the woods. And it is. The male wears Jacobean doublet, ink black with pearl drops, and fanning his broad tail, shying at nothing, and puffing his wobbling throat he throws his head back and up and sings. Sings, like a drunk, what might be an account of fumbling at clothes, undoing a top button in extremis, and of pulling, meanwhile, a final cork. It is all told through neighs and whinnies, stamps and shivers. The ladies, hidden in blaeberries, look on discreetly, professionally unimpressed, sober in the dove greys of Morningside, and showing nothing of their secret decisions vis-à-vis sex. Anders saw all this and more as the nuclear fire was burning. He watched a beta male, a little less drunk, a little less camp-butch, make an unprecedented run at the boss-man and in a huge shoulder barge drive the alpha from his dance floor. The upstart pecked the toppled bird in the head until it was dead.

By the time I told my version of that day we were walking to the canteen in the town. The sun bounced on the western road at dusk. Mosquitoes became jewellery. Coming out of the sunset an old woman walked past us in a headscarf and home-knit jumper, steering herself with a wooden staff. She wished us *dobroho večora*. She was, I realised, the first elderly person we'd seen in the Zone. We saw no other. There are no old people in Chernobyl, or children. There are no house sparrows either, only tree sparrows. No rats. Outside our hostel, two not-right cats waited every day; one with a livid green scab across the back of its neck, the other with the face of a mother in a siege. At the edge of the town where the tarmac turned to dirt, a delinquent pack of five or six feral dogs hung around most of the time. The default canine regression in the Zone is greyhound-like, long, lean and pale: ur-dogs on the wolf-path.

Two gardens are maintained in Chernobyl town. One is watched over by the angel Gabriel, the other by Lenin. Gabriel sounding his trumpet is newer, a metal skeleton made out of stiff black cabling, the sort of rods that reinforce concrete. Behind him and his silent black horn is an avenue of crosses, more than a hundred, receding for a third of a mile across wet grass. Written on each is the name of a village that had to be abandoned after 1986. Out of sight of Gabriel, Lenin stands pewter grey amid a floral clock. In his mausoleum in Red Square in Moscow his preserved head and hands with their strangely childish fingers (who knows what goes on beneath his suit?) would recognise his Chernobyl self – the gardener of men and electrifier of the Soviet Union. His local incarnation is a little less waxy but clearly a variant bottling of the same fruit. In honour of some Japanese dignitaries who had been comparing disaster notes with the Chernobyl management, someone had buffed up the bald man.

Although the plant is dead, it still needs looking after. Rainwater is getting in; a new tomb must be built on top of the old one, a fresh concrete overcoat, and the buried reburied. The town is where the graveyard shift sleeps. Immediately after the explosion in 1986 they were allowed to approach Reactor Number 4 for only forty seconds before they had to retreat and be relieved. Many died and are dying as a result, nonetheless. Liquidators, they were called. Men and women now work four days at a time on the sarcophagus that cloaks Number 4 or elsewhere on the shut plant and then leave the Zone for four days before coming back. The town and the works are militarised; everyone wears a camouflage jacket and trousers. Some twisted idioms from the old days survive. People are in uniform but no one walks done up like a soldier any more. The workers' buses are Soviet-era with round bonnets and a hatch that must be opened at their rear to ventilate their engines. But they have dainty curtains at the windows and their old stencilled military numbers have been painted over in Ukrainian toyshop blue. A middle-aged woman with lacquered hair, pearl-drop earrings and patent black shoes that peeped from her camouflaged turn-ups, cycled slowly around us on a squeaky bike, her plastic briefcase tied on the rack at the back. Between two apartment blocks, a man, in the same fancy dress, attacked the last growth of summer grass with a sickle. He raked his hay beneath the escaped metal pipes, some naked, some clad in insulating bandages, that take (in common Ukrainian practice) steam or hot water cartoonishly on stilts over roads and from building to building but seem loath to enter any of them. On the way to our dinner of *varenyky* – parcels of something like old ears and the same colour as Lenin – we were sent through a scanner turnstile, which forced us to stand like applauding robots held mid-clap in a silent film, whilst some invisible account was made of our innards. We did this every day but I don't think the machine was ever plugged in.

The day the radio news in Britain announced the Chernobyl disaster

– three or four days after the event – I saw my first swallows of that year and also my first swift. The swallows were late and the swift a little early but I hadn't been doing much birdwatching that spring. Birds had become my business and I had an appointment at the British Museum's bird collection at Tring in Hertfordshire. My job was with the dead; my task to write a report on the status and distribution of the 106 species of endemic birds of Madagascar then known. These birds have evolved over millions of years of isolation and are some of the most extraordinary in the world, but the short book I wrote about them is one of the most monochromatic and lifeless imaginable. I am no map-maker and nothing I wrote could revivify the birds. The problem was that the nearest I got to Madagascar or its endemics was walking the narrow and dark corridors of the museum, pulling open cabinets and drawers, spending forty seconds here and there in one sarcophagus after another. Lying there, mostly on their backs, were hundreds of gutted specimens, what scientists call skins, many with a stick driven up through their insides and a dab of cotton wool in their eye places: vangas, ground-rollers, mesites and couas, the bizarre and magically complete avifauna found only on Madagascar but which I knew only as stiff and sorted, eyeless and grounded, and wrapped into themselves like all dead birds, whether under a hedge or in a fridge, on a beach or in a drawer. I took tray after tray to a work-table to decipher the details written on the labels tied to the leg of each bird. These labels are passports, information for the next world, like the cards tied round the necks of evacuee children, or coins placed under the tongues of the dead. They are small, no longer than an inch and a half, and usually written by the person who had collected the bird. To collect a bird means to kill it. That ought to be interesting, the written words ought to allow you to reinflate the moment and the hollow skin that came from it. I stared at the birds as I turned them in my hands, blue couas, sicklebill vangas and scaly ground-rollers; they were beautiful but strange, airy, fading smudges, somehow further away from me at an arm's length than they ever were before or have been since. A whispered lost language in an alien script. There was nothing to assemble beyond the colourless string, the greying card, and the inky lines recording dates and weights, measurements and localities. Laid out in rows in the trays like sorted bodies after a disaster, the dead awaiting repatriation, I had no way of helping them home. In death and tethered to their facts they were, to me at least, invisible. No news from nowhere.

Driving back I switched on the radio, spreading the words of the day into the car with talk of nuclear fire and airborne contaminants detected in Sweden and heading west. I couldn't picture Chernobyl, wasn't sure where it was, but that, I saw, was the point. The sky was the same colour as it had been the day before but now was utterly changed. We didn't know it but we were joined to it all. Perhaps the wind *did* blow from the Urals. Swallows fresh out of the blue from Africa and southern Europe cut and bucked around us, as they must have been doing above the roads and villages of the Kiev region too. Nadezhda Nikolaevna Timoshenko (her surname, my mother's nickname for me, coincidentally) lived in Borshchyovka village a few miles from Chernobyl. Her memories of 26 April 1986 begin: 'It was a very warm and sunny day, very quiet and still. Some birds could be heard singing in the sky. It was just an ordinary spring day . . .'

Anders and Tim had a coloured map of the Zone and kept a copy in the car. On my lap it spread from pale green to dark red. The colours record degrees of contamination. It was exquisite to look at. Didn't Francis Bacon keep a handbook of diseases of the mouth because the plates were so beautiful? On the map, scarlet areas plume west from the reactor in a narrow tongue of intense flame. Further west, the colours pale to orange and yellow but then in several places the red resumes as isolated lesions or bruises. Cheek by jowl with green areas, where the background radiation level is unexceptional, are hot spots that thicken on the map red, dark and dangerous.

Birds in the Zone are doing their own mapping, or rather it is being done to them. Anders has counted returning warblers in Chernobyl springs and found contaminated areas quiet in April, while blackcaps and willow warblers thronged elsewhere. Perhaps they can detect the ticking of the isotopes and thereby know the contaminated areas to be already occupied. More likely there is simply nothing there for them.

I took a tape machine with me into the Zone, but it was so quiet in September I stopped trying to record. Straining to hear anything, I pushed the input level so high that all I got were buzzes and clicks, the noise the machine itself makes when it has gone haywire. Beyond that was just the sick Earth's feedback: the hiss of a dry place, the needle-thin calls of a few tits and chaffinches moving on, the mist of mosquitoes, nothing else.

Nature even when driven out with a pitchfork is said to return. We have lived in the world believing this. At Chernobyl it isn't coming back. On 5 October 1893 Tolstoy wrote in his diary: 'They say that one swallow doesn't make a summer; but, because one swallow doesn't make a summer, would that swallow which already senses summer not fly in, but wait? In that case every bud and blade of grass will have to wait, and there will be no summer.'

We drove thirty miles west of Chernobyl to Vesniane village, still locked deep in the Zone. Like everywhere else away from the town, it is totally deserted. As we left our hostel we saw three official cars on the road, then no one else all day. We put on boots and stepped carefully but we could have walked naked and loud and not frightened anyone, except perhaps a moose. Anders stumbled on a dead one in a pond on his visit here in the spring. Only three sounds marked the day, other than the tick of the radiation meter: a grey-headed woodpecker attacked a rotten telephone pole and, finding nothing, laughed his high, resigned laugh; a jay screeched mid-air, the flying Mr Punch; and once a chiffchaff let slip its thin autumn music, two near-whispered rounds of its spring tune, a song before parting.

The village lies in the middle red bruise of three on the map, between the abandoned collective farms of Novyi Myr and Lubianka. Such names! By the old milking parlour Anders's meter showed 200 to 300 times the level of normal background radiation. The same number of people – between 200 and 300 – was evacuated from the village. Overall 130,000 people were taken from the Zone. At first, seventy-four settlements were evacuated. Later, further west, an additional clearance was undertaken: forty-eight villages were abandoned, a further thirty-seven partially evacuated.

A milk churn lay on its side at the doorway to the parlour. Inside, each plastered brick stall where the cows ate and were milked was rubbed and scuffed differently, signed by their late occupants. Further in, about twenty birch trees grew up thickly from the floor through the broken roof. In the village, trees are moving across the old fields, blurring their edges to dusk, but nowhere do they grow so excitedly as up through and out of its barns and houses. Perhaps browsing moose and others are reluctant to enter old buildings to eat; perhaps the barns are floored with old manure that provides some vestigial nutrition for saplings. Beyond these explanations the walled woods rise in front of you like flags of the Zone, the heraldry of its dark green law, drawing attention to what was there before while showing the way life will increasingly grow here – clearings closed, castles hemmed from within, timber walls, the death of grass. Soviet power turned churches into granaries and stables; here a village has become a nursery for a forest. This is a country that *wants* to be trees.

The grasshoppers were not difficult in Vesniane. The sun shone and they were easy to net in the scrapes of sand ploughed out of the old meadows by the rootling tusks of wild boar. The insects like this opened ground for laying their eggs. Along the village street, birch and lime trees crowded and pressed close to the buildings. Some cottages had all but disappeared or turned tree-house: now beamed with branches and roofed with leaves, their deal-planked rooms indistinguishable from the stockade of trunks that pushed at them, green papering the walls. The village school had limes filling its playground; in its assembly hall was a row of infant chairs, yoked together and facing into the rank heart of the building, home of hungry mosquitoes. Across the street, through the trees, was the library. It had been ransacked at some point since it was abandoned and someone had filled its porch with rotting books to mulch like dying woodland flowers. Through twenty-five dry summers and twenty-five iced winters anything humanly bright had been switched off or driven away. The same or other looters had put outside every ruined house any even remotely salvageable scrap-metal object for a later collection that never happened. In its slow rot the iron-age was chasing down the nuclear: on one verge the metal handle from a manual water pump lay next to three candle holders, nearby was a child's bike, strands of wire, a pram, a bedstead, lampshades, a madness of pipes, some birdcages, a heap of mousetraps, a motorbike sidecar, and more buckets and pans than I could count. It was as if some magnet had been pulled through the village, dragging everything we had made to the roadside so that the junk might bid farewell to the departing people. Let the scanner pass over our treasure at the crossroads of Vesniane, where we cannot live any longer in the world that we have fashioned. Here is our Scythian gold, our Roman silver, our cave paintings, our ghost shirts and dream-catchers, here all of it dreck and trash and the colour of old blood, our pigment gift to the world's palette, our rust.

Grasshopper quota bagged, I turned my attention to shoes and fruit. At the village bus stop, once tiled in blue, a birch grew where villagers would have stood. On the roadside was a single green plastic slipper, nearby three separate and different soles walked through leaf mould; at the crossroads a child's shoe, furred now with a petite sock of electric moss; further into the trees a leather boot like a dead calf. One hundred and thirty thousand Cinderellas waiting for a last bus, sabotaged.

Between the shoes there were apples: overlapping constellations of grounded things. Every cottage had fruit trees and more grew along field edges and at the roadside. In September there was an abundance of fruit, half was still on the trees, half had dropped. The fallen lay where they fell, bright and undisturbed, red, yellow, green: demonstrations of the physics of cluster, roll and drop, the way things fall down and fall apart. I walked closer and red admirals that had been feeding on the fallen sweetness lifted over the fruit like small flying carpets. Spun around other trees there were pears and plums as well as apples: atomic models, planets, dwarves, moons, small and large, red, yellow and green. Some were perfect, others crabbed, some going the way of all flesh, others hurrying there, every fruit forbidden, galled and inedible, bad seeds at the heart of every one. The *pink* of a chaffinch hit a tiny metal hammer on the sky and I heard an apple fall into a soft receiving sleeve of grass. The sound summoned all the others I wouldn't hear and a thought of how, 1,000 years from now, the A14 and the other main roads and motorways of England and the once villages of Chernobyl, sick places both but lined as they are with accidental apple trees, might be identified as linear orchards, good things, threads of fruit through forests.

On a low branch of a green apple tree was a male black grouse, a poor man's capercaillie: black and brilliant and a dancer too, just smaller and slightly more sober at his lek than the horse of the woods. In Britain a dawn start and hard walking up hill is usually required to see one – here they could be found at the bus stop. I stepped too close and flushed him; his beautiful lyre-shaped tail combed the still air and hummed through the blue as he flew up to a top branch on a tall lime further along the road. A grey female I hadn't spotted on the ground, where perhaps she had been on the cider, followed him, whirring up and away.

There are wild things in the Zone like these black grouse. Moose, and wolves too. But Anders and Tim insist that there are very few. Everything they have studied bears them out. In all his travels and transects Anders has glimpsed a wolf only once. And those animals that are living here have a hard time of it. A white-tailed eagle clambered heavily into the air as we were leaving the village and whinnied to a mate and both, huge and tremendous, did their flying stable-door impersonations, calling like Pegasus through the sky. But the male may well be sterile, the female warming dead eggs summer after summer until she dies. In five days of walking through what some have wanted to call a resurgent wilderness I didn't see a single mammal. I hardly saw a bee.

The moon was alone in the sky when we finished. Half of it, only.

Chernobyl's flatness is the flatness that comes from the middle of a place; there is also a flatness that comes out of the sea. To confuse matters, the Crimean steppe, the wild grass at the southern shore of Ukraine, is flatness – a mattress – of the middle place that comes out of the sea. But because the sea here is nested within seas – the Azov to the north of the Crimea nested in the Black, the Black in the

Mediterranean – and the ocean very far away, the prevailing conditions are still interior. If the wind blows it is from the land. The air is salted from within not without.

Calandra larks are abundant on the Crimean steppe in early June. I counted 400 in one mile along the split asphalt of an old military road just inland from the Black Sea near Kerch. There were another 400 singing in the sky above. They are big and heavy-headed as grasshoppers and, similarly, look like country boys, hayseeds, chunky and grassy brown. But their song is magnificent and on the steppe it is as common as light; it carries from the fields into the towns and through each village, and it doesn't stop from dawn to dusk. In June it starts at three-thirty in the morning and ends at eleven at night and in each singing bird is an account of everything worth saying in the lark-lands. One woke me in my tent on the Baherova steppe before the sun had begun its climb, another shepherded me off the plain long after the first stars were out. The calandra is generous, good things from other singers are included in its song, and riffs on those good things too – new volleys, asides and embellishments, found tunes and footnotes to those tunes, and made up things like shopping lists and gossip, hymns and snores. Always fast and always full-mouthed, it is a jabber but done entirely without stress. As a swallow sings as if it had a beakful of flies in the way of its music, so the lark sings with dust and grass seeds rattling in its syrinx: a dry song but running with the memory of water like a streambed in summer. Lark song is steppe weather. It comes up through you from the birds singing hidden in the grass at your feet and rises to the birds hidden high in the sky until you catch them as they shudder down through yards of hot thick air on their stiffened wings, black beneath, slow-flapping and stroking slowly like a rower gathering water or a reaper cutting grass. I ate a sandwich of neon-pink salami and drank a bottle of warm beer and the same lark was singing the same extended song from my first mouthful to my last slurp.

In Marfivka village on the steppe was a shop, and for sale along with my salami and beer was a two-foot-wide brick of pig fat (no lean, just fat), dusty bottles of Ukrainian cola, and several pink mattresses. On the road continuing through the steppe and beneath the hot shouting sky, a bare-chested man in wellington boots, nylon football shorts and a cloth cap was standing between his horse and his child, a boy of about eight. Straining its neck, the horse had managed to eat the hay in the cart it was meant to be pulling. The man hit his horse between the eyes with his fisted hand and then he turned and slapped the child on its cheek. His son he hit with greater force. In the same village, just beyond a football pitch chalked into the crumbling road, a young man in hard-core cyborg nightclub kit – black plastic t-shirt, tight black cycling shorts, ant-eye sunglasses – was walking to his hay, a long-handled scythe slung over his shoulder. Civilisation and its discotheques.

I arrived hot and dusty from the steppe in Koktebel looking for a bed. The hotel was shut. '*Remont*,' the owner said, interrupting her mobile phone call on its front steps, waving me away. This condition is endemic in Crimea. Everything was being *renewed* but nothing was finished. In Kerch a brigade of elderly women in washing-up gloves scrubbed at the rusting railings, Ukrainian blue as everywhere, at the foot of their block of flats. Others swept dust with worn-out brooms into spiral patterns around chestnut trees. The water was off in Theodosia but I found a room. Just after dusk I went to the seashore there. A nightjar flapped like a stray letter, something Cyrillic, along the railway line on the front. I met a man from Armenia who had brought a green python to the sea to make money from tourists or sailors who might thrill to have a snake draped round them like a scarf. In the photograph I took, both his almond eyes and his snake's caught spits of street lamp reflection. Man and snake spend their winters in a warm apartment in Yerevan, sharing a bedroom or, if the heating fails, a bed. Next to the snake-man two prostitutes leaned on the seawall, their hands on their bony hips. In the bay beyond them and the railway track, visible through the crook of their elbows, common dolphins slipped like slivers of soap through the skin of the oily night sea. Once I'd let them follow the black scythe of the fins through my binoculars the women told me their rates: a hundred dollars to lie down, sixty dollars for anything standing up.

The next day: early into the grass. Black-headed buntings were already awake and singing on wires, black-headed wagtails leapt around the feet of some sheep, and a group of calandra larks landed ahead of me on a narrow road. In their arrival, they showed me another nightjar sitting on the verge under the full sun, its eyes dark tar bubbles below heavy lids, its head, back and tail overlapping layers of browns, obsessively worked like a madman's painting, stuffy in its complexity in the wide spaces of simpler grass. It flew awkwardly, craving dark and moths and wanting movement only when the cowled buntings and wagtails slept on the steppe. As it went swallows appeared around it, drawn to mob the freak, chittering, as they would around a cuckoo.

Every thirty miles across the plain are military listening devices pointing towards Turkey, widespread skeletons of crucified wire, like an X-ray plate of a giant bird with outstretched wings. You cannot tell if they are listening any longer. Sheep, with their heads down, goats, with their heads up, crowded around the legs of the big birds. In the empty shed of a vast and ruined collective farm was one muddy cow; its milkmaid, an old lady in boots and pinafore, sat on a recycled car seat to milk her charge by hand. As I passed I could see the chalky squirt into the tin bucket wedged between her shit-caked boots.

The Baherova plain began to shake in the heat of the day. Rose-coloured starlings, like squares of Turkish delight, lifted from the grass and fizzed towards the swimming horizon. Beneath them three displaying male great bustards were turning themselves inside out in their lather, switching themselves on by their undressing, three rival beacons bright enough even in the oven-heat and whump of sun to impress a lady or lure a traveller across the steppe. The calandra larks sang on. I became fascinated by how little they strayed from their quarter of air, their acre of grass: it was as if they sang *of* the field below them and *to* it as well, always working over the same place, and reworking. *Remont.*

The steppe is open but not flat. The bowl of Baherova, a circle of low hills cupping a four-mile-wide crater of grass, makes a beautiful amphitheatre. It runs north, joins more grass, and dips into the Sea of Azov; through binoculars I could see, as if in a mirage, brown cows cooling their legs miles away in the shallow seawater. The grass of the steppe here is continuous though not uniform: I counted eight species in four yards while thistles, herbs and purple vetches swapped places in between. In the warm wind some grass shakes, some trembles, some wobbles. The two-and-a-half-foot-high feather grass, *Stipa capillata*, is the most striking, its seed heads form hoary white plumes, eight old-fashioned-looking strands per stem. I picked a bunch to dry. Later in my car they seeded in the heat and exploded across the back seat with a crackle. Studded through the grass were burnet moths and blue butterflies I couldn't identify. Countless empty snail shells crunched beneath my every step. Rooks dug at the soil and one, rubbing against some thyme, launched a little low-slung scented cloud that climbed the hill towards me.

Walking through the feather grass on the far side of the bowl were two demoiselle cranes: new to me, specialists of the place and wonderfully made, it seemed, from the steppe. They are big, leggy and grey, with a rumpled pillow at their rear but exquisite and delicate to the fore, with silver white plumes that flow in a perfect curve from above their eyes around their faces to the top of their necks. These feathers are uncanny replicas of the steppe feather grass, and the wind blowing through Baherova lifted and blew the feathers and the feather grass in the same way, the various plumes waving in the various light. Below their pale curves, the cranes have long black stoles on their breasts like a velvet scarf reaching between their legs. The two birds walked as if attendant each on each, as if they knew without following each other's steps exactly where they were, relative to one another. Were they married? They looked it. A king and a queen surprised in their finery, wearing it for themselves, and out for a walk through their fields, which, being theirs, had come to look like them.

I slept badly that night in a tent on the steppe, put to sleep by the last lark song and woken by the first. In the few dark hours between the rising dry towers of lark music, mosquitoes passed close to my ears like cars. I hadn't realised it when camping but as I left the next morning I discovered that I had put my tent up in the grass on the edge of a ruined military base and airfield. West of where I'd been birdwatching

I followed a dirt track through the steppe leading on to an old metalled road that climbed from the basin to the flat tops. All at once my narrow route became a runway and I was driving down wide concrete lanes, bumping every hundred yards or so over the little green ribs of grass that had grown between the blocks of poured concrete. There was no fence, no signs, no people, and the steppe leapt over the criss-crossing concrete ways and carried on. There were larks as before. I headed towards some half-ruined and derelict buildings – old rusting hangars and a brick tower – that were grouped at the edge of the place and, close by, I saw the first people I'd seen for a day: some men in overalls standing around an old patched-up plane and pouring a liquid into canisters that were strapped rather provisionally to its wings. I guessed they were getting ready for some crop dusting. They didn't look up as I bumped past in my little car down the runway. It was like a scene from the beginning of time. Or the end: old machines with men in dirty clothes bending over them to keep alive something that should be dead.

Later I spoke to a Ukrainian friend about the airfield. Larisa is a kind of human metal-detector and has spent years passing her various sensitised monitors over the ruins of all sorts of Soviet and post-Soviet military darkness and other buried secrets across Crimea. At Balaklava, as we sat in a dockside cafe eating lunch, she showed me the marine caves carved out of the sandy rock across the inlet that had been the hidden berths for Soviet nuclear submarines. And Baherova base, she said, was not only a military airfield but was also one of the projected southern landing sites for the Buran, the Soviet rival to the United States' Space Shuttle – a nuclear weapon delivery device dressed up as something less nasty. The unmanned Buran flew once only, completing two orbits of the Earth and landing successfully at Baikonur in the desert steppe of Kazakhstan. The end of the cold war and the collapse of the Soviet Union aborted the development programmes of both the shuttle and the Energia, its rocket launcher. It never came to Baherova. What did, Larisa told me, was something nastier still. Nuclear waste from forty years of weapons testing at Semipalatinsk (the Soviet Union's principal test site), also on the Kazakh steppe, was removed by truck and by plane and, the rumours at least suggest, the airfield at Baherova, a closed and highly secure military establishment at the time, was one of the burial grounds. There might be dead machines entombed beneath the concrete runways now, ticking away with only their own poisonous clocks for company.

There was one last collecting site in the Zone at Chernobyl. It was to be the most astonishing of all. On the way into Prypiat, the town where the reactor's workforce had lived, we had to show our papers at another barrier. As the sleepy policeman ran his fingers down our names, a black woodpecker flew over us, coming from where we wanted to go. A carpenter-bird of big trees and deep forest, it leapt through the sky like a tool, a black hammer bouncing off the air it had tempered beneath. It landed behind us, clasping its sooty iron to the trunk of a tall pine.

After my year in Budapest I became a devotee of the frayed and failing communist empire and of the birdlife that went with it. I held on tight to my passport but relished travelling through the rubbish and the ruins. Though it was on its last legs the Eastern bloc felt unfinished and that made its people, even as they suffered, alive. I liked that. And I liked the low-watt interiors and the contrast with outdoor brightness and the birds that didn't care either way. But none of my scrapyard-pastoral adventures prepared me for the abandoned town of Prypiat where now only the black woodpecker is at home. We spent half a day there and, between the policeman on the way in and the policeman on the way out, we saw no one else. Fifty thousand people have vanished. Built to serve the plant at Chernobyl in 1970, it lived for just sixteen years. After the explosion in 1986 its population were put on buses and driven away over two days. 'Please make sure you have turned off the lights,' said the evacuation note that was issued to each household.

The town had been fully planned and purpose built: a space-age city for the happy atom plant. From the air its outline shows like a petal on a radiation sign, an inverted triangle on a stalk of road that runs from the reactors at Chernobyl. All the town buildings were boxily modern with flat roofs and austere facades. Ten-storey apartment blocks cut canyons away from the central square with lower civic structures between them. There were 160 residential buildings, a city hall, a palace of sport and culture, a hotel, a hospital, fifteen primary and five secondary schools, twenty-seven restaurants, thirty-five playgrounds and a funfair.

All the buildings are still there but now Prypiat is a forest. In a place we thought we'd made our own there are thousands upon thousands of trees. A green tide is lapping at the town. Wild trees returning to ground they were previously cleared from have met planted trees in the streets that have grown up and escaped from their concrete cordons. Everything else has stopped and is falling down and since the trees are still tenaciously alive and heading up they have taken charge. The effect is like rain inside your head. You cannot see out of yourself. A few of the roads through the town are still passable but trees narrow all of them. The asphalt surface is split as if rotten, and welters around strapping trunks. Every two- and three-storey building has been overgrown and is deep into its long dying in tree shade. Leaf ghosts camouflage grey concrete panels, where last year's emulsified foliage has printed itself on to the walls. This year's leaves are adjacent and ready. In other places the concrete is veined with green deltas of moss and water runs up the walls. The buildings seep. All the street lamps are now below the level of the green ceiling of the tree-canopy. They look tired. Rusted red stars hang from many of them like something between a bat and a discarded Christmas decoration. The upper parts of the eight- or ten-storey blocks remain above the forest but branches and leaves brush up against their lower floors like imploring children. And many of the blocks now have trees growing from their roofs or from a balcony or out of a broken window. Where, you wonder, do their roots reach? Is this what it feels like to have a bird nesting in your hair or a worm living in your head? A consoling birch cuddles a twenty-foot-high metal CCCP wreath-crest on top of one of the tallest buildings, the tree younger, smaller, more fragile than the concrete it grows from, but here for the duration.

Birnam Wood come to Dunsinane; Piranesi's crepitating Roman ruins; Mayan temples lost in the jungle; monkeys overrunning other gods in India; Max Ernst's vegetable-slime paintings; the ever-renewing Golden Bough; Ozymandias's instructions to the deaf desert; the revenge of Gaia – it all crowds in as thick as the pressing trees but nothing can truly assist with the profoundly unsettling task Prypiat puts before you. To stand in the forest that was once a town is to look *after* us. Down the wooded streets of Prypiat's arrested past you are bowled into the aftermath of man, into a future that has already arrived. I have been nowhere else that has felt as dead as here, been nowhere that made me feel as posthumous. And the strangest thing is that in this house of the dead, the dead have gone missing. To make fuller sense of it you would have to be an archaeologist of cities not yet built, or an interpreter of languages as yet unborn. Except, Prypiat is now and actually exists. Or was and did. And as bewildering as this is, this poisoned rewilding, it is all also bleakly appropriate to this concrete corner of the old empire.

'Actually existing socialism' was a sad coinage from the 1970s that described the way-station to happiness where the communist train had stopped, the best the Eastern bloc could then manage. It was meant to suggest that the radiant future was still on the timetable and that, despite difficulties – the grey cruelties of life and all the grief – what the east had was at least not what the west had. That, of course, was abundantly clear to everyone. The spurious ideological tag just rubbed the collective nose deeper into the rust. Soviet citizens were already well versed in double-speak and skilled at the clunky backwards living that was required of them. They knew the disappointment of the inevitable shortcomings of the imminent future, long before it arrived. 'Life has improved, comrades. Life has become more joyous,' Stalin famously said at the first all-union conference of Stakhanovites in 1935, having just presided over the terror-famine in Ukraine and on the verge of unleashing his great purge. 'The great shepherd' was one of Stalin's favourite epithets; grass and grasshoppers, the famished of Ukraine were forced to eat, until, when there was nothing left, they started on themselves. The louder Stalin's fanfare, the more cracked the trumpet sounded, though few dared declare it. The Finland Station was a terminus. Lenin, pickled, could last forever but no one could bring him back to life. His arm might be raised to the horizon and beyond or perhaps, as the joke used to say, he was just trying to hail a taxi. A taxi, because he'd missed the future which, long announced, turned out to have already arrived – though not at a railway station, but at a bus stop, and one where a tree grew where people might once have stood.

Lifeless neon letters marched across the pelmet of the 'Palace of Cultural Energy' at the dead heart of Prypiat. In the entrance hall there were flaking murals of science (lab-coated workers, test tubes and other laboratory kit) and agriculture (a basket of fruit and a hand severed by rot from the arm of a stout Soviet Ceres reaching to pick a red apple). I walked into a room, treading only on broken glass. Lying around an armchair pulled into its centre was a map of the best of us: cigarette butts, one sock and some scattered books about fish – the outline of a life. Someone had got up and left this room. Since it is forbidden to take anything from the Zone, I decided to leave something instead. I'd been using a postcard as a bookmark, a 1970s photograph of Wicken Fen (the windmill and reed beds, Adventurers' Fen beyond), and wrote on the back 'Field One for Field Four' and propped it on the brown armchair. Leaning against the walls of the next-door room were 1980s May Day procession portraits, ten-foot square and hand-painted, of Gorbachev and Eduard Shevardnadze and two others in uniform whom I didn't know, all blithe, optimistic, almost handsome. Their flat faces suited the place. In Prypiat everything human is thinned to screens that creak and judder through the solid and continuing trees, the apartment blocks like canvases flown in from grey skies, their broken windows like dark painted squares. Once in the foreground we are now barely part of the scenery.

One floor above the former leaders, two twenty-foot birches had grown through the parquet of a sports hall. Their green leaves throbbed in the interior light. They looked like trees brought inside to make a point. A Chekhov production could make use of them, the unsellable orchard inside us all, but that would be too easy, too glib. The trunks, the branches, the leaves have nothing to say. The Prypiat forest doesn't teach, it simply grows. It is not sublimely indifferent, not even plainly indifferent; it is just different. The real point is there is no point. There is no need for one. Overgrowth is not intrinsically menacing, it has nothing to do with us, even if we are what is overgrown. Other bosses, other regimes, pertain: yellow plums roll into life, rosehips bud like weapons. In an agricultural machine yard the huge grasshopper head of a rusted combine was tethered by three limes growing through its intricate mouth. In the vehicle workshop there were three inspection pits, a chair in the bottom of one. I climbed down and sat on it, five feet below the surface. The tiled trench seemed to close around me. I looked up and all I could see was silent green leaves.

We came out of the Exclusion Zone the next morning (though *out*, as Anders and Tim would remind me, is only relative). The sun hadn't shone for our last three days and the winter seemed keen to get on. We passed the old cooling ponds around the edge of the reactors and stopped to feed stale bread rolls to the ten-foot-long catfish that had got big on hot water. They came to the surface of the dark pond and opened their mouths, their pale jaws widening into drowned moons. Mementos of the nuclear days. As we watched I heard the creak of flying swans and six whoopers flew over, new in from the north, the colour of old snow, pulling the freeze with them. The swans alarmed a blackcap in a yellowing vine at the edge of the pond and it called a harsh cold *chack*, its concession to winter and perhaps the last thing it said before moving south. A handover of the seasons was underway for some. The politburo of cormorants, old men in old suits, stood unmoving on a gravel island.

As we crossed out of the Zone heavy rain came on. I asked Anders who his heroes were as a young naturalist. He laughed immediately at my question; he was struggling, he said, to even remember the Danish word. The clear-eyed scientific rigour of his youth shone from his face, but matters were further complicated because, he said, the Danish for *hero* is the same word as that for a species of freshwater fish found in the centre of Jutland.

The rain eased and the world was made good in front of us. We were released into it. There were bees and horses. Chickens dabbed at the roadside verges. Two dirty cows seen across an open field looked beautiful.

A cowherd with a furled umbrella under his arm moved towards them. Smallholdings were good too. A cord of cut wood was stacked between two apple trees. Old men in hats and women in headscarves walked to and from their gardens and fields; one man was carrying a white chicken under his arm, another a tin bucket bumping with muddy potatoes. Small boys rode by on grown-up bikes. In a puddle on the road, a drowned baby grass snake floated like a single cut stem of grass. Painted cottages sat warmly in the sun-bright. Orange nasturtiums fell over the wooden door of an outside privy. In gardens there were watermelons the size of boulders streaked lengthways, green and yellow, like cut fields. Concrete walls zigzagging Ukrainian blue and yellow ran along the village street. Between two plum trees a washing line was hung with pink knickers the size of small flags. Six pairs. I almost cried to see them. All the spotted flycatchers of Europe seemed to be snipping between the fruit trees and the cottage eaves in a non-stop tidying of the air. A table cut into the base of the trunk of a fat apple tree gathered windfalls from above like a ready-meal. There were hayricks and storks' nests and they looked the same. An orchard purred with bees as the sun came out. A one-legged man in a beret drove a motorbike with a sidecar down the middle of the road. A jay flew over a scarecrow. I collected my grasshoppers (the village was a control site for Anders and Tim) and picked a stem of grass; a dot of sap beaded at the break and I sucked it. Pulling wooden carts shaped like open coffins, the horses looked like they still lived in this place. After the rain they steamed. Anders asked: 'Perhaps you don't remember the smell of wet horse?'

Leaving Ukraine, you may proceed through the Green Channel at Kiev Airport if, as the sign says: 'You haven't got: Weapons, Explosives, Poisonous, Narcotic, Psychotropic, Drastic Substances and Medicine. Or Radioactive Materials. Or Flora and Fauna Objects, their parts and products obtained of them.'

I got back to England and in my waiting post was a letter from the council telling me to cut my hedge: 'I am aware that branches/foliage from trees/bushes growing within your premises are causing a partial obstruction of Happy Lane.'

Months later by chance I asked a friend what Lubianka means in Russian. Something, he said, like the place made of bark, or a basket made of bark, or a hut lined with bark, a cork-panelled room if you like, or a quiet place to sleep, or a place surrounded by trees where, whatever you said, or shouted, or wept couldn't be heard.

Autumn Fen

There are turf farms on the fens. Turf in the current sense of the word. The old diggings or turbaries where peat (also called turf) was cut for fuel are gone. Now the fen grass and its cradling fen earth are cut and shipped out in other ways. The level fields and the rich peat are good for growing lawns. Emerald-green squares alternate on the fen with arable acres and grasslands, and these brilliant smooth plots are the most disconcerting of all the fen fields.

One of the common effects of the fens is a roomy feel. You often catch them seeming spacious but hardly ever fully open. Despite appearing edgeless and held in their shallow basin by nothing more than the horizon, their fields have an interior air. The lawns of the turf fields give off this atmosphere more than anywhere else. They are like something incubated or cultured in a greenhouse without glass. The grass suggests walls that ought to be there but aren't. The lawns are so smart you expect a civic building, a crematorium, the stonework of an old university, or something comparably solid and grave to rise from them. Without a human edge their stage is very empty. Apart from a few rabbits and wagtails and the odd crow nothing ever stands on them. They are so level and smooth and the sown grass, when it comes, is so uniform and then so neatly managed, that looking at it you sense a missing dimension.

It is just *surface*. And that surface is cut by a giant lawnmower and then shaved by a machine that rolls up the lawn with a thin backing of peat into uniform widths to be stacked on a pallet and wrapped in clear plastic. Lorries drive on to the open-cast fields when the turf has been sliced from them and load it up and take it away down the lanes. The fens are unrolled like prayer-mats wherever they are required. A kind of thin topiary is effected on these farms: the needy and parodic human transformation of nature, its diminution or its prostitution, into what Marvell, in his poem 'The Mower against Gardens', called a 'green seraglio', whereby fields of grass are cut to resemble a lawn which is grown to resemble a field of grass.

On a blustery early autumn day on the fen I once saw swallows settling on a turf field. At first they came with an air of exploratory trepidation and then, as more and more of them joined in, their dangling over the field took on a playful insouciance that looked like bird fun. They flew to the grass, as they do over water, angling their bodies horizontally above it and sliding lower and lower to its surface. And because that surface was so smooth and so flat – even smoother and flatter than water – they slowed their wings and gently stepped down on to it. Then they sat around on the short turf on their short legs as if they were doing it simply because they could. I have never seen that before. But it suited the lawn. It was a temporary fiction: a playground or a holiday. And the birds knew it.

Sometime around 1815 Coleridge wrote in his notebook: 'If a man could pass thro' Paradise in a dream, & have a flower presented to him as a pledge that his Soul had really been there, & found that flower in his hand when he awoke – Aye? and what then?' The fen, too, throws up flowers from paradise once in a while.

Chalk and flint break through the eastern fen edge like an exposed skeleton. The fens themselves are boneless. But for the remains they cradle, they are fleshy, soft and giving. So stoneless indeed that, as has happened, you might sink into them: 'I have known a riding horse to be bogged and have to be shot to save it from cold and starvation.' So stoneless that the song thrushes that live in the rare fen hedges find it hard to make an anvil for breaking open the snails they love to eat, and I have seen them use the bottom rung of a metal gate for the purpose, leaving it sticky with snail guts. You cannot build on the open fen – houses lean and roads ripple on the moving surface of the soil. Only on an island could Ely cathedral be built. Only on an island would you bury your dead.

It wasn't always like this. The fen has had a wooded past as well as a marine one. When Alan Bloom and his men were attempting to deal, as he thought necessary, with Burwell Fen, opening drains, ploughing up reeds, filling the turf pits and generally scrabbling around in the earth, they found assorted relics: a trepanned human skull alongside beaver skulls, deer antlers and the jawbones of wild boar. Others found wolf remains and a 'Roman slave-chain' with a 'lock for the attachment of the log of wood'. More commonly, Bloom bumped into a buried sleeping wood itself. Lying on the blue gault clay below the surface peat of the fen was a preserved thick lattice of fallen trees, a layer of wattle through the daub. The first day they opened up the soil on Burwell Fen they hit a trunk. Parts of the fen went on to yield up to thirty trees per acre, a corner, Bloom says, of 'what was once a mighty oak forest'.

Bog oaks have long been found across the southern peat fens. They still turn up. Shrinking peat and deep working ploughs pull them to the surface and they continue to make the local news when they appear. The wooden treasure, keels of oak, lying beneath a wet treeless place have excited and exercised almost every fen writer and it is a given that fen books will pitch in to the debate around the origins of the vegetable antiquities. Often there are photographs of men standing in bare muddy fields staring into a trench with a blackened trunk lying there like a great dead thing. These oaks were splinters in the fen flesh. Clearing water not trees was thought to have fixed this place. That the wet of the fens wasn't their first story was baffling, troubling even, and the discovered woods, like the fields in drag, were attacked with a furious zeal as if there was something devilishly wrong about them.

Bloom solicits the opinions of his fieldworkers: 'one man said he was sure they floated there, washed down from the uplands in some great flood. Another said that the Romans cut them down. But the belief that they raised themselves to near the surface naturally was quite prevalent.' Bloom himself doesn't credit the fen version of Birnam Wood come to Dunsinane, the oaks' spontaneous birthing and upward climb, but the trees trigger a mixed reaction in him: they are amazing 'primeval monsters', the leftovers of a bigger world, some with trunks up to 108 feet long and four feet thick; but they are also a terrible nuisance, 'great ugly things' that offend a farming man and which must be blasted out of the ground with gelignite.

Some of the wood was hard, some soapy soft; as it dried on the fen top it often shivered to bits. Thomas Browne, writing in 1658, guessed that the 'Moore-logs' that he knew well in Norfolk were the 'undated ruines of windes, flouds or earthquakes' and older than the cypress of the ark of Noah, which was believed otherwise to be the oldest of all wood. Alan Bloom ages the trunks on Burwell Fen at 7,000 years. Eric Ennion, in his book, thinks the oaks half that. James Wentworth Day, magus of Wicken, declares their age to be 'unguessable' but guesses anyway at ten times Bloom's estimate; they are, he says, 'not less than 70,000 years old'. Charles Lucas, like Ennion and Ennion's father a doctor in Burwell (in the latter part of the nineteenth century) and also a keen local antiquarian, would prefer to have the oaks falling in a crisis at the Crucifixion, as if to deny Christ's murderers their raw material, but his literal mind won't quite allow this: 'the Fen cataclysm was certainly not then, because that was in the Spring, and the Fen trouble was not till the autumn – probably about September, as the trees were in full leaf and fruit was abundant'.

Neither the beavers of Burwell nor Roman executioners felled the trees. The oaks were horizontal long before either. And they are not only oaks: alder, birch, yew and pines have also been found. All of them pre-date the fens and, indeed, it was the fens that killed them. Most bog oaks are thought to be between 3,500 and 4,000 years old, though some older trees aged up to 6,000 years have surfaced. They grew in drier times across dozens of miles of ground that is fen now, but wasn't then. Wicken Fen thickening with carr woodland as it dries out is the bog oak story in reverse. Between 5,000 and 4,300 years ago with rising sea levels came a great flood, more properly known as an extensive marine transgression, which inundated the northern part of the fen area from the Wash southwards. The sea dropped marine silt and the fenland basin became flooded with fresh water as its drainage systems stalled. With a new gradient to climb to reach the sea, the rivers draining from the south were hindered in their progress. Wetlands spread over the waterlogged ground. The trees that are now under Burwell Fen drowned and fell into the emerging and accumulating freshwater peat, which kept them buried and preserved. In some places the trees are scattered erratically, elsewhere stands lie with their crowns all pointing to the north-east, and appear to have fallen together, perhaps in a wild storm harrowing out of the west.

Another photograph in one of the fen books shows a single bog oak lying lengthways in its trench in the foreground, while behind it at the horizon, across miles of flat grey fen, is the ghostly outline of Ely Cathedral like another fallen trunk or a beached whale: huge hopeless things under the withering sky. Seeing these tree-bodies cradled on the plain summons the moment of their collapse: a single tree falling on its own into the peat, one splash across twenty miles of new fen and then nothing but the wet ground closing over the trunk. John Clare knew that sound, two or three fallen trees away, across the fens in Northamptonshire. He has a word for it all to himself in the dictionary, a word for those downed fen trees. *Gulch* as a verb can mean to fall or plunge heavily upon, and the only citation (though spelled differently) in the OED is from Clare's 'The Village Minstrel' of 1821: 'Ne'er an axe was heard to sound, / Or a tree's fall gulsh'd the ground'.

Bloom's heaving out or blowing up of bog oaks, long after their gulch, takes its place in the great and general gutting of the fens – the removal of what is in them to make them what they are. The trees are also part of something like a conversation that has gone on along-side the digging and the draining between what is buried and what is known. Rinsing the water from the fens and drying their soil hasn't really worked in the way that Bloom and the Adventurers and others would have had it, but the attention downwards has meant that a lot of hidden things have come to light and have been spotted, prodded and poked. The eastern edge of the fens, where Burwell and other villages run along the base of a chalk ridge, is dotted with Roman settlements. In 1942, the same year that Alan Bloom was tripping over bog oaks on Burwell Fen, the Mildenhall late-Roman treasure hoard was ploughed up. A little to the north, about nine miles from Burwell, just over the county border in Suffolk, twenty-seven pieces of silver were found on a run of land at the point where it crept out of the wet. The jewel of the hoard, a great dish nearly two foot across, was made in the fourth century a long way away (the nearest likely workshop was in Trier in present-day Germany) but its half-amphibious half-pastoral relief decoration is apt for its final resting place in the earth of a field on the fen edge.

The dish, like the fen basin itself, tells stories of the meeting of the wet and the dry, the exuberant and the sober, the planned and the unpredictable. The central figure is the mask of a marine god, Neptune or Oceanus. He is a green man salted to sea with large staring eyes, a beard of toothed seaweed and four dolphins plunging through his long wild hair as through surf. Around him are two concentric friezes of anarchic bliss. The inner ring is a revel of nereids or sea nymphs and assorted seahorses, crab-men and eely things in the thick of a marine transgression or orgy. The outer, broader, ring depicts the triumph of Bacchus over Hercules 'in a vivid manner' as the British Museum catalogue says: 'Bacchus stands naked, his long hair crowned with a diadem and his foot resting on the back of a panther.' As well as the drunken and meandering Hercules there are satyrs, dancing maenads and a priapic and shaggy Pan whose skipping hooves and parted furry thighs are terrifyingly well done. The find of the great dish close to and in the same year as Bloom's bog oaks is a coincidence, of course, but the possibility that other worlds – wet or green – might exist around or beyond the world we have made plays across both sets of reliefs: the carved silver figures and the corrugated surface of the fen.

There is a further and related strangeness about the fallen trees that worries at the fenmen, and it is because of this, I think, that the oaks are lodged so often in their books. Raising them out of the earth breaks up the order of things. The fallen wood undermines our sense of how farming works and what the soil is for and, for a moment at least, it shakes our understanding of the world, suggests that the spring might sometimes fail, and catches at the permanent awkwardness of farming, the way it wants to be in step but is always tripping over, the way the surface is always determined by its undertow. Earth is made of dead things and is a place to put dead things but life springs from it. We know that. Without rot there can be no green. And green in time will feed rot. Dung heaps smoke with the life of their deaths. The peat of the fens is made from dead and rotted fen, mostly reeds and sedge. The earth is served. New reeds and sedge grow out of dead reeds and sedge. Mole-sticks grow into willow trees and scythe handles are kept fresh under water and wet grass.

Yet on Burwell Fen the peat has chosen – the trunks in the trenches show it – to keep some things unrotted, to preserve the fallen trees and even – magically it seems – some green leaves, but only so long as the tree and its leaves are kept underground. At the surface, the very place we make green things grow, the treasure – a bloom out of paradise – cannot be kept. Its gold becomes dross. It seems wrong that by bringing stuff up into our air we kill it, but the buried truth of this shivers us awake. And deep down we have known it forever, known that the growing season is only part of the year, that death rhymes with life, that Persephone comes up out of a crack in the earth but must return there, that winter is a rehearsal for oblivion, that we grow old as we think on these things, and that it is a shock each time we discover them to be true.

What lies beneath and what will it tell us? Near Whittlesey swaths of mown grass were found beneath five feet of peat. Did a sudden summer flood come and cause the mowers to leave in a hurry? Why didn't they return? At Upware a blacksmith's forge was found beneath ten feet of peat, with tools, and some metalwork ready for use and some half-finished. Where were the horses and where were the men? On Burwell Fen James Wentworth Day reports, 'they found the dead, dried and pickled body of a fenman of a thousand years ago, standing bolt upright in the remains of a dug-out canoe. His long black hair hung down the leather skin of his face and neck. His right hand was poised and crooked as though to throw a spear, whilst on his legs were still the leather buskins and cross garterings. He could not survive the outer air and crumbled too soon into desiccation and dust.'

Green suits couldn't make the Manea commune grow. Only so long as Burwell man and the fen oak leaves are buried, will he be ready to fight, and they stay green. The upper green world, our green world, turns out to be inhospitable to other green worlds. Grass grows up green but other life brought to the surface dies. On Burwell Fen Alan Bloom dug up a namesake:'we found leaves that were still almost green at the instant a tree was rolled out, leaves of some other shrub like large privet, but within minutes of exposure to sun and air they faded and crumbled away'.

Watching a 4,000-year-old green leaf die on a would-be green field is to sit once again in the little cinema on the fens where blind Milton's creation film flickers forwards or backwards (it is hard to say which) on an old white sheet hung between two hawthorns, the earth moving with death pulling free from it, while a bittern bumps somewhere in rusty reeds in the background, and countless moths are drawn to the stream of projected light.

At the end of each afternoon for an autumn week, I went on to the fen at Wicken to watch snipe on a pool. A watery flash on an old field of Alan Bloom's one-time farm had dried out enough to reveal a tongue of soft peaty mud. The snipe liked the mud. The feeding was good and the birds, which otherwise favour the cover of grass and sedge, had moved out into the open. I'd last seen them here in June when the displaying birds tossed themselves into the sky as feathered rockets, dancing and drumming like midsummer hippies at a solstice festival, but these autumn birds were different. Around six o'clock most days sunlight streamed clean and low from the west and brilliantly lit the pool and its birds. By the end of the week more than a hundred snipe were on show. There were scarcer species as well, ruff and black-tailed godwits and green sandpipers, and I confess that I was hoping for something rarer still but, through the week of watching, the snipe came to be more than enough. I spent eight solid hours looking only at them, the birds filling my vision, big in the telescope. Not that I could now accurately reproduce what I saw or properly describe the bar code of browns across their backs and wings, the tussock of dried wetland grasses, rushes and sedges, which they have taken for their plumage. Part of the genius of snipe crypsis is that, although when you see them you are in no doubt that they are snipe, the birds declaring their *snipehood* immediately and obviously (round head, beady eyes, long bill, all else streaky), the moment you look away, you cannot rebuild them as anything other than a clump of fen grass.

In the pool the snipe were at home. On an inventor's blueprint their bill would seem unrealistically ludicrous, like a bird with a trunk. Looking at them, working the ooze, that thought never crossed my mind. They fed by dipping and tip-tapping into the mud either directly or through the water. Most tip-tapped once every five seconds and, roughly once every three tip-taps they got something. They would then pull their bill halfway from the mud or the water and draw up whatever they had caught in little nibbling actions. This is the 'suction' that Byron said woodcocks used. If they had waded out into the pool, the snipes' dipping sometimes went up to their eyes. I watched them tighten their faces as they winced a little. Now and again they dipped deeper still and their heads submerged entirely, but they were less keen on this and after any plunge like that they would shake their heads clean and dry, and stop feeding for a bit. Some, straying deeper still, had to swim back for a foot or so towards shallower water, and looked as they went like hastily opened coracles made out of straw.

Whatever they were doing each bird would occasionally cock its head to one side and look up at the sky with one eye. When they weren't feeding, they preened, twisting and stretching themselves around the tip of their bill, never getting within five inches of their face. Parties of the birds put the wind up themselves sometimes and hurried off the pool, their *crisp* calls as they took flight sounding like an elastoplast being ripped from the skin of the fen. Though they fed close to one another on the ground, there was always some agitation in the air, and this infected them when they first landed again. Coming back to earth, they made curious matador-style movements for a few moments, fanning their tails and laying their beaks on to their breasts, as if half remembering their courtships. It was like seeing the end of a dance with the dancers inadvertently continuing their steps after the music has stopped.

There was something of a country-disco or a ceilidh about the whole scene. The snipe, like farmers, fresh from their fields and dressed in the colours of the acres around them, squeezed into smart-suit versions of the land they live and work in, the mud cleaned from their fingernails for one night of the year only.

The nature reserve at Wicken Fen has been preserved for more than a hundred years. But the fens being as they are, being the fens, means that *preservation* is not the right word and nor is *reserve*. Wicken might now be intended for nature but the fen is really a ruin, an abandoned open-air factory or series of out-of-town workshops with centuries of human use behind them and many different quasi-industrial lives. But because everything has been greened over, the old working fen is hard to see. The signs say it is the last of the undrained fens. And, whatever you know of the worked past of the place, its vegetated fullness today encourages you to think that the landscape must have been 'natural' in the old days even if the fen was busy: the floods kept coming, the crops were wild, there were many people on the fens but they were foraging rather than farming. We should guard against this thought. And much work has been done at Wicken itself to teach us why. The fens before the twentieth century were not really any more natural (or less) than they are now. Natural, indeed, is another of those bastard words.

Wicken was once a place where, to catch moths, white sheets were hung over bushes, and treacle smeared on corks that were nailed to posts. People came to the fen and worked the sheets for science; others did the same for cash. But the fen has also been a farm, woodpile, brickworks, turbary, charcoal kiln, fishery, and greenhouse. It was once what could be called a plant-hire centre. The harsh and durable leaves of great fen sedge, *Cladium mariscus*, a native present at Wicken for at least 5,000 or 6,000 years, made it a highly valuable crop for thatching. Before the prevalence of daily newspapers, dried sedge also made good kindling. It was carried off the fens on a shallow-boat-cum-giant-floating-haystack. It was landed at villages around the fen edge and carted to towns further afield. Testimony to sedge's importance as a crop is the host of local laws and regulations that governed quotas and harvesting dates, and ruled against the employment of sub-harvesters or hired gang-labour. Sedge cutting was lucrative and fiercely protected work. Like eels, sedge at times became fen currency: payments were made in *seggesilver*. Through the twentieth century, sedge cutting – and almost all the old functions along with the customs of the fen – came to an end. For a few years during the Second World War, some ghostly echoes of the busy and exploited countryside came back. Alan Bloom's farm in the fen nibbled at the edges of Wicken from the south-east side of Wicken Lode. Burwell Fen was drained once again – Eric Ennion's recovered wilderness dug out into 'productive' land. And on the reserve at Wicken itself, a new use was found for old trees. Charcoal made from alder buckthorns was a crucial ingredient in shell fuses and since the trees were invading the fen, they were dug for victory as well as to keep the fen fenny.

The rich flora that was found when the reserve was established at Wicken was associated with these long-running harvests of the fen. Wicken was thick with plant life *because* it had been worked. When sedge cutting was stopped and the fen 'preserved', vegetation succession led to the reduction of some species and the loss of others. This happened to the fen orchid, *Liparis loeselii*, with its delicate-fingered yellow-green flowers that entwine as if they are holding hands. It was discovered in Cambridgeshire in 1660 by John Ray, who found it 'in the watery places' of the fens, and knew it as the *Dwarf Orchies of Zealand*. It was last seen at Wicken in 1945 and is now extinct in the county. When peat cutting ended the orchid went with it, vanishing hand in hand with the turf pits.

In the middle of the twentieth century at Wicken, the botanist Harry Godwin and others realised that taking a sedge crop every three or five years, or cutting grass and rush litter annually from what was called the 'mowing marsh', 'did not arrest the main reaction of the primary succession'. In other words, unrotted vegetation accumulated, and from it peat continued to form even when the sedge was harvested. The ground rose higher above the water level and in places the fens were naturally drying out. Similarly, submerged vegetation was shallowing the water it was submerged in. Soon enough it wouldn't be sufficiently wet for water plants to grow. Trees and shrubs would have liked the way the fen was going, but because it was being cut for sedge their saplings were as well: trees couldn't become established so long as the fen was worked. When the fen was 'reserved' and no longer cut, the trees eagerly made their way. Active management has been needed ever since to stop Wicken Fen becoming Wicken Wood.

I was on the fen when summer turned to autumn. Each incoming season is made out of the ruins of the last. Summer's drying gives way to autumn's fall. A quiet and still day had come and passed. In the autumn the sun itself can look dead in the sky, as if its light has already been switched off somewhere, and all we get is the colour of the bulb. This was such a day. But then, in the late afternoon, a little local breeze cooked up close to the ground of the fen at Burwell. There is more thistle than grass in these acres in August, and I watched the dry lick of the warm air beginning to lift the thistledown. Every thistle-head had seeded and there were so many that the whole fen was draped in a long loose scarf of dirty snow. The tiny seeds on each head are dark and the plumes of down sandy pale and almost transparent. As the plant grows, both seed and plumes crowd tight together but the whole head loosens as its dries and sets and the seeds (the outermost ones first) are pushed up and out while the down froths around them. This was the day. Again the year rhymed with itself: the season now ended with thistledown in August that began with willow-down in May when the trees along the lode shook their swaddled seeds out across the fen in drifts, and I had watched a party of swallows rag-picking at the ready-made nest-lining.

On the first autumn day on the fen the wind sometimes took a whole thistle-head and sometimes just a hank of down. The loosest heads were the first to be prised from their prickly anchor but even these lift-offs involved countless local struggles, the breeze picking at the ties that held the down to its plant, the down committed to its flight but still not going willingly. Once these negotiations were over the cottony seed heads were lifted, raised, and then encouraged above the thistles and the rest of the field of grass, sorrel, loosestrife, wild carrots and docks.

As they blew, the strands snagged on one another, riding the air like soft chain-shot, wool-gathering as they went. Everything was floating towards the south-east in a silent, spreading, milky broadcast. I stepped off the bank and followed. Like snow pushed away from the earth, the down sometimes rose in the wind and climbed upwards. Other clots of spindrift thickened the spiders' webs on the fences to caricatures; or caught at the corner of the eyes of the bullocks on the field or stuck to their shitty tails; or bearded the stubble on my chin. Most of the down seemed to catch and stop on other thistle-heads within the big field, but some floated out of my sight far beyond the fen. A stray I followed with binoculars seemed to buck the breeze and move sideways over new lands where its novelty attracted a passing black-headed gull, prompting it to scoop its wings overhead and redirect its flight to try to catch at the morsel.

There was more. Thistle is goldfinch food and there were dozens of them, at least 200 all together, feeding in loose jingling flocks on the burst heads. Their expert beaks made repeated intimate delvings into the thistle hearts. The wool of the down smothered their red faces as if it were dabbing at a wound, until the birds surfaced and superbly husked the tiny seed they had picked. But the breeze and the blow distracted them and made them flighty. Group after group lifted as one from among the thistles, each pulled by the bird ahead of them and pulling those behind. Their departures and their landings released still more down and fanned the drift yet further. The golden bars along their wings caught the light like the slub of silk, and twinkling their toy piano music they moved off through the floating down like itinerant weavers flying their precious thread through the homespun, until the whole fen became a field of the cloth of gold.

Draining and pumping have finally achieved what they have been trying to do for 2,000 years: the fens at Wicken and nearby at Burwell no longer flood. But the place remains unsurrendered. Lowering water levels across the wider area have reinforced the effects of vegetation succession and of the soil being raised by accumulating peat above the water table. The fens are drying out. But where part-rotted stuff builds up the land, the wastage of the drying peat takes it away. So long as peat is waterlogged it remains intact, but if it dries, then oxygen is able to worm into its top layers and exposes them to bacterial and fungal attack (the rot truncated resumes) and to direct chemical oxidation. The wasting soil that remains changes, too. Because of its desiccation, the surface peat at Wicken had acidified to the point where more than sixty species of 'acidicolous mosses and liverworts and ferns', all new to the fen, had been reported by the time Harry Godwin wrote his book in 1978.

To my shame, I don't really know what a liverwort is. I've looked at the pictures and fingered the guides – detailing the 300 British species of these overlooked and under-sung neighbours to the mosses – and I realise I have probably trodden on some but I am not a botanist and still less a bryologist. I like the sound, though, of those who not only know but love their liverworts. One of the extraordinary facts about Burwell and Wicken is how many people have raised, on its few squares of fen ground, their liverwort flags and others equally lovely, equally obscure. These hundred fen acres have prompted an astonishing harvest of close-focused scientific discoveries and explor-atory inventories, of *slodging* or *glaiving* with a hand-lens or a notebook. So much so, that we must open a new chapter for the liverworters, the mosquito men and the followers of the harvestmen, and many like them in the great soggy encyclopaedia of the place, drying now on the washing line slung between the pylons marching across the fens. We must add their names to the pages of prospectors and projectors, the old-guard fenland drainers, the new-fangled rewetters, the bird lovers and mole haters, and all the soft-spotters, curio-gatherers and pseudo-historians in between.

This epic surveying is best captured in a book that I cannot afford to buy and could hardly read anyway, but which, because it exists, makes me happy. It proves, I think, that attention to detail is a species of love. *The Natural History of Wicken Fen* edited by Professor J. Stanley Gardiner in six parts and running to 652 pages was fully made here-abouts. Published in 1932 by Bowes and Bowes in Cambridge and printed in the city, it is a vast sponge that has taken up the greatest draught possible of peaty water and with that everything that floats in the fens. It raises a model of the place even though it is made of flat type on a flat page (perfect for the flat lands), and draws a bright map of it even though it is made of words and figures without colours or contours (perfect for the zero-line fen). In the library it barely stirs in its sleep within the leaden chest of its covers. But this book-sponge, which is also an ark and which is also a brain, could be set back down over the place and would fit it perfectly, so fully has the looking at absorbed the looked at. Here come the plants, and the Lepidoptera, Orthoptera, Paraneuroptera and Neuroptera, Hirudinea, Hemiptera-Heteroptera, spiders and harvestmen, Phytoplankton, Ichneumonidae, Mollusca, Coleoptera, Oligochaeta, Thysanura, fossil vertebrates, Collembola, Diplopoda and Chilopoda, sawflies, Copepoda, the Cambridgeshire Planarians, Cladocera, Trichoptera, Bryophyta, mosquitoes, Psocoptera, Ephemeroptera, Ostracoda, and the Entomostraca, and then, mopping it all up once again, on pages 637 to 643, the freshwater sponges of the Cam basin.

Last but not quite, for on page 644 of *The Natural History of Wicken Fen* begin the 'Omissions and Additions'. And here is the most articulate scientific incarnation imaginable of the fen trope of the open ending, the wet fade, or the dissolve. Life forms have been missed. We forgot the fungus flora! And the Diptera! And, as the professor explains, it is not entirely our fault: 'I have long tried to find a student who would be interested in the free-living nematodes of this country.' I know the feeling. You get can get laughed at if you have a pair of binoculars, let alone a butterfly net or a pooter. But, even incomplete, I love the *Natural History* for its extravagant harvest and heave-to of all the tiny things, each threshed for their truth and laid into the great floating barn of the book. Actually, I love it for being incomplete as well, for ultimately not being able to cage or net, drain or preserve the teem that passed in front of J. Omer Cooper, the Rev. C. E. Tottenham, P. W. Richards, Robert B. Benson, D. J. Lewis, G. J. Kerrich, A. G. Lowndes, G. P. Bidder, R. Moylan Gambles, and so many more. And I love it also for illuminating, if only for moments when you open their dry pages, some of the bright filaments that made up the lives of those initials and doctorates, all of them now spun into the dark along with their samples and gone down, like them, with their nets.

I did see a rarity. Not long after she had moved to the fens and we were exploring the local area together, Claire and I bumped into a vagrant, a collared pratincole, that should have been on the other side of Europe but which we flushed from the muddy scrape at Tubney Fen on our first visit there. It was exciting enough, the bird is beautiful like a large sandy swallow with an equally buoyant flight and a rather piratical hawking manner, and when the news got out people hurried from across the county to see our prize. It was the fourth ever seen in Cambridgeshire. The first record in the county was reported not far from our bird. Leonard Blomefield, great diary keeper of the turning year, sent notice of one shot on Wilbraham Fen on 21 June 1835. Like that one, lost and shot, gone into the dark, the bird we saw revealed little of itself. It had appeared from nowhere and it flew on the same afternoon when our backs were turned and without us seeing it leave. The bird had gone wrong in its journeys and perhaps was trying to correct its ways. Or was it less purposeful than that and forced to fly without direction, unable to rest, though exhausted and disoriented? Or was it sick, its compass skewed, its head screaming with bad noise? Or perhaps, more simply, the Tubney mud didn't suit. We would never know if it found its home again.

The same day, just before we spotted the pratincole, we heard a wood sandpiper whistling once and then the triplets of greenshank calls. From the overcast August sky six birds spilled down, one sandpiper and five greenshanks, tumbling towards the small pool of water on the fen. There were lambs in the field next door, newly separated from their mothers and crying miserably, and the birds' calls made them sound even more bereft and feeble. To see any migrant bird alter its flight course, to know that below it – as it flies – it has seen a place it either knows or wants to know, prickles at our sense of the Earth and the seasons. The waders lingered even less than the pratincole, the wood sandpiper merely dipped towards the mud and never landed, but the inland day on the roomed fen was released by those birds moving through it, plumbing south, tugged by the flash of silvery wet beneath them. The bar-tailed godwits I had watched coming down to feed in the spring half a mile from here arrived from the south and went on to the north; the wood sandpiper and the greenshanks came from the north and headed south. It was as simple and as good as that. The world moves, and watching those moving birds you feel it doing so.

The Fenland Research Committee, and five strips of fen known as the Godwin Plots at Wicken, followed up and extended the work of *The Natural History of Wicken Fen* by, in effect, bringing all its authors and all its life forms together into one ecosystem. The story of the fens was fully worked out from their heart. They grew it themselves. Geology doesn't come close enough to the surface of the fens: too much has happened too recently for the rocks below to pertain. The fens are too young, too plastic, too earthy and too wet. To be explained, the rubbery place needed ecology, with its understanding of the bend and give of life, of co-evolution and of the tangled mingling of things, the way dryness gives way to wet, and wet in turn makes dry.

In 1921 Cambridge University's new-formed Botany School Ecology Club got on their bikes and cycled north from Cambridge to the fens. The riders were led by Arthur Tansley, sometime clerk in the Ministry of Munitions and future student of Sigmund Freud, as well as crusading new phytologist or plant scientist. Among his *domestiques* was Harry Godwin, who later joked he was 'pitchforked' by Tansley into becoming secretary of the British Ecological Society. But at Wicken, Godwin got interested. With Tansley, in 1923, he marked out five scientists' fields, five fen plots, and began an investigation asking questions about plant succession that is still evolving today and which counts as among the world's longest-running scientific experiments. The first plot was never to be cut. The second was to be cut every four years. The third every three. The fourth every two. The fifth every year. This management, with its echoes of Biblical crop-rotation and Joseph's harvest dreams, has, over many years, produced different vegetation patterns and different degrees of succession. The plots further underline how Wicken Fen is not a natural relic of undisturbed vegetation, but the combination of wild growth and anthropogenic change, or a kind of green archaeology.

The Fenland Research Committee, which started in 1932, the year *The Natural History of Wicken Fen* was published, worked on a kind of succession of the mind. Stratigraphy was at its heart – the meaning of each layer of the fen and the different ways those archived strata might be prised apart and interpreted, and then re-laid with cumulative effect. To learn to read the ground, people had to know about pollen and the sea and ice and rivers and rot. Archaeologists were needed, biologists and geologists, professionals and amateurs. The vice-president of the committee was Major Gordon Fowler, the manager of water transportation for a sugar-beet factory. Godwin described him as 'a massive hearty man'. He had lost a leg in the First World War but, even with what Godwin called his 'ersatz' model, he remained active in 'boxing, hockey and sailing'. Fowler's specialism was roddens, the riverbeds of extinct natural waterways in the fens revealed by the wastage of the land around them, and which show as ghostly serpentine shapes or phantom limbs through crops and ploughed fields. The 'imaginative Ely schoolboy', Anthony Vine, who traced many of these long-abandoned meandering river channels, helped Fowler in his researches. They were joined by the geologist O. T. Jones with his 'quiet but withering Welsh accent'; the archaeologists C. W. Phillips, an 'amiable, generous giant', and Miles Burkitt, who had explored sites in France and Spain with the pope of prehistory, the Abbé Breuil; and the (more recently) celebrated eccentrics, the archaeologist and loony parapsychologist T. C. Lethbridge, and O. G. S. Crawford, the aerial archaeology officer of the Ordnance Survey. Meanwhile, and keeping the gentlemen and scholars on the straight and narrow, Miss Robin Andrew prepared slides of microscopic pollen. It was these, it turned out, that had the most to tell.

Godwin repeatedly took the committee and his students out into the fens, having learned much from his early bike rides. He was famous for his field trips. He walked and talked fast and there are stories of him heading enthusiastically through the densest or wettest of vegetation, resulting in a single file of students, with those at the forefront writing his comments down and passing back the information by word of mouth to the rearguard. What the last undergraduate wrote is not known.' But Godwin and the committee asked, as committees will, what kind of synthesis might be possible if you tie the head of the snake to its tail, if you bring people who know one thing together with people who know another. Out of it came the first multidisciplinary studies of any kind in Britain. Godwin's findings in post-glacial fenland have been called a 'landmark in Quaternary [i.e. the present era] research'. Just a *landmark* would be good enough in the fens.

On the south bank of Burwell Lode I watched a young man, tattooed and pierced, catching an eel. Like all fish it seemed to cool the air as it came wet up into it, but like no other fish it seemed at first to come towards its end, wanting to climb out of the water, twisting on its hook and up the line, refusing to be a fish, and performing some speeded-up account of evolution or of its own past as a sometime land-thing. One silky foot of muscle slalom. A rib of water. An electricity cable shocking itself. I shuddered to remember the country road on the bank of a lough in County Clare where my fishing life began and ended at the age of eleven, with an eel pulled by a worm on a hook from the dark water into the rainy air. And me, terrified by this snake on a string, breathing that same air as I was, and keen, so keen, to live that I couldn't touch it, couldn't still its writhing, couldn't hold it to me to take the hook from its man-mouth, couldn't even cut the line, but instead laid the rod on the road and, as the eel bucked and shimmied like something newly amputated, I picked up a grey breezeblock loosed from a jetty and with both hands launched it on to the fish. Then I first heard that particular sound, the wet fibrous crunch, which is living bone being broken. With the tip of my boot I shifted the breezeblock. The eel was down but not out. I needed it dead. There was another breezeblock and then a third before the thing stopped moving and had lost all of its living shapes and became part of the rain on the road. At the lode I left the eel swimming in the air on its hook and hurried on, asking its fisherman if he would eat it. 'Only', he said, 'if I was Polish.'

* * *

John Ray's *Flora* of Cambridgeshire was published in 1660. It was the first-ever county flora in Britain and appeared in the soggy middle of the great fen-adventuring century. Today it seems to have been pulled from a similar fen-trawling net that threw up those more recent books, *The Natural History of Wicken Fen* and Harry Godwin's *Fenland* book. The connection is fundamental: it is to do with kneeling to the wet earth and noting how everything you see there lives together. The effect of the books – on me at least – is also the same. They are works of learning and knowledge, but they are made from such a mixed unfixed place and in such a mixed unfixed way, that they are perfect fen books, and contribute brilliantly to, in Coleridge's phrase, keeping alive the heart in the head.

The *Flora* (more properly the *Catalogus Plantarum circa Cantabrigiam nascentium*) was Ray's first book; he went on to write on fishes, birds, insects and mammals, becoming the country's greatest all-round naturalist. He started out local. He was born in rural Essex; his mother was a herbalist and his father a blacksmith. But he was clever and went to Cambridge University and studied and then lectured in Greek, Mathematics and the Humanities. He knew a lot. The world began to extend away and ripple around him. He became a friend of Thomas Browne among other myth-busters and general-surveyors. Ten years after his Cambridgeshire book he wrote a British flora and, later, three volumes and 2,000 pages of an *Historia plantarum*, describing 6,000 plant species. It was Ray's botanical *Synopsis* (a successor to his British flora) that Jean-Jacques Rousseau carried as his field-guide during his British excursion in 1766.

Ray apologised for any omissions in these books, saying, what else could be expected from one mere man who 'must needs plough the whole field with his own hand'? The Cambridgeshire county *Flora*, a book made from close-looking and local fieldwork or *simpling* (the lovely term for going after – especially medicinal – flowers), was where Ray began. It was mostly written in Latin and my botanising is poor but the *Flora* still reads (translated and explained) as a marvellously fresh-air account of the county (its wetlands especially) coming into focus as flower after flower and grass after grass is picked out in front of us.

Writing later in 1696, Ray was the first to use the word *botany* and the field study of flowers dates from him, and his six years of 'long walks of exploration' into the fens and the wider county. In his preface to the *Flora* he declares that his intention on these journeys was 'to gaze with his own eyes on the nature of things' and to 'gain wisdom by [his] own experience rather than from somebody else's brain'.

Everything swam in those years while Ray knelt to the wet and scrutinised what he saw. Life shifted in front of any observer. The names of things were constantly moving off. Go and stand anywhere on the Equator if you are not from there, and watch its wildlife, and you'll get an idea of what this must have felt like. Plant nomenclature and taxonomy were as unstable as the ground that the unnamed or the misnamed grew from. The boggy elemental fens, half water, half earth, were apt expressions of the dynamism of nature. The world there was turned upside down every winter.

As a concession to the precise specificities of the general wet, Ray moves into English when he describes where he finds the flowers he found. In this way he makes an addition to the great watery plainsong of the fens. But by being faithful to the plants' places and wanting to be clear about their localities, Ray writes a world of local difference and adaptation and, so doing, prepares the ground, as it were, for particular species. One of his plants is found 'in the moory places', another 'on the boggy grounds', a third 'in the osier holts', and so on: 'where toads are found', 'in water courses', 'in moist and marshy localities', 'where waters are stagnant', 'in divers ditches', 'in a Moorish place where they digge turves', 'in damp meadows', 'in sluggish rivers', 'in infinite other ditches'.

There are crops as well as wild plants in the catalogue. There were no potatoes in the fens then, no cabbage, no beet, no celery. But Ray noticed seven varieties of wheat. And with this in mind he poked around in another *crop*, the dissected gut of a fen bustard, and 'found it stuffed with hemlock seeds; [with] only four or five grains of corn mixed with them [s]o even at harvest the bird leaves corn for hemlock'. As he writes this, we can watch how, from the grains that sat in the dead bustard's stomach, Ray can re-walk the bird's last heavy steps through the fields. A single moment, a bird's stride, is raised vividly before us.

At the end of his alphabetical list of plants, as if he knows the A to Z of things is not the best way to make sense of them, Ray gives an outline system for plant classification, and a location-by-location list, a true field-list, of the plants he found in various neighbourhoods – at Gamlingay, and Chesterton, and Ditton, and Stretham, and 'On the bank of the great Ditch called Devils ditch' and several other places. In this list we can see the beginnings of his understanding of habitat and ecosystems; the understanding that gave us, 250 years later, a great encyclopaedia of life from the few acres of Wicken Fen.

Brilliant on the liquefaction of the wetlands, Ray is very good as well on the confusion of grass. Through the words he gives to them we can watch him looking. Among the received common names he notes are the 'Hedge-hog-grass' and 'Grasse of Parnassus' (not a grass in fact, but a bog-star). But we can also *hear* his ordering eye at work as other grass names compound, build up and grow. It is as if speciation itself is happening right in front of his enquiring gaze. Indeed, Ray got closer than anybody had before to defining what we now understand to be a species (Linnaeus later paid his dues to Ray who, he acknowledged, had got there first). Look at the bunch he has picked of 'small foxtail grass' and 'lesser bastard Fox-tail-grass' and 'small rough-eared bastard Fox-tail-grass'. See how sometimes on the fen even the great naturalist was lost for words, or rather flooded with them. Pay attention to 'Water-grasse'; 'Float-grass'; 'Great water Reed-grasse'; '[o]ur great Reed-grasse with chaffie heads'; and '[t]he marsh soft Rush with a round blackish head,' you know the one, yes, the one which is found '[e]verywhere in the watery places of Hinton and Teversham moors, so that he which shall look there cannot doubt what rush we mean . . .'

Ray's little book, which was printed in Cambridge by one John Field, is so beautiful in both its precision and its vagueness, and so stuffed with looking and thinking about looking, that it makes you want to keep it with you, to use it as a true field-guide, to allow it to staunch any wound you might have, to live by it. It couldn't help us when, on my knees at my village roadside, Claire and I grappled with a dead bee orchid next to an orobanche, but it marvellously brimmed full when we got home and read that in the late 1650s there were 'hundreds' of the 'Humble-bee Satyrion' 'in a close behind the Bell Inn at Haverhill', and that the parasitic orobanche then grew 'in barley on the right hand side of the way between Cambridge and Grantchester'.

I can think of nothing more thrilling, nothing that our species has done better, than this benign capture and permanent vivifying of a season, a pathway and a field edge, and its *simpling*, or its lovable mapping of what might be in front of us. He was there and noticed what was there. And now, being all but there, we see it all, 'by the well on the hill not far from the church' or 'along the balks of the plowed fields next the closes, on the left hand of the horse-way to Cherry-Hinton ...'

Out Field

My son, Lucian, aged five, in December 2000: 'I wish I could be a bird. When I am in heaven I might be an eagle, because you can be whatever you like. Even a drawing pin. Or a piece of fluff. Or a crumb. Or a piece of grass.'

Emily Dickinson, a little older and a while ago, on grass when it dies: 'in Sovereign Barns to dwell – / And dream the Days away, / The Grass so little has to do / I wish I were a Hay – '

Older still. Sir Gawain cuts off the Green Knight's head and it rolls about a bit on the earth. As it bumps past the other knight-spectators they kick at it (as if to send it into the long grass). But the felled Green Knight picks up his own head and carries it off, and you know that when he plants it back on his shoulders it will grow again, that what was cut will not die but will come again, that the Green Knight *is* grass.

You can still catch the smell of the meadow in a city's streets. One May day, in Mount Auburn cemetery on the wooded edge of Harvard near Boston, I watched a female bobolink, a migrant grassland sparrow-like bird, resting on its way north to open fields. It landed on the carved stone wheatsheaf that lies on the tomb of one Caleb Wood. The scene made me think of Bob Dylan saying how he learned 'Baby Let Me Follow You Down' from Ric von Schmidt in the green pastures of Harvard University. Later the same day, outside the Harvard Book Store, an elderly white-haired man in a beret and a chunky Aran sweater, knitted with creamy furrows and ridges, played a tune on a silver-buttoned accordion. It was 'The Bonny Earl of Murray':

Ye Highlands and ye Lawlands,
       O where hae ye been?
They hae slain the Earl of Murray,
       And hae laid him on the green.

In *Henry V* Falstaff dies talking of green fields at the river's edge as the Thames tide turns. He doesn't appear in the play but Hostess Quickly memorably describes his off-stage last moments and his death:

> Nay, sure, he's not in hell: he's in Arthur's bosom, if ever man went to Arthur's bosom. A made a finer end and went away an it had been any christom child. A parted e'en just between twelve and one, e'en at the turning o' th' tide. For after that I saw him fumble with the sheets and play with flowers and smile upon his fingers' end, I knew there was but one way, for his nose was as sharp as a pen on a table of green fields. 'How now, Sir John?' quoth I. 'What, man? Be o'good cheer.' So a cried out. 'God, God, God!' three or four times. Now I, to comfort him, bid him a should not think of God; I hoped there was no need to trouble himself with any such thoughts yet. So a bade me lay more clothes on his feet. I put my hand into the bed and felt them, and they were as cold as any stone. Then I felt to his knees, and so up-peered and upward, and all was as cold as any stone.

The lines are not totally watertight. Hostess Quickly perhaps mistakes Arthur for Abraham whose bosom was a byword for heaven, though Arthur has a good ring of England or Lyonesse. Other lines are contested. Alexander Pope thought a stage-direction had crept into the text: 'Greenfield was the name of the property-man in that time who furnished implements, etc for the actors, *A table of Greenfield's*.' No other Shakespeare editors follow Pope but many are not happy with 'on a table of green fields'. Variant readings have been proposed and the words emended to 'and a babbled of green fields' or 'and a talked of green fields'.

I like it each way and all ways (and so did Edward Thomas: 'Almost as soon as I could babble', he wrote, 'I "babbled of green fields."').

Whatever the intended words or image, we are watching the green flash at the end of a life. The consolations of a primal experience (to be in a field . . .) are invoked and much else is configured and remembered in a few fleeting moments. An elderly man is in his bed talking of fields – the best good thing that he knows outside and which (at least in his living life) he is on the verge of forsaking forever.

Falstaff at the beginning of his ending and in a kind of easeful delirium dandles a last pastoral plaything at his fingers like a child's toy, the equivalent of a farm-set of animals and implements. He sees flowers and passes his hands over them on the rumpled meadow of his bedclothes, an embroidered pattern mistaken perhaps, but they are also the flowers of the field that will bloom on the turned earth of a grave, making Falstaff alive to his own death like the dying Keats who, having heard his burial place in Rome described, declared back to his friend Joseph Severn from his deathbed that 'he already seemed to feel the flowers growing over him'.

Keats coughed blood on to his sheets during the night of 3 February 1820. He thought its bright red meant it was arterial blood and that his tuberculosis was therefore advanced and probably fatal. In fact tuberculosis invades veins as much as arteries and all coughed blood will look bright because of its contact with oxygen in the airways. But Keats believed he had seen on his sheets what he called his 'death-warrant' and he was right. He died a little over a year later. Ten days after the coughed blood he wrote a letter to his friend James Rice:

How astonishingly does the chance of leaving the world impress a sense of its natural beauties upon us. Like poor Falstaff, though I do not babble, I think of green fields. I muse with the greatest affection on every flower I have known from my infancy – their shapes and coulours [are as] new to me as if I had just created them with a superhuman fancy – It is because they are connected with the most thoughtless and happiest moments of our Lives – I have seen foreign flowers in hothouses, of the most beautiful nature, but I do not care a straw for them. The simple flowers of our spring are what I want to see again.

*   *   *

Tolstoy is buried at Yasnaya Polyana in a clearing in the wood behind the house. Yasnaya Polyana means 'bright glade' and a sunlit circle has been found or made around his grave. He instructed it thus, though to look at it you might think that nature had decided in any case to comply with the Count. There is no stone and no cross; no lettering of any kind from any time writes its way into the ring of green.

He died on the run like King Lear. In November 1910, aged eighty-two, he fled from his wife and his wider life, his aristocratic class, the state and the religion he had come to hate, those cranky followers who crowded needily around him, his own pride and arrogance that he had never been able to shake off, and the very storm of words which he had lived in for so long. His mad flight also took him from the place that had nurtured him for almost all of his life and that, according to his son Lev, he regarded as 'an organic part of himself'. In the end not even Yasnaya Polyana could save him. The dark green leather sofa Tolstoy was born on, and which he made Sofya Andreyevna use for many of her many labours, is in his study in the white house with its green roof and window frames just down the hill from his grave. The sofa is blackened with age now and dull-polished like the old used skin that it is. Tolstoy died in a stranger's bed in an unfamiliar place. His recent biographers have no truck with his reported last words and W. H. Auden thought they sounded 'too much in character to be credible' but for a time they were said to be: 'But the peasants – how do the *peasants* die?'

Tolstoy's body was returned to Yasnaya Polyana and his funeral was the first public burial in Russia made without religious rites. A hole was scratched in the ground and topped with earth. Tolstoy, Leo or Lev the lion, had requested a pauper's burial and he was granted a simple coffin but hundreds of people followed it up the hill. At the head of the procession two peasants carried a banner made of a white sheet of coarse linen slung between two birch poles. Written on it: 'The memory of your good deeds will not die amongst us.' It was signed: 'The Orphaned Peasants of Yasnaya Polyana.'

His grave must have been repaired over the years but it is still something to look at. The path to it opens to the grassed glade with birch trees towering around, two or three of them leaning over the clearing like comforting parents reaching down to their children. Set to one side of the green is what looks like a table of turf rising little more than a foot from the ground. The entire tomb-barrow, its top, ends and sides, is clothed in grass that, even at the end of September, was still growing and vividly bright. It looked like a delicious place to sit – a table and a bench at once – and I would have if I hadn't known I would be resting on Tolstoy's remains. The raised grave seemed shorter than a body: in my mind's eye, and in the statues of him that are still everywhere in Russia, Tolstoy was taller, but as he aged he shrank. By his last years he was less than five foot four inches high.

Tolstoy is buried in these woods in this way for all sorts of reasons; his whole life took him to his end. But he told one story, a kind of green dream, about why he wanted to end up where he did. When he was about five his eldest brother, Nikolay, who was ten, told him he had discovered the secret of happiness and that it was written on a little green stick which was buried somewhere in the woods just behind their home at Yasnaya Polyana. When the stick was found and its words were read all the world would turn loving and would be at peace. Then everybody would become members of an 'ant brotherhood'. Through their childhoods Tolstoy and his brothers played at being ants, building nests and dens and huddling close, and Tolstoy never forgot the dream and explicitly asked to be buried near to where the stick might lie:

The ideal of Ant-Brothers lovingly clinging to one another, though not under two armchairs curtained by shawls, but of all mankind under the wide dome of heaven, has remained the same with me. As I then believed that there existed a little green stick whereon was written the message that could destroy all evil in men and give them universal welfare, so I now believe that such truth exists and will be revealed to men and give them all it promises.

It isn't clear if the stick was a painted piece of wood or a leafing bough but, whatever it was, when taken back into the ground it offered an endlessly renewable and happy life. So, at the edge of the clearing, it was inevitable that I bent to the earth and peeled from a fallen branch a page of birch bark and, as I pulled it away, several ants hurried like scattering letters and punctuation marks along the rotting wood and into the leaf mould. They didn't like being disturbed and as I stood up I could taste in my mouth and feel at my eyes the smarting metallic vapour that John Ray, sometime fen botanist and discoverer in 1671 of the properties of formic acid, described as *ant juyce*.

In September 1877 at Fort Robinson in the Pine Ridge area (now in northern Nebraska, south of the present-day Sioux reservation), Crazy Horse, the Sioux warrior, was killed as he resisted being taken into prison. He had surrendered at the fort a year after he had helped see Custer into the soil of the Little Bighorn. There are many stories about his death. His life up until then is remarkably unknown. He was never a talker; there is no photograph of him. But as the world closed in the voices grew up. At least twenty people who were at the fort spoke about it subsequently. He was stabbed twice with a bayonet in the stomach during a scuffle. His assailant was probably a soldier called William Gentles from County Tyrone. Still alive, Crazy Horse was wrapped in a sheet or blanket and carried to the adjutant's office where he was encouraged to lie on a cot. He refused. He was perhaps the last man in human history never to sit on a chair. He died on the office floor and Ian Frazier, in his book *Great Plains*, wants to believe that because Crazy Horse spurned the bed he died his own man, claiming his shape on the earth as the only space left to him: 'Lying where he chose, Crazy Horse showed the rest of us where we are standing. With his body, he demonstrated that the floor of an Army office was part of the land, and that the land was still his.' When Touch the Clouds saw that his friend was dead he pulled a blanket over him and said, 'This is the lodge of Crazy Horse.'

He was about thirty-seven. His parents took their dead son by travois forty miles east to the Spotted Tail Agency, which was where he had wanted to move. His body, wrapped in red blankets, was put up on a scaffold on a hill. His parents stayed with it for three days. He had done the same when his baby daughter died of cholera, climbing into her scaffold and lying next to her. A wooden fence was erected around his bier to keep it from carrion-seeking wolves. Later the body was removed to an unknown place. 'Because he possibly said that his bones would turn to rocks and his joints to flint,' Frazier writes, 'Indian boys used to search the hills for his petrified remains. No one knows for sure where Crazy Horse's bones lie.'

The Crazy Horse memorial mountain round the back of Mount Rushmore in the Black Hills is a very sad thing. The mountain top is slowly being carved into the shape of Crazy Horse riding for his life. If you pay your dollars you can go and look at the drilling and blasting. If you don't you are kept from the man and the mountain by a screen of buildings around the car park.

There is a story that before any battle Crazy Horse would paint his pony with earth unearthed by a mole and would rub a smudge of the same earth into his hair. His hope was that the black earth dug by the believed-blind black mole would make both horse and Crazy Horse harder to see.

When T. H. White loses the goshawk that he has been training, 'my lunatic from the Rhine' as he calls it, he tries to get his bird back by hiding out as a field. The story is at the heart of *The Goshawk*. He sets a pigeon as bait and tethers it to the ground. Nearby he slides under a scaffold of ash sticks covered in a sheet. He has sprinkled the sheet with grass and mustard seed and soaked it in water until it has sprouted into a growing green cloth. Sometimes he calls his hide 'the mole-hill' and sometimes 'the grave'. Hidden but primed, he is prepared to wait for days for the pigeon to lure the hawk down from its freedom and for the hawk to come close enough to be grabbed from the grave. The camouflage is good. One day three poachers walked over White without noticing what lay beneath them; one, he says, he could have caught 'by the foot'. But it doesn't work for his bird.

Around the time John Clare started writing poetry he was also saving up for an olive-green coat. He hardly ever had any spare money and was almost always what Robert Graves described as *mouse-poor*. In 1806 Clare had saved enough to buy James Thomson's long poem *The Seasons* from a bookseller in Stamford and was so thrilled he couldn't resist reading it even as he walked home. But he knew he mustn't be seen so he climbed the walls of the estate at Burghley, just outside the town, and hid away in order to read the poem. Soon he started writing himself, and to begin with he buried or cached his words on scraps of paper in holes in the wall of his cottage as if they were not to be known about or were to be held and saved, ready for later.

When his first book appeared in 1820, Clare went to London. He was anxious in the city about many things. Later he rebuked Londoners for claiming they heard nightingales singing everywhere in the capital, but when he first went there he did the same thing, misidentifying street-walking prostitutes in their grabby finery for grand ladies. He was also embarrassed by the poverty of his own wardrobe and his publisher offered him some clothes. His first biographer, Frederick Martin, detailed the camouflage he accepted: 'Clare refused to take anything, except an ancient overcoat somewhat too large for him, but useful as hiding his whole figure from the top of the head down to the heels. In this brigand-like mantle he henceforth made all his visits, unwilling to take it off even at dinner, and in rooms hot to suffocation.'

Clare didn't want to be thought a hayseed but couldn't help playing the part. An old form of his surname was *Clayer* meaning a man who mixes the soil, who marls peaty land with clay. Trying to dress for the occasion on his second visit to London in 1822 he instead gave away the cast of the place he came from, wearing a 'bright grass-coloured coat and yellow waistcoat' and getting himself called, by a magazine editor, 'our Green Man'.

When, in July 1841, Clare absconded from his first asylum in Essex and walked home to Northamptonshire, he was hungry and ate grass from the roadside. The greenery on the verge was known as *flitting grass*; the poor and commoners alike used this marginal herbage to feed their animals. Flitting meant to graze cattle on a tether. Children are attending their family's animals in this way all across Africa today. In revolutionary France, Wordsworth and his friend Michel Beaupuy were horrified by the sight of a hunger-bitten girl being half-dragged by a heifer along such a verge. The grass north of London, Clare said, tasted something like bread.

Later in Northampton Asylum, where he lived for twenty-three years (and was listed on a census first as a limeburner and then, a decade later, as a poet), Clare declared he had been at the Battle of Waterloo where his head had been shot off. He couldn't explain how he came to have it back on his shoulders again. At the same time he told this story to Dr Nesbitt, the medical superintendent, he also reported, clear as day, how his poetry 'came to him whilst walking in the fields' and that he 'kicked it out of the clods'. Writing out of the flat and unedged places of eastern England, he made a horizon with his opening lines, and then dipped below it repeatedly into the fields, noticing what was there. Clare the clayer never stopped being a fieldworker and walked, even in his asylum, like a ploughman it was said, 'one leg seeming to be always in the furrow'.

I always did leave doors open behind me and I still do. It is good to be able to see any available exit and shutting a door has forever seemed rather severe and final, the click of the handle denoting some permanent entrance into a headmaster's study or a doctor's consulting room. Bad news happens behind closed doors. I lock my front and back door but no other door within any of the three places I live is shut. When I was a child, one or other of my parents, who both had known life before central heating and who both now paid the bills for it, would shout after me as I left the room, 'Born in a barn?' But I was happy to be slandered, or to think then of what that would mean. It wasn't a comparison with Jesus that I was seeking – his barn birthplace was, in any case, a stable, with scary horses and other heavy-duty stuff, wise men crowding in and meaningfulness. But to be always on the point of going out – I liked that thought.

I've slept twice in a barn, both times after birds. Once on straw in the crowded birdwatcher's dossing-place at Salthouse, I think it was, on the North Norfolk coast after my first greater yellowlegs, a vagrant from America, in 1975. We were late, it was dark and I tripped over the sleepers already lying in rows, heads to the walls and feet to the centre, scout-tent style. I remember the stirring shrouded figures and the bliss-excitement that took me to sleep, the bird having been seen and all else therefore made good and easy. The other time was in Cornwall a year or so later and near Stithians or Siblyback reservoir, where we'd been chasing another American wader – perhaps a Baird's sandpiper, though I cannot now recall the bird for certain. We hadn't seen it. Antony, one of our carload of bird-boys, had remembered a family friend living nearby and we gatecrashed a dinner party, still slung with our binoculars and heavy in wellingtons. They sat us like tramps or beggars at the distant end of their long farmhouse table, fed us their leftovers, and then pushed us out through the rain into a barn stacked with hay, a loose cap of it just below the roof on top of a solid house of bales. We climbed up, as you might a stepped pyramid, and slept in a fragrant silvery-green pool of dusty cuttings lit from the side by moonlight bruising through clouds. Both nights I recall for the rain galloping on the metal roofs of the barns that woke me every now and then and the complementing prickle of the cut grass on my cheeks as I turned in my sleep, and for the dormitory security of the one barn and my fear in the other of sinking or even drowning into the hay, which seemed so giving and soft in its swimming strew of stems.

I shot and killed a wildebeest one day in Zambia. It was running with its herd through high tawny grass. Then it was a dirty sheet thrown down on the same field. In its abrupt passage from life to death (close in front of me and steered by my trigger-finger) and in the same second that I watched this happen down a telescopic sight (as if from the far side of the world and the other end of time) so all the pages of this book came to call: a field, its contents, its meanings and me.

I killed it because it was sick and a little lame and heading for the chop whether I delivered the final blow or not. I killed it because everyone else where I was staying on the game-farm near Choma had already gone with a gun or a crossbow after one thing or another and I could no longer say not me, not now, not yet. I killed it because my wife is South African and for a time slept with a shotgun under her bed and I thought killing something might let us know one another better. I killed it because, although I had never shot or even held a rifle before, having passed an audition with a cardboard box target wedged in a tree, I felt the dark gun tracking me as we drove out on to the open grass and targeting me until I picked it up once more. I killed it because, although I had watched hours of wildebeest passing me in the grass of the Rift Valley, mooing and mowing there, and being dead there in so many ways, I had never touched one. I killed it because I wanted to mark a field, to cut into it somehow and feel some holding anchor on its grassy floor, to enter a place and to know both it and me more alive even as I made part of it dead. I killed it though I am a student of the Ancient Mariner and his albatross, of D. H. Lawrence and his snake, of George Orwell and his elephant, and Ahab and his whale. I killed it perhaps just because I could.

My knees came close to stopping me. The shooting was to be done from the open back of a Land Cruiser so that we could approach the small herd of twenty-five or so animals and hide from them at the same time. My top half was clouded in a loose camouflage-patterned smock, with my shorts and bare legs, moony and milk-white shanks, hidden behind the cab. I had to steady myself on the bumpy ride across the plain by jamming my knees hard against the chassis. As I looked down they appeared as hopeless as two slices of flabby bread. Something of the very beginnings of my life, of Liverpool and wet days in the playground, came up to me from those knees. But by pushing them harder still into the metal I steadied myself enough, even though my calves and then my thighs juddered as if in shock. Sweat stung my eyes and I had to wipe them with my camouflaged arms to see down the gun-sight. The wildebeest moved on, passing beyond scrub and thorn trees, but the last of them was tiring and lagged a little and I knew my target. It had a limp and, though it could still run, it picked up speed more awkwardly than the others and never got beyond a broken canter. If I was a leopard I would have marked it out in the same way as had Ian. He owns the farm and knows the herd, had tested my gunnery and loaded the rifle, and was driving while quietly mouthing encouragement to both sides of the story, tightening the thread between us as he shortened it. Twice I had the beast side-on as desired and in the sight. But it moved and the moment

247

spooled from me. We drove closer and the herd stopped and Ian switched off. The electric quiet of the outer world came loud into my head and met my nervous pulse. The gun was fantastically solid and sweat had rolled again into my eyes. But looking down the sight calmed me. Years of birdwatching, of tunnel vision and of the magnification of things, helped me arrive in a place without being there and to know that I was looking, without being seen, at a living thing living. The wildebeest turned its old eyes towards me and sniffed the hot air between us. There were lines – cross-hairs – scratched on the lens and my finger was on the sickle-shaped trigger not the focusing wheel of a pair of binoculars, but I was sure that as I squeezed so the wildebeest would sharpen and come closer. That was what I felt I was doing: bringing it to me, getting a gnu with a gun.

It fell before I finished pulling. My muscles dragged behind my optic nerve. I saw a hurry-slump to the grass before I felt my tendons stretch. I heard nothing and registered no kick from the stock. My nerves were looking after that as well. Ian got out of the cab, took the gun from me and started walking into the long grass. The herd had run on over a low rise and we were alone. All the muted noises came back at once and the plain became an itching hot day. I followed Ian in a trance. We walked 163 strides.

There was a dead thing on the ground: big and dirty and already infinitely older than the living morph that had occupied its shape until a few moments ago. Without touching it I could feel the body's warmth but there was no suggestion of any engine running down or ghostly departure. The life had gone out in an instant and everything had changed. Its eyes, like matchboxes now, goatish and new blind, said the same thing. The animal's front sticky legs bent under its chest, and its nose was pushed in the sand between some clumps of grass. It had found its way to the beginning of the earth but couldn't get in.

I did my best for a photograph and tried to cuddle the corpse. Its head was heavier than the gun. I had to take both its horns in my hands and heave and hold on to them like reins. Its mane fell long and black across my pale legs and made me think of pictures of the Ramones outside CBGBs. The animal had been ill. Its hooves were worn with rot to nothing and it had been running on its nails alone. Around its anus a ring of ticks clustered like swollen fruits, already big with blood but buried in bliss in the pink opening and drinking more. At the other end of its body, blood had bubbled scarlet and frothy into the wildebeest's mouth with the final pump of its heart and, strung with slobbery drool, it came dribbling into the sand, pooling darkly as oil will beneath a cracked sump. Its puce tongue had slid out through its slack ruminant mouth. A fly was walking there already. Its teeth showed too, pearly but worn down below the gums, like bulbs uncovered in soil.

Close up its grey-brown body hair might have been the field it fell in. No matter how many apparently uniform runners started at the off, every tight-stretched pelt within the herd makes its own unique tweed. There were scars and swirls of fur, licked places, blemishes and beauty spots, wormholes and bald patches, the signature of a life written into the hills and valleys of a body. And just above its front right leg there was a new bloody nick where the bullet had gone in, finding the lungs and the heart as it ought and blowing and burning them apart before slowing through the rest of the body and coming to a halt inside the top of the front left leg. A punch brought to rest within a punchbag. I could feel the bullet beneath my finger like a loose knuckle just below the skin.

When Ian laid the wildebeest on the concrete of the farmyard his dogs licked its tongue clean of blood and then hurried to stem the bright red gulf that ran from its mouth. Once the dogs had finished on the floor they licked at my bare shins and knees for the specks of blood the wildebeest's death-breath had sprayed on me. Thirty-four portions of meat were butchered from the body. One for each of the thirty women working that day in the fields and four more for each of the compound foremen. The inedible tail was given to the butcher, Samuel, for his 'senior' wife (he has two). Worth one hundred dollars, and more valuable than all the rest of the wildebeest put together, it would be used in dances and, if put under a pillow, could banish bad dreams.

* * *

In the Hungarian novelist László Krasznahorkai's *The Melancholy of Resistance*, a vast stuffed whale travels the small towns of sea-less Hungary on the back of a truck. I once heard the writer say that when he was a child he had seen such a whale when it trundled into the backwater town of Gyula, on the edge of the Hungarian plain close to the Romanian border. Looking at the whale, he said he had thought that if *it* was possible then *everything* was.

Nicholas Redman shares an interest in the *idea* of a whale, though he might not declare it in the same way. He lives in South London not far from the River Thames. Or, rather, his workplace is there: a modern house with blinds drawn on every window, a single army-surplus camp bed in one room, and the rest of the space tight-jammed with the grey hulks of filing cabinets, stuffed bookshelves and splitting cardboard boxes. He uses an ironing board as a desk. Every available inch of the house is made from the details of as many of the whales' bones of Britain as Nick has been able to secure. The bones strewn across the country, that is, that have parted company from their bodies and that have found their way onshore and inland, a skeleton scattered as if dropped from space and made of skulls, vertebrae and ribs, some visible, many lost, a few remembered, most forgotten. In a lockup garage nearby Nick has more boxes and some rescued ribs leaning against the walls like huge half-rotten oars. 'People don't know what to do with them any more and offer them and I feel I must take them,' he told me. A blade of baleen rested on a shelf behind his head like a scythe. From all his findings he has compiled an extraordinary book called *Whales' Bones of the British Isles*, a directory and gazetteer of all of the bones that he knows and of their places. It is a book that nobody else wants as much as he does. He lists whale remains in museums but they can mostly take care of themselves and his real concern is with the farm buildings and barns roofed from bones; the fence posts and field edges made from them driven into the earth; the jawbones donated by a sea captain to the fen town of March and erected in 1850 as Melville was raising *Moby-Dick* on the other side of the sea; the grottoes of marine topiary in forgotten Victorian gardens; the slipway for boats made of a whale ribcage on Harris; the arches of ribs raised into the sky like ruined church entranceways; the half-buried vertebrae near old whaling ports, bone-yard monuments to their own slaughter; the set of jawbones made into a child's swing.

The odd thing is that Nick is not interested in *whales*. A celebrated and publically mourned northern bottle-nosed whale strayed up the Thames in 2006 and came within a few yards of his files and photographs but he didn't go to see it. It was still alive. His fascination is only for what people have thought to do with whalebones. No more than that, but no less than that either. Living whales don't interest him but his is a true work of *nature writing*, an account of how it marks the world, and an answer, like *Moby-Dick*, to its call.

Nick Redman, when I left him, was at work on various European companion volumes to his British whalebone book. Hungary will surface eventually.

I was descending through a crack in the earth, as you must, to the metro station below the Champs-Élysées in Paris and there, at the bottom of the first flight of steps, was a small rabbit, white all over apart from two brown ears, its nose snuffling freely in its slinky lollop between my feet. It stopped me in my tracks. What sort of burrow for what sort of rabbit? But there, sitting against the metro tunnel wall, was its minder, a smiling elderly Maghrebi man, who sat with an opened newspaper in front of him on which was laid one carrot with feathery green tops, his calling card, and their begging bowl – a ticket to another field, another Elysium. I took my train and first came up from the earth at Notre Dame where, at the doors of the cathedral, there was a one-eyed black African beggar, the blue of his clouding cataract as bright as the cloudless sky. He held his arm out, raised in front of him, palm up, St Francis-style, and house sparrows milled there in a halo of blurred and rusty cornlight. I went down again and got out at the Louvre. In the Tuileries, house martins were nesting under the stone flower heads that deck the underside of the Arc de Carrousel and, beyond them, a black and white goat was kneeling into a flowerbed apparently gardening.

*   *   *

One of the sweetest and greenest moments in the *Divine Comedy* comes in Canto 15 of the *Inferno* when Dante meets a friend. Brunetto Latini, the chancellor of the first popular government of Florence, was Dante's guardian after his father died and then became a tutor-figure to him. When they meet Brunetto is dead and condemned, probably for his sodomy, to hell. The damned man appears at Dante's side in the middle of a dark version of the fens, a 'solid mire' with 'fuming mist' and a 'maze of dykes' laid by an 'evil engineer'. Brunetto catches at Dante's sleeve and walks alongside him – the damned must move forever – and they speak of how they both came to be there. It is a tender talk made in the mutuality of love complicated by their shared knowledge (the fallen man and the visitor from the world of life and light), and it continues until Brunetto sees that 'fresh steam is stirring from the sand' and turns from Dante to run back to his place on the night soil of the hot fen and, doing so, Dante says, 'he seemed one of those / who run for the green cloth through the green field / at Verona . . . and seemed more like the one who wins the roll of cloth than those who lose'.

These beautiful last lines drew Robert Lowell, their translator, towards them and as well as making a version of the canto he incorporated them into two of his other poems. In his 1929 essay on Dante, T. S. Eliot wrote of the same passage: 'One does not need to know anything about the race for the roll of green cloth, to be *hit* by these lines; and in making Brunetto, so fallen, run like the winner, a quality is given to the punishment which belongs only to the greatest poetry.' I would only add that I think the *green* helps. The Palio was run outside the walls of Verona on the first Sunday of Lent. In Italian *verde* rhymes with *perde*, but green is for go and the race was towards life and the prize the best badge of it. The loser received a cockerel.

I went out into the fields down a grassed track between olive trees not far from Prato near Florence one late autumn afternoon. Somewhere above me in the sky two woodlarks sang. I couldn't see them. The woodlark's is the song I love the most of all the birds that I have heard. It is tuneful but sad, broken and slight and a little cold. On a beautifully strange LP I bought, when I lived in Budapest in the 1980s, an elderly Hungarian tenor moans a slowed-down version of a singing woodlark. It sounds as if the Earth has cracked open and this sweet, thin and true music is what breaks from its exposed heart. Since I heard the singer and his drifting notes I cannot hear the birds without thinking that theirs is the music of afterwards, a blues, the song of how things have been. Its small sprinkling noise is a modest declaration of limits and is as honest as any song I know. This is where we have arrived, it says to me: a boy standing at the side of a dance floor looking at his feet and expecting nothing.

Of course it is none of this. It is sex and the swollen gonads pushing at the syrinx and warfare over the sky's acres and the olive grove and the horse field below. But I walked under the singing, still not seeing the singers, hearing the threads let down from the sky and feeling the woodlarks only as sad. And their music came then through the chop and burr of human voices that thickened ahead of me in the strange olive wood. And none of it could I understand. On one side of the track there were Chinese men in white shirts and suit trousers crouched in the low crowns of the olives or standing on stepladders leaning against them. One man in each tree. From tree to tree they spoke to each other as they might in a room. They had short-handled rakes and combed as they talked, and the olives rained down through their words and the branches on to the plastic sheets they had laid on the grass to skirt each tree. On the other side of the track West African men in indigo-blue scarves and padded jackets were at the same work. They were taller and moved more than the Chinese and their Wolof remarks jumped loudly from one tree on to another. But the olives fell as before and the woodlarks' song came down through the little grey-green crowns of the trees with their teams of men perching in them like captured birds hung in small cages.

The woodlarks were still singing as, at the edge of a wilder wood of sweet chestnuts and oaks, I crossed the path of an irregular platoon of burly hunters dressed in camouflaged suits and carrying plastic bags of butchered meat dripping blood along the dusty track. There are wild boar in these woods and all day the horizon had popped with gunshots. The woodlarks didn't seem to mind but the woodpigeons were going

253

crazy, first clattering out of any treetop they had stopped down into, then swirling into a bigger nervousness, pulling higher above the woods and leaving the valley as quick as they could. The gunmen, their guns shouldered in cases the same pattern as their clothes, and happy with their bits of boar swinging from their hands, didn't even look up at the larks or the pigeons as they walked to their little runabout cars parked up the lane.

There are no right angles in the seasons, but there are corners and there came a day one late August when I could see round one on the fen and watch the year turning.

The local roads there are cut straight but they slump and humpback following the rise and fall of the ground beneath. Anything driving at more than twenty-five miles an hour fouls with an ugly metal snarl in the tarmac bottoms. The route I take to and from the fen has been laid in sections to give it some stretch-space and so allow for the ebbs and runs of the earth-tide's passage through the moving land. Every twenty yards or so, inch-wide trenches between the sections have opened across the road. Narrow green lines of low grass crouch in them. Crossing these dips in a car the tyres tick; on a bike the repetitive lurch throws your heart into your mouth.

With swallows moving south around me I cycled home from the fens following a tractor pulling a trailer of grain fresh hulled from one of the new harvested fields. It was heading towards the Swan Lake Grain Store where the treasure is tipped into dunes of gold, swimming alive with warmth and weight, and humming with fragrant dust in the dark of the cavernous sheds.

The bumps of the little trenches across the bucking road jiggled a line of grain from the back of the trailer, a thin curtain of English manna. In the fen wind and the machine-blow from the tractor the beads of wheat rolled towards the trenches and gathered in them, joining the grains already captured from earlier journeys. With the lowering sun the evening light made these threads across the road shine warmly. Yellowhammers had already found the golden seams. As I pedalled towards them, three flew up, lifting some of the grain's metal in the shining yellow jewellery of their faces. I stopped and watched as they returned to a glinting trench behind me towards the fen. In my bag I had a pewter flask of sloe gin, the spirit flavoured from the fen edges hereabouts, and warming to the warm moment, I dribbled a little libation, by way of a thank you, on top of the grains at my feet. As I did, I looked back to see the first mist of the autumn growing from the fields and smoking over the road and the rifts of gold, and taking everything – all that was before me – from me, until I could see only the air made thick with water from the earth.

Grass seeds and broken stems and leaves get stuck in the lining of my boots on almost every crossing of a field. When my walking herbarium gets too prickly, I pick the seeds from the weave. All the four fields have met at my feet. I shake them out, my *coup de grâce*, sowing on to my little back lawn at home the seeds from half a mile away and from thousands of miles away, reed flags and sedge-heads, Bushmen's and steppe-feather, prairie and timothy. My days.

'If you want me again look for me under your boot-soles.'
Walt Whitman

Notes and References

Place of publication London unless otherwise stated.

ix   *A man keeps and feeds a lion* – Diogenes, *7 Greeks*, trans. Guy Davenport, New Directions, New York, 1995, p. 173.

Home Field

2   *There was no possibility of taking a walk that day* and other quotations – Charlotte Brontë, *Jane Eyre*, ed. Margaret Smith, Oxford University Press, 1980, pp. 7–8. First published 1847.

3   *a language of my whole life* – Ted Hughes, interviewed in 1995, *The Paris Review – Interviews, III*, Canongate, Edinburgh, 2008, p. 293.

3   *This green plot shall be our stage* – William Shakespeare, *A Midsummer Night's Dream*, III.i.3.

3   *a uniform hieroglyphic* – Walt Whitman, 'A Child Said, What is the Grass?' *Song of Myself* (1855), poem 6, *Complete Poems*, ed. Stephen Matterson, Wordsworth, 2006, p. 27.

4   *The fields!* – John Ruskin, *Modern Painters*, Vol. III, Part IV, Ch. XIV, +51, *Ruskin Today*, ed. Kenneth Clark, Penguin, Harmondsworth, 1964, pp. 102–3. Based on a journal entry made at Vevey, 3 June 1849.

5   Seamus Heaney's 'Digging' was the first poem in his first collection *The Death of a Naturalist* (1966).

5   *Visionary dreariness* – William Wordsworth, Book Eleventh (1805) 310 and Book Twelfth (1850) 256, *The Prelude*, eds

Jonathan Wordsworth, M. H. Abrams and Stephen Gill, Norton, New York, 1979, pp. 432–3.

9   *all those creatures we behold, are but the hearbs of the field* – Thomas Browne, *Religio Medici* 1.37, *Thomas Browne: The Major Works*, ed. C. A. Patrides, Penguin, Harmondsworth, 1977, p. 107. First published 1642–3.

9   Psalm 103 in the King James version: '*As for* man his days *are* as grass.'

15   *like a very ghost of joie de vivre* – D. H. Lawrence, 'Second-Best', *The Prussian Officer and Other Stories*, ed. John Worthen, Penguin, 1995, p. 115.

17   *The land has been humanised, through and through* – D. H. Lawrence, *Sea and Sardinia*, Heinemann, 1964, p. 123. First published 1921.

Winter Fen

20   *by the height of a man in the life of a man* – Alan Bloom, *The Fens*, Robert Hale, 1953, p. 57.

21   *tench and pike, pearch and eels* – Daniel Defoe, in 1724, quoted in H. C. Darby, *The Draining of the Fens*, Cambridge University Press, Cambridge 1956, 2nd edition, p. 156.

21   *Book-Fish* – see Jennifer Westwood and Jacqueline Simpson, *The Lore of the Land*, Penguin, 2005, p. 60.

22   *great lowland plain* and *harpoon* – Harry Godwin, *Fenland: Its Ancient Past and Uncertain Future*, Cambridge University Press, Cambridge, 1978, p. 25.

28   *aftergrave* – Thomas Browne, 'A Letter to a Friend', *Thomas Browne: The Major Works*, as above, p. 402.

29   Eric Ennion's book: E. A. R. Ennion, *Adventurers Fen*, Herbert Jenkins, 1949. All quotations from Ennion in this chapter are from here. 1st edition 1942, revised 1949.

32   *wrestled for an hour* – see William Yarrell, *A History of British Birds*, John Van Voorst, 1871–4, 4th edition, rev. Alfred Newton

and Howard Saunders, vol. 3, p. 198. The event occurred at about 4 a.m. on a fine June morning.

35   *The only fish that can swim backwards is an eel* – Hilaire Belloc, 'The Sea Wall of the Wash', *Hills and the Sea*, Methuen, 1941, p. 102. First published 1906.

35   *the putrefaction of the earth* – Izaak Walton, *The Compleat Angler*, Dent, 1947, p. 156. 5th edition, 1676.

36   *all those who disobeyed* – Olive Cook, *Cambridgeshire*, Blackie, 1953, pp. 76–7.

38   *out of the ground uprose* – John Milton, *Paradise Lost*, Book VII, 456–74, *Complete Poems*, ed. John Leonard, Penguin, 1998, p. 280. First published 1667, second enlarged edition 1674.

39   *Milton! thou should'st be living at this hour* – William Wordsworth, 'London, 1802', *Selected Poetry*, ed. Nicholas Roe, Penguin, 1992, p. 200.

41   *rigid grid* – Christopher Taylor, *The Cambridgeshire Landscape*, Hodder and Stoughton, 1973, p. 110.

43   *scribbling* and *a tap on the snout* – Arthur Randell, *Fenland Molecatcher*, Routledge and Kegan Paul, 1970, pp. 17 and 34.

43   *hung . . . for traitors* – John Clare, 'Remembrances', *The Oxford Authors: John Clare*, eds Eric Robinson and David Powell, Oxford University Press, Oxford, 1984, pp. 259–60.

45   *the sink of no less than thirteen Counties* – Daniel Defoe, quoted in Dorothy Summers, *The Great Level*, David and Charles, Newton Abbot, 1976, p. 23.

51   *that long-lost, archaic companionship* – Edwin Muir, 'The Horses', *Selected Poems*, ed. Mick Imlah, Faber, 2008, pp. 73–4. Muir's gravestone, the butterfly's rest, is carved with lines from his poem 'Milton': 'his unblended eyes / Saw far and near the fields of Paradise'.

54   *I had a farm in Africa* – Karen Blixen, *Out of Africa*, Penguin, 2001, p. 13. First published 1937.

85   *Here come the Boer, we must hurry away* – quoted in Julia Martin, *A Millimetre of Dust*, Kwela, Cape Town, 2008, p. 41.

On honeyguides see: H. A. Isack and H. – U. Reyer, 'Honeyguides and honey gatherers: interspecific communication in a symbiotic relationship', *Science*, 1989, 243:1343–5. The standard text remains: H. Friedmann, *The Honeyguides*, United States National Museum Bulletin 208, Smithsonian Institution, Washington, DC, 1955. It includes a survey of references to the birds' behaviour in European literature. The earliest was a Portuguese missionary's account in a book called *Ethiopia Oriental*, written in 1569 and printed in 1609: 'when the birds find a beehive they go to the roads in search of men and lead them to the hives, by flying on before them, flapping their wings actively as they go from branch to branch, and giving their harsh cries'. The next observation was also Portuguese. The *Voyage to Abyssinia* was written in 1659, translated into French, and later into English by Samuel Johnson, who was interested in all things Abyssinian: 'the Moroc, or honey-bird [...] is furnished by nature with a peculiar instinct, or faculty of discovering honey. They have here multitudes of bees of various kinds [. . .] some place their honey in hollow trees, others hide it in holes in the ground, which they cover so carefully, that though they are commonly in the highway, they are seldom found, unless by the Moroc's help; which, when he has discovered any honey, repairs immediately to the roadside, and when he sees a traveller, sings and claps his wings; making many motions to invite him to follow him, and when he perceives him coming, flies before him from tree to tree, till he comes to the place where the bees have stored their treasure, and then begins to sing melodiously. The Abyssin takes the honey, without failing to leave part of it for the bird, to reward him for his information.'

86 Thomas Hardy, *Under the Greenwood Tree*, ed. David Wright, Penguin, Harmondsworth, 1986, p. 209.

86 Robert Herrick, 'Corinna's Going a Maying', *Cavalier Poets: Selected Poems*, ed. Thomas Clayton, Oxford University Press, Oxford, 1978, p. 42.

90 *enclosed within the garden's square* – Andrew Marvell, 'The Mower against Gardens', *The Oxford Authors: Andrew Marvell*, eds Frank Kermode and Keith Walker, Oxford University Press, Oxford, 1990, pp. 40–1.

92 *the sleeping green* – Isaac Rosenberg, 'Break of Day in the Trenches', *First World War Poems*, ed. Andrew Motion, Faber, 2003, p. 80.

92 *like autumn corn before the cutter* – anonymous witness quoted in Malcolm Brown, *The Imperial War Museum Book of the Somme*, Pan, London and Basingstoke, 1997, p. 68.

93 *Story about the mole* – Franz Kafka, *Diaries 1910–1923*, ed. Max Brod and trans. Joseph Kresh, Martin Greenberg and Hannah Arendt, Penguin, Harmondsworth, 1972, p. 317.

93 *Does a mole ever get hit* – Edward Thomas, 'War Diary', included in *Collected Poems*, ed. R. George Thomas, Faber, 2004, p. 159.

93 *You see how this world goes* – William Shakespeare, *King Lear*, IV.v.150.

93 *chief organ of sentiment* – John Constable, letter 23 October 1821 quoted in C. R. Leslie, *Memoirs of the Life of John Constable, Composed Chiefly of his Letters*, Phaidon, 1951, p. 85.

95 *an eminent town in the midst of the Level* – Dorothy Summers, as above, p. 71. See also Alan Bloom, 1953, as above, p. 267.

95 On the colony at Manea: Christopher Taylor, as above, p. 204; and www.welney.org.uk and www.utopia-britannica.org.

97 *Wypes* – name for lapwings from 1780, see J. Wentworth Day, *A History of the Fens*, Harrap, 1954, p. 74.

97 *dingy dirty green* – John Clare, 'The Pewit's Nest', cited in Jonathan Bate, *John Clare: A Biography*, Picador, 2004, p. 383.

98   *Moor-lambs* – William Yarrell, as above, vol. 3, p. 344.

98   *Gabhar-athair* – Francesca Greenoak, *All the Birds of the Air*, Penguin, Harmondsworth, 1981, p. 119.

98   *his bump* – John Skelton, 'Philip Sparrow,' line 432, *Selected Poems*, ed. Gerald Hammond, Carcanet, Manchester, 1980, p. 51.

99   *I am in one way better* – William Empson, *Some Versions of Pastoral*, Penguin, Harmondsworth, 1966, p. 19. First published 1935.

99   *pathos of distance* – Friedrich Nietzsche, paragraph 257, *Beyond Good and Evil*, trans. R. J. Hollingdale, Penguin, 2003, p. 192. First published 1886.

100   *[M]y own field* – Hilaire Belloc, 'The Mowing of a Field', *Selected Essays*, ed. J. B. Morton, Penguin, Harmondsworth, 1958, p. 38. All quotations from Belloc in this chapter are from here.

100   *you could have seen me* – D. H. Lawrence, letter to Blanche Jennings, 30 July 1908, *The Letters*, vol. 1, 1901–13, ed. James T. Boulton, Cambridge University Press, Cambridge, 1979, pp. 67–8.

100   *[m]y sheep are thoughts* – Sir Philip Sidney, *The Countess of Pembroke's Arcadia (The Old Arcadia)*, ed. Katherine Duncan-Jones, Oxford University Press, Oxford, 2008, p. 94.

102   *Nature is never journalistic* – W. S. Graham, '[Nature is Never Journalistic]', *Aimed at Nobody*, Faber, 1993, pp. 26–7. The poem continues: 'It does not tell us to tell how / It is faring now.'

104   *Methinks I have a great desire to a bottle of hay* – William Shakespeare, *A Midsummer Night's Dream*, IV.iv.24–5.

105   *Master, our young master!* – Henri Troyat, *Tolstoy*, trans. Nancy Amphoux, Penguin, Harmondsworth, 1970, p. 81.

106   *thinking that he was thinking about what he was thinking about* – John Stewart Collis, *Tolstoy*, Burns and Oates, 1969, p. 15.

106   *The gentleman must be mowed* – J. G. Frazer, *The Golden Bough*, abridged, Macmillan, 1957, vol. 2, p. 566. See also Traffic's 'John Barleycorn (Must Die)' on their 1970 album.

107   *20 April 1858* – Leo Tolstoy, *Tolstoy's Diaries*, trans. and ed. R. F. Christian, Athlone Press, 1985, vol. 1, pp. 150–1. All diary quotations in this chapter are from this two-volume edition.

108   *Bulletin of the Patients of the Yasnaya Polyana Lunatic Asylum* –

quoted in John Stewart Collis, as above, pp. 72 and 86.

108   *lost to literature* – Henri Troyat, as above, p. 265.

114   *Sunk out of knowledge* – Daniel Defoe, *A Tour Through the Whole Island of Great Britain*, ed. and abridged Pat Rogers, Penguin, Harmondsworth, 1971, p. 418.

114   *constant vigilance* – Alan Bloom, 1953, as above, p. 318.

114   *I had almost forgotten Marsh-Earths* – John Evelyn, *Terra: A Philosophical Discourse of Earth*, John Martyn, The Royal Society, 1676, pp. 20–1.

115   *On less competent authority* – John Henry Gurney, *Early Annals of Ornithology*, H. F and G. Witherby, 1921, p. 235.

Buffalo

118   *We use nails to stir the tea* – Wallace Stevens, *British Columbia Journal*, August 1903, in *Letters*, ed. Holly Stevens, University of California Press, Berkeley, 1996, p. 65.

118   *dust scatterers* – quoted in Evan S. Connell, *Son of the Morning Star*, Harper, New York, 1991, p. 86.

119   *Let them eat grass* – Andrew Myrick quoted in Connell, as above, p. 252.

119   *The white people have surrounded me* – Red Cloud, *Our Hearts Fell to the Ground: Plains Indian Views of How the West was Lost*, ed. Colin G. Calloway, Bedford St Martins, Boston and New York, 1996, p. 154.

119   *from the grass roots down* – Custer quoted in Geoffrey C. Ward, *The West: An Illustrated History*, Seven Dials, 1999, p. 292.

119   *I want a sow and a boar* – Red Cloud quoted in Ward, as above, p. 297.

121   *And me they turned inside out* – John Clare, 'The Lament of Swordy Well', *The Oxford Authors: John Clare*, as above, pp. 147–52.

121   *the bosom of a new Atlantic* – James Silk Buckingham, quoted in William Cotter Murray, 'Grass', *American Heritage*, 1968, 19:3.

122   *altered the regimental line of march* – Connell, as above, p. 357.

122   *sang a thunder song* – Connell, as above, p. 320.

123   *a fusillade of pistols* – Richard Manning, *Grasslands*, Viking, New York, 1995, p. 143.

124   *The excitement and heat made our thirst almost maddening* – Lieutenant Edward S. Godfrey, quoted in *Reno-Benteen Entrenchment Trail* guide, Western National Parks Association, 2004, p. 7.

125   *We walked on top of their internals and did not know it in the high grass* – Private John Guthrie, quoted in Connell, as above, p. 130.

125   *sadeh* – translator's note in *The Five Books of Moses*, trans. Robert Alter, Norton, New York, 2004, p. 114.

127   *This was done to improve his hearing* – Connell, as above, p. 422.

127   *double handful* – Connell, as above, p. 344.

127   *When the last stand was made* – Sitting Bull, quoted in David Markson, *Vanishing Point*, Shoemaker and Hoard, Washington, DC, 2004, p. 150.

128   *thousands of dogs* – Ian Frazier, *Great Plains*, Faber, 1990, p. 180.

128   *no longer than a hungry man* – quoted in Ward, as above, p. 302, and Frazier, as above, p. 181.

128   *It was as easy as killing sheep* – Rain quoted in Connell, as above, p. 399.

128   *It was like some Biblical exodus* – Charles Windolph quoted in Connell, as above, pp. 76–7.

129   *disembowelled, with stakes driven through their chests* – survivor Edward Pickard of F troop, quoted in James S. Brust, Brian C. Pohanka and Sandy Barnard, *Where Custer Fell: Photographs of the Little Bighorn Battlefield Then and Now*, University of Oklahoma Press, Norman, 2007, p. 127.

129   *to keep the wolves from digging them up* – Sergeant Ryan quoted in *Where Custer Fell*, as above, p. 129.

130   *A trench was dug* – Lieutenant Charles F. Roe quoted in on interpretation board at Little Bighorn battlefield. See also *Where Custer Fell*, as above.

132   *one of the first permanent structures* and *ghost herder* – *Custer National Cemetery* guide, Western National Parks Association, 2009, p. 6.

134 *saw the whole world* and *they brought back white, greyish earth* – Frazier, as above, p. 42.

135 *We tried to run but they shot us like we were buffalo* – Louise Weasel Bear quoted in Ward, as above, p. 398.

140 Leo Tolstoy, 'How Much Land Does a Man Need', *How Much Land Does A Man Need? and Other Stories*, trans. Ronald Wilks, Penguin, 1993. All quotations are from this edition.

150 Fred E. Miller's photographs are reproduced and his life sketched in *Fred E. Miller: Photographer of the Crows*, ed. Nancy Fields O'Connor, University of Montana and Carnan VidFilm, Missoula and Malibu, 1985.

Summer Fen

153 *Summer* – Coleridge, quoted in *The Charles Lamb Daybook*, Methuen, 1925, p. 135.

154 *a letter 'on the fishes eaten by our Saviour* – Samuel Johnson's 'Life of Browne', in *Thomas Browne: The Major Works*, as above, p. 496.

154 *when, or on what occasion, it was* – Dugdale quoted in Claire Preston, *Thomas Browne and the Writing of Early Modern Science*, Cambridge University Press, Cambridge, 2005, p. 126. I am much in debt to this account of a marvellous man and his mind. Other quotations from the exchange between the two men are from here or from *Sir Thomas Browne: Selected Writings*, ed. Claire Preston, Carcanet, Manchester, 1995.

154 *kild by a greyhound* – Browne quoted in Gurney, as above, p. 203.

155 *that great and true Amphibium* – Thomas Browne, part 1 section 34, *Religio Medici*, *Thomas Browne: The Major Works*, as above, p. 103.

157 *nearly every small grass meadow* – David Lack, *The Birds of Cambridgeshire*, Cambridge Bird Club, Cambridge, 1934, p. 111.

158 *tawny mowers* and other lines – Andrew Marvell, 'Upon Appleton House', *The Oxford Authors: Andrew Marvell*, as above, pp. 53–77.

159   *A sort of living doubt* – John Clare, 'The Landrail', *The Oxford Authors: John Clare*, as above, pp. 233–4.

160   *it is given to them that their sea-longing shall be land-longing* – Ronald Iain, quoted in David Thomson, *The People of the Sea: Celtic Tales of the Seal-Folk*, Edinburgh, Canongate, 2001, p. 175. First published 1954.

162   *level fields / Far from those lovely sights* and *I looked for universal things* – William Wordsworth, Book Third (1850), 94 and 109, *The Prelude*, as above, p. 97.

163   *The wide, wide fens are drear and cold* – James Wentworth Day, *A History of the Fens*, Harrap, 1954, p. 196. All the following quotations from Wentworth Day are from here.

163   *8th March 1852 Fell in with a flock of rare linnets* – quoted in Charles Lucas, *The Fenman's World*, Jarrold, Norwich, 1930, p. 78.

166   Leonard Blomefield, *A Naturalist's Calendar kept at Swaffham Bulbeck, Cambridgeshire*, ed. Francis Darwin, Cambridge University Press, Cambridge, 1922. First published 1903. Written 1846–9. All the following quotations from Blomefield are from here.

167   Georges Perec, *An Attempt at Exhausting a Place in Paris*, trans. Marc Lowenthal, Wakefield Press, Cambridge, Massachusetts, 2010. All the following quotations from Perec are from here.

170   *reading Darwin one admires the beautiful solid case* – Elizabeth Bishop, Letter to Anne Stevenson, 8 January 1964, quoted in Anne Stevenson, *Five Looks at Elizabeth Bishop*, Bloodaxe, Tarset, 2006, p. 82.

171   *live at large, and prey, like pikes* – E. P. Thompson, *Customs in Common*, Penguin, 1993, p. 163.

172   *reeds, fodder, thacks, turves* – Anti-Projector, quoted in H. C. Darby, *The Draining of the Fens*, Cambridge University Press, Cambridge, 1956, 2nd edition, p. 52.

172   *Souls of Sedge* and adjacent lines – Samuel Fortrey (attributed), quoted in Darby, *Draining*, as above, p. 90.

172   *mother* – Alan Bloom, 1953, as above, p. 153.

173   *where wee should be now plowing* – quoted in Dorothy Summers, as above, p. 94.

174 *the water, in time of extremity, may go in a large room* – quoted in Dorothy Summers, as above, p. 71.

176 James Ferguson – I owe his story to Richard Holmes.

176 On swifts and their night flights see: http://jeb.biologists.org/cgi/content/full/205/7/905.

Swallow

186 *The old is dying* – Antonio Gramsci, *Selections from the Prison Notebooks*, trans. and eds Quintin Hoare and Geoffrey Nowell Smith, Lawrence and Wishart, 1971, p. 276.

192 *a dying world, like Mars, but glowing still* – J. A. Baker, *The Peregrine*, Collins, 1967, p. 15.

197 *It was a very warm and sunny day* – Nadezhda Nikolaevna Timoshenko's testimony appeared at www.chernobyl.info. Or did. I would be keen to find where it is now.

198 *They say that one swallow doesn't make a summer* – Leo Tolstoy, 5 October 1893, *Tolstoy's Diaries*, as above, vol. 1, pp. 326–7.

Anders and Tim have published their work and findings in Chernobyl extensively over several years in a series of scientific papers. See: Anders Pape Møller and Timothy A. Mousseau, 'Biological Consequences of Chernobyl: 20 years on', *Trends in Ecology and Evolution*, vol. 21 no. 4, April 2006, pp. 202–7.

Autumn Fen

215 *green seraglio* – Andrew Marvell, 'The Mower against Gardens', *The Oxford Authors: Andrew Marvell*, as above, pp. 40–1.

215 *If a man could pass thro' Paradise* – *Coleridge's Notebooks: A Selection*, ed. Seamus Perry, Oxford University Press, Oxford, p. 127.

215 *I have known a riding horse to be bogged* – Sydney Skertchly, quoted in Dorothy Summers, as above, p. 20.

216   *Roman slave chain* – Charles Lucas, as above, p. 9.

216   *what was once a mighty oak forest* – Alan Bloom, 1953, as above, p. 173. Other following quotations from Alan Bloom are from here or from his earlier book, *The Farm in the Fen*, Faber, 1944.

217   *Moore-logs* – Thomas Browne, 'Hydriotaphia or Urne-Buriall', *Thomas Browne: The Major Works*, as above, p. 287.

217   *unguessable* – James Wentworth Day, as above, p. 78.

217   *the Fen cataclysm* – Charles Lucas, as above, pp. 7–8.

218   *Ne'er an axe was heard to sound* – John Clare, 'The Village Minstrel', cited in OED.

219   *Bacchus stands naked* – K. S. Painter, *The Mildenhall Treasure*, British Museum, 1977, p. 26.

220   *they found the dead, dried and pickled body* – James Wentworth Day, 'The Most English Corner of all England', in *Countryside Mood*, ed. Richard Harman, Blandford, 1943, p. 178.

221   *we found leaves that were still almost green* – Alan Bloom, 1953, as above, pp. 173–4.

222   *suction* – Lord Byron, Canto II, stanza 67, *Don Juan*, eds T. G. Steffan, E. Steffan and W. W. Pratt, Penguin, Harmondsworth, 1978, p. 118.

224   *in the watery places* – John Ray, *Ray's Flora of Cambridgeshire – Catalogus Plantarum circa Cantabrigiam nascentium*, trans. and eds A. H. Ewen and C. T. Prime, Wheldon and Wesley, Hitchin, 1975, p. 88. First published 1660.

224   *mowing marsh* – Harry Godwin, as above, p. 180.

227   *acidicolous mosses and liverworts and ferns* – Harry Godwin, as above, p. 181.

228   *I have long tried to find a student* – J. Stanley Gardiner, ed., 'The Natural History of Wicken Fen, Part VI', Bowes and Bowes, Cambridge, 1932, p. 646.

230   *pitchforked* – see www.jitterbrush.com.

231   *a massive hearty man* – Harry Godwin, as above, p. 45. Other following Godwin quotations are from here.

231,232 *enthusiastically through the densest or wettest of vegetation* and *a landmark in Quaternary research* – see www.jitterbrush.com.

233   *must needs plough the whole field* – John Ray, quoted in Anna Pavord, *The Naming of Names*, Bloomsbury, 2005, p. 389.

234   *long walks of exploration* – John Ray, *Flora*, as above, p. 23. Other following Ray quotations are from here.

On John Ray see also: Tim Birkhead, *The Wisdom of Birds*, Bloomsbury, 2008; David Elliston Allen, *The Naturalist in Britain*, Penguin, Harmondsworth, 1978.

Out Field

237   *in Sovereign Barns to dwell* – Emily Dickinson, poem 379, 'The Grass so little has to do', *The Poems of Emily Dickinson*, ed. R. W. Franklin, Belknapp, Cambridge, Massachusetts, 1999, p. 174.

238   *Ye Highlands and ye Lawlands* – 'The Bonny Earl of Murray', *The Oxford Book of Ballads*, ed. Arthur Quiller-Couch, Oxford University Press, Oxford, 1932, pp. 422–3. See also Five Hand Reel's sung version.

238   *Nay, sure, he's not in hell* – William Shakespeare, *Henry V*, 2.iii.7–18.

238   *Greenfield was the name of the property-man* – Alexander Pope, annotation in *The Dramatick Writings of Will. Shakspere, with the notes of all the various commentators; printed complete from the best editions of Sam. Johnson and Geo. Steevens*, John Bell, 1788, Volume 12.

238   *Almost as soon as I could babble* – Edward Thomas, quoted in introduction, *Selected Poems*, ed. Matthew Hollis, Faber, 2011, p. ix.

239   *he already seemed to feel the flowers growing over him* and *death-warrant* – Joseph Severn talking of Keats, quoted in Stanley Plumly, *Posthumous Keats*, Norton, New York, 2008, pp. 65 and 206.

239   *How astonishingly does the chance of leaving the world* – John Keats, *Letters*, ed. Robert Gittings, Oxford University Press, Oxford, 1977, p. 359.

240   *an organic part of himself* – Rosamund Bartlett, *Tolstoy: A Russian Life*, Profile, 2011, p. 12.

240   *too much in character to be credible* – W. H. Auden, *A Certain World*, Faber, 1982, p. 404.

240   *The memory of your good deeds* – John Stuart Collis, as above, p. 124.

241   *The ideal of Ant-Brothers* – John Stewart Collis, as above, p. 12.

242,243 *Lying where he chose* and *Because he possibly said* – Ian Frazier, as above, pp. 119 and 115.

242   *This is the lodge of Crazy Horse* – Larry McMurtry, *Crazy Horse: A Life*, Penguin, New York, 1999, p. 138.

243   T. H. White, *The Goshawk*, New York Review of Books, New York, 2007. First published 1951. All quotations are from this edition.

243   *mouse-poor* – Robert Graves quoted in David Markson, *The Last Novel*, Shoemaker Hoard, 2007, p. 77.

244   *Clare refused to take anything* – Frederick Martin, quoted in Jonathan Bate, *John Clare: A Biography*, as above, p. 167. Other following quotations from Clare are from here.

250   Nicholas Redman, *Whales' Bones of the British Isles*, Redman Publishing, 2004.

252   Dante, Canto 15, *Inferno*, translated in 1967 by Robert Lowell as 'Brunetto Latini' in *Dante in English*, eds Eric Griffiths and Matthew Reynolds, Penguin, 2005, pp. 373–8. All the following quotations from Dante are Lowell's version.

252   *One does not need to know anything about the race* – T. S. Eliot, 'Dante', *Selected Essays*, Faber, 1972, p. 247.

255   *If you want me again* – Walt Whitman, 'Song of Myself', poem 52, 1855, *Complete Poems*, as above, p. 69.

275   *A blade of grass is always a blade of grass* – Samuel Johnson, recorded by Hester Lynch Piozzi, *Anecdotes of the Late Samuel Johnson*, 1786, quoted in Geoffrey Grigson, *Before the Romantics*, George Routledge, 1946, p. 310.

275   *If I want to write about men* – Albert Camus, from 'Notebook I', *Selected Essays and Notebooks*, trans. and ed. Philip Thody, Penguin, 1979, p. 239.

A Fen Bookshelf

Every fen has its words. My fen chapters draw heavily on the following books, maps and documents. The literature is as deep as the peat and deeper in places. At least one major book is missing from my list. I read Graham Swift's *Waterland* not long after it came out in 1983. I was living in Cambridge and the novel occurred there like weather brought into the city wrapped in the fens to its north. It marked me then, as next to no other modern novel has, going in and staying in. I copied passages from it into my notebooks. In the last few years I deliberately haven't read it again. It was so good I can imagine it easily curtailing other attempts on the fens, raising its own contagious fogs, flooding already drowning minds.

A. K. Astbury, *The Black Fens*, Golden Head Press, Cambridge, 1958.

Dudley Barker, Central Office of Information, *Harvest Home: The Official Story of the Great Floods of 1947 and their Sequel*, HMSO, 1948.

W. H. Barrett, *A Fenman's Story*, Routledge and Kegan Paul, 1966.

W. H. Barrett, *Tales from the Fens*, Routledge and Kegan Paul, 1966.

Trevor Bevis, *Water Water Everywhere*, Trevor Bevis, 1992.

Trevor Bevis, *Flooded Fens*, Trevor Bevis, 2001.

P. M. M. Bircham, *The Birds of Cambridgeshire*, Cambridge University Press, Cambridge, 1989.

Leonard Blomefield, *A Naturalist's Calendar kept at Swaffham Bulbeck, Cambridgeshire*, ed. Francis Darwin, Cambridge University Press, Cambridge, 1922. First published 1903. Written 1846–9. See also Leonard Jenyns.

Alan Bloom, *The Farm in the Fen*, Faber, 1944.

Alan Bloom, *The Fens*, Robert Hale, 1953.

Edward Bond, 'The Fool' in *Plays: 3*, Methuen, 1999. First performed 1975.

British Geological Survey, *Soil and Drift Edition*, 1:50 000 series, Cambridge (sheet 188), 1980, and Ely (sheet 173), 1981.

Mary Chamberlain, *Fenwomen*, Full Circle, Woodbridge, 2011. First published 1975.

Caryl Churchill, 'Fen' in *Plays: 2*, Methuen, 1990. First performed 1983.

Ross Clark, *Cambridgeshire*, Pimlico, 1996.

Olive Cook, *Cambridgeshire*, Blackie, 1953.

H. C. Darby, *Medieval Fenland*, Cambridge University Press, Cambridge, 1940.

H. C. Darby, *The Draining of the Fens*, Cambridge University Press, Cambridge, 1956. 2nd edition.

Anthony Day, *Turf Village*, Cambridgeshire Libraries, 1985.

William Dugdale, *The History of Imbanking and Draining the Fens and Marshes*, W. Wittingham, 1792. First published 1662.

E. A. R. Ennion, *Adventurers Fen*, Herbert Jenkins, 1949. 1st edition 1942, revised 1949.

E. A. R. Ennion, *Cambridgeshire, Huntingdonshire and the Isle of Ely*, Robert Hale, 1951.

John Evelyn, *Terra: A Philosophical Discourse of Earth*, John Martyn, The Royal Society, 1676.

Robin Field, Val Perrin, Louise Bacon and Nick Greatorex-Davies, *The Butterflies of Cambridgeshire*, Butterfly Conservation, 2006.

Laurie Friday, ed., *Wicken Fen: the Making of a Wetland Nature Reserve*, Harley, Colchester, 1997.

J. Stanley Gardiner, ed., 'The Natural History of Wicken Fen, Part VI', Bowes and Bowes, Cambridge, 1932.

Thomas Gibbons, *An Account of a Most Terrible Fire*, James Buckland, 1769.

Harry Godwin, *Fenland: Its Ancient Past and Uncertain Future*, Cambridge University Press, Cambridge, 1978.

John Humphreys, *Hunter's Fen*, David and Charles, Newton Abbot, 1986.

John Humphreys, *Poachers' Tales*, David and Charles, Newton Abbot, 1991.

John Humphreys, *Days and Nights on Hunter's Fen*, David and Charles, Newton Abbot, 1992.

Ernie and Audrey James, *Memoirs of a Fen Tiger*, David and Charles, Newton Abbot, 1986.

M. R. James, *Collected Ghost Stories*, ed. Darryl Jones, Oxford University Press, Oxford, 2011.

Leonard Jenyns, *Fauna Cantabrigiensis*, eds Richard C. Preece and Tim H. Sparks, The Ray Society, 2012.

David Lack, *The Birds of Cambridgeshire*, Cambridge Bird Club, Cambridge, 1934.

G. Lohoar and S. Ballard, 'Turf Digging at Wicken Fen' pamphlet, n.d. (after 1989).

Charles Lucas, *The Fenman's World*, Jarrold, Norwich, 1930.

J. E. Marr and A. E. Shipley, eds, *Handbook to the Natural History of Cambridgeshire*, Cambridge University Press, Cambridge, 1904.

Sybil Marshall, *Fenland Chronicle*, Penguin, 1998. First published 1967.

Arthur Mee, *The King's England: Cambridgeshire*, Hodder and Stoughton, 1965. First published 1937.

K. S. Painter, *The Mildenhall Treasure*, British Museum, 1977.

A. K. Parker and D. Pye, *The Fenland*, David and Charles, Newton Abbot, 1976.

Rowland Parker, *The Common Stream*, Paladin, St Albans, 1976.

Nikolaus Pevsner, *The Buildings of England, Cambridgeshire*, Penguin, Harmondsworth, 1954.

Arthur Randell, *Sixty Years a Fenman*, Routledge and Kegan Paul, 1966.

Arthur Randell, *Fenland Memories*, Routledge and Kegan Paul, 1969.

Arthur Randell, *Fenland Molecatcher*, Routledge and Kegan Paul, 1970.

John Ray, *Ray's Flora of Cambridgeshire – Catalogus Plantarum circa Cantabrigiam nascentium*, trans. and eds A. H. Ewen and C. T. Prime, Wheldon and Wesley, Hitchin, 1975. First published 1660.

P. H. Reaney, *The Place-names of Cambridgeshire and the Isle of Ely*, Cambridge University Press, Cambridge, 1943.

Dorothy L. Sayers, *The Nine Tailors*, New English Library, 2003. First published 1934.

R. S. Seale, *Soils of the Ely District*, Memoirs of the Soil Survey of Great Britain, Harpenden, 1975.

John Seymour, *The Companion Guide to East Anglia*, Collins, 1972.

Rex Sly, *From Punt to Plough*, History Press, Stroud, 2003.

Rex Sly, *Soil in their Souls*, History Press, Stroud, 2010.

Margaret Spufford, 'A Cambridgeshire Community: Chippenham from Settlement to Enclosure', College of Leicester, Dept. of English Local History, Occasional Papers No. 20, 1965, Leicester University Press.

Dorothy Summers, *The Great Level*, David and Charles, Newton Abbot, 1976.

Christopher Taylor, *The Cambridgeshire Landscape*, Hodder and Stoughton, 1973.

Joan Thirsk, 'Fenland Farming in the Sixteenth Century', Dept. of English Local History, Occasional Papers No. 3, 1953, University College of Leicester.

E. P. Thompson, *Customs in Common*, Penguin, 1993.

C. J. R. Thorne and T. J. Bennett, *The Birds of Wicken Fen*, The Wicken Fen Group, Cambridge, 1982.

James Wentworth Day, *Farming Adventure*, Harrap, 1943.

James Wentworth Day, *A History of the Fens*, Harrap, 1954.

B. C. Worssam and J. H. Taylor, *Geology of the Country around Cambridge*, Memoirs of the Geological Survey of Great Britain, HMSO, 1969.

A blade of grass is always a blade of grass, whether in one country or another: let us if we *do* talk, talk about something; men and women are my subjects of enquiry; let us see how these differ from those we have left behind.

Samuel Johnson

If I want to write about men, should I stop talking about the country-side? If the sky or light attract me, shall I forget the eyes or voices of those I love?

Albert Camus

ACKNOWLEDGEMENTS

My thanks, here, to many who helped me find a way, there. In the fens: Prill Barrett and the late Gabriel Horn, Nick and Jan Davies, Laurie Friday, Martin Jenkins, Ade Long, Helen Macdonald, Ben Phalan (whose science challenges all pastoral complacency and who told me about it as he took me boating above the Earth along the lodes at Reach and Burwell), Rose Thorogood, Geoffrey Woollard, assorted anonymous fishermen and vegetable pickers. Ken Arnold, who cycled with me into the fens in the early 1980s, has been the best of friends ever since. The late Eric Ennion painted his fenny way into my heart long before I even knew where the wet places were. The Cambridgeshire Bird Club is a decent outfit. I also gained much from listening to various participants at a CRASSH conference called Communicating Cultural Knowledge of Environmental Change, in Cambridge in January 2011, and from the annual meetings of New Networks for Nature.

In Zambia: Bruce Danckwerts showed me his fields without knowing I was writing them down; Lazaro Hamusikili and Collins Moya followed honeyguides without knowing quite how much I was following them. Deepest thanks to all three. And also to Ian Bruce-Miller (who trusted me with his gun), Emma Bruce-Miller, the late John Colebrook-Robjent, the late Royce Colebrook-Robjent, Mary Counsell, Ailsa and Dan Green, Chris Wood. Troy and Squacky Nicolle have brought the Colebrook-Robjent farm back to life: it is described here as it was not as it is. In Kenya: Grahame Dangerfield and Lyn Munro, Ben Parker. In South Africa: Mark Johnston, Guy and Jay Louw, Gus and Margie Mills, Christopher and Cécile Spottiswoode.

In the United States: Bill Yellowtail was as friendly and generous as is possible and got up to full speed in a matter of minutes. His insights and honesty turned me round. Thanks also to Steve Alexander and other Custer impersonators, Jeremy Harding (who worked out for me why wolves were interesting and why Melville was too), Fraser Harrison (who first showed me how to look at the Great Plains), and Tim McCleary (who opened the Crow up for me). A Society of Authors award was very helpful in allowing me to travel to Montana.

In Ukraine: Tim Mousseau and Anders Pape Møller took me with them on trust into their field site in one of the world's most troubling places and once there were remarkably patient with my stupidities and generous with their intelligence. Earlier and elsewhere in eastern Europe: Rosamund Bartlett, Michael Hofmann, Gerard McBurney, Simon McBurney, Catherine Merridale, the late Ken Smith, George Szirtes, Miklos Zellei, Zinovy Zinik, and Larisa in Yalta. A British Council studentship in the 1980s to Budapest sent me east and I have been grateful for the kick ever since.

Thanks across the time zones and locales: Simon Armitage, Simon Bainbridge, Jeff Barrett and *Caught by the River*, John Berger, Tim Birkhead, Lesley Chamberlain, Robert Chandler, Susannah Clapp, Mark Cocker, Nigel Collar, Sam Collyns and Antonia Byatt, Christopher Cook, Jonathan Davidson, Jenny Dee and Simon Blackwell, Caitlin DeSilvey, William Earp, Paul Farley, Joe Farrell, Will Fiennes, Roy Fisher, Lavinia Greenlaw, Tessa and Eric Hadley, Alexandra Harris, Louise Henson, Matthew Hollis, Richard Holmes, Jonathan Holloway, Kathleen Jamie, Danny Karlin, Andrew Kelly, Richard Kerridge, James Lasdun, Alastair Laurence, Nigel Leask and Evelyn Arizpe, Kim Lochen, Richard Long, Michael and Edna Longley, Hayden Lorimer, the late Derek Lucas (schoolteacher, word-lover, birdwatcher), Richard Mabey and Polly Munro, Robert Macfarlane, Andrew McNeillie and *Archipelago*, Andy Martin, Andrew Motion, Stuart Murray, Jeremy Mynott, Simon Naylor, Jon Nicholls, Joseph Nichols, Tom Nichols, Adam Nicolson and Sarah Raven, Redmond O'Hanlon and the *TLS*, Alice Oswald, Chris and Helen Parker, Ian Parker, David Perry, Greg Poole, the late Peter Reading, Nicholas Redman, Christopher Ricks and Judith Aronson, Alan Ritch and his *Hay in Art* website, Robin Robertson,

Suzanne Rolt, Colin Sackett, Sukhdev Sandhu, Jo Shapcott, Owen Sheers, Christopher Somerville, Lydia Syson, Matt Thompson, Martina Thomson, Mike Walker, Marina Warner, Christopher Woodward.

At the BBC: Mike Burgess, Kate Chaney, Matthew Dodd, Sarah Goodman, Iain Hunter, Sarah Langan, Clare McGinn, Duncan Minshull, Tony Phillips, Ali Serle, Mark Smalley. In the book world: Sarah Ballard, Zoe Pagnamenta, Joe Pickering, Zoe Ross, Ellie Steel, Clara Womersley. Dan Franklin has made me feel plausible and therefore possible. My thanks also to the estate of Mario Giacomelli for granting permission for the use of the cover image: a picture I have had in my head since 1980 and which I am thrilled to be wrapped in.

In Bristol, my sons Dominic and Lucian have kept me down to earth in all the right departments; I wish I hadn't neglected them as much as I did to get this story dug but I love them for reminding me often enough that there is more to life than grass. Their mother, Stephanie Parker, has (again) been generous and big-hearted. She has done more than her share in many ways and I couldn't have written this book without that. My parents, Kate and John Dee, like my boys, have got used to me looming from behind a laptop and have been, as ever, sweet and encouraging as well as suitably hard to impress. My mother taught me to fold laundered bed-linen with her when I was about six. Something of that comes back in this book with its welcoming sheets of green. She also negotiated the plastic grass that started me off, fixed my subscription to *Farmers Weekly*, and recited poetry at me until a few lines stuck. My father, it turns out, might hail from farming stock. That nothing of this has come through our family line has allowed this book. If only a small, unmuddy, portion of his intelligence, his humour, and his appetite for jokes and ideas has rubbed off on me I would be proud.

Claire Spottiswoode made everything come to life that is here. She gave this book its juice and its heart. I have stolen places and people from her; I have tried to capture some off-cuts of her brilliant way of seeing; and, with her, I have walked and talked almost every sodding inch of these fields. She has been superb throughout and continues so.

Close Encounters of Empire

American Encounters/Global Interactions

A Series Edited by Gilbert M. Joseph and Emily S. Rosenberg

Close Encounters of Empire

Writing the Cultural History

of U.S.–Latin American Relations

Edited by Gilbert M. Joseph, Catherine C. LeGrand,

and Ricardo D. Salvatore

With a Foreword by Fernando Coronil

Duke University Press Durham and London

1998

Printed in the United States of America on acid-free paper ∞

Typeset in Times Roman with Fratiger display by Tseng Information Systems, Inc.

Library of Congress Cataloging-in-Publication Data appear

on the last printed page of this book.

This book was published with the assistance of

the Frederick W. Hilles Publications Fund of Yale University.

Frontispiece:

René d'Harnoncourt, *American Artist in Mexico,* 1932.

Gouache. Courtesy of the d'Harnoncourt family.

Photo: Philadelphia Museum of Art.

American Encounters/Global Interactions

A series edited by Gilbert M. Joseph and Emily S. Rosenberg

This series aims to stimulate critical perspectives and fresh interpretive frameworks for scholarship on the history of the imposing global presence of the United States. Its primary concerns include the deployment and contestation of power, the construction and deconstruction of cultural and political borders, the fluid meanings of intercultural encounters, and the complex interplay between the global and the local. *American Encounters* seeks to strengthen dialogue and collaboration between historians of U.S. international relations and area studies specialists.

The series encourages scholarship based on multiarchival historical research. At the same time, it supports a recognition of the representational character of all stories about the past and promotes critical inquiry into issues of subjectivity and narrative. In the process, *American Encounters* strives to understand the context in which meanings related to nations, cultures, and political economy are continually produced, challenged, and reshaped.

Contents

III: Final Reflections

Fernando Coronil

Foreword

A pathbreaking study of U.S.–Latin American relations, *Close Encounters of Empire* is also a landmark of postcolonial studies in the Americas. The product of a conference at Yale University, this unusually coherent collection of essays reflects vigorous collective discussions, painstaking scholarship, and skilled editorial work. While the individual cases examine with sophistication a wide range of imperial encounters in the Americas, the introduction and the two concluding interpretive essays relate the studies to each other and discuss their collective achievements. I will exchange the opportunity to comment further on the case studies for the chance to discuss this volume's theoretical contribution to the broader field of postcolonial studies.

The authors of these essays treat postcolonial encounters in the Americas as complex affairs involving multiple agents, elaborate cultural constructs, and unforeseen outcomes. While evidently inspired by recent developments in social theory associated with cultural and feminist studies, as well as with poststructuralism and postcolonialism, the essays also build on a long tradition of Latin American scholarship on colonialism and imperialism. The book's theoretical importance results from the diverse ways in which its authors establish, often implicitly, a dialogue among these diverse bodies of scholarship.

In the introduction Gil Joseph highlights the significance of this dialogue, noting that the collection is distinguished by the pioneering use of postmodern approaches to the analysis of U.S.–Latin American relations. As Joseph observes, while the essays are informed by a postmodern sensitivity to the formation of subaltern subjects, the ambiguities of power, and the multistranded character of historical processes, they do not abandon a more traditional concern with large-scale historical contexts and overarching political relations. Through the interplay of these approaches, the essays treat the "encounter" between the United States and Latin America as a complex interaction among unequal social actors, illuminating in new ways their modes of cooperation, subjection, and resistance under changing historical conditions.

This collection's engagement with modern and postmodern approaches is also underlined by Rosenberg and Roseberry in the two interpretive essays that close the book. Rosenberg contrasts this volume with studies that take a modernist perspective and emphasizes its affinity with post-colonial theory, postmodern studies of international relations, and culture-centered discussions of U.S. foreign relations. According to her, the recognition of the complexity and ambiguity of power systems has led to studies that reject the positivist conceits of the master narratives of modernism and that opt for the more modest goal of illuminating social reality through partial glimpses, attentiveness to localized context, and sensitivity to multiple stories and protean symbolic systems. For Roseberry, this volume's theoretical significance lies in its ability to draw on new perspectives while building on earlier modes of analysis. Seeking to bridge rather than to reinforce the gap between political economy and cultural studies that underwrites the modern-postmodern divide, Roseberry suggests that we read this book as effecting not so much a shift as a dialogue between these approaches.

Yet Latin America has been largely absent from the internal dialogue that has established the field of postcolonial studies in the metropolitan centers. Readers familiar with this field may be aware that it has been fundamentally defined by work produced about northern European colonialism in Asia and Africa, and that its critique of dominant historiographies (whether imperial, nationalist, or Marxist) has led to a significant reconceptualization of the making and representation of colonial histories (perhaps best exemplified by the scholarship of India's Subaltern Studies Group). However, both postcolonial imperialism and Latin America (as an area of study and as a source of theoretical and empirical work) are fundamentally absent from postcolonial studies' canonical texts. This volume counters both absences.

The inclusion of the Americas expands the historical referents and theoretical scope of postcolonial studies. The Americas encompass a vast territory where, since the end of the fifteenth century, European imperial powers (not only Spain and Portugal but also England, France, Holland, and Germany) have imposed various modalities of colonial control, learned from each other, and transplanted this learning to other regions. It is also the region where the United States has most forcefully practiced new modes of imperial domination as the world's major capitalist power. A lengthy postcolonial history has encouraged Latin American and Caribbean thinkers to confront imperialism's changing forms. From the perspective of the Americas, some of the pitfalls entailed by the *post* of *postcolonialism,* such as the notion that it denotes effective decolonization, are perhaps easier to avoid.

I will treat the encounter between modern and postmodern approaches that informs this collection on postcolonial encounters in the Americas as the opportunity to move beyond the limitations of either approach. The following five propositions, derived from my reading of this book, are but some tentative steps in this direction.

1. *Culture/Political Economy.* While the scholarship on U.S.–Latin American relations has traditionally centered on political economy (largely through works influenced by the dependency perspective), recent studies inspired by postcolonial theory tend to focus on the culture of imperial-subaltern encounters. Yet "political economy" and "culture" are ambiguous theoretical categories that refer both to concrete social domains and to abstract dimensions of any social domain. The traditional focus on political economy entails a neglect not only of domains outside the economy, but also of the cultural dimension of economic practices themselves. In postcolonial studies the current focus on culture has opened new areas of inquiry, yet has tended to neglect the study not only of economic and political relations, but also of the materiality of cultural practices. A recognition that the separation between culture and political economy is itself culturally constructed would help overcome this oversight.

2. *Metanarratives/Ministories.* One consequence of the various "turns" (discursive, linguistic) and "posts" (postmodernism, postcoloniality) has been the tendency to identify political economy with modernist master narratives and cultural studies with postmodern fragmented stories. While one approach typically generates unilinear plots, unified actors, and integrated systems, the other produces multistranded accounts, divided subjects, and fragmented social fields. Yet there is no reason why social analysis should be cast in terms that polarize determinism and contingency, the systemic and the fragmentary. The critique of modernist assumptions should lead to a more critical engagement with history's complexity, not to a proliferation of disjointed vignettes and stories.

3. *Fluid Subjects/Complex Wholes.* The field of postcolonial studies has focused on the range, inner complexity, and fluidity of the subjects and locations involved in imperial encounters. Yet the analytical inclusion of fluid subjects and unstable terrains must be complemented by the analysis of their articulation within encompassing social fields. These fields of power are internally ordered, and their systemic properties have effects that must be analyzed. Fragmentation, ambiguity, and disjuncture are features of complex systems, rather than their opposite. Lest we miss the forest for the trees, the task remains to understand the complex architecture of parts and whole.

4. *Borders/Bodies*. Imperial encounters entail the transcultural inter-action of the domestic and the foreign under changing historical conditions. This process does not involve the movement of discrete entities from one bounded body into another across fixed borders, but rather their reciprocal transformation. The borders between the dominant and the subaltern are multiple—from the physical frontiers that separate them to the "contact zones" where imperial and subaltern actors interact. In imperial-subaltern encounters, bodies and borders are mutually defined and transformed through asymmetrical processes of transculturation.

5. *Imperialism/Subalternity*. Imperial-subaltern encounters occur in social landscapes structured by differing modes of exploiting nature and labor. The social identities formed in these landscapes—constituted by such relations as nationality, class, ethnicity, gender, religion, race, and age—cannot be analyzed without reference to these forms of exploitation. A focus on the complex articulation of these asymmetrical relations avoids reductionist explanations that dismiss culture as a mere epiphenomenon, discursive accounts that disavow the material dimension of domination, and essentialist interpretations that celebrate as resistance any form of subaltern response and adaptation. Studies of specific postcolonial encounters must address the encompassing landscapes of power in which they unfold and the persisting colonizing effects of (post)modern empires.

The Americas have always been a site of unexpected transfigurations. It would be a welcome irony if on the social terrain of the Americas—so saturated by a history of imperialism and by reflections on it—the turn to postmodern discursive approaches converged with or emerged as a material turn, understood as a move toward a fuller recognition of the complex wholeness of social reality. By bringing excluded objects of study into view and refining the way we view them, *Close Encounters of Empire* advances the project of developing a perspective on imperialism capable of confronting its ongoing colonizing effects on territories, peoples, and knowledges. This critical perspective will permit a fuller understanding of the colonial and postcolonial past, as well as more adequate responses to the new forms of subjection and inequality of the ever-changing postcolonial present.

Preface

The idea for this book grew out of a series of discussions among the editors in the spring of 1994. Catherine LeGrand and Ricardo Salvatore were Postdoctoral Fellows in the Program in Agrarian Studies at Yale University, where Gil Joseph directed the Council on Latin American Studies. Each of us had done extensive historical research on problems of Latin American political economy and on the United States' formidable presence in the region. Each of us had also been influenced by the recent cultural and linguistic "turn" in the human sciences. In the wake of the avalanche of cultural history and criticism generated by the five-hundredth anniversary of the so-called Columbian encounter, we found it surprising that little scholarship of a similar nature existed for Latin America's postcolonial (or neocolonial) encounter with the United States during the nineteenth and twentieth centuries. To be sure, exciting work was under way across several fields and disciplines, but the cultural history of U.S.–Latin American relations remained to be written almost in its entirety. As we speculated on why the field's development had been stunted, we came to appreciate the almost total lack of communication that existed between Latin Americanists and historians of U.S. foreign relations who worked on inter-American affairs: rarely did members of the two groups of scholars attend the same professional meetings, let alone collaborate on joint projects.

As our discussions came to include a broader range of Latin Americanists (from north and south of the Rio Grande) and U.S. foreign relations historians, the three of us began to plan a research conference that would unite scholars working on the cultural history of inter-American relations across fields, disciplines, and regions. We hoped to take stock of the more innovative work being done and, hopefully, to set a future agenda for research. Following a year-and-a-half planning process, an international conference, "Rethinking the Postcolonial Encounter: Transnational Perspectives on the Foreign Presence in Latin America," was held at Yale in October 1995, sponsored by the University's Council on Latin American Studies. The event brought together fifty-two established and younger scholars of hemispheric relations: historians, anthropologists, sociologists, political scientists, and cultural and literary scholars; a cast that included North Americans, Latin Americans, Europeans, and one Australian. Four days of intense discussion and debate among this diverse, interdisciplinary cast—one Latin American participant likened the conference's own feisty "encounters" to porcupines making love—expanded and enriched frames of reference and produced a harvest of papers, eight of which have found their way into this volume.

Four-day international conferences are costly affairs. Ours was generously funded by the National Endowment for the Humanities (Conference Grant RX-21583-95), Yale's Office of the Provost, and the Kempf Memorial Fund at Yale. Special thanks go to Associate Provost Arline McCord, for her encouragement of the event from the earliest stages of planning. We are also grateful to Heather Salome, then Senior Administrator of the Council on Latin American Studies, and her assistants, Jonathan Amith, Steve Bachelor, and Delia Patricia Mathews, for ably and cheerfully managing the logistical details of the conference. We also thank the New Haven Colony Historical Society for providing its facilities and services for the working sessions.

Of course, we are particularly indebted to those colleagues whose ideas and energy ensured the success of the 1995 conference, which laid the groundwork for the present volume. Besides the writers whose work appears in these pages, we also wish to thank the following people who contributed research findings and commentaries in New Haven: Ana María Alonso, Warwick Anderson, William Beezley, Jefferson Boyer, Jürgen Buchenau, Avi Chomsky, Marcos Cueto, Emília Viotti da Costa, Julie Franks, Alejandro García Quintanilla, Paul Gootenberg, Donna Guy, John Hart, Timothy Henderson, Robert Holden, Gladys Jiménez-Muñoz, Friedrich Katz, Alan Knight, Agnes Lugo Ortiz, Francine Masiello, Louis Pérez, Daniel Nugent, Gerardo Rénique, Karen Robert, Cristina Rojas de Ferro, Jeffrey Rubin, Kelvin Santiago-Valles, William Schell, Stuart Schwartz, James Scott, Patricia Seed, Doris Sommer, Alexandra Stern, Lynn Stoner, William Taylor, Mauricio Tenorio, and George Yúdice.

The present volume is the product of several years of collaboration among the editors, contributors, and individuals mentioned above. Following the 1995 conference, contributors spent the next year revising their papers. William Roseberry and Emily Rosenberg were each invited to submit shorter concluding reflections; Fernando Coronil was asked to write a foreword; and María Suescun Pozas was asked to do a think piece on the visual arts. Joseph's introductory essay and the contributions by LeGrand, Eileen Findlay, Steven Topik, and Lauren Derby, while written more recently, owe a great deal to the stimulating deliberations in New Haven.

Four final acknowledgments are in order. We are grateful to Yale's Center for International and Area Studies, particularly its two most recent directors, Gaddis Smith and Gustav Ranis, for providing funds that supported much of the editorial and clerical costs attending preparation of the book's manuscript. The Social Science and Humanities Research Council of Canada contributed additional funding. We are indebted to Bill Beezley and Allen Wells for their meticulous readings of the manuscript. Finally, we express our gratitude to Valerie Millholland, our editor at Duke University Press, for her constant encouragement and ability to do the special things that mean so much to editors and authors.

GILBERT M. JOSEPH, CATHERINE C. LEGRAND,
AND RICARDO D. SALVATORE

I: Theoretical Concerns

Gilbert M. Joseph

Close Encounters

Toward a New Cultural History of

U.S.–Latin American Relations

It is a commonplace that Latin American history has been powerfully influenced by foreigners and foreign powers—not least by North Americans
and the United States. Not for nothing do Mexicans refer to their neighbor as the "Northern Colossus" and visit the government's "National
Museum of Interventions" (which showcases invasions of the *patria* by
European powers as well as the United States). Nor is it surprising that
throughout the hemisphere Latin Americans joke sardonically that "When
the United States sneezes [undergoes a recession], *we* get pneumonia [ex-
perience full-blown depression]." Or, that the images Cubans, Chileans,
and Central Americans nurture of North American wealth and corporate
power or CIA plots are invariably dark and larger than life—images codified by some of the hemisphere's most influential writers: José Martí, José
Enrique Rodó, Pablo Neruda, Miguel Angel Asturias, Carlos Fuentes, and
Gabriel García Márquez, to name but a few.[1]

Of course, there are also more benign legacies, heroes, and mytholo-
gies. Fidel Castro quoted Tom Paine and Thomas Jefferson long before he
invoked Lenin, and for a time played baseball as passionately as politics.
Mexican journalists report the strong influence of the U.S. New Left on
the Zapatista leader of Chiapas, Subcomandante Marcos.[2] No world leader
has enjoyed as enduring and popular a cult in Latin America as John F.
Kennedy. The intimidating Northern Colossus is also "El Norte"—"el
otro lado" (the other side)—a sanctuary for Latino immigrants and refugees; a source of insurgent support (e.g., Cuba in the 1890s, 1950s, and
since 1959; and Mexico in the 1910s); and a mecca for tourists and consumers.[3] In short, the U.S. (and broader foreign) presence is varied and
complex, and it has cast a long shadow.[4]

In seeking to understand the influence that North Americans and other
foreigners have had on the region in the post- (or, as some prefer, neo-)
colonial period, Latin Americanists first studied foreign investment and
commercial affairs, diplomacy, and military interventions—and relied
disproportionately on U.S. sources. Not surprisingly, their analyses re-

flected prevailing notions regarding the determining influence of climate, the struggle between "civilization and barbarism," the "challenge" posed by "modernization," the specter of "communist subversion," the deforming legacy of imperialism, and so forth.[5] In the 1960s and 1970s, "dependency theory" held center stage among progressive intelligentsias north and south of the Rio Grande: the structural subordination of Latin America as a periphery within the capitalist world system was held responsible for the "development of underdevelopment," understood primarily in economic terms. Like its neoclassical predecessor, "modernization/diffusionist theory," the predominantly neo-Marxian dependency school emphasized the power and influence of the "developed" world in shaping Latin America, but—as we shall see presently—the two paradigms were diametrically opposed in their interpretation of whether the results were positive or negative.

The Postmodern Challenge

Today, with theories of imperialism and dependency under attack and the once-discredited diffusionist model recycled (yet again) in "neoliberal" form by the managers of the "New World Order,"[6] Latin Americanists across a variety of disciplines and a new generation of historians of U.S. foreign relations (once known as "diplomatic historians") are challenged to study the region's engagement with the United States in innovative ways. New poststructural concerns with the intersection of culture and power, with historical agency, and with the social construction of political life are producing new questions about the nature and outcomes of foreign-local encounters.[7] Turning away from dichotomous political-economic models that see only domination and resistance, exploiters and victims, Latin Americanists (like their counterparts in African, Asian, and European studies)[8] are suggesting alternate ways of conceptualizing the role that U.S. and other foreign actors and agencies have played in the region during the nineteenth and twentieth centuries.[9] At the same time, they are integrating gendered, ethnic, and linguistic analysis in their research designs; challenging the conventional separation of "public" and "private" spheres (and thereby expanding notions of the political); unsettling such seemingly fixed categories as "the state," "the nation," "development," "modernity," and "nature";[10] and in the process rethinking the canon of such traditional genres as diplomatic, business, and military history, and international relations theory.[11]

This volume represents the first systematic attempt to take stock of this exciting watershed and, in the process, to theorize a new interpretive framework for studying the United States' formidable presence in Latin America.[12] Contributors explore a series of power-laden "encounters"— typically, close encounters—through which foreign people, ideas, commodities, and institutions have been received, contested, and appropriated in nineteenth- and twentieth-century Latin America. We should be clear at the outset: our use of the term *encounter* in conceptualizing the range of networks, exchanges, borrowings, behaviors, discourses, and meanings whereby the external became internalized in Latin America should not be construed as a euphemizing device, to defang historical analysis of imperialism. Sadly, in much of the literature on the 1992 Columbian quincentenary, the term performed just this sanitizing function.[13] Equally, it is not our intention to reify "Imperialism," validating Leninist identifications of it as the "highest stage of capitalism," or imposing other teleological conditions for its study.[14]

Rather, we are concerned in this volume with the deployment and contestation of power, with scrutinizing what Mary Louise Pratt refers to as the "contact zones" of the American empire.[15] As these essays vividly demonstrate, U.S. power has been brought to bear unevenly in the region by diverse agents, in a variety of sites and conjunctures, and through diverse transnational arrangements. Forms of power have thus been multiple and complex: simultaneously arranged through nation-states and more informal regional relationships; via business and communications networks and culture industries; through scientific foundations and philanthropic agencies; via imported technologies; and through constructions of nationality, race, ethnicity, gender, and sexuality. Contact zones are not geographic places with stable significations; they may represent attempts at hegemony, but are simultaneously sites of multivocality; of negotiation, borrowing, and exchange; and of redeployment and reversal.

We feel no obligation to rehearse the attenuated debate over whether or not the United States has been an imperial power—a debate that continues to preoccupy U.S. diplomatic historians and American studies scholars. To argue in the manner of George Kennan and subsequent generations of "realists" (and latter-day "postrevisionists") that if the United States *briefly* had an empire in the aftermath of the Spanish-American War, it promptly gave it away; that, therefore, imperialism has always been inconsequential to U.S. history;[16] that, unlike the great powers of Europe, the historical experience of the United States has been characterized by "discovery" not "imperium," "global power" not "imperialism," "unipolarity" not "hegemony" is to perpetuate false notions of "American exceptionalism" and to engage psychologically in denial and projection.[17] Such arguments also ignore structures, practices, and discourses of domination and possession that run throughout U.S. history.[18] A quarter century ago, as the United States' defeat in Vietnam became apparent, the notion that the United States was an imperial power gained wide acceptance; leading politicians like Senator J. William Fulbright openly described the nation's foreign policy as "imperialist." [19] By contrast, today, amid the continuing celebration of the defeat of the Stalinist regimes of Eastern Europe, "you need an electron microscope to find 'imperialism' used to describe the U.S. role in the world." [20]

A provocative recent collection, *The Cultures of United States Imperialism,* edited by American studies scholars Amy Kaplan and Donald Pease, dissects this "ongoing pattern of denial" among U.S. policymakers and academics and seeks to "name" the empire again.[21] The volume's contributors argue compellingly that the politics of U.S. continental and international expansion, conflict, and resistance have shaped the history of American culture just as much as the cultures of those the United States has dominated. The book makes a powerful case for restoring empire to the study of American culture(s) and for incorporating the United States into contemporary discussions of "postcoloniality."

Cultures of United States Imperialism also begins to fill the lacuna that most preoccupies contributors to this volume: the absence of cultural analysis from the overseas history of U.S. expansion and hegemony. The realist school's overriding emphasis on high politics, the balance of power, and national security interests had not gone unchallenged: beginning in the mid-1950s, William Appleman Williams and a subsequent generation of New Left, "revisionist" diplomatic historians called into question realism's paradigm of denial, focusing almost exclusively on the economic determinants of empire. In doing so, however, they neglected the role of culture in the imperial expansion of "America's frontier." [22] Kaplan writes:

> Revisionist emphasis on economic causality may have stemmed in part from the effort to endow imperialism with reality and solidity against the subjective explanations ["moral idealism," "mass hysteria" generated by the yellow press] given by those "realists" who relegated empire to a minor detour in the march of American history. The economic approach, however, embodied its own contradictions, which led to multiple debates among historians . . . about whether the fabled markets . . . were mere "illusions," as opposed to having "real" economic value. If economics is privileged as the site of the "real," then cultural phenomena

such as the belief in markets, or racialist discourse, or the ideology of "benevolent assimilation" can only be viewed as "illusions" that have little impact on a separate and narrowly defined political sphere.[23]

To combat such dichotomized, economistic thinking (which Williams himself would temper in a later volume on "empire as a way of life"),[24] the contributors to *Cultures of United States Imperialism* wrote about "those areas of culture traditionally ignored as long as imperialism was treated as a matter of foreign policy conducted by diplomatic elites or as a matter of economic necessity driven by market forces." [25] Nevertheless, given their predominant orientation as American studies scholars, and literary and cultural critics, the volume's contributors focused overwhelmingly on questions of representation and disproportionately on how U.S. imperialism had influenced or consolidated North American rather than foreign cultures. And although the editors wisely caution against theoretically segregating material and cultural/discursive analysis, the former is largely conspicuous by its absence in this otherwise absorbing volume.

While our project has much to say about the "representational machines" of empire—the technologies and discourses that conveyed empire to audiences back home (see particularly the essays by Salvatore and Poole)—it is more concerned with representation as an integral dimension of imperial encounters "on the ground." Particular attention is given in these essays to a materially grounded, processual analysis of U.S. interaction with Latin American polities, societies, and cultures. The manner in which international relations reciprocally shaped a dominant imperial culture at home, although implicit in several of the essays, is not a central concern here; even less so are the modes by which imperial relations have been contested within the United States. For these matters readers can profitably consult *Cultures of United States Imperialism.*

If terms such as *encounter* or *engagement,* which appear in many of the contributions, are not meant to affirm the neutral notion of social gatherings that much recent scholarly writing has chosen to emphasize, what do they connote? Certainly they designate the connectedness of specific material and discursive interactions in the contact zones of empire; moreover, they are multivalent. On the one hand, they index attempts by people of different "cultures" to enter into relationships that need not deny or obliterate the subjectivity of the other party: efforts to understand, empathize with, approach the other; gestures to establish some type of bond, commitment, or contract. On the other hand, *encounter* and *engagement* also connote contestation and conflict, even military confrontation (not for nothing are these terms synonymous with battles in military parlance). Indeed, the derivation of *encounter* from the Latin is itself instructive: the word fuses *in* ("in") with *contra* ("against").

Thus, these terms designate processes and practices through which the other is rendered proximate or distant, friend or adversary (or some more ambiguous, ambivalent status), practices that entail mutual constructions and misunderstandings—the recourse to "othering" and "orientalizing" that is inherent in power-laden contexts.[26] Our emphasis on close encounters in Latin American contact zones—or, as Bill Roseberry prefers in his contribution, diverse "social fields"—suggests interactions that are usually fraught with inequality and conflict, if not coercion, but *also* with interactive, improvisational possibilities. Such a perspective, according to Pratt, treats imperial relations "not in terms of separateness and apartheid, but in terms of copresence, interaction, interlocking understandings and practices." [27]

It should be clear that, without wanting to be canonic in our understanding of "culture," this volume's contributors work within a broad Gramscian tradition, examining the links between culture and power. If pressed for a portmanteau concept, we might define culture as the symbols and meanings embedded in the daily practices of elite and subaltern (or foreign and local) groups, but with the proviso that such a definition is not intended to rigidly specify what the contents of those symbols and meanings are—a static, reifying exercise at best. Rather, our definition would underscore their processual nature, and insist that both elite/foreign and popular/local understandings are constantly being refashioned. At once "socially constituted (it is a product of present and past activity) and socially constituting (it is part of the meaningful context in which activity takes place)," [28] culture—popular or elite, local or foreign—never represents an autonomous, authentic, and bounded domain. Instead, popular and elite (or local and foreign) cultures are produced in relation to each other through a dialectic of engagement that takes place in contexts of unequal power and entails reciprocal borrowings, expropriations, and transformations. Throughout this volume, the reader will encounter cultural practices and institutions such as music, art, literature, folklore, mass media, leisure pastimes, and spectacle; she will also find herself immersed in the broader cultural realm of aspirations, beliefs, values, attitudes, tastes, and habits. But if the manifestations of inter-American culture are many and diverse, their history is always interwoven with political intentions and consequences.[29]

This book's contributors include historians and anthropologists from the United States, Canada, and Latin America. An effort has been made to introduce senior scholars in the fields of Latin American studies and the history of U.S. foreign relations to each other, as well as to members of a newer generation in these fields. Moreover, in order to facilitate discussion between Latin Americanists and scholars working on similar problems elsewhere, the book is structured in the form of a dialogue between more general theoretical and comparative statements (in the introductory and concluding sections) and Latin American case studies based on recent research (in the volume's extensive middle section).

No single volume can adequately cover the waterfront—in this case, a veritable universe of multiform imperial engagements that have occupied the Americas over two centuries. We have sought to feature instructive and absorbing cases representing mainland and circum-Caribbean areas, and to include Brazil as well as Spanish America. If the Caribbean basin and Mexico receive proportionately greater attention, it is because, owing to propinquity, they remained the principal theaters of North American geopolitical and economic concern, and were most thoroughly inscribed with imperial power and influence. Not surprisingly, these areas have generated some of the most innovative scholarship, particularly work that contributes to a new cultural history of U.S.–Latin American relations.

The reader will also note that the editors have chosen to emphasize the period roughly before 1945, although several of the essays extend their chronological focus beyond World War II, some right up to the present (e.g., the contributions by Joseph, Stern, LeGrand, Klubock, Fein, Derby, Rosenberg, Roseberry, and Suescun Pozas). Clearly, the globalization of the planet, stunningly reflected in the internationalization of capital, labor, commodities, and cultural flows that has accelerated in recent decades, merits numerous volumes of its own. Nevertheless, we believe that the conceptual framework elaborated here will usefully inform such a sequel.

In this introductory essay, I first "unpack" the most influential political-economic models that Latin Americanist scholars and policymakers have employed over the last several decades to make sense of inter-American relations. To what extent do such paradigms usefully address the historical dynamics of foreign involvement in Latin America? In what respects are they deficient? I then go on to suggest how the initiative represented in this volume expands our understanding of the foreign-local encounter in Latin America.[30]

Confronting and Unpacking Historical Paradigms

Confrontation with major paradigms of world history has distinguished the field of Latin American history during the last quarter century or so.[31] Starting in the late 1960s and early 1970s, a dissident generation of social scientists began to challenge prevailing diffusionist models of development with various renditions of dependency and world-systems theory.[32] It is instructive to deconstruct these paradigms and examine the assumptions they share as well as their points of disagreement. After all, the new interdisciplinary scholarship has questioned many of these assumptions in rethinking foreign-local encounters in Latin America.

The once and future diffusionist model is based on a persistent belief that "development" — or, interchangeably, "modernization" — comes about as a result of the penetration of technology, capital, trade, democratic political institutions, and attitudes from the "developed" into the "developing" countries of the world.[33] Its proponents further assume that developing countries are themselves "dual societies" divided into a "lagging" rural sector and a "modernizing" capitalist urban sector. Just as the modernization of a developing country comes about through the diffusion of capital and ideas from developed nations, so the modernization of the lagging rural areas of the developing country comes about through the penetration of capital and ideas from its own dynamic urban centers (often referred to as "growth poles"). Thus, agents and agencies of development from the modern capitalist countries, working closely with the growing "middle class" in the receiving society, incrementally facilitate a closing of the gap, not only between developed and developing countries, but also between modern and lagging sectors of the developing nation itself.[34]

Early modernization theory, epitomized by W. W. Rostow's influential book *The Stages of Economic Growth* (1960), emphasized the cultural and psychological obstacles to growth (e.g., an ingrained fatalism), prescribing that underdeveloped countries needed only to follow the steps traversed by developed nations. The early models were additive: essentially, they postulated that merely by adding technology and capital, underdeveloped societies would progress. Later diffusionists, such as S. N. Eisenstadt, were less sanguine about surefire, unilinear solutions. They placed far greater emphasis on internal *structural* obstacles to change, particularly the syndromes of "internal colonialism" (the dominance of primate cities over poor hinterlands) and "the vicious cycle of poverty." Nevertheless, like the early theorists, they maintained an abiding belief in foreign aid and investment, open trade, export production, and technology transfer.[35]

Leftist critics of "modernization" have proposed a variety of "dissident paradigms"—new formulations of imperialism, dependency theory, and world-systems theory—which essentially stand diffusionism on its head. Although a nuanced analysis of these various alternative paradigms of development cannot be elaborated here,[36] two broad initial observations are in order. On one level, these dissident approaches have collectively administered a telling blow to the doctrine of modernization: "economic growth," "transnational integration," and "democratization" have repeatedly been accompanied by national disintegration; the growth of an exploited, marginal mass has superseded the creation or maintenance of a dynamic and prosperous middle class.[37] On a more fundamental, epistemological level, however, these dissident paradigms, despite their powerful, often compelling linkage of Latin American inequities to world-scale political-economic structures and forces, have frequently replicated the same dichotomized, bounded view of foreign-local engagement and the same penchant for teleology that undermined diffusionism.[38]

New theorists of "imperialism," for example, focus on the U.S. (or European) center's penetration of the Latin American periphery. Imperialism's main branches are held to be political, military, and economic; secondarily it involved the inexorable transfer—indeed, virtual imposition—of a kind of cultural compost, the so-called American way of life. Concerned mainly with the question of uneven power relations between nation-states and with the tensions created by exports of capital to social formations that were in a less "advanced" state of development, this view has presented the growing and multifaceted connection between the United States and Latin America as a relationship between two distinct political entities and two economies. American businessmen, diplomats, and military personnel abroad are typically portrayed as instruments of an alliance between capital and the state to conquer markets, tap cheap sources of raw materials, and consolidate an asymmetrical relationship of power.[39]

In similar fashion, dependency and world-systems models take off from a series of inequalities located in international trade and finance. They then proceed to map out a complex network of relationships by means of which local governments, ruling elites, political parties, and institutions in civil society have become involved in the reproduction of a structural condition—"dependency"—that prevented the "peripheral" countries of the region from achieving the levels of development of the northern "metropolis" or "core." While less tied to notions of the metropolis's expansion or "spillover" into the periphery than theories of imperialism (or "revisionist" U.S. diplomatic historians), dependency formulations have retained the central idea of "penetration"; this time, however, the vehicle of penetration was an ensemble of U.S. capital, technology, and culture.[40] The rationale of the capitalist system remained the same: the reproduction of a highly skewed pattern of accumulation that rewarded the productivity of the North via the exploitation and impoverishment of the South. Now, however, local actors were implicated in the relationship from the start: accomplices, or "compradors," in an "infrastructure of dependence" that drained resources and creativity, reduced the sphere of liberty, and reproduced the syndrome of poverty.[41]

Thus, the master narrative of "dependency," like that of "imperialism," has presupposed a bipolar relationship that subsumed difference (regional, class, racial/ethnic, gender, generational) into the service of a greater machinery that set limits, extracted surpluses, established hierarchies, and shaped identities. Both narratives have depicted the United States (or the "core" nations of the world-system) at the controls of a great "neocolonial" enterprise, managing a stream of flows unified by the logic of profits, power, and a single hegemonic culture. From the center flowed commodities; capital; technology; cultural artifacts; and military power, equipment, and expertise—in order to reproduce more of the same. In the periphery, these narratives often suggested, there were only forces and agents that abetted or constrained these flows. Nations were frequently personified and gendered: each had its own national interest and manly persona, and acted in compliance with it or betrayed it, depending on the degree to which dependency had advanced. Of course, by imagining national entities motivated almost exclusively by economic interest, *dependentistas* challenged the self-loathing notion, first preached by nineteenth-century elites, that the "national character" was culturally incapable of economic modernization: too indolent, improvident, and unsavvy to be a serious contender in the race for "progress." [42] Nevertheless, this one-dimensional perspective of "comprador elites" had the effect of redefining locals as foreigners, and preempted the examination of other relations, shared assumptions, and emotional and other affinities between foreign agents and local elites.[43]

The politics of resistance to imperialism and dependency was similarly encoded in the analysis: the only other option to collaboration with the capitalist system was rejection of it. For many, the only alternative to liberal modernizing reform, the only pathway to an economically balanced, socially just form of development, was socialist revolution.[44] The demonology of the imperialist other was extended not only to North American corporations, policymakers, and military agents, but also to cultural brokers and institutions of higher learning. It was from U.S. universities, after all, that the new "modernizing" (read *colonizing*) impulse seemed to have emerged; therefore, in the mid-1960s, university professors, librarians, and foundation workers were charged with constituting the new imperialist front. Walt Rostow himself was publicly attacked, charged with being a CIA agent.[45] In a 1965 conference in Mexico, organized by Andre Gunder Frank and Arturo Bonilla, one-hundred professional economists from Latin America pledged allegiance to a new program that would revamp the research and teaching agendas of economics. The signatories denounced the subordination of the region's economists to advances in "the Anglo-Saxon countries" and pledged to base their inquiry not on "an alien reality," but "on the historical experience and present-day reality of Latin America." [46] (How times have changed!)

Ironically, while many exponents of these dissident paradigms advocated revolutionary change, they conceived of two types of neocolonial subjects, neither of which was empowered to resist. For if local elites were judged to be implicated in the dependent relationship, willing members of a comprador class, then impoverished peasants and urban masses were viewed as displaced subjects, less a part of history than its victims. They waited on the sidelines for the transformative social project (and vanguard) that would initiate them into the adventure of development.

Finally, the economism of dissident paradigms relegated culture to a subsidiary role.[47] Since the comprador bourgeoisie lacked a true consciousness, their interests and tastes were essentially those of metropolitan capital, not their own. In their criticism of local elites, dependentistas constructed mediating agents who lacked real agency. It is not surprising, therefore, that the imposition of the "American way of life" became an instrumentalist corollary of the exportation of certain commodities, culture industries, forms of social relations, and technologies (e.g., Coca-Cola, Donald Duck and Disney's Magic Kingdom, radio and television, factory and *maquila* systems, "mall culture," and so forth).[48]

Writing the History of Foreign-Local Encounter

The contributors to this volume call into question several of the monochromatic assumptions of the dissident paradigms: the centripetal nature of imperialism and dependency, which risks conceiving of Latin America solely as "peripheral societies," intelligible only in terms of the impact that center nations have on them;[49] the idea of penetration; the reflexive indictments of complicity; the bipolarity of the North-South relationship; and the subsidiary role accorded to culture. Whereas theories of dependency, imperialism, and the world-system—like diffusionism—promote dichotomies that centralize and reify political-economic structures and processes, and ignore culturally embedded human subjects, we strive to "decenter" analysis, break down reifications, and restore agency to the historical narrative.

Nevertheless, our purpose in this volume is not to reject these dissident paradigms out of hand, substituting cultural analysis for structural analysis. To do so would be to indulge in the same dichotomizing we have been critical of—a process that unfortunately has witnessed the ranking of different areas of knowledge in the academy and also has underwritten the kind of mind/body, reason/nature, masculine/feminine, civilization/barbarism distinctions woven into legitimizing discourses of empire.[50] In this sense, our intention is not so much to elaborate a new paradigm as to acknowledge a heterogeneity and complementarity of approaches. By endorsing "crosstalk" between political economists and cultural critics, we might be able to supplement historical structuralism's attention to the blending of social theory and power with poststructuralism's abiding concern with questions of contingency, representation, and difference.[51]

In entertaining such a synthesis, it is useful to keep in mind that the fundamental suggestion to explore the diverse historical combinations whereby the external has been internalized in Latin America comes from Fernando Henrique Cardoso and Enzo Faletto's classic dependency text, *Dependencia y desarrollo*.[52] That dependency theorists have rarely embraced their empirical agenda, rarely specified through fine-grained research either the complex alliances of dependency or the culturally embedded social fields in which they were situated, does not invalidate Cardoso and Faletto's original insight. Indeed, in *Dependencia y desarrollo* and a select group of dependentista historical monographs, we gain real insight into how foreign influences and powers were "imbricated in the formation of *local* class relations," and how "rather than acting like puppets on a string [manipulated by omnipotent foreigners] . . . these local classes pursued particular interests . . . [and] constructed local political institutions and webs of power." [53]

At the same time, even more nuanced dependency formulations have epistemological deficiencies. Cultural critics point out, for example, that even as dependentistas criticized "alien" social science models and demanded solutions based on an "authentic Latin American reality," they were blind to their own textuality. In other words, they never questioned the received "evidence" they pressed into service from popular national history texts, never confronted these "facts" with other interpretations or alternative periodizations. Much less did they problematize the "making" of national history itself; indeed, in the 1960s and early 1970s, Latin American historiography had not yet experienced the shocks of "history from the bottom up," microhistory, gender studies, cultural studies, and deconstruction. For Cardoso and Faletto, Latin America's history was essentially "the history of capitalist accumulation," a "history of struggles, of political movements, of the affirmation of ideologies, and of the establishment of forms of domination and reactions against them." [54]

The contributors to the present volume have all been deeply influenced by dependency theory and world-systems approaches; indeed, in many cases the essays build on and refine these perspectives, rather than jettison them (see particularly the chapters by Stern, Schroeder, Klubock, Fein, and Roseberry). How, then, is this accomplished? How do we at once validate the unequal nature of Latin America's encounter with the United States and write a history that is culturally sensitive, multivocal, and interactive? We might first deconstruct this multiform engagement into its various components: for example, its business, philanthropic, textual, and aesthetic practices; its multiple agents and mediators (who invariably had multiple identities); its institutional and ideological bases of support. We can then begin to reinterpret the foreign-local encounter in a manner that takes into account, among other things, political and cultural processes of resistance, adaptation, and negotiation; the role of the state; the construction and transformation of identities; and the contingent nature ("intertextuality") of evidence. These essays examine a variety of sites or contact zones where ideologies, technologies, capital flows, state forms, social identities, and material culture meet, and where multiple messages are conveyed. Viewed as a series of communicative exchanges in which "insiders" and "outsiders" engage, act on, and represent each other, the relationships between Latin Americans and North Americans become multifaceted and multivocal.[55]

Such a perspective allows us to distinguish, say, the experiences of U.S. diplomats with local dictators from those of North American marines in contact with local *caciques,* merchants, and prostitutes (see Roorda's and Schroeder's essays in this volume); to differentiate the assumptions

and goals of U.S. labor organizers from those of the executives of multinational corporations or representatives of philanthropic organizations
(see Palmer's essay).[56] It also challenges us to rethink facile juxtaposi-
tions of "us" and "them," of "foreign" and "local." For example, a recent study of the North American colony at the turn of the century in
Mexico argues persuasively that as Mexicans were "Americanized," so
too were Americans "Mexicanized." In the process they became "integral outsiders" whose identities and interests often mirrored those of their
Mexican counterparts of the same class, and frequently put them at odds
with Washington's geopolitics.[57] In his recent novel *Four Hands,* Mexican writer Paco Ignacio Taibo II similarly underscores the permeability
of linguistic and national borders. He imaginatively recreates the labyrinth of networks and associations that bound U.S. and Latin American
leftists together throughout this century, enabling them to fight injustice
and endure decades of lost causes. In this context we also think of Mauricio Tenorio-Trillo's recent essays on "los Coyoacanes y los Nuevayores":
the community of nomadic, counterhegemonic intellectuals that operated with equal facility in Mexico City and New York during the 1920s
and 1930s—a set that included Diego Rivera, Frida Kahlo, Tina Modotti,
Edward Weston, Bertram and Ella Wolfe, Frank Tannenbaum, and Joseph
Freeman, among others.[58] Sociologist Christian Smith's recent anatomy
of the transnational interfaith community that established "Witness for
Peace" and the sanctuary movement during the height of the Nicaraguan Contra War and the insurrection in El Salvador in the 1980s raises
similar issues from the perspective of religious workers and "citizen diplomacy." [59]

   This blurring of boundaries, of who or what is "local" and "foreign,"
"inside" or "outside," characterizes contemporary critical theory across
a variety of fields; it also distinguishes most of the contributions in this
volume. Far from representing pristine, autonomous cultures moving directly into contact, like billiard balls striking each other on a felt-covered
table—and therefore easily identifiable as "internal" and "external"—
ideas, institutions, and other cultural and economic forms are more often
the messy sediments of previous exchanges. As such, they might more
meaningfully be viewed as *transcultural* products that mutually constitute,
at any point in time, the "local" and the "foreign." [60] In this regard, anthropologist Sherry Ortner writes, "Pieces of reality, however much borrowed from or imposed by others, are woven together through the logic
of a group's own locally and historically evolved bricolage." [61] Cultural
geographer Doreen Massey provides an instructive illustration:

While [it] is in some sense true [that a Kentucky Fried Chicken franchise in Paris does not qualify as part of a French national identity] it is also important to remember that the national identity of which Kentucky Fried Chicken is not part was itself formed over centuries by layer upon layer of interconnections with the world beyond what was to become France. Some of the elements which are now as obviously French as Kentucky Fried Chicken is not must once have seemed just as "alien," similarly imported from the global beyond.[62]

In similar fashion, these essays point up the shaping power that local milieus exercised on foreign actors, ideas, institutions, and commodities. Time and again, "foreign influences are introduced within preexisting social and cultural relations that reconfigure and localize or situate the foreign." [63] Catherine LeGrand, for example, forces us to rethink just how foreign and "closed" the United Fruit Company's banana enclave was in Santa Marta, Colombia (the export zone treated in García Márquez's *One Hundred Years of Solitude*). In no way did the advent of the *bananera* signify a complete break with the past: the enclave's boundaries were porous; the company had to function within a context of local social networks, practices, and meanings. LeGrand obliges us to think of enclaves as dynamic places with their own historical traditions—albeit traditions that undergo reconstruction during and after "the foreign time."

Seth Fein conflates conventional notions of "cultural imperialism" and "cultural nationalism" in Cold War Mexico. He provides an analysis of the day-to-day collaboration between U.S. and Mexican cultural workers, specifically film crews doing rural extension work with Disney and other short films on proper citizenship and modern hygiene. The collaboration was so well integrated that it becomes difficult to determine where one state project began and the other ended.

Lauren Derby raises a number of ironies in her analysis of the uproar provoked in recent years in the Dominican Republic by so-called gringo chickens. This was the local term for poultry grown in high-yield factories by domestic entrepreneurs. Rumors circulated that these chickens were riddled with worms, caused AIDS, robbed men of their potency or turned them into homosexuals, and brought infertility to women. Derby suggests that the gringo chicken became a lightning rod for controversy because it symbolized the ambivalence of national identity on the island. It mediated the nexus between foreign and homegrown, between cash and patio crops, money and morality, the United States and the Dominican Republic. Originally from North America, the gringo chicken is white and eats imported feed; nevertheless, it lives on the island and is raised by Dominican producers. In effect, the controversial bird crystallizes a dilemma every *dominicano* faces today: namely, what is "Dominican" in a context in which the national has been so interpenetrated by the foreign over the last several hundred years? Derby asks: "Where does national identity reside when U.S. firms own and control great expanses of land, beach, and property on the island and, moreover, when almost as many Dominicans live in New York City as in their own capital?"

Thus, the essays in this volume showcase historical subjects and experiences either neglected or treated in truncated fashion in diffusionist and dependency formulations. They reveal that in addition to the formidable flows of financial capital, direct investment, commodity trade, technology transfer, and military power and assistance, other currents and individuals—acting (and being acted on) as cultural mediators rather than crude instruments—shaped a dynamic, multistranded encounter between Latin Americans and North Americans. The power relations attending such mediations may have been asymmetrical, but communication typically flowed both ways and often had unintended, paradoxical consequences.[64]

Steven Palmer's essay on the Rockefeller Foundation's anti-hookworm mission in Costa Rica provides a rich example. Whatever imperial motives the foundation's directors may have harbored, the Rockefeller mission ultimately strengthened and expanded the reach of the Costa Rican state and provided resources and methods that fomented a sense of nationalism among the rural populace. In a time of fiscal crisis, the personnel and funds of empire were redirected by some of Costa Rica's leading anti-imperialist intellectuals to give a healthy boost to local initiatives in public health and public education, and to overwhelm oligarchical opposition to state-led reform.[65]

The volume's contributors also offer recent empirical research that examines the imperial aesthetic of explorers and visual artists (Poole); the cult of the airplane and other technological "spectacles" promoted by imperial impresarios and private diplomats without portfolio (Roorda and Topik); the intercultural mediations of filmmakers; and the introduction of "the movies" and other new patterns of leisure and consumption (Fein, Klubock, and Derby).[66] Each of these "flows" presented a distinct theater of interaction, a particular medium of communication, a variety of actors stating diverse sets of claims.[67] Mutual constructions ("othering"), borrowings, misunderstandings, and oppositions emerged from these interactions and were recorded under specific forms of representation.

Understanding these communications (and the gendered, racial, and class relations of power embedded in them) is a precondition for a reconceptualization of the foreign-local encounter.[68] It is a task of interpretation that requires close readings and attention to both the details of engagement and the contingent textualities and visual regimes that convey them to us. Such an intellectual project obviously also entails a search for new sources as well as a reconsideration of more standard ones. In this spirit, the book's contributors have drawn on oral histories, folk traditions, travel accounts, works of literature and art, political cartoons, popular music and humor, photographic albums, recipe books, film archives, radio and television programs, and public monuments and architecture—in addition to institutional minutes and reports, criminal court cases, official and personal correspondence, and the mainstream and alternative press.

Much more, of course, remains to be done. Latin Americanists might benefit from recent attempts by Asianists to understand how local elites and subaltern groups internalize foreign influences.[69] Changes in cultural orientation and habits of consumption tell us a great deal about the cultural history of these groups' relationships to Europe and the United States. For example, what constituted the "Grand Tour" for Latino elites? When did New York, Washington, Los Angeles, and Miami begin to replace the great centers of Europe on their sons' and daughters' itineraries? What languages did elites insist their children learn from their tutors, and in what order—and when did that order change? What comparable shifts occurred in patterns of foreign schooling? Did a local education ever confer the same cultural capital? Did a "national pilgrimage" ever come to compete with an international one as a mark of civilization and cultural consumption? What art did local elites choose to hang on their walls; which foreign novels and works of poetry did they prefer (and demand to have translated by their publishing houses)? Indeed, each elite home was a kind of archaeological site in which things were acquired and displayed— such as tapestries, silver, china, furniture, and items of dress. In excavating these sites, we can track the cultural commitments, affiliations, and identities of elites, documenting foreign "cultural occupation" of "sovereign" national landscapes with far greater precision.

Similar "cultural digs" might be undertaken for middle-class intelligentsias, working classes, and peasantries. James Scott reports that the Malay village household is a rich archaeological site: one important index is the dramatic changes that have taken place over the last quarter century in the style of calendars that hang on each family's walls. Through labor and religious migrations, wars, and economic dislocations, Asian peasants may have become more mobile and cosmopolitan than elites. Their map of the world can be reconstructed through the calendars, photos, mimeographed prayer sheets, cassette tapes, items of clothing, modest bits of household crockery, and architectural styles that they bring back from their foreign travels and fashion into their cultural repertoires.[70] Given Latin America's similar structural position in the world economy, particularly its recent record of hemispheric migration, and given similar efforts by Latin American states to make such household changes "legible" — through refined property surveys, censuses, and tax lists — Scott's insights merit serious investigation by Latin Americanists.[71]

One useful window onto Latino migrants' encounter with El Norte over several generations is the Mexican genre of humble religious paintings known as *retablos* or *ex-votos*. Painted on small sheets of tin, these brightly colored offerings represent the fulfillment of promises to a holy image of Christ, the Virgin, or a Mexican saint who has interceded on a particular migrant's behalf at a critical or threatening moment. Retablos document the joys, successes, privations, sorrows, and devotions that are emblematic of a new transnational culture born of international movement. Frequently they are displayed in the church sanctuary taped or pinned to photographs, medical paraphernalia, diplomas, examination results, drivers' licenses, and copies of immigration credentials recently obtained in the United States.[72]

Of course, the cultural venturesomeness of North American and other foreign travelers might also profitably be investigated in the realm of material culture. The "enormous vogue of things Mexican" among U.S. artists, intellectuals, and activists in the 1920s and 1930s, for example, played itself out on one level in a "discovery" of aspects of Mexico's "authentic" popular culture. Rustic and indigenous songs and dances, folk cuisine and handicrafts, the idiosyncratic murals painted on cantina walls, "primitive" retablos, children's art, and the evocative woodcuts of Mexican revolutionary artisan José Guadalupe Posada generated a powerful, romantic appeal among waves of "revolutionary tourists" disaffected with the excesses of U.S. capitalist society and modernity itself.[73] The new Mexican revolutionary state did what it could to promote these imperial desires, eager to perpetuate notions of a primordial, authentic, Mexican rural culture of which it was the legitimate custodian and beneficiary.[74]

Seeking to understand the foreign-local encounter in the manner undertaken in this volume entails the risk of multiplying endlessly the types of agents/authors and practices involved, the kinds of statements uttered, and the forms of engagement (e.g., borrowing, negotiation, "offstage" resistance, lip service, overt confrontation, and so forth). (Suggestions for mitigating this problem will be discussed presently.)[75] The benefits of such an approach, on the other hand, are to reposition "culture" (*integrated with political economy*) at the center of the foreign-local encounter, to improve our understanding of the workings of ideology and discourse in relation to power, and to produce a more diversified narrative of Latin American responses to the formidable structures and agencies of North American power. By examining the textual, visual, ritual, even theatrical dimensions of these engagements (see particularly the chapters by Poole, Topik, Roorda, LeGrand, and Derby),[76] we will be able to transcend the compartmentalized, structuralist views of inter-American relations often provided by scholars and policymakers.[77] Within the statements that narrate the multiple encounters of North Americans with their southern neighbors, we are likely to find arguments that connect the economic, political, social, and cultural imperatives of a given relation of power. Read with different underlying assumptions by different groups of "outsiders" and "insiders," these statements figure importantly as raw materials in the construction of relations of domination, resistance, collaboration, and negotiation. They also figure in the creation of antagonistic, symbiotic, or merely incongruous hybrid identities.[78]

A project such as ours faces at least three major challenges. First, there is the obvious need to locate these discrete encounters within a broader historical context of hemispheric and international affairs, state formation, and societal transformation.[79] Much as we might object to conceptualizing the foreign presence according to procrustean or teleological structural models, we must recognize that interactions between "outsiders" and "insiders" took place within boundaries shaped by the international system, capitalist expansion, and related sociopolitical phenomena (e.g., racial discrimination, sexual oppression, and authoritarian rule—or more hegemonic forms of the state).[80] In turn, such encounters shaped or reinforced larger structures and relationships. (A particularly good illustration of this is Fein's pioneering essay on how mobile film units—representing both the United States Information Service and the Mexican PRI—participated in everyday forms of interstate formation during the Cold War.) Attentiveness to the production of subjectivities and ideologies within the micro contexts *and* macro constructs postulated by social science theorists—such as the factory system, "Fordism," the rise of the multinational corporation and "mass consumer society," and, more recently, the restructuring of economic conditions based on high technology in electronics and information ("post-Fordism")[81]—should provide the basis for more nuanced periodizations of the history of U.S.–Latin American relations.[82]

Second, even as we historicize and decenter the foreign-local encounter, we must also trace out the broader patternings of power. What were the unifying elements in the vast array of statements about "us" and the "other"; about "America's mission" on the one hand, and the duty of Latin Americans to defend "Nuestra América" on the other? In particular, we might inquire into the seeming "necessity" for North Americans, alternately, to intervene, survey, display, civilize, contain, reform, democratize, and integrate Latin America. Finding the common denominators encoded in the discourse of (and about) diplomats and "money doctors";[83] soldiers and mercenaries;[84] businessmen;[85] advertisers and tourist promoters;[86] prison reformers;[87] architects and urban and rural planners;[88] world's fair organizers;[89] geographers; anthropologists; eugenicists, scientists, and physicians;[90] foundation directors and philanthropists;[91] missionaries;[92] journalists;[93] and travelers and adventurers[94]—the guiding cultural/ideological assumptions or imperatives—will refine our understanding of a critical substrate of "imperialism" and "dependency": the arrangement of ways of perceiving, visualizing, speaking to, and disciplining the other that lies at the core of all these asymmetrical relationships.[95]

Third, we need to connect these "cultural imperatives" with the process of social conflict generated by foreign-local encounters. Among other things, we need to know to what extent the resistance and intellectual and social renovation that emerged from these encounters served to transform or reinforce prevailing ideologies, strategies, and identities.[96] In a real sense, our project seeks a better cultural understanding of the contested processes of "development" and "modernity." These processes are most often studied from the top down, by focusing on development and globalizing policies orchestrated in concert by foreign and domestic elites.[97] This volume also explores the historical capacity of popular political cultures to articulate challenges and frame alternative proposals to official modernizing schemes.[98] These challenges could resonate throughout the world system, not least locally in the construction of new, often empowering, collective identities, as the chapters by Findlay, Schroeder, LeGrand, Klubock, and Derby demonstrate. Here and elsewhere in this volume, a reassessment of U.S. power and presence in Latin America obliges us to endorse Gabriel García Márquez's plea in his Nobel acceptance speech for a recognition of the region's "outsized reality." [99]

Notes

Special thanks go to my coeditors, Catherine LeGrand and Ricardo Salvatore, and to Allen Wells, Seth Fein, Michael Hunt, Emily Rosenberg, Jürgen Buchenau, William Schell, Patricia Pessar, Eric Van Young, Eric Zolov, and Agustín Laó-Montos, for bibliographic suggestions, insights, and criticisms that substantially improved this text. I am also grateful to the Woodrow Wilson International Center for Scholars, whose fellowship supported the research and writing of this essay.

1. José Martí, *Inside the Monster: Writings on the United States and American Imperialism,* trans. Elinor Randall (New York: Monthly Review Press, 1975); idem, *Our America: Writings on Latin America and the Struggle for Cuban Independence,* trans. Elinor Randall (New York: Monthly Review Press, 1977); José Enrique Rodó, *Ariel,* trans. Margaret Sayers Peden (Austin: University of Texas Press, 1988); Pablo Neruda, *Canto general* (General song), trans. Jack Schmidt (Berkeley and Los Angeles: University of California Press, 1991), esp. the selections "La United Fruit Co." and "Los abogados del dólar" (The dollar's lawyers); Miguel Angel Asturias's "banana trilogy" (published in English by New York's Delacorte Press; all volumes translated by Gregory Rabassa): *The Green Pope* (1971), *Strong Wind* (1968), and *The Eyes of the Interred* (1973); Carlos Fuentes, *The Death of Artemio Cruz,* trans. Alfred MacAdam (New York: Farrar, Straus and Giroux, 1991); and Gabriel García Márquez, *One Hundred Years of Solitude,* trans. Gregory Rabassa (New York: Harper and Row, 1970). For a provocative discussion of García Márquez's portrayal of the North American banana enclave in coastal Colombia, see LeGrand's essay in this volume.

2. For example, Fidel invoked Jefferson, Thomas Paine, and the Founding Fathers in his now classic trial defense speech in 1953, *History Will Absolve Me,* bilingual ed. (New York: Center for Cuban Studies, n.d.), 63–64; Alma Guillermoprieto, "Mexico: The Watershed Years" (lecture presented at Yale University, New Haven, Conn., 20 Nov. 1996).

3. Witness, for example, Anna Thomas and Gregory Nava's film "El Norte" (1983), which employs touches of magical realism to poignantly evoke the allure of the United States for two refugees fleeing the horrors of military repression in highland Guatemala. Also see Patricia R. Pessar, *A Visa for a Dream: Dominicans in the United States* (Boston: Allyn and Bacon, 1995). For an absorbing discussion of the tensions and contradictions generated in one U.S. city by these multiple realities and representations, see Alejandro Portes and Alex Stepick, *City on the Edge: The Transformation of Miami* (Berkeley and Los Angeles: University of California Press, 1993).

4. For a celebrated view of Latino ambivalence toward the United States, see Carlos Rangel, *Latin Americans: Their Love-Hate Relationship with the United States* (New York: Harcourt, Brace, 1977); cf. "U.S.-Mexico Wrangle: Closeness Breeds Friction," *New York Times,* 5 May 1997, 1.

5. See, e.g., Mark T. Gilderhus, "Presidential Address. Founding Father:

Samuel Flagg Bemis and the Study of U.S.–Latin American Relations," *Diplomatic History* 21 (winter 1997): 1–13. The literature is vast: this introductory essay is necessarily rather selective and focuses on trends since the mid-1960s. For three useful, comprehensive surveys that approach the field from extremely different methodological (and ideological) positions and examine (mostly North American) scholarship and attitudes since the nineteenth century, see Fredrick B. Pike, *The United States and Latin America: Myths and Stereotypes of Civilization and Nature* (Austin: University of Texas Press, 1992); Mark T. Berger, *Under Northern Eyes: Latin American Studies and U.S. Hegemony in the Americas, 1898–1990* (Bloomington: Indiana University Press, 1995); and James William Park, *Latin American Underdevelopment: A History of Perspectives in the United States, 1870–1965* (Baton Rouge: Louisiana State University Press, 1995). Also see John J. Johnson, *Latin America in Caricature* (Austin: University of Texas Press, 1980), for an exploration of more than a century (1860s to 1980) of hemispheric relations through political cartoons from leading U.S. periodicals; and George Black, *The Good Neighbor: How the United States Wrote the History of Central America and the Caribbean* (New York: Pantheon, 1988), another treasure trove of cartoon (and photographic) images that effectively punctuate the author's sardonic critique of U.S. imperialism. Two serviceable historiographical essays on U.S. relations with Latin America by diplomatic historians are Richard V. Salisbury, "Good Neighbors? The United States and Latin America in the Twentieth Century," in *American Foreign Relations: A Historiographical Review,* ed. Gerald K. Haines and J. Samuel Walker (Westport, Conn.: Greenwood Press, 1981); and Mark T. Gilderhus, "An Emerging Synthesis? U.S.–Latin American Relations since the Second World War," in *America in the World: The Historiography of American Foreign Relations since 1941,* ed. Michael J. Hogan (New York: Cambridge University Press, 1995), 424–61.

6. See, e.g., the special issue on "Liberalism's Revival and Latin American Studies" in *Latin American Perspectives,* 24, no. 1 (January 1997); and Michael Monteón, " 'Oh, Mama, Is This the End?' Chilean History and the Dependency Perspective: A Reflection on the Current Literature" (paper presented at the University of California Latin American History Conference, Riverside, Feb. 1997). For the onslaught against dependency theory within the academy, see Stephen H. Haber's introductory chapter in *How Latin America Fell Behind: Essays on the Economic Histories of Brazil and Mexico,* ed. Stephen H. Haber (Stanford, Calif.: Stanford University Press, 1997), and his more strident review essay, "The Worst of Both Worlds: The New Cultural History of Mexico," *Mexican Studies* 13, no. 2 (summer 1997): 363–83.

7. Amid the confusion of "exploded paradigms" and the rejection of "metanarratives" and "foundationalist discourses," some scholars have wondered whether we have taken refuge in less theoretically adorned history. Does this reflect a receding faith in social science methodology or merely a shift in attention to more culturally relevant themes and methods—or a bit of both? Recent studies that

wrestle provocatively with these questions are Robert F. Berkhofer, *Beyond the Great Story: History as Text and Discourse* (Cambridge, Mass.: Harvard University Press, Belknap Press, 1995); Jay O'Brien and William Roseberry, eds., *Golden Ages, Dark Ages: Imagining the Past in Anthropology and History* (Berkeley and Los Angeles: University of California Press, 1991); and Frederick Cooper et al., *Confronting Historical Paradigms: Peasants, Labor, and the Capitalist World System in Africa and Latin America* (Madison: University of Wisconsin Press, 1993); also see Florencia E. Mallon, "The Promise and Dilemma of Subaltern Studies: Perspectives from Latin American History," *American Historical Review* 99 (Dec. 1995): 1491–515.

8. See, e.g., Frederick Cooper and Ann Stoler, eds., "Tensions of Empire," special issue of *American Ethnologist* 16 (1989); Cooper et al., *Confronting Historical Paradigms;* Hans Rogger, "Amerikanizm and the Economic Development of Russia," *Comparative Studies in Society and History* 23 (July 1981): 382–420; Reinhold Wagnleitner, "The Irony of American Culture Abroad: Austria and the Cold War," in *Recasting America: Culture and Politics in the Age of the Cold War,* ed. Lary May (Chicago: University of Chicago Press, 1989), 285–301; Wagnleitner, *The Coca-Colonization of the Cold War: The United States Cultural Mission in Austria after the Second World War* (Chapel Hill: University of North Carolina Press, 1994); Richard Kuisel, *Seducing the French: The Dilemma of Americanization* (Berkeley and Los Angeles: University of California Press, 1993); and Rob Kroes, *If You've Seen One You've Seen the Mall: Europeans and American Mass Culture* (Urbana: University of Illinois Press, 1996).

9. Among the pioneering works that have influenced contributors to this volume, see Mary Louise Pratt, *Imperial Eyes: Travel Writing and Transculturation* (New York: Routledge, 1992); Amy Kaplan and Donald E. Pease, eds., *Cultures of United States Imperialism* (Durham, N.C.: Duke University Press, 1993); Daniel Nugent, ed., *Rural Revolt in Mexico and U.S. Intervention,* rev. ed. (Durham, N.C.: Duke University Press, 1998); and the essays by Emily S. Rosenberg ("Walking the Borders") and Michael Hunt ("Ideology") in *Explaining the History of American Foreign Relations,* ed. Michael J. Hogan and Thomas G. Paterson (New York: Cambridge University Press, 1991), much of which was originally published as "A Round Table: Explaining the History of American Foreign Relations," *Journal of American History* 77, no. 1 (June 1990): 93–180.

10. See, e.g., Gilbert M. Joseph and Daniel Nugent, eds., *Everyday Forms of State Formation: Revolution and the Negotiation of Rule in Modern Mexico* (Durham, N.C.: Duke University Press, 1994); Fernando Coronil, *The Magical State: Nature, Money, and Modernity in Venezuela* (Chicago: University of Chicago Press, 1997); Enrique Dussel, "Eurocentrism and Modernity (Introduction to the Frankfurt Lectures)," *boundary 2* 20, no. 3 (1993): 65–76; and Arturo Escobar, *Encountering Development: The Making and Unmaking of the Third World* (Princeton, N.J.: Princeton University Press, 1995).

11. In addition to the essays in this volume and the works cited in nn. 7–10, see,

e.g., Charles S. Maier, "Marking Time: The Historiography of International Relations," in *The Past before Us: Contemporary Historical Writing in the United States,* ed. Michael Kammen (Ithaca, N.Y.: Cornell University Press, 1980), 355–87; Charles R. Lilley and Michael Hunt, "On Social History, the State, and Foreign Relations: Commentary on the Cosmopolitan Connection," *Diplomatic History* 11 (summer 1987): 246–50; Sally Marks, "The World According to Washington," *Diplomatic History* 11 (summer 1987): 265–82; Akira Iriye, "The Internationalization of History," *American Historical Review* 94 (Feb. 1989): 1–10; Cynthia Enloe, *Bananas, Beaches, and Bases: Making Feminist Sense of International Politics* (Berkeley and Los Angeles: University of California Press, 1989); Rosemary Foot, "Where Are the Women? The Gender Dimension in the Study of International Relations," *Diplomatic History* 14 (fall 1990): 615–22; Michael Hunt, "Internationalizing U.S. Diplomatic History: A Practical Agenda," *Diplomatic History* 15 (winter 1991): 1–12; idem, "The Long Crisis in Diplomatic History: Coming to Closure," *Diplomatic History* 16 (winter 1992): 115–40; "Culture, Gender, and Foreign Policy: A Symposium," *Diplomatic History* 18 (winter 1994): 47–124 (esp. Emily Rosenberg's essay, " 'Foreign Affairs' after World War II: Connecting Sexual and International Politics," 59–70, and Amy Kaplan's commentary, "Domesticating Foreign Policy," 97–105); Jürgen Buchenau, *In the Shadow of the Giant: The Making of Mexico's Central American Policy, 1876–1930* (Tuscaloosa: University of Alabama Press, 1996); Kyle Longley, "Internationalizing the Teaching of United States Foreign Relations," *Perspectives* (American Historical Association Newsletter) 34 (Nov. 1996): 24–26, 30, 34; Lester D. Langley and Thomas Schoonover, *The Banana Men: American Mercenaries and Entrepreneurs in Central America, 1880–1930* (Lexington: University Press of Kentucky, 1995); Thomas F. O'Brien, *The Revolutionary Mission: American Enterprise in Latin America, 1900–1945* (New York: Cambridge University Press, 1996); Thomas Schoonover, " 'The Big and the Small of It': Perspective in Latin American–U.S. Business Relations," *Diplomatic History,* forthcoming; James G. Crawford, "Cross-Cultural Encounter and Entanglement: U.S. Soldiers in Philippine Society, 1898–1902" (paper presented at the Latin American Studies Association Meeting, Atlanta, 1994); Jeffrey Stark, "Against Parsimony: Post-positivist International Relations Theory and the Redefinition of Security," manuscript (published in Portuguese in *Contexto Internacional* [Rio de Janeiro] 15, no. 1 [Jan.–June 1993]); Jim George, *Discourses of Global Politics: A Critical (Re)Introduction to International Relations* (Boulder, Colo.: Lynne Rienner, 1994); Christine Sylvester, *Feminist Theory and International Relations in a Postmodern Era* (Cambridge: Cambridge University Press, 1994); the special section edited by Craig N. Murphy and Cristina Rojas de Ferro on "The Power of Representation in International Political Economy," in *Review of International Political Economy* 2 (winter 1995): 63–183; and Roxanne Lynn Doty, *Imperial Encounters: The Politics of Representation in North-South Relations* (Minneapolis: University of Minnesota Press, 1996). Also see four papers presented at the Oct. 1995 Yale conference "Rethinking the Post-colonial Encounter": Louis A. Pérez, "The Invention of Identity: A Century of the Cuban–North American Encounter" (which provides the outline of a multi-volume project in progress); K. Lynn Stoner, "Beauty, National Identity, and the Cuban Representation of Self, 1910–1920"; Donna J. Guy, "The Pan American Child Congresses, 1916–1963: Forging Multiple Pan Americanisms, Genders, and Relations between Family and the State in Latin America"; and Francine Masiello, "Gender Traffic: Women, Culture, and Identity Politics in This Neoliberal Age." Finally, see Lester D. Langley, *America and the Americas: The United States in the Western Hemisphere* (Athens: University of Georgia Press, 1989), which inaugurated a series of volumes dedicated to providing a new, culturally informed history of inter-American relations: e.g., Brenda Gayle Plummer, *Haiti and the United States: The Psychological Moment* (Athens: University of Georgia Press, 1992). For demurrers to the new scholarly trends, see Stephen G. Rabe, "Marching Ahead (Slowly): The Historiography of Inter-American Relations," *Diplomatic History* 13 (summer 1989): 297–316; Alexander DeConde, "Essay and Reflection: On the Nature of International History," *International History Review* 10 (May 1988): 282–301; and the symposium on diplomatic history and international relations theory, in *International Security* 22, no. 1 (summer 1997): 5–85.

12. The Yale conference, "Rethinking the Postcolonial Encounter: Transnational Perspectives on the Foreign Presence in Latin America," which inspired the present volume, included several papers on British and German involvement in the region. Nevertheless, owing to space limitations and a desire to achieve greater coherence, this volume focuses explicitly on the United States's presence in Latin America. Two broadly conceived essays from the October 1995 conference that provide a useful comparative dimension are Friedrich Katz, "Germany and Latin America until 1945," and Alan Knight, "British Imperialism in Latin America."

13. Marvin Lunenfeld, *1492: Discovery, Invasion, Encounter: Sources and Interpretations* (Lexington, Mass.: D.C. Heath and Company, 1991), esp. xv–xvii.

14. Cf. the lively forum of commentary and debate (mostly among "new diplomatic historians") on "Imperialism: A Useful Category of Analysis?" in the *Radical History Review* 57 (fall 1993): 1–84. The contributions by Marilyn B. Young (33–37), Linda Carty (38–45), Prasnegit Duara (60–64), and Emily Rosenberg (82–84) most closely approximate the nonreductionist, culturally informed perspective on imperialism represented in this volume.

15. Pratt, *Imperial Eyes,* esp. 6–7, and "Arts of the Contact Zone," *Profession* 91 (1991): 33–39.

16. Thus, Samuel Flagg Bemis, the dean of an earlier generation of realist diplomatic historians, devoted a chapter of his popular textbook, *A Diplomatic History of the United States,* 5th ed. (1936; New York: Holt, Rinehart, and Winston, 1965), 463–75, to "The Great Aberration of 1898." For Bemis, imperialism represented nothing more than "adolescent irresponsibility" (475); "historically ill-fitting,"

it would be "purged" long before the era of the Good Neighbor policy (Bemis, *The Latin-American Policy of the United States: An Historical Interpretation* [1943; New York: Norton, 1967], 356).

17. The classic "realist" statement is found in George F. Kennan, *American Diplomacy, 1900–1950* (Chicago: University of Chicago Press, 1951); for further discussion of "realism"/"postrevisionism" and its legacy, see Norman A. Graebner, *America as a World Power: A Realist Appraisal from Wilson to Reagan* (Wilmington, Del.: Scholarly Resources, 1984); Hogan and Paterson, *Explaining the History of American Foreign Relations*, esp. Stephen Pelz's and Melvyn Leffler's respective essays on "Balance of Power" and "National Security"; Hogan, *America in the World*, esp. the essays and commentaries by Hogan, Leffler, Bruce Cumings, and Michael Hunt in pt. 1; Seth Fein, "Hollywood and United States–Mexico Relations in the Golden Age of Mexican Cinema" (Ph.D. diss., University of Texas at Austin, 1996), chap. 1; and Emily Rosenberg's contribution to this volume. For the cultural studies critique quoted here, see Amy Kaplan, " 'Left Alone with America': The Absence of Empire in the Study of American Culture," in Kaplan and Pease, *Cultures of United States Imperialism*, 3–21 (quotations, 13). On the enduring grip of "American exceptionalism," see Ian Tyrell, "American Exceptionalism in an Age of International History," *American Historical Review* 96 (Oct. 1991): 1031–55; for strategies to overcome it in the classroom, see Carl J. Guarneri, "Out of Its Shell: Internationalizing the Teaching of United States History," *Perspectives* 35 (Feb. 1997): 1, 5–8.

18. E. J. Hobsbawm, for example, observes that while "colonial possessions have not been a significant element in [U.S. imperialism,] . . . unlike the British who abandoned political and military interventions in the 'informal' empire (e.g., Latin America in the nineteenth century), the U.S. since the nineteenth century has combined 'informal' hegemony with political control or at least the exclusion of rivals, and when necessary a military presence: first in the Caribbean area, then in the Pacific, and after 1945 worldwide" (Hobsbawm, "Addressing the Questions," *Radical History Review* 57 [fall 1993]: 73–75 [quotation, 73]). Cf. Peter H. Smith, *Talons of the Eagle: Dynamics of U.S.-Latin American Relations* (New York: Oxford University Press, 1996), esp. 7–9; and Marilyn B. Young, "Ne Plus Ultra Imperialism," *Radical History Review* 57 (fall 1993): 33–37, which repeats the rhetorical question first posed by William Appleman Williams in 1980: "Can you even imagine America as not an empire?" (36).

19. For example, see Robert W. Tucker, *Nation or Empire? The Debate over American Foreign Policy* (Baltimore, Md.: Johns Hopkins University Press, 1968).

20. Bruce Cumings, "Global Realm with No Limit, Global Realm with No Name," *Radical History Review* 57 (fall 1993): 46–59 (quotation, 47).

21. Kaplan, "Left Alone with America," 11; cf. Donald E. Pease, "New Perspectives on U.S. Culture and Imperialism," in the same volume, 22–37; Cumings, "Global Realm with No Limit," and idem, "Revising Postrevisionism, or, The Poverty of Theory in Diplomatic History," in Hogan, *America in the World*, 20–

62. For striking recent examples of such academic denial, see John Lewis Gaddis, *The Long Peace: Inquiries into the History of the Cold War* (New York: Oxford University Press, 1987); and Tony Smith, *America's Mission: The United States and the Worldwide Struggle for Democracy in the Twentieth Century* (Princeton, N.J.: Princeton University Press/Twentieth Century Fund, 1994). Cf. Gaddis's earlier receptivity to the notion of "U.S. imperialism," in the atmosphere that followed the Vietnam War: see "The Emerging Post-revisionist Synthesis on the Origins of the Cold War," *Diplomatic History* 7 (summer 1983): 171–90. In a more recent statement, his 1992 presidential address to the Society for Historians of American Foreign Relations, Gaddis granted that the United States had practiced hegemony and empire during the Cold War, but contrasted America's "open and relaxed form of hegemony" and "empire of invitation" with the Soviet Union's closed and repressive imperialism ("The Tragedy of Cold War History," *Diplomatic History* 17 [winter 1993]: 1–16 [quotations, 3–4]).

22. The classic statements of "revisionism" are William Appleman Williams, "The Frontier Thesis and American Foreign Policy," *Pacific Historical Review* 24 (Nov. 1955): 379–95; and idem, *The Tragedy of American Diplomacy,* 2d rev. and enlarged ed. (1959; New York: Dell, 1972). For a discussion of the long-running debates between revisionists and their realist and postrevisionist critics, see Paul M. Buhle and Edward Rice-Maximin, *William Appleman Williams: The Tragedy of Empire* (New York: Routledge, 1995); and Cumings, "Revising Post-revisionism." For one revisionist's swipe at cultural studies, see Bruce Kuklick, "Confessions of an Intransigent Revisionist about Cultural Studies," *Diplomatic History* 18 (winter 1994): 121–24.

23. Kaplan, " 'Left Alone with America,' " 13–14.

24. William Appleman Williams, *Empire as a Way of Life: An Essay on the Causes and Character of America's Present Predicament along with a Few Thoughts about an Alternative* (New York: Oxford University Press, 1980).

25. Kaplan, " 'Left Alone with America,' " 14. It should be noted that in the late 1970s and 1980s, diplomatic historians began to contribute works on the cultural dimensions of U.S. foreign relations: e.g., see Emily S. Rosenberg, *Spreading the American Dream: American Economic and Cultural Expansion, 1890–1945* (New York: Hill and Wang, 1982); Frank A. Ninkovich, *The Diplomacy of Ideas: U.S. Foreign Policy and Cultural Relations, 1938–1950* (Cambridge: Cambridge University Press, 1981); Frank Costigliola, *Awkward Dominion: American Political, Economic, and Cultural Relations with Europe, 1919–1933* (Ithaca, N.Y.: Cornell University Press, 1984); J. Manuel Espinosa, *Inter-American Beginnings of U.S. Cultural Diplomacy, 1936–1948* (Washington, D.C.: U.S. Department of State, 1976); Gerald K. Haines, "Under the Eagle's Wing: The Franklin Roosevelt Administration Forges an American Hemisphere," *Diplomatic History* 1 (fall 1977): 373–88; and idem, *The Americanization of Brazil: A Study of U.S. Cold War Diplomacy in the Third World, 1945–1954* (Wilmington, Del.: Scholarly Resources, 1989); cf. the agenda advanced in Kinley Brauer, "The Great American Desert

Revisited: Recent Literature and Prospects for the Study of American Foreign Relations, 1815–61," *Diplomatic History* 13 (summer 1989): 395–417. Nevertheless, although these writers expanded the scholarly agenda by focusing on the distribution of U.S. ideas, images, propaganda, and forms of entertainment, they tended to treat culture as a form of foreign policy, and to examine the manner in which diplomacy abetted the commercial and ideological penetration of American culture abroad. Such studies "presupposed the Americanization of the world (i.e., American culture simply by its presence in another country had an impact). They neither examined the quality of impact nor its limits and unintended consequences. These shortcomings were implicit in the focus of this type of work on U.S. policy rather than the reception—in political and economic or sociocultural terms—in the host nations and societies. . . . [Such studies] tended to focus only on the U.S. government's role in promoting distribution rather than [on] the media [themselves]; they ignored questions of . . . representation. . . . Such studies broadened the range of issues studied by diplomatic history more than they deepened its conceptualization." Fein, "Hollywood and United States–Mexico Relations," 7; cf. Claudio González-Chiaramonte, "American Cultural Diplomacy, Argentine Nationalism, and the Quest for a New Inter-American Community of Scholars" (paper presented at the Annual Meeting of the American Historical Association, New York, 1997).

26. The classic text on such practices is Edward W. Said, *Orientalism* (New York: Viking Books, 1978); see Nicholas Thomas, *Colonialism's Culture: Anthropology, Travel, and Government* (Princeton, N.J.: Princeton University Press, 1994), for a review of the prodigious discussion Said's book triggered. For valuable treatments of "othering" in different regional contexts, see Kelvin Santiago-Valles, *"Subject People" and Colonial Discourses: Economic Transformation and Social Disorder in Puerto Rico, 1898–1947* (Albany: State University of New York Press, 1994); Richard Drinnon, *Facing West: The Metaphysics of Indian Hating and Empire-Building* (New York: New American Library, 1980); John Dower, *War without Mercy: Race and Power in the Pacific War* (New York: Pantheon, 1986); Henry Louis Gates Jr., ed., *"Race," Writing, and Difference* (Chicago: University of Chicago Press, 1986); Catherine A. Lutz and Jane L. Collins, *Reading National Geographic* (Chicago: University of Chicago Press, 1993); and Matthew Jacobson, *Barbarian Virtues: The United States Confronts Foreign Powers and Peoples, 1876–1914* (New York: Hill and Wang, forthcoming).

27. Pratt, *Imperial Eyes,* 7; cf. anthropologists Martha Kaplan and John Kelly's notion of colonial "zones of transcourse," where contending discourses operate within a "dialogic space." "Rethinking Resistance: Dialogics of 'Disaffection' in Colonial Fiji," *American Ethnologist* 21 (Feb. 1994): 123–51; also see Benjamin Orlove, "Mapping Reeds and Reading Maps: The Politics of Representation in Lake Titicaca," *American Ethnologist* 18 (Feb. 1991): 3–38. All of these studies effectively shed light on the complex mixture of cultural dynamics in situations of power, particularly in imperial and colonial contexts.

28. William Roseberry, *Anthropologies and Histories: Essays in Culture, History, and Political Economy* (New Brunswick, N.J.: Rutgers University Press, 1989), 42.

29. Cf. the similar formulations of culture in Gilbert M. Joseph and Daniel Nugent, "Popular Culture and State Formation in Revolutionary Mexico," in Joseph and Nugent, *Everyday Forms of State Formation,* 3–23; Néstor García Canclini, "Culture and Power: The State of Research," *Media, Culture, and Society* 10 (1988): 467–97; Stuart Hall, "Notes on Deconstructing 'The Popular,'" in *People's History and Socialist Theory,* ed. Raphael Samuel (London: Routledge and Kegan Paul, 1981), 227–40; and David A. Whisnant, *Rascally Signs in Sacred Places: The Politics of Culture in Nicaragua* (Chapel Hill: University of North Carolina Press, 1995), esp. chap. 1.

30. The reader will note that many of the contributors to this volume are leery of using terms such as *postcolonial, postcoloniality,* or *postcolonial encounter.* This is not because they object to the decentering of history; the emphasis on hybrid, transnational identities; or the critique of teleological models and linear time that postcolonial theory espouses. On the contrary, many of the essays reflect just these sensibilities. Nevertheless, they also appreciate the pitfalls attending the use of such terms to indicate anything more than the period following Spanish or Portuguese imperial rule. References to "the postcolonial," in Anne McClintock's words, "may too readily license a panoptic tendency to view the globe through generic abstractions void of . . . nuance." Moreover, "the historical rupture suggested by the prefix post- belies both the continuities and discontinuities of power that have shaped the legacies of the formal European . . . empires." Important political and ideological differences *between* and *within* societies are elided, subordinated to their temporal distance from European colonialism. (Regarding these differences, see Stern's essay in this volume.) Finally, such terms are prematurely celebratory: when we consider the manner in which the region now confronts the colonizing of its markets, media, and cultures under the New World Order—see the chapters by Klubock and Derby—there may be little "post" about colonialism! For all these reasons, most contributors use the more neutral designation *foreign-local encounter.* For useful discussions of the relevance of these terms, see McClintock, *Imperial Leather: Race, Gender, and Sexuality in the Colonial Contest* (New York: Routledge, 1995), 8–17 (quotations, 11–12); J. Jorge Klor de Alva, "The Postcolonization of the (Latin) American Experience: A Reconsideration of 'Colonialism,' 'Postcolonialism,' and 'Mestizaje,'" in *After Colonialism: Imperial Histories and Postcolonial Displacements,* ed. Gyan Prakash (Princeton, N.J.: Princeton University Press, 1995); Mark Thurner, "Historicizing 'the Postcolonial' from Nineteenth-Century Peru," *Journal of Historical Sociology* 9 (Mar. 1996): 1–18; idem, *From Two Republics to One Divided: Contradictions of Postcolonial Nationmaking in Andean Peru* (Durham, N.C.: Duke University Press, 1997); and John McClure and Amir Mufti, eds., "Postcolonialism and the Third World," special double issue of *Social Text* 10, nos. 2–3 (1992). For a similar interrogation of "postimperialism," see Young, "Ne Plus Ultra Imperialism," esp.

35; and Linda Carty, "Imperialism: Historical Periodization or Present-Day Phenomenon," *Radical History Review* 57 (fall 1993): 38–45.

31. This section, particularly the critique of dependency thought, owes much to discussions with coeditor Ricardo Salvatore.

32. See, particularly, Peter Klarén and Thomas Bossert, eds., *Promise of Development: Theories of Change in Latin America* (Boulder, Colo.: Westview Press, 1986); Cristóbal Kay, *Latin American Theories of Development and Underdevelopment* (London: Routledge, 1989); Cooper et al., *Confronting Historical Paradigms,* esp. the introductory and concluding essays by Steve Stern and Florencia Mallon, respectively; and Stern's and Roseberry's chapters in this volume.

33. Regarding the model's persistence, it is instructive to compare the fundamental similarity of such recent political-economic initiatives as the Alliance for Progress (1960s), the Caribbean Basin Initiative (1980s), and the current North American Free Trade Agreement—which itself has prompted comparisons with Mexico's first great moment of export-led growth during the long regime of Porfirio Díaz (1876–1911). In a recent, award-winning book, anthropologist Arturo Escobar examines the persistence and naturalization of the model and the powerful mechanisms of control that the "development apparatus" has generated. See Escobar, *Encountering Development;* for an equally stimulating deconstruction of the model on the ground in southern Africa, see James Ferguson, *The Anti-Politics Machine: "Development," Depoliticization, and Bureaucratic Power in Lesotho* (Cambridge: Cambridge University Press, 1990). For an iconoclastic Marxian critique of such statements of "non-development" that also provides a useful archaeology and genealogy of development from the early nineteenth century on, see M. P. Cowen and R. W. Shenton, *Doctrines of Development* (New York: Routledge, 1996).

34. For classic statements of the diffusionist model, see W. A. Lewis, *The Theory of Economic Growth* (London: Allen and Unwin, 1955); W. W. Rostow, *The Stages of Economic Growth* (New York: Cambridge University Press, 1960); and Cyril Black, *The Dynamics of Modernization* (New York: Harper and Row, 1966). For influential Latin American applications, see Seymour Martin Lipset and Aldo Solari, eds., *Elites in Latin America* (New York: Oxford University Press, 1967); Jacques Lambert, *Latin America: Social Structure and Political Institutions* (Berkeley and Los Angeles: University of California Press, 1967); Richard Graham, *Britain and the Onset of Modernization in Brazil* (Cambridge: Cambridge University Press, 1968); Charles Cumberland, *Mexico: The Struggle for Modernity* (New York: Oxford University Press, 1968); Lawrence Harrison, *Underdevelopment Is a State of Mind: The Latin American Case* (Cambridge, Mass.: Center for International Affairs/University Press of America, 1985); and idem, *The Pan American Dream: Do Latin America's Cultural Values Discourage True Partnership with the United States and Canada?* (New York: Basic Books, 1997). For overviews of the model, see Robert A. Packenham, *Liberal America and the Third World: Political Development Ideas in Foreign Aid and Social Science* (Princeton,

N.J.: Princeton University Press, 1973); and Berger's far more critical account in *Under Northern Eyes,* chaps. 2-3.

35. See, e.g., S. N. Eisenstadt, "Social Change and Development," in *Readings in Social Evolution and Development,* ed. Eisenstadt (Oxford: Pergamon Press, 1973); idem, *Tradition, Change, and Modernity* (New York: Wiley, 1973); and idem, "Functional Analysis in Anthropology and Sociology: An Interpretive Essay," *Annual Review of Anthropology* 19 (1990): 243-60; cf. the discussion of "later modernization theory" in Ted C. Lewellen, *Dependency and Development: An Introduction to the Third World* (Westport, Conn.: Bergin and Harvey, 1995), 54-59, 67-69. For a recent, nuanced application by a Latin Americanist of modernization concepts, one that eschews Rostow's imitative "stages of growth" theory, see Jonathan Brown, *Oil and Revolution in Mexico* (Berkeley and Los Angeles: University of California Press, 1993).

36. Although I generalize broadly about these dissident paradigms to distinguish them from the more culturally oriented approaches represented in this volume, it is important to note that many of the contributors—myself included—cut their teeth on dependency and world-system perspectives, and their current work developed in dialogue and debate with them. For detailed discussions of these paradigms that examine competing currents within and reverberations among them, see Charles Bergquist, ed., *Alternative Approaches to the Problem of Development: A Selected and Annotated Bibliography* (Durham, N.C.: Carolina Academic Press, 1979); John Taylor, *From Modernization to Modes of Production* (New York: Macmillan, 1979); Vincent A. Mahler, *Dependency Approaches to International Political Economy: A Cross-National Study* (New York: Columbia University Press, 1980); Magnus Blomstrom and Bjorn Hettne, *Development Theory in Transition, the Dependency Debate, and Beyond: Third World Responses* (London: Zed Books, 1984); William B. Taylor, "Between Global Process and Local Knowledge: An Inquiry into Early Latin American Social History, 1500-1900," in *Reliving the Past: The Worlds of Social History,* ed. Olivier Zunz (Chapel Hill: University of North Carolina Press, 1985), 115-90; Klarén and Bossert, *Promise of Development;* Steve J. Stern, "Feudalism, Capitalism, and the World-System in the Perspective of Latin America and the Caribbean," *American Historical Review* 93 (Oct. 1988): 829-72; Kay, *Latin American Theories of Development;* Thomas J. McCormick's chapter on "World Systems" in Hogan and Paterson, *Explaining the History of American Foreign Relations;* Robert A. Packenham's biting, anti-Marxist critique, *The Dependency Movement: Scholarship and Politics in Development Studies* (Cambridge: Harvard University Press, 1992); Cooper et al., *Confronting Historical Paradigms;* Lewellen, *Dependency and Development;* Patrick Wolfe, "History and Imperialism: A Century of Theory, from Marx to Postcolonialism," *American Historical Review* 102, no. 2 (April 1997): 388-420, esp. 393-99; and Monteón, " 'Oh, Mama, Is This the End?' " Particularly good antidotes to the reification of dependency theory and political-economy approaches are found in Fein, "Hollywood and United States–Mexico Relations,"

chap. 1; Coronil, *The Magical State,* esp. chap. 2; and Roseberry's essay in this volume.

37. Such assessments have been legion: see, e.g., Mahler, *Dependency Approaches,* esp. 114, 167; José Nun, "Democracy and Modernization, Thirty Years After" (paper presented at the plenary session on "Democratic Theory Today: Empirical and Theoretical Issues," Fifteenth World Congress of the International Political Science Association, Buenos Aires, 1991); Saskia Sassen, *The Global City* (Princeton, N.J.: Princeton University Press, 1991); Arturo Escobar and Sonia Alvarez, eds., *The Making of Social Movements in Latin America: Identity, Strategy, and Democracy* (Boulder, Colo.: Westview Press, 1992); Nancy Scheper-Hughes, *Death without Weeping: The Violence of Everyday Life in Brazil* (Berkeley and Los Angeles: University of California Press, 1992); Stark, "Against Parsimony"; David Slater, ed., "Social Movements and Political Change in Latin America": Special Issues of *Latin American Perspectives* 21, nos. 2–3 (1994); Jorge A. Lawton, ed., *Privatization amidst Poverty* (Coral Gables, Fla.: University of Miami North-South Center Books, 1995); James L. Dietz, ed., *Latin America's Economic Development: Confronting Crisis,* 2d ed. (Boulder, Colo.: Lynne Rienner, 1995); Michael E. Conroy et al., *A Cautionary Tale: Failed U.S. Development Policy in Central America* (Boulder, Colo.: Lynne Rienner, 1996); Paul Farmer, "Hiding Structural Violence in Agrarian Societies: The Case of Haiti" (paper presented in the Agrarian Studies Seminar, Yale University, New Haven, Conn., Dec. 1996); and Richard Tardanico and Rafael Menjívar, eds., *Global Restructuring, Employment, and Social Inequality in Urban Latin America* (Coral Gables, Fla.: University of Miami North-South Center Books, 1997). In a recent, influential paper presented to the MacArthur Foundation/Interamerican Development Bank Conference on "Inequality Reducing Growth in Latin America's Market Economies," Carol Graham and Moisés Naim observed that amid the success of macroeconomic stabilization and market expansion, "There has been a 'rediscovery' of underdevelopment . . . a realization that something is 'missing' " (Graham and Naim, "The Political Economy of Institutional Reform in Latin America," manuscript, Jan. 1997).

38. Hence Escobar's critique in *Encountering Development* that even the most bitter *dependentista* critics of diffusionism have become prisoners of the naturalized categories generated by the development apparatus—not least the central priority of "development" in the so-called Third World. For a supporting argument regarding the staying power of liberal developmentalist discourses within the North American academy, see Berger, *Under Northern Eyes;* and Cumings, "Global Realm with No Limit."

39. See, e.g., Paul Baran, *The Political Economy of Growth* (New York: Monthly Review Press, 1957); Robert Rhodes, ed., *Imperialism and Underdevelopment: A Reader* (New York: Monthly Review Press, 1970); James Cockcroft et al., eds., *Dependency and Underdevelopment: Latin America's Political Economy* (Garden City, N.Y.: Doubleday, 1972), pt. 1; James Petras, "Chile," in *Latin America: The*

Struggle with Dependency and Beyond, ed. Ronald Chilcote and Joel Edelstein (New York: John Wiley, 1974), 495–578; and Walter LeFeber, *Inevitable Revolutions: The United States in Central America* (New York: W. W. Norton, 1984); for a more recent application by a Latin Americanist, see John Mason Hart, *Revolutionary Mexico: The Coming and Process of the Mexican Revolution* (Berkeley and Los Angeles: University of California Press, 1987). Also see a series of recent works by James Petras and Morris Morley that evolves a theory of the "imperial state" in an increasingly "internationalized" world order. These authors highlight the U.S. state's long-running commitment to the maintenance of hemispheric and global systems that support the interests of an increasingly well-integrated, international capitalist class. They question the usefulness of work that raises notions of the limited autonomy of the U.S. state from transnational capital, and they regard political (and cultural) phenomena as dependent variables and "short-term" factors. See, e.g., James Petras and Morris Morley, *U.S. Hegemony under Siege: Class, Politics, and Development in Latin America* (London: Verso, 1990); and *Latin America in the Time of Cholera: Electoral Politics, Market Economics, and Permanent Crisis* (London: Routledge, 1992); "The U.S. Imperial State," *Review* (Fernand Braudel Center), 4, no. 2 (1990); and Berger, *Under Northern Eyes,* which is heavily influenced by the theory.

40. In a recent communication, Ricardo Salvatore points out that frequent depictions of dependency as a "deep," "penetrating" reality call attention to "a language of sexual domination" that pervades its texts. For dependentistas, "Dispossession had effeminating effects on local producers; they became subservient to foreign capitalists. Those governments who resisted adopted manly postures. . . . Those who did not, acted in a womanly fashion, 'giving themselves to' (*entregándose*) foreign capital. 'Comprador' bourgeoisies were 'inviting' of foreign capital, their 'courtship' of foreigners revealed their inability to perform the manly task of autonomous industrialization. Titles like *The Rape of the Peasantry* speak clearly of the rooting of dependency theory in sexual language." Of course, the image of penetration also characterized the diffusionist paradigm as well. For a recent study that explores the influence of social constructions of gender in notions of development, see Catherine V. Scott, *Gender and Development: Rethinking Modernization and Dependency Theory* (Boulder, Colo.: Lynne Rienner, 1996).

41. See, e.g., Andre Gunder Frank, *Capitalism and Underdevelopment in Latin America* (New York: Monthly Review Press, 1967); Celso Furtado, *Economic Development of Latin America: Historical Background and Contemporary Problems* (New York: Cambridge University Press, 1970); Theotonio Dos Santos, "The Structure of Dependence," in *Readings in U.S. Imperialism,* ed. K. T. Fann and Donald C. Hodges (Boston: Porter Sargent, 1971), 225–36; Cockcroft et al., *Dependency and Underdevelopment;* Chilcote and Edelstein, *The Struggle with Dependency;* Fernando Henrique Cardoso and Enzo Faletto, *Dependencia y desarrollo en América Latina* (Mexico City: Siglo Veintiuno, 1971); idem, *Dependency and Development in Latin America,* rev. ed. (Berkeley and Los Angeles: Uni-

versity of California Press, 1979); Cardoso, "The Consumption of Dependency Theory in the United States," *Latin American Research Review* 12 (fall 1977): 7–24; Immanuel Wallerstein, *The Capitalist World-Economy* (New York: Cambridge University Press, 1979); idem, *The Politics of the World-Economy: The States, the Movements, and the Civilizations* (New York: Cambridge University Press, 1984); and idem, *The Modern World-System III: The Second Era of Great Expansion of the Capitalist World-Economy, 1730–1840s* (New York: Academic Press, 1989). For a recent application of dependency theory to Mexico, see Ramón Eduardo Ruiz, *The People of Sonora and Yankee Capitalists* (Tucson: University of Arizona Press, 1988); for the application of world-systems theory to Central America, see Thomas D. Schoonover, *The United States in Central America, 1860–1911: Episodes of Social Imperialism and Imperial Rivalry in the World System* (Durham, N.C.: Duke University Press, 1991).

42. Albert Hirschman characterized this elite discourse when he wrote about "the age of self-incrimination" (c. 1820s to World War I). See "Ideologies of Economic Development in Latin America," in *Latin American Issues: Essays and Comments,* ed. Albert O. Hirschman (New York: Twentieth Century Fund, 1961), 4–9.

43. See Albert O. Hirschman, *The Passions and the Interests: Political Arguments for Capitalism before Its Triumph* (Princeton, N.J.: Princeton University Press, 1977), pt. 1. For an antidote to models that focus exclusively on economic interest to the exclusion of passion and the aesthetic "pleasures of empire" that also underwrite (and subtly legitimate) imperial power, see Edward W. Said, *Culture and Imperialism* (New York: Knopf, 1993); Pike, *The United States and Latin America;* Helen Delpar, *The Enormous Vogue of Things Mexican: Cultural Relations between the United States and Mexico, 1921–1935* (Tuscaloosa: University of Alabama Press, 1992); and Poole's essay in this volume.

44. But cf. the work by "later dependency theorists" Fernando Henrique Cardoso and Peter Evans, which argues for a somewhat expanded horizon of development under capitalism in Brazil. See, e.g., Cardoso, "Associated-Dependent Development: Theoretical and Practical Implications," in *Authoritarian Brazil: Origins, Policies, and Future,* ed. Alfred Stepan (New Haven, Conn.: Yale University Press), 142–76; and Peter Evans, *Dependent Development: The Alliance of Multinational, State, and Local Capital in Brazil* (Princeton, N.J.: Princeton University Press, 1979).

45. Cf. Irving Louis Horowitz, *The Rise and Fall of Project Camelot: Studies in the Relationship between Social Science and Practical Politics* (Cambridge: MIT Press, 1967); and Sigmund Diamond, *Compromised Campus: The Collaboration of Universities with the Intelligence Community, 1945–1955* (New York: Oxford University Press, 1992).

46. This "Declaration of Latin American Economists" and coverage of the 1965 conference is found in Cockcroft et al., *Dependency and Underdevelopment,*

chap. II; cf. González-Chiaramonte, "American Cultural Diplomacy, Argentine Nationalism."

47. Cf. the critique found in the collection edited by Anthony King, *Culture, Globalization, and the World-System* (Binghamton: Department of Art and Art History, State University of New York, 1991).

48. See, e.g., Ariel Dorfman and Armand Mattelart, *Para leer al Pato Donald* (Valparaiso: Ediciones Universitarias, 1971); English ed.: *How to Read Donald Duck: Imperialist Ideology in the Disney Comic,* trans. David Kunzle (New York: International General, 1975); Julianne Burton, "Don (Juanito) Duck and the Imperial-Patriarchal Unconscious: Disney Studios, the Good Neighbor Policy, and the Packaging of Latin America," in *Nationalisms and Sexualities,* ed. Andrew Parker et al. (New York: Routledge, 1992), 21–41; the retrospective critique in Eric Smoodin, ed., *Disney Discourse: Producing the Magic Kingdom* (New York: Routledge, 1994); and Charles Bergquist, *Labor and the Course of American Democracy: U.S. History in Latin American Perspective* (London: Verso, 1996), chap. 4; and the more general theoretical statement in John Tomlinson, *Cultural Imperialism: A Critical Introduction* (Baltimore, Md.: Johns Hopkins University Press, 1991). Compare the chapters by Fein and Derby in this volume; Fein, "Hollywood and United States–Mexico Relations"; and Roseberry, *Anthropologies and Histories,* chap. 4, for a more culturally compelling treatment of "Americanization in the Americas." Also note the evolution of cultural analysis in Immanuel Wallerstein's most recent writings: e.g., "Culture as the Ideological Battleground of the Modern World-System," in *Global Culture: Nationalism, Globalization, and Modernity,* ed. Mike Featherstone (London: Sage Publications, 1990), 31–55; and *Geopolitics and Geocultures: The Changing World-System* (New York: Cambridge University Press, 1991).

49. Cf. Fernando Coronil, "Beyond Occidentalism: Toward Nonimperial Geohistorical Categories," *Cultural Anthropology* 11 (Feb. 1996): 51–87.

50. For incisive analyses of such discourses, see McClintock, *Imperial Leather;* Doreen Massey, *Space, Place, and Gender* (Minneapolis: University of Minnesota Press, 1994); Doty, *Imperial Encounters;* Wolfe, "History and Imperialism."

51. Cf. the forum in *Radical History Review* 57 (fall 1993), in which some contributors seek to integrate "the triptych of race-gender-class" into studies of imperialism. See especially the introduction by Van Gosse (4–6) and the commentaries by Cumings (46–59), Duara (60–64), Hobsbawm (73–75), and Rosenberg (82–83). Also see Albert Hirschman's *Propensity to Self-Subversion* (Cambridge, Mass.: Harvard University Press, 1995) for an illuminating discussion of how the combination of recent events and new theoretical insights enable a scholar to rethink and build on what he or she has written earlier.

52. Cardoso and Faletto, *Dependency and Development,* xvi; also see Cardoso, "The Consumption of Dependency Theory," 13.

53. The quotation is taken from Roseberry's essay in this volume. Two depen-

dency-oriented monographs that "internalize the external" with great explanatory power are Charles Bergquist, *Coffee and Conflict in Colombia, 1886–1910,* rev. ed. (Durham, N.C.: Duke University Press, 1986); and Allen Wells, *Yucatán's Gilded Age: Haciendas, Henequen, and International Harvester, 1860–1915* (Albuquerque: University of New Mexico Press, 1985).

54. Cardoso and Faletto, *Dependency and Development,* xviii.

55. By putting *insiders* and *outsiders* in quotation marks, we mean to problematize these terms, questioning the dichotomous, bounded notions associated with them.

56. See, e.g., Gregg Andrews, *Shoulder to Shoulder? The American Federation of Labor, the United States, and the Mexican Revolution, 1910–1924* (Berkeley and Los Angeles: University of California Press, 1991); O'Brien, *The Revolutionary Mission;* and Gilbert M. Joseph and Allen Wells, "Corporate Control of a Monocrop Economy: International Harvester and Yucatán's Henequen Industry during the Porfiriato," *Latin American Research Review* 17, no. 1 (1982): 69–99.

57. William Schell, "Integral Outsiders, Mexico City's American Colony, 1876–1911: Society and Political-Economy in Porfirian Mexico" (Ph.D. diss., University of North Carolina at Chapel Hill, 1992); cf. Jürgen Buchenau, "Not Quite Mexican and Not Quite German: The Boker Family in Mexico" (paper presented at "Rethinking the Postcolonial Encounter"); and see "Americans in Haiti Fear an Invasion," *New York Times,* 30 July 1994, 3, for a treatment of expatriate attitudes in an explosive contemporary situation.

58. Paco Ignacio Taibo II, *Four Hands,* trans. Laura Dail (New York: St. Martin's Press, 1994); Mauricio Tenorio-Trillo, "Viejos gringos: Radicales norteamericanos en los años treinta y su visión de México," *Secuencia* 21 (Sept.–Dec. 1991): 95–116; idem, "A *Gringa Vieja* in Mexico: Ella Wolfe" (paper presented at "Rethinking the Postcolonial Encounter").

59. Christian Smith, *Resisting Reagan: The U.S. Central American Peace Movement* (Chicago: University of Chicago Press, 1996); cf. Susan Bibler Coutin, *The Culture of Protest: Religious Activism and the U.S. Sanctuary Movement* (Boulder, Colo.: Westview Press, 1993), for a similar account of "border crossings" between first and third worlds that developed international notions of citizenship and ecumenical interpretations of faith.

60. The now classic "billiard ball" metaphor comes from Eric Wolf's *Europe and the People without History* (Berkeley and Los Angeles: University of California Press, 1982); it is central to Roseberry's analysis in "Americanization in the Americas" (see esp. 85ff). For conceptualizations of "transculturation" that are extremely relevant to the essays in this volume, see Pratt, *Imperial Eyes;* and Fernando Coronil's introduction to *Cuban Counterpoint,* by Fernando Ortiz (1940; Durham, N.C.: Duke University Press, 1995), ix–lvi. Sadly, "billiard ball" notions of cultural contact still weigh heavily in policy-making circles. Witness political scientist Samuel P. Huntington's clumsy understanding of cultural engagement in

his recent, disturbing salvo in the "culture wars," *The Clash of Civilizations and the Remaking of World Order* (New York: Simon and Schuster, 1996).

61. Sherry B. Ortner, "Resistance and the Problem of Ethnographic Refusal," *Comparative Studies in Society and History* 37 (Jan. 1995): 173–93 (quotation, 176); also see Arjun Appadurai, "Global Ethnoscapes: Notes and Queries for a Transnational Anthropology," in *Recapturing Anthropology: Working in the Present,* ed. Richard G. Fox (Santa Fe, N.M.: School of American Research Press, 1991), 191–210; John Borneman, "American Anthropology as Foreign Policy," *American Anthropologist* 97 (Dec. 1995): 663–72, esp. 669; Akhil Gupta and James Ferguson, "Beyond 'Culture': Space, Identity, and the Politics of Difference," *Cultural Anthropology* 7, no. 1 (Feb. 1992): 6–23; and Joseph and Nugent, "Popular Culture and State Formation," 3–23, esp. 15–18.

62. Massey, *Space, Place, and Gender,* 8. Massey's work is representative of a "new regional geography" that focuses on the "identities of place." These identities "are always unfixed, contested and multiple." Places are "open and porous" and social relations stretch beyond the place itself: "the global [is] part of what constitutes the local, the outside . . . part of the inside" (ibid., 5). Also see Massey and Pat Jess, eds., *A Place in the World? Places, Culture, and Globalization* (Oxford: Oxford University Press, 1995); and J. Nicholas Entriken, "Place and Region," *Progress in Human Geography* 18, no. 2 (1994): 227–33. For a fuller discussion and additional citations of this new current in cultural geography, see LeGrand's essay in this volume. For a practical application to contemporary ecological and agrarian problems, see Wes Jackson, *Becoming Native to This Place* (Washington, D.C.: Counterpoint, 1996).

63. The quotation comes from William Roseberry's essay in this volume.

64. Compare, however, Daniel Nugent, "Close Encounters of the Uncommunicative Kind: Pershing's Punitive Expedition to Mexico" (paper presented at "Rethinking the Postcolonial Encounter"), which argues that in certain punitive contexts of empire, communication is entirely foreclosed by imperial arrogance, racism, and brutality.

65. For other examples of unintended, unexpected, or paradoxical consequences, see especially the essays in this volume by Stern, Findlay, Topik, Roorda, LeGrand, Klubock, and Derby.

66. Regarding sports and leisure activities and new patterns of consumption, see also Louis Pérez, "Between Baseball and Bullfighting: The Quest for Nationality in Cuba, 1868–1898," *Journal of American History* 81 (Sept. 1994): 493–517; Michael F. Jiménez, " 'From Plantation to Cup': Coffee and Capitalism in the United States, 1830–1930," in *Coffee, Society, and Power in Latin America,* ed. William Roseberry, Lowell Gudmundson, and Mario Samper Kutschbach (Baltimore, Md.: Johns Hopkins University Press, 1995), 38–64; and Jeffrey M. Pilcher, "Tamales or Timbales: Cuisine and the Negotiation of Mexican National Identity, 1821–1911," *The Americas* 53 (Oct. 1996): 193–216.

67. Cf. Arjun Appadurai, "Disjuncture and Difference in the Global Cultural Economy," in Featherstone, *Global Culture,* 295–310.

68. Cf. the treatment of similar themes in the essays in *Social Text* 10, nos. 31–32 (1992).

69. The following discussion is based on James C. Scott's stimulating commentary at "Rethinking the Postcolonial Encounter."

70. Ibid.; cf. Scott's masterful ethnography of "Sedaka" in *Weapons of the Weak: Everyday Forms of Peasant Resistance* (New Haven, Conn.: Yale University Press, 1985). For a pioneering study of plebeian material culture—as well as of foreign influences on elite and popular pastimes—in turn-of-the-century Mexico, see William H. Beezley, *Judas at the Jockey Club and Other Episodes of Porfirian Mexico* (Lincoln: University of Nebraska Press, 1987).

71. Cf. James C. Scott, "Why the State Is the Enemy of People Who Move Around" (lecture presented in the International Migration and Refugee Movements Seminar, Yale University, New Haven, Conn., 2 April 1997).

72. See, e.g., Gloria K. Giffords, *Mexican Folk Retablos: Masterpieces on Tin* (Tucson: University of Arizona Press, 1974); and Jorge Durand and Douglas S. Massey, *Miracles on the Border: Retablos of Mexican Migrants to the United States* (Tucson: University of Arizona Press, 1995).

73. Delpar, *The Enormous Vogue;* Tenorio-Trillo, "Viejos gringos"; James Oles, ed., *South of the Border: Mexico in the American Imagination, 1914–1947/México en la imaginación norteamericana, 1914–1947* (Washington, D.C.: Smithsonian Institution Press, 1993); Adriana Williams, *Covarrubias* (Austin: University of Texas Press, 1994).

74. Joseph and Nugent, "Popular Culture and State Formation," 15–18; Rick A. López, "Art, Politics, and Culture in the Formation of Mexican Revolutionary Nationalism" (Ph.D. diss., Yale University, forthcoming).

75. Also see the chapters by Stern, Salvatore, and Roseberry, all of which establish interpretive frames for ordering the multiple agents and voices of Latin America's foreign-local encounter.

76. Also see Eric Roorda, "Gold Braid and Striped Pants: The Culture of Foreign Relations between the United States and the Dominican Republic, 1930–1953" (paper presented at the Latin American Studies Association Meeting, Atlanta, Mar. 1994).

77. For a sense of the compartmentalization that must be overcome, as well as some encouraging trends, see Hogan and Paterson, *Explaining the History of American Foreign Relations;* Stark, "Against Parsimony"; and Murphy and Rojas de Ferro, introduction to *International Review of Political Economy* 2 (winter 1995): 63–69.

78. Cf., for example, the multiple, hybrid personas (e.g., "The Aztec High-Tech," "The Warrior for Gringostroika") depicted in the pointed satire and radical humor of performance artist Guillermo Gómez-Peña, a student of "cultimultural" issues since he came to the United States from Mexico in 1978. Also

see Helena Solberg and David Meyer's empathetic and poignant film, "Bananas Is My Business" (1994), about the extraordinary transformation Brazilian entertainer Carmen Miranda underwent following her encounter with Hollywood.

79. Thus, the new cultural historian of inter-American relations cannot ignore the pivotal moments in North American political culture that serve as orienting points for the in-depth analysis we propose. Among these we might include the emergence of the Monroe Doctrine; the ideology of Manifest Destiny and the search for a route to California; the closing of the western frontier; the consolidation of the first transnational firms in oil, mining, and agricultural machinery; the heyday of American gunboat diplomacy and the first Pan-American Conferences; the successive invasions of Central American and Caribbean republics; the Good Neighbor Policy and the search for allies in World War II; the onset of the Cold War and the Nuclear Age; the Alliance for Progress; and the postcommunist New World Order. Indeed, the place of wars in U.S. political culture might well provide a long, distinctive thread in the fabric of our analysis of inter-American relations. Some of the best work on U.S. empire from a cultural studies perspective examines how wars both reflect and help shape class, gender, and racial dynamics in American society. See, e.g., Kaplan and Pease, *Cultures of United States Imperialism,* esp. the essays by Richard Slotkin (164–81), Vicente Raphael (185–218), and Amy Kaplan (219–36), and those in pt. 4 ("Imperial Spectacles"). Also see Eileen Findlay's essay in this volume.

Of course, we must also consider comparable markers for Central America, South America, and the Caribbean: namely, independence from the old colonial powers; the process of state and nation building that followed; the extension of export economies into the interior; the period of outward-looking economic growth in the late nineteenth and early twentieth centuries; the Great Depression; the rise and fall of import substitution industrialization; and neoliberalism and economic restructuring—among others.

80. For a persuasive overview of how "big power politics" and changes in the "international rules of the game" exerted a preponderant impact on U.S.–Latin American relations from the eighteenth century on, see Smith, *Talons of the Eagle.*

81. See, e.g., David Harvey, *The Condition of Postmodernity* (Oxford: Basil Blackwell, 1989); Featherstone, *Global Culture;* and Stuart Hall, "Brave New World," *Socialist Review* 21 (1991): 57–64.

82. For some of the challenges that attend periodization in cross-cultural contexts, see the recent forum, "Periodization in World History," *American Historical Review* 101 (June 1996): 748–82. Stern's essay in this volume provides a rough periodization of foreign-local encounter since colonial times; cf. Roseberry, *Anthropologies and Histories,* 91ff.; Keith Haynes's broader, political-economic schema in "Capitalism and the Periodization of International Relations: Colonialism, Imperialism, Ultraimperialism, and Postimperialism," *Radical History Review* 57 (fall 1993): 21–32; and Smith's attempt, in *Talons of the Eagle,* to periodize U.S.–Latin American relations within the context of epochal shifts in

international power politics. Also see Salvatore's contribution in this volume for a more restricted periodization of representational regimes.

83. Schoonover, *The United States in Central America;* John H. Coatsworth, *Central America and the United States: The Clients and the Colossus* (New York: Twayne, 1994); Eric Roorda, *The Dictator Next Door: The Good Neighbor Policy and the Trujillo Regime in the Dominican Republic, 1930–1945* (Durham, N.C.: Duke University Press, 1998); Paul W. Drake, ed., *Money Doctors, Foreign Debts, and Economic Reforms in Latin America from the 1890s to the Present* (Wilmington, Del.: Scholarly Resources, 1994); and Drake, *The Money Doctor in the Andes: The Kemmerer Missions, 1923–1933* (Durham, N.C.: Duke University Press, 1989).

84. In addition to the chapters in this volume by Topik, Schroeder, and Roorda, see Crawford, "Cross-Cultural Encounter"; Nugent, "Close Encounters of the Uncommunicative Kind"; Malcolm B. Colcleugh, "War-Time Portraits of the Gringo: American Invaders and the Manufacture of Mexican Nationalism," *Journal of the Canadian Historical Association,* n.s., 6 (1995): 81–99; and Langley and Schoonover, *Banana Men.*

85. See, e.g., Jimmy M. Skaggs, *The Great Guano Rush: Entrepreneurs and American Overseas Expansion* (New York: St. Martin's Press, 1994); Paul Dosal, *Doing Business with the Dictators: A Political History of United Fruit in Guatemala, 1899–1944* (Wilmington, Del.: Scholarly Resources, 1993); Langley and Schoonover, *Banana Men;* Brown, *Oil and Revolution;* Linda B. Hall, *Oil, Banks, and Politics: The United States and Postrevolutionary Mexico, 1917–1924* (Austin: University of Texas Press, 1995); O'Brien, *The Revolutionary Mission;* Joseph A. Fry, "Constructing an Empire? Guano, Bananas, and American Foreign Relations," *Diplomatic History* 20 (summer 1996): 483–89; Darío A. Euraque, *Reinterpreting the Banana Republic: Region and State in Honduras, 1870–1972* (Chapel Hill: University of North Carolina Press, 1996); and Steven C. Topik, *Trade and Gunboats: The United States and Brazil in the Age of Empire* (Stanford, Calif.: Stanford University Press, 1997).

86. See, e.g., Rosalie Schwartz, *Pleasure Island: Tourism and Temptation in Cuba* (Lincoln: University of Nebraska Press, 1997); Quetzil Castañeda, *In the Museum of Maya Culture: Touring Chichén Itzá* (Minneapolis: University of Minnesota Press, 1996); and Julio E. Moreno, "Constructing the 'Mexican Dream': Consumer Culture in Mexico City and the Historical Reconstruction of Modern Mexico in the 1940s" (Ph.D. diss., University of California at Irvine, forthcoming).

87. Ricardo Salvatore and Carlos Aguirre, eds., *The Birth of the Penitentiary in Latin America* (Austin: University of Texas Press, 1996).

88. Ron Robin, *Enclaves of America: The Rhetoric of American Political Architecture Abroad, 1900–1965* (Princeton, N.J.: Princeton University Press, 1996); and Karen Robert, "Inventing the Southern Metropolis: American Models of Urban Growth in Nineteenth-Century Buenos Aires," and Julie Franks, "Forging

National Institutions in the Dominican Sugar Zone, 1880–1924" (papers presented at "Rethinking the Postcolonial Encounter").

89. Robert Rydell, *All the World's a Fair: Visions of Empire, International Expositions, 1876–1916* (Chicago: University of Chicago Press, 1984); Mauricio Tenorio-Trillo, *Mexico at the World's Fairs: Crafting a Modern Nation* (Berkeley and Los Angeles: University of California Press, 1996); and Rosenberg, *Spreading the American Dream,* esp. chap. 1.

90. J. Valerie Fifer, *United States Perceptions of Latin America, 1850–1930: A 'New West' South of Capricorn?* (Manchester, U.K.: Manchester University Press, 1991), esp. chaps. 1, 4; Lutz and Collins, *Reading National Geographic;* Curtis M. Hinsley, *Savages and Scientists: The Smithsonian Institution and the Development of American Anthropology, 1846–1910* (Washington, D.C.: Smithsonian Institution Press, 1981); George Stocking, *Colonial Situations: Essays on the Contextualization of Ethnographic Knowledge* (Madison: University of Wisconsin Press, 1991); Borneman, "American Anthropology as Foreign Policy"; Peter R. Schmidt and Thomas C. Patterson, eds., *Making Alternative Histories: The Practice of Archaeology and History in Non-Western Settings* (Santa Fe, N.M.: SAR Press, 1996); Nancy Leys Stepan, *"The Hour of Eugenics": Race, Gender, and Nation in Latin America* (Ithaca, N.Y.: Cornell University Press, 1991); Marcos Cueto, ed., *Salud, cultura y sociedad en América Latina: Nuevas perspectivas históricas* (Lima: Instituto de Estudios Peruanos, 1996); David Arnold, ed., *Imperial Medicine and Indigenous Societies* (Manchester, U.K.: Manchester University Press, 1988); and Alejandra García Quintanilla, "Reshaping the Social Body: Hunger among the Yucatec Maya at the Turn of the Century" (paper presented at "Rethinking the Postcolonial Encounter").

91. In addition to Palmer's chapter in this volume, see Robert Arnove, ed., *Philanthropy and Cultural Imperialism* (Boston: G. K. Hall, 1980); Edward H. Berman, *The Influence of the Carnegie, Ford, and Rockefeller Foundations on American Foreign Policy: The Ideology of Philanthropy* (Albany: State University of New York Press, 1983); Donald T. Critchlow, *The Brookings Institution, 1916–1952: Expertise and the Public Interest in a Democratic Society* (DeKalb: Northern Illinois Press, 1985); Elizabeth Cobbs, *The Rich Neighbor Policy: Rockefeller and Kaiser in Brazil* (New Haven, Conn.: Yale University Press, 1992); and Marcos Cueto, ed., *Missionaries of Science: The Rockefeller Foundation in Latin America* (Bloomington and Indianapolis: Indiana University Press, 1992).

92. Rosenberg, *Spreading the American Dream;* David Stoll, *Fishers of Men or Founders of Empire: The Wycliffe Bible Translators in Latin America* (London: Zed Press, 1982); Soren Hvalkopf and Peter Aaby, eds., *Is God an American? An Anthropological Perspective on the Missionary Work of the Summer Institute of Linguistics* (London: Survival International, 1981); Gerard Colby with Charlotte Dennett, *Thy Will Be Done: The Conquest of the Amazon: Nelson Rockefeller and Evangelism in the Age of Oil* (New York: HarperCollins, 1995), which attempts to

link the religious, business, and political dimensions of U.S. imperialism; Jeffrey Swanson, *Echoes of the Call: Identity and Ideology among American Missionaries in Ecuador* (New York: Oxford University Press, 1995); Anne Hallum, *Beyond Missionaries: Toward an Understanding of the Protestant Movement in Central America* (Lanham, N.Y.: Rowman and Littlefield, 1996); and Avital H. Bloch and Servando Ortoll, " 'Viva México! Mueran los Yanquis!' The Guadalajara Riots of 1910," in *Riots in the Cities: Popular Politics and the Urban Poor in Latin America*, ed. Silvia M. Arrom and Servando Ortoll (Wilmington, Del.: Scholarly Resources, 1996), 195–223. Compare Emilia Viotti da Costa, *Crowns of Glory, Tears of Blood: The Demerara Slave Rebellion of 1823* (New York: Oxford University Press, 1994), for an extraordinarily rich account of British missionaries' encounter with a nineteenth-century Caribbean plantation society.

93. See, for example, Johnson, *Latin America in Caricature;* Sarah E. Sharbach, *Stereotypes of Latin America, Press Images, and U.S. Foreign Policy, 1920–1933* (New York: Garland Publishing, 1993); Christopher P. Wilson, "Plotting the Border: John Reed, Pancho Villa, and *Insurgent Mexico,*" in Kaplan and Pease, *Cultures of United States Imperialism,* 340–61.

94. Pratt, *Imperial Eyes;* Barbara M. Stafford, *Voyage into Substance: Art, Science, Nature, and the Illustrated Travel Account* (Cambridge: MIT Press, 1984); Ricardo D. Salvatore, "North American Travel Narratives and the Ordering/ Othering of South America (c. 1810–1860)," *Journal of Historical Sociology* 9 (Mar. 1996): 85–110; Jason Wilson, *The Traveller's Literary Companion: South and Central America, Including Mexico* (Lincolnwood, Ill.: Passport Books, 1995); William B. Taylor, "Mexico as Oriental: Thoughts on a History of American and British Representations since 1821" (paper presented at the Latin American Studies Association Meeting, Washington, D.C., 1991); idem, " 'Her Time is Coming': San Blas and Tepic in British and American Writings, 1822–1931" (paper presented at "Rethinking the Postcolonial Encounter"); Delpar, *The Enormous Vogue;* Oles, *South of the Border;* John A. Britton, *Revolution and Ideology: Images of the Mexican Revolution in the United States* (Lexington: University Press of Kentucky, 1995); Whisnant, *Rascally Signs,* esp. chap. 7; Deborah Poole, *Vision, Race, and Modernity: A Visual Economy of the Andean World* (Princeton, N.J.: Princeton University Press, 1997); and Poole's chapter in this volume.

95. For useful statements by foreign relations scholars, see Martha L. Cottam, *Images and Intervention: U.S. Policies in Latin America* (Pittsburgh: University of Pittsburgh Press, 1994); Eldon Kenworthy, *America/Américas: Myth in the Making of U.S. Policy toward Latin America* (University Park: Pennsylvania State University Press, 1995); Elizabeth A. Cobbs, "Why They Think Like Gringos: The Discourse of U.S.–Latin American Relations," *Diplomatic History* 21, no. 2 (spring 1997): 307–16; for a radically dissenting view, see Frederick B. Pike, *FDR's Good Neighbor Policy: Sixty Years of Generally Gentle Chaos* (Austin: University of Texas Press, 1995). For more theoretical statements from literary and cultural studies, see Kaplan and Pease, *Cultures of United States Imperialism;* Eric

Cheyfitz, *The Poetics of Imperialism: Translation and Colonization from the Tempest to Tarzan* (New York: Oxford University Press, 1991); Thomas Richards, *The Imperial Archive: Knowledge and the Fantasy of Empire* (London: Verso, 1993); David Spurr, *The Rhetoric of Empire: Colonial Discourse in Journalism, Travel Writing, and Imperial Administration* (Durham, N.C.: Duke University Press, 1993); Chris Tiffin and Alan Lawson, eds., *De-Scribing Empire: Post-Colonialism and Textuality* (London: Routledge, 1994); and McClintock, *Imperial Leather.* Also see Santiago-Valles, *"Subject People" and Colonial Discourses;* idem, "Unraveling the 'Duties to the Race' and the 'Stronger, Manlier Powers' in the U.S. Colonial Frontier of the Turn-of-the-Century Caribbean" (paper presented at "Rethinking the Postcolonial Encounter"); and the chapters by Salvatore and Poole in this volume.

96. For valuable comparative formulations of this problem, see Jean Comaroff, *Body of Power, Spirit of Resistance: The Culture and History of a South African People* (Chicago: University of Chicago Press, 1985); Ashis Nandy, *The Intimate Enemy: Loss and Recovery of the Self under Colonialism* (Delhi: Oxford University Press, 1983); and Ortner, "Resistance and the Problem of Ethnographic Refusal." For diverse Latin American treatments, see Friedrich Katz, *The Secret War in Mexico: Europe, the United States, and the Mexican Revolution* (Chicago: University of Chicago Press, 1981); Florencia Mallon, *The Defense of Community in Peru's Central Highlands: Peasant Struggle and Capitalist Transition, 1860-1940* (Princeton, N.J.: Princeton University Press, 1983); Robert G. Williams, *Export Agriculture and the Crisis in Central America* (Chapel Hill: University of North Carolina Press, 1986); Hart, *Revolutionary Mexico;* Nugent, *Rural Revolt;* Gilbert M. Joseph, *Revolution from Without: Yucatán, Mexico, and the United States, 1880-1924,* rev. ed. (Durham, N.C.: Duke University Press, 1988); Julie Franks, "The Gavilleros of the East: Social Banditry as Political Practice in the Dominican Sugar Region, 1900-1924," *Journal of Historical Sociology* 8 (June 1995): 158-81; O'Brien, *The Revolutionary Mission;* and Bloch and Ortoll, " 'Viva México!' " Some important clues also lie in the recent literature on Latin America's "new social movements": e.g., Escobar and Alvarez, *The Making of Social Movements;* Slater, "Social Movements"; Elizabeth Jelin, ed., *Los nuevos movimientos sociales* (Buenos Aires: Centro Editor de América Latina, 1985); Jelin, ed., *Women and Social Change in Latin America* (London: Zed Books, 1990); and Joe Foweraker and Ann Craig, eds., *Popular Movements and Political Change in Mexico* (Boulder, Colo.: Lynne Rienner, 1990).

97. Cf. Janet Abu-Lughod, "Going beyond Global Babble," in King, *Culture, Globalization,* 131-37. For a particularly incisive, critical analysis of development from the "commanding heights of power," which also theorizes "subaltern modernity" (i.e., development's consequences for Third World states and populations), see Coronil, *The Magical State.*

98. For other examinations of this dialectical process at work, see Kaplan and Pease, *Cultures of United States Imperialism;* Joseph and Nugent, *Everyday Forms*

of State Formation; Fernando Coronil and Julie Skurski, "Dismembering and Remembering the Nation: The Semantics of Political Violence in Venezuela," *Comparative Studies in Society and History* 33 (Apr. 1991): 288–334; Coronil, "Listening to the Subaltern: The Poetics of Neocolonial States," *Poetics Today* 15 (winter 1994): 643–58; Allen Wells and Gilbert M. Joseph, *Summer of Discontent, Seasons of Upheaval: Elite Politics and Rural Insurgency in Yucatán, 1876–1915* (Stanford, Calif.: Stanford University Press, 1996); and Bergquist, *Labor and the Course of American Democracy.*

99. García Márquez, "The Solitude of Latin America (Nobel Lecture, 1982)," in *Gabriel García Márquez and the Powers of Fiction,* ed. Julio Ortega and Claudia Elliott (Austin: University of Texas Press, 1988), 81.

Steve J. Stern

The Decentered Center
and the Expansionist Periphery

The Paradoxes of Foreign-Local Encounter

Introduction: Conceptual Dilemmas

Latin America: Whether one notes that Bolívar's panoramic vision of Spanish American destiny was premised on a vision of colonizers and other external powers, or observes that the very term derived from French imperial pretension in Mexico in the nineteenth century,[1] or notes the presence of Spaniards and colonial right in contemporary Amerindian claims of right "since time immemorial" — one cannot conceptualize Latin America, it seems, without conceptualizing a powerful foreign presence. Yet to reduce "Latin America" to a peculiar imperial extension of the foreigner's social model or the foreigner's will is also unacceptable. To do so would ignore the more endogenous social dynamics that have shaped the region's history and defied external power and desire, in dramatic and undramatic ways, in heartland territories of imperial power as well as "middle ground" regions of comparatively weak control, over the centuries.[2] It would also evade the sense of "solitude" so important to Latin Americans' cultural sensibilities,[3] and reproduce the questionable we/they dichotomies this book intends to challenge and transcend.

How, then, do we conceptualize a foreign presence that is integral yet not totalizing in its power to mold peoples and events, a foreign-local relationship that constantly draws cultural boundaries of "we" and "they" yet fails to preclude communications, mediations, and identities that confound division into "we" and "they"? How do we accomplish this conceptual challenge, as well, in dialogue with a historical sensibility that recognizes major changes over time—distinct eras in the meanings and relations of *foreign* and *local* in Latin America?

I do not pretend to offer thoroughly developed answers or hypotheses for these questions. I do propose that one constructive approach is to explore historically the paradoxes that seem to negate customary categories or apparent solutions, without necessarily falling into the assumption that such paradoxes fully undermine such categories and solutions. From this point of view, the Americas have become, with special intensity by the late twentieth century, an arena where relations between "Latin America" and the "United States" are those between an "expansionist periphery" and a "decentered center." Perhaps needless to say, such relations yield particularly complex blends of intimacy and estrangement, imposition and mediation, and group dichotomization and transculturation in matters of "we" and "they."

Unpacking Apparent Solutions

Let us begin with an intellectual autobiography of customary categories and apparent solutions. My first attempt to conceptualize the foreign presence in Latin America focused on questions of political economy in early modern times, and the adequacy of the standard historical categories— "feudalism," "capitalism," and "world-system"—many intellectuals have used to interpret colonial Latin America. This effort took the specific form of a systematic critical investigation of the usefulness of Immanuel Wallerstein's interpretation of the sixteenth century as a founding era in the creation of a capitalist world-system encompassing the Americas as well as Western and Eastern Europe. When I found Wallerstein's paradigm untenable from both explanatory and descriptive points of view, I tried to avoid nihilism by proposing starting points—my own version of "customary categories and apparent solutions"—for a new conceptual approach. The apparent solution was a triangle of interacting and internally contradictory "motors"—the European world-system, popular strategies of resistance and survival within the periphery, and mercantile and elite interests joined to American centers of gravity. "It is in the contradictory interplay between these three grand motors, and in the divisions and contradictions internal to each of them, that we will find keys to a deeper understanding of the structures, changes, and driving forces of colonial economic life." [4]

The problem with this apparent solution is at least threefold. First, the formulation, even if useful as an abstraction or a starting point, can prove misleading if the various corners of this interactive triangle remain rather "unpacked." (Indeed, in my own case, I had written the formulation as a conclusion, an abstraction based on historical case studies of colonial silver and sugar labor that first took the reader through a more "unpacked" analysis.) Once the unpacking process begins, however, internally conflictual and crosscutting dynamics may come into play that complicate or partly negate the usefulness of the original formulation. A certain decentering or pluralizing of identity, purpose, interest, and unintended by-product within the original categories begins to render them more vulnerable.

Let us reconsider the three corners of our triangle. As William Roseberry has observed, each corner itself constitutes a complex "field" of social and power relations.[5]

1. The "world-system" — or more precisely, its hegemonic representatives and institutions for a given "peripheral" region — were hardly unified or homogeneous entities, but rather arenas of power, state formation, and cultural struggle in their own right. Beyond a certain point, such dynamics may call into question how much historical force to attribute to the "world-system" (or an analogous category for the foreign presence).

2. "Popular strategies of resistance and survival" failed to preclude conflicts of interest and values and competing strategies of survival among subalterns. They also failed to preclude popular engagement of the colonizing power (through market participation or entrepreneurship, litigation or political pacts, social climbing or patronage, and the like) in ways that rendered subalterns partly complicitous with "external" projects, and they failed to preclude strategies of physical and mental "withdrawal" from the world and the projects of foreign colonizers and local elites. Beyond a certain point, such dynamics belie a vision of subaltern "resistance" in the direct sense, and force one to ask how much friction toward elite projects (whether those of the world-system or more America-centered projects) to attribute to subaltern lifeways.

3. "America-centered logics of mercantile and elite interest" existed in dialogue with more externally driven or global logics of marketplace and elite interest. Precisely for this reason, creole elites took pains to "colonize" or domesticate new imperial agents, and foreign immigrants and entrepreneurs, and to develop transatlantic webs of interest. Recently arrived foreigners, for their part, developed local relations of kinship, patronage, and interest that joined them to American centers of gravity.[6] Beyond a certain point, this blurring of identities and multiplicity of relevant market logics call into question the usefulness of a contrast between foreigners joined to world-system or international market logics, and local elites more rooted in regional or continental markets and production.

Add to such complications the emergence of crosscutting ties of kinship and patronage, and the emergence of new social categories (persons of mixed racial descent, Indian migrant fugitives, and African maroons) on the margins of the conceptual categories of the colonial order. Beyond a certain point, such mediations and shadow categories also call into question the we/they contrasts and contests of will embedded in our original triangle.

The second major problem with the formulation of a triangle of interactive yet internally contradictory motors is that the formulation was developed around questions of political economy — specifically, the political economy of silver and sugar in the colonial Americas that constituted a high priority to an emerging capitalist world-system. Yet as this book demonstrates, the issues of power, culture, and experience raised by foreign-local encounters and exchanges in the Americas are not all reducible to questions of political economy.

For purposes of argument, let us consider three large, somewhat overlapping, yet distinct domains of transnational encounter: (1) political economy and high-power politics, the classic domains of international economic history, imperial history, and postimperial diplomatic or foreign relations history; (2) moral values and assessment of self and other, a domain where issues such as Orientalism, civilization and barbarism, missionary pretense and expectation, and human rights take on dynamics of their own, despite connections to political economy and high-power politics; and (3) cultural venturousness, a domain of lived and vicarious experience of the ethnographic other's environment (tourism, travel magazines, museums), cultural artifacts or commodities (Third World crafts, First World movies), or competitive ability (international sports events or film festivals). A conceptual formulation that may be reasonably adequate or useful for understanding the transnational domains of political economy and high-power politics may be less useful for probing a transnational history of moral values or cultural venturousness. Arguably, the world system's commanders of political economy and power politics may not grant all that much priority to the interactions and identities, understandings and misunderstandings, achieved through cultural venturousness.

The third problem with reliance on the original formulation is that of historicity. Once one acknowledges the possibility of major transformations in the social dynamics and power balances of transcultural and transnational encounter, the usefulness of *any* conceptual formulation beyond a particular space/time is open to question. If, for example, the major powers within a capitalist world system acquire once unimaginable capacities of technological and informational "reach" and velocity, do such capacities imply a power balance so dramatically concentrated that the triangular metaphor becomes downright misleading?

In short, once one unpacks the corners of a triangular "solution" useful to capture a problem in early modern political economy, once one observes that issues of political economy and related issues of power politics cannot subsume an entire range of transnational encounter issues, and once one is attentive to historicity's capacity to wreck any conceptual scheme, one calls into question just how much has been solved. Perhaps the solution was useful only for a rather specific set of problems in a particular historical era. Perhaps it obscured as much as it illuminated even about the particular problems and era for which it had been formulated. Perhaps we must begin all over again to conceptualize a foreign presence that is integral yet not totalizing in its power to mold, or a foreign-local relationship that constantly draws cultural boundaries of "we" and "they" yet fails to preclude dynamics that confound division into "we" and "they."

The Value of Paradox

We need not succumb, I think, to conceptual despair. On the contrary, once one truly explores the paradoxes posed by partial negations of customary categories and apparent solutions, one finds a method that enables us to infuse a conceptual framework with the sensibilities—an awareness of historicity, of the multiplicity of human pathways and identities, of the powers of unintended consequence and desire—that clarify its historical substance and limits. Such an exploration would involve, I think, at least two interrogations: asking what specifically seemed to be the most important countervailing forces that yielded "paradox" within the foreign-local nexus that patterned a given historical era; and asking about commonality, difference, and interrelationships in the substance and consequences of such crosscurrents for different domains of transnational encounter. (These domains were summarized earlier as those of political economy and high-power politics, moral values and assessment of self and other, and cultural venturousness.)

Let us return, in this perspective, to our triangular formulation of three interacting yet internally contradictory social fields—the capitalist world-system (or more precisely, its hegemonic representatives, institutions, or interests within a given "periphery"), popular strategies of resistance and survival within the periphery, and mercantile and elite interests joined to American centers of gravity. I will explore briefly the first of the two interrogations mentioned above—specifying the countervailing forces that yielded the most powerful partial negation, or paradox, in the foreign-local nexus—within the domain of political economy and high-power politics. Space constraints will prevent me from explicit engagement of the second interrogation—attention to commonality, difference, and inter-relationships in the paradoxes evident in different domains or aspects of the foreign-local nexus. But a rich variety of chapters in this book focus on questions of moral assessment and cultural venturousness, and offer clues to the moral ambivalences and the appeals of border crossing that partly negate the structures of foreign-local categories and relationships.[7]

To some extent, our earlier "unpacking" of the three corners of our triangle yielded a paradox that seems applicable to various historical eras: a "decentering" of the power centers (whether power centers at the world-system level, or at the American region level) in their capacity to present a unified, directing force in accord with elite interests, needs, or priorities; and a certain "expansionary" quality of the periphery sector (whether at the level of regional elites or at the "popular" level of subaltern laboring folk), understood as the receiving "host" for elite projects, desires, and impositions. These dynamics, along with the emergence of crosscutting mediations and unforeseen social categories at the margins of main social categories and adaptations, tended to undermine, at least partially, the we/they contrasts and the contests of will embedded in our original triangle.

But this formulation, even if useful as a starting point, needs to be historicized. The substance and dynamics of the paradox of a "decentered center" and an "expansionist periphery" varied in ways that bore witness to historical change and transformation. For our purposes, it will be useful to distinguish *a groso modo* among three historical eras and the specific paradoxes that specify the meanings and undersides of an interacting and internally contradictory triangle of "motors."

Before we proceed, however, three caveats are needed. First, the transition dates between eras should not be construed as relatively compact dates of quick transition, but as convenient shorthand for a transition process that might span, say, some thirty to fifty years. Thus, the markers "c. 1540s" and "c. 1930s" are really midpoints of a longer process— abbreviations for a transition that might be rendered, more literally and more awkwardly, as "c. 1520s to 1560s" and "c. 1910s to 1950s," respectively. Second, the "tricks of time" in Latin America mean that the key issues and dynamics of one historical era are not so much displaced, as in a linear progression, by the key issues and dynamics of a new era. The relationship is more subtle: one of overlays of past and present, indeed reconstitutions of continuity within altered historical contexts.[8] Therefore, the dynamics of power and paradox used to characterize one historical era should not be construed as completely displaced or displacing alternatives to the dynamics of another era. Third, the rough periodization presented here is for the purpose of conceptualizing the foreign presence, with emphasis on political economy and power relations. Its degree of fit with periodizations focused on different problems or emphases remains an open question. One hopes that it embraces sufficiently important social issues to yield a chronology that is not wildly dissimilar from those developed around different themes or emphases within themes. But one also suspects a less than isomorphic fit.

Historical Eras and Paradoxes (1)

In the first post-Conquest era (c. 1540s to c. 1750s), when a transcontinental presence of the "foreigner" had become embedded (after an initial period of conquest wars, alliances, and ruptures) into the structures of local life and linked to the founding of a new kind of social order, our triangle of interacting social forces developed within a formal colonial framework hegemonized by Iberian colonial powers. Denoting the "starting" point as c. 1540s defers to the importance of a "first-generation" period of conquest wars, alliances, and ruptures that ushered in a new social order and geography, and to the importance of regional variations in timing.

In this era, the paradox that partly negated the premises of the entire triangle and its implied power balances was that of *reverse colonization and massive social leakage*. By "reverse colonization" I mean the entire array of responses whereby Indians and other subalterns colonized apparatuses of colonial control and profit-taking—the numerous ways that peoples condemned to colonization ended up invading and putting to their own use the colonial state's legal rules and political alliance games, or appropriating colonial markets and production niches in ways that furthered their own life strategies while undercutting colonial monopolies and revenues, or engaging and redeploying the meanings of Catholic religion and sacred patronage, or incorporating written decree, memory, and genre into a sense of group self, right, and destiny. This engagement and redeployment of the institutions and sites of colonial imposition constituted a kind of invasion or "reverse colonization" that partly undercut colonial powers of imposition.[9]

Reverse colonization also happened at an elite level as creole interests became increasingly adept at domesticating the colonial state apparatus — either through holding posts directly or rendering officeholders, even recently arrived foreigners, complicit with local elite practices, interests, and identities. From this point of view, the seventeenth century was not so much a period of "decline" in colonial Spanish America as a period of heightened creole rulership and relative autonomy.

Equally important as reverse colonization, by the mid–seventeenth century, was the phenomenon of massive social leakage — the processes that enabled people and commodities, identities and social worlds, to leak out of the social arrangements (including arrangements of resistance or dispute) set by the formal parameters of colonial status, right, and duty. Such leakage took an immense variety of forms. People leaked out as slaves and children of slaves who became runaway "maroons," as migratory Indians (*forasteros,* in the Andean regions) who had abandoned their tributary communities and who had become less visible to colonial tracking for tribute and labor quotas, as a growing population of mestizos and other racially mixed persons at the margins of the major categories of colonial right, obligation, and social control. Regions — their peoples, riches, and possibilities — leaked out in the vast territorial zones of uncertain imperial boundaries and overlays, where "middle ground" dynamics of mutual dependence and uncertain social control encouraged the transcultured identities and discourses, the ad hoc social arrangements and tacit agreements to overlook taboo and idiosyncrasy, associated with untamed "frontier zones." Commodities and revenues leaked out as smugglers and representatives of rival imperial powers established networks of trade and fraud that redirected ores from mints that produced debased coinage, or redirected commodities from formal fleets and registries.[10]

Reverse colonization and massive social leakage, the partial negation that calls into question the premises and power balances of our triangle of forces during the first major era of transcontinental encounter, not only undercut Iberian colonial powers of imposition. They also generated shadow processes of identity, interest, and possibility that lay outside the parameters set by our colonial triangle of social actors — social arrangements and mediations in a different dimension. (If one were to continue with the triangle metaphor, it would be as if a two-dimensional depiction of a triangle acquired a fourth corner in a third dimension, thereby creating three new triangles and a new geometrical shape.) One by-product might be a blurring of boundaries that might otherwise be taken as hard and fast: when a colonial trader sold guns to a band of maroon runaways, when an Indian social climber served as godfather or patron to a Hispanic client, the contrasts embedded in standard social categories and relations faded.

Historical Eras and Paradoxes (2)

Our second historical era will receive more extended attention because it overlaps with the chronological emphasis of this book. In this era (c. 1750s to c. 1930s), our triangle of interacting social fields developed within a framework of colonial dismantling and national state formation. The Iberian colonial framework that had hegemonized the earlier system of foreign-local interaction suffered a decisive unraveling; a set of America-centered elites set about charting a new political destiny in relations with the transforming North Atlantic world and with the dark and laboring folk on whose backs newly imagined order, progress, and community would be built; the "popular" sectors would develop their adaptation and resistance strategies in conflictual dialogue with creole elites and their pretenses and projects of rule, with imperial pretenders and newcomers of various sorts (the French, the British, the United Statesians, the Chileans, etc.), and in some instances (e.g., Indians seeking to reconstitute an imagined colonial "pact" in relations with postcolonial states) with memories of a lost Iberian past.

In this era, the paradox that partly negated the premises of our conceptual framework was that of *struggle to remake the "who" and "how" that populated a triangle of interacting social forces.* Both the identities ("who") of the main new social agents, and the basic rules ("how") by which they would live, fight, and reconcile among themselves and in relations with others, seemed subject to profoundly intense remakings. The remakings, moreover, seemed not to congeal in hegemonic outcomes that might yield long-term predictability, but to spark new rounds of remaking efforts.

At almost any moment in this era, for example, one witnesses intense struggles to redefine the peoples, interests, and principles of rule that constituted the relevant external "world-system" force. By the late eighteenth century, the competition between rival colonial powers had become fierce. In addition, the period witnessed a drive by the premier colonial powers—especially the British, Spanish, and Portuguese—to remake themselves anew, into more efficient engines of rule in a "reconquered" America. (The French case is complicated by the politics of revolution in St. Domingue and in Paris, and by territorial retreats to the British and the United States in North America, but it also implied a remaking of the imperial presence.) This "newness" of imperial rule provided a spark, of course, to the anticolonial struggles that shook the Americas.

The dismantling of most of the Iberian colonial grip from 1810 to 1824, and the realignment of many of Latin America's external links toward British economic agents and interests, failed to diminish a competition that seemed to undercut the hegemonized representation of the world system. Rival pretensions and interventions by various European powers — now supplemented by the United States and by Latin American power contenders — continued to mark the rules of the game for the new republics, federations, and empires. In addition, the failure of hegemonized representation inspired a sprinkle of foreign would-be kings, emperors, and adventurers convinced that they could set up their own personal fiefdoms or republics. The final collapse of the Spanish Empire in 1898 facilitated the launching of a newly aggressive geopolitical and economic drive by the United States to hegemonize the foreign presence in Latin America.[11] Nonetheless, the transition toward U.S. dominance of the relevant foreign presence was neither regionally even (it was most pronounced in Middle America and the Caribbean) nor smoothly accepted. Indeed, as Friedrich Katz has shown, the outbreak of the Mexican Revolution in 1910 sparked a "secret war" to determine which of the competing foreign powers might hegemonize the internal and external course of the Mexican convulsion.[12]

The struggles by creole elites to remake themselves into true regional rulers, differently aligned in a changing transatlantic world yet anchored in American centers of gravity, seemed to demand an effort to redefine the "who" and "how" that populated all three corners of a triangular foreign-local nexus. Those who aspired to lead new republics and imagined national communities faced, of course, decisions about how to define themselves. Were they the spiritual heirs of pre-Columbian glory, of an Iberian tradition deformed by colonizing tyranny exercised against creoles, of a late colonial awakening and struggle that created a new social leadership, free to experiment among and adapt several European and U.S. visions of progress and civilization to the conditions of American life and rule? Were they the racial heirs of Europe, or a hybrid race molded by the encounters of Europeans, Amerindians, and Africans in America? (Note a knotty corollary: were Amerindians and Africans equally acceptable as part of the racial mix?) Did ethnoracial malleability and cultural freedom to experiment, adapt, and fuse several versions of Europe imply that wealthy immigrant capitalists could be folded into creole families and social statuses, as "local" rather than "foreign" leaders of industry? (Note a revealing boundary: European immigrant capitalists seemed to become "native" in elite ethnoracial status more readily than Middle Eastern *árabes* or *turcos*.) Whoever the new national elites were, how could they establish workable rights of rule?[13]

These basic questions about the rights of rule (understood both as the "who" of social identity as legitimate national rulers, and the "how" of social practices in relationships of rule with others) necessarily required an effort to remake the other corners of a triangular relationship. In the various domains of foreign-local interaction, the America-centered leaders would need to channel their linkages toward preferred foreigners, the representatives of the external world's system of progress, prosperity, and power. Should the key economic and political contacts be channeled toward Great Britain, Germany, or the United States, or toward individual persons, companies, and speculators? Should models of liberalism, morality, and progress rely more on British or French inspiration? Should a sense of cultural aesthetics and venturousness revalidate the Hispanic inheritance, mimic French refinement and pretense, or establish a unique transcultural synthesis?

The necessity of remaking applied not only to the external world-system representatives, but also to the popular folk whose identities and strategies of survival and resistance would prove fundamental to national futures. Creole rulers would need to consider whether to encourage massive European immigration schemes that might "whiten" the national subaltern population, whether to define particular popular folk inherited from the older order (Indians, blacks, and mulattos; gauchos, *llaneros*, and *sertanejos*) as persons necessarily condemned to physical or cultural obliteration in the cause of national progress, and whether to proclaim racial mixing at the base of society as the special glory and possibility of a national community. Just as important, creole rulers would need to chart the boundaries and meanings of "citizenship" for subalterns in the process of state formation.[14] All of these issues implied that relationships between national elites and subaltern groups involved not merely interaction and contests of will between known social agents, but a profound desire to reconstitute altogether "who" the subalterns might really turn out to be, in ethnoracial and cultural terms, and "how" basic rules of right, obligation, and identity might channel their conditions of survival, citizenship, and resistance.

During our second historical era, intense rounds of struggle to constitute the "who" and "how" of basic social categories also engaged popular groups at the base of society. The late eighteenth and early nineteenth centuries witnessed efforts by Indians and slaves, in Andean South America and the larger Caribbean world especially, to imagine a transformed arrangement of social rule, identity, and standing. Such efforts were not limited to the massive civil wars that swept over Peru-Bolivia and Haiti in the 1780s and 1790s, respectively. The cycles of liberal opening and closure, inclusionary social mobilization followed by exclusionary repression and retreat, that marked the interior history of the independence wars; the social struggles that developed around the questions of slavery and abolition later in the nineteenth century; the complex political roads to peasant participation and exclusion in the construction of new "nations" and citizenship communities out of nineteenth-century wars against foreign invaders; the emergence, in the early twentieth century, of political coalitions that linked middle-sector agitation to crack open oligarchical political regimes, and more "popular" mobilizations by workers, peasants, and the new urban poor: all point toward repeating cycles of effort to establish a "popular" version of social identity and right that laid claim on "national" politics, identities, and rights of citizenship.[15] These were *repeating* cycles precisely because (at least until the near-end of the era) such efforts, in dialogue and rivalry with parallel efforts at social remaking and realignment by regionally anchored elites and international interests, were rarely decisive enough to lay down relatively stable, enduring markers that defined the "who" and "how" of social identity, rule, and struggle in the future. Even the Mexican Revolution yielded a certain indecisiveness before the political consolidation engineered by President Lázaro Cárdenas in the 1930s.

Struggle to remake the "who" and "how" that constituted basic social categories—the triangle of external agents, local elites, and popular groups whose relations defined power and the nexus of the "foreign" and the "local"—is the most salient partial negation of our conceptual framework during the era of Iberian dismantling and abortive national constructions. To the extent that such struggles yielded less than decisive results (fell short of hegemonic outcomes, to use the contrast between hegemonic process and outcome formulated in Florencia Mallon's *Peasant and Nation*) and seemed instead to spark new rounds of indecisive "remaking," the preconditions for an analysis of an interactive triangle of internally contradictory forces seem unfulfilled. What meaning can one find in such a framework if the key sociological categories seem exceptionally volatile?

One by-product of such volatility might be a certain chameleon effect that defied social boundaries. Yesterday's barbaric Indian became today's patriotic citizen; yesterday's tainted mulatto became today's whitening hope. (The chameleon effect could also run the other way: today's citizen-patriot could revert to tomorrow's degraded Indian-child, today's white hope could revert to tomorrow's dark, unemployable drag.) Significantly, the chameleon effect of endless social remaking could defy even boundaries between "foreign" and "local." Today's local Indian, African, or gaucho could become tomorrow's foreigner—someone bleached out or destroyed by the transforming march of historical progress, converted into a folkloric relic that is both historically "local" (native) and currently "foreign" (out of place). Today's self-styled local leader could become transposed by the pressures and lures of international war, investment, or political schemes into tomorrow's foreign agent (traitor). Today's foreign investor, worker, agricultural colonist, or interloper could become tomorrow's national capitalist, citizen, farmer-peasant, or political leader.[16]

Historical Eras and Paradoxes (3)

In a third historical era (c. 1930s onward), our triangle of interacting social forces developed within a framework of overwhelming U.S. importance as the hegemonic external presence in the Latin American world and as the wielder of unparalleled technical powers of control (powers of information monitoring and processing, of economic ownership and financial intervention, of political clientelism and socialization, of moral and cultural projection) between an imposing "center" and a receiving "periphery." Rival representatives of a relevant world-system presence were largely eclipsed. National elites contended with the United States' direct ownership and interventions in regional centers of political and economic gravity. Popular strategies of resistance and survival seemed futile unless one confronted the national question and the social question simultaneously.[17] Small wonder that this was an age that produced a kind of love-hate intimacy in relations with the United States, and a cluster of efforts to reclaim spaces—whether by enacting import-substitution schemes, promoting theories of dependency, or declaring nationalist revolutions—for a destiny less shadowed by the U.S. presence.

In this era, the paradox that partly negated the premises of the entire triangle was a *massive expansion and diversification of direct relationships, dependencies, and communications that turned territorial boundaries and directions of control into an illusion.* The result, by the late twentieth century, was an extreme decentering of the newly fortified center, an extreme expansionism by the newly vulnerable periphery, and the emergence of "globalization" dynamics that cut across the conventional, territorially rooted categories of identity and action in international relations.

The decentering of the will and coherence of the new "center" as it projected outward took many forms and derived in part from the same forces that heightened the potential for control. The mandate and possibility of control exerted by the U.S. central government after World War II—in part a result of the revenues that flowed from social prosperity, in part a result of the Cold War's platform for interventionism—diversified the kinds of overseas relationships and agendas directly and indirectly sponsored by the imperial state. The same state that stationed a diplomatic corps and intelligence agents in Latin America, and that promoted conditions favoring corporate exports and foreign investments, also sponsored Peace Corps and development projects and Fulbright programs of cultural interchange. The expansion of functions and programs promoted by the hegemonic foreign state diversified the social relations, experiences, and sympathies that United Statesians acquired abroad. Perhaps more important, the unprecedented technical capacity of a military superpower to destroy and to intervene also yielded an underside: military insecurity and political strife that limited powers to control. The Cuban missile crisis graphically demonstrated the illusion of nuclear military power during the Cold War: unprecedented power to destroy exposed the superpower to unprecedented vulnerability. The Cuban revolution, the most severe challenge to U.S. power in the Americas, would be met with schemes of political assassination and economic strangulation that failed to achieve their objectives. The Vietnam experience, a demonstration of amazing technical capacity to project power abroad, ended up (in conjunction with complex domestic social dynamics, including those associated with the civil rights movement and race relations) fracturing the political values and certainty of will that emanated from the center. Indeed, the experience fostered a political space for a skepticism that defended the unfettering of political processes and revolutions in the Third World.[18]

Add to this diversification of state-sponsored relationships abroad, and to the ironic military and political undersides of an amazing technical capacity to intervene and intimidate, the effects of prosperity and international technical capacity in "civil society." These facilitated direct relationships in politically uncontrolled or contrarian directions. Direct citizen action and transcultural experience in work brigades and sister-city projects, in fundraising and supply-donation task forces, in political and faith-based solidarity and citizen diplomacy groups, in refugee and human rights projects: the same society that seemed to exert unprecedented powers of control also seemed to have generated a multiplicity of direct contacts, sympathies, and politicization processes that divided the ability to exert unified political will and representation by a narrow circle of state representatives. Equally unsettling to a logic of centered political will, interest, and cultural influence abroad was the emergence of transnational corporations whose capacity for a global logic of investment, political interest, and personal loyalties cut across "old" logics that had been more anchored in national home territories and markets.[19]

The diversification of direct contact, dependencies, and exchanges also facilitated an unparalleled expansionism—more direct and more multidirectional—by the peoples and ideas of the "periphery." In a new world of diversified direct connection to external people, resources, and information, "demonstration effects" and cultural proselytizing could travel in South-to-South and South-to-North as well as North-to-South directions. The Cuban revolution and liberation theology might capture the imagination of the young and the socially minded in both South and North. The new world of diversified direct connections, exchanges, and dependencies also fostered a new demography in the center society. The juxtaposition of prosperity and decenterings of political will in the center, and poverty and political convulsions in the proximate periphery, sparked South-to-North expansionism and biculturalism. The new scale and diversity of Latino and Caribbean immigration congealed into permanent resident and refugee/exile communities (not small pockets of allowable new citizens, or bands of temporary *braceros* to be shipped away when inconvenient, or transitory refugees to be returned soon) that defied the physical (national borders), legal (allowable citizenship and residence), and cultural (predominant languages and ethnoracial heritage) boundaries of control exerted by the power center. Economic remittances and transnational kin webs implied a more directly integrated foreign-local nexus, and a more expanded placement of identity sites, for those who "remained" in the periphery.

In part, the failure to thwart the influx of expanded and diversified bicultural communities bore witness to expanded direct relations of complicity and dependence. Commercial employers and household heads offered work or shielding to those who accepted jobs and work conditions shunned by long-term residents and citizens of a prosperous society. Relatives residing in the United States but tied to transnational kinship and community webs might respond to a new arrival as a bearer of transnational reciprocity, connection, or obligation, or as a patron-client opportunity. Refugees and exiles might find political allies already committed to exposing the justness of their cause or the dangers of their return. Business, political, and cultural intermediaries might find their back-and-forth presence and biculturalism welcomed by those who sought international bridges in trade or investment, politics or education, sport or entertainment. (One need not romanticize such expansionism and complicities, of course. The vulnerability of immigrant workers could invite exploitation and abuse by employers, or transform transnational kinship and origin connections into ambiguous takings of advantage; the traumas of refugees could not be easily buried, above all if legal status or social claims depended on re-living the crisis that led to exile; the business of back-and-forth contact could include extralegal as well as legal activities.)

As the technical means for international financial transactions and com-modity delivery proved more fluid, and as the upper third of Latin Ameri-can populations concentrated considerable financial resources and instru-ments, the expansionism of the periphery into the center could also take on a significant economic aspect. Exports diversified and included manu-factured products, inputs, or assembly that once remained a domain of the center economy. Latin American investors and savers transacted business and acquired foreign holdings within the United States. Important trans-national purchasing zones developed along the U.S.–Mexican border and in Florida. Debt crisis and currency manipulation in the Mexican periph-ery brought to the surface the exposure and interdependence of the U.S. center.[20]

In short, the massification and diversification of direct relationships yielded strange alchemies: decentering and expansionary dynamics that undercut the known triangle of identities and power in an era when the relevant external power seemed especially hegemonic, able to eclipse rival international players and to assemble formidable technical capacities of control. The muscular giant equipped with amazing powers of control somehow seemed disposed to metamorphose into an awkward bumbler, constantly frustrated by unintelligent or misapplied uses of power lead-ing to unintended consequences. The direct relations of people, monies, information, and ideas seemed somehow to create crosscutting dynamics of globalization that defied the standard division of politically organized territories ("nations") into the familiar power asymmetries and identity boundaries.

Beyond a certain point, the negations implied by such dynamics call into question the premises of our conceptual triangle. The decentering of a center subject to an internal reshuffling of its own "local" population, the expansionism of a periphery whose reach capacity extended beyond immediate boundaries of the "local," suggest logics of "globalization" and multidirectional effect that undermine the entire structure of identification and expectation. In the realm of political economy, one of the most dramatic examples of such negation was the emergence, within the United States, of a more "Third World" style of economic modeling of prosperity and austerity: concentration of purchasing power toward a top third of the prosperous, well educated, and culturally sophisticated; competitive pressure that squeezed middle-class life into a mold of fragile aspiration and prosperity, in a shrinking middle third of respectable folk; poverty and extreme indigence in an expanding bottom third filled with relatively disposable people; and an ideology of justification premised on the necessity to compete with rivals in rich and poor countries alike.

Conclusion

To conceptualize the foreign presence in Latin America is to walk an intellectual tightrope. Our challenge is that of partial negation—both to find useful conceptual frameworks, and to infuse them with the sense of historicity, crosscurrents, and ironic undersides (a sensibility we have abbreviated as "paradox") that expose their meanings and limits.

This essay has focused on paradox and negation to refine and historicize a proposed framework—a triangle of interactive and internally contradictory "motors," or social fields, that drive Latin American political economy and, to some extent, politics. Yet it is crucial to strike a balance that avoids throwing out the proverbial baby with the bathwater: to remember that countervailing currents do not necessarily deny a structure of power and identity rules. Taken by themselves or stripped out of context, the negations discussed above invite exaggeration. One forgets that the negations are partial, that the paradoxes derive much of their meaning from the frameworks they seem to negate and unsettle. The reverse colonization by which Indians invaded the colonial state's legal labyrinth did not undo the Spanish colonial state's hegemonic presence. The leakage that turned slaves into maroons failed to stop the development of a powerful plantation sector, and of armed raids and knowledge networks that rendered maroon life difficult to sustain and subject to reversal. The remakings that unsettled the relevant social categories of postcolonial nations in formation failed to block the eventual congealing of a state run by an oligarchical elite of rulers wedded to specific international markets and patrons, and to an exclusionary politics of rule over relatively "dark" or "barbaric" peoples.

Similarly, the direct relations that projected an expansionist periphery—its peoples, resources, and ideas—into the life of a decentered center could thwart the will of a policy-making elite, but only in part. The Reagan administration often found itself detoured and frustrated in its script for Congressional lobbying and political intervention in the Central American wars of the 1980s. Sometimes, it must have seemed that House Speaker Jim Wright talked more directly to Daniel Ortega, Rubén Zamora, or Central American refugees than to Ronald Reagan. But such detours were partial. They did not block the strangulation of Nicaragua's revolution and they did not block the stalemating that turned back El Salvador's opposition.

Notes

I wish to thank the Yale conference organizers and book editors, Gilbert Joseph, Catherine LeGrand, and Ricardo Salvatore, for writing the stimulating proposal that sparked the reflections in this essay; the conference participants, especially William Roseberry and George Yúdice, for pertinent comments and suggestions; and my colleagues Florencia Mallon and Francisco Scarano for suggestions and support.

An *advertencia* for readers: Because this essay is a synthetic reflection, it avoids detailed annotations. In particular, I avoid lengthy annotations of events and patterns that will be familiar to most scholars of Latin American history, and generally limit annotations to documentation of more obscure points, and to suggestion of useful works that amplify points made in the text.

1. See John L. Phelan, "Pan-Latinism, French Intervention in Mexico (1861–1867), and the Genesis of the Idea of Latin America," in *Conciencia y autencidad históricas: Escritos en homenaje a Edmundo O'Gorman* (Mexico City: UNAM, 1968), 279–98. I am grateful to Paul Edison for helping me to track this reference.

2. Richard White, *The Middle Ground: Indians, Empires, and Republics in the Great Lakes Region, 1650–1815* (Cambridge: Cambridge University Press, 1991).

3. Among the classic expressions of this sensibility are Gabriel García Márquez, *Cien años de soledad* (Buenos Aires: Editorial Sudamericana, 1967); and Octavio Paz, *El laberinto de la soledad,* 2d rev. ed. (Mexico City: Fondo de Cultura Económica, 1959).

4. Stern, "Feudalism, Capitalism, and the World-System in the Perspective of Latin America and the Caribbean," in *Confronting Historical Paradigms: Peasants, Labor, and the Capitalist World System in Africa and Latin America,* Frederick Cooper et al. (Madison: University of Wisconsin Press, 1993), 23–83 (quote, 55). The essay was originally published in *American Historical Review* 93, no. 4 (Oct. 1988) and included a debate with Wallerstein.

5. I am grateful to Roseberry's oral comments on this point at the Yale conference on which this book is based. For a recent reflection by Roseberry on the importance of understanding peasants within "locally configured fields of power," see "Beyond the Agrarian Question in Latin America," in Cooper et al., *Confronting Historical Paradigms,* 318–68 (quote, 359).

6. Read consecutively, the last two books by the late John Leddy Phelan yield considerable insight on this point: see *The Kingdom of Quito in the Seventeenth Century: Bureaucratic Politics in the Spanish Empire* (Madison: University of Wisconsin Press, 1967); and *The People and the King: The Comunero Revolution in Colombia* (Madison: University of Wisconsin Press, 1978). More recent studies of transatlantic family networks and immigration also enrich understanding of such issues: see, e.g., Ida Altman, *Emigrants and Society: Extremadura and America in the Sixteenth Century* (Berkeley and Los Angeles: University of California Press, 1989); and Altman and James Horn, eds., *"To Make America": European Migration in the Early Modern Period* (Berkeley and Los Angeles: University of California Press, 1991).

7. In addition to the relevant case studies in this book, considerable theoretical insight on the problems of moral assessment and cultural venturousness may be found in Edward Said, *Orientalism* (New York: Pantheon, 1978); Mary Louise Pratt, *Imperial Eyes: Travel Writing and Transculturation* (New York: Routledge, 1992); and Jane Collins and Catherine Lutz, *Reading National Geographic* (Chicago: University of Chicago Press, 1993).

8. The "tricks of time" theme requires treatment in its own right. My views on this issue are developed in Stern, *The Secret History of Gender: Women, Men, and Power in Late Colonial Mexico* (Chapel Hill: University of North Carolina Press, 1995), chap. 14; and "The Tricks of Time: Colonial Legacies and Historical Sensibilities in Latin America" (paper presented at a Princeton University conference, "Empire and Underdevelopment: The Colonial Heritage of Latin America Revisited," Princeton, N.J., 2–3 Dec. 1995; [a preliminary version appears in *Princeton University Library Chronicle,* 57:3 (spring 1996)], 371–92).

9. Elsewhere, I have offered a fuller orientation to scholarship demonstrating indigenous engagement and redeployment of colonial apparatuses of control and dominance: see Stern, "Paradigms of Conquest: History, Historiography, and Politics," *Journal of Latin American Studies* 24 (quincentenary supplement, 1992), 1–34; cf. William B. Taylor, "Between Global Process and Local Knowledge: An Inquiry into Early Latin American Social History, 1500–1900," in *Reliving the Past: The Worlds of Social History,* ed. Olivier Zunz (Chapel Hill: University of North Carolina Press, 1985), 115–90.

10. On maroons, the best introduction remains Richard Price, ed., *Maroon Societies: Rebel Slave Communities in the Americas,* 2d ed. (Baltimore, Md.: Johns Hopkins University Press, 1979); on migratory Indians, the fundamental work is Ann M. Wightman, *Indigenous Migration and Social Change: The Forasteros of Cuzco, 1570–1720* (Durham, N.C.: Duke University Press, 1990); on the redraw-

ing of colonial territories and administrative rules, in the era of the Bourbon reforms, as a "second conquest" designed to combat the slippages that rendered Iberian control leaky and inefficient by the mid to late colonial period, see John Lynch, *The Spanish American Revolutions, 1808–1826* (New York: Norton, 1973), chap. 1; for a similar point from the perspective of a regional frontier, see Nancy Farriss, *Maya Society under Colonial Rule: The Collective Enterprise of Survival* (Princeton, N.J.: Princeton University Press, 1984).

11. The "newly aggressive" characterization refers to expansionism toward the south, since an aggressive east-to-west push had marked U.S. history well before 1898.

12. See Friedrich Katz, *The Secret War in Mexico: Europe, the United States, and the Mexican Revolution* (Chicago: University of Chicago Press, 1981); on U.S. interests, see also Gilbert M. Joseph, *Revolution from Without: Yucatán, Mexico, and the United States, 1880–1924,* 2d ed. (Durham, N.C.: Duke University Press, 1988); and John Mason Hart, *Revolutionary Mexico: The Coming and Process of the Mexican Revolution* (Berkeley and Los Angeles: University of California Press, 1987).

13. Among the most revealing ways to explore the efforts of creole elites to define themselves is through the lens of their perception of race and popular culture. See, e.g., Richard Graham, ed., *The Idea of Race in Latin America, 1870–1940* (Austin: University of Texas Press, 1990); Thomas E. Skidmore, *Black into White: Race and Nationality in Brazilian Thought,* 2d. ed. (Durham, N.C.: Duke University Press, 1993); George Reid Andrews, *The Afro-Argentines of Buenos Aires, 1800–1900* (Madison: University of Wisconsin Press, 1980), and *Blacks and Whites in São Paulo, Brazil, 1888–1988* (Madison: University of Wisconsin Press, 1991); Euclides da Cunha, *Rebellion in the Backlands,* trans. Samuel Putnam (Chicago: University of Chicago Press, 1944); and Domingo F. Sarmiento, *Life in the Argentine Republic in the Days of the Tyrants; or Civilization and Barbarism,* trans. Mrs. Horace Mann (New York: Hafner Publishing Co., 1960). For the related problem of the emergence of imagined national communities, see Benedict Anderson, *Imagined Communities: Reflections on the Origin and Spread of Nationalism,* 2d. ed. (London: Verso, 1991). On the differences in the propensity to transform and absorb European versus "Arab" immigrants and entrepreneurs as "insiders," I have benefited from Darío Euraque's study of Honduran elites, *Reinterpreting the "Banana Republic": Region and State in Honduras, 1870–1972* (Chapel Hill: University of North Carolina Press, 1996); as well as Peter Winn, *Weavers of Revolution: The Yarur Workers and Chile's Road to Socialism* (New York: Oxford University Press, 1986).

14. Especially relevant for such issues are Florencia E. Mallon, *Peasant and Nation: The Making of Postcolonial Mexico and Peru* (Berkeley and Los Angeles: University of California Press, 1995); and Gilbert M. Joseph and Daniel Nugent, eds., *Everyday Forms of State Formation: Revolution and the Negotiation of Rule in Modern Mexico* (Durham, N.C.: Duke University Press, 1994); see also n. 15.

15. These themes are too vast for detailed annotation. But for suggestive orientations or especially relevant works, see the following: on late colonial wars and the interior history of the independence wars, Lynch, *Spanish American Revolutions;* on social struggles and the slavery-to-abolition transition, Emilia Viotti da Costa, *Da senzala a colonia,* 2d ed. (São Paulo: Livraria Editora Ciencias Humanas, 1982); Rebecca J. Scott, *Slave Emancipation in Cuba: The Transition to Free Labor, 1860–1899* (Princeton, N.J.: Princeton University Press, 1985); on peasants and construction of new citizenship communities amid war, Mallon, *Peasant and Nation;* cf. Aline Helg, *Our Rightful Share: The Afro-Cuban Struggle for Equality, 1886–1912* (Chapel Hill: University of North Carolina Press, 1995); on middle-sector agitation and more "popular" mobilization, the most dramatic case is Mexico: see, e.g., Alan Knight, *The Mexican Revolution,* 2 vols. (New York: Cambridge University Press, 1986); Allen Wells and Gilbert M. Joseph, *Summer of Discontent, Seasons of Upheaval: Elite Politics and Rural Insurgency in Yucatán, 1876–1915* (Stanford, Calif.: Stanford University Press, 1996); and for a longterm and theoretical perspective, John Tutino, *From Insurrection to Revolution in Mexico: Social Bases of Agrarian Violence, 1750–1940* (Princeton, N.J.: Princeton University Press, 1986); and Joseph and Nugent, *Everyday Forms.*

16. Particularly revealing examples of "chameleon effects" may be discerned in Mallon, *Peasant and Nation;* Helg, *Our Rightful Share;* Skidmore, *Black into White;* and Mark Thurner, *From Two Republics to One Divided: Contradictions of Postcolonial Nationmaking in Andean Peru* (Durham, N.C.: Duke University Press, 1997). See also two recent studies on integral outsiders and immigrant communities: William Schell, "A Modern Trade Diaspora: American Integral Outsiders in Porfirian Mexico City," and Jürgen Buchenau, "Not Quite Mexican and Not Quite German: The Boker Family in Mexico, 1865–1995" (papers presented at the conference "Rethinking the Postcolonial Encounter: Transnational Perspectives on the Foreign Presence in Latin America," Yale University, New Haven, Conn., Oct. 1995).

17. This was a context that led to a blending of discourses on social emancipation and anti-imperialism. Significantly, such discourses were influential not only in Mexico, Central America, and the Caribbean—the zones of obvious interventionism by the United States—but also in more "distant" South American regions. A classic example is that of APRA and Haya de la Torre; for context and analysis, see Peter F. Klarén, *Modernization, Dislocation, and Aprismo: Origins of the Peruvian Aprista Party, 1870–1932* (Austin: University of Texas Press, 1973).

18. For a discussion of the intellectual effects of domestic and international upheavals on the historical profession in the United States, particularly on visions of the Third World, see Cooper et al., *Confronting Historical Paradigms,* esp. chap. 1.

19. In this context, criticism of transnational corporations shifted from an earlier cycle of denunciations of "imperialism," in which the agents of advanced nations exploited the peoples of poor nations, toward a critique of "globalization" that might lament a shift of manufacturing sites toward the "periphery," and a conse-

quent "deindustrialization" that undermined the living standards of select social sectors in the advanced nations. The debates on the NAFTA accords in the United States were quite revealing of this shift. See, e.g., Saskia Sassen, *Losing Control? Sovereignty in an Age of Globalization* (New York: Columbia University Press, 1996).

20. The statistics on manufactured goods as a percentage of exports from major Latin American countries are quite revealing of a certain "expansionism" by the periphery that cut against inherited schemes whereby "advanced" countries exported processed goods and "poor" countries exported raw commodities. By the 1980s and 1990s, manufactured goods accounted for between a third and a half of goods and services exported by Brazil; by the 1990s, manufactured products accounted for roughly a third of Mexican exports of goods and services, despite the continuing high profile of crude petroleum in the structure of Mexican exports; for Latin America as a whole, the manufacturing proportions in the early 1990s were similar to those of Mexico (calculations based on CEPAL [Comisión Económica para América Latina y el Caribe], *Anuario estadístico de América Latina y el Caribe/Statistical Yearbook for Latin America and the Caribbean, 1994* [Santiago, Chile: United Nations, 1995], 112–13, 124–25, 142–43, 438–39, 452–53, 476–77). On the capacity of Latin American investors to set up subsidiaries in the countries of the "center," see Peter B. Evans, *Dependent Development: The Alliance of Multinational, State, and Local Capital in Brazil* (Princeton, N.J.: Princeton University Press, 1979), esp. the opening anecdote on Hills Brothers Coffee. More recently, I recall the appearance of a *New York Times* article, shortly after Congressional passage of the NAFTA accords, noting that among the unexpected consequences of NAFTA was enhanced capacity for Mexican investor expansion into U.S. production processes.

Ricardo D. Salvatore

The Enterprise of Knowledge

Representational Machines of Informal Empire

Although the primary object of the Expedition is the promotion of the great interests of commerce and navigation, yet you will take all occasions, not incompatible with the great purposes of your undertaking, to extend the bounds of science, and promote the acquisition of knowledge. Instructions to Charles Wilkes, U.S. Exploring Expedition, 1838–1842

It can be said that most of the modern explorers did not really discover anything, since there were people already living in the regions they set out to explore. But they were the first to draw these places into the orbit of our collective knowledge. J. PERKINS, 1981, American Museum of Natural History

In this essay, I examine a set of representations of the encounter between North Americans and South Americans during the construction of the U.S. informal empire in the region. Rather than proposing a particular model or explanation about the genesis of the empire, my objective is to displace the problematic of empire to the terrain of representations, culture, and practice. The essay is exploratory, its conclusions preliminary. It attempts to map the terrain in broad strokes as a way of initiating a longer research project. The search advances in different directions: seeking analytical tools that could help conceptualize the subject matter, describing the variety of interventions that constitute the informal empire, establishing connections among these interventions, and interpreting the narratives of different cultural mediators, all the while identifying elements of continuity and change. While exploratory, the essay calls attention to the representational nature of the postcolonial encounter, focusing in particular on the construction of "South America" as a field of North American engagement. Second, the essay stresses the relevance of certain conceptual tools, among them the notion of "representational devices," as a way of organizing our own reconstruction of the phenomena under analysis. Finally, the essay tries to establish the centrality of a given imaginary for legitimating the expansionist project, something I call "the enterprise of knowledge."

Representational Devices and Practices of Empire

British colonialism in South Africa, according to John and Jean Comaroff, was a complex assemblage embodying at least three models of colonial governance, each one with its enunciators and predicaments: the state overseeing and exploring territory, the white settlers coercing the aborigines for profit, and the religious missions in charge of "civilizing" and protecting the latter.[1] Each of the three competing colonialisms stressed one aspect of the imperial impulse: the state emphasized the political and legal aspects of British rule; the settlers, the racial bases of socioeconomic coercion; and the missionaries, the ethos and practices of bourgeois Europe. None of the three discourses and interventions were reducible to another; on the contrary, each stood in contradiction with the others, carrying into the construction of empire the conflict over the meaning of "Britain." Far from constituting a monolithic and unchanging structure, British colonialism was the displacement of the ongoing tension of institutions, values, images, and practices in Britain onto the territory of South Africa.[2]

In similar fashion, we may think of the U.S. informal empire built around the period 1890–1920 as a collection of diverse discourses, multiple mediators or agents, and various and, at times, contradictory representations. Theories of imperialism and dependency have accustomed us to think of North American domination or hegemony in terms of a few interventions, namely the economic, the diplomatic, and the military. Culture, textuality, and, more generally, other types of interventions (scientific, reformist, religious, literary, etc.) received a short shrift in these conceptions.[3] We need at this juncture to reintroduce the question of diversity in the making of the North American informal empire. In part, this can be accomplished by considering other cultural mediators whose texts and visions have left an important and enduring imprint in the metanarratives of U.S. expansionism.

Many were the ambassadors of "American culture" in South America: missionaries, agricultural settlers, educators, social reformers, scientists, businessmen, labor organizers, journalists, travelers, and navy and army officers, among others. Each of them must have seen South America with different eyes and therefore textualized the North American presence in the region in distinctive ways. Despite commonalities of culture, North Americans' engagement with South American countries and their peoples varied significantly. Common cultural anxieties, the use of the same cognitive categories, and similar predispositions to see, document, and experiment did not preclude the existence of tensions in the ways these ambassadors negotiated the values, traditions, and presuppositions of the two cultures. Also diverse was the degree of these mediators' involvement with the host society and, presumably, their conceptions of the U.S. role in South America—their reasons for empire.[4]

In order to understand both the tensions and the coherence within the discourse of informal empire, we need to conceive of the latter as a collective enterprise encompassing multiple *practices of engagement,* practices that included, necessarily, the production and circulation of representations. The diversity of views, involvements, and predicaments implied by the term *engagement* can be analytically separated into professional or occupationally based interpretive communities (writers, engineers, traders, investors, priests, and so forth) and ultimately rearranged according to the distinct *practices* cooperating for the inclusion of South America within the orbit of North American knowledge (collecting, mapping, narrating, photographing, displaying, etc.).[5] An adequate reconsideration of the postcolonial encounter can no longer ignore the multiplicity of these practices of engagement or minimize the importance of representations in the constitution of these practices.

The construction of the U.S. informal empire was a collective enterprise laden with representations. Beyond the extraction of economic surplus through commerce, direct investment, or the provision of services, the empire was a pharaonic accumulation of representations. Just as an army of photographers, museum directors, land surveyors, railroad promoters, journalists, scientific explorers, and popular entertainers contributed to form the idea of "the West" that fed the transcontinental migrations,[6] the construction of "South America" as a territory for the projection of U.S. capital, expertise, dreams, and power required the channeling of massive energies into the production of images and texts. The arguments for hemispheric hegemony—and also the economics and politics of empire—had to be lodged in representations: beyond diplomatic tours, Pan-American conferences, or company towns, the Pax Americana existed in maps, paintings, geography books, novels, and natural history exhibits.

Legitimating the presence of North American capital, expertise, ideas, and values in the lands to the south demanded a double and simultaneous textual construction: describing the other (South America) in terms of a perennial deficit or vacuum, and ascribing meaning to "the mission" (the role of the North Americans in the region). Without one or the other, the expansion of U.S. capital and culture would be impaired, its legitimacy negated. Rather than being guided by a single logic, the postcolonial encounter produced a mass of representations transected by competing discourses about the other and the mission. The reasons for informal empire confronted arguments of economic interest, benevolence, moral reform, knowledge, and the "national interest." Similarly, diverse textual producers (belonging to distinct interpretive or professional communities) engendered competing visions of South America. The region was imagined as a large potential market, as an impressive experiment in racial mixture and republicanism, as a target for missionary colonization, as a reservoir of "evidence" for the natural sciences, as the site for the regeneration of "humanity," and so on.

In this essay, I want to explore the discursive formation of informal empire (as built by North American textual producers) in all its diversity, posing simultaneously the question of regularity, order, and commonality in the production and circulation of representations of South America. Both sides of the coin are important. As each cultural producer belonged to a particular professional or interpretive community in the United States —or, better, as they were involved in particular projects belonging to a certain field of power/knowledge—their encounters with South America must have left variegated representations. At the same time, conventions of genre, technologies of observation, and institutional practices of display limited the set of arguments used by different agents. Narrative and visual representations of South America, though diverse, present recurrent metaphors, familiar associations, and often interchangeable images.

Diversity and order in the production and circulation of representations of South America must be in turn related to changes in the nature of the imperial economy and state and to the development of technologies of seeing, regimes of exhibition, and practices of science. The objective is not to construe yet another reified version of empire but to propose an analytical framework that can accommodate multiple forms of imperial engagement, relate cultural anxieties and questions of political economy in the United States to the discursive production of empire, and attribute its due importance to the changing technologies of reproduction and display.[7]

Stephen Greenblatt's concept of *representational machine* can be profitably employed in this regard. A representational machine is a set of mechanisms, processes, and apparatuses that produce and circulate representations constitutive of cultural difference.[8] The term *machine* is used to indicate that texts are produced, circulated, displaced, or re-signified with the help of certain technologies of representation and display.[9] In the same way that machines are assemblages of different tools organized for the production of goods, representational machines are collections of dispositives or devices (each one with its own logic of representation) organized for the production of cultural difference. Although the production of representations is not rigidly determined by the devices used, these technologies of seeing and displaying influence the construction of alterity. A collection of devices ranging from the printed press to ethnological exhibits (from romantic novels to photography), representational technologies are the vehicles through which statements about other cultures are produced and disseminated.

By integrating two apparently distinct realms—technology and culture—Greenblatt's concept challenges us to see the complex connections between the constitutive powers of an imperial society (the economy, the state, the reformist elite, the media, the aesthetic producers) and the representations that mediate the contact between cultures. Both technology and circulation are central to Greenblatt's concept of representational machines. To translate an undifferentiated succession of local, individual, concrete events of encounter into larger, more meaningful narratives—narratives that convey meaning to formulations of nation, empire, race, or masculinity—each culture must work with and through certain representational technologies.[10] These technologies set the boundaries of what is representable and provide guidance as to how, given the parameters of the receptive culture, a certain object is to be represented.

Circulation, according to Greenblatt, is the aim of most representations of difference. Through thousands of appropriations and metamorphoses, enunciations, images, and performances produced in a given context reach various audiences or readerships, carrying with them prevailing cultural anxieties about self and other, the social system, the role of science, the right of government, and so forth.[11] The message implicit in one form of representation is rapidly incorporated into another and from there disseminated throughout the cultural field. The displacement of a given representation in turn produces a shift in its meaning: each interpretive community receives, appropriates, and reinterprets in particular ways the representational harvest of empire. This makes representational machines quite malleable, eroding in fact the rigidity implied in the term *machine*.[12]

The concept of representational machines can help us visualize the workings of the multiple representational practices that have constituted the U.S. informal empire in South America. The region became visible and apprehensible to North America only through concrete representational practices and devices (e.g., travel narratives, geographic handbooks, photograph albums, and ethnographic exhibits). These representational practices constituted the stuff of empire as much as the activities of North Americans in the economic, military, or diplomatic fields.

Though dispersed and atomistic with regard to their points of production, the mass of representations constituted a flow with a given directionality and a few sites of assemblage. World fairs, museums of natural history, and the printing press in the United States were the final points—the sites of arrangement and display—of a vast process of production and circulation of texts and images about South America. This process included the collection of animals, plants, rocks, mummies, and native artifacts from the region and their classification and display in museums, fairs, and other scientific institutions in the United States.[13] Also part of this process were other representations making South America visible or readable for North Americans: photograph albums, travel narratives, statistical handbooks, maps, sociological surveys, and so on. The latter carried "evidence" that necessitated the printing press as a mediating institution. This mass of representations was generated as a by-product of the practices of engagement of North Americans in South America, many of them facilitated by institutions in the fields of natural science, the humanities, business, social reform, and religion.

One way of conceptualizing the U.S. informal empire is to think of it as a chain of nodes or points of textual/image production, each involving a combination of technologies, practices, and forms; as an extended flow of information, visual images, arguments, and meanings going from South to North; as a process of accumulation of symbolic capital through multiple technologies of seeing, narrating, and displaying. How was this system organized? What coordinated the diversity? Were there common rules governing this process?

At a most basic level, the system organized devices of *observation* (photography, interviews, the traveler's gaze), *representation* (maps, statistical handbooks, travel narratives), and *display* (museums, world fairs). The organization of these different nodes of cultural production was loose. Different projects (science, business, diplomacy, philanthropy, religion) and practices (reporting, collecting, mapping, image-making, displaying) contributed independently to the construction and reproduction of this representational machine.[14] What united these different projects was a common attempt to insert South America into the orbit of North American collective knowledge. The obsession of North American science with comprehensive knowledge, together with the technologies of seeing and displaying characteristic of this age of mass consumption, constitute the most solid bases of this representational machine.

For analytical purposes we may think of this representational machine as composed of three departments, each in charge of a particular function. The first served *to construct the nature of the expansionist project,* that is, to present to North American visitors to South America a coherent interpretation of what they (the visitors) were doing "down there." I include here a series of enunciations that competed to legitimate the presence of North Americans and the extension of U.S. business in the region. In scientific reports, photograph albums, addresses to businessmen, or novels we can separate a distinctive set of arguments and images locating the North American (the representative of peace, commerce, progress, modernity, masculinity, etc.) in a foreign territory. A second department served *to construct the nature of "South America."* A series of representational practices (sketching, painting, photography, surveying, reporting, and collecting natural specimens, among others) translated the impressions or observations of the region's natural resources, inhabitants, customs, institutions, and beliefs into simplified enunciations and texts about the meaning of "South America." A third department made texts and images about South America *reach the North American public.* How the constructs about the other and the mission were received by U.S. science and the North American public depended crucially on the institutions and practices organizing the circulation and display of these texts and images. Museums, world fairs, and photographic exhibits—what Tony Bennett calls the "exhibitionary complex" [15]—together with illustrated magazines, travel books, maps, and handbooks, served to circulate the representational harvest of imperial engagement, conveniently tailoring it for an expanding North American public.[16]

While no central coordination guided the accumulation of images and texts (and there was certainly ample room for individual and idiosyncratic expressions), certain common understandings, restrictions, and technologies oriented the selection of arguments and the modes of representation and display. Representations about South America did not accumulate at random; they followed certain rules of enunciation and display determined in part by available technologies common to science and the arts. Moreover, textual producers worked within a delimited discursive field; their representations of South America attempted to answer questions posed by their communities of origin, questions only slightly reformulated by the experience of the encounter.

A major impetus unifying the different practices of engagement of North Americans abroad was the "enterprise of knowledge," a somewhat modified version of the Humboltian program adapted to the age of mass consumption. This proposition connected North Americans' multiple practices of engagement to the common purpose of drawing South

America into the orbit of "American" collective knowledge. In the rhetoric of informal empire, there was always a layer of South America's reality insufficiently understood or known, a vacuum of knowledge that authorized the presence of more scientific explorers, collectors, photographers, statisticians, and business promoters.[17]

From Commercial to Neo-imperial Engagement

Two periods can be clearly demarcated in the development of the representational machinery of the U.S. informal empire: a moment of *mercantile engagement* (1820–1860), when the outward impulse was driven by the expansion of commerce, and the textualization of South America proceeded by means of traditional forms of representation (travel narratives); and a moment of *neo-imperial engagement* (1890–1930), marked by increasing U.S. direct investment in the region and by the use of technologies of representation characteristic of the age of mass-produced commodities (photography, product advertising, illustrated magazines).[18] Significant transformations in the nature of business enterprise, in the cultural anxieties and imperial ambitions of the United States, and in the technologies of representation marked the transition between these two forms of engagement. Also important was the explosion of written and visual representations of South America coincidental with the emergence and diffusion of Pan-Americanism.[19]

During the first period (1820–1860), a process of capitalist accumulation in the U.S. Northeast, centered on commerce and light industry, engendered a culture constructed around the concepts of small-scale property, productive labor, and agrarian republicanism.[20] This was a culture preoccupied with the emergence of (Jacksonian) "mob politics," overtly concerned with the sudden changes in banking policy; looking for an illusory "natural order" of races; and searching for means of channeling the energies of the Second Great Awakening into various "reform" movements (abolitionism, prison reform, temperance, religious benevolence, and education reform).[21] Production rather than consumption was at the center of the cultural preoccupations of the time. The economy was less intense in representations than during the second period. Commodity merchandising depended chiefly on person-to-person interactions; the "jobber" was key to market expansion, catalogs were rare, and Barnum displays at the American Museum remained a baroque set of curiosities.

In a United States insecure about its position vis-à-vis Europe and the moral dilemma of appropriating Indian lands, knowledge and understanding of the "external world" were crucial. Thus, the representatives of U.S. culture abroad (the merchant adventurer, the scientific explorer, the missionary) were entrusted with the task of gathering information about foreign lands. They had to search for "useful knowledge" as well as for "general knowledge." The traveler-ethnographer had the responsibility of translating the "outer worlds" into a language comprehensible to North American readers, while the scientific explorer collected "evidence" on a global scale to generate vast classificatory systems intended to order the natural world.

Mercantile travelers, in particular, were supposed to gather market information about foreign lands, information that included, besides data on prices and demand, the customs, habits, beliefs, and forms of government of the countries they visited. Before the industrial and transportation revolutions brought about a comparative advantage for U.S. manufacturers, expectations of fair competition in the world market depended on the skills with which merchants collected information.[22] Complying with this imperative of culture, mercantile travelers became the first ethnographers of the "young republics"; their travel narratives, "price currents," and newspaper articles contributed to an early mapping of South America into the orbit of North American knowledge.

Travel writing was the preferred genre for textualizing the encounter between North and South Americans. Aided only by sketches, watercolors, and engravings, these texts tried to interest readers in South American landscapes and peoples by discussing issues of concern to young, educated, white, male North Americans: gender propriety, racial diversity, customs and manners, forms of government, and institutions of culture. As these encounters were limited (a reduced number of merchants, sailors, navy officers, diplomats, clergy, and entrepreneurs visited the region during the postindependence period), so were the representations of South America available to the North American public. During this period, history books, novels, travel and adventure narratives, and even journalistic reports about South America were relatively rare. Hence the insistence on the need to enhance North American knowledge of the region at a time of unprecedented expansion of commerce to South America and the Pacific, an expansion sanctioned by the official doctrine "America for the Americans."

Early travel narratives of South America written by North Americans carried into the text of the encounter the "mission" and the "character" attributed to merchants by the culture of the educated communities of the U.S. Northeast.[23] Various institutions (e.g., mercantile library associations, athenaeums, the Y M C A) had constructed the field of activities of a "good merchant" as one that embraced business, benevolence, and "useful knowledge." Consequently, mercantile travelers projected onto the textual terrain of their encounters with South America an ideology that united commerce, peace, and the search for intellectual and spiritual improvement.[24] This ideology was consistent with the Monroe Doctrine.

The same discourse that elevated the merchant to a truth seeker also contested the project of colonization and territorial annexation. Even if William Walker's filibustering in Nicaragua, Gibbon and Hendron's report of their expedition to the Amazon, and the war with Mexico over Texas and California spoke the language of Manifest Destiny, the Northeastern mercantile community rejected the project of formal empire as inimical to hard labor, domestic order, and thrift. Manifest Destiny, D. H. Haskell told an audience of mercantile men in 1848, was a petty doctrine, more appropriate to the children of the poor who saw their horizon in the Western territories than of merchants whose perspective extended to the world at large.[25] The realm of experience for the U.S. merchant was the world market, a territory where competition aided by knowledge could procure the long-desired incorporation of the "young republics" into the North American sphere of influence.

Later during the period of neo-imperial engagement (1890–1930), corporations came to dominate the U.S. economy, intensifying the process of mechanization, industrial concentration, and mass production. Business enterprise became larger and organizationally more complex, vertically and horizontally integrated, and more dependent on the scientific apparatus.[26] A rapid period of economic growth led to the concentration of population in urban areas and the development of new market institutions geared to the sale of mass-produced goods (department stores, retail chains, mail-order houses). The advertising industry, a veritable engine of new ideas about marketing and industrial design, rearranged the symbolic order toward mass consumer culture, undermining the centrality of work, landed property, and agrarian citizenship in the process.

According to William Leach a new cultural compost, marked by the democratization of desire, the revalorization of money, and the identification of consumption with happiness, emerged during this period.[27] New technologies of observing and representing "realities" became central to the organization of the perceptions of U.S. consumers: namely, the arrangement of show windows, magazines, billboards, electrical signs, advertising cards, mail-order catalogs, and so forth. Sustaining these new fields of vision were advances in the reproduction of images (chromolithography and photography) and new uses for glass and electricity in displays.[28] Capitalist production intensified its use of representations.

The advent of corporate capitalism generated its own anxieties and concerns about the United States and its place in the global order. In the 1890s popular concerns with trusts and the erosion of democracy coexisted with business anxieties about overproduction and the rising power of skilled workers.[29] By the 1920s, corporations' control of an ever-increasing fund for investment brought about a rapid mechanization of industry, creating an avalanche of new products for mass consumption. Thus, the concern shifted back toward overproduction, now examined in relation to the preferences, lifestyles, and motivations of consumers. The problem advertisers faced was how to make North Americans consume more, spend more, enjoy more.

By the 1920s reformers, managers, and professionals managed to displace the debate over class, inequality, and productive labor to the sphere of consumption.[30] Consumer society presented a terrain devoid of conflicts, a fertile soil for crafting a new engagement between corporate capital and "the people." [31] The new techniques for manufacturing desire, however, brought new criticism about the unreality of it all (the Land of Desire was also a dreamland) and the search for new sources of objectivity. Hence the renewed belief in science, and the increasing popularity of the "empire of facts" and the philosophy of pragmatism.[32] The North American fascination with science was strengthened by the activities of institutions that promoted and popularized scientific discoveries.[33] World fairs representing the achievements and promises of North American industrialization developed into a national pastime. These were the sites where the United States could deploy its imperial ambitions and its representations of the world.

Aided by new representational technologies, around the time of the Panama-Pacific Exposition (1915) the construction of the United States converged into a dream of global empire predicated on technological, military, and racial superiority.[34] The U.S. empire, a new form of global governance, was imagined through a variety of cultural practices: lawmaking, court decisions, Indian treaties, Wild West shows, science fiction, world fairs, and natural history museums, among others. From these practices emerged the sense that a new era was in the making; that the Western frontier had ended and needed to be relocated abroad; that the world population could be classified in an ascending scale of races; and that U.S. technology, having dominated nature, was the mark of the country's superiority.

The heyday of Pan-Americanism was concomitant with the invention of "consumer engineering." [35] The coincidence is important for it marks a change in the nature of the North American engagement with South America, a change directly related to the technologies of representation. Pan-Americanism, scientific philanthropy, and corsumer persuasion as the metaphor for inter-American relations developed in the intersection between the new technologies of seeing and the new requirements of science during the era of corporate capitalism. Oil prospectors, railroad builders, and bankers, the representatives of North American capital in South America, carried with them new cultural and economic imperatives: to incorporate new areas into the sphere of North American capital accumulation and knowledge, according to the new requirements of science and organized capitalism. This meant reporting about business opportunities and peoples' customs with the aid of photographs, statistics, and maps. Thus, the place and importance of South America for the informal empire were reconstructed with the aid of new visual (ideographic) representations that claimed greater accuracy and objectivity.

Pan-Americanism as Textual Explosion

Recent reinterpretations have emphasized the notion of imperialism as a cultural project, calling attention to the role played by cultural technologies and academic disciplines in the construction of an imagined territory conquerable by North American science, technology, and capital.[36] The specific place of *South America* in the new imagined empire, however, has not been sufficiently explored. As I will attempt to show, the construction of a field of involvement south of Panama operated according to different rules than those applied to Central America and the Caribbean. In South America—where military invasion, territorial annexation, and direct colonial government were not viable alternatives—the "imperatives of reason and conquest" had to be replaced by the arguments of knowledge, persuasion, and markets.

Around 1910–1915, when Pan-Americanism transformed the meaning of the Monroe Doctrine into an ideology of mutual cooperation among American states, a multiplicity of arguments coalesced to give ideological support to a new form of engagement between the United States and the southern republics. Textual producers presented the region as a site of potentially lucrative investment for North American capital, a growing market for North American goods and services, a receptacle for the surplus morality of North American reformers, a territory for missionary colonization, and a field of research for a variety of North American disciplines. It was at this time that South America became a "continent of opportunity" and also a land of "lost cities" and "ancient glories," a contradictory synthesis of future market opportunities and current backwardness.

The production and dissemination of these representations increased qualitatively and quantitatively after the opening of the Panama Canal. Scholars have noted the renewed search for investment opportunities abroad in areas like mining, petroleum, car distribution, road construction, and finance during the heyday of Pan-Americanism.[37] Less noted is the fact that during this period a series of interventions in the cultural field, private and governmental, served to redefine the nature of the North American engagement. Among these were the publications of the Pan American Union (PAU), various tours prepared and financed by the Carnegie Endowment for Peace, international conferences in diverse areas of science, and congresses of Protestant missionaries in the region. These activities reflected a new impulse (stemming simultaneously from government, science, business, and religion) to bridge the gap separating North and South America, a gap that was construed in informational and cultural terms as well as material and technological ones.

An obsession with gathering information accompanied the diffusion of North American commodities, firms, and expertise in South America.[38] The PAU pioneered efforts to create an "information industry" with regard to South America, publishing country handbooks, statistical reports, travel guides, directories, and bulletins about ports, cities, and commodity trades. At the rate of one hundred publications a year, the agency ignited something akin to an information explosion, increasing dramatically the availability of sources about the region.[39] Clearly, the PAU was not alone in this enterprise. Universities organized Latin American collections, and public libraries and reading clubs arranged courses on South America, while business groups funded "fact-finding" tours to the region.[40] The accessibly priced series *Seeing South America* summarized the editorial preoccupation of the time: to disseminate the knowledge recently acquired about the region among common North Americans.

Other practices of engagement, most notably the expansion of evangelical Christianity and scientific philanthropy, also expanded the volume of information about South Americans. Missionaries of the Social Gospel organized social surveys of their host communities, applying the most modern techniques developed by sociology.[41] Philanthropic foundations such as Carnegie, Russell Sage, and Rockefeller also contributed to the "enterprise of knowledge," providing funds for scientific exploration, publications, and the development of cooperation among scientists and educators in North and South America.[42]

The press similarly contributed, carrying articles that reproduced and modified what the U.S. public knew about the region.[43] Even more powerful was the impact of photography on popular readership.[44] The popularity of the *National Geographic Magazine* (subscriptions soared from 3,400 to 107,000 between 1905 and 1912) coincided with the increasing space devoted to photographs, especially newly introduced color photographs.[45] In keeping with his philosophy of creating vivid pictures in the reader's mind, editor Gilbert H. Grosvenor presented North Americans with colorful views of Chilean railroads, Brazilian coffee *fazendas,* the Argentine pampas, Patagonian natives, and Peruvian Inca ruins.[46] Illustrated reports used the new technologies — photography and chromatic reproduction — to produce, with a semblance of neutrality and greater objectivity, new perspectives about South America. More importantly, photographs brought home the activities of North American explorers and scientists in the region, making magazine readers participants in the expansionist project.[47]

The increased volume of visual and textual representations of South America coincided with a revival in scientific exploration. Major universities, sometimes in cooperation with the National Geographic Society and the PAU, organized research trips to South America in the fields of anthropology, archaeology, geography, geology, and astronomy. The new explorations (the field trips by Hiram Bingham in 1909, 1912, and 1914 are perhaps the best known of these cooperative ventures) produced a vast amount of visual evidence to feed the printing machine. Scientific reporting continued much as Wilkes had designed it, but now it reached a wider audience through the impulse provided by popular magazines.[48] Inserting photographs into the reports became part of the narration of the adventures of North American explorers.

Rediscovering South America

Three arguments about South America constituted the legacy of earlier textual encounters by North Americans. One was the disposition to see

South America as a land caught in a perpetual state of childhood, unable to reach the political maturity required to sustain stable and democratic governments. Another motif related to the region's atypical racial mixture, presented as a major difference vis-à-vis North America. The third was a concern with the economic "backwardness" and lack of "civilization" of the region, predicated on the two other arguments (political instability and miscegenation). Used in the nineteenth century as a pretext for indictments about the region's economic backwardness, cultural simplicity, and political immaturity, these arguments lost strength and explanatory power in the early twentieth century. Intensive information-gathering in the region, the projection of new concerns with social issues, and, quite significantly, the spread of scientific philanthropy, translated into a questioning of the stereotypes built in the previous century.

Ever since independence, North Americans perceived South America as a land of *caudillos,* incessant civil warfare, banditry, and political fragmentation.[49] Writers of this period equated political instability, the most distinguishing feature of the "young republics," with political immaturity or inexperience, talking of the new nation-states as children.[50] The first two decades of the twentieth century brought about a reconsideration of this stereotype—a change that was related to transformations in the nature of foreign business enterprise and in the technologies of representation. When Theodore Roosevelt visited Buenos Aires in 1913, he told the elite audience gathered at the Colón Theater that, after thirty years of uninterrupted progress, Argentina had achieved a certain threshold of economic progress and political stability he associated with maturity.[51] The country was no longer an infant needing the protection of a big brother but an adult nation standing on equal footing with the United States.[52] The reasons for this change seemed obvious to contemporary observers. Between 1890 and 1930, some countries in South America—most notably Argentina and Brazil—integrated their economies into the commodity circuits of the North, receiving increasing amounts of North American goods in exchange for their primary exports. As a result, South America became a female consumer fascinated with North American goods and culture, mature enough to marry North American capital and culture. Powerful countries such as Brazil and Argentina—each with respectable military forces—had gone further: they had achieved manhood.

For countries such as Ecuador, Peru, and Bolivia (and sometimes Chile), the language of infancy and manhood had also lost all relevance, not because they had reached maturity/modernity but for the opposite reason: they seemed to have regressed into a premodern, feudal time.[53] Starting in the second decade of the twentieth century, North American travelers under the influence of progressivism, the Social Gospel, and newly available images of the "real" South America discovered that Andean nations were infected with the social disease of "landlordism," that the Indian majorities remained marginalized and exploited, and that political democracy was therefore an illusion.[54]

The discourse on racial diversity and miscegenation, a central piece of the construction of South America in the early nineteenth century, also came under criticism in the new century. Geographer Isaiah Bowman, Harvard professor and director of the American Geographical Society, found in 1914 that the concept of racial mixture no longer served as an interpretive key to South America.[55] European immigration had complicated the easy association between racial mixture and degeneration. Though South Americans were all in some way descendants of the Spaniards, Indians, and Africans, they showed great national diversity of temperament, customs, and sociability not attributable to race. Some of them carried traits similar to those of Anglo-Saxons.[56] South American (white) elites claimed to be direct descendants of the best of European culture without renouncing their American heritage. In some instances, racial mixture had acquired a positive value. Brazil, due to its experience with miscegenation, came to be seen as a country experimenting with a unique "racial democracy," a vision exalted by Gilberto Freire in the 1920s.[57]

After 1910 racial visions of South America caved in under the pressure of more robust explanatory agents. Economic modernization had brought a greater source of diversity, that of commodities attracting laborers and entrepreneurs from all corners of the world: German merchants, Indian rubber hunters, Welsh sheepherders, English coffee factors, U.S. steamship owners. In the Andean countries, on the other hand, miscegenation had proved a myth: here North American observers (following the path set by Hiram Bingham and the social photographers) rediscovered the "purity" of Indian culture, which had resisted a century of European "progress" preceded by three centuries of Spanish acculturation.

The consolidation of a U.S. informal empire also changed expectations about the region's progress. Observers began to acknowledge modernity as a reality in some South American nations and found even greater backwardness in the interior of the region. On the one hand, there were the enclaves of modernity produced by foreign enterprise, company towns whose design, management, and services reflected the new conceptions of social progress. On a similar plane were urban metropolises such as Buenos Aires or Rio de Janeiro, whose sophistication, consumption habits,

and overall modernity surprised North Americans. Symmetrically opposite were the Inca ruins and other archaeological sites that served to construct the space of certain countries (Peru, Ecuador, Bolivia) as marked
by the contrast between a remote, glorious past and a present of poverty,
corruption, and oppression.[58] Modernity and antiquity, strategically allocated, produced new concerns about the diversity of South America, a
feature overlooked by previous representations.

Model company towns were spectacles of corporate modernity. Their
implantation in the middle of jungles, mountains, or deserts showed the
power of U.S. capital to defeat nature's most awesome obstacles. Agnes
Rothery, a North American visitor to South America in 1930, saw Fordlan-
dia, a new model town built by Henry Ford on the banks of the Amazon
in 1928, as such a spectacle. Here was a town equipped with the amenities
of the North American way of life (electricity, running water, sanitation,
a hospital, schools, canteens, and movies).[59] A similar message was conveyed by the photographs taken by Harry Franck of a company town built
in northern Chile by the Braden Copper Company[60]—a well-lit marvel in
the midst of the Andes—or by Percival Farquhar's photographs of Porto
Velho, a sanitary city built in the middle of the Amazon jungle according
to the dictates of industrial architecture and tropical medicine. In contrast
with these "modern American" towns were cities characterized by their
"ancient," "Catholic," "Spanish" flavor (adjectives applied to La Paz,
Quito, and Lima, for example) and many Indian villages that seemed "un-
affected by the passage of time." [61]

In part these changes in the construction of South America related to
the new representational technologies. Argentina's rise to maturity was
made visible (publicized) through a barrage of representations: statistical
handbooks, photograph albums, government reports, and scientific publications. These representations gave Argentina the semblance of modernity that neighboring countries lacked. Similarly, the old racial understanding of South America was destabilized by the new technologies of
seeing—photography in particular—by the presence of extremely diverse
and modern (urban) landscapes, and by import and export statistics that
reported the progress of production, consumption, and exchange. Moreover, it was the work of photographers and journalists that reshaped the
North American perception of Buenos Aires and Rio de Janeiro, around
the 1920s, as modern cities of sophisticated French taste, "culture," and
congested street traffic. Photographers, in conjunction with archaeologists,
road builders, and journalists, rediscovered the antiquity of Peru, transforming it into a land of "lost Inca cities," colorful Indian market towns,

and pressing social issues. Over and over, Indian subjects appear carrying heavy loads, posing in front of "ancient ruins," dancing on festive occasions—all of which conveyed to North American viewers the plight of peoples with a long tradition, who were now impoverished and powerless in the face of progress.

These new views of South America reached the U.S. public in multiple ways, none perhaps as massive and impressive as world exhibitions and natural history museums. Displays at these institutions made visible two distinct orders: on the one hand, the world of commodities, machines, and progress; on the other, the world of nature and "primitive" peoples. By showing commodities, machines, and the wonders of modern science, exhibitors intended to involve viewers in the dreams of modern consumer society. By displaying "native" customs, crafts, and mummies (if not living "natives") in relation to "more progressive" civilizations or to "nature," exhibitors attempted to engage viewers in a pedagogy of evolution.[62] Though the design for displaying commodities was similar to that for showing stuffed animals or "native" tribes, each type of exhibit aimed at a distinct pedagogy: in one case, the engagement of U.S. people with consumer culture; in the other, the construction of the United States in relation to its others.

Through the artifacts displayed in museums and at world fairs circulated similar constructs about South America. The Yale expedition to Machu Picchu, for instance, produced the Indianization of the Andean nations, creating both a genuine concern for the situation of the Indian peasantry and a negative racial rhetoric about the possibilities for economic development and democratic government in countries dominated by Indian masses. This "discovery" tying the backwardness of Peru and Bolivia to the "character" of the Indian masses found support in the various world fairs and museums in the United States, where images of Andean "Indians" carrying heavy loads pointed to the barbarism and timelessness of their wretched lives. Images of Indian America circulated freely through different representations, conveying a similar set of impressions, categories, and associations (backwardness, social injustice, Hispanic heritage, glorious antiquity).

Business, Knowledge, and Engagement

The production and circulation of representations about "South America" were not divorced from the generation of profits via direct investment abroad. In 1924 a U.S. company, charged with the construction of the Lima-Callao highway, found a huge Inca cemetery lying across its route. To complete the road, the company's technicians and laborers unceremoniously dug up the site, uncovering in the process the remains of many Indians.[63] The situation dramatized the tensions between North American business and local traditions and culture since, literally and figuratively, U.S. capital was disturbing the peace of ancient Peruvians. U.S. roads promised to awaken the energies of the Andean nation, kept dormant by centuries of primitivism and tradition, at the cost of destroying an Inca cemetery. While regretting this disturbance, the *Detroit News* celebrated the news as a contribution made by North American business to the enterprise of knowledge abroad. After all, it was an American company that made the archaeological find, adding a wealth of skulls, bones, and utensils to existing collections of Andean Americana. Used by expert archaeologists, ethnographers, and historians, the new "evidence" (though a by-product of road building) could assist the construction of more accurate representations of Inca society, serve to validate or reject existing views about Peruvian ancient history and national identity, and help to locate Peruvian "natives" within the order of human evolution.

Business and knowledge, connected since the beginnings of U.S. commercial expansion abroad, had acquired by the 1920s a high degree of interdependency. American petroleum interests, confronted with the need to evaluate the actual size of petroleum resources in South America, now sent a small army of geologists on field explorations to the coastal districts of Venezuela and Peru; to remote territories in the Amazon, Orinoco, and Paraguay river valleys; and to the Andean plateaus and forests of Bolivia.[64] In the name of business, these "oil scouts" followed the paths of former explorers, facing similar dangers and adventures in order to map with more precise instruments new territories for exploitation. Their expeditions were located in the intersection between science and business. Their geological maps and charts, while designed to evaluate the possibilities of North American business in the region, produced a visual incorporation of these new territories into the sphere of (North American) knowledge.[65]

U.S. direct investment brought more to South America than capital, technology, and management practices: it also carried with it an informational and public relations machinery that helped to map the new "realities" of the host nations. Geographical knowledge benefited from the intelligence gathered patiently by the foreign concessionaires (British, German, and American) of public utilities. They provided much-needed urban maps, statistics about sanitary conditions, and detailed population studies. Similarly, the field reports of railroad prospectors and road-building companies served to correct the earlier maps of geographers and explorers. The surveys on reading skills ordered by the Bible Society or the polls used by advertising companies to measure the market for General Motors cars also contributed to enhance the knowledge of the region. Each represented not only the applications of scientific methods of observation to business purposes but also a way of apprehending South American "realities." The cases of two railroad promoters in the 1900s (one in Bolivia, the other in the Amazon) exemplify the complex relationship between business and knowledge in the era of informal empire. In both cases, the entrepreneur-explorers were personally engaged in the production, diffusion, or application of knowledge and left a vast collection of representations (mostly photographs) of the territories and populations transected by the new railroads.

Rankin Johnson, a U.S. engineer working for the Bolivia Railroad Co. (1906–1909), carried to completion the construction of the Antofagasta railway, helping afterward to sell the enterprise to a British company. Though heavily involved in managing this difficult project, Johnson found time to undertake an ethnographic and archaeological exploration of the country that could fill this "vacuum." He used his photographic skills for a double purpose: to document the progress of the business and to collect impressions of the Bolivian peasantry.[66] Photographs of Indian peoples wearing masks during fiestas, common folks in the streets of Cuzco, market scenes in La Paz, or Indian laborers working for the railroad served to show the "human face" of Bolivia to North American viewers (the collection was intended as an album). Aymara and Quechua peasants were photographed inside, alongside, or on ruins, suggesting the blending of the "ancient" and the "modern" in the making of contemporary Peru. A few shots show Johnson cooperating with a North American scientist, digging a pile of bones and skulls from an archaeological site.

Between 1907 and 1912 Percival Farquhar, the U.S. railroad magnate, completed the construction of the Madeira-Mamoré railroad, an engineering miracle built in the interior of the Amazon basin.[67] The center of operations was Porto Velho, an American-style company town built under the sanitary regime recommended by the new tropical medicine.[68] Porto Velho was visible proof of the capacity of U.S. technology to conquer nature, under quite unfavorable conditions. Here was a company town with all the modern services—electric power and lighting, water and sewage systems, a hospital, an ice plant, a steam laundry, a wireless station, a weekly newspaper, and a baseball diamond—installed in the midst of the "impenetrable" jungle.[69] Photographs, conveniently placed in newspapers, albums, and business reports, were used to convey the success of this implanted modernity.[70]

These two cases illustrate the importance of representations in the era of corporate capitalism and, at the same time, the engagement of U.S. capitalists in the expansion of U.S. science and technology. Rankin Johnson —like the construction company building the Lima-Callao road—contributed to the archaeological and ethnographic project framed within universities and museums in the United States. Percival Farquhar, for his part, contributed to the application and spread of tropical medicine. Both used the newest representational technologies (photography) to report business progress and create the illusions of modernity and antiquity, a chief marker of difference within South America.[71] Their representations projected the image of a triumphant U.S. technology and science dominating South American nature, of a benevolent and socially sensitive corporate capitalism in peaceful relations with South American aborigines.

The connection between business and knowledge had deep roots in the culture of U.S. capitalism. Back in the period 1820–1860, mercantile library associations and other institutions such as the Boston Atheneum and the YMCA had tried to instill in young merchants the habits of reading, listening, and oratory, familiarizing them with issues of social and moral reform as well as questions of science. They had made the pursuit of knowledge a defining element of the mercantile character. The "good merchant" was a "healthy reader" and a "good scholar," a person who in his numerous travels could collect information about the world around him and use this information to educate his countrymen.[72]

Around mid-century, when the United States embarked on a massive effort to explore the world, the quest for knowledge shifted to a more ambitious project: the validation of general theories about the "natural order" of the world. The Wilkes Expedition (1838–1848), being the earliest of these endeavors, set the pattern for new practices of engagement with South America: collecting specimens of "natural history" to feed museums and exhibits in the United States. This was a truly Humboltian program, taken up by the U.S. government with the encouragement of many scientific associations and with the sponsorship of some business interests. As the instructions given to Captain Wilkes show, this activity was wholly compatible with the needs of commerce and navigation. Starting in the 1860s, many business agents in South America contributed to this project, collecting plants, animal skins, fish, rocks, and archaeological artifacts for the Smithsonian and other museums in North America.[73]

Early expansion of U.S. enterprise in South America (prior to 1890) depended on traditional technologies of representation (travel writing, engravings, watercolors). Business prospectors, the same as pleasure travelers, missionaries, diplomats, and navy officers, pursued a narrative of business knowledge that was predatory of nature and violent toward the native inhabitants. Collecting specimens, shooting animals, and felling trees were all part of the same enterprise of violently asserting the superiority of U.S. technology and the need to collect "evidence" for American museums and universities.

Business enterprise was to follow the traces left by earlier narratives and, with the help of guns, instruments, and machines, it transformed the natural environment into centers of febrile productive and mercantile activity. This mode of operation, this form of building an informal empire, the mercantile community knew, was destined for failure. The British, in command of the shipping, insurance, banking, and financial resources that appealed to South American governments and producers, were building a more credible informal empire, an empire that grew unchallenged until the turn of the century. It was then that U.S. corporate capitalism discovered new forms of interaction with South America and a wholly renovated technology of representation. Farquhar's and Johnson's photographs and business reports reveal this new type of engagement: a concern for establishing the polarity modernity/antiquity at the center of the master narrative of South America's incorporation within the orbit of North American knowledge.

The Enterprise of Knowledge

The most enduring product of the textual machine of informal empire was a set of enunciations concerning the very possibility of knowing South America: an assortment of doubts and criticism about what constituted evidence about South America, what was a proper inference, and what was the perspective and interpretive framework for analyzing the region. Knowing the region was a collective and progressive enterprise, challenged at every step by new ways of seeing, more insightful narrations, or more scientific categories and measurements. Contributors to this enterprise shared the common belief that a certain area or aspect of South America (its geography, its cities, its production, its indigenous peoples, its consumption patterns, its banking system, and so forth) had been insufficiently studied in the past and was in need of more information. Only on the terrain charted by new evidence, and classified and appropriated according to the principles of science, could the region be apprehended and new forms of involvement legitimized.

Starting from the crude instruments of nineteenth-century travelers (romantic narration and disorganized collections of "facts"), the observation of South America advanced by leaps and bounds, gaining accuracy and depth. The Exploring Expedition of 1838–1842 advanced the project of comprehensive knowledge, embarking on an ethnographic, philological, and biological classificatory project that promised a better understanding of the region's aboriginal peoples, customs, and forms of government. Compared to this attempt, the information contained in earlier travel narratives appeared crude, subjective, and inconclusive.[74] Similarly, the geographers, railway prospectors, and oil scouts of the following period (1870–1910) displaced the terrain of inquiry to new disciplines, adding new demands of precision and measurement. In the 1920s, when the "social" and "Indian" questions became relevant to North American observers, new and more detailed evidence about subaltern subjects was demanded to complete the knowledge of South America.[75] Toward the end of our period (1930s), other disciplines such as economics and psychology claimed their place in the collective enterprise of knowing South America.[76]

A similar set of utterances, repeated over and over again, had constructed the rationale for the expansionist project. To William E. Curtis and William A. Reid, the first directors of the International Bureau of the Pan American Union, South America was still terra incognita. Their efforts to generate and circulate knowledge about the region stemmed from the same assumption: the existence of a vacuum of knowledge that, if rapidly filled, could help produce a better understanding and hence better commercial interactions between North and South Americans. Private philanthropy (in this period closely associated with U.S. foreign policy) framed the extension of its cooperation to South America in quite similar terms. In 1914, with the support of the Carnegie Institution, a party of U.S. university professors visited South America. The initiative was guided by the need to better understand the region; personal contacts and the possibility of bringing home "eyewitness" accounts of the situation were presented as key in the reconstruction of hemispheric cooperation.[77] Even writers critical of U.S. interventionist policies acknowledged the need for additional knowledge about South America. To preacher, educator, and historian Samuel G. Inman, the author of influential works criticizing U.S.

foreign policies, the widespread misunderstandings of the cultural differences between Latin Americans and North Americans stood in the way of better relations.[78]

The thirst for knowledge was insatiable, or at least this was what North American textual producers believed. In 1928, preparing the readers for the coverage of Hoover's Goodwill Tour, the *Saturday Evening Post* resorted to the same commonplace: "[To] most North Americans," it declared, "South America is *terra incognita*."[79] Journalists, therefore, had a responsibility to fill the gap, reporting about the life and politics of the South American republics, so that "Americans" could understand the importance of the elected president's tour. While President Hoover paid a one-day visit to ten countries, a press corps of twenty-seven reporters and photographers translated for the U.S. public the "condition" of each nation, resorting to traditional stereotypes of sleepy villages, banana republics, corruption-ridden governments, grandiloquent Hispanic statesmen, and hospitable natives. They wrote as if they were discovering an entirely new world, hitherto hidden from the North American by business interests, the manipulations of politicians, and public apathy.[80]

In a variety of representations, the justification of the expansion of U.S. inquiry into South America followed a familiar pattern. First, enunciators stated that colonial annexation, plunder, and even the accumulation of mercantile profits were not the true objectives of the expansionist project, suggesting instead that it was the acquisition of new knowledge and the effects derived from that knowledge that were the prime movers of the enterprise. This argument, stated in multiple ways, served to establish the connection between knowledge and empire, asserting that the good, moral empire had to be validated not by conquest or imperial aggression but by the power of knowledge, or better, by the activity of knowing. If a new form of expertise could grasp South America in its true dimension, the argument went, there would be no need for direct military intervention. Knowledgeable diplomats and traders would foster peaceful communications and interactions with the southern neighbors and a better informed public would elect governments committed to peace, commerce, and humanity.

The "enterprise of knowledge," the single most important discourse unifying the activities of many North American cultural mediators, was the language of authority of the informal empire. Its invocation authorized the presence of explorers, collectors, photographers, statisticians, and business promoters in South America and naturalized the inclusion of the region within the sphere of U.S. preoccupations and concerns. In

The Imperial Archive, Thomas Richards describes how the British imagined, in the second half of the nineteenth century, an empire united by information.[81] The totality of the reach of British hegemony and power became apprehensible as a centralized collection of information about the colonies, a project located in the British Museum and Library. The dream of comprehensive knowledge—the fantasy of converting bits and pieces of information of the empire into a unique system of knowledge—became the ideological support of empire, the imaginary basis of the colonial state. The U.S. informal empire built during the heyday of Pan-Americanism participated in a similar obsession with the accumulation of information. But the dream of empire was somewhat different. The availability of new technologies of seeing at the beginning of the new century subjected the quest for knowledge to demands of greater objectivity, accuracy, and proximity. Also, the massive production of representations about South America was destined to impact the U.S. public at large, not just the scientific community or the state bureaucracy.

Conclusions

During the period 1890–1930, a variety of representational practices converged to constitute South America as a textual space for the projection of the cultural anxieties of an expansive commercial culture and power, the United States. Pan-Americanism, the ideology that replaced the Monroe Doctrine, produced a dramatic increase in the representations of South America, making the region more readable and apprehensible for the vast public created by corporate capitalism and mass consumer culture. South America became an immense source of "evidence" for validating theories and propositions of science, a confusing array of specimens and commodities displayed in museums and fairs, and the object of the curiosity of North Americans as they browsed through photograph albums and popular magazines.

New technologies of observation and reproduction (photography and chromatic reproduction) aided the transition, questioning past impressions of South America and bringing the diversity and peculiarities of its inhabitants, resources, and "culture" closer to the eyes of North Americans. From a generic Latin America emerged a different region, South America, with traces of modernity and antiquity, a compost that was no longer representable by the image of an undifferentiated "Indian" (an absolute other, incapacitated for progress and civilization). Pan-Americanism activated a new imagined scenario where the possibility of cultural assimilation of South Americans depended on the diffusion of U.S. products (e.g., cars, roads, sewing machines, rails, and radios), and where better relations between North and South depended on expanded knowledge, the concern of both science and business. This imaginary was the very stuff of the world fairs that millions of North Americans visited between 1893 and 1933.

Businessmen, teachers, social reformers, scientists, missionaries, and diplomats contributed to this collective enterprise of representation, an enterprise that derived its impetus and pattern from the experience of mid–nineteenth century scientific explorers and mercantile travelers. Business abroad was the vehicle of the scientific and technological achievements of the United States and, consequently, claimed that its activities were one with those of geographers, statisticians, ethnologists, naturalists, and other scientists. So did educators, economists, criminologists, and evangelical missionaries. Indeed, every North American engagement in South America seemed justified by the "enterprise of knowledge."

Knowledge was the virtual territory of informal empire, the instrument for placing the southern continent under the gaze of the United States. The knowledge gathered in South America fed an exhibitionary complex in the United States, imagined as a new form of governance (based on consumer persuasion, advertisement, and visual technologies) pioneered by the engineers of mass consumer culture. Not surprisingly, then, the representation of business enterprise in South America collapsed the two motivations, interest and knowledge, into one. Railroad promoters and engineers collected evidence for the natural history project and also photographs destined to build "more realistic" ethnographies of South America.

After the arguments about infant republics, Indian primitivism, and racial mixture seemed to have lost their potency to explicate South American "realities" — unsettled by the presence of massive European immigration, modern and noisy urban centers, incipient industrialization, modern forms of labor unrest, and reformist state policies — the project of knowledge continued to guide new North American cultural interventions. A truly collective enterprise cutting across social and occupational borders in the United States, the project managed during the time of Pan-Americanism to put South America on permanent display.

Notes

I thank George Yúdice, William Roseberry, Patricia Seed, and Ana María Alonso for their insightful commentaries at the Yale conference. Catherine LeGrand and Carlos Forment read early versions of this paper and helped me to edit out unfounded claims. Gil Joseph's remarks significantly improved the readability of the essay. Those who pointed me toward new and unexplored dimensions of my paper (Stuart Schwartz, Steve Stern, Emília Viotti da Costa, Eric Roorda, Alexandra Stern, Fernando Coronil, and Steven Palmer, among others) also have my appreciation.

1. John and Jean Comaroff, *Ethnography and the Historical Imagination* (Boulder, Colo.: Westview, 1992), esp. 181–213. For a similar view (competing colonialisms) in the American setting, see Catherine Hall, "White Visions, Black Lives: The Free Villages of Jamaica," *History Workshop Journal* 36 (1993): 100–131.

2. Anne McClintock, in a feminist reading of the same phenomenon, points to three distinct orders governing the narrative of British imperialism: "The male, reproductive order of patriarchal monogamy; the white economic order of mining capital; and the global, political order of empire." Unlike the Comaroffs, McClintock sees these orders not as contradictory but as reinforcing each other: "The adventure of mining capital reinvents the white patriarch . . . as the heir to imperial 'Progress' at the head of the 'Family of Man' —a family that admits no mother" (McClintock, *Imperial Leather: Race, Gender, and Sexuality in the Colonial Contest* [New York: Routledge, 1995], 4).

3. To explain the informal nature of the Pax Americana in most of Latin America (particularly in South America during the time of Pan-Americanism), dependency or neocolonialist formulations substituted economic for political and military ties (imperialism for neocolonialism or dependency) without changing the basic triad. In fact, *dependentista* critiques of "cultural dependency" hinged on basic and transcendental economic inequalities between the United States and Latin America. The analysis of cultural flows surrendered its specificity and diversity for the sake of reaffirming the primacy of the economy in shaping international relations. In this sense, dependentista perspectives reaffirmed the obsession of classical Marxist theories of imperialism for explaining inequalities of power relations at the international level in terms of economic, political, and military forces.

4. For example, the vision of South America expressed by missionaries interested in spreading the Social Gospel was undoubtedly different from that constructed by the State Department, preoccupied with generating greater cooperation for the Pan-American conferences, and equally different from the view of the Midwestern farmers who settled in Bolivia.

5. The term *engagement* has at least two meanings. On the one hand, it designates the connectedness of enunciations pertaining to different textual corpuses. One text is said to be engaged with another when some subset of its enunciations

resonate well (resemble, or have a familiarity) with those of a second text, produced at a different time or location. In this way, through a series of connecting textual operations, authors negotiate their engagement with values, traditions, and cultural presuppositions that are not their own. A second meaning of the term *engagement* refers to the attempts of people of different cultures to enter into a relationship that neither obliterates nor denies the subjectivity of the other party. Here we include all encounters in which the participants try to understand, construe, empathize, or approach each other. Establishing some type of bond, commitment, or contract (a popular connotation of the term *engagement*) seems to be a particular form of this second meaning. In this paper, I use the term *engagement* to refer both to the textual resonance that exists between two texts and to the experiential interaction between peoples of different cultures.

6. On the "picturing" of the American West to Easterners, see Peter B. Hales, *William Henry Jackson and the Transformation of the American Landscape, 1843–1942* (Philadelphia: Temple University Press, 1988). On the representation of the West to popular audiences, see Richard Slotkin, "Buffalo Bill's 'Wild West' and the Mythologization of the American Empire," in *Cultures of United States Imperialism,* ed. Amy Kaplan and Donald Pease (Durham, N.C.: Duke University Press, 1993), 164–81. The analogy between the North American western expansion of the nineteenth century and the later expansion of U.S. investments in South America appears in J. Valerie Fifer, *United States Perceptions of Latin America 1850–1930: A 'New West' South of Capricorn?* (Manchester: Manchester University Press, 1991).

7. In this essay, I avoid a discussion of resistance in its multiple manifestations or, if you will, the multiple forms of narrating experience from a "South American" perspective. I believe that prior to (or independent of) an analysis of the impact of "North American" representations on the peoples and cultures of South America, there is a need to unpack and examine the discourse of informal empire. After all, natural history exhibits, world fairs, travel books, plays, congressional documents, statistical handbooks, lectures, etc., were the means through which ordinary North Americans engaged with the cultures of South America.

8. The adjective *representational* emphasizes the nature of the inputs and outputs of this peculiar production process. Here, all that circulates are texts, images, and performances. The production process in this case refers to the representational practices that transform the views, impressions, assumptions, and prejudices that emerge from a given experience of encounter into a communicable set of utterances and images about the other.

9. Perhaps the words *assemblage* or *collection* might be preferable to the term *machine,* but I want to emphasize that images and texts about empire and other do not accumulate at random; rather, they are generated, collected, and displayed following certain rules (e.g., figures of discourse, conventions of genre, and limitations given by the technology of representation).

10. See the introduction to Stephen Greenblatt, *Marvelous Possessions: The Wonder of the New World* (Chicago: University of Chicago Press, 1991), 1–25.

11. Greenblatt applies the phrase *mimetic circulation* both to the itinerary followed by a particular text as it circulates between cultures and to the process of re-signification that occurs when a given cultural practice is re-presented through a new medium (ibid., 120).

12. Circulation evokes the other big metaphor of modernity, the market (or competition), with its associations of diversity of goods, producers (multivocality), and freedom (unconstrained speech). All of this, of course, seems to be at odds with what one normally associates with the term *machine*.

13. Laura Dassow Walls calls this the "Humboltian program," the imperative to explore, collect, measure, and bring data into a general order. See Dassow Walls, *Seeing New Worlds: Henry David Thoreau and Nineteenth-Century Natural Science* (Madison: University of Wisconsin Press, 1995), 134.

14. More appropriately, we can speak of the "museum project," the "geographical project," the "ethnographic project," the "educational project," the "missionary project," and so forth.

15. Tony Bennett, *The Birth of the Museum: History, Theory, Politics* (London: Routledge, 1995).

16. In the first set of enunciations we find the tensions characteristic of a multi-dimensional engagement (business, knowledge, moral reform): that is, arguments of economic necessity or convenience contend with those invoking benevolence or the expansion of knowledge. In the second group of enunciations, the tensions relate rather to the veracity of the representations. Stereotypes, simplifications, and falsifications appear in close proximity with claims about the validity, veracity, and relevance of the observations made. In the third group of enunciations, the educational imperatives of exhibitors predominate. Here, the hybridity of the exhibits reflects the diversity of the contributing projects (anthropology/archaeology, business/architecture, government, civic associations, the media).

17. This principle also limited the scope of representations. Whereas the construction of alterity demanded a certain degree of generalization and prejudice, the imperatives of knowledge demanded accuracy in representation. The texts narrating South America had to correspond with the "evidence" presented on the shelves of museums, in photographs, in statistics, or in illustrations.

18. Between the two moments stretches a period of transition, redefinition, and repositioning marked by the empowerment of scientists (ethnologists, naturalists, geologists, archaeologists) as designers of the new imaginary empire. Their collective construction, the "enterprise of knowledge," would survive the transition to corporate capitalism and consumer culture, influencing both the imagined relationship between science and business and the role of U.S. capitalism in the world order until the 1950s.

19. Pan-Americanism was an attempt by the U.S. administrations of the period from 1890 to 1930 to redefine the Monroe Doctrine of a protective brother into a doctrine of mutual interest among the countries of the Americas. To control the suspicion of Latin American nationals about the imperialist pretensions of the United States in the region, and to diffuse the already strong nationalist sentiments against U.S. intervention, U.S. foreign policy promoted the realization of Pan-American conferences (in a multiplicity of fields) and sponsored a series of diplomatic and cultural activities with the participation of Latin American delegates. Pivotal to these efforts to create good will among the Americas was the Pan American Union, an institution created in 1910 to replace the former International Bureau of American Republics.

20. On the centrality of productive "free" labor for antebellum culture, see Jonathan A. Glickstein, *Concepts of Free Labor in Antebellum America* (New Haven, Conn.: Yale University Press, 1991).

21. Joel Porte, *Representative Man: Ralph Waldo Emerson in His Time* (New York: Columbia University Press, 1988), 268. For a comprehensive view of "reform," see Gerald N. Grob and George A. Billias, *Interpretations of American History,* vol. 1 (New York: Free Press, 1972), 339–420.

22. In practice, it was the increasing efficiency of sailing vessels (the Yankee clipper), the discovery of gold in California, and the liberalization of trade that contributed to the expansion of American commerce in South America before 1870. Still, it was the conception of merchants' activities abroad as producers of representations (market statistics, ethnographies, adventure stories) that transformed South America into a coveted terrain for travelers, into an object of the "enterprise of knowledge."

23. Ricardo D. Salvatore, "North American Travel Narratives and the Ordering/Othering of South America (c. 1810–1860)," *Journal of Historical Sociology* 9, no. 1 (Mar. 1996): 85–110.

24. The scientific explorer, on the other hand, used a similar genre (the journal of exploration) to project onto the territory of South America an all-encompassing vision of science, motivated by religious, racial, and humanistic concerns. He carried into practice the obsession of the scientific communities of the Northeast for collecting "evidence" about nature and its order.

25. D. H. Haskell, *An Address Delivered before the Boston Mercantile Library Association, January 3, 1848* (Boston: MLA, 1848).

26. See Glenn Porter, *The Rise of Big Business, 1860–1910* (Arlington Heights, Ill.: AHM Publishing, 1973); and Alfred D. Chandler, *The Invisible Hand: The Managerial Revolution in American Business* (Cambridge, Mass.: Harvard University Press, 1977).

27. Guiding the economy was a new "commercial aesthetic of desire" geared to restructuring the perceptions of millions of American consumers (William Leach, *Land of Desire: Merchants, Power, and the Rise of a New American Culture* [New York: Vintage Books, 1993], esp. 3–12).

28. It was thanks to these technologies of reproduction and display that the notion of "Americanness," stylized and re-signified, came to be represented in products, corporate buildings, department stores, industrial exhibitions, and an array of printed texts. "The graphic arts and photography," writes Leach, ". . . ushered in a new era in the presentation of visual information between 1880 and 1910, making it more eye-catching. Any article, any painting, any photography could be readily converted by new technical processes into attractive halftone illustrations" (*Land of Desire*, 50).

29. James Livingston, *Pragmatism and the Political Economy of Cultural Revolution, 1850–1950* (Chapel Hill: University of North Carolina Press, 1994), chap. 3, esp. 57–63.

30. Business had contested quite successfully the challenge of the productive classes (de-skilling, mergers, union-breaking laws, mono-metalism) and undercut the demands for returning to a world of productive labor, small property, and popular control over money. Scientific management brought about such fragmentation of work that the notion of "productive labor" lost much of its original appeal. The merger movement witnessed the disappearance of many individual capitalists, undermining the ideology of upward social mobility. Even the criticism of modern technology, centered on the dehumanizing aspect of large-scale industry, lost strength in the face of a barrage of images that associated science, technology, and business with a future of abundance and peace (ibid., 100–102).

31. Consumer culture took root, writes James Livingston, "when the notion of 'productive labor' stopped making sense as a way of designating values, allocating social roles, and explaining class relations or political conflicts" (ibid., 95).

32. On the other hand, the dialectic of enticement and rejection produced by the "commercial aesthetics of desire" (show windows invited everyone to share the dream of possession but admitted only a few to actual enjoyment) generated new sources of class division and alienation that required novel solutions. Within this cultural context grew feminism, the Social Gospel, and Mind Cure, ideologies of toleration, incorporation, and community in a society torn by increasing divisions and exclusions.

33. The National Research Council, created in 1916, helped to engineer a closer cooperation among government, business, and science, resulting in the organization of various world fairs in the 1920s and 1930s—fairs that presented science as the leading force behind American industrial progress. Visitors to these fairs were invited to contemplate and participate in the miracles of modern science, by contrasting the GM modernist tower with Native American tepees and wigwams. See Robert W. Rydell, *World of Fairs: The Century-of-Progress Expositions* (Chicago: University of Chicago Press, 1993), esp. chap. 4, 92–114.

34. Donald E. Pease, "New Perspectives on U.S. Culture and Imperialism," in Kaplan and Pease, *Cultures of United States Imperialism,* 22. A suggestive interpretation of the transition in the dream of empire from the dispossession of Native Americans to violent ventures abroad can be found in Eric Cheyfitz, *The Poet-*

ics of Imperialism: Translation and Colonization from the Tempest to Tarzan (New York: Oxford University Press, 1991).

35. Stuart Ewen, *All Consuming Images: The Politics of Style in Contemporary Culture* (New York: Basic Books, 1988), chap. 3, 41–53.

36. See, for example, Kaplan and Pease, *Cultures of United States Imperialism;* Cheyfitz, *The Poetics of Imperialism;* Edward W. Said, *Culture and Imperialism* (New York: Vintage Books, 1993); McClintock, *Imperial Leather;* Thomas Richards, *The Imperial Archive: Knowledge and the Fantasy of Empire* (London: Verso, 1993); and Michael Adas, *Machines as the Measure of Men* (Ithaca, N.Y.: Cornell University Press, 1989). The notion of "discursive colonialism," presented by Chris Tiffin and Alan Lawson in their *De-Scribing Empire: Post-colonialism and Textuality* (New York: Routledge, 1994), is also relevant in this context.

37. On American investments in this period, see Mira Wilkins, "Multinational Oil Companies in South America in the 1920s: Argentina, Bolivia, Brazil, Chile, Colombia, Ecuador, and Peru," *Business History Review* 48, no. 3 (autumn 1974): 413–46; idem, *The Maturing of Multinational Enterprise: American Business Abroad from 1914 to 1970* (Cambridge, Mass.: Harvard University Press, 1974); Josh DeWind, *Peasants Become Miners: The Evolution of Industrial Mining Systems in Peru, 1902–1974* (New York: Garland, 1987); Dan La Botz, *Edward L. Doheny: Petroleum, Power, and Politics in the United States and Mexico* (New York: Praeger, 1991); Gilbert M. Joseph, *Revolution from Without: Yucatán, México, and the United States, 1880–1924* (Durham, N.C.: Duke University Press, 1988), esp. chap. 2; and Emily S. Rosenberg, *World War I and the Growth of the United States Predominance in Latin America* (New York: Garland, 1987).

38. Fifer, *United States Perceptions,* 5; see also chaps. 1, 4.

39. Ibid., chap. 4, esp. 153–55.

40. For contemporary reading lists, see *A Selected List of the Commercial Relations of South America Principally with the United States* (Boston: Public Library of Boston, 1918); and Corine Bacon, *South America: Topical Outlines for Twenty Club Meetings with Bibliography* (White Plains, N.Y.: H. W. Wilson, 1917).

41. Robert Speer et al., *Christian Work in South America,* vol. 2 (New York: F. H. Revell, 1926).

42. These foundations, born out of large business fortunes and forced into engineering solutions for the social evils of capitalism by episodes of class conflict and adverse public opinion, found Latin America a propitious field for extending their activities. See Robert Arnove, ed., *Philanthropy and Cultural Imperialism* (Boston: G. K. Hall, 1980). After World War II, the foundations established an agenda of issues to be discussed regarding Latin America and defined the boundaries of new fields of research (social science, development theory, and foreign area studies), fields that would authorize new expert interventions into the region. Edward H. Berman, *The Ideology of Philanthropy* (Albany: State University of New York Press, 1983), 99–125.

43. On the influence of the press in shaping U.S. conceptions of Latin America,

see Sarah E. Sharbach, *Stereotypes of Latin America, Press Images, and U.S. Foreign Policy, 1920–1933* (New York: Garland, 1993). Similar conclusions are reached in John J. Johnson, *Latin America in Caricature* (Austin: University of Texas Press, 1980), and his more recent *Hemisphere Apart: The Foundations of United States Policy toward Latin America* (Baltimore, Md.: Johns Hopkins University Press, 1990).

44. A collection of over 60,000 volumes and over 25,000 photographs at the Columbus Memorial Library helped to make South America more visible to North Americans.

45. Fifer, *United States Perceptions*, 161–62.

46. In 1913 the magazine devoted a whole issue (186 pages, 8 drawings, 2 maps, and 234 photographs) to Bingham's report on Machu Picchu. *The National Geographic Society: 100 años de aventuras y descubrimientos* (Barcelona: Edic. Folio, 1987), 151.

47. In the 1930s and 1940s, aerial photography captured the imagination of North American reporters and scientists as an innovation that could provide a more accurate and synthetic representation of South American "realities." John L. Rich's *Face of South America: An Aerial Traverse* (New York: American Geographical Society, 1942) uses the new technique of aerial photography to present a more accurate representation of South America. The pictures, taken from a long distance, promised the viewer "a clearer impression" than that afforded photographers on the ground. Aided by the National Geographical Society (and using the new 1:1,000,000 map produced by the society), Rich expected his pictures to contest the view of South America presented by other travelers (and the U.S. State Department) as the "land of opportunity."

48. The success of magazines such as *Cosmopolitan* and *McClure*—leaders of the "magazine revolution" of the 1890s—owed much to the use of photoengraving to illustrate articles of politics, scientific discovery, and travel (Matthew Schneirov, *The Dream of Social Order: Popular Magazines in America, 1893–1914* [New York: Columbia University Press, 1994], chap. 2).

49. Salvatore, "North American Travel Narratives."

50. Clearly, there were exceptions to this rule: Chile and Brazil, with their Portalian and imperial solutions, often received praise for their achievements in political stability and governability. All other nations, particularly Argentina, Uruguay, Peru, and Bolivia, lacked this stability.

51. "But times have changed. Certain of the Latin American nations have grown with astonishing speed to a position of assured and orderly political development, material prosperity, readiness to do justice to others and potential strength to enforce justice from the others. These nations are able to enforce order at home and respect abroad" (Emilio Frers, *American Ideals: Speeches of the President of the "Museo Social Argentino" Dr. Emilio Frers and of Col. Theodore Roosevelt at the Banquet Given in the Colón Theater, Buenos Aires, November 12, 1913* [Buenos Aires: Museo Social Argentino, 1914], 23).

52. Ibid., 24, 27.

53. The metaphor of Latin American infants crying, shouting, or misbehaving was key to the North American understanding of Central America and the Caribbean as well. See Johnson, *Latin America in Caricature.*

54. Edward A. Ross, *South of Panama* (New York: Century, 1915), 331.

55. Isaiah Bowman, *South America: A Geography Reader* (Chicago: Rand Mc-Nally, 1915), 7.

56. Ibid., 6.

57. American visitor Agnes Rothery, after traveling through Amazonas on the eve of the Great Depression, wrote: "Red men, black men, white men with yellow hair, and white men with black hair, and now yellow men. And Brazil absorbs them all, assimilating them after her fashion—the most conspicuous and complete example we have of a country where the equality of races proceeds without feuds, antagonisms, or prejudices" (Rothery, *South America: The West Coast and the East* [Boston: Houghton Mifflin, 1930], 287).

58. The same representational strategy, says Michael Adas, was employed in the orientalist rediscovery of India. The contrast between ancient glories and modern ruins pointed unequivocally to the existence of a period in history where the progress of civilization stopped. It was the ascendancy of Western science, during the heyday of Enlightenment, that rediscovered Indian antiquity and put it at the service of the project of Western scientific superiority (Adas, *Machines as the Measure of Men,* esp. 95–107).

59. Rothery, *South America,* 285–86.

60. Harry A. Franck, *Rediscovering South America* (Philadelphia: J. B. Lippincott, 1943).

61. The caption corresponding to the city of La Paz reads: "The ancient city of La Paz, de facto capital of Bolivia, has recently given itself a very modern aspect." The modern aspect of the city referred, of course, to the presence of automobiles, electric lights, and a few apartment buildings.

62. The mixing of objects—the presence of ethnological exhibits in world fairs and the presence of machines in museums of natural history—underscores the preoccupation of both institutions for working out the appropriate relationship between the two realms.

63. "Peru Cuts Road through Inca Burial Ground," in *South America: Continent of Opportunities,* comp. K. W. Miller (Detroit, Mich.: Evening News Association, 1925), 110–11.

64. "Petroleum Interests Look below Tropics," in Miller, *South America,* 116.

65. To this extent, the oil prospectors—like the road builders, railroad engineers, steamship navigators, and dealers in farm machinery—were participating in the same project that produced the first detailed map of Hispanic America, the ethnological collections at the Smithsonian, and the statistical handbooks published by the PAU.

66. Rankin Johnson Papers, 1853–1957, boxes 7, 8, Archives of Industrial Society, University of Pittsburgh Libraries.

67. What follows is based on Charles A. Gauld, *The Last Titan: Percival Farquhar, American Entrepreneur in Latin America* (Stanford, Calif.: Institute of Hispanic American and Luso-Brazilian Studies, Stanford University, 1964), chaps. 8, 9.

68. A system of daily intake of quinine, quarantine for incoming laborers, the use of mosquito netting, and good diets for laborers permitted—or so the medical advisers thought—a reduction in the rate of labor turnover (and mortality) to tolerable levels. This is of course a relative concept, for 1,550 graves were added to the local cemetery between 1907 and 1912. L. Werner, "All Aboard to Nowhere: The Mad Mary," *Americas* 42, no. 4 (1990): 14.

69. Gauld writes: "The company town was unmistakably American with its clean, regular streets, and its electricity, saw mill, ice plant, bakery, steam laundry, and telephones in town and two main stations" (ibid., 140).

70. Dana Merill, a photographer hired by Farquhar to document his project, left a collection of photographs showing the success of North American entrepreneurship in implanting a modern city in the middle of the Great Forest.

71. North American modernity in the Amazonian jungle and in the Atacama desert, South American antiquity in the form of Inca ruins and Caripuna "natives."

72. This discourse resonated clearly all across the culture. To Ralph Waldo Emerson (writing in 1833), his journal was his savings bank, a vault where he could deposit his discoveries about himself and the surrounding world. Knowledge, conceived as a process of social accumulation, required the contributions of all learned Americans, particularly those passionless and detached observers, at a time when the process of "civilization" was yet incomplete and the country's politics had turned into "mob" violence (Porte, *Representative Man,* 239, 254–55).

73. Rodman MacIlvaine, an engineer working on the Madeira-Mamoré railroad in 1878, spent most of his year on the construction site shooting animals for collecting purposes. His engagement with this part of South America (shooting nature, treating aborigines as nature) appeared as an enactment of his country's fascination with hunting and collecting, two activities legitimated by the project of science.

74. Though most travelers before 1870 endeavored to present their narratives of South America as a true representation of "facts," most of what they claimed as "evidence" was the result of "impressions," first notes about phenomena imperfectly observed, hastily interpreted, and narrated a long time after their occurrence.

75. Social surveys conducted by the Rockefeller Foundation in Peru as a basis for its medical research and sanitary projects contained more information about the country's poor than had hitherto been obtained.

76. To Normano, opposed to the easy and optimistic characterizations of South

America given by his contemporaries in the late 1920s, the subcontinent was still a *desert of knowledge,* a land still asking itself important questions about its identity, a territory that needed large doses of research. "Neither in South America itself nor abroad has any attempt so far been made to answer the question which Sarmiento, one of the greatest minds of South America, asked some eighty-five years ago: 'What is America? What are we?' Scientifically, perhaps even more than economically, South America is still a desert with oases near the coast. Ultimate rediscovery is to be made, not by means of prophetic pilgrimages, nor the visits of statesmen, nor banquet eloquence, but rather in the study." Arguing against the psychological interpretations that tried to reduce South America to the commonplaces of the nineteenth century (political childhood and mixed-race primitivism), now dressed in Freudian language, Normano demanded a better study of the economy of the region (including the incipient industrialization taking place in Brazil) (Normano, *The Struggle for South America* [London: Allen and Unwin, 1931], 16).

77. Direct observation was an explicit goal of this program: "The object in view was to assure the presence in various widely scattered educational institutions in the United States, of *men who had seen South America with their own eyes,* who had talked with its representative men, and who could speak with some authority concerning the problems and activities of the other American republics" (Harry E. Bard, *Intellectual and Cultural Relations between the United States and the Other Republics of America* [Washington, D.C.: Carnegie Endowment for International Peace, 1914], 1; italics mine).

78. As a result he devoted part of his life to teaching the culture and history of Latin America to North Americans (at Columbia University and the University of Pennsylvania, in the Committee on Cooperation with Latin America, etc.) (Sharbach, *Stereotypes of Latin America,* 58–64).

79. Ibid., 107.

80. "On the one hand, Hoover's press corps reacted as if they had discovered an entirely new world, and yet they relied on preconceptions they knew their readers would be able to recognize" (ibid., 179).

81. Richards, *The Imperial Archive.*

II: Empirical Studies

Figure 1. Frederic Edwin Church, *The Heart of the Andes,* 1859.
Metropolitan Museum of Art, Bequest of Margaret B. Dows, 1909.

Deborah Poole

Landscape and the Imperial Subject

U.S. Images of the Andes, 1859–1930

In the woods . . . I become a transparent eye-ball. I am nothing. I see all.
The currents of the Universal Being circulate through me;
I am part or particle of God.

RALPH WALDO EMERSON

In 1859 a doorman opens the Studio Building on 10th Street in Manhattan to let in the crowd that has been gathering outside for several hours. After showing their prepaid twenty-five-cent tickets, small groups are ushered up the stairs and through heavy black curtains. There, within the darkened studio, stands a five-by-ten-foot oil painting of a lush mountain landscape. The canvas is mounted in a thirteen-by-fourteen-foot frame carved in the form of a casement window and designed to bring the landscape's horizon line to just above eye level. A skylight above is directed so as to illuminate only the brilliant surface of the canvas. At the far left, a massive snow-capped mountain shines through a clearing in dark clouds. Nestled in the verdant plain below is a small hamlet and church. In the foreground, there is a cross before which two Indians kneel. Below them to the center right, a cascading waterfall gives way to a shimmering pool of water (figure 1).

The effect on the spectators is immediate. When confronted with its immensity, the crowd becomes hushed. Women feel faint. Both men and women succumb to the dizzying combination of terror and vertigo that they recognize as the sublime. Many of them will later describe a sensation of becoming immersed in, or absorbed by, this painting, whose dimensions, presentation, and subject matter speak of the divine power of nature. As one critic commented after seeing the painting, "The observer feels that the canvass [sic] has depth and that he is looking open eyed, out upon nature itself." [1] Later, on the painting's national tour in 1861, precautions will be taken to monitor these reactions: Spectators in Boston are advised to use opera glasses when viewing the painting.[2] Elsewhere, visitors prepare themselves for the exhibition by studying one of the several pamphlets that have been published to guide viewers on their tour of this immense and strangely refracted Andean landscape.[3]

The exhibit we have just revisited was mounted for Frederic Edwin Church's *Heart of the Andes*. During the three weeks of its New York opening, the single-painting exhibit drew over 12,000 people.[4] On some days, attendance was over 2,400.[5] In 1862, the year after its national tour, an engraving based on the painting was produced and sold well.[6] In 1863 the composer George William Warren dedicated a composition to the painting.[7] In 1864 the canvas was once again seen by record numbers of viewers in the Metropolitan Sanitary Fair at New York's Union Square. In 1909 it was acquired by the Metropolitan Museum of Art in New York, where it remains on permanent display in the American wing. A century later, in 1993, *The Heart of the Andes* was again celebrated by the Met in a one-painting exhibit designed to replicate the original conditions of its viewing.[8]

Given the numbers of people who have seen *The Heart of the Andes,* it is relatively easy to imagine that this landscape might have influenced how people residing in the United States perceived, represented, and acted on that region of western South America known as "the Andes." But how do we explain this "influence"? Should we think about the act of *seeing* in the same way we theorize such discursive practices as writing and speaking? How can we trace the influence of a picture such as Church's on the particular forms of subjectivity that have enabled and propelled the U.S. imperial mission in Latin America? Can we reduce this influence—and the painting's popularity—to the ideological enchantments of Manifest Destiny? If we adopt this ideological interpretation of the image's power, how do we then explain the very strong emotional and physical reactions that contemporary viewers felt in the presence of Church's Andean landscape? Should we think of Church's public as already formed imperial subjects? Or should we rather be thinking about how specific acts of seeing help to form particular types of social subjects?

This chapter considers some of these questions through a discussion of three Andean landscapes produced for North American audiences. The landscapes I will consider are Church's 1859 *The Heart of the Andes;* an engraving published in 1868 by the diplomat/archaeologist Ephraim George Squier; and a photograph taken in 1913 by the mountaineer, explorer, historian, and politician Hiram Bingham. I have chosen these images because each was, in its day, seen by large numbers of people. I am also interested in them as expressions of three different moments in the history of both U.S.–Latin American relations and U.S. visual culture. In terms of the U.S. experience in Latin America, the period covered by these images stretches from the heyday of Manifest Destiny, when Church and Squier visited the Andes, until the era of Pan-Americanism, when Hiram Bingham carried out his scientific explorations for the good of mankind and Yale University.[9]

Visually, these three images also suggest the possibility of periodization: Church's one-work exhibition coincided with the zenith of a nineteenth-century mass visual culture centered on dioramas, international expositions, and the rise of studio photography. Squier's printed engravings appeared during a decade when photography and engraving were becoming increasingly commodified. Finally, Bingham's three expeditions—which took place in the decades immediately preceding television, Hollywood cinema, and the visualizing practices of what Guy Debord has called the "society of the spectacle"—can be thought of as marking the close of a nineteenth-century understanding of visual modernity.[10] In discussing the relation between vision and the politics of empire in these three periods and landscapes, I am particularly interested in examining the different ways in which vision is assigned material force and agency through its relation to the body. I then consider how this relation enables the (embodied) viewing subject to exert or imagine specific types of claims on the material world.

In conclusion, I offer some suggestions regarding the importance of a study of vision to our project of rethinking the cultural bases of imperial regimes and political formations. What we see in a painting such as *The Heart of the Andes* depends in important ways on the aesthetic, philosophical, and biological discourses that teach us what it is *to see*. Visual images, however, are not mere condensations of words. Nor should we think of them as tools or "reflections" of some more or less intentioned ideological program. Vision is more complex and powerful than such a formulation would lead us to believe. In the Western tradition with which I am concerned here, its power derives in large part from the ways in which vision is inscribed within the domain of pleasure. To understand the place of culture in imperial projects, therefore, we must first look a bit more closely than we have at what Edward Said has called "the pleasures of empire." [11] Here, in the subtle, complex, and, above all, uneven workings of literature, music, and art resides the key to understanding how our identities and imaginations have been shaped by the racial discourses, administrative habits, historical narratives, and spatial configurations that form and legitimate imperial power. This chapter, then, examines how one form of visual and aesthetic practice—landscape representation—has helped to shape various sorts of "imperial subjects."

The Visual Property of Empire

It is difficult to overestimate the importance of the landscape painter in early nineteenth-century America. Men like Church's mentor, Thomas Cole, and his rival, Albert Bierstadt, were, in every sense of the words, public intellectuals. Their paintings were anxiously awaited and eagerly consumed. Their vision of the North American landscape shaped how people (then and now) would think about the future of their country and the peculiar ways in which its citizens' sense of self came to depend on constant territorial expansion.

The landscapes that Cole, Bierstadt, and Church offered to their North American viewers conformed to the reigning aesthetic principles of the picturesque. As defined by its most important British theorist, William Gilpin, the picturesque posited both a particular relationship to the land and a particular type of observing subject.[12] Briefly stated, Gilpin's notion of the picturesque prescribed that the artist should first observe and study nature. In representing nature in art, however, the artist was instructed to rework what he saw in accordance with certain principles of composition and harmony. The most important of these principles was the combination of smooth and irregular forms. Thus, in painting *The Heart of the Andes,* Church juxtaposes rounded hills and shimmering pools with craggy mountains, rough trees, zigzagging roads, or other diagonal forms. Gilpin and other picturesque theorists also suggested that landscapes might be made more pleasing to the eye when combined with such signs of a receding human presence as ruins, dilapidated fences, or, in the case of Church's canvas, a rustic cross and village.

Picturesque conventions were originally fashioned in reaction to the highly refashioned landscapes of England.[13] There, a century-long struggle over enclosure had produced a distinctively aristocratic form of pastoral in which gardens were reworked to resemble pristine nature and whole villages were sometimes moved so as not to obstruct the view from stately manor windows. North American landscape painting drew in important ways on these established conventions of the picturesque. From early on, however, U.S. artists such as Church who traveled to Europe to study art were cautioned against learning too much from Europe. They were advised instead to work for the formation of a distinctively "American" tradition. This new tradition was to be more spontaneous and individual than its European predecessor. To obtain these qualities, artists were instructed to shun European concerns with history and academic traditions. In their paintings, the historical references (principally ruins) so prominent in European picturesque art were replaced by a new icon of rusticity: the individual settler living on the edge of a wilderness and looking into the future rather than musing over the past.

The leading spokesman for this new artistic project was Ralph Waldo Emerson. For Emerson, this "American" aesthetic was to be the foundation of a new "transcendentalist" vanguard conceived in the universal language of liberal individualism, yet deeply embedded in the national context and interests of the United States. Specifically, Emerson proposed that intellectuals and artists should celebrate two principles: the autonomy of the individual and the ways in which nature taught individuals to disregard both history and tradition. "All that you call the world," Emerson advised, "is the shadow of that substance which you are." [14] He saw no need for the classic histories and written traditions that had brought Europe its greatness. Instead, for Emerson, truth was to be found through immersion in nature. The American artist or poet, in other words, was to lose himself in nature, rather than simply *observe* it as in the British picturesque.

Emerson's transcendentalist doctrine certainly helped to shape the aesthetic forms and languages of mid-nineteenth-century American landscape painters such as Church. More importantly for our purposes, however, it also fueled a swelling public interest in landscape as a vehicle for fusing religious experience with patriotic emotion. The man who steeps himself in "picturesque language," Emerson wrote, "is a man in alliance with truth and God. The moment our discourse . . . is inflamed with passion or exalted by thought, it clothes itself in images." [15] Similar convictions animated the thousands of men and women who flocked to see Church's paintings—and described their reactions in terms of out-of-body experiences, loss of self, immersion, and vertigo. To look at a landscape painting—or better still, at its original—was to realize a certain ideal of the self.[16]

But what was the particular fascination exerted by a painting of the Andes? While most U.S. painters looked to New England and the western frontier for the landscapes that could produce these effects, others looked further south. In the early 1840s Frederick Catherwood and John Lloyd Stephens mounted expeditions to the jungles of Central America; some years later James Whistler and George Catlin undertook artistic excursions to eastern South America; and in the 1850s Church himself traveled to the northern Andes.[17] These artistic expeditions coincided with a period of heightened U.S. commercial and political interest in the South American republics. In the decades prior to Church's trip, Peruvian guano had become a coveted international commodity. In the 1850s, William Walker and other filibusters had made their names meddling in the political affairs of Central American nations. Further south, three U.S. government expeditions had begun a well-publicized effort to assess the resources and navigable rivers of Brazil, Peru, and Bolivia.[18]

The paintings and sketches that Church brought back from his journeys to the Andes were both similar to and different from the landscapes he and his fellow countrymen were producing of New England and the West. Like these, the South American paintings relied on an inspirational vocabulary derived from Ruskin and Emerson, and a more or less conventional set of symbols meant to convey everything from processes of aging to moments of transcendence.[19] This aesthetic and symbolic vocabulary served to smooth the transition from North America to that relatively unknown region that Americans of the time referred to as "our southern continent."

In the particular case of the Andes, public appreciation of their "Americanness" was deepened by the work of two other men. The first was the Prussian geographer and traveler Alexander von Humboldt, whose books on the Colombian and Ecuadorian Andes were the nineteenth century's principal resource on Andean South America. Humboldt had famously described the equatorial Andes as a microcosm of the world where one could observe the entire range of climates and vegetations known to mankind. For Church (and his public), Humboldt's scientific observations of northern Andean ecology opened up not so much the possibility of studying the variety of nature as the opportunity to experience a landscape that *actually contained* the wealth of vegetation and the variety of geological formations that North American landscape artists had had to invent when constructing their allegorical and fantastic landscapes. By admiring Church's Andean scenery as a composite expression of *American* nature, contemporary viewers elided the geographic and cultural distance separating them from the Andes. *The Heart of the Andes* was, in the words of one contemporary observer, "a continental picture" that "seizes the very spirit and splendor of our most characteristic scenery."[20]

The other man who had shaped what Church's public might have known about the Andes was the U.S. historian William Hickling Prescott. Prescott's books on the Conquest of Mexico and Peru described the Conquest as a tragic but divinely ordained event by virtue of which Andean people were simultaneously deprived of their sovereignty and brought closer to a state of Christian civilization.[21] Underwriting Prescott's texts was the clear message that the next divinely ordained step in South America's progressive march toward civilization would be the fall of Spanish Catholicism and the subsequent rise of Protestantism.[22] To say that Prescott's narrative of the Peruvian conquest was the reigning paradigm for Andean history would be to grossly understate its influence. In 1859 it was the principal source of historical information on the Andes for those people who entered the Studio Building to view Church's Andean landscape. The painting's snowcapped mountain would have spelled "Humboldt" for many educated viewers. An even greater number, however, would have read the cross and hamlet in Church's Andean landscape as features of a physical and historical landscape that Prescott had inscribed within the eminent domain of North American Protestant ambition.

In the first pages of his "guide" to *The Heart of the Andes,* Church's close friend and publicist Theodore Winthrop provides a roadmap by which both Prescott's history and Humboldt's geography can be applied to Church's Andean creation. Like Prescott, Winthrop wanted to trace the progressive movement of history toward truth. In Winthrop's history, however, the episodic movement of Andean history is defined not by different types of conquerors and religions, but rather by the forms of aesthetic consciousness they bring. First in line in Winthrop's history are the sun-worshipping Incas. Once their "barbaric music" had "died away," the Andes were then first heard of again, according to Winthrop, "as a scientific convenience" for the "French Savans [sic]" who earned respect for "these mountains as pedestals for science." [23] The final two periods in Winthrop's Andean history are marked by Humboldt's scientific discovery of the Andes' natural grandeur and the even higher, culminating truth of his friend Church's aesthetic insight. "The Andes' transcendent glory," Winthrop concludes, "remained only a doubt and a dream, until Mr. Church became [their] interpreter to the northern world." [24]

For Winthrop, Church's aesthetic insight was directly derived from the one fact that set him apart completely from his predecessors in the Ecuadorian Andes. Unlike either Charles Marie de la Condamine or Humboldt, Church was a North American. Indeed, for his contemporary public, his fame rested in large part on his reputation as a "sixth generation Yankee of Yankees who was immune to European influences." [25] He was also an artist. More importantly he was *both,* and, as such, he participated in that broader movement championed by Emerson in which artists were to reject the academic and historical perspectives of European art by immersing themselves in the transcendental, divine truth of nature. While the vast majority of the paintings that supposedly provided witness to this "American" spirit portrayed New England or the West, the boundaries of nature were easily extended. Indeed, for one contemporary critic, it was Church's Andean paintings, and in particular *The Heart of the Andes,* that marked the "inauguration of this new art epoch" in which American art would surpass that of Europe. The characteristics of this new epoch, he argued, had as much to do with the "pure, bright and transparent American sky" that "brings out everything clearly and sharply to the eye," as with the "independent spirit of our artists, who refuse to be bound by the conventionalities of other [European] schools." [26]

The Andes offered painters such as Church a totally trackless and conceptually unexplored arena in which to engage this Emersonian ideal of nature and transcendence. Church himself described Riobamba as a "pathless wilderness" where he experienced the "reduction of civilized man to bare subsistence." [27] Elsewhere in the Ecuadorian Andes, he described himself as "careening, in a chariot of rock; through airy wastes beyond the reach of gravitation, with no law but my own will." [28] Church's North American viewers experienced, as we have seen, very similar sensations of disembodiment, vertigo, and loss of self in the presence of Church's vast Andean landscape. This visual encounter with nature made it possible at least to imagine the *physical* sensation of that most radical individualist: the "natural man" living outside the social compact. By giving free rein to those passions that society repressed, the visual politics of the landscape painting thus lent physical, material support to a particular interpretation of the individual and the claims he (and I use the gendered pronoun intentionally) could exert over nature.

The success of Church's paintings depended on a very similar dynamic. As an artist, he "organized everything to thrust the viewer into the pictorial space quickly and forcibly, so that the sensation of looking *at a picture* is replaced by a feeling of actually being present *in the scene.*" [29] As one contemporary reviewer noted after viewing another of Church's Andean paintings, "One feels the muscles grow tense gazing over that great Alpine panorama." [30]

Church achieved this effect through two optical techniques common to contemporary luminist painting. First, he constructed the picture in a series of receding, parallel planes. The illusion of depth created by these planes fostered that sensation of physical immersion or absorption that

Church's public *sought* in their landscape paintings. Church's genius was to heighten the almost magnetic pull such pictures exerted on contemporary viewers by further foreshortening the lower and upper registers of the picture plane. Once placed in the casement-window frame and darkened room, the overall effect was one of looking out a real window into the depths of an exotic mountain wilderness. The second, complementary trick—common to the luminist school of painting—had to do with how the painting's mirrorlike surface appeared to erase all evidence of the artist's hand. The Andean mountains, plains, and palms were presented not as creations of an intervening human mind, but rather as objects with an unmediated physical and emotional claim on the viewer's body and mind. It was this sense of immediacy and presence that fostered what contemporary viewers described as a sensation of floating out of their bodies and into the picture's alluring space.[31]

But how did these "out-of-body experiences" and physical absorption serve the needs of empire? How did they contribute to the formation of what I have called "the U.S. imperial subject"? For Emerson, as for Church, vision was a form of privilege and the "true man" was constituted through a particular act of seeing. This type of "seeing" was, in turn, characterized by two features. First, it was part of each person's physical and daily life: it became, in Emerson's words, "a part of his daily food." [32] Second, it did not dwell on the details of nature. Rather it recomposed "the details" into an "integrity of impression." [33] It is precisely here that the "imperial" subject emerges, for a landscape is no longer an earthly reality—a representation of the social relations, property rights, and labor that made up, for example, the small hacienda that Church included in *The Heart of the Andes*. "The charming landscape," in Emerson's words, may well be made up of "some twenty or thirty farms" belonging to identifiable (and nameable) individuals. "But none of them owns the landscape. There is a property in the horizon which no man has but he whose eye can integrate all the parts, that is, the poet. This is the best part of these men's farms, yet to this their land-deeds give them no title." [34]

For Emerson, as for Thomas Jefferson and John Locke, the material space of "nature" was transformed into "property" through a process in which the individual transferred some elementary essence or "property" of the self into the material world around him. For Locke (and Jefferson), this transferal underwrote the transformation of common land to private property by the investment of individual labor, since labor itself formed the essence or "property" of the (European) individual.[35] A similar logic allows Emerson to posit vision as a form of labor through which the partitioned landholdings and details that define the social landscape could be transformed into the unified horizon of a "natural" landscape.

On one level, Emerson imagined this "natural" or "desocialized" landscape as the basis for a new collective and utopian *national* relationship with both nature and God. Indeed, in many respects, the new forms of transcendental subjectivity championed by Emerson and Church were grounded in this expansive relationship to the physical world. This relationship erased the boundaries of both the individual and the human landscape in the interests of creating a substantively new—and conceptually "divine"—relationship among nature, self, and nation. On the other hand, however, the utopian collective identity envisioned by Emerson and the transcendentalists depended on a radical individualism seemingly at odds with this vision of a national, natural commonwealth. Thus, for Emerson, it was only the aesthetically atuned and solitary philosopher (or, more appropriately, seer) who was able to transcend the material and social worlds of both private property and history. Through this act of transcendence the individual could join "the poet" to ascend into the emotive world of images, commune directly with "nature," and make the distinctively imperial claim to reconfigure the landscape and, hence, own "the horizon."

The ideological and political project of Manifest Destiny relied in obvious ways on just this ability to erase the property lines (and title deeds) of real space. As the empire expanded, it also came to depend more and more on the ability of individual "imperial subjects" to imagine a personal claim or right to that space. The heated debates over homesteading and land rights that unfolded in the United States during Church's own lifetime certainly depended on such a collective or national sense of individual right. So too did the various projects for colonization and investment that New York bankers, Boston merchants, Washington politicians, beleaguered Southern slaveholders, and filibusters imagined for Andean South America.[36] What I want to suggest here is that the *aesthetic projects* of both Emerson and Church formed a very real part of this larger project we so readily recognize as nineteenth-century imperialism. They provided the visual apparatus or discipline by which such imperious claims could be not only imagined, but daily reenacted as an essential component of each person's *physical* and spiritual self.

Figure 2. Ephraim George Squier, *Desaguadero,* 1868. From *Incidents of Travel in the Land of the Incas.*

Vision and Statistics

In 1868, the popular U.S. magazine *Harper's Monthly* published an engraving of another Andean landscape (figure 2). In this scene, the snowcapped mountain occupies a more prominent place along the horizon than the mountain in Church's famous canvas. The middle distance also differs. It shows a land that is apparently barren and certainly unsettled. In the left-hand middle ground, two men stand, their backs to us, facing—and apparently contemplating—the mountain and the plain below them. The rocky ledge on which they stand falls precipitously into a sort of void. At first, the presence of these two spectators seems to offer a "point of view," a position that we might adopt so as to comprehend the scene. On closer consideration, however, it becomes clear that this picture—like Church's much larger painting—offers its viewer no easy entry into the picture's space. There is, for example, no level foreground area that invites the viewer to imagine him- or herself stepping into the scene. In the absence of such an entry point, the perspective we must assume is instead an unrealistic "bird's eye" view—a view from above that is somehow even more omniscient than the point of view we are offered by Church's Andean landscape.

The engraving also lacks the painting's brilliant colors and seductive play of light. It is monotonous and gray. There is no vegetation or other significant detail. Instead, when we attempt a closer scrutiny, our eye is drawn to the minute, obsessive lines of the engraver's tool. Whereas the earlier picture's details draw our attention to specific pieces of the landscape, the engraving's lines instead distract and disorient. They offer "noise," where the painting offers meaning. They give us nothing to hold on to. They give the illusion of failing eyesight, of an eye or lens that has failed to focus and that can therefore give us neither the depth of field nor the meaningful detail through which we are accustomed to perceiving a "scene."

Finally, the engraving differs in its arena of reception. Unlike Church's canvas, which was publicly viewed, this engraving, by Ephraim George Squier, was seen and appreciated in private. As part of the magazine, it would have been held in the viewer's lap, perhaps at arm's distance, perhaps up close. But the important point is that it would have been *held* and thus, to a certain extent, possessed by its viewer. It was small; it was portable; it could, if necessary, be removed from the binding; and it was one of many thousands of this particular Squier engraving produced, viewed, and circulated in the United States in the year 1868. The public it created was thus constitutively different from the one that had gathered nine years earlier to see Church's canvas. Whereas that public was physically gathered to share an experience, Squier's public was only tenuously linked by the knowledge that this engraving was being held, possessed, and viewed by others. The members of Church's public were, perhaps, involved in ongoing debates concerning homesteading and National Reform. Squier's late-1860s public was still recovering from a devastating civil war and in the trance of a national western expansion predicated on the laying of rails, measurement of land, plotting of homesteads, and killing of "Indians." For them the experience of an Emersonian immersion in the landscape offered less appeal than an aesthetic of control and monitored reaction.

Squier would have been known to most members of this public. He had served as a U.S. diplomat in Nicaragua and, later, as a commercial envoy charged with ameliorating a trade war with guano-rich Peru. He was also known for his archaeological theories concerning the origins of

North American Indians, and—last but not least—for his recent New York society divorce. The engraving itself appeared in a serialized account of Squier's travels and excavations in Peru titled *Incidents of Travel in the Land of the Incas.*[37] *Incidents* was the first widely read U.S. publication to be based on firsthand experience in the Andes. At a time when very little at all was known about South America in the United States, Squier's detailed descriptions filled in the blanks in Prescott's popular romantic narrative with concrete data on the ancient ruins and modern cities of Peru.

The appeal of these scientific observations was widened by Squier's engaging narrative style and by the inclusion of 259 engravings made from photographic plates by Auguste Le Plongeon and Squier himself. Although often radically embellished to fit artistic or pictorial conventions of the time, the original photographs on which these engravings were based were in many cases the first taken of such important archaeological sites as Tiahuanaco, Raqchi (Cuzco), and Pachacamac.[38]

The man who introduced these images to the U.S. public was a Methodist civil engineer and former Ohio state legislator who had already established his archaeological and political credentials with his study of the ancient burial mounds of the Ohio and Mississippi Valleys.[39] As a political intervention, Squier's work on the Mound Builders was important for its suggestions that this North American culture was at least as old as, if not older than, many preclassical European ruins. Following a decade of intense scholarly and public debate about the mounds and their builders, Squier's conclusive new evidence was, as one reviewer pointed out, a welcome "reproach" to European attacks on "the excessive modernness and newness of our country." [40]

The Mound Builders study insured that Squier's future work would be read—as all archeology has been then and now—against the backdrop of nationalist politics. Our present goal, however, is to explore the *visual* politics of Squier's work. What I therefore want to emphasize here is the visual and descriptive regime that Squier marshaled to support his interpretations of pre-Columbian American societies.

In the text of *Incidents* Squier adopts two techniques to describe the Andean landscape. The first involves the familiar technique of quantification. Throughout his journal, Squier describes the Andean landscape as a sort of inventory: it contains so many churches, so many rivers, so many fields and plains, all occupying a certain amount of space. Snowcapped mountains—which led Church to disembodied flights of fancy—are dealt with in the same fashion as other, smaller features of the landscape. They serve in Squier's view as comforting limits on the expansive views he repeatedly encounters. "The whole great table-land of Peru," writes Squier, which is "all framed in by the ranges of the Cordillera and the Andes, is presented like a map before the adventurous traveler." [41] Even when confronted with the most spectacular views, Squier retained a surprisingly quantitative approach to both the observation and description of the Andean landscape.

The second, and I think more interesting, technique builds on this commodifying impulse. In this technique Squier employs statistical language to describe his own emotional or aesthetic reaction to particular views or scenes. On first viewing the Bay of Copacabana, for example, Squier confesses that although "I am an old traveler and not given to 'sensation,' here I experienced an emotion." Ever the good engineer, Squier then promptly requests that his companion take his pulse "for the purpose of ascertaining the fact [of the emotion]." Quoting, he claims, directly from his notes, Squier then concludes that "deducting for a slight irregularity, consequent on walking up the hill rather rapidly, he discovered a percussion in the pulse, such as often attends sudden excitement." To calm his emotions (and pulse), Squier then goes to the precipice's edge, where he "occupied [him]self in timing the fall of stones into the water below." [42]

As a scientist, engineer, and Christian, Squier was not immune to the doctrines of nature preached by his contemporaries Emerson and Church. Indeed, given the cultural understandings of nature and transcendence that we have seen at work in Church's aesthetic, it is not at all surprising that Squier should assign transformative capabilities to the landscapes he encountered in the Andes. [43] What is different about Squier's aesthetic is its ruthless resort to physiology. As in the above-mentioned incident at Copacabana, the body becomes a means to discipline sensation, not, as in some stoic or masculinist philosophy, through the simple repression of emotion, but rather through the statistical—and, I will argue, *visual*—technique of partitioning and regulating the physiological evidence that, for Squier, makes up the senses. Emotion, in other words, is experienced through its materialization in such visible, measurable units as heartbeats, blood pressure, and so on. If for Church and Emerson the physical experience of seeing is anarchic and Rousseauian, for Squier it is regulated and controlled. For Squier, there is no loss of the social and physical self. Instead, vision itself is broken down into the discrete, quantifiable, and governable units of "pulse."

Squier's rigorous philosophy of vision also surfaces in the two types of visual materials with which he illustrates *Incidents*. The first type includes the numerous small woodcuts showing site plans, as well as the many skulls, potsherds, pottery, and mummies unearthed by Squier on his Peruvian travels. In these plates, Squier effectively transforms found objects into visual evidence. For such artifacts as potsherds or pottery, evidential status is attained by emphasizing the visual similarity and hence typological identity of a given set of objects. For other objects, principally skulls, equivalence and hence type are defined by breaking objects down into their constitutive measurements. These measurements are then mapped onto those of other similar objects, and the degree of correspondence is presented as proof that the objects belong to the same category or class (in the case of skulls, a "race"). In these plates, material objects are presented as objects whose "meaning" can be perceived only through a type of *statistical* vision. Like Squier's landscape aesthetic, this visual regime first breaks the surface effect of an object into a patterned array of smaller constituent units and then replots these units as a grid. They display artifacts, skulls, and potsherds as "populations" whose statistical patterning enables Squier to elaborate an interpretation of the whole.

The second type of visual material in *Incidents* consists of larger inset engravings such as the landscape reproduced in figure 2. In addition to landscapes, these engravings also portray views of modern cities and ancient ruins. The evidential value of these views, as Squier often reminds his reader, depended on both the eyewitness status of Squier himself and the realist allure of the photographs on which the engravings were supposedly based. Squier, however, never published his photographs and, indeed, seems to have placed little value on them. This may be partly due to the sad events by which his personal life came apart after the Peruvian expedition.[44]

It may equally well have been due, however, to the specific visual dynamics inherent to the two technologies. Photographs fascinated the nineteenth-century viewer with their fetishlike qualities. They were small, reproducible, and alarmingly realistic. They bore an indexical as opposed to symbolic relation to the real. Engravings, on the other hand, were one step removed from the world they represented. They too were reproducible and small. They were viewed in private. Yet their surface did not bear up to the sort of scrutiny that both the photograph and the painting invited. Instead, as we have seen, they were made up of a seemingly infinite and apparently random sequence of very small lines. Yet, when one stepped back, this randomness assumed a pattern. Squier reordered and made sense of landscapes through inventory-like descriptions, and made sense of emotions through the quantifiable rhythms of his pulse. His engravings, which made sense of the world by transforming the randomness of an engraver's lines into the pattern of a "scene," employed a similar strategy. Whereas photographs offered an aesthetic of "realism," engravings offered Squier and his readers an aesthetic of "control" and governance. As in his textual descriptions of the Andean landscape, discipline and the partitioning of emotions take precedence over the sort of untrammeled sensualism of Church's Emersonian aesthetic.

Discipline and Abstraction

The third and final mountain landscape that I want to consider here is the photograph in figure 3. It is composed in four more or less distinct planes. In the foreground the dark underbrush of a first low range of hills cuts in from the left and right. In the next plane a more distant set of peaks stretches across the entire picture space. The sides of this range are carved in ridges that lend texture to the image. Because they converge at a point more or less in the center of the middle foreground, they also provide a sort of visual anchor for the entire scene. Immediately above this point, a sharp peak then draws the eye up to the next, more distant range. This higher range features several snowcapped peaks, some lost in the clouds that form the fourth and final pictorial plane.

Taken together, the skillful arrangement of light, perspective, and form make this black and white photograph both precise and impressively abstract. It seems to contain, somehow, the essence of a mountain range: the harshness, the mass, the inaccessibility, the cold, the wavelike formation, and the sheer beauty that we associate with mountains. Many of these qualities are technologically based: As a photograph, the picture tells us that we are looking at "real" mountains, rather than at an artist's or engraver's secondhand rendering. For this reason too, the point of view we adopt in looking at the picture is necessarily that of its creator. Because we know it is a photograph, we know as well that we are looking at this scene as if through the same lens as the photographer, and thus from exactly his standpoint. Finally, because it is a photograph we are less inclined to approach the image as an aesthetic rendering. We say—as I just did—that the source of beauty in this scene is the mountains themselves, rather than the artist's hand or eye.

Despite its obvious differences, this photograph nonetheless shares certain traits with the earlier two images. It is taken from above. Its horizon line occupies more or less the same relative position as in the engraving. Because of this conjunction of point of view and horizon line, the photo-

Figure 3. Hiram Bingham, *The Most Inaccessible Corner,* 1930. Frontispiece, *Machu Picchu: A Citadel of the Incas.*

graph offers us no easy "stepping off" place in the foreground. If we were to imagine entering this photograph, we would have to do so with a para-chute. In this it is very much like the engraving. Yet at the same time, it is also like the painting in that its elevated point of view is designed to draw us *into* the scene. Whereas both this image and the painting seem to draw their distant snowcapped mountains toward us, the engraving makes us feel that its mountain is impossibly far away. It is, however, like the engraving in its aesthetic of reception. It too is small, possessable, pri-vate, and mechanically produced, rather than large, singular, and publicly exhibited. As a result, we have no good record of what contemporary viewers felt when they looked at either the engraving or the photograph.

This photograph was taken by another highly public figure: Hiram Bing-ham, who is best known today as the "discoverer" of Machu Picchu. The photograph itself was published in Bingham's most popular book, *Machu Picchu: A Citadel of the Incas* (1930), over a caption identifying the scene as "The Most Inaccessible Corner of the Most Inaccessible Section of the Central Andes." The photographer who took the picture (and wrote the caption) would also have been known to his contemporaries as a U.S. senator, a prestigious affiliate of Yale University, the heir to a famous lineage of Hawaiian missionaries, and the son-in-law of a prominent New England family.[45] Others of his Peruvian photographs had appeared in the widely read family magazine *National Geographic.* In addition, his hand-tinted lantern slides were a central attraction in the archive of images lent out to public schools, civic groups, and freelance lecturers by the American Museum of Natural History.[46] In short, like Church's painting and Squier's plate, this and others of Bingham's Andean photographs were seen by a *lot* of people.

Like Squier before him, Bingham was adept at fusing the scientific authority of his expeditions—which were sponsored by Yale University and the National Geographic Society—with the allure of the explorer and wilderness writer. Like Squier as well, his travel accounts reveal a sometimes obsessive concern with both physiology and physical discipline. Bingham's physical involvement, however, differed from Squier's in its explicit concern with self-sacrifice, pleasure, and pain. On the one hand, this new approach to travel was central to a certain modernist metaphysics of the self. On the other hand, it also pertained to that discourse of conquest and territorial possession which we consider central to imperialism. In this section, I suggest that the specific forms of visuality at work in Bingham's photographs emerge from precisely this convergence between the mountaineer's (or modernist's) concern with the body and physical discipline, and the imperialist's triumphant sense of geography and conquest. In this sense, Bingham's images combine the discrepant constructions of the embodied visual subject that we have seen in Church's and Squier's work.

Bingham opens his 1912 book *Inca Land*—in which he recounts the discovery of Machu Picchu—by describing Squier's engraving of a hanging bridge. "In the foreground" of the plate, writes Bingham, appears "a delicate suspension bridge . . . which hangs in mid-air at a great height above the swirling waters of [the Apurimac River]. In the distance, towering above a mass of stupendous mountains, is a magnificent snow-capped peak." [47]

According to his own account in *Inca Land,* it was this picture that inspired Bingham to go to Cuzco and, from there, to the little-known ruins of Choqquequirau high above the Apurimac gorge.[48] Once at Choqquequirau, however, what captured Bingham's imagination was not the immaculate Inca masonry of the walls that surrounded him, but rather the "tantalizing glimpses of snow-covered mountains" that he caught during breaks in the clouds (figure 4). "There seemed to be an unknown region 'behind the Ranges,' " Bingham recalls,

Figure 4. Hiram Bingham, *The Land beyond the Ranges*, 1912. Frontispiece, *Inca Land: Explorations in the Highlands of Peru.*

which might contain great possibilities. Our guides could tell us nothing about it. Little was to be found in books. Perhaps Manco's [the last Inca king's] capital was hidden there. For months afterwards the fascination of the unknown drew my thoughts to Choqquequirau and beyond. In the words of Kipling's "Explorer": *"A voice as bad as Conscience, rang interminable changes One everlasting Whisper day and night repeated—so: / 'Something hidden. Go and find it. Go and look behind the Ranges.' Something lost behind the Ranges. Lost and waiting for you. Go!"* [49]

The Land beyond the Ranges was, of course, Vilcabamba, where Bingham would "discover" the "Lost City" of Machu Picchu.

According to Bingham's own account, the snowcapped mountains of Apurimac provide the most important link between Squier's expedition (and engraving) and his own mission of discovery. But did the *nevados* carry the same significance for this Kiplingesque archaeologist from Yale as they did for either Squier or Church? As we have seen, snowcapped mountains figure prominently in all three of our Andean landscapes. From Church's own journals, we also know that this "prophet of Manifest Destiny" saw the volcanoes of Ecuador as manifestations of the wildest nature and, as such, as a potential source of the type of spiritual transformation (and out-of-body experience) sought by the nineteenth-century transcendentalists.

Squier's approach to the snowcapped mountains was more oblique. His only direct mention of the Apurimac nevados that so moved Bingham comes in a historical aside on the condition of Inca and colonial roads in Peru. "High mountain ranges and broad and frigid deserts, swept by fierce, cold winds," Squier informs us, "are not the sole obstacles to intercommunication in the Altos [highlands] of Peru." [50] Ever the practical traveler, Squier—the man who confirmed emotion by registering his pulse, dealt with precipitous cliffs by timing the fall of a stone, and described sweeping alpine landscapes by parceling them into measurable units—saw Bingham's "majestic Ranges" as important primarily for the inconvenience they posed for travel in the Andes. Rather than opening up new horizons of speculative (and possessive) vision as they did for Bingham, for Squier the cordilleras posed a welcome *limit* to the observing subject's view.

For Squier, mountains as a feature of the landscape were visually— and hence conceptually—divorced from the roads, ruins, and sights that marked the narrative of his itinerary. Even in the Squier engraving to which Bingham refers, the snowcapped mountain is sketched in almost absentmindedly; it forms a background feature necessary for the formal composition of the engraving, but with no immediate relationship to either the travelers or the bridge they pass.

Instead, Squier's purposeful gaze rested at eye level. His itinerary was marked by the regular, countable units of footsteps, yards, and miles. His horizon encompassed the road ahead and only those immediately tangible parts of the general landscape. In narrating his experience crossing the same bridge whose image had so impressed Bingham, Squier pays considerable attention to each and every feature of the perilously narrow road on which he must travel to reach the bridge. He is also concerned to describe the waters that surge below the bridge. But he gives not even a passing glance at the mountains that tower above him. In crossing the bridge, Squier looks down instead of up. As with the dropping of stones off a precipice in Puno, he cures his apprehension at crossing the frail bridge by taking out the sounding lines with which he can measure the canyon below.[51]

For Squier, then, it was the measuring tape that provided order to a visual experience in which novelty (and, let's face it, majesty) threatened to overcome his obsessive sense of order. Yet the regulatory concept of measurement entered hardly at all into the visual worlds of either of his fellow countrymen. Church focused on snowcapped mountains—and volcanoes in particular—as symbols of the uncontrollable (and hence inherently unmeasurable) spiritual power of nature. His visual standpoint reflected this attitude. Unlike Squier, he did not look down. Unlike Bingham, he did not project a landscape "beyond the horizon." Rather, he imagined himself in (and composed his paintings from) a disembodied position somewhere above the peaks.

In contrast to both Church and Squier, Bingham's sense of vision *started* at the horizon. Vilcabamba was first "seen" by Bingham as a mysterious—and, above all, invisible—*thing,* existing out there *beyond* the ranges. Bingham imagined this space (which he could not actually see) as if he were viewing it from above. Yet his "bird's eye" view was not, as was Church's, disembodied. Rather, it was imagined as a view obtained *as if* his body had been physically removed to a position on top of the far-off ranges. To see the Andes, Bingham—unlike Church—had to occupy *physically* (and not just spiritually) the special vantage points that would allow him to "see."

This same form of visuality informs Bingham's photographic sense of landscape as space. From his imagined position on top of the far-off ranges, Vilcabamba appeared to Bingham as a space on a map. It was a region with visible outlines (or borders), but with no distinguishing details or names. Indeed, Bingham's "archaeology" was more concerned with naming than excavating. Throughout *Inca Land,* Bingham eagerly assigns new names to topographical features, archaeological ruins, and whole regions. On the basis of these names he then constructs the historical narrative through which he will prove Machu Picchu was home to the last Inca emperor.[52]

To anchor these names in space, Bingham invokes an aesthetic of discovery in which the new horizons, revealed to the traveler, form essentially meaningless—because nameless—tracts of wilderness. His descriptions of new views are sparse and economical, as if the scenery itself defeated attempts to represent it. Unnamed topographic features become nonspecific markers of a wilderness that, in Bingham's words, "surpasses the possibilities of language for adequate description." [53]

For Bingham, the undifferentiated (and inarticulable) space of this view-from-above was at one with the depleted state of the explorer's (or viewer's) body. Throughout *Inca Land,* a view is presented as something that must be physically *achieved.* Here, in the mountainous Andes, the crucial aesthetic is elevation, which combines both the physical exhaustion of attainment and the panoramic sweep of an open vista. Much as contemporary forms of modernist abstraction separated form from content, this new travel aesthetic focused on abstracting the physical experience and achievement of travel from the actual content of what the traveler saw or observed. In a process wherein the fact of seeing began to take precedence over the object seen, the goal of travel became either to see something totally new or to see something from a different or unique perspective—a perspective that could then be claimed as one's own.

The novelty of this new aesthetic is more easily understood if we return to Bingham's largely featureless account of the panoramic view from Choqquequirau and compare it with Squier's exacting inventory of the topographic features and "sights" that fill his panoramic view of the plain of Desaguadero. First, Bingham: "As we mounted [Coropuna], the view of the valley became more and more magnificent. Nowhere have I ever witnessed such beauty and grandeur as was here displayed. . . . In the distance, as far as we could see, a maze of hills, valleys, tropical jungle, and snow-capped peaks held the imagination as though by a spell. Such were our rewards as we lay panting by the side of the little path when we had reached its highest point." [54] Bingham's superlatives tell us little about what he saw or even in what direction he was looking. Instead they tell us that this is a special, perhaps irreproducible, view that had not been seen before. It is the labor of arriving at this special view that is given more attention in Bingham's account than the view itself.

In Squier's description of a view, the priorities are altogether different. Every feature is accounted for and the satisfaction of seeing derives from the satisfaction of knowing exactly what is being seen. Another way to think about the differences between these two visual regimes is to examine the notion of itinerary and sight. Whereas Bingham "explored" and hence defined his own somewhat idiosyncratic itinerary by an arbitrarily chosen meridian on the map,[55] the majority of nineteenth-century travelers followed an established itinerary defined by a known set of "sights." [56] As they moved along these itineraries, travelers saw the same ruins, villages, and landscapes as their predecessors. For them, the goal and aesthetic of travel was to experience for themselves the seeing of objects that had already been constituted as "sights." The goal of Bingham's travels was, of course, quite the opposite. No longer content with seeing what had already been seen ("the sights"), Bingham sought to open new horizons of sight out there "beyond the ranges." Like the colonialist who wishes to possess a territory regardless of its contents and people, Bingham's goal was to stake a claim to a new and better view regardless of what that view contained. It was this aesthetic that motivated his exploration of regions such as Vilcabamba.

The extent to which Bingham was not just moved but driven by this aesthetic mission is revealed in his account of the ascent of Coropuna. Like other climbers, Bingham wished to ascend what he and others at the time thought to be the highest mountain in the Andes: Coropuna. Bingham's narrative of the ascent up Coropuna is marked by three recurring themes: the physical exhaustion of the climbers, which peaks as they reach the summit; the state (and weight) of the scientific equipment they carried to the summit; and the Indian porters' fear of the mountain itself.

As Bingham and his three companions—one American and two Peruvians—ascend the mountain, they are overcome with altitude sickness, exhaustion, and apathy. Several times Bingham comments on his inability to appreciate the beauty of the scenery or the brief glory of the Andean sunsets viewed from on high. He is aware of their beauty, yet unable to react. As they near the summit, the expedition members are drained of their humor, sensibilities, and humanity. Their existence has been reduced to the pure physical discipline necessary to attain their goal. Stripped of their abilities to apprehend the stupendous view stretching out beneath their feet, the climbers become a sort of pure expression of Bingham's modernist aesthetic. Unable to perceive the content of their hard-won view, their achievement is one of pure form: They have achieved a new and better view—a view that no one else had before experienced and that, therefore, might be claimed as a sort of territorial conquest. Bingham—following a time-honored tradition of mountaineers—is quick to stake his claim on Coropuna by planting the flags of Yale University and the United States on the snow-crowned summit.[57]

The photographs with which Bingham illustrates the Coropuna climb speak to this complex interplay of aesthetic tradition, metaphysical transcendence, and scientific rigor. In Bingham's own photography, Coropuna is shown from a distance, a desolate stretch of flat and rocky land surmounted by a massif of rock and ice. In other published photographs of the ascent, taken by H. L. Tucker, the climbers are shown in the horizontal positions that provide evidence of the physical exhaustion endured in their vertical ascent.

In his other photographs of Andean mountains, Bingham skillfully pictorializes the glacial landscape as a high contrast play of light and dark.

Such images, however, are reserved for those mountains which Bingham has not himself climbed and which remain, therefore, markers of an imaginative—rather than realized—horizon of sight. Coropuna itself, for example, is not similarly allegorized, perhaps because, as Bingham himself comments, his physical exhaustion was such that, on reaching the peak, he "could not take the least interest or pleasure in the view from the top of Coropuna." [58] Having reached the top of a mountain that he believed to be the highest in the Americas, Bingham forewent photographing the panorama spread at his feet and instead busied himself taking snapshots of the instrument readings that would assure proof of his physical accomplishment.

In a continuation (or culmination) of the aesthetic informing his other, lesser panoramas, Bingham effectively erases *all* detail in the landscape below him. His concern is to chronicle not the content of the view below his feet, but his attainment of that view. The view that Bingham saw from the peak "was desolate in the extreme . . . a great volcanic desert dotted with isolated peaks covered with snow and occasional glaciers. Apparently," he continues, "we stood on top of a dead world." [59]

Today the Quechua peasants of southern highland Peru ascribe Coropuna's power to the transient souls who live there, in a state of eternal condemnation. For Bingham as well, Coropuna's power had something to do with a transitional state between knowledge and death. There, on what Bingham—as a true Pan-Americanist—liked to describe as "the top of America," the body was reduced to near death, while the view itself was reduced to the purely physical operation by which the body, as the instrument of vision, had conquered it. By staking his claim to the view from what he believed to be the highest mountain in the Americas, Bingham, like Kipling's explorer, exerted a claim over the "empty" and desolate lands that stretched beneath his feet.

Vision and Empire

In introducing my discussion of Church, Squier, and Bingham I explained my choice of images by saying that theirs were, arguably, the most widely seen images of the Andes produced in North America. What exactly does it tell us, however, to say that these pictures were widely circulated, viewed, and thus "consumed" by a North American public? On the one hand, it suggests that visual images *probably* exercised a shaping influence on the way North Americans would come to perceive, imagine, dream about, and act on that part of Latin America known as "the Andes." The exact nature of this "influence" owes as much to the visual and material characteristics of the specific representational technologies (painting, engraving, photography) as to the sociology of vision linking image and artist to their viewing (and reading) public.

On the other hand, however, it also presents us with a peculiar sort of paradox, for no matter how "influential" we argue these images were, or how widely seen, they are images of a part of Latin America that does not, in fact, form a well-defined part of the U.S. visual imaginary. Unlike, for example, Mexico with its sleepy burros and mustachioed *bandidos,* there is no readily available inventory of stereotypes through which your "average U.S. citizen" can visually conjure the Andes. This fact about the Andes makes it a particularly interesting area to begin thinking more deeply about how particular visual regimes—as opposed to isolated stereotypes or "representations"—informed both the production and reception of images within the political culture of U.S. imperialism. By asking how the visual languages or styles (as opposed to the content) of particular images relate to the politics of their makers, their viewers, and their times, it may be possible to go beyond the relatively simple assertions that we have so far been able to make about how images operate as either purposive components or reflections of particular ideological programs.

In conclusion, I want briefly to consider three scenarios by which we might reconcile the existence of the differing—and at times contradictory—visual regimes informing the work of Church, Squier, and Bingham, with the singularity of what we have become accustomed to thinking of as "the imperial gaze." One scenario, of course, is to think of them as products of qualitatively different historical moments. To follow this scenario is to ask us to think more deeply about the way we construct our chronologies of U.S.–Latin American relations. Should such cultural forms as art and literature be considered when we define the boundaries between consecutive historical "periods"? And, if so, how should we weigh culture over, for example, politics, when particular regimes of representation or vision seem to blatantly crosscut or interrupt what we have become accustomed to thinking of as distinct historical moments? While the relatively brief sampling of landscape forms and periods presented here makes it difficult to argue convincingly for such a scenario, it is nevertheless interesting to think about what it might mean for us to reconstruct a chronology in which the salient markers were not restricted to such political and economic events as the Monroe Doctrine or Pan-Americanism. Instead, the chronology would include as well the dates and contours of such distinctive regimes of visual subjectivity as those heralded by the daguerreotype, the *carte de visite,* the stereoscope industry, the Kodak camera, and television. At the very least, the inclusion of these representational technologies and visual regimes into our history of imperialism would force us to think more seriously about the role of culture in the shaping of imperial—and imperialized—subjects.

Another scenario would call for us to think more deeply about the multiplicity of the cultural forms and visual regimes existing within the political economy and culture of imperialism.[60] In this scenario we would want to look at the substantive *differences* among Church's, Squier's, and Bingham's visual selves as evidence for the existence of multiple visual regimes coexisting in time and space. Such a scenario would allow us to reconfigure "the imperial gaze" (and hegemony itself) as a space of maneuver within which "imperial subjects" are unevenly formed by, among other things, competing visual regimes. This option, in turn, allows us to explore not only how "empire" has shaped our ways of seeing, but also how the less-controllable realms of fantasy and desire work their way around the interstices of prescribed ways of seeing.

A final scenario would see all three landscapes as expressions of a single imperial project. This scenario would privilege the striking similarities between Bingham's and Church's (dis)embodied, near-death experiences of visual transcendence and cite them as evidence for the consistent role played by vision and visual representations in the formation of U.S. imperial culture. Church's disembodied flights of fancy, Squier's obsessively statistical partitions, and Bingham's exhausting alpine adventures would all appear as part of a single discursive and political formation premised on the unquestioned right of North Americans to appropriate the South American landscape to their own, sometimes fanciful ends. The truth of such a scenario could certainly be traced in the appalling history of U.S. intervention in the political, economic, and cultural affairs of Latin Americans.

On the other hand, however, I would not want to argue that these—or any—images are bound by any single ideology or discourse. The images that men such as Church, Squier, and Bingham brought back to the United States also carried within them, as we have seen, a sensuous undercurrent of historical memory, myth, and desire. Each North American who either went, or was sent, to study the Andes or to survey their potential for investment carried with him (or, more rarely, her) aspirations and emotions that sometimes contravened the business of empire and the interests of capital. The photographers and artists who attempted to portray the Andes and their peoples had to juggle the similarly conflicting claims placed on their image-making by the rules of aesthetic proportion, the canons of scientific objectivity, the dictates of religion and metaphysics, and, finally, the immediacy of their own sympathies and physical desires. The tensions at work among these disparate domains of sentiment were experienced as part of the excitement of a modern world in expansion. Their lived and inchoate reality as feelings and emotions formed the cement linking the individual consumer of images and ideas to the very colonial and imperial enterprise of expansion that had made possible such "modern" ways of seeing.

Notes

1. On the 1859 Studio Building exhibit, see *New York Commercial Advertiser,* 30 Apr. 1859, 2; Kenneth Avery, *"The Heart of the Andes* Exhibited: Frederic E. Church's Window on the Equatorial World," *American Art Journal* 18 (winter 1986): 52–72; Gerald Carr, "Frederic Edwin Church as a Public Figure," in *The Early Landscapes of Frederic Edwin Church, 1845–1854,* ed. Franklin Kelly and Gerald Carr (Forth Worth, Tex.: Amon Carter Museum, 1987), 14–18; David C. Huntington, *The Landscapes of Frederic Edwin Church: Vision of an American Era* (New York: George Braziller, 1966), 5–6; Franklin Kelly, *Frederic Edwin Church and the National Landscape* (Washington, D.C.: Smithsonian Institution Press, 1988), 98–99; and Katherine Manthorne, *Tropical Renaissance: North American Artists Exploring Latin America, 1839–1879* (Washington, D.C.: Smithsonian Institution Press, 1989), 31–32. For contemporary accounts of the painting, see James Sommerville, *F. E. Church's Painting: "The Heart of the Andes"* (Philadelphia, n.d.); Samuel Clemens, *Mark Twain's Letters,* ed. Albert Bigelow Paine, vol. 1 (New York, 1917), 46; and Albert Ten-Eyck Gardner, "Scientific Sources of the Full-Length Landscape: 1850," *Metropolitan Museum of Art Bulletin* (Oct. 1945): 59–65. For contemporary reviews of the exhibition see *Harper's Monthly* 9 (June–Nov. 1859): 271; *New York Tribune,* 24 May 1859, 7; *New York Evening Post,* 28 Apr. 1859, 4–5; *New York Herald,* 5 Dec. 1859, 6–7; *Harper's Weekly,* 7 May 1859, 291; and *New York Times,* 28 Apr. 1859, 4–5; 4 May 1859, 4; 21 July 1859, 2; 12 Aug. 1959, 3; and 24 Nov. 1859, 4.

2. *Boston Daily Evening Transcript,* Jan. 1860.

3. The two guides were Theodore Winthrop, *A Companion to the Heart of the Andes* (New York: D. Appleton and Co., 1859); and Louis Legrand Noble, *Church's Painting: The Heart of the Andes* (New York: D. Appleton and Co., 1859).

4. Avery, *"Heart of the Andes,"* 52. The single-painting exhibition was a marketing ploy developed in Europe in the late eighteenth century and used with increasing frequency in nineteenth-century America. Church had used it previ-

ously for display of his immensely successful paintings *Icebergs* and *Niagara.* In all three exhibitions, Church used many of the same tricks of lighting and presentation employed in the popular landscape dioramas. On single-picture exhibitions, see Gerald R. Carr, *Frederic Edwin Church: The Icebergs* (Dallas, Tex.: Dallas Museum of Fine Arts, 1980); and Kenneth Avery, *Church's Great Picture: The Heart of the Andes* (New York: Metropolitan Museum of Art, 1993), 21. On contemporary landscape dioramas, see John Francis McDermott, *The Lost Panoramas of the Mississippi* (Chicago: University of Chicago Press, 1958).

5. David C. Huntington, "Landscapes and Diaries: The South American Trips of F. E. Church," *Brooklyn Museum Annual* 5 (1963–1964): 66.

6. Manthorne, *Tropical Renaissance,* 55.

7. Carr, "Frederic Edwin Church," 14. The two-piano march, titled "The Heart of the Andes: Marche di Bravura, The Andes," was first performed in New York in March 1863.

8. Avery, *Church's Great Picture.* The 1993 New York exhibit showed the painting in a frame designed after the original casement-window frame and built for a 1989 National Gallery exhibit in Washington, D.C.

9. In the Andes themselves, the period covers the years of modern liberal state formation in Ecuador, Peru, and Bolivia. While this process took different routes and assumed different rhythms in the three countries, it can be roughly summarized as a period when the short-lived military regimes (or "caudillo states") of the early nineteenth century gave way to (differing versions of) a liberal bureaucratic state. These states were led by strong regionally based elites and characterized by the political exclusion of indigenous majorities, the increasing acceptance of foreign capital, and attempts at territorial consolidation (e.g., road building, railroads, education, and military conscription). The artists and adventurers whose visual images I will consider here were drawn to the Andes, in differing ways, by the economic and political intrigues that accompanied these processes of state formation. Although it is impossible to do justice to the complex histories of both continents in a chapter that deals for the most part with an analysis of visual and aesthetic regimes, it is important to think of the three images as shaped, each in its own way, by a specific intersection of U.S. imperial ambition and the realities of the country on which that ambition was—in this case, quite literally—focused.

10. Guy Debord, *Society of the Spectacle* (Detroit, Mich.: Black and Red, 1977). See also Jonathan Crary, *Techniques of the Observer: On Vision and Modernity in the Nineteenth Century* (Cambridge: MIT Press, 1990); and Regis Debray, *Vie et mort d l'image: Une histoire du regard en Occident* (Paris: Gallimard, 1992). On the chronology of Debord's "society of the spectacle," see Jonathan Crary, "Spectacle, Attention, Counter-Memory," *October* 50 (1989): 97–107.

11. Edward W. Said, *Culture and Imperialism* (New York: Knopf, 1993).

12. William Gilpin, *Three Essays: On Picturesque Beauty, On Picturesque Travel, and On Sketching Landscape* (London, 1803).

13. On the social and historical context for the English landscape tradition, see Ann Bermingham, *Landscape and Ideology: The English Rustic Tradition, 1740–1860* (Berkeley and Los Angeles: University of California Press, 1986).

14. Ralph Waldo Emerson, "The Transcendentalist," in *The Portable Emerson,* ed. Carl Bode (New York: Penguin, 1981), 95.

15. Emerson, "Nature," in Bode, *The Portable Emerson,* 22.

16. Landscape painting and the picturesque aesthetic contributed to the origins of the tourism industry in the nineteenth-century United States; see Dona Brown, *Inventing New England: Regional Tourism in the Nineteenth Century* (Washington, D.C.: Smithsonian Institution Press, 1995).

17. See Manthorne, *Tropical Renaissance.* On Church's itinerary and diaries, see also Huntington, "Landscapes and Diaries."

18. Of particular importance for the Andean region was the Herndon Gibbon Expedition of 1851–1852.

19. For example, palm trees, which appear in nearly all of Church's Andean paintings, were understood to stand for the prodigality and fertility of South America. For other examples, see Manthrone, *Tropical Renaissance,* 13–20. On the probable influence of Ruskin on Church, see Huntington, "Landscapes and Diaries," 87; and Manthrone, *Tropical Renaissance,* 76.

20. *Harper's Monthly* 11 (June–Nov. 1859), 271. On Church's composite landscapes, see Avery, *Church's Great Picture,* 16–17. On Humboldt's influence on Church, see Avery, *Church's Great Picture,* 13–16; and Huntington, "Landscapes and Diaries," 71–72. On Humboldt's aesthetic, see Poole, *Vision, Race, and Modernity: A Visual Economy of the Andean Image World* (Princeton, N.J.: Princeton University Press, 1997), chap. 2; and Mary Louise Pratt, *Imperial Eyes: Travel Writing and Transculturation* (New York: Routledge, 1992).

21. W. H. Prescott, *History of the Conquest of Mexico* (London: George Bell and Sons, 1843), and *History of the Conquest of Peru* (New York: Harper and Bros., 1847).

22. Prescott's narrative drew on the tradition of the "black legend," which blamed fanaticism and the Catholic Church for the excesses of the Spanish conquest. In the U.S. context, the black legend of Spanish Catholicism was an integral component of early Puritan preachings and shaped popular conceptions of Latin Americans (in particular, Mexicans) as lazy, cruel, and in need of salvation. See Raymund Paredes, "The Origins of Anti-Mexican Sentiment in the United States," in *New Directions in Chicano Scholarship,* ed. Ricardo Romo and Raymund Paredes (San Diego: Chicano Studies Program, University of California—San Diego, 1978), 139–65.

23. Winthrop, *Companion,* 3. Winthrop is referring to the mission sent to Ecuador in 1739 by the French Royal Academy and led by Charles Marie de la Condamine.

24. Winthrop, *Companion,* 3–4.

25. Huntington, *Landscapes,* 10.

26. *New York Herald,* 5 Dec. 1859, 6–7. Humboldt also wrote about the "transparency" of light in the Ecuadorian Andes and its effects on visual perception.

27. Cited in Huntington, *Landscapes,* 45.

28. Cited in Huntington, *Landscapes,* 46.

29. Kelly, *Frederic Edwin Church,* 17; italics mine.

30. Cited in Huntington, *Landscapes,* 44.

31. The out-of-body experiences described by Church's public can be usefully compared to the sensations of vertigo and immersion that contemporary viewers described for the new technology of the stereoscope. See, for example, Oliver Wendell Holmes, "The Stereoscope and Stereography," in *Classic Essays on Photography,* ed. A. Trachtenberg (New Haven, Conn.: Leete's Island Books, 1980), 71–82.

32. Emerson, "Nature," 276.

33. Humboldt had called for a similar method of description based on the integrated "view." See Poole, *Vision,* chap. 2.

34. Emerson, "Nature," 10.

35. It was this transformative sense of property as a *right* grounded in (and derived from) the individual's productive labor that legitimated the settler colonialisms advocated by Locke and Jefferson. See Barbara Arneil, *John Locke and America: The Defence of English Colonialism* (Oxford: Clarendon, 1996), esp. 132–67; John Locke, *Two Treatises of Government,* ed. Peter Laslett (Cambridge: Cambridge University Press, 1970), 303–20; and William B. Scott, *In Pursuit of Happiness: American Conceptions of Property from the Seventeenth to the Twentieth Century* (Bloomington: Indiana University Press, 1977).

36. Although most filibusters went to Central America, Congress sent at least one major expedition to explore South America. This expedition, led by U.S. Navy Lieutenants Lewis William Herndon and Lardner Gibbon, was charged with the task of ascertaining navigable routes across South America and with assessing the possibilities of relocating slave populations from the United States to Brazil. Their illustrated report was widely read in the United States, and Church took a copy of it with him to Ecuador. See Lewis William Herndon and Lardner Gibbon, *Exploration of the Valley of the Amazon, Made under the Direction of the Navy Department* (Washington, D.C.: Government Printing Office, 1854); Whitfield J. Bell, "The Relation of Herndon and Gibbon's Exploration of the Amazon to North American Slavery, 1850–1855," *Hispanic American Historical Review* 19 (1939); and Manthorne, *Tropical Renaissance,* 52–53.

37. In 1877 *Incidents* was published as a single-volume book. By that time, Squier was living in an asylum on Long Island.

38. Keith McElroy, "Ephraim George Squier: Photography and the Illustration of Peruvian Antiquities," *History of Photography* 10, no. 2 (1986): 99–129.

39. Ephraim George Squier and Edwin H. Davis, *Ancient Monuments of the Mississippi Valley* (Washington, D.C.: Smithsonian Institute Press, 1848).

40. On the Mound Builder debates, see Thomas C. Patterson, *Toward a Social History of Archaeology in the United States* (Fort Worth, Tex.: Harcourt Brace College Publishers, 1995), 27–29; and Robert Silverberg, *Mound Builders of Ancient America: The Archaeology of a Myth* (Athens: Ohio University Press, 1968).

41. Squier, *Incidents,* 269.

42. Ibid., 318.

43. Squier followed Humboldt in citing the beauty of the Andean landscape as a source of the moral (and hence civilizational) impulse that created Inca society. See, for example, *Incidents,* 486.

44. Squier's high-society wife was a former actress from New Orleans, with family ties to Central America. Following a period of emotional difficulties, Squier divorced his wife in May 1873. A year later she remarried Squier's colleague and former employer, the publisher Frank Leslie. Less than a month later, Squier was declared legally insane and was placed in the care of a Long Island asylum. His brother, Frank Squier, assumed responsibility for publishing *Incidents* following Squier's hospitalization. See McElroy, "Ephraim," 99, 103.

45. Alfred M. Bingham, *Portrait of an Explorer: Hiram Bingham, Discoverer of Machu Picchu* (Ames: Iowa State University Press, 1989).

46. Archives of the Public Education Department of the American Museum of Natural History, New York. See also George Sherwood, "Free Education by the American Museum of Natural History in Public Schools and Colleges: History and Status in 1917," *Miscellaneous Publications of the American Museum of Natural History,* no. 10 (New York, 1917).

47. Hiram Bingham, *Inca Land: Explorations in the Highlands of Peru* (1912; Boston: Houghton Mifflin, 1922), 1.

48. His motives for undertaking the 1909 overland journey through Cuzco and Apurimac are represented differently in the book that chronicles that journey. In that book, Bingham describes "the chief interest of the trip" as being the exploration of the historic trade route linking Buenos Aires, Potosí, La Paz, and Lima (Hiram Bingham, *Across South America: An Account of a Journey from Buenos Aires to Lima by Way of Potosí* [Boston: Houghton Mifflin, 1911], vii–viii). This road runs through Cuzco and Apurimac. His trip to Choqquequirau was a sidetrip from his original itinerary and was made at the urging of authorities and townspeople in Abancay (Apurimac) (ibid., 291–95).

49. Bingham, *Inca Land,* 2.

50. Squier, *Incidents,* 544.

51. Ibid., 547–48.

52. See especially Bingham, *Inca Land.*

53. Bingham, *Across,* 308.

54. Ibid., 304.

55. Bingham reconciled his desire to climb the snowcapped mountain of Coropuna with Yale University's scientific demands by concocting a plan to "survey" Peru along the seventy-third meridian. This route conveniently allowed him to

include the mountaineering expedition in his "scientific" plans. See Alfred Bingham, *Portrait,* 113–14.

56. For Peru, this itinerary ran a short initial circuit from Lima to La Oroya and Cerro de Pasco, and then a longer second circuit from Mollendo to Arequipa, Puno, Sicuani, Raqchi, Cuzco, and back.

57. Much to his chagrin, Bingham was not the first U.S. citizen to climb Coropuna. Just a few days before he reached the peak, his principal rival, Miss Annie Peck, had climbed the opposite (and higher) peak, where she left a suffragette flag bearing the English words "Votes for Women." See Annie Peck, *A Search for the Apex of America* (New York: Mead and Co., 1911); and Deborah Poole, "Fotografía, Fantasía y Modernidad," *Márgenes* [Lima] 8 (Dec. 1991): 109–39.

58. Bingham, *Inca Land,* 43.

59. Ibid.

60. On multiple visual regimes, see Martin Jay, "Scopic Regimes of Modernity," in *Force Fields: Between Intellectual History and Cultural Critique* (New York: Routledge, 1988), 115–33.

Eileen J. Findlay

Love in the Tropics

Marriage, Divorce, and the Construction of Benevolent

Colonialism in Puerto Rico, 1898–1910

During the summer of 1898, U.S. soldiers tramped through the mountains and sugar fields of Puerto Rico, Cuba, and the Philippines, proclaiming themselves the liberators of downtrodden island inhabitants from the despotic rule of Spain. Several months later, the United States claimed the islands as its "protected possessions." The military intervention culminated in Spain's loss of the last shreds of its far-flung empire, catapulted the United States into an undeniable position as a world imperial power, and stifled the potentially radical direction of nationalist armed struggles that had been well under way in Cuba and the Philippines.[1]

In Puerto Rico, aspirations for national autonomy had not led to armed struggle. However, just months prior to the U.S. occupation, Liberal elites had won an Autonomy Charter from Spain after decades of political agitation. The charter decreed increased economic autonomy for the island and universal male suffrage. Despite this recent loosening of Spanish colonial control, the U.S. occupation forces were met almost unanimously with open arms in Puerto Rico. Puerto Ricans of all classes, races, and genders hailed the United States as the standard bearer of democracy and economic prosperity, and continued to support either statehood or "autonomous" colonial status for many years. Local elites dreamed of the vast markets for coffee and sugar that would be theirs once free trade with the great northern power was established; they expected that their hard-won local autonomy would be preserved under U.S. rule.

Working people's celebration of the U.S. presence had different roots. Plebeian Puerto Ricans denounced local elites as active participants in Spanish oppression of the island's poor. The United States, with its growing labor movement, its constitution that promised social and legal equality for all people, and its reputation as a great democratic nation, would surely be an unswerving ally against elite exploitation. U.S. rule, laboring people hoped, would usher in a golden era for them.[2]

Colonial officials were eager to consolidate this widespread support, for Puerto Rico played an important role in the legitimation of the U.S. imperialist project more broadly. The representation and maintenance of social stability and local popular endorsement of the U.S. presence on the island positioned Puerto Rico as a potentially compelling counter-example to the much more uncertain situations facing U.S. capitalists, military personnel, and bureaucrats in the Philippines and Cuba. In their discourses produced for North American audiences, colonial agents consistently feminized and infantilized the apparently more docile Puerto Ricans, who they insisted both needed and desired the United States' virile, fatherly imperial rule. Such representations of Puerto Ricans in familiar gendered and generational terms made Puerto Ricans' subject status vis-à-vis the United States seem more natural, comprehensible, and ultimately legitimate.[3] On the island, the attempt to maintain stability resulted in a wide array of disciplinary strategies during the early years of U.S. colonial control, ranging from criminalization of "troublesome" Puerto Rican popular practices to repression against strikers. But in order to mediate coercion effectively and gain a reasonable level of consent from the populace, discipline could not too consistently wear an openly repressive face. Thus, with relatively more success than in the other islands of its new empire, U.S. colonial rule in Puerto Rico attempted to clothe itself as a "gift to the colonized."[4] Ultimately, colonial agents hoped to cement Puerto Ricans' initial enthusiasm into a permanent desire for "Americanization."

Two important elements of these efforts were the encouragement of civil marriage and the legalization of divorce.[5] In Puerto Rico, feminist agitation did not legalize divorce, as in Europe, the United States, and much of the rest of Latin America. Puerto Rican feminists did not broach the issue of divorce during the nineteenth century. Instead, in an ironic twist of history, male U.S. colonial officials, with the eventual collaboration of local male elites, institutionalized the right to full divorce much earlier in Puerto Rico (1902) than in the rest of Latin America.[6] Colonial officials hoped that shifting the legal structures of marriage and the family in Puerto Rico would overcome the island's popular classes' deep-seated reluctance to marry (only about 50 percent of the marriageable population lived in formal wedlock). By reforming the sexual practices and definitions of the Puerto Rican poor, colonial agents and local elites sought to produce a recognizable, acceptable order in the island's domestic and public life. The benevolent paternalism of successful U.S. colonialism would ideally be both mirrored in and consolidated by the new definitions of marriage and divorce.

The official concern about sexual reform in Puerto Rico illustrates well Eric Cheyfitz's assertion that imperialism strives in many ways for the "disappearance of the other." [7] Colonial agents endeavored to homogenize their new colonial subjects sexually, to reduce diverse popular sexual practices and morals to a unified standard of heterosexual marriage and two-parent families. They also attempted to construct absolute moral oppositions between their ideas of themselves and their conceptions of Puerto Ricans, thus confirming their superiority and distance from those whom they sought to reform. This they continued to do even as they strove to remake Puerto Ricans in their own idealized self-image. Colonial observers thus simultaneously affirmed hierarchical differences and attempted to erase difference through assimilation.

U.S. colonial officials' conceptions of morality—and Puerto Ricans' divergence from them—became a focal point both for confirming Puerto Ricans' alleged inferiority and for reforming them into a more "civilized" state. This was given added urgency by fear of Puerto Rican sexual contamination of North Americans. Early U.S. strategies in Puerto Rico confirm Ann Stoler's insight that definitions of morality and sexuality lie at the heart of colonial power relations. Concerns about them express anxieties about the ambiguities of colonial rule. Sexual identities become an important way to define groups and their sociopolitical legitimacy.[8] In Puerto Rico, the dream of sexually disciplining the popular classes went hand in hand with the creation of new forms of male dominance over women. Both, it seemed to officials, were key to colonial success.

But definition of sexual arrangements in Puerto Rico did not lie only in the hands of imperial authorities and local elites. Broadening the scope of legally sanctioned marriage elicited little interest among Puerto Ricans. Access to divorce, on the other hand, unleashed a quiet flood of popular response. Married women flocked to the courts to demand divorces in the early twentieth century. Although previously ignored by Puerto Rican historians, their actions constituted one of the many popular explosions unleashed by the new colonial regime—perhaps less dramatic, but more widespread, and certainly more enduring than the famous *partidas sediciosas* who sacked Spanish properties in the wake of the U.S. occupation.[9] The surge of early-twentieth-century divorce petitions expressed Puerto Rican women's keen awareness that marriage was not necessarily a homogenizing, stabilizing institution, as colonial officials and elite Puerto Rican men insisted. Rather, bitter struggles over gendered interests and power imbalances lay at its heart. In their appeals to the courts for divorce, Puerto Rican women voiced their long-standing yearnings for more tolerable gender relations: reliable economic support, safety from male violence, and an end to the sexual double standard. Now even plebeian women had a formal forum in which to voice these demands, however diffusely, and to receive some type of legal redress, however feeble and inadequate.[10]

Implementation of divorce and other ameliorative reforms did not ensure justice on the island, however. The new, allegedly compassionate colonial order had an ominous side. The United States quickly abrogated several of the key political gains consolidated in the Puerto Ricans' 1897 autonomy agreement with Spain. Early colonial governors restricted the island's newly won universal male suffrage to only literate or taxpaying men (Puerto Rican women did not win full suffrage until 1935). The same decree that established the eight-hour workday also declared that only property owners could be members of municipal councils. The U.S. Congress's 1900 Foraker Act codified a greatly reduced space for popular participation in local governance, even as it instituted free trade and civil government. Colonial charity boards set up to dispense public relief after a devastating hurricane in 1899 soon developed a variety of methods to coerce impoverished rural Puerto Ricans into plantation labor.[11] By 1907, English had become the primary language of instruction in the newly established public school system.[12] The new judicial system was no exception to this pattern. Puerto Rican women who sought marital equity through divorce petitions eventually discovered, as did workers and other marginalized groups, that there were quite severe limits to the new colonial order, however benevolent it may have seemed at its inception.

The Uses of Puerto Rico

For the most part, both anti-imperialist protests during the 1890s and recent historical studies of early U.S. imperialism ignore Puerto Rico; the dramatic armed struggles for national sovereignty in Cuba and the Philippines placed these nations at the center of both types of analysis. As in Cuba and the Philippines, the U.S. colonial enterprise in Puerto Rico sought expanded markets for U.S. goods, profits from tropical agricultural production, and strategic positioning on both international trade routes and military control points.[13] But Puerto Rico was not simply the "silent sister" within the new U.S. empire. Its construction as the peaceful, cooperative, decidedly nonvirile colony—a counterexample to Cuba and the Philippines—played an important role in the attempts of colonial officials and advocates of imperialism to justify the United States' dominance of other peoples.

U.S. rule did, in fact, enjoy widespread support among most Puerto Ricans, at least during the first few decades after the North American invasion. However, Puerto Rico was represented in specific ways that lent particular power to attempts to legitimize U.S. imperialism. Colonial discourses about Puerto Rico equated civilization and the right to self-governance with masculinity. In the eyes of U.S. colonial officials, male Puerto Ricans were certainly not "real" men. True masculinity, and thus the right to sovereignty and self-definition, U.S. colonial agents reserved for themselves. The construction of Puerto Ricans as uniformly disordered yet docile—both feminine and childish—simultaneously established them as naturally needful and desirous of the United States' manly "tutelage," warned of their potential threat to the United States' civilized status, and sought to erase the conflict that did exist on the island.

Since Spanish troops did not hold up long in the face of combined republican-U.S. forces in Cuba and the Philippines, the United States' real political and military challenges in both countries arose after peace was declared with Spain. Then the United States had to contend with broad-based, increasingly radicalized nationalist insurgencies. Although the radical potential of the Cuban liberation movement was eventually neutralized, and the Philippine movement was finally quelled after years of fighting between U.S. troops and nationalist guerrillas, the outcomes of these conflicts were not clear for several years. Even after the formal pacification of both movements, significant upheavals continued during the early twentieth century.[14]

Puerto Rico, in comparison, seemed peaceful and trouble-free. The military governor George Davis reminded Congress in 1899 that Puerto Ricans had initially welcomed U.S. troops to the island. Davis reassured the congressmen that the situation there remained optimal for U.S. capitalists. He insisted that, unlike Cuba and the Philippines, Puerto Rico posed no danger of "revolution or open resistance," since the populace was neither "armed nor belligerent" and, he claimed, did not have a deeply rooted anti-imperialist revolutionary tradition.[15] These arguments also were made implicitly to the general public through visual images; in the political cartoons of the period collected by John J. Johnson, Puerto Rico was often portrayed as the obedient, lighter-skinned woman or child, in stark contrast to Cuba and the Philippines, which were consistently represented as rebellious, unruly, caricatured African Americans, requiring overt discipline (figures 1 and 2).[16]

The Filipinos' tenacious rejection of the U.S. presence and the Cubans' passionate struggle for independence sowed doubts among U.S.

Figure 1. "Uncle Sam to Porto Rico: 'And to think that bad boy came near being your brother!' " *Chicago Inter Ocean,* 1905. Taken from John J. Johnson, *Latin America in Caricature* (Austin: University of Texas Press, 1980), 127.

congressmen and citizens alike about U.S. imperial interventions. But if a minimum level of social stability and support for U.S. rule could be maintained in Puerto Rico, the questions raised about the validity of U.S. imperialism by armed resistance in the Philippines and the de facto denial of nationalist aspirations in Cuba might well be quelled. Puerto Rico had the potential to transform a politically questionable imperialism into an eminently legitimate "expansion," as explained by Senator Williams of Mississippi:

> What is expansion? It is stretching yourself out, carrying yourself as a nation, with all that clothes you and makes you, your Constitution and free institutions, to people somewhere else; not superimposing yourself upon somebody, but carrying your Government, its spirit, its Constitution . . . —in short, its soul as well as its body—to new parts of the world. . . . There is a field for "expansion" for the

Figure 2. William Allan Rogers, "Uncle Sam's New Class in the Art of Self-Government." *Harper's Weekly*, 27 Aug. 1898. Taken from John J. Johnson, *Latin America in Caricature* (Austin: University of Texas Press, 1980), 217.

American people. Wherever, moreover, you can find a kindred population capable of assimilation with ours, capable of understanding, appreciating, and loving our institutions, there is also a field for the Republic's expansion.[17]

Frequently constructed for the North American public and politicians as unequivocally docile as well as desirous of U.S. rule, Puerto Rico was presented as the counterexample to Cuba and the Philippines. It held out hope of being a potential showplace for imperialism—a place that persistently confirmed both U.S. colonial benevolence and colonized gratitude.

This was a pressing political necessity from 1898 to 1900, when U.S. anti-imperialists organized a nationwide movement decrying their country's denial of self-determination to the Philippines and Cuba. William Jennings Bryan, the Democratic candidate for president in 1900, made anti-imperialism one of his principal campaign issues. Anti-imperialist leagues held public meetings of protest throughout the United States and penned passionate editorials in local and national papers. They were joined by scores of prominent writers, reformers, and labor leaders such as Mark Twain, Jane Addams, and Samuel Gompers, as well as Andrew Carnegie, the Pittsburgh steel "robber baron."[18] The presence of such a vocal domestic opposition greatly complicated the domestic legitimization of the United States' new overtly imperial identity; Puerto Rico provided a potential point of reference for advocates of colonialism.

But the image of Puerto Rico as an enthusiastic model colony not only helped to refute the anti-imperialist domestic opposition. It also provided an imagined space which seemed to be free of the social conflicts and dislocations that wracked the United States. Many Anglo-Saxon Protestants felt profoundly threatened by waves of immigrants, industrialization, rapid urbanization, and increasing labor conflict. Southern whites, panicked and enraged by African Americans' modest post–Civil War social, political, and economic gains, had begun a relentless drive to reassert their dominance. Puerto Rico seemed to offer the potential for starting over, for creating the ideal paternalist society that had so tragically failed at home. The island was poverty stricken, but decidedly preindustrial. All parties on the island, including the labor movement, welcomed U.S. rule. To the U.S.-trained eye, race relations were bafflingly fluid but apparently free of the overt conflicts that so marked mainland society.[19] The land itself suggested the possibility of recapturing that paternal state of grace before the fall. Colonial Governor Allen's 1900 ode was echoed by many other authors: "Nature has here 'planted a garden' and man has only 'to dress it and keep it' to make it blossom like another Paradise."[20] A helping modern imperial hand was all that Puerto Rico lacked. As a young North American schoolteacher wrote to a confidante back home, "Oh, I want Porto Rico to be a model in every way of what the American spirit can do and create and Porto Rico is so little and . . . could be very easily handled, so that my dream of Porto Rico is very, very possible."[21] Thus, when compared to the vastness of U.S. problems, Puerto Rico became a potential colonial utopia, backward but gentle, and ever-so-manageable.

The colonial context also allowed imperial agents to assert a unified

North American identity, cleansed of domestic diversity and disputes. On the island, the meaning of *American* seemed quite clear, unlike at home. Within the United States, immigrants speaking a bewildering array of languages and practicing unfamiliar customs swelled the cities. Assertions of the country's socioeconomic progress and the U.S. right to territorial expansion were openly challenged by labor and anti-imperialist movements. Divorce itself, an important colonial social reform apparently unanimously advocated by U.S. officials in Puerto Rico, was a hotly contested issue on the mainland between 1890 and 1915. Within the United States, conservative clergy, prominent educators, powerful legal authorities such as the U.S. attorney general, and many members of the U.S. Supreme Court opposed what they saw as a general loosening of the moral bonds of society.[22] In the colonial context, however, all of the baffling variety of the United States could be distilled into "pure" American values of bourgeois Anglo-Saxon Protestantism. In short, imperial agents sought to homogenize North American as well as colonial identities. In the process, they construed Puerto Ricans as exotically "other," asserted their own superiority over their new subjects by demasculinizing them, and insisted on their right to mold Puerto Rico as they saw fit.

According to most U.S. officials and commentators, Puerto Ricans were unfit for self-governance. Variously compared to women, U.S. Southern blacks, and Chinese immigrants in colonial reports and congressional debates, Puerto Rican men were judged incapable and undeserving of full suffrage, legal, or citizenship rights, not to mention national sovereignty.[23] Men of the laboring classes did not have the virile strength of character necessary for unrestricted political participation. "Manhood suffrage presupposes a basis of real, true manhood," thundered an early military governor.[24] Although colonial officials conceded that there were a "few good men" among elite Puerto Ricans, they were represented as either too ineffectual in their efforts to preserve social order on the island or too contaminated with the despotic political practices of their former colonial masters to govern properly.[25] Thus, male Puerto Rican elites might be allies in building the benevolent colonial project, but they needed U.S. imperial tutelage as well.

Working people on the island, U.S. officials insisted, were peculiarly undisciplined. They had "no conception of thrift or economy," as did "real Americans." [26] To white North American eyes, the island's coastal plebeian communities were also indiscriminately interracial. Generations of open sexual and social racial mingling had produced a confusing "racial mass," within which blacks and whites could not be easily distinguished. Such fluid racial relations and identities were unintelligible—and consequently inferior—to white North Americans steeped in the United States' rigidly bipolar racial system.[27] The Puerto Rican laboring classes were believed to be just as unrestrained in their sexual behavior as they were in drawing racial boundaries. They seemed to have sex often, and with many people, having large families and living in consensual union rather than marrying.[28] This alleged dissoluteness marked plebeian Puerto Ricans as childish, or even pre-human. "They sin, but they sin only as animals, without shame, because there is no sense of doing wrong. . . . They are innocently happy in the unconsciousness of the obligations of morality. They eat, drink, sleep, and smoke, and do the least in the way of work they can. They have no ideas of duty, and therefore are not made uneasy by neglecting it." [29] For the most part, then, the Puerto Rican poor were represented as innocently inert, slumbering in a premoral natural state, ready to be shaped into civilized adults by the guiding hand of the United States.

Their alleged lack of discipline and morals went hand in hand with a tractable, implicitly feminine nature, U.S. commentators usually hastened to add. Workers on the island were "docile and well-disposed," "exceedingly . . . earnest people, always faithful in their work, once set to a task," having "fine memory and ability to imitate." [30] They were "lacking in originality, with little independence of thought," "weak thinkers and poor reasoners." [31] But with proper guidance, Puerto Ricans' potential as productive workers (and thus producers of profit for U.S. capitalists) was great. They were unformed clay awaiting the imperial potter. North American creativity, reason, discipline, and political tutelage would at last give them shape and direction.[32]

U.S. officials' rhetorical infantilization and feminization of Puerto Ricans in their public proclamations and reports home justified U.S. colonialism in a number of ways. The familiar gendered and generational terms in which colonial agents discussed Puerto Rico implicitly naturalized and thus legitimized the island's subordinate status. They calmed North American fears of rebellion and unrest—particularly acute, as we've seen, while facing untamed insurgencies on other islands and social discord at home. They asserted Puerto Ricans' subordinate otherness, establishing them as "backward" and the United States as "civilized." In the process, they confirmed the United States' manly superiority over its new subjects. Finally, they implied that Puerto Ricans needed—even desired—the United States to remake and rule over them. As one widely read travel writer claimed, Puerto Ricans "are like children of the poor suddenly enriched by a visit from some beneficent Santa Claus." [33] U.S. citizens could rest assured that their country possessed Puerto Rico at her own request. This colonial project was undeniably a consensual relationship. In the Puerto Rican context, even if not in Cuba or the Philippines, imperial enthusiasts could claim that U.S. rule was the embodiment of benevolent paternalism—a kind father and husband fashioning a civilized society of abundance out of an inert mass.[34]

But within this near-ritualized public insistence on Puerto Rico's passivity and lack of discipline lurked the consciousness that Puerto Ricans were not at all as uniformly docile as advocates of colonialism claimed. The island child did need to be contained; simple reinstruction was not sufficient to control her quixotic nature.[35] Puerto Ricans' passion for electoral democracy and inclusion in the U.S. polity could take unnerving turns, such as mass public debates in town squares, the election of Socialist candidates, or demands for equal citizenship status. The island's plodding, "faithful" workers quickly formed labor unions, which began to organize protests and strikes across the sugar fields and cities, calling on the United States to intervene on their behalf.[36] Women flocked to the courts to demand divorces from abusive or wayward husbands, severing the marital bond that colonial officials claimed to hold so dear. Indeed, the very flood of popular responses that celebrated the U.S. mission as the bearer of civilization and democracy—and thus legitimized its presence—threatened to hold the new colonial rulers to their self-proclaimed standard, a dangerous proposition indeed. It was a threat that the public constructions of a docile, childlike model colony sought desperately to contain.

Benevolent Discipline: Marriage and Divorce Reform

The family forms, sexual practices, and morality of island residents—particularly those of the laboring classes—were an ever-present subtext in the U.S.-authored hearings, reports, and commentaries about Puerto Rico that proliferated in the first years of North American rule. For colonial agents, moral standing was a potent marker of identity, of one's very relationship to civilization. U.S. observers and local elites alike were concerned about the high incidence of consensual unions, serial sexual relationships, and female-headed households among the popular classes on the island. All agreed that the island's 50 percent out-of-wedlock birthrate was unacceptable. A productive, properly disciplined workforce and stable political order could only be built on a base of marriage and "legitimate" families.[37] As A. C. Sharpe, the colonial attorney general for Puerto Rico, put it in 1899: "Family life is the recognized basis of true civilization. American law and institutions regard the relation of the husband and wife as one of the most sacred guarantees for the perpetuity of the state. Marriage is recognized as the only lawful relation by which Providence has permitted the continuance of the human race, and the history of mankind has proved it to be one of the chief foundations of social order." [38] Thus, the push to bring the island out of an inert, disordered state of nature and into civilized ways of life had to begin within the home. The relatively fluid popular Puerto Rican definitions of the family had to be regulated and homogenized into a unified standard. Marriage was key; it would help establish an acceptable social order under the eye of the state.

Serial monogamy and consensual union not only prevented the construction of a disciplined colonial social order, however. Their insidious effects could also destroy "civilized men's" ordered behavior. North American teachers lamented the collapse of their countrymen's morals in the colony, where they had illicit sexual relationships and drank in public, far from "the restraint of home's influence." [39] The attorney general of the United States worriedly wrote that sexual dissolution "is one of the most important questions now confronting the government and people of the U.S.—that is to say, *whether we are to be infected and contaminated by the immoralities of Porto Rico* . . . or are to raise the moral tone of those places to approach that of the U.S. . . . Tolerating and excusing universal looseness and *sending our young men out to learn the lesson that morality or immorality is a purely local question* seems to me to entail consequences which might make the acquisition of our new possessions more of a curse than a blessing." [40] Vis-à-vis the mainland, then, the diversity of Puerto Rican moral codes—and their potential attraction for North American men—became particularly dangerous. The sexual discipline so important to male U.S. bourgeois identity could be easily tainted by contact with Puerto Rican mores. Perhaps colonizer and colonized were not so radically different after all; untamed nature lurked at the edge of civilization.

The massification of marriage, thus, was a serious matter. A series of legal reforms was quickly instituted in hopes of encouraging the Puerto Rican popular classes to marry. In March 1899, the legalization of civil marriages was confirmed by decree, and municipal judges were prohibited from charging fees for performing the ceremony. Two years later, this stipulation was codified and broadened in the civil marriage reform law;

the legislation was enthusiastically endorsed by the governor, who wrote that it "is intended to and should accomplish a great moral reform on the island." [41] Hopes were still high when the following year a law was passed that granted the right to celebrate marriages to all ministers, rabbis, and judges on the island. Governor Hunt gushed that "scarcely any act of the legislative assembly was more important." [42]

However, there is no evidence that all these attempts to make marriage more accessible to the poor of Puerto Rico had any significant effect. The census data from the first decade of the twentieth century shows a relatively stable rate of marriage, hovering around 50 percent. The roots of plebeian alternative conceptions of respectability and conjugal life were much deeper than U.S. officials had ever dreamed. Many laboring Puerto Ricans were actively *un*interested in marrying—not simply prevented from doing so. It was the right to divorce, not access to marriage, that eventually provoked a popular explosion of interest.

This was the second thrust of colonial officials' attempts to lure Puerto Ricans to marriage. Accessibility was not the only key. Marriage also had to be made more attractive. As they pushed for the legalization of divorce on the island, North American officials asserted that people might be more likely to marry if they could leave a marital situation gone awry. Women, in particular, they feared, resisted marrying because it allowed them no escape.[43] The right to divorce would hopefully popularize marriage. Indeed, picking up on mainland feminist arguments, officials implied that the right to divorce would actually transform marriage. Being able to leave unworkable relationships would help ensure that the marriage contract would be based on freely chosen love. Those whose relationships endured would enjoy happy matches; those who severed the marital tie would have the chance to choose a more satisfactory partner in the future. The result would be more democratic, less "despotic" marriages—a neat analogy to the change from the Spanish to North American colonial regime.[44]

The interest in full divorce did not spring only from colonial officials, however. Petitions for relief from husbands' violence, lack of financial support, and release from unwanted relationships began to arrive at the governor's palace as soon as word spread that the new colonial administration was sympathetic to divorce.[45] Popular pressures for the full legalization of divorce were supported by many prominent members of both Puerto Rican elite-led political parties, who had long been staunch anti-clericalists and advocates of marital reform.[46]

U.S. colonial officials did not have a completely free hand in reforming divorce law on the island. Some conservative elites initially emphatically opposed the moves. However, the 1902 Civil and Penal Codes drafted by Puerto Rico's Legislative Assembly in a general overhaul of the island's legal system included greatly expanded divorce provisions. The legalization of full divorce does not seem to have generated significant debate in the assembly. Concomitantly, very little discussion of divorce appeared in the Puerto Rican press after 1901. Thus, it seems that despite the opposition of some powerful Puerto Ricans in 1899, by 1902 a consensus had been reached that a broadened application of divorce was either acceptable or unavoidable.[47]

Despite the legalization of full divorce, the new Civil Code retained a number of key patriarchal rights; they probably helped gain the support of the more conservative Puerto Rican politicians. Men's power within the family was not completely abrogated. Although wives were now allowed to represent themselves and their property in court as well as to exercise professions, husbands were still the only legal representatives of the "conjugal unit" and retained sole rights to administer marital property. Wives could not use conjugal property for anything other than the "purchase of articles for the use of the family." Every wife was also still explicitly required to "obey her husband and follow him where he elects to reside." [48] *Patria potestad,* or parental authority over children, was supposedly transformed from an exclusive male right to one shared by both husband and wife. However, the 1902 code stated that "if there should be any disagreement between the husband and the wife, the decision of the husband shall prevail in all cases relating to family affairs." [49] As in the broader colonial project, democratization and benevolent rule had their limits; the heralded legal transformation of marriage still codified male power over women.

It was probably in the area of divorce that the new Civil Code most directly affected the lives of ordinary Puerto Ricans. For most people of the laboring classes, stipulations regarding property and its control were largely irrelevant; they owned very little. However, the right to end relationships potentially affected all married couples, regardless of class. The 1902 code made all marriages civil contracts, regardless of the religion of the participants or the celebrant. Consequently, even Catholic marriages could now be legally dissolved. The grounds for divorce were also greatly expanded. They now included adultery by either spouse without gender distinctions of legal standards, "cruel treatment" by either party, habitual drunkenness or narcotics use, and the abandonment of either party for more than a year. The sexual double standard faced a potential legal challenge. Violent, unworkable, or unreliable marital relationships could now be terminated. It would not take long for the popular response to materialize.

The Demand for Divorce

Word spread quickly among those excluded from the circles of formal colonial power that the previously lifelong bonds of marriage could be broken. Soon, women and men began to stream into the courts to demand divorces. Their petitions gave voice to popular definitions of marriage that often diverged sharply from those of colonial officials. Women's anguished testimony in particular put the lie to colonial assertions that marriage was the basis of peaceful social order. Rather, their petitions illuminated the struggles over gender power relations that permeated family life.

The new judicial forum shifted the terms of these struggles. Although women still could not effectively discipline men into compliance with the marital contract, they could at least obtain officially sanctioned release from unbearable relationships. For many Puerto Ricans, especially women, divorce would become one of the institutional changes that distinguished the "época de los americanos" from "los tiempos aquellos de los españoles" and cemented strong roots of support for U.S. rule among the popular classes.[50] Although this support remained intact, broadly speaking, through the first decades of the twentieth century, it did not reliably produce the kinds of social behaviors that colonial officials desired. Puerto Ricans enthusiastically took advantage of institutional openings established by the new, "benevolent" colonial regime. They did not, however, docilely embrace the homogenizing colonial vision of family and society. Neither the civilizing effects of marriage nor men's right to uncontested power over their wives were accepted by the Puerto Rican women who filled civil courts with their divorce petitions.

Under Spanish rule, the prospects for Puerto Ricans hoping to terminate unworkable marriages had been bleak. For most of the nineteenth century, the right to divorce was not recognized. Even once civil matrimony and divorce were introduced as legal categories in 1889, the Catholic Church maintained a near monopoly over marriage and divorce matters. Battered women might win some minimal protection from husbands' abuse by filing divorce petitions and requesting placement in a "respectable" sheltering household or *depósito*. However, physical safety did not translate into autonomy. Wives in depósito, especially those of the laboring classes, were often subjected to close surveillance by placement families and the

ecclesiastical courts. And a permanent, formal rupture of the marital relationship, no matter how unbearable marriage had become, was impossible.
The small number of divorce petitions filed during the nineteenth century
reflected this harsh reality. Only twenty-six cases were pursued between
1840 and 1898, twenty-two of them by women attempting to escape violent husbands.[51]

The marital reforms codified under the new colonial regime produced
a quite different landscape. Divorce was utilized by women and men of
all social classes in the twentieth century. Despite the island's high rate
of consensual unions, plebeian Puerto Ricans did marry—enough, in any
case, to now request divorces in significant numbers.[52] As in the nineteenth century, women were the majority of the plaintiffs; they constituted
two-thirds of all divorce petitioners. The results they achieved were much
more reliable, though, than under the previous regime: by 1909, obtaining a divorce generally took only a few months, and rarely was a petition
denied. Indeed, by the end of the first decade of U.S. rule, divorce had become legal routine, a prosaic institutionalized practice.[53] This was a far cry
from the long years that nineteenth-century women petitioners spent languishing in depósito, waiting for a response from church officials, usually
to have their petitions rejected.

The response to divorce legalization was striking. Divorce petitions
steadily rose from a miniscule share (1.5 percent) of all civil cases filed
in the jurisdiction of Ponce during 1900 and 1901 (out of 651 for the two
years combined) to a fifth of all Ponce civil cases filed during 1911 (out of
a total of 253).[54] It seems safe to assume that at least in the other coastal
districts of the island that encompassed the majority of the population, the
response was similarly enthusiastic. When compared to the numbers of
divorce cases filed during the nineteenth century, these figures are even
more remarkable. More than six times as many divorce cases were filed
in a twelve-year period—and in a single judicial district—than were filed
for the entire island in the preceding sixty years. Puerto Ricans' use of
divorce also appears to have continued throughout the early twentieth
century. Although systematic archival research was not done for the years
following 1911, Ponce newspapers reported several divorces a day in the
municipality throughout 1917 and 1918.

What prompted Puerto Ricans to request divorce in ever-increasing
numbers? What were they hoping to obtain by doing so? In order to
understand divorce's popular meanings in the early twentieth century, and
its possible ramifications for colonial hegemony, we must first examine
Puerto Ricans' expectations of marriage. Steve Stern has pointed out that

familial relations in late colonial Mexico were defined through a "language of argument," not a uniform set of values such as U.S. colonial officials sought to establish.[55] Puerto Rican notions of the family followed a similar pattern. Thus, the meaning of marriage for Puerto Ricans was not based on a single marital code. Rather, marriage was a contested patriarchal pact that linked sexual, reproductive, and economic rights and obligations. Men were expected to provide economic support and protection to their children and women partners; they also claimed the right to have multiple sexual partners and to physically discipline their wives and lovers as they saw fit. Women, in exchange, provided domestic labor, sexual access, and monogamy to their husbands, as well as frequent economic contributions, if the family's survival required it. Men and women generally knew what they were expected to deliver in a marriage.

But a great deal of contention simmered under the surface of this broad consensus; men and women had different definitions of what constituted acceptable behavior and power relations within the broad parameters of gendered marital roles. Women did not seek a protofeminist gender equality within their sexual relationships. Rather, they seem to have accepted the patriarchal balance of the marital pact. Women did, however, consider men's sexual rights and freedoms conditional: they were only allowed as long as men fulfilled their economic obligation to the family. Men, on the other hand, resisted the linkages women drew between different arenas of masculine rights and responsibilities. Husbands insisted on their right to exercise absolute power over their wives, as well as the freedom to seek sexual encounters outside marriage. Men recognized, however, that women contested these assertions; such challenges, whether veiled or overt, lay at the root of the violence that often exploded within families.[56]

Thus, popular understandings of marriage acknowledged the conflicts that lay at its core. The experiences and testimony of Puerto Ricans in divorce court put the lie to colonial officials' discourse about marriage's homogenization of familial interests and its potential for stabilizing society. Women in particular knew that the quid pro quo of heterosexual partnership was an unequal exchange. They had no choice, however, but to engage in perpetual balancing acts between their need for financial survival and their desire for respectful treatment and physical safety. Divorce petitions illuminate the points at which this delicate and contentious balance snapped.

The married women who appeared in twentieth-century divorce courts protested their husbands' extramarital affairs, which drained precious financial resources and sometimes publicly humiliated them. They resisted domestic violence through familial and informal community intervention, often calling on neighborhood networks of women. They argued back, and sometimes even hit back, when their husbands' assertions of authority became too severe. Their stories and actions challenged colonial officials' assertions of marriage as the basis of social harmony.[57]

If these strategies failed to make their marriages livable, no small number of wives left their husbands, usually to start up a relationship with another man who they hoped would treat them better or provide more adequately for them and their children. Such actions were the primary causes for men's divorce petitions. Three-fifths of the forty-seven cases filed by men alleged women's abandonment of the conjugal household. All but three blamed their wives' refusals to return on the women's live-in relationships with other men. An additional fourth of male petitions alleged wifely adultery. Nine-tenths of men's divorce complaints, then, hinged on women's sexual relationships with other men. Clearly, all wives did not passively accept their husbands' claim to total sexual ownership of them.

In effect, these women's actions constituted a popular, informal divorce practice. Its roots lay in plebeian moral norms forged in an era when legal divorce had been unavailable. Some women were quite defiant in their assertion of autonomy from husbands they felt had wronged them. Rafaela Núñez responded to her husband's demands that she return to care for him: "I received your communication, and in response I wish it to remain clear that I will not return to live at your side. Not now, not ever. There is nothing more to be said." A year and a half later, she wrote again: "I see that you are insisting that I return to you. You will never obtain your objective. And as for the divorce proceedings which you have threatened, you can do what you like. I don't believe there is a court on this earth which would require me to live with such a lowlife man as you. Do not force me to write to you anymore. If they have to kill me, you will not get me to return." [58]

Other women were not nearly so assertive as Rafaela, but they went to great pains to explain that they had not stepped outside of the normative limits of wifely behavior by choice. They had been driven there. These women agreed with the popular requirement of female monogamy. But financial necessity and physical safety took precedence over absolute moral principles. And ultimately, in their responses to their husbands' accusations, "adulterous" wives asserted, however humbly, that the roots of female infidelity lay in male irresponsibility.[59]

Women also denounced men's abandonment of them in divorce court, but their grievances differed from the male petitioners'. The meaning of abandonment, like that of so many other popular concepts, was gendered. Men's abandonment was not primarily defined as sexual. Rather, it centered on their chief marital contribution—money. Although male abuse or adultery figured prominently in a significant number of women's divorce petitions, the vast majority (85 percent) cited financial and physical abandonment as the principal cause of their requests. Women of all classes appear to have chosen divorce only after all informal methods of familial and community intervention failed to enforce their husbands' compliance with their financial responsibilities. The defining issue for women in heterosexual relationships continued to be reliable access to male income. It was generally only when husbands definitively violated this aspect of the conjugal quid pro quo that wives petitioned for divorce.

Certainly, domestic violence was a constant presence in many women's lives. Thirty percent of women's twentieth-century divorce petitions described extensive beatings and cited them as important bases for the divorce request. But violent partners were not much more likely to be disciplined by the courts under U.S. rule than they had been during the Spanish colonial era. No legal or institutional protection was available to battered women short of divorce, and most women, especially mothers, were too dependent on their partners' incomes to risk that option. (Only 15 percent of all petitions were based on male violence alone.) Thus, until male financial input became totally unreliable, women generally seem to have found ways to live with their husbands' violence, keeping it in check as best they could. Numerous wives spoke of their "constant efforts to appease [their] husbands, and to maintain domestic peace." [60] Battered wives called on family members to intervene on their behalf, fled to their neighbors and friends, and as a last resort, called in the police.[61]

Similarly, men's insistence on having multiple sexual partners inflicted great pain on women. Female divorce petitioners of all classes spoke bitterly of their husbands' infidelities.[62] Mercedes Vélez testified angrily that "letting himself be dragged along by his lowest passions, [her husband] frequently fled the loving attentions of his wife in order to run about tasting the repulsive caresses of despicable prostitutes." [63] Women of the laboring classes not only suffered the emotional stress and social shame they shared with wealthier wives. They were also locked in intense economic competition with their husbands' mistresses. Cornelia Segarra traded blows and insults with Segunda Ortiz, a laundress she suspected of being her husband's lover. Segarra also recounted bitterly that her husband had struck her when she protested the money he spent on Ortiz.

"He shouted at me that only Segunda had the right to live in his room with him, and that the funds that he could have given to [his wife] he now would give only to her."[64]

The new divorce terms codified in 1902 represented a potential watershed in women's struggle against the sexual double standard. The new Civil Code's equalization of adultery standards for both sexes marked the first time that a legal challenge had been made to men's age-old patriarchal right to multiple sexual partners. Again, however, while economically dependent on their husbands, most women must have found their newly gained legal right to divorce on the basis of infidelity difficult to exercise.

Other obstacles lay in their way as well. Although a potential challenge to male privilege was now legally codified, it remained extraordinarily difficult for women to prove their husbands' adultery in a court of law. In a number of cases, numerous eyewitnesses' testimony of men's extramarital affairs was not sufficient to convict the husbands and obtain a divorce. In contrast, several men were granted divorces solely on the basis of testimony from neighbors who had "only heard through public rumor" that their wives had had affairs.[65] Consequently, unless men's adultery was paired with cessation of all financial support, popular patriarchal custom (men's "right" to multiple sexual partners) prevailed over formal legal restrictions of male sexual practice. A silent cornerstone of male honor and privilege remained largely intact.

Thus, access to male income continued to be the bottom line for most women. As long as steady male contributions to the household economy continued, wives seem to have been reluctant to permanently sever the marital bonds, despite sometimes facing severe physical abuse and persistent infidelity. This reluctance was probably exacerbated by the courts' general unwillingness to pursue charges of adultery against men. Married women did, however, struggle to carve out a more humane space for themselves within these limits. And if they encountered potential partners who appeared to offer better terms, some women were perfectly willing to leave their marriages and set up households with other men.

When husbands' financial support ceased altogether, however, women now could move to break their marital ties. And this they did, in large numbers. Eighty-five percent of all female divorce complaints listed abandonment as the primary charge. In petition after petition, women testified to the bone-grinding hardships of life without a reliable male income. Carmen Lucca had lived for several years with her mother, sister, and daughter, all of whom worked twelve to fourteen hours a day to feed, clothe, and house the family. Her husband had not contributed anything to the family's income for "as long as I can remember," even when he was gainfully employed in a bakery.[66]

Lucca's husband and several other plebeian male defendants denied that they had violated the marital contract. While admitting that they had given their wives nothing in the way of financial support for some time, they insisted that this was due to their poverty. Material barriers, then, prevented them from fulfilling their individual responsibilities as husbands. Wives and their supporting witnesses, however, scoffed at these arguments. Wives pointed to the money their husbands spent on drink and other women, as well as how *they* worked themselves to the bone to earn a few pennies a day, which they then devoted entirely to the maintenance of their families. These women insisted that familial senses of responsibility were gendered. Their husbands may have been poor, but that did not give them the right to desert their families.[67]

Carmen Lucca told the court that she wanted her "wayward" husband to live with and support her and her daughter. But since the judge did not enforce Lucca's economic claims against her husband, she demanded a divorce. Most women filing divorce petitions had similar stories. They probably would have preferred enforcement of the male end of the conjugal quid pro quo to divorce. Instead, they accepted the best they could get: permanent release from the violated contract.

As noted earlier, municipal judges seemed reluctant to grant women divorces for petitions that alleged only infidelity. This may have meant striking too close to home in censuring male privilege. But women were extremely successful in obtaining divorces based on financial abandonment: not one of these petitions in the period reviewed was denied. Thus, financial responsibility, not physical violence or sexual privilege, was the point of possible judicial discipline of men.[68]

But judges generally ordered no economic relief for working women divorce petitioners, despite their legal ability and women's desperate pleas to do so. (The 1902 Civil Code provided for successful women petitioners to be granted alimony, not to exceed one-third of their ex-husbands' incomes.) Therefore only propertied women stood to substantially gain economically from a divorce; some immediately recovered administrative rights over their own property and received half of the marital property as well.[69] Marriage had not provided women with the harmonious, if patriarchal, stability promised by colonial officials. But divorce was hardly a panacea for women's worries, either, especially for members of the working classes. Wronged wives might come to the courts seeking marital justice from the new colonial state, but they rarely found full relief.

Conclusion

Some of the most insightful recent studies of colonialism owe a great deal to the writings of Michel Foucault. This essay is no exception. In many ways, the early U.S. colonial attempt to reform the sexual mores and family definitions of the Puerto Rican popular classes illustrates well Foucault's theory of modern disciplinary power.[70] Such power, according to Foucault, abandons outright coercion in favor of a process of subjection that brings increasing numbers of individuals under its scrutiny. By combining a widening surveillance net with proliferating discourses about specific practices or groups of people, disciplinary power channels and controls meanings and practices, even as it produces new identities. Thus, disciplinary power is both restrictive and productive. It does not depend on public displays of force; rather, it penetrates into the most intimate recesses of people's lives. Ultimately, it disciplines them into *self*-discipline. It is "elegant," and ultimately very effective, creating a totalizing web of power that incites participation from all within its reach. Sexuality is often one of its "dense transfer points." [71]

Focusing on the strategies of colonial agents who worried about popular resistance to marriage in Puerto Rico might lead us to simply confirm Foucault's brilliant reconceptualization of the workings of power. Certainly, there are many parallels. Marital reform under early U.S. rule sought to tame what colonial agents and local elites saw as the working classes' sexual cacophony and to reduce it to one unison note—the respectable, "civilized" state of marriage. This, in turn, would help establish an acceptable social order more readily available to the eye of the state. The two-pronged strategy of increasing access to marriage and legalizing divorce developed by colonial agents had many sources; popular pressures as well as colonizers' interests helped produce the U.S. strategy for marital reform. In the process, the official meaning of marriage itself was transformed; new meanings of old institutions were codified by the state.

But close attention to other aspects of the move toward marital reform in Puerto Rico invites us to expand on Foucault's insights. First, early U.S. colonial strategies for widening the net of marriage, and thus fixing the popular classes' fluid sexual practices and moral definitions were not based solely—or even primarily—on the extension of surveillance. Rather, the architects of colonial legislation in Puerto Rico hoped to lure laboring peoples to matrimony, not discipline them into it. Allowing unhappy individuals to divorce would make the state of matrimony more attractive, they hoped. Thus, the near-exclusive emphasis on surveillance and subjection that has marked many Foucault-inspired studies of dominant power may be wrongheaded. Leniency and an opening of possibilities can be an integral part of disciplinary strategies.

Second, many of the intended subjects of the new disciplinary strategy refused to participate in it fully. Puerto Ricans appropriated those elements of colonial marital reform that served their interests, and rejected those that did not. They enthusiastically took advantage of the opportunities to end unworkable relationships, rushing to the courts to petition for divorce. However, they did not go on, as colonial strategists had hoped, to marry in significantly larger numbers. Puerto Ricans' responses to the colonial reforms of marriage and divorce confirm that they were neither as docile nor as disordered as their new rulers dreamed. They had their own definitions of marriage and its responsibilities. They were also quite cognizant of their own gendered interests, and did their best to advance them through whatever fissures they could find or force open in the colonial edifice. Thus, attention to diffuse popular actions can show us that disciplinary power is not always as effective as Foucault's theory implies. Certainly, its ripple effects do reach into the intimate spaces of people's lives. But people have the power to make divergent decisions and act on them, thus challenging the totalizing patterns in Foucault's conceptualization.[72]

The reform of divorce and marriage in Puerto Rico also illuminates the contradictory effects of early U.S. colonialism on women's lives in particular. In a striking parallel to the patterns that Leila Ahmed traces for European colonialism in the Middle East, colonial officials' appropriation of feminist projects from their home country helped shift the parameters of institutions that had historically restricted women's options. However much the new colonial agents may have learned (or co-opted) from feminists at home, though, they never intended frontally to challenge male power over women. The new definitions of marriage and divorce that were codified in 1902 and subsequently worked out in the courts strove to reconstruct a patriarchal family, where husbands could still exercise power over women, although less overtly.[73]

Clearly, the right to terminate abusive, shameful, or unreliable marriages was important to Puerto Rican women, who constituted the majority of divorce petitioners. Indeed, the right to divorce—heretofore ignored by historians of the construction of U.S. colonial hegemony in Puerto Rico— may have been one of the social reforms that won the U.S. colonial regime support among marginalized Puerto Ricans. Certainly, the explosion of divorce petitions—the vast majority of which were granted—in the decade following the implementation of the new Civil Code implies that this may have been so. Popular commentary in Ponce today also hints that some Puerto Rican women still associate U.S. rule with an increase in options for their sex. Several Ponce working-class women mentioned to me that their grandmothers were only able to rid themselves of violent, "useless" husbands "after the Americans came." [74] Ironically, the dissolution of formal marital relations may have been more important in cementing popular support for U.S. rule than the colonizers' attempt to stabilize society through encouraging marriage.

As I have discussed elsewhere, women yearned for more reciprocal gender relations in Puerto Rico throughout the nineteenth century. They continually struggled against men's assertion of physical and sexual rights over them.[75] After the implementation of the new Civil Code in 1902, however, women had a new weapon in their battles. For the first time, women were able to obtain some legal redress for complaints against their husbands. An unworkable marital contract could now finally be terminated.

But there were limits to the efficacy of this new arena of struggle, just as there were serious limits to the "benevolent" nature of U.S. colonialism in general; these limits were gendered. After 1902, men could rid themselves of wives who refused to submit to their claims of sexual ownership. Divorce served their interests relatively well. However, divorce did *not* protect women from male abuse. The courts were not quick to punish husbands' infidelity. Neither did they enforce men's compliance with their financial responsibilities. Release from a bad marriage was better than the extremely limited options that existed in the nineteenth century, but it certainly did not provide the full relief that most women sought. The potential (although partial) challenge to male privilege posed by the 1902 Civil Code remained largely unrealized. The colonial state was not a dependable ally for women in their struggles for justice within the family.

In 1898, Puerto Rican women had not yet managed to create effective strategies for enforcing their alternative moral codes through the state. Nor had most plebeian women articulated their desires for male fidelity, economic stability, and freedom from physical and sexual violence into self-consciously political demands. However, women in Puerto Rico did aggressively turn a new institutional opening to their own advantage as much as possible. Women's response to the increased accessibility of divorce ripped open the dream of "civilized marital unions" on which the new colonial rulers sought to build their power. The women's diffuse but insistent voices cried out to the new colonial regime that facilitating marriage was not sufficient to stabilize the family. In the family, as in the larger society, stability without justice was an empty ideal.

Notes

I would like to thank Marisol de la Cadena, Karen Dolan, Gil Joseph, and Catherine LeGrand for their support, careful reading, and insightful comments on various drafts of this chapter.

1. Historians of U.S. foreign policy have long debated the meaning of the "Spanish-American War" of 1898. Some assert that the acquisition of formal colonies marked the beginning of a new imperialist direction for the United States. Other scholars point to previous U.S. wars against Mexico and North American indigenous nations as part of a long trajectory of nineteenth-century conquest and domination of allegedly inferior "others." These historians argue that 1898 signified the culmination of a decades-long process, rather than a dramatic turning point for the United States. For recent discussions of this question, see Joseph A. Fry, "Phases of Empire: Late Nineteenth-Century U.S. Foreign Relations," in *The Gilded Age: Essays on the Origins of Modern America,* ed. Charles W. Calhoun (Wilmington, N.C.: Scholarly Resources Books, 1996), 261–88; idem, "Imperialism, American Style, 1890–1916," in *American Foreign Relations Reconsidered,* ed. Gordon Martel (London: Routledge, 1994), 52–70; Edward Crapol, "Coming to Terms with Empire: The Historiography of Late Nineteenth-Century American Foreign Relations," *Diplomatic History* 16 (fall 1992): 573–97; and Hugh De Santis, "The Imperialist Impulse and American Innocence, 1865–1900," in *American Foreign Relations: A Historiographical Review,* ed. Gerald K. Haines and J. Samuel Walker (Westport, Conn.: Greenwood Press, 1981), 63–90.

2. Historians of this period discuss the high hopes that Puerto Ricans of almost all classes held for U.S. rule. See Mariano Negrón Portillo, *El autonomismo puertorriqueño: Su transformación ideológica (1895–1914)* (Río Piedras: Ediciones Huracán, 1981), 36–51; Fernando Picó, *1898: La guerra después de la guerra* (Río Piedras: Ediciones Huracán, 1987), 73–79; Gervasio García and Angel Quintero Rivera, *Desafió y solidaridad: Breve historia del movimiento obrero puertorriqueño* (Río Piedras: Ediciones Huracán, 1986); and Angel Quintero Rivera, *Patricios y plebeyos: Burgueses, hacendados, artesanos y obreros. Las relaciones de clase en el Puerto Rico de cambio de siglo* (Río Piedras: Ediciones Huracán, 1988), 99–116.

3. Joan Scott notes this as one of the multiple ways in which gender structures the workings of "high" politics (*Gender and the Politics of History* [New York: Columbia University Press, 1988], 48).

4. The quote is from Vicente Rafael, "White Love: Surveillance and Nationalist Resistance in the U.S. Colonization of the Philippines," in *Cultures of United States Imperialism,* ed. Amy Kaplan and Donald E. Pease (Durham, N.C.: Duke

University Press, 1993), 185. Rafael argues that despite the United States' attempts at surveillance and co-optation of Filipinos, a vibrant cross-class anti-imperialist culture thrived in urban areas.

5. Other analogous reforms included the eight-hour workday, trial by jury, and the right of habeas corpus. These reforms were state concessions to marginalized groups within the United States, compromises that were later exported as part of the United States "civilizing" colonial project. For the U.S. labor movement's fight for the eight-hour workday, see David Roediger, *Our Own Time: A History of American Labor and the Working Day* (London: Verso, 1989). The struggles over divorce in the United States are delineated in Glenda Riley, *Divorce: An American Tradition* (New York: Oxford University Press, 1991); and William O'Neill, *Divorce in the Progressive Era* (New York: New Viewpoints, 1973). Nineteenth-century feminists led the initial drives to legitimize and defend divorce in the United States.

6. The 1910 International Feminist Congress in Buenos Aires made divorce one of its principal demands. At that time, only Uruguay, of all the Latin American nations attending, had legalized divorce for religious marriages. Several Latin American countries, including Chile, allegedly one of the region's most "modern" nations, still have not fully legalized divorce today. Francesca Miller, *Latin American Women and the Search for Social Justice* (Hanover, N.H.: University Press of New England, 1991), 74–75, 92; and K. Lynn Stoner, "On Men Reforming the Rights of Men: The Abrogation of the Cuban Adultery Law, 1930," *Cuban Studies* 21 (1991): 83–99.

7. Eric Cheyfitz, "Savage Law: The Plot against American Indians in *Johnson and Graham's Lessee v. McIntosh* and *The Pioneers*" in Kaplan and Pease, *Cultures of United States Imperialism,* 109. Cheyfitz was building on the vast literature on colonial discourses about colonized peoples that has emerged in the last fifteen years, inspired in large part by Edward W. Said's *Orientalism* (New York: Viking Books, 1978). Nicholas Thomas provides a good critical review in *Colonialism's Culture: Anthropology, Travel, and Government* (Princeton, N.J.: Princeton University Press, 1994), 1–65. Concerted attention to the role of gender and sexuality in colonial discourses has only begun quite recently. See Mary Louise Pratt, *Imperial Eyes: Travel Writing and Transculturation* (New York: Routledge, 1992); Inderpal Grewal, *Home and Harem: Nation, Gender, Empire, and the Cultures of Travel* (Durham, N.C.: Duke University Press, 1996); Susan Morgan, *Place Matters: Gendered Geography in Victorian Women's Travel Books about South-East Asia* (New Brunswick, N.J.: Rutgers University Press, 1996); and Anne McClintock, *Imperial Leather: Race, Gender, and Sexuality in the Colonial Contest* (New York: Routledge, 1995).

8. Ann L. Stoler, "Making Empire Respectable: The Politics of Race and Sexual Morality in Twentieth-Century Colonial Cultures," *American Ethnologist* 16 (Nov. 1989): 634–60; "Sexual Affronts and Racial Frontiers: European Identities and the Cultural Politics of Exclusion in Colonial Southeast Asia," *Com-*

parative Studies in Society and History 34 (1992): 514–51; and Frederick Cooper and Ann L. Stoler, "Tensions of Empire: Colonial Control and Visions of Rule," *American Ethnologist* 16 (Nov. 1989): 612–14.

9. For extended discussions of the assaults on wealthy landowners and their property that punctuated the months following the U.S. invasion of Puerto Rico, see Fernando Picó, *1898;* Kelvin A. Santiago-Valles, *"Subject People" and Colonial Discourses: Economic Transformation and Social Disorder in Puerto Rico, 1898–1947* (Albany: State University of New York Press, 1994), 77–99; and Blanca Silvestrini de Pacheco, *Violencia y criminalidad en Puerto Rico, 1898–1973: Apuntes para un estudio de historia social* (Río Piedras: Editorial Universitaria, 1980), 13–51.

10. My analysis of twentieth-century divorce cases is based on the judicial records from the municipality of Ponce, a principal sugar-producing region in Puerto Rico, and one of the island's economic and political centers. The data gathered cover rural areas, as well as small towns and the larger city of Ponce.

11. Stuart B. Schwartz, "The Hurricane of San Ciriaco: Disaster, Politics, and Society in Puerto Rico, 1899–1901," *Hispanic American Historical Review* 72, no. 3 (Aug. 1992): 303–34.

12. Aida Negrón de Montilla, *Americanization in Puerto Rico and the Public School System, 1900–1930* (Río Piedras: Editorial Edil, 1981).

13. For a few illustrative examples, see William Appleman Williams, *The Roots of the Modern American Empire: A Study of the Growth and Shaping of Social Consciousness in a Marketplace Society* (New York: Random House, 1969); Walter LaFeber, *The American Age: United States Foreign Policy at Home and Abroad since 1970* (New York: Norton, 1989); Walter Williams, "United States Indian Policy and the Debate over Philippine Annexation: Implications for the Origins of American Imperialism," *Journal of American History* 66 (Mar. 1980): 810–31; and Fry, "Phases of Empire."

14. For Cuba, see Aline Helg, *Our Rightful Share: The Afro-Cuban Struggle for Equality, 1886–1912* (Chapel Hill: University of North Carolina Press, 1995); and Louis A. Pérez Jr., *Cuba: Between Reform and Revolution* (New York: Oxford University Press, 1988), 129–228. For the Philippines, see Stuart Creighton Miller, *"Benevolent Assimilation": The American Conquest of the Philippines, 1899–1903* (New Haven, Conn.: Yale University Press, 1982); and Rafael, "White Love," 206–14.

15. *Hearings before the Committee on Pacific Islands and Puerto Rico of the United States Senate on Senate Bill 2264, To Provide a Government for the Island of Puerto Rico, and for Other Purposes* (Washington, D.C.: Government Printing Office, 1900), 60; and *Annual Reports of the War Department for the Fiscal Year Ended June 30, 1899: Report of Brigadier-General George W. Davis, U.S.V., on Civil Affairs of Puerto Rico, 1899* (Washington, D.C.: Government Printing Office, 1900), 549–52.

16. See, for example, the cartoons from the *Chicago Inter Ocean,* 1905, and

Harper's Weekly, 27 Aug. 1898, reproduced in John J. Johnson, *Latin America in Caricature* (Austin: University of Texas Press, 1980), 128, 217.

17. *Appendix to the Congressional Record,* 11 Apr. 1900, 153.

18. Robert L. Beisner, *Twelve against Empire: The Anti-imperialists, 1898–1900* (Chicago: University of Chicago Press, 1968); Daniel B. Schirmer, *Republic of Empire: American Resistance to the Philippines War* (Cambridge, Mass.: Schenkman Publishing Co., 1972); and Richard E. Welch Jr., *Response to Imperialism: The United States and the Philippine-American War, 1899–1902* (Chapel Hill: University of North Carolina Press, 1979).

19. See Henry Curtis's and Azel Ames's testimony at congressional hearings in 1900. They were recorded in "Industrial and Other Conditions of the Island of Puerto Rico, and the Form of Government Which Should Be Adopted for It," *Hearings before the Committee on Pacific Islands and Puerto Rico of the United States Senate on Senate Bill 2264, To Provide a Government for the Island of Puerto Rico, and for Other Purposes,* 86–88, 191–92, doc. 834-12, box 124, General Classified Files pre-1914, Bureau of Insular Affairs, Record Group 350, U.S. National Archives, Washington, D.C. (hereinafter G C F, B I A, R G 350, U S N A). Also see Representative Ebenezer J. Hill from Connecticut citing Governor Davis's report, *Appendix to the Congressional Record,* 11 Apr. 1900, 177; Governor Winthrop's testimony to the U.S. House Committee on Insular Affairs in *Committee Reports, Hearings, and Acts of Congress Corresponding Thereto: Fifty-ninth Congress, 1905–1907* (Washington, D.C.: Government Printing Office, 1908), 144–48; Henry Carroll, *Report on the Island of Porto Rico* (Washington, D.C.: Government Printing Office, 1899), 49; L. S. Rowe, *The United States and Porto Rico* (New York: Longmans, Green and Co., 1904), 99–103; Charles Morris, *Our Island Empire: A Hand-Book of Cuba, Porto Rico, Hawaii, and the Philippine Islands* (Philadelphia: J. B. Lippincott Co., 1899), 190–91; and José de Olivares, *Our Islands and Their People, as Seen with Camara and Pencil,* vol. 1 (St. Louis, Mo.: N. D. Thompson Publishing Co., 1899), 287, 335.

20. Senate, *First Annual Report of Charles H. Allen, Governor of Porto Rico, Covering the Period from May 1, 1900 to May 1, 1901,* 57th Cong., 1st sess., doc. 79, p. 28, U S N A. See also ibid., 29–41.

21. Anonymous letter to Meyer Bloomfield, 27 Dec. 1911, file 451/85, box 80, entry 5, G C F, B I A, R G 350, U S N A.

22. See, for example, Senate, *Proposal for Divorce Law for the District of Columbia, February 19, 1901,* 56th Cong., 2d sess., doc. 174, #4042, U S N A. For discussions of the U.S. debates over the morality and social utility of divorce during the Progressive Era, see Riley, *Divorce: An American Tradition,* 11–131; and O'Neill, *Divorce in the Progressive Era.* After protracted political battles, divorce had been legalized by the 1870s in almost all the states of the Union, although the allowable grounds varied widely. During the 1890s, a time of intensified agitation against divorce, numerous states placed restrictions on it, although none outlawed it altogether (Riley, *Divorce,* 34–47).

23. Puerto Rico's military governor General Davis insisted that "the people generally have no conception of political rights combined with political responsibilities." "Industrial and Other Conditions of the Island of Puerto Rico," 58, 79–81. Insular Commissioner Henry Curtis, a U.S. capitalist, and various U.S. Senate members agreed (ibid., 100, 104–7, 127). See also *Annual Reports of the War Department, Part 13: Report of the Military Government of Porto Rico on Civil Affairs from October 18, 1898, to April 30, 1900* (Washington, D.C.: Government Printing Office, 1902), 115–16; and *U.S. Senate Congressional Record*, 23 Jan. 1900, 1062.

24. *Annual Reports of the War Department, Part 13*, 116.

25. "Industrial and Other Conditions of the Island of Puerto Rico," 57–60, 79–81. See also *Annual Reports of the War Department for the Fiscal Year Ended June 30, 1899*, 549–50; *Annual Reports of the War Department, Part 13*, 116; and the speech by Senator Ross, recorded in *Congressional Record*, Senate, 23 Jan. 1900, 1062. U.S. officials' accusations of elite antidemocratic practices were transparently hypocritical. Elite leaders of both Puerto Rican political parties begged the United States to reinstate universal male suffrage and allow islanders to elect their own full legislature. Governor Davis and Congress members, however, refused. See, for example, "Industrial and Other Conditions of the Island of Puerto Rico," 178–79, 185–87, 219–21.

26. Early U.S. commentators sometimes acknowledged the extreme poverty of most Puerto Ricans, but rarely if ever supported the labor movement's demands for better wages. Rather, they placed the hope for change on altering familial consumption patterns. Personal "thrift," not higher wages, would raise the Puerto Rican working classes' standard of living. See, for example, "Industrial and Other Conditions of the Island of Puerto Rico," 55–56; and *Teacher's Bulletin*, no. 2, 1900, 14, doc. 451–16, box 78, entry 5, GCF, BIA, RG 350, USNA.

27. See the testimony of various U.S. officials to the Senate in "Industrial and Other Conditions of the Island of Puerto Rico," 88, 191–92. Also see the speech of Connecticut Representative Ebenezer J. Hill, recorded in the *Appendix to the Congressional Record*, 11 Apr. 1900, 177; and comments and questions of various representatives in *Committee Reports, Hearings, and Acts of Congress*, 144–48.

28. Carroll, *Report on the Island of Porto Rico*, 35, 663, 691–712; de Olivares, *Our Islands*, 287; Rowe, *The United States and Porto Rico*, 110–14; and the speech by Representative Ebenezer J. Hill, recorded in the *Appendix to the Congressional Record*, 11 Apr. 1900, 177.

29. Governor Davis's report, cited in the speech by Representative Hill, *Appendix to the Congressional Record*, 11 Apr. 1900, 177. Also see de Olivares, *Our Islands*, 330–31; and Schwartz, "The Hurricane of San Ciriaco," 321–23.

30. See the reports of the education supervisors of Vieques, Humacao, and Mayagüez in *Report of the Commissioner of Education for Porto Rico to the Secretary of the Interior, U.S.A., 1902* (Washington, D.C.: Government Printing Office, 1902), 75, 92, box 79, GCF, BIA, RG 350, USNA. Also see the testimony of General Roy Stone and other U.S. officials in "Industrial and Other Conditions of the

Island of Puerto Rico," 86–87, 127, 189; Carroll, *Report on the Island of Porto Rico,* 50–58; Morris, *Our Island Empire,* 206–9; and de Olivares, *Our Islands,* 297, 303–7, 333–35, 350.

31. *Report of the Commissioner of Education,* 75, 92.

32. Military governor Davis proudly described his paternal resolutions of Puerto Rican elites' childish political spats. "Industrial and Other Conditions of the Island of Puerto Rico," 57–60, 100, 107; *Annual Reports of the War Department for the Fiscal Year Ended June 30, 1899,* 549–50; and the speech by Senator Ross, recorded in *Congressional Record,* Senate, 23 Jan. 1900, 1062.

33. De Olivares, *Our Islands,* 303.

34. Puerto Rican elites argued against such generalized representations of the island's population. They asserted their right to be accepted as the United States' equal economic and political partner. Island elites concurred with colonial officials' distrust of popular control over the political process. However, most painted a much more threatening picture of the working classes. This was not surprising, considering that the majority of popular protests in Puerto Rico targeted the local elite's power and abuses, rather than U.S. rule.

35. Governor Davis's 1900 report to the president provides an illuminating example. After waxing enthusiastic about the potential for peaceful exploitation of labor and natural resources in Puerto Rico, Davis exploded in a diatribe against the threat of "full manhood suffrage" there. Class conflict would increase and the cane fields go up in smoke, he warned, causing "the paralysis of all business development. . . . Foreign capital will never jeopardize itself in Porto Rico if the island is to be governed by a horde of human beings called civilized, but who are only a few steps removed from a primitive state of nature." *Annual Reports of the War Department, Part 13,* 116. The oft-touted docility of Puerto Rico depended on unwavering colonial control.

36. See García and Quintero Rivera, *Desafió y solidaridad;* and Yamila Azize, *Mujer en la lucha* (Río Piedras: Editorial Cultural, 1985).

37. See, for example, Carroll, *Report on the Island of Porto Rico,* 693–757, 762–63, 795–96; Rowe, *The United States and Porto Rico,* 110–14; de Olivares, *Our Islands,* 287; *First Annual Report of Charles H. Allen,* 34–35; U.S. attorney general to the president, 23 June 1902, *Letters Sent Feb. 25, 1902–Aug. 31, 1906,* vol. 1, 456–58, Records of the Bureau of Insular and Territorial Affairs, 1902–1906, General Records of the Department of Justice, RG 60, USNA; and *Annual Reports of the War Department for the Fiscal Year Ended June 30, 1899,* appendix C, 686.

38. *Annual Reports of the War Department for the Fiscal Year Ended June 30, 1899,* appendix C, 701.

39. Anonymous letter to Meyer Bloomfield, 27 Dec. 1911, file 451/85, box 80, entry 5, GCF, BIA, RG 350, USNA.

40. U.S. attorney general to the president, 23 June 1902; italics mine.

41. William H. Hunt, *Third Annual Report of the Governor of Porto Rico, Cover-*

ing the Period from July 1, 1902 to June 30, 1903 (Washington, D.C.: Government Printing Office, 1903), 54.

42. William H. Hunt, *Fourth Annual Report of the Governor of Porto Rico, Covering the Period from July 1, 1903–June 30, 1904* (Washington, D.C.: Government Printing Office, 1904), 30.

43. *Annual Reports of the War Department for the Fiscal Year Ended June 30, 1899,* 687; Carroll, *Report on the Island of Porto Rico,* 35, 663, 691–712; and Olivares, *Our Islands,* 331.

44. Rowe, *The United States and Porto Rico,* 113, 164–65; Carroll, *Report on the Island of Porto Rico,* 691–93; and *Annual Reports of the War Department for the Fiscal Year Ended June 30, 1899,* appendix C, 687. Leila Ahmed discusses an analogous appropriation of feminist discourse by antifeminist male British colonial officials who condemned the use of the veil in the Middle East in order to assert British superiority over colonized men (Ahmed, *Women and Gender in Islam: Historical Roots of a Modern Debate* [New Haven, Conn.: Yale University Press, 1992], 145–64).

45. *Annual Reports of the War Department for the Fiscal Year Ended June 30, 1899,* appendix C, 686; and Perfecta Montalvo to Brigadier General George W. Davis, 10 June 1899, Archivo General de Puerto Rico (hereinafter AGPR), Fortaleza, box 24. See also Expediente 4441, 30 June 1899, AGPR, Fortaleza, box 25; "Civil Marriage, Divorce, Ecclesiastical Laws Governing Same. To War Secretary," 7 Feb. 1900, Expediente 7253, AGPR, Fortaleza, box 37; and Rowe, *The United States and Porto Rico,* 164.

46. Edward J. Berbusse provides a brief discussion of anticlericalism among Liberals. Salvador Brau, José de Diego, Mariano Abril, and Luis Muñoz Rivera, some of the "founding fathers" of Puerto Rican Liberal Autonomism, were all masons and enthusiastic advocates of the separation of church and state (Berbusse, *The United States in Puerto Rico, 1898–1900* [Chapel Hill: University of North Carolina Press, 1966], 72, 198–200).

47. I found no evidence of protests against legalization of divorce from the Catholic Church during this period. This surprising silence is attributable to a number of factors. First, the U.S. restructuring of church-state relations dealt a devastating blow to the Catholic Church. The Spanish state's direct subsidies had provided the vast bulk of the church's income; these funds evaporated after the U.S. invasion. In addition, U.S. officials and anticlerical Puerto Rican municipal officers asserted control over church property on the island. The resultant legal battles were not resolved until 1906, when the U.S. Supreme Court found in the church's favor. Until then, however, the simple day-to-day economic survival of parish priests, and the physical and juridical integrity of the church seem to have absorbed most of the hierarchy's attention. They were also kept busy defending the right of women's religious orders to staff hospitals; U.S. officials launched a campaign to purge the nuns in 1901. See Berbusse, *The United States,* 139–

41, 191–210; *Committee Reports, Hearings, and Acts of Congress Corresponding Thereto: Sixtieth Congress, 1907–1909,* 347–51, Legislative Division, Y.4, In7 6, C73, USNA, Washington, D.C.

The Catholic hierarchy did not, however, completely ignore questions of marriage and divorce. They protested moves to legalize civil marriage and to allow ministers of other faiths to celebrate weddings. Marriage, ultimately, seems to have been more important than divorce in the hierarchy's political strategies: if the Catholic Church could maintain control over the terms of marriage, divorce would not be nearly as great a threat to its power.

48. *Revised Statutes and Codes of Porto Rico Containing All Laws Passed at the First and Second Sessions of the Legislative Assembly in Effect after July 1, 1902, Including the Political Code, the Penal Code, the Code of Criminal Procedure, the Civil Code,* title 4, chap. 3 (San Juan: Boletín Mercantil Press, 1902).

49. Ibid., title 9, chap. 1. Proposed modifications in *patria potestad* provoked impassioned protests from Federales such as Julián Blanco, who argued that democratizing authority within the family would produce "the most deplorable and dissolute anarchy" ("El nuevo código civil: 6," *La Democracia,* 27 Jan. 1902, 1. See also "El nuevo código civil: 7," *La Democracia,* 29 Jan. 1902, 1). Clearly, such protests had an effect; mothers' wishes were unequivocally subordinated to fathers' in the final draft of the Civil Code.

50. "The time of the Americans," and "those long-ago times, when the Spanish ruled."

51. Eileen J. Findlay, "Domination, Decency, and Desire: The Politics of Sexuality in Ponce, Puerto Rico, 1870–1920" (Ph.D. diss., University of Wisconsin, 1995), 293–301.

52. Only one in twenty of all women petitioners came from a wealthy background. Another one in ten was from the middle class or professional sector. Two-fifths were married to artisans or day laborers, and the social standing of one-third was unidentified. Male petitioners ranged broadly. One in ten was of elite status and one in four was from the professional middling sectors. One of every six male plaintiffs was an artisan or day laborer. Almost one-half of all male plaintiffs were not identified by class.

53. This is reflected not only in the rapidity of the courts' processing of cases, but also in the increasingly formulaic nature of the language used to draw up divorce petitions. After 1906, very little witness testimony and no lengthy judicial reasoning were included in the transcripts of the cases. This contrasted sharply with the detail of charges, testimony, and sentences that characterized the early files, when the terms of divorce were still being negotiated.

54. The intervening years' divorce percentages of total civil cases filed in Ponce are as follows: 1902—4 percent (n=302); 1903—4.3 percent (n=300); 1904—2.7 percent (n=226); 1905—no record of cases filed; 1906—15.2 percent (n=250); 1907—14.3 percent (n=263); 1908—14 percent (n=223); 1909—12.4 percent (n=201); 1910—16 percent (n=233); and 1911—22 percent (n=253).

55. Steve J. Stern, *The Secret History of Gender: Women, Men, and Power in Late Colonial Mexico* (Chapel Hill: University of North Carolina Press, 1995), 131.

56. See Findlay, "Domination, Decency, and Desire," 29–96, 329–36, for a more detailed analysis of the gendered workings of power within nineteenth-century Puerto Rican families and communities. See also Stern, *The Secret History of Gender*, 55–212, for a nuanced discussion of these issues among late colonial rural residents of Morelos, Mexico.

57. "María Otero contra José Gregorio Torres sobre divorcio," 1902, A G P R, Ponce, Exp. Civ., box 15; "Doña Petronila Quiles contra Don Francisco Perez Fabio, sobre divorcio," 1903, A G P R, Ponce, Exp. Civ., box 21; "Doña Andrea Corsina Martínez y Torres contra Don Juan Antonio Olivencia sobre divorcio," 1903, A G P R, Jud., Ponce, Exp. Civ., box 27; and "Elisa Ferrer Piñiero vs. José López Súarez, divorcio," 1906, A G P R, Jud., Ponce, Exp. Civ., box 43.

58. "Don Luis Besante y Lespier contra Doña Rafaela Núñez y Fernández, sobre divorcio," 1903, A G P R, Jud., Ponce, Exp. Civ., box 20.

59. "Don Juan Martínez y Torres contra Doña Juana Evangelista Rodríguez sobre divorcio," 1903, A G P R, Jud., Ponce, Exp. Civ., box 23; "Don Luis Besante y Lespier contra Doña Rafaela Núñez y Fernández, sobre divorcio"; "Francisco Muñiz Senque versus Isabel Torres y Medina, acción divorcio," 1909, A G P R, Jud., Ponce, Exp. Civ., box 28; "Pedro Montero y Torres versus Margarita Montero, acción divorcio," 1910, A G P R, Jud., Ponce, Exp. Civ., box 35; and "Ramón Ortiz Zayas versus María Rita Ortiz née López," 1910, A G P R, Jud., Ponce, Exp. Civ., box 36.

60. "María Otero contra José Gregorio Torres sobre divorcio"; "Demanda de divorcio: Doña Elisa Giménez y Ramírez contra Don José Colón y Carrasquillo por malos tratamientos de obra," 1901, A G P R, Jud., Ponce, Exp. Civ., box 7; "Doña Bernardina del Valle y Rojas contra Don Domingo Aurelio Cruz Rivera sobre divorcio," 1903, A G P R, Jud., Ponce, Exp. Civ., box 19; "Doña Mercedes Vélez contra Don Luis Castro Arciatore sobre divorcio," 1903, A G P R, Jud., Ponce, Exp. Civ., box 24.

61. "María Otero contra José Gregorio Torres sobre divorcio"; "Doña Petronila Quiles contra Don Francisco Perez Fabio, sobre divorcio"; "Doña Andrea Corsina Martínez y Torres contra Don Juan Antonio Olivencia sobre divorcio"; and "Elisa Ferrer Piñiero vs. José López Súarez, divorcio."

62. "Ezequiela Rosa del Busto vs. Simón Pierluisi y Crau, divorcio," 1904, A G P R, Jud., Ponce, Exp. Civ., box 39. See also "Doña María de la Paz Franceschi y Antongiorgi contra su esposo, Don Antonio Sánchez y Cintrón, sobre divorcio," 1903, A G P R, Jud., Ponce, Exp. Civ., box 18; and "María F. Irizary Quiñones contra Ramón del Toro Seda sobre divorcio," 1910, A G P R, Jud., Ponce, Exp. Civ., box 47.

63. "Doña Mercedes Vélez contra Don Luis Castro Arciatore sobre divorcio." For a few other examples, see: "Doña María de la Paz Franceschi y Antongiorgi contra su esposo, Don Antonio Sánchez y Cintrón, sobre divorcio"; and "El

pueblo de Puerto Rico vs. Edmundo Steinacher: Adulterio," 1905, AGPR, Jud., Ponce, Exp. Civ., box 46.

64. "El pueblo de Puerto Rico vs. Edmundo Steinacher: Adulterio." For another example, see: "Doña María de la Paz Franceschi y Antongiorgi contra su esposo, Don Antonio Sánchez y Cintrón, sobre divorcio."

65. "María F. Irizary Quiñones contra Ramón del Toro Seda sobre divorcio"; "Doña María de la Paz Franceschi y Antongiorgi contra su esposo, Don Antonio Sánchez y Cintrón, sobre divorcio"; "Don Juan Martínez y Torres contra Doña Juana Evangelista Rodríguez sobre divorcio"; "Doña Nicolasa Torres y Ledesma contra Don Bartolomé Deffendini y Mattey, sobre divorcio," 1902, AGPR, Jud., Ponce, Exp. Civ., box 16; and "Doña Mart Estrell Rodríguez y Mateu contra Don Eugenio Montalvo y González," 1903, AGPR, Jud., Ponce, Exp. Civ., box 22.

66. "Doña Carmen Lucca y Sánchez contra Don Miguel Napoleoni Tillet sobre divorcio," 1904, AGPR, Jud., Ponce, Exp. Civ., box 40.

67. See "El pueblo de Puerto Rico vs. Edmundo Steinacher: Adulterio"; "María Angustias Anguita y Ribarte contra Ercilio de la Cruz y Rivera, sobre divorcio," 1902, AGPR, Jud., Ponce, Exp. Civ., box 12; and "Doña Carmen Lucca y Sánchez contra Don Miguel Napoleoni Tillet sobre divorcio."

68. This may have influenced women in their framing of divorce petitions. María Irizarry, for example, first requested a divorce based on her husband's public affair with his mistress. She later amended her complaint, however, to eliminate all references to her husband's adultery. Instead, she provided lengthy descriptions of his physical abuse, as well as his refusal to support her financially or live with her. María's petition for divorce was approved only three months after filing the second complaint. "María F. Irizary [sic] Quiñones contra Ramón del Toro Seda sobre divorcio."

69. See, for example, "María F. Irizary Quiñones contra Ramón del Toro Seda sobre divorcio."

70. Foucault most clearly delineated his analysis of the modern forms of power in *Discipline and Punish: The Birth of the Prison* (New York: Pantheon Books, 1978); *The History of Sexuality, Volume 1: An Introduction* (New York: Random House, 1978); and *Power/Knowledge: Selected Interviews and Other Writings: 1972-1977,* ed. Colin Gordon (New York: Pantheon Books, 1980).

71. Foucault, *History of Sexuality,* 103; and *Discipline and Punish,* 180.

72. Mary Louise Pratt, borrowing from the great Cuban intellectual Fernando Ortiz, calls such processes *transculturation.* She notes that "while subjugated peoples cannot control what emanates from the dominant culture, they do determine to varying extents what they absorb into their own, and what they use it for" (*Imperial Eyes,* 6. See also Thomas, *Colonialism's Culture,* 57-61).

73. Ahmed, *Women and Gender in Islam,* 145-64.

74. Interviews with: Doña Hipólita González, 1 Apr. 1994; Doña Ramona García, 20 Mar. 1994; and Doña Carmen Rodríguez, 24 May 1994.

75. Findlay, "Domination, Decency, and Desire," 29-167.

Steven C. Topik

Mercenaries in the Theater of War

Publicity, Technology, and the Illusion of Power during

the Brazilian Naval Revolt of 1893

In one of the most bizarre episodes of the Age of Empire, U.S. merchant Charles Flint conjured up a twelve-ship flotilla to defend the Brazilian government of Marshal Floriano Peixoto, which was under severe attack from a naval revolt and civil war in 1893 and 1894. Flint's Fleet was a striking example of nascent U.S. expansionism. Although it became the last hope of Peixoto, and the nightmare of the naval rebels, it has been swallowed up by history, leaving hardly a trace.[1] U.S. and Brazilian historians have not recognized the fleet's importance, dismissing it as a failure or ignoring it entirely because of the small amount of blood, fire, and ruin it spread. They have not realized that this lack of destruction was a result of the fleet's success. Flint was a master of theater, not a master of war. From the beginning, the fleet was intended to weave the illusion of power out of a tissue of publicity and technology.[2] In Flint's modern imperial spectacle, symbols were more important weapons than cannons.

Spectacles, of course, have long existed. The most impressive ritual ceremonies were staged as official dramas meant to sustain the divine power of the miter and the crown.[3] More secular spectacles appeared with the French Revolution, where theater created new rituals, new meanings for republican citizens.[4] A good deal of postmodern analysis has explored the importance of spectacle with the post–World War II rise of consumer culture and the mass media, and the growth of U.S. overt and covert imperialism. Michael Rogin has pointed out that "American imperial spectacles display and forget four enabling myths that the culture can no longer unproblematically embrace. The first is the historical organization of American politics around racial domination. . . . The second is redemption through violence, intensified in the mass technologies of entertainment and war. The third is the belief in individual agency. . . . And the fourth is identification with the state." One should add the belief in U.S. virility, youth, and righteousness. Rogin emphasizes that "political spectacle in the postmodern empire . . . is itself a form of power and not simply window dressing that diverts attention from the secret substance of American foreign policy." [5]

This postmodern analysis applies equally well to the subject of this essay: Flint's modernist ceremony. In 1893, the telegraph, which only recently had begun to tie together the continents, and the mass daily newspaper were the publicity agents and entertainments. Men-of-war and terrible cannons were the technological marvels of their day. Although ostensibly a private and partially covert venture, Flint's Fleet had secret official collaboration in this masculine imperial initiation rite. His mercenary squadron was to muscularly penetrate the blockade of Rio de Janeiro erected by supposed monarchists and their purported stodgy, old-fashioned European allies in order to free exotic, weak, brown Brazil from unwanted advances. The financier and merchant Flint was hitching his private cart (or ship) to what he hoped would be an expanding imperial dynamo of a centralizing American state that was coming into international manhood. It happened, though, that Brazil's Marshal Peixoto and his supporters proved to be more than passive spectators or grateful damsels at the imperial spectacle. They turned the technological magic to their own ends. They refused to cede control over the interpretation of ceremonies and events, instead historically burying the memory of Flint's aid under a layer of Brazilian nationalism and virile heroism.

Although historians have forgotten the fleet, in late 1893 and early 1894 the maritime mercenaries were very big news. They grabbed headlines in the United States and Brazil and piqued European interest. The British rightfully became deeply concerned that the fleet signaled Brazil's turn away from its longtime British allies toward fellow republicans in the United States who were asserting the Monroe Doctrine.

The mercenary fleet illustrated how, in the age of corporate liberalism, private U.S. interests could conduct foreign policy with only the occasional assistance or acquiescence of the U.S. government.[6] Indeed, to a considerable degree the government relied on private individuals (often seeking private profit) to carry out covert U.S. policy. This curious and peculiar episode also revealed the marriage of interests of the U.S. commercial, financial, military, industrial, and journalistic communities.

That union, however, was not the natural outgrowth of love or of shared perceptions of material interests. While not a shotgun wedding, staging the ceremony required some fast talking. Charles Flint and Salvador de Mendonça, Brazil's minister to the United States, worked very hard to convince these groups of their mutual interests and of the potential importance of Brazil. They used propaganda and spectacle to great effect in convincing the American people that the tottering government of Floriano Peixoto was robust and that it was in the United States' interest to support it. By assembling a fleet composed of some of the most modern and sophisticated ships and weapons in existence, they associated the military government of Peixoto in the public mind not with backward, nineteenth-century cavalry *caudillos* (of which its enemies accused it) but with the modern military-industrial complex of the twentieth century. Wonderful words and pictures in the United States' major newspapers painted Peixoto's government as the regime of the future. While this episode does not testify that image is everything, the perception of power created by publicity certainly went a long way toward creating real power.[7] The fleet never needed to fire its terrible guns; it played its part in the theater of war well enough to convince its audience—U.S. government officials who were wavering in their support for Peixoto's government, the British foreign office that was leaning toward the insurgents, and the opposing rebel admirals—of its awesome war-making might.

Brazil's participation in this inventive strategy underlined the fact that the continental-sized nation was far from a banana republic. Although militarily weak and financially strapped, Peixoto's government was nonetheless not at the mercy of Yankee imperialists. Indeed, President Peixoto's regime was one of the most nationalist and populist governments in Brazil's history. It turned to the United States as the anti-imperialist alternative that could counterweigh purported British and Portuguese aid to the insurgents. In the end, the fleet helped Peixoto's "legal" naval forces much more than it aided the expansionist-minded Yankees.

Finally, Flint's Fleet may well have been the decisive factor in saving Peixoto's government and cementing U.S.-Brazilian friendship. Derided as a "cardboard squadron" by its detractors, who believed it to be chimerical, in the end Flint's Fleet resembled much more closely the appellation that the merchant coined in his publicity campaign: the "dynamite squadron."[8]

The Birth of the Republic

Time had accelerated tremendously in Brazil between 1888 and 1893. In six brief years Brazilians had finally emancipated their slaves, overthrown the only successful monarchy in the Western Hemisphere, disestablished the Catholic Church, abolished the aristocracy, and experienced unprecedented economic development. Brazil's most radical republicans could be excused for believing that they were repeating France's bourgeois revolution of exactly one hundred years earlier.[9]

But Brazil proved unready to sustain such a fevered forward march. Ex-monarchists, *latifundiários,* foreign merchants, and some of the military—particularly the more aristocratic navy—resented the Jacobin turn of the government. A revolt at the end of 1891 replaced the republic's first president, Marshal Deodoro da Fonseca, with another army marshal, Floriano Peixoto. When Peixoto sided with the radical urban Jacobins in an authoritarian regime that attacked bankers, European merchants, and suspected monarchists, the navy revolted on 7 September 1893 and seized control of Rio's harbor. At roughly the same time, federalists resenting Rio's central control provoked a civil war starting in the southern state of Rio Grande do Sul and eventually embroiling the entire southern part of the country.

When the navy revolted, Peixoto scrambled to concoct another fleet loyal to his government. This makeshift navy was supposed to assure the allegiance of the northern part of Brazil and break the blockade in Rio. When efforts to purchase ships from Argentina failed, he commissioned his minister in Washington, Salvador de Mendonça, to seek gunboats in the United States. But President Grover Cleveland refused to sell him warships; the United States, just beginning to rebuild its long-neglected navy, had none to spare.[10]

Mendonça then faced an important decision. Should he follow the advice of Brazilian Admiral J. Maurity, who suggested that instead of wasting money cobbling together an expensive and probably worthless squadron in the United States, Mendonça should just wait until Brazil's two modern cruisers under construction in Toulon, France, were ready? Mendonça instead decided to outfit a squadron in the United States, probably less for military reasons than for the publicity value of spending a great deal of money (ultimately more than $1.5 million) for a dramatic gesture in the United States. To further demonstrate his concern for U.S. public opinion, Mendonça organized a technical advisory staff made up exclusively of current or former members of the United States Navy.[11] These men would prove invaluable in securing the assistance of influential members of the Cleveland administration. The entire Brazilian navy was marginalized from the squadron's refitting and initial command. Instead, the North American Charles Flint took over.[12] Flint's loyalty to the bottom line was more trustworthy than the Brazilian navy's questionable fidelity to the republic.

Charles Flint, Brazilian Agent

That Peixoto turned to the United States is testimony to the warm diplomatic relations that drew the two countries together; military and economic pragmatism would have dictated European ships. In the early 1890s U.S. naval architects had little experience in designing modern heavy warships, nor did North American manufacturers have practice in building them.[13] Given the political nature of the decision, however, it made sense for Mendonça to call on his friend and ally Charles Flint for assistance. After all, while the British were suspected of favoring a monarchist restoration, the United States had been the first major power to recognize Brazil's republic and had cooperated closely with Brazil in the Pan American Congress of 1889; and Brazil had been the first country to sign a trade treaty with the United States under the auspices of the 1891 McKinley Tariff. This was the first treaty ever signed between the two countries and the first trade pact Brazil had agreed to in over half a century.

Flint was a natural for the assignment. The largest U.S. exporter of locomotives and other goods to Brazil and importer of Brazilian rubber, he was well known to the Brazilian elite. He had a long-standing friendship with Brazil's minister, Salvador de Mendonça, that traced back to Mendonça's days as Brazilian consul in Flint's hometown of New York. They had worked together on a number of diplomatic initiatives such as the Pan American Congress and securing American recognition of Brazil's republic, and it was alleged that they had undertaken a number of business ventures together. Flint was a very important, though underappreciated, man. As the *Brooklyn Daily Eagle* revealed, "How real and great a power he really is in all the South American republics is a subject little known except in Washington and the capitals of the countries situated around the equator." [14]

Not only did he have a vested interest in U.S.-Brazilian relations, but he had long experience in shipping and the arms trade. Flint's father and uncle were two of the largest shipbuilders in Maine and later in Brooklyn, and Flint himself had chartered freighters for the Grace company, owned a shipping company, and was an important stockholder in the United States and Brazil Mail Steamship Company (USBMSC).[15]

He also stood out in the shadowy world of international arms and mercenaries. In 1869 Flint had helped Peru fit out two monitors and three transport ships. Then, when war broke out between Peru and Chile seven years later, he sent torpedoes to Peru. This was more than a simple business transaction: Peru served as a testing ground for the Lay torpedo company, which the trader partly owned.[16] Flint also provided state-of-the-art underwater dynamite torpedoes that could be fired from merchant ships, an experience that would serve him well more than two decades later when he converted freighters into gunboats for Brazil. In the meantime, he sent munitions to Brazil in the 1880s and, in 1891, secured arms for Peru's former enemy, Chile, when President Balmaceda unsuccessfully struggled to put down a naval revolt.[17]

Equally important, Flint had considerable standing in the United States. He was one of the most influential members of the U.S. delegation to the 1889 Pan American Congress and one of the principal architects of the reciprocity provision of the 1891 McKinley Tariff, which sought to open Latin American markets to U.S. goods. The merchant also demonstrated his pull with the State Department in 1891. Employing Pinkerton detectives, he tipped off Secretary of State James Blaine that Flint's former partners, the Graces, were supplying arms to the Chilean rebels aboard the ship *Itata*. Convincing the secretary of state to send a navy cruiser to seize the cargo, Flint simultaneously himself armed Chile's legal government.[18] The merchant was well versed in covert operations. He had his own personal telegraph line to Brazil that functioned better than those of the New York newspapers, which often relied on him for information. He frequently employed Pinkerton detectives and was not adverse to spreading money around generously to win desired favors. In short, he was a seasoned and ruthless competitor.

Flint also understood the value of overt propaganda campaigns. He had his own well-greased publicity organ. Earlier, he cooperated closely with the New York press in securing U.S. recognition of Brazil's republic, and played a large role in appointing and directing the Pan American Union's publicity director, William Curtis.[19] In 1893 Flint took control more directly of an important news vehicle when he led a syndicate that bought up the ailing *New York Times*. Flint made it clear that this was only secondarily a business venture. He wanted the paper in order to bend it to pet causes such as the gold standard and Peixoto's regime. Typical of Flint's behind-the-scenes maneuvering, he hid his reorganization of the *Times* from the public to the extent that the newspaper's own seventy-fifth anniversary edition neglected to mention him by name. However, Iphigene Ochs Sulzberger, daughter of Adolf S. Ochs and wife of Arthur Hayes Sulzberger (who together ran the paper between 1896 and 1935), remembered years later that "my one childhood recollection was overhearing some talk about an 'angel' named Charles Flint." She was later disappointed to find him "just a short man with a pointed beard and no wings at all." [20]

But though he had no wings, the New York trader enjoyed powerful international political connections that helped him get this undertaking off the ground. Flint's ties to Latin America began in his early years as a partner in the New York–Peruvian trading company of W. R. Grace and perhaps reached back to his own family's involvement in the Caribbean shipping trade. He had been consul for Costa Rica and Nicaragua, served as an agent for the Peruvian government, and was named consul general for Chile to the United States under President Balmaceda in 1891. His brother Wallace was consul for Uruguay.[21] Flint had also operated as the de facto consul for Brazil in 1890, as he often spoke to the press in Mendonça's name when the minister was absent or incapacitated by illness.

In addition to being a politically well-connected arms dealer, Flint was an important financier with close ties to haute finance. He was a business associate of Jacob Schiff, August Belmont, and J. P. Morgan, and had often gone hunting in Maine with one of the principals of the British financial house of Baring, the U.S. Navy's overseas financial agent for matériel purchases.[22]

Flint later took advantage of these ties to finance the Brazilian fleet. Because he could not easily procure North American credit in these days of deep economic depression, he had to seek a loan in Europe from the Rothschilds.[23] This was a rather natural source since N. M. Rothschild had been the Brazilian government's sole financial agent for more than forty years. It is only surprising in light of Brazilian republicans' suspicions that the Rothschilds were actively working to overthrow the republic.[24] Of course this was not necessarily a contradiction. If the London bankers were in fact aiding the rebels, it would not have been the first time that a company sought to profit from both sides of a conflict.

Flint, then, was experienced, ruthless, powerful, crafty, *and* available. It should be stressed, however, that he was a businessman, not a cultural crusader. He did not really fit the definition of an intercultural mediator. He spoke no Portuguese, and indeed had not left the United States in more than a decade. His worth came in his ability to maneuver in the United States and to convince others that his services and goods were valuable. Flint operated out of personal friendship to Mendonça and, more important, the desire to profit from good relations with the new republican administration in Rio. He was angling for concessions in Manaus and a favored position in the rubber trade. But he had no special love for republicanism. He sold ships to the czar of Russia and the emperor of Japan as well as to South American republicans. As an arms dealer, political consultant, and businessman he was dedicated to his clients and his firms, not ideals or cultural understanding.

Flint Assembles a Fleet

Unable to purchase warships from governments, and with too little time to construct new ones, Flint sought out Collis P. Huntington, who owned a large commercial fleet and was a director of the United States and Brazil Mail Steamship Company. Flint then purchased the 400-foot-long, 4,600-ton passenger liner *El Cid*.[25] Huntington readily sold Flint his newest, fastest steam liner at cost, probably because the shipper hoped to win favor with Peixoto's government to benefit two of his transport companies. The financially troubled USBMSC, which had a major subsidy from the Brazilian government, went into receivership in March 1893 after the failure of its president's attempt to extend the concession in Brazil.[26] There was still hope of resurrecting the company with Brazilian assistance, however.

The shipping magnate Huntington was not the only connection between Flint's Fleet and the USBMSC. Its president, William Ivins, had been a boyhood friend of Flint's, a partner with him in the Grace Company, and a stockholder in Flint's commercial company. Ivins was put in charge of the propaganda campaign for the mercenary fleet.[27] G. A. Burt, an important official of the shipping firm, served as Flint's recruiter and sailed to Brazil as his troubleshooter.[28] The captain of the converted *El Cid*, H. Baker, had skippered ships for the steamship company.[29] Other USBMSC employees served as navigators, accountants, and the surgeon for Flint's Fleet.[30] The "dynamite fleet" was converted to war use at the Morgan shipyard, which had belonged to the founder of the steamship line, John Roach. Ingratiating themselves with Peixoto's regime should have appealed to Huntington and employees of the shipping company: all stood to gain from the marshal's reciprocal gratitude.

Moreover, Flint and Huntington had another common interest in Brazil. At almost the same time that he was purchasing the ship from Huntington, Flint was proposing that the two men join with several other "leading express-men of this city" to extend "the express business of the United States into South and Central America." Flint reassured Huntington that "with certain governments I think I could exert considerable influence in securing desirable concessions." [31]

Flint's Fleet was brought together with great fanfare. Flint intentionally made purchases and overtures that would spark the public imagination and convince Congress and the U.S. Navy of the strength and munificence of Peixoto's government. The extravagant theater of constructing a fleet in New York was intended to capture the attention and attract the favor of the U.S. audience for the war effort thousands of miles away in Brazil. Not only Flint's *New York Times,* but newspapers all over the country breathlessly rumormongered that Flint would purchase some of the biggest, fastest, most advanced, and most luxurious ships in the United States. Flint made it his "custom" to feed this speculative frenzy by refusing "to deny or confirm any of these reports." [32] The *New York Times* boasted that, "in the opinion of many naval officers in New York," *El Cid,* after being fitted out for war, "will be the superior to any vessel in the United States Navy of her tonnage class." [33] The *Times* also boasted that not only was *El Cid* "the fastest American-built merchant steamer afloat," but she was "also the fastest vessel of her class in the world." [34] The *New York Herald* chimed in that, once armed, the converted freighter would have "a battery that may make her a match for the whole naval force commanded by the Brazilian insurgent, Admiral Mello," an evaluation carried by the *San Francisco Chronicle* as well.[35] The second cruiser Flint purchased, the *Britannia,* was, according to the *New York Herald,* the fastest, largest, and most luxurious ship ever built in Norway: "There are few more elegantly fitted up passenger ships afloat." [36] The *Destroyer* had a more appropriately fierce appellation. This 130-foot submarine was built by the same Ericcson company that had built the *Monitor* of Civil War fame. Based on the same principle, the state-of-the-art *Destroyer* had a single revolving cannon in its turret and could almost fully submerge to fire its experimental underwater torpedoes.[37] The *Feiseen,* a new seventeen-ton wooden yacht that would be converted into a torpedo boat, had set a speed record of twenty-seven knots. Flint added a new sixty-ton Yarrow torpedo boat, the thirty-ton yacht *Javelin,* which had been his own personal pleasure craft, and five new torpedo boats from the German Schichau Company.[38]

Flint maximized press coverage while mounting his fleet by making overtures to many other steamship companies as well as to some of the richest, best-known men in the country. Flint took out options on five other ships (which formerly had belonged to the USBMSC) now belonging to Huntington and Charles Pratt of Standard Oil.[39] Reports circulated that Flint was negotiating for the private yachts of James Stillman of National City Bank, Jay Gould of railroad fame, and financier J. P. Morgan. Although none of these were actually purchased, the rumors added glamour to the mercenary enterprise and sparked the imagination of devotees of society-page gossip.[40]

The mercenary squadron also won public attention by arming its ships with some of the most sophisticated and, in some cases, audacious experimental weapons in existence. Flint went to the length of taking the long train ride from New York to Chicago to buy a dozen Hotchkiss rapid-fire guns off the glistening showroom floor of the renowned Columbian Exposition. By far the most popular fair in U.S. history to that point, the Columbian Exposition was a vast theater of technology, where the latest military hardware was proudly displayed to the admiring crowds as a pronouncement of U.S. racial superiority and rising world power. For Flint, tying his expedition to the Great White City made eminent sense. He was extending across the Atlantic the optimistic Midwestern celebration of U.S. technological mastery, its virile ability to transform a barren prairie into a towering metropolis. In other publicity gestures to the crowds, Flint also purchased Howell torpedoes, and an invention of Thomas Edison— the Sims-Edison submarine electrical fish torpedo (called "submarine terrors" by the *San Francisco Chronicle*)—as well as a submarine gun. None of these had ever been tested in actual warfare.[41]

The most spectacular acquisition was the pneumatic gun, known as the dynamite gun. It fired dynamite projectiles as large as 980 pounds; with smaller shells, it had a three-mile range. Developed by a naval gunner, Captain E. L. Zalinski, the gun had been undergoing tests for years. Naval gun trials in the 1890s, like rocket launches in the 1960s, attracted large crowds and much press attention. Americans knew about the amazing new gun; it also aroused international interest. The German, Italian, Russian, Spanish, and French governments considered purchasing pneumatic guns. The U.S. Navy had built one experimental ship, the *Vesuvius,* to carry dynamite guns and ordered twelve guns for coastal defense. So far, trials had proven inconclusive aboard ship; the gun was not consistently accurate. Further tests had been canceled by the navy because of budget constraints brought on by a swelling economic depression. Naval experts were anxious to test it in live combat and welcomed the opportunity to arm Flint's Fleet. The *New York Herald* reported that if the gun proved to be a success in actual battle it would revolutionize naval warfare and the construction of warships all over the world.[42] Clearly, Flint's small fleet had succeeded in raising large expectations.

It may be that Flint and Mendonça's costly purchases were also driven by the profit motive. They were attacked in the United States and Brazil for their extravagance and were accused of war profiteering.[43] It is likely that Mendonça did in fact receive three-quarters of the profits. There is a contract to that effect in the Flint papers, but, suspiciously, the name of the beneficiary has been torn out of the document.[44] Total profits could have been as much as $312,000, a very substantial sum given that Mendonça's annual salary as minister for Brazil was under $10,000.[45] On the other hand, Mendonça denied receiving any income outside of his government salary. He attributed his fine art collection and summer house to personal savings from his salary.[46]

Whether profit was a strong motive or not for the composition of the fleet, certainly the urge to maximize publicity drove many of the purchases. Said Flint: "It was important that the new fleet should have prestige. I hoped that it would have so much prestige that no one would want to fight it." [47] The fleet was purchased and converted for war between the end of October and early December 1893, precisely the time that Secretary of State Gresham and President Cleveland began leaning toward recognizing the belligerency status of Brazil's naval rebels. Their decision was crucial to Peixoto's government. For the first time, the United States New Navy, in the form of five new cruisers, had been deployed in Rio's Guanabara Bay to show the stars and stripes and defend U.S. merchantmen. Officially remaining neutral, the United States had refused entreaties by British and Portuguese officials to recognize the naval rebels and thereby allow them to blockade Rio's harbor. Since the U.S. ships were, in the words of Portuguese commander Augusto Castilho, "five of the largest, most modern and most powerful cruisers" then afloat, the European forces abided by Washington's decision, all the while maintaining their support for the insurgents.[48] But Gresham and the U.S. commander in Brazil began to waver because Peixoto's position seemed hopeless.[49] Flint's Fleet's objective was to appear as the knight in shining armor that would interest the North American public in general, weapons manufacturers and U.S. naval officers in particular, and especially the U.S. government in supporting Peixoto's government. The fleet's actual performance in battle was a secondary consideration for its architects.

For the sake of publicity, Flint established a literary bureau to publish propaganda favorable to the squadron. It was headed by the North American William Ivins, a law partner of former secretary of the navy Benjamin Tracy and an important figure in New York politics, as well as head of the USBMSC. Flint gloated years later, "As there was censorship of all cables, we controlled the news from Brazil and Ivins fed out the news in the proportion of about one inch of news for six inches of propaganda describing the dynamite squadron." [50] Mendonça at the same time published numerous articles in U.S. newspapers appealing to the adventurous and explaining the patriotic goals of defending the Monroe Doctrine.[51]

The conversion of *El Cid* to a man-of-war at the Morgan shipyard in Brooklyn, where three shifts worked around the clock, was guaranteed to attract hundreds of onlookers and journalists. This was a very popular imperial entertainment. The circus atmosphere created such a crush that the police had to intervene. Journalists became so enamored of the project that Flint delightedly recalled a decade and a half later, "I could have manned the ships with newspaper men and put a literary battery behind the guns, so anxious were the knights of the press to accompany an expedition that so appealed to their sense of humor." [52] Reporters from the *New York Herald,* the *New York World,* and the Associated Press did in fact ship out with the fleet.[53] Overseas war correspondents were quite new to the United States, which had been connected by telegraph to Europe for less than three decades and to Latin America for less than two. Their reports were privileged in newspapers. Hence, humorous though this expedition may have appeared, the words that this "literary battery" fired off were arguably more important in winning over the U.S. government to Peixoto's side than were the cannon blasts of the Brazilian army.

At the same time, contracts were dangled before various U.S. companies to build a constituency. The *London Times* reported that "large orders for arms and ammunition for the contending forces in Brazil have been placed in the United States, giving work to various New England factories." [54] As mentioned, the Hotchkiss, Pneumatic Torpedo and Construction, Sims-Edison, and Howell Companies benefited. Dupont won a substantial contract for dynamite and gun cotton, and Winchester for ammunition. Mendonça had many other industrial suitors including a big western iron company.[55] The Morgan shipyard also profited. While these firms did not constitute the powerful military-industrial lobby they would during World War I and afterward, they did have the ear of influential men in Congress and in the navy.

In fact, impressing the U.S. Navy's high command with the seriousness of this expedition was probably one of Flint's primary goals. By rapidly converting merchantmen to gunboats and fitting out the ships with the most advanced experimental weapons, Flint was providing the U.S. Navy with combat trials. This was a time of great innovation in weaponry, but the United States lagged far behind the Europeans in experimentation; indeed, they generally waited for Europeans to conduct trials. And there had been no major naval engagements to battle test equipment since Austria fought Italy and the United States fought itself in the Civil War almost thirty years earlier.[56] The mercenary squadron's impending engagement was therefore anxiously awaited. *Scientific American* observed that "the preparing, equipping and arming of this fleet has excited much interest, and especially among naval men." [57]

Mendonça recognized the U.S. Navy's "scientific" interest in his enterprise from the outset. That is why he chose a technical staff composed of high-ranking officers who were able to convince the navy to allow Flint to purchase gunpowder, torpedoes, and even the dynamite gun, all of which the service had originally contracted.[58] As Mendonça noted, military hardware "is not for sale like a commodity and ordinarily is only manufactured on the orders and at the expense of governments." [59] Only the "goodwill" of the U.S. government allowed Brazil to assemble Flint's Fleet quickly. Indeed the navy's assistance went beyond redirecting war matériel to Flint. Secretary of the Navy Herbert also allowed Brazil to purchase the *Destroyer,* which had been commissioned by the navy and was undergoing final tests before being incorporated into the U.S. fleet.[60]

The United States went yet further in aiding Peixoto's cause, when it allowed Flint to recruit sailors for his squadron in New York. With grand promises of high pay (sailors received a $500 signing bonus plus $100 per month, while officers received $5,000 per three months), the arms merchant was able to attract over 1,000 eager applicants for the 400 positions.[61] It is no surprise that Flint's offer proved so seductive. The average *annual* income of a textile worker in 1890 was $332. Flint's U.S. and Brazil steamship line had paid sailors only $5 a month.[62]

Flint attracted a capable crew. Nearly one-half of *El Cid*'s crew and many of the men on other ships had reportedly served in the U.S. Navy. Indeed, the *New York Times* boasted that this Brazilian squadron had a greater percentage of North Americans in its crew than any ship in the U.S. Navy since the Civil War, which is possibly true.[63]

Some of the men in Flint's Fleet had high standing in the navy.[64] The captains of the ships and many of the officers were Annapolis men. Some had inherited influence, such as W. A. Russel, who was nephew to Rear Admiral Russel, while others had personal influence, such as the inventor of the dynamite gun, Captain E. L. Zalinski. Because of illness, Zalinski could not sign on for the voyage to Brazil, but he did accompany *El Cid* for initial gunnery practice supposedly at the exorbitant pay of $15,000 for one month's service. And yet others were famous for their bravery. Josh Slocum, an early-day seafaring Charles Lindbergh who had already crossed the Atlantic single-handedly and would later become the first man to circumnavigate the world solo, was first officer and navigator of the *Destroyer*.[65] The presence of fellow navy men on Flint's Fleet helped win over members of the U.S. Navy, who to that point had tended to be partial to the Brazilian naval rebels in their battle against the army. As the *New York Times* observed, "Their [the Annapolis men's] performances at Rio will be closely watched by their friends in the United States Navy." [66]

The *St. Louis Post-Dispatch* saw Flint's Fleet as a precursor of a sort of Latin American minor league where North American sailors were battle tested in the constant disputes that broke out there: "The young American seamen who receive their baptism of fire in Brazilian waters may be useful in Uncle Sam's wars that are to come. The South American and Central American republics will perhaps be utilized more in the future as training schools for our soldiers and sailors. As patrons of our ship dealers and arms and ammunition manufacturers, as well as tutors of our fighters, they may gradually become indispensible to us." [67] The "wars that are to come" to which the paper referred were probably not Latin American conflicts, but rather struggles with Great Britain that appeared to loom very near in 1893. Certainly aid to Brazil itself was not the principal issue of interest. Rather, this was a training run for future U.S. efforts to project itself as a world power.

The hiring of North American sailors to serve on Brazilian warships was probably illegal and certainly, as Flint recognized, a breach of international custom. U.S. government officials, though very much aware of the recruiting, ignored its legal implications until two men (apparently agents of the Brazilian insurgents) brought suit against Flint and Mendonça in New York. They charged that the hirings were in violation of U.S. neutrality laws, which forbade the recruitment of people for war in a country with which the United States was at peace.[68] Certainly such a construction of the law was reasonable. Given Cleveland's protests of neutrality and his reputation for seeking to avoid an aggressive foreign policy, one would have expected the North American court to prevent Flint's undertaking. But Cleveland was, in fact, not neutral. The New York district attorney ruled that there was no violation of law and refused to prosecute the case. (It probably did not hurt Flint's cause that his head of publicity, William Ivins, had recently been advocate general of New York state and was a partner in the law firm of Thomas Platt, one of the two most important politicians in New York.) Turned down in New York, the two men appealed to Cleveland. His cabinet met and decided to take no action.[69]

Flint's Fleet Departs for Brazil

Flint's Fleet was gathered, the ships converted, and the crews hired in record time. Two months after Flint began this adventure, the mercenary squadron was ready to leave New York. The pace was demanded by the exigencies of politics and publicity. (As they would later sadly discover, to make the fleet truly battle-ready—rather than simply giving it a ferocious appearance—would have required more time.) Now it was time to christen the ships. Years later, Flint recalled the quixotic edge of this ceremony, presided over by Brazil's minister, conducted by Mrs. Flint, and raptly attended by hundreds of onlookers: "The only odd feature was that there was not a man aboard the ship who had ever seen the flag before, or who could speak the language of the country for which he was faring forth so gallantly to fight." [70] Flint made no pretense of Brazilian patriotism; this was a business deal, pure and simple. The dynamite crew steeled themselves with ditties that boasted of their bravery in their battle against the Brazilian insurgent admiral, Custodio de Mello, and confessed their ignorance:

> Mello, Mello, where are you, old fellow?
> A Yankee ship and a Yankee crew is out to the sea to look
> for you.
> To knock you all to hell-o.
> We fly a flag of orange and green, Sir,
> the likes of which we've never seen, Sir.
> Our good ship's name, we cannot tell it.
> We haven't had time to learn to spell it.
> But what has a flag and a name to do
> With a Yankee ship and a Yankee crew that out on the sea
> to look for you
> To knock you all to hell-o.[71]

Ideals had nothing to do with this adventure. Neither did knowledge. The crews' masculine bravery and Yankee superiority would suffice to "knock to hell-o" any Latin, no matter who it was. As they would later painfully demonstrate, many of the crew had no more respect for the Brazilian officers on "their" side than they had for the "enemy."

The crew stumbled over their ships' names because the originals were converted to more fitting Brazilian names, mostly of indigenous origins (demonstrating florianista Lusophobia). Once the fleet steamed out of New York's harbor, it had to win over the Brazilian nationalist public as much as U.S. policymakers. Since Flint's Fleet's symbolic impact had been more important than its war-making ability from the outset, Peixoto was doubtlessly concerned about the symbolism of the ships' new names for the Brazilian audience. (He who pays calls the tune, or, in this case, names the ships.) The *Destroyer* became the *Piratinin;* the Yarrow boat became the *Moxoto,* the *Javelin* the *Poty.* More symbolically, the *Britannia* was changed first to the *America,* as the United States—linguistically, at least—eclipsed the British. Once in Brazil its name was changed again to the *Andrada,* presumably to honor a hero of Brazilian independence. Perhaps most significantly, the jewel of the fleet, the dynamite-gun-carrying *El Cid,* was renamed the *Nictheroy.* Her new name not only commemorated the capital city of Rio de Janeiro state, badly battered by the naval rebels, but it also recalled another mercenary fleet that had helped Brazil in a time of crisis.[72]

That other mercenary fleet had come to Brazil's aid shortly after the Portuguese colony declared independence in 1822. The Portuguese had sent a huge convoy of 13 warships and about 70 transports and merchant ships carrying some 5,000 troops and vast stores of military matériel to the ex-colonial capital of Bahia, to recapture the ex-colony. But before arriving, this awesome fleet received news that the English mercenary Lord Cochrane, who had already won impressive battles against the Spanish off the coast of Chile and Peru, was now commanding a Brazilian squadron that was sailing to engage it. The Portuguese fled for Lisbon rather than landing their men. Cochrane's reputation inspired such fear that the Portuguese commanders did not pause to observe that the Englishman was chasing them with a motley squadron of just nine ships. During the crossing back to Lisbon, three-quarters of the Portuguese fleet were sunk by the mercenaries; the last four ships were burned at the mouth of the river Tagus by a Brazilian ship commanded by another English captain, John Taylor. The name of his ship? The *Nictheroy.*[73]

Now Peixoto was hoping that another hired fleet, formed by another mercenary who had helped wage naval warfare in Chile and Peru, could compensate for its small size and numbers by the international reputation of its crew and its exotic weapons of destruction. In the marshal's mind, the naval rebels probably represented the Portuguese, trying to restore an exhausted political regime, while Flint was a latter-day Cochrane. (In this bourgeois age, the arms dealer had become as important as the naval warrior.) But in the sequel to Cochrane's successful raid, the North Americans replaced the British as the defenders of Brazilian sovereignty.[74]

Misadventures on the Road to Rio

Flint's Fleet would have to traverse the South Atlantic and join the battle, while rumors raged of de Mello's plots to intercept the fleet on the high seas. Fear of attack and sabotage shadowed the voyage south. There had already been numerous reports of rebel efforts to thwart the departure of the mercenary squadron.[75] A journalist on board reported that the "officers and men expected Mello at every moment. Every bay and inlet was watched with suspicion. Quarters were sounded every time a sail was sighted on the horizon."[76] To prevent disaster, the U.S. Navy's armed cruiser *New York* received secret orders to accompany the mercenaries on their trip.[77] Because the loyalty of the northeastern Brazilian state of Pernambuco was in doubt, the *Nictheroy* first landed in the northern state of Ceará before ascertaining the safety of Pernambuco.[78]

The assembling and staffing of the fleet had proved much easier and faster than would readying the men and bringing the ships into the theater of battle. Almost three months passed from that rousing day when Mendonça baptized the *Nictheroy* before the dynamite squadron faced insurgent Admiral Saldanha da Gama's men across Rio de Janeiro's Guanabara Bay. What took so long?

The particulars are clear enough. Some of the fleet, the *Andrada* and the *Piratinin,* had mechanical trouble in the crossing. The *Andrada* had to put into port at Martinique for repairs, while the *Piratinin* limped into Pernambuco to be fixed. The ships also had disciplinary problems with the crews. When the *Nictheroy* arrived in Recife, some sixty of her crew were in irons.[79] Crews of other ships proved even more truculent. These fighting men were not particular about whom they fought with, their comrades and officers included. In a long, baleful letter, the U.S. consul in Recife, David Burke, bitterly protested that "a very large number of the crew since they landed here [1 Jan.] have been drunk and disorderly on and about the streets disgracing themselves, fighting amongst themselves and a reproach and a shame and a scandal to our country and to American citizens residing here."[80] The Yankee "saviors" did not appear as goodwill ambassadors or missionaries of American civilization to the disgusted citizenry of Recife. They were just another group of loud, drunken sailors.

Many of the mercenary crew became disillusioned with this adventure and declined to sign on with the Brazilian navy to enter combat. This was true for about sixty of the *Nictheroy*'s men. Some of the dissidents distrusted the ships; others despised the Annapolis officers. Yet others desisted because they refused to be subject to the Brazilian officers who boarded in Recife. Although racism no doubt played a role for some of them, resistence to authority in general seems to have motivated many. Insubordination was a common feature of all navies at the time, in the United States, Brazil, and Great Britain. The discharged crew members were given passage by the Brazilian government back to New York, where some tried, unsuccessfully, to claim wages they believed Flint's office owed them.[81]

Clearly Peixoto was unhappy with many of the New York recruits and refused their services.[82] His problem was that the fleet, rather than impress U.S. opinion for whom it had been assembled, now had to appeal to his nationalist supporters, as well as to the large share of Brazilians undecided between the dictatorial marshal and his naval adversaries. Peixoto had to demonstrate both that his government was sufficiently strong militarily to stand up to the rebels, and that it defended national sovereignty better than the rebels whom he accused of being agents for the Portuguese and the British. A fleet manned by North Americans and Europeans could aid rebel propaganda. Nationalist resentment of foreign sailors encouraged him to seek Brazilians.[83] But distrust of his own navy left him with few alternatives. He reportedly could find no volunteers in Recife, so his recruiters were consigned to "forcibly enter houses and take them." [84] The crew that they shanghaied consisted of clerks, artisans, farmers, and longshoremen. Peixoto resorted to army officers to complement the remaining Annapolis graduates and the few Brazilian naval officers willing to serve him.[85]

Despite Peixoto's dismay at the disorderliness of some of the recruits from New York, it should be noted that on the most important ship, the *Nictheroy,* 170 of the original crew, including all but one of the officers, signed on with the Brazilian navy. Captain Baker continued to command the ship.[86] The North Americans were useful not only because they were difficult to replace with trustworthy Brazilians and because of the interest they engendered in the United States, but also because they had been trained in the use of the dynamite gun. Captain Baker, in particular, was retained because he was a close friend of Admiral Saldanha da Gama, who respected and feared the ability of the *Nictheroy*'s skipper.[87] Baker's command added seriousness and legitimacy to the *Nictheroy.*

The *Nictheroy* arrived in Recife on 14 December, but it had a long wait for the *Andrada* to make port and for the *Piratinin* to be repaired. By the middle of January all of Flint's Fleet had gathered in Recife. They were joined there by five German torpedo ships, whose German captains and crew were replaced by Brazilians. Naval experts were surprised that the small boats were able to cross the heavy Atlantic seas they encountered.[88] Peixoto found no active admiral sufficiently trustworthy to direct this expedition. Instead, he had to turn to a fifty-nine-year-old retired Brazilian commandant, Jeronymo Gonçalves, who had never commanded anything larger than a small river expedition and had been retired ten years earlier for insubordination and a slow promotion rate. (Jacobins claimed that he was retired for his republicanism.)[89] He now brought a ragtag squadron of seven small monitors, corvettes, torpedo boats, and gunboats together with three merchantmen, joined it to Flint's Fleet, and took over command of the entire legal fleet.

Despite many false starts, the squadron remained in Recife until the middle of February. The apparent reluctance to join the battle in the south was in part explained by the fact that Recife was more than just a convenient rendezvous point. Flint's Fleet had been dispatched there in part to prevent rebels from taking the northeast.[90] This populous region had never embraced the republic. Pernambuco's elite seemed to favor the naval rebels, while the masses remained apathetic. By 22 November, Consul Burke could report that "restoration of monarchy is very strongly talked of privately among a very large class of Brazilians in this city." [91]

But Flint's Fleet delayed its departure for more pragmatic reasons as well. Until the reenlisting North Americans reached terms and the Brazilian government paid for the ships, they were not going south.[92] For the mercenaries, war was a business; they would not fight unless paid first. This, together with enlisting or impressing Brazilians to replace the undesirable mercenaries, took more than a month. Although the *Nictheroy* had been accepted the day after it arrived in port, the *Piratinin* and the *Andrada* had to be modified in Recife before the Brazilian government would accept them. Even in this time of crisis, when the Brazilian government's future was seriously at risk, its officials drove a hard bargain with its intended saviors.

Once the fleet was brought together, paid for, and staffed with relatively reliable crews, it still delayed its departure. The apparent lethargy of Flint's Fleet was puzzling and frustrating to Peixoto, whose regime hung in the balance.

Despite Flint's whimsical treatment of his fleet in his memoirs, it was not a comic or irrelevant sideshow in Brazil. The opinion of North American historians notwithstanding, U.S. Admiral Benham had not broken the naval revolt in Rio de Janeiro with his New Navy men-of-war at the end of January 1894. He had only broken the rebel blockade. Indeed, many thought Peixoto's government on the verge of collapse in February. The rebel Federalists from the southern state of Rio Grande do Sul overran the neighboring state of Paraná at about the same time, creating "an indescribable panic" in Rio and frightening Paulistas who stood on Paraná's border.[93] Even rebel Admiral da Gama believed that five thousand federalist troops were about to attack the São Paulo frontier. At the beginning of February, Colonel Jardim of the army wrote to Peixoto from São Paulo, alarmed that if the legal squadron did not arrive soon, the Federalists would attack the government's weakly fortified positions by sea as well as land.[94] In mid-January a U.S. officer had inspected the insurgent *Tamandere* and found her "abundantly supplied with ammo" as well as with "plenty of food." [95] Five weeks later, the *New York Times* reported that the naval rebels in Guanabara Bay had sufficient food and arms to last for months, while as late as 19 February the *Baltimore Herald* editorialized that "there is no longer any doubt that the cause of the Brazilian insurgents is strong and may ultimately triumph." [96] Members of Peixoto's national guard were slowly changing sides and important officers were plotting to join the insurgents.[97] The largest battle of the revolt took place on 9 February, when five hundred rebels landed in the city of Niteroi and controlled it for a while. Although finally driven out, the insurgents demonstrated the threat they posed if they could be coupled with land troops.

Flint's Fleet, despite its mishaps and tardiness, played a crucial role in preventing the naval rebels and the Federalists from joining forces. Already, back in December, the insurgent leader de Mello had returned to Rio from the rebel stronghold in Desterro, Santa Catarina, without the intended reinforcements, because he feared encountering the *Nictheroy*.[98] When in January de Mello heard of the troubles Admiral Gonçalves was having with Flint's Fleet in the northeast, he sent the only two modern ships left to him, the *República* and the *Aquibadan,* north to intercept the legal forces.[99] But the *República* reportedly lost its steering a few hours out of Rio Bay and had to retreat for the rebel-held port of Paranagua for makeshift repairs. The *Aquibadan,* hearing that Flint's Fleet was finally headed south (the destination was unclear), also retreated to Paranagua, supposedly to protect the *República*.[100]

Although de Mello and other participants in the revolt, such as Admiral Alexandrino Alencar, argued that they had avoided clashing with the legal fleet out of strategic considerations, in fact, fear of the *Nictheroy*'s dynamite gun was probably their greatest concern. For all the subsequent deprecation of Flint's Fleet and its crew, the fact remained that the *Nictheroy* was almost as large as the *Aquibadan* and, more importantly, it was faster.

This was even truer now that the crippled *Aquibadan* had been unable to put in for repairs at any major naval yards, all held by the government.[101]

The insurgents were well aware of the dynamite gun. Da Gama had learned of the new weapon when he toured U.S. naval installations in 1889. He had predicted that the gun was "destined to revolutionize modern naval warfare" and had recommended that Brazil purchase two of them.[102] De Mello was apparently also in awe of the pneumatic cannon.

The "incomprehensible inaction" of the insurgent navy, which so troubled Admirals da Gama, Frederico Villar, and many others, can be explained by fear.[103] The propaganda machine engineered by Flint and Mendonça reached an audience as far south as Brazil. De Mello did not attempt to intercept Flint's Fleet on the high seas, did not take advantage of the mercenary fleet's disorganization in January, and did not seek it out, despite orders, in February. Several months later, de Mello would again demonstrate his reluctance to engage it. Clearly Flint's Fleet, paper tiger or not, lost in later accounts some of the awful threat it posed during the fighting. Historians later scoffed, but those who had to face her terrible guns and torpedoes shrank from becoming targets for the newfangled "secret weapons."[104] Even people on shore "were out of their wits as long as the *Nictheroy* was in their midst," complaining of insomnia and even retreating from the shoreline.[105]

Because of mechanical problems, brought on by both the haste of the conversion in New York and probably sabotage by rebel agents, the fleet only headed toward Rio during the beginning of March. In a remarkable coincidence, the fleet embarked on the same day that Peixoto conducted the national election for his presidential successor. Given that there is good evidence that the election was pressed on a reluctant President Peixoto by U.S. Admiral Benham, who in late January apparently held out his squadron's support in Guanabara Bay until he received promises that the vote would be carried out, chances are that Flint's Fleet's departure was also tied to the election of a new president.[106] The much-needed fleet was insurance that the marshal would be true to his word.

When the squadron arrived off Rio de Janeiro on 10 March 1894, the naval revolt was in decline but its fate was still in doubt. So much so, in fact, that Brazilian monarchist Joaquim Nabuco wrote to a friend the day the squadron steamed into Guanabara Bay that although he had long thought that Peixoto would be victorious, he now believed that the rebels would win.[107]

The arrival of Flint's Fleet convinced Peixoto to attempt to put an end to the naval revolt. The day after the fleet arrived, Peixoto informed the rebels that he would begin bombarding them with the full force of his batteries, which had been considerably strengthened in the preceding months. He recommended to the inhabitants of Rio that they flee or take other precautions.

Critics afterward sneered that the final act of the naval rebellion in Rio resembled comic opera. In fact, the citizens of Rio expected an enormous and bloody battle. One witness breathlessly recalled that "the exodus of the population assumed indescribable proportions." [108] Another recounted, "street cars became loaded with women, babies and bedding. Lines of mule carts, loaded in like fashion, passed through the streets, while men, with huge bundles on their heads and followed by their families, were seen everywhere in the main thoroughfares." [109] Everyone fled either to the temporary housing that the government had built out of harm's way or to the mountains surrounding the bay for a view of the impending pyrotechnical exposition.

The dynamite fleet, which Rio residents had been hearing about since November and whose arrival had been rumored since January, aroused great curiosity and even greater expectations. When the fleet anchored outside Guanabara Bay on 10 March, crowds of *cariocas* crammed the streetcars to go out and see it. Two days later, in a demonstration test, the dynamite gun successfully hit a target two miles away, impressing onlookers. When the fleet finally entered the bay at 4:00 PM on 13 April, it was greeted by a twenty-one-gun salute and wild cheers. "It was a moment of true delirium." [110]

Flint's Fleet set out with the objective of firing three dynamite projectiles — 2,600 pounds of dynamite — at the rebel-held Villagaignon fort. The mere threat of the dynamite gun, which had already demonstrated its capacity in Pernambuco, was sufficient to induce da Gama and his forces to surrender. According to the surgeon aboard the *Nictheroy,* Peixoto ordered that the gun not be fired for fear that its "projectiles would result in great destruction and loss of life in Rio." [111] Five hundred thirty-two rebels quit ships and forts to seek refuge aboard two Portuguese cruisers escorted out of the bay by British men-of-war. The naval revolt was broken.[112]

The news of the defeat of the naval revolt had great repercussions. Paulistas celebrated the victory of the 13 April. Meanwhile, the Federalist forces led by Gumercindo Saraiva, which were poised on the Paraná border to launch an attack on São Paulo, retreated when news arrived that the naval revolt had been crushed.[113] The Federalists estimated that the revolt had tied down some 10,000 government troops in Rio. With these troops now free to march south to São Paulo, since the government once again controlled the seas, the rebels were forced to withdraw from the São Paulo border to Rio Grande do Sul.[114]

In Rio, Captain Baker and the North American crew retired from the *Nictheroy* with only one casualty among the original recruits—a soldier killed in a Rio brawl three days after the insurgents surrendered.[115] But this was not the end of the contribution of the mercenary fleet.

After several weeks respite, the fleet left Rio for Desterro, the capital of the rebel provisional government. There it captured de Mello's largest ship, the *Aquibadan,* which lay crippled. The *Nictheroy* fired the dynamite gun two times to test it and frighten the crew of the *Aquibadan,* but Peixoto did not want the rebel battleship (soon to become a government battleship once again) blown up. Instead, torpedoes tore a hole in her hull and the *Aquibadan*'s crew, along with her captain, abandoned her.[116] Government troops then disembarked at Desterro and initiated a campaign of terror.[117] Further to the south, in Rio Grande do Sul, de Mello heard that Flint's Fleet, triumphant in Rio, had now headed south. Afraid of encountering the *Nictheroy,* de Mello abandoned over two thousand troops who were attempting to take the key port city of Rio Grande do Sul. With the government back in control of the ports of Rio, Paranagua, and Desterro, de Mello had nowhere to go in Brazil. So he steamed his remaining ships to Uruguay, surrendered, and quit the war.[118] Although guerrilla fighting continued in Rio Grande do Sul for another year, the struggle receded to a local one. The threat to Peixoto's regime had ended.

Flint's Fleet Is Feted

When Flint's Fleet returned to Rio de Janeiro it was greeted with jubilation. The twenty-third of June was declared a national holiday in the fleet's honor as Peixoto and his generals, a congressional commission, and the municipal council of Rio turned out to fete the returning heroes.[119] Peixoto credited the fleet with ending the revolt in his speech to Congress on 7 May 1894: "It is appropriate that the national navy [mostly composed of Flint's Fleet], so tarnished by some of its members, should give the final blow to this revolt." [120] The insurgent Frederico Villar lamented, "History repeats itself." As in previous revolts, "without control of the seas" they could not win.[121] However, neither Peixoto nor any of the florianista or rebel historians of the naval revolt gave Flint or any other North Americans credit for the legal squadron.[122] Florianistas adamantly maintained the nationalist character of the defeat of the rebels: patriotic Brazilians had fended off the European-backed monarchist insurgents. Rebel sympathizers refused to believe that a spur-of-the-moment mercenary fleet had defeated the pride of the Brazilian navy.

Flint's Fleet was soon forgotten in the United States as well. President Cleveland, a strong advocate of small government and localism, was anxious to fight against the expansion of U.S. naval power and imperialism. Hence he stuck to the official story of U.S. neutrality in Brazil. But despite himself, Cleveland had set a precedent for expansion. Flint's Fleet and the New Navy crusiers in Guanabara Bay proved a dress rehearsal for the assertion of the aggressive Olney Doctrine in Venezuela the next year and the Spanish-American War three years later.[123] The *Nictheroy*, later sold to the U.S. Navy and rechristened the *U.S.S. Buffalo*, fought against the Spanish in the Philippines.[124]

Conclusions

It is difficult to evaluate the true fighting capacity of Flint's Fleet, since its mettle was never tried. As the squadron set off from New York, *Scientific American* had mused that, because of the untested experimental nature of so much of the weaponry, "no fleet ever sailed with more chances for and against its success than this provisional squadron." [125] The problems with machinery and weapons lent credence to critics' denunciation of the fleet's shoddy workmanship. But rebel sabotage probably also played a part. It is worth noting that most of the ships Flint purchased for Brazil remained in the Brazilian navy for more than a decade, and the American navy purchased the *Nictheroy*, testifying to the vessels' seaworthiness.

That the fleet did not militarily defeat the rebels, except to destroy the *Aquibadan*, does not indicate failure. It fulfilled its propaganda role wonderfully. North American public opinion was swayed to the side of Peixoto, and North American naval men were impressed by the success of the fleet.[126] Europeans interpreted Cleveland's tacit support for the adventure as U.S. backing for the Brazilian government, which undercut efforts to recognize the rebels.[127] Da Gama surrendered without a fight in part because he was well aware of the destructive power of the dynamite gun. And de Mello, aboard the *República*, and Alexandrino Alencar, the captain of the *Aquibadan*, so feared the mercenaries that they refused to pursue them in the northeast and fled when the fleet tracked them.

Flint's Fleet, combined with Benham's aggressiveness, had established the United States' commitment to the Monroe Doctrine and demonstrated

the myriad of ways it could be enforced. Private entrepreneurs and mercenaries, working with tacit and sometimes active federal support, had had
a significant role to play. Moreover, the adventure demonstrated an expansion of the Monroe Doctrine: the United States was opposed not only
to European recolonization, but also to European involvement in Latin
American affairs. Indeed, even a domestically inspired attempt to return
to what North Americans perceived as a European form of government,
monarchy, now came under the doctrine's aegis.[128]

This episode further cemented the bonds between the United States and
Brazil. In 1894, Peixoto, previously so aloof, sent a cavalry troop and a
representative to the U.S. minister on Washington's birthday to pay his respects. The Fourth of July was decreed a national Brazilian holiday and
immense fireworks displays commemorated the day. Ironically, some of
the fireworks left over from the celebration were fired for the inauguration of President Prudente de Morais on 15 November. The new Brazilian
president was greeted by the confused spectacle of a grand aquatic, pyro-
technic exposition featuring the Goddess of Liberty with the Brazilian
flag in one hand and the stars and stripes of the United States in the other.
That same day, the cornerstone to a monument to James Monroe and the
Monroe Doctrine was laid in Rio.[129] Given the likelihood that Admiral
Benham had brokered Morais's election and Flint's Fleet had assured it,
the display and the monument were appropriate for the inauguration. Brazil's congress also ordered a medal struck with Cleveland on one side and
Peixoto on the other, and municipalities in Amazonas and Santa Catarina
were named "Clevelandia." [130]

Both North American and Brazilian diplomats sought to strengthen their
nations' positions. The United States successfully projected its power into
international affairs; but at the same time, Brazilians demonstrated that an
alliance could be forged that did not carry with it dependence or subser-
vience. Washington won no economic or diplomatic concessions in return
for its assistance. The nascent imperialistic urge within the United States
was blocked in Brazil by pragmatic Brazilian nationalism.[131]

Finally, this rather bizarre adventure demonstrates the importance of
private forces, unofficial methods, and symbolic gestures in international
relations. Flint and Mendonça were able to contribute considerably to
changing the direction of Brazilian history using spectacle as a show of
the appearance of force. Conjuring up a fleet calculated to capture the
public, official, and naval imagination of the United States, the two men
staged their naval theater masterfully. They employed the most modern
(if untested) technology, so that the fleet's journey south would represent

Brazil's march into the twentieth century. So successful was their production that its fame reached the insurgents in Brazil, who believed the illusion of power and surrendered before testing it.

Almost as intriguing as this modernist imperial adventure itself is the fact that Flint's entire fleet, which had blared across the front pages of major U.S. newspapers and worried the foreign offices of the great powers, disappeared so completely from memory. For reasons of state and amour propre, neither the Grover Cleveland administration in the United States, publicly dedicated to a policy of international neutrality; the nationalist government of Peixoto; nor the defeated naval insurgents would officially acknowledge the key role played by Flint's Fleet. Because the mercenaries were so successful that they triumphed without firing their guns in anger or wreaking carnage, they were ignored by naval historians, who could take no strategic or technical lessons from the fleet. Born largely as a publicity measure, the fleet's success would ironically sink from public view because it did not remain useful as a symbol for any of the principals. For very different reasons, they all chose to forget. Absent from official transcripts, the squadron was easy to miss for diplomatic historians, who rely on government-to-government interactions for their interpretations of international relations, and for political historians, who too often trust politicians.

Its disappearance from memory, however, does not mean that this floating spectacle of U.S. imperial manliness was inconsequential or chimerical. The most advanced and ferocious of weapons, the dynamite gun, mounted on the elegant deck of a converted cruise liner, created not a ridiculous bastard as critics crowed, but rather a poetic symbol of the magical, transformative ability of spectacle. Flint was not a quixotic warrior looking backward to past martial feats, but a modern financier-technocrat looking to the future. The key was not the mercenary squadron's killing force, but its seduction of the imagination. As Flint's Fleet so aptly demonstrated, the illusion of power can produce real power, and publicity can be just as important as technology in the theater of war. Even if not consciously remembered, the symbolic arsenal of Flint's Fleet would continue to be deployed in the imperial adventures of the twentieth century.

Notes

I would like to thank the editors, especially Ricardo Salvatore, and Allen Wells for very helpful suggestions.

1. An earlier version of this essay appears in Steven C. Topik, *Trade and Gunboats: The United States and Brazil in the Age of Empire* (Stanford, Calif.: Stanford University Press, 1996).

2. For the treatment, or absence of treatment, of the fleet, see Moniz Bandeira, *Presença dos Estados Unidos no Brasil (Dois Séculos de História)* (Rio: Civilização Brasileira, 1967), 144; Edgard Carone, *A República Velha,* vol. 2, *Evolução Política* (São Paulo: DIFEL, 1974), 126; José Maria Bello, *A History of Modern Brazil,* trans. James Taylor (Stanford, Calif.: Stanford University Press, 1966), 129; Ronald Schneider, *"Order and Progress": A Political History of Brazil* (Boulder, Colo.: Westview, 1991), 76; Joseph Smith, *Illusions of Conflict; Anglo-American Diplomacy toward Latin America, 1865-1896* (Pittsburgh, Pa.: University of Pittsburgh Press, 1979), 255; idem, *Unequal Giants: Diplomatic Relations between the United States and Brazil, 1889-1930* (Pittsburgh, Pa.: University of Pittsburgh Press, 1991), 24, 25; Lawerence F. Hill, *Diplomatic Relations between the United States and Brazil* (Durham, N.C.: Duke University Press, 1932); and June Hahner, *Civilian-Military Relations in Brazil, 1889-1898* (Columbia: University of South Carolina Press, 1969).

3. A fascinating discussion of these rituals in the New World can be found in Patricia Seed's *Ceremonies of Possession* (New York: Cambridge University Press, 1996) and, for a quite different social formation, Clifford Geertz's *Negara: The Theatre State in Nineteenth-Century Bali* (Princeton, N.J.: Princeton University Press, 1980). For earlier forms of ritualized power, see Marcel Mauss, "L'Esquisse de la théorie de la magie," in *Sociologie et Anthropologie* (Paris: Presses Universitaires de France, 1950), and for a long-term discussion of spectacle and power, Jean Duvignaud, *Spectacle et Société* (Paris: Editions Denoel, 1970).

4. Lynn Hunt, *Politics, Culture, and Class in the French Revolution* (London: Methuen, 1984).

5. Michael Rogin, "Make My Day," in *Cultures of United States Imperialism,* ed. Amy Kaplan and Donald E. Pease (Durham, N.C.: Duke University Press, 1993), 508, 500. See also Susan Jeffords, "The Patriot System, or Managerial Heroism," in Kaplan and Pease, *Cultures of United States Imperialism,* 535-56. For the best-known postmodern treatment of the spectacle, see Guy Debord, *Society of the Spectacle,* trans. Donald Nicholson-Smith (New York: Zone Books, 1994), 13, which preceded Rogin's observation: the spectacle is not a deliberate distortion "or a product of the technology of the mass dissemination of images. It is far better viewed as a weltanschauung that has been actualized, translated into the material realm—a world view transformed into an objective force."

6. This episode also could be seen as a continuation of the filibuster tradition of the 1850s, except that in the 1890s industrial and diplomatic interests were

more involved. For more on the concept of corporate liberalism, see Jeffrey R. Lustig, *Corporate Liberalism; the Origins of Modern American Political Theory, 1890–1920* (Berkeley and Los Angeles: University of California Press, 1982); and Martin Sklar, *The Corporate Reconstruction of American Capitalism, 1890–1916: The Market, the Law, and Politics* (New York: Cambridge University Press, 1988).

7. Debord, *Society of the Spectacle,* 19, points out, "At the root of the spectacle lies the oldest of all social divisions of labor, the specialization of power. The specialized role played by the spectacle is that of spokesman for all other activities, a sort of diplomatic representative of hierarchical society at its own court."

8. Salvador de Mendonça, *Ajuste de Contas* (Rio: Jornal do Commércio, 1899–1904), 159; Epaminondas Villalba, *A Revolta da Armada de 6 de Setembro de 1893* (Rio: Laemmert and Cia., 1894), 179–86; and Frederico Villar, *As Revoluçoes que Eu Vi (O Almirante Luiz Felipe de Saldanha da Gama),* vol. 160, Biblioteca do Exército (Rio: Gráfica Editora Aurora, n.d.), 81, 84. See also Francisco Barbosa's introduction to Sérgio Corrêa da Costa, *A Diplomacia do Marechal: Intervenção Estrangeira na Revolta da Armada* (Brasilia: Universidade de Brasilia, 1979), xvii; and Charles R. Flint, *Memories of an Active Life* (New York: G. P. Putnam's Sons, 1923), 100.

9. See Steven C. Topik, "Brazil's Bourgeois Revolution?" *The Americas* 48, no. 2 (Oct. 1991): 245–72.

10. Mendonça to Carlos de Carvalho, 23 Dec. 1894, in Missao Diplomática do Brasil no Estados Unidos (hereafter MDBEU), "Oficios 1893–1896," Arquivo Histórico de Itamaraty, Rio de Janeiro; and *New York Herald,* 15 Oct. 1893, sec. 6, p. 1.

11. Mendonça, *Ajuste de Contas,* 118. In the *St. Louis Dispatch* of 8 Nov. 1893 (p. 3), Mendonça estimated that outfitting the fleet would not exceed $1.5 million. The estimate is probably low.

12. *New York Times* (hereafter *NYT*), 29 Oct. 1893, 5.

13. Harold and Margaret Sprout, *The Rise of American Naval Power, 1776–1918* (Princeton, N.J.: Princeton University Press, 1939), 192.

14. Clipping in box 7, Flint papers, New York Public Library.

15. Lawrence A. Clayton, *W. R. Grace and Company: The Formative Years, 1850–1930* (Ottawa, Ill.: Jameson Books, 1985), 177–80, 196; Cyrus Eaton, *History of Thomaston, Rockland, and South Thomaston, Maine from Their First Exploration AD 1605; With Family Genealogies,* vol. 2 (Hallowell, Maine: Masters, Smith and Co., 1865), 227–29; and idem, "The Shipbuilders of Thomaston, VII: Flint and Chapman," *Log Chips* 2, no. 7 (July 1951): 73–76.

16. M. P. Grace to Flint, 2 Oct. 1882, box 58, Grace papers, W. R. Grace Archive, Columbia University, New York.

17. Flint had attempted to purchase the *U.S.S. Bennington* for Chile; see Flint to J. G. Blaine, 17 and 19 Mar. 1891, reel 11, James G. Blaine archive, Library of Congress; and Flint, *Memories,* 69, 81.

18. Clayton, *Grace,* 212, 213.

19. In a letter from New York dated 26 Nov. 1889, Arthur F. Bauer of the *New York Tribune* thanked Flint for helping a *Tribune* reporter "learn the exact truth about everything" (box 1, Flint papers).

20. Iphigene Ochs Sulzberger (as told to Susan W. Dryfoss), *Iphigene* (New York: Dodd, Mead, and Co., 1979), 25; *New York Times, Seventy-fifth Anniversary Edition*, 18 Sept. 1926, 5; Michael J. Devine, *John W. Foster: Politics and Diplomacy in the Imperial Age, 1873–1917* (Athens: Ohio University Press, 1981), 44; and J. Green to Flint, 20 Jan. 1893, and C. N. Miller to Flint, 16 Aug. 1893, in Flint papers.

21. William Wharton to Wallace B. Flint, 9 Mar. 1892, in box 1, Flint papers.

22. Jacob H. Schiff to C. R. Flint, 19 Jan. 1893, and August Belmont to Flint, 3 Feb. 1893, in Flint papers; and Glenn D. Babcock, *History of the United States Rubber Company* (Indianapolis: Indiana University Graduate School of Business, Bureau of Business Research, Indiana Business Report no. 39, 1966), 47.

23. Flint, *Memories*, 91. See also Felisbello Freire to N. Rothschild, 27 Oct. 1893, and Rothschild's reply of 8 Nov. 1893, in which they offer to "ask the friendly intervention of a neutral power," "Brazilian Government," XI-65-8B, N. M. Rothschild archive, London.

24. The *New York Herald* (8 Feb. 1894, sec. 8, p. 6) reported that the Rothschilds were funding the rebels.

25. Collis P. Huntington to Flint, 16 Oct. 1893, microfilm series 7, reel 52, Collis P. Huntington papers; and Flint, *Memories*, 96. According to Corrêa da Costa, the *World* had argued that Flint paid three times the worth of *El Cid*, while Huntington alleged that he charged $12,000 less than the vessel had cost him (*A Diplomacia do Marechal*, 282). See also Mendonça, *Ajuste de Contas*, 164; Villalba, *A Revolta da Armada*, 128; and *London Times*, 28 Oct. 1893, 5.

26. *NYT*, 22 Feb. 1893, sec. 2, p. 4; and 19 Mar. 1893, sec. 20, p. 5.

27. Statement of stockholders of Flint, Eddy, and the American Trading Company, box 6, Flint papers; M. Grace to Sears, 4 Mar. 1889 and 30 Aug. 1889, box 62, Grace papers; and *Dictionary of American Biography*, vol. 5, pt. 1, 522.

28. *New York Herald*, 4 Nov. 1893, sec. 3, p. 5; and Mendonça, *Ajuste de Contas*, 141.

29. Villalba, *A Revolta da Armada*, 126; and *NYT*, 29 Oct. 1893, 5.

30. The captain of the *Destroyer*, Guy Brick, had worked for Huntington's Pacific Mail Steamship Company (*NYT*, 27 Nov. 1893, sec. 5, p. 3). *Britannia*'s surgeon, Dr. Randall, had previously worked for the USBMSC (*NYT*, 12 Nov. 1893, sec. 5, p. 5).

31. Flint to C. Huntington, New York, 2 Nov. 1893, series 7, reel 52 (1856–1901), Huntington papers.

32. *St. Louis Dispatch*, 23 Nov. 1893, 1. I also found reports on the fleet's assembly in the *World, New York Herald, San Francisco Chronicle, Los Angeles Times, Fullerton Tribune*, and *Anaheim Weekly Gazette*.

33. *NYT*, 28 Oct. 1893, sec. 8, p. 3.

34. *NYT,* 27 Oct. 1893, sec. 1, p. 2. The *Marine Journal* reported on 23 Sept. 1893 that "the latest performance is that of the *El Cid* whose feat on her maiden voyage elicited well-deserved notices from the daily papers and caused no small comment at home and abroad" (Cerinda W. Evans, *Collis Potter Huntington,* vol. 2 [Newport News, Va.: Mariner's Museum, 1956], 609).

35. *New York Herald,* 28 Oct. 1893, 5; and *San Francisco Chronicle,* 28 Oct. 1893, 1.

36. *New York Herald,* 2 Nov. 1893, 8; and Flint memo, 1 Nov. 1893, box 4, Flint papers.

37. *Scientific American,* 2 Dec. 1893; Mendonça, *Ajuste de Contas,* 135; and *New York Herald,* 1 Nov. 1893, 9.

38. Villalba, *A Revolta da Armada,* 128–31; William Laide Clowes, *Four Modern Naval Campaigns, Historical, Strategical, and Tactical* (London: Unit Library, 1902), 195; *NYT,* 29 Oct. 1893, 5; and Flint, *Memories,* 92.

39. *New York Herald,* 1 Nov. 1893, 9.

40. *New York Herald,* 8 Nov. 1893, sec. 11, p. 5; *NYT,* 31 Oct. 1893, 5; and *NYT,* 2 Nov. 1893, sec. 5, p. 3.

41. *Scientific American,* 2 Dec. 1893; Flint, *Memories,* 96, 97; *New York Herald,* 27 Oct. 1893, sec. 7, p. 2, and 10 Nov. 1893, 7; *NYT,* 18 Nov. 1893, sec. 4, p. 4; and *San Francisco Chronicle,* 9 Nov. 1893, 1. For more on the Chicago Exposition, see Robert W. Rydell, *All the World's a Fair: Visions of Empire at American International Expositions, 1876–1916* (Chicago: University of Chicago Press, 1984).

42. The *New York Herald* (28 Oct. 1893, 5) noted that "One Aquibadan or Republica annihilated would be an object lesson in modern naval warfare that would be as startling to foreign naval powers as was the advent of the Monitor in 1861." See also the *San Francisco Chronicle,* 28 Oct. 1893, 1; and the *New York Herald,* 2 Nov. 1893, 8.

43. Carone, *A República Velha,* vol. 2, 126.

44. Contract in "Business Papers, 1894–1899" file, box 4, Flint papers.

45. Burke to Quincy, 20 Jan. 1894, in "Diplomatic Dispatches from United States Consuls to Pernambuco," National Archives; and *NYT,* 1 Mar. 1894, sec. 3, p. 1. The *NYT* (1 Nov. 1893, 1) estimated the cost of Flint's Fleet at $3 million, including six ships that Flint optioned but never actually purchased.

46. Mendonça, *Ajuste de Contas,* 174.

47. Flint, *Memories,* 96.

48. Augusto de Castilho, *Le Portugal et le Brésil; Conflit diplomatique* (Paris: L. Larose, 1894), 245.

49. For a detailed discussion of the role of the U.S. Navy in Guanabara Bay, see Topik, *Trade and Gunboats,* chap. 7.

50. Flint, *Memories,* 91. Some of the reporting of the revolt had mercenary rather than political ends. The Associated Press reporter invented stories because, he replied to a disgusted fellow journalist, "that is just the kind of stuff the 'Associated' wants" (*NYT,* 15 Apr. 1894, sec. 1, p. 6).

51. Flint, *Memories*, 91.

52. *Human Life*, June 1908 clipping in box 7, Flint papers. See also *New York Herald*, 13 Nov. 1893, sec. 4, p. 2.

53. Burke to E. F. Uhl, 11 Jan. 1894, "Diplomatic Dispatches to Pernambuco."

54. *London Times*, 27 Oct. 1893, 3.

55. *NYT*, 5 Nov. 1893, sec. 1, p. 4. Other orders came to the United States to outfit Peixoto's army. For example, a contract was signed for three thousand boots made in Rhode Island. Ironically, the boots were reportedly manufactured by inmates of the Rhode Island state prison (*New York Herald*, 4 Feb. 1894, sec. 9, p. 5).

56. Lance C. Buhl, "Maintaining 'An American Navy' 1865-1889," in *In Peace and War*, ed. Kenneth J. Hagan (Westport, Conn.: Greenwood Press, 1978), 148; and *Boston Journal*, in *Public Opinion* (hereafter, *PO*) 16, no. 16 (18 Jan. 1894): 377.

57. *Scientific American*, 2 Dec. 1893; and *NYT*, 9 Oct. 1893, sec. 1, p. 4.

58. Mendonça, *Ajuste de Contas*, 118.

59. Ibid., 117, 120.

60. Ibid., 117, 137.

61. Burke to Uhl, 11 Jan. 1894, "Diplomatic Dispatches to Pernambuco." Joaquim Nabuco's *A Intervenção Estrangeira durante a Revolta de 1893* (São Paulo: Companhia Editora Nacional, 1939), 233, claims that they were promised $5,000 if they lost one limb and $10,000 for two. The *NYT* (8 Nov. 1893, sec. 8, p. 1) reported that gunners were hired for $50 a day plus two months in advance and shipped out for a year.

62. Stevens to Quincy, 31 Aug. 1893, "Diplomatic Dispatches to Pernambuco"; and N. W. Aldrich, "The McKinley Act and the Cost of Living," in *Forum*, extracted in *PO* 14, no. 2 (15 Oct. 1892): 29.

63. *NYT*, 4 Nov. 1893, sec. 5, p. 1. According to the navy's Bureau of Navigation, in 1890 only 47 percent of the navy's men were native born and 58 percent were U.S. citizens (in Frederick S. Harrod, *Manning the New Navy: The Development of a Modern Naval Enlisted Force, 1899-1940* [Westport, Conn.: Greenwood Press, 1978], 17). See also Burke to Quincy, 11 Jan. 1894, "Diplomatic Dispatches to Pernambuco."

64. *NYT*, 8 Nov. 1893, sec. 8, p. 1; 9 Nov. 1893, sec. 5, p. 3; 17 Nov. 1893, sec. 7, p. 2; and 21 Nov. 1893, sec. 9, p. 3. See also *New York Herald*, 11 Nov. 1893, sec. 6, p. 6; and Mendonça, *Ajuste de Contas*, 144. James F. Vivian, in "United States Policy during the Brazilian Naval Revolt 1893-94: The Case for American Neutrality," *American Neptune* (Oct. 1981): 251, is wrong when he claims that the crew of Flint's Fleet numbered only 170 men. The *America* alone had that many men.

65. *NYT*, 14 Nov. 1893, sec. 1, p. 3; 19 Nov. 1893, sec. 1, p. 5; 21 Nov. 1893, sec. 1, p. 1; and 22 Nov. 1893, sec. 1, p. 1; *New York Herald*, 27 Nov. 1893, 5; and Mendonça, *Ajuste de Contas*, 142.

66. *NYT*, 9 Oct. 1893, sec. 1, p. 4. Compare this with the views of the monarchist Joaquim Nabuco, who wrote in *A Intervenção Estrangeira* (114) that the crew of Flint's Fleet constituted "the worst scum of Yankee filibusterism," or with

those of the leftist nationalist Moniz Bandeira, who also denounced the fleet's crew (*Presença*, 92) as "riff-raff" (*choldra*).

67. *St. Louis Post-Dispatch,* 11 Nov. 1893, 4.

68. See *New York Herald,* 3 Nov. 1893, 7, for section 5,282 of the United States Revised Statutes.

69. Report of Major W. J. C. Gadsby, 5 Jan. 1894, in MDBEU, "Oficios, 1893–1896"; *NYT,* 25 Nov. 1893, sec. 5, p. 4; Mendonça, *Ajuste de Contas,* 121; and *Dictionary of American Biography,* vol. 5, pt. 1, 522. See *NYT,* 17 Nov. 1893, sec. 1, p. 2, for the seamen's contract.

70. Flint, *Memories,* 99.

71. Ibid., 99.

72. I have come across no explanation for the choices of ship names. But the coincidence of the *Nictheroy* seems too great to have been fortuitous, given her sister ship *Andrada* (also known as the *America*), the great stock Peixoto put in symbolic titles, and the care with which he used words.

73. Leslie Bethell, "Independence," in *The Independence of Latin America,* ed. L. Bethell (New York: Cambridge University Press, 1987), 35, 36; and José Honório Rodrigues, *Independência, Revolução e Contrarevolução,* vol. 3 (Rio: Livraria Francisco Alves Editora, 1975–1976), 109, 125.

74. Peixoto did consult a descendant of Lord Cochrane about hiring mercenaries (Horace Smith, *The War Maker Being the True Story of Captain George B. Boynton* [Chicago: A. C. McClung and Co., 1911], 336).

75. Mendonça to Cassiano do Nascimento, 28 July 1894, MDBEU, "Ofícios, 1893–1896"; *Anaheim Weekly Gazette,* 16 Nov. 1893, 1; *Los Angeles Times,* 7 Nov. 1893, 1; *St. Louis Post-Dispatch,* 8 Nov. 1893, 3, and 9 Nov. 1893, 8; and *San Francisco Chronicle,* 13 Nov. 1893, 1.

76. *World,* 21 Jan. 1894, 13.

77. *NYT,* 9 Nov. 1893, sec. 5, p. 3.

78. *World,* 10 Jan. 1894, 7.

79. Burke to Quincy, 23 Dec. 1893, "Diplomatic Dispatches to Pernambuco"; *World,* 4 Jan. 1894; and Mendonça, *Ajuste de Contas,* 140.

80. Burke to Uhl, 13 Jan. 1894, "Diplomatic Dispatches to Pernambuco."

81. Burke to Quincy, 11 Jan. 1894 and 20 Jan. 1894, "Diplomatic Dispatches to Pernambuco"; and *NYT,* 23 Jan. 1894, sec. 9, p. 4.

82. He took on none of the *America*'s sailors and only one of the *Piratinin*'s. Burke to Quincy, 11 Jan. 1894, "Diplomatic Dispatches to Pernambuco"; and Mendonça, *Ajuste de Contas,* 142.

83. The *NYT* reported on 8 Jan. 1893 (sec. 1, p. 3) that longshoremen in Recife deserted barges used to coal the *Nictheroy* in order to join the insurgents.

84. Burke to Quincy, 20 Jan. 1894, "Diplomatic Dispatches to Pernambuco."

85. Villar, *As Revoluçoes,* 73; and *NYT,* 11 Feb. 1894, sec. 5, p. 1.

86. Burke to Uhl, 13 Jan. 1894, "Diplomatic Dispatches to Pernambuco." A dis-

patch from the *World's* reporter on board the *Nictheroy* (10 Jan. 1894, 7) reported that the ship took on some 200 Brazilians as well, 100 to 150 of them being cadets. The cadets were there as observers to learn about the vessel. The Brazilian commandant placed on board was only to supervise: "all orders will be given through her present officers."

87. Interview with Admiral da Gama in *NYT,* 16 Jan. 1894, sec. 3, p. 2.

88. "Professional Notes," in *Proceedings of the United States Naval Institute* 20, no. 2 (1894): 458.

89. Orozimbo Muniz Barretto, *Biografia do Almirante Jeronymo Francisco Gonçalves* (Rio de Janeiro: Typ. Leuzinger, 1894); and Brasil, Ministério da Marinha, Serviço de Documentaçao, *Almirante Jerônimo Gonçalves: Perfil do Herói, do Chefe Militar e do Cidadão* (Rio: Serviço de Documentação Geral da Marinha, 1962).

90. Flint, *Memories,* 91.

91. Burke to Quincy, 22 Nov. 1893, as well as dispatches of 11 and 15 Nov. 1893, "Diplomatic Dispatches to Pernambuco."

92. Burke to Quincy, 30 Dec. 1893, "Diplomatic Dispatches to Pernambuco."

93. Memorandum of General Solon in the Coleçao Solon, Instituto Histórico e Geográfico do Brasil, Rio de Janeiro, lata 614, pasta 19. Also see Pedro Dias de Campos, *A Revolta de Seis de Setembro (A Acção de São Paulo)* (Paris: Typ. Aillauld, Alves and Cia., 1913), 261.

94. Jardim to Peixoto, 3 Feb. 1894, in Fábio Luz and Davi Carneiro, *Floriano: Memórias e Documentos,* vol. 6, *A Invasão Federalista em Santa Catarina e Paraná* (Rio de Janeiro: Imprensa Nacional, 1941), 253.

95. Picking to Herbert, 10 Jan. 1894, United States Navy, Area 4 file, South Atlantic Squadron, 1888–1894, Record Group 45, National Archives (hereafter, USNav).

96. *Baltimore Herald,* 19 Feb. 1894, in *PO* 16, no. 21 (22 Feb. 1894): 494; and *NYT,* 23 Feb. 1894, sec. 2, p. 4.

97. Picking to Herbert, 18 Feb. 1894, USNav; *NYT,* 16 Jan. 1894, 6; and Clowes, *Four Modern Naval Campaigns,* 223.

98. *NYT,* 14 Jan. 1894, sec. 8, p. 3; and Villar, *As Revoluçoes,* 74–75.

99. Dunshee de Abranches, *A Revolta da Armada e a Revolução Rio Grandense: Correspondência entre Saldanha da Gama e Silveira Martins* (Rio: Gráfica do "Jornal do Brasil," 1955), 25, 31, 32, 51, 157.

100. Abranches, *A Revolta da Armada,* 141, 142, 147, 156–57.

101. *NYT,* 16 Jan. 1894, sec. 3, p. 2; *NYT,* 24 March 1889, sec. 16, p. 1; Mendonça, *Ajuste de Contas,* 160; and Abranches, *A Revolta da Armada,* 147.

102. *NYT,* 19 Mar. 1894, sec. 8, p. 3.

103. *NYT,* 18 Mar. 1894, sec. 3, p. 3; and Villar, *As Revoluçoes,* 73.

104. Villar, *As Revoluçoes,* 85.

105. G. Burt's interview in *NYT,* 24 Apr. 1894, sec. 8, p. 3.

106. For more on the election, see Topik, *Trade and Gunboats,* chap. 7.

107. Nabuco to Hilário de Gouveia, 10 Mar. 1894, in *Cartas a Amigos,* ed. Carolina Nabuco (São Paulo: Instituto; Progresso Editorial, n.d.), 229.

108. Villalba, *A Revolta da Armada,* 147.

109. *NYT,* 17 Apr. 1894, sec. 1, p. 5.

110. Villalba, *A Revolta da Armada,* 150–51; and *NYT,* 17 Apr. 1894, sec. 9, p. 5.

111. Interview with Dr. J. A. Tonner in *NYT,* 27 Dec. 1895.

112. Selas Terry to Sec. of Navy, 28 Apr. 1894, USNav; Augusto Forjaz, *Portugal e Brazil: Apontamentos para a História do nosso Conflicto com a República dos Estados Unidos do Brasil* (Lisboa: Typ. Castro Irmao, 1894), 1, 22; Conde de Paraty, *Portugal e Brazil: Conflicto Diplomático, Breves Explicaçoes* (Lisboa: M. Gomes, 1895), 49, 58; and Nabuco, *Intervenção Estrangeira,* 234, 235.

113. Dias de Campos, *A Revolta,* 179.

114. Luz and Carneiro, *Floriano,* vol. 6, 161; Villalba, *A Revolta da Armada,* 191; Almirante A. Thompson, *Guerra Civil do Brasil de 1893 a 1895: Vida e Morte do Almirante Saldanha da Gama,* 3d ed. (Rio: Serviço de Documentação Geral da Marinha, 1958), 199; and Nabuco, *Intervenção Estrangeira,* 239.

115. *NYT,* 24 Apr. 1894, sec. 8, p. 3.

116. "Professional Notes," in *Proceedings of the United States Naval Institute* 20, no. 3 (1894): 622–23; Edward Brinley, "The Pneumatic Gun on the Brazilian Cruiser *Nictheroy,*" *Proceedings of the United States Naval Institute* 20, no. 72 (1894): 830; Memorandum of Captain Alexandrino Faria de Alencar, in Thompson, *Guerra Civil,* 223–27; and *NYT,* 27 Dec. 1894, sec. 9, p. 5.

117. Coleção Solon, lata 614, pasta 19.

118. Mello to General Luiz Salgado, 10 and 11 Apr. 1894, in Thompson, *Guerra Civil,* 206, 207.

119. Thompson, *Guerra Civil,* 214.

120. Brasil, Presidente, *Mensagens ao Congresso Nacional,* 17 May 1894, 92.

121. Villar, *As Revoluçoes,* 84.

122. See Brasil, Min. da Marinha, *Almirante Gonçalves;* Felisbelo Freire, *História da Revolta de 6 de Septembro de 1893* (Rio de Janeiro: Cunha e Irmão, 1896); and Muniz Barreto, *Biografia,* for florianista versions; and see Custodio José de Mello, *O Governo Provisório e a Revolução de 1893* (São Paulo: Editora Nacional, 1938); Thompson, *Guerra Civil;* Villalba, *A Revolta da Armada;* and Villar, *As Revoluçoes,* for studies favorable to the insurgents.

123. The Olney Doctrine was a reassertion of the Monroe Doctrine. Secretary of State Olney announced in 1895 that "today the United States is practically sovereign on this continent, and its fiat is law upon the subjects to which it confines its interposition," in Walter LeFeber, *The Cambridge History of American Foreign Relations,* vol. 2, *The American Search for Opportunity, 1865–1913* (New York: Cambridge University Press, 1993), 124.

124. The *U.S.S. New York,* whose guns had glistened under Brazil's tropical sun

in Guanabara Bay under Admiral Benham, became the flagship of Admiral Sampson during the Spanish-American War.

125. *Scientific American,* 2 Dec. 1893.

126. Howard P. Elwell, in "Arming of the Brazilian Cruisers *Nictheroy* and *America,*" *Proceedings of the United States Naval Institute* 19, no. 68 (1893): 391, observed that "the recent conversion of the merchant vessels *El Cid* and *Britannia* . . . presents an object-lesson, the value of which can scarcely be overestimated. The two ships . . . were so quickly transformed from their peaceful condition into efficient fighting vessels . . . as to astonish naval officers."

127. The *NYT* reported on 5 Nov. 1893 (sec. 1, p. 4) that "the prompt action of the Brazilian government in purchasing ships in the United States has disconcerted these backers of the insurrectionists in Europe and they fear the collapse of their venture is inevitable."

128. Joaquim Nabuco, *Balmaceda* (São Paulo: Companhia Editora Nacional, 1927), 141.

129. Hill, *Diplomatic Relations,* 281; and *NYT,* 27 Dec. 1894, sec. 9, p. 5.

130. *NYT,* 23 June 1894, sec. 4, p. 2.

131. See Topik, *Trade and Gunboats,* for more details on the assertion of Brazilian nationalism.

Michael J. Schroeder

The Sandino Rebellion Revisited

Civil War, Imperialism, Popular Nationalism, and

State Formation Muddied Up Together in the Segovias of

Nicaragua, 1926–1934

What we ought to do is to forget all our family grudges and recognize that our legitimate enemies by race and language are the Yankee invaders.
AUGUSTO C. SANDINO (1927)

Events are the real dialectics of history. They transcend all arguments, all personal judgements, all vague and irresponsible wishes.
ANTONIO GRAMSCI (1921)

Suppression of criticism, I have come to believe, is not the best way of expressing solidarity. AIJAZ AHMAD (1992)

In mid-November 1927, as wary peasants stripped ripened corn from surviving stalks, a mounted and well-armed reconnaissance patrol of five U.S.
marines and five Nicaraguan national guardsmen headed north out of the
town of Ocotal, capital of the northern Nicaraguan department of Nueva
Segovia, toward the Honduran border. "At Las Manos, which is just across
the border in Honduras," the patrol commander later reported, "we found
15 or 18 men all armed with revolvers. They seemed to be very much perturbed by our presence. They said we were the first Americans they had
ever seen." [1] They were probably members of a local Conservative gang,
though they might have been Liberals; such armed gangs flourished in this
place and time. For the past year civil war, the first in nearly a generation,
had ravaged the region. In the words of one contemporary, the war had left
the entire north "in misery and desolation, houses on all sides filled with
grief, haciendas ruined, businesses broken, crops destroyed, men mutilated by the most horrible of tortures." [2] Six months earlier, as the corn
planting season was commencing, the 1926–1927 Civil or Constitutionalist War had been formally ended in a U.S.-brokered peace accord (the
Treaty of Tipitapa, or Espino Negro Accords of 4 May 1927), though the

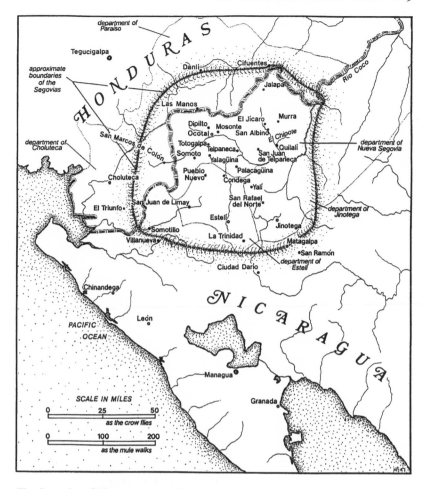

The Segovias of Nicaragua, c. 1926–1934

continuing mobilization of armed gangs across the Segovias throughout the rainy "winter" months probably made it hard to tell the difference.[3] Now, from early June 1927, for the first time in history, North Americans and Segovianos were coming into contact on a daily basis. So were two languages, two cultures, and importantly, two very different ways of organizing and practicing violence. Historically, organized violence in the Segovias had been produced by local-regional *ejércitos* (armies or gangs) in the service of one or another political faction. The power of the central state was mediated through local-regional political bosses or *caudillos* who, through these private armies, personally controlled the means of

organized violence. Now the people who made up this endlessly complicated and war-torn system suddenly found themselves standing face-to-
face with the advance guard of an invading army. It's no wonder these gang
members "seemed very much perturbed." It's hard to imagine them reading the signs (as I imagine them) and feeling at ease: the foreign tongue
and white skin, the uniforms and insignia, the exotic equipment, the shiny
new repeating rifles, the air of calm, arrogant confidence. In this seren-
dipitous encounter one can glimpse the outlines of a larger struggle, as
these gang members apparently did, of two profoundly different visions—
of morality, politics, violence, and the state—in the process of colliding.

The four groups of actors figuring in this patrol commander's report
can be read as allegories of four of the major historical processes transforming Nicaragua and the Segovias during this period: (1) ongoing civil
war between Liberals and Conservatives (represented by the armed gang);
(2) intensifying imperialist intervention (the marines); (3) rapidly if unevenly accelerating state formation (the Guardia Nacional); and (4) emergent popular nationalism and protest (the Sandinista rebels, the episode's
invisible presence, and the reason why the marines were in the Segovias
in the first place).[4] Similarly, the report's flavor of irony and contingency
can be read as emblematic of the way these four groups of actors and
four historical processes interacted over time. The marines and guardia
on patrol to Las Manos were not especially looking for gangs like the
one they stumbled into. Instead they were "hunting bandits," or Sandinistas, members of Augusto C. Sandino's Defending Army of Nicaraguan
National Sovereignty, founded only two months before.[5]

Sandino, an ardent patriot and social revolutionary, had returned from
exile in Mexico in early 1926 to join the fight against the Conservatives.
By April 1927 he had become one of the most powerful Liberal generals in the north. In May, with the Liberals poised to take Managua and
oust the unconstitutional Conservative regime of Adolfo Díaz, the United
States stepped in and brokered the peace. The treaty called for the Díaz
regime to remain in power until U.S.-supervised elections in November
1928. It also called for the establishment of a "non-partisan constabulary"
or Guardia Nacional.[6]

Sandino was infuriated. The United States had been directly intervening in Nicaraguan affairs for the better part of two decades, and now,
despite the Liberal victory in the field, the "dastardly invaders and the
nation's traitors," in his words, continued "trampling Nicaragua's sovereignty underfoot." [7] His patriotic anger also expressed a broader ideological current of anti-imperialist and leftist nationalism sweeping Central and

Latin America in the wake of the First World War and the Mexican and Russian Revolutions.[8] It also embodied a more specifically Nicaraguan anti-imperialist, anti-Yankee nationalist discourse that had emerged in the wake of the William Walker episode of the mid-1850s and had flourished since the U.S.-supported overthrow of the Liberal president Zelaya in late 1909.[9] It resonated as well with many of the grievances and aspirations of diverse groups of Segovianos. Rejecting the terms of the peace accord, Sandino marched his few remaining troops back up to the Segovias to protest the continuing U.S. occupation.

The emergence of Sandino's rebellion was thus fundamentally ironic, an unintended consequence of U.S. intervention.[10] For the next five and a half years, the peasant-worker-Indian soldiers of his Defending Army, nearly all of them Segovianos, waged a guerrilla war, centered in the Segovias, against the marines, the guardia, and their civilian supporters. In the process, a powerful new narrative of Nicaraguan history would take shape, in mortal opposition to a powerful new army—the Guardia Nacional—an army that in 1934 would crush the rebellion but prove unable to extinguish the narrative it generated. That narrative, as we know, would survive—in texts, memories, songs, stories, legends—and half a century later would provide the inspiration for the Sandinista Revolution.

This essay is offered as a contribution to a larger project devoted to rethinking the "postcolonial encounter" between the United States and Latin America. For Nicaragua, of course, that "encounter" has been shaped most of all by exceedingly lopsided relations of power: the United States has obviously influenced and changed Nicaragua far more than Nicaragua has influenced or changed the United States. The essay is therefore conceived as an intervention in Nicaraguan history and historiography. It is intended, at one level, as a kind of provocation, an effort to muddy up the waters of the master narratives of the period. These dominant stories, each informed by its own moral teleology, tend strongly to reduce contradictory social processes to linear sequences of events, shoehorning the making of history into a select handful of actors and forces and plots: U.S. imperial will versus patriotic resistance to it; heroic patriots versus evil invaders and morally bankrupt *vendepatria* (country sellers); benevolent marines versus culturally inferior natives; the forces of "order" and "civilization" versus the forces of "disorder" and "barbarism."

These dominant modes of representing the United States and Sandino, in turn, can be traced to a larger set of liberal-Marxist theoretical frames that especially in the years since World War II have dominated thinking on imperialism and "Third World" nationalisms: on the one hand, "modern-ization theory" and its kin (most notably, liberalism and neoliberalism); and on the other hand, Marxism, various neo-Marxisms, the dependency school, and world-systems analyses.[11] More recent theoretical interventions intended to transcend these dominant paradigms, that can loosely be called "postcolonialism" (especially "Colonial Discourse Analysis," subaltern studies, feminist theory, cultural studies, and other approaches still in the process of formation), have yet to be applied to Sandino's rebellion and U.S. military intervention in Nicaragua. None of these frameworks, I suggest, is by itself sufficient for understanding the richness and complexity of this period, though the Marxist and postcolonialist approaches have much to offer, and I borrow from them heavily here. Rather than confronting these narratives and their undergirding paradigms head-on (which would comprise too large a digression and, for a historian most at home in the documents, a rather tedious exercise), I aim to do so obliquely, by mapping out an alternative and, I hope, more textured account that attends to the multiplicity of contexts, agencies, and subjectivities that shaped this process of social and political-cultural change.

This essay explores how U.S. military intervention entwined with and transformed ongoing social struggles, forms of collective action, and the organization of violence in the Segovias in the 1920s and 1930s. It examines how struggles for power in the region shaped, and were shaped by, the marine intervention, and with what consequences. It shows, among other things, that Segovianos influenced the process of invasion as much as the invaders did; that Segovianos used the marines as much as the marines used them; and that native opposition to Sandino emerged out of the same social milieu and the same process of struggle that produced Sandino's army. In this way the essay also sheds new light on the rebellion's major unintended consequence: the accelerated formation of the Guardia Nacional and the extension of state power into geographic and social spaces hitherto beyond its reach.[12]

The following section offers a brief synopsis of the two major story lines that have dominated thinking on the war between the marines and Sandino, and suggests that a more compelling historical account can be crafted by combining elements of both. The remainder of the essay tries to sketch out that synthesis. It does so, first, by contextualizing struggles for power in the Segovias before the U.S. invasion. It then contextualizes the invasion and occupation, first by exploring the moral vision that informed marine actions in the field, and then by considering the contradictory effects of those actions: to galvanize support for the rebellion on the one hand, and to accelerate the formation of the Guardia Nacional on the other. The essay then explores the varied responses of Segovianos to invasion, occupation, and rebellion, before examining in greater detail the centralization of violence-making in the region as expressed in the progressive empowerment of the guardia. The conclusion briefly situates the essay's principal findings within the broader contours of Nicaraguan history, and its approach within the broader set of literatures and paradigms mentioned above.

Conventional Frames: Amplifications and Erasures

Few would disagree that intense political factionalism and polarization have characterized most of postcolonial Nicaraguan history. In but one expression of those fractures, and with some notable exceptions, the great bulk of the historical and literary representations of the period of Sandino's rebellion tend to adhere to one of two diametrically opposed master narratives.[13] The first (and probably the most familiar to non-Nicaraguans) is what might be termed the heroic or Sandinista narrative. In this story, Sandino and his rebels are represented as selfless patriotic defenders of Nicaraguan national sovereignty and social justice, a ragtag "crazy little army" of barefoot peasants and Indians sacrificing their lives for a free and independent homeland. The marines and their "collaborators" are represented as demonic brutes bent on dominating and oppressing the humble, righteous mountain folk of the region.[14] The second, what might be termed the Somocista narrative, is epitomized by and anchored in Anastasio Somoza's *El verdadero Sandino o el calvario de las Segovias* (1936). Somoza's story, which still carries considerable authority across much of Nicaragua, implicitly represents the marines and North Americans (and, by extension, the guardia) as agents of "civilization" and "modernity," bearers of "order" and "progress," while painting Sandino's rebels, in the starkest possible hues, as murderous gangs of "bandits," cutthroats, and criminals bent on the destruction of all "social order." [15] (A softer version, common in the liberal press at the time, praised Sandino's ostensible ends, national sovereignty, but decried his means, organized banditry.) While some have worked to occupy a kind of middle ground between these two poles, combining elements of both metastories, this middling terrain has remained tenuous and sparsely populated.[16]

Both master narratives capture key aspects of the period and elide others. Somoza's basic story—that Sandino and his rebels were motivated by nothing more than bloodlust and greed—is plainly wrong, and maliciously so (and for reasons that need not detain us here).[17] That said, the catalog of robberies, burnings, atrocities, and murders that is Somoza's book poses some knotty and neglected questions. The documentary evidence on which the story is based compels us to explain the violence, to recognize the extreme opposition to Sandino that emerged quickly and decisively across the region, and finally, to acknowledge that the rebellion was, in part, a regional civil and class war, waged among and between Segovianos, on their own turf and with a timeworn set of locally rooted weapons and strategies.

The Sandinista narrative inverts Somoza's emphases, suppressing or erasing rebel violence against civilians and, more generally, the civil wars embedded in the war against the marines. Instead it stresses the key slice of reality actively denied by Somoza: that the rebellion was a war of popular and national liberation waged against an invading army, a U.S.-imposed national army, local-regional and national notables whose vision of "the nation" excluded the vast majority of the region's inhabitants, and a profoundly oppressive and exploitative social and political system. It is important to emphasize that the evidence supports the heroic narrative at many levels. The U.S. Marines were invaders, and brutally violent ones. The process of armed struggle against that invasion did generate widespread and deeply felt popular patriotism and anti-Yankeeism (imagined and acted out in many different ways). It did serve to propagate a discourse of national sovereignty, social justice, and inalienable human rights among historically subordinate groups. And it did bequeath to the laboring poor an enduring field of potentially emancipatory texts and social memories, a radically new "social imaginary" expressed through a novel vocabulary and practice of popular protest and liberation from many forms of domination, oppression, and exploitation.[18]

In order to create a more *historical* understanding of this pivotal period of Nicaraguan history, these symmetrical erasures and emphases need to be brought into mutual dialogue. Sandino's struggle can be best understood as many struggles in the process of combining: a continuation and transmutation of ongoing civil wars between Liberals and Conservatives; a peasant-based, anti-Yankee, popular-national liberation movement; a class and racial-ethnic war rooted in extreme inequalities and local traditions of violence; a fight to "exterminate bandits"; a fight to make a state—or two states, as we shall see—and others besides.[19] By exploring how old and new struggles dynamically entwined, one might begin to chart out some new ways of thinking about the historic relationship between Nicaragua and the United States, and about Sandino's paradigm of national liberation—with all of its inherent limitations and "monumentally self-destructive" qualities, its intended and unintended consequences, and its emancipatory potential.[20]

Segovian Ways of War

Understanding Sandino's ideology and rebellion as something not just springing from its inventor's head but as something acted out and given meaning by men and women living and working in a particular place and time requires some understanding of Segovian history.[21] So does an understanding of the character of the intervention and the formation of the guardia in the region. In particular, one needs to inquire how struggles for power were thought about and practiced in the years before 1927. According to the historical sociologist Michael Mann, all social power ultimately derives from four overlapping sources: economic, political, military, and ideological.[22] Applying this schema to the Segovias, one can say that economic power—derived mainly from the ownership of large tracts of land—was the principal source of political and military power, which were wielded and reproduced mainly through personal control of local and regional offices of the state, family and political networks, and personal control of the means of organized violence. In the reproduction of social and power inequalities, ideological power was clearly of lesser moment than the ownership of productive resources, control of state offices, and the sustained capacity to inflict physical injury.[23]

In the 1920s (as today), the Segovias were a deeply divided and endemically violent place, where different forms of violence sprang from as many sources as there were lines of cleavage. The fault lines of party, class, and ethnicity ran deepest—in that order of consequence, it seems—but multiple fractures also laced community, family, gender, and personal relations. The reasons behind the divisions and violence were partly an expression of the same historical processes that made *political anarchy* the keywords for Nicaragua's first century of independence, and partly the result of a host of factors uniquely Segovian. Historically, the region's rugged geography and sparse dispersed population imposed severe limits on the reach of the central state. Regional geopolitics also played a key role, a result of the region's strategic location midway between Tegucigalpa and the León-Managua-Granada axis, which made the Segovias a kind of fluid frontier zone and haven for outlaws, smugglers, and "revolutionary" armies on both sides of the border. As in many other frontier regions, relative isolation from global and national markets and power networks led to a fragmentation of political space, a "localization of sovereignties" in which political power was radically decentralized and continually challenged and defended by local-regional caudillos.[24] Political power, in turn, derived from control of the local and regional offices of the state. Such offices were legion, lucrative, and bitterly contested. Battles for control of the state and its sundry offices have historically comprised the principal source of political strife and organized episodic violence in Nicaraguan history, as has long been recognized.[25] So too in the Segovias.

At the same time, battles among and between local-regional caudillos for control of state offices entwined at multiple levels with challenges from below, as subaltern groups contested elite domination in land, labor, and ethnic relations.[26] The popular explosions of the late 1840s, the Matagalpa Indian Uprising of 1881, and related expressions of popular protest in the region revealed the limits of elite dominance and the potential dangers of unrestrained factional squabbling.[27] Localized and caged struggles from below intensified from the 1880s, as the liberal revolution initiated a broad-ranging assault on the land, labor, and lifeways of the rural laboring classes. As the coffee and mining economies boomed, the violence of primitive accumulation spread decisively if unevenly across the region. These rapid, wrenching changes served to further erode the underpinnings of patron-client relations in the region, which were generally weak to begin with (especially compared to the far more densely settled Pacific littoral), as the dynamics of uneven capitalist transformation reinforced the effects of mountainous terrain, sparse population, localized agricultural frontiers, and internal migrations.[28] In sum, there is much to indicate that by the mid-1920s, a substantial proportion of the region's direct rural producers (including many dispossessed Indians), who comprised from 80 to 90 percent of its approximately 100,000 inhabitants, harbored deep and long-standing grievances against landlords, mine owners, coffee growers, cattle ranchers, and local-regional agents of the state.[29]

Here, as elsewhere, moments of rupture worked to disclose the lineaments of social relations during more "normal" times. The Civil War of 1926–1927 was one such period, the latest in a succession of violent civil conflicts in the country and region stretching back at least a century.[30] Civil wars in the Segovias historically had been waged through the organization of private armies or gangs, mobilized in patron-client fashion by local-regional caudillos. The patrons of such gangs, unlike their leaders and members, were invariably members of the dominant classes, though sometimes the lines blurred, as periods of crisis generated challenges to elite dominance both laterally and from below.[31]

If reliable evidence for these processes in the Segovias prior to 1927 is slim, the marine invasion of the Segovias did much to thicken the documentary record. One of the richest stores of evidence for the period after mid-1926 consists of the testimonies produced by the Instituto de Estudio del Sandinismo (IES) in the early 1980s, which provide a compelling glimpse into how civil warfare was thought about and practiced during the 1926–1927 Civil War, and presumably for a long time before.

As Arturo Warman writes of old-timers' memories of Emiliano Zapata's rebellion, "Their narratives are simple and concrete . . . [and] rich and prodigal in details. . . . Names play a part in them, as do the little, everyday things." [32] So too the IES testimonies. Such stories of the 1926–1927 Civil War provide a kind of window into how Liberal "revolutionary armies" in the Segovias were mobilized, organized, and culturally constructed. Several key themes are emphasized repeatedly: the importance of *personalismo, caudillismo,* and *localismo* in the formation and dissolution of Liberal "revolutionary armies"; the fluid and contradictory nature of political allegiances and identities; and the centrality of political gang violence in the region's history. Here I can do little more than take soundings from this extensive corpus of stories. Pastor Ramírez Mejía, for instance, later a captain in Sandino's Defending Army, told a long and intricate tale of his experiences in the civil war, passages of which follow:

I began serving under the command of Benito López, joining up with him near Santa María [around late October 1926]. . . . From there two other generals approached our position: Ciriaco Aguilera and Carlos Salgado. . . . They spoke to me, and I departed with five other men and joined up with them. From there I passed my command to [them]. . . . Our chiefs [Aguilera and Salgado] left us in Achuapa, and went to reach an understanding (*a tener entendimento*) with Francisco Parajón in El Sauce. . . . They returned with an understanding (*venían entendidos de él*), and from there we went to attack Chinandega. . . . [We were defeated and fled, carrying many wounded.] There was a general, at that time a colonel, José León Díaz, a Salvadoran, and we were friends with him (*éramos compañeros de él*). He came to help me with my people, he came as their chief. At that time, the organizations, those whom we recognized with their troops, were those of us who had the grade of captain. The colonels were organized in the General Staff. Those who commanded the army were the company captains, I was a company captain. . . . We entered Somoto. This López Irías had been named General in Chief of Somoto, but he had fled to Honduras. . . . So when he returned he wanted to take power from the others. So, he takes over (*le conquista*) the columns of Ciriaco Aguilera and Carlos Salgado, he won them over (*se las conquistó*). But I didn't stay around for him to take over my troops. . . . I didn't stick around to be taken over by López Irías.

After a bitter disagreement with General López Irías, Captain Ramírez and Colonel Díaz departed with their men and linked up with Sandino.[33]

From this and similar stories (and related evidence) emerges a fine-grained portrait of the language and practice of Segovian civil warfare during this period. Organized violence, an exclusively male pursuit, was produced and controlled by bands of armed men, ranging in size from five to fifty (usually around thirty, it seems), each band clustered around an individual strongman or charismatic leader, or *jefe*. Larger bands, or "armies," formed through alliances or "understandings," were basically aggregations of smaller bands. As the size of such groupings increased, cohesion diminished and internal contests for power intensified. Such groups were constantly in the process of forming and reforming, congealing and dissolving; a band would adhere, loosely and provisionally, to another such band, or band of bands, its autonomy under constant challenge. Alliances between groups were sometimes ephemeral, sometimes long-lived; betrayal was not uncommon. While most such bands were linked in some fashion to the larger Constitutionalist movement led by Juan B. Sacasa and José María Moncada, their mobilization and organization in the Segovias remained a mostly local affair. Expressions of the region's fractured political field, such collectivities remained, for the most part, small in scale, locally anchored, individually controlled, and functionally autonomous throughout the war and, in several key instances, for some time afterward. Carlos Salgado and José León Díaz, for instance, became major Sandinista jefes after the war, followed into the field by many of their subordinates and allies.

Within such a milieu, the social and political identities of individuals and families were multiple, contingent, and not uncommonly riddled with contradictions. Examples abound. One tale told by ex-Liberal soldier Lizandro Ardón included a Conservative soldier secretly aiding a Liberal friend, a Liberal sympathizer with Conservative patrons, and a Conservative uncle who helped get his Liberal nephew out of a Conservative-controlled jail.[34] A declaration from prison by leading Conservative gang leader José Torres emphasized the friction between himself and his intimate Conservative partner's long-standing Conservative patron, and between that same patron and another gang leader who was in turn described as the chief of the Conservatives in the region.[35] Families were often no less divided. After the civil war, Inés Hernández emerged as a leading Sandinista jefe, while his brother Anastacio (who some time before had killed his other brother Francisco) languished in prison for crimes committed as a leading Conservative jefe.[36] Such divisions continued through the Sandinista period. In 1929, Sandinista jefe Teodoro Molina reportedly killed three members of the Mejía family of El Roble near Somoto, while two years later three other members of the same family were reported as active Sandinistas under local jefe Julián Gutiérrez. The latter, in turn, once tried to kill a member of the Alvarado family of El Angel south of Somoto, while remaining in alliance with two other members of the same family.[37] Across the region, political identities and allegiances, like social relations of all kinds, were rife with manifold fractures and ambiguities.

Intimately related to this was the centrality of locally produced political violence in the region's history, as is especially emphasized in the IES testimonies. In a remarkable confluence of private memories, for instance, nearly sixty years after the fact, the testimonies reveal that after Emiliano Chamorro's coup d'état of October 1925, Conservative powerholders across the Segovias, most notably in the El Jícaro region, unleashed a wave of beatings, attacks, rapes, and murders in a bid to cow or eliminate their enemies among the populace. All this was the prelude to an even severer upsurge of violence a year later.[38] These waves of violence, in turn, contributed mightily to a groundswell of organized popular opposition to continuing Conservative rule, and help to explain the mushrooming of Liberal "armies" and soldiers after mid-1926. For instance, the testimonies shed new light on a neglected but crucial feature of the San Albino uprising of October 1926, an event that appears in virtually every account of the origins of Sandino's rebellion and that has long been mythologized as a pure expression of local anti-Yankee sentiment (an American, Charles Butters, owned San Albino Mine and its mythically wretched company store). According to many who remembered the period firsthand, the San Albino uprising had its origins less in the violence of mine labor or the capitalist avarice of its Yankee proprietor than in the calculated violence perpetrated by local Conservative powerholders against the civilian population in and around San Albino, Murra, and El Jícaro. Here José Paul Barahona recalls the origins of the uprising: "One day, news arrived at San Albino that the troops of Adolfo Díaz had arrived in Murra and assassinated Inés Ochoa and Lilo Leal; raped two girls, María Salomé and Concepción Cárdenas; burned the house of the old woman Luisa Mendoza; broken the leg of Lisandro Colindres; wounded Rigoberto Colindres; and captured Filiberto Barahona, who escaped and went to give warning to San Albino. It was then that we began our rebellion." In outline if not in detail, Barahona's recollections are buttressed by many others.[39] Liberal-Conservative and elite-subordinate struggles melded with Sandino's anti-imperialism at many levels, as subsequent events made clear.

In short, local and regional powerholders across the Segovias routinely used violence as a political weapon or tool, as a way to wield and maintain power. The violence their gangs produced was at once highly public, personal, political, sexualized, and locally rooted, and based on intersecting relations of party, family, class, ethnicity, and gender. Violence against bodies and families was combined with crimes against property (theft and destruction) and the system of "guarantees." The most common type of Segovian guarantee (*garantía*) was a formal promise issued by a gang leader not to attack, injure, or kill its holder, obtained through acquiescence to the gang or patron's demands; coffee growers often formed pacts to secure collective guarantees. All of these practices were as much cultural as political, intended to create power not only through the elimination of real and potential foes, but through the dispersal of a social memory and generalized sense of fear.[40]

Not surprisingly, nearly all of these ways of waging war were appropriated by Sandino's rebels in their struggle for state power. By seizing the tools of domination traditionally employed by the ruling elite, the Sandinistas in a sense "democratized" the use of collective violence by unmooring it from the vertical patron-client relations to which it had been historically tied. Yet the same tools that brought strength and empowerment also conferred weaknesses and fractures. Despite its fundamentally different aims (and despite nationalist myths to the contrary), the Defending Army was more akin to a loose confederation of armed gangs than a centralized military institution. Such gangs, mobilized by more than one hundred charismatic and well-connected local jefes, and integrated into the Defending Army's structures of authority (sometimes tightly, sometimes loosely), were riddled with factionalism and competition. Culturally specific forms of violence against the body and family—wounding and killing by machete, decapitation, and the public display of mutilated corpses—though, significantly, not rape, were among their most potent weapons, as were selective property destruction and appropriation, and the issuance and revocation of guarantees. The emerging Guardia Nacional engaged in many of the same practices, as did the marines. But before exploring how the marine intervention entwined with ongoing civil wars and forms of collective action in the region, it will be useful to explore something of the moral imagination of the marines.

Benevolent Paternalism and Racist Brutality: The Marines in the Segovias

"They were the Leathernecks, 'The Old Breed' of American regulars . . . with drilled shoulders and a bone-deep sunburn and a tolerant scorn of nearly everything else on earth." With these words Captain J. W. Thomason Jr. lovingly described his Marine Corps comrades-in-arms from the Great War. The historian Bill D. Ross seized on this imagery and applied it wholesale to the men of the First Marine Division who fought against the Japanese in World War II, though he might just as well have pinned it on the marines who served in the Segovias. Indeed, many of the First Division's gnarliest old-timers had earned their stripes in that region's "nasty little bush war" a decade before.[41] Along with their sunburn, the marines carried with them into the Segovias—as they had carried into the Philippines, Cuba, Haiti, and the Dominican Republic—a "scorn" that could be either "tolerant" or not, along with a "bone-deep" set of beliefs and assumptions about the natives, perhaps best described as fundamentally racist, culturally arrogant in the extreme, and shot through with good intentions.[42]

Born and bred in a culture awash in racist stereotypes and violence— recall the wartime and postwar urban race riots, the resurgence of the Ku Klux Klan, and the virulent nativism, anti-Semitism, and anti-Catholicism of the 1920s—these "leathernecks" formed a cohesive community of white males, mostly young, Anglo-Saxon, and Protestant, accustomed to practicing violence against "racially inferior" and culturally "backward" "bandits." They were also infused with a powerful sense of missionary zeal and moralism, a product, in part, of Wilsonianism combined with the mythologization of the U.S. role in the Great War.[43] At the same time, not all marines were the same, making it necessary to unpack the category. One especially needs to distinguish between those who believed in the morality of the intervention and those who did not—and there were some, at least, who thought the whole thing an immoral sham.[44] The average marine private, it seems clear, did not want to be in Nicaragua at all, and was especially loathe to be out on patrol "hunting bandits," which to him mainly meant going hungry, getting sore feet, and risking injury, pain, and death. Like most footsoldiers throughout history, the average marine could trace his social origins to the lower echelons of a profoundly unequal class and political system. Most senior officers, in contrast, despite similar lower-class backgrounds, tended to show more enthusiasm for the aims of the U.S. mission.

Despite their differences, however, virtually all marines shared certain presumptions about themselves and the natives they were there to help and, if need be, kill. All, the evidence suggests, remained firm in the shared belief in their own cultural and racial superiority. Most conceived of the U.S. mission as a genuinely altruistic and "civilizing" one, a way to introduce "stability" and "order" into a very "barbaric" and "disordered" country. Most also seem to have regarded themselves as a species of moral policemen, benevolent but stern father figures determined to uplift and discipline the primitive, childlike people of the region. To Marine Corps Major Julian C. Smith, for instance, the peculiar "racial psychology" of "the poorer classes of Nicaraguans" made them, among other things, "densely ignorant . . . little interested in principles . . . naturally brave and inured to hardships, of phlegmatic temperament, though capable of being aroused to acts of extreme violence. . . . A state of war is to them a normal condition." [45] Colonel Robert L. Denig, Northern Area Commander at Ocotal, in another characteristic expression of marine attitudes, compared himself to "Solomon" after helping to settle a domestic dispute, and offered his assessment of the natives in his personal diary: "They are children . . . at heart. . . . Life to them is cheap, murder in itself is nothing." [46]

Such views percolated from top to bottom, as becomes especially apparent in marine actions in the field. By imagining themselves as fair but firm disciplinarians confronting a childlike, ignorant, and inherently violent native population, the marines legitimated their own extreme violence in their prosecution of the war. "Saw a native running away and shot him dead" accurately paraphrases buried paragraphs from scores of patrol and combat reports. "Patrol killed one native who ran from them," reads one.[47] As in their other "tropical" invasions, the marines killed and terrorized rural folk systematically, deliberately, and often. This extraordinarily high level of marine (and guardia) violence is the overriding context for any understanding of the period. It is impossible to convey in so short a space the extent of the violence wreaked by the marines (and guardia) in their campaigns to annihilate Sandino's rebels and their bases of popular support. The marines' own reports provide a detailed accounting of the thousands of tons of foodstuffs they destroyed; the thousands of peasant huts torched, strafed, and bombed; the thousands of civilians injured and killed—reports that are woefully incomplete and contain marginally reliable estimates at best.

Such "Yankee brutality"—the Black Legend—is one of two major themes that dominate the Sandinista narrative of the rebellion, as expressed in literature of all kinds—memoirs, novels, songs, poems, biographies, polemics, and histories, by ex-rebels and ex-guardia alike— and especially in the IES testimonies: "They did nothing but kill the people. . . . They burned our houses, our animals, everything we had. . . . Whoever they grabbed, they killed, the Yankees did." [48] The other dominant theme, conterminous with the first, is the righteousness of the crusade to expel them.

As a nationalist trope, the Black Legend forms a key component in a complex ideological matrix. Yet it erases as much as it reveals, including the fact that the marines were generally as shrewd and pragmatic as they were brutal and ignorant, and, more to the point, that most marine-guardia violence was perpetrated by Nicaraguans serving in the guardia. By early 1930, in a prefiguring of Roosevelt's "Good Neighbor Policy," the marine withdrawal was well under way. In 1929, at its height, there were some 1,300 marines in the Segovias, some 700 in the Northern Area.[49] By February 1930, the Northern Area's contingent had dropped to 390 marines (commanding 498 Nicaraguan guardia), and by November 1930 to 222 marines (commanding 700 Nicaraguan guardia). Over the next two years the number of marines gradually diminished, while the number of guardia hovered between 650 and 800.[50] In terms of troops on patrol, after mid-1928 more than 90 percent of marine-guardia combat patrols were composed of from 5 to 35 native guardia commanded by 1 to 3 marines. The average patrol consisted of 1 marine to every 16 native guardia, and by late 1932 there were no more marines on patrol.[51]

For the Black Legend to be "true," however, the violence must be Yankee violence exclusively, or the violence of witless dupes of the Yankees. That it was neither constitutes a prime source of tension and ambiguity in the Sandinista narrative of the rebellion, a critical juncture where private memories and the "official" story collide. In 1984, more than half a century after the fact, former rebel soldier Joaquín Fajardo Arauz captured this tension and the fratricidal nature of the struggle when he was asked about the makeup of the enemy during the Battle of Labranza in 1932. "Only guardia," he at first explained, "because at that time there were few *machos* [marines]; fifty guardia with one *macho* chief." He then quickly rethought things: "Better said, they were all *macho*, because they all fought for the same opinion, even though they were Nicaraguans . . .

they were cruel with us, the same Nicaraguans. Like we say nowadays, Nicaragua has had to fight twice, with Nicaraguans and with the Yankees. We are fighting ourselves, with the other Nicaraguans being pushed by the Americans. It was happening then, and the same thing is happening now." [52] This is a rare moment in the IES testimonies. Most former rebel soldiers, in telling their stories from within the ideological framework of the larger Sandinista narrative that they themselves helped to create, tended to suppress the painful truth that their fight to free their homeland was also, in large part, a civil war with deep roots in local society.

Throughout their invasion and occupation of the Segovias, the marines thus played two very different and contradictory roles. On the one hand they served as a foil against which a new popular-national identity was created—palpable symbols of the continuing foreign domination of the country and region, a visible and often murderous enemy against which diverse social and political grievances could coalesce. It is one of the major ironies of the period (and one certainly not unique to this rebellion) that marine violence worked powerfully, and at many levels, to promote the cause it was intended to destroy. On the other hand, by working to extend the power and authority of the central state, by integrating themselves into the region's social networks in order to direct and assist in the erection of a new structure of authority and law, the marines also opened up many opportunities for diverse groups of Segovianos to exploit for their own ends. The following section explores both faces of this contradictory coin, in the context of the events and processes from which they emerged.

Power Struggles Combined:
Liberals, Conservatives, Sandinistas, Marines, Guardia

Conventional wisdom holds that U.S. intervention ended the 1926–1927 Civil War.[53] In fact the terms of the U.S.-brokered peace, while formally ending the war, also served to rechannel ongoing civil wars in new and unpredictable directions. At one level the peace accords infuriated a committed patriot and steeled his determination to resist the continuing U.S. occupation by force of arms. In response, the marines invaded and occupied the region where his troops were operating. The irony, of course, is that had U.S. policymakers simply ignored Sandino, had they let his troops sack and burn a few American properties and left it at that, the rebellion surely would have fizzled and died, leaving no organic social basis for the ideology of Sandinismo. As it turned out, their determination "to protect American lives and property," and later, "to exterminate bandits," played right into Sandino's hands—for without the invasion, and the marine atrocities that accompanied it, there would have been nothing to mobilize popular support for the rebellion or promote the nationalist and communist-anarchist ideals that inspired it.

A second irony flowed from the first. In response to the rebellion, the Guardia Nacional, also born of the May 1927 peace accords, professionalized more quickly and became larger and more powerful than it surely otherwise would have, a process explored in a later section of this essay. All the while, battles among and between Liberal and Conservative caudillos and their gangs continued. The eighteen months between May 1927 and the U.S.-supervised elections of November 1928 thus saw an intricate interweaving of old and new struggles, among and between Sandino's rebels, the invading marines and still-embryonic guardia, the triumphant (but temporarily "out") Liberals, and the beleaguered (and temporarily "in") Conservatives. The contradictory dynamics of the moment recast the political map, creating both new divisions and new confluences of interest. Most importantly here, both Sandinistas and Conservatives shared a basic interest in stymieing the intervention and preventing the 1928 elections; thus the curious phenomenon of Conservative caudillos actively aiding and abetting Sandino's rebels, who in turn lashed back against local Conservatives in revenge for years of oppression and violence.[54] On the other hand, Moncadista Liberals, the marines, and the guardia shared an interest in seeing the 1928 elections through to successful completion; thus the curious phenomenon of Sandino, the former Liberal general, excoriating and attacking his erstwhile comrades-in-arms, who were now warmly embracing the political project of the imperialists they had long denounced. After May 1927, political allegiances and identities in the region entered a state of extreme flux and ambiguity, even by Segovian standards.

As a practical matter, the marines confronted a dual mission: to stamp out both Sandino's challenge and the continuing mobilization of Liberal and Conservative gangs. Their initial successes were mixed. After Moncada's election as president in November 1928, power struggles among and between Liberals and Conservatives were being waged within a substantially transformed political and military context. Liberals now controlled the state and its offices, backed up by the guardia (in turn backed up by the marines), while the guardia aggressively garnered unto itself sole proprietorship over the means of organized violence, at least of the "official" state. Meanwhile, most of the Segovian countryside seethed in rebellion against all "official" authorities, old and new. People across the region were forced to choose sides, or at least to appear to choose sides. Most appear to have chosen Sandino's. By this time the marines-guardia and the Sandinistas had reached a kind of "strategic stalemate," with each side enjoying certain advantages and suffering certain disadvantages, and with neither able to defeat the other.[55] So it would remain till the end of the war.

The marine invasion and occupation further divided the already deeply divided region, superimposing new divisions on the old. This was expressed in countless ways, in the most minor of events—as in the June 1929 report of the commanding officer at Somoto, which reported that one Pancho Cerro of Somoto had shot and wounded the guardia *voluntario* Macario Isaguerres, and that the next day, another voluntario, Isidoro Ponce, shot and killed Pancho Cerro.[56] Whatever the conflict between these men (and the commanding officer at Somoto did not pretend to ask, though he did recommend Isidoro Ponce for commendation), it is apparent that long-simmering disputes were commonly played out under the new authority structure afforded by the guardia and its auxiliaries, including the voluntarios.

More generally, the war provided a way for Segovianos of any party, class, occupation, or gender to attack their personal or political foes by denouncing them as Sandinistas. Members of both parties did it, and often.[57] Spurned lovers sometimes did it.[58] Elaborate ruses were conceived and acted out in order to portray intra- and inter-party violence as Sandinista violence.[59] One Liberal summed it up: "There are all kinds of people around this town and in the small towns committing all kinds of cruelties that they attribute to the Sandinistas, knowing full well it is not so."[60] People across the Segovias routinely exploited the fight between the marines-guardia and the Sandinistas to advance their own agendas.

As the war dragged on, the region's social geography became increasingly divided along political-ideological and class lines. The marines and guardia remained anchored in garrisoned towns, ranging out on patrol in search of the elusive "bandits" and returning to the safety of their barracks and cantinas. Most townsfolk, local-regional notables, and many of their clients quickly and provisionally allied with them. Within the confines of garrisoned towns and ranches, and despite a good deal of permeability, the dominant culture's law, authority, and morality remained dominant.

Most of the Segovian countryside, in contrast, remained "bandit-infested," that is, Sandinista-controlled, for most of six years ("control" that was constantly contested by the marines-guardia and their allies). Within such contingently carved-out rural spaces, where Sandinismo ruled, people lived and worked in a kind of alternative moral, spiritual, and juridical universe, a sovereign, egalitarian, mystical brotherhood infused with a deeply spiritual sense of "*lo maravilloso.*" [61] Sandino's new nation was practiced as much as imagined, implemented as much as felt, and therein lay its mystery and power. Here, the historically disempowered *became* empowered through their active and radical (if selective) inversion and subversion of the dominant culture's codes of crime and punishment, of law and justice and morality. In the course of events, collective action against Conservative violence had been transformed almost seamlessly, through the prism of Sandino's teachings, into collective action against marine-guardia violence. Political, class, ethnic, and related aspirations all fed into the central motivating and unifying force of the rebellion from beginning to end: the desire to be rid of the murderous Yankee invaders. Sandino's new nation, embodying the means to this end, was also elastic enough to incorporate many other aspirations—for autonomy, land, justice, vengeance, respect. From the outset, then, the rebellion in the Segovias was as much a cultural and ideological struggle as a political and military one. At one level it was a guerrilla war between small bands of armed men whose basic aim was to kill each other. At another level the struggle centered on fundamentally opposed (if related) structures of authority, legitimacy, sovereignty, honor, morality, property, and law.

In articulating and codifying this alternative structure of authority and law, Sandino was working to create, from the outset, a kind of parallel state, or rebel republic, a juridical and moral order defined by its defiant opposition to the "official" state. Sandinista correspondence and pronouncements are replete with references to "our civil and military authorities," "the laws of our military institutions," and the "legal authority" of the Defending Army over all inhabitants of the Segovias.[62] The rebels' separate nationhood and statehood were also expressed in the rustic gold coins they minted during the first six weeks of rebellion: hefty ten-peso pieces inscribed with the words *Indios de A. C. Sandino* on one side, and on the other side the image of one such "Indio," standing atop a prostrate invader, the "Indio's" foot on the invader's chest, his right hand holding a machete, arced high in mid-swing, ready to strike down on the invader's throat.[63]

By identifying themselves as members of a separately constituted structure of authority and law, the rebels also arrogated to themselves one of the principal prerogatives of states: the right to tax, or, in the idiom employed, to levy "contributions." Over time, notifications for such "contributions" ("extortion" in the eyes of the marines-guardia and most property owners) came to be issued with increasing frequency. At one level, these forced contributions reproduced an old feature of Segovian civil conflict.[64] At the same time they added something new: the conjoining of Sandino's "patriot-traitor" dichotomy to an often bitterly ironic language of social or class protest.

Like all nationalist discourses that emerge in the context of foreign invasion, Sandino's confronted an intractable dilemma: How to deal with the invaders' supporters and allies? Like the North Americans in 1776, the Palestinians in 1996, and most everyone else in between, Sandino's revolutionary-patriotic response was to define such "collaborators" as "traitors" and thus effectively outside "the nation." His new story, or vision of the nation, was peopled by three fundamental groups of actors: "patriots" (himself and his army), "invaders" (the marines), and "traitors" (all Nicaraguans who collaborated with or supported the invasion). The category *traitor,* in turn, was routinely collapsed into that of *invader,* making *traitors and invaders* effectively synonymous, and one of the most common phrases in all of early Sandinista discourse. In Sandino's world, two diametrically opposed moral-political forces were locked in epic, mortal combat: patriots on one side, traitors and invaders on the other.

The pivot on which this "patriot-traitor" dichotomy turned was the notion of "national sovereignty," or, synonymously and more tellingly, "national honor": "patriots" defended "the nation's honor"; "traitors and invaders" violated it. "Honor," in turn, was (and remains) throughout Hispanic America a deeply gendered ideology, discourse, and set of practices centering on sexuality, male and female rights and obligations, and legitimate and illegitimate authority.[65] In this light, discourses of gender and honor are central to understanding Sandino's nationalism, its purchase on the hearts and minds of the rural poor, and its relation to contending Nicaraguan nationalisms. Sandinismo constructed "the homeland" (*la patria*) as female ("*nuestra madre patria*")—a mother-figure being brutally raped and violated by the "invaders," an image concretized in the realities of marine atrocities. "Traitors," in turn, were complicit in this despicable act.[66] For the Segovian laboring poor, Sandino's aim of "defending the nation's honor" invoked a language that found deep echoes in locally rooted languages and practices of masculinity, gender, honor, and sexuality. This helps to explain the rebels' strict codes against rape. In short, preexisting discourses of gender and honor in the Segovias made possible the rebels' imaginings of their new nation.

This new "nation," in turn, was conceived as a patriarchal family, with

Sandino, *el viejo* ("the old man") as father and patriarch. Membership in this family demanded strict adherence to two criteria: (1) membership in the "Indo-Hispanic race" (as defined primarily by language and culture), and (2) opposition to U.S. imperialism and the "Yankee invaders." In other words, whether you were a "legitimate Nicaraguan" or not depended both on where you were born and how you behaved. "Sixteen years ago Adolfo Díaz and Emiliano Chamorro killed their right to nationality," announced Sandino's first manifesto, a judgment repeated often enough during the course of the war.[67] Membership in the family-nation was revocable, contingent on actions. And the Supreme Chief was not the only rebel leader who invoked the right to decide who was "in" and who was not.[68]

By focusing attention outward, at the foreign aggressor, Sandino hoped to transcend the historic factionalism of Nicaraguan politics, "to forget all our family grudges" by forging, within the crucible of armed struggle, an entirely new family, morally superior to the old. His deeper aim, as I read it, was to revolutionize the whole of the isthmus through the process of armed struggle against the Yankees and their allies (the latter, it was hoped, would eventually disappear), to create a kind of spiritualized anarcho-communist brotherhood for all "Indo-Hispanics" — a horizontal, limited, sovereign fraternity ruled by the male laboring poor — using the "Yankees" as the external enemy against which this new community would coalesce.[69] As it turned out, part of this vision was achieved, but at a cost: in everyday practice, old "family grudges" were reproduced and new ones created.

If the deconstruction and interpretation of Sandino's texts became something of a cottage industry after 1979, insufficient attention has been paid to this nationalist idiom of "traitors" and "treason," not only for Sandino but for the vocabulary of popular protest he helped to spawn. One detects in the words and deeds of Sandinista jefes and their followers, alongside a deep love for Sandino and la patria and a deep hatred of the "Yankee invaders," a thinly veiled contempt for the wealthy and propertied, a fusion of angry social protest and popular patriotism — or perhaps more accurately, angry class protest embedded in a nationalist idiom. The war provided a strategic opening for ongoing struggles over labor and the products of labor, for all sides. Coffee growers and others routinely tried to use the marines-guardia for labor control, as discussed below. On the rebel side, consider the following excerpts from Sandinista General Pedro Altamirano's standard note to native property holders demanding "contributions" to "the cause":

It has been decreed that on this date you will give the sum of $200 as a forced contribution . . . to help the forces of the Defending Army of Nicaraguan National Sovereignty. . . . If you do not help the cause which we defend, which is the obligation of all honorable Nicaraguans to do for the good of their country, you will be obliged to abandon your property as you will be declared an enemy of the Army, and in this case, you and your family will lose all guarantees and will be subjected to whatever punishment from us that you merit as a traitor to your country. If you do not want to be attacked by our forces, you will pay the required sum, this in order that you may live in peace on your properties.[*] All orders that this Headquarters issues which are not complied with, obligate me to have them complied with by blood and fire in order that the Army will not be a laughingstock. Think carefully and well because if you do not feel inclined to help us, only God will keep your family from falling into my hands and your properties from being left in ashes. Acknowledge.[70]

Lacking the nationalist rationale, this was pure brigandage, an ancient practice of the poor against the propertied. It is noteworthy, for instance, that the word *property* is invoked here three times—once, where marked [*], in a voice that seems marked by utter contempt. It is also significant that the rebels demanded not only money but respect ("not be a laughingstock"). Rooted in popular idioms of honor and masculinity, the demand suggests a larger milieu of disrespect, of powerful men publicly ridiculing and thereby feminizing less powerful men. One senses here a new political vocabulary being grafted onto long-standing practices of rural criminality, of subaltern rejection of a "law" and a "morality" that were seen to serve only the interests of the dominant. The records of the marines and guardia fairly overflow with rebel "crimes" against property and person. This was, without doubt, as much a movement of social protest centered on labor, the products of labor, and profoundly unequal class-ethnic power relations as it was a nationalist rebellion. Early on, one marine analyst captured the "official" line on the rebels, later reproduced by Somoza: "Sandino keeps his 'cause' before the people of the countryside by operating small bandit groups under their respective jefes who personally gain by extracting small contributions. This policy, I believe, has encouraged the organization of small independent bands of thieves who are not connected with him but who assume his name in order to relieve themselves of responsibility for their acts of vandalism." [71] Such a portrayal is highly problematic. It erases crucial contexts, such as deep inequalities and marine-guardia violence; it denies any shared aspirations among the rebels ("jefes who personally gain") and the moral legitimacy of their cause; it separates too starkly nationalist ideology from class plunder, when in fact plundering the rich was often seen as entirely compatible with "offering one's life in defense of the nation's honor" and expelling the "Yankee cowards and criminals." [72] Yet parts of this portrayal are also in keeping with the interpretation being advanced here. Sandino's struggle did in fact "encourage the organization of [many] small independent bands" (though most were "connected with him" in some fashion), whose members frequently plundered the wealthy, and who employed Sandino's nationalist language to legitimate their actions. A similar dynamic obtained for family feuds, personal conflicts, and other struggles. In these and many other ways, Sandino's "patriot-traitor" dichotomy was appropriated by significant segments of the Segovian laboring poor and creatively linked to a host of much older battles—class, ethnic, family, political, personal—reproduced and reconfigured under this new semantic framework. Subaltern collective actions that the dominant culture and official state denounced as "murder and pillage" [73] were legitimated through an elastic language of popular nationalism, grafted onto much older popular discourses of honor, masculinity, and resistance to unjust authority—a creative synthesis forged from the rich tapestry of Segovian political culture, Sandino's leadership and vision, and the exigencies of a vastly unequal guerrilla war against the murderous gangs of a foreign invader.

Sandinismo thus emerged as one response to the marine invasion of the Segovias—one response among many. In untangling the various responses to the invasion and rebellion, one finds, in Michael Mann's apt phrase, a kind of "patterned mess." [74] While the evidence itself is partial and often contradictory, broad patterns do emerge. In general terms, it is clear that the rebels enjoyed enormous popular sympathy, and that a large percentage of the region's laboring poor actively aided the cause. It is also clear that the rebels had many enemies, and that a large percentage of these were not among the elite. While most Segovianos sympathized with the rebellion, a substantial proportion opposed it, as we will see. The dynamics of rebellion and war also created a host of more ambiguous spaces; more than just two polarized sides, the documents reveal many people who seem to be playing both sides of the fence, assisting each whenever necessary and offending neither whenever possible.

If we step back to consider the full spectrum of social classes in western Nicaragua and in the Segovias, however, it is evident that Sandino's base of support was considerably narrower than that cobbled together by the marines and guardia. In other words, the marines-guardia counted among their allies and supporters a significant fraction of all social classes and ethnic groups, from all parts of Nicaragua, while Sandino's rebels did not. This runs contrary to the thesis proposed by the Nicaraguan social scientist Oscar-René Vargas in 1986 and reiterated in his recent book: "Between 1930 and 1932, the petty bourgeoisie, pushed by the general deterioration of the country, began to aid the peasant rebels. This meant that the politico-moral influence of the bourgeoisie was broken; that Moncada's government did not represent more than a sector of the bourgeoisie; and that large private property and imperialism had lost ground, because their vassals, the small and medium peasants, looked for their salvation on the side of the propertyless." [75] The evidence compels a contrary conclusion, and a more supple set of categories by which to analyze Segovian (and Nicaraguan) social relations.

Who actively supported Sandino? First, few outside the Segovias and its eastern hinterlands.[76] As Knut Walter correctly observes, "In purely military and political terms, Sandino was a regional phenomenon . . . a regional caudillo." [77] While there were sporadic rebel incursions into the sparsely populated Atlantic Coast region and the more densely settled departments of Chontales, León, and Chinandega, most can be best characterized by Gilbert Joseph's phrase "revolution from without," and on the whole the rebellion remained regionally confined to the Segovias.[78] If we consider all of Nicaragua and employ the most generous estimates, we might venture that active support for the rebels was limited to around 10 percent of the population.[79] Importantly (and neglectedly), over nearly six years of war the rebels failed to generate any organic links with the popular classes of the Pacific littoral—perhaps their movement's most crippling long-term structural weakness. Throughout the war, most of the major newspapers of León, Managua, and Granada routinely denounced Sandino as a "bandit," his cause perhaps noble but his means deplorable.[80] And while significant segments of the urban artisanal and working classes generally sympathized with Sandino, there emerged no effective linkages through which such sympathies could be translated into organization and action.[81] This regional confinement of the rebellion resulted from a combination of factors: the social origins of Sandino's Liberal army in the Segovias during the civil war, the emergence of the rebels' core leadership from that original army, different agrarian histories and patron-client densities in regions adjacent to the Segovias, the geographic distance and deep cultural chasm that separated Pacific urban areas from the Segovian countryside, and a greater capacity for state repression and propagandizing in the cities and their hinterlands.

Turning then to the Segovias, and beginning at the top of the social hierarchy, it is plain that the literate and propertied, with very few exceptions, despised Sandino—mainly the result of the rebels' social and cultural "otherness" combined with their incessant demands for "forced contributions." Not uncommonly, elite perceptions of the Defending Army were laced with spleen and racism. "This is not an organized army or anything, all they are is a bunch of barefooted indians who are too lazy to work," thundered one landowner. "It would be an easy matter to hunt them up and exterminate them, if only they were shot when captured." [82] More commonly, property holders' opposition to the rebels was expressed in less strident terms. One coffee planter expressed the predominant view of his class when he observed that "after living in Nicaragua for sixteen years . . . I am in a position to say that the U.S. Marines in Nicaragua have done good to this country, mainly in maintaining peace and order, except in certain areas where the bands of General Sandino are still at large." [83]

This general antipathy toward the rebel cause extended to what Vargas calls the region's "petty bourgeoisie." Here Vargas is pointing to perhaps the region's most politically important group: that diverse, heterogeneous social class, composed of individuals, families, and family networks, occupying the expanding interstices of a historically castelike class-ethnic structure, in possession of significant cultural or material capital in comparison to the laboring poor. Professionals, merchants and traders, middling coffee growers and cattle ranchers, as well as telegraph operators, artisans, mule-team drivers, and others owning some capital other than land comprised perhaps 10 to 15 percent of the total populace, and more in towns and select subregions. The evidence is compelling that the great majority tended strongly, over time, to reject the rebels' authority and gravitate toward acceptance of the authority structure being erected by the marines and guardia. The reasons behind this tendency are not difficult to discern: for those not among the capital-less laboring poor, to ally unequivocally with the rebels was to commit the equivalent of class suicide.

Most middling farmers and ranchers fall into this category, men like Moisés González of Darailí, whose political trajectory, like that of his sons, helps reveal the tensions inherent in alliances between rebels and property holders. An old man in his seventies and a relatively prosperous first-generation coffee farmer and cattle rancher, González was a Liberal long before the civil war. At war's end he allied with Sandino, providing a strategically located base on his ranch at the crossroads of the San Rafael–Jinotega and Ocotal-Telpaneca regions. His sons Reinaldo and Moisés, and four of his nephews, joined the Defending Army. Soon after, the marines and guardia began settling into the area. In February 1928, González's nephew Luis Espinoza was killed in the famous Battle of El Bramadero.[84] By April, doubtless in response to the shifting balance of forces, González decided to cut his losses and accept, at least nominally, the authority of the marines. A garrison was established on his ranch, staffed by armed civilian volunteers. His sons applied for and received amnesties. By 1931, after numerous rebel attacks on his ranch-turned-garrison and the rebels' murder of one of his nephews, González and his sons were reportedly on Sandino's death list for "treason." All the while, González continued openly to express a profound distaste for the occupation.[85] For farmers like González, whose families comprised around 5 to 10 percent of the region, this political trajectory—from Liberal to Sandinista to reluctant marine-guardia ally—was less common than the more direct route, which bypassed the rebel phase altogether. Over the course of the rebellion, more than a dozen middling farmers and ranchers in the neighborhood of Darailí were attacked or killed for similarly "traitorous" behavior.[86] There were, in short, very few rebels among small-to-middling farmers, coffee growers, and cattle ranchers.

The same was true for merchants and professionals (lawyers, doctors, teachers, and others), less than 1 percent of the region's inhabitants but a powerful and influential group.[87] Perhaps some did assist the rebels voluntarily, but as a rule those who did lend assistance did so under duress or, less commonly, in the pursuit of profits.[88] Four or five of the bigger merchants with outlets across the Honduran border, for instance, reaped enormous sums bartering plundered Segovian property—horses, mules, coffee, clothes, record players, and other loot—for guns, ammunition, medicines, and other badly needed supplies.[89] But on the whole the merchant and professional classes deplored the rebels and their constant crimes against property, and the rebels deplored the merchants and professionals back. Even small local merchants with family connections to major rebel leaders, like Clemente Rodríguez of La Concordia, the brother-in-law of Sandino's wife Blanca Arauz, worked to keep at arm's length from the rebellion, in his case with mixed success.[90] To my knowledge, no merchants and only a small handful of Segovian professionals *became* Sandinistas, that is, embraced the rebellion's motivating ideology. The same was true of town artisans (carpenters, mechanics, shoemakers, blacksmiths, clerks, tailors, small traders, and others), perhaps 1 to 2 percent of the region's inhabitants.[91]

Similarly, only a small proportion of the permanent laborers on middling-to-large estates allied with the rebels (such laborers probably comprised less than 1 percent of the region's inhabitants). The marine-guardia archives contain many instances of permanent estate laborers threatened or killed by the rebels and assisting the forces of occupation, and comparatively few instances of their active support. The same is true of estate administrators (*mandadores*).[92]

Nor does it appear that most Indians in the surviving *comunidades indígenas* supported the rebellion. Of the country's largest comunidades—in the Pacific coastal region and extending across the highlands of Matagalpa, Chontales, and Boaco—none, the evidence indicates, offered the rebels significant or organized support. Things become more complicated in southwestern Jinotega, northwestern Matagalpa, and the western Segovias. Support for the rebels appears to have been strongest in the subregions that had experienced the progressive disintegration of comunidades over the preceding fifty or so years—especially in the zones just east of Yalí and Jinotega, and in the western Segovias near Somoto, Palacagüina, Totogalpa, and Yalagüina. The Jinotega comunidad, for example, had many Sandinista supporters, as did the San Lucas comunidad (south of Somoto); the Mosonte comunidad, on the other hand, did not. While all comunidades worked to exploit the political-military conjuncture to press demands during this period, in the great majority of cases those efforts did not include organized support for Sandino's rebels.[93]

In addition, over the course of the war the rebel movement gained very little of what can be described as local-regional literary-intellectual support.[94] In fact, the movement enjoyed much more literary-intellectual support outside the Segovias.[95] Only a very small percentage of the populace could read or write.[96] With one or two brief exceptions, there were no local newspapers.[97] Of the one or two thousand people who could be described as culturally literate, none (as far as I can tell) used their skills to promote the rebellion. As in most times and places throughout history, literacy in the Segovias was a tool of the dominant. The Sandinistas struggled to seize that tool, establishing schools in jungle camps, for instance, though till the end of the war most local jefes and the vast majority of their followers could neither read nor write.[98]

Three examples help to illustrate some larger patterns. Nicanor Espinosa, a leading Liberal lawyer in Telpaneca, published a scathing denunciation of Sandino in 1927 in the Managua newspapers (addressed to "my Segoviano friends and the companions of Sandino"). Two years later he was seized by the rebels and killed; he was last seen alive on the road to Yalagüina as their "prisoner without shoes or trousers."[99] Cipriano Rizo, secretary to the jefe político in Jinotega, was arrested and interrogated by the marines in early January 1930, suspected of stealing a mule: "[He has] a fair education, has been a strong admirer of Sandino, is strongly anti-American." Three weeks later, Rizo's coffee farm east of Jinotega was sacked and burned by rebel forces under Sandinista General Pedro Altamirano.[100] Daniel Olivas of Matagalpa, a shoemaker and publisher of a small newspaper, openly expressed spirited opposition to the intervention while remaining functionally disconnected from the rebel movement.[101] With the exception of national and transnational literary circuits outside the place and time that the rebellion was fought, this was not a movement of literate intellectuals.

In sum, then, Sandino's base of popular support never moved much beyond the unlettered and unpropertied of the Segovias. Within this heterogeneous group—again, from 80 to 90 percent of the region's inhabitants, consisting mainly of smallholding peasants, squatters, tenants, sharecroppers, seasonal estate laborers, and dispossessed Indians—popular support for the rebels was extremely deep and widespread, but far from universal.

On the flip side of this coin, active allies of the marines and guardia ran the gamut from barefoot peasants and Indians to wealthy landowners, and excluded members of no social class. In fact, a significant proportion of the marines' staunchest allies were poor and illiterate, as were most of the guardia themselves. "The enlisted men of the Guardia Nacional are practically all from the lower, uneducated classes," one memorandum explained.[102] Literacy requirements for enlistees were routinely waived.[103] As Colonel Denig's diary described it, "We have a lot of [Guardia] recruits here, Indians all. Their shoes hurt. They seem clumsy. Can't read." [104] Enlistment was voluntary, and many who sought to enlist were turned away.[105] The twelve dollars a month earned by the average enlisted man was far more than what could be earned in agricultural labor—more than the thirty cents a day he could make picking coffee, for instance.[106] In his landmark study, Richard Millett goes a long way toward explaining why so many lower-class Nicaraguans chose to serve in the guardia: "Regular pay, improved equipment, and medical care combined to make conditions for guardia enlisted men much better than the average Nicaraguan. Compared to the majority of his countrymen, the lot of the average guardia was not bad at all, and he knew it. After the first year, the forces never lacked recruits." [107] From May 1927 to December 1932, more than 5,200 men served in the guardia.[108] At least half served in the Segovias, and a substantial proportion of these were locals.[109] Many were Indians; in fact, Indian recruits were seen to possess some highly desirable qualities, despite their recruiters' deep-seated racism. "[Of] the men of the Guardia . . . those of pure Indian blood are especially proficient in many ways," wrote one intelligence analyst. "They often are expert in reading signs on the trail and in this respect are of the highest value on patrol." [110]

In addition to soldiers, the marines recruited as many as several thousand civilian spies, scouts, informants, guides, volunteers, *cívicos,* and other allies, many from the lowest echelons of rural society. Large numbers of people from all walks of life decided to exploit the opportunities opened up by the marines—people like Macario Martínez, *Capitán de Cañada* of Guasaca in Jinotega, "captain of a friendly band of well disciplined conservative indians [who] has proved himself to Marine patrols"; like Arcadio Gómez, a local ex-guardia civilian guide who applied for re-enlistment: "he knows every cowpath in this district and knows a large number of bandits, the bandits have threatened his life"; and like hundreds of nameable others.[111]

Indeed, without widespread civilian support, the marine occupation of the Segovias would scarcely have been possible. From the outset the marines and guardia were completely dependent on local individuals and communities for myriad aspects of their day-to-day operations. Most logistical problems—procuring food, horses, mules, billeting, and office space—and virtually all of the services deemed necessary, from laundresses and cooks to golf caddies and sexual partners, were generally resolved by negotiating contracts or establishing relations with local residents.[112] Not uncommonly, those providing such goods and services came to see the marine-guardia presence as an interest to be protected. "The attitude of individuals varies greatly in accordance with their relations with the marines," correctly observed one marine officer in late 1930. "Those in a position to profit financially are glad of the Marines." [113] Those at the top of the social hierarchy doubtless benefited the most, but there was a market for whoever had something to sell. Spies were paid handsomely for very dangerous work, for instance, as were guides, mule drivers, and scouts.[114] The author of another report put it this way: "It is my belief that the people of this area, although they hate and despise us they realize our presence means more wealth and greater personal safety and personal liberties to them." [115] The non sequitur here points not to widespread confusion among the populace but to a conflation of social categories: the people who hated and despised the marines were generally not the people who felt themselves wealthier and safer and freer as a result of the marine occupation.

Over time, the commanding officers of most garrisoned towns were able to stitch together dense networks of spies and informers from every social class and walk of life. Initially unable to procure even the most basic "dope" on the enemy, by the last years of the occupation the marines and guardia were reaping the benefits of a painstakingly constructed intelligence apparatus that spanned the entire north. Captain J. Ogden Brauer, stationed in Palacagüina, for instance, received regular (and extremely detailed) reports from a small army of personal spies. His methods, like those of his fellows, vacillated continuously between carrot and stick.[116] The stick was generally reserved for the countryside, the carrot for the town.

Still, cultivating friendships in the towns was an arduous task that could take some time, as Captains Frisbie, Shaw, and others learned in Jinotega in 1928. "The people of Jinotega all, or nearly all, profess to be anti-Sandino, but I doubt it," Captain Frisbie reported in late May. "No one seems willing to talk at all." A few days later he lamented that "No matter how much one tries to keep it from being so, the securing of information from residents is a personal matter." So Frisbie and his fellow officers made it personal. Six weeks later he reported that "two months ago the people were almost sullen and rarely spoke. . . . Now they are openly friendly and, wonder of wonders, some of the officers were asked to an impromptu dance at the club the other night." He added modestly, "I attribute it all to Captain Shaw's considerate and polite treatment of all natives," though his own diplomacy and tact probably played a role. As marine relations with the "better class" of townsfolk warmed, their sources of information and effectiveness grew. Relations between marines and lower-class natives were both mediated through local patron-client networks and established directly. During his first week in Jinotega, for instance, two *mozos* (laborers) stopped Captain Frisbie in the street to give him what he considered "true" information. A few months later the mozos of a prominent Liberal politician and landowner were brought before him with some important "dope." [117]

Most propertied Segovianos tended to view the marine occupation as a tolerable and necessary evil—"cordially detesting" their presence, in Salomón de la Selva's elegant characterization.[118] Many also worked to secure a marine presence on their properties. From 1928 on, petitions for marine-guardia protection poured in from across the north, from Matagalpa, Jinotega, Jalapa, Macuelizo, Mosonte, El Jícaro, Colón, La Concordia, and scores of settlements and farms.[119] At one level the occupation gave coffee growers and others a new weapon in an old struggle to better control and discipline labor. Many petitioners for marine-guardia "protection" were rightly suspected of furnishing "much misleading information . . . in an effort to have guards placed on private properties. These guards . . . are undoubtedly counted on to assist in obtaining labor and controlling this labor during the coffee season." It was commonly suspected that "some of the bandit raids have been inspired so as to give color to these reports [of banditry]"—that is, that many reported "raids" were either fabricated or prearranged—a recurring suspicion that was rarely proved.[120]

The responses of Segovianos to the marine invasion and occupation, in short, varied enormously. Very few were glad of it, a large majority hated it, large numbers fought against it, and most suffered because of it. As we know, from those sufferings and struggles was forged a new revolutionary political community, a rebel quasi-republic that effectively controlled and exercised hegemony over large parts of the north, and a new narrative of Nicaraguan history. But everything that was new was also embedded in something old. Social identities and allegiances in the Segovias, as we have seen, tended strongly to be partial, contingent, crosscutting, multilayered, and to feed into Sandino's struggle at many levels. The war, in a sense, ironically worked to simplify things. As in Vietnam, Algeria, and many other places, as the process of war unfolded, divisions sharpened, sides polarized, and any middle ground grew increasingly precarious.[121] Especially after Sandino's return from Mexico in mid-1930, all Segovianos felt increasing pressures, from both sides, to choose sides. Yet the evidence also shows that many people tried to hang on to whatever middle ground they could. A good liberal model here is of two sides squeezing the middle. But from the perspective of those being squeezed, there would seem to be at least three sides, each relentlessly pressing its own demands: (1) the rebels, (2) the marines-guardia, and (3) survival—of oneself and one's family. And in this triangular calculus, the first two sides might easily conflate, merging into a single foe—as they do in Jerónimo Aguilar Cortés's novel, for instance, and in many other texts.[122] For nearly six years, two states, essentially, battled for the allegiance of the civil populace. That populace, in turn—elite and subaltern alike—had a long history of successfully resisting the efforts of states to bring them into the orbit of their authority. Given that history, and the way events seem to have unfolded on the ground during the war, the evidence suggests that a very substantial proportion of Segovianos, following the dictates of survival and their own lights, usually tried to maintain a certain critical distance from both sides.

Relations between marines and guardia were similarly shot through with contradictions and ambiguities. "Due to differences in temperament, education, training, and language, close fraternization does not exist," one marine colonel admitted, though "in general" relations seemed to be "friendly."[123] One glowing assessment described "a splendid spirit of friendship . . . most cordial and mutually beneficial."[124] This was the commonest portrayal, and one most usefully read as bureaucratese for "we're working on it." There is abundant evidence that great social and cultural distances separated marines from native guardia. Patrol commanders, for instance, carefully avoided having too many natives and too few marines out in the bush together. "When a Guardia combat patrol exceeds sixteen men, more than one officer is quite essential," insisted one commander with extensive field experience. "This is a situation of particular pertinency in view of the state of discipline and training of the guardia and the general mediocrity, to say the least, of the non-commissioned personnel. On a long patrol where one is out of communication for days it becomes a rather serious matter."[125] Another commander put it more colorfully: "Taking the field alone with fifteen or twenty natives in bandit-infested country is a sporting proposition to be undertaken only by men not afraid of a sporting chance."[126] Marines had to be gingerly in "handling" enlisted men; too overbearing an attitude or too strict a disciplinary regimen could lead to disaster, as ten guardia mutinies attested.[127] "They handled us like dogs," lamented one Somotillo mutineer, "with blows and kicks, punishment and fines," referring here to both marines and native guardia.[128] By Marine Corps standards, desertion rates from the guardia were "heavy"—12.4 percent by one count—a fact attributed to "the comparatively unstable character of the Nicaraguan, the strenuous duty . . . [and] the lack of understanding as to the seriousness of the offense."[129]

This "seriousness" was intimately linked to one of the principal goals of the marine mission: the inculcation of a sense of "professionalism" and "duty" among the guardia, a sense of allegiance to the "imagined community" of the military, the national government, and the nation. Creating this sense of collective identity, particularly among enlisted men, remained an uphill battle. Most loyalties seem to have been directed toward the jefe and one's fellow soldiers, not to an abstraction called "duty" or "the guardia." "There is not yet MORALE in the Guardia as we understand that term," observed one senior officer in late 1929. "Some men are proud to be in the Guardia but the majority seem to have formed no ideas on the subject."[130] Three months later, another senior officer lamented that "their [the guardia's] loyalty appears almost wholly based on personal loyalty to their officers. Development of loyalty to their government as the duty of a soldier, above everything else, is not apparent in any perceptible degree yet." [131] Several years after the marine withdrawal, another officer mixed mechanical and religious metaphors to make the same point: "The individual guardia proved an active re-agent to the chemistry of leadership. . . . The 'Jefe' became the demigod of his men." [132] In order to counteract this tendency, a policy was soon developed to move enlisted men from post to post. It was hoped that such a practice would inhibit the development of exclusively *personal* loyalties and promote a more generalized sense of *organizational* loyalty. Successes were mixed, but on the whole, personal loyalties seem to have continued to outweigh other forms of allegiance.

At the same time, systematic efforts to inculcate a sense of collective identity among the guardia did achieve some partial successes. Traditions were invented, symbols constructed, rituals created—most in explicit opposition to the rebels they were trying to eradicate. Profound Sandinista hatred of the *machos* and *perros* (mules and dogs, i.e., marines and guardia) was evidently matched by an equally profound guardia hatred of the *bandoleros* (bandits).[133] This emergent sense of identity took many forms. It was expressed in the many spontaneous shouts of "¡Viva la guardia!" that punctuated the whizzing of bullets during battles. Dozens of instances resemble one patrol commander's observation that, "in the course of the fire fight some of the Guardia started a charge and shouted 'Viva la Guardia Nacional!'" He added: "That was a surprise to me." [134] Memorials were built to fallen comrades; special grave markers were erected; citations, commendations, and insignia proliferated. One marine detected among enlisted guardia a "delight in all forms of insignia." [135] After mid-1930, a "Guardia Newsletter" was published and circulated among the troops.[136]

There also emerged, in some places and times, considerable common ground between marines and guardia. Billeting, marching, and fighting together, sometimes getting wounded and killed together—it should not be surprising that a sense of common identity and shared sacrifice sometimes took root. Overall, however, the exchanges and borrowings that took place between the two militaries were more organizational and institutional than personal or individual.

In the process of suppressing a peasant rebellion, the guardia and marines combined two very different (yet in some respects hauntingly similar) ways of organizing and practicing violence. In the field, the resulting synthesis can be described as a kind of hybrid Segovian gang. The marines brought into the mix many of their own more "traditional" forms of violence making. Many marines hailed from the U.S. South, where lynchings, family feuds, and other forms of public ritual collective violence saturated the political culture.[137] These were combined with a host of more "modern" military technologies and sensibilities: field tactics, weapons and equipment, uniforms, surveillance techniques, and a sense of "discipline" and "duty." From the Segovian side came a host of traditionally Segovian practices: "guarantees," public ritual gang violence, local caudillismo. The combination of all of these ways of inflicting physical injury created a new order of organized violence, the likes of which the Segovian countryside had never seen.

One of the most horrific examples is Hanneken and Escamilla's infamous voluntarios, whose campaigns around Yalí in Jinotega department in the spring of 1929 remain legendary in the region. Captain Herman H. Hanneken had learned "bush warfare" in Haiti; the Mexican Juan J. Escamilla had been a Liberal general in the civil war. Their combined efforts cut a swath of destruction and death in the region unprecedented in its magnitude. More "modern" contributions included the rounding up and "reconcentrating" of many hundreds of civilians, accompanied by reams of detailed information on the social networks of the "bandits." More "traditional" aspects included methods of extracting information, summary executions in the bush (complete with transcripts of kangaroo trials), burnings, tortures, beatings, rapes, and murders.[138] In the years to follow, the same region suffered through Puller and Lee's even more infamous "Company M." "Chesty" Puller of World War II fame earned the nom de guerre "the Tiger of the Mountains" among the people he helped to terrorize, while stories still circulate about Lieutenant Lee throwing babies up into the air, spearing them with a bayonet, and eating their hearts.[139]

Such columns resembled Segovian gangs in many ways. The group's cohesion derived from personal loyalty to charismatic individual officers, loyalties most likely created and nurtured, in large part, through shared discourses of masculinity and gender.[140] Company M's effectiveness in the field derived from the combination of modern technologies of warfare and a host of more ancient practices designed to propagate a generalized sense of fear among the populace. Numbers alone would suggest that most of the violence was produced by natives, a conclusion not contradicted by the documentary evidence. Native guardia commonly took the initiative in firefights with rebels, and after mid-1930, green marines commonly deferred to more seasoned native guardia officers.[141]

This interpretation, of course, flies in the face of an important element of the heroic narrative, expressed by Gustavo Alemán Bolaños in 1935: "The Yankee Marines taught cruelty to the Nicaraguan soldier, violating his noble nature. They gave him lessons so he would kill human beings without mercy, so he would break the sacred law of fraternity, killing compatriots. They taught the Guardia to behave like mercenaries in their own land." [142] Compelling myth can make fallacious history. As we have seen, Segovianos required no "lessons" in "cruelty" from North Americans. What members of the guardia needed, both to advance their own individual interests and to suppress the rebellion, was to be integrated into organizational-bureaucratic structures linked fiscally to the state, and access to more modern technologies of warfare. The Nicaraguan government offered the former, the North Americans the latter.

Mapping Mountains, Mapping Bodies: State Formation in the Segovias

War making and state making have much in common. Charles Tilly, in his masterful survey of the past thousand years of European history, concludes that "war wove the European network of national states, and preparation for war created the internal structures of the states within it." [143] Much of what I have been describing was in fact part and parcel of a larger process of state formation: the fluid, contingent, and (in retrospect) inexorable process by which the central state extended its reach into social spaces that had hitherto eluded its grasp.

On the other hand, war making and state making are not the same thing. The formation of states is a complicated business, as much an ideological and cultural process as a military, political, or economic one. At one level, state formation is a function of the extension of national and transnational capitalist market networks and the growth of the state's bases of finance and taxation. At the level of culture and ideology, state formation is expressed in the state's active construction of a shared sense of its own moral legitimacy, through ritual, ceremony, iconography, educational systems, and the like. At a related and fundamental level, state formation is defined by the successful monopolization of the legitimate use of violence, the state's garnering unto itself all substantial means of organized coercion. And since states are complicated, heterogeneous, not entirely coherent actors and sites of contestation, state formation is not uncommonly an uneven, asymmetrical process.

Such was the case in Nicaragua and the Segovias. Over the course of the rebellion, market and production relations saw no radical changes; the state's tax base, bureaucracy, and administration all remained moored to more ancient, patrimonial forms.[144] At the same time, the military arm of the state became vastly more professionalized and "modern" over the course of the war, its capacity to regulate, survey, control, and dominate the populace witnessing quantum leaps forward at virtually every level. This can be seen in two principal spheres: in the guardia's growing *coercive* powers, and in its growing *surveillance* powers. The growth of both aspects of state power represents one of the most significant changes of the entire period.[145] I have already discussed the former at some length. Let us turn to the latter.

Social theorists as diverse as Anthony Giddens and Michel Foucault have explored some of the ways in which modern states work to control their citizenry through technologies of surveillance and regulation. They have observed how the state works to extend its gaze into every aspect of the citizen's daily life, through what Giddens calls "the accumulation of 'coded information' . . . [and] the direct supervision of the activities of some individuals by others in positions of authority over them." [146] Perhaps the most vivid illustration of the state's efforts to better survey and regulate the populace in the Segovias during this period is Colonel Denig's failed reconcentration program of May and June 1930. In his orders for the proposed reconcentration, Denig expressed the paradox that lay at the heart of the U.S. mission in the Segovias from beginning to end: the marine-guardia's inability to distinguish between the "honest citizens" they were trying to protect and the "bandits" they were trying to destroy. For Colonel Denig, the only logical solution was to more effectively survey, regulate, and control everyone. "There are potential bandit forces widely scattered, and over which no surveillance can be exercised," he explained. His solution was to empty the countryside into the towns, since "once having presented themselves in these towns, the natives may be kept under surveillance." [147] In addition, each reconcentrated person was to receive a card, or *boleta*. The program was soon abandoned as impractical and counterproductive, but Denig insisted that "people should be warned to preserve their cards as evidence that they complied with the proclamation." [148]

There were in fact several failed reconcentration programs and many types of boletas and efforts to issue boletas (referred to variously as cards, boletas, *Plata boletas* [those issued by voluntario General Alejandro Plata in the spring of 1929 around Yalí], *boletas de ocupación,* certificates, passes, passports, good conduct papers, good citizenship papers, and papers). After around mid-1930, possession of such papers was evidently mandatory for all inhabitants of the region, even though no centralized authority was charged with issuing them. Instead, boletas seem to have been issued locally, with each department, municipality, or military district issuing its own style, rather like "guarantees" issued by the local offices of the state, and yet another indication of the partial and uneven nature of the state's extension into the region. Related surveillance and control techniques appeared around the same time, combining both civil and military jurisdictions. By 1931, superintending the coffee harvest on *fincas* near Yalí evidently required permission from both military and civilian authorities.[149] One marine commander at Telpaneca, surrounded by a sea of smallholding peasants, even tried to arrogate to the marines the right to grant permission to plant and harvest crops. He was unsuccessful.[150] Around the same time, houses and their inhabitants were routinely searched and registered in military sweeps.[151] This was all a very uneven and messy process, but the general direction of things is clear: the gaze of the state was steadily working its way into the social fabric of the region.

One sees the centralization of the state's surveillance capabilities in the evolution of the form and content of the documents themselves, especially that vital species known as the intelligence report. In 1927 and early 1928, the guardia's intelligence apparatus was rudimentary, decentralized, nonstandardized; Jinotega had little idea of what Ocotal was doing. Reports appeared in different forms and formats and at uneven intervals; jurisdictions overlapped; efforts were duplicated. If we fast forward to 1932, we now find a single standardized intelligence report, the GN-2, issued on the first of the month and covering a one-month interval—detailed, lengthy (some nearly fifty pages), brimming with useful information. By 1932 the documents have a different, more standardized *feel;* even the typefaces nearly all look the same.

One especially sees the extension of the gaze of the state in the marine-guardia's endless exercises in mapping. Early in the war, maps of the Segovias were virtually useless. Marines on patrol frequently had little idea of where they were or where they had been. By late 1932, the labors of hundreds of patrol commanders and the Mapping Section had combined to produce an astonishingly detailed understanding of the physical (not to mention the social) landscape. The 1934 U.S. Army Map that eventually emerged out of the occupation (and on which my own interminable exercises in mapping were based) remains an impressively sophisticated and accurate text.[152] The head of B-2's Intelligence Section summed up the critical importance of mapmaking: "The compilation and gradual building up of a good map should be its [the section's] primary and lasting work."[153] So it was.

Conterminous with the mapping of the physical landscape was the mapping of the social. One sees this in endless forms, but especially in the lists upon lists of names: who lived where; who worked where and for whom; who associated with whom; who "bandit suspect" X's brothers and uncles and cousins were. The production, codification, and accumulation of this kind of information were among the top priorities of patrol commanders and intelligence analysts alike (and incidentally permit latter-day historians to mine that accumulation of data). The information Captain Hanneken squeezed from informants in the spring of 1929 is all but breathtaking in its detail and volume, and his forays into this arena were only a small piece in a much larger puzzle.

By mid-1930, as a result of the systematic application of these and related "modern" technologies of warfare, the field strength of the guardia began to far exceed the power of any previous military organization in Nicaraguan history. With a timetable set for the marine withdrawal, the marine brass, the State Department, and the Nicaraguan government routinely worked to improve and expand the guardia's bureaucratic-organizational infrastructure. The Nicaraguan National Military Academy was founded on 1 April 1930 to train a cadre of senior officers in anticipation of the marine withdrawal. After mid-1930 the academy graduated between twenty and thirty "professionalized" officers every three months.[154] Many former high-ranking military officers of both parties, and their sons, took advantage of the process, including many Zelayistas excluded from military service for the better part of two decades. By the end of 1932, many members of the traditional leading families of León, Granada, and elsewhere had been credentialed in the academy, and most of these came to populate the uppermost echelons of the guardia—another deep continuity with the past.[155]

Toward the end of the rebellion, Sandino himself seems to have been deeply confused and troubled about the guardia, denying its constitutionality, rejecting its authority, but confronted daily with the reality of its power.[156] The extent of that power was perhaps best expressed in the rebellion's denouement after Sandino's assassination in February 1934. The IES testimonies, along with much other evidence, make it abundantly clear that after Sandino's assassination, all remnants of rebel organization were destroyed and all remaining rebels either hid, fled, migrated, changed their names, surrendered, switched sides, or were killed.[157] By this time, things had come, in a sense, full circle. What began as a largely homegrown intra-elite civil war had become a regional popular-nationalist liberation movement held together by the patriotic ideal of expelling the hated Yankee invaders—the footsoldiers of an invasion intended to eradicate a movement that would never have existed without an invasion. In a relatively brief time the war against that liberation movement was effectively Nicaraguanized, by means of a new military organization that was both U.S.-imposed and indigenously Nicaraguan. After January 1933, the war once more pitted only Nicaraguan against Nicaraguan, with U.S. troops no longer directly involved, only now with a far stronger, more militarized, and more centralized state. That state soon consolidated its rule, and the result was the next forty-three years of Somocismo.

Conclusion

In recent years, scholars of diverse fields and disciplines have worked to transcend the bipolar paradigms of U.S.–Latin American relations that have long dominated popular and scholarly approaches to the subject. This heterogeneous body of scholarship has sought, among other things, to explore "the range of networks, exchanges, borrowings, behaviors, discourses, and meanings" through which the internal and external became intermeshed and "through which foreign people, ideas, commodities, and institutions have been received, contested, and appropriated in [modern] Latin America." [158]

This essay has aimed to contribute to this growing body of literature by sketching out an alternative to the metanarratives that have dominated thinking on Sandino's rebellion and the marine intervention in Nicaragua. It has focused on the contradictions, ambiguities, and ironies of the processes by which Segovianos and marines interacted, showing that there was much more to this process than heavy-handed U.S. imperial domination and heroic patriotic resistance (or benign U.S. tutelage and lower-class brigandage). It has tried to attend to the nitty-gritty of large historical processes by *tracing connections*—between the small and the large, the old and the new, the local and regional, and the national and transnational; the worlds of discourse, culture, and meaning; and the worlds of materiality, practice, and violence.

Such tracings reveal that the closer to ground-level one gets, to people living and working and struggling in a particular place and time, the more complicated, ambiguous, and contingent things become. Yet not all is an ambiguous mess; as processes unfold, patterns emerge. This essay has worked to highlight those patterns, to shed new light on how a series of old struggles in the Segovias combined with the marine intervention, and with what consequences, intended and not. On the one hand, the dynamics of the period gave rise to a new popular-nationalist social imaginary and discourse of national sovereignty, popular liberation, and inalienable human rights among historically subordinate groups. On the other hand, those same dynamics also worked to accelerate the successful monopolization of the means of organized violence by the military arm of the central state.

This essay has offered new perspectives on the formation and distinguishing characteristics of Sandino's rebellion and his paradigm of national liberation. It has argued that Sandino's nationalist ideology and practice were at once profoundly emancipatory and profoundly self-destructive. For the subordinate majority, Sandinismo's emancipatory potential lay in its vision of a more just society and a means—armed struggle—to achieve it. Yet that vision and means also carried costs. For Nicaragua as a whole, Sandinismo's self-destructive potential lay in its re-division of the "nation" and "race" it sought to remake: the conflation of "invaders" (foreigners) and "traitors" (natives) served to embed enduring civil conflict into the very core of the rebellion's ideology. Deep class, power, and ethnic inequalities and the exigencies of guerrilla war combined with this patriot-traitor dichotomy to make Sandino's rebellion as much an indigenous civil war and class-ethnic struggle as a patriotic struggle to expel the foreign invader. The moral clarity of the Sandinista vision was rooted in the stark realities of foreign invasion and marine violence. Depthless hatred of the "Yankee invaders" provided a kind of glue that bound together diverse groups and individuals in common purpose.[159] Sandino used that hatred as a means by which to propagate a vocabulary of national sovereignty and social justice among the Segovian laboring poor. Once that foreign aggressor withdrew its troops, however, there was nothing palpable left to hate except the central state and its army. The struggle to expel the invaders provided a strategic opening for subordinate groups to continue old battles under a newly emergent language and structure of authority, while the war against the Sandinistas provided a strategic opening for other individuals and groups, dominant and subordinate alike, to do much the same thing. This paper has worked to more fully understand the interplay of these contradictory effects of U.S. intervention, as part of the same process of social transformation.

In combination with other recent scholarship, the findings presented here also challenge conventional Sandinista understandings of the origins and character of the Somocista state.[160] The Guardia Nacional was not *only* a U.S. imposition, the blunt instrument of imperialist domination. (At the same time, I would insist that the guardia *was* very much an imperialist imposition.) From very early on, the guardia was an integral part of Segovian (and Nicaraguan) society, deeply embedded in the social fabric of the region (and country)—its families, communities, towns, farms, ranches, haciendas, indigenous communities, and patronage networks. Sandinismo and the guardia emerged together, out of the same process of struggle.

The story told here necessarily suffers many omissions and silences. Its regional focus has meant that national and international political-economic developments have been pushed largely into the background. A more complete story would link the processes examined here to national and transnational levels, particularly the process of state formation. This essay does not pretend to offer much more than a skeletal regional survey of Nicaraguan state formation during this period. Nor does it argue that Sandino unintentionally caused the consolidation of the central state. That state surely would have consolidated with or without Sandino, though not in the same way or by the same timeline. By the end of the 1926–1927 Civil War, the United States and a critical mass of Nicaragua's political elite were determined to put an end to the country's interminable civil wars by creating the conditions under which a strong central state could and would take shape. The formation of the guardia and the upward displacement of organized violence were going to take place with or without a peasant rebellion in the Segovias. Rather, this essay has tried to show how that imperative to make a state played out at a regional level, and how Sandino's rebellion propelled the process forward, both regionally and (to a lesser extent) nationally.

The essay has emphasized the role of organized violence in shaping the trajectory of social change in Nicaragua and the Segovias during this period, and has argued that changes and continuities in the organization of violence were key to the historical dynamics of the period. This is not because of some a priori theoretical concern with violence; it is what a protracted (and sometimes rancorous) conversation with the evidence has convinced me was so. Related factors not examined here also shaped the trajectory of Nicaraguan history during this period. The foregoing has not tried, in any sustained way, to connect the centralization of the means of coercion to capitalist transformation, a longer-term process that was also key to the formation of the Nicaraguan state. Nor has it tried to relate the Segovias or Nicaragua to isthmus-wide developments in the 1920s and 1930s, which saw the consolidation of quasi-fascist, bureaucratic-authoritarian states like Somoza's across the isthmus. It has neglected to address as well a series of macrosociological questions about the origins and shifting aims of U.S. imperialism in Nicaragua and elsewhere.[161] These omissions were deliberate: a single essay can't do everything, and the story is complicated enough as it is. The next step will be to bring the evidence and arguments presented here into dialogue with existing literatures on U.S. imperialism, transitions to capitalism, and state formation at national and isthmus-wide levels.

Finally, the story told here challenges, at least implicitly, some of the undergirding assumptions of the dominant theoretical paradigms in the human sciences. Liberalism's "traditional-modern" bipolarity and implicit teleology not only impede understanding of historical process, but efface the central political project and contradiction of liberalism (and neoliberalism) in practice: the ideological legitimation of social consensus under conditions of profound class and power inequality. Marxist, neo-Marxist, and related approaches, while contributing a host of crucial conceptual categories—irony, process, agency, struggle, and material relations in production and exchange—also strongly tend to invert and reconfigure liberalism's bipolarities (bourgeois-proletariat, feudalism-capitalism, imperialism–anti-imperialism, center-periphery), thus reproducing liberalism's teleology and disabling dichotomies. Approaches that can be considered "cultural" or "postcolonial" in one sense or another contribute to a deepened understanding of culture, language, representation, contingency, the pervasiveness and heterogeneity of power, and the social construction of meaning, but tend to reify discourse and thereby efface the manifold connections between the discursive realm and the realities of class power, state power, violence, and the ironies of historical process in on-the-ground struggles. The poststructuralist, postmodern penchant for "decentering the autonomous subject" and "subverting master narratives," part of a salutary project in many ways, needs to confront the reality that people often *do* find their centers through the agency of such narratives. Any genuinely emancipatory project needs a compelling story to mobilize people into believing that they are capable of creating a more just society. People need to envision a better future in order to create one; perhaps the point is that the narrative and vision need to be the right ones.

The foregoing attempt to muddy up the metanarratives of the period is not, as noted early on, the only one of its kind. There have long been some voices, at the margins, that have worked against the grain of the dominant stories. Juan Cortés, the protagonist in Jerónimo Aguilar Cortés's marvelously textured novel *Memorias de los yanquis a Sandino* (1972), for instance, joins the guardia to get back at the marines, who in their arrogance and "barbarism" had thrown him in jail for daring to demand his "rights." He is assigned to active duty in the Segovias and, unmoored from his family, friends, and the restraining effects of the city, undergoes a kind of despiritualization, a "transformation from a good man into a criminal guardia," becoming both a witness to and active producer of violence, devastation, and death. The realization eventually dawns that guardia and rebels have much in common; the horrors and sufferings that both visit on the humble mountain people serve to conflate the two. "There were times, in truth," confesses Private Cortés, "that I didn't know how to distinguish between us and them." After several bloody encounters with the "bandits," he is wounded, separated from his column, and captured. The "bandits" turn out to be just that—cold-blooded killers and criminals whose nationalist rhetoric is merely a smokescreen for robbery, murder, and mayhem. He eventually escapes, and the novel ends without a clear resolution, only a denunciation of the violence on all sides and a call for reconciliation.[162] Aguilar Cortés thus combines elements of both master narratives in some unexpected and ironic ways, whatever one thinks of his portrayal of the ideals motivating the rebels (my own view is that most of it is grossly inaccurate).

Abelardo Cuadra's memoirs, *Hombre del Caribe* (1977), combine elements of these narratives in a different way. Cuadra was a guardia Second Lieutenant serving in the Segovias during the rebellion.[163] Unlike Aguilar Cortés, Cuadra acknowledges the validity of Sandinista patriotism, while also recognizing the morality of the marines and the patriotism of the men who served in the guardia. The guardia's ideals, Cuadra maintains, were corrupted by its *jefe director,* Anastasio Somoza, leading to Cuadra's involvement in a plot to kill Somoza, and his subsequent imprisonment and exile.

These are but two of the handful of literary interventions that challenge and subvert the dominant narratives of the period.[164] It is a subversion that might well continue; marginalized voices need to be brought into dialogue with each other and with those at the center. For it is only in the process of displacing old centers that new ones can be created.

Notes

I would like to thank Mine Ener, Nora Faires, Ada Ferrer, Eileen Findlay, Lessie Jo Frazier, Paul Gootenberg, Bridget Hayden, Gil Joseph, Paul Kobrak, Jonathan Marwil, Rosario Montoya, and especially John Peters for their helpful comments on previous drafts of this essay. Many thanks are also due to the Yale conference organizers, and to everyone who helped make it what it was. Any errors or lapses in judgment are mine alone. Research and writing were generously supported by the Office of Research and the College of Arts and Sciences at the University of Michigan—Flint.

1. Report of Patrol, D. E. Wells, 19 Nov. 1927, Record Group 127, entry 43A, box 3, 2d Brigade B-2 Intelligence and Patrol Reports, United States National Archives and Records Administration, Washington, D.C. (hereafter NA[Record Group number]/[entry]/[box]/[file]).

2. Ignacio Vargas to Eberhardt, 18 Jan. 1927, United States Department of State, Records Relating to the Internal Affairs of Nicaragua, 1910–1929 (hereafter USDS), 817.00/4952. Open civil war in the Segovias began around October 1926, the same month as Sandino's uprising at San Albino. See Michael J. Schroeder, " 'To Defend Our Nation's Honor': Toward a Social and Cultural History of the Sandino Rebellion in Nicaragua, 1927–1934," 2 vols. (Ph.D. diss., University of Michigan, 1993), chap. 4.

3. "Winter," the rainy season, generally runs from May to November, according to the many Segovianos I spoke with during my fieldwork in the region in September and October 1990. "The Segovias," here and in the literature generally, signifies the region of north-central Nicaragua indicated on the accompanying map, embracing all of the departments of Nueva Segovia (divided into Nueva Segovia and Madríz after 1936) and Estelí, the northeastern corner of Chinandega (from Villanueva north) and northern tip of León, southeastern Jinotega, and northwest Matagalpa. Here I extend conventional definitions to include the southwestern part of Honduras stretching from Cifuentes in the northeast to El Triunfo in the southwest and stretching into Honduras for twenty or so miles. The boundaries of this region are necessarily imprecise, and more usefully conceived as geographic, social, and political frontiers, as explored more fully below. Cf. Magnus Mörner, *Region and State in Latin America's Past* (Baltimore, Md.: Johns Hopkins University Press, 1993).

4. I use the term *imperialist* deliberately here, in explicit demurral to recent critiques of the concept; see Noam Chomsky, *Agenda* (Ann Arbor, Mich.), Feb. 1991; the debate in *Radical History Review* 57 (fall 1993); and Patrick Wolfe, "Imperialism and History: A Century of Theory, from Marx to Postcolonialism," *American Historical Review* 102, no. 2 (Apr. 1997): 388–420.

5. The phrase *hunting bandits* was commonplace, e.g., Patrol Report, Kelly, 6 Jan. 1931, NA127/202/13. The Ejército Defensor de la Soberanía Nacional de Nicaragua was founded on 2 Sept. 1927. Robert E. Conrad, ed. and trans., *Sandino: The Testimony of a Nicaraguan Patriot, 1921–1934* (Princeton, N.J.: Princeton University Press, 1990), 95–97.

6. For the terms of the treaty, see Neill Macaulay, *The Sandino Affair* (Durham, N.C.: Duke University Press, 1985), 38–41.

7. Conrad, *Sandino,* 75, 83.

8. See Richard V. Salisbury, *Anti-imperialism and International Competition in Central America, 1920–1929* (Wilmington, Del.: SR Books, 1989); Sheldon B. Liss, *Radical Thought in Central America* (Boulder, Colo.: Westview Press, 1991);

Rodolfo Cerdas-Cruz, *The Communist International in Central America* (Basingstoke, U.K.: Macmillan Press, 1993); Julie Skurski, "The Ambiguities of Authenticity in Latin America: *Doña Bárbara* and the Construction of National Identity," *Poetics Today* 15, no. 4 (winter 1994); and Doris Sommer, *Foundational Fictions: The National Romances of Latin America* (Berkeley and Los Angeles: University of California Press, 1991).

9. See Instituto de Estudio del Sandinismo, *Pensamiento antimperialista en Nicaragua* (Managua: Nueva Nicaragua, 1982).

10. This has long been recognized. Most of the abundant published literature on the period is structured around this irony, from Emigdio Maraboto's *Sandino ante el coloso* (Mexico City: Editorial Vera Cruz, 1929) to Gregorio Selser's landmark *Sandino, general de hombres libres*, 2 vols. (Buenos Aires: T. I. Ricaldone, 1958), to Oscar-René Vargas's *La intervención norteamericana y sus consequencias, Nicaragua 1910-1925* (Managua: DILESA) and his *Floreció al filo de la espada: El movimiento de Sandino, 1926-1939* (Managua: Centro de Estudios de la Realidad Nacional [CEREN], 1995).

11. For compelling synthetic essays on these issues, see Frederick Cooper, Allen F. Isaacman, Florencia E. Mallon, William Roseberry, and Steve J. Stern, *Confronting Historical Paradigms: Peasants, Labor, and the Capitalist World System in Africa and Latin America* (Madison: University of Wisconsin Press, 1993).

12. In addition to published sources, this study depends particularly on two bodies of evidence: more than fifty feet of files produced and collected by the marines and the guardia from 1927 to 1932 (a remarkably rich collection that includes thousands of patrol, combat, and intelligence reports, captured Sandinista correspondence, prisoner statements, and a wealth of other material), and a series of more than seventy oral interviews with former soldiers in Sandino's army, conducted from 1980 to 1984 by the Instituto de Estudio del Sandinismo (currently the Instituto de Historia de Nicaragua, Managua, hereafter cited as the IES testimonies). The testimonies were produced as part of an IES project to recover historical memories of Sandino's struggle and promote the ideals and ideology of the 1979 Sandinista Revolution.

13. Major scholarly exceptions here include Macaulay, *The Sandino Affair;* Richard Millett, *Guardians of the Dynasty* (New York: Orbis, 1979); Donald Hodges, *Intellectual Foundations of the Nicaraguan Revolution* (Austin: University of Texas Press, 1986); Jeffrey L. Gould, *To Lead as Equals: Rural Protest and Political Consciousness in Chinandega, Nicaragua, 1912-1979* (Chapel Hill: University of North Carolina Press, 1990); Knut Walter, *The Regime of Anastasio Somoza, 1936-1956* (Chapel Hill: University of North Carolina Press, 1993); Charles R. Hale, *Resistance and Contradiction: Miskitu Indians and the Nicaraguan State, 1894-1987* (Stanford, Calif.: Stanford University Press, 1994); David Whisnant, *Rascally Signs in Sacred Places: The Politics of Culture in Nicaragua* (Chapel Hill: University of North Carolina Press, 1995); Volker Wünderich, *Sandino: Una biografía política* (Managua: Nueva Nicaragua, 1995); and Richard Grossman,

" 'Hermanos en la patria': Nationalism, Honor, and Rebellion: Augusto Sandino and the Army in Defense of the National Sovereignty of Nicaragua, 1927–1934" (Ph.D. diss., University of Chicago, 1996).

14. The literature here is extensive; for a select bibliography, consult Augusto C. Sandino, *El pensamiento vivo,* ed. Sergio Ramírez, vol. 2 (Managua: Editorial Nueva Nicaragua, 1984), 513. The phrase "crazy little army" is the Chilean Nobel laureate Gabriela Mistral's, taken by Gregorio Selser for the title of his second book on Sandino's rebellion, *El pequeño ejército loco* (Buenos Aires: Triángulo, 1958).

15. Anastasio Somoza García, *El verdadero Sandino o el calvario de las Segovias* (Managua: Tipografía Robelo, 1936); works of the same narrative include José María Moncada, *Nicaragua, sangre en sus montañas* (San José: n.p., 1985); Juan Matagalpa, *Sandino, los Somoza, y los nueve comandantes sandinistas* (n.p., c. 1984 [Hatcher Library, University of Michigan]); Humberto Belli, *Breaking Faith* (Westchester, Ill.: Puebla Institute, 1985), 3–6; and an enormous number of Nicaraguan newspaper and magazine articles and editorials (e.g., see the "summings up" in *El Centroamericano* [León], *La Noticia, La Prensa,* and *El Cronista,* [Managua] in Feb.–Mar. 1934, in the wake of Sandino's assassination; and Emilio Gutiérrez G. in *Revista Conservadora de Pensamiento Centramericano* 6, no. 33 [June 1963]: 30). Marine-centric and U.S.-centric histories that embrace this narrative include United States Department of State, *The United States and Nicaragua: A Survey of the Relations from 1909 to 1932* (Washington, D.C.: Government Printing Office, 1932); John M. Wearmouth, "The Second Marine Intervention in Nicaragua, 1927–1932" (master's thesis, Georgetown University, 1952); Lejeune Cummins, *Quijote on a Burro* (Mexico City: Impresora Azteca, 1958); General Vernon E. Megee, "United States Military Intervention in Nicaragua (master's thesis, University of Texas, 1963); Thomas J. Dodd Jr., "United States in Nicaraguan Politics: Supervised Elections, 1927–1932" (Ph.D. diss., George Washington University, 1966), and issues of the *New York Times, Marine Corps Gazette,* and *Leatherneck* from the period.

16. Most notably, in addition to the works cited above, see Sofonías Salvatierra, *Sandino o la tragedia de un pueblo* (Madrid: Europa, 1934), whose judiciousness is exceptional; Salvador Calderón Ramírez, *Los últimos días de Sandino* (Mexico: Ediciones Botas, 1934); Abelardo Cuadra, *Hombre del Caribe* (San José: EDUCA, 1977; published posthumously); Manolo Cuadra, *Contra Sandino en la montaña* (Managua: n.p., 1942); and Jerónimo Aguilar Cortés, *Memorias de los yanquis a Sandino* (San Salvador: IT Ricaldone, 1972).

17. See Whisnant, *Rascally Signs,* 356–57.

18. See Steven Palmer, "Carlos Fonseca and the Construction of Sandinismo in Nicaragua," *Latin American Research Review* 23, no. 1 (1988). It should be noted that Sandino's ideology did not attempt to overturn the oppressive and exploitative features of gender relations, though the Defending Army's strict moral codes against rape (which the evidence suggests were strongly enforced and widely ad-

hered to) did represent an abrupt departure from past practices; see Schroeder, "To Defend Our Nation's Honor," 248.

19. The phrase "exterminating bandits" appears in Recommendation for restriction for certain areas of Nueva Segovia, R. L. Denig, 10 May 1930, NA127/202/17/94.

20. Quote from Jorge Casteñeda, *Utopia Unarmed: The Latin American Left after the Cold War* (New York: Vintage, 1994), 272.

21. A strong current in the literature tends to limit analyses of Sandino's Sandinismo to the Supreme Chief's writings, utterances, intellectual formation, and belief systems; most recently, see Alejandro Bendaña, *La mística de Sandino* (Managua: Centro de Estudios Internacionales, 1994); see also Donald Hodges, *Intellectual Foundations,* esp. chaps. 1–3, and his *Sandino's Communism: Spiritual Politics for the Twenty-first Century* (Austin: University of Texas Press, 1992); David Nolan, *The Ideology of the Sandinistas and the Nicaraguan Revolution* (Coral Gables, Fla.: Institute of Inter-American Studies, University of Miami, 1984); and Hugo Cancino Troncoso, *Las raíces históricas e ideológicas del movimiento sandinista: Antecedentes de la revolución popular nicaragüense, 1927–79* (Odense: Odense University Press, 1984). Peter Worsley's admonition seems useful here: "[If we] focus our eyes exclusively or even primarily upon the leader element in the leader-follower relationship, our attention is distracted from what is sociologically [and historically] more important, to wit, the *relationship* between the two elements." Worsley, *The Trumpet Shall Sound* (New York: Schocken Books, 1968), xviii.

22. Michael Mann, *The Sources of Social Power,* vol. 2 (Cambridge: Cambridge University Press, 1993).

23. Or, in Gramscian terms, the moment of consent was subordinate to the moment of coercion; Antonio Gramsci, *Selections from the Prison Notebooks,* ed. and trans. Quintin Hoare and Geoffrey Nowell Smith (New York: International Publishers, 1971). In Tillian terms, the Segovias comprised a "coercion-intensive region" as opposed to a "capital intensive" or "capitalized coerci[ve]" one; see Charles Tilly, *Coercion, Capital, and European States, AD 990–1990* (London: Basil Blackwell, 1990), 99.

24. The phrase "localization of sovereignties" is from Pedro Francisco de la Rocha, "Revista política sobre la historia de la revolución de Nicaragua," *Revista del pensamiento centroamericano* 180 (July–Sept. 1983): 25. For a comparative treatment of the "fragmentation of sovereignties" in Europe over a thousand-year period, see Tilly, *Coercion, Capital, and European States.* For Nicaragua and Central America see Dana Munro, *The Five Republics of Central America* (New York: Oxford University Press, 1918); Humberto Belli, "Un ensayo de interpretación sobre las luchas políticas nicaragüenses (de la Independencia hasta la Revolución Cubana), *Revista del pensamiento centroamericano* 32 (Oct.–Dec. 1977); Alberto Lanuza, Juan Luis Vásquez, Amaru Barahona, and Amalia Chamorro, *Economía y sociedad en la construcción del estado en Nicaragua* (San José: ICAP, 1983). On

violence as a "background condition" in Latin American cattle frontier regions, see Silvio R. Duncan Baretta and John Markoff, "Civilization and Barbarism: Cattle Frontiers in Latin America," *Comparative Studies in Society and History* 20, no. 4 (Oct. 1978).

25. See José Dolores Gámez, *Historia de Nicaragua* (Managua: El País, 1889); for an early English-language treatment of these issues, see Munro, *The Five Republics of Central America,* esp. chap. 9. See also C. B. Carter, "The Kentucky Feud in Nicaragua," *World's Work* 54 (July 1927): 312–21.

26. Prime examples include the Matagalpa Indian Uprising of 1881, launched against landlords and the agents of a newly invigorated liberal state, and its successor in 1895, when a nativistic millenarian movement resurfaced in the same region. See Jeffrey L. Gould, "El café, el trabajo, y la comunidad indígena de Matagalpa, 1880–1925," in *Tierra, café y sociedad,* ed. Héctor Pérez-Brignoli and Mario Samper (San José: FLACSO, 1994), 279–376; and his " '¡Vana ilusión!' The Highlands Indians and the Myth of Nicaragua Mestiza, 1880–1925," *Hispanic American Historical Review* 73, no. 3 (August 1993): 393–429. See also Jaime Wheelock Román, *Raíces indígenas de la lucha anticolonialista en Nicaragua* (Managua: Nueva Nicaragua, 1985), and his *Imperialismo y dictadura* (Managua: Nueva Nicaragua, 1985).

27. On the popular explosions of the 1840s, see Pedro Joaquín Chamorro Zelaya, "Fruto Chamorro," *Revista Conservadora del Pensamiento Centroamericano* 19, no. 91 (Apr. 1968): 1–106; E. Bradford Burns, *Patriarch and Folk: The Emergence of Nicaragua, 1798–1858* (Cambridge, Mass.: Harvard University Press, 1991); and the suggestive essay by Rafael Casanova Fuertes, "Hacia una nueva valoración de las luchas políticas del período de la anarquia: El caso de los conflictos de 1845–1849," in *Encuentros con la historia,* ed. Margarita Vannini (Managua: Instituto de Historia de Nicaragua, Universidad Centroamericana, 1995), 231–48.

28. Given the centrality of patron-client relations in structuring social relations of all kinds in Nicaraguan history, the paucity of research on this topic is unfortunate. My strong suspicion is that the principal reason why Sandino's organized social base remained limited to the Segovias lay in the relative weakness of patron-client relations in the region, and the relative strength of such relations throughout the rest of western Nicaragua. See the provocative essay by Robert H. Holden, "Constructing the Limits of State Violence in Central America: Towards a New Research Agenda," *Journal of Latin American Studies* 28, no. 2 (May 1996): 435–59.

29. See Gould, "El café," and "¡Vana ilusión!"; Centro de Investigación y Estudios de la Reforma Agraria (CIERA-MIDINRA), *Nicaragua, y por eso defendemos la frontera* (Managua: CIERA-MIDINRA, 1984); and the IES testimonies.

30. On the civil wars of the nineteenth century, see Chamorro Zelaya, "Fruto Chamorro"; Burns, *Patriarch and Folk;* and José Dolores Gámez, *Historia de*

Nicaragua, and *Historia moderna de Nicaragua* (Managua: Banco de América, 1975); on struggles from below, see Wheelock Román, *Raíces indígenas.*

31. For a compelling look at one renowned popular caudillo during the 1926–1927 Civil War, see Miguel Jarquín Vallejos, *La muerte de Cabulla* (El Viejo, Nicaragua: Colección documentos históricos de El Viejo, 1984); see also Schroeder, "To Defend Our Nation's Honor," chaps. 4–5.

32. Arturo Warman, *"We Come to Object": The Peasants of Morelos and the National State,* trans. Stephen K. Ault (Baltimore, Md.: Johns Hopkins University Press, 1980), 91.

33. Testimony of Pastor Ramírez Mejía, I E S cassette no. 094-1-3, pp. 1–3 (hereafter I E S [cassette number]: [page number]). Unless otherwise indicated, all translations from the Spanish are mine. The specifics of Captain Ramírez's account are corroborated by much other evidence, including *La Noticia* (Managua), 12 Oct. 1926, which reported that 180 Liberal rebels under Ciriaco Aguilera and Carlos Salgado were active in the region south of Somoto. Captain Ramírez's name, and his brother Rufino's, also appear sporadically in marine-guardia reports, e.g., B-2 Report, 25 Feb. 1929, NA127/209/1. See also Conrad, *Sandino,* 136.

34. Lizandro Ardón Molina, I E S 032: 1–7.

35. Declaration of José Eulalio Torres, Apr. 1928, NA127/195/13/Torres, José; cf. NA127/195/5/Hernández, Anastasio.

36. NA127/195/5/Hernández, Anastasio; his brother Inés was a well-known rebel jefe; e.g. Report, Denig, 7 July 1930, NA127/209/2.

37. R-2 Report, 16 Sept. 1929, 4, NA127/209/1; and G N-2 Reports, 1 Mar. 1932, 4; 1 Nov. 1931, 13; and 1 Dec. 1931, 14, all in NA127/43A/29. One vivid metaphor for the fluidity, contingency, and multiplicity of Segovian political identities during Sandino's rebellion comes from a marine arrest report (recall that the red and black flag symbolized Sandino's cause): "The [arrested] man wore a wide black hat band. There was found a red ribbon tied with a bow and with a safety pin, which when fitted over the hat gave a red and black band. The ribbon was so tied that it fitted perfectly over the hat and could be slipped on at a moment's notice" (Report of arrest and escape of Gregorio Espinosa [Rivera], Major Rockey, 5 Apr. 1928, NA127/220/5).

38. Some episodes in the latter wave of violence, wrongly blamed on the Sandinistas, are chronicled in Somoza, *El verdadero Sandino,* 61–77; see below.

39. Including those of José Flores Gradys (I E S 058), Calixto Tercero González (I E S 095, 097), Camilo Guillén (in Claribel Alegría and D. J. Flakoll, *Nicaragua: La revolución sandinista* [Mexico City: Ediciones Era, 1982], 51–59), Luciano Gutiérrez Herrera (I E S 102), and Angel Martínez Soza, who recalled, "The days of Conservative control were wretched; if a man was a Liberal, they hanged him; if he had a woman, they raped her; and so everyone was inflamed against the Conservative rule" (I E S 060: 1).

40. See Michael J. Schroeder, "Horse Thieves to Rebels to Dogs: Political

Gang Violence and the State in the Western Segovias, Nicaragua, in the Time of Sandino, 1926–1934," *Journal of Latin American Studies* 28, no. 2 (May 1996): 383–434, esp. 407 n. 74.

41. Bill D. Ross, *Peleliu: Tragic Triumph* (New York: Random House, 1991), 19. World War II heroes who had served in the Segovias included Brigadier General (then Colonel) R. L. Denig, Major General (then Major) J. C. Smith, Lieutenant Colonel (then Captain) L. B. Puller, and Colonels (then Lieutenants) Hanneken, Edson, Ballance, Hunt, and others; see Ross, *Peleliu*. For a compelling look at the moral-mythical imagination of the First Marines in the Pacific War, see Craig Cameron, *American Samurai: Myth, Imagination, and the Conduct of Battle in the First Marine Division, 1941–1951* (New York: Cambridge University Press, 1994).

42. Excellent studies of U.S. interventions during these years include Hans Schmidt, *The United States Occupation of Haiti, 1915–1934* (New Brunswick, N.J.: Rutgers University Press, 1971); Bruce Calder, *The Impact of Intervention: The Dominican Republic during the U.S. Occupation of 1916–1924* (Austin: University of Texas Press, 1984); and Glenn Anthony May, *Battle for Batangas* (New Haven, Conn.: Yale University Press, 1991).

43. See David Steigerwald, *Wilsonian Idealism in America* (Ithaca, N.Y.: Cornell University Press, 1994); and Tony Smith, *America's Mission: The United States and the Struggle for Democracy in the Twentieth Century* (Princeton, N.J.: Princeton University Press, 1994).

44. See the personal diary of Lt. T. J. Kilcourse, USMC, item 2A47-PC169, Personal Papers Collection, Marine Corps Historical Center, Washington, D.C. (hereafter MCHC-PPC), which in its moral condemnation of the intervention foreshadows much of what would appear forty years later in Vietnam.

45. Major Julian C. Smith, USMC, et al., "A Review of the Organization and Operations of the Guardia Nacional de Nicaragua" (unpublished ms., MCHC-PPC, 1933), 26.

46. Robert L. Denig, "Diary of a Guardia Officer" (unpublished ms., MCHC-PPC, c. 1937), 21, 27, 71.

47. B-2 Report, 28 Feb. 1930, NA127/43A/4.

48. Quotes from the testimonies of Martin Blandón Rodríguez (IES 033: 10), Macario Calderón Salinas (IES 044-2-2: 3), and Cosme Castro Andino (IES 049: 6), respectively. For accounts of marine atrocities by Nicaraguans who served in the guardia, see Abelardo Cuadra, *Hombre del Caribe;* Manolo Cuadra, *Contra Sandino en la montaña;* and Aguilar Cortés, *Memorias de los yanquis a Sandino.*

49. Prior to May 1929, "the Segovias" are taken here to include military districts defined as "Department of Nueva Segovia" and "Department of Estelí"; after the guardia reorganization of May 1929, the Segovias are taken to include the Northern Area (Nueva Segovia and Estelí) and the Central Area (Jinotega and Matagalpa). See Smith et al., "A Review of the Organization and Operations of the Guardia," 7–16. The figure of 1,300 is taken from Macaulay, *The Sandino*

Affair, 151–52; the figures for the two areas are calculated from the average distribution between the two as they appear in the sources given in note 50.

50. Numbers are taken from the following sources: Distribution of Guardia Troops in the Northern Area for the week of 28 Sept. 1930, NA127/198/1; Estimate of the Situation, A. Racicot, 28 Feb. 1930, NA127/205/2/16D; Estimate of the Situation in Nicaragua, F. L. Bradman, 11 Nov. 1930, NA127/201/1; Informe consolidado mostrando la distribución de toda tropa de la Guardia Nacional de Nicaragua, 30 Sept. 1931, NA127/43A/30; Reorganization of the Northern Area, T. P. Cheatham, 10 Jan. 1932, NA127/202/1/1.3; Designation of Districts and District Combat Patrols, T. P. Cheatham, 30 May 1932, NA127/202/1/1.3.

51. Calculated from a statistical analysis of 350 patrol and combat reports; see Schroeder, "To Defend Our Nation's Honor," chap. 8.

52. IES 101-2-2:4.

53. See, for example, Macaulay, *The Sandino Affair;* and United States Department of State, *The United States and Nicaragua.*

54. There is abundant evidence for both; see Schroeder, "To Defend Our Nation's Honor," chap. 5.

55. The phrase is Mao Tse-tung's; "On Guerrilla War" (1938), reprinted in Walter Laqueur, *Guerrilla: A Historical and Critical Study* (Boston: Little, Brown, 1977), 189–97.

56. Report, Amor LeR. Sims, 19 June 1929, NA127/212/1.

57. For one convoluted example, David Villegas, Chamorrista of Jinotega, denounced the Liberal *jefe político* Rigoberto Reyes as a Sandinista in a letter to Emiliano Chamorro, lacing his lies with enough truth to make the allegations seem plausible. It appears that Chamorro instructed Villegas to write the letter so that he (Chamorro) could leak it to the marines, as the marines were ruminating over its contents within days of its composition (Villegas to Chamorro, 13 June 1928, NA127/43A/3; and Frisbie to Schmidt, 1 July 1928, NA127/220/11).

58. As for instance when Ascención Vargas of Jinotega marched into the marine garrison at Corinto Finca and accused Pedro Ramos of being a Sandinista scout; the marine lieutenant who investigated determined that "the complaint [is] due, so I believe, to a 'lovers' quarrel.' " Patrol, T. J. Kilcourse, 12 May 1928, NA127/43A/20. (This is the same Lt. Kilcourse whose personal diary denounced the intervention; see note 44.)

59. For instance, the scheme played out by Conservatives of Somoto on the night of the 1928 presidential elections, where a band of Conservatives shot off guns and shouted "¡Viva Sandino!" a mile from town as they attacked and mortally injured a political foe (Arrest and detention of Salvador Solano and Blas Tercero, Stockes, 6 Nov. 1928, NA127/220/2).

60. Paulino Castellon to Pres. Moncada, 8 Apr. 1928, NA127/220/5.

61. Among the most powerful literary representations of the moral energies of Sandinismo in the Segovian countryside are Ramón de Belausteguigoitia, *Con*

Sandino en Nicaragua (1934; reprint, Managua: Nueva Nicaragua, 1985), 140; Alfonso Alexander, *Sandino, relato de la revolución en Nicaragua* (Santiago de Chile: Ercilla, 1937); and Carlton Beals, "With Sandino in Nicaragua," *The Nation* 13, vol. 126, nos. 3270–73 (1928). See also the IES testimonies, including those excerpted in Instituto de Estudio del Sandinismo, *Ahora sé que Sandino manda* (Managua: Nueva Nicaragua, 1986).

62. See the documents in Bendaña, *La mística de Sandino*, 177–255; see also Schroeder, "To Defend Our Nation's Honor," 243–54; and Vargas, *Floreció al filo de la espada*, chap. 7. While Vargas's "dual power" thesis is, as argued here, basically right, the author goes to rather absurd lengths in trying to quantify the level of popular support enjoyed by the rebels' parallel state, at one point asserting that "The 'counter-government' had political influence over 85.13 percent of the region's population" (271).

63. See Schroeder, "To Defend Our Nation's Honor," 211–17.

64. Forced contributions were a common feature of Nicaraguan civil wars since independence; see Chamorro Zelaya, "Fruto Chamorro," 3, 4, 6. On forced contributions during the 1910–1912 civil war, see, e.g., M. Pergrina Maliaño to U.S. Consul, 28 Jan. 1910, USDS 817.00/6369.777. For an often tragicomic fictional rendition of the phenomenon, see Adolfo Calero-Orozco, *Sangre santa* (1946; reprint, Managua: Nueva Nicaragua, 1993).

65. See Steve Stern, *The Secret History of Gender: Women, Men, and Power in Late Colonial Mexico* (Chapel Hill: University of North Carolina Press, 1995), esp. 11–20, 189–213; Ana María Alonso, *Thread of Blood: Colonialism, Revolution, and Gender on Mexico's Northern Frontier* (Tucson: University of Arizona Press), esp. 73–111; and Ramón Gutiérrez, *When Jesus Came, the Corn Mothers Went Away: Marriage, Sexuality, and Power in New Mexico, 1500–1846* (Stanford, Calif.: Stanford University Press, 1991). On the patriarchal bases of postcolonial Latin American nationalisms, see Doris Sommer, *Foundational Fictions,* and Julie Skurski, "The Ambiguities of Authenticity."

66. For an analysis of gender ideology within Sandino's ranks, see Richard Grossman, "La Patria es Nuestra Madre: Género, Patriarcado y Nacionalismo dentro del Movimiento Sandinista, 1927–1934" (paper presented to the Tercer Congreso Centroamericano de Historia, San José, Costa Rica, 15–18 July 1996).

67. Quote from "Manifesto," 1 July 1927 (Conrad, *Sandino*, 74).

68. Major and minor rebel chieftains routinely arrogated this right unto themselves; one example of many is General Pedro Altamirano, discussed in note 70.

69. Benedict Anderson, *Imagined Communities* (London: Verso, 1991).

70. Reprinted in Smith et al., "A Review of the Organization and Operations of the Guardia," 250; English only. Some originals from Altamirano can be found in MCHC-PPC, J. C. Smith, box 7. Many similar letters (many in the original) can be found in the marine-guardia archives, e.g., Fulgencio Hernández to Sra. Elena Munguia, 11 Jan. 1931, NA127/209/5; and in Somoza, *El verdadero Sandino*. A 1931 letter from Sandinista jefe Marcial Rivera to Sandino suggests Altamirano's

original language in referring to being made a laughingstock: "Yo me fuí . . . a quemar la hacienda de los Nogueras para que sepan como es que se burlan de mis órdenes" (Somoza, *El verdadero Sandino,* 285).

71. Intelligence Report for the week ending 17 Sept. 1927, G. Hays, NAI27/ 198/1.

72. Conrad, *Sandino,* 100, 82.

73. Recommendation for restriction for certain areas of Nueva Segovia, Denig, 10 May 1930, NAI27/202/17/94.

74. Mann, *The Sources of Social Power,* 2:4. The conclusions advanced in this section are based on my reading of archival and published sources; for a more detailed treatment see Schroeder, "To Defend Our Nation's Honor."

75. Oscar-René Vargas, "Movimiento de Sandino: Su victoria en la derrota," in "Nuevo Amanecer Cultural," supplement to *Nuevo Diario,* 11 Oct. 1986. The same passage appears in Vargas, *Floreció al filo de la espada,* 385.

76. On the responses of the Miskitu Indians of the Río Bocay region to Sandino and the marines, see Hale, *Resistance and Contradiction,* 52–56; cf. David C. Brooks, "U.S. Marines, Miskitos, and the Hunt for Sandino: The Río Coco Patrol in 1928," *Journal of Latin American Studies* 21, no. 2 (May 1989): 311–42.

77. Walter, *The Regime of Anastasio Somoza,* 31.

78. Charles Hale detects significant popular support for Sandino among Miskitu Indians in the Bocay River region (*Resistance and Contradiction,* chap. 2); to me the evidence appears far more ambiguous. Cf. Brooks, "U.S. Marines." See also Gilbert Joseph, *Revolution from Without: Yucatán, Mexico, and the United States* (Durham, N.C.: Duke University Press, 1988).

79. My best estimate for the population of all zones that saw consistently significant rebel activity is slightly under 100,000; this excludes large parts of Matagalpa and part of Jinotega. The marines figured 73,000 for the Segovias as a whole (General Data, Northern Area, J. A. Rossell, 1 Dec. 1929, NAI27/205/2/16D). The 1930 population of Nicaragua stood at 726,000, according to sources cited in Vargas, *Floreció al filo de la espada,* 297. By these figures, the Segovias contained 13.2 percent of the country's population. If 90 percent of these could be classed as "laboring poor," and 90 percent of these actively supported Sandino, then 10.7 percent of Nicaragua's population was in active support.

80. For example, on microfilm in the Library of Congress, Washington, D.C.: *El Centroamericano* (León), July 1928–1934; *La Prensa* (Managua), Dec. 1933– 1934; and *El Diario Nicaragüense* (Mar. 1927–June 1932). Newspapers deemed overly critical of the intervention or guardia were censored or shut down, e.g., *La Tribuna* (Managua) in 1929.

81. Evidence relating to the Sandinista attack on Chichigalpa in November 1931, for example, reveals considerable popular support for the rebels (GN-2 Reports, 1 Dec. 1931 and 1 Jan. 1932, NAI27/43A/29).

82. H. Samuelson to Gen. McDougal, 10 Nov. and 6 Dec. 1929, NAI27/198/1.

83. Guillermo Hüper to USMC, 13 Apr. 1928, NAI27/43A/14; for Hüper's fate a

decade later, see Tomás Borge, *La paciente impaciencia* (Managua: Vanguardia, 1989), 72.

84. Conrad, *Sandino,* 185; anonymous report, 20 Mar. 1928, NA127/220/5.

85. Santos López, *Memorias de un soldado* (León: Frente Estudiantil Revolucionario, 1976), 12; Pedro Antonio Arauz, "El año 1927" (IES ms), 4; R-2 Reports, Managua, 26 Aug. 1928, 24 Sept. 1928, 8 Apr. 1929, 18 Jan. 1931, and 1 Mar. 1931, all in NA127/209/1&2; anonymous report, 20 Mar. 1928, NA127/220/5; Paulino Castellón to Pres. Moncada, 8 Apr. 1928, NA127/220/5; Area Commander Ocotal to Brigade Commander Managua, 19 Sept. 1928, NA127/220/6; Diligencias contra J. Salvador Gómez, 20 Feb. 1930, 5; E. L. Burwell to Area Commander, 14 June 1931, NA127/209/3; E. L. Burwell to J. O. Brauer, 11 Aug. 1931, NA127/202/1/1.3; and Somoza, *El verdadero Sandino,* 210.

86. These included Filiberto Centeno of Las Nubes, Adrián Reyes of El Tigre, Moisés Pérez of Apaguiz, Hipólito Olivas of Las Delicias, Francisco and Eusebio Fajardo of Guayucalí, Ambrosio Calero of Las Cuchillas, Timoteo Pérez of La Naranja near Santule, and Doroteo González of Ocotolillo near El Tigre; patrol, combat, and intelligence reports, NA127/above.

87. According to the 1920 census, the department of Nueva Segovia boasted 88 merchants (*comerciantes*) and 10 teachers (*maestros*) out of a total population of 42,685 (there were no categories for doctors or lawyers); the proportions for Estelí, Jinotega, and Matagalpa were comparable. Oficina Central del Censo, *Censo General de la República de Nicaragua de 1920* (Managua, 1920).

88. The marine assessment of Pastor Lobo of Ocotal was typical: "It is believed that if he has aided the bandits in the past, it has been done to protect his property from destruction by bandit groups" (T. P. Cheatham, Area Commander, 23 May 1932, NA127/202/1/1.3).

89. Since such illegal trade was of pressing concern to the marines-guardia, their archives fairly overflow with references to it. See Intelligence Reports, NA127/209/1&2; GN-2 Reports (1930–1932), NA127/43A.

90. Late in 1928, rebels sent him a note asking for "twenty pair of shoes" among other items, adding that "we believe you are in favor of our cause." Four months later, in the course of a marine investigation, Rodríguez declared his friendship for the marines. A month later rebels robbed his store of $50 in cash and $50 in liquor; the marines suspected "an element of retaliation." More than two years later he was reportedly serving as a kind of courier for the rebels. And a year later the rebels reportedly robbed one of his shipments (Pedro Antonio Arauz, "Francisco Estrada" [IES ms.], 2; General Pedro Blandón to Clemente Rodríguez, c. 28 Dec. 1928, NA127/205/1; declaration of Clemente Rodríguez, 8 Apr. 1929, NA127/43A/24; R-2 Report, 31 May 1929, 3, NA127/209/1; B-2 Report, 4 June 1929, 6, NA127/43A/4; Bandit Activities, E. Matamoros, 31 Aug. 1931, NA127/202/14; and GN-2 Report, 1 Oct. 1932, 8, NA127/43A/29).

91. For the department of Nueva Segovia, the 1920 census lists 159 carpenters (*carpinteros*), 100 shoemakers (*zapateros*), 90 students (*estudiantes*), 66 tai-

lors (*sastres*), 44 bricklayers (*albañiles*), 19 clerks (*amanuenses*), three mechanics (*mecánicos*), and a smattering of other artisans, out of a total population of 42,685; again, the numbers in the other northern departments were comparable (*Censo General,* 128, 156, 242, 269).

92. Investigating such matters was one of the principal tasks of the marines-guardia, and most signs indicate that they did it pretty well.

93. On changes within the comunidades in the Matagalpa-Jinotega highlands and their changing relations to the state in the decades before Sandino, see Gould, "El café" and "*¡Vana ilusión!*" A mapping of all known armed conflicts between Sandinista rebels and the marines-guardia (n=735), and a careful reading of relevant patrol, combat, and intelligent reports, permit one to identify with some precision the social and geographic frontiers of Sandino's rebellion. The definition of the Segovias as a region (advanced in note 3) is based, in part, on such an analysis, which reveals that in the zone of intensive coffee cultivation just north of Matagalpa and west of Jinotega, popular support for the rebels was very strong; that in the zone south and east of Matagalpa, extending south into Chontales and east into the very sparsely populated Atlantic rain forest zone, the rebels enjoyed very little organized popular support; and that only a handful of military encounters between rebels and the marines-guardia took place in regions where comunidades were most concentrated. See Schroeder, "To Defend Our Nation's Honor," chap. 8; some of the conclusions advanced in this paragraph are also based on personal communications with Jeffrey Gould.

94. The question of intellectuals in Sandino's rebellion is clearly a dicey one. Here I shy away from Steven Feierman's more expanded definition of "peasant intellectuals": peasants "who engage in socially recognized organizational, directive, educative, or expressive activities . . . all people [who] have the social function of intellectuals [as defined above]." See his *Peasant Intellectuals: Anthropology and History in Tanzania* (Madison: University of Wisconsin Press, 1990), 17–18. By this definition, Sandino's rebels obviously counted many intellectuals among their ranks. At the same time, such an expansive definition tends to obscure the connections between intellectual labor and literacy, and in this case, literacy, I would argue, was essential for "propagating the faith" among all but those within earshot of peasant-rebel intellectuals. Since the present section is more concerned with exploring the social frontiers of Sandino's base of support, Feierman's otherwise provocative and useful definition is not employed here.

95. Dozens of internationally renowned writers and intellectuals expressed support for Sandino; see the edited collections of the Instituto de Estudio del Sandinismo, *El Sandinismo: Documentos básicos* (Managua: Editorial Nueva Nicaragua, 1984), and *Pensamiento antimperialista en Nicaragua.*

96. According to the 1920 census, literacy rates in the four northern departments (Estelí, Jinotega, Matagalpa, and Nueva Segovia), defined as "saben leer y escribir," stood at 13.2 percent (27,110 out of a total population of 205,741). The census offers no definition of "saben leer y escribir," but the category prob-

ably includes everyone who could write their own name. Functional literacy rates were probably less than one-tenth of the figure given. Calculated from the *Censo General,* 128, 156, 242, 269.

97. Daniel Olivas's *El Demócrata* was a brief exception; see n. 101.

98. Testimonies of Macario Calderón Salinas (I E S 044-2-2: 9), Joaquín Fajardo Arauz (I E S 100-1-2: 3), Francisco Lara López (I E S 059: 15), and Francisco Zepeda Galeano (I E S 076-1-2: 12); see also José Román, *Maldito país* (Managua: Editorial Union, 1983), 140.

99. His indictment is reprinted in Somoza, *El verdadero Sandino,* 65; the ac-count of his capture and murder are in R-2 Report, 31 Oct. 1929, 3; and B-2 Report, 11 Nov. 1929, 5, N A I 27/209/1; also mentioned in a letter from Luis Fiallos to Pres. Moncada, 25 Nov. 1929, N A I 27/198/1.

100. Report of cooperation and sincerity of civil authorities in Jinotega, C. B. Erskine to Jefe Director, G.N., 13 Jan. 1930, N A I 27/198/1; Rigoberto Reyes to Pres. Moncada, 26 Feb. 1930, N A I 27/198/2; and Somoza, *El verdadero Sandino,* 149.

101. Olivas's *El Demócrata* was the only newspaper published in the northern departments (four hundred copies weekly); evidently only a few issues were published. He was described as follows: "Is owner of a shoe shop and cobbler by trade. Formerly a very poor man, but has made good in his business and now owns considerable property. He is a Liberal and is Anti-American and unfriendly to the Guardia" (Information on periodicals, newspapers, etc., D. A. Stafford, 4 Apr. 1930, N A I 27/43A/3). A thorough search has revealed no evidence linking Olivas to the rebels.

102. Memorandum, 3 Dec. 1929 [no author identified], N A I 27/43A/30.

103. "The requirement of reading and writing [for enlistees] has had to be waived due to the small number of the population who have this amount of education." Memorandum, 3 Dec. 1929.

104. Denig, "Diary," 19 Nov. 1929; recall that Tom Sawyer's shoes hurt because he usually ran around barefoot.

105. There were many "applicants for enlistment" who were only enlisted after proving themselves in the field as volunteer guides and scouts; e.g., Patrol Report, O'Leary, 5 July 1930, N A I 27/202/10; and Combat Report, Broderick, 13 Jan. 1931, N A I 27/202/11.

106. Report, Denig, 17 July 1930, N A I 27/202/10.

107. Millett, *Guardians of the Dynasty,* 78–79.

108. Each guardia was identified by a number; by the end of 1932 these had exceeded 5,200 (Francisco Paniagua, #5224, Patrol Report, Stevens, 9 Oct. 1932, N A I 27/202/14).

109. Enlistment papers are evidently no longer extant, but the evidence clearly indicates that many guardia who served in the Segovias were locals; dozens of patrol and combat reports contain brief references to Segovian-recruited guardia, e.g.: patrol reports of Hakala, 30 Aug. 1929, N A I 27/202/10/51; and Rimes, 17 July

1929, NAI27/212/1. For recruitment policies, see Memorandum [no author identified], 3 Dec. 1929.

110. Estimate of the Situation, A. Racicot, 28 Feb. 1930, NAI27/205/2/16-D.

111. Report, Claude, 24 May 1928, NAI27/212/1; and Patrol Report, Broderick, 13 Jan. 1931, NAI27/220/11.

112. Denig, "Diary;" from early 1928 Ocotal boasted a rudimentary golf course. The extant marine-guardia archives I have examined contain no direct references to relations between Segovian prostitutes and marines, though many sensitive documents were removed or destroyed a year prior to the marine withdrawal (Jefe Director Sheard, Secret Files, 1 Feb. 1932, NAI27/43A/30).

113. Estimate of the Situation, Bradman, 11 Nov. 1930, NAI27/201.

114. "The practice of doling out small sums of money for reliable information should be encouraged. . . . From $25 to $100.00 . . . might be justifiable. One good contact is worth a lot of time and money" (Intelligence Memorandum to all Officers, 9 Oct. 1928, NAI27/209/2). See also Memorandum, H. Schmidt, 12 Nov. 1928, NAI27/43A/4.

115. General Data, Northern Area, Rossell, 1 Dec. 1929.

116. In June 1931, Brauer reported that "bandit suspect" Ramón Centeno "refused to give any information . . . or divulge the whereabouts of any of his companions. His wife was found and thru her he was induced to talk." Soon after, Centeno "was shot attempting to escape." Six weeks later, Brauer supervised the surrender of Sandinista jefes Catalino and Marcos Olivas: "We did not harry them with questions, as they were very timorous but instead attempted to inculcate in their minds that we were their friends, that we were sent here to help them in every possible way" (I. Molina R. to Brauer, July–Aug. 1931; Special Report, 26 June 1931; Presentation of Catalino Olivas, bandit chief, 13 Aug. 1931; The body of M. A. Ortez, 20 Aug. 1931; and Intelligence, same date; all from NAI27/202/1/1.3 and /209/8).

117. Frisbie to Schmidt, 22 and 31 May; 1, 13, and 20 July; and 8 and 11 Aug. 1928, NAI27/220/11.

118. Salomón de la Selva, *La guerra de Sandino o pueblo desnudo* (1935; Managua: Nueva Nicaragua, 1985), 86.

119. On 11 Apr. 1928, *La Noticia* reported that "Major Parker . . . showed us a large file of petitions from all parts of the Republic requesting the presence of the Guardia Nacional," a claim supported by much archival evidence: e.g., a letter from "workers and natives" of Mosonte to Jefe Director G.N., 27 Dec. 1930, NAI27/202/1/1.3; letters from citizens of Jinotega and La Concordia, 14 and 15 May 1929, NAI27/202/3; a letter from "citizens and agriculturalists" of Jalapa, 15 Nov. 1928, NAI27/43A/15/16.5; and Matagalpa coffee growers resolution and response, Apr. 1930, NAI27/198/misc. 1930.

120. Matagalpa coffee growers resolution and responses, Mar.–Apr. 1930.

121. From a vast and growing literature, two older studies remain useful here: Frances FitzGerald, *Fire in the Lake: The Vietnamese and the Americans in Viet-*

nam (Boston: Little, Brown, 1972); and Peter Paret, *French Revolutionary Warfare from Indochina to Algeria: The Analysis of a Political and Military Doctrine* (New York: Center for International Studies, Princeton University, Praeger, 1964).

122. Jerónimo Aguilar Cortés, *Memorias de los yanquis a Sandino.* The level of detail and the unpredictable, spontaneous quality of marine-guardia patrol and combat reports make them fascinating windows into Segovian society and the process of war; the conclusions advanced here are based, in significant measure, on a critical reading (and rereading) of these and related documents. Sponsorship has yet to be secured for an effort to publish the choicest excerpts from these reports in a single medium-sized volume.

123. General Data, Northern Area, Rossell, 1 Dec. 1929.

124. Estimate of the Situation, Bradman, 11 Nov. 1930.

125. Patrol Report, Bales, 10 Jan. 1931, NA127/202/13.

126. Col. H. C. Reisinger, USMC, "La Palabra del Gringo: Leadership of the Nicaraguan National Guard," *United States Naval Institute Proceedings* 61, no. 2 (Feb. 1935): 218.

127. Smith et al., "A Review of the Organization and Operations of the Guardia," 109–22; and Marine Corps Casualties in Nicaragua, 1 Jan. 1927 to 2 Jan. 1933, NA127/43A/15/17.5.

128. Luis F. Peralta to father, 28 Feb. 1931, NA127/209/1.

129. Memorandum [no author identified], 3 Dec. 1929.

130. General Data, Northern Area, Rossell, 1 Dec. 1929.

131. Estimate of the Situation, Racicot, 28 Feb. 1930.

132. Reisinger, "La Palabra del Gringo," 217.

133. See Schroeder, "To Defend Our Nation's Honor," 222–26.

134. Report of Contact, Carlson, 10 July 1930, NA127/202/10. During another firefight, "Raso Daniel Figuroa displayed courage, coolness, and initiative . . . when orders were given to advance he rushed forward shouting 'Viva La Guardia!' " (Contact with Bandits, Graves, 20 Aug. 1930, NA127/202/10).

135. Reisinger, "La Palabra del Gringo," 216.

136. Copies can be found in USDS microform no. 1273, rolls 21–23.

137. See Richard E. Nisbett and Dov Cohen, *Culture of Honor: The Psychology of Violence in the South* (Boulder, Colo.: Westview Press, 1996); E. J. Gorn, " 'Gouge, and Bite, Pull Hair and Scratch': The Social Significance of Fighting in the Southern Backcountry," *American Historical Review* 90 (1985): 18–43; and Herbert Shapiro, *White Violence and Black Response: From Reconstruction to Montgomery* (Amherst: University of Massachusetts Press, 1988).

138. On Hanneken and Escamilla see Schroeder, "To Defend Our Nation's Honor," 467–71.

139. More than ten IES testimonies contain stories of Lieutenant Lee's brutality; see Schroeder, "To Defend Our Nation's Honor," 428–34.

140. I owe this latter insight to Eileen Findlay's incisive commentary on an earlier draft of this essay.

141. For example, Contact Report, Maynard, 9 Aug. 1930, NA127/202/10. In his recent book, Oscar-René Vargas claims that "in the military sphere, the characteristics of the Guardia Nacional were passivity, timidity, and waiting. Their movements were slow and conservative. . . . the troops lacked combative spirit, they were campesinos incorporated by forced drafts who saw no objective in their fight and were subject to a brutal discipline by 'drunken, dirty, illiterate officers' " (*Floreció al filo de la espada,* 403). I would submit that all of these assertions, stemming from a larger political commitment to propagating the Sandinista faith and demonizing the guardia, are entirely wrong.

142. Gustavo Alemán Bolaños, *Sandino, el libertador, biografía del héroe americano* (1951; Managua: Nueva Nicaragua, 1980), 191, where the author notes that this passage was excerpted from a series of newspaper articles published in *La Nueva Prensa* in 1935.

143. Tilly, *Coercion, Capital, and European States,* 76. Pedro Joaquín Chamorro Zelaya's survey of state-making in 1840s and 1850s Nicaragua illustrates the contingent ebbs and flows of this process; "Fruto Chamorro."

144. Oscar-René Vargas, *Floreció al filo de la espada,* makes much too much of the impact of the Great Depression on the Segovias and in fueling rebellion; while the depression did serve to dampen market-oriented economic activities across the region, it is also clear, as we have seen, that the Segovias were only partially integrated into the structures of global capitalism during this period. In fact, the basic features of market and production *relations* in the region were scarcely altered as a result of the downturn. Most rural folk simply devoted less time to seasonal wage labor and more to subsistence—hardly a radical change.

145. See, e.g., Sergio Ramírez, introduction to Cuadra, *Hombre del Caribe;* and Salvatierra, *Sandino o la tragedia de un pueblo,* 76–79.

146. Anthony Giddens, *The Nation-State and Violence* (Berkeley and Los Angeles: University of California Press, 1987), 14; and Michel Foucault, *Discipline and Punish* (Harmondsworth, England: Penguin, 1979).

147. Restriction for certain areas of Nueva Segovia, 10 May 1930.

148. Telegram, Denig to Jefe Director, all GN Northern Area, 9 June 1930, NA127/220/2.

149. For instance, Carlos Herrera in Patrol Report, Bales, 10 Jan. 1931, NA127/202/13.

150. Lt. Satterfield claimed that "[the] Alcalde of Telpaneca . . . has not the authority to grant permission to cultivate nor harvest in this district, same is granted at this headquarters" (Report of Contact, Satterfield, 20 Feb. 1931, NA127/202/11).

151. An especially egregious example is Reporte de Patrulla, Subteniente Baltazar Navarrete, 7 May 1931, NA127/202/14.

152. Memorandum, H. Schmidt, 12 Nov. 1928, NA127/43A/4. The 1934 U.S. Army Map can be found in the Map Room of Hatcher Library, University of Michigan, Ann Arbor.

153. Memorandum, H. Schmidt, 12 Nov. 1928, NA127/43A/4.

154. Estimate of the Situation, Bradman, 11 Nov. 1930. According to one report, from June 1930 to Dec. 1932, 172 cadets had reached the grade of second lieutenant; no figures are given for higher ranks (Vargas, *Floreció al filo de la espada*, 414 n. 79).

155. Recommendation of personnel for higher officers in the guardia, W. G. Sheard, 27 Aug. 1932, NA127/198/2; cf. Vargas, *Floreció al filo de la espada*, 403–6.

156. Sandino, *El pensamiento vivo*, vol. 2.

157. Pedro Antonio Arauz, "Luz y sombra" (IES ms.); testimonies of Carlos Blandón Umanzor (IES 035), Luciano Gutiérrez Herrera (IES 102), Cosme Castro Andino (IES 049), Joaqín Fajardo Arauz (IES 100), Juan Bautista Tercero García (IES 093), Sixto Hernández Blandón (IES 036), Secundino Hernández Blandón (IES 047), and Ascención Iglesias Rivera (IES 065).

158. See Gilbert M. Joseph's introduction to this volume.

159. Sandino repeatedly stressed the importance of hatred in binding his forces together, e.g.: "Because of the tremendous crimes of these human brutes [the marines], hatred exists, much hatred, the simple hatred of the patriots of Nicaragua." Conrad, *Sandino*, 154–55. So did many of his followers, e.g.: "The organization [Defending Army] maintained itself because there is no glue stronger in life than that of hate . . . hatred of the Yankees" (Testimony of Alfonso Alexander [IES 008: 1]).

160. Major contributions to this critique include Walter, *The Regime of Anastasio Somoza;* Gould, *To Lead as Equals;* Hale, *Resistance and Contradiction;* and Paul Coe Clark Jr., *The United States and Somoza, 1933–1956: A Revisionist Look* (Westport, Conn.: Praeger, 1992).

161. I note in passing here that conventional understandings of the geopolitical aims of the United States in Central and Latin America could benefit from a sustained critical dialogue with more recent scholarship that challenges the bipolar teleological liberal-Marxist models that for so long have dominated thinking on the subject. Particularly useful here are Mann, *The Sources of Social Power;* Tilly, *Coercion, Capital, and European States;* Tony Smith, *The Pattern of Imperialism* (New York: Cambridge University Press, 1981); Robert W. Cox, *Production, Power, and World Order: Social Forces in the Making of History* (New York: Columbia University Press, 1987); and Kees van der Pijl, *The Making of an Atlantic Ruling Class* (London: Verso, 1984).

162. Aguilar Cortés, *Memorias de los yanquis a Sandino;* quotes are from p. 60.

163. Cuadra's unit was instrumental in repelling Sandinista advances into León and Chinandega in July and Nov. 1931 (Report of Contact, 2d Lt. Abelardo Cuadra, 1 Aug. 1931, NA127/202/11).

164. In addition to the works cited above, see Sergio Ramírez, *To Bury Our Fathers,* trans. Nick Caistor (New York: Readers International, 1984); and Chuno Blandón, *Cuartel General* (Managua: La Ocarina, 1988).

Eric Paul Roorda

The Cult of the Airplane among U.S. Military Men and Dominicans during the U.S. Occupation and the Trujillo Regime

Airplanes flew across the Atlantic for the first time in June 1919. *Pan-American Magazine* highlighted the event with a cover story the following month, predicting that a "great volume of business" would soon be generated by "commercial aerial transportation in South and Central America." Though military aircraft had completed the transatlantic crossings, the end of the fighting in Europe meant that aviation would now be "the big factor in commerce as in war." A navy flying boat converted to carry passengers had recently flown the first commercial flight from the United States to Cuba, and though there was space for only three ticket holders aboard that craft, it clearly marked the beginning of something big.[1]

Also in 1919, the United States Marine Corps sent airplanes to occupied Haiti and the Dominican Republic to fight the Haitian *caco* and Dominican *gavillero* insurgents. Marine pilots brought new tactics to the guerrilla war: bombing, reconnaissance, and flying in formation over the principal towns to overawe the citizenry. But in addition to these bellicose employments of aircraft, the marines on both sides of Hispaniola also began to fulfill the peacetime promise of aerial technology called for by the articles in *Pan-American Magazine,* such as carrying people and mail over terrain notoriously difficult to cross on the ground. The marine flyers also performed stunts above occupied cities, dazzling the population with the unprecedented spectacle of flying machines. Whatever their errand, airplanes in the sky demonstrated to Haitians and Dominicans the technological superiority and power of surveillance possessed by the ruler of their countries, the United States.[2]

Aviation and Empire

From these beginnings in 1919, airplanes became important agents in the spread of U.S. influence in Latin America.[3] As weapons, they greatly increased the potency of U.S. intervention and the value of U.S. friendship. As carriers of people and goods, they expanded the presence of U.S. culture and society in Latin America and extended the nation's commercial reach. This intertwining of the military and civilian employments of the new technology of airplanes has been noted by Michael Sherry: "Never viewed solely as a weapon, the airplane was the instrument of flight, of a whole new dimension in human activity. Therefore it was uniquely capable of stimulating fantasies of peacetime possibilities for lifting worldly burdens, transforming man's sense of time and place, transcending geography, [and] knitting together nations and peoples." [4]

Hopes of "knitting together nations and peoples" also lay at the heart of U.S. Latin American policy, which sought a sphere of influence in the Western Hemisphere. The assumption of U.S. stewardship of the "sister republics" of the Americas was the foundation for the Monroe Doctrine, the Pan-Americanism of the late nineteenth century, and the military and economic interventions that began in 1898. The Spanish-American (and Cuban and Filipino) War inspired a fresh wave of speculation in the United States about the extent of the country's imperial potential, with "our new possessions" in Puerto Rico and Cuba seen as just the beginning of expansion to the south.[5] The prospects of dominating the region improved further with the advent of aircraft. A year after the war in Cuba and four years before the Wright brothers' first flight in 1903, the idea of drawing the Americas together through the agency of aircraft occurred to Arthur Bird, who envisioned the union of North and Latin America under the rule of Washington. In his depiction of the "United States of the Americas," huge airliners connect the cities of both continents, creating a prosperous, English-speaking whole.[6]

Pan American Airways (Pan Am) brought part of that vision into being after its establishment in 1927, thriving with a "royal charter" of U.S. government mail contracts. Despite some Latin Americans' distrust of "the Octopus of the North stretching its tentacles to devour" them, Pan Am rapidly expanded its "empire of the air" southward from its Caribbean base.[7] The same year Pan Am was founded, the U.S. Marine Aviation Force in Nicaragua became "the first organization in military history to use aircraft in organized warfare against ground troops," employing the technique of dive-bombing (pioneered in Haiti) against the forces of Augusto César Sandino. Planes routed Sandino's attack on Ocotal and later destroyed his "much vaunted strong-hold" in the mountains at El Chipote.[8]

As the examples of Pan Am and Nicaragua suggest, the airplane's twin functions of transportation and destruction made it an especially potent tool of U.S. hegemony in the Caribbean region. Capable of both "knitting together nations and peoples" and conquering them, airplanes were simultaneously symbolic of regional integration and U.S. domination, evoking both "Pan-American" ideals and Yankee aggression. Because of this duality, the airplane was more difficult to deploy as a symbol than as a weapon or a vessel; it took on a variety of contrasting identities, depending on whether it was perceived as an object of fantasy or fear, profit or oppression. Since the same machines could and did perform functions in both categories in such places as Haiti, Nicaragua, and the Dominican Republic, the overall image of the airplane was especially contradictory in these nations.

The spread of aviation technology to the Latin American republics further complicated the symbolism of airplanes. Though air transport continued to be dominated by Pan Am, and air power remained mostly in the hands of the U.S. military, national airlines and air forces came into being all around the region. The acquisition of aircraft by such countries as the Dominican Republic, where the United States maintained a virtual monopoly on airplanes until the late 1930s, had considerable nationalist significance. Though the U.S. State Department and the various aviation organizations of the U.S. military tried to control the proliferation of aircraft technology and the transmission of airplane symbolism in Latin America, this proved impossible. In the Dominican Republic, both technology and symbolism came under the control of General Rafael Trujillo, who put them to his own nationalist uses, knitting together or tearing apart where he alone saw fit.

This essay surveys the changing meanings and functions of the airplane in the Dominican Republic beginning in 1919, when the Marine Corps incorporated aerial tactics into their strategy of occupation, and continuing through the Trujillo regime (1930–1961).[9] Military and commercial aviation reached a high stage of physical and metaphorical development under Trujillo, who received his military training and to a certain extent his worldview during the eight-year marine occupation of the country (1916–1924). Among the many tools of control acquired by Trujillo as a result of his apprenticeship and later partnership with the U.S. military, airplanes proved to be among the most powerful. He employed the same basic tactics of intimidation and spectacle that the marines had, but the overall strategy that Dominican air power served was distinctly Trujillo's. An examination of the ways airplanes were presented and deployed during the "Era of Trujillo" reveals no straightforward, imperial link between the nations established by the transfer of technology from north to south, but instead a tangled mat of connections bound up in that technology, its uses, its users, and its many potential definitions.

Enthusiasm for airplanes inspired cult followings among the general population and within professional aviation circles throughout the hemisphere during the period considered here. The popular and professional fascination with airplanes was fed by the spectacular progress of aviation technology, which increased the machines' contrasting abilities to knit together and tear apart nations and peoples. Airplanes were agents of immediacy, modernity, and catastrophe in their service delivering passengers and bombs, always at faster speeds, in larger air frames. Airplanes and daring pilots were staples in popular culture in North and Latin America, with the greatest interest generated by Charles Lindbergh in the late 1920s, the Allied bombers of World War II, and the jet prototype pilots of the 1950s.[10] The airplane combined the speed and glamor of its civilian uses, embodied by the globe-trotting Pan Am Clippers of the 1930s and the "jet set" of the 1950s, with the awe and perverse romance of its military uses, which accounted for the matinee-idol personae of air force pilots in movies, comics, and novels.[11]

The more exclusive cult of professional aviators was dominated by military pilots, who comprised a special subset within the broad, transnational military culture of the Americas. Aviators of all nationalities identified themselves as an elite group, distinguished by their mastery of the most advanced and dangerous technology in existence. Pilots literally and figuratively looked down on their rivals in the traditional military services on the ground and in the water. The maverick disposition of military aviators exemplified by Billy Mitchell in the United States was characteristic of flyers in the Caribbean region, whether or not they wore a uniform. Many of the pioneer aviators in the Antilles and Central America were former military pilots, often U.S. Marines, who had served in the region and stayed there to start private air transport companies. These expatriate flyers catered to foreign tourists, showing them the sights from the air, as national airlines would do later.[12] Other U.S. military aviators with Caribbean experience remained in the service and gained high rank. These officers fostered the growth of regional air forces by providing equipment and training, though their attempts to integrate those organizations with their own had mixed results because of the differing political priorities of their Latin American counterparts.

Gold Braid and Striped Pants

Rafael Trujillo's personal connections to U.S. military men began during the marine occupation and endured and prospered after his rise to power. Despite some differences of opinion about foreign policy and air power strategy, Trujillo always got along well with his military associates in the U.S. armed services, especially the Marine Corps. U.S. diplomats who disdained Trujillo often described political relations with the Dominican Republic as strained, but this assessment did not reflect the consistent camaraderie between Trujillo and his U.S. military friends, who included such powerful officers (and aviators) as General James Breckinridge, commandant of the Marine Corps, and General George Brett, commander of the Caribbean Defense Command. The close ties enjoyed by the U.S. and Dominican militaries facilitated the transfer of air power from one to the other, despite the frequently successful obstructions of the State Department.

This difference between the diplomatic and the military versions of "bilateral" relations between the countries complicates the picture of their postcolonial encounter. Accounting for the difference leads to a cultural reading of foreign relations, one that provides a new perspective on hegemony and fills in the context for aviation rituals during the Trujillo regime. Two cultural spheres determined the texture of foreign relations with the United States in the Dominican Republic during the Trujillo regime. One was the world of the military, which included United States Marine and Navy officers who made occasional visits to the realm of their protegé, the *generalísimo*.[13] The other cultural sphere was that of the international Cuerpo Diplomático y Consular, among whom the most prominent was the head of the U.S. diplomatic mission.[14] Those wearing the gold braid of high military rank and those wearing the striped pants of formal cutaway morning suits had differing experiences and points of engagement with the "court" of the dictator, the ever-shifting circle of supporters who constituted both the national government and the "high society," or *alto mundo,* of the capital. The extent to which these individuals shared values, vocabularies, symbols, and even wardrobes, helped to determine the tenor of relations between the nations. Trujillo shared a transnational military culture with his counterparts in the U.S. Navy, Army, and especially Marine Corps that was marked by a panoply of associations of dress and comportment that helped to mediate the divisions of nationality, language, and even race that otherwise separated military men. No such connections bridged the gap between Trujillo and most of the diplomats sent to serve in Santo Domingo/Ciudad Trujillo.

Foreigners, especially resident diplomats, were bound up in Trujillo's definition of Dominican nationhood and his demonstrations of personal control. The members of the Cuerpo Diplomático, especially the representatives of the most recent colonial power, the United States, dramatized the transition of the Dominican Republic from outside domination to full sovereignty through their mandatory integration into Trujillo's official circle. The Trujillo regime, like the court of a carnival queen, placed the ambassadors in prominent display to signify the approval of the nations they represented.[15] Their presence at the numerous public events celebrating the grandeur and autonomy of Trujillo's reign also required them to exhibit a kind of personal deference to him. Trujillo did not require ritual deference from his military friends, whom he considered peers or, in some cases, mentors; often, it was Trujillo who deferred in these relationships.

When military visitors attended public events, or created such an event by visiting the capital with a warship and/or airplanes, they reported no sense of being manipulated, as diplomats so often did. Most of the U.S. diplomats who were choreographed in Trujillo's spectacles became opposed to U.S. participation in such legitimizing public displays of affection, partly because they disdained Trujillo's humble social origin, and partly because he subjected their friends in the Dominican elite to brutal and humiliating treatment. Diplomats as high in the U.S. State Department as Undersecretary Sumner Welles obstructed naval and aerial "goodwill" visits to the Dominican Republic, with some success. But as the history of the airplane in the Dominican Republic shows, disapproving diplomats were unable to disrupt the amity of military relations with Trujillo. The distance between Trujillo's military friends and his diplomatic critics in the United States provided him with extensive room to maneuver between them, and to operate in ways that do not support his reputation as a "client" of U.S. interests. In fact, as this study shows, Trujillo consolidated his dictatorship at the cost of, not in the service of, U.S. hegemony, and though he cultivated and valued the friendship of generals and admirals, he never did their bidding. Rather, he employed all the means of imperial control that he could adapt, above all the airplane, to assert his independence from the empire.

The Dominican Cult of the Airplane

The Dominican cult of the airplane under the Trujillo regime shared many of the same forms of devotion expressed by professional aviators and aviation enthusiasts in the United States. The dashing pilots and spectacular aerial performances presented by Hollywood and embodied by the flying elite of the U.S. military had their counterparts in the Dominican Republic. Just as planes, pilots, and their media representations in the United States were bound up in the assertion of national greatness and regional leadership, the airplane as constructed by the Trujillo regime was emblematic of Dominican sovereignty and progress. Members of the aviation clique of the Dominican military revered a trinity comprised of the airplane, Trujillo, and the Dominican nation, which were also intertwined in the Dominican media. Dominican flyers performed in the skies for a nationwide congregation on the numerous holidays of the trujillista public calendar, with the most lavish aerial displays reserved for 24 October, the combined birthday and name day of Rafael Trujillo, and Armed Forces Day. They convened in exclusive social spaces like the Club-Cine of the Presidente Trujillo Air Base, and held a prominent place in the alto mundo of the capital. Dominican airplanes and pilots attained the highest expression of the modernity and cultural splendor of the era. In addition, the air force was invested with the dynastic lineage of the Trujillo family; the dictator's two sons, Ramfis and Rhadamés, became the leaders of the premier fighter squadron and the tank corps, which was part of the air force.

Airplanes also projected the creed of Dominican nationalism and potency beyond the republic. They were able to communicate widely contrasting messages about Trujillo's foreign relations, ranging from inter-American congeniality to regional antagonism. Trujillo sponsored a goodwill flight around Latin America in cooperation with the Pan American Union, and promoted the development of commercial air travel to call attention to the country as a repository of Hispanic heritage and a tourist destination. On the other hand, the precocious Dominican air force became by far the largest and most threatening in the Caribbean region in the 1950s. Its demonstrations of air power menaced neighboring republics and confounded U.S. military plans for integrated regional defense.

In the process, Trujillo's air force formed a new sect that diverged from the hegemonic legacy of the former colonial power, the United States. The Aviación Militar Dominicana (AMD) assembled a syncretic blend of technologies, beliefs, and behaviors from an array of foreign aviation sources, including Sweden and Brazil in addition to the United States, but which served the political and social needs of the Trujillo regime alone. The AMD dismissed the U.S. Air Force mission to the Dominican Republic entirely in 1958, as Trujillo's international disputes worsened and his defiance of U.S. pressure stiffened. The expulsion of the air missionaries by the ranks of the converted was a step toward the outright schism of 1960, when the Organization of American States imposed collective sanctions against the Dominican Republic.

The Marine Aviation Force

The technology and ideology of aircraft first arrived in the Dominican Republic at the airfield of the U.S.-owned Consuelo sugar estate outside San Pedro de Macorís in February 1919.[16] Marine forces had been "on the ground" in the country since the summer of 1916, when Woodrow Wilson carried out his threat to take control of Dominican finances and train a new military there. U.S. Navy ships and marine landing parties occupied every major Dominican port, prompting the Dominican government to resign. Taking over administration of the country, the marine occupiers initiated an agenda of infrastructural and organizational programs that, along with similar Wilsonian colonial projects in Haiti and Veracruz, Mexico, defined a kind of Progressive imperialism. They attempted many of the same reforms advocated by Progressives in the United States: public health, public works, education, fiscal management, and civil and military service.[17]

Underlying this "explication of the Mission" of intervention was the view, widely held by U.S. policymakers, that nonwhite Caribbean populations were unable to manage their own affairs without help from the north. This "construction of the other" supported two separate and unequal sets of criteria for white and nonwhite people with regard to such vital subjects as individual freedom and the power of government.[18] While advancing its Progressive reforms and developments, the U.S. military government virtually suspended Dominican civil rights, enforcing strict censorship and employing vicious means to suppress opposition. These extreme measures were justified by the corollary belief that "the main thing" in Latin American countries was control of the army.[19] U.S. policymakers regarded a strong military as the only instrument able to impose order and material progress in the Caribbean republics, which they considered less advanced, both in terms of evolutionary and political development, than the United States. As travel writer Harry A. Franck observed of the racist marines in Haiti, "the Southerner is famed for his ability to keep the 'nigger' down, but he is less successful in lifting him up, and that is the task we have taken upon ourselves." [20] From this defense of military intervention it was but a short step to the defense of military dictatorship.

Soon after the 1916 invasion, the marines established a forward base in Hato Mayor in the mountainous eastern region of the country, where armed resistance was the most widespread and the most difficult to quell.[21] Groups of gavilleros, defined as "bandits" by the marines, eluded mounted patrols into the interior of El Seibo region and were still active nearly three years after the U.S. invasion, when the airplanes of Squadron D, First Marine Division, began operating out of San Pedro de Macorís.[22] The marine pilots saw themselves as knights coming to the rescue of the lowly "horse marines" and winning the war from above.[23] The aviation issue of *Santo Domingo Leatherneck*, "a paper by and for the Marines in Santo Domingo," included a facetious letter from "Chuck," a hick marine private, which recounted the dramatic effect the airplanes had on the nature of battle.

Our company has been chasing them birds [the gavilleros] for over a year. . . . Months ago, a bunch of aviators and there buzz wagons came down from the states. They made the trip down hear to help the rest of us leathernecks *busca* these gavillero birds. . . . Well, one day a bunch of the 44th Co. was out *busca*ing a bunch of gavilleros. . . . One of the gang says "I heard a shot." . . . Sure enough, "whang" another one. . . . Then we noticed a couple of airplanes about a mile and ½ off, circling around and around and diving strait for the tree tops. . . . Well we just put the spurs to the old plugs and say boy did we travel. When we got to the seen of the fighting we jumps off our horses and then the fun started. . . . Well we just knelt down and had some good target practice. Bobbing targets, you know. And while we was introducing them to the Springfields, one plane beats back to the hangar and gets a bomb. . . . Well this airplane flys real low over the woods and drops the bomb. We hearda bunch of yells and a crash and that wuz the end of that fight.[24]

As this exultant account suggests, aircraft provided a panoptical view of the Dominican interior that eliminated the guerrillas' greatest asset, the sanctuary of their roadless home turf.[25]

The use of airplanes against the armed opposition also accelerated the marines' campaign to unify the country under their authority. Dominican politics had previously been shaped by the ability of government opponents to operate in the remote regions of the republic, beyond the reach of the party in power. Santo Domingo was cut off from most of the rest of the country by bad roads and the scarcity of coastal shipping. This geographic separation fostered strong regional identities, which produced political leaders closely identified with their places of origin. When out of power, these regional *caudillos* were able to oppose their rivals in the capital from a safe distance. Such circumstances were partly responsible for Dominican political instability.

Seeking to impose order and centralize authority, the marines placed a high priority on building a network of roads for troops to use in putting down opposition wherever it might occur. The arrival of the Marine Aviation Force further projected the power of the U.S. military government, reaching into every corner of the territory and bringing the densest hinterland within the gaze of the occupiers. The task of gathering information about the occupied land, that imperial process termed "the enterprise of knowledge" by Ricardo Salvatore, accelerated as a result of the mapping and survey work carried out from above.[26] Airplanes simultaneously widened the colonial regime's field of vision and its field of operations, providing impetus to the marines' forceful "knitting together" of the Dominican nation and people. Trujillo would continue that process, practicing the same techniques but following a different pattern.

In addition to making the woods transparent for the guerrilla bands seeking cover there, airplanes shrank the distance between towns for military messages and passengers. Just as the economic integration of the country provided an added rationale for military road construction, the communications and transportation benefits of the aviation force complemented its war service. To illustrate this argument, *Santo Domingo Leatherneck* printed two photos under the heading "Travel in Santo Domingo—Old and New": one showed a dark-skinned man riding an ox in a canefield, the other a two-seater biplane from the marine squadron.[27] The routinization of airmail delivery around the cities of the republic increased the duties of the air squadron, which doubled in size in March 1920. Airmail runs also increased the presence of the military occupation in the lives of Dominicans, as the sight of airplanes overhead became a more frequent occurrence.

The sheer spectacle presented by airplanes also served the purposes of the U.S. occupation by impressing the citizenry. Aerial acrobatics demanded the attention of Dominicans on the ground, stirring "admiración entusiasmada" with "el loop the loop," as *Listín Diario* reported in April 1919. Such dazzlement communicated the message that the pilots "claim for themselves the sky over Macorís."[28] The romantic image of military pilots was also enhanced in the eyes of the general population by stunts, which the individual pilots used to gain the attention of specific women they admired. *Listín Diario* reported that one of the pilots passed fifteen

Figure I. Four dapper marine aviators pose for a visiting Corps photographer out-side a hangar at the military airfield near Santo Domingo in 1923. The biplane on the left bears the insignia of the ace of spades, which promotes the dashing image the flyers tried to project. Stencils on both airplanes identify them as belonging to the respective "observation squadrons" of Santo Domingo and Port-au-Prince, which were under the colonial surveillance of the United States, carried out from the skies. (RG 80-HAG-4-44, Still Photography, U.S. National Archives.)

feet over the house of one "fair young lady" on Sánchez Street every time he went out.[29] Formations of roaring de Havilland biplanes flew over the major cities in a psychological application of air power to the task of occupation, a sight that was open to different interpretations on the part of those witnessing it, depending on their attitude toward the United States and its colonial project in their nation.[30]

The popular perception of the marines was also shaped by their public drunkenness and racism, which were manifest in many ways. The Santo Domingo encampment was nicknamed the Town of Blanco, or "white," with canvas tents painted like storefronts such as "Café Luxe." [31] *Santo Domingo Leatherneck* was full of racist jokes and references to liquor, which the Volstead Act had outlawed back home. Many of these jibes tar-geted the black West Indians employed at the Consuelo sugar estate where the squadron was initially based, such as the following filler: "Did yo' all

Figure 2. Marine pilots flew low over the colonial zone of Santo Domingo to impress both visitors, like the marine photographer taking this photo, and locals, squinting up to see the droning biplanes pass overhead. On this particular day, the airplane flies low over the dilapidated palace of Diego Columbus, son of the explorer, and the seaport, where a crowd gathers alongside a visiting steamship (upper right). (RG 80-HAG-4-48, Still Photography, U.S. National Archives.)

see Miss Fanny las' night? She was the belle ob de Consuelo Ball. She jus' nach'ly hab dat rich look, jus' like she neber et nuthin' in her life but duck elbows and chicken wrisses." [32] But the Dominican citizenry was not spared, as in the poem by a private stationed at Sabana de la Mar:

> I've wooed fair señoritas,
>> In town and country sides,
> And found them every bit as sweet,
>> As Dame Humor could imply.
> I've danced at their fandangoes,
>> From taps to reveille,
> I've eaten their pears and mangoes,
>> That were picked right from the trees.

I've marvelled at the sweetness,
    Of some ole spick's guitar
As it rose from the sordidness
    Of his own filthy bar.[33]

Harry Franck noted the difference between the drinking culture of the marines, which often involved getting drunk, getting in fights, and shooting at things, and that of the Dominicans, among whom it was shameful to appear affected by alcohol.[34] Liquor remained a prominent element of the military culture of the Dominican national guard left behind by the marines, and was a reliable way to conjure up transnational camaraderie between U.S. and Dominican military men during the Trujillo regime.

Air Power and the Rise of Rafael Trujillo

Rafael Trujillo made the most of the opportunity to serve in the new constabulary established under the occupation. He enlisted in 1918, was in the first class of the military academy established to train a Dominican officer corps in 1921, and after further training in Santiago, assumed command at Barahona with the rank of captain in 1923. Here he came into contact with marine aviators operating against gavilleros in the mountains near the Haitian border, who sometimes landed at the Barahona airfield (one of a dozen runways around the country constructed by the marines). Trujillo apparently impressed the pilots he met with his efficiency and willingness to please, as he had other ranking marines who knew him, and was commended for his courtesy to fliers by Brigadier General Harry Lee, commander of the U.S. occupation forces, at the suggestion of Edwin Brainerd, who commanded the marine air squadron. Trujillo's lasting pride in this and other marine plaudits, like the regular efficiency reports praising his "fastidious" personal grooming and impeccable uniforms, is suggested by their reproduction in his 1956 military biography.[35] His personal connections with marines, including several of the aviators he had impressed, endured after the occupation ended in 1924. A number of these officers went on to high rank in the Marine Corps and became Trujillo's influential partisans later.[36]

The departure of the last marine airplane left the Dominican Republic without aircraft of any kind, but a growing public enthusiasm for aviation was heightened by Charles Lindbergh's visit to Santo Domingo in February 1928, during his Pan-American goodwill flight. Trujillo, now the commander of the Dominican military, created the Air Mail Military Institute, without planes, after Lindy's visit.[37] There were still no planes in the country in 1930, when Trujillo seized power and soon faced armed opposition led by General Cipriano Bencosme in the Cibao Valley region in the northern part of the Dominican Republic. Knowing from experience the effectiveness of air power against insurgents in rough terrain, he appealed to the marines still occupying Haiti to borrow one of their planes, a pilot, and some bombs to attack Bencosme. The marines, commanded by Trujillo's friend Colonel Richard Cutts, probably would have cooperated, but the U.S. policy of nonintervention, not to mention a good deal of animosity toward Trujillo at the State Department, prohibited such assistance.[38]

In an effort to gain an autonomous air capability, Trujillo sent pilots to train with the Cuban air force in 1930 and created the "aviation arm" of the Dominican Army in 1932, though he quickly renamed it the National Air Transport Company. This misleading title allowed Trujillo to buy two new Bellanca Pacemaker planes in the United States, despite State Department opposition. When Secretary of State Henry Stimson inquired into the purchase, Trujillo claimed that the aircraft were strictly for commercial purposes, so his $100,000 payment for the planes was permitted by the U.S. officials supervising the Dominican budget under the terms of a 1924 treaty. Only after the Pacemakers' delivery to the Dominican Republic did the State Department learn that they came equipped with bombs and machine guns.[39]

This incident established the blueprint for aviation relations with the Trujillo regime during much of its duration, including the 1930s, the late 1940s, and the late 1950s. In what became a familiar scenario, Trujillo's military associates assisted where they could to arrange aircraft sales. State Department officials objected to such sales on the grounds that the Dominican Republic could not afford airplanes, or that airplanes would only be used to attack neighboring countries, and they denied the requisite export licenses. But Trujillo usually found a way to obtain the equipment he wanted, with or without State Department authorization, by subterfuge, smuggling, or buying from another foreign country. In the case of the Pacemakers, Major Thomas Watson and Colonel Richard Cutts, the two marine officers who had developed the greatest fondness for their protegé, cautioned him that "any money . . . for armament and equipment must not appear as such, or for that purpose," lest the State Department disapprove the sales.[40] They advised Trujillo on what kind of airplanes to purchase, and corresponded with marine aviation experts and aircraft manufacturers on his behalf.[41] The result was the arrival of the two new airplanes in 1932, and the revival of air power in the Dominican Republic; this time, however, the red and blue insignias on the machines represented the Dominican, not the American, flag.

The fledgling Dominican air force, based at the former marine airfield near the capital (renamed Lindbergh Aerodrome), acquired its first three fighter planes in 1933. Two of the new planes were christened with meaningful names for the consolidating Trujillo regime: *Reelección,* in anticipation of Trujillo sweeping to a second term in office in 1934, and *Ramfis,* for his three-year-old son and political heir. These names projected Trujillo's personalism into the skies for the first time, just as his eponymous naming of public works and renaming of places on the map inscribed that personalism on the Dominican landscape. Suspicious of "foreign influence" among the fliers, Trujillo purged the American mercenary pilots that had been brought in to augment the few qualified Dominican pilots, and subsequently relied as much as possible on Dominican nationals, trained in Cuba, to fly.[42]

Dominican Air Space

The most renowned Dominican aviator was Frank Féliz Miranda, one of the first Cuban-trained pilots, who flew together with three Cuban planes in the "Pan-American Good Will Flight" sponsored by Trujillo in 1937 to publicize the Columbus Memorial Lighthouse project. The lighthouse was slated for construction near the city Columbus had called Santo Domingo, which had been rechristened Ciudad Trujillo in January 1936. Framed as a symbol of inter-American cooperation, the project was initiated at the Santiago Conference in 1923, where the American republics agreed to contribute toward its construction, and approved by the U.S. Congress in 1929.[43] Trujillo embraced the *Faro de Colón* project when he came to power, supporting an architectural contest the following year that was judged by Frank Lloyd Wright, Eliel Saarinen, and Horacio Acosta y Lara, and was won by a Scottish architect for his idea of a gigantic recumbent cross.[44] The trujillista image of Christopher Columbus was bound up with aviation through the device of the hoped-for *faro,* the winning design for which was conceived both functionally and aesthetically with airplanes, not ships, in mind. The intention of the original lighthouse

Figure 3. A model of the winning entry in the Columbus Memorial Lighthouse architectural contest, judged by Frank Lloyd Wright, is properly viewed from above, the perspective of an airplane approaching Ciudad Trujillo. A modern airport was to surround the *Faro,* which Trujillo publicized with a 1937 "goodwill" flight around Latin America and an exhibit at the 1939 World's Fair in New York. (Columbus Memorial Lighthouse Collection, Columbus Memorial Library, Organization of American States.)

idea was that the "beacon" would "stand in an airfield of ample size and equipment." The winning entry in the subsequent architectural contest was based on the monument's appearance from the air.[45]

The lighthouse project was central to Trujillo's future plans for Ciudad Trujillo as a tourist destination and a hub of commerce, and depictions of it were linked with the material "renovation" of the Dominican Republic carried out by Trujillo.[46] The Dominican Pavilion at the 1939 World's Fair in New York picked up on the connection between aviation and the "Land Columbus Loved"; the theme of its principal exhibit was "Ciudad Trujillo: Past and Present." One section of the exhibit depicted colonial Santo Domingo, while the other was arranged like the fuselage of a plane, with windows where visitors could see aerial views of the modern Ciudad Trujillo and the planned lighthouse and airport.[47] Here was the panoptical perspective on the Dominican Republic again, but with the focus on different features of the landscape below. Whereas the marine flyers had scrutinized the terrain for "bandits" and attractive women, visitors to the Dominican

Pavilion were presented with a tableau of prosperity in gleaming white buildings beside the blue ocean. Here the vision of Ciudad Trujillo comprehended not only the "past" of colonial shrines and the "present" of Trujillo's monuments and public works, but a bright future, dominated by a sprawling airport dedicated to the Great Navigator. In the trujillista construction, aviation was a modern representation of the spirit of Columbus, who typified independence, bold initiative, and leadership, all attributes of the era's aviation heroes as they were presented in popular culture.

Columbus was also the patron saint of Pan-Americanism, an ideology promoted by the U.S. Army Air Service (later Air Corps) in Latin America. Army goodwill flights in the region included a Central American flight (1924), the Pan-American Goodwill Flight (1926–1927), Buenos Aires and Bogotá Goodwill Flights (1937), and the Brazil Goodwill Flight (1939). The version of Pan-American unity purveyed by the army tours was predicated on U.S. leadership. No Latin Americans participated in them, other than cheering and helping to push seaplanes into the water. Lindbergh's 1927–1928 tour of the Caribbean region also promoted inter-American harmony; he was "hailed as the 'Columbus of the Air' " during his "gay visit" to Santo Domingo.[48]

The 1937 "Pan-American Flight" for the Columbus Lighthouse was part of this trend in public relations between the Americas, but this "goodwill flight" was initiated by Trujillo and carried out by Dominican and Cuban pilots. Like the earlier flights by Lindbergh and the U.S. Army, the Dominican version advanced the notion that the technology of air exploration, like the Spanish caravel, was bringing the Americas closer together. The four planes in the flight took the names of Columbus and his three famous vessels. The projected itinerary covered more than 21,000 air miles across every country in the hemisphere, though the flight ended halfway when all three Cuban planes crashed in a storm in Cali, Colombia.[49] The "luck and triumph" of Dominican pilot Féliz Miranda in surviving the storm helped to "immortalize Dominican Aviation." [50] Féliz Miranda and his plane *Colón* were the Dominican answer to Lindy and his *Spirit of St. Louis,* conveying a similar message having to do with "knitting together nations and peoples." [51] His plane was one of two Curtiss-Wright combat models that the State Department allowed Trujillo to purchase and export for the lighthouse promotion, which suited the publicity purposes of the Good Neighbor policy. But the inter-American solidarity evoked by Féliz Miranda differed from that of the ongoing U.S. Army "goodwill" flights; the Dominican version was predicated on the leadership of Rafael Trujillo and was related to the dictator's broader campaign for a role in Latin American affairs independent of, and sometimes in opposition to, the United States. Trujillo's foreign policy was increasingly geared to making the world notice him; launching ambitious initiatives like the "Pan-American Flight" was central to his efforts. Trujillo's quest for international publicity increased the discomfiture of those in the State Department who regarded the dictator as a kind of Frankenstein, brought to life by the marines and now terrorizing his own household and his closest neighbors.

The rapid growth of Pan American Airways during the late 1920s and 1930s demonstrated the immediacy of air travel and generated much of the excitement about it around the region, a phenomenon that was very evident in the Dominican Republic.[52] Pan Am's commitment there began with Evan Young, U.S. Minister in Santo Domingo in 1929, who helped the new airline negotiate a very favorable contract with the Dominican government. He soon left his post, and his foreign service career, to become Pan Am's vice president for public relations, and was also a founding member of the Dominican Chamber of Commerce in New York.[53] Pan Am served Santo Domingo and the water airport at San Pedro de Macorís, where one-day service from Miami began in November 1935.[54] The Dominican press followed air traffic closely; passenger lists of arrivals and departures were a regular feature among articles covering the alto mundo of the Dominican Republic, making air travel a marker of high social status.[55] Trujillo often hosted receptions and lunches at the airport for VIPs aboard Pan Am flights and foreign military aviators who were only in the Dominican Republic long enough to refuel. Like the steamships of the expanding U.S. passenger lines in the Caribbean, Pan Am planes were incorporated into the hybridized social and political life of the regime, which was a way of Dominicanizing them and reducing their influence as instruments of U.S. hegemony.

The growth and interest in commercial aviation in the Dominican Republic was intertwined with the buildup of the Dominican air force. The National Air Transport Company blurred the distinction between military and commercial functions of aircraft, with planes and pilots performing both kinds of tasks, sometimes simultaneously, as they had during the occupation. This was the case with airmail delivery, an impressive way of "showing the flag" in the far reaches of the republic and, through the device of airmail stamps, overseas. Dominican airmail stamps had destinations outside the country (including Franklin Roosevelt's stamp collection), and served as diminutive advertisements. The lighthouse, caravels, airplanes, and Columbus were often pictured, as were the expanding amenities for travel and tourism in the Dominican Republic. Various issues featured the new water airport at San Pedro (1934), a Pan Am Clipper over the obelisk on Avenida George Washington (1938), and a series on the new government-owned hotels built with Export-Import Bank credits (1950).[56] Airmail was also an easily justified reason for requesting export licenses for airplane purchases from the State Department. Colonel Charles McLaughlin, a former marine employed by Trujillo, ordered four Piper Cub Cruisers for the quasi-military Aviation School that he supervised in 1940, planes that were first put in service training pilots and delivering the mail under the auspices of a private, Trujillo-owned company, but then transferred to the air force when the Dominican Republic entered World War II immediately after Pearl Harbor.[57]

Allies in the Skies and on the Tarmac

Trujillo's quick declarations of war against both Japan and Germany kept his end of a bargain struck with the United States in military staff talks in 1940.[58] At that time, Trujillo had pledged "the land, the sea, the air, and the men of the Dominican Republic" for the defense of the hemisphere, and was promised a new airport in return. In fact, the delegations of U.S. Army, Navy, and Marine officers charged with conducting such staff talks around the Caribbean were offering assistance for aviation infrastructure wherever they went. The strategic priority in constructing a "Fortress America" was to guard the Panama Canal, so a network of improved, expanded air facilities in its vicinity that U.S. planes could use was important.[59] Pan Am constructed the airports with unpublicized funding from the U.S. government.[60] Trujillo was glad to accept the offer, but not exactly as offered. American aviation experts wanted to expand the original marine airfield at the Consuelo sugar estate, amid cane fields, which was a safer location for military aircraft to land. Trujillo wanted an expansion of the Miraflores Airport, just two miles from the center of Ciudad Trujillo, which was an easier location to integrate airplanes into his spectacles of state. Putting the new airport there also meant that all airborne visitors to the Dominican Republic would behold Ciudad Trujillo on their way down from the sky. Trujillo insisted that the construction money go to the capital's airport "for political reasons," and he won the argument.[61]

Some of the most important events in Dominican public life during the years of the Second World War, occasions that combined the politics and culture of the regime, took place at the modern urban airport constructed by Pan Am. Both of Trujillo's two inaugurations during the year

1942, when he resumed the presidency after a one-term hiatus, involved the airport and American airmen. His first, "emergency" inauguration coincided with the reopening of the improved Miraflores Airport on 10 May and the commencement of "the new Interamerican Air Service." Held on the broad tarmac with thousands in attendance, the event "eclipse[d] anything in the history of the Capital as regards political demonstrations." The day's activities served to "reaffirm and endorse" the previous dozen years of Trujillo's rule, judged Minister Robert Scotten, as well as to indicate the participants' "unreserved support" for his resumption of the presidency. "It is for this reason that the opening of the airport on this day, and the capital made of the presence of the diplomatic corps in the reviewing stand had at least potential significance." [62]

Trujillo's second inauguration of 1942 took place on the date that he had made customary, Restoration Day, 16 August. Lieutenant General Frank Maxwell Andrews, head of the Army Caribbean Defense Command based in the Canal Zone and an eminent military aviator, made a "sudden arrival" with Major General James A. Collins and six staff officers on the day of the inauguration and stayed overnight. Andrews made just the one visit to the Dominican Republic, but his preference for "direct action" for military liaison with Caribbean governments (cutting through the diplomatic channels), and his praise for Trujillo's "beautification" of the capital, quickly endeared him to Trujillo.[63] After Andrews died in an airplane crash in 1944, Trujillo announced that Miraflores would be renamed for him.[64] The Dominican Centennial celebrations of 1944, which lasted ten days and included special diplomatic delegations from twenty-two countries, commenced with the inauguration of Lieutenant General Andrews Airfield on Pan-American Aviation Day, 22 February.[65]

In comparison to the vast scale of the overall U.S. war effort, the military assistance given to the Dominican Republic during World War II was miniscule. The Lend-Lease Act, which authorized arms and equipment transfers to "any country whose defense the President deems vital to the defense of the United States," was initially funded at $7 billion in March 1941.[66] The Dominican share of this consisted of 12 coastal patrol boats, 3,000 old Enfield rifles without ammunition, some equipment for general use (marine apparel–like field hats), and 19 airplanes.[67] But this limited wartime aid, especially the great boost in airpower, influenced the Trujillo regime and helped it to accelerate the pervasive militarization of the country first set in motion by the marine occupation.

The pressing need for coastal patrols and submarine tracking in the Caribbean in 1942 speeded the allocation of Lend-Lease airplanes and a

Naval Aviation Mission to the Dominican Republic.[68] The Lend-Lease aircraft that began to arrive in April 1943 were more advanced planes than had previously been available to the Dominican Republic, and they came with trainers and mechanics attached to the U.S. Naval Aviation Mission.[69] The wartime alliance was the watershed for Dominican air power and for regional military aviation in general, says aviation historian Daniel Hagedorn: "As in most Latin American countries, the Lend-Lease cornucopia and, usually, accompanying U.S. Mission, brought the respective services a level of training, equipment and appreciation for air power that had not heretofore been achievable. The Dominican Republic was no exception. . . . The dictator himself emerged from the war years with a much more seasoned appreciation for the potential of aviation." [70] This set the stage for Trujillo's postwar buildup of the Dominican armed forces, which far outstripped the recommendations of his erstwhile American military advisors and sowed instability among the nations of the Caribbean area.

The military footing of inter-American relations during the war increased Trujillo's opportunities for "liaison" with U.S. officers, contacts that had usually been discouraged by the State Department and its diplomats "in the field." The cultural manifestations of close wartime relations abounded during the tenure of Avra Warren as chief of mission in Ciudad Trujillo. Warren shared the respect for Trujillo's accomplishments expressed by so many American military men, and he delegated complete authority for Lend-Lease acquisitions to the embassy's naval attaché, Marine Colonel Joe W. Smith.[71] After leaving the Dominican Republic in April 1944, Warren became ambassador to Panama, the primary bastion of "Fortress America," where he formed a close association with Lieutenant General George H. Brett, head of the Caribbean Defense Command after General Andrews's death.

But in the wake of Warren's warm stay as ambassador came Ellis O. Briggs, whose bitter distaste for the Trujillo regime was more in keeping with the previous fifteen years of ambivalence toward Trujillo among the U.S. diplomats most closely involved with Dominican relations. Briggs complained that the threat of submarine incursions into the Caribbean was past, leaving "no justification" for arming the Trujillo regime. On his arrival in July 1944, he said it was time for an honest "stocktaking" of U.S. policy toward the dictatorship, "because the small Caribbean countries and our relations with them constitute a sort of show-window through which our inter-American relations are carefully examined by other — and more important — nations with which we are dealing." [72] Briggs objected to the flow of Lend-Lease matériel, especially aircraft, into the country.

Colonel Smith, the naval attaché, went to Florida to arrange the delivery of six airplanes in July 1944 "without any reference whatever to the Embassy," and kept Briggs in the dark (as he had Warren) about the amount of Lend-Lease equipment already delivered. Briggs also protested the influence of Lieutenant General Brett of the Caribbean Defense Command, who formed a friendship with Trujillo.[73] Briggs's opposition revived the intragovernmental rivalry with the military over the direction of Dominican relations, this time with the focus on aircraft.

General Brett visited Ciudad Trujillo on three days' notice in July 1944, to invite Dominican officers to the Army Service Schools in Panama and to offer a U.S. Army Mission to the Dominican Republic. Brett's reception at General Andrews Airfield dominated the front page of *La Nación,* as it did when he returned four weeks later, on two days' notice to the embassy but with elaborate prior planning by the regime.[74] This time Brett brought Ambassador Warren with him from Panama, and Puerto Rico's Governor Rexford Guy Tugwell was also in attendance. As before, Brett and Trujillo discussed liaison and aviation projects without including Ambassador Briggs, who did not learn of the Dominican national airline they proposed until he read about it in the Panama Canal Zone *Star and Herald.* The article, "General Brett Sees Dominican Air Progress," related how Brett and Warren "were strongly impressed by the evidences of progressive reform" in the "up-and-coming country," where "rapid development of air transportation" was predicted by Brett.[75] The following year, Trujillo established the commercial aviation company, Compañía Dominicana de Aviación, in partnership with Pan Am. Trujillo was the new airline's major stockholder, and its pilots all held commissions in the air force.[76]

Brett's back-to-back visits prompted another strong protest from Briggs, who urged the State Department to "reassert its authority" in "the Caribbean republics," where military representatives had seized the initiative. "If my interpretation of the views of our military is correct, they regard President Trujillo and his Government with great favor, which they often make no effort to disguise. They are inclined to view Trujillo's many substantial achievements—maintenance of order, 'making the Dominicans work,' et cetera—as indicating that Trujillo is operating the best possible government in the best of all possible Caribbean worlds." [77]

The State Department subsequently resumed its prewar policy of obstructing most weapons deliveries to the Dominican Republic. No more Lend-Lease airplanes arrived after Briggs registered his opposition, though Trujillo was granted export licenses for the two transport planes he had asked Brett to obtain for the new commercial airline. These turned out to be bombers converted to carry passengers, but which could still drop bombs; the State Department had been duped again.[78]

The Dominican Air Force

The U.S. policy of "containing arms" to dictatorships in Latin America, adopted by the State Department in late 1945, signaled the end of the wartime alliance, but it marked the beginning of Trujillo's quest for military self-sufficiency.[79] Over the next three years, Trujillo built the most powerful air force in the region on the foundation left by Lend-Lease, mainly by smuggling airplanes out of the United States without export licenses from the State Department and buying others on the booming international arms market, aided by a U.S. Marine lieutenant colonel. By 1948 he had about 140 planes, including 2 smuggled B-17 "Flying Fortress" bombers, operating from at least eleven airfields around the country.[80] This air power kept neighboring Haiti in a near-constant war scare (Trujillo built five new airfields near the border), and menaced the anti-Trujillo governments in Cuba, Costa Rica, Guatemala, and Venezuela.[81] The buildup was partly in response to the threat of invasions organized by exiles and mercenaries in Cuba and Guatemala, but it was also the culmination of another aspect of the larger, ongoing drive toward sovereignty engineered by Trujillo. Having regained "financial independence" with the removal of the U.S. Customs Receivership in 1940 and the retirement of the foreign debt in 1947, and having established political autonomy at the expense of the State Department at home and in the inter-American arena, Trujillo now stood on his own in military terms as well.

The strategic considerations of the Cold War and Trujillo's success in getting the airplanes and the pilot training he needed from other countries caused the United States to reopen the arms pipeline in 1949 and send another U.S. Aviation Mission to the Dominican Republic in 1953. But Trujillo never allowed the United States to regain its monopoly on technology and expertise. He accepted offers of U.S. aid, but only on his terms. Once he accepted two dozen Thunderbolt fighters on the condition that they arrive in time to celebrate his brother Héctor's inauguration in 1952. But he also pursued airplane purchases with Sweden, Britain, Japan, Nicaragua, and Mexico, and hosted Brazilian and Swedish aviation missions, encouraging their rivalry for his attention.[82] Far from standardizing his air force as the Pentagon advocated, Trujillo sought more and different kinds of airplanes, and though it was more expensive and troublesome to do it that way, it made more sense from the angle of showmanship. The most impressive parades have the most lavish diversity. Exhibiting a variety of warplanes overhead on holidays and maintaining an eclectic group of airplanes for his personal use reflected his personal power and wealth. Standardization of his fleet along the lines advocated by the Pentagon would make Dominican air power look like a cog in the Yankee defense machine. Instead, the Dominican air force maintained competing staffs of foreign technicians and pilots. Swedish and American support teams accompanied the new generations of fighters as they arrived in the country, while mercenaries, mainly U.S. veterans working in the Brazilian aviation mission, supported the smuggled models.[83] They all contributed to the steady increase in the sophistication of the Dominican air force, which became an independent branch of the military in 1948.

The physical size of the organization was one reason why the air force became the most important component of the Trujillo government in the postwar years. Other reasons had to do with the symbolism, social life, and nepotism of the regime.

"Look! Up in the Sky!"

The symbolic vocabulary of the "Era of Trujillo" was very rich, as suggested by the interlocking images of Columbus, the lighthouse, the airplane, and the city of Santo Domingo/Ciudad Trujillo. Civil aviation communicated with these metaphors, promoting Dominican history, tourism, and nationalism at the same time. An important event in this regard was the christening of a Pan Am Clipper as *Christopher Columbus* in 1955, when the airline inaugurated direct service from New York to Ciudad Trujillo. Dominican newspapers carried front-page coverage of Trujillo's daughter Angelita pouring "baptismal water" on the nose of the plane. Front-page ads described the luxury and convenience of the new "Super 6 Clippers," capable of whisking well-to-do Dominicans to the metropolis in a few hours.[84]

Military symbolism was even more prevalent in establishing the identity of the Trujillo regime. From the predawn bugle blast on the day of his first inauguration, Trujillo had cultivated a martial ambience in the Dominican Republic through frequent parades of his armed forces in all their great variety, trotting out each new weapon acquisition to an awed populace as soon as it was out of the crate. Trucks, motorcycles, "mountain guns," gunboats, and everything else in the arsenal right down to the ambulance corps issued forth from an ever-increasing number of military bases for an ever-increasing number of Dominican national holidays, all having to do in some way with the glory of El Benefactor, Trujillo.[85] But nothing compared in potency and spectacle to airplanes droning past over a crowd, and the postwar boom in the air force had everything to do with assembling larger and more varied formations for this purpose.[86] Airplane formations had great visual power in the wake of World War II, which the Dominican press had followed with particular attention to bombing, and for some Dominicans they probably hearkened back to the marine occupation. In creating his own formations to the rhythm of the trujillista calendar, Trujillo domesticated that visual power and harnessed it for his own uses.

U.S. air power demonstrations still had the capacity to communicate hegemonic messages, but these seemed to lose something in the translation in the Dominican Republic, because they seemed to be staged for Trujillo's personal benefit. When the USAF jet flying team called the Wings of the Americas visited Ciudad Trujillo in 1954, the team included the famous young pilot Chuck Yeager, who had broken the sound barrier for the first time just a few months before. The morning performance of the Wings of the Americas team had not been announced in the press because it was a "private" one for Trujillo, as if breaking the sound barrier could be kept private. Consequently, the first sonic boom over the capital scared the wits out of the city's population, who were taken completely by surprise. The planes performed again later that day for a general audience in a "public" show at the year-old Presidente Trujillo Air Base, on the site of the old marine airfield.[87] Within a year Trujillo had acquired jets of his own from Sweden, and the noise they made over the cities and towns of the country, they made in Trujillo's name alone.

It is difficult to estimate how these displays of air power were received by the spectators. In the first place, the Dominican news media were all tightly controlled during most of the life of the regime. This fact amplifies the importance of press coverage of the air force in determining how air power fit into the policies and self-image of the dictator, but it makes such coverage unreliable as evidence of popular attitudes. Though it is safe to say, as the press reported, that the inhabitants of Ciudad Trujillo were shocked by the first sonic boom, their real emotions on hearing it are subject to speculation. The ample newspaper coverage clearly shows that Trujillo meant both the "private," surprise concussion and the "public," planned one to resound to the glory of his regime, as other loud, droning formations did every year on his birthday and Armed Forces Day, among other occasions. More obscure is what the thousands of Dominicans who

Figure 4. Rafael Trujillo attends a private air show given by the U.S. Air Force's Wings of the Americas jet fighter team in February 1954, at which pilot Chuck Yeager produced the first sonic boom over the Dominican Republic. The city's inhabitants had not expected the sound barrier to be shattered until the public air show in the afternoon, and the early morning concussion shocked them. Air Force General Reuben Hood and the U.S. ambassador sit beside Héctor and Rafael Trujillo. (R G 342-U S A F-21254-Reel 27, Motion Picture Division, U.S. National Archives.)

turned out to witness the show that afternoon thought of what they saw. Some observers must have surged with nationalist pride at the sights and sounds. Others certainly cringed at this latest demonstration of the power and influence of the dictator for whose benefit the foreign aces performed. Probably none were impartial; when the sound barrier breaks, or when a few dozen diesel fighters and big bombers pass overhead, people listen. But it is impossible to calculate the number of Dominicans who witnessed these events during the Trujillo regime with contented enthusiasm for the present order, and how many felt only hopeless despondency over its apparent omnipotence.

High Society/Alto Mundo

Trujillo showed off airplanes and hotshot pilots in other ways than aerial display, ways that helped to shape the social life of the regime and broadcast to a wide audience the pleasures and prestige of the alto mundo. The Trujillo regime was rarely at a loss for a reason to celebrate, and any holiday that was a cause for a display of weaponry was also a cause for a party, or several parties. Demonstrations of military power took place in the streets, on the ocean, and in the sky; demonstrations of social power took place in the clubs, in the government reception halls, and at the military bases. One of the most direct effects of the social transformation Trujillo effected on coming to power was his domination of the cultural venues of the capital. Having once been blackballed at the elite Club Unión, Trujillo drove the institution into extinction in the first years of his rule. He replaced that club with one of his own founding, Club Juventud, whose exclusive membership list was based not on the bloodlines of the traditional Dominican oligarchy, but on the wielders of political (and hence social) power within the regime. Even the Santo Domingo Country Club, the preserve of the Anglo-American colony and its elite Dominican associates, had to fall in with the social pace of the new ruling set. Military clubs became popular venues on the official party circuit, especially the Club-Cine at the new Presidente Trujillo Air Base, where the air force elite frequently hosted galas for the capital's in-crowd.

Military soirees received tireless attention from the Dominican media, which also proliferated during the life of the regime.[88] Trujillo started a military magazine, created two new daily newspapers, and developed national radio and television stations, all of which provided breathless coverage of the social whirl that centered on him. The radio and television stations, La Voz Dominicana, helped to glamorize the high society of the regime, indicating both progress and fashionable modernity. Aviation and electronic media were extolled together in a *décima* called "Aviación," printed in a collection of such verses praising Trujillo in 1955.

En el ramo de aviación	In the field of aviation
hay progreso superado	there's super progress now
y también el alcanzado	we're also learning how
en radio y televisión;	in radio and television;
la gran civilización	the grand civilization
del país dominicano,	of the Dominican state,
es obra del ciudadano	is the work of the great

y eximio Benefactor,	Benefactor, a citizen
quien pone todo su amor	who to the Quisqueyan
de patricio quisqueyano.[89]	the sum of his love does relate.

The Flying Trujillos

Specific airplanes added to the opulence of Trujillo's lifestyle, especially the amphibious bomber he had outfitted with luxury accommodations for his personal use in 1953. As in the employment of converted bombers for passenger service, a subtext of military strength lay behind this expression of wealth and status. The airplane, named *San Cristóbal* for Trujillo's hometown, appeared on a 1960 Dominican airmail stamp.[90]

Trujillo was not the only one to travel in a converted bomber. Porfirio Rubirosa, Trujillo's former son-in-law and the playboy alter ego of the dictator, flew in a luxurious B-25.[91] Rubirosa was also the jet-set companion of Trujillo's son Ramfis, who in the air iconography of the Trujillo regime sat at the right hand of the father as head of Aviación Militar Dominicana. The figure of Ramfis, often wearing sunglasses and a bored expression, came to represent the AMD in the media. He was frequently pictured with various "alas amigas" (winged friends) visiting from the United States, shaking hands and drinking toasts.[92] The rivalry for Trujillo's attention between the Swedish and American aviation missions was institutionalized within the "Ramfis Fighter Squadron" formed in 1952, which had a P-51 Mustang section supported by the Swedes and an F-47 Thunderbolt section supported by the USAF military assistance group.[93] Ramfis himself was not a flyer, though you would never know it from the style of his self-presentation or his portrayal in the media, which meshed with the romantic image of the young pilots being produced by the AMD's own aviation academy.[94] The heir apparent's patronage of air power (helicopters were his special interest) contributed to the importance of the technology and added to its cultlike status under the Trujillo regime.[95] Ramfis also received a great deal of the credit for the air force's obliteration of three invasion attempts by Dominican exiles in 1959, which occurred on the north coast at Maimón and Estero Hondo, and in the central mountains at Constanza. In the first two cases, fighter planes sank the invaders' boats, and, in the third, Trujillo's heavy bombers hit rebels after they landed.[96] Trujillo's other son, Rhadamés, was identified with the growing tank corps that was also part of the sprawling AMD (as was the medical corps and its modern military hospital). Trujillo's oldest daughter

Flor de Oro, the globe-trotting former wife of Porfirio Rubirosa, married a USAF pilot as the fifth of her seven husbands.

The cult of the airplane also flowed together with the cult of the saints. Each of the branches of the military had a patron saint, always female, to revere in a combined religious procession/military parade on her feast day. The Dominican navy had the Virgin of Amparo, the Artillery Corps paraded with Saint Barbara atop a caisson, and the entire armed forces and the whole Trujillo clan always turned out to glorify the overall patron of the regime, the Virgin of Altagracia.[97] The AMD's patron was Our Lady of Carmen, whose statue was paraded through the "residential barrio" of Presidente Trujillo Air Base every 16 July. The 1958 procession was led by the children of air force officers, dressed as angels with little wings on their backs and their hands clasped in prayer; it included a mass celebrated at the air base's chapel dedicated to the Virgin of Carmen, accompanied by the organist and choir of the Military Aviation Academy.[98] As in most other entertainments and rituals spicing the civic and military life of the regime, the initiative for official religious observances originated with Trujillo and reinforced his status as the patron of the spiritual, as well as the material, well-being of his people.

The Dominican air force, then, was more than just a military organization. It was also simultaneously a fraternal order, a social club, a feudal court, and a religious congregation. It even boasted the nation's best amateur baseball team, which was prominent at the annual Trujillo Tournament. Forming leagues and building stadiums to encourage baseball was another cultural aspect of trujillista state formation, in which the air force team played a glamorous part.[99] The importance of the air force to the Trujillo regime rested on a foundation of sheer technological might, but was manifested in all these other ways along lines that had become familiar under Trujillo. The parties, parades, and processions it sponsored comprised a kind of cult, but one that was entirely subsumed within the larger cult of personality of the dictator and his family.

With Friends like These. . . ?

Trujillo had another falling out with the State Department in 1957 that led the Office of Munitions Control to cut off export licenses again. Trujillo countered in 1958 by expelling the USAF Mission and the few airplanes still being supported by the military assistance program. By that time the AMD had gone over to using mainly Swedish Vampire jet fighters, confirming that there was no shortage of aircraft to be had on the international market, even without the blessing of the United States. Despite the worsening state of relations, Trujillo obtained export licenses for two dozen B-26 bombers from a Florida arms dealer at the same time the aviation mission was decamping, bolstering his defenses just as the opprobrium of his neighbors began to rain down in earnest in 1959 and 1960.[100] A kind of siege mentality characterized those years in the Trujillo regime, as José Figueres of Costa Rica, Fidel Castro of Cuba, and Rómulo Betancourt of Venezuela (whom Trujillo tried to assassinate in June 1960) mobilized regional opinion against him. This atmosphere only served to intensify the relationship among airplanes, the cultlike air force, the dictator, and the defense of Dominican territory and sovereignty against all comers. "Soy Soldado de la A.M.D.," a poem dedicated to "the valiant members of that very brilliant institution" and published in the *Armed Forces Magazine* after the 1959 invasion attempts, combined these themes:

De la Aviación soy soldado	I am a soldier of the Air Force
y a ella doy todo el brillo	I give to her the brilliance that I owe
que mi Jefe me ha brindado,	to my generous Chief, who is, of course
Rafael Leonidas Trujillo. . . .	Rafael Leonidas Trujillo. . . .
Y ganar en la batalla	And to win the battle
con tiros, bombas y aviones,	with guns, planes, and bombs
dando metralla y metralla	giving metal for metal
a un grupito de bribones. . . .	to a few bearded bums. . . .
Quiero decir a Figueres,	I want to tell Figueres
a Betancourt y a Fidel,	and Betancourt and Fidel
que tengo muchos poderes,	I have powerful militaries,
para poderlos vencer. . . .	to whip them all well. . . .
Como soy hombre sincero	I'm a man who's sincere
mi pensamiento está fijo	so my thinking is done
en alguien que tanto quiero:	about whom I hold dear:
General Trujillo hijo. . . .	General Trujillo, the son. . . .
Soy un soldado de brillo,	A shining soldier, I know,
y es grande mi corazón	my heart is big and ready
que está a la disposición	with support that is steady
de mi PATRIA y de TRUJILLO.[101]	for my FATHERLAND and TRUJILLO.

Pan Am continued to work with Trujillo as his regime sank into international troubles in the late 1950s, leading up to the inauguration of Trujillo Airport for commercial aviation in December 1959.[102] From then until Trujillo's assassination in May 1961, the Dominican Republic stood virtually alone in the community of American nations. Trujillo was increasingly regarded as the rabid dog of the hemisphere, and the Organization of American States took the unprecedented step of imposing sanctions on him in 1960. But he was defiant of outside pressure behind the shield of the Dominican air force, confident that, aside from quixotic exiles, no one would attack him directly. If there was to be any attacking, he hinted, it might be on the part of his long-range bombers against his enemies' capital cities. The Eisenhower and Kennedy administrations both supported economic sanctions and contemplated assassination attempts, but Trujillo was correct; an invasion was out of the question. Until the day of his murder on 30 May 1961, Trujillo denounced his critics and exhibited his weaponry to the world, an ally to none.

Conclusion

The magic rabbits of air power were no longer the exclusive property of U.S. military men, and were jumping out of other hats in Latin America. Now it seemed every time Trujillo doffed his bicorne at a parade, a formation of jets appeared, conjured by the generalísimo. Having apprenticed himself to some of the very first sorcerers of air power, he had compiled his own book of spells and brought great forces under his control, channeling them through his regime to attain his own objectives, not those of the putative master of the dependent states of the Caribbean, the United States. Observers in the United States often commented on the disproportionate size of the Dominican air force relative to the size of the country, but that was precisely the point of having an air force in the ideology of the Trujillo regime. Trujillo construed himself as an epochal figure, on a level with Buddha, Christ, Caesar, and Bolívar; he saw himself as disproportionately great to the little republic he ruled, a fact underlying the expansive personalism of his foreign policy.[103] Trujillo's air force, like his rhetoric, was not bound by the territory of the state, as were the other armed forces, the public works, and the Dominican social scene. Air power "defies distance," as Trujillo's defense secretary claimed in a phrase that could also mean "wards off enemies" and "boosts stature."[104] The Dominican air force was an example of a "shop-window" air force assembled for the purpose of "deterrence and prestige," which Michael Sherry has pointed out are "subjective considerations" with "discouragingly few guidelines by which to determine what is 'enough.'"[105]

Trujillo's guidelines diverged from those of the United States. The technology and ideology of airplanes in the Dominican Republic were shaped less by the global strategy of the United States than by Trujillo's interrelated goals of securing the sovereignty of his nation and enhancing his own social and political standing domestically and internationally.[106] Every airplane in the country reflected his glory and contributed to the cult of his vanity and nationalism, whether it be the fighter squadrons in formation overhead, the airliners bringing tourists to the "land Columbus loved," the flying palaces winging Trujillo family "jet-setters" to another extravagance abroad, or foreign military brass coming to visit the generalísimo. Many of the U.S. military men in the latter category belonged to their own cult of the airplane with an abiding fascination for flying machines and the status they conferred, but when translated by the Trujillo regime, their creed took on meanings that they had never intended, and which they had no way to control.

Notes

I would like to thank Catherine LeGrand, Gil Joseph, and particularly Ricardo Salvatore for their thoughtful readings of an earlier version. I would also like to thank the following people for bringing important sources to my attention: Daniel Hagedorn, Lauren Derby, A. E. Doyle, Seth Fein, and Michael Schroeder.

1. G. Douglas Wardrop, "The Future of Aeronautics" and "Aviation: The Big Factor in Commerce as in War," *Pan-American Magazine,* July 1919, 135–49.

2. The best histories of the U.S. occupation of Hispaniola are Bruce Calder, *The Impact of Intervention: The Dominican Republic during the U.S. Occupation of 1916–24* (Austin: University of Texas Press, 1984); and Hans Schmidt, *The U.S. Occupation of Haiti, 1915–34* (New Brunswick, N.J.: Rutgers University Press, 1973).

3. Emily Rosenberg, *Spreading the American Dream* (New York: Hill and Wang, 1982), 103–7; Wesley Phillips Newton, *The Perilous Sky: U.S. Aviation Diplomacy and Latin America, 1919–1931* (Coral Gables, Fla.: University of Miami Press, 1978).

4. Michael Sherry, *The Rise of American Air Power: The Creation of Armageddon* (New Haven, Conn.: Yale University Press, 1987), 2.

5. Typical of the promotional literature of U.S. imperialism that first appeared in 1898 is Trumbull White, *Our New Possessions* (Philadelphia: American Book and Bible House, 1898).

6. In Bird's vision, aerial bombardment would be outlawed. Even so, thousands of "U. S. of the A. aerial express ships . . . were employed in the government service and conveyed troops to all points in the great American Republic" (Bird,

Looking Forward: A Dream of the United States of the Americas in 1999 [1899; New York: Arno Press, 1971], 115–28).

7. Matthew Josephson, *Empire of the Air: Juan Trippe and the Struggle for World Airways* (New York: Harcourt, Brace, 1944), 53.

8. "Annual report of operations of Aircraft Squadrons, Second Brigade from July 1, 1927 to date," 20 June 1928, National Archives, Washington, D.C. (hereafter NA), General Correspondence of the Secretary of the Navy, Record Group (hereafter RG) 80, 778/a9-1 (280918).

9. For the history of the Trujillo regime, see Jesús de Galíndez, *La era de Trujillo: Un estudio casuístico de dictadura latinoamericana* (Santiago, Chile: Editorial del Pacífico, 1956; English edition, *The Era of Trujillo, Dominican Dictator,* ed. Russell H. Fitzgibbon [Tucson: University of Arizona Press, 1973]); Robert D. Crassweller, *Trujillo: The Life and Times of a Caribbean Dictator* (New York: Macmillan, 1966); and G. Pope Atkins and Larman C. Wilson, *The United States and the Trujillo Regime* (New Brunswick, N.J.: Rutgers University Press, 1972).

10. Joseph J. Corn, *The Winged Gospel: America's Romance with Aviation, 1900–1950* (New York: Oxford University Press, 1983); and Sherry, *Rise of American Air Power,* 1–75.

11. Numerous films, from *Dawn Patrol* (1930) through *Thirty Seconds over Tokyo* (1946) to *The McConnell Story* (1957), underlined this romantic attraction to intrepid pilots of dangerous aircraft. See Michael Paris, *From the Wright Brothers to Top Gun: Aviation, Nationalism, and Popular Cinema* (Manchester: Manchester University Press, 1995); and Bertil Skogsberg, *Wings on the Screen: A Political History of Air Movies,* trans. George Bisset (San Diego, Calif.: A. S. Barnes and Co., 1981). Pan Am was also romanticized in the Fred Astaire and Ginger Rogers movie *Flying Down to Rio* (1937). See Brian Henderson, "A Musical Comedy of Empire," *Film Quarterly* 85, no. 2 (winter 1981–1982): 2–16. Comic strips also glorified military fliers. Several of these appeared in newspapers in the Dominican Republic: "Jorge el Piloto," "Terry y las Piratas" (both 1940s), and "As Solar" (1950s).

12. For the role of mercenaries in aviation development in Central America, see Lester Langley and Thomas Schoonover, *The Banana Men: American Mercenaries and Entrepreneurs in Central America, 1880–1930* (Lexington: University Press of Kentucky, 1995), 161–62. For a travel account of flying with "Tex Anding, the young American ex-marine" in Haiti, see Hendrik de Leeuw, *Crossroads of the Caribbean* (Garden City, N.Y.: Garden City Publishing, 1938), 273–78. Also see Newton, *Perilous Sky,* 21–59.

13. David Long, *Gold Braid and Foreign Relations* (Annapolis, Md.: Naval Institute Press, 1988), and Richard D. Challener, *Admirals, Generals, and American Foreign Policy* (Princeton, N.J.: Princeton University Press, 1973) address the diplomatic role of the navy; Peter D. Karsten, *The Naval Aristocracy: The Golden Age of Annapolis and the Emergence of Modern American Navalism* (New York:

Free Press, 1972) discusses the institutional and social identity of its officer corps. For a general history of the U.S. Marine Corps, see Robert D. Heinl, *Soldiers of the Sea* (Annapolis, Md.: Naval Institute Press, 1962).

14. For an exploration of the "mystique" of the U.S. diplomatic ranks, see Robert D. Schulzinger, *The Making of the Diplomatic Mind: The Training, Outlook, and Style of the United States Foreign Service, 1908–1931* (Middletown, Conn.: Wesleyan University Press, 1975); and Martin Weil, *A Pretty Good Club: The Founding Fathers of the U.S. Foreign Service* (New York: W. W. Norton, 1978). For the organizational growth and professionalization of the State Department, see Richard Johnson, *The Administration of United States Foreign Policy* (Austin: University of Texas Press, 1971); Richard Hume Werking, *The Master Architects: Building the United States Foreign Service, 1890–1913* (Lexington: University Press of Kentucky, 1977); and Waldo H. Heinrichs Jr., "Bureaucracy and Professionalism in the Development of American Career Diplomacy," in *Twentieth-Century American Foreign Policy,* ed. John Braeman, Robert H. Brenner, and David Brody (Columbus: Ohio State University Press, 1971).

15. The mirroring of Trujillo's social and governmental circle by the carnaval "Reina, Embajadoras y Su Corte" was an annual event in the capital, with the queen's triumphal entrance into the city and round of parties at its primary social venues featured prominently in the press. See, for example, "El magno Desfile y el Baile al Gran Protector del Reino [Trujillo] y a las Embajadoras [de los Centros Sociales de la República]" and "El Baile de anoche en el Club Unión fue una fiesta social distinguida," *Listín Diario* (Santo Domingo), 28 Mar. 1932.

16. The 1914 "exhibition flights of a U.S. flier, Frank Burnside," had earlier "kindled interest" in aviation in the Dominican Republic (Newton, *Perilous Sky,* 15).

17. Robert E. Quirk, *An Affair of Honor: Woodrow Wilson and the Occupation of Veracruz* (Lexington: University Press of Kentucky, 1962); Frederick Calhoun, *Power and Principle: Armed Intervention in Wilsonian Foreign Policy* (Kent, Ohio: Kent State University Press, 1986); and Lauren Derby, "Teaching Freedom under Imperialism" (paper presented at the annual meeting of the American Historical Association, Chicago, Jan. 1995).

18. See Ricardo Salvatore's essay in this volume.

19. The phrase was employed by Secretary of State Henry L. Stimson to describe Trujillo to Senator William Borah (Stimson, *Diaries,* 25 Nov. 1930, 10:180–81, Herbert Hoover Presidential Library, West Branch, Iowa).

20. Harry Franck, *Roaming through the West Indies* (New York: Blue Ribbon Books, 1920), 118.

21. For the military campaign in the Dominican Republic, see Lester D. Langley, *The Banana Wars: An Inner History of American Empire, 1900–34* (Lexington: University Press of Kentucky, 1983); and Ivan Musicant, *The Banana Wars: A History of United States Military Intervention in Latin America from the Spanish-American War to the Invasion of Panama* (New York: Macmillan, 1990).

22. "Report on First Air Squadron, Marine Aviation Force," undated, United States Marine Corps Historical Center, Washington, D.C. (hereafter MCHC), Dominican Republic Reference File. For a recent study of *gavillerismo*, see Julie Franks, "The *Gavilleros* of the East: Social Banditry as Political Practice in the Dominican Sugar Region, 1900–24," *Journal of Historical Sociology* 8, no. 2 (1995): 158–81.

23. The romanticization of the Marine Corps during the interwar period often focused on aviators in the Caribbean. See, for example, Irwin R. Franklyn's novel *Knights of the Cockpit: A Romantic Epic of the Flying Marines of Haiti* (New York: Dial Press, 1931) and the movie *Devil Dogs of the Air* (MGM, 1935). This theme is treated by Craig Cameron, *American Samurai: Myth, Imagination, and the Conduct of Battle in the First Marine Division, 1941–1951* (New York: Cambridge University Press, 1994), 30–48.

24. Lieutenant Harold Miller, USMC, "Letter from 'Chuck' to his friend 'Eddie,'" *Santo Domingo Leatherneck* (San Pedro de Macorís, 1919), 9–10. The first and perhaps only issue of this magazine was subtitled the "Aviation Number," and was written by and almost entirely about the marine air squadron. A cartoon of a gavillero drawn by a marine depicted him as a pirate, with high boots marked with a skull and crossbones, and a knife between his teeth (contained in James K. Noble Collection, MCHC, Personal Papers Division, Personal Collection [hereafter PC] 15).

25. The idea of the Panopticon and the power of surveillance is developed in Michel Foucault, *Discipline and Punish: The Birth of a Prison,* trans. Alan Sheridan (New York: Pantheon, 1977), 195–230.

26. See Salvatore's essay in this volume; and Newton, *Perilous Sky,* 32.

27. *Leatherneck,* 14.

28. *Listín Diario,* 26 Apr. 1919, printed in Spanish and English in *Leatherneck,* 23–24. The aviators won converts among otherwise earthbound officers by taking them into the sky and bringing them back with acrobatic flourishes. Lieutenant Harold Miller, author of the letter from "Chuck," was taken by airplane from Hato Mayor to a suspected "bandit" camp, and though the occupants had fled before his arrival, the view of the town and the experience of doing a "steep tight spiral" while dropping from 2,500 feet left him in awe of the machine (First Sergeant Kleps, "A Short History of the 44th Company," *Leatherneck,* 32). Visiting U.S. senators were also taken aloft, as shown by photos in the Christian F. Schilt Collection, MCHC, PC 19. The Schilt photo album also includes photos of the First Air Squadron's facilities at Santo Domingo and scenes of the marine fliers "beach party dancing."

29. *Listín Diario,* 26 Apr. 1919. In this use of airplanes for courtship, the marines had a parallel in the postwar Dominican air force, which suffered some of their losses when pilots trying "to impress their girlfriends" crashed (Conversation with Daniel Hagedorn, 28 June 1995, summarizing his impressions from U.S. intelligence reports contained in RG 165, NA). For more on marine courtships, see

Listín Diario, 21, 24, and 26 Aug. 1926. Cynthia Enloe has written on what she calls the "Pocahontas myth," that "women are likely to be charmed by their own people's conquerors," in *Bananas, Beaches, and Bases: Making Feminist Sense of International Politics* (Berkeley and Los Angeles: University of California Press), 1–2.

30. For example, the flight log of marine pilot David L. S. Brewster, Mar. 1921–June 1922, includes all of the activities mentioned here (David Brewster Collection, MCHC, PC 4, folder 1).

31. John D. Bennett Collection, MCHC, PC 1296. Bennett's photo album also includes pictures of an airplane wreck, reinforcing the real danger that fueled the camaraderie of the aviators.

32. *Leatherneck,* 17.

33. Private Nix, "My Fancy Strays," *Leatherneck,* 19.

34. One of his chapters on the Dominican Republic is titled "The Land of Bullet-holes," after the clock tower in Monte Cristy, blasted by an inebriated marine during a nocturnal card game (Franck, *Roaming through the West Indies,* 189–206).

35. Ernesto Vega y Pagán, *Military Biography of Generalísimo Rafael Leonidas Trujillo Molina* (Ciudad Trujillo: Editorial Atenas, 1956), 45–56, 84–89, 173–91.

36. These included two important aviators: James C. Breckinridge, who commanded the air campaign in 1919–1920 and became the commandant of the Marine Corps, and Roy Geiger, who became a major general (Roy Geiger Collection, MCHC, PC 311). For an exhaustive account of Trujillo's ties to U.S. military men, see Bernardo Vega, *Trujillo y las fuerzas armadas norteamericanas* (Santo Domingo: Fundación Cultural Dominicana, 1992).

37. For the development of Dominican air forces, see Daniel P. Hagedorn, *Central American and Caribbean Air Forces* (London: Air-Britain, 1993), 96–111; John Dienst and Dan Hagedorn, *North American P-51 Mustangs in Latin American Air Force Service* (Arlington, Tex.: Aerofax, 1985), 2–29; and *Nacimiento y desarrollo de la Fuerza Aérea Dominicana* (Santo Domingo: Jefatura del Estado, Fuerzas Armadas Dominicanas, 1984). I am indebted to Mr. Hagedorn for sharing his extensive knowledge of Dominican air power with me, and for entrusting to me his copy of *Nacimiento y desarrollo de la Fuerza Aérea Dominicana.*

38. *Foreign Relations of the United States 1930* (Washington, D.C.: Government Printing Office, 1961), 5:724–25.

39. Stimson to Schoenfeld, 4 Feb. 1932; Schoenfeld to Stimson, 5 and 17 Feb. 1932; Scott memo, 7 Mar. 1932, NA, General Records of the Department of State, RG 59, 839.51/3677–78, 3689, and 3708.

40. Cutts to Watson, 19 Dec. 1930, MCHC, Thomas J. Watson Collection, PC 982, box 3. Watson rose to the rank of lieutenant general in the 1950s, though he had a falling out with Trujillo in 1950. Vega, *Trujillo y las fuerzas armadas norteamericanas,* 355–57.

41. Watson to Cutts, 17 Dec. 1930, MCHC, Watson Papers, box 3; Watson to

Colonel Thomas C. Turner, USMC, Aviation Section, 14 Feb. 1931; and Turner to Watson, 27 Feb. 1931, MCHC, Thomas C. Turner Collection, PC 125.

42. Hagedorn, *Central American and Caribbean*, 96.

43. *Christopher Columbus Memorial Lighthouse at Santo Domingo, Hearings before the Committee on Foreign Affairs, House of Representatives*, 70th Cong., 2d sess., 23 Jan. 1929; and Hull to Roosevelt, 13 Nov. 1935, Franklin D. Roosevelt Presidential Library, Hyde Park, N.Y., Official File 781.

44. The Columbus Memorial Lighthouse Collection at the Columbus Library, Organization of American States, Washington, D.C. (hereafter OAS), contains the records of the design competition, including drawings, correspondence, and publicity efforts.

45. General Receiver of Dominican Customs William Pulliam to Pan American Union President Leo S. Rowe, 3 June 1930, with enclosed clipping from the *Sun* (New York), 6 Feb. 1928; Joseph Lea Gleave architectural drawings and description, in "El Faro a Colón," Comité Ejecutivo Permanente del Faro de Colón (1946), OAS.

46. For the theme of Trujillo's reconstruction of (and personal identification with) the country and especially the capital after its destruction by the San Zenón hurricane of Sept. 1930, see Trujillo, *La nueva patria dominicana* (Santo Domingo: n.p., 1934). An insightful recent study of this and other related iconographical and metaphorical representations of the Trujillo regime is Andrés L. Mateo, *Mito y cultura en la era de Trujillo* (Santo Domingo: Librería La Trinitaria e Instituto del Libro, 1993). Above all, see Lauren H. Derby, "The Magic of Modernity: Dictatorship and Civic Culture in the Dominican Republic, 1916–1962" (Ph.D. diss., University of Chicago, 1998).

47. A stylish photo spread of the pavilion appeared in *Dominican Republic* magazine, June 1939, cover, 7–11; it was also described in the *New York Times*, 24 June 1939. The fair also boasted an aviation building with a "blind flying" flight simulator (*Dominican Republic*, Sept. 1938, 9).

48. For details of the Central American Flight, the Pan-American Goodwill Flight, and the Lindbergh Goodwill Flight, see Newton, *Perilous Sky*, 41–59, 85–99, 125–56. Photos of all these events are contained in the Domestic Series: Events and Activities, National Air and Space Museum Archive, Smithsonian Institution, Washington, D.C. The film *Lindbergh* (1928) concentrated on his circle route around the Caribbean, which symbolized "the binding cord of good-will," NA, Motion Picture Division, Motion Picture Distributors of America, 106.22. For Lindbergh in Santo Domingo, see *Listín Diario*, 3–4 Feb. 1928; and Newton, *Perilous Sky*, 149.

49. "Joint Statement," Dominican Minister to the U.S. Andrés Pastoriza and Cuban Ambassador to the U.S. Pedro Martínez Fraga, undated, OAS. For documentation of the flight, see Ramón A. Tejera R., *El vuelo panamericano pro Faro a Colón* (Santo Domingo: Colección Quinto Centenario, Serie Estudios 5, Editora Taller, 1992).

50. First Lieutenant Pilot Rafael Antonio Reyes Jorge, "Historial sobre aviación," *Revista de las Fuerzas Armadas,* Sept. 1954, 19.

51. See cover story on Féliz Miranda and his plane in *Dominican Republic,* July 1937, for several examples of the aviation iconography of the Trujillo regime. The *Colón* is in the collection of the Museo del Hombre in Santo Domingo. Also see George Black, *The Good Neighbor: How the United States Wrote the History of Central America and the Caribbean* (New York: Pantheon, 1988), 58–85.

52. Pan Am's expansion was rapid throughout most of Central America and the Caribbean, connecting most of the republics in the region, including the Dominican Republic, by 1929. Newton, *Perilous Sky.*

53. Newton, *Perilous Sky,* 186; Josephson, *Empire of the Air,* 55; and *Dominican Republic Actually,* Dec. 1934, 3.

54. "Monograph, Ciudad Trujillo, Dominican Republic, Office of Naval Intelligence," Dec. 1938, NA, Naval Intelligence Division, RG 38, L-9-a/22674-A; and *Dominican Republic,* Nov. 1935, 5. For a portrait of the Pan Am system in the Caribbean in the mid-1930s, including three chapters on the tourist experience in the Dominican Republic, see E. Alexander Powell, *Aerial Odyssey* (New York: Macmillan, 1936).

55. Daily issues of *Listín Diario* carried the "Llegados" and "Salidos" columns on Pan Am passengers.

56. *Scott Standard Postage Stamp Catalog, 1992,* vol. 2 (Sidney, Ohio: Scott Publishing Company, 1991), 966–67. For more on the people and places depicted on the stamps of the Trujillo regime, see *Who's Who on the Postage Stamps of the Dominican Republic* (Washington, D.C.: Pan American Union, 1945).

57. Hagedorn, *Central American and Caribbean,* 96.

58. For declarations of war, see *Listín Diario,* 9 and 12 Dec. 1941. For staff talks, see memorandum for the Assistant Chief of Staff, War Plans Division, Lieutenant Norman Randolph, 1 July 1940, NA, War Plans Division (hereafter WPD) 4115-24, RG 165 (Randolph was joined in the first round of talks by marine aviator Pedro del Valle); and Record of Staff Conversations between Representatives of the Government of the Dominican Republic and the United States of America, 17 Aug. 1940, NA, RG 165, WPD 4318.

59. David G. Haglund, *Latin America and the Transformation of U.S. Strategic Thought, 1936–1940* (Albuquerque: University of New Mexico Press, 1984); John Child, *Unequal Alliance: The Inter-American Military System 1938–1978* (Boulder: University of Colorado Press, 1980); and idem, "From 'Color' to 'Rainbow': U.S. Strategic Planning for Latin America, 1919–1945," *Journal of Interamerican Studies and World Affairs* (May 1979): 233–59.

60. Record of Staff Conversations, 17 Aug. 1940.

61. Lieutenant Colonel R. C. Smith, memo to the Assistant Chief of Staff, War Plans Division, 21 May 1941; and Orme Wilson, Liaison Officer, memo to Chief, Liaison Branch, War Department, 13 June 1941; both and related documents are in NA, RG 165, WPD 4318-3.

62. Chargé d'Affaires Edward P. Lawton to Hull, with clippings from *La Nación* (Ciudad Trujillo), 11 May 1942, NA, RG 59, 839.00/4318. The potential for increased tourism through the airport was also emphasized at its opening, with a delegation of Miami businessmen and journalists imported for the occasion on a Pan Am Clipper and Trujillo's personal yacht, *Ramfis*. Benton Jacobs, "Trujillo Plans Powerful Bid for Tourists," *Miami Daily News* article reprinted in *Dominican Republic,* Nov./Dec. 1941, 9.

63. Lieutenant General Frank M. Andrews memo to General Van Voorhis, 30 Apr. 1941; Andrews to Trujillo, 26 Aug. 1942; and Trujillo to Andrews, 31 Aug. 1942, Library of Congress, Washington, D.C., Frank Maxwell Andrews Papers, Personal Correspondence File, box 7.

64. Warren to Hull, 8 and 26 Jan. 1944, NA, RG 59, 839.7962/49 and 50.

65. Another major event of the centennial was the laying of the Columbus Lighthouse cornerstone. Warren to Hull, 7 Jan. 1944, NA, RG 59, 839.415/75; draft program of First Centennial Celebration of the Dominican Republic, enclosed with Warren to Hull, 8 Feb. 1944, NA, RG 59, 839.415/121. Pan Am ran an advertisement in *Dominican Republic* (Mar./Apr. and July/Aug. 1944) showing an enormous "Clipper of the future" unloading on a Latin American airfield, with a message of congratulations to the Dominican Republic. The text of the ad mentioned the shared interest of the United States and the Dominican Republic in Columbus and "democratic ideals," and announced increased service to Ciudad Trujillo. For a full description of the centennial and its meaning for the Trujillo regime, see Derby, "The Magic of Modernity," chap. 5.

66. Warren F. Kimball, *The Most Unsordid Act: Lend-Lease, 1939–1941* (Baltimore, Md.: Johns Hopkins University Press, 1969); and Leon Martel, *Lend-Lease, Loans, and the Coming of the Cold War: A Study of the Implementation of Foreign Policy* (Boulder: University of Colorado Press, 1979).

67. Orme Wilson, Liaison Officer, to Colonel Matthew Ridgway, 11 Feb. 1941, NA, RG 165, WPD 4318-2; Brigadier General E. Reybold to Brigadier General L. T. Gerow, 14 June 1941, and Gerow to Reybold, undated reply, WPD 4318-4; Gerow to Defense Aid Director, 11 Dec. 1941, WPD 4318-6; Secretary of the Navy Frank Knox to Commandant, USMC, 14 Aug. 1941, NA, RG 80, EF63/LII-3(22)(410813); Captain Paul Hendren to Moore Lynn, Division of Defense Aid, 25 Oct. 1941 (410911); and Commandant, USMC, to Chief of Naval Operations, 11 May 1942 (420511), General Correspondence of the Secretary of the Navy. The airplane count is from Hagedorn, *Central American and Caribbean,* 97.

68. The Naval Aviation Mission was proposed to Trujillo and accepted by him within days of Pearl Harbor, Gerow memo, 18 Dec. 1941, NA, RG 165, WPD 4318-7. The two best vessels of the Dominican Merchant Marine, the *San Rafael* and *Presidente Trujillo,* were both sunk by German submarines during May 1942.

69. Trujillo would only accept relatively advanced aircraft, turning down an offer of three rebuilt navy planes of an earlier vintage (Vought OS2Us). Admiral W. O. Spears to Chief of the Bureau of Aeronautics, 7 May 1942, NA, RG 80,

EF63/LII-3(22)(420506); and Hull to Minister Avra Warren, 14 Aug. 1942, RG 59, 839.20/108A.

70. Hagedorn, *Central American and Caribbean,* 97. The Dominican Republic was the fifteenth Latin American nation to receive a naval or military mission from the United States; the agreements were usually for a four-year term (Charles M. Barnes, Chief of the Treaty Division, memo to the Secretary of State, 23 Jan. 1943, NA, RG 59, 839.30/22).

71. Ambassador Ellis O. Briggs to Hull, 28 July 1944, NA, RG 59, 839.24/7-2844.

72. Briggs to Hull, 5 July 1944, NA, RG 59, 839.00/7-544.

73. Briggs to Hull, 28 July 1944, NA, RG 59, 839.24/7-2844. Brett "would pop into Ciudad Trujillo to go hunting with" Trujillo, reported Spruille Braden, *Diplomats and Demagogues* (New Rochelle, N.Y.: Arlington House, 1971), 279.

74. Briggs to Secretary of State, 21 July 1944, with *La Nación* clippings enclosed, NA, RG 59, 839.20III/7-2144.

75. Briggs to Secretary of State, 5 Sept. 1944, with clipping from Panama Canal Zone *Star and Herald,* 24 Aug. 1944, NA, RG 59, 839.00/5-544.

76. Hagedorn, *Central American and Caribbean,* 97.

77. Briggs to Secretary of State, 5 Sept. 1944, with clipping from Panama Canal Zone *Star and Herald,* 24 Aug. 1944, NA, RG 59, 839.00/5-544.

78. Hagedorn, *Central American and Caribbean,* 97.

79. Chester Pach Jr., "The Containment of U.S. Military Aid to Latin America, 1944–49," *Diplomatic History* 6, no. 3 (July 1982): 225–44.

80. Hagedorn, *Central American and Caribbean,* 98–100; and Dienst and Hagedorn, *North American P-51 Mustangs,* 2–4.

81. Luis Arias Núñez, *La política exterior en la era de Trujillo* (Santiago, D.R.: Pontífica Universidad Católica Madre y Maestra, 1991).

82. Hagedorn, *Central American and Caribbean,* 97–108.

83. American aviation mercenaries often had names that suited the soldier-of-fortune romance of their trade, the best being "Harrow Wild" (Hagedorn, *Central American and Caribbean,* 101).

84. *El Caribe* (Ciudad Trujillo) and *La Nación,* 13 Oct. 1955.

85. Trujillo's "coronation" is described in John Moors Cabot to Secretary of State, 21 Aug. 1930, and covered in *Listín Diario,* 17 Aug. 1930; a colorful description of the "great military display" on the day Trujillo received the French Legion of Honor is in British Minister R. G. Goldie to the Marquess of Reading, 31 Aug. 1931, *British Documents on Foreign Affairs,* part 2, series D, vol. 6: 9.

86. Some good examples of coverage of military displays including air formations come from *Revista de las Fuerzas Armadas.* These include the anniversary of Trujillo's election (May 1950); a demonstration of "fuerzas vivas" in Santiago when the enormous monument there was dedicated to him (Mar. 1954); Trujillo's birthday/saint's day (Sept./Oct. 1955); and Restoration Day (Aug. 1958), among many, many others.

87. "Piloto rompe barrera sónica y explosión causa gran alarma," *La Nación;* "Rompen Barrera del Sonido en Cielos de Ciudad Trujillo," *El Caribe,* both 12 Feb. 1954; and *Revista de las Fuerzas Armadas,* Feb. 1954, 17–35.

88. *Revista de las Fuerzas Armadas* provided the most extensive reportage of the military social life, which was closely connected to that of the diplomatic corps, but newspapers carried stories as well. See, e.g., the visit of Major General Reuben Hood, U S A F, and his wife Emma, with the traditional birthday party for the U.S. Marine Corps (Nov. 1954); and "folklore night" at Alvarado Stadium on the grounds of the air force base, in an issue featuring an article on the art of flying in formation (Mar. 1959).

89. Manuel Ramón Pérez, *Décimas sobre la era de Trujillo* (Ciudad Trujillo, 1955), 37.

90. Hagedorn, *Central American and Caribbean,* 104; and *Scott Standard Postage Stamp Catalog,* 2:967.

91. Derby, "The Magic of Modernity," chap. 6.

92. Phrase from caption of photo of Ramfis with Major General Reuben C. Hood, U S A F, *El Caribe,* 11 Feb. 1954. Ramfis was pictured on the cover of *Revista de las Fuerzas Armadas* twice, in June/July 1956 and June 1959. The rest and relaxation facility established in the mountains near Constanza was called Campamento Ramfis (*Revista de las Fuerzas Armadas,* Aug. 1955, 25–27).

93. Dienst and Hagedorn, *North American P-51 Mustangs,* 3.

94. The first graduates of the academy received their diplomas at Estancia Ramfis from Trujillo, with Chief of Staff Frank Féliz Miranda in attendance; see *Revista de las Fuerzas Armadas,* July/Aug. 1959, 20–23. Other pilots and mechanics received advanced training at U.S. flight schools in California, Texas, Alabama, and the Canal Zone. See articles in *Revista de las Fuerzas Armadas,* Aug. 1955, 23–24, 28.

95. The June 1960 issue of *Revista de las Fuerzas Armadas* carried a photo of Ramfis aloft (about a foot off the ground) behind the controls of a jet helicopter. On the same page were photos suggestive of the range of activities that combined the air force, the Trujillo family, and the public life of the nation: an Armed Forces Day reception at the Peace Fair Club; a reception for the Guatemalan polo team hosted by Captain Rhadamés Trujillo, A M D; and Rhadamés at the mass baptism of 132 children of military men at the San Rafael chapel in the National Palace.

96. *Revista de las Fuerzas Armadas,* July 1959, 7. A comedy based on the defeat of the "bearded invaders" was staged at the air base stadium, with Ramfis in prominent attendance and coverage in the military magazine (Oct. 1959, 42). An evocative fictional account of the bombing of Constanza plays an important role in a novel about the Trujillo regime by Julia Alvarez, *In the Time of the Butterflies* (Chapel Hill, N.C.: Algonquin Books, 1994), 159–68.

97. *Revista de las Fuerzas Armadas,* Nov./Dec. 1950, 27–29, 36–37. For more on the significance of the Virgin of Altagracia to the Trujillo regime, see Derby,

"The Magic of Modernity," chap. 2; and *Revista de las Fuerzas Armadas,* July 1950, I, 18–25.

98. *Revista de las Fuerzas Armadas,* Apr./May 1956, 47 (chapel dedication); and Aug. 1958, 53.

99. See the coverage of its victory in the national amateur championship of 1956, held at the new stadium in Santo Domingo with Trujillo in the first row (*Revista de las Fuerzas Armadas,* Nov./Dec. 1956, 50–52).

100. Hagedorn, *Central American and Caribbean,* 107–8.

101. Darico Martínez H., "Soy Soldado de la A.M.D.," *Revista de las Fuerzas Armadas,* Sept. 1959, 56.

102. See *Revista de las Fuerzas Armadas* articles on the party thrown for Trujillo inside the first jet to land in the Dominican Republic (Oct. 1959, 26–27); the importance of the new facilities for the continued tourism development of the country (Nov. 1959, 14–16); and the official opening of the airport (Dec. 1959, 10–11).

103. These specific comparisons were made in Juan M. Contín, *Por qué Trujillo es el lema y el emblema de la patria* (Ciudad Trujillo, 1938), a volume characteristic of the literary paeans to Trujillo produced during his rule.

104. Lieutenant General José García Trujillo, forward to Vega y Pagán, *Military Biography of Trujillo,* 12.

105. Sherry, *Rise of American Air Power,* 358.

106. The theme of the AMD exhibit in the Armed Forces Pavilion at the 1955 Peace Fair of the Free World in Ciudad Trujillo was "national conquests in the best defense of sovereignty." The exhibit featured a mural of a double line of fighter-bombers. The famous *Colón* was on display outside with a P-51 Mustang and other aircraft (*La Nación,* 2 Jan. 1956).

Steven Palmer

Central American Encounters with Rockefeller Public Health, 1914–1921

In April 1914, Costa Rica became the first Latin American state to welcome to its territory a Rockefeller Foundation program, in this case an International Health Commission (IHC) project for the eradication of hookworm disease. Over the following two years, anti-hookworm missions were established in Panama, Guatemala, Nicaragua, and El Salvador. The Rockefeller Foundation, which was created in 1913–1914 as the international extension of philanthropic work that had originated in the United States, chose to initiate operations in these countries and in the British Caribbean colonies. According to the foundation's official historian, this was because, "like the West Indies, Central America offered opportunity for a beginning in which experiments could be tried out on a small scale and in a comparatively quiet way." Moreover, she added, "its geographical position and political relations with the United States gave the Board an interest which it felt in no other country." [1]

Ominous imperial imagery: Central America as a secret biomedical laboratory and undifferentiated zone of geopolitical importance for, and close control by, the United States. As it transpired, however, the foundation's anti-hookworm program in Central America became many programs that varied widely in scope, strategy, and achievement. These programs were sometimes appropriated, often partially rejected, and occasionally dismissed by the host societies and governments. What follows is an analysis of the reception and transformation of the Rockefeller Foundation's public health mission in Costa Rica, and a preliminary comparison of Costa Rica's experience with those of the other Central American republics.

In 1914 Costa Rica was a tiny country with a population of a mere 400,000. Its political economy was dangerously reliant on the export of coffee and bananas, this latter crop produced in an enclave on the Caribbean coast overseen by the United Fruit Company. In geopolitical terms, the country was being squeezed by the expanding power of the United States: to the south was Panama and the U.S. canal; to the north was recently occupied Nicaragua. Precisely because of these general traits of hyperdependency, Costa Rica's is an interesting story about the complexity and ambiguity of the link between imperial institution and subject polity, and about the possibilities for those subject polities to shape their own destinies in their inevitable encounters with emissaries from the metropole.

Many scholars of the Rockefeller Foundation's international work have forcefully argued that its public health programs mapped and processed peoples of the Third World in the service of U.S. imperial expansion, the labor needs of agrarian capitalism, and the global hegemony of a style of scientific medicine that was finding its modern institutional and commercial form in the United States. If a general view of these programs is taken, such a characterization can hardly be disputed. Once the perspective shifts away from the grand institutional or geopolitical unities of the Rockefeller Foundation or the United States of America—and particularly if the experience of host countries comes into view—an entirely new set of questions and issues is raised about the effect of these public health ventures. What other scholars have taken to be ultimate conclusions about the Rockefeller Foundation programs are here bracketed as a given, as a point of departure for beginning what I think are more interesting and revealing studies on the many ways that these ventures affected political configurations and everyday life in a wide variety of Latin American settings.[2]

Instead of focusing on the Rockefeller Foundation itself, then, this essay explores the extent to which some Costa Rican individuals, intellectual groups, and institutions were able to transform the foundation's venture into a vehicle for realizing an already existing public health project of local making. It proceeds by calling into question a series of assumptions and stereotypes common to the literature on the Rockefeller Foundation programs, and on the spread of biomedical public health models in general. The essential argument is that, once the anti-hookworm mission was successfully established in Costa Rica, it ceased to be reducible to the ideological or institutional unity of the Rockefeller Foundation, and was reconfigured as a vital component of a local strategy and of an institutional matrix designed to advance social medicine; it also became the node of a community of public health professionals with desires and allegiances that transcended the boundaries of Rockefeller philanthropy, the nation-state, and the informal empire of the United States.

Peripheral Precedence

Latin America occupies an awkward place in the recent proliferation of studies on disease, medicine, and empire.[3] Pointing to a dramatic imposition of alien medical models coincidental with the encroachment of British and later U.S. imperial power is complicated by Latin America's prior colonial experience of transculturation. In effect, "Western medicine" was grafted onto American healing traditions from the Conquest onward. Scientific medicine and public health, as consolidated in Western Europe and the United States in the second half of the nineteenth century, were not in any direct sense arms of the imperial penetration of Latin America. Rather, this consolidation was replicated or anticipated by political and medical leaders throughout the Americas, and was to some extent refashioned to meet their own conditions and needs. Furthermore, by the time of the bacteriological revolution and the triumph of professionalism, Latin America no longer had any coherent autochthonous systems, ancient and customary, capable of waging an epistemological battle with Western medicine that might coincide, sometimes self-consciously as in the cases of Ayurvedic or Unani medicine in India, with anti-imperialist dissent. Though in Latin America scientific medicine and public health programs propelled by the germ theory were still largely confined to cities, and were accepted by only a thin stratum of society, they were by 1914 as Latin American as anything else.[4]

The Rockefeller Foundation programs in Central America have been represented by some scholars as an integral part of an asymmetrical, overwhelming imposition of alien medical and public health models. The most recent study of the evolution of health care in Costa Rica—rather a good one, too, it should be said—proposes the following picture of that process: "Two wealthy and powerful U.S. organizations, the United Fruit Company and the Rockefeller Foundation, poured money, equipment, people and technological know-how into Costa Rica. In the process, they gradually transformed the health infrastructure and dominant models of medical care along the lines of the germ-theory model of disease etiology, using disease-eradication techniques perfected during the Spanish-American war." [5]

This claim is simply wrong. The error can be illustrated by a brief look at the Central American—and particularly the Costa Rican—history of research on, and treatment of, hookworm disease. When compared to the U.S. and the Rockefeller experience with the disease, the entire isthmus becomes an excellent example of what I have chosen to call "peripheral precedence." Hookworm disease had been identified in El Salvador in 1887 and in Guatemala in 1889 by a physician of German origin, Helmut Prowe. Between 1889 and 1914, four theses had been written on the disease at the medical schools of El Salvador and Guatemala. Although Costa Rica had less than one hundred physicians at the turn of the century and no medical school, it was not without an active nucleus of medical scientists, most of them trained in Western Europe, some in other parts of Latin America, and some in the United States. As early as 1896, the patriarch of this group (and a former president of the republic), Dr. Carlos Durán, along with a research colleague, Dr. Gerardo Jiménez, had identified ancylostomiasis as endemic to certain regions of Costa Rica. Even physicians in the Central American periphery, then, discovered hookworm disease well before Charles Wardell Stiles in the United States and Bailey Ashford in Puerto Rico made their "American" discoveries of the disease in 1900.[6]

Aside from a brief program to treat Salvadoran troops, neither the Salvadoran nor the Guatemalan governments initiated programs to combat hookworm disease. In Costa Rica, however, on Durán's urging in 1907, the government sponsored a tour by two ambitious young physicians, Luis Jiménez and Carlos Alvarado. Their mandate was to determine the extent of hookworm infection in the country, and to design a treatment strategy. Based on their findings, in 1910 the government approved a not insignificant annual appropriation equivalent to U.S. $10,000 for the systematic testing and treatment of the populace. By 1913, the program was responsible for the treatment of almost 20,000 sufferers annually. The Costa Rican program actually predated the first Rockefeller campaign to treat hookworm disease in the South of the United States, which began only in 1909, after Stiles convinced the directors of Rockefeller philanthropy that the extent of affliction in the U.S. South warranted their concerted attention.[7]

In Costa Rica, the motives for undertaking this and other programs of popular hygiene were broadly similar to those that led the Rockefeller Foundation into the crusade against the hookworm. At the most basic level, hygiene was yet another realm in which to educate the popular classes in fundamental notions of reason and science. The treatment of hookworm disease was a particularly good vehicle for this, since there was an effective, quick, and relatively simple method of treatment, and the rapid relief from an acutely felt illness was an excellent form of propaganda. Obviously, a question of political economy was involved: hookworm disease, colloquially known as *cansancio* ("fatigue"), was associated with low productivity in workers. This concern, however, was merely one element in a broader hygiene project that acquired leverage by equating itself with the destiny of the nation, the purity of the race, the health of the economy, and the attainment of modernity.

The state commitment to public health programs, visible from the turn of the century onward, was advanced under the curious banner of "auto-immigration." The country's preeminent groups had long been concerned with a historical shortage of labor power. Costa Rica also had extremely high levels of infant mortality, due in large measure to amebic dysentery and other parasitic afflictions. In the official nationalist rhetoric, Costa Rica's Hispanic population had been declared homogeneous, near-white, and racially sound. However, public health reformers were motivated by a fear that without a therapeutic program to maximize the health of the laboring classes, racial degeneration would occur within what they felt was the sound (and authentically national) population group, and its "natural" growth would stagnate. A decadent people would then have to accept the further immigration of workers from population groups that had been pronounced racially degenerate (Afro-Caribbeans, Chinese, Gypsies, Arabs, and South Asians). Thus Cleto González Víquez, a two-time president (1906–1910 and 1928–1932), coined the term *autoinmigración* to refer to all public health ventures, because they would maximize the endogenous growth of the populace. Juan Bautista Alberdi's famous dictim, "to govern is to populate," had been sublated by eugenic fears: to govern was to sanitize.[8]

This remained very much a vanguard posture, however, promoted by a few influential political figures and a coterie of activist reformers, but resisted by most powerful Costa Ricans as prohibitively expensive and an intrusion of the state on domains that should remain private. Of course, it also threatened to subordinate physicians to greater state oversight and regulation, and the Faculty of Medicine fought or subverted the more ambitious public health initiatives. Vociferous resistance also came from the Juntas de Caridad, semiautonomous bastions of oligarchic prestige and economic power that administered hospitals and public relief. Nonetheless, as incipient as these modern public health ventures were in the overall scheme of things, they remind us that even in a country as marginal as Costa Rica, the Rockefeller Foundation's international public health work was in many respects epistemologically, and even programmatically, redundant. This, of course, made it relatively compatible with the established projects of these vanguard sectors of Costa Rican public power.

Imperial Blinders and Local Plans

The Rockefeller Foundation was hardly an omniscient, well-prepared imperial machine. Employees charged with setting up the program knew nothing of the Central American discoveries of hookworm disease, and they were equally ignorant of the extensive treatment of hookworm disease in Costa Rica. The foundation's advance man, Joseph White, was surprised when Guatemalan and Salvadoran physicians in public health posts informed him of the prior research on the disease in their countries, though he remained unimpressed by their opinion that ancylostomiasis was not a high public health priority. When he arrived in Costa Rica in May 1914, White was even more surprised to learn of the treatment campaign there (though it appeared to him self-evident that the campaign director, Luis Jiménez, "was by far best fitted to deal with the Commission, having been educated in Philadelphia"). White was also ignorant of the community of medical scientists in the country, and of the alliances and divisions that existed among them.[9]

This surprising lack of preparation was probably a factor of two things. First, the foundation does not appear to have worked closely with U.S. consular services, either before or after establishing operations in other countries, probably in order to minimize the perception that Rockefeller programs were an arm of U.S. foreign policy. Second, advance men like White relied to a certain degree on information given to them by local agents of the United Fruit Company, who, in his case, were "all personal friends" (White was a colonel in the Marine Hospital Service, and many United Fruit managers had also served in the Marine Corps). Indeed, in Costa Rica he even used the local general manager of the United Fruit Company to act as a conduit in extending the official Rockefeller Foundation offer to the country's minister of the interior, though this corporate cooperation later foundered, as we will shortly see. The United Fruit Company officials do not seem to have had any great insight into local public health efforts, perhaps because they had their own medical section that mostly confined itself to treating employees in the enclaves.[10]

Costa Rican politicians and public health activists, on the other hand, had a fairly good idea of what to expect from the Rockefeller Foundation's International Health Commission. Many physicians had been trained in the United States and maintained professional contacts there. Indeed, one Costa Rican physician and member of the political elite, Juan Ulloa, had been on the board of the International Sanitary Bureau of the Union of the American Republics since its creation in 1902. The bureau was more a network of information exchange than a programmatic agency, but it allowed delegates to become acquainted with the budding imperial health apparatus of the United States (the head of the Sanitary Bureau was the surgeon general of the United States). The bureau's 1909 conference was held in San José, where public health officials from all over Latin America met with the local community of activist physicians (Luis Jiménez and Carlos Alvarado presented a report on their anti-hookworm work). Costa Rican public health activists had had time to observe and to measure this colossus, and when the Rockefeller men came calling, they knew whom they were dealing with.[11]

Moreover, by 1914 anti-imperialist skepticism and resistance had become a significant and even acceptable part of Costa Rican political culture. The president of the republic at the moment of acceptance of the Rockefeller offer was Ricardo Jiménez, who had been widely applauded as recently as 1907–1908 for his nationalist denunciations of the United Fruit Company. The incoming president, Alfredo González Flores, would reveal himself to be an outspoken critic of the corruption of the political class by foreign capitalists, and of laissez-faire in general. He would actually take steps against both, actions that led to his ouster in the military coup of 1917.[12]

Anti-imperialist hostility was hardly discreet. It was one of the first things felt by Louis Schapiro, the director of the hookworm mission, on arriving in Costa Rica. In justifying to his superiors a decision to omit the name of the Rockefeller Foundation from the Departamento de Ankylostomiasis's official stationery, he noted, "I thought, with the feeling against the United States in this country, that the work would be better received by merely mentioning the International Health Commission in conjunction with the Government. There is a national suspicion of anything done by American Institutes, especially when the work is carried on free." [13] That the González Flores regime came to welcome and to work with the Rockefeller mission had a great deal to do with Schapiro himself. It also had to do with the credentials of one Costa Rican in particular, Solón Núñez, who was appointed by the government to work with the anti-hookworm department.

Double Agents and the Republic of Rational Health

The first man sent down to Costa Rica to direct the anti-hookworm mission, Henry Carter, had little success cracking the local establishment, one of the reasons that he left for another job after six months. His replacement was Louis Schapiro. The son of Polish Jews who had immigrated to the United States, Schapiro was hardly the typical "ugly American," despite the fact that his background as a physician included service in the military and the Coast Guard, and three years as a senior public health official in the occupied Philippines from 1910 to 1913. Schapiro had learned to speak Spanish quite well and, according to Victor Heiser, who had been his superior in the Philippines, had "demonstrated very unusual executive ability" and "unusual tact in getting along with all classes of people." For two years prior to arriving in Costa Rica, he had worked in the public health department of Milwaukee and as a specialist in hygiene and tropical medicine at Marquette University. Judith Walzer Leavitt has described the exceptional success of public health reformers in making Milwaukee known, by the second decade of this century, as "the healthiest city" in the United States. Schapiro's tenure there followed the brief socialist incumbency in the city council that had consolidated a model of broad community mobilization in public health. It was the product of a left-liberal coalition designed to defeat traditional politicians who had preyed on the rapid growth of the city while impeding public health initiatives.[14]

Even as Schapiro began organizing the anti-hookworm units in Costa Rica, he became intrigued by the possibility of using the public education system as the matrix of popular hygiene mobilization. He may have been the object of some calculated flattery in this regard. In April, when his assistant director, Carlos Pupo Pérez, gave a public conference on the hookworm for schoolteachers in San José and the vicinity, Schapiro was enthused by the large turnout of 174 teachers, indicating that school inspectors had done a very efficient job of publicizing the event (or of suggesting the costs of absenteeism). This was followed soon after by an official offer to Schapiro from the president and his brother, the minister of education, Luis Felipe González Flores, to organize and direct a Department of School Health.[15]

Without consulting his superiors, Schapiro accepted the post, since he thought it would "make my position here a great deal stronger, as through the Presidential Decree, all official doctors automatically come under the control of this office." A bit sheepishly, he insisted that "as soon as they can obtain a competent Costa Rican they will do so." On 2 June he concluded a report to the second in command of the IHC, John Ferrell, "I am deriving a great deal of personal pleasure and find that my position officially has been greatly strengthened by my acceptance of the Directorship of the Departamento de Sanidad Escolar." Indeed it had been: on

22 May, probably under pressure from the government, the extremely exclusionary Faculty of Medicine of Costa Rica had recognized him as an honorary member (his predecessor, Carter, had complained that doctors were "a close corporation, and do all they can to keep outsiders out of the Country"). Schapiro had impressed the Costa Ricans as approachable, competent, and flexible enough to be asked to oversee a local project long in the making.[16]

Well before the arrival of the foundation, Costa Rican health reformers had planned to piggyback the system onto the highly successful public education network, the cornerstone of the ethical state built by the Liberal reformers of the 1880s. In the words of Pupo Pérez, words that played on the old battle cry of the educational reform, this would inaugurate "the era of free and obligatory hygiene." [17] The central obstacle to this was a lack of resources, itself the product of a political class not convinced of the need to push through the necessary budget appropriations. By mid-1915, despite an executive that was singularly disposed to effect this reform, the always precarious fiscal situation of the Costa Rican state was becoming ever more bleak with the onset of the wartime recession. Schapiro was willing to take responsibility for the Rockefeller Foundation filling the void and acting as the vehicle for realizing the project.

Obviously, this hardly made him a Kurtz figure, gone "native" and no longer responsive to the imperial program. The large measure of autonomy that the foundation accorded local directors was in no small measure responsible for the wide variety of Latin American encounters with Rockefeller public health. The scope of improvisation granted to a director was particularly wide given the "demonstration model" promoted by the foundation, whereby technical and institutional frameworks would be established in the host country, and then "transplanted" through a gradual transferral of fiscal and administrative responsibility to the host state.[18] The uses a director made of his autonomy were not likely to be questioned if they could be justified as necessary for successfully making the transplant take root in the host body. They would be questioned even less when, as in the case of Schapiro, the paperwork flowed efficiently, and the end result was such an obvious fulfillment of the mission's basic mandate.

Still, it would be rash to discount the degree to which the cultural flexibility of individual directors determined the shape of different missions, and Schapiro was obviously more flexible than most in this respect. His sensitivity to host cultures was further revealed in the mid-1920s in Siam. The Rockefeller Foundation was expelled by the Thai government owing to a feeling that the organization was making the country walk down a path its government did not want to tread. They permitted only one agent to stay; it was Schapiro who, according to Heiser, had volunteered for the "thankless task," and who became "a tremendous favourite in Siam," able to engage in ambitious sanitary engineering projects, and to establish a series of health centers before he died there of a terminal illness.[19] I would suggest that we might understand Schapiro as a kind of double agent, advancing the interests of "imperial medicine," but as far as possible on the terms of those sectors of the host country's political class he considered progressive.

Schapiro soon acquired a Costa Rican partner in this double game: Solón Núñez, a young physician appointed by the government to be the assistant director of the Sanitary Department of Schools in 1916. A year later he was appointed the subdirector of the Departamento de Ankylostomiasis by Schapiro. Núñez was the key Costa Rican in the seven-year direct Rockefeller involvement, and subsequently became undersecretary of public health in 1922, and then secretary of the new Ministry of Public Health and Social Protection in 1927. His background is worth some comment, since it also brushes against the grain of the stereotypical local "collaborator" central to the assumptions of dependency theory and of proponents of cultural imperialism.

Prior to 1913, when he departed to study medicine in Geneva, Núñez was a high-profile member of a group of embittered young dissident intellectuals who had dedicated themselves to the cause of anti-imperialism and social justice. Often teachers in the country's leading schools, and grouped around radical periodicals and cultural centers for workers, this loosely affiliated network included many of Costa Rica's most inspired leftist intellectuals, like Joaquín García Monge and Carmen Lyra. Núñez had been a teacher in two rural schools, and then a school inspector, all the while increasing his profile as a critic of dominant society by taking an active role in publications like *Aurora* (1908) and *Cultura* (1910). His 1911 essay in *Renovación*, "Jesús y Tostoi," is considered a classic expression of the romantic anarchist and social Christian vision that animated the project of this generation of *ácratas* (disaffected ones).[20]

It is unlikely that Núñez had lost his anti-imperialist principles by the time he returned from his studies in Switzerland and his apprenticeship on the battlefields of France. It was clear to him, however, and to many other progressives of the day, that there was a difference between, say, the Departamento de Ankylostomiasis and the building of a U.S. canal or the annexation of the country. Direct Rockefeller control was designed to phase itself out by 1921, whereupon the state would assume complete control over the operations. The basic Rockefeller public health plan was quite compatible with that proposed by Costa Rican reformers, particularly given Schapiro's willingness to integrate the mission with the school system. The entire project promised a way of circumventing the obstacles thrown up by the retrograde elements of the medical and political establishments, and thus represented a possible shortcut to a centralized apparatus of public health that Núñez very much conceived as a socialist advance over laissez-faire. A Faustian bargain? Some said so, and Núñez caught his share of criticism for devoting himself to the mission. He never hesitated, however, and vociferously defended Schapiro on more than one occasion, insisting that the foreign physician was a great Costa Rican patriot.[21]

Ironically, then, like many of his generation who had nourished themselves on the works of the great anarchists, Núñez's energies were now turned toward imaginative leadership in expanding the role of the state. This was especially the case after 1914, when the young González Flores brothers opened the doors of state patronage positions to this brilliant generation. Its members had a sense that, if they played their cards right, they would find themselves at the social controls when the transplant was fully integrated into the local system. In many respects, this process was similar to the incorporation of progressive intellectuals into state reformism in the United States (and indeed throughout the world) at this time— proponents of social medicine like Louis Schapiro, for example.

In an important sense, however, Schapiro and Núñez were "triple agents," and their ultimate allegiance was not to an imperial institution, a nation-state, an agroexport bourgeoisie, or an embryonic, U.S.-based medical-industrial complex. Their bond and their behavior might best be understood as the result of a mutual feeling that they were citizens of a more transcendent political community: what we will call the "Republic of Rational Health," a sort of latter-day, specialist analogue of the seventeenth-century Republic of Letters. This republic, too, was universalist and devoted to the accumulation of systematic knowledge; its ideal was the maximization of human vitality through the application of that knowledge. This was a commitment to public health in the full sense of the term, since it was not bounded by any institutional borders, nor even by the nation-state: it was an identification with humanity as a whole. Núñez and Schapiro were pioneers of an international network of public health institutions staffed by bureaucrat-intellectuals, very much the first generation of the transnational, bureaucratic-intellectual, global elite with which we are increasingly familiar (and one that encompasses the functionaries of nongovernmental organizations as well). Though both were surely aware that this network had been engendered by the capital of robber barons, the imperial dreams of great powers, and the needs of commerce and industry—and remained somehow in their service—both also knew that the Republic of Rational Health was not reducible to them. The international career in social medicine had its own logic, and it was propelled by its own desire.[22]

The Campaigns

Both Lynn Morgan and Juan César García propose that the anti-hookworm campaigns targeted coffee pickers and plantation workers in Costa Rica, and that they were coordinated with the United Fruit Company's medical apparatus and the coffee oligarchy. In fact, no such direct relationship existed between the program's organization and the immediate needs of foreign or local agrarian capital. In the first year of operations, for example, campaigns were undertaken in extremely isolated peasant communities in Guanacaste and Puntarenas, and in the public schools in San José, as well as along the Pacific littoral and in coffee-growing regions of the Central Valley. The country was broken down into a grid and systematically worked through, with the intention to test and, if necessary, to treat every individual in the area. Neither the schedule nor the method were determined by the nature of agricultural production in the region, although communities could hasten the arrival of the anquilostomiasis unit by petitioning for it and promising assistance up front. As for the United Fruit Company, when a hookworm unit inaugurated its campaign in the province of Limón in June 1915, Schapiro complained to his superiors in New York that "the showing by the officials of the United Fruit Company was not that of co-operation." Schapiro only made headway in the area after meeting the governor and principal officials, the Roman Catholic priest, and the British consul to Costa Rica, who called together and secured the cooperation of the "colored ministers." [23]

Even had the United Fruit Company been cooperative in the one part of the country where it held sway (and which accounted for only a tenth of the Costa Rican populace), such complex coalition weaving would have been necessary there and elsewhere. Especially in the countryside, the anti-hookworm campaign was a kind of guerrilla war between the culture of progress and a wide variety of local cultural configurations. The greatest political resistance came from *gamonales* loathe to impose the costs of latrine building on peasants, lest it lead them to lose influence to rival political bosses. The greatest ideological resistance came from the local empirics and *curanderos,* clearly perceiving the arrival of a previously distant rival. Nonetheless, it is probably best to steer clear of romanticizing this resistance as a pure emanation of organic healing traditions under the calculated onslaught of imperial biomedicine. Herbal, spiritual, and traditional healers were merely one end of the spectrum of rural healers, which included the corner-store owner who carried on a lucrative trade prescribing foreign patent medicines for "diseases of the blood," the traveling homeopathic salesman, and even, eventually, members of the local community who had been hired on as microscopists during the campaign. It is also interesting to note that the most valuable allies of the anti-hookworm units in the rural areas were primary-school teachers, most of them women. This crucial stratum of popular female progressivism seemed to accept with gusto a mission of hygiene evangelism that led them to confront local traditions and power structures.[24]

The Department of School Health was formally a section under the direction of the anti-hookworm program. The government provided a budget for a director, part-time physicians, and full-time sanitary assistants, these latter recruited from the ranks of female teachers and trained in nursing. Because the school health work was so deeply intertwined with the propaganda activities of the anti-hookworm program, the foundation's resources were also employed to keep it administratively focused, and to subsidize its constant work with teachers, which included periodic training sessions and the supply of literature and classroom materials. As well as providing free diagnosis and prescription medicine to poor children, the school health section was the first real social work agency in Costa Rica, and the sanitary assistants increasingly undertook home visits rather than simply school inspections. By 1921, it received a larger portion of the total budget of the Departamento de Ankylostomiasis than did the actual program for the treatment of hookworm disease.[25]

Nationalism and Sovereignty

Most accounts of the dynamic between Rockefeller medicine and nationalism portray it in negative terms—that is, in terms of the nationalist backlashes provoked by the missions in host countries. In a different vein, Armando Solorzano has shown that in Veracruz the foundation's anti–yellow fever work did a great deal to legitimize the revolutionary government of Obregón, and that in its extraordinary collaboration with the socialist government in the Yucatán, it unwittingly paved the way for national integration. However, the foundation's work could also have a more intimate and complementary role in the production of the national community.[26]

In 1915, Schapiro offered to make massive quantities of hygiene literature available to the Ministry of Education. The minister responded by setting aside in the curriculum a half hour each week, "the day and the time to be uniform throughout the Republic . . . for the instruction of pupils from the literature furnished." The image of this simultaneous instruction recalls Benedict Anderson's analysis of the nation as a group of people anonymous to one another, transformed into a political community through the simultaneous sharing of identical experiences. The vehicle for these rituals need not be of creole fiber, as the employment of this imperial literature makes perfectly clear. The material resources and scale of the Rockefeller program made possible this concretization of nationalist experience throughout the republic. In a more general way, as the hygiene program became entrenched throughout the country's primary school system, the distinction between physical and moral hygiene was blurred, and both were linked to national values. Being a good Costa Rican became increasingly impossible unless one defecated in a latrine, bathed once a day, and underwent scientific examination and purification at the hands of the state. The most surreal portrait of this came from Núñez in 1931, when virtually every Costa Rican had been subjected to an examination for hookworm disease at least once in his or her life. In extolling the incorporation of this ritual by the populace, he noted that there was "a continuous stream of people to the country's laboratories in search of having their feces examined." [27]

As the state had assumed a greater burden of the cost of the Departamento de Ankylostomiasis, and as the department had proven itself to be coordinated and effective, a succession of governments had arrogated to it more authority over public health matters. On the other hand, the Faculty of Medicine and the Superior Council of Public Health, an ad hoc advisory body dominated by members of the medical and charity establishments, had lost a good deal of public confidence and prestige, especially in the wake of a chaotic response to the disastrous influenza pandemic of 1919–1920, which claimed the lives of over 2,000 Costa Ricans. In 1920, on the eve of the Costa Rican state assuming financial responsibility and administrative control over the Departamento de Ankylostomiasis, Schapiro and Núñez met with the cabinet of the new Acosta government, which had succeeded the overthrown military dictatorship of the Tinocos. They struck a secret deal to transform the Departamento de Ankylostomiasis into the Subsecretariat of Hygiene and Public Health, with Núñez at the helm. The parties agreed on what legislation would be necessary, since it meant suppressing the jurisdiction legally bestowed on the Faculty of Medicine. In return, Schapiro guaranteed further Rockefeller support for a public health laboratory in San José, the training of personnel, and other pilot projects. Thus, the moment of greatest Rockefeller subversion of Costa Rican sovereignty was also the moment that guaranteed the state jurisdiction over a hitherto unconsolidated domain.[28]

Central American Comparisons

My understanding of the anti-hookworm work in Guatemala, Panama, Nicaragua, and El Salvador is based on much more cursory evidence than my assessment of the Costa Rican program. It is clear, however, that work in these other four countries came nowhere near the extent of coverage achieved by Rockefeller-sponsored work in Costa Rica, even in absolute numerical terms. By 1921, the Costa Rican mission had examined 277,000 individuals (70 percent of the populace), inspected almost 50,000 homes, and overseen the building of 16,000 latrines. In Nicaragua, El Salvador, and Guatemala, only about 150,000 individuals in each country had been examined (25, 8, and 8 percent of the populace respectively), 15,000 homes had been inspected, and 3,000 privies had been built. The principal ingredient for the success of the work in Costa Rica—an extensive public education system—was absent elsewhere in Central America. The importance of this is reflected in the fact that the figures on the use of school infrastructure and literacy by the Costa Rican mission dwarf the extent of such work carried on by its Central American counterparts. By 1921 almost 1,000 hygiene lectures for children had been given in Costa Rican public schools, less than 200 in Guatemala, and less than 50 in El Salvador. Almost 300,000 units of literature had been distributed in Costa Rica, and less than 70,000 each in Guatemala and El Salvador, despite the fact that their populations were five times greater than that of Costa Rica.[29]

Furthermore, the mission directors in the other countries were unable to transform their institutions into nuclei of national departments of health. Neither was there any sign of strategic alliances between progressive sectors of the local intelligentsia and the Rockefeller missions of the kind so crucial to the Costa Rican encounter. Corresponding to this is a sense that the missions were never able to trade in their public image as foreign (and thus suspect) entities for a more functional national costume.

It is striking that the greater the influence of the United States within a country, the less successful was the public health work undertaken there by the imperial philanthropic institution. Although I have no figures on the Panama program, it is clear from reports that the mission was considered a failure, essentially because there was no local public health apparatus with which to work. The U.S. canal authorities had jurisdiction over public health in Colón and Panama City, and their primary efforts went toward eradicating yellow fever and maintaining potable water. The canal authorities were not interested in anti-hookworm work in rural or urban areas, and the Panamanian government was not interested in investing money or personnel in the Rockefeller project as long as control over public health matters was primarily in U.S. hands.[30]

In Nicaragua, the other satellite of the United States, the situation was not much better in terms of the insinuation of the mission into the local public health apparatus. The second director in particular, Daniel Molloy, carried out an ambitious campaign in the most populous parts of the country, and seems to have had some success in gaining popular acceptance of the mission's work, most notably among the indigenous people of Matagalpa. Support at the level of government, the medical establishment, or social reformers, however, was never forthcoming. The country's historic division between the ruling groups of León and Granada was reproduced at the level of medicine and public health, each city having its own medical school, and the central government recognizing two national boards of health (one from each domain of power). Neither group appeared particularly interested in assisting the anti-hookworm work, nor did the central government itself. In fact there is frequent mention of outright sabotage of the mission's work by these groups, and of campaigns to ensure that the mission be equated with the U.S. presence in the country.[31]

In Guatemala—and again despite close ties between Manuel Estrada Cabrera and the U.S. government—the mission got a frosty reception from *El Señor Presidente* and the local medical establishment. It also seems to have been the most ineptly run foundation project in Central America. With almost no government assistance, and with unambitious leadership, the anti-hookworm work was confined almost entirely to the agroexport plantations of the southern piedmont and coastal plain. Certain large planters agreed to assist the mission's work on their properties, and to undertake the construction of privies, in an attempt to improve labor output. Only in El Salvador did the anti-hookworm program (which did not start until 1916) eventually acquire the kind of momentum to suggest that it might have eventually rivaled the Costa Rican campaign's coverage. Although it is impossible to determine why this was so from the scant information I have available, it is worth speculating that it corresponds to the existence there of a network of positivist reformers who would become visible during the popular political mobilizations of the 1920s.[32]

Conclusion

This brief assessment of the Central American experience with hookworm disease and with the Rockefeller Foundation suggests some of the ways that rethinking the imperial encounter from a local perspective can upset entrenched assumptions. The Central American periphery actually preceded the U.S. metropole in research on, and treatment of, hookworm disease. In Costa Rica, this peripheral precedence meant that key sectors of the government and public health community were more knowledgeable about what the Rockefeller-sponsored hookworm program could offer the country than was the foundation itself, and the Costa Ricans appropriated the mission accordingly. Paradoxically, while impinging on Costa Rican sovereignty in important ways, the foundation's presence strengthened and expanded the reach of the Costa Rican state, and provided resources and methods that made more profound the sense of nation among the people of the country. Finally, a comparison with anti-hookworm work in other parts of Central America suggests that there was no positive correlation between direct U.S. geopolitical influence and the realization of the Rockefeller Foundation's imperial public health mission.

The Costa Rican campaign was the only case in Latin America where the hookworm work lived up to its original goal of acting as a catalyst for creating a centralized state agency of public health. In his 1921 summary of the Costa Rican program, Schapiro insisted that "the organization and direction of the Department of Medical Inspection of Schools . . . was the first step to centralize public health agencies towards the formation of the National Health Department." That is to say, it was the drastic modification of the original Rockefeller plan, one initiated by the Costa Rican state and made possible by Schapiro's predisposition and autonomy of action, that led to the "success" of the mission.[33]

There is no doubt that in the anti-hookworm mission the resources and prestige of the Rockefeller Foundation were employed to extend the influence of the United States, and even to tamper with Costa Rican sovereignty. Neither is there any doubt that this was part of an imperial plan to expand the network of propaganda for centralized public health systems, and to promote the idea of curative medicine alongside a more preventive model. My presentation of the program also raises the specter of issues that bedevil contemporary Latin America: the transplantation to Central America of personnel originally trained as part of Southeast Asian counterinsurgency exercises (i.e., the Philippines); and the creation of a parallel state, whereby institutions under the direction of U.S. personnel are inserted into the state apparatus of the subject country. Even the foundation's planned withdrawal, and its insistence that the host states assume the financial burden and direction of the programs, inevitably recalls more recent imperial desires of "Vietnamizing the conflict" and of "winning hearts and minds." [34]

Beside these troubling issues, however, is the argument I have presented here, that the Costa Rican state was able to meld the anti-hookworm program with its own prior public health designs, redirecting the foundation's narrowly focused original energies into a hygienicist boost of the public education system. In a time of fiscal crisis, the resources of the empire were harnessed to expand the sway of the state and to extend Costa Rican nationalism among the rural populace. The anti-hookworm commission was quite willing to ally itself with some of Costa Rica's leading anti-imperialists, and the disposition of Louis Schapiro enhanced its ability to do so. The funds and personnel of the foundation also helped overwhelm influential sectors and institutions of the political, commercial, and medical establishments who were otherwise opposed to the statist social policy then being advocated by a vanguard of public health reformers.

Notes

The author would like to thank Marcos Cueto, Ricardo Salvatore, Catherine LeGrand, Warwick Anderson, Iván Molina, and Stuart Schwartz for their assistance in refining this work. The author acknowledges the support of the Social Sciences and Humanities Research Council of Canada, and of the Vicerectoría de Investigación of the Universidad de Costa Rica, which made parts of this paper possible.

1. Catherine Lewerth, "Source Book for a History of the Rockefeller Foundation," vol. 2, Rockefeller Foundation Archives (hereafter RAC), 1949, 411.

2. A recent collection on the encounter of the Rockefeller Foundation with Latin America, taking the foundation as its principal object of analysis, is Marcos

Cueto, ed., *Missionaries of Science: The Rockefeller Foundation in Latin America* (Bloomington: Indiana University Press, 1994). The collection successfully goes beyond the often simplistic anti-imperialist, anticapitalist indictments that characterized the work of an earlier generation of students of U.S. philanthropy: in particular, Edward H. Berman, *The Influence of the Carnegie, Ford, and Rockefeller Foundations on American Foreign Policy: The Ideology of Philanthropy* (Albany: State University of New York Press, 1983); and E. Richard Brown, *Rockefeller Medicine Men: Medicine and Capitalism in America* (Berkeley and Los Angeles: University of California Press, 1979); for a more recent example, see Soma Hewa, "The Hookworm Epidemic on the Plantations in Colonial Sri Lanka," *Medical History* 38, no. 1 (Jan. 1994): 167–83. Two studies that broke the mold through more sensitive readings of the philanthropy's activities are Mary Brown Bullock, *An American Transplant: The Rockefeller Foundation and Peking Union Medical College* (Berkeley and Los Angeles: University of California Press, 1980); and John Ettling, *The Germ of Laziness: Rockefeller Philanthropy and Public Health in the New South* (Cambridge, Mass.: Harvard University Press, 1981).

3. For example, David Arnold's 1988 review essay of the state of studies of disease, medicine, and empire begins with a brief overview of the historiography treating Europe and North America in the nineteenth and twentieth centuries, and then explains that "the rest of the world has come increasingly under scrutiny as well," listing Africa, South and Southeast Asia, the Pacific region, and Australasia, but omitting Latin America. Though he does mention some specific cases from Latin America later on, they do not warrant a categorical mention, and the collection is without a Latin American case study. "Introduction: Disease, Medicine, and Empire," in *Imperial Medicine and Indigenous Societies*, ed. Arnold (Manchester: Manchester University Press, 1988), 1. Studies of Latin America are also absent from another important collection on this subject, Roy Macleod and Milton Lewis, eds., *Disease, Medicine, and Empire: Perspectives on Western Medicine and the Experience of European Expansion* (New York: Routledge, 1988). The fact that the Philippines under U.S. occupation receives attention in both collections underlines the point.

4. Guenter B. Risse, "Medicine in New Spain," in *Medicine in the New World*, ed. Ronald L. Numbers (Knoxville: University of Tennessee Press, 1987); George M. Foster, "On the Origin of Humoral Medicine in Latin America," *Medical Anthropology Quarterly* 1, no. 4 (Dec. 1987): 364–66; Poonam Bala, "State and Indigenous Medicine in Nineteenth and Twentieth Century Bengal, 1800–1947" (Ph.D. diss., University of Edinburgh, 1987); and David Arnold, "Smallpox and Colonial Medicine in Nineteenth-Century India," *Imperial Medicine*, 47.

5. Lynn Morgan, *Community Participation in Public Health: The Politics of Primary Care in Costa Rica* (Cambridge: Cambridge University Press, 1993), 17–18. This point of view is echoed by Juan César García, *Pensamiento social en salud en América Latina* (México: Interamericana McGraw Hill/Organización Panamericana de Salud, 1994), 112–13; and by Jorge Cayetano Mora Agüero, *Las Jun-*

tas Progresistas: Organización comunal autónoma costarricense, 1921–1980 (San José: Editorial PEC91, 1991), 23–24.

6. On the Central American discoveries, see Solón Núñez, "La Ankylostomiasis," *Boletín de la Subsecretaría de Higiene y Salud Pública* 1, no. 1 (May 1923): 11–15. Some of the theses are listed in Francisco Asturias, *Historia de la medicina en Guatemala,* 2d ed. (1902; Guatemala: Editorial Universitaria, 1958), 242–53, 431–34. On the numbers of physicians in Costa Rica, see Luis Dobles Segreda, *Índice bibliográfico de Costa Rica,* vol. 9, *Higiene y medicina* (San José: Imprenta Lehmann, 1927–1936; and Asociación Costarricense de Bibliotecarios, 1967), 384–402. On Ashford and Stiles, see Ettling, *The Germ of Laziness,* 29–32.

7. For Durán's 1907 proposal, see Archivo Nacional de Costa Rica, Policía, 977. For a summary of the initial Costa Rican campaign, see "Jiménez to White," 28 May 1914, RAC, Record Group (RG) 5, Series (S) 1.2, box (B) 6, folder (F) 87. On Stiles's efforts, see Ettling, *The Germ of Laziness,* 38–43. The Colombian case is an interesting halfway point in this respect, with local physicians identifying the disease in 1905 and pressing the government to initiate a dispensary campaign to treat laborers in the sugar and coffee sectors, though with limited success (systematic Rockefeller Foundation efforts against hookworm began there in 1920). See Christopher Abel, "External Philanthropy and Domestic Change in Colombian Health Care: The Role of the Rockefeller Foundation, ca. 1920–1950," *Hispanic American Historical Review* 75, no. 3 (1995): 350–51. Julyan G. Peard discusses earlier Brazilian efforts to diagnose and treat hookworm in a pioneering article on Brazilian social medicine, "Tropical Disorders and the Forging of a Brazilian Medical Identity, 1860–1890," *Hispanic American Historical Review* 77, no. 1 (1997): 1–44.

8. Steven Palmer, "Hacia la auto-immigración: El nacionalismo oficial en Costa Rica (1870–1930)," in *Identidades nacionales y estado moderno en Centroamérica,* ed. Arturo Taracena and Jean Piel (San José: Editorial Universidad de Costa Rica, 1995), 75–85.

9. On Guatemala, "White to Rose," 7 Apr. 1914; on El Salvador, "Report from Dr. P. A. Villacorta," appended to "White to Rose," 25 May 1914; and on Costa Rica, "White to Rose," 25 May 1914; all in RAC, RG 5, S 1.2, B 6, F 86 and F 87.

10. "White to Rose," 3 June 1914; and "Alvaradez [*sic*] to White," 14 Apr. 1914; in RAC, RG 5, S 1.2, B 6, F 86 and F 87.

11. Norman Howard-Jones, *The Pan American Health Organization: Origins and Evolution* (Geneva: World Health Organization, 1981), 8–13. The results of the San José conference were published as *Actas de la Cuarta Conferencia Sanitaria Internacional de las Repúblicas Americanas* (Washington, D.C.: Unión Panamericana, 1910), but the International Health Commission personnel had not read the publication prior to arriving in Central America.

12. For a complex variety of reasons, the coup was not backed by the United States, and the military regime was severely weakened by its failure to receive Washington's blessing during its two and a half years of existence.

13. "Schapiro to Ferrell," 20 Apr. 1915, RAC, RG 5, S I.2, B 7, F 106.

14. "Rose to White," 5 Oct. 1914 and 10 Oct. 1914, RAC, RG 5, S I.2, B 6, F 88; Luis Felipe González Flores, *Historia de la influencia extranjera en el desenvolvimiento educacional y científico de Costa Rica* (San José: Editorial Costa Rica, 1976), 160; and Judith Walzer Leavitt, *The Healthiest City: Milwaukee and the Politics of Health Reform* (Princeton, N.J.: Princeton University Press, 1982).

15. "Schapiro to Ferrell," 22 Apr. 1915, RAC, RG 5, S I.2, B 7, F 106; and "Luis Felipe González Flores to Schapiro," 7 May 1915, RAC, RG 5, S I.2, B 7, F 106.

16. "Schapiro to Ferrell," 7 May 1915; "Schapiro to Ferrell," 2 June 1915; and "Schapiro to Ferrell," 22 May 1915; all in RAC, RG 5, S I.2, B 7, F 106. See also "Carter to Ernst Meyer," 13 July 1914, RAC, RG 5, S I.2, B 6, F 96.

17. Carlos Pupo Pérez, *Nuestras enfermedades evitables: Principios de higiene que nadie debe ignorar* (San José: Imprenta Alsina, 1913), 4.

18. A good overview of the "demonstration model" can be found in Abel, "External Philanthropy and Domestic Change," 341.

19. Victor Heiser, *An American Doctor's Odyssey* (New York: W. W. Norton, 1936), 501.

20. Juan Bautista Frutos Verdesia, *Dr. Solón Núñez Frutos* (San José: Ministerio de Cultura, Juventud y Deportes, 1979), provides a basic biography and a selection of his writings; the importance of his youthful anarchism is discussed in Alvaro Quesada Soto, *La voz desgarrada: La crisis del discurso oligárquico y la narrativa costarricense, 1917-1919* (San José: Editorial de la Universidad de Costa Rica, 1988), 167-68.

21. For a defense of Schapiro by Núñez, see *Memoria de la Secretaría de Salubridad Pública y Protección Social: 1927* (San José: Imprenta Nacional, 1928), xi.

22. My discussion of the Republic of Letters and of its relationship to Kant's understanding of the public use of reason comes from Roger Chartier, *The Cultural Origins of the French Revolution* (Durham, N.C.: Duke University Press, 1991), 24-27.

23. Morgan, *Community Participation,* 18-19, 83; and García, *Pensamiento social,* 112-13. For a good overview of the manner in which the campaign was undertaken, see "Informe de la Sub-secretaría de Higiene y Salubridad Pública," *Memoria del Ministerio de Gobernación y Policía: 1923* (San José: Imprenta Nacional, 1924), 257-81. See also "Schapiro to Ferrell," 8 July 1915, RAC, RG 5, S I.2, B 7, F 107.

24. On the role of teachers, see "Informe del Departamento de Ankylostomiasis, 1922," *Memoria del Ministerio de Gobernación y Policía: 1922* (San José: Imprenta Nacional, 1923), 231-33.

25. This composite picture of the evolution of the Sanitary Department of Schools has been garnered from the annual reports of the Departamento de Ankylostomiasis in the *Memorias de Gobernación y Policía,* from 1915-1922. The 1921 budget information is from Dr. F. F. Russell, "Report of Inspection of Costa Rica (1921)," RAC, RG 5, S 2, B 41, F 244, 2. For a more detailed look at the links be-

tween public health institutions and other nascent agencies of moral policing, see Steven Palmer, "Confinement, Policing, and the Emergence of Social Policy in Costa Rica," in *The Birth of the Penitentiary in Latin America: Essays on Criminology, Prison Reform, and Social Control, 1840-1940*, ed. Ricardo Salvatore and Carlos Aguirre (Austin: University of Texas Press, 1996).

26. Armando Solorzano, "The Rockefeller Foundation in Revolutionary Mexico: Yellow Fever in Yucatán and Veracruz," in Cueto, *Missionaries of Science*, 52–71. An excellent treatment of the ambiguous and unexpected manifestations of nationalism in motivating biomedical research in Latin America is Marcos Cueto, "Nacionalismo y ciencias médicas en el Péru," *Quipu* 4, no. 3 (Sept.–Dec. 1987): 327–55.

27. "Report of Quarter Ending March 31, 1915," RAC, RG 5, S 1.2, B 7, F 106; Benedict Anderson, *Imagined Communities: Reflections on the Origin and Spread of Nationalism*, 2d ed. (London: Verso, 1991), 35–36; and *Memoria de Salubridad Pública y Protección Social, 1931-32* (San José: Imprenta Nacional, 1932), 9.

28. Louis Schapiro, "Hookworm Campaign in Costa Rica (1921)," RAC, RG 5, S 2, B 28, F 168, 2.

29. For Costa Rica, see "Informe del Departamento de Ankylostomiasis," *Memoria de Gobernación y Policía: 1921* (San José: Imprenta Nacional, 1922), 269, 275; for Nicaragua, "Relief and Control of Hookworm Disease in Nicaragua," RAC, RG 5, S 2, B 34, F 202, 20–21, 27; for El Salvador, "Relief and Control of Hookworm Disease in Salvador," RAC, RG 5, S 2, B 36, F 218, 12, 19, 21; and for Guatemala, "Relief and Control of Hookworm Disease in Guatemala," RAC, RG 5, S 2, B 31, F 194, 5, 10.

30. Russell, "Report of Inspection of Costa Rica," 4; and García, *Pensamiento social*, 115. Symptomatic of this is that the hookworm programs receive not a single mention in the memoirs of the Canal Zone's chief health officer during this period: Winston P. Chamberlain, *Twenty-five Years of American Medical Activity on the Isthmus of Panama, 1904-1929: A Triumph of Preventive Medicine* (Canal Zone: Panama Canal Press, 1929).

31. "Relief and Control of Hookworm Disease in Nicaragua," 32–34; "Report to Rose from Managua," RAC, RG 5, S 2, B 34, F 201; and García, *Pensamiento social*, 113.

32. "Relief and Control of Hookworm Disease in Guatemala"; and "Relief and Control of Hookworm Disease in Salvador," 5, 23–25. García, *Pensamiento social*, 111, notes the existence of a group of state medicine intellectuals in El Salvador as early as the turn of the century.

33. Schapiro, "Hookworm Campaign in Costa Rica (1921)," 2.

34. In fact, U.S. medical personnel had even used the term *Philippinization* to characterize their efforts to transfer to Filipinos the public health apparatus that was so crucial a part of occupation and counterinsurgency (Warwick Anderson, personal communication).

Catherine C. LeGrand

Living in Macondo

Economy and Culture in a United Fruit Company

Banana Enclave in Colombia

In *One Hundred Years of Solitude,* novelist Gabriel García Márquez describes the devastating impact of a U.S. banana company on the Colombian village of Macondo. The "banana company" in García Márquez's novel clearly refers to the Boston-based United Fruit Company (UFCO), founded in 1899, an early multinational that almost single-handedly created the world market for bananas. García Márquez portrays the advent of the foreign company as an overwhelming, irresistible force that bewilders and enervates the people of Macondo, leaving them helpless to forge their own communities, to generate their own meanings, even to claim their own memories. A "plague," a "hurricane," a "deluge," the foreign company submerged Macondo in a flood of money, corruption, and death; its sudden withdrawal annihilated local life.

Macondo was in ruins. In the swampy streets there were the remains of furniture, animal skeletons covered with red lilies, the last memories of the hordes of newcomers who had fled Macondo as wildly as they had arrived. The houses that had been built with such haste during the banana fever had been abandoned. The banana company tore down its installations. . . . The wooden houses, the cool terraces for breezy card-playing afternoons, seemed to have been blown away in an anticipation of the prophetic wind that years later would wipe Macondo off the face of the earth. The only human trace left by that voracious blast was a glove belonging to Patricia Brown in an automobile smothered in wild pansies.[1]

For García Márquez, foreign investment on the massive scale of the United Fruit Company brings neither modernity nor progress. Instead, it spells the end of the familiar world, and it destroys the capacity of communities to draw on their past so as to create new visions of what the future should be.

Although the novel *One Hundred Years of Solitude* ends in apocalypse, in reality the United Fruit Company did not obliterate Macondo, García Márquez's name for the Magdalena banana region.[2] After the company's withdrawal, many people migrated elsewhere, but, for those who remain, life goes on. Since 1988, I have spent several months wandering about this old United Fruit Company banana zone that lies south of the port of Santa Marta on the Caribbean coast of Colombia.

This is the place where Gabriel García Márquez was born in 1927 and where he lived with his maternal grandparents until the age of eight. During his formative years, he experienced the end of the banana boom of the 1920s and the world depression of the 1930s, when the United Fruit Company drastically cut back production, sending the area into deep recession. As a boy, he also heard tales of the great strike of 1928, which pitted 25,000 banana workers against the UFCO and which ended in the massacre of strikers by the Colombian army in Ciénaga, so vividly portrayed in *One Hundred Years of Solitude*. Decades later, García Márquez would draw on his early memories and the stories of his parents and grandparents to re-create in fiction the world of his childhood.[3]

García Márquez's representation of the fatal domination of the U.S. banana company probably also reflects the time and place in which he wrote, Latin America in the 1960s. This was the period when Chilean and Brazilian social scientists were elaborating dependency theory, a trenchant critique of how the United States and other economic powers coopted the Latin American bourgeoisie and kept the Third World underdeveloped. This was also the period when many Latin American intellectuals feared that, through its attacks on Fidel Castro, the U.S. government would wipe out a creative, locally generated reform process. These were times of pessimism and anger and also of vigorous cultural self-affirmation, manifested in part in the extraordinary literary boom, spearheaded by García Márquez's story of Macondo, which focused world attention on the unique realities of the southern continent. Nearly thirty years later, I was attracted to the old Colombian banana zone in part by my fascination with García Márquez's tales.

I was also drawn there because enclaves are the quintessential place to study the intersection of the external and the internal, the world economy and local life. As a U.S.-born historian of Latin America, I wanted to make concrete sense of the impact my country had had on one part of Colombia. From a larger viewpoint, I wanted to understand the nature of the enclave societies that American businesses, engaged in resource extraction, had carved out of Latin America. The term *enclave* commonly is used to refer to economic zones created by foreign direct investment where capital, technology, management, and sometimes labor are introduced from the outside. Enclaves such as the copper mines of Chile, Percival Farquhar's company town in the Amazon, or the United Fruit

Company banana zones along the Atlantic coast of Central America are often considered to have been "foreign" territories, molded by U.S. business culture, tied into world markets, and with little connection to the countries in which they were located.

As a graduate student of the 1970s weaned on dependency theory, I am also caught up in the present political and intellectual moment in North American universities. Structures and macrotheories are no longer in vogue, and new concerns with subjectivities, with a diversity of voices and viewpoints, and with the specificities of place and the possibility of local agency have taken center stage. Thus I came into the Magdalena area carrying the baggage of some of my old assumptions about foreign enclaves, yet at the same time seeking to understand the experiences and visions of those people who had lived through the United Fruit Company period. The ruminations of people in the zone and regional archives provide multiple perspectives that extend, complement, and sometimes contradict García Márquez's portrait of banana times. They also illuminate the ongoing cultural vitality and inventiveness of this zone of transnational intersections that nourished a Nobel Prize–winning writer.

My research centers on several questions: How did local people respond to the arrival of the foreign company? How did they react to the possibilities that connection to the world economy offered? What was it like to live in such a region transformed by foreign investment, and how did people make sense of what they were living? In such places of transnational intersection, how do people define their identities? What does community mean? And how does the foreign presence (and the boom-bust experience, so typical of enclaves) shape expressions of regionalism and nationalism?

This exploratory essay seeks answers to some of these queries by describing the impact of the United Fruit Company through local eyes. It also explores how local people related to their pre-banana past, to each other, and to the wider world during the United Fruit Company period, and what sense they made of United Fruit Company times when they were over.

This essay tells, by necessity and by choice, a rather one-sided story. The United Fruit Company (now Chiquita Brands International) does not allow researchers into its records; therefore the sources that would clarify UFCO policies and the perspectives, initiatives, and reactions of North American division managers are not available. The following account is based entirely on Colombian sources, mostly from the Magdalena banana zone; the picture I have pieced together from such sources may underestimate the company's influence. Nonetheless it is worthwhile to articulate the shift in perception that such sources induce, for they provide a useful antidote to the business histories, on the one hand, and the denunciations of UFCO imperialism, on the other, that comprise most of the existing historical literature on United Fruit Company enclaves in Latin America.[4] Perhaps because they rely heavily on U.S. sources, such publications tend to attribute sole agency to the UFCO. This essay aims to complicate the picture of enclaves by stressing the multifaceted ways in which locals initiated and responded to changes precipitated by the growth of the banana economy.

Interpreting Enclaves

Enclaves have been primarily discussed in economic terms, but until recently the social and cultural history of these regions was neglected. In the early 1970s, my fellow graduate students and I thought of enclaves as sleepy, tropical places suddenly penetrated by capitalism in the guise of a powerful foreign company. We rarely thought of enclaves as local societies at all, but rather as "factories in the field," as monocultural plantations or mines run by foreign bosses and worked by uprooted, deculturated wage laborers. Enclaves, then, were usually perceived as siphon economies with only one connection to the outside world, through the foreign company. Enclaves such as the banana regions forged by the United Fruit Company were praised as poles of modernization and denounced as imperialist outposts, but scholars working from modernization and dependency perspectives tended to agree that foreign companies held the power and did what they wished, while locals were passive, acted upon.[5]

Although the preceeding assumptions about enclave economies were widely accepted, some economists found them too dualistic: around 1970 they began to theorize how external forces could interact with local conditions to produce historically specific processes.[6] Following these economists' lead, researchers in history and the social sciences have begun to study regions of direct foreign investment through the lens of social and cultural history—as "contact zones" (to borrow Mary Louise Pratt's term), areas of intense interaction between two or more cultures in contexts of unequal power and resources.[7] The work of these investigators suggests some useful analytical perspectives through which to study the Magdalena banana region.[8]

First, the advent of the foreign company does not signify a complete break with the past: indeed, foreign companies generally must function within a context of local practices and meanings. It is important to think of enclaves as places with their own historical traditions that continue on and through the foreign time—traditions of land tenure, family networks, social markers and practices, local identities—and to question how local ways of doing things influence the social formation that evolves out of the intermeshing of local and foreign.[9]

Second, so-called enclaves are not necessarily homogeneous. Ecology, history, local rivalries, and the proximity of rural areas to cities may produce different subregional trajectories of change within a single area permeated by foreign investment. Furthermore, United Fruit Company banana enclaves were not carbon copies of each other: regions producing the same export crop under the aegis of the same foreign company may evolve very differently depending on local circumstances.[10]

Third, enclaves are socially complex places. Foreign managers and plantation workers shared this space with peasants and people in intermediate positions: lawyers, land surveyors, merchants, white-collar employees, politicians, church people, and transport workers. Some of these people were born in the place, while others came from elsewhere. What does it mean, then, to be an outsider or an insider? How do people perceive, struggle against, and adapt to each other? How do locals use the enclave for their own purposes—for economic accumulation or as political symbol and political capital? What are the possibilities and mechanisms for social mobility, and how do personal or family strategies of mobility make use of and intersect with the foreign enclave?

A final perspective is to interrogate the foundational assumption that enclaves are bounded places. To what extent did people move into and out of enclaves; what did the foreign encounter mean—in economic, social, and cultural terms—for people who spent but a part of their lives there? We also need to explore the various connections that existed between people living in enclaves and the world beyond, and the meanings that people attributed to these connections.

Land and Society: Local Trajectories

Let us turn now to the Magdalena banana enclave. The Magdalena banana-producing region included the rural counties (*municipios*) of Santa Marta, Ciénaga, and Aracataca on the northern coast of Colombia (see map). In 1894 Minor Keith, soon-to-be founder of the United Fruit Company, began buying up land there, and after 1900 the production of bananas for export markets under UFCO auspices grew rapidly. By the mid-1920s, this

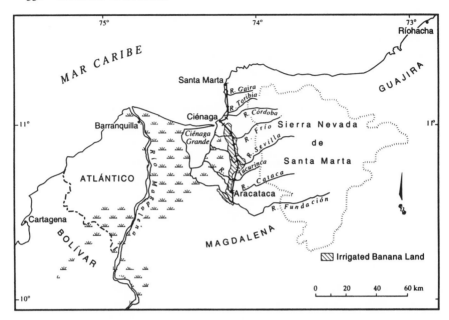

The Magadalena Banana Zone on the Caribbean Coast of Colombia, c. 1930

area had become the third largest exporter of bananas in the world, shipping more than ten million bunches a year. With the depression of 1930, the period of expansion came to a close, and the Colombian banana economy went into a series of contractions precipitated by the economic crisis, fungal diseases, and then World War II. Around 1965 the UFCO pulled out of the department of Magdalena altogether, transferring its operations 350 miles west, to the Urabá area near Panama.[11]

Of all the banana zones fomented by the United Fruit Company before World War II, only in Colombia and Jamaica did nationals produce a large proportion of the bananas exported. Who were they and how did they become banana planters? What were their strategies and forms of accumulation?

In the 1880s, a few years before banana cultivation began, there were three major areas within the larger region.[12] The first was the port of Santa Marta, a former outpost of Spanish colonial administration squeezed between the mountains and the sea. Santa Marta was home to the white colonial aristocrats who jealously guarded their Old World pedigrees and who danced only to the decorous strains of Spanish guitars. By the late nineteenth century, their descendants had become prosperous import-export merchants, facing ruin because of the rise of Barranquilla, a new port located sixty miles to the west. The second area focused on the old Indian town of Ciénaga on the shores of the great salt swamp. During the nineteenth century, this area, which also attracted runaway black slaves and a few Spanish shopkeepers, had undergone a process of *mestizaje*. Ciénaga was known as a racially mixed, self-determining, vigorously independent place of valiant Liberal fighters with strong resentments against the powerful, haughty elites of Santa Marta. In the late nineteenth century, when not fighting civil wars, the people of Ciénaga were peasants and small merchants, most of whom raised tobacco, cacao, sugar cane, and subsistence crops on the *ejidos* (common lands) that encircled the town.[13] The third subregion centered on Aracataca, a sparsely populated inland frontier area with some *colonos* (squatters) along the rivers and cattle ranging wild. Reachable only by canoe or on horseback, this was an area of *baldíos* (public lands) and *indivisos*. The indivisos were great expanses of land allocated by the Spanish king to elites from Santa Marta as a reward for fighting the Chimila Indians, whose raids had made settlement of the region impossible until the late eighteenth century. Similar to *terrenos comuneros* in other parts of the Caribbean, indivisos had many shareholders; land within indivisos could not be bought or sold because no one knew the boundaries between what one person or another owned, but *acciones* (shares) could be negotiated.[14]

Thus, there were important socioeconomic differences between the various areas in the banana-producing region, and certain rivalries based on colonial power, race, and social status set Ciénaga against Santa Marta.[15] Moreover, before bananas, private property in the region was scarce. One of the major changes that occurred with the advent of the banana economy was the privatization of land and the creation of a land market. The process of privatization was initiated and manipulated by local authorities and entrepreneurs, some of whom managed to accumulate significant amounts of capital. From 1890 to 1910, most of the ejidos of Ciénaga were privatized and the immense indivisos surveyed and divided among their co-owners. During these twenty years, from just before the advent of the United Fruit Company through the initial stage of the banana economy, much buying and selling of land occurred, mostly among Colombians.

The question is, Did privatization lead to the concentration of land in a few hands, that is, the formation of great banana plantations and the dispossession of peasant *ejidatarios* and squatters, who were turned into wage laborers? The answer is no. Apparently when the arrival of the

United Fruit Company opened new opportunities for profits by producing for international markets, local elites, middling groups, and smallholders all enthusiastically embraced banana production. In the early years, the UFCO collaborated with the powerful people of Santa Marta, extending them enormous credits so that they could go into banana production on a large scale. At the same time, the company signed banana purchase contracts with large and small producers alike, including many illiterate smallholders around Ciénaga who had no more than eight or ten acres of land in banana production.

Therefore, the basic structure of landholding that was in place in the late nineteenth century continued on through the period of privatization and through the banana period. Large banana plantations took form in the area of indivisos and baldíos in the vicinity of Aracataca, where the elites of Santa Marta astutely started up banana companies, often in partnership with the UFCO, and sold excess land in large tracts to the UFCO, but also to investors from Barranquilla, Bogotá, and France. Meanwhile in the old ejidos around Ciénaga, smallholders remained, producing with family labor both subsistence crops and bananas for export.

The advent of the UFCO, then, meant the influx of enormous sums of money, a new crop, a new connection to world markets, privatization of the land, and a quickening of the real estate market. But the particular forms this took reinforced older social structures and land tenure patterns. Many of the elites of Santa Marta entered into collaboration with the United Fruit Company and shifted their economic activities from the port to the rural interior, but the smallholders of Ciénaga also remained active. Throughout the twentieth century, a significant group of small producers persisted around Ciénaga on what had previously been ejidal land. Often we associate bananas with sugar as large plantation crops, but the very heterogeneous production structure of the Magdalena region, in which small, medium, and large national producers of bananas coexisted with the foreign company's great farms, calls to mind the structure of Colombian coffee production more than sugar.

Earlier landholding patterns also affected the rural proletariat that took form in the zone. As indivisos were privatized and public lands carved into private farms in the southern part of the banana zone, some squatters there were displaced. Very early on, they protested their dispossession through petitions to government authorities, giving rise to the conviction among the poor of the region that the elites of Santa Marta and the United Fruit Company had usurped public lands.[16] Many plantation laborers, it seems, aspired to become small independent farmers on public lands, cultivating foodstuffs for local markets and/or bananas for export. The prior existence of widespread public lands in the region, the example of the prosperous smallholders of Ciénaga, and the historical memory of struggle over public lands fueled by the growth of the banana economy made the peasant option a real one for wage workers. Many staked small claims in the foothills of the Sierra Nevada Mountains, just to the east of the banana zone, or participated in land invasions during periods of economic downturn. While some workers lived on the plantations, banana workers also resided in the southern barrios of the town of Ciénaga from whence they took UFCO trains to work each day. They connected the town to the countryside further south and the well-established smallholders of Ciénaga to the migrant proletarians and peasants of the plantation area.

To make sense of the social layout of the banana region, one more factor must be taken into account: the geography of the UFCO's presence. The United Fruit Company centered its operations in the port of Santa Marta, which connected the banana region to the world. Here the UFCO constructed an entire neighborhood of the city, called El Prado, with a social club and spacious houses in a North American style for its higher administrators. Also in Santa Marta were located the main UFCO hospital, radio and telegraph offices, the railroad terminus, and the banana docks. Although there was not much social mingling between the colonial elites of Santa Marta and UFCO executives, the company's presence was a constant of everyday life. In Santa Marta the workforce was mainly skilled port and railroad laborers. They formed a Sociedad de Artesanos y Obreros in 1915 and later identified and collaborated with the Asociación de Empleados del Magdalena.[17]

In contrast, in Ciénaga the United Fruit Company had no physical presence. It maintained warehouses and a railroad repair shop there, but no foreign managers lived in Ciénaga. Ciénaga was a dynamic, ostentatious town which, during the banana boom, developed its own indigenous, very eclectic style of architecture and its own raucous dance-hall music.[18] It was also a pugnaciously independent place of radical Liberals, small farmers, and banana workers, with an enduring history of antagonism toward Santa Marta. This singular history and social formation help to explain the ongoing tensions expressed between the inhabitants of Ciénaga and the large banana growers of Santa Marta and the UFCO based there. The Cienagueros wanted the benefits of bananas, but on their own terms. In 1920, for example, Ciénaga's municipal council passed a resolution urging congress to make the UFCO pay its workers weekly in order to save them from debt to company stores and to stimulate local commerce. The following year, the municipal council asked the national government to lend it money to irrigate 26,000 acres of land to enable the inhabitants of Ciénaga to raise bananas, sugar cane, and cacao in competition with the UFCO.[19]

Outside Connections

Clearly, to understand the forms economic and social life took once the United Fruit Company came and the specificity of local trajectories within the banana zone, it is essential to study what the Magdalena region was like before bananas. Let us turn now to a second question, that of the "boundedness" of the enclave. Did the foreign company's presence circumscribe the Magdalena banana area, cutting it off from the rest of Colombia? And was the zone linked to the outside world only through the United Fruit Company? The answer is no: there were multiple connections to the rest of Colombia and other countries.[20] Certainly the shipping link through the United Fruit Company's "Great White Fleet" was enormously important, but the banana boats connected the Magdalena zone not just to the United States, but also to other ports of the Caribbean and to Europe, where most Colombian bananas were marketed.

Even prior to the advent of the United Fruit Company, the region was not an isolated backwater. Its most prominent families were cosmopolitan people with far-flung commercial connections. In the 1880s and 1890s, for example, members of the de Mier family were based in New York, London, and Paris to handle the family's mercantile and business activities. One son remained in Paris for most of his life; Samarios say that he was a close friend of Marcel Proust. The de Vengoechea family of Santa Marta owned properties not only on the Caribbean coast but also near Bogotá, in Ecuador, and in France. And the Díaz-Granados family always had members based in Santa Marta, Bogotá, and also Quito and Guayaquil (Ecuador), where they were involved in banking activities.[21]

Not only did the elites of Santa Marta maintain their own long-standing business connections with other parts of Colombia and the world, which often involved long periods living abroad, but many people from other places also came to live in the region. In other words, UFCO managers were not the only "foreigners" present, the only foreigners who brought news of the world to this place. Workers migrated from all parts of the Caribbean coast of Colombia, including the Guajira Indian peninsula and the *palenques* (runaway-slave communities), as well as from the interior of the country. There were also smaller, spontaneous migrations from

Jamaica, Curaçao, the French Caribbean, and Spain.[22] People identified each other by the type of sandals they wore, their hats, their machetes, the way they spoke, and the kind of work they specialized in. The influx of people from all over the country produced some tensions (in Aracataca *costeños* attacked *cachacos* around 1915, killing many)[23] and new identities. For example, the "Gaiteros of Guacamayal," people from the province of Bolívar who played the *gaita,* an Indian flute characteristic of that region, became the symbol of the new community of Guacamayal that grew up along the UFCO railroad.

From the mid–nineteenth century on, foreigners had also come into the region as investors and businessmen. There were North Americans who established coffee plantations in the Sierra Nevada Mountains above Santa Marta, and British, Belgians, French, and Germans, who were land surveyors or engineers, or participated in the early tobacco trade. Some later invested in bananas, worked for the UFCO, or set up import-export businesses. These people became prominent in Santa Marta, and were often accepted into local high society and called "don." [24] Beginning after 1850, before bananas, and continuing during the early twentieth century, there was also an influx of Italians, Jewish traders from Curaçao, and Palestinians, Syrians, and Lebanese. Many of these people were merchants and shopkeepers, and they prospered. By the early twentieth century, the well-to-do of Ciénaga were mainly second-generation Italians and Jews (who soon converted to Catholicism).[25] Thus there were many "insider-outsiders" who often intermarried with the older families and soon became incorporated into local society.

Once the banana economy got under way, connections, both economic and cultural, to areas outside the banana region multiplied. The major economic connection was with the growing port of Barranquilla, capital of the department of Atlántico, to the west of the great salt swamp. Though no road existed between the Magdalena banana zone and Barranquilla until the 1950s, prior communication having only been by boat, economic relations between Barranquilla and Ciénaga were intense. Soon after 1900, some of the most prominent business families from Barranquilla bought extensive tracts of land in the southern part of the banana region and started up large-scale banana farms there. In 1908 when the UFCO began signing banana purchase contracts with local producers, the company sent a representative to Barranquilla to sign with the Barranquilla growers. Furthermore, import-export merchants in Barranquilla supplied many of the shopkeepers of Ciénaga and the banana zone, maintaining extensive credit relations with them. There also developed a domestic market for the bananas rejected by the UFCO, with Barranquilla as the distribution hub. Economic connections among Ciénaga, Aracataca, and Barranquilla were probably closer than those between Ciénaga and Santa Marta. Furthermore, many of the white-collar workers and artisans of Ciénaga were originally from Barranquilla and went back and forth.[26] A question that remains to be answered is the extent to which the growth of the banana zone contributed to the economic development of Barranquilla and the accumulation of capital that in the 1930s and 1940s would make Barranquilla the industrial center of the Colombian Caribbean coast.[27]

Not only did the business elites and skilled workers of the city of Barranquilla profit from their ties with the banana zone, but peasants from a much wider rural area of the Colombian coast were also drawn to the zone. Some migrated there temporarily or permanently as wage workers, remitting money back home. Others established themselves as peasants on public lands in the banana region. Still others sold food and clothing there: peasants from a village in the department of Atlántico, for example, regularly walked ten hours to Barranquilla and then took the overnight boat to Ciénaga to sell bread, sandals, and cotton shirts to banana workers. They returned home, their mules loaded with bananas to sell locally.[28] It seems that company stores did not supply all food demand and that widespread peasant marketing circuits moved into and out of the zone. To assume that trade did not occur because there were no good roads or railroads that connected the UFCO banana zone to other parts of the Caribbean coast is erroneous. Despite the difficulty of transport, people were mobile, and they responded with energy and creativity to market incentives. Through their efforts the banana enclave was connected in multiple ways to the larger coastal economy.[29]

During the banana period there were many cultural connections to the wider world as well. As one Cienaguero related, the advent of the UFCO set off an *afán* (eagerness, anxiety, ardor) for things foreign. But this was not an afán only for the United States.

Newspapers published in Santa Marta and Ciénaga in the 1920s expressed fascination with and a critical bent toward what was happening in the United States and Europe—literary trends, business practices, health breakthroughs, the flight of Charles Lindbergh, and so on. Also, the newspapers of Santa Marta were in direct contact with Bogotá, the nation's capital, through the telegraph, which antedated the UFCO's telegraph by twenty years. Local newspapers reprinted articles one or two days old from the Bogotano press dealing with national affairs and also with views from Bogotá on what was going on in the banana zone.[30] Just prior to the banana strike of 1928, the newspapers of Santa Marta reported at length on Sandino's resistance to the U.S. occupation of Nicaragua. (A representative from Sandino's army of liberation spoke in the port in October 1928). For the youthful newspaper editors of Santa Marta, solidarity with Sandino seemed to represent the idea of unity with Colombians of their generation in Bogotá, Cali, and elsewhere, who admired and supported the rebel.[31] It should be mentioned that the newspapers of Santa Marta also occasionally reported on conditions in United Fruit Company banana enclaves elsewhere in the Caribbean: Colombian banana growers knew what the UFCO was paying for bananas in other places and on what terms.[32]

Other connections to the outside world are evident in forms of recreation. The population of Ciénaga was enormously proud of the two large theaters private entrepreneurs built there in the 1920s that hosted Spanish operetta companies. The newspapers were full of advertisements for movies that changed every three days: Douglas Fairbanks was a favorite, as were films from France and Italy. Meanwhile, the towns of the zone were inundated with new consumption goods: in the stores of Santa Marta and Ciénaga in the late 1920s, one could buy Underwood typewriters, Parker pens, Florsheim shoes, Vicks Vaporub, Eno Fruit Salts, Bayer Aspirin, Dr. Richards Cod Liver Oil, Colgate Dental Creme, Quaker Oats, Buick Sport Roadsters, Chevrolet cars, and Firestone and Goodyear tires. If these items were not enough, more could be ordered through the Montgomery Ward catalog.[33] Traveling salesmen from the United States contacted merchants in Santa Marta and Ciénaga to act as agents for the sale of such goods, which could easily be imported on United Fruit Company boats. One could also buy French stockings, hats, and artificial flowers. And the affluent banana farmers of Ciénaga contracted Spanish and Italian stonemasons to build their mansions, while the municipal council of Ciénaga imported a French architect from Cuba to adorn the town square (the father, so it is rumored, of Cuban novelist Alejo Carpentier).

Not only did the outside world come into the banana region, but the well-to-do of Santa Marta, Ciénaga, and Aracataca went out as well. In the 1920s and 1930s, people of the upper echelons of society sent their sons to study in Barranquilla or Bogotá; the daughters went to Medellín or Curaçao. Others studied in Kingston, Jamaica. Some of the most prominent banana barons sent their male children in the 1930s to universities in the United States. The scion of one of the major families did a master's degree at Stanford, where he married an American psychology major who, having lived in Santa Marta for fifty years, is now an integral member of high society. The middle and upper classes felt it a career advantage to know English, whether to get an office job with the United Fruit Company or to deal with the UFCO on its own terms.[34]

Meanwhile, in the late 1920s and early 1930s, a colony of wealthy second-generation banana planters from Ciénaga established themselves in Brussels. Many of these families lived in Belgium for five to ten years, sometimes longer, leaving their banana farms to relatives or managers. When I asked a literary critic who had been raised in Ciénaga about stories of the banana strike passed down in his family, he replied that there were none. Instead his fantasies had centered on the enormous portrait of the queen of Belgium that hung over his bed.[35] People of more humble backgrounds call the obsession with living in Brussels "bruselosis" (a play on the term for cow disease), a kind of degeneration or effeminization of the upper classes. One person suggested that the "dandies" who had spent time in Brussels had introduced homosexuality, among other imports, into Ciénaga.

Cultural connections with the world beyond the banana zone also were manifested in several organizations with a broader reach. The most important were the Freemasons, by definition members of an international fraternal order. Local people founded lodges of Freemasons in Santa Marta and Ciénaga in 1887, prior to the advent of the UFCO; the lodge in Aracataca was established thirty years later. The early Masons were an international crew including Italians, former Jews from Curaçao, and vehemently Liberal banana planters, both large and small, many of whom had fought in the civil wars of the nineteenth century.[36] International in scope, interests, and associations, the Masons of the banana zone communicated with other Colombian and foreign lodges through the Gran Logia in Barranquilla. Members of the lodges in Santa Marta and Ciénaga included some of the British, Americans, and French long resident in the zone; U.S. employees of the UFCO who were Masons were welcome to attend meetings. The Ciénaga Lodge itself, built in 1912 during the period of Conservative party hegemony, when Masonry was illegal in Colombia, was the most imposing building in town. The Masons of Ciénaga, who numbered some 120 people in the early 1920s, avidly read books on Gnosticism and Rosicrucianism, which they carefully guarded in the Masonic library. During the banana strike, the Masons never directly criticized the United Fruit Company, but after the massacre of workers those from Ciénaga sent a strongly worded protest to the president of Colombia criticizing the government's brutality.[37]

Other groups with supraregional affiliations active in the banana zone were the Sociedad de Agricultores Colombianos (SAC) and the Rotary

Club. Whereas the national SAC was a vehicle for coffee interests during the 1920s, the regional chapter, established in 1918, functioned as a lobbying group to advance the interests of large Colombian banana growers before the national government, sometimes in opposition to the United Fruit Company.[38] The first Rotary Club in the area was established early in 1930 on the initiative of Dr. Guillermo A. Carvallo of Mexico, special envoy of the Rotary International of Chicago "to found Rotary Clubs in the world." Within the year, the Rotary Club of Santa Marta, which many local notables had joined, was proposing development projects to diversify the regional economy and promote agricultural colonization in the Sierra Nevada Mountains above Santa Marta.[39]

In sum, the banana region was not linked to the world only through the United Fruit Company. Both economically and culturally people in the zone made many connections—to Barranquilla, Bogotá, the Caribbean, and Europe, as well as the United States. Though the zone was sometimes referred to as a "state within a state," in fact the advent of the foreign company seems to have brought the banana region closer to Bogotá. The formation of a regional branch of the Sociedad de Agricultores Colombianos, a concern in Bogotá with what was happening in this region of foreign influence, the activities of several congressional commissions of inquiry—all focused national attention on the region.[40] At the same time, the banana zone became literally closer to Europe, because the banana boats (which also took passengers) drastically reduced the time and costs of travel. I would suggest that the Cienagueros' enthusiasm for things European may obliquely have signified a rejection of, or an alternative to, the United Fruit Company and its U.S. connection. At any rate, by the early twentieth century, the Colombian banana region was an enormously cosmopolitan area, much less isolated than Bogotá and the interior of Colombia.[41]

Culture and Memory

To this point we have discussed the imprint of history, subregional variations within a single enclave, and the question of boundedness. I turn now to the final issue, that of the culture of this particular banana enclave. What can identity and community possibly mean in a place that is so connected to so many outside places, in which so many people from so many places come together, and in which there is rapid economic expansion (followed by painful contraction) linked to a new crop produced almost entirely for world markets? How do people see and define themselves now that the

United Fruit Company period is over? How do they talk about the past? It should be noted at the outset that when people in Ciénaga and Santa Marta compare their banana experience to that of Urabá (the present-day center of Colombian banana production, which is wracked by violence), they say, "What makes us different from them is that we have community. The way we will keep the violence out is by cultivating and reinforcing that rootedness, that sense of community." [42]

Over the past few years, I have been asking people about their memories of the United Fruit Company banana period, about how they think the UFCO affected local life, about what changed and what didn't, what they think was good or bad. There are many answers — former company employees reminisce about the long-gone times of "green gold," the good old days of easy prosperity, while students at the local technical university write theses denouncing UFCO imperialism. But in conversations certain themes come up again and again.

What is striking about the recurrent stories is that most do not directly concern the United Fruit Company at all. Most of the cultural issues have to do not with the impact of the UFCO or direct criticisms of or reactions against it: people just do not talk much about the company. Rather most of the stories have to do with hopes, ambivalences, and strains internal to regional society but related to the rapid changes precipitated by the banana economy.[43]

First there are a set of stories focusing on money. Some people say that with the advent of the United Fruit Company, you had to buy dance partners (which was never done before); others say that the idea of buying votes dawned on local politicians only when the UFCO inundated the zone with money. Memories of banana workers dancing the *cumbia*, holding aloft burning wads of dollar bills (instead of the traditional candles) are rife, though some people doubt this really happened. There are many stories too of pacts with the devil, though the UFCO is never accused of such machinations. Rather those of whom the stories are told are poor people who overnight became rich banana planters. For their prosperity, it is said, they promised the devil one life each year, and when those who had consented to such pacts died, their wealth vanished. Various tales suggest that some planters propagated rumors that they themselves were in cahoots with the devil to intimidate their workers. The person on whom most accounts center — Manuel Varela, a "short, dark-skinned" man who in the 1920s built the great Ciénaga mansion still known as "La Casa del Diablo" — was by no means a sycophant of the UFCO. He was known as a man obsessed by technology who traveled to the United States to purchase the electric tramway that made his banana plantation the most advanced in the municipality of Ciénaga. He was also renowned for his successes in seducing poor women of the region.[44]

These devil stories point to a second theme that comes up in many conversations about the past, that of the supernatural power, the magic of the region and the people who lived there. These images are particularly potent in Ciénaga and the banana-producing areas to the south. The attraction of the zone in itself seemed magical to people from other parts of the coast: the families of young men who migrated to the banana zone held funerals for them, believing they would never return.[45] Those who did return to their villages after a stint in the banana region were changed by the experience, by the contact with the wider world that living in the banana region implied. Historian José Lobo Romero, whose father spent fifteen years as a laborer in the banana region, relates that the zone was his father's school. The father returned to his village in Atlántico having learned to read and write, and having become an atheist and an alcoholic. At home others looked up to him as a person vitally interested in national and international affairs and possessed of magical powers (he could speak to the animals, tame snakes, and find paths in the dark). Thus he returned from the banana zone a man of knowledge that embraced both older and newer forms.[46] Other stories indicate that special forms of occult practices evolved in the zone itself: it is said that just after the massacre of 1928, when many strikers were jailed, women *brujas* embedded needles in ripe bananas to incapacitate the police with stomach pains.[47]

The culture of the occult not only appealed to working people; it also permeated the more educated milieus of small and middling banana producers. In Ciénaga in the 1920s and 1930s, some radical Liberals, anarchists, and communists were also Masons, Gnostics, or herbal doctors, who sometimes cured with magnets or needles. Some were interested in Seventh Day Adventism, Theosophy, or vegetarianism as well. Ciénaga attracted various people from other places whose high standing in the community derived in part from their far travels and "universal" knowledge. Tomás Anatol, for example, practiced popular medicine and is said to have been a Peruvian Aprista who wrote poetry and had lived in Bogotá and Europe (he could also walk on water and start or stop the rain). The anarchist guru Gilberto García González, although born in Ciénaga, had traveled in Europe and India, wore a long beard and a turban, and ate on the floor. Samael Aun Weor, who came from Bogotá around 1950, made Ciénaga the center of Colombian Gnosticism for many years, before moving on to Mexico where he died.[48]

Historian Fabio Zambrano speculates that in many parts of Colombia, during the period 1886–1930, Liberals reacted against the hegemony of the Conservative party and the Catholic Church with a heterodox embrace of liberalism, spiritism, Masonry, and homeopathy, giving rise to an alternative political culture. By political culture, Zambrano means alternative forms of sociability and association that had resonance among both the educated middle groups and the working classes.[49] This seems to have been the case in Ciénaga, where such beliefs forged cultural and political bonds between certain local intellectuals and the popular classes, bonds that were probably important in the development of workers' movements in the 1920s. The ferment of ideas in Ciénaga suggests that the international spiritualist movements so popular in Europe, the United States, and the capital cities of Latin America in the late nineteenth and early twentieth centuries also resonated in the provinces.[50] Thus in Ciénaga and the banana area to the south, esoteric knowledge involved an intermeshing of older popular beliefs and practices with "universal" currents of knowledge—that is, with people and ideas from faraway (even non-Western) places.

What other themes emerged in local talk of banana times? There is a distrust of money and the sense that the economic in general is unreliable, arbitrary, external, and perhaps harmful to what is good and fundamental in local identity and social life. People express an ambivalence toward bananas. On the one hand, two historians from Santa Marta have written an entire book on the regional "language" of the banana zone that elaborates on the words of banana cultivation and their various slang uses.[51] On the other hand, a group of writers and artists in Ciénaga have articulated a utopian vision of the future with no more bananas or export crops, conjuring up instead a region joined to the mountain and the great salt swamp, blanketed by flowers.[52]

If the economy is a source of ambivalence, even consternation, people in Ciénaga express unadulterated pride in local "culture." Young professors at the Ciénaga teachers' college collect popular myths and legends; they write about the music of the zone and the yearly crocodile festival, and also proudly proclaim Ciénaga the folkloric center of Colombia.[53] With the new Colombian Constitution of 1991 that calls for the formation of administrative and cultural units intermediate between *departamentos* and municipios, local artists, intellectuals, and social activists have proposed that the old banana zone become an officially recognized and partially self-governing region.[54] But they do not define the place they live as the "banana region." Rather, they hark back to an older history inscribed in the land itself. They define the region they want to create in ecological terms, calling it "Cienaguas" (a hundred waters). In so doing, they not only advance a perspective that sees the banana period as but a blip in the millenial sweep of time; they also call for a cleaning up of the rivers and swamps that made possible the cultivation of bananas and were so terribly polluted by it. They argue that the long-term well-being of all the people of the region lies in valuing the environment over short-term economic profits.[55]

Finally, what of the great banana strike of 1928 and its tragic aftermath? There are many stories, the most important of which are collected by García Márquez in *One Hundred Years of Solitude*. No one knows how many people died in the massacre or what happened to the bodies, though it is rumored that they were dumped by night in the sea or buried in unmarked graves. Various people, however, told me they feel they live in an "important"—not a peripheral—place. Because the strike and massacre happened here and because Gabriel García Márquez wrote about them, they live in a place that is central to Colombian history and a focus of world attention.

In 1978, to commemorate the fiftieth anniversary of the banana strike, a local group of radical students and writers erected a statue to the strikers where the massacre occurred, in the train station at Ciénaga. Fifteen feet tall, the statue, by a well-known sculptor from Cali, portrays a lean, muscular man with negroid features, clothed only in a loincloth and holding a machete over his head.[56] In 1993–1994 my research assistant Adriana Corso and I asked a variety of people what they thought of the statue, seeking more opinions on the strike. We were surprised to find that the statue seems to be a touchstone for numerous issues that have little to do with the strike. Some people, especially from the wealthier classes of Santa Marta and Ciénaga, say, "He is not from this region, he is not one of us. He is black and our workers have finer features; furthermore they wear clothes and do not act in such aggressive ways." There is also a widespread rumor that the sculptor was gay and that his lover modeled for the statue. People say that the sculptor emphasized the statue's genitals; they call the statue "El Chacarón." Some women say they would like to marry the statue. A group of older women from Aracataca who led land invasions after the United Fruit Company pulled out in the early 1970s insisted that the Colombian Agrarian Reform Institute should erect a statue to them. They expressed disgust with the tiny, two-foot-tall statue they got, calling it *esa muñeca* (that doll-baby); they want a statue like the one in Ciénaga, a woman fifteen feet tall, a giant woman wielding a machete.[57]

Thus the statue in the train station is only partly about the strike of 1928; it has also become the catalyst for many stories about class, race, gender, and regional identity that have a great deal to say about subterranean and not-so-subterranean debates, assertions, and tensions in the present. At the same time, however, there is also a desire in the region to collect the stories passed down in families, to write the history of what happened during United Fruit Company times, which, as I hope this paper has made clear, was a time of bananas and much more besides. "We are the generation of the end of the millenium," people say. "We must pass down what we have lived in all its richness to our children and the generations to come as our legacy to constructing the future in ways we don't yet know." [58]

Larger Meanings

In *One Hundred Years of Solitude,* Gabriel García Márquez suggests that U.S. corporate investment in Latin America wipes out the uniqueness of place and strips a people of the ability to tell their own stories. When I was a graduate student, similar interpretations held sway among historians and social scientists. In the late 1960s and early 1970s, dependency theorists decried U.S. cultural imperialism and what they saw as the growing cultural dependency of Latin America on the United States. Meanwhile, modernization theorists optimistically predicted that, over time, the world would become more like the United States. Despite their differences, proponents of both viewpoints agreed that accelerating global integration, spearheaded by the United States, was molding the world into a homogenous civilization in which the values and practices of the marketplace would reign supreme. International market culture was obliterating the multiplicity of local values and practices and, dependency theorists added, promoting acceptance of U.S. economic domination as natural, perhaps even inevitable.[59]

We might logically assume that such homogenizing processes would be most intense in the foreign enclaves created by American multinational corporations, because these places experienced most forcefully the transformative impact of the world economy and U.S. enterprise. We might well assume that in such places local values and lifeways were eradicated.

Yet this did not happen in the Magdalena banana zone. Such a viewpoint denies the rich and vital local cultures that emerged in the Colombian banana region and perhaps in other so-called enclaves as well. This research suggests that enclaves are places with their own historical traditions; socially complex regions in which people of different national, racial, ethnic, and linguistic origins have to deal with each other; porous areas with multiple connections to their own countries and the outside world. I would stress the internal complexity of these regions and the fact that locals are actors with their own economic strategies, politics, interpretations, meanings, and memories.

To write the history of such areas only from the optic of the business history of the "dominant" foreign company is to touch only the tip of the iceberg. To conceptualize the impact of the foreign company on local society as "the penetration of capitalism" is to overlook that many people living in or attracted to the place actively embraced the opportunities opened by the connection to international markets. In order to function, foreign companies had to adapt to local contexts. The specific forms of capitalism that emerged in such places were always the product of interactions among foreign companies, local people, migrants, and national governments. At the same time that the people of Santa Marta, Ciénaga, and Aracataca collaborated with the United Fruit Company in creating the banana zone, the commodity boom and bust generated many tensions, some of which were expressed in relation to the United Fruit Company and others within local society.

Over the past two decades, thinkers from various disciplines have begun to suggest that global integration does not produce homogeneity, but instead generates diverse local trajectories and many specific hybrid cultures in Latin America, the United States, and elsewhere.[60] Anthropologist Sherry Ortner reminds us that "pieces of reality, however much borrowed from or imposed by others, are woven together through the logic of a group's own locally and historically evolved bricolage."[61] Literary critic Doris Sommer suggests that "pride of place" and locally based cultural movements signify resistance to global tendencies toward uniformity and a celebration of the richness of local human creativities that evolve in part by making the outside part of one's own.[62] Geographer Doreen Massey's perspective on the internal and external in the constitution of place is of particular relevance to the Colombian banana region. She writes:

It has in principle always been difficult and has over the centuries become more so, to distinguish the inside of a place from the outside; indeed, it is precisely in part the presence of the outside within which helps to construct the specificity of the local. . . . Instead . . . of thinking of places as areas with boundaries around, they can be imagined as articulated moments in networks of social relations and understandings where a large proportion of those relations, experiences, and understandings are . . . on a far larger scale than what we happen to define for that moment as the place itself.[63]

Through discussing links to the wider world and local identities in one United Fruit Company enclave, my aim has been to explore the ambiguous status of things foreign and to break down the often too simplistically drawn opposition between domination and resistance. I also have wanted to challenge the ahistoric, bounded notion of enclaves and to suggest that the terrain of representation may be a fruitful one to discuss both the UFCO's modernizing project and the erasure of it by local people during the last few decades.[64] Certainly the heterogeneity of this zone (which came from its variegated geography and previous history, the proliferation of social groups, the diversity of productive organization in bananas, and the multiplicity of outside contacts) contributed both to the complexity of local interactions, collaborations, and conflicts with the foreign company and to the richness of its cultural production. This was (and is) a place of cultural dynamism, open to the world, where connection to international markets created channels for the circulation of the most diverse currents of European and North American culture—currents that the people of the banana zone interpreted and appropriated in their own imaginative, idiosyncratic ways.

But if the UFCO did not wield absolute power and locals "had agency," then how shall we talk about power? To paraphrase sociologist Theda Skocpol, it is important to bring the UFCO and the state "back in." [65] In other words, we must explore how UFCO understandings and initiatives and those of the Colombian government shaped local ethnic, gender, and class relations and the multifarious responses to the foreign company. One contribution of this study has been to stress that foreign managers and plantation laborers were not the only inhabitants of the banana zone. There were also large and small banana planters, merchants, itinerant vendors, artisans, priests, prostitutes, boatmen, washerwomen, peasants producing foodstuffs for local markets, lawyers, Masons, brujas, bartenders, musicians, and many others. Between these people and among the various human settlements of the zone, there were inequalities and many forms of power and exploitation. These were complex, historically rooted asymmetries that fed into and fed off of the foreign company's influence, which derived in large part from its vast financial, technical, and communications resources. To visualize the UFCO as all-powerful, then, is to blot out the sociocultural world of the region that antedated the United Fruit Company and subsequently engaged with it. In addressing the issue of power, it is also important to realize that many people were mobile: they lived directly in the UFCO's field of influence for only limited periods of time, often changing occupations and/or moving into and out of the region. Thus although U.S. businessmen may have portrayed the areas in which they invested as modern enclaves in the North American image, wholly created by U.S. capital, such depictions perhaps purposefully ignored the existence of local societies looking back at them.[66]

This suggests another angle from which to examine the power issue, that of connections between "the relatively objective world of social and economic relations and the sometimes more subjective world of cultural identity."[67] This essay has endeavored to bring together social history focused on experience and the history of representations. The research suggests that the particularly autonomous, assertive attitude expressed by Cienagueros in their relations with the foreign company may relate directly to the fact that Ciénaga was a society of small independent farmers, literate shopkeepers, artisans, and petty bureaucrats who harbored long-standing resentments against the political power and socioracial elitism of Santa Marta, where the UFCO based its operations. An alternative perspective might be to argue that a separation existed between the economic sphere, in which the U.S. corporation exercised predominant influence through its control of credit, infrastructure, and marketing possibilities; and the cultural sphere, which remained a more independent site of commentary, veiled or only partially understood by foreign managers. Highlighting the distinction between the experiences of the past and the reconstruction of memory in the present, Argentine historian Ricardo Salvatore points to yet another possible conceptualization. In commenting on an earlier version of this essay, he suggests that perhaps

during UFCO times there was a diversity of experience, but the foreign company controlled the arena of representation (at least in Santa Marta), whereas after the Company pulled out, people took control of representation, trying to erase the memory of the Company. There seems to be a strategy of bypassing or minimizing the American company's presence as central to the region's history. Locals want to forget they were a banana zone, a site of exploitation, a territory "foreign" to the nation. The selective memory erodes the foreign from local territory, reappropriating "lo de uno" (one's own). What seems to be occurring here is a process of erasure and of selective appropriation.[68]

Salvatore rightly emphasizes the importance of historicizing perceptions and narrations. At this stage of research, my sense is that the United

Fruit Company never dominated representation, even in the port of Santa Marta, to the extent that Salvatore hypothesizes. To substantiate this, however, is problematic: attention to the methodologies of oral history and interpretation of memory, in combination with a close perusal of song lyrics, collections of jokes, politicians' speeches, broadsides, newspapers, local histories, theses, diaries, poetry, and essays produced in the zone during the banana boom period, as well as public celebrations and religious and community fiestas, will most certainly shed light on these questions.[69]

What is clear at this point is that many studies of capitalism have fetishized large foreign firms, incorrectly according them a kind of omnipotence or portraying them as the sole connection to the global economy. It is also clear that the history of Macondo did not end with the banana massacre and the departure of the United Fruit Company. Like the fictional Macondo, the old Colombian banana zone that gave birth to Gabriel García Márquez is a place of fecund intersections. Life in the area involves a generative engagement with people, ideas, and material goods external to the region and, at the same time, an ongoing reelaboration of deep-rooted local traditions and beliefs. Although local people may debate the desirability of specific contacts and changes, the fundamental attitude, at least in Ciénaga, is of a sense of self and place constituted through openness to the outside.

In August 1996 I asked poet Javier Moscarella, grandson of a Cienaguera woman and an Italian immigrant, if in his opinion the banana zone had experienced cultural imperialism. Animated, emphatic, he replied:

It is an absurdity, almost an insult to use these terms. We have always been receptive to the contributions of other societies, ever since Spanish colonial times and even before. We copy, we assimilate, we recycle into something else. We are open, but not submissive. It's impossible to dominate us. Our culture has remained intact because our subsistence technologies, our forms of sociability, and our free-thinking beliefs are our historical roots: they center us, they make us who we are. The United Fruit Company had no concerted program of cultural change. They lived over there in their chicken coops. We didn't mix with them; we (pardon my saying this) never found their white women attractive; ours, yes, but not theirs. The only power the United Fruit Company had was the power of corruption and that was circumstantial. There was money to be made and some people here took advantage of the situation.[70]

If cultural identity involves a retelling of the past by another route, then the people of the old Colombian banana zone are engaged in a creative process of recuperation and invention that incorporates the outside within as a legacy for generations to come.[71]

Notes

I wish to thank Adriana Mercedes Corso, Lucy Porras, Javier Moscarella, Rafael Darío Jiménez, Luz Paulina Travecedo, Guillermo Henríquez, Zoraida Castillo de Alfaro, Alfredo Correa, and the many people of Santa Marta, Ciénaga, and Aracataca who generously helped me toward a better understanding of regional history. I am grateful too to Karen Robert, Lauren Derby, Gil Joseph, Ricardo Salvatore, David Parker, Kris Inwood, and Doris Sommer for useful criticisms and suggestions. Paul Gootenberg and Marcelo Bucheli provided guidance to the economic literature on enclaves, and George Lovell pointed me toward the new regional geography. Financing came from the Social Science and Humanities Research Council of Canada.

1. Gabriel García Márquez, *One Hundred Years of Solitude,* trans. Gregory Rabassa (1967; New York: Harper and Row, 1970), 336.

2. Located in the northwestern part of the department of Magdalena, this area is often called the Santa Marta banana zone, even though the actual banana plantations were located south of Santa Marta in the *municipios* of Ciénaga and Aracataca. People from Ciénaga and Aracataca resent the designation as an attempt by Santa Marta, the departmental capital, to assert its preeminence. For accuracy's sake, I will refer to the region encompassing all three municipios as the Magdalena banana zone in this essay.

3. For information on García Márquez's life, see his *El olor de la guayaba: Conversaciones con Plinio Apuleyo Mendoza* (Bogotá: Editorial La Oveja Negra, 1982); and Roque Jiménez Urriola, *García Márquez en pocas palabras* (Barranquilla: Editorial Antillas, 1993).

4. See, e.g., Frederick Upham Adams, *Conquest of the Tropics: The Story of the Creative Enterprises Conducted by the United Fruit Company* (New York: Doubleday, 1914); Charles David Kepner, *The Banana Empire: A Case Study of Economic Imperialism* (New York: Vanguard Press, 1935); idem, *Social Aspects of the Banana Industry* (New York: Columbia University Press, 1936); and Stacey May and Galo Plaza, *The United Fruit Company in Latin America* (Washington, D.C.: National Planning Association, 1958).

5. For this perspective, see, e.g., Jonathan V. Levin, *The Export Economies: Their Pattern of Development in Historical Perspective* (Cambridge, Mass.: Harvard University Press, 1960); Fernando Enrique Cardoso and Enzo Faletto, *Dependency and Development in Latin America,* trans. Marjory Mattingly Urquidi (Berkeley and Los Angeles: University of California Press, 1979), xviii–xx, 69–

76; and Carlos M. Vilas, *State, Class, and Ethnicity in Nicaragua* (Boulder, Colo.: L. Rienner, 1989), 8–11, 44–54.

6. See Charles P. Kindleberger, *American Business Abroad: Six Lectures on Direct Investment* (New Haven, Conn.: Yale University Press, 1969); Raymond Vernon, *Sovereignty at Bay: The Multinational Spread of U.S. Enterprises* (New York: Basic Books, 1971); Albert O. Hirschman, "A Generalized Linkage Approach to Development, with Special Reference to Staples," in *Essays on Economic Development and Cultural Change*, ed. Manning Nash (Chicago: University of Chicago Press, 1977), 67–98; and Roberto Cortés Conde and Shane J. Hunt, eds., *The Latin American Economies: Growth and the Export Sector, 1880–1930* (New York: Holmes and Meier, 1985).

7. Mary Louise Pratt, *Imperial Eyes: Travel Writing and Transculturation* (London: Routledge, 1992), 6–7.

8. See June Nash, *We Eat the Mines and the Mines Eat Us* (New York: Columbia University Press, 1979); Barbara Weinstein, *The Amazon Rubber Boom, 1850–1920* (Stanford, Calif.: Stanford University Press, 1983); Carol A. Smith, "Local History in a Global Context: Social and Economic Transitions in Western Guatemala," *Comparative Studies in Society and History* 26 (1984): 193–228; Philippe Bourgois, *Ethnicity at Work: Divided Labor on a Central American Banana Plantation* (Baltimore, Md.: Johns Hopkins University Press, 1989); Eduardo Posada Carbó, "Imperialism, Local Elites, and Regional Development: The United Fruit Company in Colombia Reconsidered, 1900–1945" (paper presented at the 47th International Congress of Americanists, New Orleans, 1991); Juan A. Giusti Cordero, "Labor, Ecology, and History in a Caribbean Sugar Plantation Region: Piñones (Loiza), Puerto Rico 1770–1950" (Ph.D. diss., SUNY Binghamton, 1995); Aviva Chomsky, *West Indian Workers and the United Fruit Company in Costa Rica, 1870–1940* (Baton Rouge: Louisiana State University Press, 1996); Fernando Coronil, *The Magical State: Nature, Money, and Modernity in Venezuela* (Chicago: University of Chicago Press, 1997); Baron León Pineda, "Contested Identities in the Western Caribbean: The Social Development of a U.S. Company Town—Puerto Cabezas, Nicaragua" (Ph.D. diss., University of Chicago, in progress); and Thomas Klubock's essay in this volume.

9. For evocative work on this theme, see Julie Franks, "The *Gavilleros* of the East: Social Banditry as Political Practice in the Dominican Sugar Region, 1900–1924," *Journal of Historical Sociology* 8, no. 2 (June 1995): 158–81; and idem, "Transforming Property: Landholding and Political Rights in the Dominican Sugar Region, 1880–1930" (Ph.D. diss., SUNY Stony Brook, 1997). Also see Catherine C. LeGrand, "Informal Resistance on a Dominican Sugar Plantation during the Trujillo Dictatorship," *Hispanic American Historical Review* 75, no. 4 (Nov. 1995): 555–96.

10. Rebecca Scott's work comparing sugar regions after the abolition of slavery, though not specifically concerned with foreign investment, provides a useful approach for understanding variations in socioeconomic formations within a single

crop area. See Scott, "Defining the Boundaries of Freedom in the World of Cane: Cuba, Brazil, and Louisiana after Emancipation," *American Historical Review* 99, no. 1 (Feb. 1994): 70–102.

11. Good overviews of the history of the Magdalena banana region include James R. Krogzemis, "A Historical Geography of the Santa Marta Area, Colombia" (Ph.D. diss., University of California at Berkeley, 1968); Fernando Botero and Alvaro Guzmán Barney, "El enclave agrícola en la zona bananera de Santa Marta," *Cuadernos Colombianos* 11 (1977): 309–89; Judith White, *La United Fruit Co. en Colombia: Historia de una ignominia* (Bogotá: Editorial Presencia, 1978); and Manuel J. Díaz-Granados, *Geografía económica del Magdalena Grande (1946–55)* (Santa Marta: Gráficas Gutenberg, 1996). Marcelo Bucheli explains why the UFCO moved from Santa Marta to Urabá in "United Fruit in Colombia: Impact of Labor Relations and Governmental Regulations on Its Operations, 1948–1968," *Essays in Economic and Business History* [Ohio State University] 17 (1997): 65–84.

12. Historians and geographers continue to debate how to define *region*. See, for example, Joseph L. Love, "An Approach to Regionalism," in *New Approaches to Latin American History,* ed. Richard Graham and Peter Smith (Austin: University of Texas Press, 1974), 137–55; Gilbert M. Joseph, "Introduction: The New Regional Historiography at Mexico's Periphery," in *Land, Labor, and Capital in Modern Yucatán: Essays in Regional History and Political Economy,* ed. Jeffery T. Brannon and Gilbert M. Joseph (Tuscaloosa: University of Alabama Press, 1991), 1–9; Eric Van Young, "Introduction: Are Regions Good to Think?" in *Mexico's Regions: Comparative History and Development,* ed. Eric Van Young (La Jolla: Center for U.S.-Mexican Studies, University of California, San Diego, 1992), 1–36; and Magnus Morner, *Region and State in Latin America's Past* (Baltimore, Md.: Johns Hopkins University Press, 1993). The Magdalena banana region was constituted geographically by the Caribbean Sea to the north, the Magdalena River and salt swamp to the west, and the Sierra Nevada Mountains to the east, out of which flowed the seven rivers that made banana cultivation possible. Administratively the region centered on the port of Santa Marta, capital of the province (later department) of Magdalena to which Ciénaga and Aracataca were appended. As will become clear, the region was constituted too by ongoing rivalries among the three municipios, each of which defined local identities in opposition to the others. While specifying the boundaries that circumscribe regions can be useful, more relevant to this project is the "new regional geography" that emphasizes the indeterminacy of boundaries and "understand[s] regions as constructed out of wider (multiple and overlapping) processes, . . . sieved by local patterns of social organization and interpretation" (Nigel Thrift, "For a New Regional Geography 1," *Progress in Human Geography* 14, no. 2 [June 1990]: 273). The new regional geographers also are concerned with how people attribute meanings, perceive difference, and articulate identities in spatial terms. For Colombia, see the pioneering works by anthropologist Peter Wade, "A Sense of Place: The Geography

of Culture in Colombia," in *Blackness and Race Mixture: The Dynamics of Racial Identity in Colombia* (Baltimore, Md.: Johns Hopkins University Press, 1992), 51–65; historian Mary Roldán, "Genesis and Evolution of *La Violencia* in Antioquia, Colombia, 1900–1953" (Ph.D. diss., Harvard University, 1992); and idem, "Violence, Colonization, and the Geography of Cultural Difference in Colombia" (paper presented at the Latin American Studies Association meetings, Washington, D.C., Sept. 1995).

13. On Ciénaga, see J. White, *United Fruit Co.;* Pedro María Revollo, *Memorias del presbitero Pedro María Revollo: Primera parte, de 1868 a 1906* (Barranquilla: Editorial Mejoras, 1956); and José C. Alarcón, *Compendio de historia del departamento del Magdalena (de 1525 hasta 1895)* (Bogotá: El Voto Nacional, 1963). The ejidos of Ciénaga seem to have originated in a *resguardo* granted by the Spanish crown to the Indians of Ciénaga in 1757. See Lola G. Luna, *Resguardos coloniales de Santa Marta y Cartagena y resistencia indígena* (Bogotá: Banco Popular, 1993), 271–73.

14. The main sources for the discussion of the historical geography of the zone and processes of land privatization are the notary records of Santa Marta and Ciénaga, which include documentation on the ejidos of Ciénaga, the subdivision of the indivisos, the negotiation of use rights and property rights, and the transactions between the United Fruit Company and local people (credit and banana purchase agreements, UFCO land purchases, and so on). For an analysis of these notary archives, see Catherine LeGrand and Adriana Mercedes Corso, "Archivos notariales e historias regionales: Nuevas fuentes para el estudio de la zona bananera del Magdalena," *Huellas: Revista de la Universidad del Norte* [Barranquilla] (forthcoming). UFCO land purchases in the region are documented in Colombia, Archivo General de la Nación, Correspondencia de Baldíos, tomo 60, folio 16.

15. In describing local trajectories within the banana region, I intended ultimately to deal with Aracataca as well as Santa Marta and Ciénaga. However, I have not yet been able to consult the notary records of Aracataca (established as a municipality in 1915). Meanwhile, violence in the zone is making research in Aracataca and the rural areas increasingly problematic.

16. See Catherine LeGrand, "Colombian Transformations: Peasants and Wage Laborers in the Santa Marta Banana Zone," *Journal of Peasant Studies* 11, no. 4 (1984): 178–200.

17. See Notaría Primaria de Santa Marta [NPSM], 1915 #242, for the statutes of the *Sociedad de Artesanos y Obreros*. By 1928, apart from the Asociación de Empleados, workers' organizations in Santa Marta included the Sindicato General de Obreros de la "Sociedad Unión," the Union Sindical de Tipógrafos de Magdalena, and the Sociedad de Choferes (*El Estado* [Santa Marta], 5 Jan., 19 Jan., and 30 May 1928).

18. See Guillermo Henríquez Torres, "La arquitectura de Ciénaga" (videocassette); Ismael A. Correa Díaz-Granados, *Música y bailes populares de Ciénaga, Magdalena* (Medellín: Editorial Lealon, 1993); and Tomás Darío Gutiérrez Hino-

josa, *Cultura vallenata: Origen, teoría y pruebas* (Bogotá: Plaza and Janes, 1992), 408–10. Also see Rafael Caneva et al., *Presencia de un pueblo* (Ciénaga: Ediciones Mediodía, 1981); and Ismael A. Correa Díaz-Granados, *Anotaciones para una historia de Ciénaga (Magdalena)* (Medellín: Editorial Lealon, 1996). An excellent description of Ciénaga in 1907 at the beginning of the banana boom is "Informe del Alcalde del Districto de Ciénaga," 30 Sept. 1907, in *Registro del Magdalena,* año 29, no. 1281 (30 Jan. 1908).

19. Ciénaga, Archivo de la Alcaldía y el Consejo Municipal [AACM], Libro de Resoluciones y Peticiones 1920–1929, resoluciónes aprobadas el 22 de agosto, 1920 y el 17 de abril, 1921. The national government responded negatively.

20. This section is based on the notary records of Santa Marta, Ciénaga, and Barranquilla, immigration dossiers in the archive of the municipal council of Ciénaga, the newspaper *El Estado* [Santa Marta] (1920–1935), and interviews with numerous people in Santa Marta, Ciénaga, Aracataca, and Barranquilla.

21. The foreign connections of the de Mier, de Vengoechea, and Díaz-Granados families are revealed in NPSM, 1890 #14, #15; 1900 #62; 1910 #315; and 1900 #82. Gabriel García Márquez's *Strange Pilgrims: Twelve Stories,* trans. Edith Grossman (New York: Alfred A. Knopf, 1993), explores the experiences of Latin Americans traveling and living in Europe; French novelist Valery Larbaud addresses a similar theme in *Fermina Márquez,* trans. Hubert Gibbs (1917; London: Quartet Books, 1988). See also Frédéric Martínez, "La Découverte de l'ancien monde: Les Récits de voyages en orient dans le débat politique colombien (1847–1875)," in *Decouvertes et Explorateurs (Actes du VII Colloque d'Histoire au Présent)* (Bordeaux: L'Harmattan, 1994), 483–91. The notary records of Santa Marta indicate that quite a few well-to-do people from the Colombian coast went back and forth to Europe and North America.

22. See Ciénaga, AACM, Libro para Censo de Extranjeros, 1946; and AACM, Policía Nacional, Sección de Extranjeros, folders of immigration certificates.

23. See Lázaro Diago Julio, *Aracataca . . . Una historia para contar* (Santa Marta: Ediciones Aracataca, forthcoming), 65–66; and "Gabo el otro alquimista," interview with Gabriel García Márquez and his mother Luisa, by Gustavo Tatis Guerra, *El Universal Dominical* [Cartagena] 329 (3 May 1992): 8. *Cachaco* was the derogatory term used by people from the Caribbean coast to refer to people from the mountainous interior of Colombia.

24. On these immigrants, see NPSM, 1890 #17; 1895 #9, 11, 18; 1899 #61; 1900 #12, 13, 16, 23, 43, 46, 83; 1910 #248, 271, 313; and 1915 #163. Also Notaría Unica de Ciénaga [NUC] 1895 #1, 34, 46, 75; 1899 #18; 1900 #2; and 1910 #168, 169. For a stimulating discussion of the incorporation of individual Europeans into Colombian society, see Malcolm Deas, "La influencia inglesa—y otras influencias—en Colombia (1880–1930)," in *La Nueva Historia de Colombia,* ed. Alvaro Tirado Mejía, vol. 3 (Bogotá: Planeta Colombiana, 1989), 161–82.

25. See Louise Fawcett de Posada, "Libaneses, palestinos y sirios en Colombia," *Documentos* 9 (Barranquilla: CERES, Universidad del Norte, August 1991);

Isaac S. and Suzanne A. Emmanuel, *History of the Jews of the Netherlands Antilles,* vol. 2 (Cincinnati: American Jewish Archives, 1970), 822–38; and Guillermo Henríquez Torres, *El misterio de los Buendía,* vol. 1 (Barranquilla: Editorial Antillas, 1996), 66–81. On the Italians, see also N U C 1890 #53; 1892 #23, 41, 55; and 1899 #32, 49. On the Jews, N U C 1895 #21; and N P S M 1895 #27.

26. Ciénaga, A A C M, Libro de voluntarios inscritos para la defensa de la patria en el conflicto internacional colombo-peruano, Sept. 21, 1932. This book lists the occupations and birthplaces of Ciénaga's men who volunteered to fight in the war against Peru. It indicates that many railroad workers, masons, carpenters, shoemakers, sweetmakers, printers, and store employees were from Barranquilla. The Libro de entradas y salidas de extranjeros 1930–1933 reveals that many people went back and forth between Ciénaga and Barranquilla, which raises the question of connections between the labor movements in Barranquilla and the banana zone.

27. On Barranquilla, see Theodore E. Nichols, *Tres puertos de Colombia: Estudio sobre el desarrollo de Cartagena, Santa Marta y Barranquilla* (Bogotá: Banco Popular, 1973); Eduardo Posada Carbó, *Una invitación a la historia de Barranquilla* (Bogotá: Fondo Editorial CEREC, 1987); Manuel Rodríguez Becera and Jorge A. Restrepo Restrepo, "Los empresarios extranjeros de Barranquilla 1820–1990," in *El caribe colombiano: Selección de textos históricos,* ed. Gustavo Bell Lemus (Barranquilla: Ediciones Uninorte, 1988), 139–82; and Sergio Paolo Solano de las Aguas and Jorge Enrique Conde Calderón, *Elite empresarial y desarrollo industrial en Barranquilla, 1875–1930* (Barranquilla: Uniatlántico, 1993).

28. Interview with José Lobo Romero and Sara Romero de Lobo, Barranquilla, 31 July 1994. This raises the question of the development of domestic markets for export crops like coffee, bananas, and so on.

29. An excellent economic history of the Caribbean coast of Colombia, which includes a stimulating section on the U F C O banana zone, is Eduardo Posada Carbó, *The Colombian Caribbean: A Regional History, 1870–1950* (Oxford: Oxford University Press, 1996).

30. *El Estado,* 13 Jan., 4 Feb., and 30 Mar. 1928, for example.

31. Reports on Sandino appeared in *El Estado,* 11, 12, 14, 18, 19, 20, 21, and 23 Jan.; 25 and 29 Feb.; 29 Mar.; and 18 Oct. 1928. Although *El Estado* (the only newspaper from the zone for which archives exist) never criticized the U F C O directly, the editors may have done so obliquely by lauding Sandino, occasionally republishing articles from Bogotano newspapers critical of the U F C O, and editorializing against the "imperialist" designs of the United States in the Pan-American conference of 1928.

32. See *El Estado,* 13, 14, and 15 June; and 1 and 18 Aug. 1928.

33. Advertisements for these products appeared in the Santa Marta newspaper *El Estado* during 1928.

34. On students leaving Santa Marta to study, see, for example, *El Estado,* 16, 25, and 26 Jan. 1928. Also multiple interviews.

35. Interview with Ramón Illán Bacca, Barranquilla, 25 July 1994. On the Brus-

sels colony, see Guillermo Henríquez Torres, "Ciénaga: Entre la literatura y la historia," Proyecto INFIP/UTM para la Recuperación del Patrimonio Cultural del Departamento del Magdalena, Ediciones de la Organización de Estados Ibero-americanos para la Educación, la Ciéncia y la Cultura, 1986 (mimeographed), chap. 14.

36. See Américo Carnicelli, *Historia de la masonería colombiana, 1833–1940*, vol. 2 (Bogotá: Cooperativa Nacional de Artes Gráficas, 1975), 45; Muy Respetable Gran Logia "Benjamín Herrera" con sede en Santa Marta, *Constitución y estatutos* (Barranquilla: Litografía Dovel, 1984); and Respetable Logia Simbólica Benemerita y Centenaria, "Unión Fraternal," no. 45-1, Ciénaga (Magdalena), 1991–1992 (pamphlet). An excellent think piece on Freemasonry is Jean-Pierre Bastian, "Una ausencia notoria: La francmasonería en la historiografía mexicanista," *Historia Mexicana* 54, no. 3 (Jan.–Mar. 1995): 439–60.

37. Interview with Tomás Cipriano Zavaleta Herrera, Gran Masón de Ciénaga, 14 July 1994; and Archivo de la Respetable Logia "Unión Fraternal," no. 45-1, Ciénaga, minutes of the meetings of 17 and 24 Mar. 1929.

38. See *Estatutos de la Sociedad de Agricultores de la Zona Bananera* (Ciénaga: J. V. Mogollon i Cia, 1919); and *El Estado*, 6 Feb., 26 and 30 Mar.; and 2 Apr. 1928; and 3 and 28 July 1931.

39. *El Estado*, 12 Jan., 20 Aug., and 16 Oct. 1930. Founded in Chicago in 1905 as a club to "recapture some of the friendly spirit among businessmen in small communities," Rotary changed its name to the International Association of Rotary Clubs seven years later. The first Colombian Rotary was established in Bogotá in 1926–1927; by 1930 Rotarians were active in seventeen Latin American countries, including Honduras, Bolivia, and Paraguay. See *Historical Review of Rotary* (Evanston, Ill.: Rotary International, 1996); and Emily Rosenberg, *Spreading the American Dream: American Economic and Cultural Expansion, 1890–1945* (New York: Farrar, Straus and Giroux, 1982), 108–12. Today both Rotary and Lions Clubs are important in the old banana region and Barranquilla.

40. In 1923 the Colombian government established a Comisión de Baldíos in the Magdalena zone to protect public lands against usurpation and enforce water laws with the long-term aim of creating a national banana producers' cooperative (Catherine LeGrand, "El conflicto de las bananeras," in Tirado Mejía, *La Nueva Historia de Colombia*, 3:198). Later reports of commissions of inquiry were published in Colombia, *Memoria del Ministerio de Industrias al Congreso Nacional* (Bogotá: Imprenta Nacional, 1929); and *El Tiempo* [Bogotá], 15 Nov. 1930. See also *Informes que rindió a la honorable Cámara de Representantes la comisión designada para visitar la zona bananera del Magdalena* (Bogotá: Imprenta Nacional, 1935).

41. In the endeavor to make sense of the social layouts of the various subregions of the banana zone, the internalization of the foreign, and the expression of social distinctions, a visit to the local cemetery is revealing. The size, construction, and decoration of the mausoleums and monuments, the geneological information, and

the way in which a cemetery is laid out tell a great deal about the differentiations important to people in a particular time and place. In Santa Marta one finds the great old families most prominent, occasional marriages to people with foreign names, and separate spaces for the interment of Catholics, Jews, and Masons. There are two cemeteries: the "old cemetery," in which people are buried above the ground in traditional Latin American style, and the "modern cemetery," in which people are buried in the ground, U.S.-style. In Ciénaga, Jews, Catholics, and Masons were always buried in the same place, suggesting that this was perhaps a more open or tolerant society; there are two cemeteries in Ciénaga as well, but here the division is between the rich and the poor. For an innovative attempt to explore the semiotics of cemeteries (and embassies) in the context of U.S. influence abroad, see Ron Robin, *Enclaves of America: The Rhetoric of American Political Architecture Abroad, 1900–1965* (Princeton, N.J.: Princeton University Press, 1992).

42. Interview with Javier Moscarella Varela, Santa Marta, 20 July 1994. See also Jorge Yepes Henao, "Propuesta cultural de apoyo a las programas de la zona bananera," Santa Marta, Fundación Social de UNIBAN, 1994 (mimeographed). UNIBAN is one of the two associations of large Colombian banana producers presently based in Santa Marta.

43. Luise White's articles on Africa provide methodological insights for interpreting cultural responses to foreign-induced local transformations. See White, "Cars Out of Place: Vampires, Technology, and Labor in East and Central Africa," *Representations* 43 (summer 1993): 27–50; and idem, " 'They Could Make Their Victims Dull': Genders and Genres, Fantasies and Cures in Colonial Southern Uganda," *American Historical Review* 100, no. 5 (Dec. 1995): 1379–1402. Also see Candace Slater, " 'All That Glitters': Contemporary Amazonian Gold Miners' Tales," *Comparative Studies in Society and History* 36 (1994): 720–42.

44. Some say don Manuel was not a womanizer, but that he built a scientific laboratory in his country house where he did experiments with test tubes and brightly colored liquids (Interviews with Manuel Varela González de Villaumbrosia, grandson of don Manuel, Ciénaga, 17 July 1994, and others). See also Guillermo Henríquez Torres, "Mitos y leyendas de tierra y agua de los pueblos de la Ciénaga Grande del Magdalena," Ciénaga, 1986 (mimeographed), 5–9; and Carlos M. Domínguez Ojeada, *Mitos y leyendas de los pueblos de la Ciénaga Grande de Santa Marta* (Santa Marta: Ediciones Aracataca, 1991). Michael Taussig has written on devil pacts in western Colombia in *The Devil and Commodity Fetishism in South America* (Chapel Hill: University of North Carolina Press, 1980) and "The Sun Gives without Receiving: An Old Story," *Comparative Studies in Society and History* 37, no. 2 (Apr. 1995): 368–98. For interpretations of devil pacts in other times and places, see Fernando Cervantes, *The Devil in the New World: The Impact of Diabolism in New Spain* (New Haven, Conn.: Yale University Press, 1994); Jeffrey L. Gould, *To Lead as Equals: Rural Protest and Political Consciousness in Chinandega, Nicaragua, 1912–1979* (Chapel Hill: University of

North Carolina Press, 1990), 29–31, 44–45, 120, 276; Marc Edelman, "Landlords and the Devil: Class, Ethnic, and Gender Dimensions of Central American Peasant Narratives, *Cultural Anthropology* 9, no. 1 (Feb. 1994): 58–93; and Filomeno V. Aguilar Jr., "Phantoms of Capitalism and Sugar Production Relations in a Colonial Philippine Island" (Ph.D. diss., Cornell University, 1992), 312–18.

45. Interview with Elijio Valiente, Sevilla (Ciénaga), 11 Nov. 1988.

46. Interview with José Lobo Romero, Barranquilla, 31 July 1994. His father's home village was Palmar de Varela (Atlántico). On everyday occult beliefs and practices in Aracataca, see Diago Julio, *Aracataca,* 58–62; and Gabriel García Márquez, "Vuelta a la semilla," in *Hijos ilustres de Aracataca,* ed. Rafael Darío Jiménez P. (Santa Marta: Ediciones Aracataca, 1994), 60–65. Gutiérrez Hinojosa, *Cultura vallenata;* Enrique Pérez Arbeláez, *La cuna del porro: Insinuación folklórica del departamento del Magdalena en Colombia,* Separata de la *Revista de Folklore,* segunda época, 1, no. 1 (Bogotá: Editorial Antares, 1953); Gerardo and Alicia Reichel-Dolmatoff, *The People of Aritama: The Cultural Personality of a Colombian Mestizo Village* (London: Routledge and Kegan Paul, 1961); and Francisco Rada Ortíz, *Historia de un pueblo acordeonero* (Barranquilla: Editorial Mejoras, 1979), describe local religious beliefs, healing practices, and *magia popular,* including devil pacts and relations with animals, in the department of Magdalena.

47. Interview with Alvaro Navarro Girón, Barranquilla, 3 Aug. 1994.

48. Zavaleta interview; interview with Guillermo Henríquez Torres, Ciénaga, 13 July 1994; and other interviews. A glance at the Gnostic books shows sections on how to cure devil possession, how to cure the evil eye, and so on—that is, connections between Gnosticism and popular curing practices. In southwestern Colombia (Cali, Popayan, and some smaller towns), there are Gnostic healing clinics. See Fernando Urrea Giraldo, "Procesos de democratización y prácticas populares de salud: Reflexiones a partir del curanderismo urbano," in *Colombia: Democracía y sociedad,* ed. Nora Segura de Camacho (Bogotá: FESCOL, 1988), 246–50.

49. Interview with Fabio Zambrano Pantoja, Bogotá, 5 Aug. 1994. See also idem, "Historiografía sobre los movimientos sociales en Colombia: Siglo XIX," in *La historia al final del milenio: Ensayos de historiografía colombiana y latinoamericana,* ed. Bernardo Tovar Zambrano, vol. 1 (Bogotá: Editorial Universidad Nacional, 1994), 147–81.

50. On the international spiritualist movements, see Joy Dixon, "Gender, Politics, and Culture in the New Age: Theosophy in England, 1880–1935" (Ph.D. diss., Rutgers University, 1993); Frederick Crews, "The Consolation of Theosophy," *New York Review of Books* 43, no. 14 (19 Sept. 1996): 26–30; and Richard Milner, "Charles Darwin and Associates, Ghostbusters," *Scientific American* 275, no. 4 (Oct. 1996): 96–101. Their Latin American offshoots are explored in Frederick B. Pike, *The Politics of the Miraculous in Peru: Haya de la Torre and the Spiritualist Tradition* (Lincoln: University of Nebraska Press, 1986); David J. Hess, *Spiritists and Scientists: Ideology, Spiritism, and Brazilian Culture* (University Park: Penn-

sylvania State University Press, 1991); Donald C. Hodges, *Sandino's Communism: Spiritual Politics for the Twenty-first Century* (Austin: University of Texas Press, 1992); Diana DeG. Brown, *Umbanda: Religion and Politics in Urban Brazil* (New York: Columbia University Press, 1994), 15–25, 62; and Julie Skurski, "The Ambiguities of Authenticity in Latin America: *Doña Bárbara* and the Construction of National Identity," *Poetics Today* 15, no. 4 (winter 1994): 624–37. For Colombia, see Gonzalo Sánchez G., *"Los bolsheviques del Líbano" (Tolima) 1928 (Crisis mundial, capitalismo y rebelión rural en Colombia)* (Bogotá: Ediciones El Mohan, 1976), 41–44, 59; Eduardo Santa, *Arrieros y fundadores: Aspectos de la colonización antioqueña*, 2d ed. (Ibagué: Instituto Tolimense de Cultura, 1984), 93–102; Carlos Uribe Celis, *Los años veinte en Colombia: Ideología y cultura* (Bogotá: Ediciones Aurora, 1985), 81–84; and Germán Castro Caycedo, *La bruja: Coca, política y demonio* (Bogotá: Planeta Colombiana, 1994), 203–9. Mary W. Helms, *Ulysses' Sail: An Ethnographic Odyssey of Power, Knowledge, and Geographical Distance* (Princeton, N.J.: Princeton University Press, 1988), sheds light on the human tendency to associate knowledge and power with faraway places.

51. See Roberto Herrera Soto and Rafael Romero Castañeda, *La zona bananera del Magdalena: Historia y léxico* (Bogotá: Instituto Caro y Cuervo, 1979).

52. Interview with Javier Moscarella Varela and Clinton Ramírez C., Santa Marta, 10 Aug. 1994. See also Moscarella Varela, "Ciénaga hacia el siglo XXI" (mimeographed).

53. These writings are collected in the Documentation Center at the Instituto de Formación Técnica Profesional and in Ciénaga's Casa de la Cultura. See also Javier Moscarella, ed., *La cultura popular en el Caribe,* tomo 1, *Ciénaga* (Bogotá: Organización de Estados Iberoamericanos, n.d.); Consejo Regional de Planificación de la Costa Atlántica, *Mapa cultural del caribe colombiano* (Bogotá: Tercer Mundo, 1993); and Alfredo Correa de Andreis and Javier Moscarella Varela, "La cultura: Clave para el desarrollo social del sur del Ciénaga, Magdalena" (tesis de maestría, Universidad del Norte, 1990).

54. Javier Moscarella, "La subregión del Valle de Cienaguas (Magdalena) y su conformación como provincias," *Boletín de Ordenamiento Territorial* 2 (Apr. 1992): 9–12. On the process of decentralization, see Orlando Fals Borda, ed., *La insurgencia de las provincias: Hacía un nuevo ordenamiento territorial para Colombia* (Bogotá: Siglo XXI, 1988); and idem, "El reordenamiento territorial: Itinerario de una idea," *Análisis Político* 20 (Sept.–Dec. 1993): 90–98.

55. Javier Moscarella, "Ecología y región: La historia profunda de Cienaguas" (talk presented at "Sábados Sociológicos," Asociación de Sociólogos Colombianos, Sección Costa Atlántica, Barranquilla, 27 July 1994). On another Colombian regionalist movement with cultural and ecological dimensions, see Arturo Escobar, "Cultural Politics and Biological Diversity: State, Capital, and Social Movements in the Pacific Coast of Colombia," in *Between Resistance and Revolution: Cultural Politics and Social Protest,* ed. Richard G. Fox and Orin Starn (New Brunswick, N.J.: Rutgers University Press, 1997).

56. Interviews with Elías Eslait Russo, Ciénaga, 23 July 1994; Alfredo Correa de Andreis, Barranquilla, 25 July 1994; and Lucy Porras Rosa, El Rodadero (Santa Marta), 8 Aug. 1994. The impetus for the commemorative statue came from local members of the Movimiento Obrero Independiente Revolucionario aided by some people associated with the Casa de la Cultura. One individual involved in the project told me the artist had made the statue to be sent to Haiti to commemorate that country's independence, but because time and funds were short, they convinced him to send it to Ciénaga instead. This fact is not widely known in the banana zone.

57. Interview, El Retén (Aracataca), 12 Aug. 1993. A fascinating study of the women-led land invasions is Lucy Porras Rosa, "La mujer y la lucha por la subsistencia en la zona bananera del Magdalena (El Retén-Aracataca), 1947–1975" (tesis de maestría, Universidad Externado de Colombia, 1990).

58. Interview with Rafael Darío Jiménez, Santa Marta, 19 July 1994.

59. See John Tomlinson, *Cultural Imperialism: A Critical Introduction* (London: Pinter Publishers, 1991).

60. See, in anthropology, William Roseberry, *Anthropologies and Histories: Essays in Culture, History, and Political Economy* (New Brunswick, N.J.: Rutgers University Press, 1989); Akhil Gupta and James Ferguson, "Beyond 'Culture': Space, Identity, and the Politics of Difference," *Cultural Anthropology* 7, no. 1 (Feb. 1992): 6–23; in history, Michael Geyer and Charles Bright, "World History in a Global Age," *American Historical Review* 100, no. 4 (Oct. 1995): 1034–60; Gyan Prakash, "Can the 'Subaltern' Ride? A Reply to O'Hanlan and Washbrook," *Comparative Studies in Society and History* 34 (1992): 168–84; in geography, Anne Gilbert, "The New Regional Geography in English and French-Speaking Countries," *Progress in Human Geography* 12, no. 2 (June 1988): 108–28; Doreen Massey, *Space, Place, and Gender* (Minneapolis: University of Minnesota Press, 1994); Doreen Massey and Pat Jess, eds., *A Place in the World? Places, Cultures, and Globalization* (Oxford: Open University, 1995); and in literature, Doris Sommer, "The Places of History: Regionalism Revisited in Latin America," *Modern Language Quarterly* 57, no. 2 (June 1996): 119–27.

61. Sherry B. Ortner, "Resistance and the Problem of Ethnographic Refusal," *Comparative Studies in Society and History* 37 (1995): 176.

62. Sommer, "The Places of History," 119–21.

63. Massey, *Space, Place, and Gender*, 170, 154.

64. John Soluri's "Landscape and Livelihood: Toward an Agroecological History of Banana Growing in Honduras, 1870–1975" (Ph.D. diss., University of Michigan, 1998) sheds new light on the UFCO's scientific rationale for its modernizing project. A fascinating visual representation is the collection of 10,400 UFCO photographs of its Latin American operations, located in Harvard Business School's Baker Library. Also revealing are *Unifruitco*, the magazine published by and for UFCO's North American employees working in Latin America, and the descriptions of the Magdalena banana zone penned by Rockefeller Foundation

doctors involved in anti-hookworm and infectious jaundice campaigns there from 1927 to 1933. The latter reports are deposited in the International Health Division records of the Rockefeller Archive Center in Tarrytown, New York.

65. Theda Skocpol, "Bringing the State Back In: Strategies of Analysis in Current Research," in *Bringing the State Back In,* ed. Peter B. Evans, Dietrich Rueschemeyer, and Theda Skocpol (Cambridge: Cambridge University Press, 1985), 3–37. A good example of this is Steve Striffler, "In the Shadow of State and Capital: The United Fruit Company and the Politics of Agricultural Restructuring in Ecuador, 1900–1995 (Ph.D. diss., New School for Social Research, 1997).

66. The reference here is to Ricardo Salvatore's essay in this volume.

67. J. Nicholas Entrikin, "Place and Region," *Progress in Human Geography* 18, no. 2 (1994): 229. Filomeno V. Aguilar Jr. masterfully challenges this dichotomization in "Phantoms of Capitalism."

68. Ricardo Salvatore, personal communication, 6 Dec. 1995.

69. Pioneering writings on memory in Latin American history include Gould, *To Lead as Equals;* Bourgois, *Ethnicity at Work;* and Mary Ann Mahony, "The World Cacao Made: Society, Politics, and History in Southern Bahia, Brazil, 1822–1919" (Ph.D. diss., Yale University, 1993), which sets novelist Jorge Amado in the context of local contests over power and history. See also Nancy P. Appelbaum, "Remembering Riosucio: Race, Region, and Community in Colombia, 1850–1950" (Ph.D. diss., University of Wisconsin, 1997); and Lessie Jo Frazier, "Memory and State Violence in Chile: A Historical Ethnography of Tarapacá, 1890–1995" (Ph.D. diss., University of Michigan, 1997), which explores memories of workers' movements in a foreign mining enclave. For Santa Marta and Ciénaga, there are many local writings, most of which can only be found in the immediate region—in the Centro de Documentación in Ciénaga; the Casas de la Cultura in Santa Marta, Ciénaga, and Aracataca; and peoples' houses. Much has been made of the oral tradition of the Caribbean coast, but even in relatively small towns the long existence of print culture must not be overlooked. This takes the form of broadsides, local newspapers, and *microhistorias,* often directly linked to oral traditions, similar to those described by Mexican historian Luis González y González in *Invitación a la microhistoria* (Mexico City: Sepsetentas, 1973) and creatively used by Colombian sociologist Orlando Fals Borda in *Historia doble de la costa,* 4 vols. (Bogotá: Carlos Valencia Editores, 1980, 1981, 1984, 1986). Descriptions of community and religious festivals appear in the Archivo Eclesiástico of the Bishopric of Santa Marta.

70. Interview with Javier Moscarella Varela, Ciénaga, 10 Aug. 1996.

71. On this approach to cultural identity, see Stuart Hall, "Cultural Identity and Diaspora," in *Identity: Community, Culture, Difference,* ed. Jonathan Rutherford (London: Lawrence and Wishart, 1990), 222–37.

Thomas Miller Klubock

From Welfare Capitalism
to the Free Market in Chile

Gender, Culture, and Politics in the Copper Mines

In May 1983, the Chilean copper miners' federation, the Confederación de los Trabajadores del Cobre, called for a general strike in Chile's mines and for a day of national protest against the military dictatorship of Augusto Pinochet. Workers in El Teniente, the world's largest underground copper mine and one of Chile's two major mines, engaged in a wildcat strike, and members of the mining community mobilized to protest the regime's neoliberal economic policies and repression of organized labor.[1] The El Teniente strike built on a long tradition of working-class militancy in the copper mines. Following the rapid decline of the nitrate industry after the First World War, copper exports became the motor of the Chilean economy, providing close to 90 percent of its foreign earnings by 1970. As a result of the strategic location of copper in the economy, copper miners' strikes had singular impact on national events for much of the century. Strikes during the 1930s fueled the rise of the left-center Popular Front coalition and then contributed to its demise in 1947. Similarly, miners' general strikes and protests throughout the 1960s sparked a more general movement for the nationalization of the U.S.-owned mines, growing working-class discontent with the social reformist government of Christian Democrat Eduardo Frei, and the election of Socialist Salvador Allende's Popular Unity government in 1970.

In the El Teniente mine, women played a prominent role in workers' strikes and protests. Women walked the picket line, did battle with police, and met with presidents, attesting to the strength and cohesiveness of mining communities as a basis for collective action and combative working-class politics. This paper explains the remarkable solidarity between men and women, and the mining community's militancy during strikes, as a result of the gendered process of class formation in the mining enclave. The El Teniente mining community's class identity was structured by the corporate welfare strategies and the gender ideology of domesticity introduced by the North American Braden Copper Company, a Kennecott subsidiary.[2] In addition, the composition of El Teniente's working-class community was informed by and articulated with the formation of a corporatist welfare state that drew on the model of the North American copper companies' labor policies after 1938. Both capital and the state sought to build a stable and trained working class that would be prepared for labor in emerging industries and for the responsibilities of citizenship in a modern nation-state. In the copper mines, the male-headed nuclear family was to be the pillar on which this imagined community of disciplined citizens and workers would rest.[3]

Welfare capitalism and state welfare policies rotated on the axis of gender; the reformation and reorganization of working-class sexuality and family life constituted the basis for the efforts of both North American capital and the state to establish the legitimacy of their authority. By promoting new aspirations to social mobility and middle-class domesticity, the copper company, with the support of the state, sought to transform the lifestyles of working-class men and women and to incorporate them into new rhythms of work, a state-directed system of labor relations and social welfare, and a national political community based on the alliance of urban workers, the middle class, and industrial entrepreneurs. Men were offered a family wage that enabled them to exercise the authority of the wage-earning head of household and to control both the labor and sexuality of their wives and children. Women were provided with a series of guarantees in marriage: economic security, rights to their husbands' wages and benefits, education for their children, and protection from male violence. In addition, for both men and women, domesticity and the nuclear family offered access to a new universe of desires, tastes, and aspirations associated with middle-class comforts and consumption.

The establishment of a working-class community based on the nuclear family in the El Teniente mining camps, while securing a stable labor force for the company, backfired in two ways. First, men and women began to contrast the paternalist promises of social mobility with the harsh conditions of life and work in the mine and its camps. The state and the company offered miners, as both workers and citizens, the right to a family wage and a series of social benefits. Beginning in the 1930s, the mining community organized collective movements to make the rights enshrined in the gender ideology of domesticity a material reality. Miners and their families articulated demands to the copper company and the state in the language of social and economic rights. Second, the formation of a stable and cohesive working-class community in the mining enclave lent great strength to miners' collective movements. Women's economic dependence on men within the nuclear family provided new forms of solidarity between the sexes that emerged in community mobilizations during miners' strikes. Women came to identify their interests with their husbands and to organize around their rights and prerogatives as mothers and wives.[4] Thus, the working-class culture of the mining enclave and miners' militant class politics were shaped by both the gender ideology of domesticity and an associated language of rights derived from corporate and state social welfare systems.

In 1973, the bloody military coup led by Augusto Pinochet brought an end to the entwined processes of class and state formation defined by welfare capitalism and the welfare state. The replacement of corporate capitalism with a neoliberal economic ideology that was also transmitted through North American agents produced radical transformations in working-class culture and gender identities. The military regime dismantled the corporatist welfare state, set out to privatize the copper mines, and imposed a set of orthodox economic policies designed by a group of economists, known as "los Chicago boys," who had been trained in the United States. The expansion of the "market" economy, combined with the severe repression of organized labor and the political Left, undermined the material underpinnings of the mining community and destabilized gender relations within miners' families. As the structures of the mining community and nuclear family underwent drastic changes, women acquired increased economic and sexual autonomy. At the same time, the bases for powerful working-class community movements in the mining enclave were weakened, and miners found it increasingly difficult to challenge the hegemonic ideology of free-market economics. While miners and their families invoked their historic rights to economic and social security in the strikes and protests that erupted in 1983, their capacity to defend these rights was crippled by the fragmentation of their community, changes in the cultural construction of gender, and the fracturing of their class identity.

Gender and Welfare Capitalism

During the 1920s, the Braden Copper Company experienced a rapid spurt of growth in response to expanding world demand for copper. The company installed new mills in the concentrating plant and a modern smelter that greatly increased its capacity to process copper ore. The company's efforts to increase production inside the mine were impeded, however, by an unstable workforce that refused to accommodate to the rhythms of labor in a modern industrial enterprise and to submit to the company's disciplinary regime. Chilean miners, steeped in traditions of mobility, frequently deserted the mine after short stints to seek work in agriculture, burgeoning urban industries, ports, and even the nitrate mines.

Since the boom and bust cycles of Chile's agricultural and mining export economies of the nineteenth century, a significant proportion of Chilean rural, urban, port, and mine workers were itinerant *peones* who traveled the length of the country in search of work opportunities. In addition, many miners who came to El Teniente hoped to accumulate some savings and then purchase a small plot of land in the countryside or begin their own business in petty commerce in rural towns or urban centers. Few intended to stay long in the copper mine. In 1919, one North American supervisor noted that "[the miner] who lasts months is a veteran." [5] In 1922, out of a labor force of 4,638, 2,256 workers worked only two to twelve weeks in the mine before leaving their jobs. Absenteeism rates were high, as workers frequently deserted their jobs and the miners' celebration of *San Lunes* (Saint Monday) continually frustrated company supervisors. [6]

In response to its failure to build a stable and disciplined labor force, the Braden Copper Company implemented a set of paternalist social welfare policies. The company began to pay workers high wages relative to other sectors of the economy and offered workers production bonuses, work incentives, and a series of benefits, including health care and pensions. In addition, Braden created a welfare department, a center for education and social work, vocational schools, a newspaper for workers, and a network of social organizations that included soccer clubs and recreational clubs that held dances and provided workers with theater, music, and cinema. [7] Braden's corporate welfare scheme was the first introduced in Chile and reflected new management strategies that had been developed in the United States and Europe. The North American company's social welfare system provided a model both for private employers in Chile's coal and nitrate industries and for the state, as concern with "the social question" grew during the 1920s.

The company's social welfare program focused particularly on relations between men and women in the camps and on a gender ideology of domesticity. The welfare department felt that workers would tend to remain in the mine and abandon their disruptive habits if they married, lived with their families, and participated in a wide range of company-sponsored and approved social and cultural activities. It thus embarked on a campaign to transform the floating population of single workers and single women in the camps into a permanent and married workforce.

In 1922, the company welfare department proposed building more housing for married workers, since workers who had left families behind usually left the mine after a short time.[8] It also suggested buying a plot of land and constructing houses for workers, so that, according to one company manager, "our workmen would thus become more or less permanent, which is, in the main, what we are trying to arrive at." [9] The company believed that single workers, who composed the bulk of the workforce, tended to drink, gamble, fight, and eventually prove more willing to go out on strike, while married miners, more dependent on their wages and jobs, were more constant and reliable. According to the company, workers who married in El Teniente or who brought their wives and children with them tended to stay on for years, dependent on the job in the mine to support their families. A single worker or a married worker whose family lived elsewhere had more freedom to come and go, to risk unemployment in strikes, and to engage in the "vices" condemned by the company.

According to the North American company's logic, single women, who migrated to the mine in search of work as domestic servants in the camps' pensions and workers' hostels or as sex workers in El Teniente's clandestine economy of bars and brothels, contributed to unstable domestic arrangements, unhealthy recreational activities, and labor problems. A 1920 study of El Teniente noted that many "disorders of diverse kinds" were manifold in the camps because "the feminine element is not the best." Living or sexual arrangements between men and women outside of matrimony, and the presence of prostitutes or a transient population of women in the camps, were thought to contribute to other supposed vices like drinking and gambling. Workers were late or missed their shifts, the company felt, because of the influence of these women.[10]

In fact, men and women in El Teniente came from a lengthy tradition of informal sexual/romantic relationships and "consensual unions." Throughout the nineteenth century, women, as well as men, had participated in Chile's labor migrations. They left rural areas for *ranchos* on the outskirts of rural towns and mining camps and in the suburbs of urban centers, where they established their economic independence by engaging in petty commerce, selling fruit, baked goods, and alcohol. In addition, they transformed their homes into places of entertainment, bars, and brothels, and took in boarders to supplement their incomes. Women also worked as laundresses, seamstresses, and domestic servants, as well as prostitutes. Many women headed their own households and engaged in fluid, informal, and transient relationships with the large population of itinerant male peones. Few nineteenth-century working-class women lived in male-headed households.[11]

Thus women became the targets of the company's social workers, whose aim was to "educate and form good housewives so that they will not be a burden first on their fathers and then on their husbands." [12] During the first decades of operation, miners had frequently complained that women abandoned the mining camps. By providing women with recreational and educational opportunities, as well as attention from social workers, the company hoped to keep them in the camps and to train them to maintain model households with their husbands. While vocational schools for male workers provided classes in engineering, electronics, carpentry, and other "industrial arts" in order to prepare them for work in the modern industry, the vocational school for women offered classes in household cleanliness, clothes making, cooking, household budgeting, and home economics. Trained housewives would help stretch workers' wages and contribute to manufacturing a stable and "hygienic" domestic environment for their husbands.

The North American company's welfare system provided workers with the promise of social mobility and access to a life of middle-class domesticity. Workers who took vocational classes, engaged in disciplined work, and formed families could hope for high earnings and bonuses, promotions, and a life of material security and comfort, as well as a good future for their children. The company welfare department perceived women to be important targets for its messages of domesticity, consumption, and social mobility. The company paper and social workers devoted their efforts to inculcating in the camps' women the new values and aspirations of middle-class domestic life.

The Braden Copper Company's concern with regulating relations between men and women was revealed in regulations it implemented in 1917 requiring workers who lived with women to be married. The company, after studying "the advantages for order and discipline in the mine, ordered in the most resolute and determined manner the legitimization of the civil state of all its employees." [13] The regulation prohibited families or couples without a civil marriage license from occupying company housing. In order to control sexual activity in the camps, police frequently searched workers' lodgings late at night. Until the 1950s, the company implemented a policy of forcing a worker found alone with a woman either to marry or to leave his job.

The company also established a "family allowance," which became a crucial stimulus for men and women to enter into marriages. The family allowance was a bonus paid to married workers with children. The company intended the allowance to help workers with families meet the challenges of a rapidly rising cost of living and to serve as an inducement to create families. Throughout the 1920s and 1930s male workers and their female partners frequently entered into legal marriages in order to legitimize their children and thus qualify for the bonus. The miner Pedro Antonio Pinto and his partner, for example, married "to legitimize our son because it is necessary so that he can receive the family allowance and so that the conceded benefit be granted and our son's legitimacy be legally accepted." [14] The family allowance provided male workers with the economic resources to maintain their families and domestic arrangements based on the exclusion of women from the labor market.

The family allowance became increasingly important to both men and women, because women enjoyed few possibilities for wage labor and had limited educational opportunities. Women were excluded from high-paying jobs in the mining company, both below and above ground, and their education prepared them only for roles as housewives and mothers. Married women could and did engage in informal labor—taking in boarders, sewing, and laundry, or selling homemade bread and sweets. And single women could work as domestics. However, the money women earned in these activities was a fraction of male workers' lowest wages and insufficient to support a family. Women's exclusion from the formal labor market, combined with the bifurcated educational system and the family allowance, served as considerable encouragement to embrace marriage as one of the only viable strategies for subsistence.

Corporate Welfare and the Welfare State

In its efforts to reorganize gender relations and form nuclear families in El Teniente, the company received significant help from the state. During the 1920s, in response to the "social question" and a period of tumultuous labor unrest following the First World War, Chilean governments became increasingly involved in the establishment of what could be termed a proto–welfare state. This process accelerated under the governments of the Popular Front (1938–1948), which oversaw the process of import-substitution industrialization and the implementation of social reforms that were intended to benefit the urban middle and working classes. Since 1904, when the North American company began operations, the state had refused to intervene in the affairs of the copper mine, except to send troops to quell periodic swells of labor unrest. With the election of Radical Party leader Pedro Aguirre Cerda in 1938, however, the state began to regulate both labor relations in the mine and gender relations in the camps. After 1939, labor inspectors, the minister of labor, and even the president entered El Teniente's camps to review working and living conditions and to enforce labor and social legislation. Correspondingly, the local court began to play a more interventionist role in working-class family and domestic life.[15]

Reformist politicians from Chile's Radical Party and heads of Chilean industry had expressed a great deal of interest in the Braden Copper Company's social welfare programs since the early 1920s. In 1922, for example, Pedro Aguirre Cerda (sixteen years before his election to the presidency) wrote Braden as a representative of the coal industry to inquire about the company's welfare policies. Aguirre Cerda was particularly interested in Braden's claims that "welfare work tends materially to reduce strikes." [16] The company supplied Aguirre Cerda with a description of its welfare program and its supposed benefits. Because of the welfare department's activities, company representatives argued, "the worker lives better, his family is well constituted, he earns more, is better educated and more cultured. He and his family are more healthy, understand better and develop the spirit of saving, and is a better citizen." [17] And most importantly, corporate welfare's benefits were obvious in the lack of "absenteeism or social crimes." [18]

The copper company itself advocated the adoption of its social welfare policies at a national level and the construction of a state welfare system. In 1922, for example, the company commented favorably on deputy Emilio Tizzani's visit to the mine and to the Academia de Extensión Cultural de Teniente "C" as an important step in winning politicians' support for state welfare programs and for state intervention in labor-capital relations.[19] El Teniente argued for the need for legislation to regulate and harmonize labor relations: "state intervention is absolutely indispensable to solve [strikes]. The absence of special laws about these matters means that in our country strikes are an endemic and national evil." State intervention in labor-capital relations and social legislation was the solution to worker conflicts. Thus the company proposed that the state establish new programs to "inculcate in the citizens the habit of cleanliness, provide hygienic and cheap housing, control the quality of food, combat alcoholism, . . . legislate and regulate prostitution and prevent syphilis." [20] Rather than opposing state involvement in regulating social and labor conditions, the North American company promoted a new role for the state in administering workers' lives and labor-capital relations through labor legislation that would guarantee "the harmony of labor and capital," provide workers with hygienic and sanitary housing, fight alcoholism and prostitution, and foster healthy marriages.

As the Chilean state began to consider the implementation of a series of social reforms and welfare policies during the late 1920s and 1930s, social reformers looked to the Braden Copper Company's welfare program as a model. In 1936, for example, Stella Joanne Seibert Alphand presented a thesis at the Universidad de Chile, "Labor Legislation and Social Welfare in El Teniente," which argued that the Chilean government had to learn from the company's welfare program and begin to construct a similar system nationally, "a system based on ideas put in practice in the United States." Seibert located the origins of the social problem in Chile, as it was manifested in the great strikes of the first two decades of the century and incessant labor strife, in the working class's lack of training, and contended that in El Teniente, the welfare program served "to inculcate education and culture in the worker." [21] She also discussed the need to implement minimum-wage laws, an hourly limit for the workweek, a legal Sunday holiday, measures against child labor, work security laws, and indemnification for job-related injuries and illnesses. The solution to the social problem in Chile, she claimed, lay in the application of social welfare policies based on the model of the United States and its representative in Chile, the Braden Copper Company.

Seibert echoed Braden's prescriptions for confronting its own "social problem" in her solutions to the broader national problem: "to get the worker out of the filthy tenement where he lives; give to him and his children a little education and instruction; place in his muddy mind some principles of respect for hygiene, cleanliness, decency; teach him that there is something more in the world for the worker than vice, drunkenness, and abject poverty." According to Seibert, this program of social reform was little understood in Chile and "had budded from the seeds sown by the great producers of copper, with their intelligent and generous policies for their workers." [22]

The company's social reformist emphasis on family life, cultural uplift, and the improvement of living conditions in working-class neighborhoods resonated with the impulses of the Radical Party politicians who took power after 1938 at the head of a series of Popular Front coalition governments and with the new industrial employers who emerged during the accelerated industrial growth of the 1930s and 1940s. Both the state and industrial employers confronted the daunting challenge of forming a stable workforce of responsible citizens out of the large population of rural migrants who inhabited Chile's urban working-class neighborhoods. Popular Front ideology obscured class conflict with the promises of a modernizing project of domestic industrial growth from which all social classes would benefit. Workers' lives would be improved, not through a redistribution of property or income, but through a series of social reforms that offered them an improved standard of living, access to education, decent housing and health care, and better working conditions. The modern industrial economy imagined by Radical Party leaders, and by the leaders of the leftist parties who largely shared their vision, required a trained, semiskilled workforce. State reforms and employers' welfare systems were designed to meet this need.

In addition, for the Popular Front governments, the foundation of citizenship in Chile's new national community would be the nuclear family. Trained and educated male workers and female housewives who inhabited hygienic households would be prepared to exercise the rights and duties of citizenship in partnership with middle-class white-collar employees and industrial entrepreneurs. Social reformers linked the cultural improvement of the urban working class to the formation of stable domestic arrangements in which trained housewives exercised a positive moral influence on their husbands and children. The Chilean state thus implemented a series of policies during the late 1930s and 1940s aimed at guaranteeing the viability of male-headed working-class families, including social security, workers' compensation, health care, and maternity benefits.[23]

In practice, the local representatives of the Chilean state in the El Teniente mining enclave were the local court, municipal authorities, and labor inspectors. After 1938, with the election of the center-left Popular Front coalition, aldermen from the neighboring town of Machalí, regional senators and congressmen from leftist parties, and labor inspectors performed a number of investigations of living and working conditions in the mining camps. The Ministry of Labor and its inspectors began to break down the walls of the North American *feudo* in El Teniente by requiring the Braden Copper Company to adhere to national legislation of living and working conditions, labor relations, collective bargaining, and the cost of living. Government intervention to regulate the cost of living and working conditions, as well as to adjudicate labor conflicts, brought significant improvements to the mining community and eroded the total control exercised by the company over the mining camps and their inhabitants.

At the same time, however, the augmented presence of the state in the mining enclave intensified the North American company's control of the mining community's everyday social habits and strengthened the gender regime based on the male-headed nuclear family. While the North American company opposed the new intrusions of the Ministry of Labor and the enforcement of the Chilean labor code, the local court provided important support for the company's policies on gender and family life. The local court collaborated with the company welfare department and police in trying workers for crimes like drinking, gambling, and illicit sex. In addition, the court often required negligent husbands to hand over wages to their wives and thus fulfill their duties as responsible heads of household.

The court's efforts were particularly aimed at policing women's sexuality. For example, in the late 1930s, the court began for the first time to hear cases of women accused of obtaining illegal abortions. While before 1930 the court docket registered no abortion cases, despite the widespread practice of abortion through folk medicine and by midwives, by the late 1930s abortion had become a significant legal and social transgression for single women, who were castigated by arrest, dismissal, and eviction from the camps.[24] Similarly, beginning in the 1930s, women who left their husbands began to be arrested and prosecuted for the crime of "abandoning the home." While company records show that many men left their wives at will, none were arrested for abandonment. "Abandoning the home" became a particularly female crime.[25] Clandestine abortions and leaving husbands were ways in which women might exercise some control over their sexuality and their lives; the company and the state perceived these expressions of independence as threats to the community of working-class families they hoped to build.

For the first time, too, domestic violence became an important concern of the company and of the local court. While almost no domestic violence cases appear on the court record before the late 1930s, a large number appear after this time. Domestic violence was not a new legal category. Rather, traditional assault cases or cases of injuries (*lesiones*) now came to be composed frequently of incidents of conjugal violence.[26] The appearance of domestic violence cases reflected the company's and the state's new interest in regulating gender relations and the new social realities of the increasing population of married workers. Thus company social workers and the court began to receive women's complaints about their male partners' or husbands' abuses and began to step in to try to restore harmony to miners' households. Domestic violence became an ideological tool in the company's war against "working-class vice" and the "irregularity" of workers' sexual relations. The policing of domestic violence represented a new front in the larger campaign to regulate and administer working-class men's and women's domestic lives and to shape men into "responsible" heads of household and women into model housewives.

Men, Women, and the Reconstruction of Masculinity and Femininity

El Teniente's working-class men and women responded in different ways to the efforts of the state and the North American copper company to transform their lives by redefining the structure of gender relations, the household, and family life. While miners frequently rejected the company's policies on enforced marriage and its strict regulation of drinking and gambling, they embraced the dominant position, in terms of control over women's labor and sexuality, that the new arrangement of the nuclear family conferred on them. In addition, male workers increasingly pursued the promises of social mobility provided by the company's system of high wages, benefits, and vocational training. Some single women workers in the camps sought to defend their social independence by pursuing multiple sexual/romantic relationships with men and by maintaining their economic autonomy through domestic service and informal money for sex relationships, as well as prostitution. Others, however, saw in marriage to a miner a new series of rights and benefits guaranteed by both the company and the state. For these women, the repressive aspects of company and state policies on gender and sexuality represented social and economic security and protection. Thus, for both men and women, resistance to the company's strategies of social control was often eroded by the benefits of the new arrangement of gender and labor relations.

Throughout the 1930s and 1940s, miners continued to defy company regulations on drinking, gambling, and sexuality. Court records and the company archive attest to numerous cases of workers detained, suspended, fined, and even fired for smuggling and consuming moonshine and gambling. The copper company's regulation of sexual relations and family life in the camps was also frequently rejected by the workers. Workers maintained informal consensual unions with women, carried on a number of relationships at once, frequented brothels, and often falsified marriage licenses. One study found, for example, that miners often lied about their marital status or purchased false marriage licenses in Rancagua to cover up an illicit relationship.[27] In 1939, the head of the welfare department wrote to a social worker that "there exist families without legal status and many children, the products of such unions, do not have legal status; there have even arisen cases of the complete falsification of the civil marriage license book, of the union and of the registration of the children. We have also seen cases where the license of a legitimate marriage is presented in order to cover up another illegitimate union." [28]

El Teniente workers often fell short of their assigned responsibilities as husbands and fathers. The welfare department reported many cases of families neglected by workers. In 1939, company social workers reported that many miners were using the family allowance as a form of work bonus, giving limited funds to their wives for the family's sustenance.[29] The social workers found that "in general the amounts given by the married workmen to their wives for the weekly food bill is far below what they could allow." The report condemned workers for forcing their wives to take in laundry, boarders, and sewing while they spent their wages and family allowance on "wine, women, and song, . . . while their wives and children are underfed and worse clothed." In one particular case, the company fired a miner because "he fraudulently received the family allowance for his wife and children for years and neither gave it to his family nor helped them in any form." [30] The company welfare department also received complaints from miners' wives that they received only the family allowance from their husbands, who spent their wages themselves.[31] The company noted that "there has been deception by workers who registered their women and children as dependents to obtain the family allowance and then only contribute this to the family sustenance. . . . The Company doesn't want to have workers who do not fulfill their duties as husbands and fathers and who, while they leave their families with a starvation ration, spend on themselves ten times the sum they concede to their families to maintain themselves." [32]

Miners' resistance to the norms of the nuclear family were also revealed in the frequent abandonment of wives by their husbands. Many women complained to the courts in Rancagua and Santiago of abandonment, asking that they be awarded a portion of their spouses' salaries. According to one social worker's study in 1936, "cases of abandoned women with families present themselves with enormous frequency." [33] El Teniente workers were also notorious for their bigamous practices. Many miners had two wives, or at least one wife and a serious lover, one in the mine's camps and one outside the mine.[34] Bigamy was a luxury that only male workers could enjoy, since their comparatively high wages allowed them to establish more than one relationship at a time. Miners, then, did not readily conform to the pressures to transform them into reliable and responsible heads of household.

At the same time, however, by the 1930s many miners began to commit themselves to a career in mining and to marry and raise families in El Teniente's camps. The high wages and work bonuses, the family allowance, and the possibilities for limited social mobility offered by the company's social welfare system, schools, and occupational structure, particularly the possibility of promotion to a white-collar job as a skilled worker or crew chief (*empleado*), induced workers to stay on and make their lives in the mine. Inside the mine, miners developed a masculine work culture based on pride in their work and their high wages. As they stayed on to make their lives in the mine, work became a source of affirmation and dignity. For example, in terms of their new life cycle, workers defined coming to manhood through labor in the mine. As the former miner and writer Baltazar Castro remembers of growing up in the camps during the 1930s, "my aspiration was always to be transferred to the mine, to feel that I was a miner in every sense of the word." [35] Similarly, an old miner remembered how workers based their sense of militant manhood on their capacity for labor and their skill and knowledge: "Among the workers there was a certain competitiveness that made them, well, 'I'm *agallado* (strong, brave, clever) because I can carry so much, I worked this much, I advanced that much.' . . . there are workers who are truly animals for work." [36] Miners developed a work or occupational identity based on their pride in their capacity for difficult and dangerous labor and their high earnings relative to other Chilean workers.

At the same time, this accommodation to the new demands of work in the modern copper industry did not imply miners' passive acceptance of company authority. The cult of labor and physical strength that undergirded miners' intense masculine pride was reproduced in their challenging and insubordinate attitude toward their bosses. While they may have worked hard to meet company production goals and earn bonuses and overtime, miners frequently rejected the control exercised by supervisors and foremen. Workers produced an unruly work culture based on codes of behavior that emphasized solidarity among workmates and disrespect for the boss. Workers often fought with both their Chilean foremen and North American supervisors inside the mine. For example, the miner Yáñez responded to the insults of his foreman with his own flood of curses, and the two then engaged in a fistfight.[37] In 1944, one of these conflicts ended in the murder of a supervisor, Skinner, by the worker Manuel Castillo, who was "desperate from suffering so much abuse," according to the miners' union paper.[38] In another case in the early 1940s, according to company reports, a miner murdered P. M. Kinney, a mine foreman, "in revenge for a mild reprimand for failure to do his work." [39] Numerous cases of disobedience reveal workers' resistance to the strict labor discipline demanded by the company and their efforts to carve out space in the strictly regimented regime of production in the mine.[40]

The miners figured their labor as an essentially masculine activity and defined the mine as an often antagonistic and threatening presence. Thus the miners' language, lore, and myths were riddled with references to evil female spirits who threatened their safety in the mine, as well as jokes about adultery that expressed a generalized anxiety about their wives' fidelity. While they might assert dignity and manhood in their conquest of the mine through hard and skilled labor, ultimately the mine governed workers' lives. As a miner in one of Castro's stories declares, "The mine is that way, you enter her and you can't leave no matter how hard you work. She's a very vexing and chastising woman." [41]

The signification of the mine as female and labor as an essentially masculine activity reflected the masculinization of wage labor in the industrial economy of the mining enclave and women's relegation to the domestic sphere. Miners' codes of manhood at once became a basis for their assertions of pride through hard work, relatively high salaries, and physical strength, and for a workplace culture of independence and opposition to company discipline. Thus, while miners began to conform to the new requirements for productive labor in the copper industry, they maintained informal forms of resistance to company authority. While affirming their aspirations to social mobility and middle-class manhood through hard work and occupational pride, they sustained a turbulent oppositional attitude to both the company and the state, based in expressions of masculine dignity.

Women, excluded from miners' work culture and forms of solidarity and restricted to the home or domestic service, fashioned different responses to the company's efforts to regulate their sexuality. Single women workers frequently engaged in sex work to augment their earnings and rejected the attempts of both the company and their male lovers to exercise control over their social lives. Single women migrated to the mining enclave in search of wage labor in El Teniente's clandestine bars and brothels and company-owned workers' pensions and hostels. They cooked, served meals, cleaned, did laundry, sold and served illegal alcohol, and engaged in prostitution. Often, they combined the duties of domestic service with labor in the illicit economy of alcohol and sex. Most of the women who left the countryside for El Teniente were attracted not by the possibility of marriage, but by promises of wage labor. Young single women hoped to find work either in the bars, brothels, and markets in the informal settlements that sprang up outside the mining camps, or in the camps themselves, as maids and servants (*empleadas*). Like the men who entered the mine, these single women planned to work for a number of years and then return with their savings to rural towns to open their own businesses. While male workers often hoped to buy a small plot of land, the women who migrated to El Teniente often saw their future to be in petty commerce.[42]

The wages women could earn in El Teniente, however, constituted only a fraction of the male miners' lowest salary. Relegated to domestic service and a "feminized" sector of the labor market, women earned terribly low wages. While empleadas worked sixteen-hour days preparing and serving meals to hundreds of miners, washing plates and silverware, and doing laundry, they could never hope to equal their male counterparts' earnings. Their work was as strenuous and exhausting as miners' work, but the dominant ideology of gender and work placed little value on women's labor.[43]

Given the onerous and low-paying nature of domestic service, single women frequently resorted to sex work as an important economic and sexual strategy. Women could significantly improve their earnings and maximize their position with respect to men by establishing informal sexual relationships based on the exchange of sexual services for money or material goods. The empleada Mercedes Zapata, for example, was described as having gone to work in the camps "to provide the single miners her services in order to earn a little more money to start a business in Rancagua." [44]

For single women, informal sex work and domestic service represented one route to independence and a form of resistance to the company's efforts to transform them into housewives. While men assumed that they could acquire a monopoly over women's bodies and expected complete loyalty in exchange for the money and presents they gave their lovers, and while the company attempted to restrict women's sexuality, single women often refused to enter into "proper" monogamous relationships. For example, when the miner Muñoz confronted his lover, the empleada Cornejo, over her relationships with other miners and slapped her, she told him that her other relationships were no one else's business and that she was "the owner of her own body." She then complained to the police.[45] Similarly, Pilar Medina "responded insolently" to Angel Custodio Aguillera's claims of proprietorship, and when the miner beat her, she had him arrested for abuse. For some women, informal relationships with men gave them a certain measure of control over their bodies and their sexuality. They rejected men's efforts to impose monogamy on them and expressed a strong sense of independence in their conflicts with their lovers.

Despite women workers' expressions of autonomy, the company and the state established a set of social controls to restrict their behavior and punish their transgressions of the dominant gender ideology of domesticity. Thus, single women were fired and expelled from the camps if they became pregnant. In 1943, for example, the copper company fired the pregnant empleada Rosa Zúñiga, who had apparently earned extra money through sex work, "to demonstrate to these girls that they will always be the victims and that they must observe proper morals."[46] Without such a severe lesson, the company argued, "the number of women who give themselves for money would increase and little by little any notion of morality and good habits would be lost." Similarly, if a woman tried to abort an unwanted pregnancy she could be arrested. In one case, for example, an empleada was arrested after she was hospitalized following an illegal abortion. According to her fellow workers, she had had clandestine abortions before.[47]

While the local court and the company regulated single women's behavior, they did little to protect them from male violence. Thus, when a woman worker reported a rape, the female owner of a cantina where she worked cited her employee's flirtatious behavior and statement that "she was the owner of her actions and that nobody was going to interfere in her business" as signs that she "had it coming." As the cantina owner put it: "from my point of view this girl's head doesn't work right, and if what she says really happened to her, she alone is to blame since she is very backward and I know that she has had relations with a lot of people." The accused men were found innocent.[48]

The strict legal and social control of single women who either bore children or who had abortions, combined with their vulnerability to male violence, served to drive them either from the camps or into marriages with miners. The company regulations requiring men and women to formalize their sexual arrangements in marriage provided women with a certain protection and security. A company report celebrated the "great triumph" of imposing legal marriages on men and women and pointed out that one of the consequences of the prior "decayed" sexual practices was that women and children were left "without legal support."[49] Women benefited from the state's and the company's efforts to impose family responsibilities on their male partners. In marriage, women won access to their husbands' wages, the family allowance, credit at stores, and the protection of the company welfare department and the local court, which recognized their and their children's rights to economic support from their husbands. One woman recalls, for example, that in the mining camps "women married someone from El Teniente because of their economic situation." For this woman, "it was the security, not that the wages were so high, but the security." [50] In addition, marriage bestowed on single women a legitimate social position. Married women, unlike single women, could hope to receive protection from male violence from the courts and the company welfare department, which attempted to maintain the order and harmony of nuclear families in the camps.

Married women frequently turned the dominant ideology of domesticity to their own use. Women looked to the company welfare department and the camps' court to force their husbands to give them their wages and benefits. The company's attempts to control the behavior of husbands who neglected their wives and contributed little to the household budget provided married women with important support. Women drew on their rights as mothers and wives to win control of at least part of their husbands' incomes. Thus, the company's close control of family life in the camps, while certainly repressive, may at times have served married women's interests. Its stated policy of warning and then suspending or firing men who "through vice cannot fulfill their family obligations" in order to "obtain decent living conditions for a number of mothers and children who . . . suffer conditions worse than those of the unemployed" provided married women with important economic guarantees.

In the case of domestic violence, the significant role played by the company's social workers and welfare department, as well as the local court, was clear to women. Married women often took their husbands to court in order to ensure that a violent episode did not repeat itself. Many women brought charges and then dropped them, explaining that they had done so in order to prevent their husbands from getting into the habit of beating them. As one woman explained, "I was upset so I went to the police to denounce him. . . . I did it so that he wouldn't do it again." [51] Another woman testified that she had charged her husband with abuse "so that he not become accustomed to hitting me for any reason." [52] According to oral testimony, women complained to the welfare department about abusive or negligent husbands and often received aid from social workers. One woman remembers, for example, that "we were always close to a social worker . . . and if the social worker heard that a marriage wasn't functioning well, she went to the house and conversed and tried to solve the problem. . . . The social workers were around, very close, in order to help." [53]

Similarly, women appealed to the police, who at times helped women, although at other times they only talked to abusive husbands. According to the same woman, "one could go to the police without worrying . . . if they could help you, they helped you." [54] The company's efforts to regulate miners' and their families' domestic lives through the activities of the company police, social workers, and the local court provided women with support in dealing with their husbands. While miners and their wives might reject the intrusions of company social workers and the company's private police force, some women found a source of support in these social controls. Thus women in the camps, like male workers, turned to marriage and a settled family life in pursuit of the promise of middle-class domesticity and stability embedded in the company's social welfare system.

Paternalism, Community, and Politics in the Mining Camps

By the 1930s the North American company had succeeded in establishing a constant and stable labor force of married workers in the El Teniente mine. By 1937, for example, almost half of El Teniente's workers were legally married (3,503) and 3,000 women lived in the camps, a considerable increase from the 1920s.[55] Contrary to the Braden Copper Company's expectations, however, the settling of workers and their wives into stable households, rather than bringing accommodation and discipline to the workforce, coincided with an explosion of labor militancy. With the support of the newly elected Popular Front government of Pedro Aguirre Cerda in 1938 and of activists from the Chilean Communist and Socialist Parties, El Teniente workers were able to reorganize their union and engage in the first major strikes in the copper mines since 1919. The miners' union, led by militants of the Communist Party, launched five major strike movements between 1938 and 1948, and during this decade the miners engaged in innumerable wildcat work stoppages to protest working conditions and the inflated cost of living in the camps.[56]

The Braden Copper Company's social welfare program failed to produce quiescence and order because the promises of social mobility broadcast through company schools and newspapers conflicted with the harsh material realities of life and work in the camps. Workers received the company's messages that through hard work, education, and a healthy family life they could achieve a better life, represented to them in images and concepts imported from the United States. They appreciated, however, that labor in El Teniente, without collective struggle, would never lead them to that life. Every day, as they stared across the mining camps to the enclosed and guarded houses of North American supervisors and administrators, and compared them with the austerity of their own barren and cramped barracks, the company's paternalist promises rang increasingly hollow.

In oral histories old workers frequently recall the dissonance between their admiration for and aspirations to North American standards of living and forms of culture and the material realities of their own lives. Many took part in company-sponsored schools and recreational and cultural activities, and praised the North American administration, but still participated actively in union activities and joined left-wing parties that sought to nationalize the copper industry. For one worker who was a prominent soccer player on the company team, attended company vocational schools, and expressed admiration for the North American administration, the union and leftist parties were only trying to improve workers' cultural and social lives and to obtain "what the *gringos* already had." The hardship of work and life in the camps had an important effect on this worker. He recalls, for example, that life in the camps and the mine was extremely difficult, and contrasts the poverty of workers' lives with the luxury of the North Americans' homes. He notes that "in cultural and social life the *gringos* lived in a form very distinct [from the workers] which made many people dislike the *gringos*. . . . If you even looked at the *gringo* camp they would haul you up to *Bienestar* to be disciplined, and if you went near it or tried to enter, they would fire you." [57]

In interviews, workers consistently recall with bitterness the tripartite spatial division and segregation of the mine's camps into neighborhoods for North American supervisors, Chilean empleados or white-collar employees, and Chilean workers. Even workers who were enthusiastic about the North American administration felt the hardship of their material situation, the blatant inequalities that they confronted every day in the mine, and the ultimate inaccessibility of the middle-class lifestyle embodied in the lawns, houses, and golf course of the North American camp. Another union and leftist party militant remembers how in the camps "they applied North American ideas; in a Chilean city these were the norms: when a North American passed by, the *obrero,* the *empleado,* women or children had to step to one side so as not to touch him, because if they touched him, he complained with the consequence that they fired the man and made him abandon the camps." [58] Inequality and resentment were thus bred into El Teniente's workforce and took the shine off the company's paternalist policies and promises of social mobility.

The miners' sense of the racial and national discrimination embedded in the hierarchy of space in the mining camps was frequently shared by the Chilean employees who served as the mediators of both the company's disciplinary and social welfare regimes. Chileans who occupied an interstitial position in the camps and who were in charge of disseminating the company's social ideology frequently joined workers in opposing the company's authority. Chilean teachers in the company-run schools, for example, often sided with workers in their conflicts with the company and shared an equally antagonistic relationship with the company administration. Either from working-class or lower-middle-class backgrounds, they identified their interests with the mine workers and articulated a nationalist opposition to the North American company.

In 1919, for example, J. Pezoa Varas traveled to El Teniente to work as a schoolteacher. Shocked by the harsh treatment of the workforce and the blatant social inequalities of the camps, he penned a tract describing his experiences and deriding the mine's North American administrators. In *En el feudo* (Inside the fiefdom), he painted a devastating portrait of social conditions in the camps, inequalities between the North American "lords," as he called them, and Chilean workers; articulated a nationalist critique of El Teniente's "yanqui" managers; and called for the nationalization of the mine. Contrasting the "miserable dwellings" of Chilean workers, Pezoa commented on the "beauty and comforts of the [North American neighborhood], constructed intentionally far away from the lodgings for Chilean families," so that "the privileged race can live without any kind of contact with the humble uncivilized children of this country." [59]

In addition, teachers frequently shared workers' antagonism toward the company and supported them during labor conflicts. In the middle of a strike in 1946, for example, the company fired and evicted a number of schoolteachers for donating financial support to the union's strike fund. In response, the eighty Chilean teachers in El Teniente began to organize their own strike in protest, petitioning the minister of education for support. [60] Thus, many of the Chilean mediators of the company's welfare policies, far from being agents of company-imposed social control, joined the workers in their rejection of the disciplinary regime in the camps. Despite their "middling" position in the mine's social hierarchy, they articulated a strong nationalist resentment for the total control exercised by the North American company within the camps.

The miners' sense of racial and national discrimination within the enclave was exacerbated by comparisons they made between their own standard of living and the working conditions and wages of North American copper workers. The miners frequently pointed out that their wages did not approach those paid to workers in the United States, often in the same industry. In 1936, for example, *El Cobre* pointed out that copper workers in the United States had seen their wages rise by as much as 80 percent since 1900 and had had their workday lowered from ten or twelve hours to eight. North American workers earned U.S.$5.50 (at the time, around 143 pesos) a day, at least ten times more than the Chilean miners who earned an average of 9 pesos and 10 centavos daily.[61] To support this data, the paper quoted an economist from Stanford who had told the *New York Times* that "the devaluation of the [Chilean] currency signifies riches for the exporters of Chilean products that they produce cheaply, but for the poor worker of Chile it signifies ruin and misery." [62]

In 1940, the union paper, *Despertar Minero,* drew its own conclusions from a company security poster that depicted a North American copper miner. The union paper noted that in the photo the North American worker rested with his wife in a home that had "terrific bookshelves, handsome upholstered sofas and chairs, a radio and many other comforts." "But if we move to this locality," the paper continued, "we find that there are workers who don't even have chairs to sit in." Compared to workers in the United States, the union pointed out, Chilean workers earned far less, and while "the *obrero yanqui* does everything mechanized, the worker here . . . performs his job with physical force." [63] Chilean workers, the union argued, didn't even enjoy a tenth of the comfort of the *"trabajadores yanquis,"* and bookshelves, a radio, and a sofa were only a "dream for every *empleado y obrero.*" For the miners, the security propaganda posted by the company was "yet another demonstration that the demands of the workers of a company as rich and important as Braden are totally just." [64] During the strike, in a speech to the striking miners, the Communist deputy Ocampo noted that he had sent a note to the president of the CIO in the United States, one Mr. Murray, "so that the workers of that great country see the difference in treatment, in work conditions, and the astronomical difference in salaries that they pay in Chile compared to what the copper miners in the United States receive for the same work and less hours." [65]

The miners' sense that they had a right to the wages and living and working conditions of North American workers was revealed in the comments of the U.S. ambassador in Chile, Claude Bowers, during a strike in 1942. Bowers noted that "the workmen have two things in the backs of their minds: a) that workmen in the mines in the United States receive for substantially the same work wages which are several times greater, and b) that the Company is making enormous profits because of the recent increase in the price of copper and that they should obtain a good share of these." The ambassador argued that the difference in living standards between Chilean and U.S. miners "is constantly used by agitators to promote discontent." He gloomily concluded that the workers would not be convinced by the company's "rational" arguments that their wages were high in comparison with other Chilean workers and would continue to demand a greater share of Braden's profits.[66]

The schools and social and cultural institutions set up by the company created expectations of social mobility among workers. Workers who had access to education began to aspire to a new standard of living that was concretely represented to them by the North American camp and in the articles and advertisements published in the company newspapers. But the company's promise of social improvement through cultural uplift and education confronted the material limits of the workers' situation in the camps. Work remained onerous, living conditions arduous, and the possibility of joining a middle class outside the mining camps remote. The new aspirations of workers who were schooled in the company's social and educational organizations for the company's "good life" led to participation in the union and struggle with the company, rather than to accommodation and acquiescence. The social welfare policies of the company and the state gave workers a new sense of their "rights" to the family wage and a series of social benefits enshrined in the ideal of middle-class domesticity. These rights became the focus of mobilizations and collective conflicts in the mining camps.

As more women stayed in the camps and took on roles as housewives and mothers, and more men began to stay on in the camps with their families, a permanent community took shape in El Teniente that lent strength to the miners' strike movements. Married workers and their wives began to plan their lives in the mine and thus struggled to make their future there better. Men who stayed on in El Teniente participated in the elaboration of an intensely masculine and combative work culture that served as the basis for endemic labor conflicts. In addition, in their new roles as heads of household, miners strove to improve their lives and fulfill their family responsibilities by engaging in collective action.

Women played a major role in these conflicts. They organized support committees and *ollas comunes* (communal kitchens), walked the picket line with their husbands and children, and spoke at rallies. The strike, more than a collective conflict between workers and employers, was a battle between El Teniente's working-class community and the company that dominated every aspect of their lives. The miners' union recognized the importance of women's participation when it argued that a 1939 strike could not depend "exclusively on the workers . . . this mobilization must embrace all the women and families." [67] Women in El Teniente also organized a chapter of the Movimiento Pro-Emancipación de la Mujer Chilena (MEMCh), which participated actively in miners' strikes and organized political support for the Popular Front governments during these years.

The union petitions during these movements indicate the community's new sense of rights. Workers' demands included better housing, schools, recreational facilities, parks, stores, and food. In addition, the union frequently petitioned the state to intervene to control the cost of living. In the system of gender relations constructed in El Teniente, these areas of struggle all fell within the sphere of activity to which women were consigned. According to the ideology of domesticity, women had responsibility for the welfare of miners' families. Women's participation in cost-of-living committees and women's committees focused on demands that pertained to this assigned female role: consumption, food prices, and education for their children. Thus, women's desire to ensure the security and the rights promised by the company's social welfare policies and dominant gender ideology often led to their participation in collective movements. The unity of interests between men and women in labor struggles was predicated on women's economic dependence on their husbands and their subordination within the nuclear family. Miners' masculinized work culture defined militancy as an expression of manhood and produced a class identity shaped by the ideals of the male wage earner and the female housewife. This was reinforced by miners' reaffirmation of their central role as breadwinner and head of household.

Epilogue: The Mining Community, Neoliberalism, and Military Rule

The shift in El Teniente's working population to conform to the ideal of the male-headed nuclear family established a community that both enjoyed the benefits of an extensive social welfare system backed by the state and sustained a militant working-class politics in opposition to the authority of the North American company. Between 1938 and 1971, when the mine was nationalized by Salvador Allende's socialist government, workers in El Teniente continually won wage increases and benefits in semiannual collective negotiations with the state and the U.S.-owned copper company, frequently after general strikes in the copper industry. By

1971, copper miners enjoyed the highest wages of any Chilean workers; periodic automatic cost-of-living raises; the family allowance; access to company-provided health care, housing, and education; and job security for themselves and their children.

In 1973, however, a military coup placed in power one of Latin America's most repressive military dictatorships and put an end to the construction of a welfare state that had begun in 1938 and ended with the revolutionary experiment of Allende's Popular Unity government. The dictatorship of Augusto Pinochet launched state terror against working-class organizations and the Left, while imposing a draconian reorganization of the Chilean economy according to a program of neoliberal restructuring designed by "los Chicago boys." The military regime established a new model of economic policy and labor relations that dismantled the corporatist welfare state programs of the 1938–1973 period. Ironically, the regime's neoliberalism drew on North American economic ideologies and models, just as the corporatist labor relations and social welfare systems of the 1938–1973 period had drawn inspiration from the United States and its representatives in the copper industry.

The seventeen years of authoritarian rule in Chile wrought radical changes in the lives of the El Teniente copper miners, their families, and industrial workers throughout Chile. Hundreds of leftist activists were fired, and many others were arrested and tortured. The miners' tight bonds of workplace solidarity and traditions of labor militancy began to erode under the pressures of fear and repression. The effects of military repression were exacerbated in El Teniente, as in other working-class communities in Chile, by the regime's economic policies, which reduced job security, wages, and benefits for most workers. Through the use of subcontractors the new administration began to privatize a number of areas of production in the mine. By 1986, just over half the total workers employed by El Teniente (8,250) worked for nearly two hundred small private contractors. These firms paid workers half the wages earned by miners employed by the national copper company, provided no benefits, and offered little job security. Workers' efforts to unionize these small firms were easily thwarted.[68] Before 1973, children of El Teniente workers could depend on a steady job in the mine. Most miners themselves had been born and raised in the mining camps, and a career as a miner and a healthy pension were viewed by most El Teniente workers as rights guaranteed by the paternalist labor system established decades ago by the North American copper company in concert with the state. Under the military regime, neither the miners nor their children had a secure future in El Teniente, since subcontractors were able to take advantage of an ever-increasing pool of urban unemployed.

As part of its general program of "modernizing" the economy, the military regime also cut costs by reducing workers' benefits and privatizing health care and social security. El Teniente workers no longer had access to free health care. Similarly, while the North American company and the state had previously provided workers' pensions, now workers had to contribute funds from their wages to private financial groups. Finally, the regime's 1979 Labor Plan, elaborated to let "the market" govern labor relations, also took away many of the economic gains that El Teniente miners had won from the North American copper company over the years—gains that had been guaranteed by the state. The labor plan established a number of laws that severely restricted workers' unions and the rights to strike and bargain collectively.[69] In 1982, a government decree eliminated the automatic cost-of-living raises that had been part of every contract in the copper mines since 1938.

The dismantling of the material securities that miners had enjoyed since the 1940s destabilized the cohesive culture of the mining community. El Teniente miners, now living in housing projects in the city of Rancagua rather than in the mining camps, traveled two hours by bus every morning to reach the mine, leading to a significant separation of workplace and community. Whereas in the mining camps and workers' barracks the culture and experiences of the mine had infiltrated all areas of everyday life, in the city miners' neighborhoods were integrated into the broader urban environment. Miners and their families were exposed to a broad spectrum of cultural activities and influences. Their children attended public schools; housing was urban and privately owned; and the city provided alternative forms of recreation, theater, music, cinema, newspapers, and magazines.

Consumerism, stimulated by economic policies that encouraged the importation of cheap foreign manufactured goods, also played a role in transforming the culture of the mining community. By the late 1970s, Rancagua's stores were flooded with consumer items that the miners, with their relatively high wages, could afford to buy on credit; many miners fell quickly into debt. The new culture of consumption fomented by the neoliberal economy, in combination with severe political repression, transformed workers' relationships to the union and the company. The mine's administration and the workers' union now often operated as credit agencies; workers began to look to union leaders, who, through their contacts, could arrange loans. Since the 1980s, many union leaders note, miners' struggles for individual survival in the market economy and the culture of *consumismo* have superseded the culture of class solidarity that defined miners' communities for so many years.

The growth of the consumer economy and the regime's free-market policies also transformed gender relations in El Teniente's mining families. While miners confronted growing job insecurity and the erosion of their wages and benefits, miners' daughters and wives began to seek employment in the emerging service economy to supplement their families' incomes. Women in the mining community found work as saleswomen in department stores and as secretaries and office workers. Women from miners' families enjoyed a certain economic autonomy for the first time and began to exercise their power in the consumer economy. North American–produced cultural products swamped the Chilean culture industry, and women were exposed to a whole set of images, values, and desires that undermined the hegemonic hold of the ideal of the monogamous male-headed family. The consumer economy, therefore, provided women with a certain level of economic independence and new ideas about sexuality and autonomy. Few miners' daughters now define their futures in terms of marriage to a miner, as they had until the 1970s. The strict moral codes based on the ideology of domesticity that governed gender relations in the camps and within miners' nuclear families have been eroded, and women's sexual and economic subordination to men has been challenged in important ways. The economic dependence of women on men, based on the family wage and a series of social welfare benefits, united miners' families and communities during strikes and protests, but has now been undermined by the reorganization of the economy.

As El Teniente's copper mining community searches for ways to confront the radical changes wrought by a seventeen-year history of military repression and the neoliberal economic policies of a transition democratic government, the traditional bases of their militant collective action have been eroded. Copper workers have been outspoken in their rejection both of the neoliberal model and of the state's plans to privatize the copper industry by selling the large mines to foreign investors. However, miners' unions have experienced a general debilitation due to repression that has been exacerbated by their precarious position in the market economy. The union plays less and less of a role in miners' daily lives as it struggles to protect jobs and benefits from the constant threat of cutbacks and to promote alternatives to the denationalization of the copper industry.

The miners' communities and families, once the basis for a powerful labor movement in the mining camps, have lost their cohesive bonds and coherent identity. While El Teniente workers suffer increased job insecurity and reduced wages and benefits, they no longer perceive that collective action could improve this situation. Instead, they and their children look beyond the mine to new possibilities. The ideals of the male head of household and female housewife that undergirded miners' strike movements between 1938 and 1973 are neither as feasible nor as compelling as they were before 1973. Old ideas about the nature of community, class, and gender are no longer tenable in the urban world and neoliberal market economy. The miners and their families struggle to define new ways of thinking about class and community and to build an alternative to the apparently hegemonic ideology of neoliberalism that has won adherents across the political spectrum.

Notes

I would like to thank Catherine LeGrand and Gilbert Joseph for their comments on an earlier draft of this essay.

1. See Confederación de los Trabajadores del Cobre, Congreso, Punta de Tralca, 1983.

2. A number of critics have recently pointed to the importance of "engendering" histories of labor and class formation. Among these are Joan Scott, *Gender and the Politics of History* (New York: Columbia University Press, 1988); Sally Alexander, "Women, Class, and Sexual Difference," *History Workshop* 17 (spring 1984); Ava Baron, ed., *Work Engendered: Toward a New History of American Labor* (Ithaca, N.Y.: Cornell University Press, 1991); and Kathleen Canning, "Gender and the Politics of Class Formation: Rethinking German Labor History," *American Historical Review* 97, no. 3 (June 1992).

3. For analyses of gender, class, and welfare states in the United States and Europe, see Linda Gordon, "Social Insurance and Public Assistance: The Influence of Gender in Welfare Thought in the United States, 1890–1935," *American Historical Review* 97, no. 1 (Feb. 1992); Linda Gordon, *Women, the State, and Welfare* (Madison: University of Wisconsin Press, 1990); and Kathleen Canning, "Social Policy, Body Politics: Recasting the Social Question in Germany, 1875–1900," in *Gender and Class in Modern Europe,* ed. Laura Frader and Sonya O. Rose (Ithaca, N.Y.: Cornell University Press, 1996). For a pioneering study of Chile, see Karin Rosemblatt, "Por un hogar bien constituido: El estado y su política familiar en los frentes populares," in *Disciplina y desacato: Construcción de identidad social en Chile, siglos XIX y XX,* ed. Lorena Godoy, Elizabeth Hutchison, Karin Rosemblatt, and M. Soledad Zarate (Santiago: SUR/CEDEM, 1995).

4. For a similar argument about female mobilizations, see Temma Kaplan,

"Female Consciousness and Collective Action: The Case of Barcelona, 1910–1918" *Signs* 7, no. 3 (spring 1982).

5. Alejandro Fuenzalida Grandón, *El trabajo i la vida en el mineral "El Teniente"* (Santiago, 1919), 96.

6. Braden Copper Company, Welfare Department Annual Report, 1922, Archivo de la Braden Copper Company, CODELCO, Chile (hereafter ABCC).

7. See the company paper, *El Teniente,* 1920–1924, for descriptions of the company's welfare programs.

8. Welfare Department Annual Report, 1922, ABCC.

9. *Informe,* n.d., ABCC.

10. Fuenzalida, *El trabajo i la vida,* 101.

11. Gabriel Salazar Vergara, *Labradores, peones y proletarios: Formación y crisis de la sociedad popular chilena del siglo XIX* (Santiago: SUR, 1985), 256–322. Also see Elizabeth Hutchison, "Working Women of Santiago: Gender and Social Transformation in Urban Chile, 1887–1927" (Ph.D. diss., University of California, Berkeley, 1995); and Alejandra Brito, "Del rancho al conventillo: Transformaciones en la identidad popular feminina, Santiago de Chile, 1850–1920," in Godoy et al., *Disciplina y desacato.*

12. *El Teniente,* 11 Oct. 1922.

13. Fuenzalida, *El trabajo i la vida,* 95.

14. Juzgado de Letras de Menor Cuantía, Sewell, Causa Civil No. 2189, Conservador de Bienes y Raíces, Rancagua (hereafter CBRR). Also see Juzgado de Letras de Menor Cuantía, Sewell, Causa Civil No. 2200, CBRR, for a similar case.

15. See Thomas Miller Klubock, "Class, Community, and Gender in the Chilean Copper Mines: The El Teniente Miners and Working-Class Politics, 1904–1951" (Ph.D. diss., Yale University, 1993).

16. Alfred Houston to L. E. Grant, 12 Jan. 1922, ABCC.

17. "La ley seca en los centros industriales: Sus ventajes vistas en la práctica en el mineral de El Teniente," ABCC.

18. "El Departamento de Bienestar," ABCC.

19. *El Teniente,* 17 Oct. 1922.

20. *El Teniente,* 12 Oct. 1922.

21. Stella Joanne Seibert Alphand, "Legislación del trabajo y previsión social en El Teniente" (thesis, Universidad de Chile, 1936), 21.

22. Ibid., 29–30.

23. See Rosemblatt, "Por un hogar bien constituido."

24. For cases of women arrested for illegal abortions, see Juzgado de Letras de Menor Cuantía, Sewell, Causa No. 9926, 23 Mar. 1945; *Causa No. 6049,* 14 July 1940, CBRR.

25. For women arrested for abandoning their husbands, see Juzgado de Letras de Menor Cuantía, Sewell, Causa No. 5458, 5 Nov. 1940, CBRR.

26. For cases of domestic violence, see Juzgado de Letras de Menor Cuantía, Sewell, Causa No. 12047, 13 July 1948; Causa No. 6266, 14 Nov. 1941; Causa

No. 8344, 15 Sept. 1942; Causa No. 6146, 1 Feb. 1941; Causa No. 4742, 21 Nov. 1938; and Causa No. 10.955, 2 Sept. 1946, CBRR.

27. Fuenzalida, *El trabajo i la vida,* 101–2.

28. Letter to Ana Pinto Santibañez, 3 Feb. 1939, ABCC.

29. H. Mackenzie Walker to W. J. Turner, 6 Sept. 1939, ABCC.

30. Welfare department, confidential memorandum, 28 July 1943, ABCC.

31. Letter to Ana Pinto Santibañez, 3 Feb. 1939, ABCC.

32. Welfare department, letter to Presidente, Sindicato Industrial Braden Copper Company, "Sewell y Mina," 4 Sept. 1943, ABCC.

33. Seibert, "Legislación del Trabajo," 39.

34. Interview with José Donoso, Rancagua, 1993.

35. Baltazar Castro, *Mi camarada padre* (Santiago: Editorial Nascimiento, 1985), 267.

36. Interview with Domingo Quintero, Rancagua, 1991.

37. *Despertar Minero,* 25 June 1939.

38. *Despertar Minero, Primera Quincena de Noviembre de 1944.*

39. General Manager's Annual Report–1940, Braden Copper Company, ABCC.

40. See Departamento de Bienestar Social, Oficina del Trabajo, dismissal reports, 1941–1945, ABCC.

41. Baltazar Castro, *Un hombre por el camino* (Santiago: Editorial Cultura, 1950), 202.

42. The records of the local court list a large number of women arrested for selling alcohol clandestinely, for prostitution, and for operating *casas de citas,* where prostitutes could meet men. See, for example, Juzgado de Letras de Menor Cuantía, Sewell, Causas No. 6036, 11 Dec. 1940; No. 10.093, 4 June 1945; and No. 4947, 10 Mar. 1939, CBRR.

43. In 1939, women working in El Teniente's laundries earned between 5 and 7 pesos a day, in contrast to the 30-peso-a-day minimum wage for a male worker in the mine (*Despertar Minero,* 31 Aug. 1939). In 1941, domestic workers in the camps' cantinas earned between 60 and 80 pesos monthly, while the average wage for a male miner was between 30 and 45 pesos a day (*Despertar Minero,* 30 Jan. 1941).

44. Juzgado de Letras de Menor Cuantía, Sewell, Causa No. 11.082, 7 Dec. 1946, CBRR.

45. Juzgado de Letras de Menor Cuantía, Sewell, Causa No. 10.945, 28 Aug. 1946, CBRR.

46. Welfare department, letter to Presidente, Sindicato Industrial Braden Copper Company, "Sewell y Mina," 31 July 1943, ABCC.

47. Juzgado de Letras de Menor Cuantía, Sewell, Causa No. 9926, 23 Mar. 1945, CBRR.

48. Juzgado de Letras de Menor Cuantía, Sewell, Causa No. 13.599, 26 July 1951, CBRR.

49. Welfare department, "El Departamento de Bienestar," 1921, ABCC.

50. Interview with María Berrios, Rancagua, 1992.

51. Juzgado de Letras de Menor Cuantía, Sewell, Causa No. 11.342, 12 June 1947, CBRR.

52. Juzgado de Letras de Menor Cuantía, Sewell, Causa No. 11.334, 31 Mar. 1947, CBRR.

53. Interview with Nelida Carrasco Quintero, Rancagua, 1992.

54. Ibid.

55. Census de la Braden Copper Company, 1937, ABCC.

56. Klubock, "Class, Community, and Gender in the Chilean Copper Mines."

57. Interview with Javier Rosales, Rancagua, 1990.

58. Interview with Manuel Ahumada, Rancagua, 1991.

59. J. Pezoa Varas, *En el feudo: Impresiones sobre la vida obrera del mineral de El Teniente* (Rancagua: Imprenta de "La Semana," 1919), 88.

60. *El Siglo,* 10 Oct. 1946.

61. *El Cobre,* 11 Dec. 1936.

62. Ibid.

63. *Despertar Minero,* 21 Nov. 1940.

64. *Despertar Minero, Primera Quincena de Julio de 1943.*

65. *El Siglo,* 2 Mar. 1942.

66. United States Department of State General Records, RG59, 825.5045/114.

67. *Despertar Minero,* 25 Apr. 1939.

68. For a discussion of conditions in the copper industry, see Confederación de los Trabajadores del Cobre, Congreso Ordinario, Memoria, 26–28 July 1982. Also see Confederación de los Trabajadores del Cobre, Congreso Ordinario, Memoria, 6–8 Mar. 1987; and *Voz del Minero,* Dec. 1985.

69. For an analysis of the labor plan, see *Análisis* (July 1979).

Seth Fein

Everyday Forms of Transnational Collaboration
U.S. Film Propaganda in Cold War Mexico

Because the current struggle against Communism is in significant part an ideological competition for human loyalties, it has brought into the plainest view America's psychology. One of the issues it involves is the issue of a social "message" to compete with the appeal of Communism in various parts of the world. Since the American creed is a submerged faith . . . it is not a theory which other peoples can easily appropriate or understand. LOUIS HARTZ, *The Liberal Tradition in America* (1955)

The ceremony that is taking place today is similar to those that have already taken place or will take place in a large section of the state, from Tuxpam to Catemaco, and that consequently covers northern, central, and southern regions of the state. It has been organized, as a demonstration of friendship and cooperation, by the Audio-Visual Department of the Embassy of the United States of North America under the auspices of the Government of the State, contributing in this way to the intellectual, moral and civic conditions of our people. . . . You will see that it does not deal with political or religious matters, or with any other subject that may divide people, but on the contrary its purpose is to help all to cultivate the land, to care for your health, to serve your families, countrymen and friends in a better way and, in general, to make us better and more useful for the well-being of this region, of our beloved state and of the great Mexican country. GOVERNOR ANGEL CARVAJAL, Jalapa, Veracruz, 24 July 1950

The above remarks, recorded by Angel Carvajal, the governor of Veracruz, to initiate a tour by a U.S. government mobile motion-picture unit, underlined the transnational cooperation between Mexican and U.S. political elites that characterized postwar mass-cultural programs. U.S. technicians taped his speech, which was played over the U.S. embassy sound truck's loudspeaker system at the beginning of each of the 65 exhibitions presented over the 35-day tour of 61 rural towns and villages in Veracruz in the summer of 1950. Governor Carvajal invited U.S. embassy propaganda officials to organize a tour of his state, after the conclusion of a similar swing through Hidalgo state. The officially sponsored program through Veracruz—one of Mexico's largest, most socially diverse, and politically and economically important states—represented a major transnational undertaking. "Representatives of different [federal] offices of Agriculture, Statistics, Public Works, Hydraulic Resources, the Rector of the State University, and the Directors of both State and Federal Education were present" at the tour's planning meetings in Jalapa, Veracruz's capital city, where state officials arranged the film mission's itinerary.[1]

The tour itself involved representatives of the state's agriculture, education, and health departments, who accompanied the sound truck, speaking on themes illustrated by the U.S. films. An advance man supplied by the governor organized local political authorities (*presidentes municipales*) to promote and oversee each exhibition. Printed handbills and other disposable advertising as well as performances by "local musical groups," who frequently played the popular *veracruzano* song "La Bamba" at dances prior to exhibitions, encouraged large turnouts.[2] Local politicians integrated the spectacles into their own political projects, which were the building blocks of the governor's and, ultimately, the national regime's political machine. In fact, the timing of the tour was determined by the governor's desire to have it completed before he ended his term of office. The collaborative film-distribution program aimed at Veracruz's remotest rural areas was as much an instrument of the governor's own project of social modernization and political socialization as it was a means of U.S. transnational social engineering and ideological persuasion.

At one of Carvajal's weekly meetings with "organized peasantry of the state" (where, according to a U.S. observer, he responded in "patriarchal" fashion to various grievances from throughout Veracruz), the governor announced to the assembled rural folk the impending commencement of the 1950 tour. In doing so, he invoked images that resonated with the Pan-American political messages promoted during World War II in films like *Juarez* (Warner Brothers' 1939 Pan-American antifascist feature).[3] U.S. officials present reported that "the Governor told the story of the American Revolution and explained how it had served as a stimulus for Mexican independence. He mentioned the Monroe Doctrine and its death blow to European colonization and pointed out the Juarez-Lincoln friendship and American pressure against Maximilian's regime in Mexico. The Governor underlined the common interests of the two countries, declared that they must work together, and told the people of the upcoming tour." [4]

The actual programs made explicit the connection between sociocultural and political penetration. The closing of each event (like the opening recording of the governor's welcoming words) betrayed the "non-political" claims of the U.S.-Mexican facilitators. Following the usual combination of visual education and cultural films—ranging from public health, personal hygiene practices, and agricultural methods to informational shorts about U.S. history and institutions, lifestyles, recreation, and labor organization—each program ended with the projection of *President Alemán Visits the United States,* which documented the Mexican leader's 1947 Washington visit. The short, newsreel-style film underlined friendly political relations between the two nations by demonstrating the respect accorded the Mexican president in the United States. Beginning with the tour through Hidalgo, the movie was "used to close all exhibitions . . . as it typifies the same cooperative good neighborly spirit shown by the co-sponsored tour [itself]"; according to the embassy, it was "received with enthusiasm." [5] As with Carvajal's Pan-American rhetoric, amplified at the start of each exhibition during the 1950 tour, the Good Neighbor images of President Miguel Alemán in Washington provided political symbols intended to persuade provincial Mexicans of the U.S. film program's national support by promoting positive images about U.S.-Mexico relations as mutually respectful. At the same time, the film typified the Mexican state's own program, inscribed within the U.S. one, to socialize popular audiences to its authority.

The sound-truck program focused on regional and local collaboration. By 1952, cooperation of Veracruz state officials had led to the acquisition of a "locally adapted Chevrolet motion picture sound truck [by] the American consulate" for regular visits to rural hamlets, institutionalizing the U.S. presence in Veracruz. Embassy officials further reported that the administration of Carvajal's successor, Marco Antonio Muñoz, dedicated itself to "expanding the USIE [the State Department's Office of International Information and Educational Exchange] motion picture program in the [state] . . . and has promised to provide a teacher to travel with the sound truck at all times." The Veracruz newspaper *El Dictamen* described the ceremony dedicating the mobile unit as an extension of "the cultural program which Mexico and the United States are carrying out to improve Mexican agriculture and livestock as well as conservation of soil and water, which are fundamental to the welfare of humanity." As the publicity made clear, the U.S. sound truck, which the article underlined would be operated jointly, was as much a symbol of the Mexican state's commitment to social progress as it was of international good neighborliness.[6]

Theorizing Transnationalization

This essay analyzes the distribution and reception of U.S. propaganda in Cold War Mexico, focusing on collaborative modes of exhibition established by U.S. and Mexican authorities. These transnational exchanges, at both the political and social levels, resemble what Mary Louise Pratt has described, in her study of nineteenth-century cross-cultural encounters in Latin America and Africa, as " 'contact zones,' social spaces where disparate cultures meet, clash, and grapple with each other, often in highly asymmetrical relations of domination and subordination." [7] Pratt provides a useful framework for conceptualizing the international efforts by the United States and Mexico to use U.S. film as a shared instrument of modernization and sociopolitical control in pursuit of convergent social practices (promoting "progress" through education) but separate political agendas (one aimed at national and the other at transnational socialization).[8] The film program, as well as the subjects of the movies themselves, reflected the discourse of development that dominated U.S. thinking about the "Third World" in the postwar period.[9] This article attempts to move beyond questions of ideology and representation to implementation and reception, or, as Arturo Escobar has recently put it in a somewhat broader context, "the effect and modes of operation of development discourses at the local level." [10]

It is difficult, however, to so neatly separate the local from the international, given the quality and extent of transnational Mexican and U.S. collaboration. Local, national, and international factors intersect in political, sociocultural, economic, and ideological realms, demanding an analysis that considers the representation and dissemination of images and ideas not as simple imperialist impositions but as collaborative processes involving complicated, often contradictory, transnational exchanges. Such an approach offers a theoretical basis for moving beyond the conventional methodological practices of two distinct disciplines, each of which lies at the heart of this study: international communications and diplomatic (or foreign-relations) history. In different ways, across ideological positions, each field has tended to adopt an overly U.S.-centric model that disregards the contact zone even as it offers assertions about the economic, political, and cultural structures that determine development there.

Much of the theoretical discourse about "cultural imperialism," particularly regarding the influence of U.S. mass media in Latin America, has too often assumed a mechanistic relationship between economic dependence and cultural domination. It often utilizes too simple a formulation of "transnationalization" that, ironically, has focused almost exclusively on U.S. penetration, ignoring national and local factors; it tends to assert claims of cultural hegemony based only on aggregate data regarding media flows,[11] or, alternatively, on a strictly textual analysis.[12] Historical studies of film reception have generally either focused on national elite discourse (such as the views of government officials, special-interest organizations, and film reviewers) or theoretically determined historical readings of cross-cultural popular reception.[13] A lack of empirical research and methods that too often deduce conclusions derived from nationalist paradigms have limited historical research about transnational aspects of mass culture.[14] This is not to diminish the hegemonic role of U.S. mass media (and economy and foreign policy) in Latin America. Rather, it is to suggest the need for a deeper conceptualization of how that hegemonic apparatus is constructed, one that comes to terms with *how* U.S. forces interact with the ideological projects of other states, utilize symbols produced by other nations, and, most important, are popularly understood.[15]

Historians of U.S. foreign relations have shed important light on the role of mass media in U.S. foreign policy and international business practices.[16] Thus far, however, scholars have less thoroughly examined the historical interaction of U.S. culture with other states and societies. For example, Cold War foreign policy studies on the development of specific projects or outlooks in Washington have generally focused exclusively on political and economic policy rather than the more everyday cultural experiences that characterize the U.S. presence for Latin Americans, especially in the postwar period.[17] Latin American specialists have begun to examine intercultural analysis of the production and representation of Mexico in the United States, but mostly at the level of high-culture elites and institutional relations.[18] Recent work on U.S. imperialism from a cultural studies perspective has also opened up key areas of representational analysis, but has not advanced as much cross-cultural interactional study.[19] A more processual analysis of U.S. foreign relations, one that borrows from recent interdisciplinary historical research on Latin American sociopolitical change, is necessary in order to excavate the transnational history so central to the development of the Americas.[20]

William Roseberry has written that "an anthropologist interested in Latin America should have something to say about Americanization. . . . He or she should be able to reject the homogenizing stereotype without retreating into the equally stereotypic comfort of the distinctiveness of his or her 'own people.' "[21] He places in relief the false dichotomy between cultural imperialism and nationalism. His call for research that decenters the metropolis, or, alternatively, centers the periphery, in an examination of how transnational forces shape everyday experience in developing nations offers a conceptualization useful to historians of the transnational U.S. presence in Latin America (and elsewhere): "Our more automatic and unreflective ways of thinking about the conjunction of local and global historical processes are inadequate. We commonly refer to 'internal' and 'external' factors as if they could be easily distinguished and identified." [22]

In line with this concern, this article seeks to reorient the study of transnational relations by placing Mexico at the center of action where issues of political and cultural reception are concerned. Too, by listening for "silences" in relations, this work attempts to come to terms with the density of cross-cultural relations *in* Mexico rather than to make conclusions about reception or impact, that is, Americanization, based simply on the aggregate presence of U.S. mass media. This approach reconstructs the historical study of international relations as a mosaic of local, socially differentiated, transnational cultural experiences, rather than the more conventional painting of international economic and political exchanges.

World War into Cold War

In terms of U.S. foreign policy, World War II accelerated the movement from point-to-point communications and elite exchanges to an emphasis on mass media and popular culture. The war modernized U.S. foreign relations by deepening the collaboration of U.S. culture industries and various international bureaucracies. Wartime Latin America was the incubator of those policies (e.g., the production and distribution of print, radio, and film propaganda; the institutionalization of international public education and rural health programs; intellectual exchanges; and the establishment of U.S. lending libraries) that became globalized in the Cold War. The war also signified the deepening of state-to-state and transnational links between the United States and Mexico. Film was the key mass medium undergirding U.S.-Mexican sociocultural relations. It was the site where many fundamental ideological and politico-economic issues were worked out on a variety of levels significant for the overall framework of U.S.-Mexican relations.

Programs instituted by the Motion Picture Division of Nelson Rockefeller's Office of the Coordinator of Inter-American Affairs (OCIAA) ranged from the distribution of prowar/Pan-American, Hollywood, and U.S.-government-produced propaganda in Mexico to the transnational production of films by the Mexican government and the OCIAA's Hollywood apparatus. Such projects aimed to refashion the image of the Mexican state and society for consumption in the United States and Mexico as well as elsewhere in the Western Hemisphere.[23] As regards production, the OCIAA's most ambitious project involved the modernization of Mexico's commercial film industry in order to develop a source of ideologically correct and culturally authentic entertainment as political propaganda for the Spanish-speaking Americas. This wartime project linking Mexican film producers and U.S. propaganda officials facilitated the partnership of Emilio Azcárraga and RKO in establishing Estudios Churubusco as Latin America's most important postwar film and (later) television studio.[24]

After World War II, the U.S. government maintained its extensive wartime film project in Latin America, based in Mexico. In Washington, the OCIAA's culture programs were folded into State Department bureaucracies. In Mexico, the American Association, the quasi-governmental group composed of private U.S. citizens (principally businessmen residing in Mexico City) that had facilitated OCIAA wartime cultural projects through a national network of regional coordination committees, was dissolved, and the U.S. embassy and regional consulates became the implementation centers for culture programs. A series of overlapping State Department dependencies, beginning with the Office of International Information and Cultural Affairs (OIC) in 1946 and culminating with the Office of International Information and Educational Exchange (USIE) in 1949, directed visual-education and cultural propaganda programs. The State Department's International Motion Picture Division (IMP) produced the films, which were administered abroad by United States Information Service (USIS) officials based in the U.S. embassies. These functions were streamlined under the management of the United States Information Agency (USIA), formed in 1953, which represented the institutionalization of propaganda promotion as a Cold War weapon.[25]

U.S. officials in Mexico reported that film was the most extensively and effectively deployed weapon in their cultural arsenal. Aimed at the twin goals of social modernization and ideological indoctrination, the initial postwar film program mainly consisted of visual education and cultural dissemination and was not overtly political in terms of narrative content. Picking up on the wartime project, films were deemed especially useful in reaching rural and urban workers, due to the popular appeal of movies as an entertainment form and as a mobile means to communicate with illiterate (and underliterate) rural and urban audiences. In terms of content and form, the films combined social modernization with political objectives. In selling U.S. lifestyles, in promoting more efficient modes of agricultural and industrial production, and in disseminating "modern" social practices inculcating health and literacy, the USIE intended to build a social infrastructure that would forge transnational links with marginalized and potentially radicalized Mexican social sectors. U.S. planners sought to build popular support for the United States through appreciation for the service of visual education itself, and, at the same time, to demonstrate the superiority of U.S. ways and create an enduring transnational visual vocabulary:

> The regular USIE program is a long range program which tends over the years to promote understanding, friendship; to explain the United States "Way of Life"; to reach and teach each year to groups which are entering "civilization"; to influence the growing child, the new literate, the person crossing class barriers, who now has new demands and desires; to aid the student and technician; to cultivate the workers and labor unions; contact and influence the leaders and formers of public opinion. Nevertheless there are enough accounts of an almost immediate impact on individuals and on groups, quite aside from the commercial sales of United States goods, to justify the program to the most hard-headed but intelligent opponent of the program.[26]

Very specific in crafting exhibitions, U.S. officials made sure "content is always carefully selected for the particular audiences intended." [27] The two most important groups were industrial workers and peasants, the very sectors whose continued political incorporation was crucial to the Mexican state as it pursued increasingly private-sector-minded agricultural and industrial development oriented toward postwar capitalist accumulation. In pursuit of these ends, the U.S. government's and Mexican state's ideological projects converged on several levels in the transnational film program.[28]

As regards elite political consensus, the U.S. embassy reported that President-elect Miguel Alemán received regular screenings, arranged by General Zuno Hernández (who oversaw the Mexican army's extensive exhibition of USIS-distributed motion pictures), and "showed great interest in the films and organization of the work." [29] Likewise, Alemán's minister of economy, Antonio Ruiz Galindo, "expressed himself in favor of the . . . film program" and arranged regular private screenings at his home for audiences that included President Alemán, Minister of the Interior Adolfo Ruiz Cortines, the director of the national oil company (PEMEX), as well as "other Cabinet members, Senators, and leading figures in Mexico's political, intellectual, and industrial life." Among this group's favorites was Disney's wartime animated public health film *Defense against Invasion* (1944), discussed below.[30] In 1952 the embassy reported that "President-elect Ruiz Cortines continued to use USIS films in his private home until almost election time." And, during a visit by USIS sound trucks at the annual agricultural fair in Apatzingán, Michoacán, "important contacts (including ex-president Lázaro Cárdenas) were renewed," demonstrating the program's popularity across the state-party's ideological spectrum.[31]

In terms of everyday bureaucratic collaboration, the Mexican state continued to expand its wartime role distributing U.S. government films, thereby reinforcing the project carried out by the embassy and consuls through their own network of 16 mm projectors dispersed throughout the nation. As OCIAA channels receded, U.S. embassy personnel searched for ways to expand Mexican government exhibitions. The American Association reported in 1946 that the "need for more film in Mexico is fast becoming desperate." Regarding exhibition, it recommended that "with the program being put on a permanent basis it might be that the directors of the motion picture department in Washington would be interested in operation and organization of the program in Mexico, due to the very low cost of the program and the very excellent results which we are obtaining." Instead of imposing an entirely new motion-picture bureaucracy, the association suggested maintaining the existing network of projectors "operated through the cooperation of business firms and Mexican officials." [32] Increasingly in the postwar period, the Mexican state took over the wartime role U.S. transnational corporations had played in exhibiting OCIAA films.[33] The American Association, for example, served as a liaison among the Secretaría de Educación Pública, the Secretaría de Agricultura, and the State Department's IMP in meeting the demands of Mexican bureaucracies in the wake of the OCIAA's demise.[34] Through its expanding links with the Mexican state, the USIS significantly increased the invasiveness of the overall U.S. propaganda project.

In addition to its direct exhibitions and loans of films to Mexican state, civil, business, and labor organizations, by mid-1947 the USIS had over 150 projectors "on loan to Mexican government agencies [that] are operated without cost to the U.S. Government. The Mexican agencies hire the operator, and pay all the other expenses involved." Fifteen of the twenty projectors operated by the U.S. embassy were loaned, as well, to the Mexican government, "which will assume all costs of operation." Every state ministry, important agricultural organization, union, and industry, as well as elementary and secondary schools, universities, and civil and religious groups, participated in the postwar U.S. film program.[35] Mexican institutions provided detailed reports on exhibitions, allowing U.S. administrators to monitor and control national operations. By the beginning of 1948, nationwide attendance at exhibitions conducted by Mexican organizations reached over 1,200,000 persons monthly; over half of these showings were accredited to the Secretaría de Educación Pública (SEP).[36] The USIS also operated a motorized unit, part of what would become a small fleet by the early 1950s. Postwar mobile projections evolved from the OCIAA's extensive rural exhibition program, which had extended projection of U.S. propaganda films beyond the walls of the U.S. embassy, consulates, and cultural centers (such as Mexico City's Biblioteca Benjamin Franklin). These events enabled Mexican provincial bureaucracies to incorporate remote areas into the central government's mass-media project. U.S. innovations also built on long-standing links with the postrevolutionary state's political and social engineering project. For example, in many ways the USIS system represented the transnationalization of the rural education program pursued by the SEP under José Vasconcelos in the early 1920s, both in terms of infrastructure (mobile programs) and ideology (acculturation of Indians).[37]

Motorized units were equipped to project films outdoors, against buildings or on a portable screen carried in the embassy's vehicle. Of the four daily exhibitions made by the embassy's sound truck in 1947, three were sponsored by the Ministry of Public Health and the other was part of "the anti-illiteracy campaign of the Ministry of Public Education." In the early postwar period, exhibitions focused on Mexico City and its environs. Two Mexican operators working with the Filmoteca Nacional (the government's distributor for public film programs), funded by the U.S. embassy, made six daily showings, two each in primary, secondary, and night schools under the auspices of the SEP. In order to facilitate the ever-growing system, the USIS modified its production methods. It produced single fifty-minute reels containing programs of five to six short films that could be circulated more easily than multiple reels and allowed for more control of decentralized dissemination by regularizing the order and content of exhibitions.[38]

The first showing of the new one-reel programs, presented at the Cooperativo de Ejidatarios y Obreros del Ingenio del Mante, S.C.L., in Tamaulipas state, was delayed while the embassy awaited the State Department's shipment of "opening and closing footage saying: Presented by the United States Information Service." [39] The Mexican state's expansion of exhibitions of U.S. films to even the most nationalist of projects, such as Cárdenas-era social experiments in agricultural and industrial worker organization, indicated how closely its postwar project paralleled the sociocultural objectives of U.S. foreign policy. The importance of giving the USIS credit at each exhibition demonstrates how U.S. social engineering was tied to foreign policy objectives. Buying goodwill through the extension of visual education as a social service was also a way to inculcate progressive practices conducive to capitalist development and social modernization believed to be consistent with long-term U.S. influence.

Mexican collaboration was crucial to the U.S. mission. The SEP's key role in distributing U.S. propaganda dramatized the profound shifts in the state's postrevolutionary cultural policies (from the days of José Vasconcelos's promotion of nationalist public art through sponsorship of the muralist movement led by Diego Rivera, David Alfaro Siqueiros, and José Clemente Orozco, which, despite the actually more moderate economic and international policies of the Mexican state, was frequently radically anti-American and anticapitalist in its messages). By early 1948, SEP exhibitions of U.S.-government-supplied films accounted for more than half of the Mexican government's total, averaging over 600,000 viewers per month. In addition, by mid-1948 that ministry's Departamento de Alfabetismo (literacy) operated a fleet of eighteen sound trucks continuously exhibiting thirty different one- and two-hour programs prepared by the embassy's USIS staff. President Alemán's inauguration of five new SEP sound trucks, in May 1948, underlined their function as transnational instruments of Mexican as well as U.S. cultural policies.[40]

The impetus for educational collaboration did not come only from the federal government. For example, having been denied a USIS projector, the teachers' union in San Luis Potosí obtained its own and prepared to "inaugurate their program" exhibiting USIE films that the embassy was eager to supply.[41] Where SEP sound trucks did not go, the Mexican state improvised new forms of state dissemination. Later in 1948, for instance, the Mexican army made a two-month tour of remote areas of southern Mexico distributing U.S. films.[42] Although this essay is concerned with working-class and peasant audiences, it should be added that the embassy also coordinated the distribution of films aimed at modernizing important social professions, especially medicine.[43] In 1948, the Ministry of Public Health and the Institute of Inter-American Affairs (the OCIAA's successor in implementing development programs in Latin America) jointly sponsored major conferences "in Chihuahua, Monterrey, and Nuevo Laredo . . . for the special training of doctors and nurses working in health centers." They also exhibited films at a "Medical Military Congress" in Durango.[44]

Industry and Labor

While the widespread, itinerant wartime distribution of film propaganda by U.S. businessmen waned, transnational U.S. capital established new, more structured film programs aimed at expanding their interests in postwar Mexico. General Motors "requested special films to be shown at their annual salesman convention." [45] The chief of General Electric's Mexican subsidiary previewed a film about television that had been produced by his company's North American parent and donated it to the USIS to exhibit before "persons associated with television developments in Mexico." [46] U.S. corporations also produced films for USIS distribution that furthered their commercial agenda by promoting new consumption patterns that converged with the modernization goals of U.S. embassy officials and the Mexican state. For example, in July 1948 the North American general manager of Home Products of Mexico "loaned the embassy a second copy" of the ironically named *La Guardia Blanca,* a Spanish-language oral hygiene short produced in the United States by the Kolinos Tooth Paste Company, to be exhibited by USIS.[47] The film's "very good reception wherever it has been shown" led embassy officials to request twenty additional prints and to recommend it to the IMP for "world distribution through the [State] Department's program." Not only did U.S. corporations use USIS networks to extend North American social practices and economic interests in Mexico, but the Mexican state also utilized U.S. cultural infrastructure to further its postwar program to develop a modern society based in progressive capitalist social development. Toward these ends, the Ministry of Economy, a major booster of USIS exhibitions, initiated a two-year "Industrial Train" tour in the summer of 1948. In addition to its principal "exhibition of industrial equipment" to foster technological change, the train carried forty-one films provided by the embassy for "daily motion picture exhibition . . . shown in plazas outside the train." [48]

More pervasive were USIS-produced and distributed films exhibited by national and transnational capital as a means for shaping the thoughts of its growing Mexican labor force, which also represented an expanding body of potential consumers. Explosivos, S.A., a Dupont subsidiary located in the aptly named Dinamita, Durango, for example, "requested films for the workers of the plant" to be shown in "a plant theater" equipped with newly purchased 16 mm and 35 mm projectors. Dupont also "requested 2 special films for showings to their workmen and people in nearby villages" at their "chemical assembly plants in Torreon and Chihuahua." [49] Mexican businessmen also expanded their own significant collaboration in the distribution of U.S. films by facilitating exhibitions of movies deemed useful as instruments of social control and modernization. U.S. officials reported in 1948, for example, that "Enrique Huber, of Equipos Mecanicos, S.A. in Mexico City is starting a one hour weekly program for his workers." [50] In the key northeastern industrial city of Monterrey, "film totals zoomed into the stratosphere" in May 1950, as 82,125 persons attended U.S. government film exhibitions.[51] U.S. officials explained that these figures were "fattened by Servicios Coordinados, Tostadores Monterrey and other mass-production exhibitors." Over three-fourths of the attendance had been recorded at exhibitions of films loaned by USIS officials to groups like the previously mentioned Mexican industries rather than at events directly administered by U.S. operatives. Not only were the means of exhibition becoming more and more diffuse, woven into the fabric of Mexican industrial capitalism, but film itself was replacing other forms of official U.S. propaganda distributed to Mexico's proletariat. For instance, a U.S. official in Monterrey observed that, "in contrast to the film program, the use of Embassy press releases [disseminated through local newspapers] declined sharply." [52]

Provincial industrial enterprises did not escape the attention of U.S. officials. While Monterrey attendance soared, "a lumber king of South East Mexico" with holdings in the states of Campeche, Quintana Roo, and Yucatán "bought a new projector to be able to use USIE motion pictures. His first report was that the exhibitions had been 'fantastically successful.' " [53] Enlightened Mexican capitalism could serve too as a subject for U.S. propaganda production. U.S. officials proposed a film based on the enterprise of former economy minister Antonio Ruiz Galindo, "one of the most progressive industrialists in Latin America," who operated (among his other large-scale enterprises) a "model [steel furniture] factory where workers enjoy ideal working conditions" including extensive social services.[54]

Collaboration was not limited to industrial capital. Demonstrating its affiliation with the state's postwar project, emphasizing aggregate production and political subordination of workers, government-aligned organized labor—across diverse sectors and occupations—also facilitated transnational exhibitions. U.S. functionaries explained that "labor unions and other labor groups are a target the Embassy has been endeavoring with increasing success to reach. . . . In many places of the Republic the Embassy has active labor collaborators." Public affairs officials reported many conquests: in Puebla state, "an embassy sound truck accompanied the Labor Attaché to showings among unions . . . with marked success, so much so, that the Embassy was asked to cooperate in the celebration of the 20th Anniversary of the founding of the confederation of unions." U.S. government observers reported from Tamaulipas state that "a large collective sugar refinery in El Mante . . . gives many showings [of U.S. films] not only for its own personnel but in surrounding collective farms." [55] In Mexico City, by the end of 1952, the embassy reported that "13 organized labor groups are being reached . . . on a regular schedule. . . . Weekly exhibitions have been given to the laborers and employees at University City [the campus of Mexico's National Autonomous University], where 18,000 workers are employed in 3 shifts. Attendance at exhibitions has ranged from 1,000 to 4,000 workers. In addition to the film showings, pamphlets are being distributed through their foremen," who announced the programs over a campuswide loudspeaker system.[56]

The U.S. focus on labor aimed to counter perceived communist subversion rather than simply promote U.S. ideas and lifestyles. This became even more urgent following the outbreak of the Korean War. In 1950, as USIS-administered mobile-unit exhibitions moved more aggressively beyond the Federal District, a sound-truck tour of Puebla, Oaxaca, and Chiapas states "had as specific targets, chosen by the embassy's labor officer to strengthen his provincial contacts, to wean faltering labor groups from their Communistic or other extremist connections." The mission would "enable the Labor Officer to make a first hand investigation of Communism in those states. . . . With its specific target [it] was like a military offensive, in that it went directly to the point and attained its objective before unfriendly elements knew what was happening." In this case, the "target" was Salina Cruz, Oaxaca's main Pacific port, where a few weeks earlier prominent Marxist labor leader—and former head of the Confederación de Trabajadores de México (CTM)—Vicente Lombardo Toledano "had visited . . . giving speeches attacking the United States and forwarding the Communist cause." Operatives reported that the "reception was excellent" among the 3,600 persons who attended. The *lombardista* Mexico City–based national newspaper *El Popular* denounced the U.S. exhibition: "These things occurred in such a shameless fashion that one of the vehicles from which the films were projected even bore the name of the North American Embassy." [57]

Most of the exhibitions aimed at labor involved more everyday interactions intended to offset radical organizing. In this light, the embassy's film officer noted: "The Miners' Union of Real del Monte, in which there has been a raging Red and anti-Red controversy for some time, is a regular user of USIE motion pictures." And in Guaymas, Sonora, on the Gulf of

California, the embassy described how "the Consulate [film] operator . . . gives regular showings before hundreds of unionists in that important port where Communist influence is said to be strong." [58] The embassy pointed out that it distributed films to "all types of organizations," including ones like the El Angel textile workers' union where "Alejandro Carrillo, member of the Communist Party and former Assistant Governor of the Federal District, gave a campaign speech . . . for Vicente Lombardo Toledano, Presidential Candidate for the Communist Party." [59]

Since the embassy viewed oil workers as the most radically anti-American of all Mexican labor groups, it took particular pride in announcing motion-picture propaganda advances in the petroleum sector. It was pleased that the state-owned company Petróleos de México (PEMEX), which had assumed oil production and distribution following the government's 1938 expropriation and nationalization of foreign holdings, facilitated U.S. efforts at antiradical, Cold War socialization. In April 1950, PEMEX officials in the company's northern zone were working "to see how a closer coordination of efforts might be attained in film showings among the oil workers in and around Tampico," Mexico's key international petroleum port and refining center.[60] In September, U.S. operatives announced that PEMEX officials had "arranged a regular circuit of ten places of exhibition among its workers in several towns, mostly in union halls." In addition, the "temporary loan of Embassy projectors to [PEMEX] authorities in the famous Poza Rica Oil field resulted in purchase of a projector and regular exhibitions of USIE material." Completing a geographic north-south sweep of Mexico's oil region, a U.S. propaganda officer reported that "an oil workers' union in southern Veracruz is also a regular user of USIE material." [61] In 1951, the USIS boasted of a historically symbolic act of cultural collaboration: "Lazaro Cárdenas's pet union," the national oil workers' Sindicato de Trabajadores Petroleros de la República Mexicana (whose activism had stimulated the 1938 expropriation), requested installation of U.S. "film facilities for their various offices throughout the Republic." [62] The labor organization that more than any other publicly represented the postrevolutionary Mexican state's economic nationalism and political sovereignty now demonstrated, through its bureaucratic collaboration with U.S. mass-culture programmers, the ideological shift in national labor leadership and foreign policy toward the United States during the 1940s.[63]

Despite periodic international disputes over issues such as protected trade or restrictions on foreign capital in Mexico or even U.S. anticommunism in Latin America, postwar U.S.-Mexican relations were founded in a transnationalized alliance. Its logic reflected the ideological convergence of the Mexican state's antiradical political project and its accumulation-oriented industrial objectives with the goals of anticommunist-tinged, neoimperial U.S. foreign policy. Reflecting this pattern, film propaganda led to the integration of Mexican workers into U.S. systems of political persuasion and social instruction. The movies themselves demonstrated the depth of the transnationalized discourse.

U.S. officials in Mexico targeted labor as a group particularly susceptible to radical critiques of U.S. state, society, and, especially, Cold War foreign policy. As the Cold War heated up in Korea in the early 1950s, they recommended production of more politically oriented films.[64] Operatives urged development of films that showed "how unions who cooperate with management increase productivity." Organized U.S. labor, in its postwar, antiradical, corporatist mode, provided a model in USIS propaganda films such as *A Young Trade Union Member, Apprentice Training,* and *With These Hands* (a historical consideration of U.S. labor organization). Future labor films, an embassy propaganda specialist recommended, should demonstrate for Mexican workers how "the American laborer enjoy[ed] a higher standard of living than his counterpart in any other country in the world. He is a consumer as well as a producer, creating a greater demand for goods, which benefits both labor and capital." [65]

A Young Trade Union Member[66] was typical of the narrative of nonradical "democratic" organization proffered by Cold War U.S. propaganda in Latin America. As part of its effort to marginalize Marxist challenges to U.S.-aligned capitalist development, such as that mounted (at least rhetorically) by former CTM chief Vicente Lombardo Toledano's Confederación de Trabajadores de América Latina (CTAL), U.S. foreign policy extended its long-standing alliance with the American Federation of Labor (AFL).[67] The film, produced for the USIS with the cooperation of Local No. 11 of the AFL's International Association of Bridge, Structural, and Ornamental Iron Workers, relates the story of Robert Findlay, an apprentice ironworker seeking to become a journeyman through entry into the union. Individual social mobility, not class consciousness, is the film's recommendation to workers; this meant playing by the union's rules. In order to gain a better life for his kid sister, his widowed mother, and his sweetheart (whom he intends to marry once he is promoted), Robert must learn not only his trade but also the procedural practices of AFL-style membership. To gain entry into this "select circle of artisans," as the narrator explains, Robert studies the top-down procedures of union decision making. Material progress comes through obeying a labor regime of

established authorities who cooperate with capital and patriotically support the nation-state. Opinions are expressed by individual members in
"democratic" shop meetings that channel worker discourse through sanctioned representatives. Adherence to procedure rather than political debate is emphasized; the system itself is presented as inherently democratic
and therefore beyond negation. This message suited not only the antiradical policies of Cold War U.S. foreign policy (especially in the larger
industrial nations of Latin America) but also the policies of the Mexican
state and the increasingly conservative CTM, which controlled Mexican
labor through *charrismo* (government-backed bossism). For complementary reasons, the government and the confederation sought to contain internal workers' movements for union democratization, independent organization, and social justice.[68] The CTAL itself was viewed by the State
Department as a subversive international political force (a disseminator of
anti-U.S., Soviet-supported propaganda) that challenged a pro-U.S. labor
regime in Latin America.[69]

Rural Tours

U.S. planners, reflecting the day's dominant liberal ideology, believed in
Mexico's potential for economic development and social progress. In their
eyes, film programs accelerated a national process of modernization that
was transforming urban labor into a skilled, socially mobile workforce
and the peasantry into an urban proletariat. One U.S. official observed that
"the white-collar class is growing, people are going from domestic service to offices, stores, and factories. Farmers are going into industry. Class
barriers are being crossed increasingly." [70] At the same time, "the increasing growth of the tourist trade, the growing numbers of foreigners who
make their home in Mexico, the numbers of Mexicans visiting the United
States . . . are creating changes in the mentality of the Mexican masses."
USIE films would hasten modernization through the transnationalization
of everyday Mexican life and thought by disseminating U.S. information
and inculcating progressive economic practices and social values. This
was particularly important in rural Mexico, owing to its presumed lag in
integration into dominant national and transnational systems of communication. Overcoming provincial isolation would create the sociocultural
infrastructure that U.S. planners deemed crucial for economic development as well as U.S. cultural hegemony in what was feared to be a fertile
field for the cultivation of radical ideologies.[71]

Film proved particularly useful in reaching remote rural audiences with the message of progress through socialization (instead of socialism). In 1950, U.S. public affairs officials in Mexico reported that "the largest groups being reached at present through the efforts of collaborators and Embassy and Consulate operators are peasants, small farmers, ranchers and inhabitants of small towns and villages. . . . The bulk of these groups is contacted by collaborators rather than Embassy or consulate personnel." In many indigenous communities, USIE films were "interpreted on the spot into several Indian languages." [72] The liberal-progressive ideology supporting U.S. propaganda in postwar Mexico was best expressed through the goals of the motion-picture program, which sought to reach out to peasants with the same techniques used in cities and towns:

Some people wonder about the importance of the uneducated masses to the USIE. The urban Mexicans are reached easily by all the propaganda media. They are accessible to word of mouth influence as well. The reported words of an American documentary film producer, "Why teach the Indians to wash their teeth?" seems to take it for granted that the underprivileged and undereducated mass will stay so always. It must be remembered that more and more of these people are constantly being absorbed into a higher level of Mexican life. The children are extremely important and many of the leaders are anxious to teach the people to improve themselves, adults as well as the younger ones. What is the best way therefore to contact and influence all the groups which make up Mexico, the literates, the non-literates, the monolinguals, those in remote regions as well as the principal population sectors? [73]

The instrument that made these mass-cultural excursions possible was the motorized mobile exhibition unit (pictured in figure 1). Continuing propaganda practices developed during World War II, U.S. government officials coordinated tours by specially equipped vehicles to travel through areas without motion-picture equipment and/or electricity, or even adequate structures within or on which to project films. The embassy's motion-picture officer, Homer Gayne, argued for increased levels of sound-truck exhibition as the only form of mass communication that could confront underdevelopment in rural Mexico. The sound trucks would "overcome the mentality of some of these persons cut off by the barriers of language, illiteracy, electric current and lack of roads . . . that of the uneducated Mexicans in the post-conquest period." Casting USIS personnel as modern-day *conquistadores,* Gayne argued that only a cavalry of sound trucks could bring social modernization to Mexico's least integrated areas. Besides the inherent communication advantages perceived by propaganda

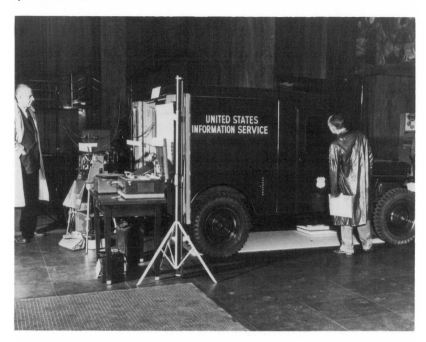

Figure 1. "Mobile motion picture unit (jeep) equipped with 16mm projector, 35mm film strip projector, tape recorder, radio receiver, two speed record player, screen, transformer, cables and films. Truck motor generates current to operate equipment. 77 such units are placed for use in isolated areas of the world to distribute U.S. Information program." This description was provided by the State Department's International Motion Picture Division in 1950, when this vehicle was launched into service. (306-PS-50-5072, National Archives Still Picture Branch)

officials in the visual appeal of film, the USIS's other major mass medium often could not overcome rural obstacles. Radio was often ineffective, owing to a variety of cultural and technological factors: monolingualism, absence of electricity, shortages of radios, or inadequate sound-wave reception.[74]

By 1953, the embassy reported that the "USIS is becoming more and more convinced that the best method for conducting its motion picture programs is by means of sound truck." With such vehicles, U.S. operatives sought to reach "the seven million illiterates [representing] roughly a quarter of the population of Mexico. . . . Many of this group can only gain any knowledge about the United States from the USIS motion pictures which are brought to them by sound truck tours." The impact of the tours was multiplied by the popularity of the films (especially animated subjects) with the "many children of school age in the audience, to which pamphlets and publications are also distributed; undoubtedly [the adult] population gets some additional knowledge through their children." [75]

Some of the most enthusiastically received productions did not aim to impart hygiene, sanitation, health, literacy, or U.S. history. Operatives reported that "each borrower wishes at least one sports film on each program." Such shorts were "invaluable in attracting new audiences. Aside from promoting contacts with new groups, such as the Syndicate of Directors of Physical Education, requests for such films have been received from State Directors of Physical Education, coaches from various Universities and others who have not formerly been on the Embassy list of borrowers. A sports film shown even in the most remote village, strangely enough, never fails to interest and attract."

During a weeklong sports festival sponsored by the Baseball Association and Department of Physical Education of Oaxaca, "USIE sports films were used and some of the more serious as well." Such productions usefully supplemented the "more serious" subjects: "Sports films serve in many ways to implement USIE objectives. It is just as important to show countries how the American public plays as it is to show how it works. American sports films show not only the need for physical stamina, a result of proper diet and habits, but also the need for cooperation, for teamwork, for the tradition of sportsmanship, and other sides of the American picture not shown in other films." [76]

The embassy's public affairs officer reported that in Mexico City, U.S. football was catching on owing to goodwill tours by U.S. clubs and contact with North American media, so much so that "one of the best ways to reach a new and large segment of the population would be through films on football." He added that "baseball films . . . are constantly used," and that soccer was also nationally popular "in smaller cities and villages." Basketball was particularly pervasive in rural villages where there were "courts, even in places with very little level ground. . . . As there is little expenditure necessary it can be played freely by the under-privileged." [77] Favorable rural reception of sports films did not depend on prior exposure to the games demonstrated. In a remote town in Puebla state, a longtime U.S. resident who projected USIE films reported that during an exhibition "the audience requested that *Aces of the Diamond* be repeated, although they are unfamiliar with the game of baseball in this community." [78] In many cases, the ground had no doubt been prepared by earlier national sports programs; the popularity of U.S. sports films, especially about basketball, no doubt had much to do with their superimposition on longer-standing SEP practices promoting progressive (i.e., U.S.-style) athletics provincially.[79]

In conducting provincial sound-truck exhibitions, U.S. officials considered the involvement of local Mexican authorities crucial in order to ensure access and legitimacy: "The Embassy is increasingly cognizant of the success of the approach of getting co-sponsorship from the highest municipal or state authority for open-air showings and special campaigns. In this manner there is no segment of the population which has a valid reason for not cooperating, as might be the case were the Embassy to allow co-sponsorship by the town priest or teacher." [80] Beginning in 1950, state governors, as in the case of Carvajal in Veracruz, began to sponsor sound-truck tours as part of their own political projects. For example, the 1950 USIE tour of Hidalgo state was temporarily delayed to await the governor's recovery from illness, so that he could participate as a cosponsor. Meanwhile, planning went ahead "to make a real event of this tour with cooperation of all municipal and state authorities in the fields of health and agriculture." [81]

U.S. operatives oversaw the exhibitions, which were carried out by Mexican personnel. Reinforcing the direct efforts of the U.S. tours, "several [Mexican] government agencies and commercial enterprises have many mobile units, motorized, on launches, and on muleback, which give free showings constantly throughout the Republic." [82] Rural exhibitions conducted by Mexican authorities demonstrated how geographically invasive and promotionally innovative the program had become. During the 1950 Veracruz tour, for example, the U.S. contingent reported that on arrival in the town of Alvarado they were informed that a recent exhibition in the town square had included films fitting the description of the sound-truck's inventory: "investigation proved that they had been shown by the teacher in charge of the Floating Cultural Mission . . . which plies the Papaloapan River, giving showings of USIE films." [83]

The outdoor exhibitions were as much a form of mass-cultural foreign policy as they were a way to absorb regional Mexican elites, whether federal or local civil officials, priests, or teachers, into U.S.-directed networks. In planning the Veracruz tour, the embassy's agricultural attaché met with "officials of the National Food Producers' Association . . . to discuss a showing at a National Congress in Túxpam." The motion picture officer arranged for "a sound-truck to be sent to give daily showings to the delegates from all over Mexico, and in the evening, showings in the public plaza to be sponsored by the Association." Several thousand people saw the films and received the USIE publications that were always distributed along with the exhibitions. Officials pronounced the event a "great success." [84] Involvement of "local personnel, well-trained, well-coordinated, well-indoctrinated and well-supervised," to lead follow-up community discussions after "open-air showings" was crucial. As one operative noted: "The presence in a village of a foreigner is apt to be a novelty, participation is liable to cause mistrust and be a drawback, arousing inherent timidity and inhibiting the *campesino's* enjoyment and full appreciation of the program." [85]

Episodic evidence, refracted through the gaze of U.S. officials, points to the impact of these exhibitions on local populations. For example, "after seeing the film *Dime Que Dientes Tienes* [Tell me about your teeth], the Mije Indians of Oaxaca exhausted the stock of tooth brushes and tooth paste in the various local stores, and everybody, young and old, were busy brushing their teeth the next day." [86] Two years later, on a 72-village tour sponsored by Oaxaca's governor that made 92 exhibitions before 61,362 spectators, the most popular film was *El Maravilloso Frijol Soya* [The versatile soybean]: "Everywhere this film was shown, members of the audience would ask the sound truck operator, and, in many cases, the Films Officer, for literature on raising soybeans." Following the mission, state agriculture officials reported record requests for soybean seed. Personal statements further indicated favorable local reception to U.S. officials: in Juchitán, "where many of the inhabitants speak only *Zapoteca,* one of the local citizens addressed the audience of 2,000 in their native language, welcoming the sound truck to the town." Afterward the man made "a speech of thanks for the valuable educational and cultural program furnished by the Embassy." [87] Toward the end of the Veracruz tour, the embassy's motion picture officer joined the U.S. film delegation at an exhibition in the town of Paso del Toro: "When interest was keen in the TVA [Tennessee Valley Authority] picture the skies suddenly opened," rapidly dispersing the approximately 500 spectators and leaving only the "bedraggled USIE personnel." As the delegation departed, an indigenous farmer commented, "What a shame—that picture was really good! When are you coming back?" [88] During the 1950 Veracruz tour, audiences varied in size from 4,500 to 200, and operators frequently noted the long distances traveled by spectators to view the films. In one case, a U.S. official reported that despite delays due to technical problems "losing several minutes, the people [about 3,000] stayed in the plaza until the end." [89]

The most widely distributed films were Disney's animated health and hygiene shorts, originally subsidized by the OCIAA during the war.[90] Among Mexican bureaucrats, their reputation spread by word of mouth, and local health officials demanded them regularly. Responding to such a request, "an American nurse married to a Mexican rancher" carried an old U.S. government "projector [probably acquired during the war] on burro-back to a town five miles away" from her own "remote village," in order to exhibit Disney's health-oriented cartoons *Tuberculosis, Defensa Contra la Invasión, El Cuerpo Humano,* and *¿Agua: Amiga o Enemiga?* She combined these with shorts on baseball, U.S. music, agriculture (including Disney's Pan-American cartoon on the virtues of corn, *The Grain That Built a Hemisphere*), and even a wartime OCIAA travelogue, *Yucatán,* to an audience of just over 200 persons composed of students from four rural schools and their parents. As often was the case, the Disney films paved the way for public health projects. "Vaccinations," the nurse reported, "were given the day following exhibition of 'Defense Against Invasion' and the response was tremendous." [91]

A note about content is called for. The images used in several of these films implicitly privileged U.S. property relations and cultural values. By depicting, for example, privately owned family farms as models for rural development, the shorts were intended to serve as instruments of social engineering to rationalize local political economies along U.S. lines. [92] Much like *A Young Trade Union Member,* these films reflected a liberal-developmentalist ideology that sought to impose U.S. ideals on Latin American development. Unlike the labor films, though, the health and literacy productions invoked (animated) Latin American representations as examples. [93] Moreover, these cartoon images reflected the unique production of the films, which had been made with the collaboration of Mexican officials for dissemination throughout Latin America. [94]

As with the labor films, we should turn to an example. *Saneamiento del Ambiente* [Sanitation of the environment] (1945), part of Disney and the OCIAA's wartime *Salud para las Américas* series, was the only health short that focused on urban rather than rural development. Also, although narratively similar to the other cartoons, its message was different in that it suggested that government intervention was necessary to confront the challenges posed by the rapid population growth and economic changes affecting cities. However, its exceptional status demonstrates clearly the dominant message and narrative structure of the social engineering shorts: the state would be the agent of modernization through moderate reform rather than radical restructuring; personal and community hygiene practices would protect the local environment, laying the groundwork for development.

Addressing the impact of rural-urban migration in Latin America in the

1940s, *Saneamiento* depicts the growth of a small town into a large city. Like the other films in the series, *Saneamiento*'s model of local development emphasizes small-property ownership by individual families. But, unlike the others, it implies that state intervention is necessary in order to secure a healthful and economically productive way of life. The film opens with a scene of a happy cityscape: an airy public square that resembles downtown Mexico City's Alameda Park.[95] The animated scene devolves quickly to the small town that supposedly existed only a few years ago in the same place. Local society grows with migration, but takes a negative path. The town turns dark, dirty, and dangerous as its population mounts. Insects and rats plague the populace. The local water supply is polluted; peasant women use a dirty river for washing clothes and for drinking water. The streets are overcrowded. Then the film offers an alternative route, the one that produced the happy and hygienic environment encountered at the film's outset. A modern dam, aqueduct, and system of water pipes serve the city, demonstrated by an animated vivisection. Sewers and covered garbage cans contain waste. The increasingly citified peasant women move from the river to a new public fountain where they draw clean water for their daily needs. Gone, too, is an unsanitary open-air market, presented as a source of disease in the film's first segment; instead, urban shopkeepers sell meat from behind shiny, new, glass-covered, refrigerated showcases that protect their food from flies and other insects. Children play in a public park. As night falls on an electrically illuminated metropolis, the narrator concludes, "Health and happiness for all inhabitants." Thus, preaching faith in the state, planning, and resources for development, the film seeks to bridge the distance between the countryside and the city. Its depiction of peasants becoming city dwellers is a rare image, as is the short's implication that not only knowledge but also official investment will solve the dilemma of rapid urbanization in developing areas.[96]

Rural Reception

Anecdotal evidence testified to the Disney health films' efficacy as instruments of social engineering. After viewing one such offering, exhibited during a sound-truck tour of San Luis Potosí state, "the Indians have finally learned that there is a way to cure [tuberculosis]." In Tamazunchale "Indians" were disseminating their new knowledge about "how to be clean and healthy," especially the lesson about the virtue of boiled water, gained from a married U.S. couple who utilized USIE films in their charity work as social missionaries to the town's impoverished inhabitants.[97] In Nayarit state a suspicious village reportedly succumbed to the inoculation appeals of Mexican health officials after being shown *Defensa Contra la Invasión.*[98] During the Hidalgo sound-truck tour, on one occasion when the local public health doctor could not attend, the USIE operator gave a short talk on vaccination before the film *Defense against Invasion.* At the end of the showing he observed a line of children waiting behind him. When asked why they were waiting, they answered that they were waiting for him to vaccinate them. On another occasion a doctor found some three hundred children at a showing where the same film was used. She at once ordered the doors closed and after the exhibition proceeded to vaccinate them all.[99]

U.S. and Mexican operatives also noted political attitudes. In Padierna, a village near Mexico City, embassy propaganda officers took part in the town's commemoration of "a decisive battle in the U.S.-Mexican war of 1847 which in previous years has given occasion for anti-U.S. outbursts." Contributing films and music to the community's ceremonies for two years, U.S. officials reported that the 1950's celebration climaxed with "a stirring speech from a senator who made history of the event and stressed the fact that we are friends now." The past, the senator said, should be overlooked for a peaceful and productive future of Mexican-U.S. cooperation.[100] The importance of using exhibitions as symbols of international friendship transcended the films' contents; the platforms on which the shorts were projected (and which also frequently served as stages for musicians and dancers who performed in conjunction with exhibitions) were usually framed with crossed U.S. and Mexican flags.[101]

Local politicians strove to demonstrate to U.S. officials the impact of the exhibitions on developing international consciousness among peasants. In one town, during the Hidalgo tour, a rumor spread that the U.S. ambassador would accompany the embassy's jeep sound truck. The tour's crew "drove up to the plaza through lines of about 1000 children on both sides. They noticed that all the houses were decorated with paper and flags. They came to a stop as all the church bells were clanging and rockets were being shot off, in front of the town authorities, the teachers and the priests, who waited, hats in hand. There were crossed American and Mexican flags, and portraits of the American and Mexican Presidents in evidence in this village in a remote region of the State." [102]

While questionable as a gauge of popular opinion, the event does illustrate (as do numerous others) the way in which local officialdom collaborated with the U.S. propaganda project. Film exhibitions were not simply events to show movies but were public spectacles, sites of transnational political collaboration and sociocultural exchange (although in ways often undetected or misunderstood by U.S. authorities, discussed below).

Reception of the films themselves demonstrated the popularity of the audio-visual form, if not necessarily its power as an ideological instrument. In some cases exhibitions represented not only the first contact villagers had with U.S. visitors (and images) but also with motion pictures. The programs were reportedly received as universally welcomed diversions in hardest-to-reach areas of the nation: in Guerrero state, one village reportedly welcomed a sound truck's U.S.-Mexican personnel as Spaniards. The U.S. film officer explained through an indigenous interpreter that they were not conquistadores but rather representatives of the Mexican federal government's project promoting modernity and democracy, seeking to legitimize the penetration of U.S. propaganda through the Mexican regime's participation.[103]

The postwar attempt at cultural conquest in Mexico was a collaborative one. It involved a neoimperial bureaucracy, represented by U.S. and Mexican technicians and experts, serving a foreign metropole based in Washington but channeled through Mexico City. U.S. public affairs officers reported not only the positive reactions of audiences but also the praise of local Mexican politicians as evidence of the exhibitions' effectiveness. During the Hidalgo tour, which reached over 60,015 spectators in 45 towns, operatives reported that "there were many requests that it be repeated. Many municipal authorities from other towns begged that their villages be included in the tour, or in the next one. Participants seemed to feel honored to be allowed to cooperate; in the entire 39 days there was not one sign of unfriendliness." [104] Typical were the numerous reports that "the authorities cooperated fully" in organizing the presentations. The publicity photographs of these events taken and disseminated by the USIS (see figures 2, 3, and 4) were self-conscious propaganda aimed at selling the progressive aims and positive reception of the tours.[105] They reflect the narrative of progress projected in the movies that supported the U.S. program's ideology; their visual construction of official U.S. rhetoric provided the justification for postwar U.S. liberalism's campaign for anti-radical development in the "Third World."

Each of the photographs relates a success story at odds with the more ambivalent picture drawn from the cumulative narrative data. The selection (perhaps also staging) of photographs that signify comprehension, appreciation, and attention favorably assessed the USIS's goals. In figures 2 and 3 the screen is absent; in each the image is focused on the audience.

Figure 2. USIS film presentation in Pátzcuaro, Michoacán, 1951. This propaganda (about propaganda) depicts the "civilizing" mission of the USIS, by juxtaposing signs of traditional life (e.g., the women in *rebozos*) with the modern (e.g., the photographer in the rear), which reminds the viewer of the event's purpose and the unseen screen's presence. As in other photographs selected for publication by the USIS, this one stages an idealized representation of reception. But the rapt expressions appear posed. Individual resistance seems to disrupt the overall surface of enthrallment; for instance, consider the expressions of the girl in the lower-right corner, the young man between the two women covered by rebozos, the young woman on the far right, and the boys on the far left, all of whom stare directly (skeptically) at the lens. (306-PSB-51-10450, National Archives Still Picture Branch)

Figure 2 is shows what seems to be attentive, even entranced, viewers at an indoor exhibition in Pátzcuaro, Michoacán. A second glance reveals cracks in the presentation of eyes focused on the screen; for instance, observe the penetrating (perhaps defiant) gaze of the woman on the lower-right side. Figure 3 is a medium-range group shot of an orderly village audience at an outdoor exhibition in San Andrés Ahuayucan, México. Figure 4 depicts inhabitants of the same village eagerly accepting print propaganda following a film presentation. As we will see, this was a critical part of the itinerant film program. The caption distributed with this

Figure 3. USIS mobile film presentation in San Andrés Ahuayucan, Mexico, July 1951. Outdoor film exhibitions often took place, as in this case, on the grounds of town schools, superimposing the U.S. project on the Mexican state's educational infrastructure. But school exhibitions did not always go as smoothly as this photograph suggests. Teachers were sometimes vocal critics of the USIS's Cold War messages. (306-PS-51-17247, National Archives Still Picture Branch)

photograph was typical of the celebratory discourse produced by USIS officials in the Mexico City embassy that accompanied these representations: "After viewing a USIS film, the audience of this small farming community near Mexico City surges out of the rural school grounds to the terrace and swarms around the table piled with USIS pamphlets of the following titles: '*La Revista Americana,*' '*Ocho Benefactores de América,*' '*Historia de un Pueblo Herman[o].*' "

While it is difficult to resist reading these photos as illustrations of the events themselves— "this is what the exhibitions looked like"—it is more appropriate to view them as products of the neoimperial representational machine (analogous to the processes Ricardo Salvatore explores in his contribution to this volume). As in many of the films aimed particularly at rural audiences, especially animated films, the USIS photos appropriated neo-imperial subjects—lower-class Indian and mestizo spec-

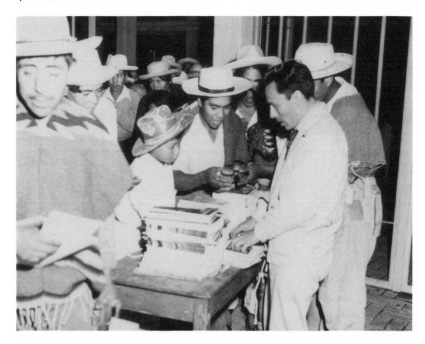

Figure 4. USIS print propaganda distribution following mobile film presentation in San Andrés Ahuayucan, Mexico, July 1951. Although literature was an integral part of the USIS mission, many recipients could not read the material distributed and often were uninterested in its contents. (306-PS-51-17248, National Archives Still Picture Branch)

tators—in producing idealized transcultural situations that were then distributed to those very subjects (as well as to other international, including U.S., publics). The production of visual representations of the film exhibitions, like the reports about the screenings, formed part of an "official story." They were integral to the collaborative mission of Mexican and U.S. authorities, demonstrating the density of postwar neoimperialism's transnational order. Propagandizing the U.S. mission, legitimizing the discourse of development, and appropriating Mexican society as subject and object required not simply international complicity, but also shared ideology and joint implementation. In terms of narrative content and as forms of visual communication, then, the photos exemplify the transculturation of U.S.-Mexican relations during the Cold War.

Politically motivated praise for the various presentations flowed in from local officials, signifying the desire to please national (and U.S.) authorities. Such positive appraisals played to bureaucratic egos, but they also represented ready acceptance of the films by local audiences. In this vein, following the 1950 tour, one municipal president wrote Governor Carvajal that "the affair was a great success, as no less than three thousand persons attended who applauded with enthusiasm your recorded words, and at the end of each film relating to the mosquito, small-pox, how to obtain better corn, and also the marvelous reception given our President Miguel Alemán in Washington, New York, and other cities of the United States." [106]

President Alemán Visits the United States, ubiquitous in USIS presentations during the Mexican leader's *sexenio,* was, not surprisingly, the film most frequently praised by local politicians. In 1952, following exhibitions by the new sound truck operated by the U.S. consulate in Veracruz, Eduardo Saloman, municipal president of Tierra Blanca, echoed messages sent from other local officials when he wrote:

Please accept my sincere gratitude for this work, for as our President Miguel Alemán said in his memorial speech before the American Congress during his visit in that country: "The seed of knowledge and mutual comprehension which should exist and has existed for a long time is one of the postulates of our country." This has been proven in a documentary film which we saw entitled *President Alemán Visits the U.S.A.* This film makes one feel that this comprehension is being gained little by little on grounds based upon mutual understanding between both countries. I want to bring to your attention that this cultural campaign was a success and we desire that these tours be more frequent for the good of my country for which they are a great necessity. This most welcome cultural tour has left a sensation of closer relations and sympathy for the meritorious work which you have started and which . . . I hope will continue indefinitely.[107]

Despite the overwhelming reports touting the receptivity of rural spectators and the cooperation of local elites, there were also signs of active and passive resistance that disappointed U.S. expectations. During one stretch of the Veracruz tour, in spite of the reported efforts of local *políticos,* attendance dropped dramatically owing to a rumor "that the [film] brigade was recruiting for the Korean War." Disclaimers issued by USIS operatives over the mobile unit's loudspeaker system were ineffective; the story persisted that the vehicle's two Mexican operatives were "raising a levy." In one town only women and children attended. USIS officials and their accompanying Mexican agriculture experts were "convinced that the rumor was purposely spread by Communists in the State Government through unfriendly teachers who are leftists." Throughout the tour monitors reported that "in certain villages teachers seemed inclined to be hostile," but that their opposition to exhibitions was overcome after viewing the educational contents of the films.[108] During a tour of Coahuila, in late 1951, "sound truck operators reported that although there was some criticism made by local professors regarding the inaugural speech of the Public Affairs Officer wherein he referred to the communist threat, this same group of professors later gave their heartiest support to the sound truck." [109] Whether the popularity of the mobile moving-picture show was as great as U.S. observers judged or not, it is clear that when there was active resistance it tended to be of an organized political nature rather than spontaneous disapproval.

Sometimes the organization of exhibitions evidently involved coercion (as well as promotion). At the start of the Hidalgo tour, in Actopán, the presidente municipal forced "prisoners, under guard of a young un-uniformed policeman carrying a rifle" to construct a structure in the town square on which a giant screen was later mounted to receive the "very large picture" from a "projection room" improvised in a pharmacy across the street. Afterward, "the prisoners shuffled back to jail and arrangements for the exhibition were continued." These were overseen by "a high-ranking police officer and five motorcycle policemen, two generals and various other police and army officials [who] reported to offer any assistance desirable." They requisitioned needed materials and cleared the area of obstructive vehicles; meanwhile "a rifle-toting municipal police-man . . . stood guard for hours over the sound-truck." Another group of "municipal policemen, all carrying rifles and none in uniform, guided the people to vantage points where they would not block the view of the authorities." Lowering by 500 the figure provided by the municipal president, a U.S. observer estimated that approximately 3,000 people attended, many of them traveling three hours by foot. The large numbers here, as in other cases, seem to have been enhanced not only by local officialdom's promotional efforts, involving hundreds of printed flyers and painted signs, but also by force. In this case, the attendance of the governor's "Oficial Mayor" to address Actopán's inaugural exhibition provided extra motivation for generating a good turnout. A speech by the U.S. embassy's motion picture officer echoed the governor's message that the exhibition symbolized the amicable structure of contemporary U.S.-Mexican relations, based in mutual respect and benevolent U.S. cooperation with Mexican programs. The "festival," as the exhibition was locally advertised, exemplified the collaborative use of film for transnational mass socialization.[110]

Despite widespread bureaucratic cooperation that produced large audiences (numbering several thousand viewers at many exhibitions), U.S.

monitors sometimes raised doubts about the quality of rural reception. Some offerings, especially historical subjects, were deemed too highbrow. And while cartoons were considered best received, in terms of interest level and message comprehension, some reports questioned whether audience enjoyment of animated visual education as popular diversion eclipsed its purpose as political and social instruction. U.S. officials became distressed, for example, when audiences, particularly children, seemingly missed intended messages and "saw only entertainment in the films." In other cases, operators had to encourage villagers to look at the screen rather than the projector, which was found to be equally interesting.[111] Instances of miscommunication, autonomous interpretations (such as laughter deemed inappropriate by officials), or resistance (for example, indigenous translators who added or substituted their own words for the film's message) are hard to mark, since they often were undetected, unreported, or misunderstood by visiting functionaries. Nonetheless, reading across the grain of the documents, we can see that they were clearly present.

If film reception was fairly diverse, distribution was less so. The contents of exhibition programs varied but retained the same general structure. For instance, over a three-day stretch, an estimated audience of 250 Zapotec Indians in San Juan Tescolula watched Spanish-language versions of four films: *National Parks of the United States, El Maravilloso Frijol Soya,* and two of the Disney-OCIAA *Salud para las Américas* cartoons, *Defensa Contra la Invasión* and *Saneamiento del Ambiente.* These four films were shown at every exhibition. The next night, after a four-hour journey over dirt roads and through ravines, the USIS unit presented basically the same program, but this time included a film on professional basketball instead of the one on U.S. national parks, to 175 Indians in Ihuitlán, "18 miles off the main road." The following evening, in Tamazulapán, four hundred people watched the film on the TVA as well as *Un Año en Corea* [A year in Korea], one in a series of newsreel-style testaments documenting the virtues of the U.S.-led mobilization to contain communism, which was exhibited with the Disney cartoons and the demonstration of basketball.[112] All the films, especially the Disney cartoons, reportedly proved popular, but the reception of the illustrated print propaganda proved more equivocal in the eyes of the tour's managers.[113]

Concern with comprehension of the literature provided at the rural exhibitions grew, as the print operation expanded over time.[114] During the 1952 Oaxaca tour, for example, over 165,000 printed items were distributed. About half were booklets that supplemented presentations with detailed information on general themes; the other half were shorter leaflets relating directly to particular films. In Oaxaca, as elsewhere, the distribution of printed materials was a key aspect of the sound-truck program. The pamphlets included: Pan-American biographical treatments of historical figures such as *Jorge Washington* [George Washington], *Colón* [Christopher Columbus], and *Libertad en el Pensamiento de 3 Gran Hombres* [Liberty in the thought of three great men]; materials propagandizing U.S. labor practices, such as *Por una Vida Mejor* [For a better life], *El Movimiento Obrero en Los Estados Unidos* [The labor movement in the United States], and *Paladines de la Democracia* [Champions of democracy]; and pamphlets promoting health, hygiene, and education, including *Cuidado del Niño* [Care of the child] and *Educación en el Hogar* [Home education]. An official opined that if the townsfolk in the three Oaxaca villages were isolated from the normal means of mass communication "(no radio antennae were observed) and [if they] are unaware of national and international events, they must be to a correspondingly greater extent involved in the affairs of their villages and surroundings. These affairs involved their two most important problems: getting enough to eat and staying healthy." Such topics were recommended because "many of the movies and their adjunctive Movie Kit leaflets fall within the limits of the interest and comprehension levels of these lower classes." By contrast, literature on historical, cultural, and political themes were judged "beyond the scope of their comprehension and interest." [115]

As with the films, U.S. officials believed that cartoons provided the most useful means of conveying printed information. The grassroots exhibition experiences of field operatives in rural sound-truck tours converged with the ideological objectives of embassy and State Department culture planners in reformulating propaganda presentations to convey Cold War messages to popular audiences. Commenting on the reception of political literature distributed during the Oaxaca tour, the U.S. embassy's print-propaganda specialist recommended that "our output of publications of the cartoon-booklet type must be increased greatly to reach the large mass of Mexicans, mostly illiterate and ill-informed of world events, who comprise about 65% of the total population. These must be carefully designed to be within the levels of interest and comprehension of this class using very basic Spanish." [116] The cartoon pamphlets' popularity as a vehicle for broader political messages "about world events" provided a model for the later production of anticommunist propaganda. The collaborative film program laid the groundwork for covertly produced, commercially distributed U.S. film propaganda, carrying anticommunist messages aimed principally at lower-class audiences. The new-style anticommunist propaganda combined forms of the cultural/visual education films with Mexican modes of mass entertainment.

As U.S. propaganda became increasingly politicized, in terms of form and narrative content, after the outbreak of the Korean War in 1950, Hollywood renewed its close wartime cooperation with U.S. government mass-culture projects in Mexico. Assisting in the distribution and production of propaganda—first with the State Department and, after mid-1953, with the newly established United States Information Agency—Hollywood's Mexican infrastructure provided the necessary legitimacy for covert projects. New techniques drew on the experiences of U.S. and Mexican operatives in the programs discussed above. Regarding distribution, for example, Hollywood's Mexican offices (RKO, MGM, Paramount, United Artists, Columbia, Warner Brothers, Fox, and Universal, represented collectively as the Film Board of Mexico) coordinated commercial distribution of United Nations newsreels about the anticommunist crusade in Korea. These were distributed (without attribution to their U.S. government origins) throughout the 35 mm circuits controlled by the U.S. companies as well as through the thousands of 16 mm provincial venues operated by the Mexican company Películas Nacionales, which functioned as an RKO subsidiary. This was supplemented, as we have seen, by sound-truck exhibitions in rural areas. As for production, in 1952–1953 the USIA undertook a series of anticommunist animated short films that made use of the popularity of the cartoon form, as demonstrated by the Disney educational series in the embassy's public programs, but incorporating Mexican visual idioms for U.S. ends. RKO executives at Mexico City's Estudios Churubusco (which the U.S. studio owned in partnership with Mexican media magnate Emilio Azcárraga) facilitated the Mexicanization of this new mode of production. These entertainment shorts emphasized conservative rural and urban social relations based in nonradical individualism, exemplified in A Young Trade Union Member (discussed above), and paternalist class relations. As with the newsreels, the cartoon production was rooted in the postwar educational/informational sociocultural project. In its own way, it reflected the ideological convergence and institutionalized collaboration of the Mexican state with U.S. foreign policy, which refashioned postwar Mexican nationalism as anticommunism.[117]

Transnational Integration

If the contours of reception remain somewhat opaque, glimpsed through the reflected gaze of U.S. operatives and their Mexican collaborators, the extent of the exhibitions is profoundly clear. By 1949, 9,000,000 Mexicans viewed USIS-distributed, USIE films each year, a figure that remained constant throughout the early 1950s; 80 percent of the program's spectators were classified as "peasants, laborers and school population." Lower-class sectors and children, groups that reportedly responded most favorably to the movies, had been reached through a flexible distribution system whereby "the great majority of showings are handled through Mexican Government, . . . labor union and other Mexican groups," including large-scale capital, schools, and a virtually national network of state governors stretching from the southern states of Tabasco and Chiapas to northern Chihuahua and Coahuila.[118]

By far the largest of the social groups targeted by U.S. propaganda planners was peasants.[119] The sound-truck tours expanded geographically in the 1950s, incorporating increasing numbers of local Mexican politicians into the U.S. system as they exposed ever-growing numbers of provincial Mexicans to USIE films.[120] For example, during the second half of 1951, an embassy sound truck visited 87 towns in the Federal District; a two-month tour of Coahuila state was completed in mid-December that made 127 exhibitions in 47 towns over 69 days; 72,460 people attended 89 exhibitions during a 60-day swing through Puebla; and in Guanajuato state, 160,550 persons attended 119 exhibitions.[121] The following year, an unprecedented four-month tour was arranged for Chihuahua. By 1952, each U.S. consulate in Mexico operated its own sound truck (Guadalajara operated two), to go along with the four that the embassy administered. Each unit utilized Mexican personnel to carry programs to hard-to-reach audiences.[122]

By (supposedly) fostering social modernization, the U.S. films served the Mexican state's development goals. By 1950, U.S. officials reported that "Mexican Government agencies cooperate fully with all U.S. agencies in Mexico." [123] National bureaucracies and their provincial branches were the largest exhibitors of U.S. films: the Ministries of Public Education, Public Health, Labor, and Agriculture as well as the military were the most prominent distributors of North American propaganda.[124] In 1951, the Ministry of Public Education organized an Audio-Visual Department, and the USIE established the agency's film library with 120 titles to be utilized by Mexican teachers for public-school exhibitions.[125] Within two years, new Audio-Visual Centers, under the SEP's auspices, had been opened or were in the process of opening in the northern cities of Ciudad Victoria (Tamaulipas), Saltillo (Coahuila), and Monterrey (Nuevo León). A U.S. official commented that Mexican education "authorities are apparently depending very heavily on USIS for film materials for all these Audio-Visual Centers," to go along with the already strong relationships "between state and Federal Departments of Education" and the U.S. film program throughout Mexico.[126]

By 1951, U.S. propaganda operatives estimated that 85 percent of their film exhibitions were conducted by Mexican officials. And the USIS recommended that "continued and intensified supervised cooperation with Mexican agencies should be a target." [127] In 1949, when the Mexican government attempted (ultimately unsuccessfully) to apply new exhibition taxes to protect Mexican commercial film production from Hollywood, the U.S. embassy protested the initial application of the measures to commercially distributed U.S. government films, pointing out that many "are used by agencies of the Mexican Government." Commercial competition was at odds with ideological collaboration, which underlined the centrality of transnational collaboration.[128]

U.S. officials considered film the key to reaching popular sectors with political propaganda. Because it could be transported to communities isolated from other forms of mass communication, it did not require literacy, and it had already established legitimacy with a wide variety of Mexican authorities. As one official put it: "Geographically there is no limit to the reach of the USIE Motion Picture Program. While the operation is centralized in Mexico and environs, and in regional operation in Guadalajara and Monterrey, its radius is extended through the use of mobile equipment, and even more so through the cooperation of Mexican agencies and organizations. It has broad appeal to all classes of people, and is especially effective in reaching the broad mass of the monolingual or illiterate rural population of Mexico." [129]

Despite aggregate success, there were qualitative concerns voiced by U.S. operatives from the outset of postwar film programs. They urged the use of commercial venues as a means to reach broader audiences in ways that called less attention to U.S. government authorship, since they were integrated into the experience of everyday commercial entertainment. A 1946 report of the U.S. consul in Tampico, Tamaulipas, for example, praised the official film program but suggested that the project would be more effective if produced as commercial films "distributed thru [sic] the moving picture organizations [Hollywood's concerns] and shown in regular theaters rather than exhibiting the 16 mm. film at special showings." [130] As we have seen, by the early 1950s the U.S. film program had moved from public cultural diplomacy to covert propaganda production, from official international sponsorship to private commercial distribution, while working within a transnational, that is, Mexicanized, framework.

The postwar film program showed how the U.S. government's film policies, which prior to World War II had focused on cultural penetration through promoting Hollywood's commercial domination, evolved during the Cold War into an independent system that still collaborated with U.S. studios but had its own ideological objectives as well. The most important culture bureaucrat was no longer the chief trade official (trying to open markets) but the public affairs officer (planning propaganda). Moreover, by the 1950s, exhibition systems involved collaboration with the Mexican state as much as they did with U.S. distributors. The alliance that instituted the film programs sheds light on the density and complexity of postwar transnational propaganda structures. The distribution project examined here also suggests that in producing a model of transnational relations, one less centered on diplomatic exchanges and foreign policy, we can explore valuable vistas at the nexus between social and political interactions in the everyday exchanges that comprise sociocultural processes in "contact zones." The OIC/USIE/USIS/USIA project, like its OCIAA predecessor, attempted to refashion Latin American social practices and to influence political behavior through transnationalized mass media. It reflected an interstate consensus on modernization, invoking a North American social vocabulary and visual idiom in pursuit of convergent (although independently motivated) goals: the incorporation of peripheral communities, marginalized social sectors, and politically disaffected groups into a hegemonic culture through new forms of audiovisual discourse.

The messages and images projected in Mexico and elsewhere, as well as the exhibitions themselves, raise questions about transnational sources of "imagined communities," identified by Benedict Anderson (and adopted by numerous mass-communications scholars) as the wellspring of national identity.[131] More sophisticated theoretical work on the impact of globalization on national sovereignty can be derived from innovative historical research on the international development of mass culture. As several recent critics have usefully suggested, the postmodern cultural situation is not sui generis but rather connected to long-term international developments. To understand today's globalization, we must excavate its historical foundations (as well as examine its present-day symbols).[132] In other words, perhaps the national (often also nationalist) paradigms frequently applied to the study of transnational media and political economy are outdated, in terms not only of present-day (so-called postmodern) communication but also that of the prior "modern" epoch. To speak of cultural imperialism without examining its actual implementation is as shortsighted as to assume that the mere existence of such a mass-communication relationship demonstrates imperialism at the level of consciousness.

It seems that, in terms of cross-cultural encounter, Louis Hartz's general skepticism about the efficacy of U.S. Cold War ideology in the developing world applies, the celebratory oratory of Mexican authorities such as Governor Carvajal notwithstanding.[133] The praise U.S. and Mexican officials showered on the exhibitions did not reflect their reception. Whether promoting modernizing social practices or more explicit political propaganda, the films interacted with national and local mentalities that often resisted or simply did not care about U.S. foreign policy, even as individuals approved of the exhibitions as sources of entertainment, information, or both. However, while the sociocultural significance of the films as a source of images, ideas, forms, and narratives should not be overestimated, it should not be underestimated either. The films not only built local alliances between Mexican and U.S. officialdom; they also shaped discourse, introduced new symbols, and spread the practice of movie viewing. Transnational links deepened, although not necessarily along the lines drawn by U.S. propaganda planners and their Mexican collaborators.

Notes

I thank Robert Divine, Alan Knight, and Steven Topik for their helpful comments on an early draft of this work. I am especially grateful to Gil Joseph for his meticulous readings of several versions of this article, greatly improving its substance and style. I also benefited from conversations with my colleagues Miriam Levin, Shawn McHale, and Ted Steinberg at Case Western Reserve University and Adan Chinchilla of the Escuela Popular in Cleveland.

1. Author's translation of the Spanish transcript enclosed in "Inauguration of Governor-Sponsored Tour of the State of Veracruz," Dorsey Gassaway Fisher (public affairs officer) to State Department (hereafter, SD), 28 July 1950, Record Group 59, central files of the Department of State, National Archives of the United States, Washington, D.C. (hereafter, NARG), 511.125/7-2850. Carvajal, a political ally of President Miguel Alemán (himself a former governor of Veracruz), was later Secretario de Gobernación, in charge, among other things, of regulation of mass media and internal political administration in the Adolfo Ruiz Cortines administration (1952–1958).

2. "Termination of Veracruz Sound-Truck Tour," Fisher to SD, 20 Sept. 1950, 5, NARG 59, 511.125/9-2050.

3. See Seth Fein, "El cine y las relaciones culturales México–Estados Unidos en los treinta," *Secuencia* 34 (Jan.–Apr. 1996): 155–95, for an analysis of the transnational context of the film, its representation of inter-American relations, and its Mexican reception. See also Paul J. Vanderwood, "The Image of Mexican Heroes in American Films," *Film Historia* 3, no. 3 (Oct. 1992): 221–44.

4. "Inauguration of Governor-Sponsored Tour of the State of Veracruz," 1–3, Fisher to SD, 28 July 1950, NARG 59, 511.125/7-2850.

5. " 'Grass Roots' USIE Cultural Mission to State of Hidalgo," Fisher to SD, 29 Mar. 1950, NARG 59, 511.125/3-2950.

6. "Delivery of Sound Truck to Veracruz Consulate," Forney A. Rankin (counselor of public affairs) to SD, 26 Mar. 1952, NARG 59, 511.125/3-2652.

7. Mary Louise Pratt, *Imperial Eyes: Travel Writing and Transculturation* (New York: Routledge, 1992), 4. Such negotiations are not limited to international relationships; see, for example, Mary Kay Vaughan's analysis of processes of political and cultural negotiation at the "point of implementation" of the Mexican state's socialist education policies during the Cárdenas years, in "The Educational Policies of the Mexican Revolution: The Response of Local Societies (1934–1940)," in the important anthology edited by John Britton, *Molding the Hearts and Minds: Education, Communications, and Social Change in Latin America* (Wilmington, Del.: Scholarly Resources, 1994), 105–26.

8. The prewar "ideological congruence" analyzed by Alan Knight in *U.S.-Mexican Relations, 1910–1940: An Interpretation* (La Jolla: Center for U.S.-Mexican Studies, University of California, San Diego, 1987), 1–20, extended beyond World War II, reinforced by new dimensions of transnational mass media. Good overviews of the Mexican state's postwar project, including its relationship to U.S. foreign policy, are Tzvi Medin, *El sexenio alemanista: Ideología y praxis política de Miguel Alemán* (Mexico City: Era, 1990); Luis Medina, *Historia de la revolución mexicana, 1940–1952: Civilismo y modernización del autoritarismo* (Mexico City: El Colegio de México, 1979); Blanca Torres, *Historia de la revolución mexicana, 1940–1952: Hacia la utopía industrial* (Mexico City: El Colegio de México, 1979); Steven Niblo, *War, Diplomacy, and Development: The United States and Mexico, 1938–1954* (Wilmington, Del.: Scholarly Resources, 1995); and Olga Brody Pellicer and Esteban L. Mancilla, *Historia de la revolución mexicana, 1952–1960: El entendimiento con los Estados Unidos y la gestación del desarrollo estabilizador* (Mexico City: El Colegio de México, 1978).

9. The best overview of these ideas is Robert A. Packenham, *Liberal America and the Third World: Political Development Ideas and Social Science* (Princeton, N.J.: Princeton University Press, 1973).

10. See Arturo Escobar's synthetic analysis of the relationship between discursive and material factors in post–World War II "First World" interventions in the "developing" world, *Encountering Development: The Making and Unmaking of the Third World* (Princeton, N.J.: Princeton University Press, 1995); quote is from p. 48.

11. The critical study of U.S. mass media as a form of cultural domination based on transnational economic power has remained greatly influenced by Herbert Schiller's works: *Mass Communication and American Empire* (Boston: Beacon, 1969) and *Communication and Cultural Domination* (New York: International Arts and Sciences, 1976). See also Emile G. McAnany, Jorge Schnitman, and Noreene Janus, eds., *Communication and Social Structure: Critical Studies in Mass Media Research* (New York: Praeger, 1981); Armand Mattelart, *Transnationals and the Third World: The Struggle for Culture* (South Hadley, Mass.: Gergen and Garvey, 1983); Rita Atwood and Emile G. McAnany, eds., *Communication and Latin American Society: Trends in Critical Research, 1960–1985* (Madison: University of Wisconsin Press, 1986); and Kaarle Nordenstreng and Herbert Schiller, eds., *National Sovereignty and International Communications* (Norwood, N.J.: Ablex Press, 1979). Recent examinations of globalization have made assumptions about the origins of transnationalization in the contemporary, say post-1970, era that could be fruitfully challenged by historical research. See, for example, Kaarle Nordenstreng and Herbert I. Schiller, eds., *Beyond Sovereignty: International Communication in the 1990s* (Norwood, N.J.: Ablex Press, 1993).

12. Ideological analysis of U.S. mass media as a window on cultural imperialism continues to build on, albeit with more sophisticated readings, the functionalist assumptions made by Ariel Dorfman and Armand Mattelart in their influential analysis of Disney in Latin America, *Para leer al pato donald: Comunicación de masa y colonialismo* (Mexico City: Siglo Veintiuno Editores, 1972). For an idea of the long shadow still cast by their work, see the provocative essays by Julian Burton-Carvajal, and Lisa Cartwright and Brian Goldfarb, in Eric Smoodin, ed., *Disney Discourse: Producing the Magic Kingdom* (New York: Routledge, 1994).

13. See, for example, Janet Staiger, *Interpreting Films: Studies in the Historical Reception of American Cinema* (Princeton, N.J.: Princeton University Press, 1992); and Eric Smoodin, " 'Compulsory' Viewing for Every Citizen: *Mr. Smith* and the Rhetoric of Reception," *Cinema Journal* 35, no. 2 (winter 1996): 3–21. For an interpretive review of the theoretical literature, see Judith Mayne, *Cinema and Spectatorship* (New York: Routledge, 1993).

14. For historical scholarship from this perspective, see Fred Fejes, *Imperialism, Media, and the Good Neighbor: New Deal Foreign Policy and United States Shortwave Broadcasting to Latin America* (Norwood, N.J.: Ablex Press, 1986); and James Schwoch, *The American Radio Industry and Its Latin American Activities, 1900–1939* (Urbana: University of Illinois Press, 1990).

15. A thought-provoking analysis of much of this literature is provided by John Tomlinson in *Cultural Imperialism: A Critical Introduction* (Baltimore, Md.: Johns Hopkins University Press, 1991); see also Frederick Buell, *National Culture and the New Global System* (Baltimore, Md.: Johns Hopkins University Press, 1994).

16. The best overview is Emily Rosenberg, *Spreading the American Dream: American Economic and Cultural Expansion, 1890–1945* (New York: Hill and Wang, 1982). See also Clayton Koppes and Gregory Black, *Hollywood Goes to*

War: How Politics, Profits, and Propaganda Shaped Movies during World War II (New York: Free Press, 1987); Holly Cowan Shulman, *The Voice of America: Propaganda and Democracy* (Madison: University of Wisconsin Press, 1990); and Allan Winkler, *The Politics of Propaganda: The Office of War Information* (New Haven, Conn.: Yale University Press, 1978). For an outline of the evolution of mass-culture policies that originated in wartime inter-American relations, but that remains, like the above books, generally an institutional history focused on Washington rather than international interaction, see Frank Ninkovich, *The Diplomacy of Ideas: U.S. Foreign Policy and Cultural Relations, 1938-1950* (New York: Cambridge University Press, 1981); an early general introduction is Gerald K. Haines, "Under the Eagle's Wing: The Franklin Roosevelt Administration Forges an American Hemisphere," *Diplomatic History* 1 (fall 1977): 373-88.

17. Very little work by "diplomatic historians" has addressed transnational dimensions of postwar inter-American relations. Most have focused strictly on U.S. foreign policy. See, for example, Stephen G. Rabe's authoritative *Eisenhower and Latin America: The Foreign Policy of Containment* (Chapel Hill: University of North Carolina Press, 1987). There are exceptions: an important recent study that focuses on nongovernmental aspects of elite relations, with implications for social analysis, is Elizabeth A. Cobbs, *The Rich Neighbor Policy: Rockefeller and Kaiser in Brazil* (New Haven, Conn.: Yale University Press, 1992). Gerald K. Haines considers a broad range of official relations, including propaganda, that transcend the usual themes covered by diplomatic studies in *The Americanization of Brazil: A Study of U.S. Cold War Diplomacy in the Third World, 1945-1954* (Wilmington, Del.: Scholarly Resources, 1989). As the title suggests, though, the study's method is limited mainly to bilateral institutional relationships; it does not address popular interactions and tends to assert one-way conclusions about the influence of the United States. Haines's chapter on U.S. propaganda, "The Projection of a Favorable American Image in Brazil," appears in Britton, *Molding the Hearts and Minds,* 210-32. On Cold War culture, see Reinhold Wagnleitner, *The Coca-Colonization of the Cold War: The United States Cultural Mission in Austria after the Second World War* (Chapel Hill: University of North Carolina Press, 1994), especially 222-71 for Hollywood's role; and Richard Kuisel, *Seducing the French: The Dilemma of Americanization* (Berkeley and Los Angeles: University of California Press, 1993).

18. Recent work on Mexico has offered very important insights about the relationship between foreign relations and elite cultural exchanges, and their impact on questions of representation. See John A. Britton, *Revolution and Ideology: Images of the Mexican Revolution in the United States* (Lexington: University Press of Kentucky, 1995); Helen Delpar, *The Enormous Vogue of Things Mexican: Cultural Relations between the United States and Mexico, 1920-1935* (Tuscaloosa: University of Alabama Press, 1992); Frederick Pike, *The United States and Latin America: Myths and Stereotypes of Civilization and Nature* (Austin: University of Texas Press, 1992); and John Coatsworth and Carlos Rico, eds., *Images of Mexico*

in the United States (La Jolla: Center for U.S.-Mexican Studies, University of California, San Diego, 1989).

19. An excellent example of this work is Amy Kaplan and Donald E. Pease, eds., *Cultures of United States Imperialism* (Durham, N.C.: Duke University Press, 1993).

20. Processual questions, relating to articulation and reception (especially regarding mass culture), still must be better addressed by historians. Local and social difference must be analyzed within a framework that integrates international issues. An important statement about these concerns is Michael H. Hunt, "The Long Crisis in U.S. Diplomatic History: Coming to Closure," *Diplomatic History* 16 (winter 1992): 115–40. An example of recent work that comes to terms with national questions in a way that might advance the study of transnational issues is Gilbert M. Joseph and Daniel Nugent, eds., *Everyday Forms of State Formation: Revolution and the Negotiation of Rule in Modern Mexico* (Durham, N.C.: Duke University Press, 1994); see also Joseph's *Revolution from Without: Yucatán, the Mexican Revolution, and the United States, 1880–1924* (Cambridge: Cambridge University Press, 1982) for an analysis of the way in which transnational capital affected popular and elite development in one region of Mexico.

21. William Roseberry, *Anthropologies and Histories: Essays in Culture, History, and Political Economy* (New Brunswick, N.J.: Rutgers University Press, 1989), 81.

22. Ibid., 88. See also Steve Stern, "Feudalism, Capitalism, and the World-System in the Perspective of Latin America and the Caribbean," *American Historical Review* 93, no. 4 (Oct. 1988): 829–72, as well as his contribution to this volume.

23. For more on these projects, see Seth Fein, "Hollywood and United States–Mexico Relations in the Golden Age of Mexican Cinema" (Ph.D. diss., University of Texas at Austin, 1996), chap. 6.

24. On the U.S. wartime mission to the Mexican industry, see ibid., chap. 5. On various media in Mexico, see José Luis Ortiz Garza, *México en guerra: La historia secreta de los negocios entre empresarios mexicanos de la comunicación, los nazis y E.U.A.* (Mexico City: Planeta, 1989). The irony of the Golden Age of Mexican cinema, in the 1940s and 1950s, is that its commercial context was transnational, to a large extent derived from wartime alliance with the United States. That transnational context led to industrial development but within a system dependent on the favorable political relations of the war. For the consequences of those processes, see Seth Fein, "La diplomacia de celuloide: Hollywood y la edad de oro del cine mexicano," *Historia y Grafía* 4 (spring 1995): 137–76; or "Hollywood, U.S.-Mexican Relations, and the Devolution of the 'Golden Age' of Mexican Cinema," *Film-Historia* 2 (June 1994): 103–35.

25. For a straightforward explication of the convoluted evolution of the Washington bureaucracies that preceded the USIA, see John Henderson, *The United States Information Agency* (New York: Praeger, 1969), 21–61.

26. "Review of the USIE Motion Picture Program in Mexico as of Decem-

ber 1950," Homer Gayne (embassy motion picture officer), 8, enclosed in NARG 59, 511.125/12-150; and "Semi-annual Evaluation Report of USIE Activities in Mexico," 15 Mar. 1951, 34, NARG 59, 511.12/3-1551.

27. "Extent of USIE Effectiveness in Mexico," William O'Dwyer to SD, 25 Jan. 1951, NARG 59, 511.12/1-2551, enclosure no. 3.

28. For an interesting contrast with earlier imperial engineering projects of the United States, see Vicente Rafael, "White Love: Surveillance and National-ist Resistance in the U.S. Colonization of the Philippines," in Kaplan and Pease, *Cultures,* 185–218.

29. "Interest of President-Elect Alemán in the Motion Picture Program," Pax-ton Haddow (American Association) to Ambassador Walter Thurston, 1 Nov. 1946, NARG 84, Embassy and Consular Records, Mexico City Embassy General Records (hereafter, MCEGR) 842, box 717.

30. "Private Showings of OIC Motion Pictures for Mexican Government Offi-cials," Fisher to SD, 23 Apr. 1947, NARG 84, MCEGR 842 OIC-MP, box 821.

31. "Semi-annual Evaluation Report of USIS Activities in Mexico," 9 Jan. 1953, 29–30, NARG 59, 511.12/1-950.

32. "Motion Picture Program in Mexico," Haddow to Guy Ray (U.S. embassy), 27 Mar. 1946, NARG 84, MCEGR 842-MP, box 717. During the world war, U.S. transnational corporations, such as Coca-Cola, Sterling Products, and Colgate Palmolive, operated their own sound trucks distributing OCIAA films to Mexican rural areas lacking the means to project motion pictures. See also Fein, "Holly-wood and United States–Mexico Relations," chap. 6.

33. In 1946, as the transition was under way from the OCIAA's coordination committee structure to the USIS program, U.S. corporations continued to exhibit government films in sound trucks as part of a State Department–directed sys-tem. For example, in December 1946, Colgate made seven exhibitions in northern Mexico, including exhibitions in Monterrey, Nuevo León, Laredo, Tamaulipas, Sabinas, Hidalgo, and Piedras Negras, Coahuila. See J. L. Lemus (Colgate-Palmolive-Peet, S.A., México, D.F.) to the American Association, 30 Dec. 1946, NARG 84, MCEGR 842, box 717.

34. See "Subjects for Motion Pictures Submitted by the 'Secretaría de Educa-ción Pública,' " Haddow to Dixon Donnelly (administrative officer, U.S. embassy), 8 Nov. 1946; see also "Request for Additional 16 mm. RCA Sound Projectors," Donnelly to SD, 30 Sept. 1946, NARG 84, MCEGR 842, box 717. In addition to Public Education and Agriculture, these requests came from the Ministries of Public Assistance and Labor.

35. See "Motion Picture Program for Fiscal Year 1948 in Mexico," Fisher (act-ing public affairs officer) to SD, 31 July 1947, NARG 84, MCEGR 842-OIC-MP.

36. See Dec. 1947, Jan. 1948, Feb. 1948, and Mar. 1948 monthly statistical Mo-tion Picture Reports compiled by Mexican officials, which tabulated exhibition figures not only bureaucratically by ministry and department, but also geographi-cally and politically by state and municipality; enclosed in "Motion Picture Re-

ports for December 1947 through March 1948," Fisher to SD, 10 June 1948, NARG 84, MCEGR 842-OIC-MP, box 821.

37. See Mary Kay Vaughan, *The State, Education, and Social Class in Mexico, 1880–1928* (De Kalb: Northern Illinois University Press, 1982), 138–40, 239–66.

38. "Motion Picture Reports for December 1947 through March 1948," Fisher to SD, 10 June 1948; and "Weekly Motion Picture Report," Haddow to Fisher, Geist, and Thurston, NARG 84, MCEGR 842-OIC-MP, box 821.

39. "Weekly Motion Picture Report," Haddow to Fisher, Geist, and Thurston, 19 May 1948, NARG 84, MCEGR 842-OIC-MP, box 821.

40. "Weekly Motion Picture Report," Haddow to Fisher and Geist, 11 May 1948, NARG 84, MCEGR 842-OIC-MP, box 821.

41. "Weekly Motion Picture Report," Haddow to Fisher, Geist, and Thurston, 8 June 1948, NARG 84, MCEGR 842-OIC-MP, box 821.

42. "Weekly Motion Picture Report," Haddow to Fisher, Geist, and Thurston, NARG 84, MCEGR 842-OIC-MP, box 821. The Mexican army and navy circulated their own supply of U.S. military training films after the war. Between 1943 and 1945, the U.S. army exhibited dozens of military titles at various Mexican installations. In 1947, the Mexican military asked for 123 titles selected from the U.S. Army catalogue to be sound-tracked in Spanish and taken on "a complete circuit of the various training camps throughout the country" and then retained for permanent use by the army, which operated "a number of 16mm. projectors" on loan from the USIS. See "16mm. Films for the Mexican Army," Haddow to General Spry (military attaché), 2 May 1947; and Spry to War Department General Staff, 6 May 1947, NARG 84, MCEGR 842-OIC-MP.

43. See, for example, "Medical Films in Use and Needed in Mexico," Fisher to SD, 9 May 1947, NARG 84, MCEGR 842-OIC-MP. This elite aspect of the U.S. film program expanded along with the larger mass-cultural projects; see, too, the reports on the 1952 Mexico City exhibitions made at the Inter-American Congress for Mental Hygiene and the Third Pan-American Meeting on Gastroenterology, in "Semi-annual Report of USIE Activities in Mexico," 9 Sept. 1952, 29, NARG 59, 511.12/9-952.

44. "Motion Picture Reports for December 1947 through March 1948," Fisher to SD, 10 June 1948, 2, NARG 84, MCEGR 842-OIC-MP, box 821.

45. "Weekly Motion Picture Report," Haddow to Fisher, Geist, and Thurston, 8 May and 8 June 1948, NARG 84, MCEGR 842-OIC-MP, box 821.

46. "Weekly Motion Picture Report," Haddow to Fisher and Geist, 18 May 1948, NARG 84, MCEGR 842-OIC-MP, box 821.

47. "Weekly Motion Picture Report," Haddow to Fisher, Geist, and Thurston, 7 July 1948, NARG 84, MCEGR 842-OIC-MP, box 821.

48. "Motion Picture Reports for December 1947 through March 1948," Fisher to SD, 10 June 1948, 3, NARG 84, MCEGR 842-OIC-MP, box 821.

49. "Weekly Motion Picture Report," Haddow to Fisher and Geist, 11 May 1948, NARG 84, MCEGR 842-OIC-MP, box 821.

50. Ibid.

51. After Mexico City and its environs, Monterrey was Mexico's most important industrial center. The highly cohesive capitalists who had built the area's wealth withstood challenges to their hegemony during *cardenismo*'s early reformist phase to emerge even stronger during the postwar period, when their political and economic goals converged more and more (although they were by no means identical) with the new rightist orientation of the national party-state. For the Monterrey group's pre–World War II development, see Alex M. Saragoza, *The Monterrey Elite and the Mexican State, 1880–1940* (Austin: University of Texas Press, 1988).

52. "Report on USIE Activities for the Month of May 1950," 4, NARG 59, 511.12/6-2050.

53. Ibid., 9.

54. "1954–1955 Prospectus Call; Response of Mission, Section 3, Motion Pictures," 29 Apr. 1953, 4, NARG 59, 511.12/4-2953.

55. "Semi-annual Evaluation Report of USIE Activities in Mexico," 12 Sept. 1950, 38, NARG 59, 511.12/9-1250.

56. "Semi-annual Report of USIE Activities in Mexico," 9 Sept. 1952, 27, NARG 59, 511.12/9-952.

57. "USIE Sound Truck [tour] through the States of Puebla, Oaxaca, and Chiapas with Embassy Labor Officer," Fisher to SD, 26 Oct. 1950, NARG 59, 511.12/10-2650.

58. Ibid.

59. "Semi-annual Report of USIE Activities in Mexico," 9 Sept. 1952, 27, NARG 59, 511.12/9-952.

60. "Trip to Tampico by Motion Picture Officer," Fisher to SD, 10 Apr. 1950, 2, NARG 59, 511.125/4-1050.

61. "Semi-annual Evaluation Report of USIE Activities in Mexico," 12 Sept. 1950, 38, NARG 59, 511.12/9-1250.

62. "Extent of USIE Effectiveness in Mexico," O'Dwyer to SD, 25 Jan. 1951, enclosure no. 3, 3, NARG 59, 511.12/1-2551. For this view of worker participation in the 1938 oil expropriation, see Jonathan Brown, "Labor and State in the Mexican Oil Expropriation," *Texas Papers on Mexico* (Institute of Latin American Studies, University of Texas at Austin, 1990).

63. For the wartime relationship, see Fein, "Hollywood and United States–Mexico Relations," chap. 6.

64. The Confederación Nacional Campesina (CNC) collaborated with the USIE project, including coordinating May Day celebrations in 1952 with the U.S. embassy's motion picture officer. See "Semi-annual Report of USIE Activities in Mexico," 9 Sept. 1952, 26, NARG 59, 511.12/9-952.

65. "1954–1955 Prospectus Call; Response of Mission, Section 3, Motion Pictures," 29 Apr. 1953, 4, NARG 59, 511.12/4-2953. The Spanish version of *With These Hands* had been requested by the embassy's labor attaché, who, on re-

viewing the film, commented, "We have been needing a film like this for years, it's worth its weight in gold"; see "Review of Film WITH THESE HANDS," William E. Webb (information officer, U.S. embassy) to SD, 13 Dec. 1950, NARG 59, 511.125/12-1350.

66. Motion Picture and Sound Recording Branch, National Archives of the United States, College Park, Maryland, 306.3977. The film was produced by Sound Masters, Inc., for the USIS.

67. See Gregg Andrews, *Shoulder to Shoulder? The American Federation of Labor, the United States, and the Mexican Revolution, 1910–1924* (Berkeley and Los Angeles: University of California Press, 1991), for the early development of this relationship.

68. See Barry Carr, "The Fate of the Vanguard under a Revolutionary State: Marxism's Contribution to the Great Arch," in Joseph and Nugent, *Everyday Forms*, 329–33, 345–50; and Ian Roxborough, "Mexico," in *Latin America between the Second World War and the Cold War, 1944–1948,* ed. Leslie Bethell and Ian Roxborough (Cambridge: Cambridge University Press, 1992), 207–9. Regarding the domestic relationship between labor and the state, see Kevin J. Middlebrook, *The Paradox of Revolution: Labor, the State, and Authoritarianism in Mexico* (Baltimore, Md.: Johns Hopkins University Press, 1995); and Medina, *Civilismo y modernización del autoritarismo,* 112–75.

69. See Fein, "Hollywood and United States–Mexico Relations," chaps. 5 , 8.

70. "Review of the USIE Motion Picture Program in Mexico as of December 1950," Gayne, 1, enclosed in NARG 59, 511.125/12-150.

71. Ibid., 2.

72. "Semi-annual Evaluation Report of USIE Activities in Mexico," 12 Sept. 1950, 37, NARG 59, 511.12/9-1250.

73. "Review of the USIE Motion Picture Program in Mexico as of December 1950," Gayne, 5, enclosed in NARG 59, 511.125/12-150.

74. Ibid., 3.

75. "Semi-annual Evaluation Report of USIS Activities in Mexico," 9 Jan. 1953, 32, NARG 59, 511.12/1-950.

76. "Acquisition of Additional Sports Films," Fisher to SD, 1 Nov. 1950, NARG 59, 511.125/11-150.

77. Ibid. Any contemporary visitor to rural areas of southern Mexico can attest that this is still the case. The PRI emblazons the basketball courts with its symbol painted in the national colors (red, white, and green).

78. "Use of USIE Film in Village in Puebla," Fisher to SD, 17 Nov. 1950, NARG 59, 511.125/11-1750.

79. Mary Kay Vaughan, "The Construction of the Patriotic Festival in Tecamachalco, Puebla, 1900–1946," in *Rituals of Rule, Rituals of Resistance: Public Celebrations and Popular Culture in Mexico,* ed. William H. Beezley, Cheryl English Martin, and William E. French (Wilmington, Del.: Scholarly Resources, 1994), 224–25.

80. "Semi-annual Evaluation Report of USIE Activities in Mexico," 12 Sept. 1950, 42, NARG 59, 511.12/9-1250. The logic was that to involve the church would arouse anticlerical/leftist ire; to include teachers (frequently anticlerical and leftist) would provoke rightists. In fact, where deemed useful, teachers and priests were involved in organizing exhibitions along with local government officials.

81. "USIE Activities for the Month of January 1950," Phillip Raine (cultural officer, U.S. embassy) to SD, 6 Mar. 1950, NARG 59, 511.12/3-650.

82. "Review of the USIE Motion Picture Program in Mexico as of December 1950," Gayne, 6, enclosed in NARG 59, 511.125/12-150; see also "Semi-annual Evaluation Report of USIE Activities in Mexico," Rankin to SD, 15 Mar. 1951, NARG 59, 511.12/3-1551.

83. "Termination of Veracruz Sound-Truck Tour," Fisher to SD, 20 Sept. 1950, 4, NARG 59, 511.125/9-2050.

84. "Semi-annual Evaluation Report of USIE Activities in Mexico," 12 Sept. 1950, 35, NARG 59, 511.12/9-1250.

85. "Review of the USIE Motion Picture Program in Mexico as of December 1950," Gayne, 9, enclosed in NARG 59, 511.125/12-150; see also "Semi-annual Evaluation Report of USIE Activities in Mexico," 15 Mar. 1951, 35, NARG 59, 511.12/3-1551.

86. *Dime Que Dientes Tienes* was one of the most widely exhibited, and reportedly most popular, of all USIE films. See "Statistical Motion Picture Report for November 1949," Fisher to SD, 8 Feb. 1950, NARG 59, 511.125/2-850; and "Statistical Motion Picture Report for January, 1959," Fisher to SD, 17 Mar. 1950, NARG 59, 511.125/3-1750. For the Mije response to the film, see "Motion Picture Section," enclosure no. 3 of "Extent of USIE Effectiveness in Mexico," 25 Jan. 1951, NARG 59, 511.12/1-2551.

87. "Motion Picture Sound Truck Tour of the State of Oaxaca," Rankin to SD, 29 Apr. 1952, 2, NARG 59, 511.125/4-2952. The tour would have been more extensive if not for an outbreak of agrarian violence that forced its premature conclusion.

88. "Termination of Veracruz Sound-Truck Tour," Fisher to SD, 20 Sept. 1950, 3–4, NARG 59, 511.125/9-2050.

89. "Grass-Roots Film Tour of State of Veracruz: First Stage," Fisher to SD, 23 Aug. 1950, 2, NARG 59, 511.125/8-2350.

90. For the popular reception of the Disney cartoons, see Ilo C. Funk (U.S. consul, Veracruz) to SD, 22 Jan. 1946, NARG 84, MCEGR 842–Information Programs; and Clarke Vyse (U.S. consul, Agua Prieta) to SD, 21 Jan. 1946, MCEGR 842–Information Programs, box 717. Several of Disney's wartime educational cartoons—¿*Agua: Amiga o Enemiga?* [Water, friend or enemy?], *La Semilla de Oro* [The grain that built a hemisphere], *El Cuerpo Humano* [The human body], ¿*Qué es Enfermidad?* [What is disease?], *La Peste Alada* [The winged scourge], and *Tuberculosis*—were among the seven most popular of the over 350 U.S. titles

distributed monthly at between 100 and 300 exhibitions each. See "Statistical Motion Picture Report for November 1949," Fisher to SD, 8 Feb. 1950, NARG 59, 511.125/2-850; and "Statistical Motion Picture Report for January, 1959," Fisher to SD, 17 Mar. 1950, NARG 59, 511.125/3-1750.

91. "Use of USIE Film in Village in Puebla," Fisher to SD, 17 Nov. 1950, NARG 59, 511.125/11-1750.

92. The author thanks Madeleine Matz of the Motion Picture and Broadcasting Division of the Library of Congress, Gary Stern of the Motion Picture and Sound Recording Branch of the National Archives, and Valerie Komor of the Rockefeller Archive Center for assistance in viewing the two principal educational series produced by Disney during the war and exhibited into the 1950s: *Salud para las Américas* and *Lectura para las Américas*. For an overview of Disney's collaboration in U.S. wartime propaganda production, see Richard Shale, *Donald Duck Joins Up: The Walt Disney Studio during World War II* (Ann Arbor: University of Michigan Press, 1982). A recent interpretation of these films is offered by Lisa Cartwright and Brian Goldfarb, "Cultural Contagion: On Disney's Health Education Films for Latin America," in Smoodin, *Disney Discourse*.

93. The Disney educational films suggest an interesting twentieth-century twist on Stephen Greenblatt's notion of "mimetic circulations" — "the underlying strategic intersection of representational forms" in the early colonial New World. See *Marvelous Possessions: The Wonder of the New World* (Chicago: University of Chicago Press, 1991), 139. Not only were the films a collaborative production enterprise between Mexican and U.S. authorities, but their representations of Mexican peasants were recycled to the very audiences depicted in the movies: thus the Mexican peasant was the subject of both production and reception.

94. Disney's wartime production of Good Neighbor propaganda and visual-education films was prominently recognized by the Mexican government. President Manuel Avila Camacho welcomed the gala Mexican premiere of *Tres Caballeros* (another OCIAA-subsidized project), approving its distribution at a private screening. See Max Gómez (RKO's Mexico City manager) to Avila Camacho, 14 Dec. 1944, and Jesús González Gallo to Gómez, 15 Dec. 1944, Archivo General de la Nación, Mexico City, Fondo Presidentes, Ramo Avila Camacho, 523.3/67. In 1943 Avila Camacho demonstrated his government's support of Disney propaganda when he awarded Walt Disney the Order of the Aztec Eagle (the highest honor Mexico bestows on foreigners) for his contributions to hemispheric solidarity; see *Variety*, 3 Mar. 1943, 6.

95. This is not surprising, given Disney's visits to Mexico to gather images for the studio's Good Neighbor cartoons.

96. Like the others in the *Salud para las Américas* series, *Saneamiento* offered a liberal alternative to radical social change. But even its moderate vision implied major new undertakings by Latin American states. The film was the only one in the series that represented "progress" as involving significant economic inputs

by the state, i.e., education and acculturation would not alone bring a better life. Reform would inevitably bring development; the question of resources went unaddressed, however.

97. "Motion Picture Section," enclosure no. 3 of "Extent of USIE Effectiveness in Mexico," 25 Jan. 1951, NARG 59, 511.12/1-2551.

98. "Semi-annual Evaluation Report of USIE Activities in Mexico," 12 Sept. 1950, 40, NARG 59, 511.12/9-1250. *Defense against Invasion* animated ways to avoid malaria through a narrative that offered political metaphors that could easily be applied to communist subversion, although they were originally aimed at fascism.

99. "First Part of USIE Tour of Embassy Jeep Sound-Truck through the State of Hidalgo," Fisher to SD, 14 Apr. 1950, NARG 59, 511.125/4-1450.

100. "Motion Picture Section," enclosure no. 3 of "Extent of USIE Effectiveness in Mexico," 25 Jan. 1951, NARG 59, 511.12/1-2551.

101. "Termination of Veracruz Sound-Truck Tour," Fisher to SD, 20 Sept. 1950, 3, NARG 59, 511.125/9-2050.

102. "First Part of USIE Tour of Embassy Jeep Sound-Truck through the State of Hidalgo," Fisher to SD, 14 Apr. 1950, 2, NARG 59, 511.125/4-1450.

103. "Review of the USIE Motion Picture Program in Mexico as of December 1950," Gayne, 3–4, enclosed in NARG 59, 511.125/12-150.

104. "Completion of 'Grass Roots' USIE Cultural Mission to State of Hidalgo," Fisher to SD, 10 May 1950, 2, NARG 59, 511.125/5-1050.

105. "Grass-Roots Film Tour of State of Veracruz: First Stage," Fisher to SD, 23 Aug. 1950, 2, and enclosed articles, NARG 59, 511.125/8-2350.

106. Ibid., 4.

107. "Semi-annual Report of USIE Activities in Mexico," 9 Sept. 1952, 34 and 33–38, NARG 59, 511.12/9-952.

108. "Termination of Veracruz Sound-Truck Tour," 2, Fisher to SD, 20 Sept. 1950, NARG 59, 511.125/9-2050.

109. "Semi-annual Report of USIE Activities in Mexico," 9 Sept. 1952, 28, NARG 59, 511.12/9-952.

110. " 'Grass Roots' USIS Mission to the State of Hidalgo," 4, Fisher to SD, 29 Mar. 1950, NARG 59, 511.125/3-2950.

111. "Semi-annual Evaluation Report of USIE Activities in Mexico," 42, 12 Sept. 1950, NARG 59, 511.12/9-1250.

112. Herschel F. Peak (acting publications officer), "USIE Field Trip to the State of Oaxaca," 12 Mar. 1952, NARG 59, 511.125/3-1252.

113. After the film on soybean cultivation, the Disney films were the most popular in the eyes of the tour's operatives; see "Motion Picture Sound-Truck Tour of the State of Oaxaca," Rankin to SD, 29 Apr. 1952, 2, NARG 59, 511.125/4-2952.

114. For example, during the 1950 Hidalgo tour only 2,240 publications were distributed, but by 1952 it was common during trips of similar duration (two months) to distribute over 100,000 pieces of literature.

115. Peak, "USIE Field Trip to the State of Oaxaca," enclosed with Rankin to SD, 12 Mar. 1952 NARG 59 511.125/3-1252.

116. Ibid.

117. For an analysis of transnational Cold War propaganda production in Mexico, see Fein, "Hollywood and United States–Mexico Relations," chap. 8.

118. "Extent of USIE Effectiveness in Mexico," O'Dwyer to SD, 25 Jan. 1951, I, enclosure no. 3, NARG 59, 511.12/1-2551; and "Psychological Offensive: Intensification of USIE Program in Mexico," 9 Nov. 1950, 5, NARG 59, 511.12/11-950.

119. For example, of the 825,690 persons who attended 2,039 U.S. exhibitions in November 1949, "Rural Audiences" led all other social categories in attendance (337,090 persons at 518 exhibitions). This category was followed by spectators described as "Miscellaneous" (212,012 at 614 exhibitions, that were most likely rural as well); next came "Government Agencies and Armed Services" (102,702 at 199 exhibitions), "Workers Groups" (83,574 at 164 exhibitions), and "Primary and Secondary Schools" (80,645 at 433 exhibitions). These were followed by smaller programs including churches and other religious organizations, professional groups, colleges and universities, business organizations, and other civil groups; see "Non-theatrical Film Distribution, November 1949," enclosed with NARG 59, 511.125/2-850.

120. The program also increased the overall Mexican spectatorship for Hollywood's commercial fare by expanding the national audience through the penetration of the countryside.

121. "Report on USIE Activities in Mexico from June 1 to November 30, 1951," 18, 27 Feb. 1952, NARG 59, 511.12/2-2752.

122. "Semi-annual Report of USIE Activities in Mexico," 9 Sept. 1952, 25, NARG 59, 511.12/9-952.

123. "Semi-annual Evaluation Report of USIE Activities in Mexico," 12 Sept. 1950, 37, NARG 59, 511.12/9-1250.

124. See, for example, "Request for Additional 16 mm. RCA Sound Projectors," Donnelly to SD, 30 Sept. 1946, NARG 84, MCEGR 842–Information Program–Motion Pictures, box 717.

125. "Film Distribution Arrangements Made with the Ministry of Education," Webb to SD, 7 Sept. 1951, NARG 59, 511.125/9-751.

126. "Semi-annual Evaluation Report of USIS Activities in Mexico," 9 Jan. 1953, 30, NARG 59, 511.12/1-953. By 1953, many USIS-distributed films regularly reached the inchoate TV audience by way of Mexico City stations, XHTV and XEW-TV; see "Transmitting Semi-Annual Evaluation of USIE Activities in Mexico," 9 Sept. 1952, 39–43, NARG 59, 511.12/9-952.

127. "Semi-annual Evaluation Report of USIE Activities in Mexico," 15 Mar. 1951, 35, NARG 59, 511.12/3-1551.

128. U.S. Embassy to Secretaría de Relaciones Exteriores, 11 Jan. 1949; and Armando C. Amador (Secretaría de Gobernación) to Mexican Embassy, Washington, D.C., 19 Feb. 1949, Archivo Concentración de la Secretaría de Relaciones

Exteriores (Mexico City), expediente 3-1626-3. See also Fein, "Devolution of the Golden Age," 119–24.

129. "Semi-annual Evaluation Report of USIE Activities in Mexico," 15 Mar. 1951, 29, NARG 59, 511.12/3-1551.

130. Francis H. Styles (U.S. consul, Tampico) to George Messersmith, 25 Jan. 1946, NARG 84, MCEGR 842–Information Program, box 717.

131. Benedict Anderson, *Imagined Communities: Reflections on the Origin and Spread of Nationalism* (New York: Verso, 1991).

132. The most compelling explication of this theme, particularly for its analysis of the relationship between political economy and international culture, is David Harvey, *The Condition of Postmodernity: An Enquiry into the Origins of Cultural Change* (Cambridge, Mass.: Blackwell, 1990).

133. Louis Hartz, *The Liberal Tradition in America: An Interpretation of American Political Thought since the Revolution* (New York: Harcourt Brace Jovanovich, 1955), 284–309. (This chapter's opening epigraph is from p. 305.)

Lauren Derby

Gringo Chickens with Worms

Food and Nationalism in the Dominican Republic

El costo de la vida sube otra vez	The cost of living goes up again
el peso que baja ya ni se ve	the peso is so low it can't even be seen,
y las habichuelas no se pueden comer	and beans, you can't eat them
ni una libra de arroz ni una cuarta	nor a pound of rice or a quarter
de café	of coffee,
a nadie le importa qué piensa usted	no one cares what you think
será porque aquí no hablamos	could it be because we don't speak
inglés	English?
ah ah es verdad	It's true
do you understand?	do you understand?
do you, do you?	do you? do you?
Somos un agujero en medio	We are a hole in the middle
del mar y el cielo	of the sea and sky
500 años después	500 years later
una raza encendida	a race in flames
negra, blanca y taína	black, white, and Taino
pero, quién descubrió a quién?	but, who discovered whom?

JUAN LUIS GUERRA and 4:40, song titled "El costo de la vida" [The cost of living], from *Areito* (1992)

¡Oh Nueva York mi dolor descamado!	Oh, New York, my immeasurable pain!
¡Oh Nueva York Humanidad sub-yacente!	Oh, New York, subjugated humanity!
por ti entendí que la primera	you taught me that the first
definición de Patria es la nostalgia.	definition of the Nation is nostalgia.

CHIQUI VICIOSO, from "Nueva York, 1992"

In June 1992 an uproar broke out in the capital of the Dominican Republic, Santo Domingo. Stories erupted that "gringo" chickens, the local term for those grown in high-yield poultry factories, were riddled with worms. The public response to these rumors was unanimous and overwhelming. The consumption of gringo chickens stopped abruptly as Dominicans shunned fast-food chicken chains like Pica Pollo and Victorina, venues normally packed at noon. These are the lunchtime favorite for the urban middle classes employed in the service sector and government on tight budgets, who live too far to return home for lunch as is customary. Because they are cheap, clean, and respectable, these are also places where the aspiring poor from the barrios can take their girlfriends in the evening. In one week, the poultry industry lost over 50 million pesos, and sent an urgent call to President Joaquín Balaguer to intervene to address their plight.[1] Pica Pollo and the hundreds of other fast-food chains serving chicken and chips in the capital were abandoned virtually overnight, and many poultry farmers were forced into bankruptcy.

Theories abounded over the origin of these rumors. Some conjecture focused on the economic rationality of the reports, alleging that there was a conspiracy afoot on the part of a competing food giant to gain market share.[2] For example, poultry farmers accused beef producers of fueling a campaign aimed at raising beef consumption, just as Dominican chicken producers accused importers of initiating the campaign so as to augment their trade. To elites, the scare simply reinforced their predisposition to see the masses as irrational and inclined toward claptrap. Others condemned this affront to the hygiene of national foodstuffs and the soothsayers who lacked faith in Dominican products.[3]

What caused this flurry of uneasiness over poultry? And why did gringo chicken become the scapegoat in this national scourge? This was not the first time that poultry had become the eye of a national scandal in the Dominican Republic. In previous years, gringo chicken had been accused of causing AIDS, infertility in women, and impotency and homosexuality in men. This hearsay first arose when stories that U.S. chicken feed was spiked with hormones began to circulate in Santo Domingo. And high-yield poultry varieties in the Dominican Republic are fed primarily with U.S. feed, which is cheaper for producers.[4] The gringo chicken, I suggest, was a magnet for controversy because it symbolized the ambivalence of national identity in the Caribbean, as the mediating nexus between foreign and homegrown (lo extranjero vs. lo criollo), cash and food crops, money and morality, market and family, and the United States and the Dominican Republic.[5] The gringo chicken (which is of North American origin, is white, and eats imported feed, but lives in the Caribbean and is grown by Dominican producers) raises a key issue every Dominican today must contend with: that is, what defines nationality in the U.S.-directed world system? What is "Dominican" in a context in which the external and the internal have for centuries been thoroughly interpenetrated and have rendered ambiguous the boundaries separating the foreign and the national?[6] Where does national identity reside when U.S. firms own and control great expanses of land, beach, and property on the island and, moreover, when almost as many Dominicans live in New York City as in their own capital?

This essay explores how food can provide a lexicon for debates over nationhood.[7] It examines how a small Caribbean nation, formed in the shadow of the Northern Colossus, expresses its ambivalence vis-à-vis the United States through the idiom of consumption. Recently scholars have focused on the hybrid and multivocal semiology of nationness as experienced in the postcolonial world. Dominicans today to be sure inhabit a fragmentary and transnational social universe.[8] As a result of high emigration rates since the 1970s, Dominicans have now become the largest Latin American migrant stream to the United States, and the largest source of recent immigrants to New York City, with one in seven nationals residing in *Nueva York,* second city of the Dominican Republic and metonym for the greater *yanqui* world.[9]

Paradoxically this experience of quotidian fragmentation has produced a desire for the concrete, one of translating disjointed worlds into mimetic fetishes that can be invoked, appropriated, and conjured. The experience of deterritorialization and powerlessness characteristic of diasporas, combined with what Richard Sennet has termed "the spectre of uselessness" under modern global capitalism, may be encouraging a particular form of fetishism in which one gains control over transnational forces by portraying them as artifacts, icons, and even foods.[10] Such fetishes may serve as alibis for place in an increasingly homeless world. Through substitution, one controls not only the representation, but that which is being represented, since some of the essence of the original is embodied in its copy. As Michael Taussig has written, "the mimetic faculty" is the process of mastering the other through its replication.[11] As Paul Stoller says, "Sympathetic magic consists of copy and contact. Sorcerers make a copy of that which they want to affect. Through its magical power the copy acquires the properties of the original, which, in turn, implies the sorcerer's mastery and power over the object."[12] During the gringo chickens episode, Dominicans rendered their relationship with the United States into a language of the body, striving to take charge of the great "shark" of the Caribbean through its absorption into idioms of daily life. And there is nothing more quotidian in the Antilles than food.[13]

This essay examines how discourses of food have articulated the boundaries of nationhood in the Dominican Republic. I examine two key moments when the relationship between the Dominican Republic and the United States was encoded as a contest between two moral economies of consumption. One system was socially regulated by the family; the other was a market economy of consumption controlled by Wall Street—the tantalizing, dangerous, and fundamentally asocial economy of the U.S. dollar. These two imaginary logics draw on the dialectical imagery that pits home, as symbolized by indigenous food crops cultivated in the garden plot, or *conuco*—the essence of the indigenous, earthen, nourishing, lo criollo—against the wild, destructive, erratic, uncontained, enticing but ultimately barren cash crops associated with a global market economy governed by the United States, of which sugar is considered the epitome. Not coincidentally, the two moments I will discuss were both moments of intense globalization: first, the late nineteenth century, when U.S. sugar farms were entering the country en masse, establishing corporate enclaves of U.S.-administered plantations, and hiring servile labor from Haiti and Jamaica to cut cane. The foreign sugar invasion and the creation of an enclave economy raised deep questions about citizenship and national identity that came to be understood through the key symbol of sugar, which stood in for the debilitating transnational force of U.S. capital, as contrasted with Dominican food crops such as the humble and homely plantain. I examine how the onslaught of the U.S.-owned sugar economy created anxieties about the loss of sovereignty that forged an image of sugar as a national nemesis and malevolent sign of commodity value. I explore the destruction wrought by sugar in the Dominican imagination as portrayed in two novels: Ramón Marrero Aristy's classic *Over,* and Francisco Eugenio Moscoso Puello's *Cañas y bueyes* [Sugar and oxen].[14] Here global capital, encoded as American and embodied in sugar, was perceived as a corrosive force that ripped apart community and razed social hierarchy. Money and morality were perceived as antithetical logics. Cash was a solvent of society, in sharp contrast to the morality of a traditional social order based on hierarchy and difference.

I also discuss sugar's foil, that quintessential emblem of creole identity, the plantain, through the writings of its greatest muse, essayist, and social critic, José Ramón López. López wrote the influential 1896 treatise on food, race, and the Dominican nation titled "La Alimentación y las Razas" [Food and the races], in which he argued that the staple food of the peasantry, the starchy plantain, was the reason behind the lack of progress of the poor—not their racial mixture.[15] López was answering European racial theorists such as Joseph Arthur de Gobineau, who in penning theories of racial determinism consigned thoroughly mulatto societies such as Brazil and the Dominican Republic to national degeneration.

Second, I analyze another moment when a rhetoric of consumption provided the lexicon for Dominicans' complex and ambivalent sentiments toward the United States: the Christopher Columbus Quincentenary celebrations in 1992, when politically the Dominican Republic was seeking to position itself at the center of the Americas, as the first site of contact and then settlement for Columbus and his entourage. The boundaries of the Dominican nation were simultaneously challenged by riots in Washington Heights, New York City, as Dominicans there (*dominicanos ausentes*) protested police brutality and U.S. ethnic stereotypes of Dominicans as drug traffickers, piquing ambivalence on the island over whether the community overseas was sufficiently "respectable" to be considered extended kin of the nation. Economically, this was a period of intense discussion over *neoliberalismo,* the market-driven global order—the late 1980s vision articulated by Margaret Thatcher, Ronald Reagan, and George Bush, which culminated in free-trade agreements in Latin America such as NAFTA. It was also the culmination of a long-term economic recession, a result of plummeting prices for exports such as sugar, tobacco, and coffee, and the shift toward export free-trade zones and tourism, enclave industries which have failed to ameliorate the deepening unemployment crisis and increasingly have skewed the distribution of income. The scandal over gringo poultry erupted in the midst of this debate over states versus markets, one that translated locally into the relative virtues and vices of control by the nation-state versus transnational capitalism. I probe the cultural logic behind these images of decay, and why gringo chickens became the "epistemological category" through which Dominicans resisted the challenge they perceived to their nationhood.[16] In sum, I demonstrate how, first, sugar and plantain, and later, gringo versus creole chicken, have provided key oppositions for framing the dialectics of national identity in the Dominican Republic, and the tensions surrounding being creole in the global arena of the Americas. An underlying theme is the story of how lo criollo has shifted from being a pejorative term, signifying a lack of European civilization in the nineteenth century, to its positive evocations today of hearth and home in an increasingly transnational world. I suggest that consumption has become a key arena in which anxieties over the dissolution of place in the transnational condition are expressed, and boundaries redrawn.

Food and Identity

Why should food metaphors become the medium of choice for communicating popular sentiments toward the United States? Perhaps because ingestion provides a graphically compelling image of power relations, and one that speaks to people because it derives from everyday life.[17] Eating is also an activity that makes sense across the class divide. Moreover, it concerns the body, particularly the boundary between corporal interiors and exteriors, which often becomes charged when anxieties surround the body politic.[18] The Dominican Republic, however, is not alone in its penchant for understanding relations of power in terms of eating. Johannes Fabian has shown that the Luba of Zaire conceive of power through the image of ingestion, a vision that conveys power not as a function but as a property.[19] This conception is quite different from postmodern theories that stress power's dispersion, its indeterminacy, and its ineffable nature in the postcolonial era. The image of power as eating is an effective means of expression, because it displays the violence behind modern techniques of domination, which often conceal hidden brutalities.[20] This notion of power also assumes agency. The image of consumption thus puts teeth back into the notion of power.

Foodstuffs provide a key idiom for several genres of identity in the Dominican Republic. Typically, food tropes are powerful as well as popular because they play on several tensions, one being the fact that they hover on the borderline between metaphor and metonymy, between being a tool for understanding and being an agent of mimetic subversion.[21] That is, foods are good to think with, but, given the right circumstances, they can also stand in for the thing itself.[22] In the Afro-Caribbean religion of Dominican *vodú,* an offering of the gods' foods can signify their presence or can induce their arrival. In a parallel vein, nostalgia for one's *patria chica,* or region of origin, can be summoned up by those foods that are signs of the province. Regional identities are often marked by food, most commonly important regional products. For example, the symbol of the southwestern town of Barahona is the plantain, which is said to be tastier as well as bigger than plantains from other regions—even though since the 1920s the primary product of Barahona has been sugar. But sugar until recently has been produced by foreign firms, hence augmenting the valence of nostalgic creole authenticity for the Barahona plantain. Here, sugar is the foil against which the plantain is defined.

In Dominican popular culture, foodstuffs are frequently deployed as sexual symbols and are often gendered. At times, erotic sparring in the street can take advantage of conflations between taxonomies of food, gender, and region. For example, a young man from Barahona might gesture his elbow, indicating just indeed how long plantains from his town are (i.e., bigger than a man's hand and forearm together), and glossing this as a felicitous comment on his sexual potency, as a good *barahonero*. The gendering of fruits in particular leads to certain taxonomic taboos: menstruating women, for example, may not eat certain fruits evocative of masculinity, particularly the phallic banana and the white milky flesh of the *guanábana* or uglifruit, which invokes semen. Pregnant and lactating women are prohibited from foods evocative of fertility, like avocados, because of their large seed.[23] Eggs are considered aphrodisiacs, particularly those of the tiny quail or large duck. Ambulant street vendors of produce (who are generally male) often play on the erotics of their cargo in their catcalls to the maids, housewives, and children who buy their goods, using particularly the "male" vegetables and fruits as props for flirtation and raucous joking.[24] Indeed, they will let the vegetables "say" things that would be disrespectful for them to utter to steady customers.

But if gender counts in the vegetable world, it matters even more in the animal kingdom. And poultry provides the basis for a cluster of central metaphors in Dominican culture. First, hens and cocks are said to have different nutritional qualities. Hens evoke fertility. Even chicken soup is classified by gender, as *caldo de gallina* (chicken soup made from the hen) is required for strengthening women on the verge of childbirth, whereas offering soup from the cock at that time would be an act of malice.[25] Roosters are also considered a poor man's food, and undercapitalized petty entrepreneurs will often buy up the refuse from cockfighting establishments for use in their *friquitín* (street fried-food stand).[26] Moreover, the chicken provides the paradigmatic template of femininity and masculinity, albeit in exaggerated, idealized form. For example, a favorite carnival costume in Santo Domingo is called *roba la gallina* (steal the hen), and consists of a man dressed up to look like a pregnant woman, with a huge pillowed stomach, bust, and butt. Although he typically wears a wig, an apron, and exaggerated facial makeup, and walks in a fashion that calls attention to his cushioned protrusions, he must let his male identity show through, often by sporting high sneakers and allowing his legs to remain hirsute. Unlike a true transvestite who would shave his legs and wear heels, this is patent dissimulation—a spectacle, not mimesis. As he passes, people chant repeatedly, *"Roba la gallina, baila con ella"* (steal the hen, dance with her). This character plays on the theme of multiple identities and their transformation, slipping from male to female, and from mother to father to embryonic child. This protean character offers commentary on several aspects of femininity: on the female social role of the housewife, the *gallina* or nesting female spouse, the ideal wife who maintains the homestead; as well as on the beckoning sexuality of the female body; and, finally, on female procreative power. These multiple meanings ascribed to femininity are mocked through their simultaneous conjuring since they are mutually exclusive: the señora or middle-class housewife, the whore, and the mother. Of course, this image also invokes the horror of blurred gender boundaries, and, fears of homosexuality.

Even more than the hen, the cock provides a key code of masculinity that reverberates in many areas of daily life. If foods gendered as female are associated with taboos, with social and personal order, those associated with men most often involve rule breaking. For example, the quintessential men, that is to say, the patriotic, honorable, and brave men who have helped make the nation through taking up arms and fighting for their ideals— "men of great political prestige . . . and great ideals" —are called *gallos,* or cocks.[27] Certain *caudillos* and statesmen have earned nicknames that resonate with this hard-earned title of male prestige, such as President Ramón Cáceres (1906–1911), who earned the name "Gallo Colorao," or piebald creole cock, which is said to be particularly fierce. The term *gallo* clearly plays on a phallic reference, and this can be seen in the stories about gallos, which often include sexual innuendo and invocations of male power and virility.[28] The heroic gallo emerges most clearly in relation to an oppressive force, be it another political party, a gang, a local villain, or the United States; a rhetoric of aggression is used as symbolic armor, and sociopolitical penetration is transcoded as "male sexual violation," as José Limón has demonstrated for Mexico.[29] The urban barrio variant of the gallo in Santo Domingo is called the tiger-cock, *el tíguere gallo,* who must be valient, ready to use force when necessary, the epitome of bodily control, a good drinker, and athletic.[30]

In this predominantly mulatto society, *comida típica,* or authentic Dominican food, often glosses the racial mixing that in the popular imagination is characteristically Dominican. *Sancocho,* a soup containing several varieties of meat and tubers, is a key sign of Dominican society, as is the triad of beans, rice, and meat, nicknamed the *bandera dominicana* (the Dominican flag).[31] The most evident racial metaphor is *moros con cristianos,* or Moors and Christians, the nickname for the black beans and rice mixture that is so dear to the Dominican heart. Moros con cristianos as the comida criolla par excellence exemplifies how Dominicans perceive their own brand of racial mixing: blacks and whites retaining their own identity but clearly intimately bound up together, a variant on the Brazilian mythic "racial democracy." [32]

Dominican food is such a powerful conveyor of nationality that one could almost say that to eat Dominican is to be Dominican. Invariably the first query foreigners are faced with in the Dominican Republic is whether one has eaten comida criolla, and even more important, whether one enjoys it or not. This became the stock theme in a series of local rum advertisements in 1992 that were exceedingly popular, featuring a blond gringa woman whose first encounter with things Dominican occurs in a New York cab. In the first installment, her Dominican cab driver happens upon a merengue street band when letting her off, and looks dreamily into space, signaling his imaginary transport to the Dominican Republic. When she inquires ignorantly what that music is, he quips, "Americana, tú no sabes nada" (American, you don't know anything). In the second installment, she visits the Dominican Republic, and on the airline home (of course, Air Dominicana, the national airline) she asks for *concon*. Dominicans cook their rice very slowly in a heavy iron pot, so as to encourage the formation of a crunchy layer along the pot's lining. This browned, crispy rice is called "concon" and is savored, and served separately. To Dominicans, the fact that the gringa asks for concon indicates her dominicanization, her symbolic assimilation into the Dominican cultural universe. The *americana* is enlightened through her initiation into the lexicon of Dominican nationality.

Sugar and the Evils of Excess

C. L. R. James, the great West Indian social critic, has said that the Caribbean has a peculiar sense of nationness that stems from the ontological status of islands.[33] The fact that these are countries without borders accounts for the fact that foreigners are encountered as strangers—as exotic, fascinating, and somewhat threatening. While this may be true, the sharp ambivalence Dominicans feel toward the United States is a product of the nation's having come of age in the epoch of U.S. imperialism. In the nineteenth century, when the rest of Latin America had achieved independence, the Hispanic Caribbean was still split over the relative advantages and disadvantages of autonomy. Ultimately in Cuba, the late-nineteenth-century jewel of the Spanish colonial empire, a popular independence war took shape; however, Puerto Rico and the Dominican Republic, which had failed to realize Cuba's highly successful sugar bonanza, were forced to bargain from a position of weakness and sought annexation to the United States as a pragmatic trade-off between political goals and the economic realities of micronationhood in the North American backyard. Furthermore, Dominicans at mid-century were still fearful of neighboring Haiti, which had made several military incursions into Dominican terrain around the time of the Haitian revolution (1804) and later occupied its Spanish-speaking neighbor (1822–1844). In fact, in 1861, when the Dominican Republic was reannexed to Spain, Dominican president Buenaventura Báez went so far as to argue that annexation to the United States signified salvation, because it would force Haiti to respect Dominican rights.[34] Decades after the rest of Latin America had moved beyond colonialism, the Dominican Republic was taken once again by Spain, as elites sought a bulwark against Haiti's powerful army. Then, just after the Dominican Republic finally became independent in 1865, the country once again narrowly missed annexation in a deal that would have swapped U.S. protectorate status for use of the northern bay of Samaná, where the United States was interested in building a naval base. In sum, all Dominican governments after 1821 sought foreign stewardship, protection, or aid of one kind or another.[35]

Caribbean nationhood has been at best partial, contested, and fractured due to the realities of geopolitics in the U.S. backyard. After the debate over trusteeship died, the United States felt no qualms about direct interference in other arenas. As the national debt grew unwieldy by the 1890s and the Dominican Republic fell behind in repayments, a New York firm became de facto treasurer; then, in 1907, the U.S. government took over customs in an effort to collect revenue, exercising fiscal control until 1941. Later, the United States occupied the Dominican Republic twice to quell political instability: from 1916–1924, and again in 1965 to end civil war over the contested presidency of reformist Juan Bosch.

Although Dominican autonomy has been delimited in myriad ways by foreign intervention, concerns over transnationalism and the impact of global markets on the nation first became articulated in the Caribbean over sugar. Around the turn of the twentieth century, sugar became the key motif of global capitalism because of the way this one crop single-handedly transformed the Dominican economy. At first sugar loomed distantly on the horizon like a mirage. Similar to the phantasmagoric visions of grandeur spawned by gold, guano, bananas, or petroleum elsewhere in Latin America, some saw sugar as the ultimate answer to the ailing economy and a guarantee of national development. Apart from the Panama Canal, which inspired comparisons with the colonial Bolivian mining center of Potosí regarding its potential to reroute global markets toward Latin America, in the Caribbean nothing became a numen for potential future enrichment quite like sugar. In fact, Cuban poet Nicolás Guillén went so far as to declare, "without sugar there is no country." [36] Certainly sugar had its naysayers, yet even its critics perceived it, in Catherine LeGrand's words, as virtually "synonymous with contact with the outside world, with capitalism, and with modernity." [37] Sugar, and the cluster of meanings it came to represent, became a key "metaphorical construct" through which the turn-of-the-century transformation of the Dominican economy and society was understood and explained.[38]

Why would sugar be singled out as the master trope in the Dominican Republic representing both the positive and negative aspects of global capital? Certainly, first and foremost, due to the scale of the transformations it engendered. The sugar industry ushered in a new wave of urban development, railroad construction, local ancillary manufactures from rum to cigars, and cosmopolitan culture. Overnight, provincial hamlets such as La Romana and San Pedro de Macorís became cities; a transnational polyglot public culture was forged as a result of the immigration of West Indians, Haitians, Cubans, Puerto Ricans, and Americans; a proletarian workforce was created; and consumption patterns were revolutionized as U.S. goods became more readily available to a larger portion of the population. Sugar came to stand in for a host of changes associated with the market and commodity culture: from proletarianization to urbanism, from conspicuous consumption to alienation. At a time when most of the Dominican economy lay outside the sphere of market exchange, sugar came to represent both the magic and the terror of the marketplace: the seduction of self-transformation through the acquisition of commodities, as well as the resultant fears of dissimulation, as the familiar suddenly became strange. Commodification created problems of misrecognition as established social identities were subject to change.[39]

Several features helped sugar acquire a unique status both as a commodity and as a substance. Sugar itself was used as a form of currency in the colonial West Indies.[40] And while Dominicans had cultivated sugar since the early colonial period, the new sugar boom was almost entirely a foreign affair. By 1930 almost all the local *ingenios,* or plantations, were foreign owned. The sugar industry was also the most technologically sophisticated industry in the country. Another property rendering sugar distinctive was that it was not locally consumed until the U.S. occupation, when it became a marker of elite status. The local appetite for sweets had been quenched until the turn of the century by rough-hewn *melao* or unprocessed molasses or honey, not refined sugar; these were the preferred sweeteners in desserts and drinks. Indeed, in the 1890s esteemed Cuban traveler José Martí recorded the local Dominican saying that honey was "better than sugar, [and] made for coffee." [41] Yet this notwithstanding, by 1910 sugar was the country's largest export crop. Sugar was the sole commodity that was produced by foreign companies, primarily through foreign labor, and yielded a crop that was sold largely in overseas markets. This rendered it a particularly appropriate prism through which to ponder the status of national identity in the wake of transnational capital flows.[42]

Just as sugar for some became the focal point for utopian dreams of progress, it was equally vilified as representing the quintessence of global capitalism and the vagaries of the dollar. Sugar came to symbolize the mercurial and ultimately transitory nature of value in the money economy. Like a fine confection, it was alluring yet ultimately ephemeral. The problem with sugar lay in its hyperindustrial character: the way in which the mechanical nature of the boiling and grinding process disguised the labor involved in its production; the fact that ultimately it was men, not machines, that cut the cane and thus actually created the fine white powder. Partly it was the highly technical nature of this new production form that rendered sugar suspect in all of its manifestations. Many Dominican observers were averse to technology that challenged the skill and craftsmanship of artisanal methods of manufacture. Take the newly redesigned U.S.-made tobacco-rolling machines that began to attract attention in 1903. As they began to replace Cuban cigar hand-rolling, they were chastised as a product of "American cupidity, the desire to produce as much as possible in a short time with as little effort as possible." [43] (Cuban resistance to the machines, however, was equally chided for its atavism and backwardness by Dominicans.) By contrast, when late-nineteenth-century Dominican writers described indigenous cane producers, they sought to endow the firms with a human face, downplaying their technical wizardry and highlighting their paternalism. They described each ingenio in terms of the family history and identity of the men who founded it, and named the kind acts of generosity bestowed on their cane farmers (*colonos*) and workers.[44]

Indeed, Dominican disgust with U.S. efforts to tamper with nature to increase productivity date from this period, a time when efforts to improve the genetic stock of various comestible plant and animal species became vogue worldwide. Some Dominicans went as far as to urge local municipal councils to ban the importation of adulterated foodstuffs, calling them fraudulent and a public health hazard. Dominicans railed at efforts to alter the natural attributes of such products, labeling them "gross and criminal adulterations." Imported, genetically engineered milk was considered particularly suspect and was said to have an inordinately high water content and scarce nutritive value.[45] Of course, sugar was indirectly implicated in this charge, since it was the sugar economy that had opened up the domestic food market to U.S. imports. Moreover, refined sugar became a symbol of the Frankenstein-like pretentions of a country that saw no limits to its ability to tamper with nature's secrets.

Above and beyond the hideous artifice of the form of its production, sugar did more than provide a key image revealing the true nature of U.S. commodity culture: it was seen as embodying it. Nor was this the only alimentary arena in which beliefs concerning national and racial character were applied directly to foodstuffs. One critic praised the efforts of a public works minister who had imported Italian queen bees, claiming that Italian bees were more gentle, strong, and hard-working than Spanish or creole bees, and capable of one hundred times their production.[46] Indeed, this experiment included the early introduction of high-yield chickens (*gallinas ponedoras*), advocates for which claimed they had ten times the value and productivity of local breeds, and which were heralded as the answer to the local poultry industry's deficiencies.[47] Some even went so far as to contend that the introduction of U.S. products and production methods would encourage the Dominican peasantry to take on certain U.S. virtues, such as industry and frugality, through the adoption of sedentary agriculture. As one essayist wrote, the industrial production of sugar could be a means to demonstrate to the rural *gavillero* or bandit "the prodigousness of this land; its machines would demonstrate the power of intelligence of the settled man; and the smoke of its chimneys, dispersing in the atmosphere, would represent the vagaries and inconsistency of the future of his little-understood politics. The guerrilla, regenerating himself with time, would exchange the gun, with which he killed his brothers, for the hoe." [48]

Yet sugar certainly had its critics as well. Some Dominican intellectuals, such as Pedro Bonó, issued tirades against sugar—now a potent symbol of the United States, and one associated with the new monied economy and the culture of the marketplace, a corrosive force that appeared to dissolve social unity. All this, of course, was opposed to the traditional crop, tobacco, which came to symbolize "dominicanity" and the old order.[49]

The harshest indictments against sugar, however, were made through the language of literature. Indeed, the novels *Cañas y bueyes* by F. E. Moscoso Puello and *Over* by Ramón Marrero Aristy blame sugar for virtually every national flaw: from landgrabbing to corruption, from indolence to violence. The difference in the two treatments lies not in the severity of the charges, but rather in their perception of which groups proved most sharply victimized by sugar monoculture—cane farmers or merchants—and precisely how sugar ruined them.[50]

In the naturalist perspective of Moscoso's *Cañas y bueyes,* sugar destroyed the nation by razing the lush, green undergrowth of the *monte,* or backwoods, without which Dominicans could not survive. Similar to Thomas Hardy's anthropomorphic vision of the heath in his literary masterpiece *Return of the Native,* the monte was portrayed here as the moral and spiritual sustenance of the pueblo, the cradle and hearth of true *dominicanidad,* "their milieu, tradition, and fortune." [51] People cried when the forests, venerated and adored, which had sustained Dominicans from their days as rebel *cimarrones* (runaway slaves) and *monteros* (woods hunters), were slashed in order to plant cane. The monte was where the peasantry grew its garden vegetables, hunted for wild boars, and ranged unfenced cattle; thus it represented the security of an assured food supply outside the sphere of market exchange. The cutting of the monte was the closing of the Dominican frontier, and it left no alternative to becoming a vendor in a plantation bodega, a *colmado* (corner grocer), or a colono. In Moscoso's treatment, everyone is degraded by the onslaught of sugar: the wealthy landowner José Contreras loses his land and cattle, just as the country's "lack of progress, backwardness, disorganization, and, above all, its racial inferiority" is blamed on sugar. As one character declares in a moment of exasperation, "In no part of the world are people more exploited than here. Peons, workers, grocers—we are all enslaved." Moscoso presents a complex vision of the sugar plantation as an alien environment that pollutes all those who enter its domain, with no particular individual to blame. Sugar is a force that sucks everyone into its vortex, forcing them into complicity with its rules and terms.[52]

While turn-of-the-century portrayals of sugar's impact were more nuanced in their view that at times the owner of a particular sugar mill could humanize the impact of the crop and the fates of those who cultivated it, these later depictions positively vilify sugar. Here sugar is a form of social arsenic, one that dissolves the former standards of value—land and cattle—on which the previous social order had been grounded, and in the process ruins individuals, couples, families, and even the extended family of the nation.[53] Social prestige had accrued to clans in proportion to the quantity of skilled professionals, landed property, and stock that they possessed; indeed, such families were said to hold more "worth." [54] Cattle, land, and honor were the key "inalienable possessions" defining personhood in the old order. Drawing on Annette Weiner's formulation, these were goods to be kept outside the sphere of exchange due to their indisputable singularity; they were "transcendent treasures . . . symbolic repositories of genealogies and historical events." [55]

Indeed, there were many sayings indicating that land and cattle were forms of symbolic currency. For example, it was said that "he who has cattle earns by night and by day." [56] According to another maxim, if land was the "only fortune," oxen was "capital" itself.[57] Furthermore, land, which in the former communal system had been held collectively, was now calculated through a system of shares called *pesos,* thus explicitly invoking a form of currency, yet one that was nearly impossible to divide into individual ownership, thereby hindering land sales.[58] Before the advent of sugar, cattle and land had been only partially commodified, perhaps due in part to their incalculable value in the popular imagination. As if to mark their inalienable identity, plots as well as oxen were known not by their owners, but rather by their nicknames (such as *Malas Mujeres—* Bad Women—or Rosita), as if they, like people, were inviolable.

By stark contrast, sugar was the commodity form par excellence, its value ultimately void. This idea was reinforced through the popular perception that all those who gained cash by working in the sugar industry seemed to lose it in the end, either through women, gambling, exaction, drinking, or spending sprees. If land and cattle were the quintessence of value, in the sense that they should not be sold, sugar money was precisely its opposite—fast money with no staying power that failed to result in the accrual of wealth to its owner. As one day laborer in Moscoso's novel comments, "the money of the plantation stays there; it just dissolves like salt in water." [59]

Ramón Marrero Aristy's novel *Over* reinforces this vision of the venal and illusory nature of sugar profit by focusing on the fiscal subculture of the sugar plantation. Whereas Marrero portrays a system that dehumanizes all, from the upper echelons of the Dominican managerial staff to the lowliest Haitian cane cutter, this text focuses on the culture of profit making, the system of extortion by which the sugar firm exacted an informal "tax" on all transactions within the domain of the mill, popularly termed "over." From cane weighing by the ton to rice sales by the ounce, the ingenio demanded an off-the-books profit, one rendered all the more onerous for company *bodegueros* in particular, due to the fact that their inventory never quite measured up to its purported weight, leaving them squeezed on both ends. The author's focus on "over" seems to imply not only that, in accord with Marx's dictum, all capitalism is theft, but, moreover, that capitalism is an entirely foreign affair—made in the United

States with the collaboration of Syrian itinerant traders, Haitian and Jamaican cane cutters, and U.S. and Cuban know-how.

Unlike *Cañas y bueyes,* which focuses on the interstitial Dominican cane farmers who, as producers for the sugar mill, mediated between the foreign-owned plantation and local constituencies, there is no room in *Over* for ambiguity in the relationship between local and foreign actors. Here the story is told in black and white. The sole indication of a blurring of boundaries is the sprinkling of English words throughout the text (i.e., *over, payroll, míster*), which have made their way into Dominican Spanish, indexing the involuntary insinuation of aspects of an originally exotic sugar culture into Dominican soil. Even though the protagonist is repelled by the systematic injustice exacted by the system of "over," he is nonetheless drawn into its logic against his will, becoming in the end the prototypical alienated and inhumane figure he so abhorred on his arrival.[60] This stark portrait depicts the firm as a total institution crushing the very spirit of local society: here the ingenio is, indeed, "another republic," with its own laws, structure of political authority, and even money, since it was ingenio *vales,* or tokens, that were accepted at the plantation bodegas, not cash.[61] If Dominicans saw the plantation system as fundamentally usurious, as one producing an "unlawful surplus" or an "illegitimate excess," this novel explains why.[62]

If the portrayal of U.S. corporate capitalism as a rapacious force quite literally devouring Dominicans and their humanity seems overblown, keep in mind that the U.S. enterprises formed overseas at the turn of the century were often quite explicit about establishing correspondences between monetary and human value. If Dominicans resented feeling dehumanized by their transformation into objects or factors of production, it was not entirely in their imaginations. Michael O'Malley has charted the correspondences between the languages of race and money in the nineteenth-century United States, arguing that free-market economic thought was deployed to essentialize notions of racial difference.[63] The most explicit case of race being put into the service of corporate profit making overseas was perhaps the Panama Canal Zone, where the labor force was segmented into "gold" and "silver" tiers based on race and citizenship, with distinct salaries, housing, and commissaries.[64] Another example is the U.S. firms' importation of migrants — Haitians and West Indians — as contract workers to serve as cheap labor for the cane and banana harvests throughout Central America and the Caribbean.[65] While defiled as the lowliest in the ethnically stratified labor force, they were nonetheless marked as different, as a kind of commodified caste, since they were paid in U.S. currency. This augmented an association between blackness and money that had originated during slavery, when slaves were the foundational commodities defining the social order.[66] Thus sugar came to embody a chain of signification linking the United States, money, whiteness (and blackness)—all associated as elements foreign to Dominican creole essence and seen as privileged in certain ways, yet simultaneously mistrusted as alien, threatening, and socially dangerous. In the words of the author of *Cañas y bueyes,* "money inspires respect and fear." [67]

As Arjun Appadurai claims, a particular style of fetishism develops in enclave economies in which locals observe only a small portion of the trajectory of the commodity and as a result tend to project onto it extraordinary attributes.[68] It is the consumption side of the equation that was missing in this case: Dominicans produced sugar for a market that remained invisible to them. Ironically, however, sugar became an emblem of consumption pathology: the expression of a system that appeared ravenously to devour the labor on which it depended, as well as the essence of nationhood, the nation's citizenry and borders. Thus, in *Over,* it is sugar that appears to be swallowing Dominicans, as is powerfully expressed in the graphic image of a mill worker chewed up and spit out by a sugar processing machine, reduced from personhood to a heap of unidentifiable flesh. The narrator's wife exclaims, "Over has swallowed your life! It owns you!" As in Andean fat-stealing narratives, modernity is harnessed to serve a logic common to witchcraft narratives, in which the values of fertility and life itself are turned inside out, and in which the production of value is transformed into its very destruction.[69]

There is apparently something particularly heinous for Dominicans about the profit logic of the plantation making its way into the subculture of the colmado or bodega, the corner grocer's, the key site of *Over.* Perhaps this is because of the way the colmado corresponds to food, and the nurturing and nourishing of the family to relations of kin and trust. The colmado is closely tied to the domestic sphere, "the only space where people breath, curse and dream as they like." [70] During the day, it is an extension of the kitchen, where women buy the daily meal ingredients before lunch or dinner, often staying to chat with the attendants who know and ask about family matters; the colmado thus invokes maternal care, sustenance, and bounty. The frequency of daily visits and resultant intimacy of the colmado injects something of the spirit of the gift into transactions, as exemplified by loyal customers being rewarded with *ñapa,* or a little extra, as an investment on their return, or by the custom of buying on credit. In this view, the colmado belongs to another "regime of value"; it should remain distinct from the omnivorous sugar, the ultimate sign of commodity exchange. This opposition between cash and food may well date originally to slavery, when what Sidney Mintz calls the "provision ground marketing complex," the conuco or garden plot, was the basis of family subsistence and autonomy from the harsh world of the cane fields.[71] Even today, sugar workers struggle to grow food crops on every available bit of soil around their living quarters, representing a tiny modicum of self-determination in otherwise abject circumstances. The symbolism of food as an emblem of the hearth is sufficiently charged that various Dominican regimes have sought to harness this powerful populist sign of home and nation and affix it to the state. For example, the Trujillo regime in the 1930s conducted a nationalist campaign to encourage Dominicans to eat locally grown (as opposed to imported) rice, and advertisements cast Dominican rice consumption as a patriotic act that would help combat national dependency. Creole rice water was even touted as a panacea for weak or sick children.[72]

Food, Race, and Nation

While U.S. commodities such as sugar had become imperial signs by the 1920s, traditional food crops have not always been innocent harbingers of dominicanidad and signs of a glorious and pristine nation. Indeed, what might arguably be termed the national foodstuff, the plantain, was in the 1890s subject to intense scrutiny and a barrage of criticism. José Ramón López, essayist and social reformer, wrote "La alimentación y las razas" in 1896, an essay that defined an epoch of Dominican social thought, even though López's disparaging view of the Dominican nation has caused him to be remembered with some ambivalence in the history of Dominican letters.[73] The text is a riposte to social Darwinism and the determinist theories of de Gobineau and Oswald Spengler that conceived of race as the embodiment of national culture, and thus the prime index of a country's potential for development. This conflation of race and nation was particularly pernicious for countries with a predominance of racial mixture, which in this view had no future but one of degeneration. To his credit, López sought to decouple the nineteenth-century link between race and nation, reframing the issue from one of nature to one of culture. The explanation for the Dominican Republic's lack of progress was to be found not in the genetic composition of *la raza* but in diet. Unfortunately, however, in his drive to de-essentialize nation, López re-essentialized class.

López's argument provides a new twist to the old adage that you are what you eat—that identity is constituted through food. After a survey of the globe's dietary routines, he concluded that eating poorly and not enough had produced the malfeasance emanating from Italy and the Middle East; and that nations like Turkey, India, and China would remain stuck in the past until the masses were fed a more regular and balanced diet. Here he took issue with the racialist theories of Cesare Lombroso, the Italian criminologist who contended that certain races (Italians and Jews) were inherently prone to recidivism and criminality.[74] The Spanish colonizers had waged a war of attrition against the swarthy Indian and African, successively reducing their rations, degenerating the races, and compromising them physically and mentally. The Dominican Republic needed a "food apostle" to teach the people how to eat; the middle class preferred their rancid but imported margarine, the poor their anemic plantain, and everyone's nutritional deficit was demonstrated by Dominicans' propensity for coffee and alcohol. For lack of consumption, Dominicans were consumed by vices.

As liberal reformers such as López invested their faith in state formation and urban development, the countryside became the criterion of alterity against which progress was gauged.[75] And the peasant and his plantain became the distillation of rural barbarism. Avid for progress and civilization, Dominican liberals blamed the lack of national development on the peasantry, who, as a result of their hunger and nutritional deficiency, were plagued by a "lack of foresight, violence, and duplicity," as well as hopeless indolence.[76] Poor diet had produced the amorality of the countryside, an ethic of lies, dissimulation, intrigue, and excessive sensuality. The gravest problem, according to López, was the irregularity of the meal, a factor which had reduced the nation to a state of animality. The peasants, most notably the monteros, or mountain dwellers, who engaged in shifting cultivation and who ate great quantities of wild pork, were among some of the most afflicted. For them, the problem "hasn't been limited to the physical and mental degeneration of the race, or the abundance of cretins and peabrains; it has also rendered epidemic the most repugnant of diseases," such that there are entire towns in the interior rotten with contagion.[77] Under a tutelary regime, the state would instruct the peasantry in matters of culture, teaching them to keep their metaphorical house in order, especially at table.[78] Small property holding would be enforced, both to tie the peasantry into the monetary economy and to promote their civilization.

This discussion of the work of José Ramón López was intended to help clarify why the plantain continues to provide such a powerful symbol of Dominican national identity. The fact that the plantain symbolizes the peasantry explains why plantain is said to *embrutecer,* to make stupid, and why *platanizar* (literally, "to platanize") is such a derogatory term.[79] The multivalence of the *plátano* is its national-cum-class resonance; since the eighteenth century the plantain, roasted, boiled, or mashed, has been the quintessential rural Dominican food. Depending on the context, the plantain can either index national nostalgia or it can be a term of denigration for either the urban or rural poor. In a brawl, it might be used to gloss the Dominican nation positively in terms of its masculine virtues, such as virility, courage, honor, and readiness to fight. The plantain today, however, is often paired with the cornflake—held to be the American national starch—as positively and negatively valued national parameters: if the United States has brains, the Dominican Republic has other virtues, such as capacity for love, valience, and most of all, respect.

Trouble on the Other Island

If sugar became a symbol of a new level of globalization of the Dominican economy in the 1890s because of the establishment of foreign-owned and staffed enclaves driven by the cash nexus, the twentieth century would prove the harbinger of an even greater transnationalization of the country. By 1955, dictator Rafael Trujillo (1930–1961) had in effect nationalized the sugar industry by buying out the majority of the U.S. and Canadian concerns.[80] However, the move toward tourism and the establishment of export free-trade zones on the island, combined with a new Dominican migration stream to the United States since 1961, resulted in a qualitatively distinct level of globalization of the economy. The principal sources of foreign exchange today, tourism and export subcontacting in free-trade zones, are far more impermeable enclaves than sugar ever was, given the total absence of linkages with the larger economy. They have not even spawned the despised ingenio bodega. Both the tourist hotels and the free-trade zones are maintained like fortresses: built like military camps, the *zonas francas* require identification to enter, and the swank hotels frequently prohibit local residents from even using their beaches. More extensive foreign investment has increased land values and helped push Dominicans out of traditional agricultural enterprises, and combined with structural adjustment measures, has contributed to spiraling unemployment rates reaching some 20 to 50 percent of the male labor force today.[81] NAFTA's passage in 1994 provided a strong incentive for manufacturers, capital, and jobs to flee the Caribbean for a far more profitable Mexico.[82]

The net effect has been extensive emigration, particularly since the 1970s. In 1990 estimates of the total Dominican population in the United States ranged from 500,000 to 1.5 million persons, rendering the Dominican Republic New York City's largest source of immigration.[83] As a result, the Dominican community has now achieved the status of a thoroughly binational "ethnoscape," one for which national identity is no longer co-incident with national terrain.[84]

Yet the fact of an increasingly deterritorialized society has created an increasing sense of unease among local elites. While Dominican migrants tend to be drawn from the most educated segment of the local population, local elites nonetheless insist on their lower-class status (a prejudice which in part stems from the fact that most migrants take lower-working-class jobs in the United States).[85] This bias is a result of the sense of displacement caused by the frequent visits paid by *Dominicanyorks* to the island as tourists flaunting their access to dollars. Emigrés contributed nearly one-third of the total revenues gleaned from tourism, for example, in 1985. Additionally, return migrants form an increasingly significant portion of "foreign" investment in the Dominican Republic, particularly in industries like construction, in which it is estimated that some 60 percent of housing is now purchased by Dominicans overseas. Today remittances have far surpassed sugar and other traditional export commodities, becoming by the late 1980s the nation's second largest foreign exchange earner. Luis Guarnizo goes as far as asserting that migrants are the "single most important social group contributing to the local economy." [86] As a result, Dominicanyorks are increasingly perceived as a threat to the local power structure, a fact that placed Dominicans on the island in a dilemma when riots broke out in Washington Heights, New York City, in July 1992.

The riots forced Dominicans on the island to come to terms for the first time with their compatriots overseas through the eyes of the United States. Just weeks after the Los Angeles riots, which erupted in response to the verdict in the Rodney King police brutality case, violence broke out in Washington Heights, the heart of the Dominican community in Queens, in upper Manhattan. A young Dominican man, José García, was shot by police during a scuffle, setting off a week of street riots, looting, and protests over a forty-square-block area. Demonstrators carrying Dominican flags and chanting "policías, asesinos" (police, assassins) rushed the 34th Police Precinct, where the offending officer was based. In response, the police mobilized more than two thousand reinforcements who, wearing their riot gear and wielding batons, were sent in to break up the protesters and compose the crowds. With the King incident fresh on everyone's

Figure 1. Demonstrators marching through the streets of Washington Heights, 7 July 1992. The Chief of Police, David Scott, is in the background. Photographer: Adam Fernandez.

mind, Mayor David Dinkins visited the area frequently and pleaded for calm. In the aftermath, the neighborhood was a shambles, awash in broken glass, overturned cars, smoldering trash bins, shattered storefronts, and garbage strewn in every direction—ardent testimony to community rage. All told, some twenty people were injured (of whom ten were police officers), twenty-four people were taken into custody, and two abandoned buildings were set on fire.[87] The greatest tragedy was the death of a twenty-two-year-old father of two who fell five flights during a rooftop police chase. The eruption took everyone by surprise, since New York had escaped the popular conflagrations of Los Angeles and Chicago in the wake of the King episode.

The particular forms of protest were meaningful, drawing on traditional Dominican idioms of popular religiosity marking mourning, loss, and bereavement. A portion of West 162nd Street was transformed into a memorial for García, with hundreds of white candles sketching García's nickname, Kiko, on the ground, and forming two large crosses outside the building where he died.[88] The use of García's nickname (*apodo*) sent a message, since names are considered an extension of one's person in the Dominican Republic and can be jealously guarded. Residents challenged the official persona the police had defined for García through the use of Kiko, a nickname that signaled his community identity, the persona he was to friends and family. The apodo also embodies the collective identities of kin and barrio (neighborhood), since it is a gift one receives from the group while a child.[89] It is thus an especially important resource to a group living in a marginal subculture, one that is impugned, reviled, and persecuted by the larger society. Certainly, the politics of official personhood has an especially charged valence in a community containing many illegal immigrants lacking proper visas, some of whom adopt false public identities to camouflage their involvement in illegal drug commerce.[90] The Catholic imagery of the candles and the crosses underscored García's innocence and his martyrdom, as residents sought to transform his image from the rough, armed drug dealer that police invoked, to a victim of ethnic prejudice. Of course, the white candles also invoked the Barón del Cemetario, guardian of the cemetery and keeper of the keys to the afterworld in Dominican vodú. The Barón is particularly popular among Dominicanyorks who beseech his assistance, for example, when applying for U.S. visas.[91] As one Dominican teenager, Clara Cruz, poignantly exclaimed, "They shot him like a dog, but worse than a dog, because Americans, they respect their dogs, but they don't respect their Dominicans." [92]

Washington Heights is a community of two realities. It is an axis of poor but hard-working Dominican immigrants with tremendous pressure to provide for their families in both New York and Santo Domingo. The majority have fought to succeed within the system. The area has hundreds of small colmados owned by struggling Dominicans, and many men from the area work in New Jersey factories. Washington Heights even campaigned for redistricting to elect its own city councilman. Yet the zone is also called the "cocaine capital of New York," with a brisk trade in drugs over the George Washington Bridge.[93] Dominican gangsters are credited with pioneering the mass marketing of crack cocaine in the United States. "Yayo" Polanco-Rodríguez masterminded a drug marketing empire modeled on the Medellín cartel protected by hit squads in the 1980s. Hand in hand with the rise in illicit commerce has been a surge in violent crime: the 34th Precinct now leads the city in yearly homicides.[94] The rift between residents and the police, though, is only exacerbated by the involvement of some Dominicans in drugs; the problem starts with the illegality of many who overstay their visas. The nest egg they hope to secure, however, often recedes like a mirage on the horizon. Nevertheless, in parts of the city, drugs have become synonymous with Dominicans, especially those from the eastern town of San Francisco de Macorís, the purported

Sicily of the Dominican Republic. In large part, the violence exploded as a result of this contest of images, the tension between residents' and the police's versions of who García was, and thus what the community was. The police contended that García was armed, and that Officer O'Keefe shot him in self-defense. García's family and witnesses claim that García was unarmed and resisting physical abuse when he was shot.[95]

The incident presented an interpretive challenge for Dominicans on the island, many of whom harbored strongly equivocal feelings about the "dominicanos ausentes," who are viewed with a mixture of envy and disdain. The official response was outrage, and the mayor of Santo Domingo and the Dominican ambassador in New York swiftly protested. A group from San Francisco de Macorís, the province the *New York Times* had dubbed the seat of the Dominican narcotraffic mafia, demonstrated outside the U.S. embassy in Santo Domingo. Curiously, however, the condemnations focused not so much on police brutality, but on the image of the Dominican community in New York, the stereotype that being Dominican was synonymous with being a drug dealer, with being a "delinquent." The protesters decried this claim as a hunt for scapegoats that violated "honest and hard-working Dominican citizens"; they countered that Dominicans were imbued with good Christian and democratic values.[96] However, these protests begged the question of exactly whose honor was at stake — that of the Dominicans overseas, or perhaps that of the nation being defended from its purported representatives in New York.

The Value of Nations and the Crisis of Values

Part of the problem was that the Washington Heights riots occurred during a moment of profound crisis in Santo Domingo, one for which the Dominicanyork became a potent symbol. The Columbus Quincentenary in 1992 became the eye of a maelstrom of controversy over how best to represent Dominican national identity. On one level, the debate raged over the meaning of the "discovery," and the putative importance historically of Indian and African ethnic input in this thoroughly mixed, creole society. Tensions ran high because of the government's desire to present a unified national image coinciding with Pope John Paul II's visit to officiate a mass in this birthplace of New World Christianity, and the violent protests challenging the official deployment of resources for the multi-million-dollar Columbus lighthouse in the teeth of the economic recession. Some estimated that the government spent $40 million per month for five years to build this exorbitant monument.[97] A second controversy swelled over proposals to create a Latin American free-trade zone. But under the surface raged another set of issues: how to define the boundaries of *lo criollo* in a thoroughly transnational context.[98]

As Roy Porter has demonstrated, corporal images often float from models of society to models of economy. In this case, the debate over neoliberal economic policies set off a range of associated fears of boundless runaway inflation. Indeed, inflation became a trope for the loss of national value and boundaries, glossed as values, morals, and honor. Complaints surged over the devaluation of the icons of citizenship through their proliferation: everything from the Dominican peso, identity cards, public sector paychecks, and U.S. dollars to university diplomas.[99] The culture of corruption was causing the "decomposition, . . . putrefaction and annihilation" of the nation, and "corroding the entrails of the country."[100]

The expressive language employed reveals the organic root metaphor at work, as the weak Dominican peso was said to be "hemorrhaging" against the dollar.[101] If money was the blood of nationhood, symbolizing the circulation of national value, promiscuous spending created "inflationary orgies."[102] Fears raged that the American dollar was becoming the very lifeblood of this tiny island nation. Indeed, one prominent economist, much to his compatriots' horror and dismay, even went so far as arguing for the disbanding of the national currency, the suppression of the Central Bank, and the adoption of the U.S. dollar as the national currency. Although the proposal was initially suggested as a drastic means of enforcing responsible banking practices, the response was singular: "the government would lose its moral credibility."[103] Parallel to this proposal was one seen as equally nefarious, and somehow linked: that of allowing dual citizenship for Dominicanyorks.[104] Compromising on issues of currency and nationality, rendering them ambiguous, would foment the current process of "denationalization," crippling the moral fiber of national essence. This perception of runaway inflation, though, was patently not merely economic, even though high unemployment and inflation did particularly affect the middle class during this period.[105] This was a symbolic inflation of nationhood, the perception of a decline in national value due to its transnational dispersion.

Elias Canetti has written of the metaphorical slippage between notions of money and of identity in inflationary moments. Inflation cheapens the worth of citizens in homological relation to the loss of real value previously backing currency. In other words, inflation can cause a crisis of national signification, as the signs of nationhood suddenly depreciate. In the Dominican case, inflation also deflated the system of class distinction.[106] The very signs of professional identity undergirding middle-class respectability came to be seen as "counterfeit signifiers" creating a wave of anxiety as the signs of class identity became unmoored. The difference between the tíguere (lit. tiger) and the *doctor* faded into obscurity, just as the rift between "organic" and "inorganic" currency widened.[107] Without these anchors of *profesionalismo,* the defining parameters of the middle class were blurred.

The Dominicanyork, the ultimate tíguere, the figure of the quintessential Dominican trickster, came to symbolize the anxieties of social mobility for a declining middle class.[108] Partly this vision resulted from a shift from a largely middle-class migrant stream to the United States in the 1970s to a predominantly lower socioeconomic group in the late 1980s, one that bourgeois Dominicans on the island were less inclined to feel proud of as national emissaries. This ambivalence was glossed linguistically on the island by the growing use of the more distant term *Dominicanyork* by the late 1980s, in contrast with the more inclusive earlier category of *dominicano ausente.* Another contradiction, of course, was the way in which some of these so-called lower-class Dominicans actually appeared to be wealthier than the local middle class. Dominicanyorks had surplus prestige due to the accoutrements of consumer spending in the United States; the bourgeoisie on the island had only the distinction of being thoroughly criollo. Another key symbol of bourgeois decline was the fact that due to the deepening economic crisis, the Dominican middle class was having trouble ensuring that their midday dinner included meat at all (even the relatively cheap pollo gringo), the food category that separated them from their class inferiors who ate only beans and rice.

The social crisis of Dominican society was articulated not only as a loss of national values, but as a world rotting from within. Anxiety over the blurred boundaries of nationhood was expressed in an idiom of defilement, as *corruption* became the keyword in the debate over the state of the nation, expressed as the perversion of traditional values of honor, propriety, respect, and family.[109] Materialist values, embodied in the culture of consumption, were polluting the nation, penetrating its borders through the Dominicanyork. A dual symbol, the Dominicanyorks have come to be synonymous with middle-class identity; yet they are simultaneously perceived as venal agents of "transculturation," bringing foreign customs, language, and habits into the national body. The image of the typical Dominicanyork is "one who returns after being away only a short time, his thick neck, ears and arms covered with shiny metal, with a lot of ostentation, and cars that here one only sees a handful of very rich driving. . . . [He is one] with huge, extravagant houses and every kind of gadget: electric garage doors, alarms, doberman dogs, with the shirt open to the navel and terrifying pistols at the waist." [110]

Trafficking in drugs and money, Dominicanyorks are self-serving individualists antithetical to the "essential values" of family and morality in the eyes of the local middle class—values such as "honesty, dignity, honor and shame." [111] They are dangerous because they are perceived as more affluent than the bourgeoisie, but lack the *buenas costumbres* that are an essential part of middle-class respectability and comportment. [112] They are also accursed due to their involvement in illicit business transactions shrouded in secrecy, through which they appear to make money out of magic. [113]

The notion of family indexes the "respectable" bourgeoisie on the island, an identity defined against the Dominicanyork, who appears to act alone. The decay of the nation is evidenced in the putrefaction of the family through its Americanization, as society is "converted into a type of serialized machine, where each one puts his or her efforts into making money quickly." An "ambivalent, aggressive and competitive" world has been formed in which one only survives through deceit (*engaño*). Survival of the nation-family will only be achieved through the "solidification of a moral base," through rectitude over terpitude. This discourse carried gendered undertones as well: *la corrupción* was a temptation with a feminine resonance, and it took a good upright father figure to resist. [114]

An example of this slippage between the symbolic domains of currency and identity, of economic and personal value, was the soaring popularity of *curanderismo,* or popular healing, in 1992. Just as the nation, the peso, and the state lost legitimacy, so did the medical establishment. One particular *curandero,* Dany, sparked national controversy in large part due to President Balaguer's efforts to repress him. [115] Dany quickly became extraordinarily popular, drawing pilgrims from a wide range of social backgrounds. At first his fame derived from his claim that Magic Johnson had been referred to him due to his expertise with terminal diseases such as A I D S. [116] Yet there were multiple, class-specific ways in which the concept of inflation was understood and applied in this case. Some critics called his remarkable popularity a result of the crisis in health care—the lack of affordable, quality health care for the poor. [117] To the marginalized themselves, Dany's popularity stemmed from their disgust and disenchantment with the pedigreed doctors who overcharged and treated them like dirt. Yet to the middle class, the figure of the curandero conjured up visions of illegitimate wealth. In this discourse, curanderos were money-grubbing shysters, "false prophets" stealing money from the irrational masses, the gullible peasant innocents.[118] Nonetheless, Dany persevered, receiving cross-class support and even becoming a popular antihero, particularly after the campaign began for his suppression.[119]

What was uppermost on everyone's minds in 1992, however, was the U.S. proposal of making the whole of Latin America into one gigantic free-trade zone.[120] A new global vision was being formulated by the United States—that of a world order driven by markets, not states—a proposal that did not go unchallenged in Latin America. Critics decried the opportunism of the larger economies, which supported open economic borders when it served their interests, and created trade barriers when they deemed fit. Most of all, the tyranny of the dollar was perceived as the definitive death knell of the Dominican national project.[121]

Gringo Chickens with Worms

This brings us back to where we began, the use of food taxonomies in marking regional, class, or national identities. *Lo criollo* is a relational term, one that invokes home and its associations, such as authenticity, warmth, and family. Lo criollo today is very much associated with wholesome Dominican foodstuffs, as opposed to the vacuous "dessert crops" of tobacco, coffee, and sugar—cash crops grown for international markets, and often by foreign firms, for money not for love.[122] Another set of associations is the contrast between the gift economy of family and friends, of blood kin, as opposed to the monetized economy of others. Finally, associated with sustenance, lo criollo is nutritious, grown with loving care in the *patio* for the family, as opposed to cash crops produced for the world of commerce, strangers, and the cold calculations of the market. In the nineteenth century, before the Dominican Republic was fully integrated into the global economy, it was the peasant who stood out as the confidence man, the trickster who seemed to dissimulate in the face of liberal elites bent on "capturing" his labor for burgeoning national economic markets. By the 1920s, however, the perspective had changed. The *flaneur* then came to be represented, first, by the figure of the U.S. sugar company man, and finally by the Dominicanyork, figures eliciting jealousy and desire, but who ultimately are seen as counterfeit Dominicans. Lo criollo had a negative valence in the nineteenth century, since it was the product of a Europhile elite that looked at the nation through the deprecating lens of racial determinism. By 1992, however, lo criollo had been revalorized due to its appropriation by the popular rumor mill, which viewed the nation from below.

Returning to the mystery of the gringo chickens with worms, things should now make a bit more sense. There is something deeply scandalous about gringo chickens. They are animals produced like machines. They are born to die, in enormous coops, and are never allowed to roam. Gringo chickens by homology also represent how Dominicans see life in the United States—confined in high-rises and trapped by the tentacles of the state. By contrast, the patio chicken represents the family because it is grown in the public extension of the house. It is typically Dominican because it is allowed free range. It represents the neighborhood because it is considered public property within the barrio; a neighbor has the right to kill one for an evening sancocho, a soup for *los muchachos del barrio,* the neighborhood guys.[123] Industrially produced poultry originally derived from U.S. methods, although since the mid-1970s they have been adopted by Dominican firms. The gringo chicken is cheaper and more beautiful (pure white, as opposed to the motley piebald—i.e., mulatto—Dominican bird), but lacks nourishment. It fills you up, but in an empty way. Most importantly, the gringo chicken, plain and simple, lacks *sabor,* or taste.

The *huevo criollo* (the creole egg) has certain properties the gringo egg does not. Quality, for one; and of course, fertility. Moreover, the huevo criollo has magical powers. It can be used, for example, in ritual purification (*despojo*), to absorb the malevolent spirits in a house by placing a raw egg in a red soda and leaving it in the corner. Danballa Uedo, a "cool" force in Dominican vodú, has a proclivity for eggs, which reflect his even-tempered, transcendental perfection.[124] The "hot" gods also appreciate boiled huevos criollos as gifts in the "dry plate" (*plato seco*) ritual offering. In San Juan de la Maguana, there is even a recipe for making a *bacá* that uses a creole egg. A bacá is a devilish spirit that can augment wealth and luck, and that is reknowned for its capacity to transmogrify into different beings, human and animal. You cross a black and a white chicken, and sleep with the resultant egg under your arm for some time, reciting prayers. The bacá will then hatch from the egg. Prototypically feminine, the gallina criolla, or creole hen, thus, is ripe, fecund, and unspoiled, as opposed to the masculine pollo gringo, which is barren. Indeed, *comer gallina* (to eat chicken) is a gloss on necking, smooching, or respectably making out (everything short of the sinful act of intercourse).

The biggest year yet of legal Dominican immigration to the United States was 1992.[125] In a way, the gringo chicken became an "incarnated

sign" in the idiom of commodity resistance, a key symbol of the changing relationship between the Dominican Republic and the United States.[126]
Cheaper than homegrown patio chickens, the gringo chicken has rendered criollo poultry a luxury by effectively pushing it out of the mass
market since its introduction in the 1960s. This logic parallels what has
happened to the Dominican economy during the same period. While U.S.
firms used to engage in direct investment on the island, in sugar or fruit
plantations, today the only growth sectors of the Dominican economy are
tourism and export free-trade zones—industries based on circulation, not
production. These are industries perceived as parasitical, using local labor
but not producing "Dominican" products. In a way, the gringo chicken,
like the Dominicanyork, is a poignant reminder that the nation itself, like
the pollo criollo, has become superfluous, a luxury product, highly valued
but largely irrelevant in the contemporary economy. This is especially
the case when so many families subsist largely through remittances from
relatives in Nueva York. The gringo chicken, then, represents the national
displacement many Dominicans feel, particularly around Christmastime,
when relatives from el Norte come home to show off their fancy cars, and
fashion themselves the chic bourgeois they wish they were in upper Manhattan. The very image of gringo chickens with worms, furthermore, uses
the language of defilement to debase a new status economy defined on
Madison Avenue, not El Conde, the main shopping thoroughfare in Santo
Domingo. It is also a language of pollution that Dominicans learned first
from the U.S. Marines.

The gringo chicken scandal established an extended degustatory commentary on consumer capitalism. Gringo chickens expressed the contradictions of Caribbean nationhood in a sea of American commodity flows.
Operating through the magic of what Taussig calls "mimetic excess,"
Dominicans conjured and then exorcised the evils of imperialism by remaking it into something tangible, as well as noxious, and then expelling
it.[127] As Achille Mbembe has argued, it is the "banality of power" in the
postcolony (and the not-so-postcolony) that encourages resistance through
a language as quotidian as lunch food, one that calls particular attention
to the arbitrary and perishable character of power.[128] And rendering the
magnificent American eagle—the imperial bird of that classic icon of
value, the dollar bill—into rotten chicken was great fodder for the popular laughter mill. Yet registering anxieties over state sovereignty through
food in the era of transnational flows is not a phenomenon limited to the
Third World. During the "mad-cow disease" scare, Britons articulated

their loss of trust in government by refusing to consume that great symbol of Englishness, roast beef. And in Australia, biscuits were at the center of debates over the potential loss of national identity when Campbell's Soup, a U.S. company, bought the firm that produces the beloved Iced Vo-Vo, a marshmallow-coconut cookie that is synonymous with childhood there.[129] Perhaps the loss of place under transnationalism has created a proclivity for grounding identity in the body, where boundaries are defined by what we eat.

The rumors that gringo poultry had worms exhorted Dominicans to stop consuming that which they felt was consuming them—the United States. Draconian as it was, this prescription was perhaps the only means to arrest even temporarily the insatiable desire for U.S. products, the cycle of hunger and emptiness that we in the United States take so much for granted.[130] The rumors also created a comforting boundary between things Dominican and things American if only in one tiny sphere, while simultaneously railing against both the Dominican middle class and the Dominicanyork for trying to be American by eating gringo. It was much better to eat pollo criollo in a sancocho at home, than to consume gringo chicken in a fast-food Pica Pollo. But most of all, the gringo chicken scandal expressed the ambivalent sentiments Dominicans feel toward a transnational modernity that comes embossed with the U.S. logo, even if, like Eddie Bauer trousers, it was assembled in the Dominican Republic.

Notes

I am indebted to Julio Cesar Santana for his assistance in collecting the materials analyzed here, as well as for sharing his deep understanding of Dominican popular culture with me. I am also grateful to Barbara Babcock, Julie Franks, Martha Ellen Davis, Raymundo González, Cesar Herrera, John MacAloon, Frank Ramagosa, Carmen Ramos, Daniel Rothenberg, Constance Sutton, and Neici Zeller for their comments and suggestions, and most especially Gilbert Joseph and Catherine LeGrand, who provided trenchant criticisms on several drafts; as well as Lisa and Carlo Middione, who for years have sought to convince me of the centrality of food. I also thank Andrew Apter for his insights on issues of value and the nation form. Fieldwork was funded by grants from the Social Science Research Council and Fulbright Hays.

1. Geraldino González, "Se recupera consumo 'Pica Pollo': Granjeros apelan," *Listín Diario,* 13 July 1992. In the first epigraph, the song's title, "The Cost of Living," puns on the sense that commodities were expensive and people were

cheap (i.e., commodities). The remainder of the song links inflation, national identity, and corruption with the impotence of professional medicine, a theme treated below. The Tainos were the largest group of autochthonous Indians found on the island when Columbus arrived.

2. Sara Pérez, "El pobre pollo: Sí tiene quien le escriba," *Hoy,* 6 July 1992.

3. "Editoriales: Los pollos," *Hoy,* 1 July 1992.

4. Pérez, "El pobre pollo."

5. On ambivalence and the nation form, see Homi K. Bhabha, "Introduction: Narrating the Nation," in *Nation and Narration,* ed. H. K. Bhabha (New York: Routledge, 1990), 1–8. Thus the gringo chicken parallels the role of the UFO, which, Luise White argues, encodes anxieties about racial transgression; see her "Alien Nation," *Transition* 63 (1994): 24–33.

6. I am following William Roseberry's call to examine the "internalization of the external in Latin America," in his "Americanization in the Americas," *Anthropologies and Histories: Essays in Culture, History, and Political Economy* (New Brunswick, N.J.: Rutgers University Press, 1994), 80–124.

7. Some of the classic anthropological studies of food include Mary Douglas, "Deciphering a Meal," in her *Implicit Meanings: Essays in Anthropology* (London: Routledge and Kegan Paul, 1975), 249–75; Mary Douglas and Baron Isherwood, *The World of Goods* (New York: Basic Books, 1979); Marshall Sahlins, "Food Preference and Taboo," in his *Culture and Practical Reason* (Chicago: University of Chicago Press, 1976); and Jack Goody, *Cooking, Cuisine, and Class: A Study in Comparative Sociology* (Cambridge: Cambridge University Press, 1982). An excellent contemporary treatment of consumption is the collection edited by John Brewer and Roy Porter, *Consumption and the World of Goods* (New York: Routledge, 1993). On the fashioning of a national identity through cuisine, see Arjun Appadurai, "How to Make a National Cuisine: Cookbooks in Contemporary India," *Comparative Studies in Society and History* 30, no. 1 (Jan. 1988): 3–24.

8. From the Dominican Republic, situated between Cuba and Puerto Rico in the Greater Antilles; not from Dominica, near Granada in the Lesser Antilles.

9. Larry Rohter, "New York–Raised Lawyer to Lead Dominican Republic," *New York Times,* 2 July 1996. For more on Dominican migration to the United States, see Patricia Pessar, *Visa for a Dream: Dominicans in the United States* (Boston: Allyn and Bacon, 1995); Sherri Grasmuck and Patricia Pessar, *Between Two Islands: Dominican International Migration* (Berkeley and Los Angeles: University of California Press, 1991); Eugenia Georges, *The Making of a Transnational Community: Migration, Development, and Cultural Change in the Dominican Republic* (New York: Columbia University Press, 1990); and Luis E. Guarnizo, "*Los Dominicanyorks:* The Making of a Binational Society," *Annals of the American Academy of Political and Social Science,* May 1994, 70–86. On the formation of transnational communities in New York and elsewhere, see Constance R. Sutton and Elsa M. Chaney, eds., *Caribbean Life in New York City: Sociocultural Dimen-*

sions (New York: Center for Migration Studies, 1987); and Nina Glick Schiller, Linda Basch, and Christina Blanc-Szanton, eds., "Towards a Transnational Perspective on Migration: Race, Class, Ethnicity, and Nationalism Reconsidered," *Annals of the New York Academy of Sciences,* vol. 645 (New York: New York Academy of Sciences, 1992).

10. Richard Sennet, "Something in the City: The Spectre of Uselessness and the Search for a Place in the World," *Times Literary Supplement,* 22 Sept. 1995, 13–15.

11. Michael Taussig, *Mimesis and Alterity: A Particular History of the Senses* (New York: Routledge, 1993).

12. As Paul Stoller describes Taussig's argument in *Embodying Colonial Memories: Spirit Possession, Power, and the Hauka in West Africa* (New York: Routledge, 1995), 41.

13. Evidence of this is the centrality of the rural *pulpería,* or corner food store, in the *costumbrista* novel; see R. Emilio Jiménez, "La pulpería rural," in his *Al amor del bohío* (1927; reprint, Barcelona: I. G. Manuel Pareja, 1975), 296–99. On fetishism and power, see Taussig, *Mimesis;* and Achille Mbembe, "The Banality of Power and the Aesthetics of Vulgarity in the Postcolony," *Public Culture* 4, no. 2 (spring 1992): 1–30.

14. Ramón Marrero Aristy, *Over* (1940; reprint, Santo Domingo: Taller, 1989); and Francisco Eugenio Moscoso Puello, *Cañas y bueyes* (1936; reprint, Santo Domingo: Asociación Serie 23, 1975).

15. José Ramón López, "La alimentación y las razas," in his *Ensayos y artículos* (1896; reprint, Santo Domingo: Ediciones de la Fundación Corripio, 1991).

16. Luise White, "Cars out of Place: Vampires, Technology, and Labor in East and Central Africa," *Representations* 43 (summer 1993): 27–50, esp. 29.

17. Mbembe, "The Banality of Power," 8–9, discusses the use of corporal images in popular notions of power.

18. Several key examples of this growing literature are Mary Douglas, *Purity and Danger: An Analysis of the Concepts of Pollution and Taboo* (1966; reprint, New York: Routledge and Kegan Paul, 1984); George Mosse, *Nationalism and Sexuality: Middle-Class Morality and Sexual Norms in Modern Europe* (Madison: University of Wisconsin Press, 1985); Andrew Parker et al., eds., *Nationalisms and Sexualities* (New York: Routledge, 1992); and Lynn Hunt, ed., *Eroticism and the Body Politic* (Baltimore, Md.: Johns Hopkins University Press, 1991).

19. Johannes Fabian, *Power and Performance: Ethnographic Explorations through Proverbial Wisdom and Theater in Shaba, Zaire* (Madison: University of Wisconsin Press, 1990), 24. Haitians also frequently express relations of power in terms of eating. In response to the prospect of an imminent U.S. intervention, Haitians said they would "eat the *blancs*" if the United States intervened (Rick Bragg, "Haiti's New Militia Drills with Sticks," *New York Times,* 11 Aug. 1994).

20. I am following part of Geertz's argument about the Balinese cockfight; see Clifford Geertz, "Deep Play: Notes on the Balinese Cockfight," in his *Interpretation of Cultures* (New York: Basic Books, 1973), 412–53, esp. 443–44.

21. George Lakoff and Mark Johnson, *Metaphors We Live By* (Chicago: University of Chicago Press, 1980), 36–37.

22. John Brewer and Roy Porter, introduction to Brewer and Porter, *Consumption and the World of Goods*, 5.

23. Avocados can be eaten, but must be eaten in combination with something else. Prepubescent girls in their *período de desarrollo* may not eat raw fruit either, until they menstruate.

24. Ambulent street vendors of raw fruits, legumes, and vegetables are typically male, while street sellers of cooked items, such as candies, *friquitín* (fried meat), plantains, and *batata* (sweet potato), are always female. For more on the *friquitín*, see Rafael Damirón, *Estampas* (1938; Santo Domingo: Ed. Alfa Y Omega, 1984), 67–72.

25. During the forty-one days after childbirth, chicken soup is also used as a barometer of the mother's health: if she sweats when drinking it, she is weak. See Pérez, "El pobre pollo."

26. Damirón, *Estampas*, 69.

27. Arturo Bueno, *Santiago: Quién te vió y quién te ve*, vol. 1 (Santiago: Impresora Comercial, 1961), 336.

28. Ibid., 336–38. Bueno writes that Cáceres challenged his political opponent Juan Isidro Jiménez by saying, "Apriétose bien los pantalones, que ya voy para ésa" (Hold on to your pants, I'm coming to take care of it). The sense of masculine entitlement is well expressed in popular sayings about gallos, such as the mother's mocking refrain, "yo tengo gallos, quien tenga gallinas que las cuide" (I have cocks, those who have hens better take care of them) (Gema García Hernández, "Hombre/mujer," *Listín Diario*, 2 Mar. 1992).

29. José E. Limón, "Carne, Carnales, and the Carnivalesque," *Dancing with the Devil: Society and Cultural Poetics in Mexican-American South Texas* (Madison: University of Wisconsin Press, 1994).

30. Lipe Collado, *El tíguere dominicano* (Santo Domingo: El Mundo, 1992), 94–96.

31. See "Platos Nacionales" and "Los Sancochos Nocturnos" in Jiménez, *Al amor*, 310–14, 92–98. Interestingly, Cuba claims the sancocho (called there *ajiaco*) as a national metaphor as well; see Fernando Ortiz, "Los factores humanos de la cubanidad," in his *Estudios etnosociológicos* (Havana: Editorial de Ciencias Sociales, 1991), 10–30, 15.

32. Jiménez even calls the sancocho "el aliado de nuestra democracia," referring to a cross-class cultural populism—i.e., all Dominicans, from the working man to the flaming aristocrat, love to eat their sancocho (*Al amor*, 89). For an example of the Dominican ideology of racial democracy, see Rafael Damirón, *Nosotros* (Ciudad Trujillo: Impresora Dominicana, 1955), 83–87, 113–15.

33. C. L. R. James, personal communication, June 1984.

34. Detlev Julio K. Peukert, "Anhelo de dependencia: Las ofertas de anexión

de la República Dominicana a los Estados Unidos en el siglo XIX," *Jahrbuch für Geschichte von Stat, Wirtschaf und Gesellschaf Lateinamerikas* 23 (1986): 315. See also Mu-Kien Adriana Sang, *Buenaventura Báez: El caudillo del sur (1844–1878)* (Santo Domingo: INTEC, 1991), 113–46; and William Javier Nelson, *Almost a Territory: America's Attempt to Annex the Dominican Republic* (Newark: University of Delaware Press, 1990).

35. Peukert, "Anhelo de dependencia," 311, 314–15.

36. Nicolás Guillén, *El diario que a diario,* quoted in Vera M. Kutzinski, *Sugar's Secrets: Race and the Erotics of Cuban Nationalism* (Charlottesville: University Press of Virginia, 1993), frontispiece.

37. Catherine C. LeGrand, "Informal Resistance on a Dominican Sugar Plantation during the Trujillo Dictatorship," *Hispanic American Historical Review* 75, no. 4 (Nov. 1995): 555–96, esp. 559.

38. Fernando Coronil, introduction to Fernando Ortiz, *Cuban Counterpoint: Tobacco and Sugar* (Durham, N.C.: Duke University Press, 1995), xxvii.

39. I have been inspired by the treatment of commodity culture in Jackson Lears, *Fables of Abundance: A Cultural History of Advertising in America* (New York: Basic Books, 1994).

40. Adam Smith, *An Inquiry into the Nature and Causes of the Wealth of Nations,* ed. Edwin Cannan (1904; reprint, Chicago: University of Chicago Press, 1976), 27.

41. José Martí, *Apuntes de un viaje (Mi visita a Santo Domingo)* (Santo Domingo: Editora Universitaria, 1992), 47. I wish to thank Neici Zeller for bringing this citation to my attention.

42. For more on the Dominican sugar industry, see José del Castillo, "The Formation of the Dominican Sugar Industry," in *Between Slavery and Free Labor: The Spanish Speaking Caribbean in the Nineteenth Century,* ed. Manuel Moreno Fraginals, Frank Moya Pons, and Stanley L. Engerman (Baltimore, Md.: Johns Hopkins University Press, 1985), 215–35. For a treatment of sugar as a transnational cultural force, see Sidney W. Mintz, *Tasting Food, Tasting Freedom: Excursions into Eating, Culture, and the Past* (Boston: Beacon Press, 1996), and his *Sweetness and Power: The Place of Sugar in Modern History* (New York: Viking Penguin, 1985). On turn-of-the-century technological advances in the sugar industry, see Manuel Moreno Fraginals, "Plantation Economies and Societies in the Spanish Caribbean, 1860–1930," in *The Cambridge History of Latin America,* ed. Leslie Bethell, vol. 4 (Cambridge: Cambridge University Press, 1988), 187–232.

43. "Sobre la industria tabacalera," *Listín Diario,* 15 Oct. 1903. For more on Dominican ambivalence regarding U.S. technology, see LeGrand, "Informal Resistance."

44. Juan J. Sánchez, *La caña en Santo Domingo* (1893; Santo Domingo: Taller, 1976), 43–57.

45. "Urgente," *Listín Diario,* 9 Oct. 1903. During this period, the Ministry of

Public Works began introducing high-yield varieties of many products, including American poultry (although British pigs had been imported in the nineteenth century).

46. "Agricultura," *Listín Diario,* 10 Oct. 1903.

47. "Gallinas ponedoras," *Listín Diario,* 8 Oct. 1903.

48. Sánchez, *La caña,* 64.

49. Bonó's work predates Fernando Ortiz's classic text *Cuban Counterpoint,* which draws on the same symbolism of tobacco and sugar to express a contemporaneous process in Cuba. For more on Bonó, see Raymundo González, "Notas sobre el pensamiento socio-político dominicano," *Estudios Sociales* 20, no. 67 (Jan.-Mar. 1987).

50. Julie Franks argues in her dissertation that actually many Dominican landowners (particularly cane farmers) in the eastern provinces used the cover of the foreign sugar invasion as a means of extending their landed properties and regional control during a moment when local criticism was focused on foreign sugar corporations and their abuses. She asserts that while there had been political struggles before the late nineteenth century, sugar added an economic dimension to the conflicts. Thus, while these novels tend to portray Dominicans as innocent victims of alien corporate greed, the picture was far more complex. See Franks, "Transforming Property: Landholding and Political Rights in the Dominican Sugar Region, 1880-1930" (Ph.D. diss., SUNY Stony Brook, 1997).

51. Moscoso, *Cañas,* 9.

52. Ibid., 36, 178.

53. This argument about nationalist allegory is developed in Doris Sommer, *One Master for Another: Populism as Patriarchal Rhetoric in Dominican Novels* (New York: University Press of America, 1983), and her *Foundational Fictions: The National Romances of Latin America* (Berkeley and Los Angeles: University of California Press, 1991). Interestingly, sugar was condemned by some European consumers as well; see Simon Schama, *The Embarrassment of Riches: An Interpretation of Dutch Culture in the Golden Age* (New York: Alfred A. Knopf, 1987), 165. On cattle-based regimes of value, see Jean Comaroff and John Comaroff, "Goodly Beasts, Beastly Goods," in their *Ethnography and the Historical Imagination* (Boulder, Colo.: Westview Press, 1992), 127-54.

54. Moscoso, *Cañas,* 156.

55. Annette B. Weiner, *Inalienable Possessions: The Paradox of Giving-while-Keeping* (Berkeley and Los Angeles: University of California Press, 1992), 33. I am grateful to Claudio Lomnitz for bringing this point to my attention.

56. Moscoso, *Cañas,* 18.

57. Ibid., 80, 92.

58. For more on the system of *terrenos comuneros,* see Franks, "Transforming Property."

59. It was also said that "once they leave the cane, the Devil carries them off" (Moscoso, *Cañas,* 206). Thus, sugar money in the Dominican case corroborates

Michael Taussig's findings regarding the perception of profits from Bolivian mines and Colombian sugar as negatively charged and even diabolical; see his *Devil and Commodity Fetishism in South America* (Chapel Hill: University of North Carolina Press, 1980).

60. I am indebted to Doris Sommer's analysis regarding the use of English in Dominican Spanish. Additionally, I agree with her argument that in the novel the crushing horrors of the sugar industrial monopoly stand in for the tyranny of the Trujillo dictatorship (which lay outside the bounds of permitted political discourse); see *One Master*, 125–60. I would add that portraying the protagonist as a victim also serves to rationalize his collusion with the *trujillato* as part of the logic of a regime based on drawing political subjects into positions of complicity against their will.

61. Moscoso, *Cañas*, 250.

62. Jacques Le Goff, *Your Money or Your Life: Economy and Religion in the Middle Ages* (New York: Zone Books, 1998), 26.

63. Michael O'Malley, "Specie and Species: Race and the Money Question in Nineteenth-Century America," *American Historical Review* 99, no. 2 (Apr. 1994): 369–95.

64. Michael L. Conniff, "Afro–West Indians on the Central American Isthmus: The Case of Panama," in *Slavery and Beyond: The African Impact on Latin America and the Caribbean*, ed. Darién J. Davis (Wilmington, Del.: Scholarly Resources, 1995), 147–72; and Conniff, "Black Labor on a White Canal: West Indians in Panama, 1904–1980" (Albuquerque: University of New Mexico, Latin American Institute, Research Paper Series No. 11, 1983).

65. For more on Haitian migration to the Dominican sugar sector and Haitian-Dominican labor and social relations, see Samuel Martínez, *Peripheral Migrants: Haitians and Dominican Republic Sugar Plantations* (Knoxville: University of Tennessee Press, 1995); Martin Francis Murphy, *Dominican Sugar Plantations: Production and Foreign Labor Integration* (New York: Praeger, 1991); and Frank Moya Pons et al., *El batey: Estudio socioeconómico de los bateyes del Consejo Estatal del Azúcar* (Santo Domingo: Fondo para el Avance de las Ciencias Sociales, 1986). On the atrocious treatment faced by Haitians on Dominican sugar estates, see Maurice Lemoine, *Bitter Sugar: Slaves Today in the Caribbean* (London: Banner Press, 1985). For more on banana migration, see Philippe Bourgois, "West Indians and the Banana Industry: Panama, Costa Rica," *Cimarrón* 2, nos. 1–2 (spring/summer 1989): 58–86.

66. For more on the association between Haitians and money in the Dominican Republic outside the sugar sector, see Lauren Derby, "Haitians, Magic, and Money: *Raza* and Society in the Haitian-Dominican Borderlands, 1900–1937," *Comparative Studies in Society and History* 36, no. 3 (1994): 488–526.

67. F. E. Moscoso Puello, *Cartas a Evelina* (1941; Santo Domingo: Editora Cosmos, 1974), 100.

68. Arjun Appadurai, "Introduction: Commodities and the Politics of Value,"

in *The Social Life of Things: Commodities in Cultural Perspective,* ed. A. Appadurai (Cambridge: Cambridge University Press, 1986), 54.

69. Marrero, *Over,* 210. For more on Andean fat-stealing mythology, see Nathan Wachtel, *Gods and Vampires: Return to Chipaya,* trans. Carol Volk (Chicago: University of Chicago Press, 1994).

70. Marrero, *Over,* 172.

71. Sidney Mintz, "Slavery and the Rise of Peasantries," *Historical Reflections* 6, no. 1 (1979): 213–53.

72. The domestic rice campaign was part of Trujillo's plan of import substitution industrialization (Richard Turits, personal communication, 15 Aug. 1996); see Orlando Inoa, *Estado y campesinos al inicio de la era de Trujillo* (Santo Domingo: Librería La Trinitaria, 1994). I appreciate Catherine LeGrand's first having brought this point to my attention.

73. López, *Ensayos y artículos.* For contextualization and critical commentary, see Michiel Baud, "Ideología y campesinado: El pensamiento social de José Ramón López," *Estudios Sociales* 19, no. 64 (Apr.–June 1986): 63–81; Raymundo González, "Notas sobre el pensamiento socio-político dominicano"; and idem, "Ideología del progreso y campesinado en el siglo XIX," *Ecos* 1, no. 2 (1993): 25–44. See also *El gran pesimismo dominicano: José Ramón López* (Santiago: UCMM, 1975); and Fernando I. Ferrán B., "Figuras de lo dominicano," *Ciencia y Sociedad,* 10, no. 1 (Jan.–Mar. 1985): 5–20.

74. Gina Lombroso-Ferrero, *Criminal Man, According to the Classification of Cesare Lombroso* (New York: Putnam, 1911).

75. See González, "Ideología del progreso"; and William Roseberry, "Images of the Peasant in the Consciousness of the Venezuelan Proletariat," in *Proletarians and Protest: The Roots of Class Formation in an Industrializing World,* ed. Michael Hanagan and Charles Stephenson (New York: Greenwood Press, 1986), 149–69.

76. González, "Ideología del progreso," 33. I am indebted here to González, who argues that the discourse of the lazy peasant arose during the 1780s Bourbon Reforms, and was the obverse and complement to the liberal ideology of progress; see González, "Ideología del progreso." *Indolence* referred to a peasantry that subsisted through shifting agriculture and hunting, and resisted settlement—the bane of liberal reformers bent on incorporating the peasantry into the market economy.

77. Ibid., 20.

78. Ibid., 36, 46. Concretely, López called for the creation of schools of practical agronomy in the provinces, where the peasantry would be taught, quite simply, "to live": to eat well and at regular intervals, to dress properly, to wear shoes, to live in clean houses, and to follow the rules of hygiene.

79. Plantains are also called *embruteína,* literally, stupid food (the antithesis of our carrots, i.e., brain food). Martha Ellen Davis found that these terms are used in the Canary Islands as well, thus indicating that the denigration of the plantain may well be of Spanish colonial precedence (personal communication). The term

aplatanados also is used to designate the process of creolization in Cuba (see Ortiz, "Cubanidad," 13).

80. LeGrand, "Informal Resistance," 560.

81. Kathy McAfee, *Storm Signals: Structural Adjustment and Development Alternatives in the Caribbean* (Boston: South End Press, 1991), 4.

82. Larry Rohter, "Impact of NAFTA Pounds Economies of the Caribbean," *New York Times,* 30 Jan. 1997.

83. These figures include both legal and illegal Dominican immigrants, as well as individuals of Dominican ancestry, in the United States (Patricia Pessar, personal communication, Dec. 1996). For more on New York City immigration patterns, see "Immigrant Influence Rises in New York City in 1990s," *New York Times,* 9 Jan. 1997.

84. Arjun Appadurai, "Global Ethnoscapes: Notes and Queries for a Transnational Anthropology," *Modernity at Large: Cultural Dimensions of Globalization* (Minneapolis: University of Minnesota Press, 1996), 48–65.

85. Guarnizo, *"Los Dominicanyorks,"* 75.

86. Ibid., 77–79.

87. Virginia Byrne, "Protestan muerte dominicano Nueva York," *Listín Diario,* 8 July 1992; and James Dao, "Tension in Washington Heights: Amid Dinkins Calls for Peace, Protesters Skirmish with Police," *New York Times,* 8 July 1992. See also the graphic coverage: "Disturbios en Manhattan," *Hoy,* 9 July 1992; and "Manifestantes," *Hoy,* 8 July 1992.

88. James Dao, "Angered by Police Killing, A Neighborhood Erupts," *New York Times,* 7 July 1992.

89. In contrast to the pseudonym, which is self-chosen. See Octavio Amiama de Castro, "Ensayusculos a vuela pluma: Seudónimos y sobrenombres," *Listín Diario,* 15 Aug. 1992.

90. Another layer of significance to naming in the Dominican Republic is that the practice of using only the nickname (apodo, or *sobrenombre*) among friends became entrenched under the daily repression of the Trujillo dictatorship (1930–1961), in order to conceal public identities from the secret police. The use of a nickname is a marker of intimacy and friendship. Also, in Dominican vodú, the name is considered part of the body and can be used in charms and amulets as a sign of personhood, as can nails and hair.

91. I am indebted to Carlos Andújar for this information. Andújar has made a film about the worship of the Barón among Dominicans seeking U.S. visas.

92. Dao, "Tension in Washington Heights."

93. James Bennet, "A Neighborhood Bonded by Turmoil," *New York Times,* 7 July 1992.

94. Ibid. See also Clifford Krauss, "Wealthy, Wanted, and Untouchable: Notorious Drug Suspect Lives Good Life, Beyond Reach of U.S.," *New York Times,* 14 Nov. 1996.

95. James Dao, "Tension in Washington Heights." There were also conflicting

versions of the story behind the man who died during the rooftop chase; see James Bennet, "Stories Differ on Fatal Fall from Rooftop," *New York Times,* 7 July 1992.

96. Saúl Pimentel, "Ariza protesta a The New York Times por editoral ofende dominicanos EU," *Listín Diario,* 11 July 1992; "Defiende honestidad colonia criolla en EU," *Hoy,* 11 July 1992; O. Mata Vargas, "Corporán comunica a Dinkins preocupación por muerte," *Listín Diario,* 10 July 1992; and Domingo Páez, "Protestan por muerte de dominicanos en NY," *Hoy,* 11 July 1992.

97. Mark Kurlansky, *A Continent of Islands: Searching for the Caribbean Destiny* (New York: Addison-Wesley, 1992), 3. Balaguer completed the lighthouse that Trujillo commenced; for more on this, see Roorda, this volume.

98. The link between the Columbus celebrations and the challenge to national identity is explicit in Luchy Placencia, "Dice pretenden destruír identidad nacional," *Hoy,* 7 Sept. 1992. This line of argument was associated with those critical of Balaguer, such as affiliates of popular organizations like the Christian Base Communities.

99. "Circulan billetes de RD $100 falsos," *Listín Diario,* 18 Feb. 1992; "Fraude gigantesco y rutinario," *Listín Diario,* 26 May 1992; "Policía evita pongan circular U.S.$ falsos," *Listín Diario,* 26 May 1992; and Pilar Moreno, "Falsean títulos 5 universidades," *Hoy,* 1 Feb. 1992.

100. Arturo Uslar Pietri, "Una cultura de la corrupción," *Listín Diario,* 11 May 1992.

101. "Fraude gigantesco."

102. José Luis Alemán, "Bernardo, Banco Central y Gobierno," *Listín Diario,* 5 Mar. 1992. On the interpenetration of notions of blood and money in another context, see Fernando Coronil, "The Black El Dorado: Money Fetishism, Democracy, and Capitalism in Venezuela" (Ph.D. diss., University of Chicago, 1987).

103. Máximo M. Pérez, "Vega pide eliminar Banco Central," *Listín Diario,* 16 June 1992; Alemán, "Bernardo, Banco Central."

104. Most dominicanos ausentes do not naturalize as Americans for reasons of pride, even after as many as thirty years in the United States (Chiqui Vicioso, "Nueva York: Luces y sombras," *Listín Diario,* 3 Sept. 1992). For samples of the debate over dual citizenship, see Pelegrín Castillo Seman, "Propuesta peligrosa," *Hoy,* 31 July 1992; Servio Tulio Almanzar Frías, "Doble nacionalidad," *Hoy,* 5 June 1992; Héctor Luzón, "Proponen forma preservar la ciudadanía dominicana," *Listín Diario,* 30 Aug. 1992; and "Doble nacionalidad debe ser producto reforma a Carta," *Hoy,* 29 May 1992. Dual citizenship was finally legalized in 1995.

105. Frank Romero Alvarez, "Desarrollo sin inflación," *Hoy,* 16 Nov. 1992. Nonetheless, the loss of value of Dominican money was a constant complaint, one author arguing that the Dominican peso had become "a pygmy or a figure from the imaginary island of Liliput from *Gulliver's Travels,* where everyone only measures six inches in height" (Jacinto Gimbernard Pellerano, "¿Cuánto es en dinero de verdad?" *Listín Diario,* 6 May 1992).

106. See the section titled "Inflation and the Crowd," in Elias Canetti, *Crowds*

and Power (1962; New York: Farrar, Straus and Giroux, 1988), 183–88. The "crisis of values" also revived a traditional discourse that money causes the loss of respect and honor due to the loss of individual agency; see Jaime A. Viñas-Román, "Opinión pública y el poder corruptor del dinero," *Listín Diario,* 29 Sept. 1992.

107. In Spanish, currency is termed *emisiones orgánicas* or *no orgánicas* (organic and inorganic emissions) as a means of distinguishing inflationary from noninflationary money. Thus, they are perceived as more than different forms of spending, but actually as different forms of money. However, as Coronil demonstrates, this is more than just a figure of speech—it indexes an epistemology of money. The notion of a counterfeit signifier is from Jean-Joseph Goux, *Symbolic Economies: After Marx and Freud,* trans. Jennifer Curtiss Gage (1973; Ithaca, N.Y.: Cornell University Press, 1990), 102. Evidence of the fascination with *tigeraje* is found in the series of articles in *Hoy* on the subject by Lipe Collado in June 1994, which were reprinted in his book *El tíguere dominicano.*

108. As Karen Halttunen has argued in another context; see her *Confidence Men and Painted Women: A Study of Middle-Class Culture in America, 1830–1870* (New Haven, Conn.: Yale University Press, 1982). For more on the figure of the tíguere, see Christian Krohn-Hansen, "Masculinity and the Political among Dominicans: 'The Dominican Tiger,' " in *Machos, Mistresses, Madonnas: Contesting the Power of Latin American Gender Imagery,* ed. Marit Melhuus and Kristi Anne Stolen (London: Verso, 1996), 108–33.

109. Douglas, *Purity and Danger,* 124.

110. Ubi Rivas, "¿Son iguales todos los dominican-yorks?" *Hoy,* 8 Feb. 1992.

111. María Elena Marqués-Portela de Viñas, "Reflexiones sobre la corrupción y la crisis de valores," *Listín Diario,* 3 June 1992; and R. A. Font Bernard, "Sabatinas: Nuestra vocación extranjerizante," *Hoy,* 1 Aug. 1992. On the positive, middle-class valence of Dominicanyork identity, see Grasmuck and Pessar, *Between Two Islands,* 201. For more on Dominican migration, see Georges, *Transnational Community.*

112. Marqués-Portela de Viñas, "Reflexiones sobre la corrupción." On the decline of the Dominican middle class, see P. R. Thompson, "¿Se nos muere la clase media?" *Hoy,* 25 June 1992.

113. Apart from drugs, the most highly publicized illicit financial activity is the illegal Lotto. See "Juego ilegal basado en Lotería RD genera US$ milliones en barrio NY," *Listín Diario,* 28 Apr. 1992.

114. Quotes are from Marqués-Portela de Viñas, "Reflexiones sobre la corrupción." On the gendering of *la corrupción* as female, to be countered by the male virtues of "decisión, valor y firmeza," see Jaime A. Viñas-Román, "El despeñadero de la corrupción," *Listín Diario,* 30 Aug. 1992. See also Juan A. Arias F., "Drogas," *Hoy,* 26 June 1992; Roque N. Muñoz P., "Corrupción," *Hoy,* 19 Mar. 1992; Arturo Uslar Pietri, "Una cultura de la corrupción," *Listín Diario,* 11 May 1992; and Jaime A. Viñas-Román, "Temo ser tragado," *Listín Diario,* 7 June 1992. Part of the concern over corruption during this period had to do with a speech by

Balaguer (27 Feb. 1992), which appeared to justify or even condone bribery on the part of public sector employees. The president argued that "corruption came hand in hand with abundance and progress"; see Rafael G. Santana, "Ejecutivo vincula actos corrupción a la abundancia," *Listín Diario,* 28 Feb. 1992. Corruption during this period was a major topic all over Latin America due to scandals in Venezuela and Brazil.

115. As a result of Balaguer's repression, Dany became a political issue, and members of the leftist PLD party came out in his support; see Pedro Germosen, "Afirma es torpe tratamiento a curandero," *Hoy,* 21 May 1992.

116. D. Saint Hilaire, "Curandero espera devolverle salud a Magic Johnson sin recompensa," *Listín Diario,* 14 May 1992.

117. Rafael Kasse Acta, "Curanderismo y medicina," *Hoy,* 27 May 1992.

118. There was an avalanche in the press against Dany, "el brujo de Maizal," whose real name was Humberto Grullón Denis (and to his detractors, Humberto Ortiz Mercado—with an accent on *mercado,* or market). For example, see Teofilo Bonillo, "Pide aplicar medidas contra curanderos," *Hoy,* 22 May 1992; and Emilio Reyes Ledesma, "El brujo de Maisal," *Hoy,* 21 May 1992. Although his critics maligned him for representing the barbarism and backwardness of the country, in fact Dany specialized in "modern" ailments such as cancer and AIDS, not exorcisms or witchcraft; see Sergio Sarita Valdez, "Hechicería y curanderismo," *Hoy,* 21 May 1992.

119. In the end, after being banned by the public prosecutor of Mao and the secretary of health, Dany personally appealed to Balaguer, and after intervention by Emma Balaguer de Vallejo, the president's sister, who herself was a practicing *santera* (priestess of the Afro-Cuban popular religion Santería) until her untimely death in 1992, he was allowed to resume his practice after relocating to Maizal, Esperanza. See Osiris Gómez, "Curandero reabre 'consultorio' pese prohibición de autoridades," *Listín Diario,* 22 May 1992; and Ubi Rivas, "Curanderos están de moda," *Hoy,* 27 May 1992.

120. José Serulle Ramia and Jacqueline Boin, "Tratado de Libre Comercio: Expectativas y temores," *Hoy,* 26 Sept. 1992.

121. Mario Arvelo Caamaño, "Una receta envenenada," *Hoy,* 21 June 1992.

122. For example, in 1992, the Supermercado Nacional of Santo Domingo staged a display for Independence Day titled "Arriba República Dominicana" (Up with the Dominican Republic). Employees dressed in folkloric hand-woven straw hats played bachata and perico ripiao (rural music) over the loudspeakers, and, most of all, promoted national products, particularly food. The slogan was "Consume lo nuestro! Gran festival Dominicano Gastronómico-Cultural."

123. Jiménez, *Al amor,* 90, asserts that the sancocho actually requires a chicken stolen from the barrio.

124. Martha Ellen Davis, *La otra ciencia: El vodú dominicano como religión y medicina populares* (Santo Domingo: Editora Universitaria UASD, 1987), 242.

125. "Editoriales: Discurso esclarecedor," *Listín Diario,* 26 Mar. 1992.

126. Appadurai, "Introduction," 30, 38.

127. Michael Taussig, "Sympathetic Magic in a Post-Colonial Age," in his *Mimesis*, 250–55.

128. Mbembe, "The Banality of Power."

129. John Darnton, "The Logic of the 'Mad Cow' Scare," *New York Times,* 31 Mar. 1996; and Thomas L. Friedman, "Politics in the Age of NAFTA," *New York Times,* 7 Apr. 1996.

130. For a harsh critique of U.S. consumerism, see Jaime A. Viñas-Román, "Temo ser tragado." In contrast, Georges describes the positive valuation of consumer goods induced by return migrants (*Transnational Community,* 209). For European reactions to U.S. consumerism, see Victoria de Grazia, "The Arts of Purchase: How American Publicity Subverted the European Poster, 1920–1940," in *Remaking History: Discussions in Contemporary Culture,* ed. Barbara Kruger and Phil Mariani (Seattle: Bay Press, 1989), 221–58.

III: Final Reflections

Emily S. Rosenberg

Turning to Culture

This collection of essays, dealing with Latin American–U.S. relations, addresses issues concerning categories, boundaries, and sites of power. Many of the contributions avoid a focus on nation-state policies. They critically probe the often unsystematic politics of capital, culture, and social connections that scholars focusing largely on high politics have often called an inter-American "system." [1] They challenge paradigms and categories (such as liberalism/modernization, imperialism/dependency) that have long discursively framed historical investigations of this region.

This concluding analysis seeks to contextualize the contributions in this volume within the broader field of the history of U.S. foreign relations. I suggest that these essays can be fruitfully read as being theoretically compatible with three new and interrelated scholarly projects: postcolonial theory, postmodern international relations theory, and the new focus on culture in the history of U.S. foreign relations, a turn that attends closely to questions related to language, symbolic meanings, and constructions of race, gender, and nationalities. After some initial description of these three approaches, this essay will examine more closely how the individual articles in this volume contribute to these emerging, highly diverse bodies of scholarship that are recasting the ways of seeing the U.S. role in the hemisphere and the world.

Postcolonial investigations, especially those indebted to literary theory, have been transforming the study of global relationships. Focusing initially on formal European empires in Africa, India, Asia, and Latin America, postcolonial theorists explored the cultural mixing that empire building induced, the subsequent arrangement and rearrangements of hierarchies of power and authority, and the continual transformation of relational identities—national, group, and individual—that emerged within the interplaying discourses of discipline and resistance. The term *postcolonial* may imply the kinds of economic and cultural networks that the word *neocolonialism* describes, but the theoretical discourses and genealogies of the two terms are quite different: neocolonialism is generally associated with a Marxist, materialist, modernist, positivist orientation; postcolonialism is usually associated with postmodern theory.[2]

In studies of Latin American–U.S. relations, the term *postcolonial* presents special problems, both because of the dispute in U.S. historiography over what constitutes a U.S. "empire" and because *postcolonial* in Latin American studies has connoted the period following independence from Spain and Portugal. Putting aside the semantical difficulties of the term itself, however, many issues in Latin American–U.S. relations during the twentieth century connect well to the concerns of postcolonial theory. As with histories of European empires, relationships within the Western Hemisphere deal with the extension, out from the metropole, of complex networks of capital, military "assistance," and media; the substantial (but always shifting) disparities in power; and the construction of hierarchies through the reinforcement of racial/ethnic/cultural distinctions. Both within European empires and within the nexus of Latin American–U.S. relations, symbiotic processes of centralization and decentralization have emerged: integrative, imperial forces that pressed for homogenization and predictable rationalization continuously vied with (and helped give rise to) differentiation, disruption, and resistance. In addition, although many postcolonial theorists have concerned themselves with European imperial space, being "postcolonial" is broader than any particular geographical or temporal site. Diasporic diffusion, immigration, migration, and the cultural mixing resulting from changes in communications networks makes much of the world—certainly much of the Western Hemisphere over the past four centuries—appropriate for postcolonial theory. Postcoloniality is part of a postmodern condition of multiple identifications and fluctuating significations.

Cultures of United States Imperialism, edited by Amy Kaplan and Donald Pease, has recently introduced postcolonial theory, particularly literary theory, into the history of U.S. foreign relations.[3] The essays in *Cultures* explore the relationships between U.S. expansionism and the cultural consolidation of national identities at "home." Some articles probe the ways in which discourses of race, gender, and nation delineate "foreign" cultures—both inside and outside of U.S. borders. Other articles, exploring the issue of subjectivity, address the construction of transcultural or resistant identities. Most of the contributors approach their historical topics through literary theory. The essays in the present volume, which deal with some of the same themes of postcoloniality, now build on the Kaplan and Pease volume by highlighting the work of historians with specific expertise in the history of Latin America.

Postcolonial theory synchronizes with a similar turn toward postmodern international relations theory in political science. Historians of U.S. foreign relations have often looked to international relations for methodological paradigms that might help to structure historical investigations. During the post–World War II period, for example, the discourse of realism became prominent in both political science and historical studies.[4] Since then, historians have employed other political science models, particularly those that might loosely be grouped under rubrics such as "global society," "world systems," and "bureaucratic politics."[5] Within the last decade, however, critical scholarship influenced by feminist and postmodernist theory has challenged these positivist paradigms. Postmodern international relations theory—developed especially in the work of critical theorists such as Richard Ashley, R. B. J. Walker, Christine Sylvester, James Der Derian, Michael Shapiro, David Campbell, and others—has only begun to have an impact on historical discourses. But the concerns parallel those in postcolonial theory and are theoretically compatible with many of the perspectives and methodologies in this volume.

In a useful overview of postmodern international relations theory, Jim George explores four major ways in which the new critical scholarship challenges orthodoxies. It has sought to interrogate and historicize the "great texts" of the international relations tradition, a project that attacks the discourse of ahistorical, universalized "truths" on which the discipline, and especially the great realist works, have grounded claims to being political *science*. It has deconstructed other discursive building blocks of realism: concepts such as sovereignty, anarchy, and security; and dichotomies such as foreign/domestic and self/other. It has questioned those post–Cold War policies that seemed shaped by older discourses about the meaning of "strategy" and "security." And it has called for a new politics of resistance appropriate to the reconfigured forms of power that are both more, but in some ways also less, organized than before.[6]

By injecting questions that have been associated with postcolonial and postmodern international relations theory into histories of Latin American–U.S. relations, the essays in this volume also contribute to one of the most dynamic developments in foreign relations history: the use of new critical perspectives from cultural history to investigate a variety of topics relating to cultural interactions.[7] To assess this "cultural turn" in foreign relations, which has gained momentum only recently, a brief digression into the historiography of U.S.–Latin American relations might be helpful.

In some ways, emphasizing "culture" in investigating hemispheric relations is an old theme. Two of the most widely used English-language textbooks on Latin American history, written during the first two decades of the twentieth century by William Warren Sweet of the University of Chicago and Hutton Webster of Stanford University, structured their "knowledge" largely around the cultural differences attributed to racial "type." Affected by the biological determinism of Western scholarship at the time, these historians surveyed the demographics of the southern continent, carefully and "scientifically" asserting that people of Indian and African descent were backward, that mestizos were unstable, and that Latin American whites were sentimental and impulsive. They therefore concluded that Latin Americans as a whole were morally deficient and incapable of developing modern businesses or stable governments. Acceptance of U.S. culture through Pan-Americanism provided the only hope for progress in Latin America.[8]

Although these texts continued to be widely used in U.S. schools even into the 1940s, another "cultural" framework for interpreting Latin American–U.S. relations also emerged. During the 1920s and 1930s, Herbert Bolton and his students at the University of California broke with parts of the anti-Spanish, "black legend" tradition and emphasized the positive aspects of the Spanish legacy and the "essential unity" of nations of the hemisphere. Stressing parallel histories, the Bolton school examined cultural similarities and affinities: the effects of Old World colonization, republican revolutions, and hoped-for progressive destinies. The assumption of common cultures and futures, however, may have been less a departure from the earlier tradition than it may at first appear. As David Weber has pointed out in his astute evaluation of the Bolton school, Bolton and his students tended to emphasize and exalt the Spanish heritage when exploring America's "common history," leaving other discourses of racial hierarchy largely unchallenged.[9]

During and immediately after World War II, the most influential historians of Latin American–U.S. relations turned away from cultural themes toward an examination of political and strategic structures. In 1943 Samuel Flagg Bemis published his widely used text *The Latin American Policy of the United States,* a chauvinistic work unsympathetic to Latin America.[10] Influenced more by the Boltonian discourses of "common histories," Arthur P. Whitaker traced the history of what he called a "Western Hemisphere idea"; Dexter Perkins synthesized his monumental history of the Monroe Doctrine; and J. Fred Rippy's many works examined hemispheric relationships.[11] All of these scholars wrote within the context of outside "threats" to the United States and, presumably, to the hemisphere during World War II and the early Cold War era. Despite different political perspectives and policy prescriptions, all were concerned with maintaining political structures that would keep Latin American and U.S. interests both friendly and compatible. Like the foreign policy "realists," whose scholarship dominated the decade, strategic questions and concerns lay at the center of their studies.

After 1960, a decisive shift occurred. Scholarship became much more critical of U.S. dominance and focused increasingly on issues of political economy. In part, this scholarship revived an earlier critical legacy. During the late 1920s and 1930s, the first significant critical examinations of Latin American–U.S. economic relationships had appeared under the series title "Studies in American Imperialism," funded by the Garland Foundation and guided by the socialist historian and economist Scott Nearing.[12] This short-lived series, however, fell victim to wartime concerns. J. Fred Rippy, for example, had written his first book for Nearing's series but went on to build his career as one of the leading authorities of hemispheric relations along the lines of the more political and strategic subjects in vogue during the World War II era. In the late 1950s and 1960s, however, the radical orientation, with its concentration on political economy and use of the word *imperialism,* revived. William A. Williams, Walter LaFeber, and others of the "Wisconsin School" proclaimed that empire had been "a way of life" for the United States. These so-called revisionist historians examined in detail what Walter LaFeber called "the New Empire"—that is, the turn toward U.S. economic domination as a substitute for territorial acquisition in the twentieth century. They argued that economic advantage—creating an open door for trade and investment—lay at the heart of U.S. policy.[13]

The debates over "revisionism," together with the efforts by many historians to produce a "synthesis" that accommodated both economic and strategic foundations of policy, set the discursive frameworks of scholarship for more than two decades.[14] Through the 1980s and beyond, most writers on Latin American–U.S. relations primarily positioned their interpretations in the context of questions about economic motivations and structures. During the 1980s, historical discussions began to recenter more around dependency scholarship, which had been elaborated in Latin America among neo-Marxist scholars during the 1970s, and around "corporatism"—the national and then transnational stretch of functional groups such as business, labor, and professional elites.[15] Both dependency and corporatism highlighted the importance of transnational elites, but, as with the disputes over the Wisconsin School, the focus remained on political economy.

Thus, most of the histories within the dominant postwar traditions—realism, the "open door" school, corporatism, and dependency—were framed largely by the positivist discourses of political and economic history. Dozens of fine monographs in English during these decades examined the growth of U.S. power in the hemisphere, focusing on specific U.S. interventions or on particular economic connections: especially notable are works by Samuel Baily, Jules Benjamin, Charles Bergquist, Cole Blaiser, Bruce Calder, Mark Gilderhus, David Healy, Stanley Hilton, Richard Immerman, Gilbert Joseph, Friedrich Katz, Walter LaFeber, Lester Langley, Thomas Leonard, Frank McCann, Thomas Paterson, Louis Pérez, Stephen Rabe, and W. Michael Weis. Many of these studies were based on multiarchival research; most took a critical stance toward U.S. policy. The growth of U.S. economic interests and the persistent U.S. fear that radical movements in Latin America might threaten property rights or provide strategic advantage to communist movements provided a common theme. This overwhelming emphasis on the materialist basis of U.S. domination eclipsed attention to cultural connections within the hemisphere.

During the 1970s, however, a widespread backlash against U.S. cultural predominance in the world began to emerge: UNESCO championed demands for a "New World Information Order" that would break Anglo-American dominance of the news and entertainment industries, and scholars such as Herbert Schiller, particularly in the discipline of communications, began to study what they called "cultural imperialism" or "media imperialism." [16] These trends coincided with publication of what must surely be one of the most influential works in Latin American–U.S. cultural relations: Ariel Dorfman and Armand Mattelart's *How to Read Donald Duck: Imperialist Ideology in the Disney Comic.* Dorfman, who tried to put his ideas into practice as the Minister of Culture under the socialist government of Salvador Allende in Chile, subsequently expanded on this theme of cultural imperialism in *The Empire's Old Clothes.*[17] Writing in the tradition of the Frankfurt School and reflecting on what he saw as U.S.-based cultural conspiracies to unseat Allende, Dorfman's book presented a scathing indictment of how U.S. popular culture (Disney, *Reader's Digest,* and the "Lone Ranger") infantilized common people, spread capitalist culture and consumerism, and prevented "authentic" cultural communities from developing an alternative to individualistic and competitive social relationships.

The works of Schiller and Dorfman were part of a growing discourse that applied the premises of dependency theory to the realm of cultural products and, particularly, to media. Interest in the spread of U.S. media into Latin America grew, although scholars in communications studies, not in history, were the most enterprising researchers of the subject.[18]

Although the claims of "cultural imperialism" opened up vibrant new areas for investigation, its theoretical basis began to erode as cultural theorists investigated the creation of "meanings." Antonio Gramsci's writings stimulated more complicated theories of hegemony based on consent rather than coercion. Stuart Hall and others began to reassess popular culture as a site of struggle, not simply a site of oppression; Stanley Fish, Janice Radway, and others emphasized the importance—and variability—of audience reception; Benedict Anderson and Eric Hobsbawm threw into question the category of "nation" and examined notions of "authenticity" and "national culture." [19] Categories of "race" and "nation," which had framed the discourses of many of the earliest studies of Latin American–U.S. relations, became problematized in postcolonial theory. Taking cues from these and many other theorists and from the tremendous vitality in cultural history and criticism that exploded in the 1990s, a growing number of scholars turned toward the study of transnational cultural interactions. As exemplified in this book, such investigations both build on and complicate the old "cultural imperialism" framework. They also go beyond the decades-old preoccupation with strategic interest and political economy, by asking fresh questions in new ways.

There are many subjects and methodologies associated with this new cultural turn in the history of U.S. foreign relations. Some work addresses the variety of symbolic systems that comprise the languages of power. Studies by Robert Rydell on race and world's fairs; Edward Linenthal on historical monuments and memorials; Ron Robin on imperial architecture; Michael Sherry on air power; Frank Costigliola and Robert Dean on gender; and Frank Ninkovich and Reinhold Wagnleitner on "informational diplomacy" exemplify the cultural turn over the past decade. In the field of Latin American–U.S. relations specifically, John Johnson, George Black, Fredrick Pike, Paul Vanderwood, and Eldon Kenworthy have worked on myth and image; Gerald Haines, on informational policies; and Alan Klein, Gilbert Joseph, and Louis Pérez, on baseball. Lester Langley is the general editor of a book series that promises more attention to a variety of cultural dimensions.[20]

Some of the new works in international history have also moved the focus away from nation-states onto transnational cultural networks. Akira Iriye has long advocated more attention to transnational cultural interconnections.[21] In a 1989 essay on U.S.–Latin American relations, Stephen Rabe noted the growing attention to a wide variety of transnational exchanges.[22] And in 1991 Ian Tyrrell suggested that a "new transnational history" would help break the discourses of "American exceptionalism" still embedded in the field of U.S. foreign relations.[23] Transnational frameworks highlight what state-centered scholarship often tends to suppress: the cross-border cooperation among many functional or interest groups and also the racial and cultural diversity that exists not just *among* states but *within* them. Cultural mixing was assisted through historical waves of migration or immigration, through more than a century of business relationships, and through processes of cultural hybridization accelerated by international social organizations and popular media. Drawing on these themes, all kinds of studies have been enriching the field of "transnational history": emphasis on the African-American diaspora (work by Paul Gilroy, Judith Stein, James Campbell, Brenda Gayle Plummer, and Penny Von Eschen), transnational women's networks (Ian Tyrrell and Leila Rupp), transcontinental environmental histories (Alfred Crosby, Donald Worster, and Mark Lytle), and the huge number of studies in the history of global communications. Specifically in Latin American–U.S. relations, transcultural themes have also emerged: artistic movements (Helen Delpar and Shifra Goldman), entrepreneurial culture (Paul Drake, Elizabeth Cobbs, and Thomas O'Brien), anti-imperialist ideologies (Richard Salisbury), labor movements (Gregg Andrews), and drug control (William Walker). In transnational history, it may be difficult to make distinctions between what is "domestic" and "foreign," what is "inside" and "outside."

New work centering on cultural interactions has not met with a uniformly warm welcome within the field that used to be called "diplomatic history." Addresses given by the presidents of the Society for Historians of American Foreign Relations over the past four years—by John Gaddis, Warren Kimball, and Melvyn Leffler—have viewed a "cultural turn" in foreign relations with varied responses ranging from hostility to skepticism. Their perspectives seem to suggest that questions in the field should inevitably revolve around states, their policies, and their geopolitical and economic assets. New kinds of international interactions, they imply, are unimportant unless they clearly serve those arenas of investigation; moreover, they suggest that something as fuzzy as "culture" cannot be subjected to rigorous kinds of empirical proof and is too vague to be factored into cause-and-effect relationships. Others disagree. Michael Hogan, Bruce Cumings, and Michael Hunt, for example, see no reason for barring more substantive breadth and greater theoretical depth.[24] If histories of U.S. foreign relations are about global power relationships, how can it enrich the field to read Niccolò Machiavelli and Karl von Clausewitz but not Michel Foucault; to ponder Samuel Huntington on "clash of cultures" but not Edward Said; to consider Immanuel Wallerstein on economic systems but not Joan Scott on gender systems? By probing how various regimes of power inscribe themselves within culture, this volume confirms the worth of the "cultural turn."

It might now be useful to probe in greater depth the connections between the essays in this volume and what have been central concerns of postcolonial theory, postmodern international relations theory, and the cultural turn in the history of U.S. foreign relations.

One technique of postcolonial theory has involved delving into the colonial past to understand how the colonizers' needs for national self-definition, together with global disparities in power, helped structure imperial knowledge about the colonized subject. Elaborating the concept of "other," as developed in Edward Said's seminal work *Orientalism,* scholars interested in the origins of postcolonial relationships have probed a variety of European cultural institutions: novels, zoos, exhibitions, travel literature, painting.[25] Ricardo Salvatore provides a rich examination of such sources in the context of U.S. relations with Latin America. Businessmen, reformers, scientists, travelers, educators, missionaries, and economists, he argues, all placed South America under their gaze and fed an "exhibitionary complex" within the United States's burgeoning consumer culture. Pan-Americanism thus organized a vast "enterprise of knowledge," a "representational machine" that obsessively accumulated images and texts and thereby constructed the "nature" of South America for U.S. audiences.

Deborah Poole's essay likewise explores the "imperial gaze." Analyzing three visions of the landscape of the Andes produced in the United States during a period that saw a waxing of U.S. imperial ambitions in the Western Hemisphere, she crafts a subtle examination of the discourses through which "imperial subjects" could lay claim to that distant space and of the ways in which representations of such claims may have changed over time. Through sketches, photographs, measures, and maps, U.S. artists and scientists created a basis of imperial knowledge. She also emphasizes, however, that the discourses of the gaze are not singular in meaning. They simultaneously express a less controllable "sensuous undercurrent" of fantasy and desire toward the imperial object, a theme suggestively explored in recent works by Helen Delpar and Fredrick Pike.[26]

Steven C. Topik, who also deals with the power of representations, is primarily concerned with formulations of political/military spectacle. He examines Charles Flint's mercenary squadron, privately outfitted in the United States without objection by the Cleveland administration and sent to support the Brazilian government of Marshal Floriano Peixoto against the naval insurgency that wracked Brazil in 1893–1894. Like Perry's steamboats in Japan in the 1850s or Theodore Roosevelt's Great White Fleet, this squadron emblemized modernity and power so spectacularly that its actual military effectiveness never had to be invoked or tested. Overblown publicity accompanying the squadron's departure for Brazil temporarily grabbed headlines and helped shape a "perception of power" about the ability of the Peixoto government to withstand the rebel threat, about the new naval role the United States might play in the hemisphere, and about the future of a U.S.-Brazilian alliance.

All of these essays illuminate the representational technologies of U.S. predominance. Through such representations, imperial regimes attempt to enforce a sharp dichotomy between the modernized self and premodern others. Postcolonial, postmodern theory, by contrast, tries to disrupt the dichotomy by blurring the lines between past and present. "Cultural traditions" and "traditional cultures" are both scrutinized as discourses that construct a continuum from "traditional" to "modern." [27] And as the categories marking this continuum have been challenged, so the notion of any linear, "progressive" trajectory to history becomes more tenuous. Robert Berkhofer has recently examined how history, under these influences, is moving *Beyond the Great Story,* once the staple of historical production.[28]

The alternative to modernist historical metanarratives, according to Berkhofer, will be new forms of historical writing that can open space for multiple perspectives. Michael Schroeder's and Catherine LeGrand's essays build on this project by disrupting stable narratives and refusing to repress the multiplicity of "stories" about the past or to cast groups of people into single molds. Schroeder refuses to categorize the Sandinistas of the 1920s as either heroic peasants fighting for "tradition" against imperialism or as "bandits" fighting "modernization." Instead, he situates them within their own local politics—in which their meanings and significances take on various forms depending on the perspectives and alliances of the teller. Similarly, Catherine LeGrand's fascinating interviews with the current residents of the United Fruit Company's enclave that Gabriel García Márquez fictionalized as "Macondo" confirm the variety of perceptions that mock deterministic frameworks such as "imperialism" and disrupt categories such as "enclave" or "dependency." If historians cannot hope to capture all of the complexity of multiple stories, a problem that Berkhofer acknowledges, at least many no longer pretend that simply one will do.

Challenging boundaries not only of time and narrative trajectories but also of space, critical theory has directed attention to what constitutes "national" and "foreign." What is "inside"? What is "outside"? And how are the boundaries between the two culturally constructed and policed? What are the technologies that hold difference in place? What are the resistances that subvert them? Drawing from Eric Hobsbawm, Benedict Anderson, Charles Taylor, Sander Gilman, and others, such questions often focus attention on the shaping of collective and individual identities: public pageantry, the role of print media, the construction of "self" and "other," and the spread of ethnic and racialized images.[29] Such investigations of identity formation can erase the difference between domestic and international history by problematizing the ways in which culture might, or might not, be constructed and contained within nation-states. Such investigations suggest how, despite the discursive walls that nation-states and subgroups try to create around themselves, boundaries remain fluid. As William Cronon, Richard White, Patricia Limerick, and other practitioners of the "new" history of the U.S. West have emphasized, frontiers and boundaries are not only lines that divide but also zones of interaction where identities blur.[30] If borders strive for distinctiveness and division, they also invite penetration and diffusion.

Many of these essays elaborate this dual process by which national identities are formed both in accordance with, yet also against, inside/outside distinctions. And as historians highlight the multiplicity and complexity of interactions in many different sites, they tend to smother any simplistic paradigms. They "muddy up," to use Michael Schroeder's phrase, the large frameworks of liberalism versus dependency that tended to organize the field in the past. As Steven Palmer's notion of "peripheral precedence" suggests, center and periphery may be shifting terrain, and what is periphery in some respects may, in fact, take precedence in other areas. Who is the agent? Who is the receiver? Who decides which is which? And what is exchanged? Money? Forms of organization? Medical knowledge? Meanings of all sorts? In how many of these areas need groups of people on the "periphery" take a "lead" before the discourse of periphery must drop away altogether? Subjectivity—who claims it and who claims to assign it—is unstable and infinitely slippery. Steve Stern calls this complexity the "decentered center" and the "expansionist periphery," and he astutely calls for the need to historicize—to periodize and contextualize—interactions among groups and nations.

Presenting an example of peripheral precedence, Palmer examines the Rockefeller Foundation's public health mission in Costa Rica and finds little to support the notion of an imperialistic, U.S. imprint. On the contrary, he finds that Costa Rican experts, who were more knowledgeable about hookworm than were their U.S. sponsors, tapped foundation funds to shape their own agendas: advancing social medicine, forging activist public health programs, and extending the reach of the nationalist state among the rural populace. The hookworm campaigns of the Ministry of Education, far from demonstrating the importation of foreign and imperialistic medical practices, helped forge nationally observed rituals of moral hygiene that reinforced a national political community. He also suggests that relationships among professional, transnational groups not only might fail to correlate with power relationships between their respective states, but that they might even run in counterintuitive directions. He hypothesizes, for example, that cooperation in matters of public health may have been easier to effect in countries less suspicious of U.S. power (such as Costa Rica) than in countries experiencing a backlash against more direct, visible U.S. interventions (such as Nicaragua).

Seth Fein also deals with the issue of transnational elites. He examines the U.S. government's film-distribution program in Veracruz, designed as a tool of propaganda in the Cold War, and shows how it also became a way to project the local governor's own messages about the authority of the Mexican state. Cooperation and collaboration between transnational elites in both countries produced complicated "zones of contact," in which U.S. messages extolling consumption and "free labor" were interwoven with information extolling practices of public hygiene that, reminiscent of the Costa Rican campaigns discussed by Palmer, enhanced the reach and preeminence of the national state. Fein also raises doubts about how many of the so-called propaganda messages were actually *received* by targeted audiences.

As Fein's essay suggests, questions of identities and boundaries pose even more complicated questions about the processes of cultural reception. Building on theories about response in literary studies, such as those elaborated by Stuart Hall and Stanley Fish, many recent histories of U.S. foreign relations have tried to reassess the multiple impacts of the flows of cultural products that, in the dependency and imperial paradigms, were assumed to produce dominance. Reinhold Wagnleitner, Richard Pells, Richard Kuisel, and Rob Kroes, among others, show the complexity of responses to U.S. informational policies in the Cold War era in Europe. As Kroes writes, "Americanization then should be the story of an American cultural language traveling and of other people acquiring that language. What they actually say in it is a different story altogether." [31] Or as the poet Javier Moscarella says in his critique of the concept of cultural imperialism (as quoted in LeGrand's piece), "we assimilate, we recycle into something else. We are open, but not submissive. It's impossible to dominate us." LeGrand, like Kroes, challenges the dichotomy between domination and resistance, and suggests that zones of contact between far-flung places (even in cases of severe power disparities) could be places not simply of silencing and erasure but of cultural syncretism, even dynamism (as García Márquez's own background and astonishing creativity suggests).

Eric Paul Roorda also explores the issues of reception and multiple meanings in his fascinating analysis of the symbolism of the airplane, introduced into the Dominican Republic in 1919 to assist U.S. military intervention. He shows how General Rafael Trujillo, who learned the magic of aerial intimidation and imperial spectacle during the U.S. occupation, then redeployed this technology to construct a larger-than-life vision of Dominican nationalism that was intertwined with his personal vanity and prestige. Roorda ingeniously unravels the ways in which signifiers of military might (in this case airplanes) can "float" and attach themselves to different regimes of power.

Lauren Derby moves meaning production to the lunch table, examining food as a site for contests over national definition in the Dominican Republic. She first explores the negative representation of sugar, associated with the social disruption introduced by global capital, as contrasted with the symbolism of the plantain, the homey staple of the creole, the family, and the poor. She then examines the diffusion in 1992 of the idea that white, factory-produced "gringo chicken" had worms, the subsequent informal popular boycott of the fast-food chains that served this meat, and the contrasting symbol of darker, decentrally grown, creole chicken. Culinary discourses carry meanings about economic organization and national identity.

Two other essays turn attention to the gendered subtext of U.S. power in Latin America. Like imperial rule in the European colonial context, discourses of political dominance have been intertwined with assumptions about "proper" sexual practice, morality, and gender relations.[32] Thomas Klubock, analyzing the interlocking discourses about class and gender, examines the gender system that accompanied the male-wage, union-based, industrial work system during the era of "welfare capitalism" in the U.S.-owned Chilean copper mines, and he elucidates the transitions that then accompanied the rise of neoliberal forms of corporate capitalism. Eileen Findlay looks at the legalization of divorce introduced by the U.S. occupation of Puerto Rico in 1902. Supported by U.S. officials and local elites as a means of overcoming the reluctance of working-class Puerto Ricans to marry, the measure was part of a larger project to confine sexuality to marriage and to order gender relations in "acceptable" ways.

Both essays suggest, however, that the process of shaping gender norms and practices involved much more than the simple imposition of ideas from above. Lower-class women themselves, with little direct access to a sustainable wage and also few levers of power against the husbands or partners who could choose to have multiple liaisons or to abandon altogether economic responsibility toward them, seized some benefits from the North American emphasis on "stable" nuclear families. Redeploying the messages of U.S.-originated educational campaigns to fit their own circumstances, women might find congenial discourses that would work against the sexual double standard, threats of male violence, and economic insecurities.

All of these examples suggest what Steve Stern calls processes of "engagement and redeployment" of the institutions of imposition, or what Stephen Greenblatt terms "mimetic circulation." The tools of empire—from professional expertise to military hardware, to products of daily consumption, to gender norms—may be exported and even sometimes acquired. But how they are reshaped and then used by local cultures may be "a different story altogether."

Histories of foreign relations, as this volume suggests, are being reshaped by the new emphases in historical studies on postcoloniality, postmodernity, and cultural analysis. Modernist assumptions (both liberal and Marxist) about the centralizing and rationalizing momentum in international life are challenged by reversals: a decentering of organized capital, states made uneasy by transnational flows of people and capital, and cultures that variously accept, reshape, differentiate, and redeploy.[33] Such assumptions are also "muddied up" by the proliferation of meanings and floating signifiers churned up by the communications revolution. Within these investigations, power remains the central concern. But power systems are now assumed to be multiple and complex, arranged simultaneously through nation-states and regional relationships; through networks of capital, communications, and technology; through constructions of sex, gender, ethnicity, race, and nationality. As this volume exemplifies, histories that capture these reversals and complexities avoid the universalist, objectivist master narratives of modernism and often tend self-consciously toward more modest goals: to illuminate through partial glimpses, to attend to localized context, to deal sensitively with multiple stories and protean symbolic systems.

Notes

1. Gordon Connell-Smith, *The Inter-American System* (London: Oxford University Press, 1966); and more recently, Peter H. Smith, *Talons of the Eagle: Dynamics of U.S.–Latin American Relations* (New York: Oxford University Press, 1996), both organized their outstanding overviews of Latin American–U.S. relations around the idea of a changing "system."

2. Two influential collections are Bill Ashcroft, Gareth Griffiths, and Helen Tiffin, eds., *The Empire Writes Back: Theory and Practice in Post-colonial Literatures* (London: Routledge, 1989); and Patrick Williams and Laura Chrisman, eds., *Colonial Discourse and Post-colonial Theory: A Reader* (London: Harvester Wheatsheaf, 1993). An excellent critique of the term *postcolonial* (from an author who nonetheless builds on its theoretical substance) appears in Anne McClintock, *Imperial Leather: Race, Gender, and Sexuality in the Colonial Contest* (New York: Routledge, 1995), 9–17. A highly useful examination of various theoretical stances on imperialism is Patrick Wolfe, "History and Imperialism: A Century of Theory, from Marx to Postcolonialism," *American Historical Review* 102 (Apr. 1997): 388–420.

3. Amy Kaplan and Donald E. Pease, eds., *Cultures of United States Imperialism* (Durham, N.C.: Duke University Press, 1993).

4. See, for example, George F. Kennan's highly influential work, *American Diplomacy, 1900–1950* (Chicago: University of Chicago Press, 1951); and work by Norman A. Graebner, such as his *America as a World Power: A Realist Appraisal from Wilson to Reagan* (Wilmington, Del.: Scholarly Resources, 1984).

5. Oli R. Holsti, "International Relations Models," in *Explaining the History of American Foreign Relations,* ed. Michael J. Hogan and Thomas G. Paterson (New York: Cambridge University Press, 1991), 57–88.

6. Jim George, *Discourses of Global Politics: A Critical (Re)Introduction to International Relations* (Boulder, Colo.: Lynne Rienner, 1994).

7. For some overviews of this literature, see Akira Iriye, "Culture and International History," in Hogan and Paterson, *Explaining the History,* 214–25; Melvyn P. Leffler, "New Approaches, Old Interpretations, and Prospective Reconfigurations," *Diplomatic History* 19 (spring 1995): 173–96; Walter LaFeber, "The World and the United States," *American Historical Review* 100 (Oct. 1995): 1015–33; Emily S. Rosenberg, "Cultural Interactions," in *Encyclopedia of the United States in the Twentieth Century,* ed. Stanley I. Kutler (New York: Charles Scribner's Sons, 1996), 695–717; and idem, "Walking the Borders," in Hogan and Paterson, *Explaining the History,* 24–35.

8. William Warren Sweet, *A History of Latin America* (New York: Abingdon Press, 1919); and Hutton Webster, *History of Latin America* (Boston: D. C. Heath and Co., 1924). "Report on the Teaching of Latin American History," *Bulletin of the Pan American Union* 61 (June 1927): 547–51, reports the most widely used texts.

9. David J. Weber, *The Spanish Frontier in North America* (New Haven, Conn.: Yale University Press, 1992), 353–56.

10. See Mark T. Gilderhus, "Founding Father: Samuel Flagg Bemis and the Study of U.S.–Latin American Relations," *Diplomatic History* 21 (winter 1997): 1–14.

11. Arthur P. Whitaker, *The Western Hemisphere Idea: Its Rise and Decline* (Ithaca, N.Y.: Cornell University Press, 1954); Dexter Perkins, *Hands Off: A History of the Monroe Doctrine* (Boston: Little, Brown, 1941); and J. Fred Rippy, *Globe and Hemisphere: Latin America's Place in the Post-war Foreign Relations of the United States* (Chicago: H. Regnery Co., 1958).

12. The books were Margaret Marsh, *The Bankers in Bolivia: A Study in American Foreign Investment* (New York: Vanguard Press, 1928); Leland H. Jenks, *Our Cuban Colony: A Study in Sugar* (New York: Vanguard Press, 1928); Melvin M. Knight, *The Americans in Santo Domingo* (New York: Vanguard Press, 1928); and J. Fred Rippy, *The Capitalists and Colombia* (New York: Vanguard Press, 1931). See also Scott Nearing and Joseph Freeman, *Dollar Diplomacy* (New York: Benjamin Huebsch and the Viking Press, 1925).

13. Stephen Pelz, "Balance of Power," in Hogan and Paterson, *Explaining the History*, 111–40, provides an overview of realist works. The most influential statements of the "open door" economic interpretation are William A. Williams, *The Tragedy of American Diplomacy* (Cleveland, Ohio: World Publishing Co., 1959), and idem, *Empire as a Way of Life* (New York: Oxford University Press, 1980); and Walter LaFeber, *The New Empire: An Interpretation of American Expansion, 1860–1898* (Ithaca, N.Y.: Cornell University Press, 1963). The best overview is provided by Lloyd C. Gardner, ed., *Redefining the Past: Essays in Diplomatic History in Honor of William Appleman Williams* (Corvallis: University of Oregon Press, 1986). For a historical perspective on economic interpretations in American foreign relations, see Emily S. Rosenberg, "Economic Interest and United States Foreign Policy," in *American Foreign Relations Reconsidered, 1890–1993*, ed. Gordon Martel (London: Routledge, 1994), 37–50.

14. Perhaps the two most influential efforts to create a "synthesis" include John Lewis Gaddis, "The Emerging Post-revisionist Thesis on the Origins of the Cold War," *Diplomatic History* 7 (1983): 171–90; and Melvyn P. Leffler, "National Security," in Hogan and Paterson, *Explaining the History*, 202–13.

15. Michael J. Hogan, "Corporatism," in Hogan and Paterson, *Explaining the History*, 226–36; Louis A. Pérez Jr., "Dependency," in ibid., 99–110; and Thomas J. McCormick, "World Systems," in ibid., 89–98.

16. Herbert I. Schiller, *Communication and Cultural Domination* (White Plains, N.Y.: International Arts and Sciences Press, 1976); see also Jorg Becker et al., eds., *Communication and Domination: Essays to Honor Herbert I. Schiller* (Norwood, N.J.: Ablex, 1986).

17. Ariel Dorfman and Armand Mattelart, *How to Read Donald Duck: Imperialist Ideology in the Disney Comic,* trans. and intro. by David Kunzle, 2d ed. (New

York: International General, 1984); and Ariel Dorfman, *The Empire's Old Clothes: What the Lone Ranger, Babar, and Other Innocent Heroes Do to Our Minds* (New York: Pantheon, 1983).

18. In the tradition of "cultural imperialism," see especially Fred Fejes, *Imperialism, Media, and the Good Neighbor: New Deal Foreign Policy and United States Shortwave Broadcasting to Latin America* (Norwood, N.J.: Ablex, 1986). Other works that center less around the "imperialism" thesis are Gaizka S. De Usabel, *The High Noon of American Films in Latin America* (Ann Arbor, Mich.: UMI Research Press, 1982); Richard Shale, *Donald Duck Joins Up: The Walt Disney Studio during World War II* (Ann Arbor, Mich.: UMI Research Press, 1982); and James Schwoch, *The American Radio Industry and Its Latin American Activities, 1900–1939* (Urbana: University of Illinois Press, 1990).

19. Various discursive traditions of "cultural imperialism" are examined and critiqued in John L. Tomlinson, *Cultural Imperialism* (Baltimore, Md.: Johns Hopkins University Press, 1991).

20. Lester D. Langley, *America and the Americas: The United States in the Western Hemisphere* (Athens: University of Georgia Press, 1989).

21. Akira Iriye, "The Internationalization of History," *American Historical Review* 94 (Feb. 1989): 1–10.

22. Stephen G. Rabe, "Marching Ahead (Slowly): The Historiography of Inter-American Relations," *Diplomatic History* 13 (summer 1989): 297–316.

23. Ian Tyrrell, "American Exceptionalism in an Age of International History," *American Historical Review* 96 (Oct. 1991): 1031–55.

24. For a convenient summary of these positions, see Michael J. Hogan, "State of the Art: An Introduction," in *America in the World: The Historiography of American Foreign Relations since 1941,* ed. M. Hogan (New York: Cambridge University Press, 1995), 3–19.

25. Recent examples include Mary Louise Pratt, *Imperial Eyes: Travel Writing and Transculturation* (London: Routledge, 1992); McClintock, *Imperial Leather;* Harriet Ritvo, *The Animal Estate: The English and Other Creatures in the Victorian Age* (Cambridge, Mass.: Harvard University Press, 1987); and Annie E. Coombs, *Reinventing Africa: Museums, Material Culture, and Popular Imagination* (New Haven, Conn.: Yale University Press, 1994).

26. Helen Delpar, *The Enormous Vogue of Things Mexican: Cultural Relations between the United States and Mexico, 1921–1935* (Tuscaloosa: University of Alabama Press, 1992); and Fredrick B. Pike, *The United States and Latin America: Myths and Stereotypes of Civilization and Nature* (Austin: University of Texas Press, 1992).

27. See, for example, Eric Hobsbawm and Terence Ranger, eds., *The Invention of Tradition* (Cambridge: Cambridge University Press, 1983); and Jay O'Brien and William Roseberry, eds., *Golden Ages, Dark Ages: Imagining the Past in Anthropology and History* (Berkeley and Los Angeles: University of California Press, 1991).

28. Robert F. Berkhofer, *Beyond the Great Story: History as Text and Discourse* (Cambridge, Mass.: Harvard University Press, 1995).

29. Hobsbawm and Ranger, *The Invention of Tradition;* Benedict Anderson, *Imagined Communities: Reflections on the Origin and Spread of Nationalism* (London: Verso, 1983); Charles Taylor, *Sources of the Self: The Making of the Modern Identity* (Cambridge, Mass.: Harvard University Press, 1989); and Sander Gilman, *Inscribing the Other* (Lincoln: University of Nebraska Press, 1991).

30. See, for example, William Cronon et al., *Under an Open Sky: Rethinking America's Western Past* (New York: Norton and Co., 1992).

31. Rob Kroes, *If You've Seen One You've Seen the Mall: Europeans and American Mass Culture* (Urbana: University of Illinois Press, 1996), 128.

32. See, for example, Anne McClintock, *Imperial Leather;* Vron Ware, *Beyond the Pale: White Women, Racism, and History* (London: Verso Press, 1992); essays by Anne Laura Stoler and others in *Gender and the Crossroads of Knowledge: Feminist Anthropology in the Postmodern Era,* ed. Micaela di Leonardo (Berkeley and Los Angeles: University of California Press, 1991); and Gail Bederman, *Manliness and Civilization: A Cultural History of Gender and Race in the United States, 1880–1917* (Chicago: University of Chicago Press, 1995).

33. Michael Geyer and Charles Bright, "World History in a Global Age," *American Historical Review* 100 (Oct. 1995): 1034–60, examines these "reversals." A very different attack on claims about the homogenizing effects of American cultural expansion, which comes from a conservative and more culturally essentialist position, is presented in Samuel P. Huntington, "The West and the World," *Foreign Affairs* (Nov./Dec. 1996): 28–46.

William Roseberry

Social Fields and Cultural Encounters

This book engages two broad issues. The first concerns the complex and multistranded "encounters" between the United States and Latin America during the postcolonial centuries. The second critically examines prevailing theoretical interpretations of these encounters. The issues are intertwined in interesting ways. One interpretive question concerns the analytical weight that should be given to "foreign" influences, forces, and powers in Latin American settings. Several essays stress the shaping power of local contexts, the ways in which foreign influences are introduced within preexisting social and cultural relations that reconfigure and localize or situate the foreign. Thus, as Catherine LeGrand argues, even an enclave economy as infamous as a United Fruit Company banana zone is not *just* a foreign enclave. The relative presence and weight of the company is uneven throughout the banana zone, and local farmers and elites respond to and take advantage of the company's presence in different ways. Thus specific communities, and cultures, emerge within the zone. Similarly, Michael Schroeder argues that the consequences of another well-known example of Yankee power—the marine occupation of Nicaragua in the 1920s—need to be understood in the specific context of the Segovias, and a complex social organization and culture of organized violence to which marines and other actors had to adapt.

Other essays upset our understanding of "foreign" and "local" altogether, examining the construction of representations of Latin American peoples by North Americans, as part of larger projects of scientific exploration and discovery, commercial expansion, and personal quests for the exotic (Ricardo Salvatore and Deborah Poole). Here the focus shifts to the United States and the construction of "representational machines" that depict particular images of Latin America stripped from any context other than that required by the representation itself. The "foreign" and "local" are undercut in a different way in LeGrand's essay. As part of her study of a particular social and cultural field, she depicts a local elite which has constructed its own foreign webs of relationships—elsewhere in Colombia, elsewhere in Latin America, and then beyond Latin America altogether to particular European and North American capitals. Lauren Derby's essay shifts the focus between the Dominican Republic and Washington Heights in a complex and sophisticated reading of the social and cultural politics of food.

This, in turn, raises another dimension of the essays collected in the book. Their emphasis throughout is on multistranded encounters. This means, first, that *encounter* is not singular, as in *the* U.S. presence in, say, Venezuela. Rather, as Ricardo Salvatore and Gilbert Joseph stress, the meetings are almost as variable as the individuals, institutions, and agencies involved—government agents, merchants, plantation owners, mining corporations, skilled workers and technicians, managers, missionaries, tourists, and retirees.[1] It means, second, that our understanding of these encounters will remain impoverished if we see only one dimension of them—the economic, say, or the political, or "imperialism."

The emphasis on multiplicity and on dimensions of experience that cannot be reduced to the economic and political is one of the characteristic features of cultural studies. One way of reading the book, then, would be to see it as representing a shift from older theoretical models that were embedded in political economy and that overemphasized the shaping influence of foreign powers toward cultural studies with its emphasis on multiplicity, indeterminateness, and the ambiguities of power. To do so would, I think, miss one of this volume's most important contributions, which is to build and expand on earlier understandings and modes of analysis by means of dialogue and argument, rather than simply to supplant or displace them.

Indeed, as we look at some of the issues that are central to this book, we see that they do not fit easily into a before and after, political economy versus cultural studies, construction. For example, the relative weight and shaping role of local contexts in encounters between the United States (or other foreign powers) and particular Latin American societies have long been a subject for discussion and debate. Our understanding of this complex problem would be impoverished if we ignored the debates and caricatured earlier scholars as having produced flat, one-sided models of foreign domination. Let us consider two earlier debates that are of direct relevance to the issues confronted in this book.

We might begin with dependency and world-systems perspectives, which can be seen as foils for many of the arguments herein pursued. These frameworks emerged in argument with a field of studies, inadequately labeled then and now as modernization theory, that was: (*a*) implicitly or explicitly evolutionist (that is, modernity was an identifiable endpoint of a singular historical trajectory, and Latin American and other "traditional" or "undeveloped" peoples were a bit slow in moving along that trajectory); (b) innocent with regard to power, especially foreign, and especially U.S., to the extreme of putting on blinders when it came to examining U.S. "influence"; and (c) in sociological and anthropological studies, "culturalist" in the sense of ignoring economic and political relations and realities. Dependency and world-system perspectives challenged the evolutionism by positing underdevelopment as a new kind of social reality and condition (not a stage) that had to be understood in relation to the development of modernity itself. They challenged the innocence with regard to foreign power by placing the relation with foreign powers at the center of analysis, and they rejected culturalism in favor of strictly political, and especially economic, analyses.

It is now commonplace to note that the emphasis on foreign and especially U.S. power was often too simplistic and mechanical; that it paid too little attention to relations, processes, and resistances that could not fit within, or pressed against, or undermined a bipolar power relation; and that it paid too little attention to relations, processes, powers, and resistances more specific to, and internal to, particular countries and regions. To recognize and understand these relations, processes, powers, and resistances, in turn, it is necessary to go beyond political and economic analysis strictly conceived. Thus, with regard to two of the fundamental arguments of dependency perspectives, we find serious problems that affect even one of the lasting contributions of dependency thought—the rejection of evolutionism in favor of a more relational perspective. To the extent that relations were seen simply in terms of power politics, or never left the terrain of capitalist economics, the critique of evolutionism was undercut.

Yet we need to recognize a set of arguments *within* dependency and world-system perspectives. One of the most important from early on concerned the relative weight of foreign power. If at one extreme we find a catastrophist version that made foreign power determinant, we find simultaneously an argument against this view from within dependency perspectives (and eventually going beyond them in interesting ways), as in, for example, Fernando Henrique Cardoso and Enzo Faletto's emphasis on the distinct ways in which particular states have absorbed and internalized foreign forces, investments, and powers within specific processes of class and state formation, and so on. The framework they outline provided a basis for comparative studies that concentrated on particular Latin American states and the distinct ways in which foreign influences and powers had been imbricated in the formation of *local* class relations. Rather than acting like puppets on a string, however, these local classes pursued particular interests in alliance, competition, or struggle with other local classes; they constructed local political institutions and webs of power. While particular Latin American settings were placed in contexts dominated by foreign powers, then, analyses inspired by this framework concentrated on the *different* ways "external" forces were "internalized." [2]

This was not the only line of debate, or the only approach available to the "local." In his original argument with Immanuel Wallerstein, Steve Stern posits a "triangle" of forces or motors—the world system, popular strategies of resistance and survival in the periphery, and mercantile and elite interests joined to U.S. centers of gravity.[3] In this critique, his analysis of forces and relations within each of these poles, and in their interrelation, is primarily a political economic one. In his essay for this book, Stern revisits that analysis and finds it inadequate in that (*a*) it does not "unpack" each of the three points of the triangle in terms of their internal contradictions, tensions, relations, and resistances; (*b*) it was pursued too much within the realm of political economy; and (*c*) it pays insufficient attention to historicity, or the fact that the relative weight of each of the poles in the triangle is likely to be different at particular moments and conjunctures.

These three reservations are important, and lead directly to the themes of this book. But they show a direct line of dialogue and critique from world-systems theory to a framework that suggests a more subtle model for understanding the interplay of global and local forces and relations and finally to one that opens even more on a wider range of local powers and resistances, as well as multistranded relations between foreign and local currents, forces, and powers, and more open conceptions of politics and economics. Because of the dialogue, and the understanding that one moves theoretically by engaging theoretically, structures are neither ignored nor taken for granted. Instead, one comes away with a richer, more detailed sense of structure through an examination of limits, paradoxes, "leakages," and so on.

Let us now move to an older literature and debate that attempted to conceptualize the role of external relations and forces in specific settings, one that figures much less importantly in present-day lists of citations. I have in mind a discussion among social anthropologists in the 1930s and 1940s grappling with the problem of practicing ethnography in colonial situations. Some of the most interesting debates concerned the conception of the "local" itself, as evidenced in Max Gluckman's classic essay, *Analysis of a Social Situation in Modern Zululand.* The essay begins with a detailed description of the dedication of a bridge in the Mahlabatini District of Zululand in the Union of South Africa, in 1938. The description of the ceremony and associated interactions, the presence of "Europeans"

and "Africans," of "Zulu" and "European" officials and administrators of
varying rank, of "Christian" and "pagan" Africans, and of the intermix-
ing of "European" and "Zulu" rituals and performances in the ceremony
led Gluckman to conclude that the ceremony revealed and "crystallized
some of the social structure and institutions of present-day Zululand." [4]
Most important, in his view, the structured and profoundly unequal pattern of interaction among groups at the bridge indicated that they existed
within, and could only be conceived as part of, a single "community."
That community was not marked by homogeneity and shared value but by
conflict and inequality, beginning with the color bar. Commencing with
this structure of interaction, Gluckman then turned to a historical analysis
that attempted to trace the development of modern Zululand and account
for the groups, relations, and tensions that were present and crystallized
at a bridge in 1938.

That is, along lines similar to those pursued by Cardoso and Faletto,
but now concentrating not on a state but on a ritual occasion in a colonial backwater, Gluckman was postulating the *internalization* of external
forces and relations. The aim of the analysis was to dissolve boundaries
by exploring the ways in which foreign influences were reconfigured in
new territorial settings.

Gluckman's analysis did not escape criticism. Bronislaw Malinowski, in
particular, took issue with Gluckman's claim of a common community,
opening a larger debate regarding the study of race relations and colonialism in southern Africa. In a review of Malinowski's posthumously published *The Dynamics of Culture Change: An Inquiry into Race Relations
in Africa,* which, among other things, criticized earlier work by Gluckman and Isaac Schapera, Gluckman engaged the question of inclusion of
"European" agents and institutions within "tribal" orbits, an inclusion
that Malinowski found particularly offensive. According to Malinowski,
"Nor can industrial enterprise be regarded as part of a tribal unit. It would
be a strange African tribe which would embrace the gold mines of the
Rand with their gigantic plant; the stock exchange of Johannesburg, and
the banking system stretching from Cape to Cairo. The communication
systems, railroads and planes . . . all this is part of culture contact. But the
concept of an extended African tribe, into which this could be squeezed
in order to produce a unified tribal horizon, falls to the ground as soon as
it is stated." [5] To which Gluckman responded with an extended example:

No one has said that the Rand mines, etc., were within the embrace of an African tribe or could be "squeezed" into "a unified tribal horizon." We state that the

Rand mines and the African tribe which suppies their labour are both parts of a single social field; that the administrator who represents a government in London ruling over settlers and Africans, and the chief who rules over only a tribe whose members are in constant relationships with settlers and with government, are both parts of a single political body. For example, the son of a Zulu councillor was selected by the Zulu paramount to work for him, a signal honour for the father. The youth ran away from home. His father upbraided the youth for spoiling his name with the paramount. The youth retorted that the chief paid him nothing— look at his clothes; the Native Commissioner was better than the chief, since he paid those he employed. Afraid of his father's wrath and desirous of money, the youth ran away to a sugar-cane plantation—it might well have been the Rand mines. He could only flee from the paramount because the latter's writ of compulsion was limited by government. Here we have a right of the chief to call for labour which honours a father, the son desiring money and asserting a "preference" for the administrator because he pays, the development of a family conflict, and the solution of the conflict by flight to an enterprise of European capital. I quote this simple example to make explicit our conception of tribal group and Rand mines, of administrator and chief, as parts of a single social field.[6]

Let us now move from the details of this anthropological debate from the 1930s and 1940s and draw certain implications for the analysis of social fields. Although Gluckman's use of the word *community* to describe the inclusion of "European" individuals, institutions, rituals, norms, and rules within what he was later to describe as the same "social body" or "social field" signaled a point of confusion for Malinowski, it remains an important choice of words. Gluckman was, in fact, describing a new kind of community, forged not simply in "contact" between separate and discrete "cultures"—changed but nonetheless still discrete through the contact—but also, and more fundamentally, through an ongoing set of relationships that were part of the daily material and cultural reality of Zulu "tribesmen." His example of the chief's son who ran away to a sugar-cane plantation is especially apposite. The structure of social relations, and the actions of individuals within that structure, make no sense if central elements of the structure are analytically excluded.

Full development of this viewpoint requires a more detailed history and sociology of social fields, including a study of the development of particular commodity markets and circuits, as well as the forms and relations through which labor is mobilized and surplus labor appropriated. The framework traces *both* the historical development of capitalism as a global force and system *and* the local sedimentation of forces, relations, and contradictions that creates the specificity of particular locales. In this understanding, the social field places the local within larger networks, and therefore requires a knowledge of those networks. But the networks themselves are uniquely configured, socially and historically, in particular places at particular times. The local is global, in this view, but the global can only be understood as always and necessarily local.

I raise the example of the social field not to claim that it resolves all of our problems or provides a magical, methodological fix. Nor do I wish to suggest that Gluckman's *Analysis of a Social Situation* can be taken as a model of the sort of analysis we should undertake today. It was an interesting attempt, and in many ways it suggests a road not taken in social anthropological analysis, but it is as marked by the historical, social, political, and racial assumptions of the time in which it was written as are other texts. I do want to suggest that the analysis of historically specific social fields may provide a useful starting point for thinking through the kinds of problems considered in this book.

The enclave situations described by LeGrand and Thomas Klubock are especially apt settings for this sort of analysis. In attempting to resolve one set of labor problems, Braden Copper in Chile promoted and rewarded nuclear families, with unforeseen consequences for labor relations at the mining camps and in local politics. Similarly, as Eileen Findlay's discussion shows, the extension of marriage and divorce laws to Puerto Rico shortly after the U.S. acquisition of the island meant rather different things, and responded to different imperatives, in U.S. and Puerto Rican social fields. Whatever the intention of U.S. policymakers, the laws were *localized,* and used by actors maneuvering for position in settings and situations the policymakers could not imagine. And Steven Palmer's study of the Rockefeller Foundation's campaign against hookworm in Costa Rica, especially the Costa Rican government's incorporation of Louis Schapiro, provides a particularly apt example of the internalization of the external.

These examples, along with other essays in the book, demonstrate the possibility of extending the metaphor beyond the more strictly political and economic terms with which I first presented it. Indeed, an expanded model of social fields may prove useful for exploring the theoretical issues that inform the book.

First, it retains a notion of structuration without either imposing a pre-existing structure or collapsing the historically specific and particular within a global (capitalist, colonial, or neocolonial) structure. Instead, an understanding of structure requires a complex mapping of institutions, social formations, communities, individuals, corporations, administrative entities, identities, and ideologies, in specific social, cultural, and political spaces.

Second, the notion of structure that emerges is one that stresses context, relation, and history, along lines suggested above.

Third, though its field is "local," it includes within that field, within the structure of local social and cultural relations, aspects of the "external" or "global," *localized* in specific, particular relation.

Fourth, in related fashion, its notion of boundaries is exceptionally fluid, not only in that its concentration on relation allows it to include within particular boundaries sets of apparently external or foreign or outside powers, institutions, individuals, and so on, but because it does not specify in advance the appropriate boundaries of fields (community, region, plantation, enclave, or state). The very definition of appropriate boundaries (which in turn are seen as permeable membranes rather than impermeable barriers)[7] depends on specific historical/political/cultural problems.

In Gluckman's usage, the analysis of the constitution of a social field led him to a particular kind of history, a history of colonialism and missionization tied to an understanding of the constitution of the color bar in South Africa. Yet it stuck with the "harder" realities of that history, the more easily graspable aspects of social and political structure and relation. These remain an essential part of any history of a social field, but the essays in this book remind us that they are insufficient. We must also get at what Stern calls the complex overlays of past and present, at various kinds of social leakage, "decentering," and "expansionism." We also need to try to understand the complex culture and politics of the "representational machine" at particular moments, and the formation of actors who carry with them particular identities and ideologies; particular, internally contradictory understandings of class, race, and gender, of civilization and barbarism; and so on. Salvatore and Poole explore in rich detail the constitution of a set of images and representations of South America within and among U.S. audiences and settings in the nineteenth and early twentieth centuries.

Together, these papers point toward the necessity of a kind of history that at once deepens our understanding of social fields and may go a good way toward undermining the effectiveness of the metaphor. To truly understand these representations, Salvatore suggests, we have to turn toward a political and cultural history of their home base. Salvatore's and Poole's projects do not offer histories of the represented—of the processes, relations, powers, and resistances present in South American fields in the nineteenth and early twentieth centuries—but of the representing. When we turn to particular Latin American fields and examine the actions of particular individuals (merchants, missionaries, travelers, consuls, and so on), we need to understand that they carry with them not simply a set of instrumental ideas about the actions they are undertaking (the buying of coffee, the processing of sugar, the mining of copper, the saving of souls), but also a whole complex of ideas and representations about civilization and barbarism, white and dark, male and female, progress and backwardness, the understanding of which requires the re-siting of those individuals in North American (or English or German) social fields. Of course they remain actors, and constructors (in relation with others) of "structure" within, say, South or Central American fields. Thus, the kind of analysis pursued by Salvatore and Poole cannot take the place of the analysis of the constitution of historically specific social fields. Instead it points to the complexity of relation, representation, and ideology that needs to be considered in the analysis of individuals, the creation of enclaves, the formation of institutions, or the exercise of powers.

While such complexity might have disanimated both Gluckman and his critics, it provides the necessary starting point for any attempt to understand postcolonial encounters between Latin American societies and foreign powers. This book offers exciting evidence of the understandings that are possible.

Notes

1. See also William Roseberry, *Anthropologies and Histories: Essays in Culture, History, and Political Economy* (New Brunswick, N.J.: Rutgers University Press, 1989), 84–91.

2. See, for example, Fernando Henrique Cardoso and Enzo Faletto, *Dependency and Development in Latin America* (Berkeley and Los Angeles: University of California Press, 1979); Cardoso, "The Consumption of Dependency Theory in the United States," *Latin American Research Review* 12, no. 3 (1977): 7–24. For a recent comparative study of the "internalization of the external" in coffee-growing areas, see William Roseberry, Lowell Gudmundson, and Mario Samper Kutschbach, eds., *Coffee, Society, and Power in Latin America* (Baltimore, Md.: Johns Hopkins University Press, 1995).

3. Steve Stern, "Feudalism, Capitalism, and the World-System in the Perspective of Latin America and the Caribbean," *American Historical Review* 93 (1988): 829–72.

4. Max Gluckman, *Analysis of a Social Situation in Modern Zululand* (1940, 1942; reprint, Manchester: Manchester University Press, 1968), 12.

5. Bronislaw Malinowski, *The Dynamics of Culture Change: An Inquiry into Race Relations in Africa* (New Haven, Conn.: Yale University Press, 1946), 15, 16; cited in Max Gluckman, "Malinowski's Functional Analysis of Social Change," in *Order and Rebellion in Tribal Africa* (New York: Free Press, 1963), 215.

6. Gluckman, "Malinowski's Functional Analysis," 215–16.

7. The image of permeable membranes and impermeable barriers comes from Jackson Lears's discussion of hegemony, "The Concept of Cultural Hegemony," *American Historical Review* 90 (1985): 567–93.

María del Carmen Suescun Pozas

From Reading to Seeing

Doing and Undoing Imperialism

in the Visual Arts

TO THE READER: DIRECTIONS FOR ASSEMBLAGE

This visual essay consists of three interdependent parts.

The first two are a group of eleven images (which include the outside

cover and frontispiece as well as the foldout you may already have

found inside the back cover) and the captions that accompany each

image. I encourage the viewer/reader to dwell on the images

themselves and explore the captions before delving into

the third part, the text itself.

Seal of the Defending Army of Nicaraguan National Sovereignty, 1927.
Marine Corps Historical Center, Washington, D.C., Personal Papers
Collection, Box "Sandino."

Crafted at Sandino's request, this stark image of one man about to slit the throat of another is a remarkable material vestige of the Sandino revolt against the U.S. Marine occupation of Nicaragua. Forging Nicaragua does not take place in a middle ground or space of negotiation: the patriot meets the invader/traitor, who symbolizes U.S. imperialism, in a violent struggle to reclaim the Nicaraguan nation.[1] The standing figure is perhaps one of Sandino's troops or a peasant supporter, or even Augusto César Sandino himself, carrying a machete and a *mochila* and wearing the big hat that later came to invoke Sandino in the popular imagination. On the ground probably lies a U.S. Marine or any Nicaraguan who stood against the *patria* Sandino predicated and urged his followers to defend with their lives. Sandino's rebel army engraved this seal on one side of the coins it minted in 1927 with gold from the San Albino mine recently confiscated from its Yankee owners. To ensure the readability of the image, the other face of the coins is inscribed "Indios de A. C. Sandino" and "R. de N. [República de Nicaragua] 10 pesos oro." Like Sandino's three written manifestos, the seal and the coins first circulated on the eve of the initial military clash between Sandino's forces and the U.S. Marines on 16–17 July 1927. Printed in newspapers, the manifestos mainly reached a literate audience of town-dwellers, while the coins may have had particular meaning for the rural population of the Segovias, where Sandino took his stand. We do not know if these coins were used in commercial transactions, but certainly they held symbolic significance. Like coins and printed money everywhere, Sandino's coins might have symbolized, at both the material and the visual levels, the collectively shared expectations of a group of people and their desire to create an autonomous economic, political, and cultural order. What the coins meant and how they appealed to the imagination of those through whose hands they passed is an open question. Also open is the issue of how meanings attached to the coins changed over time as "myth" and "reality" moved them into spheres other than the economic.

Sykes, *My, How You Have Grown!*
Philadelphia Evening Public Ledger, 1923.
Courtesy of *Philadelphia Inquirer*.

The position of the actors expresses the reorganization of hemispheric relations after World War I. Uncle Sam steps forward to take the place previously occupied by Europe in Latin American affairs. Here Latin America attracts Uncle Sam's attention in the guise of an attractive, white, upper-class female, thus suggesting that Uncle Sam endorses a diminished adulthood for Latin America, stripped of independence and self-determination. The cartoonist here plays on perceptions of women prevalent in the United States at the beginning of the twentieth century, disregarding that the position and status of women at home were evolving in response to industrialization, urbanization, and the suffrage movement, among other influences.[2]

René d'Harnoncourt, *American Artist in Mexico,* 1932. Gouache.
Courtesy of the d'Harnoncourt family. Photo: Philadelphia Museum of Art.

Like the American artist in Mexico, Latin Americanists inevitably stand as "informed tourists" before the landscape and enthralling views that the field of U.S.–Latin American relations offers to our historical imaginations. We hope that our sins of omission as well as commission will not be regarded as stereotyping practices because of their selectiveness and limitations, but rather as sensible attempts to further understanding of the position Latin Americans occupy in the rhetoric and practice of empire.

Joaquín Torres-García, *Inverted Map of South America,* c. 1936.
Ink drawing, reproduced in *Círculo y Cuadrado* [Montevideo] 1 (May 1936).
Courtesy of Cecilia de Torres. © Joaquín Torres-García/Kinémage,
Montreal, 1997.

On returning from several years in Europe, this Uruguayan artist encouraged his compatriots to value pre-Columbian traditions by advancing the idea that "Our North is the South." [3] In the period of the Great Depression, when nationalist feelings were intensifying throughout Latin America, Torres-García erased the United States and Canada from his map of "the North." He replaced them with the America that extends below the Rio Grande, drawn upside down. If the "North" was somehow superior, the place to look to for guidance and example, the place whose models had to be followed by Uruguayan artists who wanted to be written into the history of art and by Latin Americans who wanted to be "modern" and "civilized," then Torres-García said we must turn our South into our "North."

Jorge González Camarena, *Visit Mexico,* c. 1943. Poster.
Photo: Prints and Photographs Division, Library of Congress, Washington, D.C.

In 1943 the Mexican government's Tourist Department commissioned a travel poster intended to attract U.S. visitors. Following the example of the political cartoonist Sykes, this Mexican artist genders Mexico female and offers her to the U.S. viewer. Despite changes brought by the Mexican Revolution, Mexico was constructed abroad, as much as at home, as an alluring place where picturesque peasants still toiled the land. For almost two decades Mexican muralist Diego Rivera had immortalized the image of rural women carrying bouquets of flowers framed by their braided hair. Camarena plays knowingly with these motifs; he feeds the viewer's imagination with the stereotypes and idioms of a visual language that aimed at speaking the Revolution in what by then were institutionalized terms. In Camarena's poster, Mexico is not only embodied by the ripe young woman but by the fruits themselves, addressing both the male tourists' longing for an escapade as well as the potential investor, nostalgic perhaps for the regime of Porfirio Díaz, who promoted Mexico as a land whose fruits were available to any who would capitalize its soil. Camarena's and Rivera's iconography appealed both to a foreign audience longing for myths and to a government that sought to improve its image abroad and strengthen the domestic economy by promoting the tourist industry.

José Gamarra, *El Progreso de una Ayuda,* 1969.
Collection of the artist. Photo courtesy of the artist.

In response to the Cuban Revolution, which had occurred but two years earlier, President John F. Kennedy launched the "Alliance for Progress" in 1961. Along with a socioeconomic development program intended to spearhead social change across Latin America, the U.S. government gave Latin American governments help in fighting guerrilla movements by training military and police forces and funneling south new military technologies. For this reason, many Latin Americans, including this Uruguayan-born artist, viewed the so-called Alliance as "aid" intended mainly to bring "progress" in securing U.S. strategic interests in Latin America. Gamarra (who has lived in France since 1963) takes up time and again the theme of imperial encounters in his paintings, highlighting the parallel histories of conquest, colonization, and imperialism, past and present.

Have a Coca-Cola = ¿Qué Hay, Amigo?
(WHAT GIVES, PAL?)

...or making pals in Panama

Down Panama way, American ideas of friendliness and good neighborliness are nothing new. Folks there understand and like our love of sports, our humor and our everyday customs. *Have a "Coke"*, says the American soldier, and the natives know he is saying *We are friends* . . . the same friendly invitation as when you offer Coca-Cola from your own refrigerator at home. Everywhere Coca-Cola stands for *the pause that refreshes,*—has become the high-sign of kindly-minded people the world over.

* * *

In news stories, books and magazines, you read how much our fighting men cherish Coca-Cola whenever they get it. Yes, more than just a delicious and refreshing drink, "Coke" reminds them of happy times at home. Luckily, they find Coca-Cola — bottled on the spot — in over 35 allied and neutral countries 'round the globe.

It's natural for popular names to acquire friendly abbreviations. That's why you hear Coca-Cola called "Coke".

COPYRIGHT 1944, THE COCA-COLA COMPANY

Have a Coca-Cola = ¿Qué Hay, Amigo? 1944. Printed with the permission of the Coca-Cola Company. "Coca-Cola," "Coke," and the contour bottle are registered trademarks of the Coca-Cola Company. Courtesy of Industry and Consumer Affairs, The Coca-Cola Company, Atlanta.

Coca-Cola as the "global high-sign" has become the trope for "U.S." throughout Latin America. For many it stands for the overt denial of difference; Coca-Cola is perceived as an instrument for the "Americanization," that is, homogenization of the continent. Since 1914, with the opening of the transoceanic canal, Panama has figured as a strategic post in U.S. national defense. Thus it is not by chance that in this poster Panama was to be brought back home and made familiar to the general audience supporting U.S. participation in World War II and the U.S. military presence in Panama. Between 1933 and 1947, "Good Neighbor" rhetorics permeated U.S. popular culture. Picking up on the motto, the Coca-Cola Company incorporated it into advertising campaigns with the confidence that it would appeal to patriotic North Americans. Just as such advertising aimed at reinforcing the U.S. audience's positive perception of itself, it also attempted to undo the image U.S. citizens held of Latinos as unfriendly and untrustworthy. "Have a 'Coke,' says the American soldier" to native Panamanians, who know this means "We are friends." Both through its image and its nuanced text, this poster extends U.S. frontiers well below the Rio Grande, blurring the distinction between "here" and "there," and between "us" and "them." This uniformizing impulse has long been identified by Latin Americans as being of the imperial kind.

Cildo Meireles, *Insertions into Ideological Circuits: 1. Coca-Cola Project,* 1970. Printed stickers on Coca-Cola bottles. Variable dimensions. Collection of the artist. Courtesy of the artist and Galerie Lelong, New York.

At a time when the Brazilian urban guerrilla had kidnapped the U.S. ambassador, this Brazilian artist undertook to short-circuit one of the most important symbols of U.S. imperialism and capitalism in Latin America. He also urged his fellow citizens to subvert the military regime's censorship by making political use of the unimpeded circulation of commodities. In Brazil in the 1960s and 1970s, people bought Coca-Cola in glass bottles that had to be returned and were then refilled and sold again. By absconding with these bottles and transforming them, Meireles's installation was a call to oppose both U.S. economic imperialism and tacit U.S. support for the Brazilian dictatorship. He inscribed "Yankees Go Home" on empty Coke bottles before returning them; below this, a second legend appears: "Register information and critical opinions on the bottles and return them to circulation" ("Gravar nas garrafas informações e opiniões criticas e devolve-las a circulação"). By inscribing these two legends on the most salient manifestation of cultural and economic imperialism of the time, Meireles obliges us to read them as part of the same story of national sovereignty. This means that the U.S. beverage must be consumed "critically," as the surface on which formally censored ideas could be voiced and the military government's ban on freedom of expression subverted. Likewise, national characteristics could be inscribed into what many perceived as a U.S. imperialist mechanism to promote cultural uniformity; the Coca-Cola bottle could be turned into an instrument of self-expression. Ironically, one of the first places this photograph was exhibited was in the United States, in Kynaston L. McShine's "Information" exhibition of Conceptual Art at the New York Museum of Modern Art in 1970. Surprisingly, this work was later shown in Brazil at an exhibition organized by the Coca-Cola Company, to which artists from all over Latin America were invited.

Antonio Caro, *Colombia,* 1976. Enamel paint on metal sheet. White lettering on Coca-Cola-red background. Museo de Arte Moderno, Santafé de Bogotá, Colombia. Courtesy of the artist.

Coca-Cola was the symbol of U.S. imperialism across Latin America, particularly in the 1960s and 1970s. Taking up the two most salient motifs of Coca-Cola advertisement (color and lettering), Colombian artist Antonio Caro seems to pose the question, "Where do 'they' stand and where do 'we'?" This superimposition of "Colombia" and the Coca-Cola logo points not just at U.S. imperialism but at how "we" and "they" cannot be disentangled one from the other. By engaging subjects in actions, empire must be addressed as a practice that brings mutual transformation rather than mere obliteration of one of the parties.

José Bedia, *The Little Revenge from the Periphery,* 1992.
Acrylic, found objects. 96 inches diameter. Detail.
Photo: Frumkin/Adams Gallery installation, 1992 (re-created
for Cartographies exhibition organized by Winnipeg Art Gallery, 1993).
Courtesy of George Adams Gallery, New York.

A member of the Afro-Cuban Palo Monte religious faith in Havana, this Cuban-born artist has worked in close contact with Afro-Cuban and Amerindian communities for many years. His involvement with American Indian cultures and religions dates from 1985, when he first visited the Lakota Nation in South Dakota at the invitation of Cherokee artist Jimmie Durham. In 1973 Bedia made a pencil drawing of a Native American warrior aiming his rifle at an unseen target. Twenty years later "The Little Revenge from the Periphery" revealed the target: surrounded by members of First Nations from across the globe, the white man is pierced by arrows, swords, and axes, symbols of the power now turned back against him. Not only does this installation reverse the logic and dynamic of power between center and periphery, but it implies that the construction of meaning now lies in the hands of those who, in previous narratives, were deprived of access to it.[4]

(c)

(d)

(Facing pages, broken into four sections for reproduction here.) Michael Lebrón, *The North and the South,* 1993. Photomural. 3,300 cm by 300 cm (101 feet by 9.75 feet). © ATW ("Against the Wall") Communications. Courtesy of the artist.

Mural text:

AFTER A HARD WEEK'S WORK, YOU'RE READY FOR

Every year, the Coors family, owners of Coors Brewing Co., gives financial

THE RIGHT PLACE WITH THE RIGHT ONE, WHY

support to groups like The National Forum Foundation, Morality in Media,

MAKE THE RIGHT MOMENT THE RIGHT'S MOMENT?

and The Free Congress Foundation.[1] They contribute to a culture that shapes

DOES COORS LIGHT HAVE THE TASTE THAT'S

the views of religious and political extremists.[2] When you buy Coors products,

SILVER SMOOTH? OR IS IT THE SILVER BULLET

do you help them turn back civil rights, censure high school textbooks, weaken

THAT AIMS THE FAR RIGHT'S POLITICAL AGENDA

labor laws and environmental protections, promote homophobia, and

AT THE HEART OF AMERICA? WANT THE AWESOME

meddle in foreign affairs? Why did Joe Coors himself, for example, buy

FACTS? THEN READ BETWEEN THESE LINES.

an aircraft for the Nicaraguan contras?[3] Where are the contras today?

"Once, we were glad to have Joe Coors and his friends on our side," says El Loco,[4] a former contra commander. "Together, we fought the hard and dirty fight[5] that helped Nicaraguans get to the voting booth to make The Right's Choice for a Better Nicaragua! Now the shooting war is over; today, I can walk into my favorite Managua bar and say, 'No more of that industrial strength Nicaraguan cerveza for me. Gimme the great taste of Coors Light!' But Nicaraguan families are poorer than ever. With 55% unemployed,[6] we scour garbage heaps for food in villages that remain ravaged by war. After 30,000 dead,[7] what happened to all that promised U.S. aid? What does it really mean to say that Coors Light is The Right's Beer now?"

This advertisement is an art installation paid for by Michael Lebron and produced by The ATW Communications Group. It does not reflect the views of TDI, Amtrak, LIRR, New York City Transit Authority, Adolph Coors Co., Coors Brewing Co., the Adolf Coors Foundation, or their associates. The ATW Communications Group is solely responsible for its content. 1992 ATW Communications Group.

1. Coors Foundation Annual Report, 1988; Internal Revenue Service form 990PF, Schedule 9A, November 1989–1991. 2. Russ Bellant, *The Coors Connection: How Coors Family Philanthropy Undermines Democratic Pluralism* (Boston: South End Press, 1991). 3. Joe Coors's testimony to the congressional committee investigating the Iran-Contra Affair, 21 May 1987. 4. Pseudonym. 5. Reed Brody, *Contra Terror in Nicaragua: Report of a Fact-Finding Mission. September 1984–January 1985* (Boston: South End Press, 1985). 6. Francisco Rosales, UNO Minister of Labor, Managua, Nicaragua, 29 Oct. 1992. 7. *Los Angeles Times,* 21 Feb. 1990.

The U.S.-born artist of Costa Rican descent Michael Lebrón designed this photomural for the "Spectacular," which is an advertising billboard on the rotunda of the Amtrak railroad terminal at Penn Station in New York City. After Lebrón had paid a $37,000 two-month rental fee, Amtrak withdrew its permission to use the space just three days before the mural was to be installed in December 1992, on the grounds that the installation was "political." The artist sued Amtrak, appealing to the U.S. Constitution's First Amendment on freedom of speech. The purpose of Lebrón's court suit, as reported in the *New York Times* and the *Washington Post,* was to force Amtrak to display the piece, which, according to the artist, is no more or less political than any commercial advertisement is. Lebrón's was a visual parody of the Coors Light slogan, "It's the right beer now," a piece of, in the artist's words, "critical realism for a consumer corporatist society." [5] The selection of Coors as the focus was not arbitrary. In the summer of 1987 the U.S. press had revealed that Joseph Coors of the Coors Brewery Company had purchased aircraft for the U.S.-sponsored Contras seeking to overthrow the Sandinista government in Nicaragua. This was but one of several right-wing political causes that the Coors family had funded in the United States and abroad during the 1980s. Lebrón calls his photomural "the Guernica of our time." Yet it has never been publicly displayed in the United States. The work was exhibited only once, at the Fifth Havana Biennial in Cuba in 1994, in a museum space for an art audience, clearly not the audience for which it was intended. Since the artist's desire had been to jolt North Americans into a deeper awareness of how they themselves are embedded in a web of imperial practices, he meant to reach audiences at home, the thousands of people who congregate around Penn Station each day who should and do have a say in influencing what the United States does in Latin America. Meanwhile, Lebrón's court case grinds on.

How can the subject of U.S.–Latin American relations be addressed without taking a quick glance at one of the most powerful and alluring orders of the twentieth century, the order of the image? This section has several purposes. First, it highlights the works of Latin American artists who engage head-on with the question of U.S. imperialism, addressing a multiplicity of U.S.–Latin American encounters of the "imperial kind." Second, it aims to show the reader/viewer how a specific form of discourse, that of visual representation, can contribute to conceptualizing the various processes we call imperial encounters. Images provide mechanisms of articulation through which the theme may, on the one hand, be problematized and exposed in its complexity or, alternatively, be simplified so that some sets of meanings are privileged and others subsumed in an ongoing "othering" process that produces an "outsider" versus a "unifying us." I want to stress that as socially constituted practices, the present set of images themselves must be understood as practices of empire and as interpretive acts. Their engagement as interpretive processes has two interrelated dimensions. One is at the level of their materiality as paintings, posters, sketches, or installations, whose internal elements build visual languages that tell a story at many levels. The other involves the structures, contexts, and experiences that deeply imprint an artist and a work of art, that is, the influences that socially constitute it.[6] Images shape and are shaped by material (and social, political, and cultural) conditions, both at the moment of their production and at the moment of their circulation and reception in various times and places. Finally, the third purpose of this section is to encourage the reader/viewer to engage with the multiple dialogues opened by the present ensemble of images. Such dialogues occur within each image, between them, and with their framings, that is, the above-mentioned material, social, political, and cultural orders.

This visual essay came together as a puzzle does when only a few pieces are left: almost by itself. No effort was made to cover specific countries, and the final distribution over a seven-decade time span, from 1927 to 1993, was but fortunate happenstance. Rather, my guiding intention in selecting these works was to bring together materials from Latin America and the United States that spoke to each other. Any pool of images from Latin America that elaborates on the issue of imperialism must be studied in conjunction with images of Latin America produced in the United States. (I would contend that the reverse is also true.)

I want to urge the reader to engage with each image as an essay in its own right. To understand how images signify is not an easy task. It demands first and foremost that the viewer be willing to let the images catch his or her eye "unawares" in the idiom of visual language. By this I mean that an interpretive process is embedded in each image, in images in relation to other images, and in the group of images as a whole. My hope is that the present material will fire our imaginations and enlarge the interpretive process by engaging the viewer in what for historians may be a new language and a new way of seeing.

The collection of images brought together here elaborates on the notion of encounter. The images render problematic the unidimensional notion of empire by pointing in multiple directions; they expose in their own paradoxical ways the paradoxes of empire. "From reading to seeing" is thus an abbreviation for an exegetical exercise by which all of the elements that contribute to and make up the images are considered and in which we, as viewers, play a role in the process of *interpretive structuration*. This is equivalent to saying that, beyond merely showing, images are capable of doing (and undoing) things. That is, images engage with the multifaceted dimensions of empire by elaborating on tensions that originate at the heart of imperial political and economic systems. This is what allows us to view socially constituted images not as inanimate objects, as "windows into the past," but as active agents engaged in activities well described by the notion of encounter: paradoxical movements simultaneously "with" and "against" a particular social, political, economic, cultural, and aesthetic frame.[7] Drawing on the tools of discourse analysis and theories of representation, this visual essay opens a spatial dimension within which to probe and multiply the points of contention and convergence that U.S.-centered accounts of U.S.–Latin American relations have generally failed to recognize.

Considering each image, a subgroup of them, or the whole set of images helps illustrate what this "doing and undoing of empire" is all about. The material gathered for this essay includes the images presented in this section as well as the book cover, frontispiece, and foldout. Taken together, these visual representations are meant to work as a *transformation group,* that is, to work both with and in opposition to each other.[8] Grouping them is an exercise in building complexity, for although they can be sorted according to their most salient features, groups inevitably overlap. For instance, one possible grouping, centered on the Coca-Cola motif, sets Cildo Meireles's and Antonio Caro's works against the Coca-Cola Company advertisement. A second combination, which suggests a critical perspective on what many Latin Americans view as the deceptive media techniques of multinational beverage companies, involves viewing Meireles's, Caro's, and Michael Lebrón's works against the Coca-Cola Company poster. It is also instructive to place Lebrón's 1993 mural side by side with the 1927 seal of Sandino's army, for both address the ongoing intervention of the United States in Nicaraguan internal affairs; or to view Lebrón, as an anti-ad, against the Coca-Cola Company poster. Sykes's political cartoon and the "Visit Mexico" tourist poster both gender Latin America female in accordance with early-twentieth-century U.S. images of the attractive, subservient female and the Mexican tendency to portray Mexico as a woman (e.g., *La Malinche*). At the same time, the "Visit Mexico" poster might be paired with the d'Harnoncourt painting as stereotyped renditions of the Mexican landscape and its people, one by a Mexican and the other by a U.S. artist.

And the combinations have not been exhausted. Lebrón's "North and the South" and Torres-García's "Inverted Map of South America" play with the North-South dichotomy as part of a much more extended critique of the economy of ideas and commodity culture. Furthermore, both Lebrón's and Torres-García's works can be grouped with Caro's, Meireles's, José Bedia's, and José Gamarra's as different elaborations on a contentious encounter between the United States and Latin America. Taken together, these works signal an element of continuity in Latin American artists' perceptions of asymmetrical power relations between the United States and Latin America. Gamarra and Meireles most clearly play with the shifting meanings consumer goods present when they are "short-circuited." Toys and Coca-Cola bottles have a double face: turned into ideological weapons they can simultaneously entertain and threaten your life by undermining local consumption (and cultural) patterns and entrenching military values.

Though these images and groupings make many trenchant observations on the notion of imperial encounters, they bring no resolution, no closure of meaning. While Caro seems to criticize the U.S. presence in the configuration of Colombian identity, he gives equal weight to the elements he takes from the Coca-Cola logo, on the one hand, and "Colombia," the symbol of national unity and sovereignty, on the other. In Gamarra's sky, full of camouflaged objects dropped by a U.S. plane on a tropical landscape, we perceive weapons that seem to be toys and then shift again to become weapons, interspersed with a strange assortment of objects from everyday life. Try as we might, it is impossible to fix the quality of these objects or to attach one meaning to them. The two inscriptions on Meireles's Coca-Cola bottles trigger a flickering association between the Yankees and oppressive conditions at home. Yet the artist's refusal to make explicit a logical connection between them creates a gap that can only be filled by the reader/viewer/consumer's attribution of meaning. The two inscriptions might be collapsed into one so that they serve as a critique of U.S. invasion via patterns of consumption, or they might instead be read as separate yet interconnected aspects of Brazilian life in the 1960s. As Lebrón's Coors Light beer can/bullet streaks across space from left to right, the scene on the right immediately sends us back to where the story originates, which in turn returns us to the Nicaraguan village where the movement begins again. Thus the artist shows the interconnectedness of the realms of experience of the North American consumer and the Nicaraguan peasant. Furthermore, Lebrón's stance with respect to the media is paradoxical: his ad–anti-ad game aims at undermining commercial advertisement by employing its characteristic modes of address, particularly the monumental size of the billboard and its invasion of public space. The Sykes political cartoon is no less confounding: Latin America is positioned at the center of the composition, yet "her" centrality is offset by the economy of the look within the image and between the image and the external viewer. The success of the cartoon rests on its ability to address the male viewer, turning female observers into transvestites.

Images like Sykes's demonstrate that reversals and displacements are not necessarily effective. Much as the central position of Latin America in Sykes's cartoon is displaced to the periphery by the onlookers, we should be attentive to the fact that even if Latin Americans turn the map upside down, as Torres-García does, "our" (Latin Americans') South probably would not become "their" (North Americans') North. Furthermore, regarding Sandino's seal through the lens of gender, it becomes evident that the force of reversal can be undermined by its attempt to adopt the grammar of "othering" to speak for itself. Thus Nicaragua, embodied in the figure of the rebel, is gendered male vis-à-vis the vanquished, feminized "other" (the foreigner). The previous hierarchical order is not contested by the image, but simply restaged, this time to assert the place of the emergent nation.

Caro's "Colombia," in contrast, resists this impulse to gender Latin America female or male. As opposed to what happens in Sandino's seal or Sykes's cartoon, Caro's "Colombia" visually interweaves the two symbols that stand for the North and the South so that they cannot be disentangled. Thus he points to the multifaceted, interactive continuum of the North-South axis and to the pitfalls inherent in categorizations posited in terms of dyadic oppositions.

The preceeding observations highlight but a few of the many paradoxes that constitute our images' contribution to a critique of unidimensional accounts of encounters of the imperial kind. Unraveling the paradoxes inherent to this set of images as a *transformation group* provides insight into how empire is made, that is, constructed as a one-way relation between dominator and dominated, where the former subsumes the latter. Simultaneously, probing the paradoxes provides insight into how empire can be undone, that is, complicated, by revealing the interdependence of the United States and Latin America. It is this proliferation of meanings, this impossibility of closure, that strikes us as the most compelling aspect of this ensemble of images.

One purpose of this essay has been to suggest alternative ways of seeing and interpreting so as to bring the visual arts more squarely into the historian's field of vision. Clearly important to comprehending visual modes of expression as practices of empire is the question of reception. What public were specific images initially intended for, and how did they circulate? What role should the devices that frame an image, such as newspapers, museums, multinational companies, or rebel movements be attributed in our attempts to interpret images as signifying practices? How have viewers across time and space engaged with these images, and how do we contribute to the production and reproduction of empire by circulating them? Sykes's cartoon and Meireles's and Bedia's installations must be examined in light of such queries. Did Sykes's audience laugh? With whom in the cartoon did they identify, that is, how was the economy of the look organized within the picture *and* without? Did Meireles's Coca-Cola bottles circulate? How many and where? Have Native Americans and Afro-Cubans had access to Bedia's work? Does the work itself demand interpretation from their perspectives? It is essential that in approaching images as acts of interpretation, we consider as well how various U.S. and Latin American publics received them. Only by doing so can we move toward more nuanced, more socially embedded accounts of the viewing activity as a practice of empire.

To conclude, this essay opens chronologically with Sandino's seal and ends in an unexpected manner with Lebrón's Coors Light anti-ad. But does it really end? The sense of urgency provoked by the two images that bracket this visual essay evokes both the uneasy place occupied by historians at the crossroads of our practice and the course of events that make up the daily substance of U.S.–Latin American relations. Our contribution can be compared to a chess match. Ending the match does not change the rules of the game.[9] As these images reveal, no effort to refine our conceptual apparatus in accordance with contemporary lines of inquiry will spare people the suffering they experience living in abject poverty or under conditions of exploitation or political repression, where freedom of expression often comes at a very high price. We must be willing to accord images the place they merit in historical narratives, not merely as illustrations or discursive aids, but as central to the historian's construction of evidence about the past, about people's outlooks, and about their lives.

Notes

Composed after this book was completed, this essay is intended as a response "from within" as much as a dialogue with the book. I thank the editors for their invitation to contribute this visual essay, especially Gilbert Joseph for the enthusiasm with which he received the present collection of images and Catherine LeGrand for her invaluable support throughout the various stages of thinking and writing.

1. For discussion of Sandino's construction of dichotomous social categories in his three manifestos, the seal, and the coins, see Michael J. Schroeder, " 'To Defend Our Nation's Honor': Toward a Social and Cultural History of the Sandino Rebellion in Nicaragua, 1927–1934" (Ph.D. diss., University of Michigan, 1993), 211–17.

2. See the stimulating essay by John J. Johnson, "Latin America as Female," in his book *Latin America in Caricature* (Austin: University of Texas Press, 1980), 72–73.

3. Joaquín Torres-García, "The School of the South," in *El Taller Torres-García: The School of the South and Its Legacy*, ed. Mari Carmen Ramírez (Austin: University of Texas Press, 1992), 53. (This essay was first published in Montevideo, Uruguay, in February 1935.)

4. On Bedia's work, see Robert Farris Thompson, "Sacred Silhouettes," *Art in America*, July 1997, 69; and Charles Merewether, "Displacement and the Reinvention of Identity," in *Latin American Artists of the Twentieth Century*, ed. Waldo Rasmussen et al. (New York: Museum of Modern Art, 1993), 147.

5. Michael Lebrón, "Amtrak: On the Right Track Now?" *AIGA Journal of Graphic Design* 13, no. 2, the "Outsiders Issue." See also Todd S. Purdum, "The Adman as Artist (Or Is It Vice Versa?)," *New York Times*, 28 Jan. 1993, sec. C, 1, 8; and Joan Jedell, "What's It All About, Michael?," *Art Direction*, Dec. 1993, 65.

6. To be more precise, we might conceptualize these images as "indexes" that signify the physical connection existing between them and events in the history of U.S.–Latin American relations. By "indexes," I refer to Charles S. Peirce's classification of signs into "indexes," "icons," and "symbols," in his essay "Logic as Semiotic: The Theory of Signs," in *Semiotics: An Introductory Anthology*, ed. Robert E. Innis (Bloomington: Indiana University Press, 1985), 13.

7. For elaboration on this "strategic" model of interpretation, see Claude Lévi-

Strauss, *The Way of Masks,* trans. Sylvia Modelski (Seattle: University of Washington Press, 1982), 144.

8. For the notion of "transformation" in painting see Hubert Damisch, *The Origin of Perspective,* trans. John Goodman (Boston: MIT Press, 1994), 288.

9. In his book *Fenêtre jaune cadmium, ou les dessous de la peinture* (Paris: Editions du Seuil, 1984), Hubert Damisch adopts the metaphor of chess to describe painting in terms of "the match" and "the game" (154). Here I extend Damisch's metaphor to activities whose parameters are relatively well established, such as those of the historian and image-making itself.

Contributors

Fernando Coronil is a Venezuelan anthropologist, trained at the University of Chicago, who now teaches in the Anthropology and History Departments at the University of Michigan. His work creatively challenges the categories commonly used to think about the state and the economy. Of late he has been concerned with systems of meaning and with issues of space and memory in postcolonial situations. His influential essay "Dismembering and Remembering the Nation: The Semantics of Violence in Venezuela" appeared in 1991 in *Comparative Studies in Society and History*. His book *The Magical State: Nature, Money, and Modernity in Venezuela* was published in 1997 by the University of Chicago Press.

Lauren Derby is Harper Instructor in the Social Sciences at the University of Chicago, where she completed her doctorate in Latin American history in 1998. Her research focuses on popular culture and the state in the Dominican Republic, Haiti, and Cuba. She is the author of "Haitians, Magic, and Money: *Raza* and Society in the Haitian-Dominican Borderlands, 1900–1937," which appeared in *Comparative Studies in Society and History* in 1994 and won the 1994 Conference on Latin American History Award. Her dissertation explores civic culture and public life during the regime of Rafael Trujillo (1930–1961) in the Dominican Republic.

Seth Fein teaches modern U.S. and Latin American history at Georgia State University. A specialist on U.S. foreign relations and culture in the twentieth century, he wrote his dissertation at the University of Texas on Hollywood and U.S.-Mexican relations in the Golden Age of Mexican cinema (1996). He has published articles on international mass culture, U.S. foreign relations, Mexican development, and film in the journals *Studies in Latin American Popular Culture, Film-Historia, Historia y Grafía, Nuevo Texto Crítico,* and *Secuencia,* and chapters in the books *Mexico–Estados Unidos: Encuentros y desencuentros en el cine* (1996) and *Visible Nations: Latin American Cinema and Video,* ed. Chon Noriega (forthcoming).

Eileen J. Findlay is Assistant Professor of Latin American History at American University. Since completing her doctorate at the University of Wisconsin at Madison in 1995, she has published several articles on sexuality in late-nineteenth- and early-twentieth-century Puerto Rico. She is finishing a book about the history of morality, political culture, and social movements in Puerto Rico that will be published by Duke University Press.

Gilbert M. Joseph is Professor of History at Yale University and editor of the *Hispanic American Historical Review*. He is the author of *Revolution from Without: Yucatán, Mexico, and the United States, 1880-1924* (rev. ed., 1988; Spanish ed., 1992), *Rediscovering the Past at Mexico's Periphery* (1986), *Summer of Discontent, Seasons of Upheaval: Elite Politics and Rural Insurgency in Yucatán, 1876-1915* (with Allen Wells, 1996), and numerous articles on modern Mexico, U.S. involvement in Latin America, and the history of rural crime and protest. He is also the coeditor of *Yucatán y la International Harvester* (with Allen Wells, 1986), *Land, Labor, and Capital in Modern Yucatán: Essays in Regional History and Political Economy* (with Jeffery Brannon, 1991), *Everyday Forms of State Formation: Revolution and the Negotiation of Rule in Modern Mexico* (with Daniel Nugent, 1994), and *I Saw a City Invincible: Urban Portraits of Latin America* (with Mark Szuchman, 1996). He is currently writing a social and political history of modern Mexico.

Catherine C. LeGrand teaches Latin American history at McGill University. She is the author of *Frontier Expansion and Peasant Protest in Colombia, 1850–1936* (1986; Spanish ed., 1988) and several articles on social conflicts in regions of export agriculture, and serves on the editorial board of the *Canadian Journal of Latin American and Caribbean Studies*. She is now engaged in two parallel research projects focusing on foreign investment and local responses in the Caribbean. The first is a microhistory of a Canadian-owned sugar plantation in the Dominican Republic, and the second is a regional study of the United Fruit Company banana zone in Colombia.

Thomas Miller Klubock is Assistant Professor of Latin American History at Georgetown University. He completed his doctorate at Yale University in 1993 with a thesis on gender, working-class culture, and politics among Chilean copper miners. His book *Contested Communities: Class, Gender, and Politics in Chile's El Teniente Copper Mine, 1904–1951* will be published in 1998 by Duke University Press.

Steven Palmer (Ph.D., Columbia University, 1990) is a Canadian cultural historian who has written on nationalism in Central America and, more recently, on the development of social policy in the region. He has published important articles on the construction of Sandinismo in Nicaragua and the invention of nations in Costa Rica and Guatemala, and is coeditor, with Iván Molina Jiménez, of *Heroes al gusto y libros de moda: Sociedad y cambio cultural en Costa Rica, 1750–1900* (1992) and *El paso del cometa: Estado, política social y culturas populares en Costa Rica, 1880–1950* (1994). Presently he is completing a book on social policy and popular culture in Costa Rica from 1900 to 1940. Having taught at the Universidad de Costa Rica, the University of Iowa, and Memorial University in Newfoundland, at present he is a writer and performer on *The Great Eastern,* heard weekly on the radio network of the Canadian Broadcasting Corporation.

Deborah Poole is Associate Professor of Anthropology at the Graduate Faculty of the New School for Social Research. She has done field and archival research on religion, social organization, political violence, and visual traditions in the Peruvian Andes. Her publications include *Unruly Order: Violence, Power, and Social Identity in the Highland Provinces of Southern Peru* (1994) and *Vision, Race, and Modernity: A Visual Economy of the Andean Image World* (1997). She is also coauthor, with Gerardo Rénique, of *Peru: Time of Fear* (1992).

Eric Paul Roorda is Assistant Professor of History at Bellarmine College in Louisville, Kentucky. He did his graduate work at Johns Hopkins University, where he received a Ph.D. in U.S. diplomatic history in 1990. He was a Fulbright scholar in the Dominican Republic, and has taught for the Johns Hopkins School for Advanced International Studies in China, Long Island University's "SEAmester" program in the Caribbean, and the Williams College–Mystic Seaport American Maritime Studies Program. His article on U.S. perceptions of the Dominican massacre of Haitians in 1937 appeared in 1996 in *Diplomatic History*. His book *The Dictator Next Door: The Good Neighbor Policy and the Trujillo Regime in the Dominican Republic, 1930–45* is forthcoming in 1998 from Duke University Press.

William Roseberry is Professor of Anthropology at the New School for Social Research. His first book, *Coffee and Capitalism in the Venezuelan Andes* (1983), established new standards for the writing of historical ethnography. He has gone on to do comparative research on the peasantry and the political economy of development in Venezuela, the southern Andes, Mexico, and England. Several of his influential theoretical essays have been collected in *Anthropologies and Histories: Essays in Culture, History, and Political Economy* (1989). He has also coedited *Golden Ages, Dark Ages: Imagining the Past in Anthropology and History* (with Jay O'Brien, 1991) and *Coffee, Society, and Power in Latin America* (with Lowell Gudmundson and Mario Samper Kutschbach, 1995).

Emily S. Rosenberg is DeWitt Wallace Professor of History at Macalester College in St. Paul, Minnesota. Her first book, *Spreading the American Dream* (1982), examined American economic and cultural expansionism from 1890 to 1945. She has subsequently published numerous articles bringing issues of culture and gender into the study of U.S. foreign relations and has also coauthored two widely used texts, *In Our Times: America since World War II* (5th ed., 1994) and *Liberty, Power, Equality* (1996). She has served on the executive board of the Organization of American Historians, the Department of State's Advisory Committee on Historical Diplomatic Documentation, the Minnesota Humanities Commission, and the Council of the Society for Historians of American Foreign Relations, of which she is now president. Her current work examines U.S. foreign financial policies in the age of "dollar diplomacy."

Ricardo D. Salvatore is Professor of History at the Universidad Torcuato Di Tella in Buenos Aires. He has been a fellow at the Institute for Advanced Studies (Princeton) and at the Program for Agrarian Studies (Yale University), and has taught at various universities in Argentina and the United States since receiving his doctorate in economics from the University of Texas in 1987. His articles have appeared in the *Journal of Interdisciplinary History, Social Science History, Journal of Historical Sociology, Hispanic American Historical Review, Journal of Economic History, Agricultural History, Peasant Studies, Dispositio, Desarrollo Económico, Revista de Historia de América, Sociedad,* and *Delito y Sociedad,* among others. He is coeditor, with Carlos Aguirre, of *The Birth of the Penitentiary in Latin America,*

1830–1940 (1996), a collection of essays on the history of prisons, criminology, and social control. Presently he is writing a book on the cultural and social history of peasants and workers in Buenos Aires province during the Rosas era (1829–1852) and is also doing research on the narratives and images of South America produced by North Americans.

Michael J. Schroeder spent half again as many years as a roofer and carpenter as he spent in graduate school at the University of Michigan (Ph.D., 1993). He has been four times to Nicaragua and has spent several months in the Segovia mountains, including a month clearing weeds and planting beans with a peasant family near Jinotega. His article, "Horse Thieves to Rebels to Dogs: Political Gang Violence and the State in the Western Segovias, Nicaragua in the Time of Sandino, 1926–1934," published in the *Journal of Latin American Studies* in 1996, won Honorable Mention for the 1996 Conference on Latin American History Award. He is completing a book titled "Tragedy, Redemption, Power: The Sandino Rebellion in Las Segovias and Nicaragua, 1926–1934," and ruminating about further contributions to a social and cultural history of memory and power in the Segovias. He teaches U.S. and Latin American history at the University of Michigan—Flint.

Steve J. Stern is Professor of History at the University of Wisconsin, Madison. He has authored *Peru's Indian Peoples and the Challenge of Spanish Conquest* (1982) and *The Secret History of Gender: Women, Men, and Power in Late Colonial Mexico* (1995), and edited *Resistance, Rebellion, and Consciousness in the Andean Peasant World* (1987). With Frederick Cooper, Alan Isaacman, Florencia Mallon, and William Roseberry, he also coauthored *Confronting Historical Paradigms: Peasants, Labor, and the Capitalist World System in Africa and Latin America* (1993), a provocative critique of both "orthodox" and "dissident" models of development. His edited collection, *Shining and Other Paths: War and Society in Peru, 1980–1995,* is forthcoming from Duke University Press. Presently he is moving out of the colonial period, with a new research project on the construction of historical memory in twentieth-century Chile.

María del Carmen Suescun Pozas is a joint doctoral candidate in Art History and History at McGill University. She specializes in comparative approaches to Latin American, European, and North American cultural practices and the visual arts. Her dissertation involves a close reading of Latin American visual culture and its multiple historical interactions with ideological and artistic currents coming out of Europe and North America. As a Colombian residing in Canada, she daily grapples with the challenges that Latin American cultural production poses for an artist and art historian who is simultaneously speaking from within and writing from without, and who is eager to assume and push to their limits the contradictions inherent to such a paradoxical enterprise.

Steven C. Topik is Professor and Chair of the History Department at the University of California, Irvine. In addition to numerous articles on modern Brazilian and Mexican political-economic themes, he is the author of *The Political Economy of the Brazilian State, 1889–1930* (1987) and *Trade and Gunboats: The United States and Brazil in the Age of Empire* (1996), and the coeditor of *The Second Conquest? Latin American Export Economies in the Age of Imperialism* (with Allen Wells, 1998). He is writing a history of coffee from 1400 to the present.

Index

Library of Congress Cataloging-in-Publication Data

Close encounters of empire: writing the cultural history of U.S.–Latin American
relations/edited by Gilbert M. Joseph, Catherine C. LeGrand, and Ricardo D.
Salvatore; with a foreword by Fernando Coronil.
p. cm.—(American encounters/global interactions)
Includes index.
ISBN 0–8223–2085–1 (cloth:alk. paper).
ISBN 0–8223–2099–1 (pbk.:alk.paper)
1. Latin America—Relations—United States. 2. United States—Relations—Latin
America. 3. Latin America—Civilization—American influences. I. Joseph, G. M.
(Gilbert Michael). II. LeGrand, Catherine. III. Salvatore, Ricardo Donato. IV. Series.
F1418.C64 1998
303.48'28073—dc21   98-27624 CIP